Poetry Criticism

Guide to Gale Literary Criticism Series

When you need to review criticism of literary works, these are the Gale series to use:

If the author's death date is:

You should turn to:

After Dec. 31, 1959
(or author is still living)

CONTEMPORARY LITERARY CRITICISM

for example: Jorge Luis Borges, Anthony Burgess,
William Faulkner, Mary Gordon,
Ernest Hemingway, Iris Murdoch

1900 through 1959

TWENTIETH-CENTURY LITERARY CRITICISM

for example: Willa Cather, F. Scott Fitzgerald,
Henry James, Mark Twain, Virginia Woolf

1800 through 1899

NINETEENTH-CENTURY LITERATURE CRITICISM

for example: Fedor Dostoevski, Nathaniel Hawthorne,
George Sand, William Wordsworth

1400 through 1799

LITERATURE CRITICISM FROM 1400 TO 1800
(excluding Shakespeare)

for example: Anne Bradstreet, Daniel Defoe,
Alexander Pope, François Rabelais,
Jonathan Swift, Phillis Wheatley

SHAKESPEAREAN CRITICISM

Shakespeare's plays and poetry

Antiquity through 1399

CLASSICAL AND MEDIEVAL LITERATURE CRITICISM

for example: Dante, Homer, Plato, Sophocles, Vergil,
the Beowulf Poet

Gale also publishes related criticism series:

CHILDREN'S LITERATURE REVIEW

This series covers authors of all eras who have written for
the preschool through high school audience.

SHORT STORY CRITICISM

This series covers the major short fiction writers of all nationalities
and periods of literary history.

POETRY CRITICISM

This series covers poets of all nationalities, movements, and periods of
literary history.

ISSN 1052-4851

Poetry Criticism

Excerpts from Criticism of the Works of the Most Significant and Widely Studied Poets of World Literature

VOLUME 1

Robyn V. Young
Editor

91-03360

 Gale Research Inc. · *DETROIT · NEW YORK · LONDON*

Since this page cannot legibly accommodate all the copyright notices, the Acknowledgments constitute an extension of the copyright page.

While every effort has been made to ensure the reliability of the information presented in this publication, Gale Research Inc. does not guarantee the accuracy of the data contained herein. Gale accepts no payment for listing; and inclusion in the publication of any organization, agency, institution, publication, service, or individual does not imply endorsement of the editors or publisher.

Errors brought to the attention of the publisher and verified to the satisfaction of the publisher will be corrected in future editions.

Contents

Preface

At various points in literary history, poetry has been defined as "jigging veins of rhyming mother wits" (Christopher Marlowe); "the spontaneous overflow of powerful feelings" (William Wordsworth); "the opening and closing of a door, leaving those who look through to guess about what is seen during a moment" (Carl Sandburg); and "a momentary stay against confusion" (Robert Frost). The study of poetry produces a natural curiosity about the political, social, moral, and literary trends of a particular time period and is an essential element of a well-rounded liberal arts curriculum.

Poetry Criticism (PC) was created in response to librarians serving high school, college, and public library patrons who noted an increasing number of requests for critical material on poets. Like its Gale predecessor in genre-oriented studies, *Short Story Criticism (SSC)*, which presents material on writers of short fiction, *PC* is designed to provide users with substantial critical excerpts and biographical information on the world's most frequently discussed and studied poets in high school and undergraduate college courses. Each *PC* entry is supplemented by biographical and bibliographical material to help guide the user to a greater understanding of the genre and its creators. Although major poets and movements are covered in such Gale Literary Criticism Series as *Contemporary Literary Criticism (CLC), Twentieth-Century Literary Criticism (TCLC), Nineteenth-Century Literature Criticism (NCLC), Literature Criticism from 1400 to 1800 (LC),* and *Classical and Medieval Literature Criticism (CMLC), PC* offers more focused attention on individual poets than is possible in the broader, survey-oriented entries on writers in these Gale series.

Scope of the Work

In order to reflect the influence of tradition as well as innovation, poets from various nationalities, eras, and movements will be represented in every volume of *PC*. For example, the present volume includes commentary on Emily Dickinson, one of the most popular and widely read American poets of the nineteenth century; Charles Baudelaire, considered one of the world's greatest lyric poets, whose *Les fleurs du mal* continues to elicit scholarly attention and debate; Langston Hughes, the Harlem Renaissance poet whose verse reflects the aspirations and disappointments of modern African-Americans; and John Donne, the English scholar and artist whose secular and divine poems have generated contrasting critical opinion during the past four hundred years. Since many of these poets have inspired a prodigious amount of critical explication, *PC* is necessarily selective, and the editors have chosen the most important published criticism to aid readers and students in their research.

Students, teachers, librarians, and researchers will find that the generous excerpts and supplementary material provided by *PC* supply them with vital information needed to write a term paper on poetic technique, examine a poet's most prominent themes, or lead a poetry discussion group. Twelve to fifteen authors will be analyzed in each volume, and each author entry presents a historical survey of the critical response to that author's work. Some early reviews are included to indicate initial reaction and are often written by the author's contemporaries, while current analyses provide a modern view. The length of an entry is intended to reflect the amount of critical attention that the author has received from critics writing in English and from foreign critics in translation. Critical articles and books that have not been translated into English are excluded. Every attempt has been made to identify and include excerpts from the most significant essays on each author's work. In order to provide these important critical pieces, the editors will sometimes reprint essays that have appeared in previous volumes of Gale's Literary Criticism Series. Such duplication, however, never exceeds fifteen percent of a *PC* volume. Finally, because of space limitations, the reader may find that some important articles are not excerpted. Instead, these pieces may be found in the author's further reading list, with complete bibliographic information followed by a brief descriptive note.

Organization of the Book

A *PC* author entry consists of the following components:

- The **author heading** cites the name under which the author wrote, followed by birth and death dates. If the author wrote consistently under a pseudonym, the pseudonym will be listed in the author heading and his or her legal name given in parentheses on the first line of the biographical and critical introduction. Uncertainty as to a birth or death date is indicated by question marks.

- The **biographical and critical introduction** contains background information designed to introduce a reader to the author and to the critical discussions surrounding his or her work. Parenthetical material following the introduction provides references to other biographical and critical series published by Gale, including *CLC, TCLC, NCLC, LC, CMLC,* and *SSC, Children's Literature Review, Contemporary Authors, Dictionary of Literary Biography,* and *Something about the Author.*

- A **portrait of the author** is included when available. Many entries also contain illustrations of materials pertinent to an author's career, including holographs of manuscript pages, title pages, dust jackets, letters, or representations of important people, places, and events in the author's life.

- The list of **principal works** is chronological by date of first publication and lists the most important works by the author. The first section comprises poetry collections and book-length poems. The second section gives information on other major works by the author. For foreign authors, the editors have provided original foreign-language publication information and have selected what are considered the best and most complete English-language editions of their works.

- The **critical excerpts** are arranged chronologically in each author entry to provide a useful perspective on changes in critical evaluation over the years. All individual titles of poems and poetry collections by the author featured in the entry are printed in boldface type to enable a reader to ascertain without difficulty the works under discussion. For purposes of easier identification, the critic's name and the publication date of the essay are given at the beginning of each piece of criticism. Unsigned criticism is preceded by the title of the journal in which it originally appeared. Publication information (such as publisher names and book prices) and parenthetical numerical references (such as footnotes or page and line references to specific editions of a work) have been deleted at the editor's discretion to provide smoother reading of the text.

- Critical excerpts are prefaced with **explanatory notes** as an additional aid to students and readers using *PC.* The explanatory notes provide several types of useful information, including: the reputation of a critic, the importance of a work of criticism, and the specific type of criticism (biographical, psychoanalytic, historical, etc.).

- Whenever available, **insightful comments from the authors themselves and excerpts from author interviews** are also included. Depending upon the length of such material, an author's commentary may be set within boxes or boldface rules.

- A complete **bibliographical citation,** designed to help the interested reader locate the original essay or book, follows each piece of criticism.

- The **further reading list** appearing at the end of each entry suggests additional materials for study of the author. In some cases it includes essays for which the editors could not obtain reprint rights.

Other Features

- A **cumulative author index** lists all the authors who have appeared in *PC, CLC, TCLC, NCLC, LC, CMLC,* and *SSC,* as well as cross-references to the Gale series *Children's Literature Review, Contemporary Authors, Contemporary Authors New Revision Series, Contemporary Authors Autobiography Series, Dictionary of Literary Biography, Dictionary of Literary Biography Yearbook, Concise Dictionary of American Literary Biography, Something about the Author, Something about the Author Autobiography Series,* and *Yesterday's Authors of Books for Children.* Users will welcome this cumulated index as a useful tool for locating an author within the Literary Criticism Series.

- A **cumulative nationality index** lists all authors featured in *PC* by nationality, followed by the number of the *PC* volume in which the author appears.

- A **cumulative title index** lists in alphabetical order all individual poems, book-length poems, and collection titles contained in the *PC* series. Titles of poetry collections and separately published poems are printed in italics, while titles of individual poems are printed in roman type with quotation marks. Each title is followed by the author's name and the corresponding volume and page number where commentary on the work may be located. English-language translations of original foreign-language titles are cross-referenced to the foreign titles so that all references to discussion of a work are combined in one listing.

A Note to the Reader

When writing papers, students who quote directly from any volume in the Literary Criticism Series may use the following general formats to footnote reprinted criticism. The first example pertains to material drawn from periodicals, the second to material reprinted from books:

[1] David Daiches, "W. H. Auden: The Search for a Public," *Poetry* LIV (June 1939), 148–56; excerpted and reprinted in *Poetry Criticism,* Vol. 1, ed. Robyn V. Young (Detroit: Gale Research, 1991), pp. 20–2.

[2] Pamela J. Annas, *A Disturbance in Mirrors: The Poetry of Sylvia Plath* (Greenwood Press, 1988); excerpted and reprinted in *Poetry Criticism*, Vol. 1, ed. Robyn V. Young (Detroit: Gale Research, 1991), pp. 289–301.

Suggestions Are Welcome

Readers who wish to suggest authors to appear in future volumes, or who have other suggestions, are cordially invited to contact the editors.

Acknowledgments

The editors wish to thank the copyright holders of the excerpted criticism included in this volume, the permissions managers of many book and magazine publishing companies for assisting us in securing reprint rights, and Anthony Bogucki for assistance with copyright research. We are also grateful to the staffs of the Detroit Public Library, Wayne State University Purdy/Kresge Library Complex, and the University of Michigan Libraries for making their resources available to us. Following is a list of the copyright holders who have granted us permission to reprint material in this volume of *PC*. Every effort has been made to trace copyright, but if omissions have been made, please let us know.

COPYRIGHTED EXCERPTS IN *PC*, VOLUME 1, WERE REPRINTED FROM THE FOLLOWING PERIODICALS:

The American Book Review, v. 6, March-April, 1984. © 1984 by *The American Book Review.* Reprinted by permission of the publisher.—*The American Scholar,* v. 15, Spring, 1946. Copyright 1946, renewed 1973 by The Phi Beta Kappa Society. Reprinted by permission of the publishers.—*Another Chicago Magazine,* v. 16, 1986.—*Antaeus,* v. 5, Spring, 1972 for an interview with W. H. Auden by Daniel Halpern. Copyright © 1972 by Daniel Halpern. Reprinted by permission of Curtis Brown, Ltd. for the Literary Estate of W. H. Auden and by Daniel Halpern.—*The Atlantic Monthly,* v. 225, May, 1970 for "The Poet in Praise of Limestone" by Frank Kermode. Copyright 1970 by The Atlantic Monthly Company, Boston, MA. Reprinted by permission of the author.—*Book World—The Washington Post,* August 2, 1981. © 1981, *The Washington Post.* Reprinted by permission of the publisher.—*Callaloo,* v. 9, Winter, 1986. Copyright © 1986 by Charles H. Rowell. All rights reserved. Reprinted by permission of the publisher.—*The Centennial Review,* v. XIII, Spring, 1969 for "Sylvia Plath: The Trepanned Veteran" by Robert Boyers; v. XXIV, Fall, 1980 for "The Sources of the Spoon: Edgar Lee Masters and the 'Spoon River Anthology' " by James Hurt. © 1969, 1980 by *The Centennial Review.* Both reprinted by permission of the publisher and the author.—*CLA Journal,* v. VI, March, 1963; v. XI, March, 1968. Copyright, 1963, 1968 by The College Language Association. Both used by permission of The College Language Association.—*Commentary,* v. 57, April, 1974 for "Sylvia Plath Reconsidered" by John Romano. Copyright © 1974 by the American Jewish Committee. All rights reserved. Reprinted by permission of the publisher and the author.—*Commonweal,* v. XCII, April 24, 1970. Copyright © 1970 Commonweal Publishing Co., Inc. Reprinted by permission of Commonweal Foundation./v. LXVI, June 21, 1957. Copyright © 1957, renewed 1985 Commonweal Publishing Co., Inc. Both reprinted by permission of Commonweal Foundation.—*Concerning Poetry,* v. 19, 1986; v. 20, 1987. Copyright © 1986, 1987, Western Washington University. Both reprinted by permission of the publisher.—*Critical Inquiry,* v. 5, Winter, 1978 for "Naming as History: Dickinson's Poems of Definition" by Sharon Cameron; v. 13, Summer, 1987 for " 'Soul at the White Heat': The Romance of Emily Dickinson's Poetry" by Joyce Carol Oates. Copyright © 1978, 1987 by The University of Chicago. Both reprinted by permission of the publisher and the author.—*Criticism,* v. VII, Fall, 1965 for "Emily Dickinson: The Transcendent Self" by Hyatt H. Waggoner. Copyright, 1965, Wayne State University Press. Reprinted by permission of the publisher and the Literary Estate of Hyatt H. Waggoner.—*Diacritics,* v. II, Fall, 1972. Copyright © Diacritics, Inc., 1972. Reprinted by permission of the publisher.—*Essays in Criticism,* v. XXV, July, 1975 for "Auden's Last Poems," by F. W. Bateson. Reprinted by permission of the Editors of *Essays in Criticism* and the Literary Estate of F. W. Bateson.—*The Georgia Review,* v. XLIII, Winter, 1989 for "Stalking the Barbaric Yawp" by Diane Wakoski. Copyright, 1989, by the University of Georgia. Reprinted by permission of the publisher and the author.—*Harper's Magazine,* v. 244, January, 1972. Copyright © 1972 by *Harper's Magazine.* All rights reserved. Reprinted by special permission.—*The Iowa Review,* v. 8, Winter, 1977 for "Sylvia Plath and Confessional Poetry: A Reconsideration" by M. D. Uroff. Copyright © 1977 by The University of Iowa. Reprinted by permission of the publisher and the author.—*Italian Americana,* v. 1, Autumn, 1974. Copyright © by Ruth Fablo and Richard Gambino. Reprinted by permission of the publisher.—*John Donne Journal: Studies in the Age of Donne,* v. 6, 1987. Reprinted by permission of the publisher.—*Kansas Quarterly,* v. 7, Summer, 1975 for "Langston Hughes: A Kansas Poet in the Harlem Renaissance" by Cary D. Wintz. © copyright 1975 by the *Kansas Quaterly.* Reprinted by permission of the publisher and the author.—*Keats-Shelley Journal,* v. XV, Winter, 1966. © Keats-Shelley Association of America, Inc. 1966. Reprinted by permission of the publisher.—*The Kenyon Review,* n.s. v. 6, Winter, 1984 for "Separateness and Solitude in Frost" by Patricia Wallace. Copyright 1984 by Kenyon College. All rights reserved. Reprinted by permission of the author.—*MELUS,* v. 8, Fall, 1981. Copyright, MELUS, The Society for the Study of Multi-Ethnic Literature of the United States, 1981. Reprinted by permission of the publisher.—*The Midwest Quarterly,* v. XVI, October, 1974. Copyright, 1974, by *The Midwest Quarterly,* Pittsburg State University. Reprinted by permission of the publisher.—*The University of Mississippi Studies in English,* n.s. v. III, 1982. Copyright © 1982 The University of Mississippi. Reprinted by permission of the publisher.—*The Nation,* New York, v. 187, October 11, 1958. Copyright 1958, renewed 1986 *The Nation* magazine/The Nation Company, Inc. Reprinted by permission of the publisher.—*Negro American Literature Forum,* v. 5, Winter, 1971 for "The Blues Poetry of Langston Hughes" by Edward E. Waldron. Copyright © Indiana State University 1971. Reprinted with the permission of Indiana State University and the author.—*New Pages,* n. 9, Spring-Summer, 1985. Copyright © 1985 New Pages Press. Reprinted by permission of the publisher.—*The New Republic,* v. III, September 11, 1944 for "Frost: A Dissenting Opinion" by Malcom Cowley.

Authors to Be Featured in *PC*, Volumes 2 and 3

Anna Akhmatova, 1888–1966 (Russian poet, translator, and essayist)—Generally considered Russia's finest female poet, Akhmatova is often regarded as Boris Pasternak's successor in the Silver Age of Soviet literature. Although her life under Stalinism was marred by tragedy, Akhmatova is acclaimed for her ability to recreate her experiences in poems which reveal a love of nature and humankind.

Robert Browning, 1812–1889 (English poet and dramatist)—One of the most prominent poets of the Victorian era, Browning is chiefly remembered for his mastery of the dramatic monologue and for the diversity and scope of his works. In "Fra Lippo Lippi," "Andrea del Sarto," and his masterpiece, *The Ring and the Book,* Browning advanced the art of the dramatic monologue to new levels of technical and psychological sophistication.

Hart Crane, 1899–1932 (American poet and essayist)—Often compared to William Blake, Samuel Taylor Coleridge, and Charles Baudelaire, Crane sought salvation through art from the spiritual torment of human existence. His major work, *The Bridge,* has undergone substantial critical reevaluation since its publication in 1930.

Federico García Lorca, 1898–1936 (Spanish poet, dramatist, critic, and essayist)—One of Spain's most important twentieth-century poets, García Lorca combined his knowledge of Spanish and classical literature with folk and gypsy ballads to create an idiom at once traditional, modern, and personal. His verse attests to the beauty and excitement of life experienced close to a natural order.

Horace, 65–8 B.C. (Roman poet and prose writer)—Horace served as Principal Poet of Rome and the Imperial Court during the reign of Emperor Augustus. His *Satires* and *Epodes* remain among the most renowned verse in world literature.

Claude McKay, 1889–1948 (American poet, novelist, short story writer, journalist, essayist, and autobiographer)—The first prominent writer of the Harlem Renaissance, McKay searched among the black working class for his subject matter and for a means of preserving the creativity of the African spirit in an alienating world. McKay was successful in converting anger and racial protest into such poems as "If We Must Die," an eloquent piece which reaffirms the African-American's willingness to die for freedom.

Arthur Rimbaud, 1854–1891 (French poet)—Rimbaud is regarded as an important forerunner of the Symbolist movement and a major influence on twentieth-century poetry and poetics. His major works, *Les illuminations* and *Une saison en enfer,* demonstrate his contributions to the development of the prose poem and his innovative use of the subconscious as a source of literary inspiration.

Walt Whitman, 1819–1892 (American poet, essayist, novelist, short story writer, journalist, and editor)—One of America's seminal poets, Whitman sought to reach the common people whom he felt were ignored by a literature written for the elite. His masterpiece, *Leaves of Grass,* remains a classic in American letters.

Additional Authors to Appear
in Future Volumes

Addison, Joseph 1672–1719
A.E. (ps. of George William Russell) 1867–1935
Aeschylus 525–456 B.C.
Aiken, Conrad 1889–1973
Akhmadulina, Bella 1937–
Aldington, Richard 1892–1962
Aleixandre, Vicente 1898–1984
Alighieri, Dante 1265–1321
Angelou, Maya 1928–
Armah, Ayi Kwei 1939–
Arnold, Matthew 1822–1888
Ashbery, John 1927–
Baraka, Imamu Amiri 1934–
Barker, George 1913–
Barnes, Djuna 1892–1982
Behn, Aphra 1640–1689
Bell, Marvin 1937–
Belloc, Hilaire 1870–1953
Benét, Stephen Vincent 1898–1943
Benét, William Rose 1886–1950
"Beowulf Poet" c. 8th cent.
Berryman, John 1914–1972
Betjeman, Sir John 1906–1984
Bishop, Elizabeth 1911–1979
Blake, William 1757–1827
Bly, Robert 1926–
Bogan, Louise 1897–1970
Borges, Jorge Luis 1899–1986
Bontemps, Arna 1902–1973
Bradstreet, Anne 1612–1672
Brodsky, Joseph 1940–
Brontë, Emily 1818–1848
Brooks, Gwendolyn 1917–
Brown, Sterling Allen 1901–1989
Browning, Elizabeth Barrett 1806–1861
Brutus, Dennis 1924–
Burns, Robert 1759–1796
Byron, George Gordon, Lord Byron 1788–1824
Caedmon d. c. 680
Cardenal, Ernesto 1925–
Carroll, Lewis 1832–1898
Cavafy, C. P. 1863–1933
Césaire, Aimé 1913–
Char, René 1907–1988
Chaucer, Geoffrey c. 1343–1400
Ciardi, John 1916–1986
Clarke, Austin 1896–1974
Coleridge, Samuel Taylor 1772–1834
Cotter, Joseph Seamon, Sr. 1861–1949
Crane, Stephen 1871–1900
Creeley, Robert 1926–
Cullen, Countee 1903–1946
cummings, e. e. 1894–1962
Day Lewis, Cecil 1904–1972
De La Mare, Walter 1873–1956
Deutsch, Babette 1895–1982

Dickey, James 1923–
Dodson, Owen 1914–1983
Doolittle, Hilda 1886–1961
Dove, Rita 1952–
Dryden, John 1631–1700
Dunbar, Paul Lawrence 1872–1906
Duncan, Robert 1919–1988
Eberhart, Richard 1904–
Eliot, T. S. 1888–1965
Elytis, Odysseus 1911–
Emerson, Ralph Waldo 1803–1882
Evans, Mari 1923–
Gautier, Thophile 1811–1872
"Gawain Poet" fl. 1370
Ghalib, Asadullah Khan 1797–1869
Gibran, Kahlil 1883–1931
Ginsberg, Allen 1926–
Giovanni, Nikki 1943–
Glück, Louise 1943–
Goethe, Johann Wolfgang von 1749–1832
Goldsmith, Oliver 1728–1774
Graves, Robert 1895–1985
Gray, Thomas 1716–1771
Grimké, Angelina Weld 1880–1958
Grimké, Charlotte L. Forten 1837?–1914
Guest, Edgar A. 1881–1959
Guillén, Jorge 1893–1984
Guillén, Nicolas 1902–1989
Hagiwara, Sakutaro 1886–1942
Hall, Donald 1928–
Hammond, Jupiter 1711?–1806
Hardy, Thomas 1840–1928
Harper, Frances Ellen Watkins 1825–1911
Harte, Bret 1836–1902
Hayden, Robert 1913–1980
Heaney, Seamus 1939–
Herbert, George 1593–1633
Herbert, Zbigniew 1924–
Herrick, Robert 1591–1674
Hölderlin, Friedrich 1770–1843
Homer fl. 9th or 8th cent B.C.
Hopkins, Gerard Manley 1844–1889
Housman, A.E. 1859–1936
Hughes, Ted 1930–
Hugo, Richard 1923–1982
Hugo, Victor 1802–1885
Hulme, T. E. 1883–1917
Hunt, Leigh 1784–1859
Ignatow, David 1914–
Isherwood, Christopher 1904–1986
Ishikawa, Takuboku 1885–1912
Jackson, Laura Riding 1901–
Jarrell, Randall 1914–1965
Jeffers, Robinson 1887–1962
Johnson, James Weldon 1871–1938

Jonson, Ben 1572–1637
Jordan, June 1936–
Kerouac, Jack 1922–1969
Kinsella, Thomas 1928–
Kipling, Rudyard 1865–1936
Kizer, Carolyn 1925–
Knight, Etheridge 1931–
Koch, Kenneth 1925–
Kumin, Maxine 1925–
Lamartine, Alphonse Marie de 1790–1869
Larkin, Philip 1922–1985
Lawrence, D. H. 1885–1930
Levertov, Denise 1923–
Levine, Philip 1928–
Lindsay, Vachel 1879–1931
Longfellow, Henry Wadsworth 1807–1882
Lorde, Audre 1934–
Lowell, Amy 1874–1925
Lowell, Robert 1917–1977
Loy, Mina 1882–1966
Lundkvist, Artur 1905–
Lytton, Edward Robert Bulwer 1831–1891
Macaulay, Thomas Babington 1800–1859
MacLeish, Archibald 1892–1982
MacNeice, Louis 1907–1963
Madhubuti, Haki R. 1942–
Marlowe, Christopher 1564–1599
Martial 42?–102? A.D.
Marvell, Andrew 1621–1678
Matsuo, Basho 1644–1694
Meredith, George 1828–1909
Meredith, William 1919–
Merrill, James 1926–
Merwin, W. S. 1927–
Millay, Edna St. Vincent 1892–1950
Milosz, Czeslaw 1911–
Milton, John 1608–1674
Moore, Marianne 1887–1972
Nash, Ogden 1902–1971
Nemerov, Howard 1920–
Neruda, Pablo 1904–1973
Niedecker, Lorine 1903–1970
Nishiwaki, Junzaburo 1894–1982
O'Hara, Frank 1926–1966
O'Hehir, Diana 1922–
Okigbo, Christopher 1932–1967
Olson, Charles 1910–1970
Olson, Elder 1909–
Ovid 43 B.C.–18 A.D.
Owen, Wilfred 1893–1918
Pastan, Linda 1932–
Pasternak, Boris 1890–1960
Patchen, Kenneth 1911–1972
Petrarch 1304–1372

Pope, Alexander 1688-1744
Pound, Ezra 1885-1972
Prokosch, Frederic 1908-1989
Pushkin, Aleksandr 1799-1837
Randall, Dudley 1914-
Ransom, John Crowe 1888-1974
Rexroth, Kenneth 1905-1982
Rilke, Rainer Maria 1875-1926
Rodgers, Carolyn M. 1945-
Roethke, Theodore 1908-1963
Rosenthal, M. L. 1917-
Rossetti, Christina 1830-1894
Rossetti, Dante Gabriel 1828-1882
Rukeyser, Muriel 1913-1980
Sanchez, Sonia 1934-
Sandburg, Carl 1878-1967
Sanders, Ed 1939-
Sappho c. 6th cent. B.C.
Sassoon, Siegfried 1886-1967
Schwartz, Delmore 1913-1966
Scott, Sir Walter 1771-1832
Senghor, Léopold Sédar 1906-
Sexton, Anne 1928-1974

Shelley, Percy Bysshe 1792-1822
Sidney, Sir Philip 1554-1586
Simpson, Louis 1923-
Sitwell, Edith 1887-1964
Smart, Christopher 1722-1771
Smith, Dave 1942-
Snodgrass, W. D. 1926-
Snyder, Gary 1930-
Sorrentino, Gilbert 1929-
Spender, Stephen 1909-
Spenser, Edmund c. 1552-1599
Stafford, William 1914-
Stein, Gertrude 1874-1946
Stevens, Wallace 1879-1955
Swenson, May 1919-1989
Swift, Jonathan 1667-1745
Swinburne, A. C. 1837-1909
Tagore, Sir Rabindranath 1861-1941
Taneda, Santoka 1882-1940
Tate, Allen 1899-1979
Tennyson, Alfred, Lord Tennyson
    1809-1892
Thomas, Dylan 1914-1953

Thoreau, Henry David 1817-1862
Tolson, Melvin B. 1900?-1966
Toomer, Jean 1894-1967
Tzara, Tristan 1896-1963
Vergil 70-19 B.C.
Verlaine, Paul 1844-1896
Vigny, Comte Alfred Victor de 1797-
    1863
Wakoski, Diane 1937-
Walcott, Derek 1930-
Warren, Robert Penn 1905-1989
Weiss, Theodore 1916-
Whalen, Philip 1923-
Wheatley, Phillis c.1753-1784
Wilbur, Richard 1921-
Williams, Sherley Anne 1944-
Williams, William Carlos 1883-1963
Winters, Yvor 1900-1968
Wordsworth, William 1770-1850
Wright, James 1927-1980
Yeats, William Butler 1865-1939
Yevtushenko, Yevgeny 1933-
Zukofsky, Louis 1904-1978

W. H. Auden

1907-1973

(Full name: Wystan Hugh Auden) English-born American poet, critic, essayist, dramatist, editor, translator, and librettist.

Auden is recognized as one of the preeminent poets of the twentieth century. His poetry centers on moral issues and evidences strong political, social, and psychological orientations. In his work, Auden applied conceptual and scientific knowledge to traditional verse forms and metrical patterns while assimilating the industrial countryside of his youth. He thereby created an allegorical landscape rife with machinery, abandoned mines, and technological references. Commentators agree that Auden's canon represents a quest for a systematic ideology in an increasingly complex world. This search is illuminated in its early stages by the teachings of Sigmund Freud and Karl Marx and later by philosopher Søren Kierkegaard and theologian Reinhold Niebuhr. Auden's poetry is versatile and inventive; ranging from terse, epigrammatic pieces to book-length verse, it incorporates the author's vast knowledge and displays his efforts to discipline his prodigious talent. Affirming Auden's influence on twentieth-century poetry, Seamus Heaney commented: "Auden was an epoch-making poet on public themes, the register of a new sensibility, a great sonneteer, a writer of perfect light verse, a prospector of literature at its most illiterate roots and a dandy of lexicography at its most extravagant reaches."

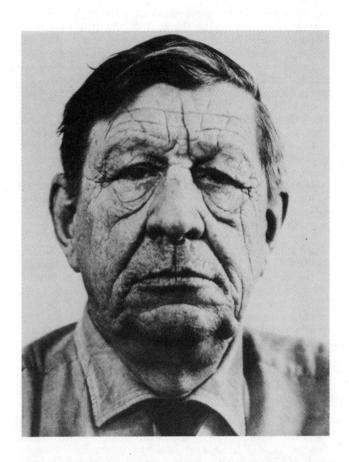

Auden was born and raised in heavily industrial northern England. His father, a prominent physician whose knowledge extended into the mythology and folklore of his Icelandic ancestry, and his mother, a strict Anglican, both exerted strong influences on Auden's poetry. Auden's early interest in science and engineering earned him a scholarship to Oxford University, where his fascination with poetry caused him to change his field of study to English. His attraction to science never waned, however, and scientific references are frequently found in his poetry. While at Oxford, Auden became familiar with modernist poetry, particularly that of T. S. Eliot, which was to influence his early writing. It was also at Oxford that Auden became the pivotal member of a group of writers that included Stephen Spender, C. Day Lewis, and Louis MacNeice, a collective variously labeled the "Oxford Group" or the "Auden Generation." These authors adhered to various communist and anti-fascist doctrines and expressed in their writings social, political, and economic concerns, all of which are evident in Auden's work of the 1930s.

In 1928, Auden's first book, *Poems,* was privately printed by Stephen Spender. During the same year, T. S. Eliot accepted Auden's verse play *Paid on Both Sides* for publication in his magazine *Criterion.* This play, along with many poems from the 1928 collection, appeared in an early revision of Auden's *Poems* that was published on Eliot's urging in 1930. Critics noted that these early poems display the influences of Thomas Hardy, Laura Riding, Wilfred Owen, and Edward Thomas and commended the collection for its ability, in M. D. Zabel's words, to "evoke a music wholly beyond reason, extraordinarily penetrating and creative in its search for significance behind fact." Stylistically, these poems are fragmentary and terse, relying on concrete images and colloquial language to convey Auden's political and psychological concerns. In his next volume, *The Orators: An English Study,* Auden implemented modernist and surrealist techniques to detail and satirize fascism and the stagnation of British life and institutions, although much of the work consists of private allusions, jokes, and references to his friends. Despite its abstruseness, *The Orators* was praised for its adventurous experimentation with literary styles and lively and original use of English verse and prose. During the next few years, the pieces Auden published in periodicals and anthologies evidenced a gradual change in his verse style. Many of these poems are collected in *Look, Stranger!* (published in the United States as *On This Island*), in which Auden's development of a highly disciplined style is expressed in the volume's dedication to Erika Mann: "Since the external disorder, and extravagant lies, / . . . What can truth treasure, or heart bless, / But a narrow strictness?" These poems are written in an intensely formal style that appears to eschew Romantic idealism and modernism and is seemingly intended to offset contemporary chaos. The change in Auden's approach prompted Gavin Ewart to comment:

"Mr. Auden's verse has undergone a considerable simplification and a more severe formal discipline, emerging both concise and emotive, in the political poems of very great powers and in the love poems . . . of very great sympathy and tenderness."

Auden's poems from the second half of the 1930s evidence his many travels during this period of political turmoil. "Spain," one of his most famous and widely anthologized pieces, is based upon his experiences in that country during the civil war. *Letters from Iceland,* a travel book written in collaboration with MacNeice, contains Auden's poem "Letter to Lord Byron." This long epistle to the author of *Don Juan* derives from that work the metaphor of the journey for artistic growth and displays Auden's mastery of ottava rima, a stanza of eight lines of heroic verse with a rhyme scheme of *abababcc. Journey to War,* a book about China written with Christopher Isherwood, features Auden's sonnet sequence and verse commentary "In Time of War." The first half of the sequence recounts the history of humanity's move away from rational thought, while the second half addresses the moral problems faced by humankind on the verge of another world war.

Auden left England in 1939 and became a citizen of the United States. His first book as an emigrant, *Another Time,* contains some of his best-known poems, among them "September 1, 1939," "Musée des Beaux Arts," and "Lay Your Sleeping Head, My Love." *Another Time* also contains elegies to A. E. Housman, Matthew Arnold, and William Butler Yeats, from whose careers and aesthetic concerns Auden was beginning to develop his own artistic credo. A famous line from "In Memory of W. B. Yeats"— "Poetry makes nothing happen"—presents Auden's complete rejection of romantic tenets. Auden's increasing concentration on ethical concerns in *Another Time* points to his reconversion to Christianity, which he had abandoned at age 15. His reconversion was influenced by his disillusionment with secular political solutions, his reading of the works of Kierkegaard, and his personal friendships with Niebuhr and theological writer Charles Williams. These concerns are central to *The Double Man* and *For the Time Being. The Double Man* contains "New Year Letter," a long epistolary poem outlining Auden's readings of Christian literature, while *For the Time Being* features two allegorical pieces that present in prose and verse the author's views on art and life. The title poem of *For the Time Being* is a rendering of the Nativity that utilizes technical language derived from modern science and psychology in order to rationalize Christian faith. Even more ambitious is *The Sea and the Mirror: A Commentary on Shakespeare's "Tempest,"* considered by many critics to be Auden's best extended poem. Taking characters from *The Tempest, The Sea and the Mirror* represents, according to Herbert Greenberg, "Auden's conception of the true function of art; both mimetic and paradigmatic, its purpose is not only to show us as we truly are but also, by its example of order, to suggest that we might be different and better."

Auden's next volume, *The Collected Poetry,* in which he revised, retitled, or excluded many of his earlier poems, helped solidify his reputation as a major poet. *The Age of Anxiety: A Baroque Eclogue,* winner of the Pulitzer Prize for poetry, features four characters of disparate backgrounds who meet in a New York City bar during World War II. Written in the heavily alliterative style of Old En-

glish literature, the poem explores the attempts of the protagonists to comprehend themselves and the world in which they live. The characters fail to attain selfrealization and succumb to their immediate desires rather than adhering to a spiritual faith. Auden's next major work, *Nones,* includes another widely anthologized piece, "In Praise of Limestone," and the first poems of the "Horae Canonicae" sequence. This sequence, and another entitled "Bucolics," are contained in *The Shield of Achilles,* for which Auden received the National Book Award. These works, though less overtly Christian in content, are serene meditations on human existence informed by the philosophy of Martin Heidegger, historical events of the Christian church, and elements of nature. *Homage to Clio,* in similar fashion, begins the sequence "Thanksgiving for a Habitat," which appeared in its entirety in *About the House* in 1965. In these poems, Auden expressed the conflict between the private and public spheres of an artist's life.

In his later years, Auden wrote three more major volumes—*City without Walls and Other Poems, Epistle to a Godson and Other Poems,* and the posthumously published *Thank You, Fog: Last Poems.* All three works are noted for their lexical range and humanitarian content. Auden's penchant for altering and discarding poems has prompted the publication of several anthologies since his death. The 1976 *Collected Poems* is faithful to Auden's last revisions, while *The English Auden: Poems, Essays, and Dramatic Writings, 1927-1939* includes the original versions of Auden's early writings as well as portions of his dramatic and critical pieces. Included in *The English Auden* is an uncompleted work, *The Prolific and the Devourer,* an epigrammatic piece written in the manner of Blaise Pascal and William Blake.

Auden's career has undergone much reevaluation through the years. While some critics contend that he wrote his finest work when his political sentiments were less obscured by religion and philosophy, others defend his later material as the work of a highly original and mature intellect. Many critics echo the assessment of Auden's career by the National Book Committee, which awarded him the National Medal for Literature in 1967: "[Auden's poetry] has illuminated our lives and times with grace, wit and vitality. His work, branded by the moral and ideological fires of our age, breathes with eloquence, perception and intellectual power."

(For further information on Auden's life and career, see *Contemporary Literary Criticism,* Vols. 1, 2, 3, 4, 6, 9, 11, 14, 43; *Contemporary Authors,* Vols. 9-12, rev. ed., Vols. 45-48 [obituary]; *Contemporary Authors New Revision Series,* Vol. 5; and *Dictionary of Literary Biography,* Vols. 10, 20.)

PRINCIPAL WORKS

POETRY

Poems 1928; revised editions, 1933, 1960, 1965
Paid on Both Sides: A Charade 1930; published in periodical *Criterion*
The Orators: An English Study 1932; revised edition, 1967

Look, Stranger! 1936; also published as *On This Island,*
    1937
Letters from Iceland [with Louis MacNeice] 1937; revised
    edition, 1969
Spain 1937
Selected Poems 1938
Journey to a War [with Christopher Isherwood] 1939; re-
    vised edition, 1973
Another Time 1940
Some Poems 1940
The Double Man 1941; also published as *New Year Let-
    ter,* 1941
Three Songs for St. Cecilia's Day 1941
For the Time Being 1944
The Collected Poetry of W. H. Auden 1945
The Age of Anxiety: A Baroque Eclogue 1947
Collected Shorter Poems, 1930-44 1950
Nones 1951
Mountains 1954
The Shield of Achilles 1955
The Old Man's Road 1956
A Gobble Poem 1957
Selected Poetry 1959; revised edition, 1971
Homage to Clio 1960
W. H. Auden: A Selection 1961
The Common Life 1964
About the House 1965
The Cave of the Making 1965
Half-Way 1965
The Platonic Blow 1965
Collected Shorter Poems, 1927-57 1966
Marginalia 1966
Portraits 1966
A Selection by the Author 1967
Collected Longer Poems 1968
Selected Poems 1968; revised edition, 1979
Two Songs 1968
City without Walls and Many Other Poems 1969
Academic Graffiti 1971
Epistle to a Godson and Other Poems 1972
Selected Poems [with Leif Sjoeberg] 1972
Thank You, Fog: Last Poems 1974
Collected Poems 1976
*The English Auden: Poems, Essays and Dramatic Writings,
    1927-1939* 1977

OTHER MAJOR WORKS

The Ascent of F6: A Tragedy in Two Acts (drama) 1931
The Dance of Death (drama) 1934
The Dog beneath the Skin; or, Where Is Francis? (drama)
    1936
The Oxford Book of Light Verse [editor] (anthology)
    1938
The Rocking-Horse Winner (radio play) 1941
The Enchafed Flood (essays and criticism) 1950
The Dyer's Hand, and Other Essays (criticism) 1962
Selected Essays (essays and criticism) 1964
A Certain World: A Commonplace Book (annotated per-
    sonal anthology) 1970
Forewords and Afterwords (essays and criticism) 1973

Malcolm Cowley (essay date 1934)

[*An American critic, editor, poet, translator, and historian, Cowley prepared critical editions of the works of Nathaniel Hawthorne, Walt Whitman, and Ernest Hemingway. He also contributed literary essays to the* New
Republic *and other periodicals. In the following excerpt,
he briefly examines the early poetry of Auden and Stephen Spender, noting particularly the "damnable and
perverse obscurity" of Auden's work.*]

There has been a great beating of drums and clashing of
cymbals to announce [Stephen Spender and W. H.
Auden]; perhaps there has been more noise than is justified by their work so far. . . . [Neither poet] has yet written a long poem that belongs with the English classics,
even with those of the second rank. But they have done
something else, something that seemed next door to the
impossible: they have brought life and vigor into contemporary English poetry.

They appeared in a dead season when all the serious young
men were trying to imitate T. S. Eliot and weren't quite
bringing it off. Eliot himself, after writing *The Waste
Land,* had entered a territory that was supposed to be watered with springs of spiritual grace, but most travelers
there found that the waters were subterranean and the soil
brittle with drought. Reading his new poems was like ex-
cavating buried cities at the edge of the Syrian desert; they
were full of imposing temples and perfectly proportioned
statues of the gods, but there was nothing in the streets
that breathed. Say this for Spender and Auden: they are
living in an actual London; they walk over Scotch moors
that are covered with genuine snow; they are not in the
British Museum pressed and dried between the pages of
a seventeenth-century book of sermons.

Still more important, they do not stand alone. They are
merely the vanguard of a group that includes Charles
Madge, John Lehmann, Cecil Day-Lewis (in some ways
the most promising of all), Richard Goodman, Julian Bell
and others. All of these poets are young, gifted in their
various fashions, and seem to know what they are doing.
All of them are able to write about political issues, not
dryly or abstractly, but in terms of human beings. Most
of them are radical without being proletarian. It is a matter of simple good sense that a proletarian poet ought to
begin by being proletarian, just as a Catholic poet ought
to be Catholic; otherwise he runs the risk of becoming as
empty and affected as the hangers-on of the Oxford Movement. These young men, graduates of the English universities, don't pose for the newsreel men in the role of mechanics, dressed in greasy overalls; but nevertheless their
sympathies are with the workers, and their sympathies
have sharpened their perception of what is going on in the
world around them. They are able to convey the sense of
violence and uncertainty that we gulp down with the
headlines of our morning papers, and of disaster waiting,
perhaps, outside our doors.

So far Auden and Spender are the only members of the
group whose work has appeared in this country (and incidentally their publisher deserves credit for giving them
two handsome volumes). In a curious way they remind me
of two recent American poets. Auden suggests E. E. Cummings: he has the same crazy wit, the same delight in playing with words and the same indifference to whether he

is being understood. Spender suggests Hart Crane, more by a quality of outpouring emotion than by any specific mannerism. Auden, with his sharper tongue and quicker eyes, has more to teach his fellow poets, but Spender, on second reading, is the one I prefer. (p. 189)

W. H. Auden is a battle poet. His boyhood was spent among rumors of war, troop movements, lists of officers dead on the field of honor; his career as a poet belongs to the gray depression years. In his poems he has made a synthesis of these two adventures. The results of unemployment are projected forward into another war, this time a war between social classes fought against a background of decaying industrialism. He gives us a sense of skirmishes in the yards of abandoned factories, of railroads dynamited, ports silted up, high-tension wires fallen to the ground, of spies creeping out at night or stumbling back to drop dead of their wounds (it is curious how often he mentions spies) and always a sense of mystery, of danger waiting at the corner of two streets:

> But careful; back to our lines; it is unsafe there,
> Passports are issued no longer; that area is closed.

Along with this goes a sanguinary sort of wartime humor that is best illustrated in his burlesque account of a revolution in England. On the second day of fighting, "A white-faced survivor informs the prison governor that the convicts, loosed, storming the execution shed, are calculating the drop formula by practical experiment, employing warders of various weights." On the third day, famine attacks the upper classes—"For those who desire an honorable release, typhoid lice, three in a box, price twopence, are peddled in the streets by starving corner boys." There are pages of Auden that have the irresponsible savagery of the Dada Manifesto.

His principal fault, I think, is his damnable and perverse obscurity. Partly this is the result of his verse technique, of his habit of overusing alliteration and thus emphasizing the sound of words at the expense of what they signify. Partly it is the result of literary tradition—the famous tradition of "opacity" that Eliot and Pound did so much to spread, and the plain-reader-be-damned tradition that was part of Dadaism and Superrealism. There are times when Auden deliberately befogs his meaning, and other times when he obviously doesn't mean anything at all; he is setting down his perceptions for their value in themselves and if they don't fit together into a unified picture, well, so much the worse for the reader. But there is another reason for his obscurity, a psychological reason having to do with his own position in that class war about which he is always writing. By birth and training Auden belongs with the exploiters. When he says "we," the people to whom he refers are the golf-playing, every-morning-bathing, tea-at-the-rector's-taking type of Britons. When he says "they," he is thinking of the workers; but he admires "them" and despises "us." He believes that his own class is decaying from within, is destined to be overthrown, and he looks forward to this event with happy anticipation:

> If we really want to live, we'd better start at once to try;
> If we don't, it doesn't matter, but we'd better start to die.

And that, I think, is the principal source of his ambiguity: he regards himself as a class traitor, a spy, a Copperhead. For this reason he is forced to speak in parables, to use code words like a conspirator in a Vienna cafe who wants to deliver a message but knows that the bulls are listening. He is on his guard, wary—till suddenly he gets tired of being cautious and blurts out a condemnation of everything he hates. I like him best when he is least self-protective.

What shall we say of both these poets? They have a good many obvious faults, their appeal is partly a snob appeal (and this is true of Auden in particular), but there is life in them always, and reading them is a stimulating experience. They are opening up a new territory. The best of them is the feeling that they will call forth other poets, not merely to follow in their footsteps, but perhaps to go beyond. (p. 190)

> *Malcolm Cowley, "Spender and Auden," in* The New Republic, *Vol. LXXX, No. 1034, September 26, 1934, pp. 189-90.*

Edith Sitwell   (essay date 1934)

[*An English poet, biographer, and critic, Sitwell evidenced a deep interest in the sound and rhythm of poetry. She wrote often on this subject and carried out daring experiments in her verse. She first received public attention in 1916 as the editor of* Wheels *(1916-21), a series of anthologies of contemporary poetry that offered readers an alternative to the sentimental work of certain popular poets of the era. Her own works, which are colored with idiosyncratic imagery and highly personal allusions, reflect her belief that meaning is of secondary concern in poetry—second to sound and rhythm. Throughout her career, Sitwell used her influence to draw attention to younger writers, including Wilfred Owen, Dylan Thomas, and Allen Ginsburg. In the following excerpt from her* Aspects of Modern Poetry, *she offers a mixed review of Auden's poetic canon.*]

Mr. Auden has an able mind, but, unhappily, he writes uninteresting poetry, or, at least, his poetry nearly always lacks interest. When therefore, we are told by an admiring reviewer that, since the publication of his first volume, [*Poems*], two or three years ago, "it has been generally recognized that he is one of the four or five living poets worth quarrelling about"—and that "Here is something as important as the appearance of Mr. Eliot's poems fifteen years ago"—I can only reply that this is sheer nonsense. Mr. Eliot's poems, from the very beginning, showed signs of that genius which fires and ennobles his work—had always, too, an integral being, an intense visual and tactile sense, had depth, wisdom and passion.

The meaning of Mr. Auden's poems is frequently so obscure that it defies detection, and, it is this obscurity, I imagine, which has frightened certain timid critics into this excessive admiration. He is unfortunate, inasmuch as a great deal of nonsense is talked about his work, and that his most fervent admirers contradict each other about his aims. A usually intelligent reviewer, for instance, explained to us that *The Orators* "is quite definitely not a book to be apprehended intellectually. . . . Read as passively as possible, just a body sensitized to words, without letting intellect interfere. . . . Don't bother to think at first, just listen. Then it will all begin to stand out like the red Cliffs of Parnassos. . . . " Another critic, however, announces that "here is thought stripped to its essentials."

My own impression is that Mr. Auden has a real capacity for feeling, and considerable rhythmical sense, but that he is too apt to be carried away by the necessities of pattern-making, and that these patterns are superimposed on the material; they are, as well, oral alone, and have nothing to do with the visual sense.

Mr. Auden's greatest danger, in his longer poems, is that he is led towards disintegration, not cohesion, of matter and of manner. A certain critic said of him that "We must wonder if Book II, the **'Journal of an Airman,'** is perhaps a kind of life of [T. E.] Lawrence, reduced to elements and then built up again." I find that whereas Mr. Auden frequently reduces his subject to fragments, he does not always reduce them to elements (the latter being at times a valuable process). Still less often does he rebuild the fragments. Mr. Auden does not organize his experience. It must be said, too, that his material is too often of a purely temporary interest, has no universal significance. And in this failure to sift, and then reorganize the experience, lies one of the major dangers of the poetry of our time. It is especially Mr. Auden's danger. In the power of assimilating details into a whole, in the visual and the tactile sense, Mr. Auden is, at the moment, almost entirely lacking. *The Orators,* for instance, is not an organic whole. It may be claimed that it represents the disintegration of the world in its present state, but it shows merely lack of fusion, looseness of interest, "the belief," to quote Mr. John Sparrow, "that experience hitherto taken to be the raw material of art, should be accepted as its finished product."

Here then, in Mr. Auden, we have the raw material of art; and sometimes, but very rarely, the finished product.

What interest, for instance, can this passage, which occurs [in] *The Orators,* arouse in the mind of the reader:

> I'm afraid it sounds more like a fairy story
> There was a family called Do;
> There were Do-a, Do-ee, and other Do-s
> And Uncle Dick and Uncle Wiz had come to stay with
>   them
> (Nobody slept that night.)
> Now Do-a loved to bathe before his breakfast
> With Uncle Dick, but Uncle Wiz . . .
> Well?
> As a matter of fact the farm was in Pembrokeshire,
> The week the Labour Cabinet resigned.
> Dick had returned from Germany in love.
> I hate cold water and am very fond of potatoes.
> You're wondering about these scratches?

I am not! I am wondering at the simple credulity of the critics and the public in allowing themselves to be gulled by such unattractive nonsense. We can see, in the following lines, how much the absence of the visual sense, and the tactual sense, affects, to its detriment, Mr. Auden's poetry. This poem (I cannot quote it in its entirety) is admirably formed, as far as structure goes; the last (unquoted) verse brings it to a perfect whole as far as thought and movement and climax are concerned, but the absence of the visual and tactual senses, of any delight in physical beauty, renders the poem tasteless in the sense in which food cooked without salt is tasteless.

> From the very first coming down
> Into a new valley with a frown
> Because of the sun and a lost way,
> You certainly remain: to-day

> I, crouching behind a sheep-pen, heard
> Travel across a sudden bird,
> Cry out against the storm, and found
> The year's arc a completed round
> And love's worn circuit re-begun,
> Endless with no dissenting turn.
> Shall see, shall pass, as we have seen
> The swallow on the tile, spring's green
> Preliminary shiver, passed
> A solitary truck, the last
> Of shunting in the Autumn, But now
> To interrupt the homely brow,
> Thought warmed to evening through and through
> Your letter comes, speaking as you,
> Speaking of much but not to come.

Here indeed is a blind world, a world in which the objects would not taste if we put them to our mouths, or smell if we held them to our noses. Is this a poetry of pure thought? If so, can it be claimed that the thought is of any value in this case?

In spite of these great disadvantages, however, Mr. Auden's poems do, at moments, express a very real and poignant emotion, and the body he chooses for his expression is on these occasions adequate and moving. Take, for instance, this passage from *Paid on Both Sides*:

> Always the following wind of history
> Of others' wisdom makes a buoyant air
> Till we come suddenly on pockets where
> Is nothing loud but us; where voices seem
> Abrupt, untrained, competing with no lie
> Our fathers shouted once. They taught us war,
> To scamper after darlings, to climb hills
> To emigrate from weakness, find ourselves
> The easy conquerors of empty bays:
> But never told us this, left each to learn,
> Hear something of that soon-arriving day
> When to gaze longer and delighted on
> A face or idea be impossible.
> Could I have been some simpleton that lived
> Before disaster sent his runners here;
> Younger than worms, worms have too much to bear.
> Yes, mineral were best: could I but see
> These woods, these fields of green, this lively world
> Sterile as moon.

This fragment, until the tragic expressiveness of the last six lines, has a phrasing, a texture, a diction, which are deliberately threadbare and flat to suit this wearied and hopeless dirge for an outworn world. We can compare this purposeful threadbareness and flatness, so suitable to the theme and to the emotion expressed, with the unsuitable flat threadbare texture of "The Shropshire Lad," where the theme is usually eager and believing youth brought to disaster by circumstances, and with the knowledge that death lies at the end of the road, yet keeping his soul undimmed and unstained. (pp. 238-43)

> *Edith Sitwell, "Envoi," in her* Aspects of Modern Poetry, *1934. Reprint by Books for Libraries Press, 1970, pp. 227-264.*

Stephen Spender (essay date 1937)

[*Spender rose to prominence during the 1930s as a Marxist lyric poet and was a close associate of Auden, Christopher Isherwood, C. Day Lewis, and Louis MacNeice. Like many other artists and intellectuals of his day, he became disillusioned with communism after World War II. His later work is concerned chiefly with aspects of self-knowledge. Spender evidenced a deep and abiding concern with poetic and artistic theory. He argued that art contains "a real conflict of life, a real breaking up and melting down of intractable material, feelings and sensations which seem incapable of expression until they have been thus transformed. A work of art doesn't say 'I am life, I offer you the opportunity of becoming me.' On the contrary, it says: 'This is what life is like. It is even realer, less to be evaded, than you thought. But I offer you an example of acceptance and understanding. Now, go back and live!'" In the following excerpt from an essay first published in* New Verse *in 1937, Spender discusses the political side of Auden's poetry.*]

When I was at Oxford, I did not understand Auden's poems, yet they gripped my imagination, and, although I have a very bad memory for poetry, I found myself involuntarily remembering lines and phrases of his. It was something analytical, objective, self-consciously clinical, deliberately impersonal which fascinated me. In those days, his fantasies of the necessary impersonality of poets led him at once to a distrust of politics and to extravagance. I remember him once saying that "the poet" would "enjoy," in a civil war, lying on a roof and shooting at his best friend, who was on the other side. I was always interested in politics, but his interests were poetry, psychoanalysis and medicine. I think he disapproved of my politics, just as, at that time, he disapproved of my writing prose or going to concerts to hear classical music.

Auden "arrived at" politics, by way of psychology. His early poems begin by being preoccupied with neurosis in individuals, but this gradually extends (at the time when he had left Oxford and gone to live in Berlin) to an interest in the epoch and capitalist society. At first though this interest was clinical; he was content to state what he beautifully and profoundly saw without implying an attitude or a remedy.

Yet the strength of socialism or communism and its appeal to the poet lies in the fact that the mere statement of social realities today, if it goes far enough, both suggests a remedy and involves one in taking sides. For example, in postwar and pre-Hitler Berlin, one began by noticing symptoms of decadence, suffering and unemployment; one looked further and one saw beneath the decay of the liberal state, the virulent reaction of the Nazis and the struggle for a new life of the Communists. The one side stood for the suppression of the very objectivity which the poet required, perhaps also his life, certainly his intellectual standards; the other, however painful and disillusioning its birth pangs, promised finally a world in which one could see and tell the truth.

From the point of view of the working-class movement the ultimate criticism of Auden and the poets associated with him is that we haven't deliberately and consciously transferred ourselves to the working class. The subject of his poetry is the struggle, but the struggle seen, as it were, by someone who whilst living in one camp, sympathises with the other; a struggle in fact which while existing externally is also taking place within the mind of the poet himself, who remains a bourgeois. This argument is put very forcibly by Christopher Caudwell in the last chapter of his book *Illusion and Reality.* Whilst accepting its validity as a critical attitude, may we not say that the position of the writer who sees the conflict as something which is at once subjective to himself and having its external reality in the world—the position outlined in Auden's Spain—is one of the most creative, realistic and valid positions for the artist in our time? (pp. 9-10)

Stephen Spender, "Oxford to Communism," in New Verse, *Nos. 26-27, November, 1937, pp. 9-10.*

Edmund Wilson   (essay date 1937)

[*Considered one of America's foremost literary critics in the twentieth century, Wilson wrote widely on cultural, historical, and literary concerns. He is often credited with bringing an international perspective to American letters through his discussion of European literature. Wilson examined the social and historical implications of a literary work, particularly literature's significance as "an attempt to give meaning to our experience" and its value "for the improvement of humanity." In the following excerpt, originally published in the* New Republic *in 1937, Wilson reviews Auden's* On This Island.]

Mr. Auden himself has presented the curious case of a poet who writes an original poetic language in the most robust English tradition, but who seems to have been arrested at the mentality of an adolescent schoolboy. His technique has seemed to mature, but he has otherwise not grown up. His mind has always been haunted, as the minds of boys at prep school still are, by parents and uncles and aunts. His love poems seem unreal and ambiguous as if they were the products of adolescent flirtations and prep-school homosexuality. His talk about "the enemy" and "their side" and "our side" and "spying" and "lying in ambush" sounds less like anything connected with the psychology of an underground revolutionary movement than like the dissimulated resentments and snootiness of the schoolboy with advanced ideas going back to his family for the holidays. When this brilliant and engaging young student first came out for the class struggle so strongly, it seemed an audacious step; but then he simply remained under the roof of his nice family and in the classroom with his stuffy professors; and the seizure of power he dreams of is an insurrection in the schoolroom: "I should like to see you make a beginning before I go, now, here. Draw up a list of rotters and slackers, of proscribed persons under headings like this. Committees for municipal or racial improvement—the headmaster. Disbelievers in the occult—the school chaplain. The bogusly cheerful—the games master—the really disgusted—the teacher of modern languages. All these have got to die without issue. Unless my memory fails me there's a stoke hole under the floor of this hall. The Black Hole we called it in my day. New boys were always put in it. Ah, I see I am right. Well look to it. Quick, guard that door. Stop that man. Good. Now boys hustle them, ready, steady—go."

With all this—and at times out of all proportion to the interest of what he has had to say—Mr. Auden's imagery and language have been remarkable for an energy, a felicity, a richness, a resource, a nerve, which have made him a conspicuous figure. He certainly has more of what it

Auden during his schooldays.

in that earlier work the great idiom of English poetry at its most vigorous, its liveliest and freest, telescoping the whole tradition, from the emphatic alliteration of Anglo-Saxon through the variety and ease of the Elizabethans to the irony and bizarre imagination of the generation just before his own. But in **On This Island** it seems to me that the rhythms of the lyrical and reflective poems let one down by approximating too closely to the deliberate loose-ness of the satirical ones; and the off-rhymes begin to get on one's nerves. (Near-rhymes and negligent rhythms are, I suppose, a symptom of blurred emotions. There are mo-ments when Louis MacNeice sounds like a serious Ogden Nash.)

It has come to be a depressing feature of the literary scene at the present time—noticeable also in this country—that writers who had hitherto seemed able to stand on their own feet have begun flopping over on one another and imi-tating one another's idiom—without there necessarily being any question of the normal attraction of the weaker toward the stronger. Thus Auden, whose voice we have known and liked, disconcerts us by suddenly falling into the accents of Housman or Yeats or the palest of the later Eliot. Thus Louis MacNeice, who seems to me perhaps (except Auden himself) the most gifted of the Auden group, the master of a lyric impressionism that differs from the work of the rest, appears, in a recent number of the English magazine *New Verse,* to have toppled over on Auden and to have become almost indistinguishable from him. (pp. 669-72)

> *Edmund Wilson, "The Oxford Boys Be-calmed," in his* The Shores of Light: A Liter-ary Chronicle of the Twenties and Thirties, *Farrar, Straus and Giroux, 1952, pp. 669-73.*

takes to become a first-class poet than anybody else of his generation in England or, so far as I can think, in the Unit-ed States. And in one department Mr. Auden is entirely and brilliantly successful: he has invented a new satire for the times. The most satisfactory part of his work seems to me that which includes such skits as *The Dance of Death,* with its cheap and weary rhythms; the satiric-elegiac cho-ruses of *The Dog Beneath the Skin;* and such poems as the one, in [*On This Island*], in which he describes the Cam-bridge intellectuals,

> Who show the poor by mathematics
> In their defense
> That wealth and poverty are merely
> Mental pictures, so that clearly
> Every tramp's a landlord really
> In mind-events.

He is especially good at calling the roll of the lonely, the neurotic, the futile—of all the queer kinds of individuals who make up the English upper classes. No one else has given us just this sense, at once pathetic and insipid, of the slakening of the social organism and the falling apart of its cells.

But, once having taken their stand, once having put them-selves on record, we get the impression that Mr. Auden and his associates are at a loss as to what to do next. In some ways they appear to be retrograding. Thus the idiom of Auden in this latest book seems to me to be actually less personal than it was in his earlier poetry. He had revived

David Daiches (essay date 1939)

[*Daiches is a prominent English scholar and critic who has written extensively on English and American litera-ture. He is especially known for his in-depth studies of such writers as Robert Burns, Robert Louis Stevenson, and Virginia Woolf. His criticism is best characterized as appreciative; it is attached to no single methodology. Summarizing his conception of the critic's role, Daiches wrote in 1950: "Literature exists to be read and enjoyed, and criticism, at least in its pedagogical aspect, exists in order to increase awareness and so to increase enjoy-ment." In the following excerpt, Daiches documents what he labels Auden's "search for a public" for his poet-ry.*]

To whom could a poet like Auden appeal? With a new technique and a new attitude going hand in hand, symbols would have to be determined by the poet's point of view and would therefore be unintelligible—poetically unintel-ligible as well as intellectually puzzling—to those who were unable to see the force of those symbols. "Comrade" has a cheering sound to those who agree that we ought to get together and do something to improve social condi-tions, but to those who do not share this view it is a dis-tasteful word, suggesting Marxist dogma at its most vio-lent. When Auden says

> Make me some fresh tea, fetch me some rugs,

we understand this as a symbol of social futility only if we share Auden's assumptions about the nature of contemporary society. The problem of "what attitude?" and the problem of "which audience?" are very closely related.

It is therefore natural that we should find in Auden's 1930 volume [*Poems*] a certain confusion on both these points. His symbolism wavers: sometimes he is addressing a group of his personal friends and using symbols intelligible to them alone, and at other times he is addressing an indeterminate audience using symbols some of which are broadly enough based to have a fairly wide appeal but others of which are carried over from the first group and are therefore only confusing. The attitude of the poems wavers similarly. The comparative obscurity of the charade *Paid on Both Sides* arises from the fact that Auden himself had not yet thought through the ideas he intended it to express. Poem after poem indicates that the author is searching for his own standpoint:

> Here am I, here are you:
> But what does it mean? What are we going to do?

The dissatisfaction with the present condition of society is indicated clearly and consistently, but there are only vague and conflicting hints as to what is to be done about it. And whom is he addressing? Who is it that has to take this action? It is "we" and not "they", "they" being modern decadents and hypochondriacs, and "we" being—who? The very structure of the poems, such as the one beginning "Since you are going to begin today" with the swift transition from point to point of one who is searching for his own standpoint, indicates this uncertainty. As we read through the volume a few prevailing ideas emerge. "Death of the old gang" is a necessity (but "the old gang" is a highly ambiguous symbol), invalids and decadents, who are all regarded as shamming (which conflicts with his view that society is really diseased), must be pulled out of their bathchairs, and all kinds of psychological maladjustment must be rectified. On the whole, these poems give the impression of a man of genuine poetic gifts and possessing to a quite uncanny extent the power to do new things with words, who is not quite sure what he wants to say, and who is even less decided about whom he wants to speak to. The latter problem, we feel, is the more urgent: once he finds his audience—either a real or an ideal audience; it does not matter which, for the problem is simply to give consistency to his symbolism and coherence to his attitude—he will be able to speak more clearly.

With *The Orators* in 1932 we have the next stage. Here we see Auden's dilemma more clearly still. The obscurity in this book is the obscurity of a poet who does not want to be obscure but cannot help himself: he is halfway between the private coterie and the public group in his search for an audience, and thus both his attitude and his symbols will be Janus-faced, facing two ways. The three line dedication to Stephen Spender is illuminating:

> Private faces in public places
> Are wiser and nicer
> Than public faces in private places.

He would rather write for a larger group in terms intelligible only to a smaller group, so that members of the smaller group will have the pleasant surprise of recognizing "private faces in public places", than employ the reverse method and run the risk of leveling his friends to the common state of apprehension of ordinary folk. That he should formulate his problem in terms of this alternative is significant.

In *The Orators* we see a destructive and a constructive purpose wrestling for supremacy. Sometimes Auden takes the line of least resistance and states the situation as a simple conflict between schoolboys and their teachers, or as a vague struggle between disease and health, the latter never being clearly defined. At other times he seeks to seize on more concrete aspects of the conflict. But always his myth-making—and Auden's mythopoeic faculty is, in its way, as strong as Shelley's—is obscured by his doubts concerning the public for whom he is constructing his myths. We see some progress, however, towards the crystallizing of attitude and audience. In the Public School imagery of the **"Address for a Prize-day"** we see the first step forwards in his decision to fight the Public School Spirit with its own weapons. (Considering how many typical qualities of the English Public School product Auden has retained we can see something almost masochistic in this decision.) It is in the **"Address"** too, that we see formulated the theme of the whole book: "What do you think about England, this country of ours where nobody is well?" The "you" here are schoolboys: Auden is addressing the educated youth of his country. But the identity of the speaker is not yet fixed. The movement towards identifying his public with some kind of idealized conception of the schoolboy is illustrated not only by the predominant imagery of *The Orators* (imagery from school life, school sports, and O. T. C. activity) but also by the dedication of the second of the *Six Odes* to "Gabriel Carritt, Captain of Sedbergh School XV", of the fifth of the odes to his pupils, of the fourth to the young son of Rex Warner, and by the suggestion that salvation is to come from the young:

> John, son of Warner, shall rescue you.

There is a new simplicity of diction and symbolism in *The Dance of Death* (1933). In his journey from the coterie to a larger public Auden has now gone far enough to be less disturbed by the risk of "public faces in private places". But there is still uncertainty about the audience addressed. The allegory, a simple and obvious one in itself, is complicated in parts by a use of ambivalent imagery which is the last thing one wants in a simple dramatic allegory. Auden may try to disguise this hesitancy as irony, but irony has no place in a straightforward socio-political parable, and its employment here is suspicious. It is all very well for Karl Marx to be deflated into a joke at the conclusion of the play, but for a poet who is about to deliver a message to suddenly lose confidence and indulge in horse-play instead indicates a confusion of purpose that does not conduce to poetic effectiveness. Auden as a personality shows this same combination of prophet and clown which is a natural refuge for a man in doubt about his audience: this quality in him seems to be a permanent legacy of his period of sojourn between two stools.

In 1936 Auden published *Look, Stranger!* (in America, entitled *On This Island*) and here we find the conflict to a large degree solved. The simple and highly effective strain of description and meditation which runs through these poems, the subtle clarity and plastic handling of language which he displays, seem to indicate that at last he has found a public, that he knows to whom he is speaking. As a result both his attitude and his expression of attitude has been clarified. His public, like the public envisaged by most poets, is an ideal one, yet sufficiently grounded in reality to provide him with a consistent and impressive symbolism and a new strength of purpose. It might be called simply the ideal schoolboy. He is addressing those who will make the future, the alert youngster who observes his environment and is dissatisfied and requires more information about the present and direction for the future if he is to be able to do anything effective about it. Auden is demonstrating and illustrating and warning. There is the past, history and tradition, "our fathers"; there is the present, to be diagnosed; there is the future, to be built. All three are discussed as though to one who will have to do the re-building. This does not mean that all the poems are actually addressed to schoolboys, or even worded for that kind of an audience; it means simply that by envisaging that kind of audience he has been able to clarify both his own attitude and his use of symbols, and having attained that new clarification he can write to whom he wishes. Words like "we" and "they" acquire both intellectual and emotive meanings. The whole texture of the poetry is tightened as well as clarified as a result of Auden's having translated this vague feeling of being involved in transition into concrete terms: the poet fixing his attitude by addressing his younger contemporaries in the light of what the past was and what the future must be made to be. If he turns to address one of his own generation, such as Christopher Isherwood, he still carries with him the confidence he won in fixing his own attitude and ideal audience. We can see now how *The Orators* served as a training ground. Even when addressing the "Lords of limit", it is for his pupils' sake:

> Oldest of masters, whom the schoolboy fears
> Failing to find his pen, to keep back tears . . .

> At the end of my corridor are boys who dream
> Of a new bicycle or winning team;
> On their behalf guard all the more
> This late-maturing Northern shore,
> Who to their serious season must shortly come.

That he is no longer between two stools, but living in a clearly apprehended moment in history, he makes clear in his poem to Isherwood:

> This then my birthday wish for you, as now
> From the narrow window of my fourth floor room
> I smoke into the night, and watch reflections
> Stretch in the harbour. In the houses
> The little pianos are closed, and a clock strikes.
> And all sway forward on the dangerous flood
> Of history, that never sleeps or dies,
> And, held one moment, burns the hand.

Though this is to a friend, there is no private symbolism here, no fear of "public faces in private places". Auden the schoolmaster has his pupils to thank for his solution of this problem. *Letters from Iceland,* essentially a *jeu d'esprit,* and put together in rather exceptional circumstances, lies perhaps outside the present argument. (pp. 149-56)

David Daiches, "W. H. Auden: The Search for a Public," in Poetry, *Vol. LIV, No. 3, June, 1939, pp. 148-56.*

Randall Jarrell   (essay date 1941)

[Jarrell was an acclaimed American literary critic and poet. He was, according to Robert Lowell, "almost brutally serious about literature." He is perhaps best known for his war poems and his often acerbic reviews of the literary works of his contemporaries. In the following excerpt, he analyzes the "general position" Auden made for himself in his early poems and compares it with the attitude evident in his later poems.]

The date is *c.* 1930, the place England. Auden (and the group of friends with whom he identifies himself) is unable or unwilling to accept the values and authority, the general world-picture of the late-capitalist society in which he finds himself. He is conscious of a profound alienation, intellectual, moral, and aesthetic—financial and sexual, even. Since he rejects the established order, it is necessary for him to find or make a new order, a myth by which he and his can possess the world. Auden synthesizes (more or less as the digestive organs synthesize enzymes) his own order from a number of sources: I. Marx—communism in general. 2. Freud and Groddeck: in general, the risky and non-scientific, but fertile and imaginative, side of modern psychology. 3. A cluster of related sources: the folk, the blood, intuition, religion and mysticism, fairy tales, parables, and so forth—this group includes a number of semi-Fascist elements. 4. The sciences, biology particularly: these seem to be available to him because they have been only partially assimilated by capitalist culture, and because, like mathematics, they are practically incapable of being corrupted by it. 5. All sorts of boyish sources of value: flying, polar exploration, mountain-climbing, fighting, the thrilling side of science, public-school life, sports, big-scale practical jokes, "the spies' career," etc. 6. Homosexuality: if the ordinary sexual values are taken as negative and rejected, this can be accepted as a source of positive revolutionary values.

Auden is able to set up a We (whom he identifies himself with—rejection loves company) in opposition to the enemy They; neither We nor They are the relatively distinct or simple entities one finds in political or economic analyses, but are tremendous clusters of elements derived from almost every source: Auden is interested in establishing a dichotomy in which one side, naturally, gets all the worst of it, and he wants this *all the worst* to be as complete as possible, to cover everything from imperialism to underlining too many words in letters. A reader may be indifferent to some or most of Their bad points, but They are given so many that even the most confirmed ostrich will at some point break down and consent to Auden's rejection. Auden wants a total war, a total victory; he does not make the political mistake of taking over a clear limited position and leaving to the enemy everything else. Sometimes his aptitude for giving all he likes to Us, all he doesn't like to Them, passes over from ingenuity into positive genius—or disingenuousness. I am going to treat this We-They opposition at the greatest length—a treatment of it is practically a treatment of Auden's early position; and I shall mix in some discussion of the sources of value I have listed.

Auden begins: The death of the old order is inevitable; it is already economically unsound, morally corrupt, intellectually bankrupt, and so forth. We—the Future, They—the Past. (So any reader tends to string along with Us and that perpetual winner, the Future.) Auden gets this from Marxism, of course; but never at any time was he a thorough Marxist: it would have meant giving up too much to the enemy. He keeps all sorts of things a Marxist rejects, and some of his most cherished doctrines—as the reader will see—are in direct contradiction to his Marxism. At the ultimate compulsive level of belief most of his Marxism drops away (and, in the last few years, *has* dropped away); his psychoanalytical, vaguely medical beliefs are so much more essential to Auden—"son of a nurse and doctor, loaned a dream"—that the fables he may have wanted to make Marxist always turn out to be psychoanalytical. But Marxism as a source of energy, of active and tragic insight, was invaluable; it was badly needed to counteract the passivity, the trust in Understanding and Love and God, that are endemic in Auden. Marxism has always supplied most of the terror in his poetry; in his latest poems all that remains is the pity—an invalid's diet, like milk-toast.

Obviously They represent Business, Industrialism, Exploitation—and, worse than that, a failing business, an industrialism whose machines are already rusting. Auden had seen what happened to England during a long depression, and he made a romantic and beautifully effective extension of this, not merely into decadence, but into an actual breakdown of the whole machinery, a Wellsish state where commerce and transportation have gone to pieces, where the ships lie "long high and dry," where no one goes "further than railhead or the end of pier," where the professional traveler "asked at fireside . . . is dumb." The finest of these [is **"Poem XXV"**] in *Poems:* history before the event, one's susceptible and extravagant heart tells one. (Incidentally, this vision is entirely nonMarxist.) Here Auden finds a symbol whose variants are obsessive for him, reasonably so for the reader, another machine's child: *grass-grown pitbank, abandoned seam, the silted harbors, derelict works*—these, and the wires that carry nothing, the rails over which no one comes, are completely moving to Auden, a boy who wanted to be a mining engineer, who "Loved a pumping-engine, / Thought it every bit as / Beautiful as you." The thought of those "beautiful machines that never talked / But let the small boy worship them," abandoned and rusting in the wet countryside—the early Auden sees even his machines in rural surroundings—was perhaps, unconsciously, quite as influential as some political or humanitarian considerations.

Auden relates science to Marxism in an unexpected but perfectly orthodox way: Lenin says somewhere that in the most general sense Marxism is a theory of evolution. Auden quite consciously makes this connection; evolution, as a source both of insight and image, is always just at the back of his earliest poems. (This, along with his countryishness—Auden began by writing poetry like Hardy and Thomas—explains his endless procession of birds and beasts, symbols hardly an early poem is without.) [**"Poem IV"** in the same collection] is nothing but an account of evolution—by some neo-Hardyish *I* behind it—and a rather Marxist extension of it into man's history and everyday life. The critical points where quantity changes into quality, the Hegelian dialectic, what Burke calls neo-Malthusian limits—all these are plain in the poem. There are many examples of this coalition of Marxism and biology; probably the prettiest is [**"Poem IX"**] a poem with the refrain, "Here am I, here are you: / But

what does it mean? What are we going to do?" The *I* of the poem is supposed to be anonymous and typical, a lay-figure of late capitalism; he has not retained even the dignity of rhetoric, but speaks in a style that is an odd blank parody of popular songs. He has finally arrived at the end of his blind alley: he has a wife, a car, a mother-complex, a vacation, and no use or desire for any. All he can make himself ask for is some fresh tea, some rugs—this to remind you of Auden's favorite view of capitalism: a society where everyone is sick. Even his instincts have broken down: he doesn't want to go to bed with Honey, all the wires to the base in his spine are severed. The poem develops in this way up to the next to the last stanza: "In my veins there is a wish, / And a memory of fish: / When I lie crying on the floor, / It says, 'You've often done this before.' " The "wish" in the blood is the evolutionary will, the blind urge of the species to assimilate the universe. He remembers the fish, that at a similar impasse, a similar critical point, changed over to land, a new form of being. Here for the millionth time (the racial memory tells the weeping individual) is the place where the contradiction has to be resolved; where the old answer, useless now, has to be transcended; where all the quantitative changes are over, where the qualitative leap has to occur. The individual remembers all these critical points because he is the product of them. And the individual, in the last stanza, is given a complete doom. . . . But his bankruptcy and liquidation are taken as inevitable for the species, a necessary mode of progression; the destructive interregnum between the old form and the new is inescapable, as old as life. The strategic value in Auden's joining of Marxism and evolution, his constant shifting of terms from one sphere to the other, is this: the reader will tend to accept the desired political and economic changes (and the form of these) as themselves inevitable, something it is as ludicrous or pathetic to resist as evolution.

When compared with the folkish Us, They are complicated, subtle in a barren Alexandrian-encylopedia way. They are scholarly introspective observers, We have the insight and natural certainty of the naive, of Christ's children, of fools, of the third sons in fairy stories. They are aridly commercial, financial, distributive; We represent real production, the soil. They are bourgeois-respectable or perverted; We are folk-simple, or else consciously Bohemian so as to break up Their system and morale—there is also a suggestion of the prodigal son, of being reborn through sin. They represent the sterile city, We the fertile country; I want to emphasize this, the surprisingly *rural* character of most of Auden's earliest poems, because so far as I know everyone has emphasized the opposite. They are white-collar workers, executives, or idlers—those who neither "make" nor "do"; We are scientists, explorers, farmers, manual laborers, aviators, fighters and conspirators—the real makers and doers. Auden gets Science over on Our side by his constant use of it both for insight and images, by his admiration of, preoccupation with the fertile adventurous side of it; he leaves Them only the decadent complexity of Jeans or "psychological" economics.

Since Auden has had to reject Tradition, he sets up a new tradition formed of the available elements (available because rejected, neglected, or misinterpreted) of the old. There are hundreds of examples of this process (particularly when it comes to appropriating old writers as Our ancestors); the process is necessary partly to reassure oneself, partly to reassure one's readers, who otherwise would have to reject Our position because accepting it necessitated rejecting too much else. One can see this working even in the form of Auden's early poetry: in all the Anglo-Saxon imitation; the Skeltonics; the Hopkins accentual verse, alliteration, assonance, consonance; the Owens rhymes; the use of the fairy story, parable, ballad, popular song—the folk tradition They have rejected or collected in Childs. Thus Auden has selected his own ancestors, made from the disliked or misprized his own tradition.

In *The Orators* Auden shows, by means of the regular Mendelian inheritance chart, that one's "true ancestor" may be neither a father nor a mother, but an uncle. (His true ancestor wasn't the Tradition, but the particular elements of it most like himself.) This concept is extremely useful to Auden in (1) family, (2) religious, and (3) political relations. (1) By this means he acquires a different and active type of family relationship to set up against the inertia of the ordinary bourgeois womanized family. (2) God is addressed and thought of as Uncle instead of Father: God as Uncle will help revolutionary Us just as naturally and appropriately as God as Father would help his legitimate sons, the Enemy. This Uncle has a Christ-like sacrificial-hero representative on earth, who is surrounded with a great deal of early-Christian, secret-service paraphernalia. This hero is confused or identified with (3) the political leader, a notably unpolitical sort of fantasy-Hitler, who seems to have strayed into politics with his worshipers only because he lives in an unreligious age. There is hardly more politics in early Auden than in G. A. Henty; what one gets is mostly religion, hero-worship, and Adventure, combined with the odd Lawrence-Nazi folk-mysticism that serves as a false front for the real politics behind it—which Auden doesn't treat.

When Auden occasionally prays to this Uncle he asks in blunt definite language for definite things: it is a personal, concrete affair. In his later poetry Auden is always praying or exhorting, but only to some abstract eclectic Something-Or-Other, who is asked in vague exalted language for vague exalted abstractions. Once Auden wanted evils removed by revolutionary action, and he warned (*it is later than you think*). Today—when he is all ends and no means, and sees everything in the long run—he exhorts (*we all know how late it is, but with Love and Understanding it is not too late for us to . . .*) or prays (*Thou knowest—O save us!*). Most of this belongs to the bad half of what Burke calls secular prayer: the attempt, inside any system, to pray away, exhort away, legislate away evils that are not incidental but essential to the system. Auden used to satirize the whole "change of heart" point of view; "do not speak of a change of heart," he warned. He had a deceived chorus sing vacantly: "Revolutionary worker / I get what you mean. / But what you're needing / 'S a revolution within." He came to scoff, he remained to pray: for a general moral improvement, a spiritual rebirth, Love. Remembering some of the incredible conclusions to the later poems—*Life must live,* Auden's wish to *lift an affirming flame*—the reader may object that this sort of thing is sentimental idealism. But sentimental idealism is a necessity for someone who, after rejecting a system as evil, finally accepts it—even with all the moral reservations and exhortations possible. The sentimentality and idealism, the vague abstraction of such prayers and exhortations, is a *sine qua non:* we can fool ourselves into pray-

ing for some vague general change of heart that is going to produce, automatically, all the specific changes that even we could never be foolish enough to pray for. When Auden prays for anything specific at all; when he prays against the organization of the world that makes impossible the moral and spiritual changes he prays for, it will be possible to take the prayer as something more than conscience-and face-saving sublimation, a device ideally suited to make action un-urgent and its nature vague. (pp. 326-32)

Just how did Auden manage to change from almost-Communist to quite-liberal? He did *not* switch over under stress of circumstance; long before any circumstances developed he was making his Progress by way of an old and odd route: mysticism. In Auden's middle period one finds a growing preoccupation with a familiar cluster of ideas: All power corrupts; absolute power corrupts absolutely. Government, a necessary evil, destroys the governors. All action is evil; the will is evil; life itself is evil. The only escape lies in the avoidance of action, the abnegation of the will. I don't mean that Auden wholly or practically accepted all this—who does? But he was more or less fascinated by such ideas (completely opposed to Marxism; fairly congenial with a loose extension of psychoanalysis), and *used* them: If all government is evil, why should we put our trust in, die for a choice of evils? If all action is evil, how can we put our faith in doing anything? If the will itself is evil, why select, plan, do? Life is evil; surely the contemplation of ideal ends is better than the willing and doing of the particular, so-often-evil means.

The reader may object that the method of change I suggest is too crude. But let me quote against him the changer: "The windiest militant trash / Important Persons shout / Is not so crude as our wish . . ." What is the mechanism of most changes of attitude?—the search for any reasons that will justify our believing what it has become necessary for us to believe. How many of us can keep from chorusing with Bolingbroke, *God knows, my son, by what bypaths and indirect crook'd ways I met this*—position? Marxism was too narrow, tough, and materialistic for the Essential Auden, who would far rather look dark with Heraclitus than laugh with Democritus. Auden's disposition itself (Isherwood says that if Auden had his way their plays would be nothing but choruses of angels); the fact that he was never a consistent or orthodox Marxist; the constant pressure of a whole society against any dangerous heresy inside it; Auden's strong "medical" inclinations, his fundamental picture of society as diseased, willing itself to be diseased (a case to be sympathized with, treated, and talked to *à la* Groddeck); his increasing interest in metaphysics and religion; the short-range defeatism, the compensatory long-range optimism that kept growing during the interminable defeat of the '30's; these, and more, made Auden's change inevitable. (p. 333)

These earliest poems are soaked in Death: as the real violence of revolutionary action and as a very comprehensive symbol. Death is Their necessary and desired conclusion; often poems are written from Their increasingly desperate point of view. Death belongs to Us as martyrs, spies, explorers, tragic heroes—with a suggestion of scapegoat or criminal—who die for the people. It belongs to Us because We, Their negation, have been corrupted by Them, and must ourselves be transcended. But, most of all, it is a symbol for *rebirth:* it is only through death that We can leave the old for good, be finally reborn. I have been astonished to see how consistently most of the important elements of ritual (purification, rebirth, identification, etc.) are found in the early poems; their use often seems unconscious. The most common purification rituals (except that of purification by fire) are plain. There is purification through decay: physical and spiritual, the rotting-away of the machines and the diseased perversions of the men. There are constant glaciers, ice, northern exploration—enough to have made Cleanth Brooks consider the fundamental metaphorical picture of the early poems that of a new ice age. There is purification by water: in the second poem in *On this Island* a sustained flood-metaphor shifts into parent-child imagery. There is some suggestion of purification through sin. There is mountain-climbing: from these cold heights one can see differently, free of the old perspectives; one returns, like Moses, with new insights. This is akin to the constantly used parable of the fairy-tale search, the hero's dangerous labors or journey. And the idea of rebirth is plainest of all, extending even to the common images of ontogenetic or phylogenetic development; of the foetus, new-born infant, or child; of the discontinuities of growth. The *uncle* is so important because he is a new ancestor whom We can identify ourselves with (Auden recommends "ancestor worship" of the true ancestor, the Uncle); by this identification We destroy our real parents, our Enemy ancestry, thus finally abolishing any remaining traces of Them in us. These ideas and their extensions are worth tracing in detail, if one had the space. Here is a quotation in which rebirth through death is extremely explicit; seasonal rebirth and the womb of the new order are packed in also. Auden writes that love

> Needs death, death of the grain, our death,
> Death of the old gang; would leave them
> In sullen valley where is made no friend,
> The old gang to be forgotten in the spring,
> The hard bitch and the riding-master,
> Stiff underground; deep in clear lake
> The lolling bridegroom, beautiful, there.

I want my treatment of Auden's early position to be suggestive rather than exhausting, so I shall not carry it any further; though I hate to stop short of all the comic traits Auden gives the Enemy, wretched peculiarities as trivial as saying *I mean* or having a room called the Den. The reader can do his own extending or filling in by means of a little unusually attractive reading: Auden's early poems. My own evaluation of Auden's changes in position has been fairly plain in my discussion. There are some good things and some fantastic ones in Auden's early attitude; if the reader calls it a muddle I shall acquiesce, with the remark that the later position might be considered a more rarefied muddle. But poets rather specialize in muddles—and I have no doubt which of the muddles was better for Auden's poetry: one was fertile and usable, the other decidedly is not. Auden sometimes seems to be saying with Henry Clay, "I had rather be right than poetry"; but I am not sure, then, that he is either. (pp. 335-37)

Randall Jarrell, "Changes of Attitude and Rhetoric in Auden's Poetry," in The Southern Review, *Louisiana State University, Vol. VII, No. 2, Autumn, 1941, pp. 326-49.*

AUTHOR'S COMMENTARY

It is impossible, I believe, for any poet, while he is writing a poem, to observe with complete accuracy what is going on, to define with any certainty how much of the final result is due to subconscious activity over which he has no control, and how much is due to conscious artifice. All one can say with certainty is negative. A poem does not compose itself in the poet's mind as a child grows in its mother's womb; *some* degree of conscious participation by the poet is necessary, *some* element of craft is always present. On the other hand, the writing of poetry is not, like carpentry, simply a craft; a carpenter can decide to build a table according to certain specifications and know before he begins that the result will be exactly what he intended, but no poet can know what his poem is going to be like until he has written it. The element of craftsmanship in poetry is obscured by the fact that all men are taught to speak and most to read and write, while very few men are taught to draw or paint or write music. Every poet, however, in addition to the everyday linguistic training he receives, requires a training in the poetic use of language. . . .

It has been said that a poem should not mean but be. This is not quite accurate. In a poem, as distinct from many other kinds of verbal societies, meaning and being are identical. A poem might be called a pseudo-person. Like a person, it is unique and addresses the reader personally. On the other hand, like a natural being and unlike a historical person, it cannot lie. We may be and frequently are mistaken as to the meaning or the value of a poem, but the cause of our mistake lies in our own ignorance or self-deception, not in the poem itself.

(essay date 1962)

John G. Blair   (essay date 1965)

[*Blair is an American academic and scholar. In the following excerpt, he studies the modernism of Auden's poetry.*]

Even without knowing the author's name, any reasonably sensitive reader of a poem by W. H. Auden would speedily be aware that he was looking at a "modern" poem. Regardless of how traditional the stanza form might be, the tone, diction, and imagery work together to make a poem unmistakably post-Victorian. Take, for example, a recent nursery-rime limerick, **"The Aesthetic Point of View"** (1960):

> As the poets have mournfully sung,
> Death takes the innocent young,
>   The rolling-in-money,
>   The screamingly-funny,

And those who are very well hung.

The innocently conventional diction of the first lines gives way gradually through the colloquial feminine rimes of lines three and four to the jolt of obscene slang in the last line. The poem is apparently frivolous, hardly worthy of a "serious" poet; yet frivolousness is its essential point. Following Kierkegaard, the poem implicitly condemns the essential frivolity and amorality of the aesthetic point of view, which is concerned only with how interesting or striking a situation is.

This little poem is instructive beyond its limited merit, for it reveals a tension central to Auden's mode, a tension between moral seriousness and the inescapable amorality of poetic artifice. The poem has a serious moral implication, but its admonition to those inclined to overvalue the aesthetic point of view is embedded in a form and style that do not even nod in the direction of serious moral contemplation. From the beginning Auden has wanted his skill in playing with words to stimulate efforts toward moral reform in his readers, but by the middle 1930's, when the basic terms of his characteristic mode had reached maturity, he was conscious of two crucial problems. First, he felt compelled to reject the direct communication of moral truth as a presumptuous assertion of his own will to power, analogous in politics to fascism. At the same time, his probing of the human psyche convinced him that direct preaching at an audience was simply ineffective. Highly self-conscious himself, he saw that modern readers would have to be trapped into self-awareness by indirect means. Since about 1935, then, most of his developments in manner and technique grow out of his search for more effective, though always indirect, didactic means. His philosophical position has changed over the years, but the root problems of writing a poem in his mode have not. In every poem he seeks a poetic strategy which can surprise, shock, or seduce his reader into serious self-examination, but simultaneously he seeks to avoid prejudging the terms in which the self-assessment should take place.

To state the tension another way, he must create a poetic mirror which is incisive, memorable, and inescapable, while insisting only that the reader should see in it his own deepest self. Paradoxically, one of Auden's difficulties in achieving this elusive end is his brilliance of technique. Each new poetic deftness, contrived to circumvent or cut through a reader's defenses, may allow him to be satisfied with himself for perceiving that brilliance. The poetic technique which makes didactic effectiveness possible may be just that instrument which defeats itself. Wrestling with this paradoxical aesthetic-moral problem has been Auden's major concern as a mature writer and an important stimulus to his inventiveness. The basic stances he has developed to deal with the problem constitute his poetic mode. In general orientation and method, the resulting poetry is clearly "modern." His poems are characteristically ironic and indirect, impersonal, and largely "anti-poetic."

Auden, of course, is not the innovator of these modern tendencies, as he himself is characteristically aware. He is a second-generation modern who formed his conception of poetry as a disciple of T. S. Eliot and *The Criterion*. During his Oxford years, starting in 1926, Auden appropriated the theories of Eliot which define the general out-lines of the modern mode, and then went on to carry the same principles further than his master. (pp. 11-13)

Among the ancestors Auden has claimed and honored by imitation, some are Continental or American but most are English. With the exception of two major groups, his imagination moves freely over the entire scope of English poetry, appropriating whatever it finds useful. He can paraphrase the Anglo-Saxon "Battle of Maldon," or turn a meter of Tennyson's to a new use with equal facility. He is equally adept at complex traditional forms like the sestina and simple fluid forms like the clerihew and the ballad. In addition, the knowledge of the poetic tradition exhibited in Auden's reviews and anthologies is imposing. In every case of close parallelism between an Auden poem and an earlier piece, he is almost certainly conscious of the precedent.

Two groups of English poets are conspicuously missing from the long list of those Auden has imitated or alluded to—the Metaphysicals and the Romantics. Metaphysical habits of imagination do appear in his work, but more noticeably in a general inclination toward "wit" than in direct imitation of particular forms or settings. Auden may have deliberately turned his attention to pre-Elizabethan verse in order to avoid becoming dominated by the models made fashionable through Eliot's sponsorship. He may also have been influenced toward medieval poetry by his Oxford tutor, Nevill Coghill, to whom he dedicated *The Dyer's Hand* in 1962. At the same time, Auden's later work has revealed such a strong native inclination toward moral allegory that he may have responded almost instinctively to poets like Langland.

Auden's studious avoidance of the Romantics is understandable since he is fond of developing his own views in explicit rejection of their ideas. Auden chose Shelley as his particular scapegoat and has torpedoed him in print periodically since 1934. **Letters from Iceland** (1937) is shot through with criticism of the Wordsworthian attitude toward nature. Only Burns, Byron, and Blake does Auden recognize, and he chooses to imitate their satiric or light verse rather than their more serious poems.

Outside these two major groups, Auden's borrowing has been both wide and judicious. It is a tribute to his poetic integrity that he rarely allows his borrowing to do his work for him. Like Eliot he consistently makes a new poem out of the fragments he borrows. Eliot, however, especially in his earlier poems, usually employs quotations from the past for ironic contrast with the corrupted world of the present, whereas Auden habitually selects allusions which reinforce the dominant mood of his own poem. Auden's reader is less specifically dependent on his knowledge of the original context of quotations or allusions, especially those whose source is in a foreign language.

Auden summarizes his attitudes toward the tradition as follows: "In poetry as in life, to lead one's own life means to relive the lives of one's parents and, through them, of all one's ancestors; the duty of the present is neither to copy nor to deny the past but to resurrect it." In large measure he has succeeded in bringing about the rebirth of the past described in this mature statement. The poems in which he fails come mainly from his earliest writings when he was uncertain just who his true ancestors were and how he could successfully recreate them in poetry. Too often, for example, Auden's early imitations of Langland and his suppression of articles and connectives in the manner of a literal translation of Anglo-Saxon seem strained mannerisms. Similar devices used fifteen years later in *The Age of Anxiety* (1947) have a startling poetic evocativeness.

In "Tradition and the Individual Talent" Eliot pointed to the whole literature of Europe from Homer as the tradition the poet should have ready at hand. While Eliot's interests led him to concentrate on French and Italian writing, Auden's Icelandic family background influenced him to study Germanic literature. Christopher Isherwood reports that he was raised on the sagas, and certainly their influence on his early poems is marked. In 1928 Auden went from Oxford to Germany and saw there the plays of Bertolt Brecht, which were to be a major influence on the dramas he wrote with Isherwood in the middle 1930's. Rilke became an important model for his use of the sonnet form and reinforced his own tendency to use physical objects as a projection of human qualities. Like Eliot, Auden has more recently found inspiration in Dante, but his orientation continues to be primarily Germanic. (pp. 15-18)

Besides the persistent concern for poetic ancestors, Eliot formulated for Auden other anti-Romantic attitudes as well. Most pervasive in Auden's poetic theory and practice is the impersonality enunciated by Eliot: "Poetry is not a turning loose of emotion, but an escape from emotion; it is not the expression of personality, but an escape from personality." Stephen Spender reports Auden's view during the Oxford years in similar terms: "He told me that the subject of a poem was only the peg on which to hang the poetry. A poet was a kind of chemist who mixed his poems out of words, whilst remaining detached from his own feelings. Feelings and emotional experiences were only the occasion which precipitated into his mind the idea of a poem." If Spender's memory is accurate, Auden was even thinking in a chemical metaphor for impersonality analogous to Eliot's in "Tradition and the Individual Talent."

Auden has continued to see the poet's task as impersonal; we have his continued delight in the impersonal "rules" of complex poetic forms to reinforce his numerous extra-poetic statements. In 1954, for example, he succinctly reiterates his anti-Romantic bias. "Poetry demands that the poet piously submit his precious personality to impersonal limitations; he cannot say anything he likes but only what they permit him to say." An attempt to evaluate such a poetry from a Romantic point of view is bound to miss some elements that are essential to its nature. Joseph Warren Beach is certainly on tenuous ground when he suggests that **"In Memory of W. B. Yeats"** and **"September 1, 1939"** are, among others, "earnest, direct, and manly" expressions of the poet's personal feelings. In none of his poems can one feel sure that the speaker is Auden himself. In the course of his career he has demonstrated impressive facility in speaking through any sort of dramatic persona; accordingly, the choice of an intimate, personal tone does not imply the direct self-expression of the poet. It is precisely self-control and rationality that lead Auden to choose Dante as his chief judge. He can hope for sympathetic understanding from the Dante who, out of "Amor Rationalis," sees that men he personally likes may require a place in the Inferno. Heaven, says Auden, may be "full of people you don't like." When a poet like Auden embraces restraint of his personal impulses as a means to his art, a Romantic reading, attuned to the expression of personality, may miss the poem's essential character as suprapersonal performance.

Auden's response to the problems of tradition and personality should demonstrate the kind of consistency that constitutes his characteristic mode. While he adopted different poetic ancestors as his ideas changed, he has never worked for long outside the context of some poetic precedent. He sometimes, especially during his first decade of writing, adopted an intimate or confessional tone, but the perspective of his whole work reveals this voice as only one of many through which he can dramatize his views. Similarly, the impersonal relation of poet to poem is evident in his progressive tendency through the 1930's and 1940's to submit his impulses to the rational control implicit in allegory. Auden's poetry, as much as that of any romantic, is the product of a unique encounter with the world, but, unlike the Romantic, he does not ask acceptance of his vision because it is unique or because it is his.

A related opposition to Romanticism centers around the third major problem for Auden as modern poet—the search for an audience. Where the Romantic emphasizes self-expression, Auden seeks communication. As he put it in 1936, "Those who have no interest in communication do not become artists either; they become mystics or madmen." But one must be able to locate an audience to communicate anything successfully, and this problem was a crucial one for Auden for many years. Characteristically he is aware and perhaps even hyperconscious of his audience. Many of his changes in style and manner have been stimulated by the attempt to isolate and engage different sorts of audiences. The problem has been less acute since 1940 and his projected audience has changed relatively little. Though he may have wanted a more popular audience, he has settled most often for the educated and somewhat sophisticated literary public—say, readers of the *New Yorker*. His frequent reliance on American slang may limit some of his more recent poems to readers on this side of the Atlantic, just as the English schoolboy slang in his poems of the early 1930's handicaps the non-British audience. Still, he is clearly aiming at an urban and urbane reader who will respond to the expression of moral seriousness through deft and witty verbal play.

During the last half of the 1930's, however, Auden's postulated audience was somewhat different. He sought a relatively unsophisticated "proletarian" audience. With characteristically easy transition from politics to poetry Auden remarks: "The social virtues of a real democracy are brotherhood and intelligence, and the parallel linguistic virtues are strength and clarity." The result in Auden's poetry was a startling change toward transparency in meaning and conventional rimed stanzas in form.

It has been dangerously easy to attribute these poetic changes in the middle 1930's to a conversion to communism. Indeed, Auden encouraged such interpretations of his newly acquired techniques by speaking of poetry in political terms, by publishing in the left press in England, and by accepting Marxist analyses of social phenomena in his extra-poetic statements. The influence of Marxism on his poetry should not, however, be overemphasized. Auden himself recognized his inability to reach a truly proletarian audience. "Personally, the kind of poetry I should like to write but can't is 'the thoughts of a wise man in the speech of the common people.' ' " The audience he could and did reach in the late 1930's was that of the educated middle class with left-wing or revolutionary sympathies. However, the simple concern for changing the status quo or even opposition to fascism in Germany and Spain do not make one a Communist. Stephen Spender's comments are worth noting because of his close contact with Auden in this period: "He had a firmer grip of Marxist ideology, and more capacity to put this into good verse than many writers who were closer to Communism. This led to the legend that he went through a Communist phase. But his poem, **'A Communist to Others,'** is an exercise in entering a point of view not his own. It is his summing up of conversations with Communists rather like the ones I used to have with Chalmers in Berlin." Marxism was only indirectly an influence on Auden's poetry. It did indicate a relatively well-defined audience to whom or through whom Auden felt he could make his private vision public.

There are also some purely aesthetic factors influencing the new-found transparency of Auden's poetry in this period. In the middle 1930's he began to rely more than ever before on anti-Romantic impersonality in organizing his poems. In 1935 he met Benjamin Britten and began writing songs and ballads, the words for music which were to culminate in the libretto for Stravinsky's opera, *The Rake's Progress* (1951). Songs require relatively simple and easily grasped imagery and in that sense can appeal to a wider reading public. They are also, in Auden's conception, of all kinds of poetry "the least personal and most verbal." A further commitment to impersonality is evident in Auden's new interest in light verse. He edited *The Oxford Book of Light Verse* in 1936 and began to produce his own *vers de société*. In Auden's hands, light verse, as in **"The Aesthetic Point of View"** . . . , becomes a sharp, impersonal instrument which attacks the self-deception of men, poets or not, who believe they can be "seriously" sincere. . . . (pp. 19-24)

Before 1935 or so, Auden was still in the process of working out the lineaments of the mode which has become characteristically his, but in the perspective of his work as a whole his anti-Romantic leanings are clear. His initial strategy to avoid the "honest manly style" was primarily to cloak his poems in obscurity. Eliot had predicted that modern poetry must be "difficult"; Auden, from 1926 till roughly 1935, seemed sometimes to take Eliot at his word and to manufacture obscurity so that he could be "modern." It is easy to share the exasperation of Malcolm Cowley in 1934 when he concluded: "His principal fault, I think, is his damnable and perverse obscurity" [see excerpt dated 1934]. There are two essential types of obscurity in Auden's early verse. First is obscurity created by his manipulation of language, especially syntax and occasionally diction; second is obscurity resulting from the small, self-contained audience Auden felt he could write for.

Syntactical obscurity results most commonly from the suppression of connectives or the indefinite reference of pronouns. Syntactical short-cuts and a parallel suppression of the full context of poetic statements lead to confused symbolism in a number of poems. Take the following stanza, first published in 1930, for example:

A neutralizing peace
And an average disgrace

Are honour to discover
For later other.

The sense of the stanza is reasonably clear; it can be paraphrased as follows: it is a worthwhile achievement for your descendants to remember if you manage to accomplish even a limited goal, not victory but "a neutralizing peace." In the context of the entire poem, however, the stanza fails to make sense because the poem sets up no oppositions that could be resolved in "a neutralizing peace." All the preceding stanzas offer for the brave is defeat by the enemy and disgrace at home. If there is a context in which this frustration could be considered a "neutralizing peace," the suppression of that frame of reference makes the symbolism impenetrably obscure.

Auden's interest in the clipped, disconnected style has two important motivations. First is simply a demand for attention by startling phraseology. Second, and more important, is the impulse described by Richard Hoggart: "It is the verse of a young man prepared to experiment widely with forms and manners of expression, but particularly suspicious of lushness, and anxious to evolve a hard, cerebral style." The anti-Romantic starkness of expression is the more startling because so many of the themes of these early poems reveal attitudes traditionally associated with Romanticism. There is nostalgia for childhood, yearning for a trust in the unconscious and the flesh after D. H. Lawrence and Blake, and a considerable measure of trust in the perfectibility of man. This incongruity of theme and poetic expression illustrates the complexity of Auden's growth. Not until near 1940 did his themes become as consistently anti-Romantic as his mode of presenting them. In fact, starting from the initial impact of Eliot, Auden's progressively greater anti-Romanticism may well reflect a more or less conscious revolt against Romantic impulses he found within himself.

The second major source of obscurity in this earliest period is the small audience that Auden felt he could reach. Again and again in his analyses of the problems of the modern poet, Auden laments the lack of a homogeneous society with shared beliefs or at least shared images and symbols that a poet could draw on. In 1936 he put it thus: "The problem of the modern poet, as for everyone else today, is how to find or form a genuine community, in which each has his valued place and can feel at home." There was only one place in the England of 1930 where Auden could feel at home and that was in the group of his college friends, including, most prominently, Stephen Spender, C. Day Lewis, Christopher Isherwood, Rex Warner, and Edward Upward. Understandably, Auden concludes that amusing one's friends is a primary motivation for an artist:

Art, if it doesn't start there, at least ends,
Whether aesthetics like the thought or not,
In an attempt to entertain our friends;
And our first problem is to realise what
Peculiar friends the modern artist's got; . . .

The particular friends that Auden had were witty, intelligent, and highly educated; they were acquainted with all the latest theories, especially in psychology. The obscurity that results from writing for the coterie appears in private allusions and esoteric theorizing. However opaque some of these poems seem to a reader from outside the group, it seems probable that the poems do have intelligible meaning. Stephen Spender insists that: "Every line of his poetry—which has been called obscure—*means* something in the sense that it has an immediate relation to some real event which he interprets as a psychological or spiritual or sociological symptom." If Spender is right, then presumably one could understand presently opaque images if he knew either the real events or the theoretical systems for isolating symptoms. Auden himself criticizes obscurity in a way that suggests he would not consciously indulge in it. "One must begin by distinguishing between riddle, which is, I believe, a fundamental element in poetry, and obscurity, which is an aesthetic vice." The difference, he suggests, is obvious to the crossword puzzle addict, who responds to an answer with either "What a fool I was. Of course that's it," or "The clue was unfair. Four or five other words would fit it equally well." Those poems that an outsider can decipher suggest that most of the "obscure" poems are not intrinsically so. However, they can be criticized for failing to make their vision available to more than a handful of people.

There is one further sort of obscurity in the early poetry which is better understood as an imitation of Eliot than as a practice peculiar to Auden. A number of early poems, including Auden's most ambitious early work, *The Orators* (1932), are constructed with a "logic of the imagination" as opposed to a "logic of concepts." These Auden poems are obscure in the manner of *The Waste Land;* like it they attempt "to find the verbal equivalent for states of mind and feeling" by presenting a succession of images without explicit conceptual relation.

The Orators is only partially successful and Auden soon thereafter abandoned the associational logic of a succession of images. He became interested less in simply defining the state of the world and more in expressing a thesis as to what should be done. As a result, Auden after the early 1930's characteristically uses images to illustrate a diagnosis of the contemporary situation. Thus he puts images to a more clearly conceptual use in a typical poem of the late 1930's, **"Dover 1937"**:

> Steep roads, a tunnel through the downs are the
>   approaches;
> A ruined pharos overlooks a constructed bay;
> The sea-front is almost elegant; all this show
> Has, somewhere inland, a vague and dirty root:
> Nothing is made in this town.

The poet's interest here is in defining and communicating a conceptualized insight into the contemporary malaise with all its uncreative passivity and triviality. As time has passed, Auden has tended to make his themes even more conceptually clear; **"New Year Letter"** (1941), for example, is virtually rational discourse in verse after the manner of Dryden. In general, one may say that Auden's movement away from Eliot's mode of associational organization represents a more complete commitment to anti-Romanticism than Eliot himself made. Another indication is Auden's frequent choice of allegory with its associated control of emotive faculties by rationality. Bringing what one accepts or rejects to full consciousness is Auden's mature ideal for both artist and man. (pp. 25-30)

John G. Blair, in his The Poetic Art of W. H. Auden, *Princeton University Press, 1965, 210 p.*

Justin Replogle   (essay date 1969)

[*In the following excerpt, Replogle explores the meter, diction, and syntax of Auden's poetry.*]

Auden's dazzling prosodic skill is acknowledged by everybody. Admirers talk about his mastery of nearly every metrical and stanzaic practice known to English poetry (and of several unknown), while detractors gleefully emphasize the same point as proof that Auden, the Good Gray Academic Poet, is a huge museum of outmoded prosody. Since more than anything else, rhythmical effects are peculiar to individual works, in one giant generalization I will pass over practices that may produce the most exciting effects in each poem: Auden's rhythmical skill, it seems to me, is almost completely traditional or an extension of practices introduced by his recent predecessors. Though his prosody is one of his great accomplishments, close analysis will show that he relies heavily on the rhythmical expectations established during centuries of English poetic development. His prosodic practices reveal what is obviously true of his temperament, that his own aesthetic excitement almost never comes from *avant-garde* art. Like most other admirers of past poetry, he clearly gets great pleasure from the skill with which a performer handles familiar technical devices. This has always been one of the most important sources of aesthetic delight in all the arts. Until expectations have been established by witnessing a great many similar performances, no reader can respond with excitement to an extraordinarily skillful exhibition. Auden's own habits show that he, like all good readers, responds aesthetically to a skillfull performance quite apart from the performer's subject. This is part of what he means by poetry being a game. Like all the other arts it is a performing art, with the creator as performer. Every knowledgeable reader knows about the relative difficulty of certain practices (rules, Auden likes to call them), and will respond emotionally when a poet's skill makes difficulties seem easy. Even modern Romantic critics like Kenneth Rexroth or Karl Shapiro, while they deplore "rules," would surely understand and approve of Auden when he says, " . . . the formal structure of the poem 'I Remember, I Remember' [by Phillip Larkin], in which the succession of five-line stanzas is regular but the rhyming is not, being used both within the stanza and as a link across the stanza break, gives me great pleasure as a device, irrespective of the poem's particular contents." If that is not all art is, it is that as well. And just such a taste for prosodic technique for its own sake is, I think, the best general explanation of Auden's own practice.

Whatever its traditional roots, though, Auden's prosody conforms to the main stream of twentieth-century practice by freely using prose and speech rhythms. In his syllable-stress poems, his general practice is enough like that of his metrical predecessors to be passed over without comment. But his prose or speech rhythms deserve special attention, since they play a large part in creating one of his characteristic voices. Of course the pleasing struggle between metrical rhythms and those of speech and prose has always caused a good bit of the excitement in English poetry. And Auden's poetry contains all the varieties of this struggle: poems where syllable-stress rhythm dominates, poems where syllable-stress and speech rhythm are about equally powerful, poems where speech rhythms are played off against strong-stress patterns learned from Hopkins and Anglo-Saxon literature, and poems where speech or prose rhythms nearly obscure metrical patterns. In a great many poems, especially after 1940, foot and stress patterns succumb to their much stronger opponent. Speech or prose rhythms prevail, and no one exceeds Auden's virtuosity in running these across the most unlikely meters. One of the most unlikely, for instance, is in a playful monologue in *For the Time Being.* Here an extremely colloquial speech rhythm ("For having reasoned—'Woman is naturally pure / Since she has no moustache' ") flows through ten-line stanzas of intricately patterned four- and five-foot lines (4,5,5,4,5,5,5,4,5,5) rhyming abcacbddff. This rigorous stanza design in no way aids the colloquial speech. Quite the opposite. Its formidable demands make speech more difficult. Its creator is the poet who believes art to be partly a game. His aesthetic delight arises from self-imposed rules made increasingly difficult, and most knowledgeable readers will respond to this with a similar pleasure.

Whether accompanied by formal patterns or not, Auden's speech rhythms nearly always have heavy stresses. Unlike Pound (who consciously explored the far reaches of rhythmical flatness), Auden's speech rhythms usually have stresses as strong as (and sometimes stronger than) his metrical rhythms. Because of this it is not always possible to decide what formal pattern governs some of the later poems. Is Auden counting syllables, feet, or stresses? Some lines, for instance, in the acknowledged syllabic poem **"In Praise of Limestone,"** are syllabic anomalies and seem to be governed by stresses. (Counting elided vowels as single syllables will not explain away all the syllabic deviations.) In contrast, foot and stress poems sometimes appear to be governed by syllable count. The cause of all this is not Auden's faulty ear, but that he hears something more pre-emptive than line pattern. Whatever their formal shape, many poems after 1940 contain an unmistakably similar voice, with its own strong speech rhythm. In various poems this same voice runs across lines that are technically six feet, five feet, four feet, three feet, even two feet, or syllabic. (It even appears in the prose included in poetry volumes.) The line unit, almost never dominant in these, often eludes the ear, and sometimes even analysis. In a given poem Auden may theoretically be writing thirteen-syllable lines, but he is mostly listening to a speech voice that sometimes may use fourteen or fifteen syllables or speak in six-stress units. The rhythms of this voice are so outstandingly distinctive that surely the voice itself can be singled out for identification. The voice rhythms are used by both Poet and Antipoet for all sorts of verse— high, low, or middle style—and I am tempted to guess that both voice and rhythms owe something originally to Marianne Moore. (Auden says he read her poetry for the first time in 1935.) Though short syllabic lines can often be heard (that is, the reader can hear or feel the proper number of syllables instead of stresses or feet) in long lines of the sort Miss Moore likes, the syllable count itself is often an intellectual rather than an auditory game. What the reader hears is not a repeated number of syllables but a distinctive speech rhythm. This is just what the reader hears in Auden's syllabic poems as well, and to my ear the voice in these poems sounds similar to that in Miss Moore's poetry, as though when he borrowed her prosody he also borrowed part of her voice (perhaps the one is nearly the sole cause of the other). I say this only as a descriptive aid. When speech rhythms dominate in Auden

they often create a distinctive voice. The voice first became distinctive in the late 1930's and early 1940's. Originally it sounded something like Miss Moore's poetic voice, and Auden used it in both syllabic and nonsyllabic poems and in prose. But no amount of abstract description can classify this voice as well as a few illustrations. Here is the voice:

> . . . to become a pimp
> Or deal in fake jewelery or ruin a fine tenor voice
>   For effects that bring down the house could
> happen. . . .
>
> **("In Praise of Limestone")**

>   To manage the Flesh,
>   When angels of ice and stone
> Stand over her day and night who make it so plain
> They detest any kind of growth, does not encourage. . . .
>
> **("Mountains")**

> To practise one's peculiar civic virtue was not
> So impossible after all; to cut our losses
> And bury our dead was really quite easy. . . .
>   (The Narrator in *For The Time Being*)

> To break down Her defences
>   And profit from the vision
> That plain men can predict through an
>   Ascesis of their senses,
> With rack and screw I put Nature through
>   A thorough inquisition. . . .
>   (The First Wise Man in *For The Time Being*)

> As long as there were any roads to amnesia and anaesthesia still to be explored, any rare wine or curiosity of cuisine as yet untested, any erotic variation as yet unimagined . . . there was still a hope. . . .
>   (Simeon in *For The Time Being*)

The formal line patterns here (each different, the last prose) all quickly capitulate to the overpowering speech stresses of a voice nearly identical in each passage. This voice appears in a great many poems after 1940 and is an important and obtrusive feature of Auden's style, one created largely by rhythm. So powerful is this rhythm in creating a distinctive voice, that by the time of *Homage to Clio* it makes sense to say that in all of Auden the Grand Persona speaks in two distinct voices (used in variation by all his speakers), one created by dominant metrical, the other by dominant speech, rhythm. Poet and Antipoet make their speeches out of both. Despite the vast number of shared features these voices have (diction, imagery, and so forth) rhythm alone makes them very unlike. For instance:

> Within a shadowland of trees
> Whose lives are so uprightly led
> In nude august communities,
> To move about seems underbred. . . .
>   **("Reflection in a Forest")**

• • • • • • • • • • • • • • • • • •

> Out of a gothic North, the pallid children
>   Of a potato, beer-or-whiskey
> Guilt culture, we behave like our fathers and come
>   Southward into a sunburnt otherwhere. . . .
>   **("Good-bye to the Mezzogiorno")**
>   (pp. 182-86)

A large part of all English poetry depends on evocative diction for much of its effect, and without it Auden must use something else to give verbal excitement to what otherwise would be flat sentences of direct conceptual statement. Since the most obvious thing he does is to animate concepts, his poetry is filled with the moving, dancing ideas that animate allegories small as an epithet and large as a volume, and set in motion all the related verbal practices that attend them. This way of intensifying language has been very much out of fashion (at least in theory) since Coleridge labeled it Fancy and called it a lesser thing than Imagination, and Auden has suffered at the hands of critics who, knowingly or not, share this preference, probably more common now than in Coleridge's time. Auden himself has accurately described Fancy as a "conscious process" involving in its analogical method a "one to one correspondence . . . grasped by the reader's reason," while Imagination, he says, is a process emphasizing the "less conscious side of artistic creation . . . the symbolic rather than the decorative or descriptive value of images." A symbol "is an object or event . . . felt to be more important than the reason can immediately explain . . ." Whatever he may prefer in his theoretical prose, in poetry Auden employs the resources of Fancy: embellishment, decoration, invention, ornament. A great many twentieth-century readers respond to these words as Kenneth Rexroth does, when he says that "Bad poetry always suffers from the same defects: synthetic hallucination and artifice. Invention is not poetry. . . . Poetry is vision, the pure act of sensual communion and contemplation." That "invention" and "ornament" have such pejorative associations again shows how much twentieth-century readers are fashioned by the nineteenth-century tastes they so often deplore. For of course Dr. Johnson thought Rexroth's "bad poetry" the very best sort: " 'A work more truly poetical,' " he said of *Comus,* " 'is rarely found; allusions, images and descriptive epithets embellish almost every period with lavish decoration!' " This is not the place to engage in lengthy polemics or to assess the caprices of changing fashions. But if some doubtful reader of Auden is put off by the very nature of his poetry (no one would claim it is everywhere successful, of course), he should recall that all poets must make their artifacts out of either conceptual or emotive diction, and there is no reason a priori to believe one better than the other. (pp. 195-96)

Syntax, more than anything else, creates an oratorical voice. A 1939 poem opens with "Not as that . . . Napoleon, rumour's dread and centre, / Before whose riding all the crowds divide. . . . " This period runs on until the eighth line, a truly Miltonic postponement of subject and verb. Only slightly less imposing are the opening lines

> Will you turn a deaf ear
> • • • • • • • • • •
> Yet wear no ruffian badge
> Nor lie. . . .

By "oratorical" syntax I mean the syntax in just such lines as these. With their lengthy periods, declarative and declamatory questions, and such miscellaneous formulations as "Yet . . . Nor," such sentences are almost never used by two individuals speaking to each other, but only by speakers addressing much larger audiences. The syntax shows what even the meaning of the words may try to deny. For instance, one Auden speaker talks like this:

> And since our desire cannot take that route which is straightest,
> Let us choose the crooked, so implicating these acres,

These millions in whom. . . .

Auden pretends that this is a lover speaking to his beloved, the "my darling" of a previous stanza. But we never doubt that these sonorities (astounding between two lovers) are meant for the ears of some vast public who will find such constructions appropriate. "Consider this and in our time," another speaker begins, clearly from the podium, and even in middle-style poems speakers usually adopt such oratorical voices. "Here on the cropped grass of the narrow ridge I stand," though a traditional first line for English meditative poetry, is, however traditional, far too theatrical to be put to an individual in conversation or in a letter to a friend. Letter or conversation demand "I am standing here on the cropped grass of a narrow ridge"—at least. (Even "cropped" alone probably makes the sentence "literary" and oratorical.) One familiar generalization, then, is: the more periodic and inverted the syntax, the more consciously patterned, the higher the oratory.

A majority of Auden's poems have a voice at some level of oratory, whatever their subject or other stylistic feature. "To-day no longer occupied like that, I give,"; "Deaf to the Welsh wind now, I hear." Whether appropriate to the subject or not, voices ringing out in these periods produce the emotional effects a poet with conceptual diction cannot get from his words alone, and the handy, and usually lengthy, inverted sentences make possible a wide variety of rhythmical complexity. Looked at this way, one of Auden's problems in the 1930's can be described as a syntax—or voice—problem. His oratorical syntax enabled him to create emotional voices and excellent rhythms, but its very existence automatically created a persona sometimes too sententious and formal for the occasion. If he wanted to bring his Poet down off the Parnassian peaks, Auden had to rebuild his syntax. The syntax of conversational speech generally runs to short sentences with a subject-verb-object arrangement or no clear grammatical arrangement, not to oratorical inversions and lengthy periods grammatically polished. Swinging from one extreme to the other, for a time in the late 1930's Auden's Poetic speakers came forth in . . . exaggerated short declarative statements. . . . They reached a degree of compulsiveness in **"In Time of War"** that added another eccentric manner to that already mannered work:

> They wondered why the fruit had been forbidden;
> It taught them nothing new. They hid their pride,
> • • • • • • • • • • • • • • • • •
> They knew exactly what to do outside.
>
> They left. . . .

Along with this new syntax came some of the choppy rhythms always threatened by short sentences with parallel structure. Auden was already a master of rhythms that could be made from oratorical speech, but he had not learned how to make this new style work. To get some kind of rhythmical flow across these maddeningly short and similar sentences, he began sticking them together with that weakest of connectives, "and." In the first 112 lines (eight sonnets), "and" turns up forty-four times at the head of a line. In *Another Time* he tried occasionally to remedy matters by pasting the oratorical "O" onto these nonoratorical sentences: "O in these quadrangles where Wisdom honours herself." Sometimes that helped; sometimes it simply made the speech an incongruous mixture. But the excessively simple syntax began to fade. A higher oratory returns in **Another Time** and remains in the later poetry. Thus most of Auden's poetry could be described as fundamentally oratorical (the major cause, I suspect, of the peculiar belief that he is our most pedagogical poet).

But not all his poems, even the Poetic ones, have high oratory in them. Among the exceptions are those late poems where Auden again tries to develop a plain, nonoratorical voice:

> The sailors come ashore
> Out of their hollow ships,
> Mild-looking middle-class boys. . . .

A poem that begins like this is certainly not a declamation from some high podium. But if it is not high oratory it is certainly not conversation either. It might accurately be called low oratory, part of the long tradition of poetic speech that presents the illusion of informality and conversation, but in reality always aims at a large audience from a public platform, which if low is always there.

Yet if much of his poetry is oratorical, Auden certainly knew how to write the syntax of face-to-face talk, informal and personal: "The fact is, I'm in Iceland"; "You must admit, when all is said and done"; "I don't know whether / You will agree, but"; "And then a lord—Good lord, you must be peppered [with fan mail]." It must be clear by now that nonoratorical syntax and other colloquial features are the very things that often separate the Antipoet's voice from that of the Poet. I say "often" because while the Poet nearly always orates, the Antipoet does not always use the syntax of face-to-face talk. A good share of his syntax is oratorical too—parodied oratory. He mocks the Poet's style:

> For in my arms I hold
> The Flower of the Ages,
> And the first love of the world.
> • • • • • • • • • • • • • •
> The didactic digit and dreaded voice
> Which imposed peace on the pullulating
> Primordial mess. Mourn for him now,
> Our lost dad. . . .

I have remarked in various contexts that Auden never found a comfortable style for his Poetic voice. He dared not let it become too ornate. The Antipoet would burlesque it. Neither could he seem to lower it with ease, even though he obviously had a knack for writing colloquial speech. Now we can speculate about the cause (the stylistic cause, at least) of Auden's problem. Apparently he could not separate certain kinds of speech from certain kinds of speakers. Colloquial voices seem to be so firmly part of Auden's joking, farcical sense of life's foolishness that he can seldom speak colloquially without being comic. In other words, the Poet cannot borrow the Antipoet's vernacular idiom without getting the rest of his mocking, comic behavior as well. However informal he may be, the Poet cannot maintain sobriety and speak conversationally at the same time, so Auden's Poetic voice, even at its least formal, fails to be completely informal and always sounds a bit stiff. On the other side, Auden's Antipoetic self cannot speak formally without self-parody, self-mockery. Only when Poet and Antipoet are combined in the speakers of the middle-style and high comic poems can Auden successfully combine oratory with the most unbuttoned conversational syntax, sobriety with horseplay, and all with an emotive and intellectual profundity. These speakers mock themselves and their style, but their very self-contradictions and incongruities are the poem's intellectual and emotional message. (pp. 203-07)

> *Justin Replogle, in his* Auden's Poetry, *University of Washington Press, 1969, 258 p.*

Frank Kermode   (essay date 1970)

[*Kermode is a renowned English literary critic. He is perhaps best known for his studies of English Renaissance literature and reviews of the works of his contemporaries. According to James Gray, he* "*belongs as observer to the whole world of literature, and as critic only to himself.*" *In the following essay, he examines the evolving form, technique, and subject matter of Auden's verse, particularly* City without Walls.]

Auden is the twentieth-century poet in something like the way Tennyson was the nineteenth-century poet. He was born ninety-eight years after Tennyson, his first book appeared one hundred and one years after Tennyson's, and anybody of about fifty or over who reads poetry must feel, as a Victorian in the same case felt a century ago, that his whole reading life coincides with one important career. It is difficult to explain how much this colors one's mind, but it certainly has an effect on the sentiments. It is a relation like a very old friendship, which may not be as active and exciting as newer ones, and which one may on occasion casually traduce, but always in the knowledge that it can never end. Just so might a man have been irritated by *The Princess* and bored by *Maud,* only to acquiesce, perhaps with a sigh, in *The Idylls of the King.*

Differences must, however, be declared, and they are many. Auden will write no *Idylls* and bore us with no Doubt; he has made himself ineligible for the Laureateship and the House of Lords, and he is unlikely to give private readings to the Queen of England. Tennyson claimed to be the greatest master of the English language since Shakespeare, but added that he had nothing to say. Auden is a great master, and there is virtually no limit to what he has to say. The parallel remains: this for some who are aging is the voice, the demeanor, of our aging century. Once taut and cold, that voice could speak to the accompaniment of a blue stare learnt from a school bully, shout in-jokes aloud, express like a surgeon in one breath our sickness and his assured, jargon-protected knowledge. Now the voice is more benign, the look more tolerant, and we can share the knowledge if we want to. But there is no question that it is the same voice, or that it is a twentieth-century institution.

This gives him no Tennysonian centrality; Auden is the poet of our pluralism, a very singular person indeed. He has formed no school, is seriously eclectic ("His guardian angel / has always told him / What and Whom to read next"), and has precisely defined for himself and us—to whom he is therefore important—the unimportance of what he is doing. He agrees with Nietzsche that "we have Art in order that we may not perish from the Truth." He is very private, himself polices his limits and his lacks, rejoices in his immense technical resource, and takes what he wants when he wants it; from Groddeck long ago, or Lorenz now; from Graves long ago, and now, in **City Without Walls,** from John Hollander (because he knows a good comic verse form when he sees it). Forty years ago, in **Paid on Both Sides,** he inserted a whole chunk from a mummer's play and left us to explain to ourselves how it fitted the plot, which was about a feud. More fluent and amenable today, he still expects his "handful of readers" to to be able to "rune." (p. 67)

Auden finds in maturity good reasons to support a conviction of his youth, that there is much to be said for "light" verse, for verse that uses the intelligence, for verse that remembers the gaiety possible to the natural man. This emphasis displeases some readers, especially some who were among his earliest admirers; for thirty years or more they have been complaining that he did not know how seriously to take himself, though in fact the course of his career is one long demonstration that he takes himself seriously enough to know exactly that. The wit and craft of his later poetry, rightly taken, continue this demonstration.

He at first wrote as if charged with creating mystery or uttering prophecy, and since he began in the twenties, there is nothing surprising about that; but it became clear that he was more a Dryden than a Yeats. The parallel with Dryden is indeed obvious, and is suggested in a general way by Auden's intensely professional approach to his craft and the vastness of his linguistic and conceptual resources. More specifically, he is, like Dryden, occasional poet, translator, playwright, librettist (perhaps the best of our time), songwriter, master of the styles of argument, a more important critic than his idiosyncratic prose discourse allows some people to see, and a wit. In this last capacity he has preserved longer than Dryden did the fantastic strain of his youth, and occasionally this takes one back behind Dryden to the Donne of the funeral elegies, or his imitators. The new book contains an epithalamium quite as conceited as seventeenth-century examples of the genre, and in its day quite as modern.

To enjoy it you need all your wits and at least one first-rate dictionary (Auden's own, he tells us, are "the very best that money can buy"). Consider, for example, these stanzas, addressed to a kinswoman on her marriage.

> May Venus, to whose caprice
> all blood must buxom,
> take such a shine to you both
> that, by her gifting,
> your palpable substances
> may re-ify those delights
> they are purveyed for:
>
> cool Hymen from Jealousy's
> teratoid phantasms,
> sulks, competitive headaches,
> and Pride's monologue
> that won't listen but demands
> tautological echoes,
> ever refrain you.

Only the deities are commonplace, and the good wishes; all are forced to share the poem with some strange words and themes. The verb "to buxom" is obsolete, and means "to obey." It sits snugly beside "take a shine to," for each is its own kind of slang, one proper to goddesses and one to ordinary lovers. The rest of the stanza means that he hopes this will enable their bodies to make actual the plea-

sures for which they are provided. "Teratoid" means monstrous, pathological, used here for its original as well as its medical sense, and instantly cut down to size by "sulks." As all echoes are tautological, that word here rather nicely applies to itself as well as to the echoes. In the remainder of the poem we are counseled to thank Mrs. Nature—sometimes called Dame Kind and a member of Auden's make shift pantheon, with Dame Philology, Dame Algebra, and occasional less substantial allegorical figures—for bringing humanity to the point where the Auden clan get together for the marriage; a huge evolutionary effort, an epic of survival, must be celebrated by human beings so assembled, but as persons they also owe thanks to

> the One for Whom all
> enantiomorphs
> are super-posable, yet
> Who numbers each particle
> by its Proper Name.

"Enantiomorph," I see, is a term used mostly by crystallographers, but in general meaning, according to the *O.E.D. Supplement,* "a form which is related to another as an object is related to its image in a mirror: a mirror image." Webster, under "enantiomorphous," seems closer to our mark: "similar to but not superposable; related to each other as a right-handed to a left-handed glove." The point is that for God enantiomorphs *are* superposable, though he does not fail to distinguish the individuality of each created thing. The Proper Name, thus capitalized, is an indication of one respect in which poets, insofar as they resemble Adam, are made in God's image: for "whatsoever Adam called every living creature, that was the name thereof, which is to say, its Proper Name. Here Adam plays the role of the Proto-poet. . . ."

The argument of the epithalamium is at once flip and serious, and yet it is an argument, not just a bunch of witty, avuncular good wishes. Two "nonesuches," two Proper Names, have decided to "common" their lives, always a "diffy" undertaking, and one with a long strange history; a marriage is a symbol of the superposability of enantiomorphs (if it works), and the ceremony provides a good moment to joke about the physical and also the spiritual adventures of *homo sapiens.*

The reading of such poetry is an experience about as different as possible from that of reading, say, Wallace Stevens, even though he looks more "philosophical" and also has a very personal lexicon; the difference is that Auden's meanings are exactly defined by the unusual words: *nauntle, dindle, ramstam, noodling* are from the dialect dictionary; *depatical, olamic* are more learned. When Auden speaks of

> the *baltering* torrent
> sunk to a *soodling* thread,

or of the Three Maries *sossing* over the seamless waves, he is not, as you might suppose, inventing the words. If he remarks that "the insurrected eagre hangs / over the sleeping town" we may have to look up *eagre,* but once we've done that we know what he's talking about. In the poem beginning

> On and on and on
> The forthright catadoup
> Shouts at the stone-deaf stone—

I had lazily assumed that a catadoup was some sort of bird, but actually it is a Nile cataract, and this naturally makes a difference to the poem. Hence the importance of those dictionaries. (pp. 68-9)

Once, in serious mood, Auden catalogued our Anxieties. "The basic human problem," he said, "is man's anxiety in time; e.g., his present anxiety over himself in relation to his past and his parents (Freud), his present anxiety over himself in relation to his future and his neighbors (Marx), his present anxiety over himself in relation to eternity and God (Kierkegaard)." This characteristically triadic formulation belongs, however, to 1941, to the period of *New Year Letter* and the other poetry of that time. Since then the task of the poetry has been modified; broadly speaking, it is to celebrate what is present rather than what makes anxious; to see (with knowledge) and name (with language) whatever in the multitudinous world presents itself before you, wherever you stand. Auden always admired Hardy for "his hawk's vision, his way of looking at life from a very great height." This enabled him "to see the individual life related not only to the local social life of its time, but to the whole of human history." There are bold modern attempts to do likewise; for example, Virginia Woolf's *Between the Acts*. Auden's is different, more exact and knowing, less comprehensive and "musical." The most he does is to sketch the grand gestures, as in the paleobotanical splendor of the lines on

> that preglacial Actium when the huge
> Archaic shrubs went down before the scented flowers
> And earth was won for color—
>
> (*About the House*)

which neatly superimpose a historic upon a prehistoric battle, one time scale on another, so that even readers who wonder whether poets need to bewilder us with "scientific" information may have, for a second, a sharper sense of where they stand in the longer perspectives of time. Thus a lifelong love of technical language for its own sake pays off. The material isn't, as it were, orchestrated in a Woolfian way, nor is there anything like the immemorial moaning that Tennyson combines with geology. There is not even any anxiety; without music, without magic, he professes accuracy in respect of what it is to stand in the Arctic Circle, in a Manhattan Kitchen, or in an Austrian house.

Primarily he is a city poet. He thinks of the city in relation to geology, human evolution, and history; he remembers too that a City is emblematic of a community bound by need and love, so that the actual lower-case city is far from being the same thing. He further reflects that there are great differences between poems and cities and societies:

> A society which was really like a good poem, embodying the aesthetic virtues of beauty, order, economy and subordination of detail to the whole, would be a nightmare of horror for, given the historical reality of actual men, such a society could only come into being through selective breeding, extermination of the physically and mentally unfit, absolute obedience to its Director, and a large slave class kept out of sight in cellars.

(He saw in his youth that totalitarian aesthetics, like those of Hulme, Pound, Eliot, and Yeats, had a tendency to be reflected in totalitarian politics.) Such preoccupations not surprisingly promote a special interest in the celebrant of

the city and its antecedents, in the work of seeing and making which he does under his particular roof. And so Auden, without ceasing to be reticent, writes more and more (wryly, ironically, yet charitably) about himself.

This does not shorten the historical perspective, or diminish the sense of standing on a world of rock and soil. The myth of the limestone Eden, which is recurrent but which we now associate principally with the beautiful **"In Praise of Limestone,"** published in 1962, has not lost its force. But in that poem the preference for limestone led to generalizations about human types with other preferences. Now the tone grows more personal, the poems more directly concerned with the curiosity that upon a particular middle-aged man, shaped thus, dressed thus, should devolve the professional task of praise. It is long enough, I admit, since he required that "the shabby structure of indolent Flesh / Give a resonant echo to the World"; but there is a new element of amused wonder that the spirit, no longer orgulous or bold, and established in still shabbier flesh, should "conform to its temporal focus of praise." In *About the House,* published in 1966, the poet meditated on the quality of the space each room represented. The study is cut off from "life-out-there," however "goodly, miraculous, lovable" it may be; in it poems are written, and the poet serves "this unpopular art which cannot be turned into / background noises for study / or hung as a status trophy by rising executives." And a poem may be, at best, "a shadow echoing / the silent light," no more than that; but it is a great deal. And to be doing something so relatively impressive and so privileged can seem odd, especially if one happens to be doing it in the middle of an incorrigible, indifferent metropolis.

So the new book opens with a poem in alliterative five-line stanzas about the fantastic forms of Manhattan, and the inhabitants of this cliff full of folk, mechanically working nobodies whose reaction to Nothing is expressed in meters almost as old as the language:

> Small marvel, then, if many adopt
> cancer as the only offered career. . . .

The meditation is building up a sardonic picture of a postwar world when it is interrupted by a voice "at three A.M. / in mid-Manhattan"—which censures his *Schadenfreude;* a little psychomachy ensues, and the poet is advised to go to bed.

Teasing, moral, the meanings float down metrical streams; we should, we are told, "look at / this world with a happy eye / but from a sober perspective." There is an occasional regression to old moods and styles, as in the joke-menace of "Song of the Ogres"—

> Little fellow, you're amusing.
> Stop before you end by losing
> Your shirt . . .

but by and large the new book is about the Poet at Sixty. The concluding poem is called **"Prologue at Sixty."** Characteristically it contemplates its author, first as a member of the human race:

> Name-Giver, Ghost-Fearer,
> maker of wars and wisecracks,
> a rum creature, in a crisis always,
> the anxious species to which I belong

and then as random particle and Proper Name, the descendant of Nordic pirates, inhabitant of Austria within the limits of the Roman Empire; member of a culture which has grasped the relation between flesh and spirit, and which in principle accepts the duties of acknowledging happy eachness and of bearing witness "to what is the case." To the meaningful landscapes of his life he now adds bits of New York; a New Yorker, sixty, turning first to the obituary columns of the *Times,* he still has some hope of being able to share the city with the alien young.

The little seventeen-syllable *obiter dicta* which have for a few years past scattered themselves across his work are sometimes directly about the Poet: "He thanks God daily / that he was born and bred / a British Pharisee"; "The way he dresses / reveals an angry baby, / howling to be dressed." And so selected crotchets are revealed: the Poet is not vain, except about his knowledge of meter and his friends; he wishes he were Konrad Lorenz, and that he had written the novels of Firbank; he expects lights to turn green for him when he reaches a crossing. He has little to complain of, living as he does, "with obesity and a little fame," among Americans, of whom it may be said that they resemble omelets: "there is no such thing as a pretty good one."

These little sketches contribute selectively to an image of the Poet as benign, as saying Yea but not loudly, tamed by age, domestic in his own kitchen, given to amusingly rueful speculations about verse, sex, God. Do we see in him any of the lineaments, however modified, of the Poet of our youth, of *Lions and Shadows*—the chill genius working all day behind darkened windows, a gun in his desk; the technical virtuoso who could write a double ballade on the names of toothpastes; Stephen Spender's guru; C. Day Lewis' accompanist on the harmonium, or Louis MacNeice's sardonic traveling companion in Iceland, the brilliant joker of the *Letter to Lord Byron*? Where is the public school mythopoet, the boy who cut up his poems and stuck together only the best, terse lines, so that sometimes they sounded like an urgent telegram received in a nightmare—

> Coming out of me living is always thinking,
> Thinking changing and changing living,
> Am feeling as it was seeing?

Is there any trace of the louche **"Letter to a Wound,"** or the tone, borrowed from cruel bullying prefects out of the world of *If . . .*, that conveyed to us so valued a *frisson* in **"The Witnesses"**? Where is our deliciously minatory prophet, studding with epithets he made his own a clever child's vision of disaster—

> The sinister tall-hatted botanist stoops at the spring
> With his insignificant phial, and looses
> The plague on the ignorant town.
>
> Under their shadows the pitiful subalterns are sleeping,
> The moon is usual; the necessary lovers touch?

Where is the voice, so certain of its priorities and its audience, that advised us of our duty in *Spain,* that battered sixpenny pamphlet, its red now fading on our shelves, that is never reprinted? We say nothing of the shouting, brawling Odes, the poems spoken from behind a clinician's mask, or the *gemütlich* apocalypse of **"Out on the lawn I lie in bed. . . ."** I do not know how we can hear them

in the present voice, or see them in the present face of Auden, except by the same imaginative effort we should need to restore our own uncrumpled faces and uncracked voices. But something endures, too deep for time to eradicate; it is a rhythm of thought, convolute, indirect, persistent. One hears it in the Prologue to *Look, Stranger!,* **"O love, the interest itself in thoughtless heaven . . ."** with its long-drawn sentences, the beautiful conceit of Newton,

> who in his garden watching
> The apple falling towards England, became aware
> Between himself and her of an eternal tie;

in the last seventeen lines, of which I cannot say whether my admiration is actual or remembered from my eighteenth year. Certainly they represent a sort of controlled aspiration at the end of a magniloquent poem; and now, quietened by religious certainties, lacking the long breath of youth, he ends with that still. The Love of the early poetry now speaks its Name; there is less threatening, less exaltation, but these are among the qualities that would show up in a voice print and establish the identity of the boy and the man chatting quietly in Manhattan or Kirchstetten.

Looking on that portrait and on this, we see what lies between them: a life. Living it, the Poet decided that poetry was a game, a shadow. This has, somewhat absurdly, been held against him; he suffers as much as Dryden from irrelevant censures. It is the mark of a bore, or, to use an Auden word, a *juggins,* to suppose that something is supremely important because you can do it well. Gardeners, scholars, athletes often bear this mark. But, as the Poet's friend Marianne Moore decisively remarked, there are things that are important beyond all this fiddle. St. Thomas Aquinas and Pascal were aware that there were things more important than their things, and Wittgenstein did not think that what cannot be said is less important than what can. All these people took their business very seriously. Games are not trivial in Wittgenstein, and Auden is not trivializing poetry when he calls it a game. Nor is he less serious because the manic threats of *The Orators* became the controlled dismissive gestures of Antonio in *The Sea and the Mirror,* the decayed city of *The Dog Beneath the Skin* merged into a benign survey of modern Manhattan. His visions of the Unjust City were made actual in the forties; we do not need those fantasies now. They belonged to their time, and it is not blindness or weakness that abandons them in favor of a wary calm. Also there is no need, when you really know, to seem knowing. The Poet will not be betrayed into a vulgar sadness; and he coexists, in the same skin, with an average sensual man. What we hear in the voice is a life; in the face we may even see an analogue of that limestone landscape, cut by intelligible streams, containing features that in themselves suggest poems, as, within the outcrops of the Poet's favorite rock, goddesses lie in wait for the chisel. That is, for many of us, a landscape we grew up with. And if some slip away to sterner slopes, productive plains, or to experiences more oceanic, many others will remain, and will certainly praise limestone. (pp. 69-71)

Frank Kermode, "The Poet in Praise of Limestone," in The Atlantic Monthly, *Vol. 225, No. 5, May, 1970, pp. 67-71.*

Monroe K. Spears   (essay date 1970)

[Spears is an American professor of English literature. He is the author of many published critical commentaries, including books on Auden and Hart Crane. In the following excerpt from his Dionysus and the City: Modernism in Twentieth-Century Poetry, *he explores the city as metaphor in Auden's poems.]*

The City has been a prominent feature of Auden's moralized landscape from the beginning. In the early poetry it is a natural symbol for civilization, order, collective responsibility as opposed to escapist and isolationist islands. Thus **"Paysage Moralisé"** concludes with the exhortation that we "rebuild our cities, not dream of islands"—islands "where love was innocent, being far from cities" in our unreal and sentimental imaginings. When Auden took up residence in New York in 1939, he chose to live his myth almost like Yeats in his tower with its winding stair. **"New Year Letter"** is based upon a parallel between two types of *civitas,* art and society: "To set in order: that's the task / Both Eros and Apollo ask." (In the elegy on Freud, Eros is called "builder of cities.") In **"New Year Letter,"** the only existing order is that of art—the *"civitas of sound"* produced by a passacaglia of Buxtehude; but this exists inside the order represented by Elizabeth Mayer's New Year's Eve party: a small group of civilized persons, cosmopolitan, mostly exiles, existing precariously in the huge anonymous city and coming together briefly to form a temporary order of art and civilization. At the end of the poem, after much inconclusive exploration of the problem of relating internal and external ideas of order (though concluding firmly that art "cannot be / A midwife to society / For art is a *fait accompli*"), the poet looks out at the "ironic points of light" in the darkened city and imagines them to represent scattered individuals who participate in the same internal order of art and civilization, and he prays that he will in response "show an affirming flame." In *For the Time Being, The Age of Anxiety,* and numerous shorter poems of the 1940s, the City image is a fusion of ancient Rome and the modern city, suggesting a parallel between our own naturalistic civilization and that of decadent Rome: both cultures reject, in the name of reason, the Absurd of Christianity, which alone can give meaning to history as well as to individual life. **"The Fall of Rome"** portrays our secular culture in terms of the collapsing Roman one; **"Under Sirius"** presents the ironically-named Fortunatus in Rome in the dog-days of history, uncertain what to wish for, longing for yet fearing the supernatural.

"Memorial for the City" (1949) is Auden's most systematic development of the symbol. The first section contrasts the naturalistic and Christian attitudes toward history and time. The world as it appears to animals or cameras is one in which time is the enemy and human events are without significance; only Nature is "seriously there" because she endures. But human beings, even "now, in this night / Among the ruins of the Post-Vergilian City" know, because of the Christian revelation, that the "crime of life is not time," that we are not to pity ourselves nor to despair. The second section describes man's attempts to build a City. The Middle Ages achieved the Sane City, but it became corrupt; Luther denounced it, pointing out a "grinning gap / No rite could cross," and the City became insecure and divided. In the Renaissance "poets acclaimed the

raging herod of the will." Later, reason and science (based upon the false belief that Nature "had no soul") brought civility and prosperity; the French Revolution aimed at the Rational City, based on natural goodness, seeking the prelapsarian man. In spite of all disasters, the same goal of the Glittering and Conscious City has been pursued ever since. The third section returns to the present: the end result of this progress is the "abolished City," in which civilization has broken down completely, leaving the barbed wire and ruins of war. The ultimate cause is that this secular ideal falsifies human nature, "the flesh we are but never would believe." The last section, "Let Our Weakness speak," personifies human weakness. This weakness, the despair of logicians and statesmen, is the irreducible core of individuality which protects man while it infuriates the social planners, the Apollonians ("As for Metropolis, that too-great city; her delusions are not mine").

The symbol of the City dominates the volume *Nones,* in which the shorter poem we have been discussing appeared, and it is extremely important in the next volume, *The Shield of Achilles.* The title poem contrasts to the "Marble well-governed cities" of Homer's world the modern featureless plain on which an "unintelligible multitude" is ordered about by a faceless voice citing statistics, victims are tortured and executed by "bored officials," and a juvenile delinquent loiters "who'd never heard / Of any world where promises were kept, / Or one could weep because another wept." It is a grim picture of the complete breakdown of the ideal of community and civilized society, the most extreme contrast of ancient and modern. But Auden does not usually take so glum a view of the modern predicament; he does not give up hope or abandon the ideal, however improbable it appears. The first section of **"Memorial for the City"** ends:

> As we bury our dead
> We know without knowing there is reason for what we
>   bear,
> That our hurt is not a desertion, that we are to pity
> Neither ourselves nor our city;
> Whoever the searchlights catch, whatever the loudspeak-
>   ers blare,
> We are not to despair.

In **"Winds"** (*Bucolics*) he takes a much lighter tone: weather "Is what nasty people are / Nasty about and the nice / Show a common joy in observing: / When I seek an image / For our Authentic City, / . . . I see old men in hall-ways / Tapping their barometers, / Or a lawn over which / The first thing after breakfast, / A paterfamilias / Hurries to inspect his rain-gauge." And in **"Sext"** (*Horae Canonicae*) he describes the human capacity for vocation, for ignoring the appetitive goddesses and "forgetting themselves in a function." Without those "nameless heroes" who first took this step, we humans would be "Feral still, unhousetrained, still / wandering through forests without / a consonant to our names, / slaves of Dame Kind, lacking / all notion of a city" (but also, being still animals, incapable of sin: "and at this noon, for this death, / there would be no agents"). (pp. 82-5)

[The] section of *The Dyer's Hand* called "The Poet and the City" presented Auden's latest reflections on the relation between art and society. In the relation of the poet to the city, one of the most damaging modern developments has been the emergence of a passive, uncommitted, abstract "public," or crowd, created by the growth of populations and the development of mass media. The "appearance of the Public and the mass media which cater to it have destroyed naïve popular art." The sophisticated "highbrow" artist survives, because his audience is too small to interest the mass media; but the "audience of the popular artist is the majority and this the mass media must steal from him if they are not to go bankrupt." This they do by offering not popular art, but entertainment, to be consumed and replaced. "This is bad for everyone; the majority lose all genuine taste of their own, and the minority become cultural snobs." (p. 86)

The analogy between the order of art and the order of society that Auden explored in **"New Year Letter"** and elsewhere he reduces to an even sharper contrast. The good poem is analogue to Utopia or Eden, not to a historical society: a "poetic city would always contain exactly the same number of inhabitants doing exactly the same jobs forever"; a society which was really like a good poem would be a "nightmare of horror," and a poem which was really like a political democracy would be "formless, windy, banal, and utterly boring." On the other hand, in our age "the mere making of a work of art is itself a political act." The existence of functioning artists reminds "the Management of something managers need to be reminded of, namely, that the managed are people with faces, not anonymous numbers, that Homo Laborans is also Homo Ludens."

Although Auden has thus rigorously distinguished between the realms of poetry and politics, he has never become indifferent toward the collective human enterprise nor despaired of it. The ideal of civility and community dominates his latest volume, **About the House,** with its sequence called **"Thanksgiving for a Habitat."** These poems celebrate the House, and in that obvious sense the ideal has become very much more personal, the symbol shrunk from civil to domestic. Since **"New Year Letter,"** as we have seen, Auden has conceived of the City as embodied in scattered individuals who participate in civility, and not embodied in any actual society.

"On Installing an American Kitchen in Lower Austria" is retitled **"Grub First, Then Ethics"** and incorporated into the cycle. Celebrating the art of cookery (which Auden has called in prose "one art in which we probably excell all other societies that ever existed . . . the one art which Man the Laborer regards as sacred"), the poem offers a humorous and minimal defense of our civilization. The last stanza puts explicitly the image of the City as composed of scattered individuals—and their houses:

> the houses of our City
> are real enough but they lie
> haphazardly scattered over the earth,
> and her vagabond forum
> is any space where two of us happen to meet
> who can spot a citizen
> without papers. So too, can her foes. Where the
> power lies remains to be seen,
> the force, though, is clearly with them: perhaps only
> by falling can She become
> Her own vision, but we have sworn under four eyes
> to keep Her up—all we ask for,
> should the night come when comets blaze and meres
> break,
> is a good dinner, that we

may march in high fettle, left foot first,
to hold her Thermopylae.

The House poems continue this notion, for the House is more than personal: it is an outpost and repository of civilization. The poems regard it characteristically through long perspectives of history, archaelogy, geology, and biology, counterpointing such formal themes with the easily personal and humorous. (pp. 86-88)

> *Monroe K. Spears, "The Nature of Modernism: The City," in his* Dionysus and the City: Modernism in Twentieth-Century Poetry, *Oxford University Press, Inc., 1970, pp. 70-104.*

W. H. Auden [INTERVIEW WITH Daniel Halpern] (interview date 1971)

[In the following interview, held in New York City in 1971, Halpern questions Auden about the social, literary, and personal influences that helped shape his poetry.]

[Halpern]: Christopher Isherwood once described you as being "a sturdy, podgy little boy, precociously clever, untidy, lazy, and with the masters, inclined to be insolent. His playbox was full of thick scientific books on geology and metals and machines . . . " Does that sound like you?

[Auden]: Well, you see we knew each other when I was eight and he was ten; we were at school together. It was true enough, I guess. I'm not quite as podgy, I hope, and I don't think I'm lazy. I did like to shock my elders. My first day of school, where Isherwood was, the headmaster's wife asked me how I liked school; I said that I liked coming to school to see the various types of boys. That shut her up.

Weren't you quite sophisticated in the ways of sex at a rather early age?

This is a slightly bad thing. You know, Freud talks about the latency period? That I never experienced! That's all I can say.

Your father was a doctor, so there were a great many medical books at your disposal, which you read, of course.

Of course. Actually, the single most embarrassing experience of my life was when I was twelve. My father was at the war and my mother thought she ought to tell me the facts of life. Well, she was very embarrassed and I was even more embarrassed. I didn't tell her that I knew them all completely! (p. 135)

Aside from your medical knowledge, you were also fairly well versed in Psychology. Did you try this out on your friends?

I suppose one did, yes. But it was just fun. I was always interested in psychosomatic things, and I always sort of teased people: "Why have you got this?" or "Do you know why you did that?"

Let's talk now about some of your early influences.

Hardy was the first one. Then I got interested in Edward Thomas. I discovered that Edward Thomas had started

writing quite late. I think he was over forty when he
began, and he had been started by Robert Frost; so then
I got interested in Frost quite early, when he wasn't very
well known. I've always liked his work.

In The Dyer's Hand *you used C. S. Lewis's phrase, "good
drab" to describe his work.*

I don't mean that in a derogatory way at all.

*What about Laura Riding? She's been fairly neglected up
till now.*

Yes, she was an influence. She wouldn't have anything
published for a long time. (pp. 135-36)

*In discussing the development of self criticism, you suggest
that it must be born pretending to be somebody else; the
poet has to get a literary transference upon some poet in particular.*

That's what I meant about Hardy. You find out that if you
can do a convincing imitation of a poet, you've gotten
away from writing poetry in general. And this was Hardy,
for me. I've had lots of influences ever since, of course. But
what I wrote during this time was quite clearly imitative—
anyone who read it would say at once, oh yes, you've been
reading Hardy. I hope that later on people don't know
what I've been reading.

*And after this period of apprenticeship, hopefully, one's own
voice begins to emerge.*

Yes, but that takes time. I think I was twenty when I wrote
the first poem that I kept.

*How do you feel about those first poems now? Say the ones
that appeared in* **The Orators?**

I think they're all right. I have no objection to them. The
only thing is, one gets tired of warhorses that appear in all
the anthologies; it's not that you think there's something
wrong with them, but you don't want to hear about them
again. (p. 136)

"September 1, 1939" *comes to mind.*

That is a case of a poem which I call unauthentic. That
is to say, it may be good or bad, I don't know, but I do
know that I shouldn't have written it. The rhetoric is too
high-flown. It's not in my handwriting and it's a forgery.
I might add here that truth in poetry is very important to
me. I think you must feel, when you read a poem, that it
says something about life which you recognise to be true.
This seems to me enormously important. There's a certain
thing I dislike very much in poetry: when somebody says
something not because he believes it to be true, but because he thinks it sounds poetically effective. I think Yeats
sometimes did that, and I don't like it.

*Did you have other writers you could show your work to
during those early days?*

Naturally one had friends like Isherwood and other people
who one always showed one's stuff to, and one listened to
what they had to say. But I don't think anyone ever studied under somebody, as they do now. Students naturally
read each other's work, but you couldn't say you studied
under somebody, because there weren't such things as
"creative writing" courses in those days. The other thing
that surprises me nowadays is when students want courses

in contemporary literature, because when I was an undergraduate we regarded contemporary literature as something *we* had to discover. I think we were reasonably well
informed; we wouldn't have dreamt of going to our teachers and saying, "Could we have a course in Eliot or
Joyce?" You looked for these things yourself! It was such
fun finding people: "Oh, have you read this . . . " We had
enormous fun. (pp. 136-37)

*Did you ever feel that you were racing, in a sense, against
time? That you had to get a certain number of books read
within a certain period of time?*

No, I don't think so. I've been lucky, in that some instinct
always tells me what to read next. But I've always read
what I wanted. Naturally, at the university one had to
read books one wouldn't normally have read, but generally speaking, I've just read what I liked.

How do *you feel about your education?*

I can't complain. The only thing that was badly taught
was mathematics—languages and science were taught
very well. The result is I can't follow in mathematics. I like
reading science, but I'm stumped when it comes to the
mathematical parts. (p. 137)

*What is your reaction to the neglect of form in most of the
poetry that's being written today?*

I disapprove and would have nothing to do with it myself.
I will continue to write in forms; I think they're making
a mistake. First of all they don't realise what *fun* they're
missing by neglecting form. I look on poetry as a sort of
rite or game of a fairly solemn kind, but it's fun to do. I
prefer to the word "poet" the word that medieval people
used, which was really a direct translation of the Greek:
they call themselves "Makers", like carpenters. You make
a verbal object, and this should be the first thing you think
about. You like a table to stand up and not fall down. It's
intended to last.

*In your interview with Stanley Kunitz, you said that you
couldn't imagine not counting syllables when you are writing a poem.*

There are all kinds of things you can count. One is syllabic
count, which you have to count out to see if it's right.

*Do you look first to see how a poem is made before you read
what it has to say?*

Yes, that's the first thing I look at, to see what the poet's
up to formally. Then of course you have to think about
what it says. My only criticism of my critics is that when
I've done something metrically which I'm rather proud of,
they never notice. I don't think that most of them know
the difference between a bacchic and a choriam, but I
think if you're going to write about poetry you should.

*Your test for critics is whether or not they know four forms:
a sestina, a villanelle, an englyn and a drott-kvaet.*

I'm one of the few people who have written a drott-kvaet
in English, because they're very difficult to do. It's a scholarly Scandinavian form. The englyn is a Welsh form.
These are things critics should know and enjoy—the playful things involved in complicated forms.

Are there any younger poets you follow with interest?

Well, I don't know how young they are. I have one or two young people I know who publish nothing but seem to me to have talent. I'm interested in what they're doing. I help them and we get along all right. You have to remember that if you write poetry yourself a great deal of what you read is going to be poetry of the past, or things other than poetry. For example, I don't take any literary magazine; I do take *Scientific American* and I do take *Natural History,* because I can learn something from them.

But aren't you curious about what's being written now?

One hasn't the time!

How do you feel about explication and the digging for symbolism in poetry?

All that bores me stiff, because poems aren't written in code by an expert, although some poems are more difficult than others. Poems mean what they say! There are critics whom I admire enormously. Auerbach I admire very much; C. S. Lewis I admire very much; Valéry I admire very much; Chesterton is a very good literary critic, I think.

A few years ago you said that the characteristic style of modern poetry is the intimate tone of voice, the speech of one person addressing one person, not a large audience. Has this changed?

No, this I still feel. Supposing you're reading aloud—there may be 1,000 people there, but you think of yourself as speaking to one person.

You also said that many of the people you write for are dead now.

People I *consciously* think about. After all, you hope that some people will read you who are not yet born. You write for whoever likes it. What else can you say? When I say that the people I consciously think of are dead, it is that I think of the old masters looking over my shoulder, and I say, "Do you approve?" The reaction one hopes for from a poem is that the reader will say, "Of course I've always known that, but I've never realised it before." That is what one ideally hopes for.

Is there anything to say concerning the role of political poetry?

About this I would say, by all means let people, if they want to, if they feel like doing it, write what's now called an engagé poem. That's fine. So long as they don't think by writing it they will change the course of history, because they won't. It's slightly embarrassing to me now, for example, that in the 'thirties I wrote a certain number of things about Hitler and other things, which I don't take back for a moment, I think that what I said was quite true. But if I think who benefited, the only person who really benefited from it was me, because it gave me a certain literary reputation. But nothing I wrote prevented one Jew from being gassed or spared the war by five seconds. This is slightly embarrassing to think about. The only things that are effective, when there are political or social evils are: (1) political action, and (2) absolutely straight journalistic reportage for the facts—you must know what the facts are. This can be very important. But neither of these has anything to do with the arts. I think there is a slight modification that one should make. In the case of a coun-

try like Russia, which has never had a free press, a writer can sometimes have a political effect, because he says something which people can't hear anywhere else, and the fact that he risks his liberty and perhaps his life to say it, gives him a moral authority. In the West, none of us can have this, because we can say what we like about Vietnam and we're not going to get shut up. As far as we're concerned, we must not imagine that we can affect anything by this. After all, if you look back, the political and social history of Europe would be what it has been if Goethe, Dante, Shakespeare, Michaelangelo, Mozart, Beethoven and whom you like, had never lived. We'd have missed an awful lot of pleasure, but the political and social history would have been more or less the same. Fairly recently I did write a short poem about the invasion of Czechoslovakia. I was living very near to it and I was quite moved by what was going on. But I don't kid myself that writing it is going to do any good. I did discover that a number of people in Russia had read the poem.

Would you agree with Spender, when he says that you have a philosophy based on a religious view of life?

Yes, I think that's true, but it's really for other people to decide. Certainly everything I've written since 1940 has been theologically orthodox. That's about all I can say. It doesn't mean that I talk directly about religious subjects, necessarily, but the value is implied. Really, I think of myself as a comic poet. I always try to make jokes.

But has this religious view of life changed your feeling about writing poetry?

I don't think it has changed that. I probably look at life a little differently, which means that probably what I write is a little different as a result, but my interpretation of the world depends on certain beliefs I have.

So you decided that the beliefs you held were no longer of value to you.

I thought this would be a truer view of life than what I had before. I don't think of this change as a weakness, but as a lucky gift. Basically I was what could be called a Liberal Humanist.

You were called other things: A Spiritual Physician, and a Lunatic Clergyman. Have you heard those before?

Oh yes. I believe I really invented them myself. I don't think I'm particularly lunatic, though. Looking back now, as I wrote in my *Commonplace Book,* it is always amusing to think of alternate careers to the one you've actually had, in which you think you possess the talents that could have made you successful. I feel that if I hadn't decided to be a poet, I could have been an Angelican bishop by now. Yes, I can see myself as a bishop. This is an amusing thing to play with. There's another thing, and I wonder what you feel about this. Imagine yourself a contemporary male friend of your future father; and then a contemporary female friend of your future mother. Your future father comes to you and says, "I'm thinking of marrying this girl, what do you think?" And your future mother comes to you and says, "I'm thinking of marrying this man, what do you think?" One would probably have said no. Now, this is rather odd, because if one's advice was taken, then one wouldn't exist. You think about this and see what answer you give. I have found that most people give the same answer I do. Not that my parents' marriage was unhappy; it wasn't, but one would simply have said no.

I think I would have said yes.

You really would? I think you're in a minority. I'm not talking about relationships, though. You might have said, "Look here, Papa (your future Papa), you're interested in sports. Do you really want to marry this girl who's interested in literature?"

No, I think it was a real match.

Well, fine, but I think you'll find you're the exception. It's not that one's criticising their marriage if one would have said no; it's simply what you would have advised had you been a contemporary.

What about you?

If I had been a contemporary of my father's, I'd have said: "I think you want a girl who is a little easier, and gentler." And I think I would have said to my mother, "You need somebody who's a little stricter." (pp. 138-41)

Do you have much to do with young people now?

I see some. Of course, a thing that happens when you get to my age, is that often when I am with young people, I can get on with them better than their own parents' generation can, because I've become a grandpa already. It's always easier in that way.

How do you feel about the "drug scene" here?

I deplore it, but personally I think they should legalise pot. Though I don't approve of the young smoking it, particularly. I see it as something used to produce a sort of ego inflation, which I think is bad for them. But as long as it isn't legalised, it's worse, because they have to mix in illegal circles with people who *are* on harder things. And though I don't approve of their taking it, I think legalising it would be the sensible thing to do.

What about pot as an aid to writing?

If they think it will help them to write, it won't. I mean, they may get fun out of doing it, but that's all. All drugs, even the harmless ones like pot, deprive people of a real wish to communicate. They talk, but they talk nonsense.

You don't think it's an attempt to communicate on a "higher level"?

No. I'm all for ordinary communication.

How do you feel about poets such as Baudelaire, who smoked opium?

I don't think it taught him much about poetry, although he might have had fun taking it. It's very interesting to hear recordings of what highly articulate and intelligent people say under the influence of LSD. Absolute nonsense!

Have you ever taken LSD?

Oh yes, that's a complete frost. It was rather funny. I would only take it under medical supervision, so the doctor came at 7:30 in the morning and gave me the dose. Well, I sat there, I sat there, I sat there, waiting for something to happen; *nothing* would happen, except some slight schizoid associations in my body. At 10:30, when

the effect was supposed to be maximum, we went around the corner to Second Avenue to have some ham and eggs. I was staring out of the window and I thought, *now* something is beginning to happen, because I thought I saw my mailman making signals. When we got home the doorbell rang and there was my mailman, who said, "I waved at you and you took no notice!" So, I decided LSD was not for me. (pp. 142-43)

How do you feel about [the "Auden Group"] label?

I object to the word "group". This is an invention of journalists, really. We all happened to be more or less the same generation, we happened to be personal friends; now, naturally people of more or less the same age, living in the same world, are going to have certain things in common, but what they have in common is the least interesting; what is interesting is the way in which they differ. But one knows how this labeling happens. Let's say a reviewer has to review three poets in one review, so he cooks up something like a group of writers in the 'thirties, or whatever it is. Well, this is very annoying! Of course we all happen to be friends, but to talk about a "group" is wrong.

I remember your initial reason for going to Berlin, if I may quote you: "I had an unconscious bias in favor of Germany because, when I was a little boy in prep-school during the first World War, if I took an extra slice of bread and margarine, some master was sure to say: 'I see, Auden; You want the Huns to win,' thus establishing in my mind an association between Germany and forbidden pleasures."

The basic thing I think though was when I went down from Oxford and my parents said I could have a year abroad. . . . Well, the intellectual generation just before mine was attracted to French culture, so I thought if I was going to go, I was not going to Paris. That was really the reason. It so happened that it was a fortunate time to be in Berlin. Rather exciting. (p. 144)

Let's move back to writing for a moment. In much of the Auden literature one thing that recurs is the idea of isolation of the individual.

I don't feel particularly isolated. I must say I have very good friends and I'm not conscious of being isolated. I like to be alone for most of the day, but that's something else.

Do you still feel that "aloneness" is man's real condition?

Yes. In one sense everyone is alone.

In the old existential sense?

Yes, but I think existentialism has done all it can, and is now a danger. I think it's a form of gnosticism. It doesn't pay proper attention to the body.

Would you say that you have an "approach to poetry"?

One likes to make verbal objects. At any given point one has certain kinds of subjects that interest one; I think it's frightfully important to be one's age. There are certain things you should write at a certain period; when you've learned how to do that, then you've got to do something else. You can get an idea for a poem which you have to turn down for one of two reasons: I'm sorry, no longer, or I'm sorry, not yet. And then there are the problems connected with language—whether it's metrical or diction or whatever it is. The language interest looks for the sub-

Auden, Stephen Spender, and Christopher Isherwood at Rugen Island in 1931.

ject it can incorporate, the subject looks for the right kind of form. When these things come together you can write a poem.

Do you agree that the most poetical of all scholastic disciplines is philogy? That every poet must presuppose, sometimes mistakenly, that the history of the language is at an end?

Yes. Sometimes you're mistaken because you get comic changes that happen when a word has changed its meaning. For example, you can't write about fairies any more in a poem; you have to call them elves. This is because particular changes have taken place in the word. This is a case where language changes and then you do get funny double entendres. I couldn't live without the big O.E.D.; I have one set here and one set in Austria. (pp. 145-46)

Do you feel, from the contacts that you have had with younger poets, that things are different for them than they were for you?

I am a little alarmed about a lot of the things I read. Again, it's the lack of form, my being a passionate formalist, because I take a rather hedonistic view about all this—surely everyone knows you can't play a game without rules, although the rules can be varied from one game to another. But why writing should be any different I cannot see. What I am convinced of is that a poem shouldn't be

self expression, and I agree with Valéry, who said, "A poet is someone whose imagination is stimulated by arbitrary restrictions." So often they make you have second thoughts, which you discover are often better than your first ones. What you find, funny enough, happening when people ignore form, is that far from making each poet more original, they sound more like each other. I'm sure this happens. There are a few people, like D. H. Lawrence for example, who you feel had to write in free verse. But they are the exception, I think.

To put that another way, I'll quote from The Dyer's Hand: "The poet who writes free verse is like Robinson Crusoe on his desert island. He must do all his cooking, laundry, darning and washing himself. . . . More often the result is squalor, dirty sheets on the unmade bed and empty bottles on the unswept floor!"

Yes, I think that's still true, but there are the exceptions and Lawrence was an obvious one.

I would like to know about how proper names have become so important for you. You say that proper names can't be translated, that they are a kind of poetry.

Proper names *are* poetry in the raw; it's why the early epic poets had half their work done for them—they spoke to an audience who had the same myths, the same landscapes, the same names. But now you hardly dare use a proper name without thinking. Should I gloss it? It's very difficult to use them now. It makes our task a great deal more difficult than it was for those early epic poets. I had an interesting experience in 1934. I wrote a poem which included the name Garbo. I thought: Well, everyone knows her, and they did at that time. And yet, when Hogarth did a selection of my poems after the war, he felt it necessary to gloss it. But I think poetry consists in trying to give proper names to appearances. (p. 147)

You have also written a great deal about sacred objects? What is your concept of "sacredness"?

An object is sacred that arouses in you a feeling of awe and reverence. Now the feeling may range all the way from joyous happy wonder, to panic rage. But there is this feeling of awe in it that's common to all experiences of an object's being sacred or luminous, or whatever word one likes to use.

This idea of sacredness seems to have been something that was very significant in your early work.

It still applies, although I handle it differently now.

Spender talks of an "external human authority" in your work. What is your conception of this? What does it mean to you?

I don't exactly know what Stephen means there. When we met I didn't believe in God, but naturally, things have changed since then. I don't know what he meant, except that I was rather an intellectual bully—I used to bully my friends.

But as for a belief in God?

I was brought up in a pious home; when I was sixteen, which is not uncommon, I decided all this was nonsense and I didn't come back to the church until I was 32.

What brought you back?

A variety of things. Hitler had something to do with it. One had to ask oneself, of Hitler and those others, "If I think these people are wrong, why do I think they're wrong?" One just assumed that the ordinary "humanist values" were something that anyone who was sane would know about. But it turned out not to be so. I remember hearing Hitler speak. He said: "When I come to power I promise you every German girl shall get a German husband," and they cheered wildly. Another person who was important in my life was somebody who I was convinced was a saint. Charles Williams. Actually, I met two people in my life who I thought were saints. The other was a woman. They both had the same affect, utterly different as they were. When you were in their presence you felt ten times as nice, ten times as intelligent, even ten times as good looking as you really were. It was only when you went out that you realised: I'm not that nice, I'm not that intelligent, I'm not that good looking.

Who was this woman?

Dorothy Day, who ran the Catholic Worker. But when I did come back to the church I was driven absolutely up the wall by this liturgical reform nonsense. My own parish church went mad because I used to go to the Russian Orthodox, where I didn't understand a word!

This might be a good time to ask about your involvement with Homer Lane, the American "healer".

I never met him myself, but I knew a patient of his. He was also a patient of Grodeck's, in whom I got interested after Homer Lane.

He wrote The Book of the It?

Yes, and *The World of Man*. They were involved in the relationship between body and mind, which they were so good on. The whole psychosomatic thing I found extremely interesting.

Speaking of the mind/body relationship, I hear that you enjoy cooking.

I'm not a very good cook, but I try to cook things I enjoy eating. I'll cook for myself when I'm here alone; it's plain cooking, but it's all right. And it's such a saving of money, of course. I think everyone now has to learn to cook, because all the good restaurants are geared to people with expense accounts. Unless you cook or are very rich you're condemned to eat in cafeterias, and presently you'll begin to think that that's how food ought to taste.

What kind of things do you enjoy cooking?

Well, tonight we're having fish. . . . (pp. 148-49)

W. H. Auden and Daniel Halpern, in an interview, in Antaeus, *Vol. 5, Spring, 1972, pp. 135-49.*

F. W. Bateson   (essay date 1975)

[*An English critic, scholar, and educator, Bateson edited* The Cambridge Bibliography of English Literature *and founded the periodical* Essays in Criticism. *He also wrote on the poetry of William Wordsworth and was active in criticism of twentieth-century letters. In the following excerpt, he reviews Auden's* Thank You, Fog, *placing it within the context of the author's literary career.*]

'You were silly like us.' The half-line from the moving poem on Yeats's death has the disconcerting memorability that was then Auden's special peculiar talent. Eliot, one of his early models and earliest admirers, might have called it 'surprise', a quality that is described in *Homage to John Dryden* as 'essential to poetry'. But what is meant or hoped to surprise may often seem to an unsympathetic reader merely silly. This indeed is the basis of the Public Prosecutor's case in Auden's lively *Partisan Review* article 'The Public v. the Late Mr. William Butler Yeats' (written within a week or two of the poem). Yeats, the Prosecutor said, had edited that absurd *Oxford Book of Modern Verse*, he admired peasants but only as long as they remained poor, he began with fairies and proceeded from them to 'legends of barbaric heroes with unpronounceable names', before finally reaching 'the mumbo-jumbo of magic and the nonsense of India'. It is true that Auden provides a 'Counsel for the Defence' in his article, as the poem had ended the line about Yeats's silliness ('Your gift survived it all'). But in both poem and article the apologia comes too late and is too muffled.

Silly like *us*? The first person plural includes, as it was clearly intended to, Auden himself. No doubt his silliness is different in kind and degree from Yeats's (which was more innocent and sometimes more profound), but it is an irritant, an apparent irresponsibility. That Auden was aware of this mote (not, I think, a beam) in his own eye is suggested, to take one example, by his later comment on **The Orators,** which has in its 'Prologue' and 'Epilogue' alone two of the best poems he ever wrote, though considered as a whole it is in no doubt, as Auden put it, a 'fair notion' fatally injured by 'incompetence or impatience'. The observation occurs in the Preface to **Collected Shorter Poems, 1930-1950** (1950). The *1927-1957* collection of **Shorter Poems** (1966) achieves a silliness more difficult to excuse than the lapses into automatic writing in **The Orators**—which is still surely, as John Hayward proclaimed it to be in *The Criterion* on its original publication, 'the most valuable contribution to English poetry since *The Waste Land*'. The silliness I am referring to in *1927-1957* is the strange animus against the definite article, 'a German characteristic', as the Foreword calls it, which Auden tells us he has now done his best to eliminate from the poems written in the 1930's. He had perhaps been reading G. Rostrevor Hamilton's *The Tell-Tale Article* (1949), in which these poems of Auden's are said, incorrectly, to be over-indulgent in definite articles. **"Oxford,"** which was printed in *The Listener* in February 1938 and was probably written the preceding summer, is one of the worst sufferers. In **"Another Time"** (1940) the first three lines run:

> Nature is so near: the rooks in the college garden
> Like agile babies still speak the language of feeling;
> By the tower the river still runs to the sea and will run . . .

In the *1927-1957* collection this has become:

> Nature invades: old rooks in each college garden
> Still talk, like agile babies; the language of feeling,
> By towers a river still runs coastward and will run . . .

The six definite articles have been reduced to one. But what is substituted for them really won't do. It isn't only *old* rooks who use the language of feeling, nor are they to be found in *each* Oxford college garden. And Magdalen is the only college to have a tower with a river running by it. In any case, like it or not, the definite article is fundamental to modern English speech; its use has become more necessary (as that of inversion has become less justifiable) as English becomes less and less an inflected language. (Like Latin, Anglo-Saxon didn't have a definite article.) In the remote past when I was an editor of *Oxford Poetry* my stylistic models were Graves and Richard Hughes, and the poetry editor of *The Spectator,* which printed several of my undergraduate poems, tried to dissuade me, I remember, from their *telegraphese*. She (it was Amabel Williams-Ellis, the editor-cum-proprietor's daughter) was right; Oxford poets for three or four years before Auden's dramatic arrival at Christ Church did leave too many definite articles out. All recent English poetry seems to demand about one *the* per line; **"Oxford"** as it happens in its earlier version didn't even have that, there being only 28 of the 'German' invaders in its 45 lines.

Many worthy people I know find this sort of Audenic silliness, in which the later prefaces particularly abound, intensely irritating. Leavis, for example. The 'Retrospect' that he added in 1950 to *New Bearings in English Poetry* generalizes and overstates the defect as evidence of a persistent 'immaturity', which is then defined as Auden's own

'uncertainty as to the degree of seriousness he intended'. Applied to the early and obscure **Paid on Both Sides**—the one work of Auden's Leavis actually specifies either in the 'Retrospect' or the more generous *Scrutiny* review (June 1934)—the comment is no doubt valid. But the uncertain seriousness of the best of the later poems *was* intended. Auden's principal achievement indeed has been to break down the Romantics' barrier between Poetry and Light Verse. That Leavis was not unappreciative of the potentialities of Serious Light Verse is clear from the original and at the time daring enthusiasm he displays for *Peter Bell the Third* in the essay on Shelley. But while applauding the 'vividness of imagination' and 'verbal vigour' displayed in **Paid on Both Sides** he has remained curiously blind to the persistence and development of these qualities in the poems Auden wrote between 1930 and 1940. The critical trap of Arnoldian 'high seriousness', a quality in which Arnold found both Chaucer and Burns regrettably deficient, is clearly still an easy one to fall into.

Auden's occasional silliness must be seen in its historical context, which is that of *Dadaisme* and Surrealism, *Finnegans Wake*, Gertrude Stein's lyrics, Pound's *Cantos*, Eliot's strange *After Strange Gods*. There was a dottiness in the literary air in the inter-war years. There was also a local difference. Although Oxford's examiners found fit, quite unjustifiably, to award Auden only a Third in the English Literature Finals (Geoffrey Grigson also got a Third the same year), his intellectual essence has always been Oxonian. Leavis, of course, is Cambridge, product and prophet. Today I suppose you can be either an Oxford man or a Cambridge man without the difference being noticed, but in the 1930's Oxford and Cambridge were not speaking the same critical language. Auden's finest lyrics coincide by a happy accident with the golden age of *Scrutiny*. But, though Auden wrote six reviews for Leavis's journal, his sociological and psychological interests give them an odd look in *Scrutiny*'s severely ethical pages. In his indispensable *Reader's Guide to W. H. Auden* John Fuller has called attention to 'the unusual amount of unfair criticism' the clever allegorical ballad **"Miss Gee"** (written 1937) has received; but the only unfair critics he cites are in fact Leavis ('a pointless unpleasantness') and Kathleen Raine, also very much of that Cambridge. Other examples could be listed.

So far as these two pre-World War II intellectual climates can be reduced to a formula we may say that Cambridge wanted private poetry whereas Oxford preferred a public poetry. The Public Prosecutor, representing the Oxford Public, had proposed three critical minima in Auden's imaginary case against Yeats: a great poet must have (i) 'a gift of a very high order for memorable language', (ii) 'a profound understanding of the age in which he lived', (iii) 'a working knowledge of and sympathetic attitude towards the most progressive thought of his time'. By this triple standard—which I still find self-evidently inexorable—at least half of **Look, Stranger!** (1936) and **Another Time** (1940) is great poetry. And, to be brutally blunt in the best Cambridge manner, if you actually prefer the Pound pastiches of Bottrall to such a poem as **Look Stranger's** superb Prologue ('O love, the interest itself in thoughtless Heaven') you are merely displaying local prejudice. (I have to admit that Auden left this poem out of the *1927-57* collection of his **Shorter Poems**—but that was for political reasons.) This particular poem had appeared in the *New Statesman* only two months before Auden's first review in *Scrutiny*—which was sarcastically headed, as it happens, 'Private Pleasure'. (pp. 383-86)

I have found nothing in **Thank You, Fog** to revive my earlier enthusiasm. It is 'Parnassian', in the sense in which Hopkins used the term of Tennyson's *Enoch Arden.* I cannot find a line in it that I expect to remember with any such increasing intensity of admiration that I have for one line from the Epilogue to **The Orators:**

> That gap is the grave where the tall return.

In a way Auden has been my generation's Lost Leader more disturbingly even than Eliot. But at least the pretentious obscurity of the long New York poems slipped away in the last three or four collections. As a literary historian, as I confess myself to be, the poem that interested me most in this thin final volume is the autobiographical **"A Thanksgiving".** Here Auden's successive models or mentors are listed in the chronological order of their impact upon his verse. He began, we learn, by sitting at the feet of Hardy, Edward Thomas, and (more surprisingly) Frost. But 'Falling in love altered that' and now '*Yeats* was a help, so was *Graves*'. With the coming of the Depression of the 1930's 'there to instruct me was *Brecht*'. But the brutalities of Hitler and Stalin 'forced me to think about God', when

> Wild *Kirkegaard, Williams* and *Lewis*
> guided me back to belief.

Finally, back again in Oxford, he has turned to '*Horace*, adroitest of makers' and (of all people) '*Goethe*, devoted to stones'. The many exclusions from this list are of some interest—no mention, for example, of early heroes like Blake, D. H. Lawrence and Freud, or of stylistic models like Owen, Hopkins, Rimbaud and Rilke. The parallel with Horace, however, especially the Horace of the *Odes*, may provide a critical clue to the final poems. How much Latin Auden had isn't clear. John Fuller was only able to provide one possible specific borrowing. In **"Lakes"** the *estranging sea* appears in quotation marks. The acknowledgement may perhaps include on to *Oceano dissociabili* (*Odes*), but primarily it is clearly to Arnold's 'estranging sea' ('To Marguerite—Continued'), which does derive from Horace. What seems to have particularly fascinated Auden in Horace is not the diction but the prosody. The adroitness with which he combines and varies line-lengths and sentence-lengths as well as the stress equivalents of iambs, spondees, dactyls and anapests would have been admired by Tennyson and Swinburne, even perhaps by Hopkins. The vocabulary on the other hand is much wider and more daring than Horace's. The first stanza of **"A Thanksgiving"**, before we get to Hardy, Thomas and Frost, is typical of this lighter side of the Horatian Auden:

> When pre-pubescent I felt
> that moorlands and woodlands were sacred:
> people seemed rather profane.

Oderat profanum vulgus. Why, however, does the second line extrude? Because, as the later verses guarantee, it must scan: x/- xx/- xx/- -/x (a half-foot at the beginning and end of the line with two dactyls and a spondee intervening, a total equivalent to four Latin feet). The first line, on the other hand, consists of only two dactyls and a final stressed syllable, as the first line of the third verse confirms

('Falling in love altered that'). The third line also consists of two dactyls and a stressed monosyllable. What will interest the prosodist most, however, is not the accentual patterns in themselves but their use as a way of underlining what is semantically crucial, while *underplaying* whatever is less important in what the poem says. (In other words, metrics as pointers to meaning.) Thus of the thirteen first person singulars (*I* or *me*) each regularly receives only a half-stress. Although in common speech *I* is a long diphthong and *me* a long vowel, which therefore invite emphasis, Auden's metre has de-emphasized them into a non-egotistical humility. The fact has a moral as well as a technical instructiveness.

It is true that something of the early silliness persists in the collection's title—chosen by Auden himself according to Edward Mendelson, who provides a preliminary 'Note', which also informs us that 'the book contains the poems that Auden completed after leaving New York in the Spring of 1972. **"Thank You, Fog"** is the title of the first poem. Auden, it seems, has been spending a misty Christmas in a Wiltshire manor-house and is delighted to have exchanged New York's 'smog' for English fog—a graceful way of explaining in verse, though hardly in poetry, what the 'Note' tells us in prose.

Auden died on 29 September 1973 (Mendelson; 28 September according to *Who's Who*). He had been born on 21 February 1907 and was therefore sixty-six when he died. But he had perhaps aged prematurely. What I miss in all his later poems is the 'profound inner disturbance; a turbid pressure of emotions from below' that Leavis acutely recognized in the early work (*Scrutiny*, June 1934). Still the technical wizardry, the range of tone and diction, and above all the poetic manipulation of abstract thought—a theme which would demand a greater philosophical expertise than I can command—were retained to the end. Whether they satisfy the Public Prosecutor's triple standard is, of course, another matter. I suppose they don't. (pp. 387-90)

F. W. Bateson, "Auden's Last Poems," in Essays in Criticism, *Vol. XXV, No. 3, July, 1975, pp. 383-90.*

George T. Wright   (essay date 1981)

[*In the following excerpt, Wright surveys Auden's character as a poet.*]

What kind of poet is W. H. Auden? Critics have often condemned him for not being one kind or another, but they have seldom succeeded, even when they have wanted to, in describing the kind he *is.* During a career that spans two continents and several faiths, his poetry has seemed, from phase to phase, to alter not merely its loyalties but its character. Is it really British or American? really Freudian, Marxist, or Christian? Is Auden mainly a satirist, a Romantic, a journalist, a song writer, or what? Every new poem or new style of his seems to challenge what we thought we knew about him. Randall Jarrell, with delicate malice, once placed at the head of an article hostile to Auden a quotation he attributed to Heraclitus: *We never step twice into the same Auden.*

Two or three characteristics, however, seem fairly permanent. For one thing, although Auden, sometimes very obviously, borrows techniques or mannerisms from dozens of other writers, he has to an extraordinary degree the poet's ability to make what he borrows his own, to mold it into something we think of as recognizably Auden. All readers will probably see as essential qualities of his style a quickness and lightness of touch; a cleanness of phrase and sentence; a caustic wit; and ironic hardness that, even as it recommends love as the answer to modern anxiety and injustice, is seldom in danger of sentimentality. At times Auden's wit is so exuberant and zestful as to produce, in the service of the most serious ideas, fanciful and even outrageous extravaganzas. At other times the wit is restrained and the verse austere; his writing achieves an Augustan, a Latin, a rococo, elegance.

But, in spite of the feeling we have of an undeniable precision, most readers of Auden have had the experience, after reading one of his poems, of being thoroughly mystified—the thing doesn't make sense; the point vanishes between two stanzas; and the reader is left with a blurred image, an obscure situation, a half understood, possibly misunderstood point. It may be that Auden intends this uncertainty as a way of saying that, among all our precise instruments for measuring, computing, refining, we still have no sure knowledge of where we are. But among the causes of Auden's obscurity are some which account in large part for both the blur and the zest of his writing: his concern at once with inner experience and with society, his frequent shifts in perspective, his readiness to interpret anything as a parable of human experience, and his tireless experimentation.

Although Auden's poems always probed the illnesses of modern society he usually approached this subject through the examination of inner motives and conflicts. A consistent student of the inner life—of anxiety, guilt, fear, self-doubt, anguish, love—he brought himself for a time in the 1930s to maintain that our inner lives could be put right only if certain social changes occurred; but he always found more congenial the opposing view that, whatever its causes, the center of our *malaise,* as well as the focal point of any cure, is the lonely human being. His work tends to make the outer world symbolic of an inner reality that is the scene of all finally significant action or at least the testing ground on which all action must be tried out and evaluated. Intellectual as Auden's poetry often seems—removed, detached, impersonal—the center of it is nevertheless the inner man who is thinking, feeling, comparing, refining, mocking, doubting, believing. As Auden puts it in a poem of the 1930s: "For private reasons I must have the truth."

Still, from another point of view the *public* reasons are important. Skeptical of utopias, critical of society's administrators and managers, Auden is always alert to the contradictions between the personal and the public; and his poetry constantly shifts its angles of vision in order to show graphically the distance between the feeling inner self and what that self looks like from the point of view of the state, or of an objective observer. Even such an observer is at successive moments a social scientist, an interplanetary visitor, a psychoanalyst. The perspectives are often different, often changing; but all of them are needed to correct one another, to fill out Auden's view of the whole man: anguished self, citizen, organism, outsider.

Outer perspectives, however, may be fairly clear (although

some of their intricate combinations can be puzzling); it is the *inner* perspective that often makes poems hard for us to focus. In the early work Auden uses syntactical ellipsis to give us that hard, gruff, urgent sense of meaning deeper than words: "Can speak of trouble, pressure on men/Born all the time, brought forward into light/For warm dark moan." Frequently, too, both here and later, the syntax, though always crisp, is very involved; in fact, no other modern poet uses such various or such elaborate sentences.

Auden's poems are also full of unexplained pronouns, concepts, jokes, and contexts. Especially in the early poems (1928-32) we have a decisive sense of something happening, but not in a clearly defined place or time or situation. Many of these early poems revolve around the fighting of some unspecified war or an unexplained exile, but we do not know exactly who the enemy is, or what war we are engaged in, what its purpose is, or what we hope to gain. Although we may sometimes identify the cause with Marxist revolution (and early readers often did), we are not told enough to justify this identification; and the war is usually more intelligible as a conflict between inner forces of a Freudian kind, perhaps between a child and his elders.

The deliberate blurring is necessary to Auden's aims in these poems. The effect is that of dream-symbolism; for Auden, in exploring the inner life, is trying to present objects and events which are strong in felt, not reasoned, significance. What is important in the early poems is not the intellectual exposition of a social or psychological doctrine but the feeling that accompanies ambiguous commitment: what it feels like to go into voluntary, purposeful, if regretful, exile or partly to see one's way out of smothering anxieties and guilts. Even later on, when Auden's poetry becomes more discursive, the inner reality is still central. As with more obvious stream-of-consciousness techniques, Auden's aim is to avoid explaining what the feeling self already knows and he presents landscapes, statements, and dream-imagery as correlatives of inner anxiety or polished corruption. Indeed, much of the best of Auden's work is expressionist in character; and even the rational statements, however analytical they sometimes become, normally function in poetic structures which distort outer reality to conform to the self's feelings of anguish, dread, hope, faith, or worry.

For example, the opening stanza of this poem seemed quite opaque when I first read it:

> Wrapped in a yielding air, beside
> The flower's soundless hunger,
> Close to the tree's clandestine tide,
> Close to the bird's high fever,
> Loud in his hope and anger,
> Erect about his skeleton,
> Stands the expressive lover,
> Stands the deliberate man.

Gradually I realized that Auden is speaking of man in general and of the universe that surrounds him: the air that stirs as he moves; the plant life whose thirst, when we come to think of it, is unlike that of other thirsty things in being silent; trees in which the sap rises like a tide (the image echoes one of Rainer Maria Rilke's), but also silently and secretly; birds that seem intense and live in the air above us—hence the pun "high fever."

Later on Auden speaks of this man as

> The brothered and the hated
> Whose family have taught him
> To set against the large and dumb,
> The timeless and the rooted,
> His money and his time.

And, because I have read Auden's essays of this period, I see at once that he is not condemning the strong man's exploitation of the less gifted—"the large and dumb" working class, for example. No, the "timeless and the rooted" clearly refers, respectively, to animals and plants. As with "high fever," the juxtaposition of money and time is a passing joke, which temporarily distracts us from seeing, and later adds emphasis to the fact, that "time" means "conception of time." And when we see this, we see that "money" signifies something like "the human capacity to deal with symbols and hence to develop elaborate social structures," which we then use to lay waste the natural world. (pp. 21-5)

Another permanent feature of Auden's work is his delight in parables, in all literary or mythological structures that symbolize the relations between parts of the self or the self's relation to elements of society or nature: the unidentified war, the Marxist conception of history, the Christian picture of a world fallen but capable of redemption through miracle. Fairy tales, fantasies, dreams, or any stylized model of events may express for him certain fundamental spiritual conditions in the life of men for which he is always seeking analogues and symbols—the relations between members of a family, between master and servant, between doctor and patient, or the relations that hold in quests, in detective stories, in legends and landscapes.

Auden thus subordinates the usual practical, objective categories of value, of time, and of political order in favor of a world of parabolic relationships that are symbolic of real but inner conditions. He subordinates appearance to what he feels is deeper reality. The surfaces of life are still important to him, for it is through the physical and the immediate that a man works out his salvation. But, although in Auden's perspective one actual event may be empirically more important than another, *any* apparently trivial object, action, or system of relationships—a room, a meal, a forest—may have a capacity for illuminating our lives far beyond what we would expect from its modest position in ordinary life.

Holding such a view, Auden is remarkably attentive to the surfaces of ordinary life; for anything may, if we look at it right, suddenly glow with meaning. Looking at it right involves submitting it to sometimes bizarre perspectives, deliberately deranging our usual rational or sensory categories—having Caliban talk like Henry James, or locating a pastoral poem in a city bar. This kind of derangement is constant in Auden; it enters almost always into his imagery and is largely responsible for the blur of meaning that both intrigues and perplexes. It reminds us that his poetry, however rational in tone and structure, is faithful to its source in that unconscious that never gets logical categories straight, that his verse is often wildly playful, and that he is hopelessly in love with variety, improvisation, experiment.

Experiment, like other important things, may look trivial at first, may *be* so at first; but the trivial may lead us to the richest sort of meaning. Auden's experiment often begins in parody and ends in conversion; indeed, Christopher Isherwood recalls in his autobiographical *Lions and Shadows* how Auden (whom he calls "Weston") used to change his personality with his hats:

> There was an opera hat—belonging to the period when he decided that poets ought to dress like bank directors, in morning cut-aways and striped trousers or evening swallow-tails. There was a workman's cap, with a shiny black peak, which he bought while he was living in Berlin, and which had, in the end, to be burnt, because he was sick into it one evening in a cinema. There was, and occasionally still is, a panama with a black ribbon—representing, I think, Weston's conception of himself as a lunatic clergyman; always a favourite role.

On a bus trip into the country one day in 1926, Auden embarrassed Isherwood not only by his hat (which raised snickers) but also by his pretentious pronouncements

> in resonant Oxonian tones: "Of course, intellect's the only thing that matters at *all.* . . . Apart from Nature, geometry's all there *is.* . . . Geometry belongs to man. Man's got to assert himself against Nature, all the *time.* . . . Of course, I've absolutely no use for colour. Only form. The only really exciting things are volumes and *shapes.* . . . Poetry's got to be made up of images of form. I hate sunsets and flowers. And I loathe the *sea.* The sea is formless. . . .

But, Isherwood tells us, such pomposities "never for a moment made me feel . . . that Weston himself was a sham. He was merely experimenting aloud; saying over the latest things he had read in books, to hear how they sounded." And Auden continued to do so throughout his poetic career. He mimics the tones, the verbal habits, even the imagery of other writers, of older verse forms, and of political, scientific, or religious points of view. But this mimicking is not always, or even typically, hostile. It may even be, at first, a form of reverence, an awestricken trying on of a new hat to see what it feels like on the head. And who knows? The hat may turn out to fit, to be the right one for the experimenter. Without the experiment, he might never have found the hat. Several of Auden's poems in 1939 and 1940 show him "trying on" Christianity before he actually became a Christian. As he states in *The Age of Anxiety,* "Human beings are, necessarily, actors who cannot become something before they have first pretended to be it. . . . "

But trying on a hat—or a style or a Church—whatever its serious side, is also amusing; and, as one of the age's great wits, Auden is rarely far from a joke. The jokes sometimes undermine serious purposes, and his poems of the 1930s in particular often suffer from an uncertainty of feeling: there are too many tones, and we don't know how to take them. Any sincere stance Auden assumes in a poem—Freudian, Marxist, or even Christian—is always in danger of being ridiculed by that other, comic side of him. And perhaps his most remarkable achievement is that, despite his almost unmanageable multiplicity of attitudes, he has not wasted his talents in ironic play but has worked through to new forms, new ironic structures, which do justice to the critical qualifications of the ironic intelligence, and yet affirm.

Auden, then, is a thoroughly serious poet, and a thoroughly amusing one. Never only one thing at once, he keeps shifting his own perspectives on the world and, in the process, reveals different sides of himself. His formal variety is astounding: he performs authentically as satirist, song writer, epigrammatist, didactic poet, meditative poet, elegist, odist; in long lines or short, sonnets or sestinas, octosyllabic couplets or four-stress alliterative verse, loose meter or strict, iambics or syllabics, and all kinds of rhyme. He develops styles and abandons them, a sign not of instability but of versatility—of wide, deep, and various interests. From the oracular early poems to the more direct analyses of social illness; from the quiet music of the early songs to the abstract imagery of the later 1930s that culminates in the earnest poems on Yeats and Freud; and from these to the elegance of **"New Year Letter"** and *The Sea and the Mirror,* and to the balanced Latin opulence of his more ambitious poems of the last three decades, Auden's poetry is continually changing.

Within these periods, even within single poems, the poetry is rarely single; it plays off mood against mood, reinforces wisdom with wit, enriches its textures with quick changes in feeling. For art, to Auden, is a mixed, a paradoxical, affair. It is play, but play is worth dying for; and yet it is, too, "in the profoundest sense, frivolous. For one thing, and one thing only, is serious: loving one's neighbor as oneself." Auden's poetry keeps bringing together the sense of everything as of intense significance, and the sense of everything as trivial and frivolous. But each attitude is coherent only in the light of the other.

In fact, as it explores both the rationalities and suddennesses of the inner life, Auden's poetry asserts as its basic insight the connectedness of everything, even of the most unlikely things. The techniques of wit, the shifting images, the unexpected turns that the prosody often takes, all stress the surprise that life is—"O what authority gives / Existence its surprise?"—its playfulness, its magic, its outlandish order. Inner life and outer spectacle, landscape and self, society and feeling—all are discovered to be connected in mysterious, puzzling, disturbing, yet marvelous ways.

Indeed, the world, touched anywhere, will expose these underground connections—if they are approached with just the right attitude of serious play. Words, ideas, feelings are fun to fool around with, to arrange, to order. They are the landscape of this world, whether it be Freud's or God's; and Auden always loved to name, to map, and to anatomize this landscape. Ultimately, this kind of happy tinkering amounts to reverence: to enjoy the world is perhaps to make the most pious use of it. As Auden's career proceeded, he passed from the nightmare conception of man divided from his own best self by overpowering shadows to the more sanctified fairy tale of man born to evil but capable of enchantment by Grace. Freudian inquisitor and Marxist prophet gave way to the more congenial role of ashamed but hopeful Christian. (pp. 25-9)

> *George T. Wright, in his* W. H. Auden, *revised edition, Twayne Publishers, 1981, 232 p.*

Stan Smith   (essay date 1985)

[*Smith is an English authority on twentieth-century British poetry. In the following excerpt from his 1985 study of Auden, he discusses some of the principal themes in Auden's longer poems.*]

'Whether, as some psychologists believe,' Auden wrote in his commonplace book *A Certain World,* 'some women suffer from penis envy, I am not sure. I am quite certain, however, that all males without exception, whatever their age, suffer from penis rivalry, and that this trait has now become a threat to the future existence of the human race':

> Behind every quarrel between men, whether individually or collectively, one can hear the taunt of a little urchin: 'My prick (or my father's) is bigger than yours (or your father's), and can pee further.'
>
> Nearly all weapons, from the early spear and sword down to the modern revolver and rocket, are phallic symbols . . .
>
> Today our phallic toys have become too dangerous to be tolerated. I see little hope for a peaceful world until men are excluded from the realm of foreign policy altogether and all decisions concerning international relations are reserved for women, preferably married ones.

It is a commonplace enough thought. For an Auden so hostile to *kitsch* philosophizing to give it a separate entry among his *obiter dicta* means it is none the less genuine. In the long poems of the forties, confronted by the enormities of that war he had expected for a decade, Auden came to submit the whole phallic ethos of male power to a new and damning scrutiny. Naomi Mitchison had written of 'the curious, archaic maleness' of *Paid on Both Sides,* but had added, 'there is nothing anti-feminist about it, but something in one jumps out to welcome it.' Certainly the young men in that play are forced into a closed circle of killing in the name of their dead fathers by the urgings of their all-too-live mothers. But the alternative to the treadmill of vendetta is presented by that strange hermaphrodite figure the Man-Woman, who appears as a prisoner behind barbed wire to reproach a world where sexual differentiation itself seems to be the cause of violence.

"Letter to Lord Byron" had dismissed somewhat cavalierly the utopian 'dream . . . of being both the sexes'. In more serious vein a 1939 poem from *Another Time,* **"The Riddle"**, spoke of the fall into sexual duality, which had created 'the fallen man and wife', as the source of all contradiction and inequality. Only in the beloved's eyes can we learn at last to say:

> All our knowledge comes to this,
> That existence is enough,
> That in savage solitude
> Or the play of love
> Every living creature is
> Woman, Man, and Child.

New Year Letter had been dedicated to a mother-figure, and was in one sense a confession of phallic incompetence in a world at war, dominated by the penis rivalries of a patriarchal order. *For the Time Being* is dedicated to the memory of his real mother, whose death in 1941 left Auden desolate. The personal crisis, compounded by a breakdown in the relation with Kallman, coincided with the global one. *For the Time Being* was written between October 1941 and July 1942 (in December 1941, after the bombing of Pearl Harbour, the United States entered the war); *The Sea and the Mirror* between August of 1942 and February 1944; *The Age of Anxiety* was begun in July 1944 and completed in November 1946. The world of these poems is like the 'politically powerless' and 'cynical' Panhellenic world which Auden found in C. P. Cavafy's poetry.

The Sea and the Mirror is usually seen as a meditation on art; but it is equally concerned with the idea of power. The Stage Manager's opening address to the Critics speaks of an "authority" which can no longer give 'Existence its surprise' but multiplied to 'ghosts who haunt our lives' is still 'handy with mirrors and wires' at keeping us in our subject-positions, with a combination of habit, wonder and terror. This 'world of fact we love' may well be 'unsubstantial stuff'; but to face up to this is to take us into that realm of silence beyond even factitious meanings, 'On the other side of the wall'. It is this realm that the Narrator of *For the Time Being* fears, preferring even 'The nursery bogey or the winecellar ghost' and the 'violent howling of winter and war' to its unconditional challenge. All these, by comparison, offer a juke-box tune of consolation that fills out and denies that silence. It is the conviction of *The Sea and the Mirror,* however, that it is only in the silence outside discourse, beyond power, that meaning resides, for the silence is ripeness, 'And the ripeness all'.

The Sea and the Mirror is itself a postscript, imagining what might happen to the various characters of Shakespeare's *Tempest* after the play has ended. It opens with an address to departing critics. Prospero has broken his rod of power; Shakespeare has, in the play's final speech, craved our indulgence and departed. As Caliban explains to the Audience in the elaborate Jamesian prose which comprises the second half of the work, we may call for the author, 'the all-wise, all-explaining master' we believe in. But all we will get is the ugly brute Caliban himself, left behind on the island as the captains and the kings depart, the mere echo of 'our so good, so great, so dead author.'

Like Cavafy's Panhellenic world, Prospero's island is a place where the supposedly 'self-governing' kingdoms of the sovereign 'individual' stand revealed as satellites of a power which is always elsewhere, but which shows its hand in every tug of the puppet's wires. For Prospero language itself is a mere 'gift / In dealing with shadows':

> But now all these heavy books are no use to me any more,
>   for
> Where I go, words carry no weight; it is best,
> Then, I surrender their fascinating counsel
>   To the silent dissolution of the sea
> Which misuses nothing because it values nothing;
>   Whereas man overvalues everything
> Yet, when he learns the price is pegged to his valuation,
>   Complains bitterly he is being ruined which, of course,
>   he is.
> So kings find it odd they should have a million subjects
>   Yet share in thoughts of none, and seducers
> Are sincerely puzzled at being unable to love
>   What they are able to possess.

This reality beyond words is 'The lion's mouth whose hunger / No metaphors can fill' of the Preface. We may, like the clown, 'Double [our] meaning', but all the inflationary *doubles entendres* of discourse cannot stuff this emptiness. We are left with an inflationary spiral in which price is the mirror-image of valuation, in a bitter parody of those laws of supply and demand which play over the surface of reality, ignoring questions of ultimate or intrinsic worth, and bankrupting us in their endless play.

The implicit contrast here, between market price and use-value, runs through the poem. Dealing in shadows as the stockbroker deals in commodities, Prospero has cut himself off from that 'Common warmth and touching substance' in which alone a real world is touched. Prospero's power to command has been that of the manager, valid only in so far as his word can command his workers, the mental skills of Ariel and the manual energy of Caliban. It is in *their* labour-power that Prospero's expropriating magic is based. Kings may hold power over their subjects but they cannot enter into communion with their subjectivities, any more than the seducer can ever really know the object he possesses and by possessing turns into an exchangeable commodity. In the essay 'Balaam and His Ass,' which contains a series of reflections on *The Tempest,* Auden offers a definition of the seducer Don Giovanni as one himself 'inconspicuous as a shadow' whose 'pleasure in seducing women is not sensual but arithmetical; his satisfaction lies in adding one more name to his list . . . [S]o far as any finite motive is concerned, he might just as well have chosen to collect stamps.' Prospero's motive, too, has been the accumulation of power for its own sake, turning a means into an end.

The language of finance subverts the most innocent words ('dear', for example) and puts a distance between event and interpretation. It is disenchantment with his *déraciné* magic that leads Prospero to ask, in one of his interspersed songs, *'Dare even Pope or Caesar know / The price of faith and honour?'* For Gonzalo too the gulf between signifiers and signifieds is where the subject falls into loss:

> Not in me the credit for
> Words I uttered long ago
> Whose glad meaning I betrayed;
> Truths today admitted, owe
> Nothing to the councillor
> In whose booming eloquence
> Honesty became untrue.

'Credit' and 'owe' add a new timbre to the idea of a 'booming eloquence'. By the same token, Gonzalo froze his assets, 'by speculation froze / Vision into an idea.'

Fact and value seem at odds in these fallen consciousnesses. When Ferdinand comes to address his love sonnet to Miranda, she is a 'Dear Other' who participates with him in the accumulation of capital, 'From moment to moment as you enrich them so / Inherit me', caught up in those inflationary spirals which Prospero fears may bring their own Wall Street Crash—'Will Ferdinand be as fond of a Miranda / Familiar as a stocking?' But it is Trinculo who epitomizes most effectively this world of exchange values where relations between subjects have turned into relations between signs. Trinculo's detachment from the world of mechanic, merchant and king is profound:

> There lies that solid world
> These hands can never reach;
> My history, my love,
> Is but a choice of speech.

Everywhere signifiers have substituted for the things they signify. When a terror shakes Trinculo's tree, 'A flock of words fly out'. Trapped in language none of these characters can evade the power relations imposed upon them by Prospero's wand, that ultimate signifier and source of power. This explains the key antithesis of the poem, indicated in the title. For although as Caliban indicates in his address the mirror is Shakespeare's metaphor for art, held up to the sea of nature, there are more complex resonances. Alonso advises his son to ascend his throne majestically while keeping in mind the sea that dissolves all hierarchies of value dear to the subject:

> the waters where fish
> See sceptres descending with no wish
> To touch them . . .
> . . . the sands where a crown
> Has the status of a broken-down
> Sofa or mutilated statue:
> . . .
> The cold deep that does not envy you,
> The sunburnt superficial kingdom
> Where a king is an object.

He warns against expecting sense from the words subjects speak to princes. Such language is the 'prince's ornate mirror', giving back only reflections of his own conscious wishes. It is from the embarrassments of his own 'darkness' and dreams, the sea of the unconscious, that revelation may instead come, breaking the closed circle of reflections in which the mirrors of language trap him. Otherwise he will disappear 'To join all the unjust kings'. True power, Alonso proposes, lies not in a cold detachment that seeks mastery. This will in the end destroy. It lies instead in the 'dissolution of your pride'. In the same way, waking from a dream 'Where Prudence flirted with a naked sword, / Securely vicious', Sebastian finds proof of mercy in the fact that he wakes *without* a crown. The sestina works its changes upon the key words as if to remind of that closed circle from which only Failure and Exposure free him: 'Caught unawares, we price ourselves alive', in a mirror inversion of the Sleeping Beauty story. A break with the closed circuits of self-reflection offers true positionality: 'Just Now is what it might be every day, / Right here is absolute and needs no crown,/Ermine or trumpets, protocol or sword.' 'It is defeat gives proof we are alive.'

When the 'conjuror' artist comes to dismiss this Ariel 'whose obedience through all the enchanted years has never been less than perfect', he will be transfixed with horror to find reflected in Ariel's eyes not 'a conqueror smiling at a conqueror' but a 'gibbering fist-clenched creature with which you are all too unfamiliar . . . the only subject that you have, who is not a dream amenable to magic but the all too solid flesh you must acknowledge as you own'. He comes face to face, that is, with himself as Caliban, not the 'all-forgiving because all-understanding good nature' he had imagined himself. Like Caesar in *For the Time Being,* he finds power revealed to be trickery, the magic wand of Prospero a phallic toy:

> Can you wonder then, when . . . your spirits, because you are tired of giving orders, have ceased to obey, and you are left alone with me, the dark thing you could never abide to be with, if I do not yield you kind answer or admire you for the achievements I was never allowed to profit from . . . ?

In 'Balaam and His Ass' Auden proposed that 'In a stage production, Caliban should be as monstrously conspicuous as possible, and, indeed, suggest, as far as decency per-

mits, the phallic. Ariel, on the other hand . . . should, ideally, be invisible, a disembodied voice.' What the supposedly disinterested, spiritual voice of bourgeois art serves, in the end, is the principle of phallic power, Caliban pretending to be Prospero, the dog beneath the skin.

Auden's reading of *The Tempest* is not the traditional one. It is, he says, 'a disquieting work', for whereas the other last plays 'end in a blaze of forgiveness and love'—

> in *The Tempest* both the repentance of the guilty and the pardon of the injured seem more formal than real . . . more the prudent promise of the punished and frightened, 'I won't do it again. It doesn't pay,' than any change of heart: and Prospero's forgiving is more the contemptuous pardon of a man who knows that he has his enemies completely at his mercy than a heartfelt reconciliation . . . He has the coldness of someone who has come to the conclusion that human nature is not worth much, that human relations are, at their best, pretty sorry affairs . . . One might excuse him if he included himself in his critical skepticism, but he never does; it never occurs to him that he, too, might have erred and be in need of pardon.

In Auden's text this blind spot is revealed in the easy assumption Prospero makes that, unlike Caliban, his brother Antonio can be brought back within the circle of reconciliation.

> All by myself I tempted Antonio into treason;
> However that could be cleared up; both of us know
> That both were in the wrong, and neither need be sorry.

Antonio, however, feels himself the contemptuous victim of a theatrical imposture in which everybody has been cast into predetermined roles by the actor-manager Prospero. Now, he says sarcastically, 'As all the pigs have turned back into men / . . . we can all go home again' and 'take life easily now as tales / Write ever-after'. But he declares himself different from the others, 'Your loyal subjects all, grateful enough / To know their place and believe what you say'. Power, Antonio says, is not so easily demitted:

> Break your wand in half,
> The fragments will join; burn your books or lose
> Them in the sea, they will soon reappear,
> Not even damaged: as long as I choose
> To wear my fashion, whatever you wear
> Is a magic robe; while I stand outside
> Your circle, the will to charm is still there.

Antonio's denial of his assigned place maintains Prospero in his position of pride and melancholy. The significance of this relation is suggested by the comments in 'Balaam and His Ass' on the role of dialogue in presenting 'a human personality in its full depth, its inner dialectic, its self-disclosure and self-concealment'. The soliloquy is inadequate for this because it is really 'a dialogue in the form of a monologue', addressed to the audience and so, we suspect, out to con us. A dialogue requires two voices, and, if it is to express 'the inner dialogue of human personality', must be of a specific kind. The pair must be similar, of the same sex, but also polar opposites, and inseparable. Only the master-servant relation satisfies all these conditions, and it defines all the relations of power that obtain under Prospero's auspices.

It extends, for example, to that between Miranda and Ferdinand, who, like all lovers—Auden notes in his essay—instinctively use the master-servant metaphor. Behind each relation lie the conflicting wishes of the divided 'volitional ego', wishes that, 'since the Fall, instead of being dialectically related, have become contradictory opposites': the wish to command, and the wish 'to have something to obey, to be the servant of '. This irresolvable contradiction often issues in the illusory solution represented by the myth of Narcissus, who 'falls in love with his reflection; he wishes to become its servant, but instead his reflection insists upon being his slave.' This is why Miranda's Dear One is hers only 'as mirrors are lonely', and why so much of her language of love involves the same kind of shifting, flux-ridden transformations we find in Stephano's song. She and Ferdinand run the risk of the kind of narcissism represented by Tristan and Isolde, in Auden's description, 'Indifferent to each other as persons with unique bodies and characters', important to each other only as externalized icons of their own desire.

For the Time Being is subtitled 'A Christmas Oratorio', the last word teasingly close to Auden's first work for several voices, *The Orators.* In the friction between oratorio and oratory lies the whole theme of the work. The voice of power in *For the Time Being* speaks with the same accents as the **"Address for a Prize Day"** in the earlier work, and it follows the same trajectory. In both cases an apparently rational, authoritative and controlling sensibility breaks down towards its conclusion into incoherence, self-justification and contradiction, in a highly libidinized scenario of catastrophe and massacre, revealing, as Auden still believed, that liberalism could easily don a brown shirt, and was, indeed, the final authorizing voice of Fascism. 'Civilisation must be saved even if this means sending for the military, as I suppose it does', says Herod, in weary recognition of the inevitable, excusing his decision to massacre the innocents. Herod is strong on the Law. It is part of that litany of losses he rehearses that will follow from allowing the Christ child to live. Reason will be replaced by Revelation; instead of Rational Law, 'Knowledge will degenerate into a riot of subjective visions'; Justice will give way to 'Pity as the cardinal human virtue, and all fear of retribution will vanish'; 'Idealism will be replaced by Materialism.' 'Naturally', Herod adds, 'this cannot be allowed to happen.'

Herod's bad faith stands self-revealed when he stumbles into contradiction, evincing two equally powerful but unhappily contradictory arguments for going ahead with the massacre. If, he says, Christ is allowed to demonstrate that a sinless life is possible, 'God would expect every man, whatever his fortune, to lead a sinless life in the flesh and on earth. Then indeed would the human race be plunged into madness and despair.' That passing allusion to 'fortune' indicates how little this is a question about 'nature'. He has just argued quite the opposite, revealing his true attitude to the lower orders: if Christ lives, 'Every corner-boy will congratulate himself: 'I'm such a sinner that God had to come down in person to save me. I must be a devil of a fellow." Every crook will argue: "I like committing crimes. God likes forgiving them. Really the world is admirably arranged." ' Herod's real motives, justifying the maintenance of a status quo of which he is a major beneficiary, is revealed in his contemptuous references to those 'materialistic Masses' whose need, 'Diverted from its normal and wholesome outlet in patriotism and civic and

family pride . . . will be driven into totally unsocial channels where no education can read it'. Protecting 'this little civilized patch' against 'the old barbaric note' means, in reality, defending the power and privileges of an Empire. The coherent, powerful figure of authority gives himself away in the collapse from mealy-mouthed smugness to hysterical plaintive whine which concludes this special pleading:

> Ask anyone you like. I read all the official dispatches without skipping. I've taken elocution lessons. I've hardly ever taken bribes. How dare He allow me to decide? I've tried to be good. I brush my teeth every night. I haven't had sex for a month. I object. I'm a liberal. I want everyone to be happy. I wish I had never been born.

Herod preserves the delusion that he is simply a liberal private citizen with a job to do, instead of a wielder of power and authority. That is, he passes the buck. It is only in the contradictions of his rhetoric, self-loathing and self-pity, that we can read another story. In the words of the opening sequence, 'the miracle cannot occur' so long as his language refuses its contradictions, insists on its correctness and clarity. 'Unless you exclaim—"There must be some mistake"—you must be mistaken.' Only in the doubling back of discourse of 'The Meditation of Simeon' can the Real be found, for 'The Real is what will strike you as really absurd.' Instead of what Simeon calls the 'flip cracks and sententious oratory' of official discourse, the true Word is one in which power is diffused so widely that it turns into the non-coercive, democratic discourse of which the Angels sing:

> As the new-born Word
> Declares the old
> Authoritarian
> Constraint is replaced
> By His Covenant,
> And a city based
> On love and consent
> Suggested to men,
> All, all, all of them.

The Narrator is himself revealed as a party to the discourse of power, when he invites us to remain formal believers while practically submitting to the power of Caesar, offering us the shallow confidence of a word that is 'ever legible', with a 'Meaning unequivocal', where even sin, in his specious logic, is valid as a 'sign' of Goodness. In *Modern Canterbury Pilgrims* Auden was to inveigh against 'an obscuring of the Word behind the splendors of the flesh, reduction of spiritual life to a mechanical and automatic routine of physical acts.' This helps us to see why Auden deliberately chose the polyphonic form of the oratorio to present his vision. Throughout the poem revelation is multiplied and dispersed into many consciousnesses. There is no central controlling consciousness where truth resides. Only in the always undisclosed child is the Word one and unitary. All claims to unequivocal meaning must be false.

The repetition of words and phrases can give a gloomy air of eternal return to the poem, a sense that nothing will ever break out of these mechanical and automatic routines in which the flesh is trapped. But there is a different kind of repetition, like that use of ploche, anaphora and parison in Gabriel's address to Mary, where meaning overflows the words, and the paronomasic repetition of such key concepts as 'love', 'choose', 'know', 'flesh' spins a surplus of meaning like that of 'the Word / Who utters the world out of nothing', revealing 'The truth at the proper centre / . . . Of language and distress'. In the same way, there is a distinction between the genuine polyphony of those who respond positively to the annunciation and birth—the shepherds and wise men—and the orchestrated uniformity of those who resist it, worshipping instead the old principle of power. The former sing with antiphonal voices, the latter in a monotonous co-ordinated chant, as in the Fugal-Chorus of **"The Summons"**, with its banally intoned repetition, 'Great is Caesar', full of lists and catalogues.

"The Temptation of St Joseph" is to succumb to this patriarchal discourse, seeing himself in the traditionally offered terms as a pathetic victim, cuckolded by the coming of the Lord, so that even in accepting meekly what has happened he ratifies the old oppressive order. But Joseph has to go beyond this, cauterize all those last reflexes of phallocratic power. He must answer all the questions himself, neither deferring to nor blaming the one of whom he asks 'Father, what have I done?' Joseph has to seek absolution for all those crimes in which the male principle has perpetually reinscribed itself in the discourse of power, a catalogue of which expresses everywhere the—

> gallantry that scrawls
> In idolatrous detail and size
> A symbol of aggression of toilet walls.

He has, that is, to atone for a history which is a series of campaigns in that 'Sex War' of which the soldiers sing after Herod's soliloquy. To avoid conscription to that war, Joseph must accept not only that 'Today the roles are altered; you must be / The Weaker Sex whose passion is passivity.' He must also undergo that symbolic emasculation of which Rachel speaks after the soldiers' ribaldry: "Somewhere in these unending wastes of delirium is a lost child, speaking of Long Ago in the language of wounds.'

To redeem that lost child he must take the holy family back in a **"Flight into Egypt"** which is also, in classically Freudian terms, a return through the mirror-phase in which the gendered subject is constructed, 'through the glass / No authority can pass', to a realm where placement under the sign of the father is abolished. The voices in the desert lament that once 'All Father's nightingales knew their place, / The gardens were loyal: look at them now'. The **"Temptation of St Joseph"** had told us that 'Upon the nursery floor / We gradually explore/Our members till our jealous lives' discover 'A vague but massive feel / Of being individual'. At the same time, entry into individuality is entry into 'a long life of lies'. Only in dissolving the phallic core of selfhood, by contrast, can the collective truth be recovered in this flight. At the heart then of that revelation offered and refused every Christmas lies a 'future . . . freed from our past', a 'new life' in 'a great city that has expected your return for years'. The city remains a vision of an authentic socialism, beyond patriarchy, beyond the repressive and repressed selves of that prudent,

Auden at Christ Church, Oxford, in the late 1960s.

incestuous bourgeoisie revealed to be bankrupt in the **"Temptation"**.

Exile from the true city is the source of the restlessness, envy and self-contempt that afflicts all the four allegorical characters of *The Age of Anxiety,* wandering in search of their absconded selves when the real object of their quest should be another way of living. The narrator tells us that in wartime 'everybody is reduced to the anxious status of a shady character or a displaced person'. But this merely compounds a larger, ontological crisis for a creature with 'no one-to-one correspondence between his social or economic position and his private mental life'. The allegorical form itself—each of the characters is supposed to represent one of Jung's four faculties of the psyche, Intellect (Malin), Feeling (Rosetta), Intuition (Quant) and Sensations (Emble)—is a way of representing this self-belatedness, in which the characters live in perpetual arrears, not understanding what is happening to them until it is too late. At the beginning of Part Five, when they have returned exhausted from their journeyings, each would rather go home alone to bed, but refuses to say so out of deference to all the others. In this collective estrangement of their individual wishes no one is satisfied. This is a figure, in miniature, of the larger self-estrangement that afflicts a world at war, dividing peoples and driving them to mutual destruction, as in Malin's memory of one of his bombing-raids:

> Conscious in common of our closed Here
> And of Them out There, thinking of Us
> In a different dream, for we die in theirs
> Who kill in ours and become fathers.

This war, as Malin records at the opening of **"The Seven Ages"**, begins in the primal Oedipal guilt of symbolic parricide and incest:

> already there is
> Dread in his dreams at the deed of which
> He knows nothing but knows he can do,
> The gulf before him with guilt beyond,
> Whatever that is, whatever why
> Forbids his bound; till that ban tempts him;
> He jumps and is judged: he joins mankind,
> The fallen families, freedom lost,
> Love become Law.

With *The Age of Anxiety,* Auden worked his way through that crisis of Oedipal revolt against the particular life that had animated all his early work. But it would be wrong to see this as a Prospero-like reconciliation, as acceptance and contentment. The subversive worms still niggle and wriggle in the gut of his world. In the Freudian terms appropriate to this poem, anxiety is always associated with the fear of castration. The response of the homosexual Malin, attracted to young Emble, is to decide not to enter into competition for him with Rosetta. Yet his sense of being on trial persists. In 1946, Auden concluded his essay on 'K's Quest' with a bleak view of a world where one is always on trial for a crime that cannot be named, but which bears all the hallmarks of the Oedipal insurrection. Kafka's K, he says, 'has a name consisting of only one letter and no position in the world'. The other characters have many-lettered names and occupations, or rather, they seem to have to K:

> For what Kafka seems to be saying is: 'What is generally called individuality is nothing of the kind,

but only the *persona* or mask of action which is all we can know about others; individuality is something that can only be known subjectively, and subjectively individuality is the simplest brute fact that the "I" which feels and knows and acts can never be defined by what it feels and knows and acts; it can be reduced to the barest minimum of a single letter, but to nothing, never.' Man, therefore, can never know the whole truth, because as the subject who knows, he has to remain outside the truth, and the truth is therefore incomplete.

> From this follows the paradox that K's only guarantee that he is following the true way is that he fails to get anywhere. If he succeeded in getting his way, it would be proof that he had failed.

Lacking a full name and a position in the world, K is not inscribed under the name of the Father. A castrate subject, he cannot enter into the penis-rivalry of the urchin, for without a patronym how can he claim 'My prick (or my father's) is bigger than yours (or your father's)'? Yet, as for Ransom and the Airman, the wound can be the source of a more authentic identity; failure and weakness may be the only way to be Truly Strong. The subject who knows remains outside the truth, as Antonio and Prospero do in their different ways. Yet he has, nevertheless, a place in the world, even if it is only that gap between Ariel's 'one evaporating sigh' and the reiterated 'I' of the Prompter, no more than the preordained echo of a disembodied voice. It is here that, like Prospero, doubting or disputing all those particular meanings in which he might be fixed,

> Trembling he takes
> The silent passage
> Into discomfort.

(pp. 152-67)

Stan Smith, in his W. H. Auden, *Basil Blackwell, 1985, 227 p.*

FURTHER READING

Bayley, John. "W. H. Auden." In his *The Romantic Survival: A Study in Poetic Evolution,* pp. 127-85. London: Constable, 1957.

> Surveys the major forms and themes of Auden's poetry, offering commentary on psychological aspects of selected works.

Beach, Joseph Warren. "The Poems of Auden and the Prose Diathesis." *The Virginia Quarterly Review* 25, No. 3 (Summer 1949): 365-83.

> Discusses what Beach terms the "admixture of the specifically or intrinsically prosaic" in Auden's verse, emphasizing the poet's range of personal and formulaic expression.

Bradbury, John. "Auden and the Tradition." *The Western Review* 12, No. 4 (Summer 1948): 223-29.

> Explores Auden's pattern of development as a poet. Bradbury maintains that Auden's work must be judged by standards deriving from "Langland and Chaucer,

from Dryden and Swift," not from "Spenser and Keats, Blake, Donne, and Mallarmé."

Brophy, James D. *W. H. Auden.* Columbia Essays on Modern Writers, edited by William York Tindall, No. 54. New York: Columbia University Press, 1970, 48 p.
Isolates and describes the principal verse forms of Auden's poetry.

Buell, Frederick. *W. H. Auden as a Social Poet.* Ithaca, N.Y.: Cornell University Press, 1973, 196 p.
Discusses the formation of Auden's social vision during the 1930s.

Callan, Edward. "W. H. Auden: The Farming of a Verse." *The Southern Review* III, No. 2 (April 1967): 341-56.
Examines the craftsmanship of Auden's poems.

Carpenter, Humphrey. *W. H. Auden: A Biography.* Boston: Houghton Mifflin Co., 1981, 495 p.
In-depth study of Auden's life and literary works. Carpenter notes of the biography: "It is not a book of literary criticism. I have not usually engaged in a critical discussion of Auden's writings. But I have tried to show how they often arose from the circumstances of his life, and I have also attempted to identify the themes and ideas that concerned him."

Cowley, Malcolm. "Auden in America." *The New Republic* 104, No. 1375 (7 April 1941): 473-74.
Close, mixed review of *The Double Man,* contending that readers unfamiliar with Auden's recent work "will find on reading it that they are entering an unfamiliar and uncomfortable but stimulating world of ideas."

Frankenberg, Lloyd. "W. H. Auden." In his *Pleasure Dome: On Reading Modern Poetry,* pp. 301-15. Boston: Houghton Mifflin Co., 1949.
Examines Auden's poetic technique, emphasizing qualities of sound and meter.

Hampshire, Stuart N. "W. H. Auden." In his *Modern Writers and Other Essays,* pp. 19-29. New York: Alfred A. Knopf, 1970.
Praises the "weight and variety" of Auden's poetry, noting particularly the author's wit and inventiveness.

Hardy, Barbara. "W. H. Auden, Thirties to Sixties: A Face and a Map." *The Southern Review* V, No. 3 (Summer 1969): 655-72.
Attempts to elucidate the personal, private side of Auden's poetry, commenting on eros, love, and the tension between private and public worlds.

Hollander, John. "Auden at Sixty." *The Atlantic* 220, No. 1 (July 1967): 84-87.
Traces the shifting themes and concerns of Auden's verse, from his schoolboy poems to the works of late middle age.

Isherwood, Christopher. "A Conversation on Tape." *The London Magazine* n. s. 1, No. 3 (June 1961): 41-58.
Transcript of an interview with Auden conducted at Isherwood's California home in 1960. The discussion treats the two authors' personal working habits and centers upon current social, political, and literary events.

James, Clive. "Auden's Achievement." *Commentary* 56, No. 6 (December 1973): 53-8.
Discusses the impact of Auden's homosexuality upon

his verse and comments on his "innovations in technical bravura."

Johnson, Richard. *Man's Place: An Essay on Auden.* Ithaca, N.Y.: Cornell University Press, 1973, 251 p.
Attempts to demonstrate that Auden's poetry is best understood in the light of its "underlying humanistic impulses."

Leavis, F. R. "Mr. Auden's Talent." *Scrutiny* V, No. 3 (December 1936): 323-27.
Reviews *Look, Stranger!* and *The Ascent of F6,* focusing on irony and satire in the former work.

MacNeice, Louis. "Letter to W. H. Auden." *New Verse,* Nos. 26-27 (November 1937): 11-13.
Brief commentary on the method and intent of Auden's poems.

Mander, John. "Must We Burn Auden?" In his *The Writer and Commitment,* pp. 24-70. London: Secker & Warburg, 1961.
Rigorous study of Auden's critical reputation as a poet.

Mendelson, Edward. *Early Auden.* New York: Viking Press, 1981, 407 p.
Book-length history and interpretation of Auden's work up to 1939.

Moore, Marianne. "W. H. Auden." In her *Predilections,* pp. 84-102. New York: Viking Press, 1955.
Appreciative reading of Auden's major poems. Moore offers this characterization and appraisal of the poet: "Inconvenienced, aided, attacked, or at large; a waveworn Ulysses, a Jerome among his documents; a misinterpreted librettist; or a publisher's emissary insistently offered at luncheon a dish of efts, Mr. Auden continues resolute."

Newman, Michael. "The Art of Poetry XVII: W. H. Auden." *The Paris Review* 14, No. 57 (Spring 1974): 32-69.
Transcript of a 1972 interview with Auden, emphasizing biographical matters.

Powell, Dilys. "Advance Guard." In his *Descent from Parnassus,* pp. 167-221. London: Cresset Press, 1934.
In-depth appraisal of the rise and influence of poets of the "Auden Generation," with extensive commentary on poetic innovations attributable to members of the group.

Rowse, A. L. *The Poet Auden: A Personal Memoir.* London: Methuen, 1987, 138 p.
Highly personal account of the critic's long acquaintance with Auden.

Schwartz, Delmore. "The Two Audens." In his *Selected Essays of Delmore Schwartz,* edited by Donald A. Dike and David H. Zucker, pp. 143-52. Chicago: University of Chicago Press, 1970.
Reprint of an essay first published in the *Kenyon Review* in 1939. Schwartz documents shifts in Auden's poetic voice, particularly from irony "and the need of destruction" to love.

Scott-James, R. A. "Modern Poets." In his *Fifty Years of English Literature, 1900-1950, With a Postscript—1951 to 1955,* pp. 210-39. London: Longmans, Green and Co., 1956.
Explores Auden's role in the development of movements in modern British poetry.

Spears, Monroe K. "The Dominant Symbols of Auden's Poetry." *The Sewanee Review* LIX, No. 3 (July-September 1951): 392-425.

Isolates six "major clusters" of symbols in Auden's poetry: "War, the Quest, Paysage Moralisé, Psychosomatic Disease, Eros-*Agape*-Logos, and the City." Spears cites examples of these symbols in a number of poems, especially *The Age of Anxiety.*

———. "In Memoriam W. H. Auden." *The Sewanee Review* LXXXII, No. 4 (Fall 1974): 672-81.

Impressionistic character study of Auden, with brief commentary on selected poems.

Spender, Stephen. "W. H. Auden (1907-1973)." *Partisan Review* XL, No. 3 (1973): 546-48.

Memorial tribute, finding Auden's "great originality" in his "endlessly fertile invention of symbols."

Stead, C. K. "Auden's 'Spain'." *London Magazine* 7, No. 12 (March 1968): 41-54.

Close reading of Auden's "Spain," emphasizing the political content of the poem.

Charles Baudelaire

1821-1867

French poet, critic, translator, essayist, novelist, and dramatist.

Baudelaire is considered one of the world's greatest lyric poets and his masterpiece, *Les fleurs du mal* (*The Flowers of Evil*), ranks among the most influential volumes of French poetry. A critical and popular failure at the time of its publication, *The Flowers of Evil* is now esteemed for its innovative, efficacious verse. Its flagrant portrayal of controversial and diverse subjects, amoral tone, and diabolic evocations of degradation and despair attest to the eloquence of Baudelaire's versification of the modern spirit. In *The Flowers of Evil,* Baudelaire analyzed in often shocking terms erotic love, the urban underclass and environs of Paris, and the conflicts within his own soul. His depiction of spiritual discontent has prompted some critics to discern a Catholic philosophy in his work. While others have perceived satanic overtones, most critics acknowledge a vague mystical quality about his verse. Scholars note that Baudelaire firmly believed that individuals, if left to their own devices, are inherently evil and inevitably damned—only that which is artificial can be construed as absolutely good. To Baudelaire, the function of poetry was to inspire and express beauty as distinctly separate from the natural or moral world. Commentators agree that these aesthetic assumptions constituted Baudelaire's poetic and artistic principles.

Born in Paris in 1821, Baudelaire had a happy childhood until age six, when his father died. In the year following his father's death, Baudelaire grew very close to his mother; he later remembered their relationship as "ideal, romantic . . . as if I were courting her." When Madame Baudelaire married Jacques Aupick, a military officer, in 1828, Baudelaire became deeply resentful. Initially he had excelled in school, but as he grew older he increasingly neglected his studies in favor of a dissipated, rebellious lifestyle. In 1841, the Aupicks sent him on a two-year trip to India. His experiences abroad failed to reform him as his parents had hoped but proved to be literarily productive—it was during this time that he experimented with verse and wrote the first poems that would be included in *The Flowers of Evil.*

When Baudelaire returned to Paris, he received a sizable inheritance and briefly lived the life of a frivolous dandy. According to Baudelaire, the dandy was one who glorified the ego as the ultimate spiritual and creative power—a heroic individualist revolting against a decadent society. At this time, Baudelaire fell in love with Jeanne Duval, a Parisian woman of African descent. Though she cared little for poetry, Duval inspired the verse that formed the "Black Venus" cycle, his first series of love poems. The sensuality of these early verses eventually erupted in a volatile passion which dominated his writing as well as his life. When his relationship with Duval deteriorated, he denounced romance and became introspective and solemn. However, Baudelaire continued to write and also began to experiment with opium and hashish, which inspired his

"Poeme du haschisch." In 1855, Baudelaire published several poems in the journal *Revue des deux mondes.* Condemned by some critics as scandalous, his work nevertheless was esteemed by such noted literary figures as Victor Hugo and Algernon Charles Swinburne.

Upon publication of *The Flowers of Evil* in 1857, Baudelaire was critically attacked, and even author and critic Charles Sainte-Beuve, a close friend, refused to praise the book. Subsequently, Baudelaire and his publisher, Auguste Poulet-Malassis, were prosecuted and convicted of immorality. Six poems deemed morally offensive were removed from the book and published later the same year in Belgium as *Les épaves.* These poems scandalized Paris with their detailed eroticism and graphic depiction of lesbianism and vampirism. For both the 1861 and the posthumously published 1868 editions of *The Flowers of Evil,* some poems were added and others reworked, but the ban on the suppressed poems was not lifted in France until 1949. After the publication of the 1861 edition, Baudelaire's publisher went bankrupt, and in an attempt to regain both his reputation and his financial solvency Baudelaire traveled to Belgium on a lecture tour. The tour was unsuccessful, however, and Baudelaire returned to Paris in 1866, whereupon he suffered a debilitating stroke. His mother, with whom he had recently reconciled, nursed him until his death in 1867.

The Flowers of Evil comprises poems which were written over a period of several years. These poems combined the passion of Romanticism with a Parnassian perfection of form, yet their subject was wholly original. Like Théophile Gautier, to whom he dedicated the volume, Baudelaire sought to depict "l'horreur et l'extase de la vie," the horror and ecstasy of life, in his own verse. Baudelaire found beauty in the horrific, particularly exploring the perplexities of a soul both sinful and repentant. Henri Peyre suggested that "the poems embrace despair, paralysis, feverish soaring into the unreal, a death wish, a morbid playing with sensation." Organized in six sections—"Spleen et idéal," "Tableaux parisiens," "Le vin," "Fleurs du mal," "Révolte," and "La mort"—*The Flowers of Evil* juxtapose the concept of a perfect existence with the knowledge of the futility of that ideal. Critics note that despite his religious ambivalence, Baudelaire profoundly felt the presence of both Satan and God and satanic imagery pervades *The Flowers of Evil*. With these recurrent images Baudelaire effectively evinced the conflict between temporal pleasure and spiritual redemption. The conclusion of *The Flowers of Evil* poignantly details Baudelaire's notion of humanity's final endeavor—the search for peace in death.

Baudelaire's most controversial pieces in *The Flowers of Evil* are his love poems. In addition to the "Black Venus" cycle, he included poetry written for his two other mistresses, Apollonie Sabatier and Marie Daubrun. Sabatier, the "White Venus," inspired a cycle of reverent, celestial verse reminiscent of his early adoration of his mother. The "Green Venus" poems, however, depict Baudelaire's unrestrained passion for Daubrun. Evoking a sensuality similar to the "Black Venus" cycle, these pieces are more sexually explicit and display elements of sadism. Collectively, the love poems provide an important and, to some, disturbing commentary on Baudelaire's conflicting feelings about women. Critics speculate that from the time of his mother's remarriage, he never had an enduring or successful relationship with any woman.

Baudelaire is acknowledged as one of the first French poets to delineate the plight of the urban underclass. Unlike his Parnassian predecessors who located beauty in *objets d'art,* Baudelaire discovered artistic possibilities among the outcasts of Parisian society. Their misfortune became a metaphor for his conception of original sin and vivified the paradox of good and evil. The beauty and cruelty of Parisian existence, Baudelaire contended, mirrored the complicated and irrational nature of all humanity. Scenes of the Parisian underworld are vividly depicted in his *Petits poemès en prose: Le spleen de Paris* (*Poems in Prose from Charles Baudelaire*). Comparable to the lyrical imagery and language of *The Flowers of Evil,* this work conveys in melancholy tones a desire to escape the misery of earthly existence. Critics note that the stylistic innovations of Baudelaire's prose poems strongly influenced the poetry of Stéphane Mallarmé, Paul Claudel, and Arthur Rimbaud.

Twentieth-century critical interpretations of Baudelaire's poetry are varied, yet most critics agree that *The Flowers of Evil* is among the greatest achievements in world literature. Commentators acknowledge Baudelaire's contributions to Symbolist poetry and have shown that his influence extended to the works of T. S. Eliot and W. B. Yeats. Contemporary scholars have highlighted the religious aspects of Baudelaire's verse—some have maintained that *The Flowers of Evil* is essentially religious poetry. Others have focused upon Baudelaire's juxtaposition of classicism and romanticism, demonstrating that the classical qualities of his balanced versification, adherence to traditional poetic form, and objective appreciation of beauty counterbalance the romantic elements suggested by his reliance on intuition and exaltation of the emotions and senses. The underlying meaning of Baudelaire's poetry continues to intrigue critics and readers alike. Perhaps T. S. Eliot best indicated the lasting appeal of Baudelaire's lyrics: "The possibility of damnation is so immense a relief in a world of electoral reform, plebiscites, sex reform and dress reform, that damnation itself is an immediate form of salvation—of salvation from the ennui of modern life, because it at last gives some significance to living."

(For further information on Baudelaire's life and career, see *Nineteeth-Cenutury Literature Criticism,* Vol. 6)

PRINCIPAL WORKS

POETRY

Les épaves   1857
Les fleurs du mal   1857, 1861, 1868
  [*The Flowers of Evil,* 1909]
Petits poemes en prose: Le spleen de Paris   1869
  [*Poems in Prose from Charles Baudelaire,* 1905]

OTHER MAJOR WORKS

La fanfarlo   (novel)   1847
Histoires extraordinaires [translator; from the short stories of Edgar Allen Poe]   (short stories)   1856
Nouvelles histoires extraordinaires [translator; from the short stories of Edgar Allen Poe]   (short stories)   1857
Adventures d'Arthur Pym [translator; from the novel *The Narrative of Arthur Gordon Pym* by Edgar Allen Poe]   (short stories)   1858
Les paradis artificiels: Opium et haschisch [translator; from the autobiography *Confessions of an English Opium Eater* by Thomas De Quincey]   (autobiography and poetry)   1860
Curiosités esthetiques   (criticism)   1868
Oeuvres complètes. 7 vols.   (poetry, letters, essays, and criticism)   1868-70
L'art romantique   (criticism)   1869
*Journaux intimes   (diaries)   1887
  [*Intimate Journals,* 1930]
Lettres: 1841-1866   (letters)   1905
The Letters of Charles Baudelaire   (letters)   1927
The Mirror of Art: Critical Studies   (criticism)   1955
Art in Paris, 1845-1862: Salons and Other Exhibitions Reviewed by Charles Baudelaire   (criticism)   1965

---

*This work includes the diaries "Fusées" and "Mon coeur mis à nu."

Charles Augustin Sainte-Beuve   (essay dates 1860 and 1862)

[Sainte-Beuve is considered the foremost French literary critic of the nineteenth century, noted for his literary and historical erudition. His "Causeries du lundi"—weekly newspaper articles which appeared every Monday morning over a period of several decades—are the best known of his extensive body of critical writings. He began his career as a champion of Romanticism, but eventually he formulated a psychological method of criticism that considered each author's life and character integral to the comprehension of the author's work. In the first excerpt, from a work originally published on February 20, 1860, Sainte-Beuve views Baudelaire's poetry as representing the last vestiges of Romanticism. In the second excerpt, from an essay initially published on January 20, 1862, he reluctantly acknowledges Baudelaire's creative ability.]

Baudelaire is one of the oldest among those whom I call my "young" friends: he knows how highly I prize his subtle mind and his curious, clever talent. If I had discussed [*Les Fleurs du mal*], however, he would not have been spared advice, remonstrances, and even chidings; he would have been subjected to a sermon. Occasionally, he forgives me such sermons. I would have said to him: "Let me give you one piece of advice, which may surprise those who don't know you: you are too distrustful of passion—of natural passion; it is a theory with you. You rely too much on the intelligence, on thinking things out. Let yourself go, don't be so afraid of being like everyone else, of being too common; your expression will always be refined enough to set you apart."

Still, I should not have wanted to appear more prudish than I am, or than is fitting in one who perpetrated his own youthful poems and has read the poets of every age. I should have added frankly: "I like more than one piece in your volume. **"Les Tristesses de la lune,"** for example, is a pretty sonnet that could almost be the work of some English poet, a contemporary of the young Shakespeare. Even the stanzas of **"À celle qui est trop gaie"** seem to be exquisitely done. Why is this piece not in Latin—or rather, in Greek—and included under the heading "Erotica" in the *Anthology?* The learned Brunck would have given it a place in his *Analecta veterarum poetarum;* the Président Bouhier and La Monnoye, that is to say, men of authority and unimpeachable morality (*castissimae vitae, morumque integerrimorum*) would have commented it without embarrassment, and we should set our own seal to it, signaling it to lovers of poetry, with Horace's line, *"Tange Chloen semel arrogantem."* I would have told him all that and many other things, making allowance for the fact that he as well as some others (like Bouilhet and Joséphin Soulary, recent author of some very distinguished sonnets,) come late, when the school to which they belong has already given and produced so much, when it is exhausted, so to speak, when the old voices of the past are falling silent, save for one great voice [Victor Hugo, in *La Légende des siècles*]. These and a few others are honorably carrying on the tradition, adorning the decline and final sunset of the Pléiade. . . .

• • • • •

When M. Baudelaire presented himself as a candidate, some asked whether he was intending a practical joke on the Academy, making a kind of epigram. Some wondered whether his real purpose was not to remind the Academy that it was high time it considered admitting Théophile Gautier, his teacher, a distinguished writer, clever in all the genres of diction. M. Baudelaire's name had to be spelled for more than one member of the Academy, completely ignorant of his existence. It is not as easy as you might suppose to prove to Academicians who belong to political circles that *Les Fleurs du mal* contains some pieces truly remarkable for their talent and their art, nor to explain to them that among the author's little prose poems **"Le Vieux Saltimbanque"** and **"Les Veuves"** are gems, and that, all told, M. Baudelaire has managed to build for himself, out at the very farthest point of a neck of land reputed uninhabitable and beyond the frontiers of known romanticism, a bizarre kiosk of his own, ornate and contorted, but at the same time dainty and mysterious. Here Edgar Poe is read, exquisite sonnets are recited, hashish is taken for the purpose of analyzing the experience afterward, and opium and every other more dangerous drug is served in cups of the most exquisite porcelain. This kiosk, of a singular marquetry construction, expresses a deliberately composite originality and for some time now has been calling attention to the farthest outpost, to the Kamchatka of romanticism. I call it *"la folie Baudelaire."* The author is content to have done something impossible, to have reached a point no one supposed it possible to go. Is this to say, however, when it has all been explained to the best of one's ability to somewhat surprised, highly respectable colleagues, that such curiosities, novelties, and refinements are to be looked upon as conditions for admissions to the Academy? Does the author himself seriously believe so? What is certain, is that M. Baudelaire gains by being seen: where one may expect to meet a strange eccentric, one finds oneself in the presence of a courteous, well-spoken, exemplary candidate, a very nice young man, who has a fine feeling for language and is entirely classical in his forms. (pp. 276-78)

> *Charles Augustin Sainte-Beuve, "Baudelaire," in his* Selected Essays, *edited and translated by Francis Steegmuller and Norbert Guterman, Doubleday & Company, Inc., 1963, pp. 275-79.*

Algernon Charles Swinburne   (essay date 1862)

[Swinburne was an English poet, dramatist, and critic who is remembered for his lyric poetry and his rejection of Victorian mores. With this essay, Swinburne brought Baudelaire to the attention of English-speaking readers by praising his delicate verse and technical skill. Unlike many critics who considered Les fleurs du mal *immoral and repellent, Swinburne found the poems to be truthful, graceful, and founded upon a "distinct and vivid background of morality."]*

[M. Baudelaire] has more delicate power of verse than almost any man living, after Victor Hugo, Browning, and (in his lyrics) Tennyson. The sound of his metres suggests colour and perfume. His perfect workmanship makes every subject admirable and respectable. Throughout the chief part of [the *Fleurs du Mal*], he has chosen to dwell mainly upon sad and strange things—the weariness of pain and the bitterness of pleasure—the perverse happiness and wayward sorrows of exceptional people. It has the languid lurid beauty of close and threatening weather—a heavy heated temperature, with dangerous hothouse scents in it; thick shadow of cloud about it, and fire of molten light. It is quite clear of all whining and windy lamentation; there is nothing of the blubbering and shrieking style long since exploded. The writer delights in problems, and has a natural leaning to obscure and sorrowful things. Failure and sorrow, next to physical beauty and perfection of sound or scent, seem to have an infinite attraction for him. In some points he resembles Keats, or still more his chosen favourite among modern poets, Edgar Poe; at times, too, his manner of thought has a relish of Marlowe, and even the sincerer side of Byron. From Théophile Gautier, to whom the book is dedicated, he has caught the habit of a faultless and studious simplicity; but, indeed, it seems merely natural to him always to use the right word and the right rhyme. How supremely musical and flexible a perfect artist in writing can make the French language, any chance page of the book is enough to prove; every description, the slightest and shortest even, has a special mark on it of the writer's keen and peculiar power. The style is sensuous and weighty; the sights seen are steeped most often in sad light and sullen colour. As instances of M. Baudelaire's strength and beauty of manner, one might take especially the poems headed **"Le Masque," "Pärfum Exotique," "La Chevelure," "Les Sept Vieillards," "Les Petites Vieillas," "Ilrumes et Pluies"**. . . .

[The sonnet titled **"Causerie"** is a complete] specimen of the author's power. The way in which the sound and sense are suddenly broken off and shifted, four lines from the end, is wonderful for effect and success. M. Baudelaire's mastery of the sonnet form is worth remarking as a test of his natural bias towards such forms of verse as are most nearly capable of perfection. . . . Not the luxuries of pleasure in their simple first form, but the sharp and cruel enjoyments of pain, the acrid relish of suffering felt or inflicted, the sides on which nature looks unnatural, go to make up the stuff and substance of this poetry. Very good material they make, too; but evidently such things are unfit for rapid or careless treatment. The main charm of the book is, upon the whole, that nothing is wrongly given, nothing capable of being re-written or improved on its own ground. Concede the starting point, and you cannot have a better runner.

Thus, even of the loathsomest bodily putrescence and decay he can make some noble use. . . .

Another of this poet's noblest sonnets is that **"A une Passante,"** comparable with a similar one of Keats, "Time's sea hath been five years at its slow ebb," but superior for directness of point and forcible reality. Here for once the beauty of a poem is rather passionate than sensuous. . . .

There is noticeable also in M. Baudelaire's work a quality of *drawing* which recalls the exquisite power in the same way of great French artists now living. His studies are admirable for truth and grace; his figure-painting has the ease and strength, the trained skill, and beautiful gentle justice of manner, which come out in such pictures as the *Source* of Ingres. . . .

It may be worth while to say something of the moral and meaning of many among these poems. Certain critics, who

will insist on going into this matter, each man as deep as his small leaden plummet will reach, have discovered what they call a paganism on the spiritual side of the author's tone of thought. Stripped of its coating of jargon, this may mean that the poet spoken of endeavours to look at most things with the eye of an old-world poet; that he aims at regaining the clear and simple view of writers content to believe in the beauty of material subjects. To us, if this were the meaning of these people, we must say it seems a foolish one; for there is not one of these poems that could have been written in a time when it was not the fashion to dig for moral motives and conscious reasons. Poe, for example, has written poems without any moral meaning at all; there is not one poem of the *Fleurs du Mal* which has not a distinct and vivid background of morality to it. Only this moral side of the book is not thrust forward in the foolish and repulsive manner of a half-taught artist; the background, as we called it, is not out of drawing. . . .

[Those] who will look for them may find moralities in plenty behind every poem of M. Baudelaire's; such poems especially as **"Une Martyre."** Like a mediaeval preacher, when he has drawn the heathen love, he puts sin on its right hand and death on its left. (p. 999)

[We] may note a few others in which [a] singular strength of finished writing is most evident. Such are, for instance, **"Le Cygne," "Le Poison," "Tristesses de la Lune," "Remord Posthume," "Le Flacon," "Ciel Brouillé," "Une Mendiante Rousse"** (a simpler study than usual, of great beauty in all ways, noticeable for its revival of the old fashion of unmixed masculine rhymes), **"Le Balcon," "Allegorie," "L'Amour et le Crâne,"** and the two splendid sonnets marked xxvii. and xlii. We cite these headings in no sort of order, merely as they catch one's eye in revising the list of contents and recall the poems classed there. Each of them we regard as worth a separate study, but the **"Litanies de Satan",** as in a way the key-note to this whole complicated tune of poems, we had set aside for the last. . . .

Here it seems as if all failure and sorrow on earth, and all the cast-out things of the world—ruined bodies and souls diseased—made their appeal, in default of help, to Him in whom all sorrow and all failure were incarnate. As a poem, it is one of the noblest lyrics ever written; the sound of it between wailing and triumph, as it were the blast blown by the trumpets of a brave army in inrretrievable defeat. . . .

[**"Litanies de Satan"** is not] more finished than the rest; every verse has the vibration in it of naturally sound and pure metal. It is a study of metrical cadence throughout, of wonderful force and variety. . . . We know that in time it must make its way. . . . (p. 1000)

Algernon Charles Swinburne, "Charles Baudelaire: 'Les fleurs du mal',' in The Spectator, *No. 1784, September 6, 1862, pp. 998-1000.*

Théophile Gautier   (essay date 1872)

[*Gautier, to whom Baudelaire dedicated* The Flowers of Evil, *holds an important place in French letters as a transitional figure between Romanticism and Realism. Like Baudelaire, he adhered to the doctrine which he expressed as "art pour l'art," or art for art's sake. In the following excerpt, taken from an essay in his* The Complete Works of Théophile Gautier, *he maintains that in* The Flowers of Evil *Baudelaire wished to excite "in the reader's mind the senation of the Beautiful." Further, he states that though the volume's intention and execution are Romantic, Baudelaire should not be confined to any literary school or movement. He praises the work's musical meter and prosody, and terms* The Flowers of Evil *"new and unexpected."*]

[Baudelaire] loved what is inaccurately called the decadent style, which is simply art that has reached the extreme point of maturity which marks the setting of ancient civilisations. It is an ingenious, complex, learned style, full of shades and refinements of meaning, ever extending the bounds of language, borrowing from every technical vocabulary, taking colours from every palette and notes from every keyboard; a style that endeavours to express the most inexpressible thoughts, the vaguest and most fleeting contours of form, that listens, with a view to rendering them, to the subtle confidences of neurosity, to the confessions of aging lust turning into depravity, and to the odd hallucinations of fixed ideas passing into mania. This decadent style is the final expression of the Word which is called upon to express everything, and which is worked for all it is worth. (pp. 39-40)

When Baudelaire is not engaged in expressing a yet untold side of the soul or of things, he makes use of so pure, clear, correct, and accurate a tongue that the most critical can find nothing in it to blame. This is particularly noticeable in his prose, in which he treats of matters more generally current and less abstrue than in his verse, which is almost always extremely condensed. (pp. 42-3)

[Baudelaire] did not believe that man was born good, and he admitted original sin as an element that is ever to be found in the depths of the purest souls, sin, that is an evil counsellor urging man to do what is harmful to him, precisely because it is deadly to him and for the sole pleasure of running counter to law, without any other inducement than disobedience, apart from any sensuality, any profit, any charm. . . . He might have engraved as a motto on his seal the two words, "Spleen and Idealism," which form the title of the first part of [*The Flowers of Evil*]. If it be urged that his bouquet is composed of strange, metallic-leaved flowers, with intoxicating perfumes, their calyxes filled with bitter tears or aqua-tofana instead of dew, his answer is that scarce any others grow in the black loan, saturated with rottenness like the soil of a graveyard, which is formed by the decrepit civilisations, in which the corpses of former ages are dissolving amid mephitic miasmata. (pp. 43-5)

[Baudelaire] believed art should be absolutely autonomous, and refused to admit that poetry had any end other than itself, or any mission to fulfil other than that of exciting in the reader's mind the sensation of the Beautiful, in the strictest meaning of the word. . . . He banished from poetry, to the utmost of his power, eloquence, passion, and the too accurate reproduction of truth. (pp. 46-7)

These principles may surprise one, when reading certain poems of his in which he seems to have deliberately set out to be horrible; but if they be carefully examined, it will be seen that the horrible is always transformed by the character and the effect of it, by a Rembrandt-like flash, by a grand stroke, like that of Velasquez, that reveals the high breeding under the foul difformity. (p. 47)

Although few poets have been endowed with more spontaneous originality and inspiration, Baudelaire, no doubt through disgust at the sham lyricism that pretends to believe that a tongue of fire settles upon the head of the writer who is striving hard to rime a stanza, maintained that a true writer called up, directed and modified at will the mysterious power of literary production. . . . (p. 51)

Baudelaire's nature was more subtle, complex, logical, paradoxical, and philosophical than that of poets in general. The æsthetics of his art preoccupied him greatly; he had a wealth of systems which he endeavoured to apply, and he planned out whatever he did. In his belief, literature should be *predetermined,* and the share of the *accidental* restricted as much as possible. (pp. 55-6)

The Flowers of Evil was a happy title, and happy titles are far more difficult to hit upon than is believed. It summed up in brief, poetic fashion the general idea of the book and indicated its tendency. Although quite plainly Romanticist in its intention and its execution, Baudelaire cannot be connected by any very visible bond with any one of the great masters of the school. His verse, with its refined and erudite structure, its occasionally too great conciseness, clothing objects as with a suit of armour rather than with a garment, appears at the first reading to be difficult and obscure. (p. 57)

The volume opens with a poem addressed **"To the Reader,"** whom the poem, contrary to custom, does not attempt to win over, but to whom he speaks the harshest of truths, accusing him, in spite of his hypocrisy, of having all the vices he blames in other men, and of bearing in his heart the great modern monster, Weariness, which with bourgeois cowardice, idiotically dreams of Roman ferocity and debauchery, like the bureaucratic Nero, the shopkeeping Heliogabalus it is. (pp. 58-9)

In **"Elevation"** we see the poet soaring in the very vault of heaven, beyond the starry spheres, in the luminous ether, on the very confines of our universe which has vanished like a cloudlet in the depths of the infinite, drinking in deeply the healthy rarefied air free from the foul odours of earth and perfumed by the breath of angels. For it must not be forgotten that Baudelaire, though he has often been accused of materialism—a reproach fools never fail to address to men of talent—is on the contrary endowed to an eminent degree with the gift of *spirituality,* as Swedenborg would say. He also possesses the gift of *correspondence,* if I may still use these mystical terms; that is, he is able to discover through a secret intuition relations invisible to other people, and thus to connect by unexpected analogies, which a *seer* alone can note, objects apparently utterly removed from and most opposed to each other. Every true poet is endowed with this quality to a greater or less degree, for it is the very essence of his art.

No doubt, in this book devoted to the representation of modern depravity and perversity, Baudelaire has placed repugnant pictures, in which vice laid bare wallows in all the hideousness of its shame; but the poet, filled with utter disgust, with indignant contempt, and with a return to the ideal that is often lacking in satirists, stigmatises and brands with a red-hot iron the unhealthy flesh, plastered over with unguents and powder. Nowhere does the thirst for pure, untainted air, for immaculate whiteness, for spotless azure, for inaccessible light manifest itself more ardently than in those poems which have been charged with immorality; as if the flagellation of vice and vice itself were one and the same thing, or a man were a poisoner because he had described the toxic pharmaceutics of the Borgias. (pp. 60-1)

[Baudelaire] more than once dedicated to cats beautiful poems—there are three in *The Flowers of Evil*—in which he sings of their moral and physical qualities, and he very often brings them in as characteristic accessories in his compositions. Cats are as numerous in Baudelaire's verse as dogs are in Paolo Veronese's paintings, and are equivalent to a signature. (p. 65)

Diverse female figures show in Baudelaire's poems, some veiled, others semi-nude, but to none can a name be given. They are types rather than persons; they represent the *eternal woman,* and the love the poet expresses for them is *abstract love,* and not *concrete love,* for we have seen that his theory did not admit individual passion, which he looked upon as too crude, familiar, and violent. (pp. 65-7)

At the end of *The Flowers of Evil* come a number of poems on "Wine" and the different forms of intoxication it produces, according to the kind of brain on which it acts. It is unnecessary to say that these are not bacchanalian songs in which the fruit of the vine is honoured, or anything resembling them. They are terrible and hideous descriptions of drunkenness, but unprovided with a Hogarthian moral. The painting needs no inscription, and one shudders at **"The Workingman's Drink."** **"The Litanies of Satan,"** the god of evil and the prince of this world, are a cold piece of irony of the kind the poet indulges in, and which it would be a mistake to consider impious. Impiety did not form part of Baudelaire's nature, for he believed in a higher law established by God from all time, the least violation of which is punished in the severest way, not in this world only, but also in the next. (pp. 69-70)

I must draw attention to some of the most remarkable poems in *The Flowers of Evil,* especially the one called **"Don Juan in Hades."** It is a tragically grand picture, painted with a sober masterliness of colouring upon the sombre flaming background of the infernal regions. (pp. 70-1)

The serene melancholy, the luminous peace, and the slumbrousness of the poem entitled **"The Former Life,"** form a pleasant contrast to the sombre descriptions of monstrous modern Paris, and testify to the fact that by the side of the blacks, bitumens, browns, umbers, and siennas on the artist's palette, there is a whole range of cool, light, transparent, delicately rosy, ideally blue hues like those in the distances in Paradise Breughel's pictures, which are fitted to reproduce Elysian landscapes and the mirages of dreams.

The feeling for the *artificial* should be mentioned as characteristic of the poet. By this must be understood a creation due wholly to art and whence nature is excluded. . . . [A striking instance of this curious tendency is] the poem called **"A Parisian Dream."** (pp. 71-2)

Is it not strangely fanciful, this composition made up of rigid elements among which nothing lives, breathes, or moves, in which no blade of grass, no leaf, no flower, breaks the implacable symmetry of fictitious forms invented by art? Does not one seem to be in an untouched Palmyra or Palenque which has remained intact and erect in some dead planet from which the atmosphere has vanished?

Unquestionably such fancies are fantastic, anti-natural, bordering on hallucination, and they betray a secret desire for impossible novelty, but for my part I prefer them to the sickly simplicity of so-called poems that embroider with old faded wools upon the canvas of worn-out commonplaces, trite, trivial, and idiotically sentimental patterns. . . . Barbarism is superior to platitude, to my thinking, and Baudelaire has this advantage, so far as I am concerned: he may be bad, but he is never vulgar; his faults are as original as his qualities, and even when he is unpleasant, it is because he has willed to be so, in accordance with long matured æsthetics and reasoning. (pp. 73-4)

Baudelaire rightly considered that metre, disdained by all who lack feeling for form,—and there are plenty such nowadays,—is most important. (p. 75)

[While] he accepted the chief improvements or reforms introduced by Romanticism, such as richness of rimes, the displacement at will of the cæsura, the running into or encroaching upon the next line, the use of exact or technical terms, the fulness and firmness of rhythm, the casting of the great Alexandrine in one unbroken length, and the whole of that careful mechanism of prosody and cadence in stanzas and strophes, Baudelaire nevertheless exhibits in his verse his own peculiar architectonics, his own individual formulæ, his own easily recognised structure, his own professional secrets, his own knack. . . . (p. 77)

Baudelaire often seeks to produce his musical effects by the use of one or more peculiarly melodious lines that form a refrain, and that reappear in turns, as in the Italian stanza called sextain. . . . He uses this form, which has something of the faint swing of a magical incantation dimly heard in a dream, in subjects of sorrowful remembrances and unfortunate love. The stanzas, with their monotonous soughing, bear the thought away and bring it back, rocking it the while as a flower fallen from the bank is rocked in the regular volutes of the billows. (p. 81)

From the structure of the verse let us pass to the woof and warp of the style. Baudelaire weaves in it threads of silk and gold with strong, rough threads of hemp, as in those stuffs of the East, at once superb and coarse, in which the most delicate ornaments are embroidered in a delightfully fanciful way upon a ground of harsh camel's-hair or coarse cloth, rough to the touch as sail-cloth. The most coquettish refinements, the most subtle, even, are thrown side by side with grim brutalities, and the reader passes suddenly from the boudoir with its heady scents and its voluptuously languorous conversations, to the vile pothouse where drunkards, mingling blood with their wine, are knifing each other for the sake of a street Helen.

The Flowers of Evil are the finest gem in Baudelaire's poetic crown. It is in them that he sounded a note wholly his own, and proved that even after the incalculable number of volumes of verse, which seemed to have exhausted every possible subject, it was still possible to bring to the light something new and unexpected, without necessarily indulging in absurdities or causing the whole procession of universal history to file past as in a German fresco. (pp. 84-5)

Medically speaking, *The Artificial Paradises* constitute a very well written monograph of hascheesh, and science might find in it reliable information; for Baudelaire piqued himself on being scrupulously accurate, and not for the world would he have allowed the smallest poetic imagery to slip into a subject that was naturally adapted to it. He specifies quite correctly the peculiar character of hascheesh hallucinations, which does not create anything, but merely develops the particular temperament of the individual while exaggerating it to its highest power. What is seen is one's own self, enlarged, rendered more acutely sensitive, excited beyond all reason, outside the confines of time and space, of which the very notion vanishes, in surroundings that are real to begin with, but which are speedily deformed, intensified, exaggerated, and in which every detail, extreme in its intensity, assumes supernatural importance, that, however, is readily apprehended by the hascheesh eater, who perceives mysterious relations between images often incongruous. (pp. 103-04)

Baudelaire brought out a precious, dainty, and odd side of his talent. He has managed to get closer to the inexpressible, and to render the fleeting shades that hover between sound and colour, and thoughts that resemble motives of arabesques or musical themes.

This form is applied successfully not to physical nature only, but to the most secret motions of the soul, to fanciful melancholy, to the splenetic hallucinations of nervous temperaments. The author of *The Flowers of Evil* has drawn marvellous effects from it, and it is surprising at times to find that speech manages to show objects apparently impossible to describe, and hitherto never *reduced* by verbs, now through the transparent gauzy veils of dreams, now with the sudden sharpness of a sunbeam that brings out vividly, in the bluish openings in the distance, a ruined tower, a mountain crest, or a clump of trees. It will be part of Baudelaire's glory, if not his greatest claim to it, to have brought within the possibilities of style numbers of objects, sensations, and effects, unnamed by Adam, the great nomenclator. No writer can wish for higher praise, and he who wrote the *Short Prose Poems* [*Petits poèmes en prose*] undoubtedly deserves it. (pp. 122-23)

> *Théophile Gautier, "Charles Baudelaire," in his* The Complete Works of Théophile Gautier, *Vol. XII, edited and translated by F. C. De Sumichrast, Bigelow, Smith & Co., 1903, pp. 17-126.*

Lafcadio Hearn   (essay date 1883)

[*Considered one of America's leading Impressionistic critics of the late nineteenth century, Hearn produced a large body of work that testifies to his love of the exotic and the beautiful. His sketches, short stories, and novellas demonstrate a vision of evil and the supernatural reminiscent of the works of Edgar Allan Poe and Baudelaire. In addition, his writings about Japan sparked international interest in that nation's cultural life. In the following excerpt, taken from an essay originally published in the* New Orleans Times-Democrat *in 1883 and reprinted in his* Essays in European and Oriental Literature, (1923), *Hearn highlights the Oriental and tropical influences evident in Baudelaire's poetry, especially in the "Jeanne Duval" poems.*]

Baudelaire had traveled over half the world before he attempted authorship;—and in his eyes, says Theodore de Banville, "there seemed to linger something of the strong light and the clear immensity of those far horizons which he had seen"—the lands of further India, Ceylon and the Malay peninsula, and the Indo-Chinese countries beyond. In some respects Baudelaire was certainly the most remarkable personage of his literary epoch.

In 1857 Baudelaire's collected poems were first brought out in book-form by Levy, of Paris, to the astonishment and horror of the public. *Flowers of Evil* is the translation of the title the volume still bears; and the alarm caused by the appearance and odor of these fantastic blossoms soon took active shape in a legal effort to eliminate the new vegetation from French literary soil. The book survived the attack, but it did not leave the courts unscathed;—several of the most extraordinary pieces, such as the **"Metamorphoses du Vampire,"** were suppressed, and have never, we believe, been republished. The press became afraid of the new author, and for the rest of his life he experienced the greatest difficulty in persuading either journals or reviews to accept a piece signed with his name. After his death he obtained full justice, and the introduction of his complete works, [*Oeuvres completes de Charles Baudelaire,*] written by Theophile Gautier, is certainly the finest critical article ever penned by that magician of language.

In its present shape, the volume contains 151 brief poems, resembling nothing else in the French language—marvelously original, audacious, terrible, but so exquisitely composed that it is doubtful whether they will ever cease to live. They have served as models of expression to Swinburne; and there is hardly a striking image or a strange thought in the earlier work of the great English lyrist which may not be found in the *Flowers of Evil.* And this astounding jewelry of verse, wrought as Gautier declares, with diamond-words,—with ruby, sapphire, emerald words, "words also which shine like phosphorus when rubbed,"—was formed into designs so hideous that a great critic did not hesitate to say there were only two things left for the author to do—"become a Christian or blow his brains out."

The frightful piece **"Une Charogne"** describing the corruption of a corpse in such fashion as no other writer, ancient or modern, ever dared to do before or since, and the unspeakable revolting **"Une Martyre"** represent the two extremes which brought the book to trial—the horrors of death and of vice described with fantastic cynicism and obscene truth. Strangely blended with these horrors the reader will find beauties of weird thought equal to the fancies of Poe (whom Baudelaire so well translated), and splendors of tropical imagination which seem the creations of hasheesh. Baudelaire could never forget the vast East,—the odors and colors and glories of Indian lands,—the statuesque grace of Javanese women,—the mighty vegetation of primeval forests. All that is tender and beautiful in his book has a tropical perfume,—potent enough to intoxicate the reader's brain.

The Flowers of Evil (*Fleurs du Mal*) wrote Gautier in speaking of Baudelaire's extraordinary volume of poems, in no wise resemble those which usually form the bouquets of modern poetry. Their colors are metallic, their foliage black or glaucous, their calixes strangely striated; and theirs also is the vertiginous perfume of those exotic flowers which may not be smelt of without peril. They have sprung from the black soil of putrefying civilization;—they seem to have been brought to us from Java or from Hindostan. . . . This poet feels an intense passion for exotic singularity. Throughout all his poems,—dominating their caprices infidelities, and griefs,—obstinately reappears one strange figure—a venus moulded in African bronze, tawny but beautiful, *nigra sed formosa,* a species of black Madonna whose niche is always decorated with crystal suns, and bouquets of pearls. It is to her that he always returns after his voyage into the Land of Horror, to ask of her if not happiness, the boon of appeasement or oblivion. That savage mistress dumb and dark as a sphinx,—with her soporific perfumes and torpedo-caresses,—seems a symbol of true nature or primitive life to which the human heart turns when weary of the complications of civilized existence.

Who this swarthy beauty was remained a mystery to the world at large for many years. Gautier hinted that she was only an ideal savage woman,—a sombre Eve specially created for the imaginary paradise of the poet. But the portraits of her which appear not only in the *Flowers of Evil,* but likewise in the *Prose Poems,* are so *naturally* minute that a careful study of Baudelaire would convince most readers to the contrary. "Supple and cajoling like the black panther of Java" this woman really lived, and lived in Paris, and exercised unconsciously a wonderful influence upon the life and the work of the poet, who never wearied singing of her beauty.

She must have been the model for the **"Dorothee"** of the *Prose Poems;* she may have served for that of the Serpent Woman (of the infernal bouquet), and that of the Malabaress whose "dreams are full of humming birds," and whose eyes pensively seek through the foul fogs of Paris "for the ghosts of absent cocoa-palms." She is also the Dorothee of that wonderful bit of light and music and perfume **"Bien lion d'ici."** [He] sings of her hair,—"an aromatic forest, an ebony-sea whose blue-black billows bear him in fancy to far tropical ports full of golden glow, and odors of musk and cocoa." . . . (pp. 57-61)

The mystery is rather brutally revealed in the *Souvenirs* of Theodore de Banville: "As one may readily become convinced of by reading Baudelaire, the poet never really loved but one woman—that Jeanne whom he never ceased to sing of in so magnificent a way. She was *a colored girl,* of very lofty stature, and quite attractive with her dark, superb, ingenuous head, crowned with a mass of *violently*-curling hair. There was something at once divine and yet animal in her queenly carriage, full of savage grace." Where the half-breed came from, however, we are not informed. Perhaps she was of that really superb type which inspired a celebrated French sculptor for his symbolic statute, *L'Afrique.*

Perhaps Baudelaire himself might have brought her back to Europe from some remote colony of the Indian or African sea; for he was wont to do very strange things during his travels. Having been once sent with letters of credit and recommendation to some outlandish country, he wea-

ried of his Creole hosts, and went off to the mountains to live among the savages, who cooked these extraordinary dishes for him of which we have a souvenir in the seventeenth of his prose-poems,—the "crabs stewed with rice and *saffron.*"

At all events, Jeanne was Baudelaire's model;—the word-painter sought from her all that the colorist seeks from living types, and yet something more,—the sense of tropical life, the indefinable and mysterious beauty created by interblendings of race, the type of savage grace, the dusky outward impassiveness that marks fantastic passion. She was the swarthy Aphrodite of his Indian Eden,—his bayadere, Javanese, Malabaress,—his tropical witch who evoked for him at will memories of far-away coasts, echoes of strange Eastern life, phantoms of Asiatic or African suns, luminosities and odors of equatorial ports and primeval woods. Utterly unconscious of the part she occupied in his life, the girl naturally believed her admirer mad;—wont, as he was, to dress her in oddly colored costumes of costly stuffs, and compel her to pose for him, while he recited poetry to her in a tongue which she could not understand—perhaps his own poetry also, in which he threatens to return after death to give her "kisses colder than the moon." Little did he then guess how soon death would come or in how dreary a shape,—slow paralysis of mind and body. Bitter-souled and brilliant of fancy like Heine, like Heine also he died,—though, perhaps even more miserably, speechless and thoughtless as any of those Orient idols whereof he had sung. Whether the dark woman tended him thus helpless, does not yet appear, nor has any mention been made of her fate—possibly and painfully suggested, no doubt, to many minds by the image of the **"Malabaress"** "trembling in the snow and sleet" of winter, and vainly gazing through the pallid Paris fogs for the ghosts of absent cocoa-palms. (pp. 62-4)

Lafcadio Hearn, "The Idol of a Great Eccentric (Baudelaire)," in his Essays in European and Oriental Literature, *edited by Albert Mordell, Dodd, Mead and Company, 1923, pp. 55-64.*

François Mauriac   (essay date 1920)

[*Mauriac is considered one of the notable Roman Catholic authors of the twentieth century. Most of his works offer vivid depictions of his native region of Bordeaux, France, and feature individuals tormented by the absence of virtue in their lives. A recipient of many honors and literary prizes during his lifetime, Mauriac was elected to the Académie Française in 1933 and was awarded the Nobel Prize in literature in 1952. In the following excerpt, he proposes that* Les fleurs du mal *represents "the cry not of a reconciled Christian, but of a sinner who cannot be resigned to sin."*]

I know that you keep a place for the poet
In the happy ranks of the heavenly hosts,
And that you invite him to the eternal feast
Of Thrones and Virtues and Dominations. . . .

Because Charles Baudelaire died some fifty years ago, journalists throw themselves on the great memory avidly. I dread for it indiscreet friendships more than I do insults. One commentator asserts that the Catholic was but a subtle mystifier, another swears that that debauchee died a virgin. Fine subjects indeed for articles! But let us ask Charles Baudelaire alone to show us "his heart laid bare." We Catholics shall not reject that sorrowful brother without close scrutiny. Down to his dying day, he listened to his poor soul and he confessed it. The flowers of evil are the flowers of sin, of repentance, of remorse and penitence. He suffers, but he knows why.

> Blessed be Thou, O God, who givest suffering
> As a divine remedy to our impurities,
> And as the best and the purest essence
> Which prepares the strong for holy delights.

He is humiliated, but "those humiliations have been graces sent by God" (*Mon Coeur mis à nu*); Pascal likewise had written: "To offer oneself to inspirations through humiliations." Baudelaire prays, like a child of the Church:

> The man who says his prayers at night is a captain who places sentinels; he then can sleep. . . . Every morning, make my prayer to God, the reservoir of all strength and of all justice, to my father, to Mariette [the maid he had as a child] and to Poe as intercessors; pray them to impart to me the strength I need to fulfill all my duties and to grant my mother a life long enough so that she may witness my transformation. . . . Trust God, that is to say, justice itself for the success of my projects; make every night a new prayer, to ask God for life and strength for my mother and myself. . . . Do not punish me in my mother and do not punish my mother because of me. . . . Grant me the strength to do my duty immediately every day and thus to become a hero and a saint.

Elsewhere Baudelaire wrote: "Beads are a medium, a vehicle; they are prayer put within the reach of all." The sorrow of men of genius, of the beacons, as he calls them, appears to him through the centuries like one indefinite prayer:

> For it is truly, O Lord, the best proof
> We may give of our dignity,
> This ardent sob which rolls from age to age
> And dies on the shore of Your eternity!

The revelations which we owe to his friend Nadar and to the two women who were loved by Baudelaire seem to leave scant doubt as to what his strange ideal was: he wanted to possess the loved one in chastity. In his eyes, woman always remains "my child . . ., *my Sister . . .*" Eyes radiant with light go in front of him as he says:

> Escaping every snare and every grave sin.

(pp. 30-2)

Jules Lemaître asserts that Baudelaire's thoughts are but a pretentious and painful stammering and that no less philosophical head can be imagined. Neither a philosopher nor a scientist, I agree. But because he believes in the dogma of original sin, the poet holds the key to the universal enigma. Lemaître derides this maxim which he quotes: " . . . The one and supreme voluptuous delight of love lies in the certainty of doing *evil*. Man and woman well know, from their birth, that in evil all that is voluptuous has its roots." I do not see that there is matter for laughter here. Those few words illuminate the human heart better, for me, than all the confusions and postures of theatrical peo-

ple. Lemaître assures us that the Catholicism of *Les Fleurs du mal* is scarcely Christian, impious and sensuous. Facile blasphemies, deliberately exaggerated, will not avert us from those poems, where a poor soul, torn with remorse, is hungry and thirsty for perfection and knows the price of sorrow. True, he is fond of making his title of Catholic sound aloud, as a young lord does with his noble name. He takes glory in his baptism in a France "where everyone resembles Voltaire." To me, such pride appears legitimate. I am not scandalized by such spiritual dandyism. Still a danger lurks there. Today also, the vulgarity of the free-thinking middle class may well lure some young Catholics to laud God for having made them such admirable creatures. I fear ostentatiousness for them more than human respect.

But to that Catholic attitude, and that religious dandyism, there corresponds in Baudelaire a heart truly pursued by Grace. A few experiences with opium and hashish, a few excesses with alcohol do not alter the fact that "the frightening grip of God" weighed on that soul. Whenever I read his poems, I have the feeling that they do not bear their true title. With those three words, "Flowers of Evil," at the very threshold of his book, that great poet slanders himself. I remember how, at fifteen, I opened in secret that forbidden collection of poems, but almost nothing in that music disturbed my child's heart. Sin maintained all its ugliness in it; man severed from God was abandoned to his solitude and misery; the heart kept its craving for love, its need to possess someone beyond the blood, beyond the flesh.

Echoes responding to Pascal's lyricism are audible in Baudelaire's poetry. "Man does not know at what rank to place himself," Pascal wrote. "He is clearly lost and fallen from his true estate, and he can not retrieve it. He seeks it everywhere restlessly and unsuccessfully, through impenetrable darkness." Amid that impenetrable darkness where Baudelaire gropes his way as a wanderer of original sin, he is guided by a love unknown to Pascal: Beauty. But he fears it and he hates it, when it asserts itself as carnal and criminal. He merely wishes that it might open in front of him the gate

> Of an infinite which I love and never have known.

His yearning for "the voyage," for "elsewhere," do they not transcend the world? It is beyond the setting suns that the ships of the **"Invitation au voyage"** carry the poet, and woman does not lead him away from the unattainable horizon:

> And nothing, neither your love, nor the boudoir, nor the hearth
> Equals for me the sun radiant over the sea.

The last of the *Fleurs du mal,* **"Le Voyage,"** in a manner unequalled in its splendor, expresses that need of the human heart to escape from the finite. First it is the earthly departure that is sung in the poet's lines, that desire to

> Cradle our infiniteness on the finite seas,

to destroy memory, to obliterate the trace of kisses; but the world is too small, the poet only yearns for the ultimate crossing. He weighs anchor for ever, he trusts death to lead him to God. . . . That celestial Father whom we hope, after a martyrdom without name, Charles Baudelaire at last found.

If they do not deserve their title, *Flowers of Evil,* Baudelaire's poems are indeed sickly flowers, as he himself called them in his dedication to Gautier. But Catholicism is balance. Holiness is health itself. There exists a subtle temptation which consists in loving, in the Church, a source of delights, a moving vision of the world and of oneself, the evil pleasure of challenging a prohibition and of disobeying someone; that taste for sinning can be perceived in Baudelaire even by the least attentive of readers. Before he became resigned to the strait gate, the poor poet scratched his hand at too many of its bars. His very purity, which I have praised, is undeniably suspect. It is given to man to discover a worse quest in abstinence, and, if he did not sin through his body, his intellectual debauchery knew no restraint. (pp. 32-4)

Baudelaire's posthumous writings also served as lights on Claudel's way, and we see grace cross the soul of the "accursèd poet" for remote ends. He did not remain untouched by its burning mark. Grace wrought a miracle in him that such a lover of Beauty might not be satisfied with the world of shapes. Among the perfumes, the colors, the sounds, Baudelaire, in order to broaden the universe in which he feels stifled, creates correspondence. He sees nature as a forest of symbols. He prolongs his life in the realm of appearance with the imagined splendor of an "anterior life." But it is in vain; and he forsakes all the appearances to the extent of only tolerating a bare and stripped landscape, a landscape, as he puts it in his prose poems, "made with light, and the mineral and the liquid to reflect them." His poems, like vessels sailing to far-off seas, intoxicate the restlessness of wandering hearts. They suggest a flight toward impossible climates and they constrain us to love death like a supreme departure. They can be summed up in the cry which everyone of us, at some time in his youth, has uttered: "Anywhere out of the world!"—the cry, not of a reconciled Christian, but of a sinner who cannot be resigned to sin. What is refused to Baudelaire, to his ilk, to his brethren, by merciful powers, is the gradual acceptance and the habit of sin; he returns to his nausea, but he is aware that it is but nausea. The most alluring blandishments of the prince of this world do not dim his clear-sightedness. Baudelaire's work illustrates Fausts's derisive remark in Goethe's tragedy: "What hast thou to give, poor demon? Thou hast only food which does not satiate."

Never satiated, his thirst always unslaked, aggravated by that trickery of sin, by that deceitful decoy of the senses, why does he not surrender to God the father? Because, on the path of the prodigal son, in the night, the lamps of evil houses burn. It cannot be doubted that the poet used and abused drugs, the criminal delights of which he described for us in his *Artificial Paradises.* But never does he lose the lucidity of one who has not renounced true religion: in more than one passage the *Artificial Paradises* evince a passionate and Pascalian logic. In the entrancing resort to poisons, Baudelaire denounces, as Pascal might have done, the perversion of the taste for the infinite: "Alas! man's vices, full of horror as they may be imagined to be, contain the proof (were it but in their infinite expansion!) of his passion for the infinite: but that passion is often waylaid. . . . Everything leads to reward or to punishment, two forms of eternity. The human spirit brims over with passions . . . " ("The Taste for the Infinite," in *Artificial Paradises*).

Conscious and remorseful lucidity, such is the torment to which grace condemns the poor poet gone astray. Even when he writes on hashish and opium, he knows with absolute certainty that he sits under the watchful gaze of the Trinity and, not to lose heart altogether, he utters a cry of hope toward God in one of his prose poems:

> O Lord, my God, you, the servant, you, the Master; you who established law and freedom, you, the sovereign that tolerates; you, the judge that forgives; you who are full of motives and of causes and who perhaps placed in my spirit the taste of horror in order to convert my heart, like the healing at the edge of a blade. . . .

I know not whether, at the deathbed of Baudelaire, the prayer for the commending of the soul to divine mercy was recited. But his soul deserved, more than any other, that such a testimonial be granted it: "Although it sinned, it denied neither the Father nor the Son nor the Holy Ghost; it believed in them." Some teachers of youth worry: Shall we invite every adolescent to drink, without discernment, from those turbid waters? There are, not only in the commonplace vituperations of preachers, books which are harmful. But the peril is twofold: one consists in inducing young people, for the love of art, to indulge in morbid reading; the other was not eschewed by the priests whose textbooks fostered in me, when I was sixteen, a nefarious sense of irony. To the poison of Balzac and of Flaubert, those pious educators opposed the antidote of the most insipid Sunday School literature. Neither Baudelaire nor Verlaine, needless to say, was granted a single mention in their books, nor any of the poets whom we cherish.

There is no ground for smiling light-heartedly at such pious deceit: I know what storm brews in a young heart when it deems itself exiled, through its faith, from all the paradises whose odor it breathes; when the notions of mediocrity, of childish silliness are married in his thought with religious practice. What! The highest geniuses of the last century and of ours have, according to Nietzsche's phrase, "dropped in collapse at the foot of Christ's cross," and you propose edifying and insipid beverages, as specifically Catholic, to the teenager? I grant that he should be put on his guard against modern writers; that, until he is fortified in his faith, reading them should be forbidden him, in the name of that demanding truth which obliges us to forsake the remotest occasions for sinning; and yet I hold that we should teach young souls the immense role of God in contemporary art, showing them that the lyricism of Baudelaire, of Verlaine, of Rimbaud, Jammes, Claudel, in different degrees, proceeds from the Father, like that of Bossuet and of Pascal. (pp. 34-6)

As he neared the end of his life, Baudelaire, deep in the pangs of suffering, found the strength to submit to God. He died a penitent. To be sure, such a death does not exorcize the work of the poet. But in its very blasphemies, that work is the advancement of a heart which, in order to reach God, follows the longest road. Everything delays the poet, because he sees what others do not perceive; solitude, silence, "the incomparable chastity of the azure sky," long avert his gaze from what lies beyond them. The "mute language" of flowers, of skies, of the setting sun cover up the inner voice of God. They may be mistaken and mad in that temporary blindness of theirs. But let us repeat in humility the prayer of Baudelaire's **Poems in Prose:** "O Lord, take pity upon the mad ones! O Creator! can there exist monsters in the eyes of him alone who knows why they exist, how they became thus, and how they might not have thus become monsters?" (p. 37)

François Mauriac, "Charles Baudelaire the Catholic," translated by Lois A. Haegert, in Baudelaire: A Collection of Critical Essays, *edited by Henri Peyre, Prentice-Hall, Inc., 1962, pp. 30-7.*

T. S. Eliot (essay date 1930)

[*An American-born British writer, Eliot was one of the most influential poets and critics of the first half of the twentieth century and is best remembered as the author of* The Waste Land (*1922*). *In the following excerpt, he views Baudelaire as "essentially Christian," yet asserts that Baudelaire displays a "theological innocence;" his primary concern is the problem of good and evil in the Christian tradition, but he is confused by both concepts. Eliot judges Baudelaire to the "greatest exemplar in* modern *poetry" for his "renovation" of verse and language as well as for his "renovation of an attitude towards life. . . ."*]

It was once the mode to take Baudelaire's Satanism seriously, as it is now the tendency to present Baudelaire as a serious and Catholic Christian. . . . I think that the latter view—that Baudelaire is essentially Christian—is nearer the truth than the former, but it needs considerable reservation. When Baudelaire's Satanism is dissociated from its less creditable paraphernalia, it amounts to a dim intuition of a part, but a very important part, of Christianity. Satanism itself, so far as not merely an affectation, was an attempt to get into Christianity by the back door. Genuine blasphemy, genuine in spirit and not purely verbal, is the product of partial belief, and is as impossible to the complete atheist as to the perfect Christian. It is a way of affirming belief. This state of partial belief is manifest throughout the *Journaux Intimes.* What is significant about Baudelaire is his theological innocence. He is discovering Christianity for himself; he is not assuming it as a fashion or weighing social or political reasons, or any other accidents. He is beginning, in a way, at the beginning; and being a discoverer, is not altogether certain what he is exploring and to what it leads; he might almost be said to be making again, as one man, the effort of scores of generations. His Christianity is rudimentary or embryonic. . . . His business was not to practise Christianity, but—what was much more important for his time—to assert its *necessity.* (pp. 373-74)

[Baudelaire] was one of those who have great strength, but strength merely to *suffer.* He could not escape suffering and could not transcend it, so he *attracted* pain to himself. But what he could do, with that immense passive strength and sensibilities which no pain could impair, was to study his suffering. And in this limitation he is wholly unlike Dante, not even like any character in Dante's Hell. But, on the other hand, such suffering as Baudelaire's implies the possibility of a positive state of beatitude. (pp. 374-75)

From the poems alone, I venture to think, we are not likely to grasp what seems to me the true sense and significance of Baudelaire's mind. Their excellence of form, their perfection of phrasing, and their superficial coherence, may give them the appearance of presenting a definite and final state of mind. In reality, they seem to me to have the external but not the internal form of classic art. . . . Now the true claim of Baudelaire as an artist is not that he found a superficial form, but that he was searching for a form of life. In minor form he never indeed equalled Théophile Gautier, to whom he significantly dedicated his poems: in the best of the slight verse of Gautier there is a satisfaction, a balance of inwards and form, which we do not find in Baudelaire. He had a greater technical ability than Gautier, and yet the content of feeling is constantly bursting the receptacle. His apparatus, by which I do not mean his command of words and rhythms, but his stock of imagery (and every poet's stock of imagery is circumscribed somewhere), is not wholly perdurable or adequate. His prostitutes, mulattoes, Jewesses, serpents, cats, corpses, form a machinery which has not worn very well; his Poet, or his Don Juan, has a romantic ancestry which is too clearly traceable. Compare with the costumery of Baudelaire the stock of imagery of the *Vita Nuova . . . ,* and you find Baudelaire's does not everywhere wear as well as that of several centuries earlier. . . . (pp. 375-76)

To say this is only to say that Baudelaire belongs to a definite place in time. Inevitably the offspring of romanticism, and by his nature the first counter-romantic in poetry, he could, like any one else, only work with the materials which were there. It must not be forgotten that a poet in a romantic age cannot be a "classical" poet except in tendency. If he is sincere, he must express with individual differences the general state of mind—not as a *duty,* but simply because he cannot help participating in it. For such

Baudelaire in dandyish dress, painted by Emile Deroy when Baudelaire was in his early twenties.

poets, we may expect often to get much help from reading their prose works and even notes and diaries; help in deciphering the discrepancies between head and heart, means and end, material and ideals.

What preserves Baudelaire's poetry from the fate of most French poetry of the nineteenth century up to his time, and has made him . . . the one modern French poet to be widely read abroad, is not quite easy to conclude. It is partly that technical mastery which can hardly be overpraised, and which has made his verse an inexhaustible study for later poets, not only in his own language. (p. 376)

[His] invention of language, at a moment when French poetry in particular was famishing for such invention, is enough to make of Baudelaire a great poet, a great landmark in poetry. Baudelaire is indeed the greatest exemplar in *modern* poetry in any language, for his verse and language is the nearest thing to a complete renovation that we have experienced. But his renovation of an attitude towards life is no less radical and no less important. In his verse, he is now less a model to be imitated or a source to be drained than a reminder of the duty, the consecrated task, of sincerity. From a fundamental sincerity he could not deviate. The superficies of sincerity . . . is not always there. . . . [Many] of his poems are insufficiently removed from their romantic origins, from Byronic paternity and Satanic fraternity. The "satanism" of the Black Mass was very much in the air; in exhibiting it Baudelaire is the voice of his time; but I would observe that in Baudelaire, as in no one else, it is redeemed by *meaning something else*. He uses the same paraphernalia, but cannot limit its symbolism even to all that of which he is conscious. . . . Baudelaire is concerned, not with demons, black masses, and romantic blasphemy, but with the real problem of good and evil. It is hardly more than an accident of time that he uses the current imagery and vocabulary of blasphemy. In the middle nineteenth century. . . , an age of bustle, programmes, platforms, scientific progress, humanitarianism and revolutions which improved nothing, an age of progressive degradation, Baudelaire perceived that what really matters is Sin and Redemption. It is a proof of his honesty that he went as far as he could honestly go and no further. To a mind observant of the post-Voltaire France . . . , a mind which saw the world of *Napoléon le petit* more lucidly than did that of Victor Hugo, a mind which at the same time had no affinity for the *Saint-Sulpicerie* of the day, the recognition of the reality of Sin is a New Life; and the possibility of damnation is so immense a relief in a world of electoral reform, plebiscites, sex reform and dress reform, that damnation itself is an immediate form of salvation—of salvation from the ennui of modern life, because it at last gives some significance to living. It is this, I believe, that Baudelaire is trying to express; and it is this which separates him from the modernist Protestantism of Byron and Shelley. It is apparently Sin in the Swinburnian sense, but really Sin in the permanent Christian sense, that occupies the mind of Baudelaire.

Yet. . . , the sense of Evil implies the sense of good. Here too, as Baudelaire apparently confuses, and perhaps did confuse, Evil with its theatrical representations, Baudelaire is not always certain in his notion of the Good. The romantic idea of Love is never quite exorcised, but never quite surrendered to. In *Le Balcon*. . . , there is all the romantic idea, but something more: the reaching out towards something which cannot be had *in,* but which may be had partly *through,* personal relations. (pp. 377-79)

[In] the adjustment of the natural to the spiritual, of the bestial to the human and the human to the supernatural, Baudelaire is a bungler compared with Dante; the best that can be said, and that is a very great deal, is that what he knew he found out for himself. In his book, the *Journaux Intimes,* and especially in *Mon cœur mis à nu,* he has a great deal to say of the love of man and woman. . . . Baudelaire has perceived that what distinguishes the relations of man and woman from the copulation of beasts is the knowledge of Good and Evil (of *moral* Good and Evil which are not natural Good and Bad or puritan Right and Wrong). Having an imperfect, vague romantic conception of Good, he was at least able to understand that the sexual act as evil is more dignified, less boring, than as the natural, "life-giving," cheery automatism of the modern world. (pp. 379-80)

[Baudelaire's] human love is definite and positive, his divine love vague and uncertain: hence his insistence upon the evil of love, hence his constant vituperations of the female. In this there is no need to pry for psychopathological causes, which would be irrelevant at best; for his attitude towards women is consistent with the point of view which he had reached. Had he been a woman he would, no doubt, have held the same views about men. He has arrived at the perception that a woman must be to some extent a symbol; he did not arrive at the point of harmonising his experience with his ideal needs. The complement, and the correction to the *Journaux Intimes,* so far as they deal with the relations of man and woman, is the *Vita Nuova,* and the *Divine Comedy.* . . . But—I cannot assert it too strongly—Baudelaire's view of life, such as it is, is objectively apprehensible, that is to say, his idiosyncrasies can partly explain his view of life, but they cannot explain it away. And this view of life is one which has grandeur and which exhibits heroism; it was an evangel to his time and to ours. (p. 381)

T. S. Eliot, "Baudelaire," in his Selected Essays, *Harcourt Brace Jovanovich, Inc., 1950, pp. 371-81.*

Jean Prévost   (essay date 1953)

[*Prevost was a French novelist, critic, and essayist esteemed for his lively style and lucid thought. In the following excerpt, he discusses the themes of Baudelaire's poetry, particularly the themes of death, evil, and love in* Les fleurs du mal.]

Baudelaire certainly does not have the extreme variety of subjects, of themes, and of tones found in Victor Hugo. But his poetical themes are broader and more numerous than those of Lamartine, for example: The *Fleurs du mal* offers horizons of an amplitude seldom in any other single volume. There would have been scant, if any, gain in the book's being two or three times larger; if Baudelaire, for sheer mass, equalled Hugo, he would be hardly tolerable. Under the variety of topics, an extreme suppleness of form, a distinctive unity of tone and of feeling is perceptible, with the same tension and the same will. Baudelaire's contemporaries did not fail to notice it, when they mockingly compared him to Boileau, and Sainte-Beuve, unjust as he was in his estimate of the poet's greatness, nevertheless saw his deliberate attempt to transform and transpose. Different as Baudelaire may be from Pascal, aesthetic impressions akin to those produced by the *Pensées* are frequently experienced by those who reread the *Fleurs du mal.* Each of them in his own realm probes our feelings and our thoughts with a very acute knife, cutting narrow and deep furrows into the quick. Both are anatomists rather than contemplators of life; in a few words, they reach straight to the bone, and strip it of all flesh.

Listing the themes of Baudelaire's poetry would not be enough. First and foremost one must ask how the poet *wants* to transform that theme, and to which others he wishes to marry it. A survey of the simple themes, or of those which seem simple at first, could be made fast enough. Again like Pascal, and like all those who load their thought and their looks with passion, Baudelaire feels, sees, understands through antitheses. The most important picture of Baudelairean themes can only be had through contrasting touches.

Naturally it happens that the poet receives or undergoes dreams which he has not organized; even if he has perhaps provoked them through hashish or laudanum, he has not organized their visions. Let us consider the poem **"Rêve parisien"**: nothing appears clearer or simpler, provided we do not look for sources too high or too far, in the clouds or in regions beyond the spirit, of what the poet actually found in a precise craftsmanship and in the resources of his art. That weird vision owes little or nothing to De Quincey, E. A. Poe, Novalis, or Gautier, whose vision was distorted (in the case of the first two through intoxication). Baudelaire is clearcut, even when he describes what is vague.

In **"Rêve parisien,"** the poet sees nothing but his hotel-room. But the perspectives are distorted: the tables, the door, the shelves, the plinths, the plaster moldings on the ceiling, the mantelpiece become prestigious structures. To a vague and magnifying perception, all that shines becomes metal if it is very small, a sheet of water if it is larger. Thus the mirror on the wall can be in turn huge polished glass and a waterfall rushing down from the sky; a few bottles around a wash basin are enough to suggest a colonnade around a garden pond; the little vault of the fireplace, above a metal plate which vaguely shines, becomes an arch or a tunnel above an ocean. The lines on the ruled paper are turned into rivers which come down from the sky; the small fragment of sky which can be seen from the window is projected afar, into the infinite, and instead of standing upright, appears to stretch horizontally; it is a boundless sea, weirdly contained on its sides. And if nothing vegetal appears in that vision, it is because the poet does not have the slightest bunch of flowers in his room; he is honest and refuses to alter anything in that perception so simply and vastly distorted.

It must be distorted a second time, or rather it must be given a shape at last, and pass from a false perception into a work of art. Then only, along with the customary rhymes which associate the images ("crise" and "cristallise," "fééries" and "pierreries," "diamant" and "firmament"), images will appear which have been borrowed from Baudelaire's predecessors, in poetry, or perhaps in painting and engraving. For every sight which he contemplates or interprets, the poet is prepared by all the images he has seen, all the words he has heard.

"La Chambre double," one of the prose poems, with similar simplicity describes another aspect, a humbler one, of the reveries provoked by intoxication. This time, the phial of laudanum is mentioned; it interposes only a happy mist between reality and the poet's eye; it makes the shape of the furniture and the settling more harmonious; its sole task of hallucination, a very modest one, is to spread a veil of muslin between the windows and the bed. The loved woman is dreamt; she is scarcely believed to be present; even the dream seems to wonder about its own presence. The vision as a whole does not create objects, but merely transposes values and invests every commonplace object with an appearance of beauty.

The same "moral message" emerges from **"Rêve parisien"** and **"La Chambre double"**—that which is also proposed by Thomas De Quincey's confessions. The dream which has been voluntarily caused by the dreamer and to which he submits must be followed by a desolate awakening, a bleak and frozen return to earth. . . . But if Baudelaire knew, underwent passively, and recorded the dreams caused by artificial paradises, his dreams are vastly different. These, more vaporous and subtle than the others, are impervious to change and are not followed by that forlorn awakening; they emerge at the mind's highest peak of lucidity.

The idea of death, on which the *Fleurs du mal* ends, remains more real and more religious than that of God for the poet. Even in that idea, which might appear to be monolithic and without any diverse hues, similar to the mat black of painters, he finds contrasts. He consents to rest in **"La Fin de la journée,"** but seems to have doubts about doing so in **"Le Squelette laboureur"**; with exaltation, he affirms survival in **"La Mort des amants"**; he denies it in **"Le Mort joyeux,"** which sounds like a challenge to fear and to faith. The vague hope of a glorious blossoming transfigures the end of **"Bénédiction"** and of **"La Mort des artistes"**; but **"Le Rêve d'un curieux"** tells us that even our thirst for the beyond must be frustrated.

The man for whom nature was monotonous and narrow, and who saw the world through a few artists rather than in its original nudity, vaguely expected from death something which no longer would look like what was known, which would not be our shadow or our reflection on things, but a novel sensation. **"Le Voyage"** thus truly deserves to be the final poem of the book, the one in which the stages of the poet's life are, one after the other, most clearly marked: memoirs, in a word, but at the same time the memoirs of all of us. Once again, this time all encompassed in one poem, the world as he has seen it unrolls before our eyes; life, like the sea, wearies us with its monotonous and dazzling brightness. Let us close our eyes, first to rest them, then to implore wildly for newness, "du nouveau." Spiritual flame has extinguished the sumptuous spectacle of nature, and the sun is now only an inner one:

> If the sky and the sea are black like ink,
> Our hearts which you well knew are filled with bright rays!

That enchanted and disappointed review of human things sacrifices everything to a last hope, the only one which life cannot take away. The world, so lovely in its images, has shrunk and wilted; love is a stain which obstinately lingers; the lightness of departures, full of fresh hopes when one set out at the dawn of one's life, appears madness to him whose dreams have regularly foundered on rocky reefs. Even the splendor of the Orient, not unlike the grey sadness of our cities, fails to conceal the powerless human misery. The only folly which comes up to our mad expectations is that of opium. One hope alone will restore to the poet the cheerful joy of his earlier departure; in the midst of the vain tumult of old temptations, it will blow like an off-shore breeze, the only chance of freshness; death is the only certitude left to man, and the poet attempts to make it the only hope.

Along with poems in which Baudelaire yearns for the good or for nothingness, there are some in which complacency in plunging into evil is triumphant. His conscientious examinations now appeal to God, now to the Devil. So exacting, so perfect in playing his part is the latter, that he ceases to be the enemy and becomes the object of a desolate cult.

In **"L'Horreur sympathique,"** the misery of the unhappy libertine is relieved by his pride. There, as in **"Le Rebelle,"** the soul agrees to persist in its evil incarnation. The damned one in **"Le Rebelle"** is content with saying: "I do not want." The libertine in **"Horreur sympathique"** refuses to moan; he wants neither the brightness nor the certainty promised to the elect by faith; on the contrary, he is "avide de l'obscur et de l'incertain." What matters it to him if he is expelled from Paradise? At last, he will confess his pride and his taste for Inferno. The two poems are close to each other: the taste for Inferno is but a fierce taste for freedom; in spite of all hopes, in spite of all the rewards promised to docile submission, I want to choose what appeals to me, "to prefer myself to my happiness."

"L'Irrémédiable" shows another voluptuous aspect of evil, another pride: no longer that of independence, but of lucidity. Yes, I have seen myself, I have gazed clear-sightedly at all the evil that is in me, and here I am, God of myself, fully aware of my good and of my evil. In its first part, the poem is a series of comparisons, borrowed from Vigny's "Eloa," Poe, and De Quincey. These comparisons which all bring the reader back to the poet recall the pieces entitled **"Spleen,"** in which the soul, melting in melancholy images of the world, seems to surrender. But the Devil appears, and the poet's admiration for that character who "always does well all that he does" gives a clearer outline to despair. Thus the second half of the poem is introduced, in which the mournful joy of lucidity will give itself free play:

> Unique relief and glory—
> Conscience in Evil.

Examination of conscience does not necessarily constitute an exercise toward virtue for Baudelaire. A particular examination impels to energy and hard work; a general examination leads to despair, and to the acceptance of that despair. The Socratic "Know thyself," basis of all virtues, here becomes awareness of and consent to evil; the monastic meditation which leads to good resolutions is utilized against laziness, but it accepts and it exalts the vast realm of sins. We do not have to judge it from the point of view of a moralist, but from that of a lover of poetry. Bound as it was to the constant quest for new and adequate trans-

lation into words, it made the poet more acutely aware of his own particular being. It led him to borrow the language of religion for very secular descriptions, to merge into one the two desires to know himself and to judge himself. When he observes man, he starts with himself; lyricism and lucidity are thus married.

It appears that once at least Baudelaire experienced romantic passion of the kind which transfigures the loved one into an angelic creature. Most of the poems sent to "La Présidente," as she was called by her friends, or written for her, seem like the rites of a cult. The poet occasionally offered the same fervor to Berthe or to Marie, "the child, the sister," but then without pretending to lower himself before them. Does he find in this experience the great "romantic love," and are not those poems as beautiful as the great love elegies by Musset, Lamartine, or Hugo, closely allied to them in their inspiration?

For the romantics, passion is an exchange. The words and the feelings of the loved woman appear to occupy the first place there. She is almost like Dante's Beatrice or Petrarch's Laura, the inspirer, she to whom the poet owes his genius. The inspirer is aware of her role and of her mission, so that her beauty seems but a paltry thing compared to the loftiness of her mind or the impulses of her heart.

Not so with Baudelaire. "La Présidente," for him, is not a living goddess but a nearly mute idol. He calls her Angel, but praises chiefly the merits of a filly in her: splendid eye, beauty, blooming and contagious health. Curiously enough, the confessions in the *Journals* and the other love poems in **Les Fleurs du mal** evince an enduring taste, first instinctive and then reasoned, for the thin, much painted, rather sad-looking type of woman. Does he offer his adoration to this healthy and plump woman precisely because she is not "his type," because he can sympathize with that healthy and overflowing vigor without feeling any desire for it? Doubtless this woman, whom he had long known, a good partner at smoking and hashish parties, the mistress of several of his friends, held little mystery for him at the time when he decided to make her his idol. Biography allows us to see in that "love" only a poetical raw material, a pretext for sonnets; the written work confirms it. From his idol, he received only one confidence, out of which he made the stanzas of **"Confession."** He succeeded there in hiding the extreme banality of the avowal under the description of a Paris night and a simple and faultless rhythm. We owe it to his genius to imagine that, by himself, he would have treated the same theme more profoundly. Elsewhere, she is not supposed to speak ("Taisez-vous, ignorante! âme toujours ravie!"), but at times the demon in her speaks, at times the phantom of the idol; in other words, to the woman herself, the poet prefers the image of her which he makes or unmakes at will.

Poet that he was, he sought two things in Madame Sabatier whom he treated as a work of art rather than as a real being. As early as 1853, in one of the first poems which he sends to her, he shows it ingenuously. First, her refreshing and salutary atmosphere, the contagion of health and cheerfulness which might impart tone and vigor to him. He does not wish to possess her; he wants rather, at times, to share in her robustness and her easy-going gaiety; he wants to believe in the contagion of physical good as the ancients did:

David on his death bed would have implored health
From the emanations of your enchanted body. . . .

But chiefly he asks from her a continuous surprise, an ever-renewed opportunity for contrasts with himself. Obsessed with himself and his own problems, in her he finds his perfect opposite. It may be a chance to forget himself; more often still, an opportunity for comparing and opposing himself to her. That series of methodically developed contrasts is the theme of **"Reversibilité."** The beloved hardly appears; only her vaguest virtues are celebrated; she is the motionless wall against which the foam of her worshipper's contrary passions, the tide of his impure suffering, beats. The last stanza devotes three lines to her. There the real woman appears as if she were a sum of abstractions, a being of reason, an Angel, whose prayers the poet implores in concluding.

In most of the sonnets which come later, Baudelaire does not even ask the loved woman to participate in her own cult. She does not even need to understand herself, to wonder what kind of beauty she represents for the poet. Baudelaire celebrates her eyes; he has taken them as his guides; thanks to them, for a moment he ceases to be demoniacal or Christian. He allows himself to surrender to a love of simple and superficial gaiety, to admiration for the most natural and blossoming beauty. In a word, under a softer and more refined shape, with a suave quality which his elder and master did not have, he seems to profess the aesthetic and pagan religion of Théophile Gautier; he instills into it a mysticism without content, made solely of remote intentions and of purified images. Nothing designates the loved one in particular. These chants of adoration could be equally addressed to all women whose eyes are normal: for example . . .

They walk in front of me, those eyes filled with light

In **"Le Flambeau vivant,"** or the similar lines in **"L'Aube spirituelle."** According to the poet's own declaration, **"Harmonie du soir"** is a flower from the same bouquet of laudatory hymns: one may wonder whether it celebrates a living creature. A Spaniard, more accustomed than a Frenchman to a poetry of dolorous filial tenderness, might suppose that the poem is addressed to a mother rather than a mistress. The "Présidente" is more exactly depicted in **"Allégorie,"** if it is she who is designated in that poem, as evidence leads us to believe. There Baudelaire magnifies his model, but does not idealize it.

Upon receiving her copy of *Les Fleurs du mal* and rereading the poems which the poet had said were devoted to her, Mme. Sabatier never wondered why, in that volume of verse, she was more vague and indistinct, less real than Jeanne Duval. She apparently did not ask: "But have these pretty lines anything in common with me? Can I see and recognize myself there?" She did not wonder, because she was one of those women who assume a modest air when the name of *beauty* is merely uttered in their presence. She did not understand that she served Baudelaire only as an embodiment of the ideal, and that, in such an ideal, the poet had put nothing of himself: he had only put the very opposite of himself. (pp. 170-77)

Jean Prévost, "Baudelairean Themes: Death, Evil, and Love," in Baudelaire: A Collection of Critical Essays, *edited by Henri Peyre, Prentice-Hall, Inc., 1962, pp. 170-77.*

AUTHOR'S COMMENTARY

I know that those who are passionately fond of sublime language expose themselves to the hatred of the masses; but no respect for humanity, no false modesty, no workers' charters, no universal suffrage, will ever oblige me to mouth the incomparable cant of this century, or to confuse ink with virtue.

For some considerable time, illustrious poets have divided the spoils of the most fertile provinces of the poetic domain. I have found it diverting, and all the more congenial because of the difficulty of the task, to extract *beauty* from *Evil*. [*Les fleurs du mal*], essentially innocent, was written for no other purpose than to entertain me and to give a free rein to my intense love of challenge.

Some people have told me that the poems are capable of causing harm; I did not delight in this. Others, kinder souls, have told me that they might do some good; this did not make me gloomy. The fears of the former and the hopes of the latter equally astonish me and serve only to prove to me once again that the present age has forgotten all our old traditional classical notions of literature. . . .

I had originally intended to reply to numerous criticisms, and, at the same time, to explain a few simple points obscured by the light of modernity. What is poetry? What is its purpose? I had meant to talk of the distinction between the Good and the Sublime; of the Sublime in Evil; of how rhythm and rhyme satisfy man's eternal need of monotony, symmetry and surprise; of the adaptation of style to subject; of the vanity and danger of inspiration, etc., etc., but this morning I was imprudent enough to read one or two newspapers, and was instantly overcome by a torpor of some twenty atmospheres' weight, and grew weak before the terrifying futility of trying to explain anything to anyone. Those who know will sympathize with me, and for those who cannot or will not understand, all explanations, however weighty, would prove fruitless.

(essay date 1857)

Wallace Fowlie   (essay date 1957)

[Esteemed for his broad intellectual and artistic sympathies and his acute understanding of French literary creativity, Fowlie is considered one of the most comprehensive scholars of French literature. His works include translations of the major dramatists and poets of France as well as critical studies of leading figures and movements in modern French letters. In the following ex-

cerpt, Fowlie considers Baudelaire the first modern poet "because of his awareness of disorder in the world and in himself."]

Some years seem to count more than others in the development of the creative human spirit. The year 1857, a century ago, gave to France *Madame Bovary,* which was promptly condemned, and a few months later, ***Les Fleurs du Mal,*** for which Charles Baudelaire was fined five hundred francs and from which he was ordered to delete six poems. It was the year when Dostoevsky and Tolstoy received their first real recognition, and when Richard Wagner completed the second act of *Tristan.*

Today ***Les Fleurs du Mal*** is one of the most frequently edited books in world literature, the most often edited book after the Bible, it is claimed. It is undoubtedly the book which has been translated most often, into the largest number of languages, during the past fifty years. It would seem that Baudelaire has become the poet we can't escape from. All civilized Europeans not only know his name, but read him. They read him because he speaks directly to them. The introductory poem, **"Au Lecteur,"** which is a study of modern man's spiritual malady, an analysis of his famous *ennui,* ends with the challenging apostrophe, "Hypocrite reader, who are like me, who are my brother!"

Paradoxes abound when one tries to establish reasons for Baudelaire's presence among us. For example, no poet has ever been closer to Paris in his art than Baudelaire. And yet no poet yet produced by France has been less dominated by patriotism or fashions or customs. By being deeply and pervasively the poet of one city, Baudelaire has become the most universal French poet. He is the poet of a single book, but many of the poems have become so familiar that they now participate in that part of our heritage which seems unalterable. (p. 304)

Long before the publication of ***Les Fleurs du Mal,*** Baudelaire had been looked upon in Paris as a dandy, a mystifier, and, even more than that, a poet who wrote about vermin, rotting bodies, assassins and worms. Two years before the book, in 1855, eighteen of his most remarkable poems were published in *La Revue des Mondes,* and called forth violent and vituperative attacks. At the poet's death, in 1867, the accounts stressed sensational details in his life, his eccentricities, his diabolism, his dandyism. It is true that Baudelaire, as long as he could afford it, lived the role of dandy in the Hôtel Lauzun on the Ile-Saint-Louis, that he often shocked the French bourgeoisie with his immorality and cynicism, that he cultivated an attitude toward Satanism and the Gothic tale or *roman noir.*

But today, thanks to the accessibility of all of his writings, we know that far more important than the exterior dandyism of his appearance and behavior was the "inner dandyism" of his spirit, his feelings of horror and ecstasy. Baudelaire is the first "modern poet" not because of his behavior and dress, but because of his awareness of disorder in the world and in himself. Satanism is at the center of his work, not by histrionic black magic values, but by the poet's horror of man's fate and his obsession over guilt. The pathology of Baudelaire's sado-masochism has been elaborately studied in recent years, but it reveals very little unless it is considered in terms of his entire spiritual life.

When Baudelaire was writing his earliest poems, about 1845, his principal references and directions came from

romanticism. He felt close affinity with the enthusiasms of Gautier and Banville, with the esoteric interests of Nerval, with the macabre interests of Pétrus Borel. These men—more than the so-called leaders of the romantic movement; Hugo, Lamartine, Vigny—helped Baudelaire to define modern art by its secrecy, its spirituality, its aspiration toward the infinite. He was among the first to define romanticism as a way of feeling (*une manière de sentir*). The examples of Delacroix, Poe and Wagner confirmed the intuitions of Baudelaire concerning the modern form of melancholy and nostalgia. In his search for beauty through the "forests of symbols" where every element is hieroglyph, he practiced the art of symbolism instinctively, long before it reached its consecration in theory and manifesto.

In France today—and this is generally true for the past quarter of a century—the most persistent problem in Baudelaire criticism concerns the poet's spirituality and religious drama. Many of the Catholic critics, Stanislas Fumet, Charles du Bos, Jean Massin, have with considerable justice pointed out that Baudelaire addresses the fundamental part of his message to Christians and that without Catholic dogma *Les Fleurs du Mal* would not have been written. Contradictions which obscure every phase of the study of Baudelaire are particularly forceful in the problem of his religious experience. His understanding of Christianity is constantly being contradicted by his theories of eroticism, examples of his pride, and even outbursts of blasphemy. There are passages in letters to his mother which reveal even a doubt concerning the existence of God. A major error has been committed many times: that of making Baudelaire into a saint, of canonizing him and drawing him into Catholicism. Another error, equal in its excesses, and often perpetrated, is that of distorting Catholicism to fit Baudelaire's measurement and Baudelaire's weaknesses.

Today critical inquiry about him almost infallibly stresses spiritual values. Rather than concentrating on his sensuality, which was far more limited than once believed, it is studying the breadth and complexity of his intelligence and his mind's very central religious obsessions. This in itself is a severe judgment on the nineteenth century, which condemned *Les Fleurs du Mal* in 1857 on charges of immorality and yet applauded the childish obscenities of so many other writers. Baudelaire's personal modesty and reticence were well known in his own day. Gautier, in particular, said that Baudelaire in his metaphysically-minded conversations usually spoke of his ideas, that he very seldom referred to his feelings and never spoke of his actions.

The spiritual source of romanticism and of Baudelaire's poetry is the will to reach some degree of happiness or self-achievement either in this life or another, but Baudelaire's lucid intelligence made him more scrupulous and more jealous of his ideas than most romantics engaged in the quest for self-realization. Whenever any degree of peace or happiness came within sight, a fear that he was deceived grew in him and tended to defeat the promise. The beauty of his mistress never appeared perfect to him for long. His heart always ended by changing it into a lure or a trap. Irony tempered his heart and his writing at moments when his feelings or his words might have become over-intense or frenetic. His heart's truth was tenderly and despairingly explored by his mind. Nevertheless, Baudelaire testifies today to the most violent and the most irresistible aspirations of the romantic spirit, aspirations which are perhaps still dominant in the contemporary creative artist. (pp. 304-05)

Wallace Fowlie, "First Modern Poet," in The Commonweal, *Vol. LXVI, No. 12, June 21, 1957, pp. 304-05.*

Norman H. Barlow   (essay date 1964)

[*In the following excerpt, taken from his* Sainte-Beuve to Baudelaire, *Barlow maintains that Baudelaire's* Petits poèmes en prose (Poems in Prose) *are based on a "sense of spiritual animation . . . that transcends the sordid reality of the metropolis."*]

According to Baudelaire's letter of January 15, 1866, the spirit of Joseph Delorme was apparent not only in the "Tableaux parisiens" of the *Fleurs du Mal,* but also in his *Petits Poèmes en prose,* which bore the subtitle *Spleen de Paris.* As evidence of the close relationship between Baudelaire's two chronicles of Parisian life, the first four verses of the epilogue to the poet's prose poems clearly re-affirm the essential poetic function of the *Fleurs:*

Le cœur content, je suis monté sur la montagne
D'où l'on peut contempler la ville en son ampleur,
Hôpital, lupanars, purgatoire, enfer, bagne

Où toute énormité fleurit comme une fleur.

The poet's achievement in both works is a projection of the individual psychic *moi* through the souls inhabiting Paris. The best and most frequently cited items in the *Spleen de Paris* suggest a conception of modern heroism similar to that conveyed by Baudelaire in his "Tableaux parisiens." The order of poetry is founded on the same sense of spiritual animation—an extended *ribote de vitalité*—that transcends the sordid reality of the metropolis.

In these exquisite prose poems, which are inspired by human or animal characters observed on the Parisian scene, Baudelaire chronicles the common man's normal pursuit of his humble destiny. Modern Adam and Eve are depicted in the suffering of their daily struggle with hardship, in their illusions, in the satisfaction of their material needs and sensuous desires, in their automatic response to the call of routine duties. In his chronicles the author is necessarily concerned with the cripples of this world, both the physically afflicted and the downcast in spirit. Besides evoking his compassion, the experiences of the citizens of Paris enhance Baudelaire's own consciousness of the horrors of life. He suspects, too, that these lame souls share with him a heroic aspiration to the sublime.

Baudelaire explains in the prose poem **"Les veuves"** that the poet of modernity disdains as source of his inspiration the "turbulence dans le vide" represented by the happiness of the fortunate. Such a poet's field of interest lies rather in the suffering victims of the *horreur de la vie.* In this particular composition the author credits Vauvenargues with a description situating the *veuves* in their characteristic milieu and emphasizing their nature as cripples. . . . The substance of poetic creation, Baudelaire continues, is to be found in the facts or legends comprising the universal drama of human existence. . . . A similiar conception of the true poetic substance is revealed in **"Les bons chiens,"** where *bons* is equated with *pauvres* or *crottés.* In this prose poem the composer invokes the aid of a less fastidious and bolder muse to help him portray the outcasts of the animal world. . . . He rejects the pampered pets of the privileged classes to embrace the more valid pedigree of suffering. . . . (pp. 190-92)

The humble citizenry of the capital periodically seeks respite from the crushing struggle against the maleficent powers of life. In **"Le vieux saltimbanque"** Baudelaire achieves a particularly dramatic effect by depicting the extreme misery of a decrepit old entertainer against the ebb and flow of the populace, who attempt to assuage their defeats in the frantic gaiety of the carnival. . . .

In the midst of plenty, the accusing faces of the needy inspire in the fortunate either shame or embarrassed annoyance. The heart of those who indulge in the pleasures of luxury is sometimes softened toward the wretched. But this tenderness is not necessarily communicable; **"Les yeux des pauvres"** reveals how, at a certain elegant new café, the seed of hatred is sown between two lovers because of a compassion that the couple do not share. The six eyes which are the innocent cause of the quarrel symbolize for Baudelaire the perpetual drama of the *éclopés* of Paris. . . . (p. 193)

For the common people death is the only permanent release from the progressive martyrdom of spiritual erosion imposed by the daily physical struggle, but there are temporary reliefs. In **"Le crépuscule du soir,"** the approach of night brings relaxation from monotonous drudgery. . . . The citizens enslaved on the relentless treadmill of passing time may otherwise relieve their burdens in the oblivion afforded by the various intoxicants recommended in the prose poem **"Enivrez-vous."** . . . Moreover, the struggling masses are not subject to despair. In **"Chacun sa chimère,"** each traveler bears willingly the burden of his own cherished illusion, which impels him to pursue his gloomy destiny. . . . (p. 194)

In extracting his poetic substance from the diffuse chronicle of human ills, Baudelaire remains faithful in the *Petits Poèmes en prose* to the aesthetic principle of his *Fleurs du Mal.* He seeks what is potentially sublime in the atrociously abnormal. Two examples from the Parisian prose poems illustrate his technique. In **"Mademoiselle Bistouri,"** the case history of what conventional society would regard as a very unhealthy prostitution of the flesh yields a glimpse of the divine omnipresence which serves as a key to Baudelaire's poetic intention. . . . In **"Le joujou du pauvre,"** the atrocious live rat is the unforgettable symbol of the sublime, drawn albeit from the squalor of raw life. This terrible plaything brings happiness to the innocent "marmot-paria" and is coveted by the rich boy stifled in the boredom of artificial luxury. Through the iron barrier of a garden railing this shared interest draws together two widely separated social beings into a common humanity.

Some among the *Petits poèmes en prose* do not participate in the external projection of ennui effected in Baudelaire's chronicle of the Parisian populace. In one group of introspective compositions the background of the metropolis provides a psychological décor for the author's personal spleen. This atmosphere sharpens his consciousness of the duality in which his own soul alternates between the *hor-*

reur and the *extase* of man's experience. In **"La chambre double,"** the poet's ecstatic dream of an ideal paradise—equivocal gift, perhaps, of some treacherous narcotic—is interrupted by the entry of a ghost. This specter symbolizes the destruction of the spirit wrought by the anguish of earthly existence. . . . With the specter reappears tyrannical Time, bringing his satanic retinue of memories, regrets, fears, anxieties, nightmares, anger, and neuroses. The poet is shocked out of his languid dream world to confront the sinister squalor of his actual abode. . . . In **"A une heure du matin,"** the victim of spleen seeks in the solitude of his apartment an escape from the horrors of the day's routine. There he meditates upon the shortcomings of other men and upon his own vile acts or omissions. . . . Another composition, **"Le mauvais vitrier,"** reveals what kind of unreasoning madness may be born in the spiritual desert of ennui. The victim of a pathological or satanic practical joker is the entirely fortuitous exterior target of an interior spirit of destruction. . . . The moral enormity of this incident is intensified by the fact that the crime itself affords but a moment of perverse enjoyment to the perpetrator.

The atrocious impulses and abject moods of personal spleen suggest, however, the spiritual alternative in the potential ecstasy of the sublime. In **"A une heure du matin,"** the poet, in order to banish "le mensonge et les vapeurs corruptrices du monde," invokes the spiritual intercession of his loved ones. To restore his battered self-respect, he begs the divine gift of poetic creativity. In similar tone, the same night which in **"Le crépuscule du soir"** brings a respite in the struggle of the harried workingman brings also to the poet a sweet deliverance from the anguish of the day. His soul regains its liberty in a supernatural world of imagination and, perhaps, artistic inspiration.

Baudelaire unfolds in his prose poems a drama peopled by characters the essence of whose heroism is their total engagement in the anguish of spiritual bipolarity. Their author presents them in the midst of their sordid struggles with the evil forces of man's world—in temptation and in sin—but he conveys the impression that they never surrender the essential nobility which is their heritage from the Divine Creator. Their immersion in the horror of earthly existence does not drown their aspiration toward the sublime, and they are always open to the visitation of God's grace. The heroic type is well illustrated by the decrepit old woman of **"Un cheval de race."** . . . In **"Les veuves,"** the poet draws a striking contrast between one of his heroines and the triviality of her surroundings. The occasion is a military band concert, and at first the author finds incredible the presence of such a noble character among the poor, who greedily feast upon the entertainment from beyond the barrier. . . . But harsh economic necessity has forced this respectable widow to forego a privileged seat, for the sake of a son whose needs are her sole concern. . . . The prose poem **"Les bons chiens"** portrays the drama of creatures moved by carnal instincts, material needs, and a sense of duty. The heroic role of these characters is their very pursuit of their particular destiny, with seeming resignation to the changing adversities of their environment. . . . (pp. 194-99)

The obvious compassion of the poet for the sufferings of his fellow "parias" is not however blind to the need for a drastic psychotherapy in order to dispel the dangerous inferiority complex produced by their habitual dejection. The beggar in **"Assommons les pauvres"** has to be provoked into proving himself worthy of the respect which society has so long denied him. He is given a sense of his dignity by the "énergique médication" of his retaliation to physical affront. The therapist offers him constructive advice for the future. . . . (pp. 199-200)

Baudelaire most clearly explains the poetic essence of his *Petits poèmes en prose* when he comments in **"Les foules"** on the rare privilege enjoyed by the poet of modernity. . . . To create the poetry of Paris . . . is to participate in an indescribable orgy, in a "sainte prostitution" of the spirit, which gives itself entirely, poetry and charity, to the unforeseen incidental reality and to the passing stranger. Artistic creation and love of fellow man are thus joined in the poet's tribute to the "éclopés de la vie."

Through this spiritual prostitution that takes place in the "bain de multitude," the poet lives and suffers in personalities other than his own. For example, in the sordid degradation of his "vieux saltimbanque" he perceives the reflection of his own probable destiny. . . . (pp. 200-01)

The metropolis is full of similar stories, factually authentic, and of legends, true only in the artist's imagination. It does not matter, writes Baudelaire in **"Les fenêtres,"** whether the incidental reality exterior to himself is true or untrue, providing that it gives him a keener awareness of his own existence and a deeper understanding of the purpose of that existence in a creation unlimited in time or space.

The order of poetry in Baudelaire's *Petits poèmes en prose* is effectively summarized by a remarkable coincidence of meaning evidenced in three passages chosen from different prose poems. The last stanza of the epilogue to the collection confirms the author's strong conviction concerning the rich poetic material offered by Parisian life:

> Je t'aime, ô capitale infâme! Courtisanes
> Et bandits, tels souvent vous offrez des plaisirs
> Que ne comprennent pas les vulgaires profanes.

The poet of modernity has the special gift of sensitivity to the spiritual drama inherent in the exterior reality of the metropolis. We are reminded in **"Les foules"** that many human beings do not share this poetic perception. . . . The tragedy of popular insensitivity is as widespread, suggests Baudelaire, as the human race. As for Paris, the fatuous vulgarity of the common mind seems to him well characterized by the encounter in **"Un plaisant"** between the irresponsible reveller and the harassed, but obedient, donkey:

> L'âne ne vit pas ce beau plaisant, et continua de
> courir avec zèle où l'appelait son devoir.
>
> Pour moi, je fus pris subitement d'une incommensurable rage contre ce magnifique imbécile, qui me parut concentrer en lui tout l'esprit de la France.

The drunkard is insulated by his intoxication from the spiritual current of the human drama. The animal, on the contrary, symbolizes those human beings who, in accepting the ferocious challenge of worldly horror, create their own particular roles in heroic patience and endurance. (pp. 201-02)

Norman H. Barlow, "Baudelaire's 'Petits

poems en prose'—'Poetry and Charity',*" in his
Sainte-Beuve to Baudelaire: A Poetic Legacy,
Duke University Press, 1964, pp. 190-202.

Henri Peyre (lecture date 1967)

[*A French-born American, Peyre was respected as one of
the foremost critics of French literature. He has written
extensively on modern French writers, most notably in*
French Novelists of Today *(rev. ed. 1967). In the following excerpt, he examines "the sensual, the sentimental, and the cerebral" aspects of Baudelaire's love poetry.*]

Baudelaire's love poetry, unlike that of others, has successfully shunned one of the perils of that theme in literature, and perhaps of love itself as expressed in letters,
terms of endearment, compliments, scenes and gestures in
real life; monotony. It embraces the domains of the sensual, the sentimental, and the cerebral. (p. 16)

As a rule, Baudelaire eschewed the coarser sensuality of
the poets of the seventeenth century, such as Théophile,
whom his friends revived and praised; scorn of the woman
as Martial in Latin and the libertine poets of 1610-1640
had crudely professed may have entertained Flaubert and
friend Louis Bouilhet, among Baudelaire's contemporaries, but it ill fitted the gravity of the singer of evil as a
proof of original sin tainting man's corrupt nature. Even
the final wrathful stanzas of **"A celle qui est trop gaie"**
evince respect for the woman whose healthy cheerfulness
unnerved her poet-lover.

The sensuality present in the volume of poems (it is not
found in the poems in prose or in any of Baudelaire's stories or essays on opium and hashish) is often that which
appealed to the Petrarchists once, and to the Surrealists
more recently. Like them, Baudelaire sketches enumera-
tions of the physical charms of the woman: unlike them,
he dwells seldom on the cheeks and the teeth and even the
neck which, in some Italian paintings, could be made so
poetically languid. The "gorge," as the French used to
designate the broad and bulging front in women which
least deserves to be compared to a narrow pass, occasionally serves as a pretext for a more precise evocation of a
beauty à la Rubens. **"Le Beau Navire,"** in which the
woman harmoniously walking is likened to a majestic ship
unfurling its sails, is the most curiously sustained catalogue of the beauties of the ample woman addressed. It
must have been written for Marie Daubrun who, presumably, felt flattered to see her arms pictured as powerful serpents, capable of stifling "precocious Hercules." Her
shoulders also are fat ("grasses" rhymes conveniently in
French with "grâces"). But the breastplates of her bosom
are especially conspicuous, in lines which are not, in my
opinion, too successful as poetry but curiously baroque in
their far-fetched imagery:

Ta gorge triomphante est une belle armoire
Dont les panneaux bombés et clairs
Comme les boucliers accrochent des èclairs;

Boucliers provoquants, armès de pointes roses!

Your triumphant bust is a splendid wardrobe
Whose bulging and clear panels
Like shields catch lightning;

Provoking shields, armed with rosy points!

The only other piece in which the poet indulged a similar
catalogue of a woman's physical charms is clearly a buffoonery and was published under that general category in
the posthumous edition of **Les Fleurs du Mal,** "Le Mon-
stre." Its tone is humorous and deliberately vulgar and it
reveals Baudelaire as a master of sarcasm. Generally,
however, a thin or lean woman appears to have better corresponded to his ideal of feminine beauty. He would have
relished Modigliani's women and, had he known his
works better, those of Lucas Cranach. "La maigreur," he
wrote, and the French substantive conveys more than
thinness or leanness, "is more bare, more indecent than
fatness." A poet whom he knew, August Lacaussade, had
advanced, perhaps with involuntary humor, that "on est
plus près du cœur quand la poitrine est plate" ("One is
closer to the heart when the breast is flat").

In the same poem, **"Le Beau Navire,"** Baudelaire alluded
to the swinging rhythm of the woman's gait, conveyed
somewhat in an unusual and skillfully balanced stanza,
and to the legs of the woman, expert at tormenting or teasing the desires of the male. Repeatedly, he is fascinated by
the rhythm of a woman's walk, enhanced by the gowns
then worn by Parisian ladies, with flounces and festoons,
"sweeping the air" or gracefully held and swung by the
woman's hand. Baudelaire, however, never stresses the geometry of feminine legs as a promise of higher secrets to
tantalize the male observer. Proust remarked in his article
on Baudelaire that the poet often accused of morbidity
chastely stops at the knees of the woman; like the suppli-
ant before an Egyptian statue of a goddess, or even more
like a child yearning for motherly solace, he asks to lay his
weary forehead on the woman's lap: "Ah! Laissez-
moi, le fronte posè sur vos genoux" (**"Chant d'automne"**) or, at
the end of **"Le Voyage,"** "Dit celle dont jadis nous bai-
sions les genoux" ("Ah! let me, my brow laid on your
lap . . . says she whose knees we once kissed").

The woman's hair set Baudelaire's fancy roaming more
than any other part or accessory of the female body. Every
culture has its peculiar love ritual and stresses, in its poetry, one or another aspect of the person courted and lauded. English love poetry appears to have shied away from
the uppermost part of a woman standing, the hair. Baudelaire's fascination with the hair, rapturously conveyed in
"La Chevelure" and in the prose poem in which he hails
a whole hemisphere in the waving hair of his mistress,
proved contagious. . . . The hair was, to the singer of
Jeanne Duval, a receptacle of perfumes which conjured up
exotic lands. It was, as for the Greek sculptors of old and
several modern French painters, the most changeable and,
blown by the wind like "the bright hair uplifted from the
head of some fierce Maenad," in the Shelleyan phrase, the
most alive element of a woman's personality. . . . For
Baudelaire, even the fragrance of the hair is hardly a pretext for sensuous reveries; he cherishes Jeanne Duval's
dark tresses because they are replete with memories which
he wants to treasure and to revive, and because of the
dreams of travels, presumably solitary, which the hair provokes:

Tu contiens, mer d'ébène, un éblouissant rêve
De voiles, de rameurs, de flammes et de mâts.

You contain, sea of ebony, a scintillating dream

Of sails and rowers, of pennants and of masts.

Even more than the hair, the eyes of the woman, half veiled with languor or dimmed with tears, seldom brightly alive or saucily provoking, more often dreamy and indolent, are the theme of Baudelaire's most poetical hymns. The eyes of Mme Sabatier or those of Marie Daubrun (he easily transferred to one the poems written for, or on, the other), rather than the colder gaze of his mulatto mistress, have inspired those lines. Coldness there is, in those eyes of a Gorgon-like woman, inexpressive, petrifying, "charming minerals": if the hair appealed to the poet's "vegetable love," the metallic eyes, recalling the statuesque Beauty in the sonnet **"La Beauté,"** affirmed the woman's closeness to inanimate stone. In **"Le Serpent qui danse,"** where the woman is likened both to a snake and to a ship, he celebrates her eyes in unusual fashion:

Tes yeux, où rien ne se révèle
De doux ni d'amer,
Sont deux bijoux froids où se mêle
L'or avec le fer.

Your eyes, where nothing sweet or bitter is revealed,
are two cold jewels in which gold and iron are mixed.

In **"Le Poison,"** the same green eyes, lakes in which his soul trembles to see itself reflected in reverse, emit a venom.

Elsewhere the color of the eyes is less clearly determined. It reflects the changing moods of the mysterious person and perhaps the paleness of the sky on days when clouds tarnish the sun's brightness. One of the most tender invocations to the loved one in the whole volume occurs at the opening of **"Ciel brouillé":**

On dirait ton regard, d'une vapeur couvert;
Ton œil mystérieux (est-il bleu, gris ou vert?)
Alternativement tendre, rêveur, cruel,
Réfléchit l'indolence et la pâleur du ciel.

One would say your gaze is veiled in a mist; Your mysterious eye (is it blue, grey or green), alternately tender, dreamy, cruel, reflects the indolence and the paleness of the sky.

Less original is the idealized celebration of the eyes as the windows of the soul or as the luminous and living torches guiding the worshipping lover, as in the rapturous sonnet **"Le Flambeau vivant,"** in the least natural manner of Edgar Allan Poe or of the rapturous and disembodied canzone of the *Vita Nuova.* Any sensuality is excluded from those Baudelairian raptures inspired by Mme Sabatier, or any suggestion of desire. Once at least, in the most expertly musical of all his poems, **"Le Jet d'eau,"** the poet, purifying but retaining the sensual element, alluded to the eyes of the woman after love has fulfilled her: they are half closed and dazed, and rocked by the sound of the fountain, in the courtyard, which, ascending in the air and descending rhythmically, prolongs the ecstasy which the two lovers experienced.

Tes beaux yeux sont las, pauvre amante!
Reste longtemps sans les rouvrir,
Dans cette pose nonchalante
Où t'a surprise le plaisir.
Dans la cour le jet d'eau qui jase
Et ne se tait ni nuit ni jour

Entretient doucement l'extase
Où ce soir m'a plongé l'amour . . .

Your lovely eyes are weary, poor lover! Stay a long while without opening them again, in that nonchalant pose in which pleasure by surprise seized you. In the courtyard the babbling fountain, which night and day runs on, softly prolongs the ecstasy into which tonight love plunged me.

Most often however, more probably than in any other great poet's work, unfilfilled love, with its exasperation of desire, is the subject of Baudelaire's poems, and the part played by the senses is extenuated in them. Goethe, in his *Xenien,* extolled the "delicious poison of unfulfilled love," "das Gift der unbefriedigten Liebe," which burns and cools, corrodes the marrow of the bone and renews it. But the marked restraint showed by Baudelaire in avoiding any frank delineation of love fully accomplished is not the only means through which he controls sensuality in his poetry. Jean Prévost, in his posthumous book, the best in French on Baudelaire, has shrewdly analyzed some of the devices he used to underplay the role of desire in love and to deprive the war of the two sexes of any suggestion of brutality. His few poems on a nude body, especially **"Les Bijoux"** which frightened the courts of justice in 1857, are characteristically cold, even colder than Manet's "Olympia" which likewise revolted the timorous onlookers of the French Second Empire. The reclining woman wearing her jewels as a foil for her nudity becomes a work of art, but arouses neither desire nor fear of those failures which the poet dreaded.

Another feature of the Baudelairian feminine ideal is sadness. The poet could conceive beauty only as "ardent and melancholy." Cheerfulness irritated him, presumably as slightly vulgar and detracting from the Jansenist gravity with which love should be imprinted. The variegated colors of the woman's dresses and her insolent health, in **"A Celle qui est trop gaie,"** drive her admirer to anger and wickedness. He prefers his female companion to be clad with a mantle of sadness and ennobled by it.

He also prefers her not to be too talkative. There are no dialogues in Baudelaire's love poems, not even in **"Confession"** where he records a few complaints whispered by the woman on the role which she must constantly put on (the complaints are trite, it must be admitted) or in the opening lines of **"Sempereadem"** in which, again, the woman wonders why she is invaded by gloom. He answers her by an invitation to silence. . . . She is but a child and should know that men prefer to intoxicate themselves with a lie, which is only possible if their female partner keeps her lips sealed. "Be lovely and be sad," he bids the woman; "Sois belle! et sois triste! Les pleurs / Ajoutent un charme au visage / Comme le fleuve au paysage" ("Tears add a charm to the face, as the river does to the landscape"). That very original poem in octosyllabic lines is entitled **"Madrigal triste";** it expresses insistently the poet's requirement of tears "as warm as blood" and of silence in the beloved. . . . Being able to dream about love rather than to act it is Baudelaire's preference.

Indeed, a pathetic fear runs through that strange love poetry where sensuality is repeatedly subdued and the impetuosity of desire offset or annihilated: it is the fear of passion and of anything which might disrupt the regular order of life and the poet's normalcy. Here again, the contrast between Baudelaire and his successors is striking. He wrote magnificently on hashish and opium, but to condemn those artificial paradises and the disorder which they stir, in severely moralistic tones. After him, Rimbaud, then the Surrealists, did not hesitate to proclaim as "sacred the disorder of their minds." Rather than possession, passion, and domination, mutual understanding is what Baudelaire prizes in his relations with women. Too much may be made, and has been made, of his close dependency upon his mother. The words "a complex" need not be pronounced, and contribute little in the way of an explanation. But, again like Proust, and with more slyness (for he had to implore his mother for money incessantly), Baudelaire cajoled and deceived his mother, and looked for maternal tenderness and protection in the women whom he addressed in verse.

> Et pourtant aimez-moi, tendre cœur! Soyez mère . . .

> And yet love me, tender heart! Be a mother . . .

he begs her in **"Chant d'automne."** In several poems, he invokes, in the same breath, the mistress as a sister, yearning for fraternal affection and gentle understanding more than for passionate love, as in **"Chant d'automne":**

> Amante ou sœur, soyez la douceur éphemère
> D'un glorieux automne ou d'un soleil couchant

> Lover or sister, be the ephemeral sweetness
> Of a glorious autumn or of a setting sun

Sensuality is ever present in that poetry of love, but also ever held in check, feared or sublimated. The two other features which make up the originality of Baudelaire are his stress on the cerebral element in modern man which analyzes and complicates desire, and the resort to imagination which raises obstacles and heightens love, otherwise a vulgar and almost animal affair in the eyes of a poet. (pp. 16-27)

Baudelairian love, fearful of unleashing desire, anxious to disarm it, deprives the senses so as to enrich the intellectual element in love. Such a process of intellectualizing results in a new and more insidious superexcitation. Hence that lack of power to love, which Benjamin Constant had been the first to probe in *Adolphe:* the inner force which might have been projected on to the partner and perhaps have spent itself in carnal fulfillment is thrown back upon the lover himself and devours his thoughts and his nightmares. Hence also the enhancing of eroticism, of which one facet is the lover's eagerness to observe and thus to share his partner's experience in the love act, while analyzing his own. In almost religious language and in austere and abstract terms, Baudelaire depicted the two Lesbian women, in the amplest and most majestic piece in the volume (**"Femmes damnées"**), performing a gloomy ritual. A will to be worshipped as the giver of pleasure impels Delphine, the older and stronger of that feminine couple, as she watches her accomplice and victim:

> Elle cherchait dans l'œil de sa pâle victime
> Le cantique muet que chante le plaisir
> Et cette gratitude infinie et sublime
> Qui sort de la paupière ainsi qu'un long soupir.

> She looked, in the eye of her pallid victim,
> For the mute canticle which pleasure sings,
> And that infinite and sublime gratitude
> Which comes out of the eyelid like a long sigh.

That cerebral introspection is not that of a detached observer who might relish watching the workings of his brain and the mechanism of his self-delusion. It never shakes itself free from moral judgment and from the conviction that love is evil and that celebrating its rites, or merely being tempted to yield to it, is fundamentally becoming a prey to Satan's machinations. T. S. Eliot in England and some ardent French Catholics have depicted Baudelaire as "a Christian born out of his due time," or even as a saint. His sensibility certainly was permeated by that conception of Christianity which brandishes woman as a snare of the Devil and love as a form of metaphysical evil. The most terrifying lines in the *Fleurs du Mal* are not the conventional ones in which the woman is vituperated against as a vampire, but the picture of consciousness delving into its own recesses, becoming also the moral conscience which judges and condemns, facing evil ironically cursed and cherished:

> Tête à tête sombre et limpide,
> Qu'un cœur devenu son miroir!
> Puits de vérité clair et noir
> Où tremble une étoile livide,

> Un phare ironique, infernal,
> Flambeau de grâces sataniques,
> Soulagement et gloire uniques,
> —La conscience dans le Mal!

> Sombre and limpid confrontation,
> A heart which is its own mirror!
> Clear and black well of truth
> In which a livid star trembles,

> Ironical and infernal beacon,
> Torch of Satan's graces,
> Unique solace and glory,
> —Consciousness in Evil itself!

The three forms assumed by evil thus pictured as an active force are aggressiveness in love unleashed by either of the two partners, self-destruction wrought by the male in his masochist wrath, and the attraction of death as the one logical goal and end of love.

The poems alluding to the woman's blood-sucking fury and to her perversely capricious onslaughts on the male's physical energy and on his quietude belong to a tradition of vampirism, of which the late and minor French romantics were the inheritors. They do not constitute the deeper part of Baudelaire's love poems. Cursing the female enemy dispenses the poet from lending to her any character. But two of the most masterly pieces in *Les Fleurs du Mal* show the man wreaking his revenge upon the insatiable woman. One, **"A Celle qui est trop gaie,"** has already been alluded to: its octosyllabic lines grouped in stanzas of four create an impression of glee even where the poet's thirst for chastisement of the overly gay woman ascends to the tragic, animal-like inflicting of a wound. The other one, **"Une Martyre,"** was singled out by Paul Bourget, as early as 1883, as "the most powerful in the volume." Nothing in Poe or in Swinburne, or in Elizabethan dramatists like Ford and Webster, could match the lurid and ironical grandeur of the scene. The martyr is not a martyr to faith, not even to love: she lies, amid a voluptuous and refined setting, beheaded: the crime has just taken place and the pillow is soaked with her blood. . . . In no other Flower of Evil have dramatic force and pictorial vividness been so harmoniously blended; in none has "the tempestuous

Baudelaire's self-portrait. It has been suggested that Baudelaire drew this likeness while under the influence of hashish.

The awareness of the obstacles of aggression and self-destruction which Baudelairian love requires in order to avoid insipidity dramatizes the sensual reveries of the poet; his cerebral eroticism adds spice to the monotony of a love which would be free from self-hatred and from sadism. Death, however, is the supreme fulfillment. . . . (pp. 27-31)

Too much has been made, and not only by the critics who, for several decades after his death, viewed him as decadent, of the nostalgia of the mud in Baudelaire's poetry. The movement toward the lower and murky depths in us, with its delving into abysses of sensuality and of fear, is indeed one of the original features of his delineation of love, which makes other poets appear timorous in comparison and poor in symbolic secrets. But the Baudelairian correspondences rise boldly above such frightened contemplation of the flesh and of the demoniacal. The poet displayed equal courage when he dared, Icarus-like, soar into the empyrean and even, Ixion-like, embrace clouds of ethereal phantoms. From the modern city and its turbulence, from its mud and its dens of evil, he was proud of having extracted, like a chemist, the epic poetry and the purest gold. We may well mourn his never having completed the sketch for an epilogue to *Les Fleurs du Mal* which would have closed on the famous lines:

> Car j'ai de chaque chose extrait la quintessence;
> Tu m'as donné ta boue et j'en ai fait de l'or.

> For I have, from each object, extracted the quintessence;
> You gave to me your mud, I turned it into gold. . . .

Literally, the poet is a forger of gods and of goddesses. Through damnation, he gropes for salvation. Through the flesh, tortured, maligned, scorned, he reaches toward spirituality. "Dans la brute assoupie un ange se réveille" from **"L'Aube spirituelle"**: "In the slumbering brute an angel awakens." Some critics have endeavored to sum up Baudelaire in that process of bipolarity, showing him, by dint of highly scientific terms and of counts of his verbal devices, oscillating from a negative to a positive pole. No mechanical interpretation of that sort can suit the man who condemned all systems as much too comfortable structures of half lies.

Simply, by the side of aggressivity which may lurk in sensual union, and of the cerebrality which revels in exacerbating it, there exists also in the Baudelairian man the sentiment which prolongs passion; there is generosity and the assumption of a duty on the part of the male lover. In that extraordinarily pure and tender elegy, **"Le Balcon,"** addressed to the mulatto woman, he does not hesitate to invoke her, in the second line, as "ô toi, tous mes devoirs." No love poem in Musset, Hugo, Nerval, Verlaine, or Apollinaire is impregnated with that reasonable tenderness which Baudelaire invested with restrained imagery, always eschewing the vulgarity which we tend to associate with sentimentality. The famous Platonic elevation at the end of **"Une Charogne,"** the **"Hymne"** which invokes Mme Sabatier as "l'ange, l'idole immortelle" ("the angel, the immortal idol"), the plaintive stanzas probably composed for Marie Daubrun (**"Chant d'automne"**) do not emit a harsh note as the poet's vituperations of scorn and hatred often did. Death itself has lost its sting and its hope of being victorious. Love is triumphant.

Its triumph is achieved through understanding the part-

loveliness of terror," of which Shelley speaks apropos of the Medusa attributed to Leonardo da Vinci, been so terrifying.

Baudelaire never heard of Sader Masoch, his contemporary who published in French magazines a few years after the poet's death. But self-destruction was practiced long before it received the name of that strange Austro-Hungarian. The sonnet **"La Destruction,"** the starkest of the masochistic poems, with a Demon maddening and humiliating the victim, is hardly a love poem, even if it may be read as referring to onanism. **"L'Heautontimoroumenos,"** entitled after a play by Menander done over in Latin by Terence, is less graphically concrete. The punishment which the executioner-poet wants to inflict on his mistress is mental rather than physical; it is paralleled by the even more furious punishment which, as a vampire of himself, he wreaks upon himself. He suffers in her body as well as in his own.

> Je suis la plaie et le couteau!
> Je suis le soufflet et la joue!

> I am the wound and the knife!
> I am the slap and the cheek!

ner, submitting to her with humility, transfiguring her through imagination, and also through the alchemy of memory. With Baudelaire, then with Apollinaire, Proust, Alain Fournier, Mauriac, whose imagination is too weak or too firmly held in check by the writer, memory replaces imagination in the elaboration of the work of art. Those typically modern men cannot forget all that lies behind them, in their childhood and in their dreams of fond security in that "green paradise." Proust repeats that the only true paradises are the lost ones. Baudelaire could not be consoled for having been exiled from the bliss once dreamed of: he pictures the poet as essentially "a nature exiled in the world of imperfection, and wanting to conquer immediately, on this very earth, a revealed paradise" (*New Notes on E. A. Poe*). Like Proust again, and unlike either Bergson or Sartre for whom living is acting and molding the future, Baudelaire's inner gaze is fascinated by the past. The lover embracing the body of his mistress does not, in the poem **"Un Fantôme,"** necessarily experience pleasure; he plucks the exquisite flower of memory. Like the perfume which intoxicates us through restoring and enshrining the past into the present,

> Ainsi l'amant sur un corps adoré
> Du souvenir cueille la fleur exquise.

(pp. 33-5)

Baudelaire would have been a more complete poet of the dramatic conflicts of sentiment with the relentless analytical power of the intellect if he could have added the gifts of a novelist to those of a poet. Perhaps none of the women whom he loved could render him the service which Proust declares to be the most valuable any loved being can do us: that of making us suffer so as to help us deepen our awareness of ourselves. His life, harried with debts and sordid struggles against family, friends, and a public which did not understand him, did not present him with a partner who might have forced him and herself to apply to each other. . . . (pp. 38-9)

As it is, driven by his Catholic sensibility and by contradictions which, unlike a more Olympian genius like that of Goethe, he could never reconcile into a majestic, and selfish, synthesis, Baudelaire left us the most heartrending picture which French literature has of "l'homme désaccordé," the modern man attuned neither to the world or to others nor to himself. He repeated in his prose works that he saw the human being as a "homo duplex." He was convinced he had been doomed, and damned, from the beginning of Time. But that very disharmony inside himself enabled him to express the plight of the human creature, everlastingly building up illusions around love and forever in need of artists and writers audacious enough to shatter into pieces "ces miroirs déformants de l'amour, où chacun cherche à se puiser," in Jean Cocteau's phrase ("those distorting mirrors of love, in which everyone seeks to draw himself as from a well"). (p. 39)

Henri Peyre, "Baudelaire as a Love Poet," in Baudelaire as a Love Poet and Other Essays, *edited by Lois Boe Hyslop, The Pennsylvania State University Press, 1969, pp. 3-39.*

John Porter Houston (essay date 1969)

[*Houston was an American educator and author whose critical studies focused on nineteenth-century French literature and poetry. In the following excerpt, taken from his book* The Demonic Imagination, *Houston analyzes Baudelaire's poetry in terms of rhetoric, allegory, and analogy.*]

Baudelaire's poetry is nearly always recognizable as his own: there are certain underlying principles beneath the varied surface. The first of these is obviously archaism: Baudelaire is alone among nineteenth-century French poets in his dedication to renaissance and neoclassical rhetoric. Hugo's use of baroque conceits in *Ruy Blas* and Gautier's emulation of medieval Italian in "Le Triomphe de Pétrarque" are merely episodes in their development as poets; even Mallarmé tired of traditional figures of speech after having magnificently revived them. For Baudelaire, epithet, personification, and allegory—to name only a few favorite devices—remained identified with poetry itself. Our first task will therefore be the examination of what the value of rhetoric was for him.

If one closely studies a good many of the [poems in] *Fleurs du mal,* it becomes apparent that adjectives and participles are more numerous than finite verbs, that the syntax is not characterized by elaborate clauses; in short, that despite all differences in vocabulary and subject, Baudelaire's style, like Vigny's, continues the phrasal, epithetical tendencies of the abbé Delille's manner. But in Baudelaire's case, of course, we have no reason to expect such a filiation: unlike Vigny, who became a poet in an age of neoclassicism and never had sufficient verbal imagination to free himself from Delille and Chénier, Baudelaire started writing in the late 1830's, after the advent of modernism. Between him and Vigny lie not only some twenty-odd years but also the *genre romantique* as practiced by Gautier and the *bouzingos.* One might expect Baudelaire to have pruned his verses of the adjectives *beau, charmant, vaste, grand, immense,* which we find everywhere in them. But he did not, and we must determine what charms eighteenth-century diction had for him.

For many of Baudelaire's contemporaries, of course, the *ancien régime* was coming to seem like an enchanted age. Traces of this can be found in Hugo, Gautier, and Nerval. The Watteau revival was underway in the mid-century, and, by the time of Verlaine and the Goncourts, nostalgia for the eighteenth century was widespread. Baudelaire seems to have felt a very particular identification with the days before 1789. . . . Two reasons for this bond between the poet and the past come readily to mind: Baudelaire admired the idea of aristocracy—at least after 1848—and he associated his childhood with the eighteenth century. But there are deeper, sounder reasons for Baudelaire's imitation of neoclassical diction.

Of all the nineteenth-century French poets, Baudelaire had probably the most delicate sense of tone; he realized more fully than any other what subtle effects could be obtained from deliberately faded and insipid language. **"Les Petites Vieilles"** . . . is probably the most audacious, lengthy, and brilliant example of conscious *fadeur* in *Les Fleurs du mal,* but elsewhere there are equally studied uses of old-fashioned poetic diction. The following lines, thought to be early Baudelaire, are especially relevant:

> Je t'adore à l'égal de la voûte nocturne,
> O vase de tristesse, ô grande taciturne,
> Et t'aime d'autant plus, belle, que tu me fuis,
> Et que tu me parais, ornement de mes nuits,
> Plus ironiquement accumuler les lieues
> Qui séparent mes bras des immensités bleues.

Voûte nocturne, belle, tu me fuis, and *ornement* suggest the language of the *fête galante,* the tradition of erotic pastoral. *Vase de tristesse* is probably modelled on *vas electionis* or the *vas spirituale* of the Litany of the Holy Virgin; it has, in any case, a ceremonious solemnity of tone. Of course, these words and expressions are embedded in a far more intricate context than an eighteenth-century poet would have created: the identification of Jeanne Duval with the moon is both genuine and ironic, as Baudelaire expressly puts it. This first verse-paragraph is intended to build up a mood of *galanterie* which the second one will destroy. . . . The shift to the vocabulary of *bas-romantisme* produces an effect we are accustomed to in more recent ironic poets; Baudelaire seems to have been the first in France to have consciously juxtaposed dissimilar poetic styles.

The second archaizing rhetorical device that we must consider is personification, and it also is more characteristic of the late eighteenth-century poets than of Racine or Corneille. Baudelaire had one curious bond with the eighteenth-century estheticians, which is generally overlooked: he was fascinated by the possibility of *painting pictures with words,* just as the *ut pictura poesis* school could not resist philosophically rather dubious parallels between the plastic arts and literature. One of the more concrete *transpositions d'art* that emerged from the generally hazy theories of *ut pictura poesis* was the equivalence established between sculpture and personification. The kind of sculpture that could be "translated" by personification is necessarily quite iconographic in tendency: Michelangelo provides us with a handy example since he both sculpted Night and wrote lines for her to speak. Baudelaire's sonnet **"La Beauté"** ("Je suis belle, ô mortels, comme un rêve de pierre") is conceived directly in this tradition of story-statues and statue-characters. Aside from poems like **"La Beauté,"** which are built around one central abstract personage, so many passing personifications occur in Baudelaire's work that we must consider it an essential element of his style. When the personifications accumulate we are in the presence of one form of allegory, as in the late sonnet **"Recueillement."** (pp. 91-4)

There are other kinds of allegory than that based on personification. The classical distinction is between the practice of Guillaume de Lorris and that of Dante: the first part of the *Roman de la Rose* concerns figures named Liesse, Bel Accueil, Male Bouche, and so forth, while Dante's narrative is literal as well as symbolic. Baudelaire had a taste for all forms of symbolism: one can extract several theories of it from the sonnet **"Correspondances,"** and his critical essays are filled with references to the Book of Nature and Universal Analogy. Most writers tend, in my opinion, to ascribe to Baudelaire a far too coherent and detailed theory of symbolism, but, be that as it may, his poetic practice shows a great range of symbolic modes. To begin with the simplest example, traditional kinds of analogical poems, which we discussed earlier in reference to Gautier's work, abound in *Les Fleurs du mal;* **"L'Albatros"** follows this pattern.

More distinctive is what we may call the emblematic poem. An emblem is a pictorial representation which is presumed to contain elliptically a wealth of meaning; it is obtrusive, pregnant with significance and, as such, demands to be interpreted. *Emblem* is a word Baudelaire was fond of. . . . The renaissance emblems were didactic or sententious and drew on a long iconological tradition. Baudelaire's, of course, are either private or belong to the common romantic iconology.

An emblem is presented with a kind of fascinating focus, which distinguishes it from the initial term of an ordinary analogical poem. The emblem is, as it were, the basic unit of a certain kind of allegory, urging solution of its enigma. **"Le Masque"** offers perhaps the most orthodox example of an emblem, but a poem like **"Un Voyage à Cythère"** is somewhat more characteristic of Baudelaire's practice. Here the corpse hanging from the gibbet stands out from the surrounding landscape, since it alone is fraught with meaning, and the poet perceives it as an intended object of contemplation. . . . There is a frankly didactic note in this handling of the emblem, which we may consider another aspect of Baudelaire's fondness for the moods and conventions of earlier poetry. Furthermore, the allegorical gloss at the end of the poem, far from seeming mechanical, is the most intense and dramatic part of it.

When emblems combine to make more sustained allegories, the element of symbolic setting becomes particularly important. The opening lines of the *Inferno* provide a classic example of a landscape which prepares one for allegory, and Baudelaire was familiar with Dante. Although there is no lengthy allegory in *Les Fleurs du mal,* **"Les Sept Vieillards"** has all the traditional aspects of one, including arithmosophy. Its beginning establishes a background suitable for an apparition:

> Fourmillante cité, cité pleine de rêves,
> Où le spectre en plein jour raccroche le passant!
> Les mystères partout coulent comme des sèves
> Dans les canaux étroits du colosse puissant.

The poetic word *cité* rather than *ville* serves to establish the particularity of this metropolis, and its canals are specifically mentioned in order to recall the elaborate fluvial system of Dante's hell. Prostitutes grabbing at the arm of passers-by (the special sense of *raccrocher*) were a characteristic sight of Paris streets, and here they are replaced by phantoms. Baudelaire's sense of the allegorical mode is seldom displayed so thoroughly, but we can conclude, I think, that he understood it intimately. Goethe's famous distinction between allegory, which is bad, and symbol, which is good, would have meant little to Baudelaire.

Although Baudelaire wrote a great deal—if somewhat vaguely—about symbolism, he was less inclined to discuss the concomitant matters of metaphor and simile. Yet the rhetorical virtuosity he displayed in handling the latter suggests that he must have had elaborate and complex theories about these stylistic details. First of all, we notice not only the great density of Baudelaire's imagery, but the extraordinary number of ways he found to convey analogies. Three short poems will illustrate this variety. The first is **"La Cloche fêlée,"** which, while perhaps of no great weight in *Les Fleurs du mal,* is a fascinating piece of rhetoric.

Perhaps the first thing we should observe is that there is

no cracked bell mentioned in the poem; the title draws together two different analogical patterns, which are not joined in the body of the sonnet. . . . The initial comparisons are clear, if not straightforward. The adjectives applied to the bell compare it to a man, an analogy which the soldier simile, introduced casually and as if by afterthought, strengthens. The relationship between the sound of the bell and memory is not underscored, yet it is essential to what will follow. At the beginning of the tercets the previous comparison of the sturdy bell to a healthy old soldier is complemented by the equation of the speaker to a cracked bell:

> Moi, mon âme est fêlée, et lorsqu'en ses ennuis
> Elle veut de ses chants peupler l'air froid des nuits,
> Il arrive souvent que sa voix affaiblie
>
> Semble le râle épais d'un blessé qu'on oublie
> Au bord d'un lac de sang, sous un grand tas de morts,
> Et qui meurt, sans bouger, dans d'immenses efforts.

The *semble* is one of Baudelaire's favorite ways of avoiding expressions such as *comme, être pareil à,* and so forth; the verb creates an analogy while avoiding the most commonplace grammatical signs of it. Here Baudelaire is using a double comparison: when the speaker tries to sing like a bell, he sounds like a dying soldier. The military image, which initially appeared insignificant, ends by effacing the bell and swelling up to fill all the second tercet. The system of analogies is complex since there is a sound bell resembling a healthy soldier, and a speaker whose soul is cracked and gives forth the sounds of a dying soldier. The *cloche fêlée* of the title unites the two antithetical chains of similes.

Another, and very effective form of analogy, which Baudelaire imitated from *La Comédie de la Mort,* consists of a simple predicate nominative after *être.* "Causerie" uses this in conjunction with more traditional metaphors and similes. . . . The sequence of images is notable for the sharpness of each one and their contrasting relations: the external sky and the inner sea are doubly antithetical, while the speaker's heart is at once a place and something devoured. The heart-place image dominates the first tercet, where, instead of its being empty, the implications of the adjective *saccagé* are developed: palaces are ransacked by crowds. The second tercet then works a change on the direction of the imagery: fire replaces pillage, the women-beasts are mentioned once more, and the heart has again become an organ. This fondness for sudden changes of metaphor accounts in part for Baudelaire's predilection for sonnets and quatrains: the stanzaic divisions provide convenient articulations for a series of images. In this respect, Baudelaire is often reproached with lack of *souffle,* as if all metaphors should be prolonged. There is, on the contrary, an admirable effect of density produced in poems like "Causerie."

One of Baudelaire's favorite comparisons is between a woman and a climate or landscape. In "Ciel brouillé" he uses four different verbs as equivalents of "is like" to build up to a climax in which a person *is* a climate. . . . With the apposition *paysage mouillé* the woman becomes a landscape. At this point the initial analogy is inverted: at first she merely reflects real weather; now she creates the weather, which reflects her. Rhetorically, the shift is very subtle; it might be represented schematically as follows: A is like B; A is B; B is part of A. Logical twists in the use of analogy are extremely important for the subsequent development of French poetry: Mallarmé and Rimbaud were to exploit causal inversions with great brilliance. One other type of logical shift consists of reversing the expected initial and secondary terms of a comparison. (pp. 95-9)

One of Baudelaire's greatest poems begins with an elaborate tangle of unexpected analogies; "Le Cygne" initially presents its theme in deceptive terms. . . . The initial statement appears to be contradicted by the following lines: the poet speaks not of Andromache but of the buildings which used to fill the Place du Carrousel before 1852. The analogy would seem to be between Andromache beside the "false" Simois, which was built in Epirus to console her for the destruction of Troy, and the poet, who sees the changing face of his own city. Her heart did not change with the fall of Troy, and the poet seems to feel some similar regret for the past. Yet there is a strange contradiction in the verb *féconder:* instead of the new look of the Place du Carrousel reminding him of Andromache, the classical legend has reminded him of what is before his eyes. The normal causality of association has been reversed: the more remote image suggests the more immediate one.

The system of analogies is both clarified and complicated by the next stanzas. . . . What appeared to be the initial comparison of Andromache and the speaker, sustained by the reference to destruction of buildings, has given way to an analogy between Andromache and the swan, the latter's native lake and Troy, the false Simois and the dry gutter. The chain of associations still remains logically peculiar, but poetically justified. The traditional image of Andromache is introduced first and the unusual one of the swan is slowly elaborated to a climax. The missing link in the associations is the present bare look of the Place du Carrousel which recalls the swan, which, in turn, recalls Andromache. But there persists the secondary association between Andromache's recollections of Troy and the poet's memories of the old Carrousel. The complexity of these relations depends on the order in which they are introduced. As if to show how much less vivid the logical order is, Baudelaire begins the second part of the poem by reintroducing all his images in a rational pattern. . . . From the new Paris to the old, from the swan to Andromache, the logic of association is intact. (pp. 100-02)

Baudelaire's experiments with spatial ambiguities are abundant, but nowhere, perhaps, so elegantly elaborated as in "La Chevelure." The first stanza presents us with the image of a small object, the head of hair, enclosed in a dark bed alcove. . . . The magnificent conceit of shaking memories out of the hair suggests expansion and growth, for, as the sea-sky analogy of the verb *moutonner* implies, the large is contained by the small. The hair next becomes a forest. . . . Odor is, as it were, the catalyst which permits the hair to metamorphose into a whole world. The paradox of the container and contained is then expressly stated. . . . All of Baudelaire's customary ecstatic imagery is deployed . . . sea, sky, and light, and the correspondences between odor, sound, and color. The tropics become in these gorgeous lines the lost paradise of the past remembered in the night-bound hell of a European city. The merely exotic is transcended by the moral and esthetic force of Baudelaire's thought. Finally the hair becomes a tent, whose ceiling is the warm blue sky. . . . The tent which contains the infinity of the ether is the final point of evolution of Baudelaire's imagery, and is followed by a brief recollection of the exotic port mentioned earlier. This leads us back to the bed alcove and, for the first time, to the woman whose hair is the point of departure for the poem. . . . The second-person pronoun has switched dramatically from *vous* to *tu*. The tent of hair has dwindled into a mane, and the woman, appearing as an oasis as opposed to a broad sky, and a gourd as opposed to the sea, represents a shrinking of the poet's mind from imaginative scope into the tiny elements of reality. The evocation of the past has recondensed, so to speak, into the well of the oasis and the contents of the drinking gourd. The supporting imagery of *parfums* throughout the poem has given coherence to the implied analogy between remembering and vaporization of liquids.

The spatial imagery of **"La Chevelure,"** like that of **"Le Mauvais Moine,"** and many other *Fleurs du mal* has a temporal aspect which is worth emphasizing. By an analogy with mind and body, memories are represented as being contained: sometimes it is within an object like the head of hair, sometimes within a kind of mental space like "la forêt où mon esprit s'exile." In one of the "Spleen" poems (**"J'ai plus de souvenirs . . ."**) the speaker identifies himself with containers holding objects associated with remembrance. . . . The past is thus being shut up in enclosed spaces, which, furthermore, are structures—chests, pyramids, and vaults—suggesting death or by-gone days. With a sudden dramatic shift, the speaker is now himself contained, as he looks out on the surrounding present. . . . The present and future stretch out drearily to the horizon. The subject of the poem is not stated but must be inferred from the imagery: its theme is regret, the poisoning of the present by the past. This time pattern is characteristic of Baudelaire, for whom the categories of the future and potentiality seldom had imaginative relevance. (pp. 103-06)

The dimensions of time and space are not the only ones which Baudelaire reinterprets and recreates in his verse. There is also in *Les Fleurs du mal* a sense of relationship between individual minds and souls which is unique in nineteenth-century French poetry. This system of bonds, identifications, and antipathies constitutes the dramatic aspect of Baudelaire's work: he is given neither to the solipsism of much lyric poetry nor to the conventionalized declamation before an audience of readers, such as we have seen in Hugo and Vigny. Laforgue spoke of Baudelaire's intimate, "confessional" tone, but the term is too narrow: what Baudelaire achieves through the persistent presence, overt or implied, of a second-person singular is a feeling of personality and situation which can only be compared with theater, where our chief concern is the interplay of idea and emotion among the dramatis personae.

The poetry of the second-person singular, which addresses itself to an individual and is merely overheard by the public, has taken so many forms in the history of literature that we can here suggest only its manifestations in France. The love poem and, to a lesser degree, the satire and devotional lyric, are the principal genres in which *you* is as important as *I* or *they*. But love poems, vituperations, and prayers tend strongly toward conventional patterns of image and idea, so that often they fall short of a truly dramatic effect. To take a simple illustration, "Mignonne, al-

lons voir si la rose . . ." is so completely conceived in the tradition of *carpe diem* poems that we think no more of the person it is addressed to than we would meditate on Horace's Leuconoe, Lalage, Cinara, or similar shadowy recipients of ritual tribute. On the other hand, Maurice Scève's lady—and Catullus'—seem like the magnetic fields holding together their poets' work. The personalities of Délie and Lesbia are, of course, mere illusions wrought of poetic style: in Scève's case the strangeness of his language gives individuality to his mistress, while Catullus achieved the same effect through violent shifts of tone unexpected in a "classical" writer.

Baudelaire's great contribution to the poetry of *tu* and *vous* lies in his exploitation of dialogue. He was certainly not the first French poet to adapt the patterns of conversation to verse, for Musset's "Souvenir" shows expert manipulation of the colloquial, but he was, of all the romantic poets, the one who most consistently used the relationship between *I* and *you* for dramatic purposes. The last lines of **"Au Lecteur"** are exemplary:

> Tu le connais, lecteur, ce monstre délicat,
> —Hypocrite lecteur,—mon semblable,—mon frère!

The generalities of the previous stanzas prepare us in no way for so blunt a shift: the poet has been declaiming before an audience, as poets will; now the public disintegrates into a group of isolated individuals, each of whom becomes the specific object of the poet's words. Discourse yields to conversation and, appropriately enough, Baudelaire adapts to verse the dash, which in French anticipates dialogue.

The characteristic thing about Baudelaire's use of dialogue is that we hear only one side of it, without, for that, the poem becoming monologue: the sense of the *other person* remains acute, and we always feel that she, for it is usually a woman, is about to reply. We need not attempt to catalogue all of Baudelaire's uses of half-dialogue: they range from the vituperative love poems addressed to Jeanne Duval (for which we may find baroque antecedents in Sigogne) to prayers like **"Réversibilité"** and traditional eulogies. However, we can examine with some profit the poem beginning **"La servante au grand coeur"** . . . whose second person does not place it in the famous cycles of the Black, White, and Green-eyed Venuses, as critics persist in naming Baudelaire's muses. . . . Four words, "jealous," "ungrateful," "friends," "family," serve to establish the tense relations between the speaker and his listener: instead of violent recriminations, his remarks are inspired by guilt, which, in turn, detaches him from her. Though she is so intimate a part of his life as to have taken part in some sordid domestic clash, he addresses her with the formal *vous*, as is done in many stiff, hypercorrect French families. Attachment to her—her sex is elegantly revealed by the feminine ending of *jalouse*—and loathing of her cruelty are fused in an ambivalent mood. The occasion for the speaker's anguish is subtly implied: the time is October, All Soul's Day is approaching, and, with the advent of the time when Catholics think of their dead, he guiltily remembers some cowardice on his part and some pain on that of the old servant. The subdued tone of the speaker's words is rendered by the thoughtful, halting movement of the syntax. The first sentence is colloquial in structure; a noun, placed at the beginning, is caught up and syntactically ordered by the pronoun *lui* in the third line, a pattern common in speech and demonstrative of the devious way in which language follows thought. The rest of the verse-paragraph consists of one long complex sentence which shows Baudelaire rivaling Hugo in ability to write a cohesive series of alexandrine couplets. It is commonly said that Baudelaire lacked the capacity for elaborating sentence structure within the framework of verse. **"La servante au grand coeur"** . . . , which everyone ascribes to Baudelaire's early years, proves quite adequately that, had he not preferred stanzas to verse-paragraphs—for various effects of design—he could have excelled in the freer form.

The concluding portion of **"La servante au grand coeur"** . . . is likewise one long sentence-paragraph. . . . The question mark at the end of the poem brings our attention back to the *vous* of the first line: the speaker delicately needles his listener, who, by implication, has contributed to the old servant's sorrowful death. The latter's gentleness has made her an easy object of undeserved persecution, and the tormentor is now being arraigned. The key word here is *maternel;* the servant was the speaker's true mother, and the listener is either an unnatural mother or a vicious mistress. That Baudelaire allows this ambiguity to remain is characteristic of the elegance and concision with which he builds up dramatic situations: it does not matter who the *you* is; we realize that she is an imperfect woman in contrast to the mother figure of the old servant.

With regard to the verse-paragraphs of **"La servante au grand coeur"** . . . as with Baudelaire's use of time patterns and his distribution of metaphor, we can observe an unusually acute concern on his part for introducing clear divisions within poems. This is hardly a peculiarity of Baudelaire's, since any poem of several lines must consist of parts within the whole, but yet Baudelaire makes a much more obvious use of structuring devices than his contemporaries. His versification reflects this tendency. Judged by superficial textbook standards the prosody of *Les Fleurs du mal* is not more "modern" or "free" than that of other mid-nineteenth-century poets. In the domains of line-length, rime, enjambment, and caesura, Baudelaire innovated no more, no less than any French romantic poet. At the same time, however, anyone who has carefully read the major nineteenth-century poets knows that there is something different about the prosodic patterns of *Les Fleurs du mal,* something that we do not find even in such expert versifiers as Gautier, Leconte de Lisle, or Hugo himself. What distinguishes Baudelaire's work, I think, is a delicate care for the poem as a visual object: Baudelaire, reluctant to publish, seems, along with Flaubert, to have been the first French writer to realize the importance of space and typography for the reader. Blank separating spaces are essential to his style. Many simple illustrations come to mind: Baudelaire loved short stanzaic forms to order his inspiration; in particular he like the *quintil,* often with a framing line, because of its look of fullness in comparison with the commonplace quatrain; he patiently elaborated more sonnet forms than any other French poet, and, finally, Baudelaire indulged in numerous isolated experiments in prosodic patterns, none perhaps constituting a major discovery, but all of them fascinating. The common denominator of all Baudelaire's verse forms seems to be an attempt to make the poem look interesting or unusual on paper. From a purely phonetic

standpoint he did little that was new, but the impact of his verse is served by typographic devices which are as powerful in their effect as more purely prosodic innovations.

The single detached alexandrine which stands at the beginning of the second "Spleen" poem is a fine example of the use Baudelaire made of blank space as a psychological and rhythmic entity. The almost banal words "J'ai plus de souvenirs que si j'avais mille ans" acquire a foreboding weight, which they would not have if joined to the following rime line. Even Hugo, the greatest nineteenth-century master of the alexandrine verse-paragraph, seldom achieved such dramatic results. Elsewhere spacing creates unusual effects within ordinary prosodic forms. The last line of the *quintil* in **"Le Goût du néant"** acquires a gnomic force by its typographical detachment:

> Esprit vaincu, fourbu! Pour toi, vieux maraudeur,
> L'amour n'a plus de goût, non plus que la dispute;
> Adieu donc, chants du cuivre et soupirs de la flûte,
> Plaisirs, ne tentez plus un coeur sombre et boudeur!
>
> Le Printemps adorable a perdu son odeur!

The brusqueness of the movement is accentuated by the blank. In **"Abel et Caïn"** the quatrain is broken up into two-line groups:

> Race d'Abel, dors, bois et mange;
> Dieu te sourit complaisamment.
>
> Race de Caïn, dans la fange
> Rampe et meurs misérablement.

The rhetorical pattern demands separation of the apostrophes to the two races, but *rimes plates* would have made the verse disintegrate. The form Baudelaire chose points up at once the parallelisms and antitheses between Cain's and Abel's descendants. Where the one group has food, the other has mud, and so forth: the rime serves an ironic purpose. Furthermore this odd form contains a delicate reminiscence, in rhythm and rime, of the old-fashioned French form of the Decalogue:

> Un seul Dieu tu adoreras
> Et aimeras parfaitement.
> . . . .
> Tes père et mère honoreras
> Afin de vivre longuement.

Baudelaire is creating in **"Abel et Caïn"** a demonic version of Scriptures, in which Abel's descendants are identified with an unjust God.

Baudelaire's prosodic inventions are small enough, but they are important insofar as they attest his care for all manner of detail in verse. Although he is the only major nineteenth-century French poet whose work is not central to the history of versification, it is nevertheless impossible to think of the richness of romantic stanzaic forms without poems like **"Harmonie du soir"** or **"L'Irréparable"** coming to mind. (pp. 108-13)

John Porter Houston, "Baudelaire: Innovation and Archaism," in his The Demonic Imagination: Style and Theme in French Romantic Poetry, *Louisiana State University Press, 1969, pp. 85-124.*

Charles Chadwick   (essay date 1971)

[*Chadwick is a British author, essayist, and critic of French literature. In the following excerpt taken from his book* Symbolism, *he describes Baudelaire's "Symbolist approach to poetry," focusing on* Les fleurs du mal.]

The double Symbolist concept that reality is no more than a facade, concealing either a world of ideas and emotions within the poet, or an ideal world towards which he aspires, is associated in the case of Baudelaire with the doctrine outlined in his celebrated sonnet **"Correspondances."** Sensations, for Baudelaire, are not merely sensations; they can convey thoughts or feelings of, for example, corruption, wealth or triumph:

> Il est des parfums . . . .
> . . . corrompus, riches et triomphants

and objects are not simply objects but are the symbols of ideal forms lying concealed behind them:

> La Nature est un temple où de vivants piliers
> Laissent parfois sortir de confuses paroles.
> L'homme y passe à travers des forêts de symboles . . .

There are a number of poems in Baudelaire's one volume of poetry, *Les Fleurs du Mal,* first published in 1857 and followed three years later by a second, considerably enlarged edition, which illustrate the first of these two related concepts. **"Harmonie du Soir,"** for example, might appear at first reading to be simply a description of a landscape since it consists almost entirely of a series of images—the setting sun, the fading perfume of flowers, the dying note of a violin:

> Now come the days when, trembling on its stem,
> Each flower is scented like an incense bowl;
> Sounds and perfumes swirl through the evening air;
> The senses turn in a slow and languid dance.
>
> Each flower is scented like an incense bowl;
> A violin trembles like a broken heart;
> The senses turn in a slow and languid dance;
> The sky is sad and splendid like an altar.
>
> A violin trembles like a broken heart,
> A loving heart that hates the vast and dark abyss;
> The sky is sad and splendid like an altar;
> The sun has sunk in its own congealing blood.
>
> A loving heart that hates the vast and dark abyss
> Gathers every vestige of the hallowed past;
> The sun has sunk in its own congealing blood . . .
> My memory of you gleams like a sacred shrine.

The final line, however, ['My memory of you gleams like a sacred shrine'], provides the clue indicating that these repeated images, all possessing as a common factor the notion of something beautiful that has passed away, are in fact objective correlatives whose purpose is to re-create in the reader the emotion experienced by the poet at the memory of a past love affair.

Precisely the same process is followed, though in order to recreate a very different emotion, in the first of the four poems entitled "Spleen" where all the images again have a common factor though it is quite unlike that of **"Harmonie du Soir"**:

> The god of rain, in anger against the city,

> Pours down floods of cold and darkness
> On the pale inhabitants of the nearby cemetery
> And waves of death on the fog-ridden suburbs.
>
> My cat, trying to find a place to rest,
> Twists and turns his thin and sickly body;
> The soul of an old poet haunts the rooftops
> With the sad voice of a trembling ghost.
>
> The church bell tolls and the smoking log
> Hisses alongside the wheezing clock,
> While in a stale-smelling pack of playing cards,
>
> A gloomy legacy from a crippled old hag,
> The handsome Knave of Hearts and the Queen of Spades
> Coldly talk about their long-dead love.

Once more it is the final line, and even the last two words, which provide the clue as to what the poem is really about. It is only then that one fully realizes that the purpose of all the preceding images in their various ways is to make the reader feel the cold hand of death that has descended on the love affair between the knave of hearts and the queen of spades who can be taken to represent Baudelaire and his coloured mistress Jeanne Duval, dragging out a miserable existence long after the relationship between them had ceased to have any warmth and any real meaning. Far from being a mere description of a sad and mournful scene "Spleen" is therefore an attempt and, in its own way, as successful an attempt as **"Harmonie du Soir"**, to re-create in the reader, through an accumulation of symbols, an emotion experienced by the poet.

Human Symbolism of this sort plays a considerable part in Baudelaire's poetry, but perhaps an even more important part is played by transcendental Symbolism. To some extent the two overlap in that **"Harmonie du Soir"**, for example, may be said to evoke not only a feeling of perfect happiness but also, at least by implication, a picture of paradise. Similarly "Spleen" may be regarded as depicting a scene from hell (a kind of hell that heralds in some degree Sartre's *Huis Clos*) as well as conveying a mood of black despair. Other poems, however, lay greater stress on the transcendental aspect of Symbolism and endeavour to penetrate beyond reality to an ideal world. In **"La Chevelure"**, for example, it is not Jeanne Duval's hair that really fascinates Baudelaire, nor the fact that its jet-black colour and wavy texture remind him of a voyage he had made shortly before through the Indian Ocean to Mauritius. . . . (pp. 8-11)

This is not simply a case of present reality nostalgically recalling past reality. Had Baudelaire really wanted to return to the tropics, his family, who had insisted on his making his original voyage in the hope of calling a halt to the Bohemian life he had begun to lead in Paris, would no doubt have been only too glad to send him there. What he is really looking for is a non-existent paradise and it is this for which he finds a symbol in a past memory concealed within a present reality. Once more there is a common factor to the various images in the poem and what they transmit to the reader is the notion of eternity and infinity, conveyed by such expressions as 'tout un monde absent, lointain, presque défunt', 'un éblouissant rêve', 'un ciel pur où frémit l'éternelle chaleur', 'infinis bercements', 'l'azur du ciel immense et rond' and 'l'oasis où je rêve'.

An even more idealized picture of a future paradise is presented in **"L'Invitation au Voyage"** where this time the objective correlative of Baudelaire's immaterial world is a Dutch landscape, though he had never in fact been to Holland, and still more perhaps than in **"La Chevelure"** there is a certain quality of eternity and infinity about the phrasing, especially the refrain three times repeated:

> Là, tout n'est qu'ordre et beauté,
> Luxe, calme et volupté.

Elsewhere he looks back with longing towards his childhood and to what he calls in **"Moesta et Errabunda"** 'Le vert paradis des amours enfantines', yet another guise under which the ideal world appears in *Les Fleurs du Mal.*

In giving poetic form to these various symbolic representations of paradise Baudelaire is escaping from reality through the medium of poetry. He is in fact creating a kind of second reality and his distant, absent world, his dazzling dream, his pure skies shimmering with eternal warmth, his land of order and beauty, luxury, calm and voluptuousness reside in his poetry which fixes this ideal world not only for the poet himself but also for his readers.

Thus the poet becomes a divine figure, able to see through the wall of reality to the paradise beyond and able to transmit his vision to others. He is endowed with the capacity, as the poem **"Elévation"** puts it, to understand 'le langage des fleurs et des choses muettes'. He does in fact belong by nature to this paradise and is an exiled figure here on earth according to **"Bénédiction"**, the opening poem of *Les Fleurs du Mal,* which makes an almost explicit analogy between the poet and Christ and is closely linked with other poems in *Les Fleurs du Mal* which stress the angelic nature and divine mission of art and the artist.

These essentially optimistic poems are, however, virtually limited to the first few in *Les Fleurs du Mal,* and although the long opening section is entitled "Spleen et Idéal," the movement of this section is actually in the opposite direction, from 'idéal' to 'spleen', from a supremely optimistic belief that a paradise exists beyond the real world and can be perceived and re-created by the poet, to a profoundly pessimistic recognition that reality may not, after all, be a 'correspondance du ciel' but rather a 'correspondance de l'enfer'. 'C'est le diable qui tient les fils qui nous remuent'—'it is the devil who pulls the strings which control us'—contends Baudelaire in the poem **"Au Lecteur"** which serves as a preface to his volume and warns the reader that the optimism of the first few poems will soon be dissipated. By the time he has neared the end of "Spleen et Idéal" he no longer conceives of himself as a divine being for whom a place is reserved in heaven, as he had done in **"Bénédiction"** but as:

> Une Idée, une Forme, un Etre
> Parti de l'azur et tombé
> Dans un Styx bourbeux et plombé
> Où nul œil du ciel ne pénètre.

Reality no longer conceals a radiant paradise but a gloomy inferno which Baudelaire now glimpses, not only in a poem such as "Spleen", but more clearly in, for example, **"Les Sept Vieillards"** where a terrifying procession of seven crippled old men appear to him out of hell.

At the end of *Les Fleurs du Mal* Baudelaire is thus no longer sure exactly what is the nature of the world lying beyond reality. In the final verse of the closing poem, **"Le Voyage"**, when his one desire is to bring to an end his jour-

ney through life, defined in retrospect as 'une oasis d'horreur dans un désert d'ennui', he acknowledges that it is to an unknown destination that he will be setting off, that it may be either heaven or hell that is awaiting him. . . . (pp. 12-14)

Both transcendental Symbolism and human Symbolism form part of what have been called 'correspondances verticales' involving movement from the plane of material objects and the sensations they provoke to the plane of abstract concepts and personal feelings, from sights and sounds and smells to the notions or emotions they inspire. There also exist, however, in Baudelaire's poetry, what have been called 'correspondances horizontales' or movements on the same plane from one physical sensation to another. In the lines from the sonnet **"Correspondances"** that have been quoted, Baudelaire not only contends that perfumes can be 'corrompus, riches et triomphants', he also claims that:

> Les parfums, les couleurs et les sons se répondent.
> Il est des parfums frais comme des chairs d'enfant,
> Doux comme les hautbois, verts comme les prairies.

Perfumes can therefore have the same quality as the soft feel of children's flesh, or as the gentle sound of oboes, or as the green colour of fields. This process of sense transference, or synaesthesia, has often been remarked upon in *Les Fleurs du Mal,* especially in those poems addressed to Jeanne Duval where the perfume of her hair stimulates

Jeanne Duval, sketched by Baudelaire. The Latin inscription at the bottom translates as: "Seeking whom she may devour."

visual images of tropical lands, or the sound of ships in distant harbours. But this correspondence between the different senses is in fact no more than a variation on the general process of repetition that is fundamental to Baudelaire's poetry and which brings it close to music. Since his aim is not to tell a story or to define an idea, but to create an emotion or to convey an impression, he accumulates outward symbols which constantly reiterate and reinforce the essential inner theme of the poem. An obvious way of doing this and, at the same time, of avoiding monotony, is to find images belonging to the different senses, rather as a composer calls in the different instruments of an orchestra. But there is no basic difference between, on the one hand, **"Harmonie du Soir"**, for example, where a feeling of past happiness and the impression of a paradise lost are conveyed through images which make a threefold appeal to the sense of smell, the sense of hearing and the sense of sight, and, on the other hand, the last three verses of **"Le Cygne"** where a feeling of captivity and the impression of a world without hope are conveyed through an accumulation of images that are entirely visual:

> I remember the thin, consumptive negress
> Trudging through the mud and looking, weary eyed,
> For the long-lost palm trees of proud Africa
> Beyond the endless prison-wall of fog.
>
> I think of all those who have lost something
> Forever and forever; of those who drink their tears
> And are suckled by sorrow as their foster-mother.
> I think of orphans as shrunken as dried flowers.
>
> Thus in the dense forest where my mind roams,
> An old memory echoes like a hunting horn.
> I think of sailors lost on desert islands,
> Of captives, of prisoners and of many more . . .

It was no doubt this Baudelairian characteristic of insistently repeating the same thing in various guises, not infrequently with an actual system of refrains, as in **"Harmonie du Soir"**, that led the leading nineteenth-century French critic, Ferdinand Brunetière, to say of him disparagingly: 'Ses vers suent l'effort. Ce qu'il voudrait dire, il est très rare qu'il le dise. Le pauvre diable n'avait rien, ou presque rien du poète que la rage de le devenir.' ('His lines reek of straining after effect. He rarely manages to say what he is trying to say. The poor devil had nothing of the poet about him except the desperate longing to become one.') It is true that Brunetière revised this judgement in later years, but it is a measure of the originality of *Les Fleurs du Mal* that one of the authoritative literary figures of the day should at first have so signally failed to understand and appreciate the Symbolist approach to poetry. (pp. 14-16)

> *Charles Chadwick, "Baudelaire's 'Correspondences'," in his* Symbolism, Methuen, 1971, *pp. 8-16.*

Francis S. Heck   (essay date 1982)

[*Heck is an American educator and essayist on French letters. In the following excerpt, he demonstrates how Baudelaire's poetic style transforms and sublimates sensual pleasure into "a spiritual emotion."*]

The dichotomy between spiritual aspiration and physical love is perhaps nowhere so evident as in the works of Baudelaire. For the poet, the effects of original sin make physical beauty attractive; nevertheless his experience constantly warns him of the illusion of beauty. Baudelaire is, of course, a poet and not a theologian; hence, he treats this "lie" in a literary, and primarily a poetic context, even though its moral aspects cannot be completely ignored. The duality of the poet manifests itself in his ambivalent attitude toward beauty: he is attracted to it in terms of physical desire but, because of his spiritual yearning, he is at the same time repulsed by the presence of physical beauty.

A study of the illusion of beauty in Baudelaire's works reveals the intimate spirit of the man, his very soul laid bare. Marcel Raymond insists, moreover, that "Baudelairean poetry, in addressing itself less to the heart than to the soul, or the profound self . . . seeks to affect, beyond our range of feeling, the more obscure domains of the spirit." In his works, therefore, Baudelaire envisions beauty with the mixed emotions of attraction and repulsion; attraction because of its evocation of the spiritual nature of man, and repulsion due to its rapport with man's physical yearnings.

In his essay on Théodore de Banville, Baudelaire sees in modern art generally "an essentially demonic tendency," or the depiction (by writers such as Byron and Poe) of "the hidden Lucifer implanted in every human heart." The devil in the human heart evinces the lie concerning beauty. The devil might also take the form of a most beautiful woman in the eyes of the poet: "Sometimes, knowing of my great love for Art, he assumes the form of the most seductive of women" (in the poem, **"La Destruction"**). In its 1855 version, the poem was entitled **"La Volupté"** (Sensual Pleasure), a fact that emphasizes the equation between *volupté* and *destruction*. Concomitant, then, with the concept of the illusion of beauty is that of *volupté*.

Volupté is the means by which physical beauty is communicated to the poet. For him, "all *volupté* is a manifestation of the state of nature, which is in its essence evil, the evil." That which is both natural and evil also engenders a repulsion on the part of the poet; hence, *volupté* in the life of the poet explains how he is mutually attracted and repulsed by the lie of beauty. In **"Hymn to Beauty"** (1860), the poet in a unique image observes the forces of attraction and repulsion in operation: "The panting lover, bent over his beloved, seems like a dying man caressing his tomb." From the objective position of the poet-observer, *volupté* is manifest by the anticipation of physical pleasure on the part of the lover, but the scene is equally repulsive and morbid as the lover, in the act of caressing his beloved, is at the same time envisioned as a dying man in the act of stroking his grave. These two verses are typically Baudelairean, inasmuch as they suggest the viewpoint of experience, the more objective reality at which a mature person arrives only after considerable time and after profound meditation.

Another example of the attraction-repulsion theme occurs in **"The Metamorphoses of the Vampire"** (1852), wherein the poet himself assumes the role of victim with respect to beauty. The exquisite description of *volupté* in the first part of the poem has its counterpoint in the ghoulish horror of the second part. In the latter part, as the poet, under the spell of attraction toward beauty, turns toward the woman: "in order to return her kiss, I saw nothing but a slimy object whith flanks like goatskin, all full of pus." The obvious repulsion inherent in the scene suggests again the machinations of the devil, since he could assume a repulsive form as easily as he could assume the form of "the most seductive of women." In its macabre style, the poem is a veritable paean to the lie of beauty because in the course of the poem the woman is transformed from a beauty to a skeleton.

Baudelaire's duality concerning beauty, and especially his insistence upon the illusion of beauty, is characteristically anti-Romantic. The poet denigrates the Romantic attitude toward love and beauty by revealing the lie endemic to human beauty. In **"The Mask"** of 1859, for example, he avows to the "perfect beauty" that "your lie intoxicates me." In the poem, **"Semper Eadem"** (1860), he says quite candidly to the woman: "Let, oh let my heart be intoxicated by a *lie,* let me plunge into your beautiful eyes as into a beautiful dream." Woman, in keeping with the title of the poem, is always the same, whether it is a question of Jeanne Duval, Mme. Sabatier, . . . Marie Daubrun, or any other woman. In **"The Love of the Lie"** (1860), moreover, the poet once more reveals the contradiction in his attitude with regard to the lie of beauty: "But isn't it enough that you are the appearance, in order to gladden *a heart fleeing the truth?"* (italics mine). Here, Baudelaire accepts the illusion, and he chooses to ignore reality; it is a situation where the heart is divorced from the head (i.e. the heart accepts what the mind would reject). Baudelaire is all too human, but at the same time he is completely lucid with regard to the attraction of this lie in his life. (pp. 39-41)

For Baudelaire there is an irrevocable dichotomy between physical love and spiritual sentiments. By virtue of the poet's insistence upon the illusion of physical love, he literally gives the lie to an entire generation of Romantic lovers who, in spite of all their experience in love, still adhere to the hope of achieving an apotheosis of *volupté* in this life. Years before the appearance of Gustave Flaubert's parody of Romantic love in *L'Education sentimentale* (1869), Baudelaire already evokes the sensation of the emptiness that ensues after one is addicted to physical love "when our hearts have once had their harvest, living is an evil" in **"Semper Eadem."**

To solve this problem, Baudelaire at first decides to accept the emptiness in his role as the docile martyr of sensual pleasure; that is, he will surfeit himself with physical beauty to the point of oblivion ("powerful oblivion dwells on your lips and Lethe flows from your kisses") in **"Le Lethe."** If beauty had no other representative for him than Jeanne Duval, then this journey toward oblivion would be the sole course to take. Opposed to Jeanne's physical attraction, however, the poet sets up in his mind and heart an altar to spiritual beauty (symbolized by Mme. Sabatier, at least until 1857). As a result of these opposing forces infused into his work, "his aesthetics are not founded upon a refusal, but upon a combat." This combat assumes the form of a transposition of the ardor of his physical desires into a work of art which will endure. Art, then, dispels the emptiness of sensual pleasures.

For Baudelaire, therefore, beauty is really pure only when it is transposed into art. Otherwise, "beauty represents an absolute deception." In this process of transposition, *volupté* must become sublimated into a sensation which will be divorced as much as possible from physical desires.

The poem, **"Voyage to Cythera,"** discloses that, as early as 1852, Baudelaire suggests the need to sublimate *volupté.* The early part of the poem is replete with the poet's anticipation of sensual pleasure to be enjoyed on the isle that he is approaching:

> Where the young priestess, a lover of flowers, was advancing, her body burning with secret, ardent desires, while her robe was exposed to the passing breezes.

Instead of the young priestess of love, however, the poet sees on the shore only a gibbet, on which is suspended the remains of a disemboweled corpse. Immediately, the poet realizes that the corpse is a symbol of himself, hanging on a symbolic gibbet. He is condemned to hang there metaphorically: "in expiation for your imfamous cults," that is, the cult of Venus in the allegory and the cult of the illusion of beauty in real life. The realization of his own attachment to the cult of *volupté* draws the prayer-cry at the end of the poem: "Oh Lord! give me the strength and the courage to observe my heart and my body without disgust." This disgust is directed against himself because he has offered his heart and his body to the cult of sensuality; he now realizes that this sensuality must be eradicated, or re-directed.

Ten years later in the prose poem, **"At One o'Clock in the Morning,"** the poet again utters a prayer-cry of the same intensity: "Fortify me, sustain me, remove from me the lie and the corrupting vapors of the world." The "lie" is quite evidently the lie of beauty, which gives rise to the "corrupting vapors" (a euphemism for *volupté*). In these two examples, the initial phase in the course of sublimation of *volupté* has begun, with the awareness of the problem on the part of the poet. This opening phase is dominated by the desire, as is stated in Baudelaire's study of Wagner's music, "transforming my *volupté* into consciousness." (pp. 41-3)

In this second stage of the sublimation, there is a liaison effected between *volupté* and *tristesse.* Ardor is counterbalanced by lassitude and characterized by the sentiment of melancholy; in the process, the original equation of *volupté* and sensuality is greatly modified. It is not only suffering and sadness that is introduced in **"Le Masque,"** but what Jean Prevost labels aesthetic despair, the conclusion that life itself is a condemnation and that beauty is synonymous with sorrow.

Now, in the consideration of beauty, the poet is attentive to "spiritual needs;" the memories of mutual past joys and sorrows effect a metamorphosis to a *volupté* saturated with sorrow and remorse." Such a *volupté,* nurtured by suffering, forms a polarity to that of the lover "panting," bending over his beloved. This new form of *volupté,* in its complexity, is indicative of an evolution in which mind, heart, and soul have converted the ardor of human passion into an emotion that assumes intense, spiritual qualities.

The experience of sorrow and remorse has so fortified the poet that, in terms of art, *volupté* has been sublimated. In the poem, **"Meditation"** of 1861, "the poet removes himself from places of pleasure while his spirit becomes more and more detached from *volupté."* (*Volupté* is used here in its original meaning of sensuality.) Baudelaire addresses his sorrow with parental tenderness, or in other words, with the *volupté* modulated and purified by years of suffering. The "dead years in outdated dresses," as well as the "moribund sun" refer to the poet's anterior life style, to his attachment to *volupté* in the initial phase of his adult life. These symbols of a bygone period are now detached from the person of the poet because they are now "dead" and "moribund," as they are about to sink into the sea of oblivion: "Look at the dead years descending." The counter movement to the descent of these dying elements is "smiling Regret," which is in the act of surging upward from the sea in order to surround the poet. It is the poet who, at the end of the poem, is "sage" (in its double meaning of wise and behaved), as he calmly awaits death with a sense of *volupté* so expurgated that death is envisioned as "sweet Night."

In death, the sublimation of *volupté* is complete. In **"Death of the Lovers"** (1851), for example, "pleasure and love are both mutually experienced and not exclusive of one another." Pleasure, though, can no longer exist as *volupté* in the physical sense, and in death the lovers are completely devoid of the illusion of Beauty, which is endemic to physical love in the world of the flesh. The first tercet of the sonnet expresses this mystic parting of the lovers:

> Some evening full of pink and mystic blue
> we shall exchange one flashing look,
> overflowing with farewells like one long sob.

The tone of the poem is that of the opposite pole of the erotic.

Through awareness, sadness, suffering, and the feeling of regret, therefore, *volupté,* in this final, expurgated state, emerges as an element eminently spiritual. In its terminal stage of evolution, *volupté* represents a distinct antithesis to the illusion of beauty.

The study of the illusion of beauty in Baudelaire's work might serve as a counter-argument against those critics (e.g. A. E. Carter) who consider the poet's preoccupation with sex as evidence of "a certain immaturity of mind." Baudelaire, though, is no more immature in this respect than is Freud. The poet's use of the macabre and the horrible (his *bas-romantisme,* or romanticism of the lower depths) frequently serves to emphasize the illusion of physical pleasure; his reaction to the illusion is quite literally a "flower from evil."

Because of his reaction, and in the course of the sublimation of *volupté,* Baudelaire adopts the role of the dandy in society. This role is marked by the inherent sentiment of being disinterested, that is, "an effort, an asceticism with the goal of perfection, without any mental reservation in regard to profit or recompense." Desirous of renouncing physical passion because of its inherent deceit, while at the same time adamant in his resolution to maintain his purity and his integrity, the poet withdraws more and more from society into a cult of the self, in spite of a genuine, but abstract, love for the poor. In *My Heart Laid Bare,* physical love (e.g. love for women) is placed on the level of the postulation toward Satan, which is equated with "animal nature" or the "joy of descending." This position is in direct opposition to the concept of the dandy, who disdains contact with such "animal nature." In general terms, the dandy speaks like the anti-sensual voice in **"The Voice"**: "Come, oh come travel in dreams, beyond the possible, beyond the known." For the dandy, therefore, the world is no longer "a cake full of sweetness"; he is acutely aware

of his difference from the more common pleasure seekers, as he remains constantly alone with his "wound" and his "fatality."

"To a Passing Woman" of 1860, for example, illustrates Baudelaire's dandyism. At first reading, it might seem that the poet, at the end of the poem, has nothing but regret, inasmuch as the unknown woman and he have not become lovers: "You whom I could have loved, you who were aware of it." This conclusion, however, neglects to consider the steps in the poet's reaction to the woman. Even though he stares at her as though transfixed, he is at the same time lucidly aware that she represents: "The sweetness that entices and the pleasure that kills." In spite of the physical attraction, therefore, he is also to some extent repulsed by the realization of the consequences of the omnipresent illusion in human passion. Accordingly, by referring to the woman as "fleeing beauty," he maintains his distance from her. The benefit that he derives from this encounter is not at all physical, but spiritual, because the woman's look alone "caused me to be suddenly re-born." By remaining free from human passion, the poet confirms his dandyism, his detachment from *volupté* (nonsublimated, of course). Because of this spiritual turn of thought, the feeling of regret at the end of **"To a Passing Woman"** is akin to the "*volupté* saturated with sorrow" of *Fusees.*

In **"The Voyage,"** the poem in which "all the threads of the book are deliberately recalled and drawn together," Baudelaire assigns important roles to the illusion of beauty and to *volupté.* There is here a consistency on the part of the poet, who, instead of contradicting himself, reveals the contradictions of the human heart in general.

"The Voyage" starts with the Romantic notion of life as an ideal voyage and of the travelers who set out with "light hearts":

> *Those whose desires have the form of clouds and*
> *who,* as the raw soldier dreams of cannon fire,
> *dream of voluptés* which are unconfined, changing
> and unknown, and concerning which the human
> spirit has never known the name. (italics mine)

These words express the exultation of youth embarking upon life's adventures for the first time, seeking "voluptés," or life's sensual pleasures.

The desire for sensual pleasures fills every sojourn with anticipated *volupté* (an "Eldorado"), but in the light of reality: "The imagination, anticipating an orgy, finds only a reef at the break of day." Here, the reefs that replace the orgy of sensual pleasures are a repetition of the "illusion" that was already seen in **"Voyage to Cythera"** in which the gibbet with the corpse replaced the anticipated vision of the sensual priestess. The exultation of youth is gradually diminished by the constant contact with reality, which more and more obfuscates the Romantic *volupté.*

Disappointment is the key word for the middle sections of this long poem. As soon as the travelers experience physical pleasures, their thirst for new, more exotic, *voluptés* becomes an obsession: "Costumes which are an intoxication for the eyes; women whose teeth and fingernails are painted." Their prerequisites for sensual pleasures become more and more exacting, but the end result betrays their keen deception, as they denounce all their adventures and loves as: "the boring spectacle of immortal sin." At this stage, there no longer exists any vestige of youth; it is the voice of experience which now speaks. *Volupté* at this stage corresponds to sadness.

In the seventh and eighth parts of the poem, Baudelaire draws a twofold conclusion. The first part of his conclusion suggests the lie of beauty (as well as everything else on the human level), when the poet envisions life as: "an oasis of horror in a desert of boredom." The stark pessimism of the statement evolves out of the personal experiences of the travelers, just as the poet's own experiences are the direct cause for the realization of the existence of the illusion. The second part of the conclusion is the observation that there is yet one final voyage to make, namely, that on the "Sea of Darkness" or death. Now, *volupté* is completely sublimated, as is attested by the voices, still "charming" but also "funereal"; they propose: "the miraculous fruits which your heart starves for." For the spiritually starved, these are miraculous enjoyments not to be possessed during their life on earth.

The final stanza of **"The Voyage"** is a direct appeal to death itself: "Death, aged captain, it is time, hoist the anchor." As in the first stanza of the poem, again it is with enthusiasm (now born of experience, sorrow, and regret) that: "Inasmuch as this fire burns our brains, we want to plunge to the depths of the abyss, Hell or Heaven, what does it matter, to the very depths of the Unknown in order to find the *new*." F. W. Leakey underlines the total *dépaysement* and the denunciation of sin ("Man in his most general and endemic sinfulness") in these final verses of the poem. Leakey's insistence upon the nihilism of the poet, however, is viable only insofar as human nature is concerned; Baudelaire's aspiration is to attain a level beyond the bounds of human nature (i.e. in death), an existence wherein all attachments to nature will have been obliterated, and wherein, moreover, the illusion of beauty will have been replaced by the new. At this final stage, the illusion itself will have ceased to exist.

Baudelaire's literary work is not intended to be a religious tract; its function is eminently poetic. The ending of **"The Voyage,"** for example, which leaves unanswered many questions concerning heaven and hell, good and evil, is nevertheless artistic, since the poet cannot be more specific without being unfaithful to his poetic vision. As a poet, it is Baudelaire's objective to reveal the presence of the illusion of beauty, and its operation by means of *volupté*, in an artistic manner. By means of art, *volupté* is tranformed and eventually sublimated into a spiritual emotion. In real life, Baudelaire is unable to achieve this goal with the desired degree of "order and beauty, luxury, calmness and *volupté*." In art, however, he "managed artistically to do what he was incapable of in his life: to order his dualistic vision of the world and to move beyond it," a process which bestows upon his work "a dimension of meaning, which all the flaws in its structure cannot diminish." (pp. 43-7)

Francis S. Heck, "The Illusion of Beauty and Volupté in the Works of Baudelaire," in Renascence, Vol. XXXV, No. 1, Autumn, 1982, pp. 39-48.

FURTHER READING

Auden, W. H. Introduction to *Intimate Journals,* by Charles Baudelaire, translated by Christopher Isherwood, pp. 13-28. Hollywood, Calif.: Marcel Rodd, 1947.
Discusses Baudelaire's conception of the individual in society, noting that Baudelaire's dandyism was a strong element of his creative persona.

Aynesworth, Donald. "Humanity and Monstrosity in *Le Spleen de Paris:* A Reading of 'Mademoiselle Bistouri'." *Romantic Review* LXXIII, No. 2 (March 1982): 209-21.
Explores the artistic values of fragmentation in Baudelaire's *Poems in Prose,* maintaining that "the prose poems appear as a kind of esthetic monstrosity, fragmented, never finished, designed solely to entertain or distract."

Benjamin, Walter. *Charles Baudelaire: A Lyric Poet in the Era of High Capitalism.* Translated by Harry Zohn. London: NLB, 1973, 179 p.
Examines the structure and content of *The Flowers of Evil,* focusing on Baudelaire's poetic vocabulary and incorporating a broad cultural analysis of mid-nineteenth-century France.

————. "On Some Motifs in Baudelaire." In his *Illuminations,* edited by Hannah Arendt, translated by Harry Zohn, pp. 155-200. New York: Schocken Books, 1969.
Considers the philosophical implications of *The Flowers of Evil* as an indictment against modern society, concluding that Baudelaire "indicated the price for which the sensation of the modern age may be had: the disintegration of the aura in the experience of shock."

Berman, Marshall. "Baudelaire: Modernism in the Streets." *Partisan Review* XLVI, No. 2 (1979): 205-33.
Maintains that Baudelaire, more than any nineteenth-century artist, experienced "modernity as a basis for self-definition," defining modernity as a form of self-awareness which did not exist before Baudelaire's lifetime.

Bowie, Malcolm; Fairlie, Alison; and Finch, Alison, eds. *Baudelaire, Mallarme, Valery: New Essays in Honour of Lloyd Austin.* Cambridge: Cambridge University Press, 1982, 456 p.
Collection of essays treating various aspects of Baudelaire's verse and prose poems.

Cargo, Robert T. *Baudelaire Criticism, 1950-1967: A Bibliography with Critical Commentary.* University, Ala.: University of Alabama Press, 1968, 171 p.
An annotated bibliography listing Baudelaire studies that were published between 1950 and 1967.

De Casseres, Benjamin. "Baudelaire: Ironic Dante." In his *Forty Immortals,* pp. 206-11. New York: Joseph Lawren, 1926.
Considers Baudelaire's artistic nature, contrasting him with Dante Alighieri. De Casseres notes that, while Dante's Hades is fictional and theological, Baudelaire's conception of hell is real and psychological.

Emmanuel, Pierre. *Baudelaire: The Paradox of Redemptive Satanism.* Translated by Robert T. Cargo. University, Ala.: University of Alabama Press, 1970, 189 p.
Views Baudelaire as a Christian and analyzes his artistic creations as the manifestation of his spiritual aspiration.

Friedrich, Hugo. "Baudelaire." In his *The Structure of Modern Poetry: From the Mid-Nineteenth Century to the Mid-Twentieth Century.* Translated by Joachim Neugroschel, pp. 19-38. Evanston, Ill.: Northwestern University Press, 1974.
Explores Baudelaire's contributions to modern poetry.

Hemmings, F. W. J. *Baudelaire the Damned: A Biography.* New York: Charles Scribner's Sons, 1982, 251 p.
An insightful biography, focusing on the issue of Satanism as evidenced in Baudelaire's writings and personal philosophy.

Huxley, Aldous. "Baudelaire." In his *Do What You Will,* pp. 171-202. London: Chatto & Windus, 1929.
Analyzes the satanic imagery of *The Flowers of Evil,* maintaining that "Baudelaire was not merely a satanist; he was a bored satanist . . . the poet of ennui."

Isherwood, Christopher. Preface to *Intimate Journals,* by Charles Baudelaire, translated by Christopher Isherwood, pp. 5-12. Hollywood, Calif.: Marcel Rodd, 1947.
Brief biographical note.

Kuhn, Reinhard. "The Draining of the Clepsydra." In his *The Demon of Noontide: Ennui in Western Literature,* pp. 279-329. Princeton, N.J.: Princeton University Press, 1976.
Probes the element of ennui in Baudelaire's verse.

Monroe, Jonathan. "Baudelaire's Poor: The *Petits Poèmes en Prose* and the Social Inscription of the Lyric." *Stanford French Review* IX, No. 2 (Summer 1985): 169-88.
Argues that Baudelaire's prose poems illustrate the "self-alienation of the human subject, the perception that the self is an object existing for others than the self."

Morgan, Edwin. *Flower of Evil: A Life of Charles Baudelaire.* New York: Sheed & Ward, 1943, 179 p.
Focuses on the negative aspects of Baudelaire's life, concentrating on his relationship with Jeanne Duval and his mother.

Peyre, Henri, ed. *Baudelaire: A Collection of Critical Essays.* Twentieth Century Views, edited by Maynard Mack, Vol. 18. Englewood Cliffs, N. J.: Prentice-Hall, 1962, 184 p.
A collection of essays by the foremost commentators on Baudelaire. Includes two essays excerpted above: François Mauriac (1920) and Jean Prévost (1953).

Quennell, Peter. "Charles Baudelaire (1821-1867)." In his *Baudelaire and the Symbolists,* 2nd rev. ed., pp. 1-55. London: Weidenfeld and Nicolson, 1954.
A study of Baudelaire and his literary successors, demonstrating how he influenced the direction of Symbolist poetry. Considers Baudelaire "one of the noblest spirits of the nineteenth century, both as an insightful critic and visionary poet."

Rexroth, Kenneth. "Baudelaire, *Poems.*" In his *Classics Revisited,* pp. 173-76. 1968. Reprint. New York: New Directions Books, 1986.
Brief essay focusing on the "modern sensibility" of Baudelaire's lifestyle and poetry.

Shanks, Lewis Piaget. *Baudelaire: Flesh and Spirit.* 1930. Reprint. New York: Haskell House Publishers, 1974, 265 p.
General biographical study.

Starkie, Enid. *Baudelaire.* London: Faber and Faber, 1957, 622 p.
The definitive biography in English. According to Starkie, Baudelaire's writing indicates his desire to rid himself of vice and to reflect "the beauty of God's creation," an interpretation that had been presaged by the commentary of T. S. Eliot and Wallace Fowlie. [See excerpts dated 1930 and 1957, respectively.]

Turnell, Martin. *Baudelaire: A Study of his Poetry.* Norfolk, Conn.: New Direction Books, 1953, 328 p.
Examines the meaning and artistic value of *The Flowers of Evil,* particularly its prosody and syntax, and appraises Baudelaire's consequent impact on French poetry.

Welch, Cyril, and Welch, Liliane. *Emergence: Baudelaire, Mallarme, Rimbaud.* State College, Pa.: Bald Eagle Press, 1973, 134 p.
Recognizes Baudelaire as one of the first French poets to break with classical poetic style, arguing that his primary accomplishment was the development of poetry as an extension of human existence rather than pure imaginary creation.

Emily Dickinson

1830-1886

(Full name: Emily Elizabeth Dickinson) American poet.

Dickinson is regarded as one of the greatest American poets. Although almost none of her poems were published during her lifetime and her work drew harsh criticism when it first appeared, many of her short lyrics on the subjects of nature, love, death, and immortality are now considered among the most emotionally and intellectually profound in the English language. Dickinson's forthright examination of her philosophical and religious skepticism, her unorthodox attitude toward her gender, and her distinctive style—characterized by elliptical, compressed expression, striking imagery, and innovative poetic structure—have earned widespread acclaim, and, in addition, her poems have become some of the best loved in American literature. Thomas Wentworth Higginson, Dickinson's mentor, commented that "the main quality of [her] poems is that of extraordinary grasp and insight, uttered with an uneven vigor, sometimes exasperating, seemingly wayward, but really unsought and inevitable." Today an increasing number of studies from diverse critical viewpoints are devoted to her life and works, thus securing Dickinson's status as a major poet.

Dickinson was born in Amherst, Massachusetts, where she lived her entire life. Dickinson's father, Edward Dickinson, was a prosperous lawyer who served as treasurer of Amherst College and also held various political offices. Her mother, Emily Norcross Dickinson, has been described as a quiet and frail woman. Dickinson's formal education began in 1835 with four years of primary school. She then attended Amherst Academy from 1840 to 1847 before spending a year a Mount Holyoke Female Seminary. Her studies, including courses in the sciences, literature, history, and philosophy, were largely informed by New England Puritanism, with its doctrines of a sovereign God, predestination, and the necessity for personal salvation. Dickinson, however, was unable to accept the teachings of the Unitarian church attended by her family, and despite her desire to experience a religious awakening, remained agnostic throughout her life.

Following the completion of her education, Dickinson lived in the family home with her parents and younger sister, Lavinia, while her older brother, Austin, and his wife, Susan, lived next door. Although the details of her life are vague, scholars believe that Dickinson first began writing poetry seriously in the early 1850s. Her otherwise quiet life was punctuated by brief visits to Boston, Washington, D.C., and Philadelphia in the years from 1851 to 1855. Biographers speculate that during one stay in Philadelphia Dickinson fell in love with a married minister, the Reverend Charles Wadsworth, and that her disappointment in love triggered her subsequent withdrawal from society. While this and other suggestions of tragic romantic attachments are largely conjecture, it is known that Dickinson became increasingly reclusive in the following years, spending her time primarily engaged in domestic routine and long solitary walks.

Biographers generally agree that Dickinson experienced an emotional crisis of an undetermined nature in the early 1860s. Her traumatized state of mind is believed to have inspired her to write prolifically: in 1862 alone she is thought to have composed over three hundred poems. In the same year, Dickinson initiated a correspondence with Thomas Wentworth Higginson, the literary editor of the *Atlantic Monthly*. During the course of their lengthy exchange, Dickinson sent nearly one hundred of her poems for his criticism. While Higginson had little influence on her writing, he was important to her as a sympathetic adviser and confidant. Dickinson's reclusiveness intensified during 1869, and her refusal to leave her home or to meet visitors, her gnomic remarks, and her habit of always wearing white garments earned her a reputation for eccentricity among her neighbors. Her isolation further increased when her father died unexpectedly in 1874 and she was left with the care of her invalid mother. The death of her mother in 1882, followed two years later by the death of Judge Otis P. Lord, a close family friend and Dickinson's most satisfying romantic attachment, contributed to the onset of what Dickinson described as an "attack of nerves." Later, in 1886, she was diagnosed as having Bright's disease, a kidney dysfunction that resulted in her death in May of that year. Only seven of Dickinson's poems were published during her lifetime, all anonymously and some apparently without her consent. The editors of the periodicals in which her lyrics appeared made significant alterations to them in an attempt to regularize the meter and grammar, thereby discouraging Dickinson from seeking further publication of her verse. Subsequently, her poems found only a private audience among her correspondents, family, and old school friends. Her family, however, was unaware of the enormous quantity of verse that she composed. After Dickinson's death, her sister Lavinia was astounded to discover hundreds of poems among her possessions. Many were copied into "fascicles," booklets formed from sheets of paper stitched together, but a large number appeared to be mere jottings recorded on scraps of paper. In many instances Dickinson abandoned poems in an unfinished state, leaving no indication of her final choice between alternate words, phrases, or forms.

Despite the disordered state of the manuscripts, Lavinia Dickinson resolved to publish her sister's poetry and turned to Higginson and Mabel Loomis Todd, a friend of the Dickinson family, for assistance. In 1890 *Poems of Emily Dickinson* appeared, and even though most initial reviews were highly unfavorable, the work went through eleven editions in two years. Encouraged by the popular acceptance of *Poems*, Todd edited and published two subsequent collections of Dickinson's verse in the 1890s as well as a two-volume selection of her letters. Family disputes over possession of manuscripts hindered the publication of further materials, yet over the next fifty years, previously unprinted poems were introduced to the public in new collections. It was not until 1955, with the appearance of Thomas H. Johnson's edition of her verse, that Dickinson's complete poems were collected and published together in an authoritative text.

Nearly eighteen hundred poems by Dickinson are known to exist, all of them in the form of brief lyrics (often of only one or two quatrains), and few of them titled. In her verse, Dickinson explores various subjects: nature, her preoccupation with death, her skepticism about immortality, her experience of love and loss, the importance of poetic vocation, and her attitude toward fame. Drawing on imagery from biblical sources, particularly from the Book of Revelation, and from the works of William Shakespeare, John Keats, and Elizabeth Barrett Browning, Dickinson developed a highly personal system of symbol and allusion, assigning complex meanings to colors, places, times, and seasons. Her tone in the poems ranges widely, from wry, laconic humor to anguished self-examination, from flirtatious riddling to childlike naïveté. Dickinson's diction is similarly diverse, incorporating New England vernacular, theological and scientific terminology, and archaisms. The meters of her poems are characteristically adapted from the rhythms of English hymns or nursery rhymes. Dickinson's experimentation with half rhyme, slant rhyme, assonance, consonance, and tonal harmony defied the poetic conventions of her day, as did her idiosyncratic capitalization and punctuation, especially her use of dashes for emphasis or in place of commas. The terse, epigrammatic, and elliptical aspects of Dickinson's style further distinguish her poetry from the mainstream of nineteenth-century American verse.

Most nineteenth-century critics viewed Dickinson's poetry with a combination of disapproval and bewilderment, objecting to her disregard for conventional meter and rhyme, her unusual imagery, and her apparent grammatical errors. By the turn of the century, Dickinson had acquired an enthusiastic popular following, but she was still regarded as a sentimental poet of minor importance. Interest in her eccentric life-style and alleged love affairs was the main focus of Dickinson scholarship over the next several decades, but there were also some serious critical assessments, especially by the New Critics, who concentrated on the technical aspects of her poetry. The single most important development in Dickinsonian scholarship was Johnson's 1955 edition of the complete poems. Numerous studies of her works have followed, utilizing linguistic, psychological, philosophical, historical, and feminist approaches. Studies of Dickinson's language and style often center on the complex interplay of her diction and imagery with her innovative meter and rhyme. Her adept use of images drawn from nature and literature has also been widely examined. Dickinson's unorthodox religious beliefs, her relation to the Romantic and Transcendental movements, and her personal philosophy of skepticism as expressed in her poems have been the main concerns of other research. In the 1970s and 1980s, feminist critics have explored such issues as the difficulties Dickinson encountered as a woman poet, the significance of her decision to withdraw from society, her use of language as a means of rebellion, and her importance to contemporary women writers.

Although Dickinson engendered no particular school of poetry, poets as diverse as Amy Lowell, Hart Crane, and Adrienne Rich have acknowledged her verse as an influence on their writings. Dickinson has continued to elicit fascination for both readers and scholars. For her originality, range, and emotional depth, Dickinson is now among the most universally admired and extensively studied figures in English literature. As Joyce Carol Oates has written, "Here is an American artist of words as inexhaustible as Shakespeare, as vigorously skillful in her craft as Yeats, a poet whom we can set with confidence beside the greatest poets of modern times."

(For further information on Dickinson's life and career, see *Nineteenth-Century Literature Criticism*, Vol. 21; *Something about the Author*, Vol. 29; *Dictionary of Literary Biography*, Vol. 1; and *Concise Dictionary of American Literary Biography: Realism, Naturalism, and Local Color, 1865-1917.*)

PRINCIPAL WORKS

POETRY

Poems of Emily Dickinson   1890
Poems by Emily Dickinson, second series   1891
Poems by Emily Dickinson, third series   1896
The Single Hound: Poems of a Lifetime   1914
The Complete Poems of Emily Dickinson   1924
Further Poems of Emily Dickinson   1929
Unpublished Poems of Emily Dickinson   1935
Bolts of Melody: New Poems of Emily Dickinson   1945
The Poems of Emily Dickinson. 3 vols. 1955
The Complete Poems of Emily Dickinson   1960

OTHER MAJOR WORKS

Letters of Emily Dickinson. 2 vols.   (letters)   1894

Emily Dickinson Face to Face: Unpublished Letters with
    Notes and Reminiscences (letters) 1932
The Letters of Emily Dickinson. 3 vols. (letters) 1958

Thomas Wentworth Higginson (essay date 1890)

[*In the following excerpt from his preface to the 1890
collection* Poems by Emily Dickinson, *which he edited
in conjunction with Mabel Loomis Todd, Higginson
comments on the personal style of Dickinson's poetry
and praises her "wholly original and profound insight
into nature and life."*]

The verses of Emily Dickinson belong emphatically to
what Emerson long since called "the Poetry of the Portfolio,"—something produced absolutely without the
thought of publication, and solely by way of expression of
the writer's own mind. Such verse must inevitably forfeit
whatever advantage lies in the discipline of public criticism and the enforced conformity to accepted ways. On
the other hand, it may often gain something through the
habit of freedom and the unconventional utterance of daring thoughts. In the case of the present author, there was
absolutely no choice in the matter; she must write thus,
or not at all. A recluse by temperament and habit, literally
spending years without setting her foot beyond the door-
step, and many more years during which her walks were
strictly limited to her father's grounds, she habitually concealed her mind, like her person, from all but a very few
friends; and it was with great difficulty that she was persuaded to print, during her lifetime, three or four poems.
Yet she wrote verses in great abundance; and though curiously indifferent to all conventional rules, had yet a rigorous literary standard of her own, and often altered a word
many times to suit an ear which had its own tenacious fas-
tidiousness. (p. 416)

This selection from her poems is published to meet the desire of her personal friends, and especially of her surviving
sister. It is believed that the thoughtful reader will find in
these pages a quality more suggestive of the poetry of William Blake than of anything to be elsewhere found,—
flashes of wholly original and profound insight into nature
and life; words and phrases exhibiting an extraordinary
vividness of descriptive and imaginative power, yet often
set in a seemingly whimsical or even rugged frame. They
are here published as they were written, with very few and
superficial changes; although it is fair to say that the titles
have been assigned, almost invariably, by the editors. In
many cases these verses will seem to the reader like poetry
torn up by the roots, with rain and dew and earth still
clinging to them, giving a freshness and a fragrance not
otherwise to be conveyed. In other cases, as in the few
poems of shipwreck or of mental conflict, we can only
wonder at the gift of vivid imagination by which this recluse woman can delineate, by a few touches, the very crises of physical or mental struggle. And sometimes again
we catch glimpses of a lyric strain, sustained perhaps but
for a line or two at a time, and making the reader regret
its sudden cessation. But the main quality of these poems
is that of extraordinary grasp and insight, uttered with an
uneven vigor sometimes exasperating, seemingly way-

ward, but really unsought and inevitable. After all, when
a thought takes one's breath away, a lesson on grammar
seems an impertinence. As Ruskin wrote in his earlier and
better days, "No weight nor mass nor beauty of execution
can outweigh one grain or fragment of thought." (pp. 416-
17)

> *Thomas Wentworth Higginson, in an excerpt
> from* Ancestors' Brocades: The Literary
> Debut of Emily Dickinson, *by Millicent Todd
> Bingham, Harper & Brothers Publishers,
> 1945, pp. 416-17.*

Mabel Loomis Todd (essay date 1891)

[*The wife of a professor at Amherst College and a friend
of the Dickinson family, Todd played an important role
in the editing and publication of Dickinson's poetry. In
the following excerpt from her preface to* Poems by
Emily Dickinson, *second series (1891), she describes
Dickinson's style and how her poems came to be published.*]

The eagerness with which the first volume of Emily Dickinson's poems has been read shows very clearly that all our
alleged modern artificiality does not prevent a prompt appreciation of the qualities of directness and simplicity in
approaching the greatest themes,—life and love and
death. That "irresistible needle-touch," as one of her best
critics has called it, piercing at once the very core of a
thought, has found a response as wide and sympathetic as
it has been unexpected even to those who knew best her
compelling power. This second volume, while open to the
same criticism as to form with its predecessor, shows also
the same shining beauties.

Although Emily Dickinson had been in the habit of sending occasional poems to friends and correspondents, the
full extent of her writing was by no means imagined by
them. Her friend "H. H." must at least have suspected it,
for in a letter dated 5th September, 1884, she wrote:—

> MY DEAR FRIEND,—What portfolios full of verses
> you must have! It is a cruel wrong to your "day and
> generation" that you will not give them light.
>
> If such a thing should happen as that I should out-
> live you, I wish you would make me your literary
> legatee and executor. Surely after you are what is
> called "dead" you will be willing that the poor
> ghosts you have left behind should be cheered and
> pleased by your verses, will you not? You ought to
> be. I do not think we have a right to withhold from
> the world a word or a thought any more than a
> *deed* which might help a single soul. . . .
>   Truly yours,
>   HELEN JACKSON

The "portfolios" were found, shortly after Emily Dickinson's death, by her sister and only surviving housemate.
Most of the poems had been carefully copied on sheets of
note-paper, and tied in little fascicules, each of six or eight
sheets. While many of them bear evidence of having been
thrown off at white heat, still more had received thoughtful revision. There is the frequent addition of rather perplexing foot-notes, affording large choice of words and
phrases. And in the copies which she sent to friends, sometimes one form, sometimes another, is found to have been

used. Without important exception, her friends have generously placed at the disposal of the Editors any poems they had received from her; and these have given the obvious advantage of comparison among several renderings of the same verse.

To what further rigorous pruning her verses would have been subjected had she published them herself, we cannot know. They should be regarded in many cases as merely the first strong and suggestive sketches of an artist, intended to be embodied at some time in the finished picture. (p. 418)

As a rule, the verses were without titles; but **"A Country Burial," "A Thunder-Storm," "The Humming-Bird,"** and a few others were named by their author, frequently at the end,—sometimes only in the accompanying note, if sent to a friend.

The variation of readings, with the fact that she often wrote in pencil and not always clearly, have at times thrown a good deal of responsibility upon her Editors. But all interference not absolutely inevitable has been avoided. The very roughness of her own rendering is part of herself, and not lightly to be touched; for it seems in many cases that she intentionally avoided the smoother and more usual rhymes.

Like impressionist pictures, or Wagner's rugged music, the very absence of conventional form challenges attention. In Emily Dickinson's exacting hands, the especial, intrinsic fitness of a particular order of words might not be sacrificed to anything virtually extrinsic; and her verses all show a strange cadence of inner rhythmical music. Lines are always daringly constructed, and the "thought-rhyme" appears frequently,—appealing, indeed, to an unrecognized sense more elusive than hearing.

Emily Dickinson scrutinized everything with clear-eyed frankness. Every subject was proper ground for legitimate study, even the sombre facts of death and burial, and the unknown life beyond. She touches these themes sometimes lightly, sometimes almost humorously, more often with weird and peculiar power; but she is never by any chance frivolous or trivial. And while, as one critic has said, she may exhibit toward God "an Emersonian self-possession," it was because she looked upon all life with a candor as unprejudiced as it is rare.

She had tried society and the world, and found them lacking. She was not an invalid, and she lived in seclusion from no love-disappointment. Her life was the normal blossoming of a nature introspective to a high degree, whose best thought could not exist in pretence.

Storm, wind, the wild March sky, sunsets and dawns; the birds and bees, butterflies and flowers of her garden, with a few trusted human friends, were sufficient companionship. The coming of the first robin was a jubilee beyond crowning of monarch or birthday of pope; the first red leaf hurrying through "the altered air," an epoch. Immortality was close about her; and while never morbid or melancholy, she lived in its presence. (p. 419)

> *Mabel Loomis Todd, in an excerpt from* Ancestors' Brocades: The Literary Debut of Emily Dickinson *by Millicent Todd Bingham, Harper & Brothers, 1945, pp. 417-19.*

Ella Gilbert Ives   (essay date 1907)

[*Ives was a teacher, poet, and alumna of Mount Holyoke College. The following excerpt is taken from an essay originally published in the* Boston Evening Transcript *in 1907; it was the first extended commentary on Dickinson in the twentieth century. Ives extols the poet's originality as well as her "brevity and searching quality."*]

Many obvious, many contradictory things, have been said about this profound thinker and virile writer on a few great themes. Those who cling to the old order and regard perfect form essential to greatness, have had their fling at her eccentricities, her blemishes, her crudities; they place her with the purveyors of raw material to the artistic producers of the race. They deny her rank with the creators of permanent beauty and value. Others such as hail a Wagner, a Whitman, or a Turner, as an originator of new types and a contributor of fresh streams of life blood to art or literature, accept Emily Dickinson as another proof of Nature's fecundity, versatility and daring. All acknowledge in her elements of power and originality; but especially a certain probing quality that penetrates and discloses like an X-ray.

By long-accepted standards, doubtless, she does not measure up to greatness. The first bullet was an innovation to one who drew the long bow. He did not know what to make of hot shot without the whiz and the grace of the arrow—least of all when it struck home and shattered his pet notions. Emily Dickinson's power of condensation, the rhythmic hammer of her thoughts, whether in prose or verse, is so phenomenal that it calls for a new system of weights and measures. Perhaps there is nothing essentially new here. Franklin merely identified an acquaintance of Noah's when he flew his kite; Newton, had he talked the apple over with Eve, might have found her intelligent on the fall; but both philosophers drew as near to originality as mortal is ever permitted to draw by the jealous gods. Emily Dickinson, whatever her size, is of nobody's kind but her own. The nearest approach to a family resemblance in her intellectual physiognomy is a feminine idiosyncracy, the counterpart of Thoreau's masculine one; but it begins and ends in mere suggestion. I make bold to attach "Dickinsonian" to such verse as this:

> We play at paste,
> Till qualified for pearl.
>
> ---
>
> The truth never flaunted a sign.
>
> ---
>
> The vane a little to the east
> Scares muslin souls away.
>
> ---
>
> No squirrel went abroad;
> A dog's belated feet
> Like intermittent plush were heard
> Adown the empty street.

Also to this prose: "Enough is so vast a sweetness, I suppose it never occurs, only pathetic counterfeits." . . . " 'Tis not what well conferred it, the dying soldier asks, it is only the water." . . . "We dignify our faith when we can cross the ocean with it, though most prefer ships." . . . "The golden rule is so lovely it needs no police to enforce it." . . . "Thomas's faith in anatomy was stronger than his faith." . . . "How vast is the chastisement of beauty, given us by our maker!" . . . "Was he not an aborigine of the sky?" . . . "Memory's fog is rising." . . . "A morning call from Gabriel is always a surprise. Were we more fresh from Eden we were expecting him—but Genesis is a 'far journey'." . . . "It is true that the unknown is the largest need of the intellect, though for it, no one thinks to thank God." . . . "We must be careful what we say. No bird resumes its egg." . . . "Truth, like ancestors' brocades, can stand alone." . . . "To multiply the harbors does not reduce the sea." . . . "Not what the stars have done, but what they are to do, detains the sky." (pp. 71-3)

Her poems must be seen whole in their sky, and must be touched to yield their lightning. Some of them are ragged-edged clouds, but hanging in an atmosphere and drifting one way—toward God and eternity. Touch them and you get an electric shock. The recurrent themes are life, love, death, immortality; but especially the veiled majesty of death. Did any other peer so curiously, so insistently, into the unseen, with such a baffling sense of impotence and folly?

> At least to pray is left, is left,
> O Jesus! in the air
> I know not which thy chamber is—
> I'm knocking everywhere.
>
> Thou stirrest earthquake in the south,
> And maelstrom in the sea;
> Say, Jesus Christ of Nazareth,
> Hast thou no arm for me?
>
> ———
>
> Death is a dialogue between
> The spirit and the dust,
> "Dissolve," says Death. The Spirit, "Sir,
> I have another trust."
>
> Death doubts it, argues from the ground.
> The Spirit turns away,
> Just laying off, for evidence,
> An overcoat of clay.

I would that this writer on the mysteries had possessed a more joyous temper and greater certitude; but she could rise no higher than her faith, being first of all, sincere. On the sweet, safe level of the grass, the plane of the low-flying robin and bluebird, she is serene and poised. Of all

> The simple news that Nature told,
> With tender majesty

she is a delightful bearer; a voice that has tones of pure gladness. What abandon of joy in what an Englishman calls "A Woman's Drinking Song!"—**"I taste a liquor never brewed."** If language could intoxicate, the second stanza were such a draught:

> Inebriate of air am I,
> And debauchee of dew,
> Reeling, through endless summer days,
> From inns of molten blue.

And how her mind plays holiday in these lines:

> He ate and drank the precious words,
> His spirit grew robust;
> He knew no more that he was poor,
> Nor that his frame was dust.
> He danced along the dingy days,
> And this bequest of wings
> Was but a book. What liberty
> A loosened spirit brings!

And her heart—she fails herself to find a plummet for sounding its depths, though she tries in such lines as these:

> Alter? When the hills do.
> Falter? When the sun
> Question if his glory
> Be the perfect one.
> Surfeit? When the daffodil
> Doth of the dew;
> Even as herself, O friend!
> I will of you.

As to her philosophy—and one can suck wisdom from her writings—I know no space so small more packed with nutriment than this quatrain:

> The pedigree of honey
> Does not concern the bee;
> A clover, any time, to him
> Is aristocracy;

Or these stanzas:

> I'm nobody! Who are you?
> Are you nobody, too?
> Then there's a pair of us—don't tell!
> They'd banish us, you know.
>
> How dreary to be somebody!
> How public, like a frog,
> To tell your name the livelong day
> To an admiring bog!

(pp. 73-5)

It is the brevity and searching quality (in inverse ratio) of Emily Dickinson's poetry that render it unique, and augur permanence, not so much that it lights the pathway, as that it explores the heart and touches the quick of experience. Her verse is never didactic, yet always earnest; too serious for wit, yet having the very kernel of wit—surprise—to an extraordinary degree. This dressing up of the primal emotions in strange, often outlandish garb, or exhibiting them naked yet not ashamed, has a singular effect, and throws the mind back with questioning upon the writer herself, and the influences that made her what she was—the loneliest figure in the world of letters. (pp. 76-7)

I have not dwelt upon Emily Dickinson's faults; they speak for themselves, and sometimes with such a din that the virtues cannot be heard. Granted that her poetry is uneven, so rugged of rhyme and rhythm that it jolts the mind like a corduroy road—I prefer it to a flowery bed of ease. Many can lull, but few can awake. (p. 78)

> *Ella Gilbert Ives, "Emily Dickinson: Her Poetry, Prose and Personality," in* The Recognition of Emily Dickinson: Selected Criticism Since 1890, *edited by Caesar R. Blake and Carlton F. Wells, The University of Michigan Press, 1964, pp. 71-8.*

Amy Lowell   (poem date 1925)

[*Lowell was a leading proponent of Imagism in American poetry. Like the French Symbolists before her, Lowell experimented with free verse forms and, influenced by Ezra Pound, developed a style characterized by clear and precise rhetoric, exact rendering of images, and metrical innovations. Although she was popular in her own time, current evaluations of Lowell accord her more importance as a promoter of new artistic ideas than as a poet in her own right. In the following excerpt from her "The Sisters," originally published in* What's O'Clock *(1925), she cites Dickinson as an inspiration and as one of her "spiritual relations."*]

Taking us by and large, we're a queer lot
We women who write poetry. And when you think
How few of us there've been, it's queerer still.
I wonder what it is that makes us do it,
Singles us out to scribble down, man-wise,
The fragments of ourselves. Why are we
Already mother-creatures, double-bearing,
With matrices in body and in brain?
I rather think that there is just the reason
We are so sparse a kind of human being;
The strength of forty thousand Atlases
Is needed for our every-day concerns.

                                                              (p. 459)

. . . I go dreaming on,
In love with these my spiritual relations.
I rather think I see myself walk up
A flight of wooden steps and ring a bell
And send a card in to Miss Dickinson.
Yet that's a very silly way to do.
I should have taken the dream twist-ends about
And climbed over the fence and found her deep
Engrossed in the doing of a hummingbird
Among nasturtiums. Not having expected strangers,
She might forget to think me one, and holding up
A finger say quite casually: "Take care.
Don't frighten him, he's only just begun."
"Now this," I well believe I should have thought,
"Is even better than Sapho. With Emily
You're really here, or never anywhere at all
In range of mind." Wherefore, having begun
In the strict centre, we could slowly progress
To various circumferences, as we pleased.
We could, but should we? That would quite depend
On Emily. I think she'd be exacting,
Without intention possibly, and ask
A thousand tight-rope tricks of understanding.
But, bless you, I would somersault all day
If by so doing I might stay with her.
I hardly think that we should mention souls
Although they might just round the corner from us
In some half-quizzical, half-wistful metaphor.
I'm very sure that I should never seek
To turn her parables to stated fact.
Sapho would speak, I think, quite openly,
And Mrs. Browning guard a careful silence,
But Emily would set doors ajar and slam them
And love you for your speed of observation.

                                                        (pp. 460-61)

Amy Lowell, in a poem from The Complete Poetical Works of Amy Lowell, *Houghton Mifflin Company, 1955, pp. 459-61.*

Harold Monro   (essay date 1925)

[*Monro was a well-known poet, publisher, and editor. In the following excerpt, originally published in* The Criterion *in 1925, he criticizes Dickinson's lack of poetic expertise, noting that even in her good poems there is a "large splendid awkwardness," and concludes that she does not appear to be "candid" in her poetry.*]

At a first impression Emily Dickinson's tiny lyrics appear more like the jottings of a half-idiotic schoolgirl than the grave musings of a fully educated woman. This kind of verse, I thought to myself, may go down in America, but, when imported to England, we inevitably apply to it the test of comparison with the poems of Emily Brontë, Christina Rossetti, Mary Coleridge, Michael Field. Her poems are splendid blunders. How much better they could have been if she had specialized in her craft. She was intellectually blind, partially deaf, mostly dumb, to the art of poetry. Consequently seven out of ten of her lyrical jottings are plainly failures.

Emily Dickinson has been overrated, but not so far overrated as a first survey of her selected poems might indicate. Her style is clumsy; her language is poor; her technique is appalling, and there is no excuse (except that very excuse of faulty technique) for the frequent elementary grammatical errors. There is only one rhyme (and that a doubtful one) in the poem which ends with the line—

Flinging the problem back at you and I

so that one almost feels that her editor might have taken it upon himself to correct so elementary and unnecessary a mistake.

Some twentieth-century authors, we know, ignore the rules of grammar just for fun, or as a little surprise to their readers; but there is no reason to suspect these motives in Miss Dickinson. No twentieth-century levity in her. Moreover, her lyrics have been described as "the finest poetry by a woman in the English language." (p. 121)

It would be ridiculously easy to belittle Emily Dickinson by unfavorable quotation. At her worst she is positively comic; but her worst is as distant from her best as the half-idiotic schoolgirl from, let us say, Keats. There are very few lyrics quite flawless, but as we progress in the art of understanding her, we begin to find even in many of the flaws a kind of large splendid awkwardness, something innocently audacious, grotesque, and abnormal. The woman who wrote the following:

AFTERMATH

The bustle in a house
The morning after death
Is solemnest of industries
Enacted upon earth,—

The sweeping up the heart,
And putting love away
We shall not want to use again
Until eternity.

(clumsy enough, but redeemed entirely by a magic of pathos and loveliness), could also allow (to choose only one from many possible examples) the following to stand:

But I, grown shrewder, scan the skies
With a suspicious air,—
As children, swindled for the first,
All swindlers be, infer.

She seems to be afraid. She dwelt in seclusion, social, physical, and psychological. She gives the impression of wanting to keep some secret. Clarity of thought is constantly veiled in obscurity of expression. She was not candid; she does not seem to have been moved by any overruling instinct for truth. And we compare her unavoidably with her contemporary, Emily Brontë, whose infatuated desire

to be faithful to her every aspect of truth overcame all timidity. (p. 122)

> Harold Monro, "Emily Dickinson—
> Overrated," in The Recognition of Emily
> Dickinson: Selected Criticism since 1890, ed-
> ited by Caesar R. Blake and Carlton F. Wells,
> The University of Michigan Press, 1964, pp.
> 121-22.

**"If I read a book [and] it makes my whole
body so cold no fire ever can warm me I
know *that* is poetry. If I feel physically as
if the top of my head were taken off, I
know *that* is poetry. These are the only
way I know it. Is there any other way."
—Emily Dickinson to T. W. Higginson,
1870**

Allen Tate   (essay date 1928-32)

[*Tate is considered one of the most influential American
critics of the twentieth century. His criticism is closely
associated with two critical movements, the Agrarians
and the New Critics. The Agrarians were concerned with
political and social issues as well as literature, and were
dedicated to preserving traditional Southern values. Although the various New Critics did not subscribe to a single set of principles, all believed that a work of literature
had to be examined as an object in itself through a process of close analysis of symbol, image, and metaphor.
In the following excerpt, Tate discusses Dickinson and
her poetry in the context of her historical period, especially in terms of the movement away from theocracy.
Although he notes that "she had all the elements of a
culture that has broken up," Tate offers a highly positive
evaluation of Dickinson's style. These comments were
first published in the* Outlook *(1928) and the* Symposium *(1932).*]

Great poetry needs no special features of difficulty to make
it mysterious. When it has them, the reputation of the poet
is likely to remain uncertain. This is still true of Donne,
and it is true of Emily Dickinson, whose verse appeared
in an age unfavorable to the use of intelligence in poetry.
Her poetry is not like any other poetry of her time; it is
not like any of the innumerable kinds of verse written
today. In still another respect it is far removed from us.
It is a poetry of ideas, and it demands of the reader a point
of view—not an opinion of the New Deal or of the League
of Nations, but an ingrained philosophy that is fundamental, a settled attitude that is almost extinct in this eclectic
age. Yet it is not the sort of poetry of ideas which, like
Pope's, requires a point of view only. It requires also, for
the deepest understanding, which must go beneath the
verbal excitement of the style, a highly developed sense of
the specific quality of poetry—a quality that most persons
accept as the accidental feature of something else that the
poet thinks he has to say. This is one reason why Miss
Dickinson's poetry has not been widely read.

There is another reason, and it is a part of the problem peculiar to a poetry that comes out of fundamental ideas. We

lack a tradition of criticism. There were no points of critical reference passed on to us from a preceding generation.
(pp. 197-98)

Still another difficulty stands between us and Miss Dickinson. It is the failure of the scholars to feel more than biographical curiosity about her. We have scholarship, but
that is no substitute for a critical tradition. Miss Dickinson's value to the research scholar, who likes historical
difficulty for its own sake, is slight; she is too near to possess the remoteness of literature. Perhaps her appropriate
setting would be the age of Cowley or of Donne. Yet in
her own historical setting she is, nevertheless, remarkable
and special.

Although the intellectual climate into which she was born,
in 1830, had, as all times have, the features of a transition,
the period was also a major crisis culminating in the war
between the States. After that war, in New England as
well as in the South, spiritual crises were definitely minor
until the First World War.

Yet, a generation before the war of 1861-65, the transformation of New England had begun. When Samuel Slater
in 1790 thwarted the British embargo on mill-machinery
by committing to memory the whole design of a cotton
spinner and bringing it to Massachusetts, he planted the
seed of the "Western spirit." By 1825 its growth in the
East was rank enough to begin choking out the ideas and
habits of living that New England along with Virginia had
kept in unconscious allegiance to Europe. To the casual
observer, perhaps, the New England character of 1830
was largely an eighteenth-century character. But theocracy was on the decline, and industrialism was rising—as
Emerson, in an unusually lucid moment, put it, "Things
are in the saddle." The energy that had built the meeting-
house ran the factory.

Now the idea that moved the theocratic state is the most
interesting historically of all American ideas. It was, of
course, powerful in seventeenth-century England, but in
America, where the long arm of Laud could not reach, it
acquired an unchecked social and political influence. The
important thing to remember about the puritan theocracy
is that it permeated, as it could never have done in England, a whole society. It gave final, definite meaning to
life, the life of pious and impious, of learned and vulgar
alike. It gave—and this is its significance for Emily Dickinson, and in only slightly lesser degree for Melville and
Hawthorne—it gave an heroic proportion and a tragic
mode to the experience of the individual. The history of
the New England theocracy, from Apostle Eliot to Cotton
Mather, is rich in gigantic intellects that broke down—or
so it must appear to an outsider—in a kind of moral decadence and depravity. Socially we may not like the New
England idea. Yet it had an immense, incalculable value
for literature: it dramatized the human soul.

But by 1850 the great fortunes had been made (in the rum,
slave, and milling industries), and New England became
a museum. The whatnots groaned under the load of knick-
knacks, the fine china dogs and cats, the pieces of Oriental
jade, the chips off the leaning tower at Pisa. There were
the rare books and the cosmopolitan learning. It was all
equally displayed as the evidence of a superior culture.
The Gilded Age had already begun. But culture, in the
true sense, was disappearing. Where the old order, formi-

dable as it was, had held all this personal experience, this eclectic excitement, in a comprehensible whole, the new order tended to flatten it out in a common experience that was not quite in common; it exalted more and more the personal and the unique in the interior sense. Where the old-fashioned puritans got together on a rigid doctrine, and could thus be individualists in manners, the nineteenth-century New Englander, lacking a genuine religious center, began to be a social conformist. The common idea of the Redemption, for example, was replaced by the conformist idea of respectability among neighbors whose spiritual disorder, not very evident at the surface, was becoming acute. A great idea was breaking up, and society was moving towards external uniformity, which is usually the measure of the spiritual sterility inside.

At this juncture Emerson came upon the scene: the Lucifer of Concord, he had better be called hereafter, for he was the light-bearer who could see nothing but light, and was fearfully blind. He looked around and saw the uniformity of life, and called it the routine of tradition, the tyranny of the theological idea. The death of Priam put an end to the hope of Troy, but it was a slight feat of arms for the doughty Pyrrhus; Priam was an old gentleman and almost dead. So was theocracy; and Emerson killed it. In this way he accelerated a tendency that he disliked. It was a great intellectual mistake. By it Emerson unwittingly became the prophet of a piratical industrialism, a consequence of his own transcendental individualism that he could not foresee. He was hoist with his own petard.

He discredited more than any other man the puritan drama of the soul. The age that followed, from 1865 on, expired in a genteel secularism, a mildly didactic order of feeling whose ornaments were Lowell, Longfellow, and Holmes. "After Emerson had done his work," says Mr. Robert Penn Warren, "any tragic possibilities in that culture were dissipated." Hawthorne alone in his time kept pure, in the primitive terms, the primitive vision; he brings the puritan tragedy to its climax. Man, measured by a great idea outside himself, is found wanting. But for Emerson man is greater than any idea and, being himself the Over-Soul, is innately perfect; there is no struggle because—I state the Emersonian doctrine, which is very slippery, in its extreme terms—because there is no possibility of error. There is no drama in human character because there is no tragic fault. It is not surprising, then, that after Emerson New England literature tastes like a sip of cambric tea. Its center of vision has disappeared. There is Hawthorne looking back, there is Emerson looking not too clearly at anything ahead: Emily Dickinson, who has in her something of both, comes in somewhere between.

With the exception of Poe there is no other American poet whose work so steadily emerges, under pressure of certain disintegrating obsessions, from the framework of moral character. There is none of whom it is truer to say that the poet *is* the poetry. Perhaps this explains the zeal of her admirers for her biography; it explains, in part at least, the gratuitous mystery that Mrs. Bianchi, a niece of the poet and her official biographer, has made of her life. The devoted controversy that Miss Josephine Pollitt and Miss Genevieve Taggard started a few years ago with their excellent books shows the extent to which the critics feel the intimate connection of her life and work. Admiration and affection are pleased to linger over the tokens of a great

life; but the solution to the Dickinson enigma is peculiarly superior to fact.

The meaning of the identity—which we merely feel—of character and poetry would be exceedingly obscure, even if we could draw up a kind of Binet correlation between the two sets of "facts." Miss Dickinson was a recluse; but her poetry is rich with a profound and varied experience. Where did she get it? Now some of the biographers, nervous in the presence of this discrepancy, are eager to find her a love affair, and I think this search is due to a modern prejudice: we believe that no virgin can know enough to write poetry. We shall never learn where she got the rich quality of her mind. The moral image that we have of Miss Dickinson stands out in every poem; it is that of a dominating spinster whose very sweetness must have been formidable. Yet her poetry constantly moves within an absolute order of truths that overwhelmed her simply because to her they were unalterably fixed. It is dangerous to assume that her "life," which to the biographers means the thwarted love affair she is supposed to have had, gave to her poetry a decisive direction. It is even more dangerous to suppose that it made her a poet.

Poets are mysterious, but a poet when all is said is not much more mysterious than a banker. The critics remain spellbound by the technical license of her verse and by the puzzle of her personal life. Personality is a legitimate interest because it is an incurable interest, but legitimate as a personal interest only; it will never give up the key to anyone's verse. Used to that end, the interest is false. "It is apparent," writes Mr. Conrad Aiken, "that Miss Dickinson became a hermit by deliberate and conscious choice"—a sensible remark that we cannot repeat too often. If it were necessary to explain her seclusion with disappointment in love, there would remain the discrepancy between what the seclusion produced and the seclusion looked at as a cause. The effect, which is her poetry, would imply the whole complex of anterior fact, which was the social and religious structure of New England.

The problem to be kept in mind is thus the meaning of her "deliberate and conscious" decision to withdraw from life to her upstairs room. This simple fact is not very important. But that it must have been her sole way of acting out her part in the history of her culture, which made, with the variations of circumstance, a single demand upon all its representatives—this is of the greatest consequence. All pity for Miss Dickinson's "starved life" is misdirected. Her life was one of the richest and deepest ever lived on this continent.

When she went upstairs and closed the door, she mastered life by rejecting it. Others in their way had done it before; still others did it later. If we suppose—which is to suppose the improbable—that the love-affair precipitated the seclusion, it was only a pretext; she would have found another. Mastery of the world by rejecting the world was the doctrine, even if it was not always the practice, of Jonathan Edwards and Cotton Mather. It is the meaning of fate in Hawthorne: his people are fated to withdraw from the world and to be destroyed. And it is one of the great themes of Henry James.

There is a moral emphasis that connects Hawthorne, James, and Miss Dickinson, and I think it is instructive. Between Hawthorne and James lies an epoch. The temptation to sin, in Hawthorne, is, in James, transformed into the temptation not to do the "decent thing." A whole world-scheme, a complete cosmic background, has shrunk to the dimensions of the individual conscience. This epoch between Hawthorne and James lies in Emerson. James found himself in the post-Emersonian world, and he could not, without violating the detachment proper to an artist, undo Emerson's work; he had that kind of intelligence which refuses to break its head against history. There was left to him only the value, the historic rôle, of rejection. He could merely escape from the physical presence of that world which, for convenience, we may call Emerson's world: he could only take his Americans to Europe upon the vain quest of something that they had lost at home. His characters, fleeing the wreckage of the puritan culture, preserved only their honor. Honor became a sort of forlorn hope struggling against the forces of "pure fact" that had got loose in the middle of the century. Honor alone is a poor weapon against nature, being too personal, finical, and proud, and James achieved a victory by refusing to engage the whole force of the enemy.

In Emily Dickinson the conflict takes place on a vaster field. The enemy to all those New Englanders was Nature, and Miss Dickinson saw into the character of this enemy more deeply than any of the others. The general symbol of Nature, for her, is Death, and her weapon against Death is the entire powerful dumb-show of the puritan theology led by Redemption and Immortality. Morally speaking, the problem for James and Miss Dickinson is similar. But her advantages were greater than his. The advantages lay in the availability to her of the puritan ideas on the theological plane.

These ideas, in her poetry, are momently assailed by the disintegrating force of Nature (appearing as Death) which, while constantly breaking them down, constantly redefines and strengthens them. The values are purified by the triumphant withdrawal from Nature, by their power to recover from Nature. The poet attains to a mastery over experience by facing its utmost implications. There is the clash of powerful opposites, and in all great poetry—for Emily Dickinson is a great poet—it issues in a tension between abstraction and sensation in which the two elements may be, of course, distinguished logically, but not really. We are shown our roots in Nature by examining our differences with Nature; we are renewed by Nature without being delivered into her hands. When it is possible for a poet to do this for us with the greatest imaginative comprehension, a possibility that the poet cannot himself create, we have the perfect literary situation. Only a few times in the history of English poetry has this situation come about, notably, the period between about 1580 and the Restoration. There was a similar age in New England from which emerged two talents of the first order— Hawthorne and Emily Dickinson.

There is an epoch between James and Miss Dickinson. But between her and Hawthorne there exists a difference of intellectual quality. She lacks almost radically the power to seize upon and understand abstractions for their own sake; she does not separate them from the sensuous illuminations that she is so marvelously adept at; like Donne, she *perceives abstraction* and *thinks sensation.* But Hawthorne was a master of ideas, within a limited range; this narrowness confined him to his own kind of life, his own society,

and out of it grew his typical forms of experience, his steady, almost obsessed vision of man; it explains his depth and intensity. Yet he is always conscious of the abstract, doctrinal aspect of his mind, and when his vision of action and emotion is weak, his work becomes didactic. Now Miss Dickinson's poetry often runs into quasi-homiletic forms, but it is never didactic. Her very ignorance, her lack of formal intellectual training, preserved her from the risk that imperiled Hawthorne. She cannot reason at all. She can only *see.* It is impossible to imagine what she might have done with drama or fiction; for, not approaching the puritan temper and through it the puritan myth, through human action, she is able to grasp the terms of the myth directly and by a feat that amounts almost to anthropomorphism, to give them a luminous tension, a kind of drama, among themselves.

One of the perfect poems in English is **"The Chariot,"** and it illustrates better than anything else she wrote the special quality of her mind. I think it will illuminate the tendency of this discussion:

> Because I could not stop for death,
> He kindly stopped for me;
> The carriage held but just ourselves
> And immortality.
>
> We slowly drove, he knew no haste,
> And I had put away
> My labor, and my leisure too,
> For his civility.
>
> We passed the school where children played,
> Their lessons scarcely done;
> We passed the fields of gazing grain,
> We passed the setting sun.
>
> We paused before a house that seemed
> A swelling of the ground;
> The roof was scarcely visible,
> The cornice but a mound.
> Since then 'tis centuries; but each
> Feels shorter than the day
> I first surmised the horses' heads
> Were toward eternity.

If the word great means anything in poetry, this poem is one of the greatest in the English language. The rhythm charges with movement the pattern of suspended action back of the poem. Every image is precise and, moreover, not merely beautiful, but fused with the central idea. Every image extends and intensifies every other. The third stanza especially shows Miss Dickinson's power to fuse, into a single order of perception, a heterogeneous series: the children, the grain, and the setting sun (time) have the same degree of credibility; the first subtly preparing for the last. The sharp *gazing* before *grain* instills into nature a cold vitality of which the qualitative richness has infinite depth. The content of death in the poem eludes explicit definition. He is a gentleman taking a lady out for a drive. But note the restraint that keeps the poet from carrying this so far that it becomes ludicrous and incredible; and note the subtly interfused erotic motive, which the idea of death has presented to most romantic poets, love being a symbol interchangeable with death. The terror of death is objectified through this figure of the genteel driver, who is made ironically to serve the end of Immortality. This is the heart of the poem: she has presented a typical Christian theme in its final irresolution, without making any final statements about it. There is no solution to the problem; there can be only a presentation of it in the full context of intellect and feeling. A construction of the human will, elaborated with all the abstracting powers of the mind, is put to the concrete test of experience: the idea of immortality is confronted with the fact of physical disintegration. We are not told what to think; we are told to look at the situation.

The framework of the poem is, in fact, the two abstractions, mortality and eternity, which are made to associate in equality with the images: she sees the ideas, and thinks the perceptions. She did, of course, nothing of the sort; but we must use the logical distinctions, even to the extent of paradox, if we are to form any notion of this rare quality of mind. She could not in the proper sense think at all, and unless we prefer the feeble poetry of moral ideas that flourished in New England in the eighties, we must conclude that her intellectual deficiency contributed at least negatively to her great distinction. Miss Dickinson is probably the only Anglo-American poet of her century whose work exhibits the perfect literary situation—in which is possible the fusion of sensibility and thought. Unlike her contemporaries, she never succumbed to her ideas, to easy solutions, to her private desires.

Philosophers must deal with ideas, but the trouble with most nineteenth-century poets is too much philosophy; they are nearer to being philosophers than poets, without being in the true sense either. Tennyson is a good example of this; so is Arnold in his weak moments. There have been poets like Milton and Donne, who were not spoiled for their true business by leaning on a rational system of ideas, who understood the poetic use of ideas. Tennyson tried to mix a little Huxley and a little Broad Church, without understanding either Broad Church or Huxley; the result was fatal, and what is worse, it was shallow. Miss Dickinson's ideas were deeply imbedded in her character, not taken from the latest tract. A conscious cultivation of ideas in poetry is always dangerous, and even Milton escaped ruin only by having an instinct for what in the deepest sense he understood. Even at that there is a remote quality in Milton's approach to his material, in his treatment of it; in the nineteenth century, in an imperfect literary situation where literature was confused with documentation, he might have been a pseudo-philosopher-poet. It is difficult to conceive Emily Dickinson and John Donne succumbing to rumination about "problems"; they would not have written at all.

Neither the feeling nor the style of Miss Dickinson belongs to the seventeenth century; yet between her and Donne there are remarkable ties. Their religious ideas, their abstractions, are momently toppling from the rational plane to the level of perception. The ideas, in fact, are no longer the impersonal religious symbols created anew in the heat of emotion, that we find in poets like Herbert and Vaughan. They have become, for Donne, the terms of personality; they are mingled with the miscellany of sensation. In Miss Dickinson, as in Donne, we may detect a singularly morbid concern, not for religious truth, but for personal revelation. The modern word is self-exploitation. It is egoism grown irresponsible in religion and decadent in morals. In religion it is blasphemy; in society it means usually that culture is not self-contained and sufficient, that the spiritual community is breaking up. This is, along with some other features that do not concern us here, the perfect literary situation.

Personal revelation of the kind that Donne and Miss Dickinson strove for, in the effort to understand their relation to the world, is a feature of all great poetry; it is probably the hidden motive for writing. It is the effort of the individual to live apart from a cultural tradition that no longer sustains him. But this culture, which I now wish to discuss a little, is indispensable: there is a great deal of shallow nonsense in modern criticism which holds that poetry—and this is a half-truth that is worse than false—is essentially revolutionary. It is only indirectly revolutionary: the intellectual and religious background of an age no longer contains the whole spirit, and the poet proceeds to examine that background in terms of immediate experience. But the background is necessary; otherwise all the arts (not only poetry) would have to rise in a vacuum. Poetry does not dispense with tradition; it probes the deficiencies of a tradition. But it must have a tradition to probe. It is too bad that Arnold did not explain his doctrine, that poetry is a criticism of life, from the viewpoint of its background: we should have been spared an era of academic misconception, in which criticism of life meant a diluted pragmatism, the criterion of which was respectability. The poet in the true sense "criticizes" his tradition, either as such, or indirectly by comparing it with something that is about to replace it; he does what the root-meaning of the verb implies—he *discerns* its real elements and thus establishes its value, by putting it to the test of experience.

What is the nature of a poet's culture? Or, to put the question properly, what is the meaning of culture for poetry? All the great poets become the material of what we popularly call culture; we study them to acquire it. It is clear that Addison was more cultivated than Shakespeare; nevertheless Shakespeare is a finer source of culture than Addison. What is the meaning of this? Plainly it is that learning has never had anything to do with culture except instrumentally: the poet must be exactly literate enough to write down fully and precisely what he has to say, but no more. The source of a poet's true culture lies back of the paraphernalia of culture, and not all the historical activity of an enlightened age can create it.

A culture cannot be consciously created. It is an available source of ideas that are imbedded in a complete and homogeneous society. The poet finds himself balanced upon the moment when such a world is about to fall, when it threatens to run out into looser and less self-sufficient impulses. This world order is assimilated, in Miss Dickinson, as medievalism was in Shakespeare, to the poetic vision; it is brought down from abstraction to personal sensibility.

In this connection it may be said that the prior conditions for great poetry, given a great talent, may be reduced to two: the thoroughness of the poet's discipline in an objective system of truth, and his lack of consciousness of such a discipline. For this discipline is a number of fundamental ideas the origin of which the poet does not know; they give form and stability to his fresh perceptions of the world; and he cannot shake them off. This is his culture, and like Tennyson's God it is nearer than hands and feet. With reasonable certainty we unearth the elements of Shakespeare's culture, and yet it is equally certain—so innocent was he of his own resources—that he would not know what our discussion is about. He appeared at the collapse of the medieval system as a rigid pattern of life, but that pattern remained in Shakespeare what Shelley called a "fixed point of reference" for his sensibility. Miss Dickinson, as we have seen, was born into the equilibrium of an old and a new order. Puritanism could not be to her what it had been to the generation of Cotton Mather—a body of absolute truths; it was an unconscious discipline timed to the pulse of her life.

The perfect literary situation: it produces, because it is rare, a special and perhaps the most distinguished kind of poet. I am not trying to invent a new critical category. Such poets are never very much alike on the surface; they show us all the varieties of poetic feeling; and like other poets they resist all classification but that of temporary convenience. But, I believe, Miss Dickinson and John Donne would have this in common: their sense of the natural world is not blunted by a too rigid system of ideas; yet the ideas, the abstractions, their education or their intellectual heritage, are not so weak as to let their immersion in nature, or their purely personal quality, get out of control. The two poles of the mind are not separately visible; we infer them from the lucid tension that may be most readily illustrated by polar activity. There is no thought as such at all; nor is there feeling; there is that unique focus of experience which is at once neither and both.

Like Miss Dickinson, Shakespeare is without opinions; his peculiar merit is also deeply involved in his failure to think about anything; his meaning is not in the content of his expression; it is in the tension of the dramatic relations of his characters. This kind of poetry is at the opposite of intellectualism. (Miss Dickinson is obscure and difficult, but that is not intellectualism.) To T. W. Higginson, the editor of *The Atlantic Monthly,* who tried to advise her, she wrote that she had no education. In any sense that Higginson could understand, it was quite true. His kind of education was the conscious cultivation of abstractions. She did not reason about the world she saw; she merely saw it. The "ideas" implicit in the world within her rose up, concentrated in her immediate perception.

That kind of world at present has for us something of the fascination of a buried city. There is none like it. When such worlds exist, when such cultures flourish, they support not only the poet but all members of society. For, from these, the poet differs only in his gift for exhibiting the structure, the internal lineaments, of his culture by threatening to tear them apart: a process that concentrates the symbolic emotions of society while it seems to attack them. The poet may hate his age; he may be an outcast like Villon; but this world is always there as the background to what he has to say. It is the lens through which he brings nature to focus and control—the clarifying medium that concentrates his personal feeling. It is ready-made; he cannot make it; with it, his poetry has a spontaneity and a certainty of direction that, without it, it would lack. No poet could have invented the ideas of **"The Chariot"**; only a great poet could have found their imaginative equivalents. Miss Dickinson was a deep mind writing from a deep culture, and when she came to poetry, she came infallibly.

Infallibly, at her best; for no poet has ever been perfect, nor is Emily Dickinson. Her precision of statement is due to the directness with which the abstract framework of her thought acts upon its unorganized material. The two ele-

ments of her style, considered as point of view, are immortality, or the idea of permanence, and the physical process of death or decay. Her diction has two corresponding features: words of Latin or Greek origin and, sharply opposed to these, the concrete Saxon element. It is this verbal conflict that gives to her verse its high tension; it is not a device deliberately seized upon, but a feeling for language that senses out the two fundamental components of English and their metaphysical relation: the Latin for ideas and the Saxon for perceptions—the peculiar virtue of English as a poetic language.

Like most poets Miss Dickinson often writes out of habit; the style that emerged from some deep exploration of an idea is carried on as verbal habit when she has nothing to say. She indulges herself:

> There's something quieter than sleep
> Within this inner room!
> It wears a sprig upon its breast,
> And will not tell its name.
>
> Some touch it and some kiss it,
> Some chafe its idle hand;
> It has a simple gravity
> I do not understand!
>
> While simple hearted neighbors
> Chat of the "early dead,"
> We, prone to periphrasis,
> Remark that birds have fled!

It is only a pert remark; at best a superior kind of punning—one of the worst specimens of her occasional interest in herself. But she never had the slightest interest in the public. Were four poems or five published in her lifetime? She never felt the temptation to round off a poem for public exhibition. Higginson's kindly offer to make her verse "correct" was an invitation to throw her work into the public ring—the ring of Lowell and Longfellow. He could not see that he was tampering with one of the rarest literary integrities of all time. Here was a poet who had no use for the supports of authorship—flattery and fame; she never needed money.

She had all the elements of a culture that has broken up, a culture that on the religious side takes its place in the museum of spiritual antiquities. Puritanism, as a unified version of the world, is dead; only a remnant of it in trade may be said to survive. In the history of puritanism she comes between Hawthorne and Emerson. She has Hawthorne's matter, which a too irresponsible personality tends to dilute into a form like Emerson's; she is often betrayed by words. But she is not the poet of personal sentiment; she has more to say than she can put down in any one poem. Like Hardy and Whitman she must be read entire; like Shakespeare she never gives up her meaning in a single line.

She is therefore a perfect subject for the kind of criticism which is chiefly concerned with general ideas. She exhibits one of the permanent relations between personality and objective truth, and she deserves the special attention of our time, which lacks that kind of truth.

She has Hawthorne's intellectual toughness, a hard, definite sense of the physical world. The highest flights to God, the most extravagant metaphors of the strange and the remote, come back to a point of casuistry, to a moral dilemma of the experienced world. There is, in spite of the homiletic vein of utterance, no abstract speculation, nor is there a message to society; she speaks wholly to the individual experience. She offers to the unimaginative no riot of vicarious sensation; she has no useful maxims for men of action. Up to this point her resemblance to Emerson is slight: poetry is a sufficient form of utterance, and her devotion to it is pure. But in Emily Dickinson the puritan world is no longer self-contained; it is no longer complete; her sensibility exceeds its dimensions. She has trimmed down its supernatural proportions; it has become a morality; instead of the tragedy of the spirit there is a commentary upon it. Her poetry is a magnificent personal confession, blasphemous and, in its self-revelation, its honesty, almost obscene. It comes out of an intellectual life towards which it feels no moral responsibility. Cotton Mather would have burnt her for a witch. (pp. 198-213)

Allen Tate, "Emily Dickinson," in his On the Limits of Poetry, Selected Essays: 1928-1948, *William Morrow & Co., 1948, pp. 197-213.*

George F. Whicher   (essay date 1931)

[*Whicher is an American literature scholar and the author of* This Was a Poet: A Critical Biography of Emily Dickinson *(1939), a highly regarded early biography of Dickinson. In the following excerpt, he asserts that Dickinson's main interests were the mind and sensuous experience. According to Whicher, "her special faculty was to stand . . . undismayed in the midst of the mind's convulsions."*]

Had [Dickinson] belonged to an earlier generation, she might have lapsed into a mystical fervor of self-abnegation, for the Puritan mind has always been partial to martyrdom. Vestiges of the familiar attitude are apparent in her poems; in exalted moments she does sublimate and transfigure her renunciation, speak of herself as "Queen of Calvary," and look to another life for recompense of her woes. But the God of her fathers, when she most wished to lean on Him, was disconcertingly not there. She was baffled by the emptiness, but did not hesitate to record that it was emptiness. For the continued emergency of her life "microscopes were prudent," and under the searching intensity of her vision the seeming granite of traditional faith crumbled into incoherent sand. She enjoyed playing with the fine inventions of orthodox belief, sometimes in a mood of mockery that makes her seem almost contemporary with the "bad girl" poets of the nineteen-twenties. Elsewhere the unfulfilled need of heaven wrings her heart.

"Protestantism," as Lowell was remarking, "had made its fortune and no longer protested." It had no reassurances to offer in a soul's crisis. But there were other sources to keep the spirit alive. When the reservoirs of faith run dry, men may refresh their souls with the spiritual sanity that, like dew, lies on the little things of earth, on grass and stone, tree and flower. In fullness of physical contact with nature there is a healing power, as Wordsworth and other beleaguered poets after him had discovered. The senses, the old enemies of the soul, may in a time of soul's distress become its ministers. To sensuous experience and to the working of man's mind, if one can command detachment enough to regard the mind's activities as a second kind of

external experience, those who wish to live freshly in an age of exhausted formulas must turn. These are the realities that do not have to be believed into being. Emily Dickinson's poetry is compounded of these two elements.

For the cultivation of the senses she relied on the simplest things. The forms of art were almost unknown to her, but there was always unspoiled nature, viewed not in its cosmic but in its small and intimate aspects. Thunderstorm, snow, and sunset were favorite themes, yet nearly always related to some angle of her house and garden. She did not generalize successfully. "Nature rarer uses yellow than another hue" is one of the oddest observations ever made by a poet with eyes sensitive to color and a meadow outside her window. Her miracles of exactitude were renderings of motion and atmosphere: the tone and tempo of a bee in clover, the whir of a humming-bird's wings, the air of a bluejay, a snake's movement in the grass. For these tiny fragments of fact she found perfect expression. One feels that she watched them with the intensity of interest that a soldier under fire is said to feel in the smallest inconsequential things around him, or an invalid in the crawling of a fly on the window pane. They may have been for her a relief for piercing memories, the equivalent of Hamlet's tablets.

Her sensitivity to outward nature is remarkable, but her most extraordinary gift was her power to discriminate shades and varieties of "inner weather." In her psychological poetry the New England genius for introspection surpassed itself in pure objectivity. That curious thing, her mind, so amusing, so tormenting, endlessly fascinated her attention. She recorded its movements in quaint phrase and homely metaphor that hold in solution the finer essence of wit. Her startling, wry precision amuses us when it is applied to light or indifferent subjects, but the same way of speaking is characteristic of all her poems, even the most poignant and profound. "We make a thing humorous," says Professor Cazamian, "by expressing it with a certain twist, a queer reserve, an inappropriateness, and as it were an unconsciousness of what we all the time feel it to be." That is almost exactly the quality of Emily Dickinson's writing, the tone that she never relinquishes even when she cries from the depths. God is "burglar, banker, father"—the three epithets sound the gamut from laughter to tears. Her special faculty was to stand thus undismayed in the midst of the mind's convulsions, some unshaken particle in her consciousness ready to note with ironical detachment the reeling of the brain. In the strict sense of the word, a sense divorced from all association with the comic, she was a supreme *humorist* of agony.

The phrase will at least remind us that Emily Dickinson's poetry is based on a vital paradox to which no reader can remain indifferent. In the play of mind she found a center about which she was able to integrate her personality. Beside her small perfect circle lies the vast incomplete arc of Whitman. In their different ways both bear witness that even in the drift and distraction of modern times an individual life may attain meaning. For Emily Dickinson that meaning lay in shifting the object of search from the mystic's goal of eternity to the scientist's goal of reality. We recognize in her the last stage of the Puritan's progress from the seventeenth century to our own times. (pp. 386-88)

George F. Whicher, "Poetry After the Civil

War," *in* American Writers on American Literature, *edited by John Macy, Horace Liveright, Inc., 1931, pp. 374-88.*

R. P. Blackmur (essay date 1937)

[*Blackmur was a leading American literary critic of the twentieth century. His early essays on the poetry of such contemporaries as T. S. Eliot, W. B. Yeats, Wallace Stevens, and Ezra Pound were immediately recognized for their acute and exacting attention to diction, metaphor, and symbol. Consequently, he was linked to the New Critics, who believed that literature was not a manifestation of sociology, psychology, or morality, and could not be evaluated in the terms of any nonliterary discipline. Rather, a literary work constituted an independent object to be closely analyzed for its strictly formal devices and internal meanings. Blackmur distinguished himself from this group of critics, however, by broadening his analyses through discussions which explored a given work's relevance to society. In the following excerpt from an essay that originally appeared in the* Southern Review *in 1937, Blackmur offers a negative assessment of Dickinson's language and imagery. He emphasizes that her poems are "exercises, and no more," and that if some succeed, it is by accident.*]

[Something] over two-thirds of Emily Dickinson's nine hundred odd printed poems are exercises, and no more, some in the direction of poetry, and some not. The object is usually in view, though some of the poems are but exercises in pursuit of an unknown object, but the means of attainment are variously absent, used in error, or ill-chosen. The only weapon constantly in use is . . . the natural aptitude for language; and it is hardly surprising to find that that weapon, used alone and against great odds, should occasionally produce an air of frantic strain instead of strength, of conspicuous oddity instead of indubitable rightness.

Let us take for a first example a reasonably serious poem on one of the dominant Dickinson themes, the obituary theme of the great dead—a theme to which Hawthorne and Henry James were equally addicted—and determine if we can where its failure lies.

> More life went out, when He went,
> Than ordinary breath,
> Lit with a finer phosphor
> Requiring in the quench
>
> A power of renownéd cold—
> The climate of the grave
> A temperature just adequate
> So anthracite to live.
>
> For some an ampler zero,
> A frost more needle keen
> Is necessary to reduce
> The Ethiop within.
>
> Others extinguish easier—
> A gnat's minutest fan
> Sufficient to obliterate
> A tract of citizen.

The first thing to notice—a thing characteristic of exercises—is that the order or plot of the elements of the poem is not that of a complete poem; the movement of the parts is downward and toward a disintegration of the effect wanted. A good poem so constitutes its parts as at once to contain them and to deliver or release by the psychological force of their sequence the full effect only when the poem is done. Here the last quatrain is obviously wrongly placed; it comes like an afterthought, put in to explain why the third stanza was good. It should have preceded the third stanza, and perhaps with the third stanza—both of course in revised form—might have come at the very beginning, or perhaps in suspension between the first and second stanzas. Such suggestions throw the poem into disorder; actually the disorder is already there. It is not the mere arrangement of stanzas that is at fault; the units in disorder are deeper in the material, perhaps in the compositional elements of the conception, perhaps in the executive elements of the image-words used to afford circulation to the poem, perhaps elsewhere in the devices not used but wanted. The point for emphasis is that it is hard to believe that a conscientious poet could have failed to see that no amount of correction and polish could raise this exercise to the condition of a mature poem. The material is all there—the inspiration and the language; what it requires is a thorough revision—a re-seeing calculated to compose in objective form the immediacy and singleness of effect which the poet no doubt herself felt.

Perhaps we may say—though the poem is not near so bad an example as many—that the uncomposed disorder is accepted by the poet because the poem was itself written automatically. To the sensitive hand and expectant ear words will arrange themselves, however gotten hold of, and seem to breed by mere contact. The brood is the meaning we catch up to. Is not this really automatic writing *tout court?* Most of the Dickinson poems seem to have been initially as near automatic writing as may be. The bulk remained automatic, subject to correction and multiplication of detail. Others, which reach intrinsic being, have been patterned, inscaped, injected one way or another with the élan or elixir of the poet's dominant attitudes. The poem presently examined remains too much in the automatic choir; the élan is there, which is why we examine it at all, but without the additional advantage of craft it fails to carry everything before it.

The second stanza of the poem is either an example of automatic writing unrelieved, or is an example of bad editing, or both. Its only meaning is in the frantic strain toward meaning—a strain so frantic that all responsibility toward the shapes and primary significance of words was ignored. "A temperature just adequate / So Anthracite to live" even if it were intelligible, which it is not, would be beyond bearing awkward to read. It is not bad grammar alone that works ill; words sometimes make their own grammar good on the principle of ineluctable association—when the association forces the words into meaning. Here we have fiat meaning. The word *anthracite* is the crux of the trouble. Anthracite is coal, is hard, is black, gives heat, and has a rushing crisp sound; it has a connection with carbuncle and with a fly-borne disease of which one symptom resembles a carbuncle; it is stratified in the earth, is formed of organic matter as a consequence of enormous pressure through geologic time; etc., etc. One or several of these senses may contribute to the poem; but because the context does not denominate it, it does not appear which. My own guess is that Emily Dickinson wanted the effect of something hard and cold and perhaps black and took *anthracite* off the edge of her vocabulary largely because she liked the sound. This is another way of saying that *anthracite* is an irresponsible product of her aptitude for language.

The word *phosphor* in the third line of the first stanza is a responsible example of the same aptitude. It is moreover a habitual symbol word rather than a sudden flight; it is part of her regular machinery for concentrating meaning in a partly willful, partly natural symbol. Phosphor or phosphorus—in various forms of the word—is used by Emily Dickinson at least twelve times to represent, from the like characteristic of the metal, the self-illumining and perhaps self-consuming quality of the soul. The "renownéd cold," "ampler zero," and "frost more needle keen," are also habitual images used to represent the coming or transition of death as effected seasonally in nature and, by analogue, in man. Examples of these or associated words so used run to the hundreds. The "gnat" in the fourth stanza with his "minutest fan" (of cold air?) is another example of a portmanteau image always ready to use to turn on the microcosmic view. In the word *Ethiop* in the third stanza we have a mixture of a similar general term—this time drawn from the outside and unknown world—and a special significance released and warranted by the poem. Ethiops live in tropical Africa; and we have here a kind of synecdoche which makes the Ethiop himself so full of heat that it would take great cold to quench it. That the contrary would be the case does not affect the actuality of the image, but makes it more intriguing and gives it an odd, accidental character. The misconception does, however, bring out the flavor of a wrong image along with the shadow of the right one; and it is a question whether the flavor will not last longer in the memory than the shadow. Another nice question is involved in the effect of the *order* of the verbs used to represent the point of death: *quench, reduce, extinguish, obliterate.* The question is, are not these verbs pretty nearly interchangeable? Would not any other verb of destructive action do just as well? In short, is there any word in this poem which either fits or contributes to the association at all exactly? I think not—with the single exception of "phosphor."

The burden of these observations on words will I hope have made itself plain; it is exactly the burden of the observations on the form of the whole poem. The poem is an exercise whichever way you take it: an approach to the organization of its material but by no means a complete organization. It is almost a rehearsal—a doing over of something not done—and a variation of stock intellectual elements in an effort to accomplish an adventure in feeling. The reader can determine for himself—if he can swallow both the anthracite and the gnat—how concrete and actual the adventure was made.

Perhaps determination will be assisted by a few considerations on Emily Dickinson's vocabulary as a whole and how it splits up under inspection into different parts which are employed for different functions, and which operate *from*, as it were, different levels of sensibility. It is not a large vocabulary compared to Whitman's, nor rich like Melville's, nor perspicuous like Henry James's, nor robust like Mark Twain's. Nor is it a homogeneous vocabulary; its unity is specious for the instance rather than organic for the whole of her work. Its constant elements are mostly found, like most of the poems, in arrangements, not in

compositions. The pattern of association is kaleidoscopic and extraneous far more frequently than it is crystalline and inwardly compelled. What it is, is a small, rigidly compartmented vocabulary of general and conventional groups of terms, plus a moderately capacious vocabulary of homely, acute, directly felt words from which the whole actualizing strength of her verse is drawn. The extraordinary thing is how much of the general and conventional vocabulary got activated by the homely word. In the fragment about renunciation, "piercing" and "letting go" are examples. The depressing thing is how much of the conventional vocabulary was not activated by the homely word but distracted by the homely word strained odd.

Let us list a few of the conventional types that turn up most often and most conspicuously. The most conspicuous of all is the vocabulary of romance royalty, fairy-tale kings, queens and courts, and the general language of chivalry. Emily Dickinson was as fond as Shakespeare of words like *imperial, sovereign, dominion,* and the whole collection of terms for rank and degree. Probably she got them more from Scott and the Bible and the Hymnal than from Shakespeare. There is none of Shakespeare's specific and motivating sense of kings and princes as the focus of society, and none of his rhetoric of power; there is nothing tragic in Emily Dickinson's royal vocabulary. On the other hand, there is a great deal of vague and general assumption that royalty is a good thing and that escape into the goodness of it is available to everyone: like the colorful escape into romance and fairy-tale. Besides this general assumption, and more important, there is continuous resort to the trope of heavenly coronation for the individual and a continuous ascription of imperial titles and a chivalric, almost heraldic, code to God and the angels, to flowers and bees. This vocabulary, taken as a whole, provides a mixed formula which rehearsed like a ritual or just a verbal exercise sometimes discovers a poem and sometimes does not. I extract one stanza as example.

> He put the belt around my life,—
> I heard the buckle snap,
> And turned away, imperial,
> My lifetime folding up
> Deliberate as a duke would do
> A kingdom's title-deed,—
> Henceforth a dedicated sort,
> A member of the cloud.

Other vocabularies include words taken from sewing and the kinds of cloth used in women's clothes—*stitch, seam, needle, dimity, serge, silk, satin, brocade,* etc.; legal words—*tenant, rent, litigant, title,* etc.; the names of jewels—*diamond, ruby, pearl, opal, amethyst, beryl,* and *amber;* words taken from the Civil War—*bayonet,* various images of musket and cannon fire, and of the soldier's heroism; words taken from sea-borne commerce—*port, harbor,* various kinds of ships and the parts of ships; the names of distant places—especially of mountains and volcanoes; and, not to exhaust but merely to stop the list, words taken from the transcendental theology of her time. It should be noted that only the first, second, and possibly the last of these groups named or activated anything she found in her daily life; but they had, like the vocabulary of royalty, everything to do with the stretching of her daily fancy, and they made a constant provision, a constant rough filling and occupation, for what did actually concern her—her prevision of death and her insight into the spiritual life. This is another way of saying that in what is quantitatively the great part of her work Emily Dickinson did not put the life of meaning into her words; she leaned on the formulas of words in the hope that the formulas would fully express what she felt privately—sometimes the emotion of escape and sometimes the conviction of assent—in her own self-centered experience. This is partly the mode of prayer, partly the mode of nonce-popular romance (which must always be repeated), and partly the mode of the pathetic fallacy applied to form—the fiat mode of expression which asserts that the need is equivalent to the object, that if you need words to mean something then they will necessarily mean it. But it is not except by accident the mode of the rational or actualizing imagination. The extraordinary thing in Emily Dickinson is, to repeat, that fragmentary accidents occur so often, and the terrible thing is that they need not have been accidents at all. The net result may be put as a loss of consistent or sustained magnitude equal to the impulse. We have a verse in great body that is part terror, part vision, part insight and observation, which must yet mostly be construed as a kind of *vers de société* of the soul—not in form or finish but in achievement.

This is to say that control was superficial—in the use, not the hearts, of words. We saw an example in the word *anthracite* a little above. Let us present two more examples and stop. We have the word *plush* in different poems as follows. "One would as soon assault a plush or violate a star . . . Time's consummate plush . . . A dog's belated feet like intermittent plush . . . We step like plush, we stand like snow . . . Sentences of plush." The word is on the verge of bursting with wrong meaning, and on account of the bursting, the stress with which the poet employed it, we are all prepared to accept it, and indeed do accept it, when suddenly we realize the wrongness, that "plush" was not what was meant at all, but was a substitute for it. The word has been distorted but not transformed on the page; which is to say it is not in substantial control. Yet it is impossible not to believe that to Emily Dickinson's ear it meant what it said and what could not otherwise be said.

The use of the word *purple* is another example of a word's getting out of control through the poet's failure to maintain an objective feeling of responsibility toward language. We have, in different poems, a "purple host" meaning "soldiers"; "purple territories," associated with salvation in terms of "Pizarro's shores"; "purple" meaning "dawn"; a "purple finger" probably meaning "shadow"; a purple raveling of cloud at sunset; ships of purple on seas of daffodil; the sun quenching in purple; a purple brook; purple traffic; a peacock's purple train; purple none can avoid—meaning death; no suitable purple to put on the hills; a purple tar wrecked in peace; the purple well of eternity; the purple or royal state of a corpse; the Purple of Ages; a sowing of purple seed which is inexplicable; the purple of the summer; the purple wheel of faith; day's petticoat of purple; etc., etc. Taken cumulatively, this is neither a distortion nor a transformation of sense; it is very near an obliteration of everything but a favorite sound, meaning something desirable, universal, distant, and immediate. I choose the word as an example not because it is particularly bad—it is not; it is relatively harmless—but because it is typical and happens to be easy to follow in unexpanded quotation. It is thoroughly representative of Emily Dickinson's habit of so employing certain favorite words that

their discriminated meanings tend to melt into the single sentiment of self-expression. We can feel the sentiment but we have lost the meaning. The willing reader can see for himself the analogous process taking place—with slightly different final flavors—in word after word: for example in the words *dateless, pattern, compass, circumference, ecstasy, immortality, white, ruby, crescent, peninsula,* and *spice.* The meanings become the conventions of meanings, the asserted agreement that meaning is there. That is the end toward which Emily Dickinson worked, willy-nilly, in her words. If you can accept the assertion for the sake of the knack—not the craft—with which it is made you will be able to read much more of her work than if you insist on actual work done.

But there were, to repeat and to conclude, three saving accidents at work in the body of Emily Dickinson's work sufficient to redeem in fact a good many poems to the state of their original intention. There was the accident of cultural crisis, the skeptical faith and desperately experimental mood, which both released and drove the poet's sensibility to express the crisis personally. There was the accident that the poet had so great an aptitude for language that it could seldom be completely lost in the conventional formulas toward which her meditating mind ran. And there was the third accident that the merest self-expression, or the merest statement of recognition or discrimination or vision, may sometimes also be, by the rule of unanimity and a common tongue, its best objective expression.

When two or more of the accidents occur simultaneously a poem or a fragment of a poem may be contrived. . . .

> Presentiment is that long shadow on the lawn
> Indicative that suns go down;
> The notice to the startled grass
> That darkness is about to pass.

If the reader compares this poem with Marvell's "To His Coy Mistress," he will see what can be gotten out of the same theme when fully expanded. The difference is of magnitude; the magnitude depends on craft; the Dickinson poem stops, Marvell's is completed. What happens when the poem does not stop may be shown in the following example of technical and moral confusion.

> I got so I could hear his name
> Without—
> Tremendous gain!
> That stop-sensation in my soul,
> And thunder in the room.
>
> I got so I could walk across
> That angle in the floor
> Where he turned—so—and I turned how—
> And all our sinew tore.
>
> I got so I could stir the box
> In which his letters grew—
> Without that forcing in my breath
> As staples driven through.
>
> Could dimly recollect a Grace—
> I think they called it "God,"
> Renowned to ease extremity
> When formula had failed—
>
> And shape my hands petition's way—
> Tho' ignorant of word
> That Ordination utters—

My business with the cloud.

If any Power behind it be
Not subject to despair,
To care in some remoter way
For so minute affair
As misery—

Itself too vast for interrupting more,
Supremer than—
Superior to—

Nothing is more remarkable than the variety of inconsistency this effort displays. The first three stanzas are at one level of sensibility and of language and are as good verse as Emily Dickinson ever wrote. The next two stanzas are on a different and fatigued level of sensibility, are bad verse and flat language, and have only a serial connection with the first three. The last stanza, if it is a stanza, is on a still different level of sensibility and not on a recognizable level of language at all: the level of desperate inarticulateness to which no complete response can be articulated in return. One knows from the strength of the first three stanzas what might have been meant to come after and one feels like writing the poem oneself—the basest of all critical temptations. We feel that Emily Dickinson let herself go. The accidents that provided her ability here made a contrivance which was not a poem but a private mixture of first-rate verse, bad verse, and something that is not verse at all. Yet—and this is the point—this contrivance represents in epitome the whole of her work; and whatever judgment you bring upon the epitome you will, I think, be compelled to bring upon the whole.

No judgment is so persuasive as when it is disguised as a statement of facts. I think it is a fact that the failure and success of Emily Dickinson's poetry were uniformly accidental largely because of the private and eccentric nature of her relation to the business of poetry. She was neither a professional poet nor an amateur; she was a private poet who wrote indefatigably as some women cook or knit. Her gift for words and the cultural predicament of her time drove her to poetry instead of antimacassars. Neither her personal education nor the habit of her society as she knew it ever gave her the least inkling that poetry is a rational and objective art and most so when the theme is self-expression. She came, as Mr. Tate says [see excerpt dated 1928-32], at the right time for one kind of poetry: the poetry of sophisticated, eccentric vision. That is what makes her good—in a few poems and many passages representatively great. But she never undertook the great profession of controlling the means of objective expression. That is why the bulk of her verse is not representative but mere fragmentary indicative notation. The pity of it is that the document her whole work makes shows nothing so much as that she had the themes, the insight, the observation, and the capacity for honesty, which had she only known how—or only known why—would have made the major instead of the minor fraction of her verse genuine poetry. But her dying society had no tradition by which to teach her the one lesson she did not know by instinct. (pp. 40-50)

R. P. Blackmur, "Emily Dickinson: Notes on Prejudice and Fact," in his Language as Gesture: Essays in Poetry, *Harcourt Brace Jovanovich, 1952, pp. 25-50.*

Donald F. Connors   (essay date 1942)

[*In the excerpt below, Connors lauds the breadth of Dickinson's poetry and notes her insight in poems dealing with nature, love, and meditation.*]

To make a prairie it takes a clover
    and one bee,—
One clover, and a bee,
And revery.
The revery alone will do
If bees are few.

In the case of Emily Dickinson the revery alone did suffice, and it is the factor largely responsible for the significance of her poems and letters. In the work of no other writer do we find thought and its expression so utterly dependent upon introspection and so many rewarding things springing from it.

The range of her speculation was very wide—from a cricket's chirping to the thunder of infinity—but she possessed a degree of comprehension which enabled her to inclose diversity within circumference and to measure Being in the vital drama of the common day. Dominant in her treatment of all themes is the note of human appeal—no matter how trivial or profound her meditation, it is always of the heart. Essences assume a friendly guise in the world of Emily, and the homely and the commonplace are revealed in true perspective. (p. 624)

She is unique among poets in that her mood is always lyrical; one finds a *person* in her poems rather than ideas examined objectively. This is largely due to the life of seclusion which she led and to her habit of looking inward. Joy and pain she weighed in terms of experience, and her concepts of God were her own. Despite this, her poems are filled with universal appeal. "Parting is all we know of heaven, and all we need of hell," she writes; and there is understanding for all in her words. Under similar circumstances a less gifted writer might have become egocentric and boring, but not Emily. Her words are homely and genuine, and they awaken a responsive chord in the heart of the reader. Suffering gave her vision, and when she speaks of the numbing effect of anguish she finds the words for an experience we all have known.

After great pain a formal feeling comes—
The nerves sit ceremonious like tombs;
The stiff Heart questions—was it He that bore?
And yesterday—or centuries before?

The feet mechanical go round
A wooden way
Of ground or air or Ought,
Regardless grown,
A quartz contentment like a stone.

This is the hour of lead
Remembered if outlived
As freezing persons recollect
The snow—
First chill, then stupor, then
The letting go.

The reader of Emily Dickinson's poems is soon aware of an uplifting effect received from them; she writes with conviction and persuasion. Allen Tate characterizes her work as quasi-homiletic but never didactic [see excerpt dated 1928-32]. The richness of her existence—seeing things in nature which others did not see, serving God with gladness, loving with intensity and self-discipline, recognizing and weighing the reality of immortality—leaves its mark upon the reader. How different from the life of the pedant, or the puritan, or the materialist! It is little wonder that her poetry was strange music to ears accustomed to the decadent literary performances of the Gilded Age. Nor is it in spirit aligned with the verse of the contemporary poets, who are so often agnostic and despairing. Death held no Calvinistic terrors for her, and of life she was "the little tippler." The clash of powerful opposites was present in her, and she had the ability to express penetrating thoughts in simple words and with a mind functioning so as to supply point and climax where life itself seemed to lack these qualities. She was a rebel—rebelling from all that was falsely constricting but never from the Divine Law which she recognized.

No one would hesitate to call Emily Dickinson an outstanding writer on nature. Her letters contain many lovely descriptions of the seasons of the year; and hills, woods, and meadowland fill her poems. Although she sees "New Englandly," as she says, there are deeper tones in her poetry than those which emanate from mere local color or provincialism. The metaphysical note in her writing links her with Wordsworth and Lucretius, and she sings of the Massachusetts countryside with the buoyancy of Herrick. In the end, she is closer in some ways to foreign writers than she is to her fellow-New Englanders. With Emily, beauty for its own sake was enough; she did not feel compelled to justify it with a utilitarian purpose, nor did she hold to the puritan tradition that verse should point a lesson.

Dominant in her nature poems is the friendly spirit. As in the case of St. Francis of Assisi, Brother Sun and the birds were very dear to her. Of the latter she once wrote: "It is lonely without the birds to-day, for it rains badly, and the little poets have no umbrellas." Many birds she mentions, and often with humor and insight. There are "buccaneering" bluebirds, jays who "bark like blue terriers," and even a Jesuitical oriole. Emily found nature an open book which she did not need either Emerson or Thoreau to teach her how to read. The "murmur of a bee" yielded her a witchcraft, and from the lips of such a tiny teacher as the moth she learned many a lesson. Reading her poems, one gathers the impression that she, too, was an inhabitant of the grass, with the flowers and the cricket, and, like the bee, a "debauchee of dew."

As Emily sings of nature, the full force of her creative genius comes into play. Countless images flow from her pen, and always they are new and arresting: frost becomes a "blond assassin," butterflies wear vests like Turks, a fly is a "speck piano," and a snake, "a whip-lash unbraiding in the sun." The pictures are remarkable, both for the beauty and fidelity of their expression and for the air of simple wonder which they contain. In the lines beginning, "I'll tell you how the sun rose," all the sights of sunrise and sunset are gently revealed in words which are as meaningful to children as they are to grown-ups.

But in describing Indian summer, Emily and the world of nature about her seem suddenly to have matured—almost to have grown old. Here one finds no gay picturing of the loveliness of summer, but instead deep feelings born of the sorrow attendant upon its departure. Summer was Emily's favorite season of the year, and the theme of tragedy surrounding a parting that is inevitable is a recurrent one in her work. As a nature poem it bears favorable comparison with the best that English poets have to offer, but it is also significant for what it reveals about its author. A series of symbols portraying both outer and inner experience fill the poem, the opening stanzas representing the day, the closing ones, the heart of the poet. The mounting feeling is kept in check by a familiar attitude on the writer's part—superiority to fate or courage in the face of impending disaster.

> These are the days when birds come back,
> A very few, a bird or two,
> To take a backward look.
> These are the days when skies put on
> The old, old sophistries of June,—
> A blue and gold mistake.
>
> Oh, fraud that cannot cheat the bee,
> Almost thy plausibility
> Induces my belief,
>
> Till ranks of seeds their witness bear,
> And softly through the altered air
> Hurries a timid leaf!
>
> Oh, sacrament of summer days,
> Oh, last communion in the haze,
> Permit a child to join,
>
> Thy sacred emblems to partake,
> Thy consecrated bread to break,
> Taste thine immortal wine!

Nature afforded Emily Dickinson many happy hours of reflection and, departing, left with her a vital remembrance of the common day.

If Emily Dickinson was a great nature poet, she was also a great poet of love. One is struck by the intensity of her passion, the pathos of it, and the spiritual strength which it gave her, but particularly by the harmonious way that it fitted into her orbit of living. Love bore her an identity of soul and taught her the ways of immortality. With the passage of the years, her meditations grew more spiritual and the syntheses of ideas more complete. Heaven became a place peopled by the friends she knew at home, and earth and paradise merged. Again the power of revery asserts itself in a form of transcendental thinking, drawing her away from worldly interests to an awareness of Order and the Divine Plan.

There is no need to dwell here upon the facts behind her love poems. These have been commented upon many times. Readers of her poetry find that the "Amherst heart is plain and whole and permanent and warm." But, when we know how closely she read her Bible, it is not likely that she overlooked "The Song of Songs." Generally her passion is expressed in hushed tones, but there are occasions when her voice is filled with wild abandon. Ecstasy is present in the luxurious phrase, "Rowing in Eden," and agony in "Empress of Calvary." As Amy Lowell has remarked, in her poem "The Sisters" [see excerpt dated 1925], the Massachusetts poet had ties with Sappho, Mrs. Browning, and that other Emily—Emily Brontë. The range of her feelings was not narrower than theirs, nor was her passion less intense.

The pathos of her love is evident in the way she treasures memories of the past. "Remembrance," she writes, "is more sweet than robins in May orchards." And, on one occasion, we find her bargaining with fate for a glimpse of her lover's face, pretending that she may get what she wants if she offers enough. She spent existence for "a single dram of Heaven," living out the lonely years "in the smallest parlor in the world," her heart. What fierce tragic tones there are in the words—"Mine by the right of the white election!" But the thought is futile and the mood devastating. It was easier for her after she had learned the lessons of sacrifice.

The habit of introspection led at times into abstruse fields of thinking, where her vision is the product of pseudo-mystical experience and the literal meaning eludes the reader. Musing over her favorite topics—Life, Nature, Love, Time and Eternity—she saw them as one, with Love the point of convergence. This tendency makes her words enigmatic at times, as well as epigrammatic. In the absence of dates for her poems, it is difficult to trace the progress of her thought with certainty. However, examination of three of them—the first, beginning **"I'm wife. . . . I'm woman now,"** the second, **"Title divine is mine the Wife without the Sign,"** and the third, **"A wife at daybreak I shall be"**—suggests a series of steps in a pilgrimage away from earthly love to a devotion to Omnipotence. Support for this theory is found in such poems as the one beginning **"God is a distant, stately Lover"** and in the lines in which she professes herself "Bride of the Father and the Son, Bride of the Holy Ghost!" Viewed in this light, the following represents Emily's breathless anticipation of Paradise, the apex of her love poems, and the fulfillment of her life of sacrifice.

> A wife at daybreak I shall be,
> Sunrise, hast thou a flag for me?
> At midnight I am yet a maid—
> How short it takes to make it bride!
> Then, Midnight, I have passed from thee
> Unto the East and Victory.
>
> Midnight, "Good night"
> I hear them call.
> The angels bustle in the hall,
> Softly my Future climbs the stair,
> I fumble at my childhood's prayer—
> So soon to be a child no more!
> Eternity, I'm coming, Sir,—
> Master, I've seen that face before.

The metaphors used here appear in other poems where there is no doubt about the nature of the subject treated. "Daybreak," "Midnight," "East," "Victory," and "Good night" are the symbols she employs when speaking of time and eternity. The flag requested of Sunrise is unquestionably "Eternity's white flag," and the personification in the closing lines rounds out the allegory. The involved symbolism is best explained in Emily's words: "Love. . . . nicknamed by God Eternity."

The pictorial element in her nature poems is matched by a quality of insight in the realm of metaphysics. Length and breadth become meaningful words and circumference, a reality. Like all poets, she revealed her mind in images, and the vision was particularly strong, coming as it did from both creative and interpretive powers of imagination.

Loss of friends was the greatest spiritual suffering she knew, and her notes of condolence are filled with graphic phrases. "Poor little widow's boy," she writes in one letter, "riding to-night in the mad wind, back to the village burying-ground where he never dreamed of sleeping!" The intensity of her greatest loss is in the prayer—"Burglar, banker, father, I am poor once more!" From the pain she experienced upon the death of friends arose a concept of heaven as a large house where she and they would dwell together forever. "Home," she writes, is "a bit of Eden," "a holy thing," and "the definition of God."

Although the death of others moved her deeply, her own she regarded with a calm mind. Recognizing it as the necessary link between two states of being, she painted portraits which are pleasant. Death is represented as a gentleman who stops and offers a ride in his carriage. The Soul "and Death, acquainted, meet tranquilly as friends." The courage which she showed so often in smaller things helped her to face life, death, and resurrection with faith and expectancy.

> Exultation is the going
> Of an inland soul to sea,—
> Past the houses, past the headlands,
> Into deep eternity!

Eternity is often represented as a sea, and the Soul journeys to Judgment attended by "a Single Hound—Its own Identity." The dominant note in her poems on time and eternity is one of unswerving faith in the soul's immortality. This is why death and mortality held no fears for her, and joy was in her life.

Stopping by the landmarks of her poetry, we find ourselves uplifted by her life-poems, moved by her love poems, and taught to see more clearly by her poems on nature and immortality. Within this fourfold circle of experience we perceive the core of Emily's being, and—"This was a Poet!" (pp. 626-33)

Donald F. Connors, "The Significance of Emily Dickinson," in College English, Vol. 3, No. 7, April, 1942, pp. 624-33.*

Richard Chase   (essay date 1951)

[*A distinguished American literary critic, Chase is the author of* The American Novel and Its Tradition *(1957), an influential study examining the "romance" tradition in American fiction. In this work, Chase contended that American fiction was not strictly realistic, but rather abstract, symbolistic, and more concerned with action than characterization, a definition which inspired a reappraisal of American literature. Although at one time associated with the New Critics, Chase wrote that he leaned "rather to the historical, moral, or naturalistic approach of such contemporary critics as Lionel Trilling and Edmund Wilson." In the following excerpt, he explores the psychology of Dickinson's poems, concluding that "her intellectual bent is intuitive and radically realistic."*]

[The psychology Dickinson] reveals in her poems, though narrow, is both profound and convincing. She thought that the soul of man, to remain healthy and sane, must subject itself to a "strict economy." To establish and preserve its integrity, the soul must be ready to close the valves of its attention, to seek its "polar privacy" and remain immovable and proud. Yet within its established confines the soul has a double character. A hunting, pursuing, watchful function of the soul is seen to be separable from the soul itself.

> Adventure most unto itself
> The Soul condemned to be;
> Attended by a Single Hound—
> Its own Identity.

In this poem the object-finding or externally operative part of the mind while recognized as separate is paradoxically said to be identical with the mind's self-generated moralizing guardian. But in poems such as **"My soul accused me"** and **"Me from Myself to banish"** the moralizing part of the mind is said to be autonomous and imperial. Of the soul in its accusatory aspect, she writes that it is easier to endure fire than the soul's disdain. What may happen when the "single Hound" part of the soul lapses in its vigilance is described in **"The soul has bandaged moments."** Here the soul is said to be transfixed when confronted by a ghastly apparition which strokes, with its long fingers, her freezing hair. Or the temporary abeyance of the "single Hound" may result not in fright at some eruptive sexualized image but in pure euphoria, the sense that the soul has burst "all the doors" and "dances like a bomb abroad." The watchful hound may have the quality of destiny or of the Puritan conscience but its reign is precarious, the soul it guards being subject to eruptions of uncontrollable energy.

Emily Dickinson considered sanity, one might say that she considered existence itself, to be just barely possible. Reason, she repeats in her poems, is hemmed in and threatened by madness. It is a frail bark on a profound and imminently tumultuous sea. It is the quiet momentarily imposed upon Etna or Vesuvius. Its path through the abyss is a narrow "groove"; once let it swerve and it is exposed to the terrors of the deep. In the psychological scheme of her poems, Emily Dickinson regarded all consciousness as derivable from and as typified by the consciousness of death and immortality. Fortunately, as she says in **"I never hear that one is dead,"** the "daily mind" does not "till" the abyss of death, for if it did it would go mad. Consciousness guides the soul. Yet it is a measure of man's desolation and the precariousness of his existence that consciousness, fully understood as consciousness of death, appears to us as an "awful stranger."

If we wished to pursue a Freudian analogy, we should say that her fine poem called **"As one does sickness over"** (with its account of how "one rewalks a precipice" and "whittles at the twig" that had barely saved one from extinction) can be fruitfully read as a poetic treatment of the realms of psychology which extend "beyond the pleasure principle." Like Freud, she sensed the quality of destiny in the human mind that makes it recapitulate in fancy or hallucination the occasions of its suffering. There is as little nonsense in her idea of dreams as in Freud's. "Dreams are a subtle dower" but they clearly set themselves apart from "reality" by flinging us back into "the precinct raw / Possessed before." She knew the relation of neurosis with creative efficiency: "It is easy to work when the soul is at play."

In Whitman's house of the soul there are no doors, and hardly any house. But Emily Dickinson believed that if sanity was to be preserved and a meaningful existence made possible, the soul must indeed be a house with a door, a door which is left "ajar." This is one of her most revealing images, by which she imagines not only the mind but also nature. In the following poem we encounter one of those apparently vague personifications ("the heaven") which tend to weaken even some of her best poems—"the heaven" here means, one gathers, "the revelation of truth under the aspect of death":

> The soul should always stand ajar
> That if the heaven inquire,
> He will not be obliged to wait,
> Or shy of troubling her.
>
> Depart, before the host has slid
> The bolt upon the door,
> To seek for the accomplished guest—
> Her visitor no more.

The ambiguities of "the accomplished guest," which include God, death, grace, a "tutor," a lover, are a topic for later consideration. Here I am speaking only of the "strict economy" the poet attributes to the mind, and wish to emphasize the severity with which she presents the precarious possibility that the soul can acquire (what she elsewhere calls) its royal diadem through the reception of ineffable experience, "the accomplished guest."

"Doom is the House without the Door," wrote Emily Dickinson. For Whitman, houses themselves were doom. A house for Thoreau was not considerable by spiritual man if it was more complex, structured, and intricate than a shack by the pond, every nail and slab of which was known personally by the builder. There was no house through the walls of which Emerson's soul might not be expected to dilate. For though he wrote (in a manner that must have interested Emily Dickinson) that "every spirit builds itself a house; and beyond its house a world; and beyond its world a heaven," the building of the house was less remarkable than the speed with which its confines were transcended. But the American writers with whom Emily Dickinson has her closest kinship have all made profoundly symbolic use of the house, as we recall from Poe's "Fall of the House of Usher" and "The Black Cat," Melville's *Pierre*, "I and Chimney," and "Jimmy Rose," Hawthorne's *The House of the Seven Gables*, and Henry James's "The Jolly Corner," among several other of his fictions.

A house is one of our poet's favorite symbols of the mind. In such poems as **"Remembrance has a rear and front"** and **"One need not be a chamber to be haunted,"** we discern her idea that consciousness presents itself to us as a dual discourse, having a latent content behind the manifest content; that the garret of a house is like the abode of the mind's ego-functions and that the cellar is symbolic of the unconscious; that the "prudent" who carry a revolver to ward off external enemies are misguided if they do not also guard against the "superior spectre" who may be stalking the corridors of their own minds.

The critic who tries to explicate Emily Dickinson's ideas cannot help making her sound more speculative and theoretical than she actually was. The reader must discount and translate as he judges proper. One must agree with the emphasis, at least, of Mr. Allen Tate's remark [see excerpt dated 1928-32] that she "cannot reason at all. She can only *see,"* so long as we remember that Mr. Tate is speaking of "reasoning in verse form" as this is done, for example, in the lesser poems of Tennyson. She had great intellectual power and her poetry is eminently considerable, so Mr. Tate notes, as a "poetry of ideas." But part of the economy of her mind was her own clearly expressed knowledge that she could not "organize." She was incapable of systematic abstract thought, just as she was incapable of organizing a closely knit poem of any but the shortest length. Her intellectual bent is intuitive and radically realistic. Her greatness as a poet issues from the fact that, though she had little power of systematic speculation and little enough aptitude for poetic coherence, her mind instinctively moved towards those severe separations and exclusions and that closely limited vision of things which she called the "strict economy" of the soul. (pp. 127-31)

Richard Chase, in his Emily Dickinson, *William Sloane Associates, 1951, 328 p.*

Thomas H. Johnson   (essay date 1955)

[*Johnson's contributions to Dickinson criticism include his scholarly editions of her poetry and letters and the respected study* Emily Dickinson: An Interpretive Biography, *from which the following excerpt is drawn. Johnson describes Dickinson's notions of beauty, the role of the poet, and poetry; he also surveys some of her influences, stressing that "she found the Bible her key to meaning."*]

Emily Dickinson's aesthetic credo is most substantially revealed in her concept of beauty, and the philosophy of all her Puritan past is transmuted into art in her poems on the nature of beauty. Like salvation, it comes as a grace, an infusion from without, an emanation which the creature passively receives and is powerless to win by effort to attain it. It is not merely similar to God's love, but is in fact God's love for man. It is the love which possesses those who are willing to pass through the straight pass of suffering to discover the redemption which offers immortality.

> I died for Beauty—but was scarce
> Adjusted in the Tomb
> When One who died for Truth, was lain
> In an adjoining Room—
>
> He questioned softly "Why I failed"?
> "For Beauty," I replied—
> "And I—for Truth—Themself are One—
> We Brethren, are," He said—
>
> And so, as Kinsmen, met a Night—
> We talked between the Rooms—
> Until the Moss had reached our lips—
> And covered up—our names—

Beauty inheres, it cannot be fashioned or formed. "Beauty—be not caused—It Is." An ecstatic experience, like heaven, cannot be defined.

> The Definition of Beauty is
> That Definition is none—
> Of Heaven, easing Analysis,
> Since Heaven and He are One.

Yet the beholder or listener must be willing to possess:

> To hear an Oriole sing
> May be a common thing—
> Or only a divine.
>
> It is not of the Bird
> Who sings the same, unheard,
> As unto Crowd—
>
> The Fashion of the Ear
> Attireth that it hear
> In Dun, or fair—
>
> So whether it be Rune,
> Or whether it be none
> Is of within.
>
> The "Tune is in the Tree—"
> The Skeptic—showeth me—
> "No Sir! In Thee!"

She is not thinking of death, but of the encroachment of the supernal, when she exclaims:

> Beauty crowds me till I die
> Beauty, mercy have on me
> But if I expire today
> Let it be in sight of thee—

The experience of beauty is a moral quality, won through redemptive suffering:

> Must be a Wo—
> A loss or so—
> To bend the eye
> Best Beauty's way—
>
> But—once aslant
> It notes Delight
> As difficult
> As Stalactite—
>
> A Common Bliss
> Were had for less—
> The price—is
> Even as the Grace—
>
> Our lord—thought no
> Extravagance
> To pay—a Cross—

The bliss won easily is not beauty. Though the word as she uses it connotes the sensations received by observing the natural order in the world about us, she is talking about its redemptive quality. The discernment of beauty is an intellectual experience, in the sense that it can be perceived only by those who in fact take on the image of God. "Is it Intellect that the Patriot means when he speaks of his 'Native Land'?" she wrote Higginson. In the beginning was the word, she is always aware, and the magic of language constantly elates her.

> Strong Draughts of Their Refreshing Minds
> To drink—enables Mine
> Through Desert or the Wilderness
> As bore it Sealed Wine—
>
> To go elastic—Or as One
> The Camel's trait—attained—
> How powerful the Stimulus
> Of an Hermetic Mind—

The poet, by consenting to the preordained suffering whereby creation is achieved, gains status, and the language he utters, being of God, bestows immortality. Such a concept is by no means original with Emily Dickinson, who knew her Shakespeare intimately.

> Essential Oils—are wrung—
> The Attar from the Rose
> Be not expressed by Suns—alone—
> It is the gift of Screws—
>
> The General Rose—decay—
> But this—in Lady's Drawer
> Make Summer—When the Lady lie
> In Ceaseless Rosemary—

Most of the poems that equate beauty with immortality were written in 1862 and 1863. That which is beautiful is experienced both by the heart and the mind. We cannot comprehend its immensity nor be estranged from it. Our destiny is involved in it. What Emily Dickinson knew about Jonathan Edwards came to her by way of the Valley tradition, which stressed his sterner doctrines. She would probably have been surprised to know that the quatrain she wrote in the late seventies is a twenty-word summary of Edwards' thoughts on the subject, expressed one hundred and twenty years before in his greatest essay, *The Nature of True Virtue*.

> Estranged from Beauty—none can be—
> For Beauty is Infinity—
> And power to be finite ceased
> Before Identity was leased—

On the artist is bestowed the gift that invests him with enduring rank.

> The One who could repeat the Summer day
> Were greater than itself—though He
> Minutest of Mankind should be—
>
> And He—could reproduce the Sun—
> At period of going down—
> The Lingering—and the Stain—I mean—
>
> When Orient have been outgrown—
> And Occident—become Unknown—
> His Name—remain—

Among artists she best understood poets, and had intimate knowledge of the poetic process. It is coeval with love, she knows, but it cannot be explained: "For None see God and live." Her own dedication to poetry she expressed in 1862, the year that she wrote most of her verses on the function and status of the poet. "The Soul selects her own Society—Then—shuts the Door." The poet is blessed, but isolated. Her letter to the world from which she is shut away will transmit such news about nature as she has received through her senses.

> This is my letter to the World
> That never wrote to Me—
> The simple News that Nature told—
> With tender Majesty
> Her Message is committed
> To Hands I cannot see—
> For love of Her—Sweet—countrymen—
> Judge tenderly—of Me

It is expected of the poet that he will distill amazing sense from ordinary meanings, extract attar from the familiar, which otherwise would perish. Such is the theme of **"This was a Poet,"** with its conclusion that:

> Of Pictures, the Discloser—

> The Poet—it is He—
> Enables Us—by Contrast—
> To ceaseless Poverty.
>
> Of Portion—so unconscious—
> The Robbing—could not harm—
> Himself—to Him—a Fortune—
> Exterior—to Time—

To be a poet is:

> A privilege so awful
> What would the Dower be,
> Had I the Art to stun myself
> With Bolts of Melody!

She is concerned with craftsmanship in **"Myself was formed—a Carpenter,"** and with the destiny of the poet in **"The Martyr Poets did not tell,"** and **"I reckon—when I count at all— / First—Poets."** But her final words on the subject she spoke in 1864. They exemplify as art the concept of fame that she had expressed to Higginson two years earlier—that if it belonged to her she could not escape it. Circumference is her business.

> The Poets light but Lamps—
> Themselves—go out—
> The Wicks they stimulate—
> If vital Light
> Inhere as do the Suns—
> Each Age a Lens
> Disseminating their
> Circumference—

It is of primary importance to bear in mind that when Emily Dickinson wrote her first letter to Higginson, asking him to pass judgment upon the poems she enclosed, her aesthetic theory was fully established. Though she protested in every letter which she wrote during the ensuing months that she was grateful for his "surgery," that she needed his frank criticism and would obediently follow his precepts, the fact is that she never at any time conformed to his injunctions. The prescriptions that he wrote out were intended for a beginner who, he implied, had a great deal to learn before she could qualify as a poet worthy of public attention.

Clearly Emily Dickinson had no formal theory of poetics, in the sense that she could have written a critique in the manner of Poe. But she had a developed and consistent idea of the manner in which the poet is inspired. Her ideas are conventional to the degree that they are in the main stream from Plato to Emerson. The poet is a seer; his inspiration comes as a grace, overleaping regular channels; he is thus a man possessed, who reveals truth out of the agony of his travail; and the anguish of such possession enables the receiver to partake of reality and reveal at least a fragment of the mysteries that the heart perceives. Such possession cannot be made comprehensible to others by instruction. Uncontrolled, it leads into the sheer nonsense of automatic writing. She had no more success than any other artist has ever had in giving form to every creative impulse. But her successes, she seems to have felt by 1862, were increasingly evident. She persistently labored to file her lines so that the images would be exact and sharp. She was aware that form is inherent in the created object, and she achieved control when her perceptions gave shape to the object before her pen touched paper. The abandoned worksheet drafts are examples of imperfectly wrought images; that is, of language uncontrolled by an inherent form. Her successful poems were those in which both elements coalesce. Her failures, almost without exception, are the poems in which the form was not first inherent. (pp. 142-49)

The immediate sources of Emily Dickinson's inspiration sprang from the associations she most deeply cherished and about which she felt greatest awe. First was the world about her, the moods of nature, the creatures of earth and air that scamper and soar, and the buds that bloom and fade. Equally important were friends, always held in a brittle remembrance by her acute consciousness that death at any moment can occur. And lurking behind every thought to which she gave expression was the abiding wonder, the craving for assurance, about the sempiternal. Her relation to nature, death, and immortality she made the "flood subject" of all she wrote. How did she clothe the ideas? What was the metaphor of her thinking?

Basically the words and phrases by which she makes one idea denote likeness to another are cast from the images which she absorbed from the Bible. It was the primary source, and no other is of comparable importance. Even when she draws her figures of speech from the language of the sea, of trade, of law, or of science, they usually suggest that they have passed through the alembic of the King James version of biblical utterance.

> The Sweets of Pillage, can be known
> To no one but the Thief—
> Compassion for Integrity
> Is his divinest Grief—

The theme of compassionate love draws for its metaphor upon the most famous incident of such love. At the moment of Christ's supreme trial, He extends mercy to the repentant thief. There are several score of poems where the biblical metaphor is direct and self-evident. But the shaping of her thought in terms of biblical incident, events, and precept is apparent in almost every poem that she wrote. She transmuted universals into particulars by means of such figures of speech: "location's narrow way," "the smitten rock," "broad possessions," "this accepted breath," "the scarlet way," "the morning stars," "the straight pass of suffering," "the apple on the tree," "the sapphire fellows," "moat of pearl," "the fleshy gate," "this meek apparelled thing," "the primer to a life." All are drawn from the Bible, and require on the part of the reader a like familiarity if the full import is to be rendered. Let two examples suffice. The first stanza of a poem in which she imagines herself dead, and speculates on how the living might show their grief, goes thus:

> 'Twas just this time, last year I died,
> I know I heard the Corn,
> When I was carried by the Farms—
> It had the Tassels on—

The year is at its full. Apples are ready for garnering, "And Carts went stooping round the fields/To take the Pumpkins in." The expression "I heard the Corn" does not mean that in her mind's ear she hears it growing. The line echoes Hosea 2.22, wherein the corn (and wine and oil) cry to be harvested. It is typical of her method to combine a metaphor drawn from a universal cultural heritage with objects familiar to her daily experience: carts, pumpkins, and cornfields.

She drew from about thirty books of the Bible. The three books that echo most persistently in her poems and letters are Matthew, Revelation, and Genesis—in that order. They are followed closely by John, I and II Corinthians, Exodus, and Psalms. She breathed the atmosphere of biblical lore, and inevitably the figures with which she clothed her ideas are permeated with it. . . . Several words in the first stanza [of **"Just lost, when I was saved!"**] have biblical association in a general way, including *lost, saved, girt, Eternity, breath.* The imagery in the remaining three stanzas derives from Revelation, chapters 1, 4, and 5, and from I Corinthians. The pale reporter is John at Patmos who fell as dead at Christ's feet. The beginning of John's vision occurs before the door that opened into heaven. God's purpose and promise is set forth in the book sealed to human knowledge. It is in Corinthians that the idea is made explicit concerning the limits of human wisdom: "Eye hath not seen, nor ear heard . . . the things which God hath prepared for them that love him." The poem, written about 1860, may be her first to give immediacy to the theme that she never ceased to ponder: our nearness to ultimate reality would lead us to believe that we could surely discover it by determined effort, yet we must accept the inevitable, realizing that we cannot win through to an understanding of it during our mortal years.

It is not too much to say that in almost every poem she wrote, there are echoes of her sensitivity to the idiom of the Bible, and of her dependence upon its imagery for her own striking figures of speech. The great reservoir of classical myth she rarely drew upon. Since she never uses figures of speech for embellishment, she preferred those which for her had the power to evoke deep emotion. She found the Bible her key to meaning, and shaped her words and symbols by way of the stories and precepts in its reduceless mines. (pp. 151-53)

> *Thomas H. Johnson, in his* Emily Dickinson: An Interpretive Biography, *Cambridge, Mass.: The Belknap Press of Harvard University Press, 1955, 276 p.* * [*The excerpts of Emily Dickinson's work used here were originally published in her* The Complete Poems of Emily Dickinson, *Little, Brown and Company, 1960*].

Richard Wilbur (lecture date 1959)

[*Wilbur, considered one of the major modern American poets, is also a teacher, critic, dramatist, translator, and an editor. His writings include* The Beautiful Changes and Other Poems *(1947),* The Poems of Richard Wilbur *(1963),* Walking to Sleep: New Poems and Translations *(1969),* Responses: Prose Pieces 1953-1976 *(1976), and* The Mind-Reader: New Poems *(1976). In the following excerpt from a lecture delivered at Amherst College in 1959, he explores the way in which Dickinson renders her "sense of privation" in a positive light. To Wilbur, she was an intensely self-conscious poet and her habitual distancing of herself should be interpreted "not [as] an avoidance of life but an eccentric mastery of it."*]

At some point Emily Dickinson sent her whole Calvinist vocabulary into exile, telling it not to come back until it would subserve her own sense of things.

Of course, that is not a true story, but it is a way of saying what I find most remarkable in Emily Dickinson. She inherited a great and overbearing vocabulary which, had she used it submissively, would have forced her to express an established theology and psychology. But she would not let that vocabulary write her poems for her. There lies the real difference between a poet like Emily Dickinson and a fine versifier like Isaac Watts. To be sure, Emily Dickinson also wrote in the metres of hymnody, and paraphrased the Bible, and made her poems turn on great words like Immortality and Salvation and Election. But in her poems those great words are not merely being themselves; they have been adopted, for expressive purposes; they have been taken personally, and therefore redefined.

The poems of Emily Dickinson are a continual appeal to experience, motivated by an arrogant passion for the truth. "Truth is so rare a thing," she once said, "it is delightful to tell it." And, sending some poems to Colonel Higginson, she wrote, "Excuse them, if they are untrue." And again, to the same correspondent, she observed, "Candor is the only wile"—meaning that the writer's bag of tricks need contain one trick only, the trick of being honest. That her taste for truth involved a regard for objective fact need not be argued: we have her poem on the snake, and that on the hummingbird, and they are small masterpieces of exact description. She liked accuracy; she liked solid and homely detail; and even in her most exalted poems we are surprised and reassured by buckets, shawls, or buzzing flies.

But her chief truthfulness lay in her insistence on discovering the facts of her inner experience. She was a Linnaeus to the phenomena of her own consciousness, describing and distinguishing the states and motions of her soul. The results of this "psychic reconnaissance," as Professor Whicher called it, were several. For one thing, it made her articulate about inward matters which poetry had never so sharply defined; specifically, it made her capable of writing two such lines as these:

>   A perfect, paralyzing bliss
>   Contented as despair.

We often assent to the shock of a paradox before we understand it, but those lines are so just and so concentrated as to explode their meaning instantly in the mind. They did not come so easily, I think, to Emily Dickinson. Unless I guess wrongly as to chronology, such lines were the fruit of long poetic research; the poet had worked toward them through much study of the way certain emotions can usurp consciousness entirely, annulling our sense of past and future, cancelling near and far, converting all time and space to a joyous or grievous here and now. It is in their ways of annihilating time and space that bliss and despair are comparable.

Which leads me to a second consequence of Emily Dickinson's self-analysis. It is one thing to assert as pious doctrine that the soul has power, with God's grace, to master circumstance. It is another thing to find out personally, as Emily Dickinson did in writing her psychological poems, that the aspect of the world is in no way constant, that the power of external things depends on our state of mind, that the soul selects its own society and may, if granted strength to do so, select a superior order and scope of consciousness which will render it finally invulnerable. She

learned these things by witnessing her own courageous spirit.

Another result of Emily Dickinson's introspection was that she discovered some grounds, in the nature of her soul and its affections, for a personal conception of such ideas as Heaven and Immortality, and so managed a precarious convergence between her inner experience and her religious inheritance. What I want to attempt now is a rough sketch of the imaginative logic by which she did this. I had better say before I start that I shall often seem demonstrably wrong, because Emily Dickinson, like many poets, was consistent in her concerns but inconsistent in her attitudes. The following, therefore, is merely an opinion as to her main drift.

Emily Dickinson never lets us forget for very long that in some respects life gave her short measure; and indeed it is possible to see the greater part of her poetry as an effort to cope with her sense of privation. I think that for her there were three major privations: she was deprived of an orthodox and steady religious faith; she was deprived of love; she was deprived of literary recognition.

At the age of 17, after a series of revival meetings at Mount Holyoke Seminary, Emily Dickinson found that she must refuse to become a professing Christian. To some modern minds this may seem to have been a sensible and necessary step; and surely it was a step toward becoming such a poet as she became. But for her, no pleasure in her own integrity could then eradicate the feeling that she had betrayed a deficiency, a want of grace. In her letters to Abiah Root she tells of the enhancing effect of conversion on her fellow-students, and says of herself in a famous passage:

> *I* am one of the lingering bad ones, and so do I slink
> away, and pause and ponder, and ponder and
> pause, and do work without knowing why, not
> surely, for this brief world, and more sure it is not
> for heaven, and I ask what this message *means* that
> they ask for so very eagerly: *you* know of this depth
> and fulness, will you try to tell me about it?

There is humor in that, and stubborness, and a bit of characteristic lurking pride: but there is also an anguished sense of having separated herself, through some dry incapacity, from spiritual community, from purpose, and from magnitude of life. As a child of evangelical Amherst, she inevitably thought of purposive, heroic life as requiring a vigorous faith. Out of such a thought she later wrote:

>   The abdication of Belief
>   Makes the Behavior small—
>   Better an ignis fatuus
>   Than no illume at all—

That hers *was* a species of religious personality goes without saying; but by her refusal of such ideas as original sin, redemption, hell, and election, she made it impossible for herself—as Professor Whicher observed—"to share the religious life of her generation." She became an unsteady congregation of one.

Her second privation, the privation of love, is one with which her poems and her biographies have made us exceedingly familiar, though some biographical facts remain conjectural. She had the good fortune, at least once, to bestow her heart on another; but she seems to have found her life, in great part, a history of loneliness, separation, and bereavement.

As for literary fame, some will deny that Emily Dickinson ever greatly desired it, and certainly there is evidence mostly from her latter years, to support such a view. She *did* write that "Publication is the auction / Of the mind of man." And she *did* say to Helen Hunt Jackson, "How can you print a piece of your soul?" But earlier, in 1861, she had frankly expressed to Sue Dickinson the hope that "sometime" she might make her kinfolk proud of her. The truth is, I think, that Emily Dickinson knew she was good, and began her career with a normal appetite for recognition. I think that she later came, with some reason, to despair of being understood or properly valued, and so directed against her hopes of fame what was by then a well-developed disposition to renounce. That she wrote a good number of poems about fame supports my view: the subjects to which a poet returns are those which vex him.

What did Emily Dickinson do, as a poet, with her sense of privation? One thing she quite often did was to pose as the laureate and attorney of the empty-handed, and question God about the economy of His creation. Why, she asked, is a fatherly God so sparing of His presence? Why is there never a sign that prayers are heard? Why does Nature tell us no comforting news of its Maker? Why do some receive a whole loaf, while others must starve on a crumb? Where is the benevolence in shipwreck and earthquake? By asking such questions as these, she turned complaint into critique, and used her own sufferings as experiential evidence about the nature of the deity. The God who emerges from these poems is a God who does not answer, an unrevealed God whom one cannot confidently approach through Nature or through doctrine.

But there was another way in which Emily Dickinson dealt with her sentiment of lack—another emotional strategy which was both more frequent and more fruitful. I refer to her repeated assertion of the paradox that privation is more plentiful than plenty; that to renounce is to possess the more; that "The Banquet of abstemiousness / Defaces that of wine." We all know how the poet illustrated this ascetic paradox in her behavior—how in her latter years she chose to live in relative retirement, keeping the world, even in its dearest aspects, at a physical remove. She would write her friends, telling them how she missed them, then flee upstairs when they came to see her; afterward, she might send a note of apology, offering the odd explanation that "We shun because we prize." Any reader of Dickinson biographies can furnish other examples, dramatic or homely, of this prizing and shunning, this yearning and renouncing: in my own mind's eye is a picture of Emily Dickinson watching a gay circus caravan from the distance of her chamber window.

In her inner life, as well, she came to keep the world's images, even the images of things passionately desired, at the remove which renunciation makes; and her poetry at its most mature continually proclaims that to lose or forego what we desire is somehow to gain. We may say, if we like, with some of the poet's commentators, that this central paradox of her thought is a rationalization of her neurotic plight; but we had better add that it is also a discovery of something about the soul. Let me read you a little poem of psychological observation which, whatever its date of

composition may logically be considered as an approach to that discovery.

> Undue Significance a starving man attaches
> To Food—
> Far off—He sighs—and therefore—Hopeless—
> And therefore—Good—
>
> Partaken—it relieves—indeed—
> But proves us
> That Spices fly
> In the Receipt—It was the Distance—
> Was Savory—

This poem describes an educational experience, in which a starving man is brought to distinguish between appetite and desire. So long as he despairs of sustenance, the man conceives it with the eye of desire as infinitely delicious. But when, after all, he secures it and appeases his hunger, he finds that its imagined spices have flown. The moral is plain: once an object has been magnified by desire, it cannot be wholly possessed by appetite.

The poet is not concerned, in this poem, with passing any judgment. She is simply describing the way things go in the human soul, telling us that the frustration of appetite awakens or abets desire, and that the effect of intense desiring is to render any finite satisfaction disappointing. Now I want to read you another well-known poem, in which Emily Dickinson was again considering privation and possession, and the modes of enjoyment possible to each. In this case, I think, a judgment is strongly implied.

> Success is counted sweetest
> By those who ne'er succeed.
> To comprehend a nectar
> Requires sorest need.
>
> Not one of all the purple Host
> Who took the Flag today
> Can tell the definition
> So clear of Victory
>
> As he defeated—dying—
> On whose forbidden ear
> The distant strains of triumph
> Burst agonized and clear!

Certainly Emily Dickinson's critics are right in calling this poem an expression of the idea of compensation—of the idea that every evil confers some balancing good, that through bitterness we learn to appreciate the sweet, that "Water is taught by thirst." The defeated and dying soldier of this poem is compensated by a greater awareness of the meaning of victory than the victors themselves can have: he can comprehend the joy of success through its polar contrast to his own despair.

The poem surely does say that; yet it seems to me that there is something further implied. On a first reading, we are much impressed with the wretchedness of the dying soldier's lot, and an improved understanding of the nature of victory may seem small compensation for defeat and death; but the more one ponders this poem the likelier it grows that Emily Dickinson is arguing the *superiority* of defeat to victory, of frustration to satisfaction, and of anguished comprehension to mere possession. What do the victors have but victory, a victory which they cannot fully savor or clearly define? They have paid for their triumph by a sacrifice of awareness; a material gain has cost them a spiritual loss. For the dying soldier, the case is reversed: defeat and death are attended by an increase of awareness, and material loss has led to spiritual gain. Emily Dickinson would think that the better bargain.

In the first of these two poems I have read, it was possible to imagine the poet as saying that a starving man's visions of food are but wish fulfillments, and hence illusory; but the second poem assures us of the contrary—assures us that food, or victory, or any other good thing is best comprehended by the eye of desire from the vantage of privation. We must now ask in what way desire can define things, what comprehension of nectars it can have beyond a sense of inaccessible sweetness.

Since Emily Dickinson was not a philosopher, and never set forth her thought in any orderly way, I shall answer that quotation from the seventeenth-century divine Thomas Traherne. Conveniently for us, Traherne is thinking, in this brief meditation, about food—specifically, about acorns—as perceived by appetite and by desire.

> The service of things and their excellencies are spiritual: being objects not of the eye, but of the mind: and you more spiritual by how much more you esteem them. Pigs eat acorns, but neither consider the sun that gave them life, nor the influences of the heavens by which they were nourished, nor the very root of the tree from whence they came. This being the work of Angels, who in a wide and clear light see even the sea that gave them moisture: And feed upon that acorn spiritually while they know the ends for which it was created, and feast upon all these as upon a World of Joys within it: while to ignorant swine that eat the shell, it is an empty husk of no taste nor delightful savor.

Emily Dickinson could not have written that, for various reasons, a major reason being that she could not see in Nature any revelations of divine purpose. But like Traherne she discovered that the soul has an infinite hunger, a hunger to possess all things. (That discovery, I suspect, was the major fruit of her introspection.) And like Traherne she distinguished two ways of possessing things, the way of appetite and the way of desire. What Traherne said of the pig she said of her favorite insect:

> Auto da Fe and Judgment—
> Are nothing to the Bee—
> His separation from His Rose—
> To Him—sums Misery—

The creature of appetite (whether insect or human) pursues satisfaction, and strives to possess the object in itself; it cannot imagine the vaster economy of desire, in which the pain of abstinence is justified by moments of infinite joy, and the object is spiritually possessed, not merely for itself, but more truly as an index of the All. That is how one comprehends a nectar. Miss Dickinson's bee does not comprehend the rose which it plunders, because the truer sweetness of the rose lies beyond the rose, in its relationship to the whole of being; but she would say that Gerard Manley Hopkins comprehends a bluebell when, having noticed its intrinsic beauties, he adds, "I know the beauty of Our Lord by it." And here is an eight-line poem of her own, in which she comprehends the full sweetness of water.

> We thirst at first—'tis Nature's Act—
> And later—when we die—

> A little Water supplicate—
> Of fingers going by—

> It intimates the finer want—
> Whose adequate supply
> Is that Great Water in the West—
> Termed Immortality—

Emily Dickinson elected the economy of desire, and called her privation good, rendering it positive by renunciation. And so she came to live in a huge world of delectable distances. Far-off words like "Brazil" or "Circassian" appear continually in her poems as symbols or things distanced by loss or renunciation, yet infinitely prized and yearned-for. So identified in her mind are distance and delight that, when ravished by the sight of a hummingbird in her garden, she calls it "the mail from Tunis." And not only are the objects of her desire distant; they are also very often moving away, their sweetness increasing in proportion to their remoteness. "To disappear enhances," one of the poems begins, and another closes with these lines:

> The Mountain—at a given distance—
> In Amber—lies—
> Approached—the Amber flits—a little—
> And That's—the Skies—

To the eye of desire, all things are seen in a profound perspective, either moving or gesturing toward the vanishing-point. Or to use a figure which may be closer to Miss Dickinson's thought, to the eye of desire the world is a centrifuge, in which all things are straining or flying toward the occult circumference. In some such way, Emily Dickinson conceived her world, and it was in a spatial metaphor that she gave her personal definition of Heaven. "Heaven," she said, "is what I cannot reach."

At times it seems that there is nothing in her world but her own soul, with its attendant abstraction, and, at a vast remove, the inscrutable Heaven. On most of what might intervene she has closed the valves of her attention, and what mortal objects she does acknowledge are riddled by desire to the point of transparency. Here is a sentence from her correspondence: "Enough is of so vast a sweetness, I suppose it never occurs, only pathetic counterfeits." The writer of that sentence could not invest her longings in any finite object. Again she wrote, "Emblem is immeasurable—that is why it is better than fulfilment, which can be drained." For such a sensibility, it was natural and necessary that things be touched with infinity. Therefore her nature poetry, when most serious, does not play descriptively with birds or flowers but presents us repeatedly with dawn, noon, and sunset, those grand ceremonial moments of the day which argue the splendor of Paradise. Or it shows us the ordinary landscape transformed by the electric brilliance of a storm; or it shows us the fields succumbing to the annual mystery of death. In her love-poems, Emily Dickinson was at first covetous of the beloved himself; indeed, she could be idolatrous, going so far as to say that his face, should she see it again in Heaven, would eclipse the face of Jesus. But in what I take to be her later work the beloved's lineaments, which were never very distinct, vanish entirely; he becomes pure emblem, a symbol of remote spiritual joy, and so is all but absorbed into the idea of Heaven. The lost beloved is, as one poem declares, "infinite when gone," and in such lines as the following we are aware of him mainly as an instrument in the poet's commerce with the beyond.

Of all the Souls that stand create—
I have elected—One—
When Sense from Spirit—files away—
And Subterfuge—is done—
When that which is—and that which was—
Apart—intrinsic—stand—
And this brief Tragedy of Flesh—
Is shifted—like a Sand—
When Figures show their royal Front—
And Mists—are carved away,
Behold the Atom—I preferred—
To all the lists of Clay!

In this extraordinary poem, the corporeal beloved is seen as if from another and immaterial existence, and in such perspective his earthly person is but an atom of clay. His risen spirit, we presume, is more imposing, but it is certainly not in focus. What the rapt and thudding lines of this poem portray is the poet's own magnificence of soul—her fidelity to desire, her confidence of Heaven, her contempt of the world. Like Cleopatra's final speeches, this poem is an irresistible demonstration of spiritual status, in which the supernatural is so royally demanded that skepticism is disarmed. A part of its effect derives, by the way, from the fact that the life to come is described in an ambiguous present tense, so that we half-suppose the speaker to be already in Heaven.

There were times when Emily Dickinson supposed this of herself, and I want to close by making a partial guess at the logic of her claims to beatitude. It seems to me that she generally saw Heaven as a kind of infinitely remote bank, in which, she hoped, her untouched felicities were drawing interest. Parting, she said, was all she knew of it. Hence it is surprising to find her saying, in some poems, that Heaven has drawn near to her, and that in her soul's "superior instants" Eternity has disclosed to her "the colossal substance / Of immortality." Yet the contradiction can be understood, if we recall what sort of evidence was persuasive to Emily Dickinson.

"Too much of proof," she wrote, "affronts belief"; and she was little convinced either by doctrine or by theological reasoning. Her residual Calvinism was criticized and fortified by her study of her own soul in action, and from the phenomena of her soul she was capable of making the boldest inferences. That the sense of time is subject to the moods of the soul seemed to her a proof of the soul's eternity. Her intensity of grief for the dead, and her feeling of their continued presence, seemed to her arguments for the reunion of souls in Heaven. And when she found in herself infinite desires, "immortal longings," it seemed to her possible that such desires might somewhere be infinitely answered.

One psychic experience which she interpreted as beatitude was "glee," or as some would call it, euphoria. Now, a notable thing about glee or euphoria is its gratuitousness. It seems to come from nowhere, and it was this apparent sourcelessness of the emotion from which Emily Dickinson made her inference. "The 'happiness' without a cause," she said, "is the best happiness, for glee intuitive and lasting is the gift of God." Having foregone all earthly causes of happiness, she could only explain her glee, when it came, as a divine gift—a compensation in joy for what she had renounced in satisfaction, and a foretaste of the mood of Heaven. The experience of glee, as she records it, is boundless: all distances collapse, and the soul expands

to the very circumference of things. Here is how she put it in one of her letters: "Abroad is close tonight and I have but to lift my hands to touch the 'Hights of Abraham'." And one of her gleeful poems begins,

'Tis little—I could care for Pearls—
Who own the ample sea—

How often she felt that way we cannot know, and it hardly matters. As Robert Frost has pointed out, happiness can make up in height for what it lacks in length; and the important thing for us, as for her, is that she construed the experience as a divine gift. So also she thought of the power to write poetry, a power which, as we know, came to her often; and poetry must have been the chief source of her sense of blessedness. The poetic impulses which visited her seemed "bulletins from Immortality," and by their means she converted all her losses into gains, and all the pains of her life to that clarity and repose which were to her the qualities of Heaven. So superior did she feel, as a poet, to earthly circumstance, and so strong was her faith in words, that she more than once presumed to view this life from the vantage of the grave.

In a manner of speaking, she *was* dead. And yet her poetry, with its articulate faithfulness to inner and outer truth, its insistence on maximum consciousness, is not an avoidance of life but an eccentric mastery of it. Let me close by reading you a last poem, in which she conveys both the extent of her repudiation and the extent of her happiness.

The Missing All, prevented Me
From missing minor Things.
If nothing larger than a World's
Departure from a Hinge
Or Sun's extinction, be observed
'Twas not so large that I
Could lift my Forehead from my work
For Curiosity.

(pp. 3-15)

Richard Wilbur, "Sumptuous Destitution," in his Responses: Prose Pieces 1953-1976, *Harcourt Brace Jovanovich, Inc., 1976, pp. 3-15.*

Hyatt H. Waggoner   (essay date 1965)

[*Waggoner is a respected scholar of American literature whose writings include, among many others,* Hawthorne: A Critical Study *(1955) and* William Faulkner: From Jefferson to the World *(1959). In the following excerpt, he discusses Dickinson's "lack of consistency in belief," arguing that what appears to be inconsistency in her work is actually growth and redefinition.*]

Critics who wish to find a single meaning in Dickinson's work—the "real" or "deeper" meaning they usually call it—need only select the poems that "prove" their point and ignore the rest. Is she a poet of faith, resting her faith on an Emersonian intuition? We have **"I never saw a moor"** and many others like it to prove the point. Does she reject all faith for empirical observation? We have

"Faith" is a fine invention
When Gentlemen can *see*—
But *Microscopes* are prudent
In an Emergency

in which she uses the Biblical metaphor of *seeing with the eyes of faith* to suggest that those who—like herself presumably—don't *have* faith had better turn to some other means of seeing. The poem might be used to introduce a great many in which she asks, in effect, what is the *evidence?*

Is she a "modern," "one of us," a humanistic naturalist like Wallace Stevens, as a whole book has argued? Then cite this:

> The Props assist the House
> Until the House is built
> And then the Props withdraw
> And adequate, erect,
> The House support itself
> And cease to recollect
> The Auger and the Carpenter—
> Just such a retrospect
> Hath the perfected Life—
> A past of Plank and Nail
> And slowness—then the Scaffolds drop
> Affirming it a Soul.

Here she seems to be saying not just that she is getting along fine without faith—the "Props"—but that as Nietzsche was saying at the same time, the death of God is necessary for the achievement of true selfhood. This rejection of "props" prepares us for the rejection of "balm" in a poem Johnson places on the same page of *The Complete Poems:*

> Ourselves we do inter with sweet derision.
> The channel of the dust who once achieves
> Invalidates the balm of that religion
> That doubts as fervently as it believes.

If it were argued that because Johnson tentatively assigns the two poems I have just quoted to 1869, the "humanism" they express was the point of view toward which she was moving, after having lost first her father's faith and then Emerson's, what should we say about **"And with what body do they come?"** which belongs to 1880? The poem affirms faith in immortality:

> "And with what body do they come?"—
> And they *do* come—Rejoice!
> What Door—What Hour—Run—run—My Soul!
> Illuminate the House!

Based on First Corinthians, 15:35-36 ("But some men will say, How are the dead raised up? and with what body do they come? Thou fool, that which thou sowest is not quickened, except it die.") this poem was sent in a letter to Perez Cowan, Dickinson's favorite "Cousin Peter," to console him for the death of a daughter. Must we suppose that the poet didn't really "mean" this poem, that her desire to console was stronger than her honesty, so that she knew herself to be writing merely comforting nonsense?

To answer that the poet never "means" his poems, that as an artist-craftsman he simply *uses* ideas and points of view for the sake of making poems, and that *this* is his "business," will not *do* when we are discussing Dickinson any more than if we were discussing Emerson or Thoreau or Whitman. For all of them, poetry is a form of, or a means to, illumination, and the poet is a seer or visionary first of all, and only secondarily, if at all, a "craftsman," an "artificer." Fantastic distortions result when we view romantic poets through the lens of Eliot's "impersonal" theory of

art. The question "*Did* she mean it?" or "*How* did she mean it?" is not at all an irrelevant response when we read **"And with what bodies do they come?"** after reading **"Ourselves we do inter with sweet derision."** Dickinson's conception of poetry is clearly enough expressed in a good many poems that offer no difficulties of interpretation— **"This was a Poet," "I would not paint—a picture," "I found the words to every thought," "To pile like Thunder to its close,"** and **"I dwell in Possibility,"** for example. The view is familiar, and she never qualifies or complicates it: the artist's concern is with the ineffable, and his poems are revelations of truth, the kind of truth only the imagination can glimpse.

We are left, then, with Dickinson's lack of consistency in belief as a problem. There are two considerations that may help us to reduce the size of the problem. The first involves considering once again her Emersonian heritage, the second, looking for signs of *growth* in her work.

Two poems will take us quickly into the first, the Emersonian, consideration. In the first, she writes a comment on Emerson's "Days": the real reason why we get only "herbs and apples," the practical gifts, instead of "stars, and sky that holds them all," is not, as Emerson had implied, that we *choose* wrongly, but that Nature *gives* us no choice, will not let us inside the show, *keeps* its meanings to itself:

> Dew—is the Freshet in the Grass—
> 'Tis many a tiny Mill
> Turns unperceived beneath our feet
> And Artisan lies still—
>
> We spy the Forests and the Hills
> The Tents to Nature's Show
> Mistake the Outside for the in
> And mention what we saw.
>
> Could Commentators on the Sign
> Of Nature's Caravan
> Obtain "Admission" as a Child
> Some Wednesday Afternoon.

But two poems later in the Johnson edition we read this, which is in effect a comment on the comment:

> My cocoon tightens—Colors tease—
> I'm feeling for the Air—
> A dim capacity for Wings
> Demeans the Dress I wear—
>
> A power of Butterfly must be—
> The Aptitude to fly
> Meadows of Majesty implies
> And easy Sweeps of Sky—
>
> So I must baffle at the Hint
> And cipher at the Sign
> And make much blunder, if at last
> I take the clue divine—

What this says in effect is that we are not necessarily forever to be kept outside. We may "take the clue divine" and come to read nature's Signs correctly, if we have an "Aptitude to fly." In another mood now, the poet blames herself, where before she had blamed the nature of things. Emerson could have told her—*did* tell her—that responding intuitively to nature's meanings was not at all like doing algebra, so that to "cipher at the Sign" would be a sure way of remaining outside the mystery. The two poems belong together as parts of a dialogue. In the second the faithful self answers the skeptical self, saying, as Prufrock would say much later, that she too much debates these matters. Emerson would have approved the second poem as much as he would have deplored the first.

The problem of "consistency" tends to disappear when we look at her poems this way. They are inter-dependent, a *body* of work, no one of them attempting to present "the whole Truth," not aiming at general "truth" abstractly considered at all indeed, not attempting, even in their entirety, *as* a body of work, to construct a "philosophy," but recording movements of the mind responding to "the revelation of the new hour." . . . Alice James's *Diary* is a helpful analogue. Dickinson's poems were *her* diary. Both women were interested in creating a record of what it felt like to live day by day awaiting death. Both felt the sharpest obligation to truth, but the truth they were interested in was the truth of *experience*. One could experience ideas as well as things. One watched ideas go through the mind, watched emotions forming, watched even the debate one carried on with oneself. One might think of Dickinson's poems as a record of a continuous dialogue between parts of herself, aspects of her mind, segments of her complex heritage; except that there are not just the two speakers required by dialogue but always a third, a watcher and listener, amused or dismayed, aware of the limitations of what can be conveyed by words, superior to all dialogue. This ultimate self watches the self writing in the diary or engaging in poetic debate. This self is absolute.

> Lad of Athens, faithful be
> To Thyself,
> And Mystery—
> All the rest is Perjury—

The "lad of Athens" is probably Dionysius the Areopagite, of whom we read in Acts 17:34 that he was one of those converted by Paul's preaching on Mars Hill in Athens. Prior to his conversion, he was presumably also one of those whom Paul accused of worshipping a "God Unknown." The poem, which Johnson tentatively dates only a few years before the poet's death, tells us both how well she understood what Emerson had meant by "self-reliance" and how much the idea continued to mean to her to the end. The self to which one must be faithful was deeper than the rational or the believing self, deeper than all proof and all argument, a self, as he had said, with no known or knowable circumference. Not to rely on *this* self would be to refuse all ultimate responsibility. *This* self might entertain any sort of argument, consider any sort of evidence, face any fact, and remain, as Whitman put it, "imperturbable." No merely rational contradiction could embarrass it.

The poem also tells us what Emerson had meant by his warning against a "foolish consistency." The thrust of his aphorism is against our superficial selves, our social and conventional and worldly selves, which he fears may prevent our being true to the deeper self. The thrust is against the claim of propositional reason to be the arbiter of truth, against the kind of concern for *logical* consistency that would prevent us from changing our minds, once we had become committed to a proposition, against being imprisoned in our own categories. If in fact, as he said, "there is no circumference to us," then the only consistency that matters might better be called by another name, perhaps

integrity. Emerson's warning is in effect a plea, a plea for openness, for growth, for never closing the circle.

"Philosophic" consistency would not be expected of a poet who held such ideas as these. Even when she argued against him, Dickinson was true to Emerson's principles. *Everything* is perjury that does not spring from faithfulness to the self that transcends all argument and all knowing.

If her only consistency was the consistency of growth, we ought to be able to say something about the direction of that growth, perhaps even discern its stages. Until recently, this was impossible, but now that we have all the letters and all the poems, most of them dated, we can at least make a start. But it will have to be a very tentative one, partly because I shall have to assume the correctness of Johnson's dating of letters and poems, but even more because the subject is large enough, and complex enough, for a book that has yet to be written. A "perhaps" should be understood as preceding all the major assertions in what follows.

Reading all the poems at one time, so that one has them more or less in mind all at once, has resulted, in this reader, in several preliminary impressions. Apart from the love poems and occasional poems—saying goodbye to a friend, writing a thank-you note in verse—the majority of her poems may be classified as relating to one of three subjects on which she carried on an inner debate. She debated with her father on the subject of the validity of his faith, she debated with Emerson on the validity of *his,* and she debated with both of them, her *two* fathers as it were, on the question of whether there could be any valid faith at all, as they both thought.

Logically, she had won the debate with her father at least as early as 1859, but the debate continued for many years, for her victory was of the mind only, not the heart, and she found herself drawn back again and again to questions she had already resolved. Some of her finest poems on this subject date from as late as the early seventies. Meanwhile the debate with Emerson had begun in the early sixties, at a time when personal crises made her feel that pain and limitation ought to be given a central place in any description of experience, not ignored or mentioned only as an afterthought in what she came to feel was Emerson's way. By 1875 she had made all the criticisms of Emerson's doctrines she was ever to make. **"Unto the Whole—how add?"** was so devastating a critique of the master's faith considered as a *religion* that it left nothing more to be said; and for once she *said* nothing more in this vein. Though some of her later poems might have been written by Emerson himself, they ignore the more metaphysical aspects of his doctrine. His somewhat pantheistic "Idealism" had ceased to be an issue for her.

The third subject of the inner dialogue recorded in her poems, the debate in which her skeptical self opposed both her fathers, began in the early sixties, reached its peak in the late sixties and early seventies, and then was dropped entirely. Among the poems dated by Johnson in the years from 1879 on until her death in 1886, not one of them returns to the question of whether *any* sort of religious faith is possible for one both informed and honest with himself. "Faith" in these last poems comes to be thought of as a "venture" of the soul with no expectation of "proof" from either a sacred Book or the sign language of nature. Whereas both her father and Emerson had thought that their very different faiths had rested on some sort of *revelation,* divine or natural, and would have agreed that without revelation there could *be* no faith, Dickinson came to believe that, far from being required by anything we could "know" about a reality outside ourselves, faith was simply a "first necessity" of our being, resting on nothing but need.

Redefining faith as commitment in the manner of later Existentialists was agonizingly difficult. Against both the fathers she had urged lack of evidence, an insufficiency of revelation. Increasingly in the sixties she had found God faceless and nature silent, until by 1868 she could announce, "That odd old man is dead a year," and in the following year anticipate Frost's "Design," with which this book began:

> A Spider sewed at Night
> Without a Light
> Upon an Arc of White.
> If Ruff it was of Dame
> Or Shroud of Gnome
> Himself himself inform.
> Of Immortality
> His Strategy
> Was Physiognomy.

In the same year she had written what is perhaps her most despairing poem, beginning **"The Frost of Death was on the Pane"** and concluding

> We hated Death and hated Life
> And nowhere was to go
> Than sea and continent there is
> A larger—it is Woe—.

It was out of such despair as this that her redefinition of faith came, and with it, a new acceptance of life as tragic but not necessarily meaningless. The new definition is best expressed in an early poem, written at a time when she already knew theoretically what her heart could not yet accept:

> Faith—is the Pierless Bridge
> Supporting what We see
> Unto the Scene that We do not—
> Too slender for the eye
> It bears the Soul as bold
> As it were rocked in Steel
> With Arms of Steel at either side—
> It joins—behind the Veil
> To what, could We presume
> The Bridge would cease to be
> To our far, vacillating Feet
> A first Necessity.

When in the years after 1879 she returned to the subject of the nature of faith itself, she reaffirmed the definition she had first achieved at a time when it could not help her. A little poem of 1881 will serve as an example of many similar ones:

> Not seeing, still we know—
> Not knowing, guess—
> Not guessing, smile and hide
> And half caress—
> And quake—and turn away,
> Seraphic fear—
> Is Eden's innuendo

"If you dare"?

Her new "proveless" faith did not cancel anything she knew. It left her as aware as ever of "transport's instability" (contra Emerson), of the impossibility of imagining "costumeless consciousness" (contra her father and personal immortality), aware of what it meant to "cling to nowhere" waiting for the "Crash of nothing." Yet it did have two effects. More often now she returns to Emersonian sentiments like those of **"A Route of Evanescence,"** which dates from this period. Emerson might have written

> Estranged from Beauty—none can be—
> For Beauty is Infinity—
> And power to be finite ceased
> Before Identity was leased.

Or this:

> No matter where the Saints abide,
> They make their Circuit fair
> Behold how great a Firmament
> Accompanies a Star.

The other effect was on the tone of her references to the Bible. Though she still thought it as a whole "an Antique Volume—/ Written by faded Men / At the suggestion of Holy Spectres," more often now she wrote of Christ sympathetically—

> Obtaining but our own Extent
> In whatsoever Realm—
> 'Twas Christ's own personal Expanse
> That bore him from the Tomb—

or with gentle humor—

> The Savior must have been
> A docile Gentleman—
> To come so far so cold a Day
> For little Fellowmen—
>
> The Road to Bethlehem
> Since He and I were Boys
> Was leveled, but for that 'twould be
> A rugged billion Miles—.

More often now the *example* of Christ seemed relevant to her:

> How brittle are the Piers
> On which our Faith doth tread—
> No Bridge below doth totter so—
> Yet none hath such a Crowd.
>
> It is as old as God—
> Indeed—'twas built by him—
> He sent his Son to test the Plank,
> And he pronounced it firm.

Her finest expression of what Christ had come to mean to her would probably have pleased even her father, if he had still been alive to read it and she had shown it to him:

> The Road was lit with Moon and star—
> The Trees were bright and still—
> Descried—by the distant Light
> A Traveller on a Hill
> To magic Perpendiculars
> Ascending, through Terrene—
> Unknown his shimmering ultimate—
> But he indorsed the sheen—

And he would certainly have agreed with the emphasis in the final lines of one of her greatest poems of this period:

Glass was the Street—in tinsel Peril
Tree and Traveller stood—
Filled was the Air with merry venture
Hearty with Boys the Road—

Shot the lithe Sleds like shod vibrations
Emphasized and gone
It is the Past's supreme italic
Makes this Present mean—.

And so she arrived at the simple, almost doctrineless, but existentially meaningful faith she expressed most succinctly two years before her death:

Though the great Waters sleep,
That they are still the Deep,
We cannot doubt—
No vacillating God
Ignited this Abode
To put it out—.

(pp. 314-23)

Hyatt H. Waggoner, "Emily Dickinson: The Transcendent Self," in Criticism, *Vol. VII, No. 4, Fall, 1965, pp. 297-334.*

Elizabeth Jennings (essay date 1965)

[*Jennings is an English poet, critic, and editor who established her literary reputation during the 1950s as part of The Movement, a group of "angry young men" including such writers as Kingsley Amis, Thom Gunn, and Philip Larkin, who used literature as a means of social protest. Critics have praised her scope, richness of style, and technical variety. In the following excerpt, she comments on Dickinson's personal, intense tone, and writes that, though her subjects are few, "they are presented completely, entirely accessible to the reader."*]

Emily Dickinson seems to have been one of those poets who have extracted the largest possible amount of material from the most outwardly meagre and restricted personal experience. Yet she constructed neither a world of pure fantasy nor a series of exquisite objects which, in the manner of Marianne Moore, might be loaded with agitating emotions or pressed into an ecstatic stillness which poetry surrounds but seldom penetrates. Limited in subject-matter and in metrical cadence though they are, her poems somehow give the effect of largeness, of reverberations. The simple quatrains which Emily Dickinson usually employs seem to be not merely neat, box-like forms holding and sustaining poetic *trouvailles,* but rather delicate poetic structures which have the power of suggesting shadows or, to change the metaphor, produce momentous and memorable echoes.

But her skill—and it is great—is not the most noticeable thing about Emily Dickinson's poetic *œuvre.* She is one of those poets who depend finally on personal honesty, on the faithful re-creation of a unique experience and lays that experience, with all the nerves exposed, before her readers.

Her subjects are few and constantly repeated—death, love, frustration, self-questioning, loneliness—but they are presented completely, entirely accessible to the reader. Emily Dickinson is also, in a very real sense, a voice rather

than simply a person, and it is for this reason that she can describe experiences which might, in the hands of less painstakingly honest poets, be self-pitying or mawkish. She works at that heightened level where passion is so undiluted that it can become almost something impersonal. It is not surprising that she was a prolific poet, one who worked at white-heat, continually examining and presenting the same subjects, the same obsessions. At the very centre of her work, herself both the subject and object of her poems, she wrought, out of her own highly individual and nervous self-analyses, a poetry which, paradoxically, generates a universal not a merely personal or particular passion. It is this power which places her among the major American poets.

As R. P. Blackmur has said in his study of Emily Dickinson [see excerpt dated 1927]:

The greatness of Emily Dickinson is not . . . going to be found in anybody's idea of greatness, or of Goethe, or intensity, or mysticism, or historical fatality. It is going to be found in the words she used and in the way she put them together.

And, while commenting on a particular poem, he continues, 'There is no forensic here, nor eloquence, nor justness; it is a bare statement amounting to vision—vision being a kind of observation of the ideal' (p. 35). This is fine, sensitive criticism but I would quarrel with two further comments which Blackmur has made on this poet. One is the remark, 'It [one of her poems] has nothing to do with wisdom, there is no thinking in it', and the other is 'Success was by accident, by the mere momentum of sensibility'. Now the first statement quoted above seems to be everywhere disproved in the poems themselves. They are full of 'thinking' but the thinking is poetic not philosophical, intuitive not organised or discursive. As for Blackmur's remark about Emily Dickinson's accidental successes—this is a criticism which might fairly be levelled against any lyric poet. Blackmur is, I believe, here confusing accident with intuition, chance with the suddenly discovered and surprising truth or felicity. And, furthermore, to use the word 'mere' to qualify the fine phrase 'momentum of sensibility' is surely to belittle all lyric poetry which works by the exercise of concentrated energy in order to find the right word, the fitting cadence. In this sense, *all* lyrical poems are happy accidents but 'accident', in this context, does not seem either a useful or proximate critical term; it obscures far more than it enlightens.

Nevertheless, Blackmur's study is one of the finest introductions to Emily Dickinson's poetry, largely because he is a critic who is entirely at the disposal of the poems he examines. If he blames the state of literature and religion in Emily Dickinson's own time for being the chief cause of her literary limitations, this is at least a generous judgment even if it is not one to which the co-operative reader of the poems is likely to give his full assent.

It is interesting to see, therefore, that another fine American critic, Allen Tate [see excerpt dated 1928-32], approaches Emily Dickinson in a way entirely opposed to that of R. P. Blackmur. He sees the religious climate in which she lived—that of a 'puritan theocracy'—as the atmosphere in which her particular kind of poetry could function most effectively. Thus he declares, 'It gave an heroic proportion and a tragic mode to the experience of the individual . . . it had an immense, incalculable value for literature: it dramatized the human soul'.

These are large words and perhaps they overstate their case; yet at least they gave a plausible reason why Emily Dickinson's sort of poetry could be written in the latter half of the nineteenth century in America. Such general observations about society and religion are not value judgments, they neither clarify nor annotate the poems themselves. They are, in fact, extra-literary reflections, useful scaffoldings, not pathways into the poetry. But they do clear the ground round the poems and enable the reader to examine them on their own terms.

It has been suggested already that Emily Dickinson's poems are notable for their nakedness, for their fearless presentation of experiences which are deeply, and often painfully, personal. But this poet was such a finely adjusted instrument for recording experience that the findings of vision, pain or pleasure which appear in her verse often have a universal application. And it is, oddly enough, sometimes a kind of wry wit which makes this generalising power so effective, as in the following short poem:

> To hang our head ostensibly,
> And subsequent, to find
> That such was not the posture
> Of our immortal mind
>
> Affords the sly presumption
> That in so dense a fuzz
> You too take cobweb attitudes
> Upon a plane of gauze.

It is difficult, I think, to see how any critic could claim that Emily Dickinson had no *thinking* power when they have the evidence of such a poem as this before them.

If Emily Dickinson often seems epigrammatic, even aphoristic, her ideas and her wit are not reproving or admonishing. She is, in one sense, always speaking to herself. It is as if we, her readers, were privileged to overhear her meditations and her arguments with herself. This is intense poetry in the very best sense, taut and vibrant not with emotions and ideas which the poet has already formulated outside the poems, but alive with the very process of thought and feeling. A vision is thus caught on the wing, not trapped but held and halted momentarily, just long enough for the poem to be written.

James Reeves, in his sensitive introduction to a selection of the poems [see Further Reading list], goes far towards explaining the nervous honesty of Emily Dickinson's work when he says:

> She did not withdraw from the world because she hated it: there was nothing in her of the grand romantic manner, rejecting society because the palate had become jaded. Her isolation was a calculated choice, the loss weighed against the gain, with a clear conviction of the necessity and worth of what she had to do.

Reeves is also eager to point out that there was nothing escapist about Emily Dickinson's attitude to life. On the contrary; if she appears to have been retiring and almost eremitical, it was because such an existence enabled her to live more fully, to face her personal predicaments with more dedication and more fearlessness. For her, language

was what prayer is to the religious contemplative. She has indicated this in the following eight-line poem:

> The soul unto itself
> Is an imperial friend,
> Or the most agonising spy
> An enemy could send.
>
> Secure against its own,
> No treason it can fear.
> Itself its sovereign, of itself
> The soul should stand in awe.

Emily Dickinson usually restricts herself to the quatrain or the six-line stanza, but if she thus severely limits herself in the matter of form, she compensates for this limitation by her extremely skillful use of half- and quarter-rhymes and also by her extraordinarily apt and original handling of language. Her poems are fresh not simply because they are quite unlike anyone else's but because they seem to have appropriated a poetic speech and vocabulary hitherto unknown in American or English verse. She has a complete mastery of both sensuous and abstract words, and the success of her best lyrics is often due to a cunning juxtaposition of these two modes of language. She is one of the very few poets who can shock and delight as easily and directly by her handling of abstractions as by the justness and decorum of her concrete imagery. Let me give an example of what I mean by quoting one of her poems:

> Exultation is the going
> Of an inland soul to sea,
> Past the houses, past the headlands,
> Into deep eternity.
>
> Bred as we, among the mountains,
> Can the sailor understand
> The divine intoxication
> Of the first league out from land?

Death is the subject of many of Emily Dickinson's poems, and death for her is as near, as familiar, as commonplace even, as love-affairs are in the poems of less self-sufficient poets. Yet she is not a domestic poet, not a writer who has found a comfortable niche among matters and subjects which are usually thought to be the special province of women poets. Her poems are as bare as Emily Brontë's, as ecstatic as some of Blake's shorter lyrics. If her poems are short, if she is economical and extremely severe with herself, this is because her subjects are so large that they are more effectively presented, more resonant, if they are only hinted at rather than considered at length or extended into long meditations. Her visions are so elusive that to be truthful to them, to suggest the momentariness of their coming and going, she too must be brief but also precise. So in the following twelve-line poem, she tells us more about the questing, visionary mind than many other poets have succeeded in doing in a complete *œuvre:*

> The soul selects her own society,
> Then shuts the door.
> To her divine majority
> Present no more.
>
> Unmoved she notes the chariots pausing
> At her low gate;
> Unmoved, an Emperor be kneeling
> Upon her mat.
> I've known her from an ample nation
> Choose one,

Then close the valves of her attention
Like stone.

Allen Tate has some useful things to say about this power
of Emily Dickinson's to ensnare and hold an elusive idea:

> It is a poetry of ideas [he says]; and it demands of
> the reader a point of view—not an opinion of the
> New Deal or of the League of Nations, but an in-
> grained philosophy that is fundamental, a settled
> attitude that is almost extinct in this eclectic age.
> Yet it is not the sort of poetry of ideas which, like
> Pope's, requires a point of view only. . . .

Thus Emily Dickinson's poems would seem to demand
not only an open sympathy from the reader but also the
deepest and most sensitive kind of poetic response. She
asks for a total engagement, not necessarily a complete
surrender but certainly an acquiescence of the mind and
an alertness of the senses. As has been said already, this
is a poet who extorted the largest possible amount of poetic material from the most apparently meagre personal experience. The explanation of this phenomenon is, of
course, that Emily Dickinson had an intensely rich inner
life. One might almost say that what mountains were to
Wordsworth and what social life was to Pope, the movements of her own mind and heart were to Emily Dickinson. (pp. 97-102)

*Elizabeth Jennings, "Idea and Expression in
Emily Dickinson, Marianne Moore and Ezra
Pound," in* American Poetry, *edited by Irvin
Ehrenpreis, Edward Arnold (Publishers) Ltd.,
1965, pp. 97-113.*

David T. Porter   (essay date 1966)

[*Porter is an American literature specialist and contributor to literary reviews. In the following excerpt from his
book-length study of Dickinson, he sums up her achievement in the early poetry.*]

[In Dickinson's early poems], we discern the distinctive
qualities of her creative mind: an audaciousness born of
irrepressible candor, a startling sensitivity that was yet
sufficiently controlled to be refracted through the instrument of irony and wit, a tragic understanding not to be
compromised by the promise of heaven or the onslaught
of despair, a latent nervous energy the more remarkable
for its disciplined release. We discern, too, the distinctive
qualities of her art: its bold disregard of conventional
shapeliness, the surprise of its novel verbal strategies, its
seizure of the significant image, its disconcerting integrity
in psychological disclosures, its firm control of powerful
emotion.

Like filings in a magnetic field, those early poems which
assert her genius define the emotional contours of the central theme of aspiration. In them she savors the distance
between desire and its goal. Where specific poems have a
dramatic immediacy as performance, the speaker, in one
or the other attitude of her divergent roles or in an attitude
constituted of both, is distinct and impressive. In several
of these compositions of highest achievement, the metrical
base provides occasion for the irony, and the central metaphorical construct of motion and stasis orders the perceptions. Throughout, instances of rhyme variation and stylistic mannerism that we now recognize as Emily Dickin-

son's unique mode of expression charge the poems with
urgency, create the feelings of spontaneity and sincerity,
and make us constantly aware of the immanence of the
creative personality.

In diverse ways, each element contributes to the concision
and accompanying complexity of her expression, and ultimately to that fine interior control she exercises over the
emotional vitality within her poems. Indeed, in her finest
poems the emotional experience reaches an intensity that
necessarily reveals at the same time the stylistic control
which prevents those feelings from lapsing into intemper-
ance. Her success in confining the centrifugal pressures of
emotions within an aesthetic framework represents perhaps her highest achievement as an artist. That achievement of control which would not stifle the intensity she intended to express undoubtedly posed her most challenging
problem. The questing condition and the recurrent recognition that mortality forever denies ideal fulfillment are
states inherently subject to the extremes of emotion. Yet,
even though for Emily Dickinson the emotions mediated
her experience, her art allowed her to order those potentially destructive psychic responses.

The principal method by which she resolved this problem
of control is her absolute distillation of expression, which
provides not only a formal control but so closely circum-
scribes emotions that they cannot trail off into self-
indulgence. This ability of extreme condensation attests
also to her powers of psychological insight, for with the
greatest economy of terms she could reach directly to the
core of a particular feeling. This habit of the elliptic expression, however, sometimes fragments her compositions. The early works provide numerous examples of the
precise and piercing expression, yet these fragments of genius sometimes constitute the single effective element of
otherwise unsuccessful poems. Foreshadowings of her
consummate artistry reside in these brilliant expressions
which typify her poetic mode.

A complete gathering of her markedly felicitous and distinctly Dickinsonion phrases would be an extensive one,
for early in her career the ability to compact articulation
in deceptively simple terms is fully developed. Among her
reflections on death, for example, she distills in two lines
the recognition of the inevitability of death:

> Good night, because we must,
> How intricate the dust!

In rebellious pose, she concentrates in political metaphor
the recognition of the uncommitted state of her soul, declaring that

> Imps in eager Caucus
> Raffle for my Soul!

She imaginatively constructs in homely metaphor the experience of death in the absence of any guiding faith:

> Dying! Dying in the night!
> Wont somebody bring the light
> So I can see which way to go
> Into the everlasting snow?

Early, too, she was capable of pressing her reflections on
the precise moment of death into remarkably concise expressions. She seems repeatedly to have applied herself to
formulating an answer to the problem posed in the line

which begins an otherwise unsuccessful poem: "She died—*this* was the way she died." Fixing upon the image of the open eyes glazed in death, she defines that condition as

> . . . but our rapt attention
> To Immortality.

She precisely objectifies the abstract terms by picturing the final physical convulsion:

> A throe upon the features—
> A hurry in the breath—
> An extasy of parting
> Denominated "Death."

The qualities of utter finality and motionlessness she describes succinctly as

> The quiet nonchalance of death—
> No Daybreak—can bestir.

Defined irreverently in the terms of commerce, death is

> . . . just the price of *Breath*—
> With but the "Discount" of the *Grave*—
> Termed by the *Brokers*—"*Death*"!

Death personified is a frighteningly efficient workman. He is:

> Industrious! Laconic!
> Punctual! Sedate!
> Bold as a Brigand!

Like the frost's, his work is irreversible, and so the gestures of grief the mourner offers

> Were useless as next morning's sun—
> Where midnight frosts—had lain!

The lifeless body, dispossessed even of gender in its new state, yet becomes of greatest worth when lost. Its value grows

> Vast—in it's fading ratio
> To our penurious eyes!

Emily Dickinson's obsessive recognition of the absolute disjunction which death causes demanded the creation of a new word for the condition of the dead, who exist

> . . . while we stare,
> In Leagueless Opportunity,
> O'ertakeless, as the Air.

> (pp. 156-60)

These varied examples of her fresh and arresting technique, however, are little more than dissociated fragments of her genius. The poems in which this artistry is sustained are the superior achievements and, indeed, are the ultimate products of those early attempts at refining an authentic voice. (p. 163)

Perhaps her most artful metaphorical excursion in the early period is to be found in the poem **"A Clock stopped."** The figure of man as a clock puppet conveys the satirical recognition that man lives his "Dial life" according to the gestures of a clock face. The tragic knowledge is that the force is inhuman, with power neither to create nor restore the life it tyrannizes. The poem . . . proclaims the absolute change that death effects: when man dies into another life, into a scheme of timelessness, no skill of this earth can

call him back from "Degreeless Noon," through the "Decades of Arrogance" to this "Dial life" again:

> A Clock stopped—
> Not the Mantel's—
> Geneva's farthest skill
> Cant put the puppet bowing—
> That just now dangled still—

> An awe came on the Trinket!
> The Figures hunched, with pain—
> Then quivered out of Decimals—
> Into Degreeless Noon—

> It will not stir for Doctor's—
> This Pendulum of snow—
> The Shopman importunes it—
> While cool-concernless No—

> Nods from the Gilded pointers—
> Nods from the Seconds slim—
> Decades of Arrogance between
> The Dial life—
> And Him.

This poem slays with stunning directness the cozy dream of recapturing what is lost to time by turning back the clock. Out of that cliché Emily Dickinson compounded a telling commentary on man's routine of life, the drama of his death, and the nature of the immensity of that change. (pp. 167-68)

[Ultimately] the totality of her art in the early years is greater than the sum of the individual elements that go into its makeup. Her expressive skills combined to effect a concision, a specific gravity, as it were, not often encountered in English poetry. Her elliptic expression is all the more remarkable for embodying the complexity which it does. That complexity and the intensity of the feeling with which she informs her best works from this period are, in turn, the more remarkable for being under firm control. Long before she wrote to Higginson to inquire if her poetry "breathed," Emily Dickinson had reached on several occasions that high level of lyric expression at which extraordinary emotional impulses are matched and dominated by even more extraordinary discipline. Beyond this accomplishment, she had by 1862 developed her unique ability to dissociate feelings from the limitations of specific causal experiences. Her poems exist independent of the confining facts of exterior experience, and become thereby increasingly universal. She distilled the essential psychic responses to experience—those feelings that are communicable most fully intact. That she displayed this consummate artistry in a substantial body of early work, and that in an even greater number of poems she successfully experimented in usages outside the poetic conventions of her time, provides irrefutable testimony to the judgment that she composed with purpose and conviction. (p. 175)

> *David T. Porter, in his* The Art of Emily Dickinson's Early Poetry, *Cambridge, Mass.: Harvard University Press, 1966, 206 p.* * [*The excerpts of Emily Dickinson's work used here were originally published in her* The Complete Poems of Emily Dickinson, *Little, Brown and Company, 1960*].

Sharon Cameron   (essay date 1979)

[*Cameron is an American literature scholar whose writings include* The Corporeal Self: Allegories of the Body in Melville and Hawthorne *(1981) and* Writing Nature: Henry Thoreau's "Journal" *(1985). The following excerpt is taken from the chapter "Naming as History" included in Cameron's* Lyric Time: Dickinson and the Limits of Genre *(1979). The portion reprinted below focuses on the weaknesses in Dickinson's "definition" poems.*]

For Emily Dickinson, perhaps no more so than for the rest of us, there was a powerful discrepancy between what was "inner than the Bone—" and what could be acknowledged. To the extent that her poems are a response to that discrepancy—are, on the one hand, a defiant attempt to deny that the discrepancy poses a problem and, on the other, an admission of defeat at the problem's enormity—they have much to teach us about the way in which language articulates our life. There is indeed a sense in which these poems test the limits of what we might reveal if we tried, and also of what, despite our exertions, will not give itself over to utterance. . . . [Her] poems disassemble the body in order to penetrate to the places where feelings lie, as if hidden, and they tell us that bodies are not barriers the way we sometimes think they are. Despite the staggering sophistication with which we discuss complex issues, like Dickinson, we have few words, if any, for what happens inside us. Perhaps this is because we have been taught to conceive of ourselves as perfectly inexplicable or, if explicable, then requiring the aid of someone else to scrutinize what we are explicating, to validate it. We have been taught that we cannot see for ourselves—this despite the current emphasis on our proprioceptive functions. But Dickinson tells us that we can see. More important, she tells us how to name what we see.

Naming, defining, creating propositions—a significant group of Dickinson's poems are engaged in these strenuous tasks, and fulfill them with varying degrees of perplexity and success. . . . (pp. 26-7)

But there are problems with naming in Dickinson's poetry. The names Dickinson gives us for experiences are frequently the most striking aspect of her poetry, and they occur often, as one might expect, in poems of definition. The problem they ask us to consider is precisely their relationship to the context in which they occur. Definitions in Dickinson's poems take two forms. The first group of statements contain the copula as the main verb, and their linguistic structure is some variation of the nominative plus the verb "to be" plus the rest of the predicate. The characteristics of the predicate are transferred to the nominative, and this transference becomes a fundamental aspect of the figurative language, as the following examples indicate:

God is a distant—stately Lover—

Mirth is the Mail of Anguish—

Crisis is a Hair / Toward which forces creep

The Lightning is a yellow Fork / From Tables in the sky

Safe Despair it is that raves— / Agony is frugal.

Water, is taught by thirst.

Utmost is relative— / Have not or Have / Adjacent sums

Faith—is the Pierless Bridge

Drama's Vitallest Expression is the Common Day

The previous assertions are global in nature, encapsulating the totality or whole of the subject under scrutiny. The following group of assertions attempt to establish a single aspect or identic property of the thing being defined:

A South Wind—has a pathos / Of individual Voice—

Pain—has an Element of Blank—

Remembrance has a Rear and Front—

Or they personify characteristic actions and attributes of the subject under consideration, distinguishing and so defining them:

The Heart asks Pleasure—first—

Absence disembodies—so does Death

The Admirations—and Contempts—of time— / Show justest—through an Open Tomb—

Many of these assertions are frankly aphoristic:

A Charm invests a face / Imperfectly beheld—

Perception of an object costs / Precise the Object's loss—

for in both groups, feeling and experience are abstracted from the context that prompted them, and from temporal considerations; the words are uttered in the third person present tense and may lack definite and indefinite articles, all of these strategies contributing to the speaker's authority, as they make a claim to experiential truth that transcends the limitations of personal experience. The distinctions between the two groups may seem to exist more in formulation than in function. Nonetheless, given a range of utterance, the former assertions lie at the epigrammatic extreme and occur with more frequency in the poems (it is thus with them that I shall be most concerned); the latter assertions, which appear with increased frequency in the letters, by their very admission of partiality, come closer to confessing their evolution from a particular incident or context.

The function of a successful formulation, one that says reality is one way and not another, is that it have no qualification; that it be the last word. The problem in many of Dickinson's poems is that it is the first word. It was Emerson who called proverbs "the literature of reason, or the statements of an absolute truth without qualification," and there is a sense in which statements like "Capacity to Terminate / Is a Specific Grace" or "Not 'Revelation'— 'tis that waits / But our unfurnished eyes" preclude further statement because any statement will qualify them.

Hobbes, in *The Leviathan*, makes the following observation about names and definitions:

> Seeing then that truth consists in the right ordering of names in our affirmations, a man that seeketh precise truth had need to remember what every name he useth stands for . . . or else he will find himself entangled in words, as a bird in lime-twigs. . . . And therefore in geometry (which is the only science which it hath pleased God hitherto to bestow on mankind), men begin at settling the significations of their words; which settling of

signications they call *definitions*, and place them in the beginning of their reckoning.

Geometric constructions are not, however, metaphoric ones, and it is important to note that in poems such definitional knowledge is credited best when it occurs at the end of a speaker's reckoning. Perhaps this is because, unlike Hobbes, we believe that, at least in poems, definitions are neither arbitrary nor conventionally agreed-upon assignations. Wrested from experience, they imply a choice whose nature is only made manifest by its context.

But Dickinson's names and definitions not only posit themselves at the beginning of poems, they also shrug off the need for further context, for it is difficult to acknowledge the complexity of a situation while stressing its formulaic qualities—unless the point of the formulation is to reveal complexity. In fact, definitions are often predicated on the assumption that experience can be expressed summarily as one thing. The detachable quality of some of Dickinson's lines receives comment as early as 1892 when Mabel Loomis Todd writes:

> How does the idea of an "Emily Dickinson Yearbook" strike you? . . . My thought is that with isolated lines from the already published poems, many of which are perfect comets of thought, and some of those wonderful epigrams from the *Letters*, together with a mass of *unpublished* lines which I should take from poems which could never be used entire, I could make the most brilliant year-book ever issued. . . . If I do not do it, some one else will want to, because ED abounds so in epigrams—.

One of her first biographers, George Whicher, comments: "Her states of mind were not progressive but approximately simultaneous." R. P. Blackmur summarizes the situation less charitably when he speaks of Dickinson's poems as "mere fragmentary indicative notation," and in a statement cited only in part in the Introduction, he explains himself: "The first thing to notice—a thing characteristic of exercises—is that the order or plot of the elements of the poem is not that of a complete poem; the movement of the parts is downwards and towards a disintegration of the effect wanted. A good poem so constitutes its parts as at once to contain them and to deliver or release by the psychological force of their sequence the full effect only when the poem is done" [see excerpt dated 1937]. For how a poem tells the time of the experience it narrates directly determines the crucial relationship between what we might distinguish as the mechanism of that poem's closure and its true completion, which would be perceived as a "natural" end even were the utterance to continue beyond. We have different modes of reference to the movement that leads to the coincidence of closure and internal completion within a given poem. We speak of a poem's progressions, of emotions if not of actions, of its building. We are thus presuming that a poem has development, a sense of its own temporal structure. When a poem remains innocent of the knowledge of an ordering temporality, the poem and its meaning are problematic. . . . (pp. 29-32)

There are frequent instances in Dickinson's definitional poems where the poem's conclusion follows poorly from its beginning. Sometimes, as in the following poem, it is redundant and hence gratuitous:

> Hope is a subtle Glutton—

> He feeds upon the Fair—
> And yet—inspected closely
> What Abstinence is there—

> His is the Halcyon Table—
> That never seats but One—
> And whatsoever is consumed
> The same amount remain—

The second stanza glosses the first. It explains the fact that Hope's table is prosperous (a restatement of line 2), and that Hope's consumption in no way depletes the fare of reality, since Hope feasts only in supposition (an idea contained in the last two lines of the first stanza). The problem with the restatement is that it is not particularly interesting. Similarly, the opening of the following poem has an exactitude that its conclusion lacks:

> Longing is like the Seed
> That wrestles in the Ground,
> Believing if it intercede
> It shall at length be found.

> The Hour, and the Clime—
> Each Circumstance unknown,
> What Constancy must be achieved
> Before it see the Sun!

Similes recognize that we fail at direct names because we fail at perfect comprehension, and that certain experiences evade mastery and hence definition—the best we can do is approximate or approach them; a simile is an acknowledgment of that failure and contains within it the pain of imperfect rendering. What is evocative about the simile in [the poem above] is the way in which it gets the verb to enact the tension between being, which is manifest, and presence, which is hidden. This tension is precisely the essence of longing, and externalizing it reveals the conflict: it can never be perfectly rendered because, half-hidden with its object, it can never be perfectly apprehended. Dickinson is using the word "intercede" to suggest that surfacing of longing which would be tantamount to its acknowledgment, its open coming between the speaker and an instigating source. What might be "found" at such a moment is not simply the shape of the buried feeling, but also its object, which, one presumes, is similarly absent or unavailable. In the poem's following lines, however, both the representation of tension between presence and being and the recognition that it is this tension that makes longing so difficult to represent are abandoned, and the simile is "extended" with little regard for the significance of its original distinction. Here, then, as in the previous poem, the most complex part of the assertion is the name itself. In such an instance, an explanation of, or rationale for, the genesis of the name after the fact of it cannot help but affect the reader as gratuitous.

As in the following poem, the definition exists for the purpose of dismissing the situation with which it purports to deal:

> Remorse—is Memory—awake
> Her Parties all astir—
> A Presence of Departed Acts—
> At window—and at Door—

> Its Past—set down before the Soul
> And lighted with a Match—
> Perusal—to facilitate—
> Of its Condensed Despatch

Remorse is cureless—the Disease
Not even God—can heal—
For 'tis His institution—and
The Complement of Hell—

The emphasis in the first two stanzas is on the excruciating sense in which we can be inhabited by a past that will not stay still. Remorse awakens memory and memory prevents calmness (perhaps literally prevents sleep, as the metaphor in the first line suggests) by lighting our minds with unwanted thoughts. Remorse (for that is the match) illuminates the past so that the flash revealed to us is simply accusatory. If we did not distort the past by condensing it, if we knew not to simplify, the accusation would be less clear. The speaker is defining a situation in which our experiences play upon our minds in such a way that we cannot doubt them to be ours, yet robbed of their specificity, we cannot see them as they in fact happened to us. The hell of remorse is that it blinds us to the real meanings of our experiences and simultaneously convinces us that the distortion we are seeing in place of that meaning is reality.

Our sense of the speaker in the first two stanzas is that of someone who is naming or defining an experience in order to achieve mastery over it. But in the third stanza, control is secured as a consequence of ascribing blame, so the focus of the poem narrows to exclude experience. The definitions in the first two stanzas are concerned with the quality of remorse. In them the speaker makes clear the way in which remorse is experiential hell. The definition in the third stanza is concerned with its cause. There we are told about the way in which it is a complement of theological Hell. That remorse is God's institution may be a matter of fact or, more important, a matter of belief, but it shifts the speaker's role in the experience by predicating an agent for the affliction. A relationship exists between these two factors but the poem is not positioned with respect to that relationship.

In the following poem, a disjunction between the initial naming in line one and the lines that follow it leads the reader to interpretive despair, for there is no way to figure the confusion that ensues:

Doom is the House without the Door—
'Tis entered from the Sun—
And then the Ladder's thrown away,
Because Escape—is done—

'Tis varied by the Dream
Of what they do outside—
Where Squirrels play—and Berries die—
And Hemlocks—bow—to God—

If the statement in line one is literal, it perhaps refers to the grave. But it need not be literal, perhaps cannot be literal, as line two suggests. Maybe then the speaker is using "Doom" as a metaphor for an inevitability one may come to dwell in (like a house) but be unaware of (and therefore enter like a doorless house). The second stanza, far from clarifying these concerns, only confuses them, for the shape of the two realities implicitly being compared remains too ambiguously sketched for the reader to see a coherent picture.

The lack of explicit connection between the statements in a definitional poem sometimes results in speech that is almost unintelligible:

Experience is the Angled Road
Preferred against the Mind
By—Paradox—the Mind itself—
Presuming it to lead

Quite Opposite—How Complicate
The Discipline of Man—
Compelling Him to Choose Himself
His Preappointed Pain—

The distinctions are so coiled here that it is difficult to understand them. One way of interpreting the first stanza is to assume that experience is chosen above the mind (preferred against it) even though (and this is the paradox) the mind itself states its preference for experience. But it is not clear what the mind presumes experience will "lead / Quite Opposite [to]," since the line breaks in the middle of the thought. If we infer that the object of the implicit preposition is "pain," this is still awkward sense, and it is certainly awkward syntax. The real problem, however, is that the focus of the poem shifts in stanza two. There "The Discipline of Man," an idiosyncratic but in no way interesting (because not made relevant) periphrasis for the mind, is called "Complicate," and this is then stated as the reason man chooses his "Preappointed Pain," itself an unexplained paradox. "Preappointed," moreover, has resonances of a final judgment, though whether of salvation or damnation is not clear. These resonances come from the word itself and our inferences about how Dickinson might be likely to use it rather than from the poem's context. While there is too little linguistic specificity to substantiate inference, one wonders if the speaker is choosing between the immediacy of this world and the promise of the next only to discover that any choice must confront the inevitability of pain. The problem with my reading is that while the mind has been rendered as complex, it has not been so rendered in terms of these specific issues. The problem with the poem and particularly with that suggestive last phrase is that it insinuates my reading without confirming it.

The poems about which I have been speaking have become progressively more difficult to understand, and the efforts at understanding them progressively less rewarding. In **"Hope is a subtle Glutton"** we found that the poem repeated without elaborating upon its initial name; in **"Longing is like the Seed"** and **"Remorse is Memory awake"** that complex situations were stated only to be dismissed by the poems' conclusions; in **"Doom is the House without the Door"** and **"Experience is the Angled Road"** that context and conclusion bore such an ambiguous relation to the initial names that we literally could make no sense even of the names themselves. The problem with these poems and with the many like them is twofold. First, they raise the question of the point in an experience at which one's awareness of it yields a name. For whether a name seems gratuitous or appropriate is contingent upon its relationship to the rest of the experience being narrated. Second, there is the problem of how a given speaker manifests the need of, or reason for, the name at which she arrives. It is not here my intention to theorize on criteria for fictional coherence, but it ought to be obvious that one credits speech in direct presence, and no less in poems, that issues out of a discernible and describable situation and that is functional in nature. . . . (pp. 34-8)

Sharon Cameron, in her Lyric Time: Dickinson and the Limits of Genre, *The Johns Hopkins University Press, 1979, 280 p.*

Cheryl Walker   (essay date 1982)

[*In the following excerpt from her book-length study of American women poets before 1900, Walker details the hallmarks of Dickinson's style, stressing her contributions to the writings and careers of later female poets: "After Emily Dickinson's work became known, women poets in America could take their work seriously."*]

[What] distinguishes Emily Dickinson from other women poets is her skill with words, her use of language. She retained her compression despite pressure from her closest friends and critics, people like Samuel Bowles and T. W. Higginson, who would have made her more discursive. She introduced unusual vocabulary into women's poetry—vocabulary borrowed from various professions mainly closed to women, like law, medicine, the military, and merchandising. I agree with Adrienne Rich that she knew she was a genius. Nothing else could explain her peculiar invulnerability to contemporary criticism of her work.

Dickinson wrote many poems about violation. The integrity of some poems was literally violated by editors who made unauthorized changes before printing them. But the poet triumphed in the end. She created a unique voice in American poetry and would not modulate it, even for Higginson who directed her to writers like Maria Lowell and Helen Hunt Jackson as models.

Like Lowell and Jackson, Dickinson did not look down on the female poetic subjects of her day. She used them; but she used them in what would come to be perceived as a poetic assault on the feminine conventions from which they sprung. She was not, for instance, taken in by the propaganda of "true womanhood." She saw behind the virtue of modesty the caricature of the double-bind.

> A Charm invests a face
> Imperfectly beheld—
> The Lady dare not lift her Vail
> For fear it be dispelled—
>
> But peers beyond her mesh—
> And wishes—and denies—
> Lest Interview—annul a want
> That Image—satisfies—

Perhaps Dickinson's ambivalent relation to the world has more to do with this lady "who dare not lift her Vail" than has previously been perceived. What this poem captures is the feelings of a woman who must obtain what she wants through deception and manipulation. Thus it does not simply represent the familiar Dickinson wisdom that hunger tantalizes where satiety cloys. This woman's feelings become part of the substance of the poem. They are fear (of male rejection), curiosity, and desire. The lady must finally deny her desires, sublimate her will to power, and assume a passive role. **"A Charm"** might also serve as a commentary on a poem written three years earlier.

> Our lives are Swiss—
> So still—so Cool—
> Till some odd afternoon
> The Alps neglect their Curtains
> And we look farther on!

Italy stands the other side!
While like a guard between—
The solemn Alps—
The siren Alps
Forever intervene!

We recognize the theme of the unattained, so close to the hearts of women like Lucy Larcom and Elizabeth Oakes-Smith. Here, however, the barriers both forbid assault and invite it. They are both awesome and enticing. Like the lady who "peers beyond her mesh," this speaker hasn't accepted the limitations on her experience. Though undemonstrative, she remains unreconciled.

The insights made available by the comparison of these two poems can help us even when we examine the particular language that made Dickinson unique. Take, for example, the following poem written during her most creative period.

> I had not minded—Walls—
> Were Universe—one Rock—
> And far I heard his silver Call
> The other side the Block—
>
> I'd tunnel—till my Groove
> Pushed sudden thro' to his—
> Then my face take her Recompense—
> The looking in his Eyes—
>
> But 'tis a single Hair—
> A filament—a law—
> A Cobweb—wove in Adamant—
> A Battlement—of Straw—
>
> A limit like the Vail
> Unto the Lady's face—
> But every Mesh—a Citadel—
> And Dragons—in the Crease—

This is a poem about the forbidden lover, and as such it reminds us of what Dickinson could do with conventional female subjects. Although this is not one of Dickinson's best poems, it exhibits many of her characteristic innovations and therefore makes an interesting focus for discussion. Does this poem have roots in real experience or was it merely an exercise?

In the second Master letter, probably composed about this time and intended for a recipient we can no longer identify, the poet asked: "Couldn't Carlo [her dog], and you and I walk in the meadows an hour—and nobody care but the Bobolink—and *his*—a *silver* scruple? I used to think when I died—I could see you—so I died as fast as I could—but the 'Corporation' are going Heaven too so [Eternity] wont be sequestered—now [at all]—". Here we find the familiar impossible attachment forbidden by "the Corporation," the constituted powers. It is an attachment that can only be indulged in secret, in some "sequestered" place. This Master letter has too much unrefined feeling in it to be the product of a merely literary pose, and I suggest that the poem was also written out of felt experience, although the structural properties this experience assumed may well have been influenced by the vocabulary of secret sorrow.

Dickinson begins "I had not minded—Walls" in the subjunctive, one of her characteristic modes. Thus, she establishes the initial grounds of the poem as those of the non-real, the if. The first two stanzas posit a set of circumstances that would allow for fulfillment, the enticement of the view. . . . The last two stanzas, in contrast, describe the limitations on fulfillment that forever intervene.

Typical of Dickinson's language, the poem contrasts short Anglo-Saxon words with longer Latinate ones. "Block," "eyes," "groove," "law," and "mesh," for example, are all Anglo-Saxon and convey even in their brevity a sense of abrupt limitation. "Recompense," "universe," "filament," "citadel," and "dragon," on the other hand, are Latinate words: softer and more excursive. They have feminine endings. Using the same short vowel sounds as the Anglo-Saxon words, they nevertheless convey an opposite sense of possibility. Although the words themselves do not always mean what their sounds convey ("citadel" being used to suggest an obstacle instead of a possibility), there is at the levels of both meaning and sound a sense of opposition: desire vs. frustration. Dickinson's language operates on the basis of paired antitheses. Other pairings include the concrete vs. the abstract (face/recompense), the material vs. the immaterial (rock/silver call), and the hard vs. the soft (adamant/cobweb). Her code is conflict.

Thus far we might compare her use of language to Shakespeare's, which also depends upon doublings, paradoxes, contrasts. However, Dickinson, though she loved Shakespeare, chose to be more obscure, and she did this largely by breaking linguistic rules out of a commitment to compression. The first stanza, for instance, might be paraphrased: I would not have minded walls. Were the universe to have been entirely made up of rock and were I to have heard his call from afar, it would have seemed to me merely a short distance, the other side of the block. This, of course, reduces the impact of Dickinson's compression. "Block" in her poem affects one like a pun, reminding us of "rock" earlier, as well as of the geographical meaning of "block," a city street division.

Dickinson was criticized in her day for this kind of compression. It flew in the face of most contemporary poetry, which aimed at comprehensiveness through discursive exposition. Emerson was probably her closest friend here, but even he did not break rules as flagrantly as she. Her editors also grumbled at her rhymes. "His" and "eyes" did not seem like rhyming words to them.

The structure of this poem represents a final contrast to the conventions of her time. In "Acquainted with Grief," Helen Hunt Jackson posits an unnatural occurrence by personifying grief. However, once this given is accepted, the poem never departs from its established world. Dickinson, however, reverses expectations everywhere. She begins in the realm of "if," making all the details of this realm concrete and existential: *walls, rock, block, tunnel, groove,* and *face* are part of her real world of experience. Nevertheless, when the tense shifts from the subjunctive to the present, suddenly we have paradoxes that do not belong to an experiential realm: a cobweb woven in adamant, a mesh that is a citadel, and finally, dragons, mythical beasts belonging to the world of imagination.

Furthermore, in the sequence filament/law, cobweb/adamant, and battlement/straw there is a reversal of terms in the final pair. The first two move from the insubstantial to the substantive, the last one from the substantive back to the insubstantial. "Adamant" is echoed in "battlement," but the "law" becomes "straw."

The structural progression from the real to the surreal is recognizably characteristic of Dickinson. And here the lines, "A limit like the Vail / Unto the Lady's face," become significant. Like the veil, the limitations Dickinson describes are restrictive in the real world. The seemingly insubstantial "hair" is tougher than rock, and like the veil of restrictions women must accept, to pass beyond these limitations forces one to encounter terrible dragons. However, a citadel, the *Oxford English Dictionary* tells us, is a "fortress commanding a city, which it serves both to protect and to keep in subjugation." Like the prison, this image reminds us of Dickinson's Houdini-like ability to wriggle out of confining spaces, to convert limitations into creative resources. Dragons are at least interesting to contemplate. The lady's veil—the symbol of Dickinson's sense of social, legal, and literary restrictions—provided her with a certain recompense. Thus the reversal in the third stanza, where limiting law becomes insubstantial straw, works.

Ultimately, Emily Dickinson transformed her closed world into a creative space. If there is a disappointment in this poem, it comes in the second stanza where "the looking in his eyes" seems a rather weak way of describing this triumph. But whatever its limitations, this poem shows us the way an artist like Dickinson could make interesting use of motifs such as the secret sorrow and the forbidden lover. Her vision was "slant," and therefore to us thoroughly refreshing.

Recently it has become fashionable to see Emily Dickinson as a woman who lived in the realm of transcendence, secure in the space she created for the exercise of her power. Although I am sympathetic with this view, I would like to add a word of caution. No one can read Dickinson's poems and letters in their entirety without a sense that the ground for security was forever shifting under her feet. She did not resort to references to fear only out of coyness. She felt it. She wrote: "In all the circumference of Expression, those guileless words of Adam and Eve never were surpassed, 'I was afraid and hid Myself'". And elsewhere: "Your bond to your brother reminds me of mine to my sister—early, earnest, indissoluble. Without her life were fear, and Paradise a cowardice, except for her inciting voice." To rejoice that she found ways of evading the subjugation of the spirit that her society enforced upon its women should not mean ignoring her sense of vulnerability, which was real, which was tragic. In Dickinson's preoccupation with the imagery of royalty, we find her desire to exercise the full range of her talents; we find her will to power. In her preoccupation with falling, surrendering, confinement, and violation, we find her fears. Knowing what she had to give up, recognition within her lifetime, the chance to remain within the world she devoured information about through her friends and her newspaper, we can only be glad that at moments she had the perspective to write:

> The Heart is the Capital of the Mind—
> The Mind is a single State—
> The Heart and the Mind together make
> A single Continent—
>
> One is the Population—
> Numerous enough—
> This ecstatic Nation
> Seek—it is Yourself.

The puzzle of Emily Dickinson's work is finally not a

question of the identity of the Master or the extent of her real experience, but one of tradition and the individual talent. Although the concern with intense feeling, the ambivalence toward power, the fascination with death, the forbidden lover and secret sorrow all belong to this women's tradition, Emily Dickinson's best work so far surpasses anything that a logical extension of that tradition's codes could have produced that the only way to explain it is by the single word, genius. She was "of the Druid." That a great many poems like **"I tie my Hat—I crease my Shawl"** are in places not much above the women's poetry of her time is only to be expected. What Emily Dickinson did for later women poets, like Amy Lowell who wanted to write her biography, was remarkable: she gave them dignity. No other aspect of her influence was so important. After Emily Dickinson's work became known, women poets in America could take their work seriously. She redeemed the poetess for them, and made her a genuine poet. (pp. 111-16)

> Cheryl Walker, "Tradition and the Individual Talent: Helen Hunt Jackson and Emily Dickinson," in her The Nightingale's Burden: Women Poets and American Culture before 1900, *Indiana University Press, 1982, pp. 87-116.*

Joyce Carol Oates (lecture date 1986)

[*Oates is an American fiction writer and critic who is perhaps best known for her novel* them, *which won a National Book Award in 1970. Her fiction is noted for its exhaustive presentation of realistic detail as well as its striking imagination, especially in the evocation of abnormal psychological states. As a critic, Oates has written on a remarkable diversity of authors—from Shakespeare to Herman Melville to Samuel Beckett—and is appreciated for the individuality and erudition that characterize her critical work. In the following excerpt from a lecture given at the University of North Carolina (Chapel Hill) in 1986, she analyzes Dickinson's style and themes, noting that her "greatness as a poet . . . lies in the amplitude of her poetry."*]

Emily Dickinson is the most paradoxical of poets: the very poet of paradox. By way of voluminous biographical material, not to mention the extraordinary intimacy of her poetry, it would seem that we know everything about her: yet the common experience of reading her work, particularly if the poems are read sequentially, is that we come away seeming to know nothing. We would recognize her inimitable voice anywhere—in the "prose" of her letters no less than in her poetry—yet it is a voice of the most deliberate, the most teasing anonymity. "I'm Nobody!" is a proclamation to be interpreted in the most literal of ways. Like no other poet before her and like very few after her—Rilke comes most readily to mind, and, perhaps, Yeats and Lawrence—Dickinson exposes her heart's most subtle secrets; she confesses the very sentiments that, in society, would have embarrassed her dog (to paraphrase a remark of Dickinson's to Thomas Wentworth Higginson, explaining her aversion for the company of most people, whose prattle of "Hallowed things" offended her). Yet who is this "I" at the center of experience? In her astonishing body of 1,775 poems Dickinson records what is surely one of the most meticulous examinations of the phenomenon of human "consciousness" ever undertaken. The poet's persona—the tantalizing "I"—seems, in nearly every poem, to be addressing us directly with perceptions that are ours as well as hers. (Or his: these "Representatives of the Verse," though speaking in Dickinson's voice, are not restricted to the female gender.) The poems' refusal to be rhetorical, their daunting intimacy, suggests the self-evident in the way that certain Zen koans and riddles suggest the self-evident while being indecipherable. But what is challenged is, perhaps, "meaning" itself:

> Wonder—is not precisely Knowing
> And not precisely Knowing not—
> A beautiful but bleak condition
> He has not lived who has not felt—
>
> Suspense—is his maturer Sister—
> Whether Adult Delight is Pain
> Or of itself a new misgiving—
> This is the Gnat that mangles men—

In this wonder there is a tone of the purest anonymity, as if the poet, speaking out of her "beautiful but bleak condition," were speaking of our condition as well. Dickinson's idiom has the startling ring of contemporaneity, like much of Shakespeare's; she speaks from the interior of a life as we might imagine ourselves speaking, gifted with genius's audacity and shorn of the merely local and time-bound. If anonymity is the soul's essential voice—its seductive, mesmerizing, fatal voice—then Emily Dickinson is our poet of the soul: our most endlessly fascinating American poet. As Whitman so powerfully addresses the exterior of American life, so Dickinson addresses—or has she helped create?—its unknowable interior.

No one who has read even a few of Dickinson's extraordinary poems can fail to sense the heroic nature of this poet's quest. It is riddlesome, obsessive, haunting, very often frustrating (to the poet no less than to the reader), but above all heroic; a romance of epic proportions. For the "poetic enterprise" is nothing less than the attempt to realize the soul. And the attempt to realize the soul (in its muteness, its perfection) is nothing less than the attempt to create a poetry of transcendence—the kind that outlives its human habitation and its name.

> Dare you see a Soul *at the White Heat?*
> Then crouch within the door—
> Red—is the Fire's common tint—
> But when the vivid Ore
> Has vanquished Flame's conditions,
> It quivers from the Forge
> Without a color, but the light
> Of unanointed Blaze.
> Least Village has its Blacksmith
> Whose Anvil's even ring
> Stands symbol for the finger Forge
> That soundless tugs—within—
> Refining these impatient Ores
> With Hammer, and with Blaze
> Until the Designated Light
> Repudiate the Forge—

Only the soul "at the white heat" achieves the light of "unanointed Blaze"—colorless, soundless, transcendent. This is the triumph of art as well as the triumph of personality, but it is not readily achieved.

Very often the "self" is set in opposition to the soul. The

personality is mysteriously split, warring: "Of Consciousness, her awful Mate / The Soul cannot be rid—" And: "Me from Myself—to banish— / Had I Art—" A successful work of art is a consequence of the integration of conscious and unconscious elements; a balance of what is known and not quite known held in an exquisite tension. Art *is* tension, and poetry of the kind Emily Dickinson wrote is an art of strain, of nerves strung brilliantly tight. It is compact, dense, coiled in upon itself very nearly to the point of pain: like one of those stellar bodies whose gravity is so condensed it is on the point of disappearing altogether. How tight, how violent, this syntax!—making the reader's heart beat quickly, at times, in sympathy with the poet's heart. By way of Dickinson's radically experimental verse—and, not least, her employment of dashes as punctuation—the drama of the split self is made palpable. One is not merely told of it, one is made to experience it.

Anything less demanding would not be poetry, but prose—the kind of prose written by other people. Though Dickinson was an assured writer of prose herself, "prose" for her assumes a pejorative tone: see the famously rebellious poem in which the predicament of the female (artist? or simply "female"?) is dramatized—

They shut me up in Prose—
As when a little Girl
They put me in the Closet—
Because they liked me "still"—

Still! Could themself have peeped—
And seen my Brain—go round—
They might as wise have lodged a Bird
For Treason—in the Pound—

Himself has but to will
And easy as a Star
Abolish his Captivity—
And laugh—No more have I—

Prose—it might be speculated—is discourse; poetry ellipsis. Prose is spoken aloud; poetry overheard. The one is presumably articulate and social, a shared language, the voice of "communication"; the other is private, allusive, teasing, sly, idiosyncratic as the spider's delicate web, a kind of witchcraft unfathomable to ordinary minds. Poetry, paraphrased, is something other than poetry, while prose *is* paraphrase. Consequently the difficulty of much of Dickinson's poetry, its necessary strategies, for the act of writing is invariably an act of rebellion, a way of (secretly, subversively) "abolishing" captivity:

Tell all the Truth but tell it slant—
Success in Circuit lies
Too bright for our infirm Delight
The Truth's superb surprise
As Lightning to the Children eased
With explanation kind
The Truth must dazzle gradually
Or every man be blind—

Surely there is a witty irony behind the notion that lightning can be domesticated by way of "kind explanations" told to children; that the dazzle of Truth might be gradual and not blinding. The "superb surprise" of which the poet speaks is too much for mankind to bear head-on—like the Medusa it can be glimpsed only indirectly, through the subtly distorting mirror of art.

Elsewhere, in a later poem, the poet suggests a radical distinction between two species of consciousness. Two species of human being?—

Best Witchcraft is Geometry
To the magician's mind—
His ordinary acts are feats
To thinking of mankind.

The "witchcraft" of art is (mere) geometry to the practitioner: by which is meant that it is orderly, natural, obedient to its own rules of logic; an ordinary event. What constitutes the "feat" is the relative ignorance of others—nonmagicians. It is a measure of the poet's modesty that, in this poem and in others, she excludes herself from the practice of witchcraft, even as she brilliantly practices it. Dickinson is most herself when she stands, like us, in awe of her remarkable powers as if sensing how little she controls them; how little, finally, the mute and unknowable Soul has to do with the restless, ever-improvising voice. "Silence," says the poet, "is all we dread. / There's Ransom in a Voice— / But Silence is Infinity. / Himself have not a face." (pp. 163-69)

If one were obliged to say what Emily Dickinson's poems as a whole are about, the answer must be ambiguous. The poems are in one sense about the creation of the self capable of creating in turn this very body of poetry. For poetry does not "write itself "—the mind may feed on the heart, but the heart is mute, and requires not only being fed upon but being scrupulously tamed. Like virtually all poets of genius, Emily Dickinson worked hard at her craft. Passion comes unbidden—poetry's flashes of great good luck come unbidden—but the structures into which such flashes are put must be intellectually interesting. For the wisdom of the heart is after all ahistorical—it is always the same wisdom, one might say, across centuries. But human beings live in time, not simply in Time. The historical evolution of one's craft cannot be ignored: in creating art one is always, in a sense, vying for space with preexisting art. Emily Dickinson is perhaps our greatest American poet not because she felt more deeply and more profoundly than other people, or even that she "distilled amazing sense from ordinary Meanings," but that she wrote so well.

Dickinson discovered, early on, her distinctive voice—it is evident in letters written when she was a girl—and worked all her life to make it ever more distinctive. She was the spider, sometimes working at night in the secrecy of her room, unwinding a "Yarn of Pearl" unperceived by others and plying "from Nought to Nought / In unsubstantial Trade—" but she was far more than merely the spider: she is the presence, never directly cited, or even hinted at, who intends to dazzle the world with her genius. Literary fame is not precisely a goal, but it *is* a subject to which the poet has given some thought: "Some—Work for Immortality— / the Chiefer part, for Time— / "He—Compensates—immediately— / The former—Checks—on Fame—" And, more eloquently in these late, undated poems that might have been written by an elder poet who had in fact enjoyed public acclaim:

Fame is a bee.
    It has a song—
It has a sting—
    Ah, too, it has a
wing.

And:

> Fame is a fickle food
> Upon a shifting plate
> Whose table once a
> Guest but not
> The second time is set.
>
> Whose crumbs the crows inspect
> And with ironic caw
> Flap past it to the
> Farmer's Corn—
> Men eat of it and die.

Dickinson's specific practice as a writer might strike most people as haphazard, if not wasteful, but clearly it was the practice most suited to her temperament and her domestic situation. During the day, while working at household tasks, she jotted down sentences or fragments of sentences as they occurred to her, scribbling on any handy scrap of paper (which suggests the improvised, unplanned nature of the process). Later, in her room, she added these scraps to her scrapbasket collection of phrases, to be "used" when she wrote poetry or letters. Both Dickinson's poetry and prose, reading as if they were quickly—breathlessly—imagined, are the consequence of any number of drafts and revisions. As biographers have noted, a word or a phrase or a striking image might be worked into a poem or a letter years after it was first written down: the motive even in the private correspondence is to create a persona, not to speak spontaneously. And surely, after a point, it was not possible for Dickinson to speak except by way of a persona. She addresses posterity—in fact, us, her admiring readers—over the shoulder, so to speak, of her unsuspecting correspondents. "Master," feeling the weight of a lonely woman's fantasy of passion and submission, could not have guessed how he was codified, a character in a drama not of his own devising.

In any case, the result is a body of poetry like no other. Its silences are no less potent than its speech. Slant meaning and slant rhyme contribute to the poems' suggestion of dramatic situations of the most teasing subtlety—here is a life that is a "Loaded Gun," yet writ so small it can fit into a woman's sewing basket, along with other scraps of material. From time to time there emerge mysterious "Representatives of the Verse"—"supposed persons"—an "I" that may be an attitude rather than a specific person—but, so far as literal meaning is concerned, one poem will cancel out another. It is perhaps this very drama that constitutes the poems' true subject: the self's preoccupation with the Soul, and the anguish and delight of its roles. The method is diaristic in practice, the scrupulous recording of the "unremitting Bass / And Blue Monotony" of daily domestic life, even as it analyzes those terrible times (moments? hours? days? entire seasons?) in which the heart turns "convulsive" in learning "That Calm is but a Wall / Of unattempted Gauze / An instant's Push demolishes / A Questioning—dissolves." The quest is no less epistemological than personal and emotional. It is at that point of juncture that the quest becomes our own as well as the poet's.

If Emily Dickinson suffered a breakdown of some kind, as a number of the poems vividly suggest, the experience is brilliantly translated into art. Indeed, these poems of disintegration and halting reintegration are among her most

powerful, making her the unwitting precursor of any number of contemporary poets. . . . (pp. 180-83)

Dickinson's greatness as a poet, however, lies in the amplitude of her poetry. She is the celebrant not only of hazardous states of the psyche but of the psyche's possible wholeness, that mysterious integration of the personality that has its theological analogue in the concept of grace. As the work of art most succeeds when a delicate balance is struck between that which is known, and conscious, and that which is not yet known, and unconscious, so the psyche seems to be at its fullest when contradictory forces are held in suspension. This mystical state is frequently the subject of lyric poetry because it is so notoriously difficult to describe except in the briefest of spaces. As a state of mind rather than an arid intellectual concept it is evanescent, though its power to transform the entire personality has been documented (by, among others, William James in his classic of American psychology, *The Varieties of Religious Experience*). If the mystical experience is attached to an external source it tends to have a public character, often aggressively so: one is converted, saved, born again. One becomes then a proselyte for the new belief. If the mystical experience is a consequence of the individual's own efforts—bound up, perhaps, with the intense but initially undefined desire to create art—it tends to have a deeply introspective and private character; and if there is any significant "external" object it is likely to be nature. The mystical impulse is to transcend time—and nature, unlike human beings, does not appear to age.

There are numerous poems that suggest that Emily Dickinson realized, at various points in her life, such states of wholeness and integration. If these poems are not among her most memorable, it is primarily because "ecstasy" and "bliss" are not readily exportable experiences: it is tragedy, as Yeats observed, that breaks down the dikes between human beings. But one cannot doubt the poems' sincerity:

> You'll know it—as you know 'tis Noon—
> By Glory—
> As you do the Sun—
> By Glory—
> As you will in Heaven—
> Know God the Father—and the Son.
>
> By intuition, Mightiest Things
> Assert themselves—and not by terms—
> "I'm Midnight"—need the Midnight say—
> "I'm Sunrise"—Need the Majesty?
>
> Omnipotence—had not a Tongue—
> His lisp—is Lightning—and the Sun—
> His Conversation—with the Sea—
> "How shall you know"?
> Consult your Eye!

And even more explicit still, this poem of more than twenty years later:

> Take all away from me, but leave me Ecstasy,
> And I am richer then than all my Fellow Men—
> Ill it becometh me to dwell so wealthily
> When at my very Door are those possessing more,
> In abject poverty—

On the whole, however, Emily Dickinson's naturally skeptical imagination—her "Sweet Skepticism," as she calls it—saves the great body of her work from the dogma of mere statement. The self-righteous, hectoring, frequently insufferable smugness of most religious (and "mystical") verse is contrary to her temperament:

> Of Paradise' existence
> All we know
> Is the uncertain certainty—
> But its vicinity infer,
> By its Bisecting
> Messenger—

Though "God" is frequently evoked in the poetry, one is never quite certain what "God" means to Dickinson. A presence? an experience? an outdated tradition? In these late undated poems the poet takes a heretic's playful stance:

> God is indeed a jealous God—
> He cannot bear to see
> That we had rather not with Him
> But with each other play.

And:

> A Letter is a joy of Earth—
> It is denied the Gods—

Death—that obsessive theme of the poetry!—did not intimidate Dickinson at the end. Her final letter, written on her deathbed to her cousins Loo and Fanny Norcross, is a perfect little poem, typically Dickinson, a gesture of the gentlest irony:

> Little Cousins,
>   Called back—
>   Emily.

(pp. 185-88)

Dickinson of course has no heirs or heiresses. In the minuteness of their perceptions and the precision of their images one might think of Marianne Moore, Elizabeth Bishop, the early Anne Sexton, and, certainly, Sylvia Plath, but so far as the development of American poetry is concerned, Emily Dickinson really leads nowhere since she herself is the highest embodiment of the experimental method she developed. Genius of her kind is simply inimitable. In this too Dickinson is Whitman's opposite: Whitman's heirs are ubiquitous. Whitman transformed American poetry forever, Dickinson sets an aesthetic standard no other poet dares approach. She is perfection, an end stop, as perhaps she anticipated: "Nobody!" as the emblem of the absolutely inviolable, incomparable self.

What one absorbs from Dickinson's poetry is something more valuable than an artistic method—a quality of personality and vision unlike any other; a heightened sense of the mind's uncharted possibilities; a triumphant sense that the solitary soul, confronted with the irrefutable fact of mortality, can nonetheless define its own "Superior instants." Here is an American artist of words as inexhaustible as Shakespeare, as ingeniously skillful in her craft as Yeats, a poet whom we can set with confidence beside the greatest poets of modern times. Out of hunger, pain, anguish, powerlessness—the paradoxical abundance of art. (p. 189)

> *Joyce Carol Oates, " 'Soul at the White Heat':*
> *The Romance of Emily Dickinson's Poetry,"*
> *in her* (Woman) Writer: Occasions and Op-
> *portunities, E. P. Dutton, 1988, pp. 163-89.*

FURTHER READING

Anderson, Charles R. *Emily Dickinson's Poetry: Stairway to Surprise.* New York: Holt, Rinehart and Winston, 1960, 334p.
    A respected scholarly explication of selected poems. Anderson touches on Dickinson's views on art, nature, the self, death, and immortality.

Baldi, Sergio. "The Poetry of Emily Dickinson (1956)." *The Sewanee Review* 68, No. 1 (July-September 1960): 438-49.
    Discusses the language and themes of Dickinson's poetry, noting that her special characteristic is "the interiorization of reality."

Barker, Wendy. *Lunacy of Light: Emily Dickinson and the Experience of Metaphor.* Ad Feminam: Women and Literature, edited by Sandra M. Gilbert. Carbondale: Southern Illinois University Press, 1987, 214p.
    A feminist study of light and dark imagery in Dickinson's poetry.

Bickman, Martin. "Kora in Heaven: Love and Death in the Poetry of Emily Dickinson." *Emily Dickinson Bulletin* No. 32 (1977 Second Half): 79-104.
    A Jungian analysis of Dickinson's poetry about love and death. Bickman suggests that these "poems chart a journey from a limited, ego-centered awareness to a consciousness that encompasses the entire psychic realm."

Blake, Caesar R., and Wells, Carlton F., eds. *The Recognition of Emily Dickinson: Selected Criticism since 1890.* Ann Arbor: University of Michigan Press, 1964, 314p.
    Reprints significant early reviews and later critical studies through 1960.

Bloom, Harold, ed. *Emily Dickinson.* Modern Critical Views. New York: Chelsea House Publishers, 1985, 204p.
    A collection of previously published essays on Dickinson by such critics as Charles R. Anderson, Sharon Cameron, and Shira Wolosky.

Bogan, Louise. "A Mystical Poet." In *Emily Dickinson: Three Views* by Archibald MacLeish, Louise Bogan, and Richard Wilbur, pp. 27-34. Amherst, Mass.: Amherst College Press, 1960.
    Comments on Dickinson as a visionary poet.

Buckingham, Willis J., ed. *Emily Dickinson, an Annotated Bibliography; Writings, Scholarship, Criticism, and Ana, 1850-1968.* Bloomington, Ind.: Indiana University Press, 1970, 322p.
    A comprehensive listing of materials relating to Dickinson through 1968.

Cunningham, J. V. "Sorting Out: The Case of Emily Dickinson." *The Southern Review* V (n. s.), No. 2 (Spring 1969): 436-56.
    Reexamines Dickinson's poetic style and her attitude toward death and the afterlife.

Dandurand, Karen. *Dickinson Scholarship: An Annotated Bibliography, 1969-1985.* Garland Reference Library of the Humanities, Vol. 636. New York: Garland Publishers, 1988, 203p.

A bibliography updating the work of Buckingham (see entry above).

Diehl, Joan Feit. "Dickinson and the American Self." *ESQ* 26, No. 1 (1st Quarter 1980): 1-9.

Discusses Dickinson's estrangement from both mainstream nineteenth-century American values and the new notion of the self being forged by such writers as Emerson and Thoreau.

Donoghue, Denis. *Emily Dickinson.* Minneapolis: University of Minnesota Press, 1969, 44p.

Brief comprehensive overview of Dickinson's life and poetry.

Ferlazzo, Paul J. *Emily Dickinson.* Twayne's United States Authors Series, No. 280. Boston: Twayne Publishers, 1976, 168p.

A general introduction to Dickinson's life and poetry.

————, ed. *Critical Essays on Emily Dickinson.* Critical Essays on American Literature, edited by James Nagel. Boston: G. K. Hall & Co., 1984, 243p.

Reprints criticism by important Dickinson critics.

Frye, Northrop. "Emily Dickinson." In his *Fables of Identity,* pp. 193-217. New York: Harcourt Brace Jovanovich, 1963.

Discusses Dickinson's literary reputation, style, and themes.

Gilbert, Sandra M. "The American Sexual Politics of Walt Whitman and Emily Dickinson." In *Reconstructing American Literary History,* edited by Sacvan Bercovitch, pp. 123-54. Cambridge, Mass.: Harvard University Press, 1986.

Demonstrates that, while both forged a new kind of American poetry, Whitman continued to remain close to paternalistic, male-dominated genres, whereas Dickinson and her successors moved away from them.

Griffith, Clark. *The Long Shadow: Emily Dickinson's Tragic Poetry.* Princeton, N.J.: Princeton University Press, 1964, 308p.

An analysis of Dickinson's handling of such themes as dying, dread, love, irony, and immortality in her poetry.

Juhasz, Suzanne, ed. *Feminist Critics Read Emily Dickinson.* Bloomington, Ind.: University of Indiana Press, 1983, 184p.

A collection of essays on Dickinson written from feminist perspectives.

Knights, L. C. "Defining the Self: Poems of Emily Dickinson." *The Sewanee Review* XCI, No. 3 (Summer 1983): 357-75.

Describes the role that observing and describing nature played in Dickinson's self-definition.

MacLeish, Archibald. "The Private World." In *Emily Dickinson: Three Views* by Archibald MacLeish, Louise Bogan, and Richard Wilbur, pp. 13-26. Amherst, Mass.: Amherst College Press, 1960.

A discussion of Dickinson's poetic forms.

Martin, Wendy. "Emily Dickinson: "A Woman—white—to be." In her *An American Triptych: Anne Bradstreet, Emily Dickinson, Adrienne Rich,* pp. 79-164. Chapel Hill, N.C.: University of North Carolina Press, 1984.

Examines Dickinson in the context of New England culture, pointing out that, "although Emily Dickinson's poetry contains the kernel of the modern sensibility, . . .

it also recapitulates the Puritan mission to build the city on a hill."

Miller, Cristanne. *Emily Dickinson: A Poet's Grammar.* Cambridge, Mass.: Harvard University Press, 1987, 212p.

Studies the language of Dickinson's poetry in relation to the poet's conception of the power of words, her cultural background, and her feminine identity.

Moldenhauer, Joseph J. "Emily Dickinson's Ambiguity: Notes on Technique." *The Emerson Society Quarterly* No. 44 (1966 3rd Quarter): 35-44.

Concludes that "because of Emily Dickinson's preoccupation with the difficulties of understanding, semantic and thematic tension rules her poems."

Noverr, Douglas. "Emily Dickinson and the Art of Despair." *Emily Dickinson Bulletin* No. 23 (1973 First Half): 161-67.

Explores Dickinson's treatment of despair in her poems, asserting that it should be viewed in a psychological rather than religious context.

O'Brien, Anthony. "Emily Dickinson: The World, the Body and the Reflective Life." *The Critical Review* No. 9 (1966): 69-80.

Posits that "the private landscape of her inner thought, and the bodily life, are most usually combined in Emily Dickinson with views of the outer world."

Pearce, Roy Harvey. "Emily Dickinson." In his *The Continuity of American Poetry,* pp. 174-86. Princeton, N.J.: Princeton University Press, 1961.

Cites Dickinson as the apex of the "egocentric" style typical of nineteenth-century American writers.

Pollak, Vivian R. *Dickinson: The Anxiety of Gender.* Ithaca, N.Y.: Cornell University Press, 1984, 258p.

Suggests that "Dickinson's identity crisis was, broadly speaking, a crisis of sexual identity, that her poetry associates love and social power, and that, as the laureate of the dispossessed, Dickinson is also the laureate of sexual despair."

Ransom, John Crowe. "Emily Dickinson: A Poet Restored." *Perspectives USA* No. 15 (Spring 1956): 5-20.

A review of Johnson's *The Poems of Emily Dickinson* (1955) with interspersed commentary on several of Dickinson's poems. Ransom sums up by writing that "all [Dickinson's] disabilities worked to her advantage."

Reeves, James. "Introduction." In his *Selected Poems of Emily Dickinson,* pp. ix-lii. London: William Heinemann, 1959.

A comprehensive introduction to Dickinson's life and works.

Rosebaum, S. P., ed. *A Concordance to the Poems of Emily Dickinson.* The Cornell Concordances. Ithaca, N.Y.: Cornell University Press, 1964, 899p.

A concordance to Johnson's 1955 edition of Dickinson's poetry.

Rupp, Richard H., ed. *Critics on Emily Dickinson.* Readings in Literary Criticism, Vol. 14. Coral Gables, Fla.: University of Miami Press, 1972, 128p.

Reprints a selection of biographical, explicatory, and critical essays.

Sewall, Richard B. *The Life of Emily Dickinson.* 2 vols. New York: Farrar, Straus and Giroux, 1974.

A respected biography.

————, ed. *Emily Dickinson: A Collection of Critical Essays.*

Twentieth Century Views, edited by Maynard Mack. Englewood Cliffs, N.J.: Prentice-Hall, 1963, 183p.

A collection of Dickinson criticism reprinted from earlier publications.

Stonum, Gary Lee. "Emily Dickinson's Calculated Sublime." In *The American Sublime,* edited by Mary Arensberg, pp. 101-30. Albany, N.Y.: State University of New York Press, 1986.

Explores Dickinson's use of mathematical terms and ideas as a strategy for delineating the Romantic sublime.

Warren, Austin. "Emily Dickinson." *The Sewanee Review* LXV, No. 4 (October-December 1957): 564-86.

Discusses Dickinson's language, imagery, and themes, praising the power of her poetry "to register and master experience."

Weisbuch, Robert. *Emily Dickinson's Poetry.* Chicago: University of Chicago Press, 1975, 202p.

A critical examination of Dickinson's rhetoric, metaphysical concerns, and complex vision of life.

Whicher, George Frisbie. *This Was a Poet: A Critical Biography of Emily Dickinson.* New York: Charles Scribner's Sons, 1939, 337p.

A highly regarded early biography of Dickinson.

Wilner, Eleanor. "The Poetics of Emily Dickinson." *ELH* 38, No. 1 (March 1971): 126-54.

A detailed analysis of Dickinson's style with special emphasis on her subjectivity.

Wilson, Suzanne M. "Structural Patterns in the Poetry of Emily Dickinson." *American Literature* 35, No. 1 (March 1963): 53-59.

Comments on the different types of structure Dickinson used for her poetry, concluding that "the major structural plan or ordering of logical elements conforms to that most commonly found in the sermon."

Winters, Yvor. "Emily Dickinson and the Limits of Judgment." In his *In Defense of Reason,* pp. 283-99. New York: Swallow Press, 1947.

Considers the difficulties inherent in critical evaluation of Dickinson's poetry as he examines several individual lyrics.

John Donne

1572-1631

English poet, epigrammist, and sermonist.

Donne is considered one of the most accomplished, if controversial, poets of the seventeenth century. His life and work are often perceived as a study in contrasts, evincing both a sensual rake who celebrated the joys of lovemaking in his secular verses and a severe Christian humanist who calmly contemplated mortality and the subservience of humanity to God in his divine poems. Donne inspired the School of Donne, also known as the metaphysical school of English verse, whose members include Andrew Marvell, Henry Vaughan, George Herbert, and Richard Crashaw, among others. Reacting against the traditions of Elizabethan love poetry, the School of Donne poets eschewed classical or romantic allusions, attempting instead to portray the complexities and uncertainties of everyday life. Their poetry is characterized by complex, witty conceits, sudden, even jarring paradoxes and contrasts, strong imagery that combines the ornate with the mundane, and contemplations melding the natural world with the divine. Modern scholars consider Donne a gifted, versatile poet and laud such works as "A Valediction: Forbidding Mourning," "Death Be Not Proud," and "Hymn to God My God, In My Sicknesse," for their wit, religious sensitivity, and profound insight into human nature.

Donne was born into a Roman Catholic family in 1572. His father was a prosperous London merchant and his mother was the daughter of dramatist John Heywood and a relative of Catholic martyr Sir Thomas More. Donne began studies at Oxford in 1584 but was forced to leave in 1587 without taking a degree because of his faith. For several years thereafter Donne pursued a legal career at the Inns of Court in London, and it was there that the duality of his temperament and interests first became evident. Donne was known both as a free-spending libertine and as a serious scholar of legal and religious issues of the day. While studying law, Donne wrote his *Elegies* and *Satyres,* which reflect variously his wit, dandyism, and gravity. Upon completing his degree in 1596, Donne accompanied the earl of Essex on two naval expeditions against the Spanish, after which he wrote of his experiences in the poems "The Storm," "The Calm," and "The Burnt Ship." Donne returned to England the following year and embarked upon a promising career, serving as secretary to Sir Thomas Egerton. His hopes for success vanished, however, after he secretly married Egerton's sixteen-year-old niece, Ann More, in 1601. More's father was enraged and ordered Donne dismissed from his brother-in-law's service and imprisoned. Sometime afterward, Donne sadly wrote an epigram describing his lot: "John Donne / Ann Donne / Undonne."

Released from prison in 1602, Donne had little chance of obtaining gainful employment. He spent the next thirteen years enduring long stretches of poverty during which he desperately sought patronage to support his wife and their twelve children. In 1615, Donne was ordained an Anglican priest. Thereafter he composed little poetry, devoting

himself instead to writing sermons and fulfilling his clerical duties. During the years immediately following his ordination, Donne held several important posts, culminating in his appointment as Dean of St. Paul's Cathedral in 1621. Two years later he suffered an attack of spotted fever, during which he believed himself dying and thus wrote "Hymn to God the Father" and "Hymn to God My God, In My Sicknesse," two poems of hopeful resignation. After years of intermittent illness, Donne died in 1631.

Although Donne's secular and religious verses have often been interpreted as contradictory in nature, most modern commentators argue that his poetry reveals a fundamentally consistent perception of humanity and the universe. While Donne was an outspoken, innovative poet given to realistic, often brash descriptions, he worked within a traditional Christian framework throughout his life. Included in his poetic canon are *Elegies, Satyres, Songs and Sonnets,* and *Divine Poems.* During his lifetime, Donne was probably best known for his *Elegies,* which are modeled upon Ovid's *Amores* and are characterized by witty, forthright discussions of sensuality. In "Elegy XIX: To His Mistress Going to Bed," for example, the narrator openly admires his mistress as she disrobes. Others, including "Elegy II: The Anagram,' in which Donne asserts that an old, unattractive woman will make a better wife than a young, beautiful one, are regarded as overstated defenses of outrageous ideas. In the collection *Satyres,* Donne uses a single persona throughout to present various arguments in a series of dramatic monologues. According to N. J. C. Andreasen, these pieces present "an idealistic defense of spiritual values against the creeping encroachment of six-teenth-century materialism." For example, in "Satyre II," the speaker reveals religious and moral failings that are spawned, he asserts, from the materialistic pursuits of cor-rupt lawyers.

Donne's most highly regarded verses are his *Songs and Sonets.* Although most of these poems contain the playful, exaggerated voice of the elegies, they are also usually more serious in their complex presentation of love and relation-ships. Such poems as "The Canonization," "The Ecsta-sie," and "A Valediction: Forbidding Mourning" abound in unexpected metaphors, original imagery, and startling paradoxes. Donne narrated these poems in a tone of im-mediacy and passion in which thought and feeling are inti-mately joined. In "The Flea," for example, the speaker seeks to coax a desirable woman to his bed, telling her that the flea she just caught has sucked her blood as well as his; their blood has already been mixed within the flea, fore-shadowing—he hopes and hints—a more complete and enjoyable intercourse to come. Donne's *Divine Poems* re-flect his understanding and acceptance of the Jesuit tradi-tion of liturgical prayer and private meditation. Such reli-gious verses as the seven sonnets that comprise *La Corona* examine various mysteries of faith and are concerned with questions of morality and mortality. "Goodfriday 1613: Riding Westward," illustrates Donne's concern with hu-manity's relationship with God and is considered one of his most richly symbolic meditations.

The first collection of Donne's verse was not published until two years after his death, the poems having previous-ly circulated in manuscript only. Entitled *Poems,* this vol-ume was prefaced with elegies by Izaak Walton, Thomas Carew, and other contemporaries of Donne. These writers represented one side of early criticism of Donne's poet-ry—those who honored him as a master. Another early view was first voiced by Ben Jonson, who faulted Donne's poetry for its profanity and innovative meter and dispar-aged the first *Anniversarie* as obsequious. Jonson's critical opinion was adopted by critics for nearly two centuries. In his "A Discourse on the Original and Progress of Sat-ire" (1693), John Dryden used the term "metaphysical" for the first time to describe Donne's poetry, characteriz-ing Donne as more a wit than a poet. Other scholars seized upon this commentary, with Samuel Johnson eventually writing a crushing critique of Donne's poetry in his "Life of Cowley" (1779). In this famous essay, Johnson used the term "metaphysical" as one of abuse to describe poets whose intentions were, he contended, to flaunt their clev-erness and to deliberately construct paradoxes so outland-ish and inadvertently pretentious as to be ludicrous, inde-cent, or both. Predominantly negative assessments of Donne's poetry continued until the early nineteenth cen-tury, when his verse finally began to receive popular and scholarly acceptance.

During the late nineteenth and early twentieth centuries, positive critical interest in Donne's poetry was renewed. Samuel Taylor Coleridge, Robert Browning, and Thomas De Quincey were instrumental in focusing a favorable light on his works. In 1912, the first definitive edition of Donne's poetry appeared. Edited by H. J. C. Grierson, this collection settled questions of spelling, authenticity, and misattribution, and sparked further critical interest in Donne's poetry. In 1921, T. S. Eliot wrote that Donne and the Metaphysicals were poets of signal stature who had been to their age what the twentieth-century Modernists were to theirs. Eliot argued that the Metaphysicals had written complex, emotionally charged celebrations of the joys, sorrows, and dilemmas of their own age, an era of both licentiousness and virtue. Not all modern criticism of Donne's work was favorable, however. C. S. Lewis, for example, a literary traditionalist and longtime nemesis of Eliot, found the love poetry vastly overrated, while several other commentators faulted the meter, structure, and sub-ject matter of selected poems. From mid-century to the present, Donne's poetic canon has been scrutinized ac-cording to the methods of various critical schools, with representatives of the New Critics, the deconstructionists, and others offering diverse interpretations of the works.

Once considered the story of an abrupt transformation from worldly audacity to Christian conformity, Donne's life and career are today seen in terms of an artistically sensitive man's spiritual growth in a lifelong search for meaning and wholeness. Many scholars have emphasized the importance in reading Donne of taking into account the cultural mores and atmosphere of his age. He is seen as an exceptional poet and the forerunner of many modern poets, notably the Modernist innovators of the first half of the twentieth century. Perhaps Thomas Carew, writing three centuries ago, wrote the most eloquent summary of Donne's accomplishments, concluding his elegy: "*Here lies a King that rul'd as hee thought fit / The universall Monarchy of wit; / Here lie two Flamens, and both those, the best, / Apollo's first, at last, the true Gods Priest.*"

(For further information on Donne's life and career, see *Literature Criticism from 1400 to 1800,* Vol. 10.)

PRINCIPAL WORKS

POETRY

The First Anniversarie. An Anatomie of the World. Wherein By Occasion Of the untimely death of Mistris Elizabeth Drury, the frailtie and decay of this whole World is represented 1611
The Second Anniversarie. Of the Progres of the Soule. Wherein, By Occasion Of the Religious death of Mis-tris Elizabeth Drury, the incommodities of the Soule in this life, and her exaltation in the next, are Contem-plated 1612
Devotions upon Emergent Occasions, and Several steps in my sickness 1632
†*Poems* 1633
Works. 6 vols. (poetry, essays, sermons, devotions, epis-tles, and prose) 1839

OTHER MAJOR WORKS

Pseudo-Martyr (essay) 1610
Ignatius His Conclave; or, His Inthronisation in a Late Election in Hell: wherein many things are mingled by way of satyr; concerning the disposition of Jesuits, the

creation of a new hell, the establishing of a church in the moone (essay) 1611
Deaths Duell (sermon) 1632
Juvenilia; or, Certaine paradoxes, and problems (prose) 1633
LXXX Sermons (sermons) 1640
ΒΙΑΘΑΝΑΤΟΣ. *A declaration of that paradoxe, or thesis, that self-homicide is not so naturally sinne, that it may never be otherwise. Wherein the nature, and the extent of all those lawes, which seeme to be violated by this act, are diligently surveyed* (essay) 1646
‡*Essayes in Divinity* (essays) 1652
Selected Passages from the Sermons (sermons) 1919
The Showing forth of Christ: Sermons of John Donne (sermons) 1964

*These works are collectively referred to as *The Anniversaries.*

†In later centuries, this first edition of Donne's poetry was succeeded by other, more authoritative editions, notably those issued in 1895 and 1912. H. J. C. Grierson's 1912 edition is considered definitive and contains *Songs and Sonets, Epigrams, Elegies, Heroicall Epistle, Epithalamions, Satyres, Letters to Severall Personages, An Anatomie of the World, Of the Progresse of the Soule, Epicedes and Obsequies upon the Deaths of Sundry Personages, Epitaphs, Infinitati Sacrum, Divine Poems, Holy Sonnets,* Donne's Latin poems and translations, and poems of questionable authorship attributed to Donne in early editions.

‡This work was published with a 1652 printing of *Juvenilia; or, Certaine paradoxes, and problems.*

Ben Jonson (conversation date 1618-19)

[*In the following excerpt from a series of conversations with William Drummond of Hawthornden held between December 1618 and January 1619, Jonson expresses mixed thoughts on Donne's poetic skill. Some of Jonson's remarks reprinted below are among the most famous recorded assessments of Donne's poetry.*]

Certain informations and maners of Ben Johnsons to W. Drummond [in which Jonson stated that]:

> Dones *Anniversarie* [*An Anatomie of the World*] was profane and full of Blasphemies: that he told Mr. Donne, if it had been written of the Virgin Marie it had been something; to which he answered, that he described the Idea of a Woman, and not as she was.
>
> Done, for not keeping of accent, deserved hanging.

(p. 5)

[He] esteemeth John Done the first poet in the World, in some things: his verses of the Lost Chaine ["**Elegie XI: The Bracelet**"] he heth by heart; and that passage of the "**Calme**," That dust and feathers doe not stirr, all was so quiet. Affirmeth Done to have written all his best pieces ere he was 25 years old.

(p. 11)

Done said to him he wrott that Epitaph on Prince Henry ["**Elegie upon the untimely death of the in-**

comparable Prince Henry"] Look to me, Fath, to match Sir Ed: Herbert in obscurenesse.

(p. 12)

[The] conceit of Dones Transformation or "Μετεμψυχωσιξ" ["**The Progresse of the Soule**"] was, that he sought the soule of that Aple which Eva pulled, and thereafter made it the soule of a bitch, then of a shee wolf, and so of a woman: his generall purpose was to have brought in all the bodies of the Hereticks from the soule of Cain, and at last left it in the bodie of Calvin: Of this he never wrotte but one sheet, and now, since he was made Doctor, repenteth highlie, and seeketh to destroy all his poems.

(pp. 12-13)

Done himself, for not being understood, would perish.

(p. 18)

Ben Jonson, in his Ben Jonson's Conversations with William Drummond of Hawthornden, *edited by R. F. Patterson, 1923. Reprint by Haskell House Publishers Ltd., 1974, 60 p.*

Thomas Carew (poem date 1633)

[*Carew was one of the Cavalier poets, whose number also includes Robert Herrick, Sir John Suckling, and Edmund Waller. Influenced primarily by Ben Jonson and Donne, he is best known for his early love poetry, notably "The Rapture." In the following poem, Carew praises Donne's accomplishment, concluding with lines that are among the most famous ever written on Donne's poetic stature.*]

Can we not force from widdowed Poetry,
  Now thou art Dead (Great DONNE) one Elegie
To crowne thy Hearse? Why yet dare we not trust
Though with unkneaded dowe-bak't prose thy dust,
Such as the uncisor'd Churchman from the flower
Of fading Rhetorique, short liv'd as his houre,
Dry as the sand that measures it, should lay
Upon thy Ashes, on the funerall day?
Have we no voice, no tune? Did'st thou dispense
Through all our language, both the words and sense?
'Tis a sad truth; The Pulpit may her plaine,
And sober Christian precepts still retaine,
Doctrines it may, and wholesome Uses frame,
Grave Homilies, and Lectures, But the flame
Of thy brave Soule, that shot such heat and light,
As burnt our earth, and made our darknesse bright,
Committed holy Rapes upon our Will,
Did through the eye the melting heart distill;
And the deepe knowledge of darke truths so teach,
As sense might judge, what phansie could not reach;
Must be desir'd for ever. So the fire,
That fills with spirit and heat the Delphique quire,
Which kindled first by thy Promethean breath,
Glow'd here a while, lies quench't now in thy death;
The Muses garden with Pedantique weedes
O'rspred, was purg'd by thee; The lazie feeds
Of servile imitations throwne away;
And fresh invention planted, Thou didst pay
The debts of our penurious bankrupt age;
Licentious thefts, that make poëtique rage
A Mimique fury, when our soules must bee
Possest, or with Anacreons Extasie,
Or Pindars, not their owne; The subtle cheat
Of slie Exchanges, and the jugling feat

Of two-edg'd words, or whatsoever wrong
By ours was done the Greeke, or Latine tongue,
Thou hast redeem'd, and open'd Us a Mine
Of rich and pregnant phansie, drawne a line
Of masculine expression, which had good
Old Orpheus seene, Or all the ancient Brood
Our superstitious fooles admire, and hold
Their lead more precious, then thy burnish't Gold,
Thou hadst beene their Exchequer, and no more
They each in others dust, had rak'd for Ore.
Thou shalt yield no precedence, but of time,
And the blinde fate of language, whose tun'd chime
More charmes the outward sense; Yet though maist
    claime
From so great disadvantage greater fame,
Since to the awe of thy imperious wit
Our stubborne language bends, made only fit
With her tough-thich-rib'd hoopes to gird about
Thy Giant phansie, which had prov'd too stout
For their soft melting Phrases. As in time
They had the start, so did they cull the prime
Buds of invention many a hundred yeare,
And left the rifled fields, besides the feare
To touch their Harvest, yet from those bare lands
Of what is purely thine, thy only hands
(And that thy smallest worke) have gleaned more
Then all those times, and tongues could reape before;
But thou art gone, and thy strict lawes will be
Too hard for Libertines in Poetrie.
They will repeale the goodly exil'd traine
Of gods and goddesses, which in thy just raigne
Were banish'd nobler Poems, now, with these
The silenc'd tales o' th' Metamorphoses
Shall stuffe their lines, and swell the windy Page,
Till Verse refin'd by thee, in this last Age,
Turne ballad rime, Or those old Idolls bee
Ador'd againe, with new apostasie;
Oh, pardon mee, that breake with untun'd verse
The reverend silence that attends thy herse,
Whose awfull solemne murmures were to thee
More then these faint lines, A loud Elegie,
That did proclaime in a dumbe eloquence
The death of all the Arts, whose influence
Growne feeble, in these panting numbers lies
Gasping short winded Accents, and so dies:
So doth the swiftly turning wheele not stand
In th' instant we withdraw the moving hand,
But some small time maintaine a faint weake course
By vertue of the first impulsive force:
And so whil'st I cast on thy funerall pile
Thy crowne of Bayes, Oh, let it crack a while,
And spit disdaine, till the devouring flashes
Such all the moysture up, then turne to ashes.
I will not draw the envy to engrosse
All thy perfections, or weepe all our losse;
Those are too numerous for an Elegie,
And this too great, to be express'd by mee.
Though every pen should share a distinct part,
Yet art thou Theme enough to tyre all Art;
Let others carve the rest, it shall suffice
I on thy Tombe this Epitaph incise.

Here lies a King, that rul'd as hee thought fit
The universall Monarchy of wit;
Here lie two Flamens, and both those, the best,
Apollo's first, at last, the true Gods Priest.

                                          (pp. 385-88)

Thomas Carew, "An Elegie Upon the Death of
the Deane of Pauls, Dr. John Donne," in
Poems *by J. D., John Marriot, 1633, pp. 385-*
88.

Samuel Johnson   (essay date 1779)

[*Johnson is an outstanding English literary figure and*
a leader in the history of textual and aesthetic criticism.
He was a prolific lexicographer, poet, and critic whose
lucid and extensively illustrated Dictionary of the English Language *(1755) and* Prefaces, Biographical and
Critical, to the Works of the English Poets *(10 vols.*
1779-81; reissued in 1783 as The Lives of the Most Eminent English Poets) *were new departures in lexicogra-*
phy and biographical criticism. As a literary critic John-
son was neither a rigid theorist nor a strict follower of
neoclassical rules, tending instead to rely on common
sense and empirical knowledge. In the following excerpt
from an essay originally published in the first edition of
his Lives, *Johnson describes and denigrates the meta-*
physical poets, using "metaphysical" as a term of abuse
and illustrating his arguments with examples from
Donne's poetry.]

Wit, like all other things subject by their nature to the
choice of man, has its changes and fashions, and at different times takes different forms. About the beginning of the
seventeenth century appeared a race of writers that may
be termed the metaphysical poets; of whom, in a criticism
on the works of Cowley, it is not improper to give some
account.

The metaphysical poets were men of learning, and to show
their learning was their whole endeavour; but, unluckily
resolving to shew it in rhyme, instead of writing poetry,
they only wrote verses, and very often such verses as stood
the trial of the finger better than of the ear; for the modulation was so imperfect, that they were only found to be
verses by counting the syllables.

If the father of criticism has rightly denominated poetry
an imitative art, these writers will, without great
wrong, . . . lose their right to the name of poets; for they
cannot be said to have imitated any thing; they neither
copied nature nor life; neither painted the forms of matter,
nor represented the operations of intellect.

Those, however, who deny them to be poets, allow them
to be wits. Dryden confesses of himself and his contemporaries, that they fall below Donne in wit, but maintains
that they surpass him in poetry. (pp. 12-13)

Critical remarks are not easily understood without examples; and I have therefore collected instances of the modes
of writing by which this species of poets, for poets they
were called by themselves and their admirers, was eminently distinguished.

As the authors of this race were perhaps more desirous of
being admired than understood, they sometimes drew
their conceits from recesses of learning not very much frequented by common readers of poetry. (p. 16)

Thus *Donne* shews his medicinal knowledge in some en-
comiastick verses [**"To the Countes of Bedford. 'Madame,**
reason is' "]:

In every thing there naturally grows
A Balsamum to keep it fresh and new,
If 'twere not injur'd by extrinsique blows;
Your youth and beauty are this balm in you.
But you, of learning and religion,
And virtue and such ingredients, have made

A mithridate, whose operation
Keeps off, or cures what can be done or said.

Though the following lines of Donne [from **"To the Coun-tesse of Bedford, 'This twilight of ' "**], on the last night of the year, have something in them too scholastick, they are not inelegant:

> This twilight of two years, not past nor next,
> Some emblem is of me, or I of this,
> Who, meteor-like, of stuff and form perplext,
> Whose what and where, in disputation is,
> If I should call me any thing, should miss.
>
> I sum the years and me, and find me not
> Debtor to th' old, nor creditor to th' new,
> That cannot say, my thanks I have forgot,
> Nor trust I this with hopes; and yet scarce true
> This bravery is, since these times shew'd me you. . . .

Yet more abstruse and profound is *Donne's* reflection upon Man as a Microcosm [in **"To Mr. R. W. 'If as mine is' "**]:

> If men be worlds, there is in every one
> Something to answer in some proportion
> All the world's riches: and in good men, this
> Virtue our form's form, and our soul's soul is.

(p. 17)

The tears of lovers are always of great poetical account; but Donne has extended them into worlds. If the lines [which follow, from **"A Valediction: of weeping"**] are not easily understood, they may be read again.

> On a round ball
> A workman, that hath copies by, can lay
> An Europe, Afric, and an Asia,
> And quickly make that, which was nothing, all.
>
> So doth each tear,
> Which thee doth wear,
> A globe, yea world, by that impression grow,
> Till thy tears mixt with mine do overflow
> This world, by waters sent from thee my heaven
> dissolved so.

On reading the following lines [from **"An Epithalamion, Or mariage Song on the Lady Elizabeth, and Count Pala-tine being married on St. Valentine's day"**], the reader may perhaps cry out—*Confusion worse confounded.*

> Here lies a she sun, and a he moon there,
> She gives the best light to his sphere,
> Or each is both, and all, and so
> They unto one another nothing owe.

(pp. 19-20)

Who but Donne would have thought that a good man is a telescope?

> Though God be our true glass, through which we see
> All, since the being of all things is he,
> Yet are the trunks, which do to us derive
> Things, in proportion fit, by perspective
> Deeds of good men; for by their living here,
> Virtues, indeed remote, seem to be near.

(p. 20)

That prayer and labour should co-operate, are thus taught by Donne:

> In none but us, are such mixt engines found,
> As hands of double office: for the ground

We till with them; and them to heaven we raise;
Who prayerless labours, or without this, prays,
Doth but one half, that's none.

By the same author, a common topick, the danger of pro-crastination, is thus illustrated:

> —That which I should have begun
> In my youth's morning, now late must be done;
> And I, as giddy travellers must do,
> Which stray or sleep all day, and having lost
> Light and strength, dark and tir'd, must then ride post.

All that Man has to do is to live and die; the sum of hu-manity is comprehended by Donne in the following lines:

> Think in how poor a prison thou didst lie;
>
> After, enabled but to suck and cry.
> Think, when 'twas grown to most, 'twas a poor inn,
> A province pack'd up in two yards of skin,
> And that usurp'd, or threaten'd with a rage
> Of sicknesses, or their true mother, age.
> But think that death hath now enfranchis'd thee;
> Thou hast thy expansion now, and liberty;
> Think, that a rusty piece discharg'd is flown
> In pieces, and the bullet is his own,
> And freely flies: this to thy soul allow,
> Think thy shell broke, think thy soul hatch'd but now.

They were sometimes [as in **"Twicknam garden"**] indeli-cate and disgusting. (pp. 24-5)

> Hither with crystal vials, lovers, come,
> And take my tears, which are Love's wine,
> And try your mistress' tears at home;
> For all are false, that taste not just like mine.

This [from **"Elegie VIII: The Comparison"**] is yet more indelicate:

> As the sweet sweat of roses in a still,
> As that which from chaf'd musk-cat's pores doth trill,
> As the almighty balm of th' early East;
> Such are the sweat-drops of my mistress' breast.
> And on her neck her skin such lustre sets,
> They seem no sweat-drops, but pearl coronets:
> Rank sweaty froth thy mistress' brow defiles.

(p. 26)

To the following comparison [in **"A Valediction: forbid-ding mourning"**] of a man that travels, and his wife that stays at home, with a pair of compasses, it may be doubted whether absurdity or ingenuity has the better claim:

> Our two souls therefore, which are one,
> Though I must go, endure not yet
> A breach, but an expansion,
> Like gold to airy thinness beat.
>
> If they be two, they are two so
> As stiff twin-compasses are two;
> Thy soul the fixt foot, makes no show
> To move, but doth, if th' other do.
>
> And though it in the centre sit,
> Yet when the other far doth roam,
> It leans, and hearkens after it,
> And grows erect, as that comes home.
>
> Such wilt thou be to me, who must
> Like th' other foot, obliquely run.
> Thy firmness makes my circle just,
> And makes me end, where I begun.

In all these examples it is apparent, that whatever is improper or vicious, is produced by a voluntary deviation from nature in pursuit of something new and strange; and that [Donne and the metaphysical] writers fail to give delight, by their desire of exciting admiration. (p. 28)

Samuel Johnson, "Cowley," in his Lives of the English Poets, *Vol. I, 1906. Reprint by Oxford University Press, 1955-56, pp. 1-53.*

Samuel Taylor Coleridge   (essay date 1811)

[*Coleridge was at the intellectual center of the English Romantic movement and is among the most important literary critics in world literature. His is also one of the original proponents of modern psychological criticism. Coleridge theorized that works of literature derive from and are determined by inspiration rather than by external rules. During the spring of 1811, Coleridge wrote his impressions of Donne in the margins of a copy of Donne's collected poems that belonged to Charles Lamb. In the following excerpt from this marginalia, Coleridge offers diverse judgments of Donne's work.*]

To read Dryden, Pope, &c., you need only count syllables; but to read Donne you must measure *time,* and discover the time of each word by the sense of passion. (p. 133)

Doubtless, all the copies I have ever seen of Donne's poems are grievously misprinted. Wonderful that they are not more so, considering that not one in a thousand of his readers has any notion how his lines are to be read—to the many, five out of six appear anti-metrical. How greatly this aided the compositor's negligence or ignorance, and prevented the corrector's remedy, any man may ascertain by examining the earliest editions of blank verse plays, Massinger, Beaumont and Fletcher, &c. Now, Donne's rhythm was as inexplicable to the many as blank verse, spite of his rhymes—*ergo,* as blank verse, misprinted. I am convinced that where no mode of rational declamation by pause, hurrying of voice, or apt and sometimes double emphasis, can at once make the verse metrical and bring out the sense of passion more prominently, that there we are entitled to alter the text, when it can be done by simple omission or addition of *that, which, and,* and such "small deer"; or by mere new placing of the same words—I would venture nothing beyond.

"The Triple Fool"

And by delighting many, frees again
Grief which Verse did restrain.

A good instance how Donne read his own verses. We should write, "The Grief, verse did restrain"; but Donne roughly emphasized the two main words, Grief and Verse, and, therefore, made each the first syllable of a trochee or dactyl:—

Grīef, whĭch / vērse dĭd rĕ / strāin.

"Song"

Ănd wē joīn to't ŏur strēngth,
Ănd wē teāch ĭt ārt ănd lēngth.

The anapest judiciously used, in the eagerness and haste to confirm and aggravate. This beautiful and perfect poem proves, by its title **"Song"**, that *all* Donne's poems are equally *metrical* (misprints allowed for) though smoothness (*i.e.,* the metre necessitating the proper reading) be deemed appropriate to *songs;* but in poems where the writer *thinks,* and expects the reader to do so, the sense must be understood in order to ascertain the metre.

"Satire III". If you would teach a scholar in the highest form how to *read,* take Donne, and of Donne this satire. When he has learnt to read Donne, with all the force and meaning which are involved in the words, then send him to Milton, and he will stalk on like a master, *enjoying* his walk.

On Donne's Poem "The Flea"

Be proud as Spaniards. Leap for pride, ye Fleas!
In Nature's *minim* realm ye're now grandees.
Skip-jacks no more, nor civiller skip-johns;
Thrice-honored Fleas! I greet you all as *Dons.*
In Phoebus's archives registered are ye,
And this your patent of nobility.

"The Good Morrow"

What ever dies is not mixt equally;
If our two loves be one, both thou and I
Love just alike in all; none of these loves can die.

Too good for mere wit. It contains a deep practical truth, this triplet.

"Woman's Constancy." After all, there is but one Donne! and now tell me yet, wherein, in *his own kind,* he differs from the similar power in Shakespeare? Shakespeare was all men, potentially, except Milton; and they differ from him by negation, or privation, or both. This power of dissolving orient pearls, worth a kingdom, in a health to a whore!—this absolute right of dominion over all thoughts, that dukes are bid to clean his shoes, and are yet honored by it! But, I say, in this lordliness of opulence, in which *the* positive of Donne agrees with *a* positive of Shakespeare, what is it that makes them *homoi*ousian, indeed: yet not homoousian? (pp. 133-35)

[**"The Sun Rising"**]. Fine, vigorous exultation, both soul and body in full puissance.

"The Indifferent"

I can love both fair and brown;
Her whom abundance melts, and her whom want betrays;
Her who loves loneness best, and her who sports and
plays;
Her whom the country formed, and whom the town;
Her who believes, and her who tries;
Her who still weeps with spungy eyes,
And her who is dry cork and never cries;
I can love her, and her, and you, and you;
I can love any, so she be not true.

How legitimate a child was not Cowley of Donne; but Cowley had a soul-*mother* as well as a soul-*father,* and who was she? What was that? Perhaps, sickly court-loyalty, conscientious per accident—a discursive intellect, *naturally* less vigorous and daring, and then *cowed* by king-worship. The populousness, the activity, is as great in C. as in D.; but the *vigor,* the insufficiency to the poet of active fancy without a substrate of profound, tho' mislocate thinking,—the willworship, in squandering golden hecatombs on a fetisch, on the first stick or straw met with at rising—this pride of doing what he likes with his own, fearless of an immense surplus to pay all lawful debts to self-subsisting themes, that rule, while they cannot create, the moral will—this is Donne! He was an orthodox Christian only because he could have been an infidel *more* easily; and, therefore willed to be a Christian: and he was a Protestant, because it enabled him to lash about to the right and the left, and without a *motive*, to say better things for the Papists than they could say for themselves. It was the impulse of a purse-proud opulence of innate power! In the sluggish pond the waves roll this or that way; for such is the wind's direction: but in the brisk spring or lake, boiling at bottom, wind this way, that way, all ways, most irregular in the calm, yet inexplicable by the most violent *ab extra* tempest.

"Canonization". One of my favourite poems. As late as ten years ago, I used to seek and find out grand lines and fine stanzas; but my delight has been far greater since it has consisted more in tracing the leading thought thro'out the whole. The former is too much like coveting your neighbour's goods; in the latter you merge yourself in the author, you ·become He.

"A Fever"

> Yet I had rather owner be
> Of thee one hour, than all else ever.

Just and affecting, as *dramatic; i.e.,* the outburst of a transient feeling, itself the symbol of a deeper feeling, that would have made *one* hour, *known* to be *only* one hour (or even one year), a perfect hell! All the preceding verses are detestable. Shakespeare has nothing of this. He is never *positively* bad, even in his Sonnets. He may be sometimes worthless (N. B., I don't say he *is*), but nowhere is he *unworthy.*

"A Valediction forbidding Mourning". An admirable poem which none but Donne could have written. Nothing was ever more admirably made out than the figure of the Compass. (pp. 136-38)

"The Extacy". I should never find fault with metaphysical poems, were they all like this, or but half as excellent.

"The Primrose". I am tired of expressing my admiration; else I could not have passed by **"The Will"**, **"The Blossom"**, and **"The Primrose"**, with **"The Relique"**. (p. 138)

> *Samuel Taylor Coleridge, in his* Coleridge's Miscellaneous Criticism, *edited by Thomas Middleton Raysor, 1936. Reprint by The Folcroft Press, Inc., 1969, pp. 131-45.*

William Hazlitt   (essay date 1819)

[*Hazlitt was one of the most important literary critics of the Romantic age. He was a deft stylist, a master of the prose essay, and a leader of what was later termed "impressionist criticism"—a form of personal analysis directly opposed to the universal standards of critical judgment accepted by many eighteenth-century critics. Hazlitt utilized the critical techniques of evocation, metaphor, and personal reference—three innovations that greatly altered the development of literary criticism in the nineteenth and twentieth centuries. In the following excerpt from* Lectures on the English Comic Writers *originally published in 1819, Hazlitt lambastes Donne's poetry.*]

Donne, who was considerably before Cowley, is without his fancy, but was more recondite in his logic, and rigid in his descriptions. He is hence led, particularly in his satires, to tell disagreeable truths in as disagreeable a way as possible, or to convey a pleasing and affecting thought (of which there are many to be found in his other writings) by the harshest means, and with the most painful effort. His Muse suffers continual pangs and throes. His thoughts are delivered by the Caesarean operation. The sentiments, profound and tender as they often are, are stifled in the expression; and 'heaved pantingly forth,' are 'buried quick again' under the ruins and rubbish of analytical distinctions. It is like poetry waking from a trance: with an eye bent idly on the outward world, and half-forgotten feelings crowding about the heart; with vivid impressions, dim notions, and disjointed words. The following may serve as instances of beautiful or passioned reflections losing themselves in obscure and difficult applications. He has some lines to a Blossom, which begin thus:

> Little think'st thou, poor flow'r,
> Whom I have watched six or seven days,
> And seen thy birth, and seen what every hour
> Gave to thy growth, thee to this height to raise,
> And now dost laugh and triumph on this bough.
> Little think'st thou
> That it will freeze anon, and that I shall
> To-morrow find thee fall'n, or not at all.

This simple and delicate description is only introduced as a foundation for an elaborate metaphysical conceit as a parallel to it, in the next stanza.

> Little think'st thou (poor heart
> That labour'st yet to nestle thee,
> And think'st by hovering here to get a part
> In a forbidden or forbidding tree,
> And hop'st her stiffness by long siege to bow:)
> Little think'st thou,
> That thou to-morrow, ere the sun doth wake,
> Must with this sun and me a journey take.

This is but a lame and impotent conclusion from so delightful a beginning.—He thus notices the circumstance of his wearing his late wife's hair about his arm, in a little poem which is called the Funeral:

> Whoever comes to shroud me, do not harm
> Nor question much
> That subtle wreath of hair, about mine arm;
> The mystery, the sign you must not touch.

The scholastic reason he gives quite dissolves the charm of tender and touching grace in the sentiment itself—

> For 'tis my outward soul,
> Viceroy to that, which unto heaven being gone,
> Will leave this to control,
> And keep these limbs, her provinces, from dissolution.

Again, the following lines, the title of which is **"Love's Deity,"** are highly characteristic of this author's manner, in which the thoughts are inlaid in a costly but imperfect mosaic-work.

> *I long to talk with some old lover's ghost,*
> *Who died before the God of Love was born:*
> *I cannot think that he, who then lov'd most,*

Sunk so low, as to love one which did scorn.
But since this God produc'd a destiny,
And that vice-nature, custom, lets it be;
I must love her that loves not me.

The stanza in the Epithalamion on a Count Palatine of the Rhine, has been often quoted against him, and is an almost irresistible illustration of the extravagances to which this kind of writing which turns upon a pivot of words and possible allusions, is liable. His love-verses and epistles to his friends give the most favourable idea of Donne. His satires are too clerical. He shews, if I may so speak, too much disgust, and, at the same time, too much contempt for vice. His dogmatical invectives hardly redeem the nauseousness of his descriptions, and compromise the imagination of his readers more than they assist their reason. The satirist does not write with the same authority as the divine, and should use his poetical privileges more sparingly. 'To the pure all things are pure,' is a maxim which a man like Dr. Donne may be justified in applying to himself; but he might have recollected that it could not be construed to extend to the generality of his readers, *without benefit of clergy.* (pp. 51-3)

> *William Hazlitt, "On Cowley, Butler, Suckling, Etherege, Etc.," in his* Lectures in the English Comic Writers with Miscellaneous Essays, *E. P. Dutton & Co., 1910, pp. 49-69.*

Arthur Symons (essay date 1899)

[*Symons was a poet, dramatist, short story writer, and editor who was one of the most important critics of the modern era. Symons laid the foundation for much of modern poetic theory in his 1899 study* The Symbolist Movement in Literature. *The following essay was originally published in 1899 as a review of Edmund Gosse's critical biography* The Life and Letters of John Donne *(1899). Here, Symons admires Donne's ability to convey a wide variety of emotions in his poetry and both praises and faults Donne for being a realistic writer who broke with tradition.*]

[Donne's] first satire speaks contemptuously of 'giddy fantastic poets,' and, when he allowed himself to write poetry, he was resolved to do something different from what anybody had ever done before, not so much from the artist's instinctive desire of originality, as from a kind of haughty, yet really bourgeois, desire to be indebted to nobody. . . . 'He began,' says Mr. Gosse with truth [in his *The Life and Letters of John Donne* (2 vols. 1899)], 'as if poetry had never been written before.' To the people of his time, to those who came immediately after him, he was the restorer of English poetry.

> The Muses' garden, with pedantic weeds
> O'erspread, was purged by thee,

says Carew, in those memorial verses [see excerpt dated 1633] in which the famous lines occur:

> Here lies a king that ruled as he thought fit
> The universal monarchy of wit.

Shakespeare was living, remember, and it was Elizabethan poetry that Donne set himself to correct. He began with metre, and invented a system of prosody which has many merits, and would have had more in less arbitrary hands.

'Donne, for not keeping of accent, deserved hanging,' said Ben Jonson [see excerpt dated 1618-19], who was nevertheless his friend and admirer. And yet, if one will but read him always for the sense, for the natural emphasis of what he has to say, there are few lines which will not come out in at all events the way that he meant them to be delivered. The way he meant them to be delivered is not always as beautiful as it is expressive. Donne would be original at all costs, preferring himself to his art. He treated poetry as Æsop's master treated his slave, and broke what he could not bend.

But Donne's novelty of metre is only a part of his too deliberate novelty as a poet. As Mr. Gosse has pointed out, . . . Donne's real position in regard to the poetry of his time was that of a realistic writer, who makes a clean sweep of tradition, and puts everything down in the most modern words and with the help of the most trivial actual images.

> To what a cumbersome unwieldiness,
> And burdensome corpulence my love hath grown,

he will begin a poem on **"Love's Diet."** Of love, as the master of hearts, he declares seriously:

> He swallows us and never chaws;
> By him, as by chain'd shot, whole ranks do die;
> He is the tyrant pike, our hearts the fry.

And, in his unwise insistence that every metaphor shall be absolutely new, he drags medical and alchemical and legal properties into verse really full of personal passion, producing at times poetry which is a kind of disease of the intellect, a sick offshoot of science. Like most poets of powerful individuality, Donne lost precisely where he gained. That cumulative and crowding and sweeping intellect which builds up his greatest poems into miniature Escurials of poetry, mountainous and four-square to all the winds of the world, 'purges' too often the flowers as well as the weeds out of 'the Muses' garden.' To write poetry as if it had never been written before is to attempt what the greatest poets never attempted. There are only two poets in English literature who thus stand out of the tradition, who are without ancestors, Donne and Browning. Each seems to have certain qualities almost greater than the qualities of the greatest; and yet in each some precipitation of arrogant egoism remains in the crucible, in which the draught has all but run immortally clear.

Donne's quality of passion is unique in English poetry. It is a rapture in which the mind is supreme, a reasonable rapture, and yet carried to a pitch of actual violence. The words themselves rarely count for much, as they do in Crashaw, for instance, where words turn giddy at the height of their ascension. The words mean things, and it is the things that matter. They can be brutal: 'For God's sake, hold your tongue, and let me love!' as if a long, presupposed self-repression gave way suddenly, in an outburst. 'Love, any devil else but you,' he begins, in his abrupt leap to the heart of the matter. Or else his exaltation will be grave, tranquil, measureless in assurance.

> All kings, and all their favourites,
> All glory of honours, beauties, wits,
> The sun itself, which makes time, as they pass,
> Is elder by a year now than it was
> When thou and I first one another saw.
> All other things to their destruction draw,

Only our love hath no decay;
This no to-morrow hath, no yesterday;
Running, it never runs from us away,
But truly keeps his first, last, everlasting day.

This lover loves with his whole nature, and so collectedly because reason, in him, is not in conflict with passion, but passion's ally. His senses speak with unparalleled directness, as in those elegies which must remain the model in English of masculine sensual sobriety. He distinguishes the true end of such loving in a forcible, characteristically prosaic image:

Whoever loves, if he do not propose
The right true end of love, he's one that goes
To sea for nothing but to make him sick.

And he exemplifies every motion and the whole pilgrim's progress of physical love, with a deliberate, triumphant, unluxurious explicitness which 'leaves no doubt,' as we say, 'of his intentions,' and can be no more than referred to passingly in modern pages. In a series of hate poems, of which I will quote the finest, he gives expression to a whole region of profound human sentiment which has never been expressed, out of Catullus, with such intolerable truth.

When by thy scorn, O murderess, I am dead,
And that thou think'st thee free
From all solicitation from me,
Then shall my ghost come to thy bed,
And thee, feign'd vestal, in worse arms shall see:
Then thy sick taper will begin to wink,
And he, whose thou art then, being tired before,
Will, if thou stir, or pinch to wake him, think
Thou call'st for more,
And, in false sleep, will from thee shrink;
And then, poor aspen wretch, neglected thou
Bathed in a cold quicksilver sweat wilt lie
A verier ghost than I.
What I will say, I will not tell thee now,
Lest that preserve thee; and since my love is spent,
I'd rather thou should'st painfully repent,
Than by my threatenings rest still innocent.

Yet it is the same lover, and very evidently the same, who winnows all this earthly passion to a fine, fruitful dust, fit to make bread for angels. Ecstatic reason, passion justifying its intoxication by revealing the mysteries that it has come thus to apprehend, speak in the quintessence of Donne's verse with an exalted simplicity which seems to make a new language for love. It is the simplicity of a perfectly abstract geometrical problem, solved by one to whom the rapture of solution is the blossoming of pure reason. Read the poem called **"The Ecstasy,"** which seems to anticipate a metaphysical Blake; it is all close reasoning, step by step, and yet is what its title claims for it.

It may be, though I doubt it, that other poets who have written personal verse in English, have known as much of women's hearts and the senses of men, and the interchanges of passionate intercourse between man and woman; but, partly by reason of this very method of saying things, no one has ever rendered so exactly, and with such elaborate subtlety, every mood of the actual passion. It has been done in prose; may one not think of Stendhal, for a certain way he has of turning the whole forces of the mind upon those emotions and sensations which are mostly left to the heat of an unreflective excitement? Donne, as he suffers all the colds and fevers of love, is as much the sufferer

and the physician of his disease as we have seen him to be in cases of actual physical sickness. Always detached from himself, even when he is most helplessly the slave of circumstances, he has that frightful faculty of seeing through his own illusions; of having no illusions to the mind, only to the senses. Other poets, with more wisdom towards poetry, give us the beautiful or pathetic results of no matter what creeping or soaring passions. Donne, making a new thing certainly, if not always a thing of beauty, tells us exactly what a man really feels as he makes love to a woman, as he sits beside her husband at table, as he dreams of her in absence, as he scorns himself for loving her, as he hates or despises her for loving him, as he realises all that is stupid in her devotion, and all that is animal in his. 'Nature's lay idiot, I taught thee to love,' he tells her, in a burst of angry contempt, priding himself on his superior craft in the art. And his devotions to her are exquisite, appealing to what is most responsive in woman, beyond those of tenderer poets. A woman cares most for the lover who understands her best, and is least taken in by what it is the method of her tradition to feign. So wearily conscious that she is not the abstract angel of her pretence and of her adorers, she will go far in sheer thankfulness to the man who can see so straight into her heart as to have

found something like a heart,
But colours it and corners had;
It was not good, it was not bad,
It was entire to none, and few had part.

Donne shows women themselves, in delight, anger, or despair; they know that he finds nothing in the world more interesting, and they much more than forgive him for all the ill he says of them. If women most conscious of their sex were ever to read Donne, they would say, He was a great lover; he understood.

And, in the poems of divine love, there is the same quality of mental emotion as in the poems of human love. Donne adores God reasonably, knowing why he adores Him. He renders thanks point by point, celebrates the heavenly perfections with metaphysical precision, and is no vaguer with God than with woman. Donne knew what he believed and why he believed, and is carried into no heat or mist as he tells over the recording rosary of his devotions. His *Holy Sonnets* are a kind of argument with God; they tell over, and discuss, and resolve, such perplexities of faith and reason as would really occur to a speculative brain like his. Thought crowds in upon thought, in these tightly packed lines, which but rarely admit a splendour of this kind:

At the round earth's imagined corners blow
Your trumpets, angels, and arise, arise
From death, you numberless infinities
Of souls, and to your scattered bodies go.

More typical is this too knotted beginning of another sonnet:

Batter my heart, three-person'd God; for you
As yet but knock; breathe, shine, and seek to mend;
That I may rise, and stand, o'erthrow me, and bend
Your force, to break, blow, burn, and make me new.

Having something very minute and very exact to say, he hates to leave anything out; dreading diffuseness, as he dreads the tame sweetness of an easy melody, he will use only the smallest possible number of words to render his thought; and so, as here, he is too often ingenious rather than felicitous, forgetting that to the poet poetry comes first, and all the rest afterwards.

For the writing of great poetry something more is needed than to be a poet and to have great occasions. Donne was a poet, and he had the passions and the passionate adventures, in body and mind, which make the material for poetry; he was sincere to himself in expressing what he really felt under the burden of strong emotion and sharp sensation. Almost every poem that he wrote is written on a genuine inspiration, a genuine personal inspiration, but most of his poems seem to have been written before that personal inspiration has had time to fuse itself with the poetic inspiration. It is always useful to remember Wordsworth's phrase of 'emotion recollected in tranquillity,' for nothing so well defines that moment of crystallisation in which direct emotion or sensation deviates exquisitely into art. Donne is intent on the passion itself, the thought, the reality; so intent that he is not at the same time, in that half-unconscious way which is the way of the really great poet, equally intent on the form, that both may come to ripeness together. Again it is the heresy of the realist. Just as he drags into his verse words that have had no time to take colour from men's association of them with beauty, so he puts his 'naked thinking heart' into verse as if he were setting forth an argument. He gives us the real thing, as he would have been proud to assure us. But poetry will have nothing to do with real things, until it has translated them into a diviner world. That world may be as closely the pattern of ours as the worlds which Dante saw in hell and purgatory; the language of the poet may be as close to the language of daily speech as the supreme poetic language of Dante. But the personal or human reality and the imaginative or divine reality must be perfectly interfused, or the art will be at fault. Donne is too proud to abandon himself to his own inspiration, to his inspiration as a poet; he would be something more than a voice for deeper yet speechless powers; he would make poetry speak straight. Well, poetry will not speak straight, in the way Donne wished it to, and under the goading that his restless intellect gave it.

He forgot beauty, preferring to it every form of truth, and beauty has revenged itself upon him, glittering miraculously out of many lines in which he wrote humbly, and leaving the darkness of a retreating shadow upon great spaces in which a confident intellect was conscious of shining.

> For, though mind be the heaven, where love may sit,
> Beauty a convenient type may be to figure it,

he writes, in the **"Valediction to his Book,"** thus giving formal expression to his heresy. 'The greatest wit, though not the best poet of our nation,' Dryden called him [see Further Reading list]; the greatest intellect, that is, which had expressed itself in poetry. Dryden himself was not always careful to distinguish between what material was fit and what unfit for verse; so that we can now enjoy his masterly prose with more equable pleasure than his verse. But he saw clearly enough the distinction in Donne between intellect and the poetical spirit; that fatal division of two forces, which, had they pulled together instead of apart, might have achieved a result wholly splendid. Without a great intellect no man was ever a great poet; but to possess a great intellect is not even a first step in the direction of becoming a poet at all.

Compare Donne, for instance, with Herrick. Herrick has little enough of the intellect, the passion, the weight and the magnificence of Donne; but, setting out with so much less to carry, he certainly gets first to the goal, and partly by running always in the right direction. The most limited poet in the language, he is the surest. He knows the airs that weave themselves into songs, as he knows the flowers that twine best into garlands. Words come to him in an order which no one will ever alter, and no one will ever forget. Whether they come easily or not is no matter; he knows when they have come right, and they always come right before he lets them go. But Donne is only occasionally sure of his words as airs; he sets them doggedly to the work of saying something, whether or no they step to the beat of the music. Conscious writer though he was, I suppose he was more or less unconscious of his extraordinary felicities, more conscious probably of how they came than of what they were doing. And they come chiefly through a sudden heightening of mood, which brings with it a clearer and a more exalted mode of speech, in its merely accurate expression of itself. Even then I cannot imagine him quite reconciled to beauty, at least actually doing homage to it, but rather as one who receives a gift by the way. (pp. 94-108)

> *Arthur Symons, "John Donne," in his* Figures
> of Several Centuries, *1916. Reprint by Books
> for Libraries Press, 1969, pp. 80-108.*

H. J. C. Grierson   (essay date 1929)

[*Grierson was a Scottish educator and scholar who was a leading authority on John Milton, Sir Walter Scott, and Donne. He compiled what is considered the most complete and authoritative collection of Donne's poetry,* The Poems of John Donne *(1912), a well-researched and annotated collection that settled critical controversies about definitive versions of poems and of poems falsely attributed to Donne. In the following excerpt from his introduction to a 1929 edition of this collection, Grierson surveys Donne's* Elegies *and* Songs and Sonnets.]

Sensual Donne has been called, but it is not quite the right word. Hot-blooded and passionate he was, with a passion in which body and soul are sometimes inextricably blended, again in open conflict, and again conceived in abstract separation from one another, but sensual in a more general and deliberate way, without the appeal of passion, he is not. His poetry has nothing to say of the pleasures of eating and drinking, like that of his friend Ben Jonson, and the impression one gathers from poems, records, and letters is of one indifferent or even ascetic in regard to such pleasures. Even the most audacious of the *Elegies,* compared with similar exercises by Carew and others, are agitated and aerated by a passionate play of wit that makes a difference, the absence of which, the more frigidly sensuous tone, marks clearly as *not* by Donne many poems that have been attributed to him. It is noteworthy too how little stress Donne lays on beauty in his love-poems, the aesthetic element in passion. The feeling for pure beauty was somewhat defective in his composition. The want of it is the most definite limitation to the high quality of his poetry.

Not sensual nor sensuous but passionate is the note of the young Donne and his verse, an intense susceptibility to the fascination of sex, a fascination that at once allures and repels, enthralls and awakens a spirit of scornful rebellion. He ranges through the whole gamut of passion from its earthliest to its most abstractly detached moods. For there are different strata in the love poems thrown down together in such confused order by the first editors. At the one extreme are poems of seduction and illicit love with its accompaniment of passion and scorn. Such are most of the *Elegies,* and in the *Songs and Sonets* a concentrated outburst as **"The Apparition,"** or so finely woven a web of thought as **"The Extasie,"** though the latter, as the poet warms to his theme, as the wheels of his chariot grow hot with driving, becomes a vindication of the interconnexion and interdependence of soul and body, which was to be a cardinal principle of Donne's religious thought at a later period. One may, if one pleases, descry through these poems a liaison with a married woman, an intrigue with an unmarried girl in **"The Perfume,"** or one may read them as witty and paradoxical elaborations of general theses suggested by Donne's naturalistic revolt against the insincerities of Petrarchian sonnetteers,—the fickleness of women, his own delight in change, the folly of confining love by rules and relationships, sophisticated justifications of seduction, scorn of women's affected constancy, and of the physical basis of love which no refinements and hyperboles of love-poets can disguise. Some breathe, even if the main theme be the same, a purer and more simply passionate note, the twelfth Elegy [**"His parting from her"**] which seems to tell of a wife passionately loved in secret though over them hung the

> husband's threatening eyes
> That flam'd with the oily sweat of jealousy,

and a large body of the songs as **"I wonder by my troth"**, **"For God's sake hold your tongue and let me love"**, **"If yet I have not all thy love"**, **"Oh do not die"**, **"Twice or thrice had I loved thee"**, **"All kings and all their favourites"**, **"I'll tell thee now, dear love, what thou shalt do"**, **"Whoever comes to shroud me do not harm"**, **"Take heed of loving me"**, **"So, so break off this last lamenting kiss"**. Some of these may, though I rather doubt it, belong to a later period when Donne was the lover and wooer of Ann More. To a later period certainly belongs a small group of songs, and perhaps the sixteenth Elegy, [**"On his Mistris"**]. The songs are **"Sweetest love, I do not go"**, **"As virtuous men pass mildly away"**, and **"A Valediction: of weeping."** These were written after his marriage when business of one kind or another called Donne away from his home. They are a beautifully patterned expression of the depth and sweetness of the affection which united the sorely tried couple and contrast strangely with some of the poems with which they stand cheek by jowl.

There remains a group of songs that present somewhat of a problem. They show us Donne in the, rather unusual for him, traditional attitude of the Petrarchian wooer of a fair but obdurate Laura, a lady whom he reproaches, not for fickleness or sensuality or a halfhearted reluctance to yield to love, but for a too impeccable coldness:

> O perverse sex where none is true but shee,

Who's therefore true because her truth kills mee.

These poems are **"Twicknam Garden,"** the sombre and powerful **"Nocturnall upon St. Lucies Day,"** **"The Blossome,"** **"The Primrose,"** **"The Relique,"** and **"The Dampe"**. None of the *Elegies* is in this key. In them the tone is set, not by Petrarch, but by Ovid.

It would be easier, probably, to accept the explanation which I have already ventured to propound if one might eliminate **"The Blossome,"** **"The Primrose,"** and **"The Dampe,"** for in these there is a strain of the more familiar Donne, sardonic and sensual. Apart from these, and perhaps including them, I am disposed to argue that the change of tone in this group of poems represents a difference in the social status of the persons addressed, that he is here, like other poets, adopting the Petrarchian convention to pay compliments to the noble ladies of his acquaintance. The class of women to whom, or on whom, he had composed the *Elegies* and *Songs and Sonets* of a similar kind had been that common object of young lawyers' and courtiers' freer advances and more audacious wit, the wives and daughters of citizens, women of Donne's own rank and station. In the group under consideration, as in the **"Letter to the Countesse of Huntingdon,"** the persons addressed, actual or ideal, more probably the first, are of a higher rank. It may be an accident that the titles of three of them, **"Twicknam Garden,"** **"A Nocturnall upon St. Lucies Day,"** and **"The Primrose"** suggest a connexion with the Countess of Bedford and Mrs. Magdalen Herbert. . . . I have a lurking suspicion that **"Twicknam Garden,"** and **"St. Lucies Day,"** were exquisite and passionate compliments to his great lady-patron, Lucy, Countess of Bedford, who occupied Twickenham Park from 1608 to 1617. Nor need even the devout Mrs. Herbert, of whose earlier years we know little, have felt indignant on the receipt of such an impassioned compliment as **"The Relique"**.

> These miracles we did; but now alas,
> All measure and all language I should pass,
> Should I tell what a miracle she was.

It is more difficult to imagine her the person addressed in **"The Primrose"** and **"The Dampe."** If a reference to her is ruled out, on the strength of what we know of her from Walton and on general considerations, then these poems may be the product of the years in which Donne began, as a member of Sir Thomas Egerton's household, to move in a more exalted sphere than that which the young law-student had frequented in his more unregenerate days. They are the compliments he paid to ladies like the Countess of Huntingdon and others, charming because passionate compliments with just a touch of more daring suggestion which quite possibly these not too prudish young ladies would not resent. They heard in the theatre and at Court abundance of such frank speech as a later age would not have tolerated. It is after all convention that regulates both the length of a lady's skirt and the kind of compliments one may pay her. Lady Bedford would have been more scandalized at the thought of going through the street in the attire of a Highland regiment than at some freedom of language in a kind of poetry which everyone understood to be purely conventional.

The conflict of moods which the first group of these poems betrays, the war of sense and spirit, the awareness of body and soul as complementary and yet antagonistic, becomes more intelligible against such a background as I have suggested, the revolt against a too strong superimposed bias. Donne's nature had revolted, asserted its claim to life and experience. But experience is bitter as well as sweet— sweet in the mouth but bitter in the belly. Independence humiliates as well as exalts. The emancipated instincts realize their limitations. The spiritual and ascetic impulses reassert their claim when passion has spent itself. Strife and bitterness succeed, finding vent in scornful satire and an exaggeration of sensuality or an equally extravagant and abstract idealism, till the tumult subsides, feeling gathers strength again, and body and soul are merged in the passion of the moment. 'The imagination of a boy is healthy and the mature imagination of a man is healthy; but there is a space of life between in which the soul is in a ferment, the character is undecided, the way of life uncertain, the ambition thick-sighted: thence proceeds mawkishness and all the thousand bitters which these men I speak of necessarily taste of in going over these pages.' So says Keats in the preface to *Endymion.* There were factors and elements in the ferment of Donne's soul which Keats did not know till he was a dying man; and the instinct for beauty was too uncertain in the older poet, too arrogantly controlled by a restless intellect, for him ever to attain to the peace of great imaginative work, though he perhaps comes nearest to it in the beautiful prose of some of the passages in his sermons.

But Donne was no ordinary young man carried by a swing of the pendulum from a too strict education to a life of debauchery and then again to repentance. The movement which these poems reflect in its excesses was one of thought as well as feeling, and the thought remained a central one in all his later development, even if he never succeeded in working it out to a balanced and harmonious conception of life. The dualism of body and soul he refused to accept as the absolute one to which medieval thought, influenced by Neo-Platonism, had tended. The body is not simply evil, the spirit good, sense a corrupter and misleader, the soul pure and heavenward aspiring. Man is body and soul, and neither can be complete without the other. To separate them absolutely is heresy alike in love and in religion:

> Love's not so pure and abstract as they use
> To say which have no mistress but the Muse;
> But as all else being elemented too,
> Love sometimes would contemplate, sometimes do.

The same thought in its religious bearing was to recur in many of his poems and letters and sermons:

> A resurrection is a second rising to that state from
> which anything is formerly fallen. Now though by death
> the soul do not fall into any such state as that it can
> complain (for what can that lack which God fills?), yet
> by death the soul falls from that for which it was infused and poured into man at first, that is to be the
> form of that body, the king of that kingdom; and therefore when in the general resurrection the soul returns to
> that state for which it was created and to which it hath
> an affection even in the fulness of the joys of Heaven;
> then when the soul returns to her office, to make up the
> man, because the whole man hath, therefore the soul
> hath a resurrection.

Just so Blake pictures the passionate reunion of soul and body.

But Donne was not yet a preacher penitent for his early excesses. The experience through which he passed in these early years is really a typical though salient instance of the movement of thought and feeling which we call the Renaissance. It is the movement, thrown into sharp relief by the peculiar character of Donne's upbringing, from conceptions of life and morality which made the joys of another world the goal of life and the measure of man's conduct to conceptions in which this world and man's sensible nature are at least constituent elements in the good for which he strives. (pp. xviii-xxiv)

> *H. J. C. Grierson, in an introduction to* The Poems of John Donne, *edited by H. J. C. Grierson, Oxford University Press, London, 1929, pp. xiii-xlvii.*

Leonard Unger   (essay date 1950)

[*Unger is an American essayist, poet, and academic who has written and edited several critical studies. In the following excerpt from his* Donne's Poetry and Modern Criticism, *he examines imagery, conceits, and structure in "The Good Morrow," "The Canonization," and "Twicknam Garden" to determine whether the* Songs and Sonets *should be defined as metaphysical.*]

The opening lines and title of **"The Good Morrow"**, as well as other parts of the poem, indicate that it is addressed by a lover to his loved one after a night of love. Speculation on what the lovers did until they loved is in the form of a conceit; the lovers are equated with suckling children:

> . . . were we not wean'd till then?
> But suck'd on countrey pleasures, childishly?

The poem does not develop by an extension of this conceit nor are references to infancy or the stages of human growth made again as statements upon the condition of the lovers, past or present. Instead, the conceit is followed by an alternative conceit; previous to this love the lovers were as infants, or their unawareness was a condition of sleeping in the legendary den of the seven sleepers. So the speculation runs. But there is hardly a development of thought in the sequence of these two conceits, and there is no linkage between them in figurative terms. And since the two conceits are independent of each other and yet reiterative in statement, their possibilities of precision and significance of detail become less likely when it is affirmed concerning both of them that "T'was so." First the conceits are on a par with each other and then they are lumped together, so that what issues from them is a general implication, not a conceptual argument developed by a single figure or even a series of figures. In the closing lines of the stanza the speaker turns from the pre-love condition to the present: except for his love, he says, all pleasures are fancies, and all his former experience of beauty was but a dream of the loved one. These statements, although suggestive of conceits, are hardly more than the idioms of hyperbole. They do not continue previous references in the poem, nor are they recalled in later references.

As the lover's speech continues in the second stanza there is no continuation of either argument or terminology from the first stanza. It is not until the fourth line that the figurative language of a conceit occurs. Following the generalization,

> For love, all love of other sights controules,

there comes the particular example,

> And makes one little roome, an every where.

The conceit is constituted by the identification of a room with the world. Other geographical references follow this conceit, but the conceit itself is not in any way extended. The lines that follow,

> Let sea-discoverers to new worlds have gone,
> Let Maps to other, worlds on worlds have showne,

are rhetorical imperatives exclaimed by the lover in expression of his indifference to and independence of affairs other than his own. There is nothing figurative in these statements. Their terminology, however, serves as a referential background for the conceit used in the final line of the stanza:

> Let us possesse one world, each hath one, and is one.

This time each of the lovers is identified with a world. To call this trope a conceit is perhaps questionable, unless one means by a conceit any metaphor or other figure that is not utterly conventional.

The third stanza opens with literal description: the lovers' faces are reflected in each other's eyes. The second line, "And true plain hearts doe in the faces rest," is hardly less literal, since the word *heart* is considered synonymous with *affections* rather than figuratively representative of *affections.* In the next two lines we do have a conceit:

> Where can we finde two better hemispheares
> Without sharpe North, without declining West?

This is not the first use of geographical terms. Previously it was said that each lover was a world, that each possessed a world. However calculated and noticeable the use of two "geographical" conceits may be, one is in no way the logical extension or justification of the other. The conceits stand independently side by side; one does not continue from the other. A connection between them is suggested by the fact that each makes reference to the same material, but the connection is general, even vague. Moreover, the second conceit, though it develops its own meaning, does not add meaning to the first. The second conceit says that the faces in which hearts rest are hemispheres, but of a kind that presents no perils to mariners. The implication is that the lovers have nothing to fear from each other and may be confident about the course of their love. The poem ends with a new conceit:

> What ever dyes, was not mixt equally;
> If our two loves be one, or, thou and I
> Love so alike, that none doe slacken, none can die.

Here the conceit is constituted by the application of a proposition from physical science to the relationship of the lovers. If their love is a single unity or is made of equal parts, then, like similar mixtures, the relationship will hold fast and neither party will cease loving the other. The idea of equal parts may refer to the hemispheres of the earlier conceit, but the connection between the two conceits is so slight it can hardly be considered that one is the extension of the other. If one attempts to include the hemi-spheres in the conceit of the mixture, it becomes apparent that no meaningful resolution is possible, although the final conceit is otherwise a development in the meaning of the poem.

This examination of **"The Good Morrow"** is not an attempt at evaluating the poem. Our concern is to discover which statements about the structure of metaphysical poetry are borne out by it. The only statement that is found to be wholly valid with regard to **"The Good Morrow"** is that the conceit often occurs. It can also be said that the ideological burden of the poem is to a considerable extent conveyed by the use of tropes, though not consistently. An obvious, or superficial, wit inheres in the conceits and such devices as the hyperbole of the first stanza and the rhetorical imperatives of the second. Another kind of wit, less local and rhetorical, may be considered as present in the poem. This wit consists in the contrast between the two *worlds:* the world of the lovers, and the geographical world. It is, moreover, not merely a verbal wit, for each world represents an attitude—the worldly attitude and the lover's attitude. There is, then, a complexity of attitudes in the poem. But the lover, who speaks the poem, gives no hint of being involved in an ironical situation, of entertaining any complexity of attitudes. He dismisses the geographical world and affirms the world of love.

The first stanza of **"The Canonization"** constitutes an apostrophe to anyone who might try to distract or persuade the lover from his loving. The lover, implying that he is determined upon loving, suggests that his critic admonish him upon other grounds, or that the critic attend to his own advancement, but at any rate leave the lover undisturbed. Aside from the apostrophe, there is no figurativeness in this stanza, and there is no development or addition of statement after the first line. A wittiness results from grouping together the several specific actions, each of which might be performed as alternatives to criticizing the lover; from the critic's point of view it is irrelevant and absurd to consider such alternatives. Though the stanza is from one point of view repetitious, though it contains no trope or material that is to be figuratively elaborated, its wit does characterize the speaker and establish a tone.

This tone is maintained with little change throughout the second stanza, which is similar to the first in its construction and scarcely different in its statement. The speaker continues the argument for his love, this time in the manner of rhetorical interrogations. He asks what injuries may be charged against his loving, and then, in the form of questions, lists specific possibilities: have his sighs drowned ships? have his tears flooded grounds? have his lover's-chills affected the weather? have his lover's-fevers affected the health of society? These possibilities, by the extent of their exaggeration, border upon metaphor, but the obvious function of the exaggeration is the absurdity which makes for wit. An additional element in the wit is the fact that the issues raised by the lover are irrelevant to—are a digression from—sensible arguments which might be brought against him. The same kind of wit is produced by the literal statement of the lines concluding the stanza:

> Soldiers finde warres, and Lawyers finde out still
> Litigious men, which quarrels move,
> Though she and I do love.

This observation, though it may be witty by its absurdity in the apparent argument, is on another level of reading not absurd at all, though still witty.

With these final lines of the second stanza it becomes obvious that the lover is doing more than making a witty appeal for permission to continue his loving undisturbed. He is saying that his loving has no effect upon soldiers, lawyers and litigious men; and he is implying, here and throughout the preceding part of the poem, that the values of the lover and those of the world are wholly different and unconnected. In the first two stanzas the speaker has illustrated the thesis that it is absurd to make worldly values bear upon the lover. His absurd defiance of the world is, indirectly, the suggestion of a serious defiance, and this practice of indirection is witty. It should be noticed that this wit does not depend upon the particular devices used for overt absurdity. Like the wit of **"The Good Morrow"**, it proceeds from the contrast of the two attitudes: that of the world, and that of the lover. Here, however, the lover does not easily dismiss the world. He is cognizant of the contrasting attitudes as being in conflict, and he is opposing one to the other. He is insisting upon a complexity of attitudes, arguing that one attitude should not be confused with or subordinated to the other. Throughout the rest of the poem he continues to argue for the merit and self-sufficiency of the lover's world, the lover's attitude.

The third stanza begins with the lover's statement of his indifference to what others think of or call the lovers. And the stanza continues with the lover's own suggestions as to how they may be characterized: they are tapers, dying at their own cost; in them may be found the Eagle and the Dove; finally, they are comparable to the riddle of the Phœnix:

> The Phœnix ridle hath more wit
> By us, we two being one, are it.
> So to one neutrall thing both sexes fit,
> Wee dye and rise the same, and prove
> Mysterious by this love.

These comparisons, particularly the latter, may be regarded as conceits. There is, however, no connection between the conceits in so far as their terms are concerned; but each one does make the witty point of the paradoxical—the mysterious—nature of the lovers' relationship.

None of the earlier conceits is drawn upon in the fourth stanza, which begins with the statement that the lovers can die by love, a possibility suggested in the preceding stanza. The statement is without metaphor and says in effect that when the lovers have died, their legend may not be fit for tombs and hearse, but it will be fit for verse. In the lines that follow, the subject is further developed, this time with an abundant use of metaphor:

> And if no peece of Chronicle wee prove,
> We'll build in sonnets pretty roomes;
> As well a well wrought urne becomes
> The greatest ashes, as halfe-acre tombes,
> And by these hymnes, all shall approve
> Us *Canoniz'd* for Love:

Though there are several metaphors here, the passage is not constituted by a single conceit; we do not have logical extension in the terms of an initial image or other metaphorical situation. There is, however, no lapse of metaphorical statement. The conceits follow immediately upon

each other and are joined to each other by obvious association. One example of such association is the shift from *verse* to *sonnets* to *hymns*. Another example: the sonnets containing the story of the lovers are like pretty rooms in which the lovers themselves are contained; the sonnets—or pretty rooms—are like a well wrought urn, as distinguished from some monument of greater proportions. And finally, having shifted from sonnets to hymns, the passage ends with the statement that the lovers are canonized. This conclusion is reached by no argument, it is not contained within a metaphorical development: as we have already observed, it proceeds simply by an obvious association.

The conceit of canonization continues throughout the final stanza of the poem. This continuation of the conceit may be regarded as a single segment of extension, for the extension is effected by a statement, comprising the whole stanza, which invokes the lovers as canonized—as saints:

> And thus invoke us; You whom reverend love
> Made one anothers hermitage;
> You, to whom love was peace, that now is rage;
> Who did the whole worlds soule contract, and drove
> Into the glasses of your eyes
> So made such mirrors, and such spies,
> That they did all to you epitomize,
> Countries, Townes, Courts: Beg from above
> A patterne of your love!

The elements contained in this stanza are themselves tropes proper to the religious invocation which is the embracing conceit: the lovers had a hermitage—one another—in which they found peace and performed the miracle of contracting the world. The stanza ends with a request to the lovers that they "beg from above" a pattern of their love, which is their special function as saints.

We may turn now to observation of the general structure of the poem in its entirety. It may be said of the last three stanzas of **"The Canonization"** that the conceit is frequent. A negative argument could be made, however, on the basis that there are no conceits in the first two stanzas. At any rate, even if the issue of frequency could be settled in the affirmative, this affirmation would contribute little of importance to the more complicated and systematic definitions of metaphysical poetry which several critics have ventured.

Our analysis has shown that **"The Canonization"** is not built on a single extended metaphor that is coterminous with the poem. One could argue that the embracing metaphor is constituted by the situation out of which the poem is supposedly uttered—the lover in defense of his loving—and that the poem has implications beyond its obvious verbal reference; but then such argument must make allowance for dramatic monologues and poems with other kinds of unity to be included under *metaphysical*, and as a result the term and its definition become meaningless and unprofitable. It is true that the conceit that gives the poem its title has considerable extension, but it is unanticipated and unpredictable until reached in the poem; the extent of the conceit is too slight in relation to the rest of the poem to justify its being regarded as characterizing the general structure of the entire poem.

According to our analysis of the first two stanzas, one cannot say of **"The Canonization"** that it departs at no point from the manner of the conceit, or that a prose restatement of the poem's meaning is within the poem always expressed by a trope. There are, however, passages in the poem made up wholly of conceit following upon conceit, and often it is a conceit or sequence of conceits which expresses whatever thought may be inferred or restated from the poetry. Our analysis confirms that **"The Canonization"** is witty in that it contains the devices of wit: the absurd apostrophes of the first stanza, the exaggerations and rhetorical questions of the second, and the associations and conceits in the remaining stanza. We observed, moreover, that there is in the poem wit which results from a complexity of attitudes, which is conceptual originally, and which does not follow from local rhetorical device.

Donne's **"Twicknam Garden"** is, in its title and structure, unlike many of his other poems. For instance, poems having some figurative use of titles within the poetry are **"The Sunne Rising"**, **"The Flea"**, **"The Will"**, and other poems, and even **"A Nocturnall upon Saint Lucies Day"**, which is peculiarly similar to **"Twicknam Garden"** in several respects. Unless we seek in the biography of the poet for additional meanings, the title of this poem is to be taken simply and literally: the speaker of the poem is to be present in the garden and makes references to its details.

The garden, then, may be regarded as an immediate material of the poem. Another immediate material would be the speaker's feelings, his emotional condition. These two materials are introduced and developed side by side: the poem begins

> Blasted with sighs, and surrounded with teares,
> 　　Hither I come to seeke the spring, . . .

And not until the end of the poem does the speaker pursue any argument or set up any extended metaphor as a seeming fulfillment to the direction of the whole poem. He continues speaking in the terms with which the poem begins, and the terms are actually what the poem is about—the garden and his emotion. The speaker actually discusses the relationship between these; he refers to the garden as it is seen in the light of the emotion and, thus seen, as it reflects the emotion. We have, consequently, an essentially dramatic poem: a speaker in a specific situation making utterances about the situation:

> Blasted with sighs, and surrounded with teares,
> 　　Hither I come to seeke the spring,
> 　　And at mine eyes, and at mine eares,
> Receive such balmes, as else cure every thing;
> 　　But O, selfe traytor, I do bring
> The spider love, which transubstantiates all,
> 　　And can convert Manna to gall,
> And that this place may thoroughly be thought
> 　　True Paradise, I have the serpent brought.

Although the dramatic situation of the speaker is to be taken literally, his utterance does none the less contain figurative expressions. The speaker, given over to sighs and tears, comes to the garden at the spring season, seeking some relief. The garden, with its pleasant aspects of sight and sound, would work a healing effect upon him but for the fact that he has brought the "spider love." Here we have the first conceit of the poem. This conceit—love as a spider—is extended, but with the extension the metaphor changes its terms. The emotion of love, like the spider, corrupts the pleasures of the garden. And, like reli-

gious love, it "transubstantiates" these, only with an ironical difference; for instead of providing healthy spiritual nourishment, this love changes a provident remedy—manna—into unpalatable bitterness. The speaker leaves this complex figure and continues his irony, saying that he has brought along the serpent in order that this garden may be considered a true paradise, for the traditional paradise—the Garden of Eden—had a serpent in it. This statement is far more complicated dramatically than it is rhetorically. It is in sheer irony that the speaker says he has brought the serpent purposefully. Though with the addition of the serpent the garden is made comparable to the traditional paradise, no paradisaical benefits are implied: one garden is like the other because both are invaded by evil. We see, thus, that the *serpent* is related to the general logic of its context: it is conveyed by the speaker to the garden, and this is said as part of a consistent comment upon the garden.

But how, in the first place, is the presence of the serpent to be explained? Certainly it is not to be pictured as part of a physical setting suggested by the poem. (Of course, it is there in the garden, but not in a physical sense, not as an image.) Obviously, the serpent represents that emotion of the speaker which makes it impossible for him to appreciate the pleasures of the garden, which turns these to displeasures. (One may be reminded of "a serpent in the breast".) This equation between serpent and emotion is, however, not stated. We have, consequently, an implied metaphor: a symbol is used in the place of the thing symbolized while there is no grammatical connection between the two—the thing symbolized, in fact, being omitted. An effect of the poetry is this suggestion of the nature of the emotion: we may have here something comparable to the technique of symbolist poetry. The emotion is the *subject* of the poem, and the speaker, in order to specify its character, must go beyond the statement that all is not well with him; to characterize the emotion he must discuss it in terms other than itself. And such terms are the peculiar aspect of the garden, the spider, and the serpent. All these are meaningful in that they suggest characterizations of the emotion. It is, I believe, terms such as these that would be important in a consideration of poetic effect. A symbolist poem of comparable terms would be "difficult" in so far as one could not determine the *subject* of which the terms are characterizations, the theme by which they cohere.

In the second stanza of the poem the speaker continues referring to his emotion by elaborating upon the fact that he is unable to appreciate the pleasant garden; a dismal garden would be more tolerable to his mood:

> 'Twere wholsomer for mee, that winter did
> 　　Benight the glory of this place,
> 　　And that a grave frost did forbid
> These trees to laugh, and mocke mee to my face;
> 　　But that I may not this disgrace
> Indure, nor yet leave loving, Love let mee
> 　　Some senslesse peece of this place bee;
> Make me a mandrake, so I may groane here,
> 　　Or a stone fountaine weeping out my yeare.

Here again it is apparent that the passage is not constituted by conceit—one or more. There is, of course, some figurativeness, but the meaning or effect of the passage depends upon its dramatic significance, figurative or not. Everything the speaker says, like the mention of the serpent in the first stanza, serves to intimate the quality of his emotion. The stanza begins with a conditional statement: a winter garden would be more tolerable and fitting to his feelings than a spring garden; in such a garden the trees would not laugh and mock him to his face, as they do now. The laughing, mocking trees are a metaphor (or personification), but this metaphor does not determine or extend the structure of the poem. And it is no criticism of the passage to say this. The trees become terms in a figurative expression because they are part of a situation that the speaker observes to be ironical. Here the figurativeness is dramatic rather than structural, as we have been using that word. It is dramatically significant that the speaker should make the figure, and the intimation already noted continues. It does, indeed, continue through the entire stanza. The spring garden remains unchanged, of course, so the speaker requests of "Love" (obviously the deity) that, in order not to endure "this disgrace" of mockery and yet to cease not from loving, he be made a "senseless peece" of the garden—a groaning mandrake (of folklore) or a weeping stone fountain. There is no logic and certainly no feasibility to the request. How, as a senseless object, though "groaning" or "weeping", would he continue to love? The question is a confusing one if we try to follow it literally and rationally. But this is beside the point. Because it is thus confusing, the more obviously is the question, again like other parts of the poem, connotatively an intimation of the speaker's emotion. And here, too, we may notice, there is some figurativeness, but it is incidental in the passage and subordinate to it. This is not to say that it is a detachable ornament; it is an element of the intimating rhetorical question that we have discussed.

In this second stanza there is some development of the subject of the poem, and this advance is contained in the phrase "nor yet leave loving." Such characterization of the emotion, which has been called "spider" and "serpent", suggests its tension and complexity. It should be noticed, however, that in the poem as we have read it thus far there has been no development of idea through argument or extended metaphors (cf. **"A Valediction: Forbidding Mourning"**, **"The Extasie"**, **"A Lecture upon the Shadow"**) but rather a developmental reference to the emotion which is the subject of the poem.

The opening of the third and final stanza is, in a way, comparable to extended metaphor, and the whole stanza differs, by its argumentative nature, from the first two.

> Hither with christall vyals, lovers come,
>   And take my teares, which are loves wine,
>   And try your mistresse Teares at home,
> For all are false, that tast not just like mine;
>   Alas, hearts do not in eyes shine,
> Nor can you more judge womans thoughts by teares,
>   Then by her shadow, what she weares.
> O perverse sexe, where none is true but shee,
>   Who's therefore true, because her truth kills mee.

The metaphor extended is that of the speaker as a weeping stone fountain, this having been suggested at the end of the preceding stanza. Extension of this metaphor, however, does not consist in elaboration but rather in maintained reference to the initial metaphorical situation. The speaker bids lovers to come with vials and take the tears which he, as fountain, is weeping. He calls the tears "loves wine", thus implying that they are a liquid accompaniment to the occasion of love and that they belong to a class within

which distinctions may be made, as the connoisseur distinguishes among wines. The lovers are to compare these tears with those of their mistresses in order to discover the genuineness of the latter: "For all are false, that tast not just like mine." Thus the speaker exclaims upon the genuineness and seriousness of his own emotion; and at the same time suggests the source and experiential context of the emotion. That he has been personally affected by the nature of woman is emphasized by the "Alas" which introduces his dictum: woman's heart and thought are no more to be learned from her eyes and tears than is what she wears from her shadow. In other words, women are dissemblers, making for inconsistency, illogicality and disorder. They are a "perverse sexe", for, in the experience of the speaker, one of them by being true causes him to suffer. Her trueness consists in that she does not love him and gives him this plainly to understand. Hence in a perverse and ironical sense of true, she is true in her attitude of not being his true love.

If we look back now over the stanza we find in it several metaphors: the speaker as fountain, tears as wine, the taste of tears as an indication of sincerity, and eyes as reflecting the heart. No one of these metaphors, however, includes all the others or provides the terms which are used in an expression of the central thought or subject of the poem. And though the metaphors are close upon each other, there is no logical extension of imagery. For example, the lovers' tasting the tears of their mistresses is not important as an image. If we want to make a comparable description for the development of the stanza, we might call it an associational procession of ideas. The concluding passage of the stanza ("O perverse sexe . . . ") contains no metaphor ("her truth kills me" is hardly considerable for its figurativeness); nor can the passage be figuratively connected with any preceding metaphor.

It was observed above that the final stanza differs somewhat from the others. These stanzas, we noticed, made no argument, developed no idea, but as a dramatic utterance made reference to the garden and the emotion of the speaker, thus apparently characterizing the emotion. But in the final stanza there is argument and development of idea: women are generally false, and one woman's "truth" is peculiar in that it affects the speaker painfully. These ideas offer themselves for consideration as ideas, and because of this the stanza is not so apparently a characterization of the speaker's emotion, which in the earlier stanzas is unmistakably the subject. Such observation may be in the nature of a criticism. There is a possible reading of the last stanza, and I believe it to be not unjust, which would make this criticism less strictly applicable. This reading would take the stanza as a dramatic utterance comparable to the others, despite the obtrusivenes of its ideas. That is, it would be found significant beyond its specific structure and immediate references, significant primarily in its reference to and characterization of the speaker's emotion.

We have found that no single characterization of metaphysical poetry is wholly borne out by any of the three poems we have examined. It is true that there are some conceits in each of these, and it may therefore be said that the conceit often occurs; but, as we have observed before, this is unpretentious beside the other definitions and would probably be found acceptable by proponents of these definitions. (pp. 22-37)

Leonard Unger, in his Donne's Poetry and Modern Criticism, *Henry Regnery Company, 1950, 91 p.*

JOHN DONNE, IN A LETTER TO SIR HENRY GOODYER

I have made a meditation in verse, which I call a **"Litany"**; the word you know imports no other than supplication, but all Churches have one form of supplication by that name. Amongst ancient annals—I mean some eight hundred years—I have met two Litanies in Latin verse, which gave me not the reason of my meditations, for in good faith I thought not upon them then, but they give me a defence, if any man to a layman and a private impute it as a fault, to take such divine and public names, to his own little thoughts. The first of these was made by Ratpertus, a monk of Suevia, and the other by St. Notker, of whom I will give you this note by the way, that he is a private saint for a few parishes; they were both but monks, and the Litanies poor and barbarous enough, yet Pope Nicolas the V. valued their devotion so much, that he canonised both their poems, and commanded them for public service in their Churches. Mine is for lesser chapels, which are my friends; and though a copy of it were due to you now, yet I am so unable to serve myself with writing it for you at this time (being some thirty staves of nine lines), that I must entreat you to take a promise that you shall have the first, for a testimony of that duty which I owe to your love and to myself, who am bound to cherish it by my best offices. That by which ["**A Litany**"] will deserve best acceptation is, that neither the Roman Church need call it defective, because it abhors not the particular mention of the blessed triumphers in heaven, nor the Reformed can discreetly accuse it of attributing more than a rectified devotion ought to do.

(letter date 1609)

Helen Gardner   (essay date 1952)

[An English essayist and academic, Gardner has written criticism on a variety of authors and subjects, including well-received studies and editions of Donne's poetry. In the following excerpt from her general introduction to a 1952 edition of The Divine Poems of John Donne, *Gardner compares* La Carona *and "A Litany" with the* Holy Sonnets *in her study of Donne's religious poetry.]*

With the probable exception of **"The Cross,"** for which no precise date can be suggested, and which is more a verse-letter than a divine poem, the earliest of Donne's Divine Poems appears to be **La Corona.** **La Corona** is a single poem, made up of seven linked sonnets, each of which cel-

ebrates not so much an event in the life of Christ as a mystery of faith. Those brought up in a different tradition might well wonder why Donne should devote one sonnet of his seven to the Finding in the Temple, and omit all reference to the events of the Ministry, except for a brief reference to miracles. The emphasis on the beginning and close of the life of Christ is characteristic of mediaeval art, whether we think of a series of windows like those at Fairford, or of the mediaeval dramatic cycles. It was dictated by the desire to present with simplicity the Christian scheme of man's redemption. The popular devotional equivalent of this emphasis upon the plan of salvation was the meditation on the Fifteen Mysteries of the Rosary, and reference to them explains at once why Donne would find it natural to pass directly from the Finding in the Temple to the events of Holy Week. Habits of prayer, like other early habits, can survive modifications of a man's intellectual position. It is doubtful whether Donne felt there was anything particularly Catholic in concentrating on the Mysteries of the Faith, or in addressing his second and third sonnets to the Blessed Virgin, or in apostrophizing St. Joseph in his fourth; but it is also doubtful whether anyone who had been brought up as a Protestant would have done so.

La Corona has been undervalued as a poem by comparison with the **Holy Sonnets,** because the difference of intention behind the two sets of sonnets has not been recognized. The **La Corona** sonnets are inspired by liturgical prayer and praise—oral prayer; not by private meditation and the tradition of mental prayer. They echo the language of collects and office hymns, which expound the doctrines of the Catholic Faith, recalling the events from which those doctrines are derived, but not attempting to picture them in detail. Instead of the scene of the maiden alone in her room at Nazareth, there is a theological paradox: "Thy Makers maker, and thy Fathers mother." The scandal of the Cross is presented not by a vivid picture of its actual ignominy and agony, but by the thought that here the Lord of Fate suffered a fate at the hand of his creatures. The petitions with which the last three poems end, though couched in the singular, are petitions which any man might pray. Each is the appropriate response to the mystery propounded. It is not surprising to find that the first sonnet of the set is a weaving together of phrases from the Advent Offices in the Breviary, and that the second draws on the Hours of the Blessed Virgin. As always happens with Donne, direct dependence on sources weakens as he proceeds. But the impulse with which he began **La Corona** is clearly visible in the first two sonnets. His "crowne of prayer and praise" was to be woven from the prayers and praises of the Church. It is possible that he chose to use the sonnet, a form he had used before this only for epistles, because he wished to write formally and impersonally: to create an offering of beauty and dignity. **La Corona** is perhaps no more than a religious exercise, but it is an accomplished one. The sonnets are packed with meaning, with striking and memorable expressions of the commonplaces of Christian belief. The last line of each, repeated as the first line of the next, is both a fine climax and a fine opening. Unlike the majority of Elizabethan sonneteers, Donne has chosen the more difficult form of the sonnet. He follows Sidney in limiting the rhymes of the octave to two, and employs Sidney's most favored arrangement of those rhymes in two closed quatrains. He alternates between two arrangements of the rhymes of the sestet. His seventh sonnet presented a problem; if it contrasted with his sixth, it would be the same as his first. He chose the lesser evil, and repeated the form of the sixth sonnet in the seventh, in order to make the last lead round again to the first and form a circle.

"A Litany," which is probably the next important divine poem, is less successful than **La Corona,** but more interesting. Donne has cast his "meditation in verse" into the formal mould of a litany. On the other hand, he has employed a stanza of his own invention. The contrast between the simple traditional outline of the poem and the intricacies of the separate stanzas is the formal expression of the poem's ambiguity. It appears impersonal, but is, in fact, highly personal. It tells us much, though indirectly, of its author's mind at the time when it was written, not least because it is in some ways uncharacteristic of him. It has the special interest of poems which are the product of a period of transition, when in the process of reshaping a personality some elements are stressed to the exclusion of others. "A Litany" is remarkable for a quality that is rare in Donne's poetry, though it is often found in his letters and sermons: sobriety. Although it is the wittiest of the Divine Poems, startling in paradox, precise in antithesis, and packed with allusions, its intellectual ingenuity and verbal audacity are employed to define an ideal of moderation in all things. Sir Herbert Grierson called it "wire-drawn and tormented." "Wire-drawn" it may be called with justice; it analyzes temptations with scrupulosity, and shows a wary sense of the distinctions that divide the tainted from the innocent act or motive. But "tormented" seems less just, even if we confine the word to the style. The ideal which is aspired to is simplicity of motive, "evennesse" of piety, and a keeping of "meane waies." Something of this ideal is already realized in the deliberate care with which the aspiration is expressed. At first sight the poem may appear overingenious. On further acquaintance it comes to seem not so much ingenious as exact; less witty, and more wise.

We know from Donne's letter to Goodyer, in which he refers to its composition, that "A Litany" was written during an illness and in a mood of dejection [see letter dated 1609]. The "low devout melancholie" of **La Corona** has deepened into a sin from which Donne prays to be delivered in the first verse. . . . It is a casuist's poem and shows traces both of the current debate on the Oath of Allegiance and of Donne's personal searchings of conscience in his years of failure, when he was still hoping for worldly success and, if Walton is right, had already been offered and had rejected advancement in the Church. Donne, who was "subtle to plague himself," must have been conscious of the contrast between his relatives, who for conscience' sake had chosen exile, imprisonment or death, and himself. He had conformed to the Established Church and was using his powers in its defence, and had even been offered a means of maintenance in its ministry. The rather exaggerated stress in "A Litany" on the compatibility of the service of God with "this worlds sweet" may reflect his need, at this time, to assure himself that the way that appears easier is not, for that reason, necessarily wrong. Intransigence may even, he hints, be a form of self-indulgence, an easy way out of the strain of conflicting duties:

> for Oh, to some

> Not to be Martyrs, is a martyrdome.

But if this seems an oversubtle explanation, there is another reason why Donne should at this period pray more strongly to be delivered from contempt of the world than from overvaluing it. The temptation to despise what one has not obtained and to cry, because one has been unsuccessful, "the world's not worth my care" is strong to ambitious natures. It must have been strong to Donne who had by nature both the melancholy and the scorn of the satirist. If we remember the circumstances of his life at Mitcham—his anxiety for his wife whom he had brought to poverty and for the future of his growing family, his inability to find secure employment and his broken health—the petitions of "A Litany" gain in meaning. We see the passionate and hyperbolical Donne, the proud and irritable young man of the Satires and Elegies, attempting to school himself to patience, not rejecting with scorn a world that has disappointed him, but praying that he may accept what life brings in a religious spirit. His declarations that happiness may exist in courts, and that the earth is not our prison, show an affinity with the contemporary movement in France, which Bremond described under the name of "l'humanisme dévot." They also contrast most interestingly with the pessimism of some Jacobean writers, particularly Webster, with whom Donne is often compared. The dying Antonio's cry, "And let my Sonne, flie the Courts of Princess," and Vittoria's last words, "O happy they that never saw the Court," only sum up the constant Senecan despising of the world in Webster's two greatest plays. "A Litany" has none of this cynicism. It is, whatever else we may say of it, a singularly unbitter poem, although it was written at a bitter time.

In many ways it is the most Anglican of the Divine Poems and continually anticipates Donne's leading ideas as a preacher. Although we may see in his restoration of the saints, whom Cranmer had banished from the Litany, a further sign of his loyalty to "the ancient ways," his own praise of his poem in his letter to Goodyer makes the typical Anglican claim of avoiding both excess and defect:

> That by which it will deserve best acceptation, is,
> That neither the Roman Church need call it defective, because it abhors not the particular mention of the blessed Triumphers in heaven; nor the Reformed can discreetly accuse it, of attributing more then a rectified devotion ought to doe.

We may also see in the whole poem a habit of mind which has been shaped by the practice of systematic self-examination, and thinks more in terms of particular sins and failings than in terms of general and total unworthiness; but the particular sins which Donne prays to be delivered from are not the traditional sins. There is no trace of the old classifications under which the conscience can be examined: sins against God and sins against my neighbor, or the seven deadly sins and their branches. Instead the sins in "A Litany" can all be referred back to two general philosophic conceptions: the conception of virtue as the mean between two extremes, and the related conception of virtue as the proper use of all the faculties. Donne anticipates here that ideal of "reasonable piety" which is so familiar later in the century in the manuals of the Caroline divines. The resolute rejection of otherworldliness, the antiascetic and antimystical bias of the poem, the concentration on "a daily beauty" and the sanctification of ordinary life, with the consequent ignoring of any conception of sanctity as something extraordinary and heroic, the exaltation of the undramatic virtues of patience, discretion, and a sober cheerfulness—all these things are characteristic of Anglican piety in the seventeenth century and after. In comparison with the Roman Catholic books of devotion, which they frequently drew upon and adapted, the Anglican manuals seem to some tastes rather dry, with their stress on edification and "practical piety" and the "duties of daily life." **"A Litany"** has something of this dryness. It has neither the warmth of mediaeval religious devotion, nor the exalted note of the Counter-Reformation. It reflects the intellectuality which Anglicanism derived from its break with mediaeval tradition and its return to the patristic ages.

But in spite of its many felicities in thought and expression, its beauty of temper, its interest in what it tells us of Donne's mind, and its historical interest as an early expression by a writer of genius of a piety characteristic of the Church of England, **"A Litany"** cannot be regarded as a wholly successful poem. It is an elaborate private prayer, rather incongruously cast into a liturgical form. Donne's letter to Goodyer shows he was aware of the discrepancy between such a "divine and publique" name and his "own little thoughts." He attempted to defend himself by the examples of two Latin litanies which he had found "amongst ancient annals." The defense is not a very cogent one. The litanies he refers to, although written by individuals, are genuine litanies, suitable for general use. Donne's poem could hardly be prayed by anyone but himself. Although he preserves the structure of a litany (Invocations, Deprecations, Obsecrations, and Intercessions), he does not preserve the most important formal element in a litany, the unvarying responses in each section. His opening invocations to the Persons of the Trinity have each a particular petition in place of the repeated "Miserere nobis." He is, of course, debarred by his membership of a Reformed Church from using the response "Ora pro nobis"; instead he exercises his ingenuity in finding suitable petitions for each group of saints to make, or for us to make as we remember them. There is some awkwardness in this "rectified devotion," which, accepting that the saints pray for men, avoids direct requests for their suffrages while suggesting fitting subjects for their intercessions; and the absence of any response makes these stanzas formally unsatisfactory. With the Deprecations, Obsecrations, and Intercessions, he makes use of the responses "Libera nos" and "Audi nos"; but he treats them as refrains to be modified according to each stanza, as he had loved to adapt and twist refrains in his love-poetry. In one place he goes so far as to invert his response, and beg the Lord not to hear. One may sympathize with Donne's desire to find a form for his meditation; but the incompatibility between the material of the poem and the chosen form is too great. The form has had to be too much twisted to fit the material, and the material has been moulded to the form rather than expressed by it.

Most critics have agreed in regarding *La Corona* and **"A Litany"** as inferior to the *Holy Sonnets,* which give an immediate impression of spontaneity. Their superiority has been ascribed to their having been written ten years later, and their vehemence and anguished intensity have been connected with a deepening of Donne's religious experience after the death of his wife. There can be no question

of their poetic greatness, nor of their difference from *La Corona* and **"A Litany"**; but I do not believe that greatness or that difference to be due to the reasons which are usually given. The accepted date rests on an assumption which the textual history of the sonnets does not support: the assumption that the three *Holy Sonnets* which the Westmoreland manuscript alone preserves were written at the same time as the other sixteen. These three sonnets are, as Sir Herbert Grierson called all the *Holy Sonnets,* "separate ejaculations"; but the other sixteen fall into clearly recognizable sets of sonnets on familiar themes for meditation. They are as traditional in their way as *La Corona* and **"A Litany"** are, and as the three Hymns are not. The Hymns are truly occasional; each arises out of a particular situation and a personal mood. But in theme and treatment the *Holy Sonnets,* if we ignore the three Westmoreland sonnets, depend on a long-established form of religious exercise: not oral prayer, but the simplest method of mental prayer, meditation. To say this is not to impugn their originality or their power. Donne has used the tradition of meditation in his own way; and it suits his genius as a poet far better than do the more formal ways of prayer he drew upon in *La Corona* and **"A Litany."** Yet although, with the possible exception of the Hymns, the *Holy Sonnets* are his greatest divine poems, I do not myself feel that they spring from a deeper religious experience than that which lies behind **"A Litany."** The evidence which points to a date in 1609 does not seem to me to conflict with their character as religious poems; on the contrary it accords rather better with it than does the hitherto accepted date.

Many readers have felt a discrepancy between the *Holy Sonnets* and the picture which Walton gives of Donne's later years, and between the *Holy Sonnets* and the sermons and Hymns. There is a note of exaggeration in them. This is apparent, not only in the violence of such a colloquy as **"Batter my heart,"** but also in the strained note of such lines as these:

> But who am I, that dare dispute with thee?
> O God, Oh! of thine onely worthy blood,
> And my teares, make a heavenly Lethean flood,
> And drowne in it my sinnes blacke memorie.
> That thou remember them, some claime as debt,
> I thinke it mercy, if thou wilt forget.

At first sight the closing couplet seems the expression of a deep humility; but it cannot be compared for depth of religious feeling with the **"Hymn to God the Father,"** where, however great the sin is, the mercy of God is implied to be the greater. . . . (pp. 123-30)

The almost histrionic note of the *Holy Sonnets* may be attributed partly to the meditation's deliberate stimulation of emotion; it is the special danger of this exercise that, in stimulating feeling, it may falsify it, and overdramatize the spiritual life. But Donne's choice of subjects and his whole-hearted use of the method are symptoms of a condition of mind very different from the mood of *La Corona* or even from the conflicts which can be felt behind **"A Litany."** The meditation on sin and on judgment is strong medicine; the mere fact that his mind turned to it suggests some sickness in the soul. The "low devout melancholie" of *La Corona,* the "dejection" of **"A Litany"** are replaced by something darker. In both his preparatory prayers Donne uses a more terrible word, despair. The note of anguish is unmistakable. The image of a soul in meditation which the *Holy Sonnets* present is an image of a soul working out of its salvation in fear and trembling. The two poles between which it oscillates are faith in the mercy of God in Christ, and a sense of personal unworthiness that is very near to despair. The flaws in their spiritual temper are a part of their peculiar power. No other religious poems make us feel so acutely the predicament of the natural man called to be the spiritual man. None present more vividly man's recognition of the gulf that divides him from God and the effort of faith to lay hold on the miracle by which Christianity declares that the gulf has been bridged.

Donne's art in writing them was to seem "to use no art at all." His language has the ring of a living voice, admonishing his own soul, expostulating with his Maker, defying Death, or pouring itself out in supplication. He creates, as much as in some of the *Songs and Sonnets,* the illusion of a present experience, throwing his stress on such words as "now" and "here" and "this." And, as often there, he gives an extreme emphasis to the personal pronouns:

> Take mee to you, imprison mee, for I
> Except you'enthrall mee, never shall be free,
> Nor ever chast, except you ravish mee.

The plain unadorned speech, with its idiomatic turns, its rapid questions, its exclamatory Oh's and Ah's, wrests the movement of the sonnet to its own movement. The line is weighted with heavy monosyllables, or lengthened by heavy secondary stresses, which demand the same emphasis as the main stress takes. It may be stretched out to

> All whom warre, dearth, age, argues, tyrannies,

after it has been contracted to

> From death, you numberlesse infinities.

Many lines can be reduced to ten syllables only by a more drastic use of elision than Donne allowed himself elsewhere, except in the Satires; and others, if we are to trust the best manuscripts, are a syllable short and fill out the line by a pause. This dramatic language has a magic that is unanalyzable: words, movement, and feeling have a unity in which no element outweighs the other.

The effect of completely natural speech is achieved by exploiting to the full the potentialities of the sonnet. The formal distinction of octave and sestet becomes a dramatic contrast. The openings of Donne's sestets are as dramatic as the openings of the sonnets themselves: impatient as in

> Why doth the devill then usurpe in mee?

or gentle as in

> Yet grace, if thou repent, thou canst not lacke;

or imploring as in

> But let them sleepe, Lord, and mee mourne a space.

Though the *turn* in each of these is different, in all three there is that sudden difference in tension that makes a change dramatic. Donne avoids also the main danger of the couplet ending: that it may seem an afterthought, or an addition, or a mere summary. His final couplets, whether separate or running on from the preceding line, are true rhetorical climaxes, with the weight of the poem

behind them. Except for Hopkins, no poet has crammed more into the sonnet than Donne. In spite of all the liberties he takes with his line, he succeeds in the one essential of the sonnet: he appears to need exactly fourteen lines to say exactly what he has to say. Donne possibly chose the sonnet form as appropriate for a set of formal meditations, but both in meditation and in the writing of his sonnets he converts traditional material to his own use. He was not, I believe, aiming at originality, and therefore the originality of the *Holy Sonnets* is the more profound.

With the exception of **"The Lamentations of Jeremy,"** in which Donne, like so many of his contemporaries, but with more success than most, attempted the unrewarding task of paraphrasing the Scriptures, the remainder of the Divine Poems are occasional. The poem **"Upon the Annunciation and Passion"** is very near in mood and style to *La Corona.* As there, Donne writes with strict objectivity. He contemplates two mysteries which are facets of one supreme mystery, and tries to express what any Christian might feel. On the other hand, **"Good Friday, Riding Westward"** is a highly personal poem: a free, discursive meditation arising out of a particular situation. The elaborate preliminary conceit of the contrary motions of the heavenly bodies extends itself into astronomical images, until the recollection of the Passion sweeps away all thoughts but penitence. As in some of the finest of the *Songs and Sonnets,* Donne draws out an initial conceit to its limit in order, as it seems, to throw it away when "to brave clearnesse all things are reduc'd." What he first sees as an incongruity—his turning his back on his crucified Savior—he comes to see as perhaps the better posture, and finally as congruous for a sinner. The poem hinges on the sudden apostrophe:

> and thou look'st towards mee,
> O Saviour, as thou hang'st upon the tree.

After this, discursive meditation contracts itself to penitent prayer. The mounting tension of the poem—from leisurely speculation, through the imagination kindled by "that spectacle of too much weight for mee," to passionate humility—makes it a dramatic monologue. So also does the sense it gives us of a second person present—the silent figure whose eyes the poet feels watching him as he rides away to the west.

"Good Friday" is the last divine poem Donne wrote before his ordination and it points forward to the Hymns. They also arise from particular situations, are free, not formal meditations, and have the same unforced feeling. They are the only lyrics among the Divine Poems, and it is not only in their use of the pun and conceit that they remind us of the *Songs and Sonnets.* They have the spontaneity which *La Corona* and **"A Litany"** lack, without the overemphasis of the *Holy Sonnets.* In them Donne's imagination has room for play. Each sprang from a moment of crisis. The **"Hymn to Christ"** was written on the eve of his journey overseas with Doncaster, a journey from which, as his Valediction Sermon shows, he felt he might not return. It is a finer treatment of the subject of the sonnet written after his wife's death in the Westmoreland manuscript. While the sonnet is general and reflective, in the Hymn his imagination is fired by his immediate circumstances and he translates his thoughts into striking and moving symbols. The **"Hymn to God the Father"** was written, according to Walton, during Donne's grave illness of 1623, and

the **"Hymn to God my God, in my sickness,"** whether it
should be dated during the same illness or in 1631, was
written when he thought himself at the point of death. In
both the conclusion is the same: "So, in his purple wrapp'd
receive mee Lord," and "Sweare by thy selfe." Donne's
earliest poem on religion, the third Satire, ended with the
words "God himselfe to trust," and it is fitting that what
is possibly his last divine poem, and certainly one of his
best known, should end with the memory of the promise
to Abraham, the type of the faithful. For the Divine
Poems are poems of faith, not of vision. Donne goes by a
road which is not lit by any flashes of ecstasy, and, in the
words he had carved on his tomb, "aspicit Eum cujus
nomen est Oriens." The absence of ecstasy makes his divine poems so different from his love poems. There is an
ecstasy of joy and an ecstasy of grief in his love-poetry; in
his divine poetry we are conscious almost always of an effort of will. In the **Holy Sonnets** there is passion and longing, and in the Hymns some of the "modest assurance"
which Walton attributed to Donne's last hours, but there
is no rapture. (pp. 130-34)

Donne was a man of strong passions, in whom an appetite
for life was crossed by a deep distaste for it. He is satirist
and elegist at the same period, and even in the same poem.
The scorn of the satirist invades the world of amorous
elegy; his gayest poems have a note of bitterness, his most
passionate lyrics are rarely free from a note of contempt,
even if it is only a sardonic aside or illustration. In his love-
poetry he set the ecstasy of lovers over against the dull,
foolish, or sordid business of the world, or exalted one
member of her sex by depreciating all the rest, or, in revulsion from the "queasie pain of being belov'd and loving,"
turned on his partner with savagery or mockery. But he
was also a man of strong and loyal affections: a good son,
a devoted husband, a loving father, and a warm and constant friend. From the beginning there is this other side to
Donne. In moral and psychological terms, Donne's problem was to come to terms with a world which alternately
enthralled and disgusted him, to be the master and not the
slave of his temperament. Like Wordsworth in his middle
years, he came to long for "a repose that ever is the same."
He did not look to religion for an ecstasy of the spirit
which would efface the memory of the ecstasy of the flesh;
but for an "evennesse" of piety which would preserve him
from despair. In the boldest of the **Holy Sonnets** it is in
order that he may "rise and stand" that he prays to be
overthrown, and in order that he may be ever chaste that
he prays God to ravish him. The struggles and conflicts
to which the Divine Poems witness did not lead to the secret heights and depths of the contemplative life, but to the
public life of duty and charity which Walton describes.
That Donne had to wrestle to the end is clear. Like Dr.
Johnson, with whom, in his natural melancholy and as a
practical moralist, he has much in common, he remained
burdened by the consciousness of his sins and aware of his
need for mercy at the judgment.

Donne's divine poems are the product of conflict between
his will and his temperament. They lack, therefore, the
greatness of his love-poetry, whose power lies in its "un-
chartered freedom": in the energy of will with which he
explores and expresses the range of his temperament. In
his love-poetry he is not concerned with what he ought or
ought not to feel, but with the expression of feeling itself.
Passion is there its own justification, and so is disgust, or

hatred or grief. In his divine poetry feeling and thought
are judged by the standard of what a Christian should feel
or think. As a love poet he seems to owe nothing to what
any other man in love had ever felt or said before him; his
language is all his own. As a divine poet he cannot escape
using the language of the Bible, and of hymns and prayers,
or remembering the words of Christian writers. Christianity is a revealed religion, contained in the Scriptures and
the experience of Christian souls; the Christian poet cannot voyage alone. The truths of Donne's love-poetry are
truths of the imagination, which freely transmutes personal experience. They are his own discoveries. The truths of
revelation are the accepted basis of his religious poetry,
and imagination has here another task. It is, to some extent, fettered. Donne anticipated Johnson's criticism of
"poetical devotion," and was perhaps his own best critic,
when he wrote to Sir Robert Carr, apologizing for his
poem on Hamilton:

> You know my uttermost when it was best, and even
> then I did best when I had least truth for my sub-
> jects. In this present case there is so much truth as
> it defeats all Poetry. . . . If you had commanded
> mee to have waited on his body to Scotland and
> preached there, I would have embraced the obliga-
> tion with more alacrity.

But although the Divine Poems are not the record of discoveries, but of struggles to appropriate a truth which has
been revealed, that truth does not "defeat all Poetry," but
gives us a poetry whose intensity is a moral intensity.
Some religious poetry, Herbert's perhaps, can be regarded
as a species of love-poetry; but Donne's is not of that kind.
The image of Christ as Lover appears in only two of his
poems—both written soon after the death of his wife. The
image which dominates his divine poetry is the image of
Christ as Savior, the victor over sin and death. The
strength with which his imagination presents this figure is
the measure of his need, and that need is the subject of the
finest of his religious poems. (pp. 134-36)

> *Helen Gardner, "The Religious Poetry of John
> Donne," in* John Donne: A Collection of Crit-
> ical Essays, *edited by Helen Gardner, Pren-
> tice-Hall, Inc., 1962, pp. 123-36.*

N. J. C. Andreasen   (essay date 1963)

[*In the following excerpt from an essay originally published in* Studies in English Literature *in 1963, Andreasen theorizes that Donne's early* Satyres *are based
upon a "single thematic principle of organization" that
reconciles contrasts between the sacred and the profane
both in Donne's poetry and in his personality.*]

Because Donne's **Satyres** are among his earliest works,
they have a special interest for anyone who wishes to study
the poetic techniques which he tried during his literary apprenticeship. Yet, oddly enough, no detailed study has
been made of them. Critics have commented on them in
passing, it is true, but the enormously varied nature of the
responses these **Satyres** have aroused suggests that a more
careful examination of them is needed. . . . For Donne's
Satyres, important because of their historical interest, are
also of considerable intrinsic literary merit as well.

These five satires, far from being incoherent, are all built upon a single thematic principle of organization; they are all concerned with presenting an idealistic defense of spiritual values against the creeping encroachment of sixteenth-century materialism. Donne's dramatic situations, satiric pose, diction, and imagery are all employed, in each of the five satires, to point up this contrast between the sacred and the profane. Each individual satire is put together with great care, and each depicts a different kind of materialistic deviation from the spiritual ideal. Each individual satire illuminates the others, for the whole sequence rests upon a single unifying principle which is treated from five different aspects. Once we realize that the *Satyres* are a dramatization of the contrast between the sacred and the profane, their obscurity vanishes, their roughness is justified, their organic unity is clear, and their vivid humor is delightful.

Before looking at the individual satires more closely, however, we would do well to observe in general the satiric methods which are employed in all of them. Following the precedent set by the former masters of satire, whether Horace or Chaucer, Donne has made them all dramatic in tone and technique. Each has a speaker who delivers a tirade to a listening adversary. The adversary often merely listens without responding, but he may occasionally break in and turn the dramatic monologue into a dialogue. Both speaker and antagonist are living characters, revealing their personalities by their comments on society and upon one another. The personality of the speaker is characterized more fully, however, since he reappears in each satire, while his antagonist changes from satire to satire. Their conversation is played against some background such as a street full of passers-by or a royal court full of courtiers, and this background provides a setting for the drama and an inspiration for the angry remarks of the speaker. Sometimes a situation is also briefly sketched in; in the first satire, for example, the studious protagonist is enticed away from his books by a foppish young friend. This combination of setting, situation, living characters, and interaction among them, makes each satire a drama-in-miniature.

Donne produces continuity from satire to satire through the pervasive presence of the speaker himself, who consistently defends the spiritual values of simplicity, peace, constancy, and truth. This idealistic protagonist, who combats the materialistic and profane antagonists he encounters, is a satiric mask which Donne adopts, just as Swift later puts on various masks in his various satires. But Donne's use of the mask is somewhat different from its use in, for example, *Gulliver's Travels*. Unlike Swift, Donne speaks directly through his mask, permitting his protagonist to advocate the very position Donne himself wishes to advocate. Nevertheless, the *Satyres* are literature rather than life and the fully characterized protagonist is Donne's spokesman rather than Donne himself, however much Donne's own views shimmer behind him. So I shall distinguish between the two by referring to the mask as the protagonist, the speaker, or Donne's spokesman.

This protagonist has a personality in his own right. In accordance with the over-all thematic purpose of defending spiritual values against creeping materialism, he is presented as a retiring scholar who is occasionally persuaded to venture out of his study to observe the sights which arouse his wrath. The first lines of the first satire set forth this aspect of his personality:

> Away thou fondling motley humorist,
> Leave mee, and in this standing woodden chest,
> Conforted with these few bookes, let me lye
> In prison, and here be coffin'd, when I dye;
> Here are Gods conduits, grave Divines; and here
> Natures Secretary, the Philosopher;
> And jolly Statesmen, which teach how to tie
> The sinewes of a cities mistique bodie;
> Here gathering Chroniclers, and by them stand
> Giddie fantastique Poets of each land.

Although these lines might also suggest that he has a touch of the misanthrope, a suggestion further substantiated by the harsh terms that he sometimes uses to condemn vice, we gradually realize that, like all outspoken idealists, he only hates men insofar as they fail to conform to the spiritual realities which he envisions. He is betrothed to his "Mistresse Truth," his "Mistresse faire Religion." He wishes to commend these mistresses to other men and to chastise them for giving their devotion to mistresses more earthly and more inconstant. Thus when he slips into angry vituperation, as he sometimes does, it is not because he hates mankind, but because he hates mankind's failure to fulfill the spiritual potentialities which make them fully human and mankind's tendency to dwell on more transient values. But he never permits anger to interfere with his awareness that mockery is the best weapon. The speaker, in spite of the fact that he is a contemplative scholar, can also debate skillfully with the most quick-witted worldling. In the first satire, for example, he begins by preaching gray-beardedly to his degenerate young friend; but when the ambitious youth continues to ogle noblemen, sophisticates, and prostitutes, the protagonist drops gray-bearded piety and uses the crude humor that the fop is more capable of comprehending. Their dialogue runs:

> But Oh, God strengthen thee, why stoop'st thou so?
> Why? he hath travayld; Long? No; but to me
> (Which understand none,) he doth seeme to be
> Perfect French, and Italian; I replyed,
> So is the Poxe. . . .

The fop's eyes and mind have wandered off while the protagonist is delivering his crushing retort, however, and so he neither answers it nor is deterred from lechery and ambition. As we follow him through the five satires, the speaker thus reveals himself as an idealistic but troubled scholar, eager to give paternal advice to others; he is sometimes angered by their failure to heed it or by the social abuses he observes, sometimes aroused to mockery, sometimes to astonished bitterness, never to inarticulate silence.

In addition to the continuity provided by the personality and idealism of the protagonist himself, a further link and a further sharpening of the contrast between the spiritual and the material is provided by a system of interlocking imagery which recurs within individual satires and from satire to satire. This imagery forms two main strands, one abstract and the other grossly material; the two strands become joined in the later satires as concrete imagery, especially water, is used both for its visual suggestiveness and for its abstract spiritual significance. The abstract strand of imagery is essentially conceptual and is drawn from religion and religious philosophy, employing the ideas of sin, law, conscience, virtue, and truth. In the first satire, for example, the pious protagonist playfully extends the concept of adultery when he warns his young friend not to desert him for someone who is nobler or better dressed when they venture out on the street together:

> For better or worse take mee, or leave mee:
> To take, and leave mee is adultery.

He concludes his warning by metaphorically making himself an indulgent priest and his young friend a repentant sinner:

> But since thou like a contrite penitent,
> Charitably warn'd of thy sinnes, dost repent
> These vanities, and giddinesses, loe
> I shut my chamber doore, and come, lets goe.

And later when the young friend wanders off after a brightly-dressed fellow fop, the protagonist calls him "my lost sheep."

But since Donne's object is to depict and chastise the bestial aspects of man which may interfere with the fulfillment of the spiritual ideal, there is a second strand of imagery, concrete and vivid, which is drawn from man's physical life. Through these images Donne emphasizes the coarser aspects of gratifying the senses by eating, drinking, love-making, being clothed, and obtaining money. It is this strand which has tended to repel or offend critics, for Donne is trying to make vice vividly repulsive and succeeds in doing just that. In condemnation of the bad poets who borrow and steal from the stored nourishment of others' brains, for example, his spokesman says:

> But hee is worst, who (beggarly) doth chaw
> Others wits fruits, and in his ravenous maw
> Rankly digested, doth those things out-spue,
> As his owne things; and they are his owne, 'tis true,
> For if one eate my meate, though it be knowne
> The meate was mine, th'excrement is his owne. . . .

This is one of the most brutal images in all the five *Satyres.* It would be difficult to find a phrase more ugly to the ear than "Others wits fruits." But it would also be difficult to make more vivid the ugliness of literary fraudulence.

Such superb ability to make vice repulsive to both the ear and mind is its own answer to those who object to the unpleasantness of the *Satyres.* It is motivated not by hatred of mankind, nor by Manichaean contempt for the physical, but by hatred of sins and evils to which man's incipient bestiality may lead. It proceeds by making that incipient bestiality vividly apparent. But the superficial negativeness of the *Satyres* is redeemed by their affirmation of the high human values of truth, constancy, and virtue. And their superficial ugliness is redeemed by the lightning speed of their movement and the intellectual humor of their wit. In spite of all the condemnation and vituperation which they contain, they are driven on by a rollicking *jeu d'esprit* which the reader can hardly fail to find delightful.

With these general principles of organization and technique in mind, we can observe their operation in individual satires in more detail; for the five satires, whether they are intended to be organically joined to one another or not, share the same structure and the same fundamental attitude toward life. Each satirizes a different aspect of society: I, the opportunism and lechery of a young rake; II,

corrupt lawyers; III, religion; IIII, courtiers and the court; and V, officers and suitors. I is closely related to IIII, and II is closely related to V; III, containing the great paean to Truth, is central in both position and theme.

The first satire is concerned with contrasting the constancy which adherence to virtue produces and the inconstancy which results from commitment to profane and material values. This contrast is dramatized through the personalities of the admonitory protagonist and the madcap young rake who has appeared and is trying to drag him away from his studies. Their opposition is apparent from the outset; after surveying the books in his library, the contemplative scholar asks:

> Shall I leave all this constant company,
> And follow headlong, wild uncertaine thee?

In terms of virtues and vices the protagonist stands for simplicity, peaceful contemplation, and the constancy which they possess and produce; the antagonist for fashion, lechery, and social-climbing, and the inconstancy which they possess and produce.

The imagery is directly related to the theme, drawn from religion, fashions in clothing, and prostitution. . . . Virtue is simple, bare, and unchanging; it is achieved by conferring with God and with the Muses, reflected in a contemplative life and coarse clothing. But the young rake, however much he may enjoy nakedness at some moments, is as fickle and inconstant as the fashions which he follows. The protagonist attempts to convince him of his error by appealing to religious doctrine: prelapsarian Adam wore no clothes at all and desired to put them on only after he had fallen from grace; and until souls shed in death the bodies with which they are clothed in life, they cannot ascend to the bliss of heaven.

But the young fop is almost incorrigibly committed to the material value of fashion, and the protagonist is also aroused to rebuke him for judging his friends by their appearance. . . . As Donne's spokesman implies, to judge people so cursorily on superficial appearances is a form of superstition, a quality shared by the over-scrupulous, over-precise, and hypocritical Puritans. But the protagonist knows his young friend well enough to realize that he is not likely to heed these warnings and admonitions. Before venturing out, he predicts the fop's behavior on the street in lines which compress and combine the now-familiar inconstancy images of whores and fashions:

> But sooner may a cheape whore, who hath beene
> Worne by as many severall men in sinne,
> As are black feathers, or musk-colour hose,
> Name her childs right true father, 'mongst all those. . . .
> Then thou, when thou depart'st from mee, canst show
> Whither, why, when, or with whom thou would'st go.

Part of the irony of the poem derives from the fact that the protagonist, aware of the inconstancy of the young man's friendship, goes off with him anyway after having charitably warned him of his sins. He admits that he sins against his own conscience in going, but this admission only increases his effectiveness as a protagonist. By admitting that he too sins, he establishes himself as an honest and human man, a man who can be believed and whose charitable warnings should be heeded, all the more because they grow out of his own experience of sin.

When they go out on the street, his prediction comes true. Although they follow a wall on their walk and the protagonist takes the outside track to prevent his friend from running off, the young man is still able to ogle and grin. He looks around with amorous smiles for every painted fool, servilely stoops before the great, and completely ignores the men who are grave and virtuous. As they walk and the protagonist comments on what he sees and his friend's behavior, we are given a fast-moving, vivid, panoramic, and dramatic view of Elizabethan London, its inhabitants, and its vices. The action is fully visualized, from the foppish "many-coloured Peacock" whom the young man chases momentarily to the seductive beloved whom he spies in a window and chases at greater length. The drama is further increased by several dialogues which break into the protagonist's monologue of complaint. . . . The satire comes to a natural end when the young man runs off to visit his inconstant beloved and finds her surrounded with other young men. Pressing his case, he is beaten up by them. At last he is forced to do something constantly, although not by choice; as the protagonist remarks ironically:

> He quarrell'd fought, bled; and turn'd out of dore
> Directly came to mee hanging the head,
> And constantly a while must keep his bed.

In the second satire, dealing with corrupt lawyers, Donne treats vices far more serious than the inconstancy produced by social-climbing, fashion-fascination, and lechery. In this satire his object of attack is fraud, a spiritual sin rather than a sin of the flesh, although rooted in the material because it is rooted in a desire for secular wealth and power. For this reason, the imagery of prostitution continues, but is given a new twist. Donne uses it to build up gradually to the accusation that those who commit fraud are spiritual prostitutes who sell their souls for secular gain. The main object of attack is the lawyer who uses fraud on his clients, and this form of fraud is personified in Coscus, the young man who plays the antagonist in this satire. But Coscus is also a former poet, and the protagonist is thus led to attack those poets who are frauds and spiritual prostitutes, those who write for Lords for the sake of advancement or because it is the fashionable thing to do, those who plagiarize the fruits of others' wits and produce mere excrement. After his side-glance at the abuses of poetry, however, he goes on to say:

> . . . these do mee no harme, nor they which use
> To out-doe Dildoes, and out-usure Jewes;
> To out-drinke the sea, to out-sweare the Letanie. . . .

Although at first glance this may seem "light-hearted tolerance of sin," he makes it clear a few lines later than he is simply after bigger game. These sins are their own punishment, he tells us; his vehemence against Coscus is aroused because this lawyer uses his position and profession to harm others as well. Following traditional moral theology, he regards compound sins and spiritual sins as the worst of all and attacks them with more virulence than the simple sins of lechery and gluttony.

Having thus set up his ethical and moral standard, the protagonist now summons up the figure of Coscus for indictment and judgment. Again, the scene is depicted dramatically, employing personal interaction and dialogue. (pp. 411-18)

The first two satires are long in their condemnation of vice, short in their praise of virtue, often coarse in diction and imagery, and highly visual, dramatic, and concrete. The third satire marks a partial departure from many of these characteristics. The first two, with their manifold skirmishes with every manifestation of vice within eye-range, have some of the superficial chaos of an impressionistic montage. Not so with **"Satyre III,"** every line of which has an obvious organic and thematic appropriateness. Unlike every other satire in the group, this one is a soliloquy conducted in meditative isolation. In place of the usual interlocutor, the protagonist counsels with his own better self. He begins in a state near despair, reasons himself through a series of negative possibilities, and finally rises to an affirmation which enables his will to act, concluding with a great paean to Truth.

His theme in this satire is "our Mistresse faire Religion." Setting himself a series of questions and then answering them, he distinguishes between the secular courage of straw which enables men to explore the unknown seas of a brave new world or to fight battles from the wooden sepulchers of ships and the genuine spiritual courage which prompts them to explore the mysteries of religion and do battle with the Devil himself. Bidding himself to seek true religion, the protagonist looks around to find it, but discovers instead only a confused variety of warring creeds. Mirreus chooses Roman Catholicism; Crantz, Genevan Calvinism; Graius, English Anglicanism; Phrygius, no religion; Graccus, all. What is truth, he asks himself, and pauses for an answer. Believing that man must choose only one religion, and that the right one, he suggests a way to go about choosing, though he does not completely resolve the problem of which religion is the right one. His basic appeal is to tradition:

> . . . ask thy father which is shee,
> Let him aske his; though truth and falsehood bee
> Neare twins, yet truth a little elder is. . . .

But most important is the sincerity and persistence of the search itself. Truth, like all ideals, resides at the top of a rugged pinnacle, and the ascent to it is a difficult one:

> On a huge hill,
> Cragged, and steep, Truth stands, and hee that will
> Reach her, about must, and about must goe;
> And what the hills suddennes resists, winne so;
> Yet strive so, that before age, deaths twilight,
> Thy Soule rest, for none can worke in that night.

Thus the protagonist affirms the supreme importance of the individual search for spiritual truth; for him the claim upon every man to save his immortal soul is a far higher one than the secular claims to excel in fashion, to scramble for place, to gratify physical desires; this belief is, of course, the motivation behind the vehemence with which he attacks secular abuses in the other satires. Parallel to this view of the importance of the spiritual search is his assertion that God's law stands above mere human law; if there is a conflict between them, then the individual must choose to follow God's law. Material and secular power is viewed in all these satires as a great potential threat and temptation, for it causes men to use human law to gratify their own evil desires, to ignore the supremacy of divine law, and to blind themselves to more immutable and constant spiritual values. So, returning to the water imagery which he used at the beginning of this satire, he concludes with a superbly effective image which unites all the varying emphases of the five satires:

> As streames are, Power is; those blest flowers that dwell
> At the rough streames calme head, thrive and do well,
> But having left their roots, and themselves given
> To the streames tyrannous rage, alas, are driven
> Through mills, and rockes, and woods, and at last almost
> Consum'd in going, in the sea are lost:
> So perish Soules, which more chose mens unjust
> Power from God claym'd, then God himselfe to trust.

At the top of the cragged and steep hill where truth stands, all is peaceful, calm, and good; religion, divine power, and virtue—all the immutable values—reside there. But if men abandon this height for the tyrannous rage of secular desires and injustices, they are buffeted and tossed and torn, perishing in the sea of iniquity. This underlying attitude toward secular and spiritual matters, common to all five satires, ultimately works to give them a unity greater even than their carefully conceived dramatic structure creates.

From this high point, the protagonist descends in the fourth satire to consider again the purgatory which is secular life and to chastise the folly of secular desires and accomplishments. More particularly, he satirizes the court and courtiers. Having been led away by a foppish bore to visit the court, he writes this satire as a recollection in tranquility after he has escaped from its temptations; thus he is able to unite the drama of his visit with reflections on its significance. The antagonist of this satire who incarnates most of the sins Donne wishes to condemn is a threadbare young courtier, a personification of most of the characteristics of the Gallicized or Italianate Englishman. He babbles on about his ability as a linguist, his knowledge of fashion, his love of a Lord. Their dialogue is extremely humorous, since the protagonist mocks his egoism at every turn, and the young fop is too obtuse and self-centered to understand him. When he boasts of his knowledge of languages, he is told that his skill is an anachronism, that he would have made a good interpreter to the bricklayers of the Tower of Babel. When he exclaims, "'Tis sweet to talke of Kings," the protagonist recommends him to the company of the keeper at Westminster Abbey. Still the bore sticks like a burr, and still he echoes the cry of the sixteenth-century pseudo-sophisticate:

> He's base, Mechanique, coarse,
> So are all your Englishmen in their discourse.

Changing his subject matter, the young worldling begins to talk of court life, unwittingly giving a detailed and accurate account of its iniquities; he speaks of the sale of offices, entailed until the Day of Judgment; which ladies paint themselves; who loves whom, and who boys and goats; who is going bankrupt because of ostentation; why the wars thrive ill.

Finally ridding himself of the bore by lending him a crown, the protagonist still cannot rid himself of the awful vision of court life, and so he goes on to give his own description of it. The technique is a clever one, since we are given dual views of court life—that of the admiring inside-dopester and that of the revolted man of honor; yet both the admirer and the despiser present pictures which disgust. The protagonist (who is much brighter than the fop) gives an account full of epigrammatically devastating touches:

> As fresh, and sweet their Apparrells be, as bee
> The fields they sold to buy them. . . .

He objects to the same qualities at court as were personified in the young fop himself—affectation, corruption, and false values—all the result of emphasizing secular aspirations instead of spiritual ones. Those who live at court are:

> . . . men that doe know
> No token of worth, but Queenes man, and fine
> Living, barrells of beefe, flaggons of wine. . . .

Totally disheartened with it all, he returns to the sea imagery with which he concluded the last satire, calling upon preachers ("Seas of Wit and Arts") to drown the sins of the court. He, a dweller in the peace and isolation of the stream's head, is but a tiny brook, sufficient only to wash his own stains away.

The fifth satire returns again to the theme of the law, already considered in the second satire. This time, however, the object of attack is officers who take advantage of suitors, rather than lawyers who deceive their clients. The protagonist now speaks to a young man who has fruitlessly bribed corrupt officials and who quietly listens to the angry tirade. And, as in **"Satyre II,"** the speaker also regards this perversion of the law as the prostitution of a worthy ideal; he pleads:

> Oh, ne'r may
> Faire lawes white reverend name be strumpeted,
> To warrant thefts. . . .

But he knows too well that it has been strumpeted already. The young man has bribed a judge without success, and the money he used for bribery was itself ill-gotten. The protagonist taunts him:

> Why barest thou to you Officer? Foole, Hath hee
> Got those goods, for which erst men bar'd to thee?
> Foole, twice, thrice, thou hast bought wrong, and now
> hungerly
> Beg'st right. . . .

Having stripped others of their wealth, the young man has now been stripped of his own by the judge. Ironically, this time the youth himself has been unjustly treated.

But the protagonist's anger is directed more toward the officers than toward the wretched suitor. His attack on them is linked to the previous satires through a pervasive use of stream and sea imagery. Now it is Law, God's Law, which dwells at the stream's head; officials who abuse the power delegated to them by God suck in and drown those who appeal to the law:

> . . . powre of the Courts below
> Flow from the first maine head, and these can throw
> Thee, if they sucke thee in, to misery. . . .

He sees all mankind as a world:

> . . . in which; Officers
> Are the vast ravishing seas; and Suiters,
> Springs; now full, now shallow, now drye; which to
> That which drownes them, run. . . .

When officers abuse their delegated power to increase their own wealth, there are only two possible ways to deal with them: to swim against the stream by protesting, the likely result of which is fruitless exhaustion; or to build golden bridges over it through fees and bribes, the likely result of which is the fruitless drowning of the money, a result only slightly better than the drowning of the suitor through exhausted opposition. These considerations bring the protagonist to proclaim an impassioned denunciation of the perversion of divine power for secular ends:

> Judges are Gods; he who made and said them so,
> Meant not that men should be forc'd to them to goe,
> By meanes of Angels; When supplications
> We send to God, to Dominations,
> Powers, Cherubins, and all heavens Courts, if wee
> Should pay fees as here, Daily bread would be
> Scarce to Kings. . . .

God's justice is free, not bought with bribery; God may use angels as mediaries between Himself and mankind, but He never intended that His counterparts on earth be appealed to through metallic angels. The angels of God and the angels of man should not be used so differently, but they are. And so again we find in this satire the customary contrast between the righteous ideal, and the way in which it has been perverted by man's greed for material wealth and power.

Close analysis indeed reveals that these *Satyres* are finely unified works of art in their own right, not incoherent and unpolished as some critics have described them. Donne has wrought them with care, consciously using roughness when it is necessary for his purpose, but also infusing a lofty strain of idealism which compensates for the necessary roughness. Imagery, drama, and dialogue are all united to work toward a single end: a contrast between the spiritual values which men ought to seek and the material and secular temptations which cause men to ignore or pervert the spiritual idea. The *Satyres* show that Donne was an accomplished craftsman even in his apprentice work.

Although interesting in their own right, the *Satyres* have an important secondary interest for the Donne specialist because of what they reveal about the techniques and fundamental assumptions which inform his other better-known poetry. The *Satyres* are among Donne's earliest works, and they anticipate many of the themes of his religious poetry, indicating that there was no great dichotomy between the rakish "Jack Donne" and the pious Dr. Donne. They reveal that the young Donne was deeply concerned with moral questions, that the *contemptus mundi* strain to which he gave expression in the *First* and *Second Anniversaries* was not a passing mood but a continuing preoccupation. The young man who wrote the *Satyres* saw very early that the Things of the Spirit offered more enduring satisfactions than the Things of the World. Still more important, however, is what the *Satyres* tell us about Donne's experimentation with technique. They provide concrete evidence for the view of some modern critics, predominantly Leonard Unger [see excerpt dated 1950], that many of the *Songs and Sonets* are to be read as dramatic monologues spoken by a *persona*, not as direct statements of Donne's own personal experience. Donne was in his very early twenties when he wrote these satires; their protagonist is an older man who gives grey-bearded advice to young men about town. Although this protagonist seems to state Donne's own views, none of Donne's contemporaries would have identified him as John Donne. The fact that Donne used the techniques of the mask and the dramatic monologue in the *Satyres* gives us some partial evidence for what has hitherto been presented as a use-

ful hypothesis or an unproved impression, that the *Songs and Sonets* (many of which were written at about the same time) may also be read as dramatic monologues. Perhaps the phantom of Jack Donne, resurrected to account for their cynicism and lustiness, can at last be laid to rest and these poems can again be read as poetry rather than autobiography. (pp. 419-23)

> *N. J. C. Andreasen, "Theme and Structure in Donne's 'Satyres',"* in Essential Articles for the Study of John Donne's Poetry, *edited by John R. Roberts, Archon Books, 1975, pp. 411-23.*

Richard E. Hughes   (essay date 1968)

[*Hughes is an American essayist, editor, and academic. In the following excerpt from his* The Progress of the Soul: The Interior Career of John Donne, *Hughes postulates that the* Anniversaries *are not about Elizabeth Drury, (the deceased daughter of Sir Robert Drury, one of Donne's most important patrons), but instead about Donne and his metaphysical experiences of death and rebirth.*]

[A] great many things are completed in the *Anniversaries.* The fragmented history of *The Progresse of the Soule* is mended here, the evanescent woman of the love poetry is captured here, and the incomplete cycle of meditation in the *Holy Sonnets* is finished here. A very great number of Donne's earlier themes are brought into harmonious collaboration in the *Anniversaries.* The mortally wounded Adam of *The Progresse of the Soule* reappears:

> Man all at once was there by woman slaine,
> And one by one we'are here slain o'er againe
> By them. . . .
>
> ### (*The Progresse of the Soule*)

> One woman at one blow, then kill'd us all,
> And singly, one by one, they kill us now.
>
> ### (*Anatomy of the World*)

The senescent sun of **"The Sunne Rising"** and **"A Lecture upon the Shadow"** intrudes in the *Anatomy* ("seeming weary with his reeling thus, / He meanes to sleep, being now falne nearer us"). The recollections of Dante that are observable in the fourth satire and in *Ignatius His Conclave* appear again, and St. Bernard, who plays a role in the *Essays in Divinity* and *La Corona,* is involved in the background of the poem, as are St. Augustine's trinitarianism and the Augustinian seven stages of redemption. The Ignatian meditation informs the structure of the *Anniversaries* even more entirely than in the meditative sonnets, and with a fuller acceptance by Donne of the spiritual effort envisioned by Ignatius.

To paraphrase one of Donne's own images: the *Anniversaries* like adamant have drawn random pieces of iron from his previous work. But these poems are no *omniumgatherum,* a receptacle for shreds and patches from other writings. The contrary is true: these are among the most cunningly assembled of all his poetry, the strongly focused vision of a poet who hardly knew how to be diffuse. It seems to me that a central question must be asked of the *Anniversaries:* what was the catalyst that pulled all the separate intuitions together? Why should the kaleidoscopic fragments of Donne's imagination suddenly be fixed in the numinous symbol of a mysterious "She" who draws into herself the substance of Donne's earlier thought?

We need to bear in mind Donne's continual excitement over the way events collapse into one another, revealing in a sudden flash a pervasive unity in the world. The work of his maturity is filled with wonder over the marvelous congruences that of a sudden show different places, objects, and times rushing together, charismatically asserting a pattern that underlies all experience. His was an imagination that could delight in the Annunciation and the Passion falling on one day:

> Th'Abridgment of Christs story, which makes one
> (As in plaine Maps, the furthest West is East)
> Of th'Angels Ave,' and *Consummatum est.*

He could find both Adams met in him, and think that Christ's Cross and Adam's Tree stood in one place, beginnings and endings occurring in an identical space time. He could conceive of man's life as a real and entire recapitulation of all history: "I was built up scarce 50. yeares ago, in my Mothers womb, and I was cast down, almost 6000. years agoe, in *Adams* loynes; I was *borne* in the last Age of the world, and *dyed* in the first."

Donne is quintessentially a poet in the way he perceived such mysterious juxtapositions, mandalas in experience. These epiphanies were, for Donne, manifestations of a significance that gives the lie to the profane illusion of directionless and inchoate existence. Donne was no monist, but he did believe that there were moments when creation surrendered its original design to human view. It is Seth's wisdom; and such moments (which become more and more frequent in the middle years) are not to be thought of as peripheral or as arbitrarily designed by Donne. They are a central condition of his poetry and his greatest prose, a starting point rather than a way station. And he does not invent them; he recognizes them as atypical but very real facts of experience.

It was, I believe, just such an unsolicited manifestation that set the *Anniversaries* in motion. On December 13, 1610, the Feast of St. Lucy, the first reports of Elizabeth Drury's death were abroad. For an imagination not alert to such announcements of a pattern working itself out in human affairs, this would be a coincidence, nothing more. For Donne, the death of a virginal fourteen-year-old on this liturgical festival and almost on the eve of her marriage was an indisputable declaration, a demand being made on him. He sensed a plan underlying the jumble of history, and to comprehend it fully he needed to articulate it in his poetry. The simple coincidence became the charged symbolic core around which Donne's major ideas and intuitions arranged themselves: a solar system whose center involves Lucy, the patroness of light.

At no time in his life was Donne's synthesizing power so imaginatively operative as at this moment. On this December 13, 1610, and in the days of composition that followed, Donne's creative energies must have been reaching back, absorbing, assimilating, until he had perfected one of the most complex and richest symbolic statements in English poetry. We can only sequentially and willfully attempt to retrace what was an instinctive poetic response; and it would be vain to imagine that we can entirely elucidate the causes and the full scope of the symbolic ordering

that goes on within the *Anniversaries.* Like all great poems, they finally frustrate the invasions of rational analysis. But, fragmentary though our reconstruction must be, we can see the traces of the developing symbol.

First, the poems are not eulogies in the usual sense of the word. To relate them to the encomiastic tradition, along with Donne's elegies to Cranfield, Lord Harington, or Lady Markham, ignores the difference between the public character of such "Epicedes and Obsequies" and the essentially private character of the *Anniversaries.* That they are meditations has been amply demonstrated by Professor Martz. We may go beyond Professor Martz; they are meditations in a much deeper, more fully realized way than are the meditative sonnets, accepting as they do all the implications of the meditative structure. *The First Anniversary,* which is earthbound, is a pentad, a five-part statement, with each part divided into three units (meditation, eulogy, refrain and moral). This is in keeping with the typical Jesuit exercises which "normally involve a series of five exercises daily for a period of about a month, each meditation being precisely divided into points, usually into three points." But *five* also represented for Donne incompleteness, an entity needing to be joined to something else to achieve perfection. . . . *The Second Anniversary* completes and fulfills *The First Anniversary,* showing as it does "The Progres of the Soule" into eternity. Eternity was represented by Donne as *seven,* as we can see in the *Holy Sonnets* and in the sermon at Whitehall on March 8, 1621/2; and *The Second Anniversary* is a heptad, a seven-part whole.

The repose of Donne, the assurance of redemption, inheres in the whole tenor of *The Second Anniversary,* and it is a long-awaited transformation. A significant doctrinal shift occurs in these poems: in *Pseudo-Martyr* and in the meditative sonnets, Donne took the most arduous Protestant stance on the question of man's cooperating in God's plan for redemption. The ultimate object of meditation, the full exercise of man's faculties as a way of requickening the trinitarian image of God within, is never achieved in the sonnets, for it seemed to Donne to be a presumptive defiance of his own fallen nature. But in the *Anniversaries,* the triple spiritual effort is fully operative. . . . While still dependent on bestowed and undeserved grace, man may will to be redeemed, and accept God's prevenient grace. This less anxious doctrine of man's estate is first assumed in the *Anniversaries.*

In other words, the very completeness of the meditative act in these poems suggests the private quality; the subject and the auditory are not Elizabeth and Sir Robert Drury, but John Donne. As the subject of *The Progresse of the Soule* was finally, I believe, to have been Donne himself, so the real subject of the *Anniversaries* is Donne. I cannot think that it was Donne's first intention to present the *Anniversaries* to Sir Robert. Like the sonnets, they were originally conceived of as private meditations, the pursuit, through poetry and prayer, of self-understanding. . . . The only poem about Elizabeth is **"A Funerall Elegie,"** which was printed along with *The First Anniversary* in 1611, and then in the 1612 edition. It is true that in 1610 "Drury was in need of a poet, Donne of a patron," but the grace-offering was not, in Donne's original plan, *An Anatomy of the World,* but the 106 lines of **"A Funerall Elegie."**

Not a great deal of attention has been paid to the elegy, nor is there much reason that there should have been. It is hardly more distinguished than the other competent epicedes that Donne wrote under pressure or need or command. E. K. Chambers' notion that the elegy was written first and then expanded into the *Anniversaries* has been credibly challenged, and it's probable that Donne turned aside from his major and private work to indite this conventional lament for the real Elizabeth. For **"A Funerall Elegie"** is a pastiche of bits of the symbolism of *The First Anniversary* and stereotyped funereal themes, all pressed into the service of much-needed patronage. No tomb is rich enough to hold the precious girl; even less so (in a reversal of the Horatian *monumentum perennius*) can his verse contain her, particularly since her death has crippled all things of this world. She was the music that harmonized the world, but it may be she has entered into a greater harmony through death. So delicate that she seemed heavenly while she lived, she has preserved her delicacy by dying. Not even fifteen years of age, she was so exemplary in virtue that she can be a pattern for the living. This is adroit, but it is in a different range of poetry from the *Anniversaries.*

The death that is lamented in **"A Funerall Elegie"** is, then, the literal death of Elizabeth Drury: stubborn details that describe only her are obvious ("Much promis'd, much perform'd, at not fifteene"). But the death of the *Anniversaries* themselves is not hers. On December 13, 1610, the center for which Donne had been looking for ten years was offered in a girl's death, and his intellectual and emotional life leapt into symmetry. Donne dated his own death in 1601: writing to Wotton from France, early in 1612, Donne spoke of his "Metaphoricall death," and remarked:

If at last, I must confesse, that I dyed ten years ago . . . yet it wil please me a little to have had a long funerall, and to have kept my self so long above ground without putrefaction.

His marriage, the collapse of his fortunes, and especially the grim vision of the first *Progresse of the Soule* were Donne's first death. The later poetry is at times a counterinsurgence against death:

All other things, to their destruction draw,
    Only our love hath no decay; . . .
                                    (**"The Anniversarie"**)

Love, all alike, no season knowes, nor clyme,
Nor houres, dayes, months, which are the rags of time.
                                    (**"The Sunne Rising"**)

We dye and rise the same, and prove
    Mysterious by this love.
                                    (**"The Canonization"**)

The self-abnegation that characterizes true love ritualizes and makes benign the death that permeates the world:

When love, with one another so
    Interinanimates two soules,
That abler soule, which thence doth flow,
    Defects of lonelinesse controules.
                                    (**"The Exstasie"**)

If our two loves be one, or, thou and I
Love so alike, that none doe slacken, none can die.
                                    (**"The Good-morrow"**)

But even love may be marked by death:

Love is a growing, or full constant light;
And his first minute, after noone, is night,
                                    (**"A Lecture upon the Shadow"**)

and woman may play the Judas, throwing man back into his own loneliness:

Perchance as torches which must ready bee,
Men light and put out, so thou deal'st with mee,
Thou cam'st to kindle, goest to come; Then I
Will dreame that hope againe, but else would die.
                                    (**"The Dreame"**)

Love may even become death itself:

Little think'st thou
That it will freeze anon, and that I shall
To morrow finde thee falne, or not at all.
                                    (**"The Blossome"**)

(. . . each such Act, they say,
Diminisheth the length of life a day)
                                    (**"Farewell to Love"**)

Love promises to control defects of loneliness and achieves nothing but a perverse alchemy, not the desired "abler soule" of **"The Exstasie,"** but the "pregnant pot" of **"Loves Alchymie."** The whole complex question of self-discovery and self-annihilation, the snarled metaphysical puzzle of Being and not-Being, is explored in the later love poetry, and eventually Donne is driven back into his own isolation. The proud privacy of the *Satires,* the insistent selfishness of the *Elegies,* the rambunctious singularity of the early love poetry merges into the defiant duets, the "abler interinanimated" souls, of the post-1601 period. But the expectation that submerging the lonely alienated *I* into a protective *I-Thou* pact will be recreative: this proves delusive. It is as if between **"The Exstasie"** and **"Loves Alchymie"** Donne tried to secularize St. John's text, "Except a corn of wheat fall into the ground and die, it abideth alone; but if it die, it bringeth forth much fruit" (John 12:24), and hoped through the images of a mutual selflessness in love to find a shield against the disorder of existence as he envisioned it in *The Progresse of the Soule.* The seductive appeal of a literal death is tied to a lie in *Biathanatos,* forcefully rejected in *Pseudo-Martyr.* In the *Essays in Divinity,* **La Corona,** and **"A Litanie,"** Donne approaches another way of surrendering his own loneliness to a corporate sanctuary, but only fitfully succeeds in conjuring up a communion with others (an imaginary congregation at prayer). Then, in the first six of the holy sonnets, Donne achieves a fusion between his own spiritual career and universal history. The universal-narrative, personal-dramatic movement of those sonnets reveals a central myth: the recapitulation of patterned destiny in each individual life. But Donne did not complete the pattern in the sonnets. He pulled back from the seventh and final stage of the myth and, prior to the penitential sonnets, remained convinced of his inability to re-enact in himself the entire drama of resurrection. The title of one of his poems, **"Resurrection, imperfect,"** is an ironic commentary on those sonnets. What should have been a group of seven sonnets is a group of six; as did Augustine, Donne saw redemption as seven successive stages, but instead of the redemptory *seven,* Donne's sonnets reflect the apocalyptic *six:* "And all that dwell upon the earth shall worship him, whose names are not written in the book of life of the Lamb slain from the foundation of the world. . . . Here is wisdom. Let him that hath understanding count the number of the beast: for it is the number of a man; and his number is Six hundred threescore and six" (Revelation 13:8, 18).

The mythic structure of a human life was demonstrated to Donne in the coincidence of Elizabeth Drury's death and St. Lucy's festival. The disconnected episodes of St. Lucy's martyrdom, Elizabeth's death, his own metaphorical death in 1601, and his own meditated resolutions arranged themselves in concentric circles around a central and illuminated focal point. In the *Anniversaries,* Donne describes a hierophany, a structured image of an eternal archetype working itself out in human affairs. The poet who worked brilliantly with the symbolism of light in the later love poetry, of whose extant sermons sixteen are on the Gospel of St. John (a number exceeded only by those sermons on the Psalms and on St. Paul's epistles), and whose epitaph identifies the watched-for Christ with the light from the east has created in the *Anniversaries* one of the most cogent and detailed studies of the symbolism of *light* in order to capture for himself, once and for all, the experience of a total unity in the world. The St. John of the Gospel of light and the epistle of love is ubiquitous in both poems. (pp. 196-207)

That St. Lucy was the energizing source of Donne's symbolism is clear from the situational references in *The First Anniversary.* Behind the whole procession of those incarnate versions of the mysterious *femina* is Donne's reiteration that the setting of the poem is St. Lucy's Day, the winter's depth, the shortest day and longest night, the commemorative day of St. Lucy's martyrdom. He alludes to the woman's continuing example on this short-lived day, December 13:

> For there's a kind of world remaining still,
> Thou shee which did inanimate and fill
> The world, be gone, yet in this last long night,
> Her Ghost doth walke; that is, a glimmering light,
> A faint weake love of vertue and of good
> Reflects from her, on them which understood
> Her worth; And though she have shut in all day,
> The twi-light of her memory doth stay; . . .

His poem is written at the collapsed end of the year and is an *anniversary* tribute, a yearly remembrance:

> Accept this tribute, and his first yeares rent,
> Who till his darke short tapers end be spent,
> As oft as thy feast sees this widowed earth,
> Will yearely celebrate thy second birth,
> That is, thy death.

It's been usually assumed that these lines were directed to Elizabeth Drury and, incredibly, to her patronizing father; Donne would never have been so clumsy as to relegate his poetry to a literal rent payment. The woman whose "feast" is celebrated on the day of "darke short tapers" is St. Lucy, who, like Elizabeth, was scarcely fifteen years old, dead before a projected marriage, dying on December 13. The anniversary is, subordinately, Elizabeth's, more importantly St. Lucy's, and most importantly it became Donne's own.

But there is more than specific allusion to the time of the year to connect the poem with St. Lucy. The world bears all of Lucy's wounds. Ordered by the officer of Diocletian, Paschasius, to renounce her Christianity in fourth-century Syracuse and refusing, Lucy was exposed to public prostitution, then tormented by fire. Surviving both ordeals, she was blinded (in some versions, self-blinded) and then stabbed through the throat. But in her legend, it was not she who suffered, but the world that administered the torture. Thrown into a brothel, she kept her virginity; heaped with burning coals, she remained unburned; throat-pierced, she continued to prophesy and pray; blinded, she became apotheosized into the patron saint of sight and a symbol of divine illumination. In the *Golden Legend,* Lucy's reproofs to Paschasius as he orders each of her trials are that she will suffer no corruption from the brothel, no domination from the fire, and will be unsilenced by the sword. Donne's catalogue of the sickness in the world is prefaced by the lament,

> Her death did wound, and tame thee than, and than
> Thou mightst have spar'd the Sunne, or Man; . . .

The purity of the world, unlike Lucy's, has been corrupted ("Her death hath taught us dearely, that thou art / Corrupt and mortall in thy purest part"). Sight has become blear and purblind ("Sight is the noblest sense of any one, / Yet sight hath onely color to feed on, / And color is decayd"). The world has been burnt to a cinder and has become nearly mute. Lucy, on the other hand, is a continual affront to the polluted, blind, burned, and silent world. A memory of her virtue remains and, virginal, she plays no part in the coital death of mankind. Her ordeal by fire was an alchemical purification, not an incineration. While the world feels "this consuming wound, and ages dart" and the cosmos has been "empayld," she is all harmony and proportion, she is sight, color, and song. In very large terms, she is the response to the divided soul of *The Progresse of the Soule.* (pp. 208-11)

Even with all the details in the poem emphasizing the December 13 anniversary and the recital of the wounds of St. Lucy, she is not at the exact center of the poem. That place is reserved for Donne's own experience of rebirth, the climax of his own progress. He views his own resurrection, not in purely personal terms, but in genuinely mythic terms, as the recreation of a universal pattern whose outline was most clearly enunciated in the first epistle and the Gospel of St. John. St. Lucy's martyrdom, and all the hagiographic details of her legend, evidently struck Donne as a *type* of the rebirth motif in St. John and as an analogue of his own experience. That Elizabeth Drury should have died on the feast of the longest night, that St. Lucy on this same day should have fulfilled St. John's message, that his own career might find its symbolic counterpart in the Elizabeth-St. Lucy-St. John complex, all operating in a timeless simultaneity: these are the generators of the poem.

In the first epistle of St. John, the same one on which Donne drew for the last of his meditative sonnets ("Father, part of his double interest"), Christ gave another commandment to his followers: "Again, a new commandment I write unto you . . . because the darkness is past, and the true light now shineth" (I John 2:8). This new commandment, which belongs to the generation of light, is love, and the absence of love is darkness (I John 2:8-11). After the identification of love and light, John's epistle continues:

> Love not the world, neither the things that are in
> the world. If any man love the world, the love of

the Father is not in him. For all that is in the world,
the lust of the flesh, and the lust of the eyes, and the
pride of life, is not of the Father, but is of the world.
And the world passeth away, and the lust thereof:
but he that doth the will of God abideth forever
(I John 2:15-17).

The parallels between the epistle and the life of Lucy are
evident, so evident that I believe Donne read her legend
as a historic fulfillment of Christ's injunction. It is not
merely that Lucy, *lux, lucis,* is equivalent to John's central
image; it is that each detail of what Donne calls "thy second birth, / That is, thy death" is so reflective of St. John's
whole epistle. The fifteenth verse ("love not the world")
is enacted in Lucy's giving her entire patrimony to the
poor. The three temptations of the world (lust of the eyes,
flesh, and pride of life) are epitomized in her blinding, the
assaults on her virginity, and the inquisitorial court of
Paschasius. The sixteenth verse (the world passes, but the
righteous abide) is recapitulated in Lucy's apotheosis
("Her Ghost doth walke; that is, a glimmering light"). St.
Lucy endured her own darkness, as did Nicodemus in the
third chapter of St. John's Gospel, to whom Jesus came
at night and proclaimed, "Ye must be born again" (John
2:1-7). The rebirth at night, and a host of implications that
Donne saw in the idea, provided him later on with a
sweeping *propositio:*

> Here is the compass, that the essential Word of
> God, the Son of God, *Christ Jesus,* went: He was
> God, *humbled in the flesh;* he was Man, *received
> into glory.* Here is the compasse that the written
> Word of God, *went,* the Bible; that begun in *Moses,*
> in darknesse, in the *Chaos;* and it ends in Saint
> *John,* in clearnesse, in a Revelation. Here is the
> compass of all time, as time was distributed in the
> Creation, *Vespere & mane;* darknesse, and then
> light: the Evening and the Morning made the Day.

The progress from dark to light is the movement from the
first to the second *Anniversary.* Donne's contempt for the
"sicke world" alternates with his reflection on the *light*
that has been "shut in all day" on this feast day, and the
contemplation of that light provides him with

> the matter and the stuffe of this,
> Her vertue, and the forme our practise is.

Lucy is a double reflection, first of St. John's epistle of
light and rebirth, and secondly of Donne himself, the
"forme" of his "practise." "Thy feast" becomes a remembrance of "thy second birth," which at the same time becomes his own "second birth." It would seem that Donne,
quite literally, accepted December 13 as his own anniversary or *natalia,* a day that means birthday, commemorative festival, restoration to one's birthright, and recollection of martyrdom. The things that lead me to believe this
are a letter to Goodyer, the subject of several of his sermons, and, most importantly, **"A Nocturnall upon S. Lucies Day, being the shortest day."** (pp. 212-14)

[It is] the **"Nocturnall upon S. Lucies Day"** that is most
representative of Donne's accepting December 13 as the
specific occasion of his rebirth. While there is a remote
possibility that Donne wrote the poem as early as 1606
during a serious illness of his wife Ann (but the poem specifically refers to the woman's death, and Ann did not die
at that time) or in 1612 during the Countess of Bedford's
illness (but the poem bespeaks an intimacy that is foreign

to all of his verses on the Countess), it is practically certain
that **"A Nocturnall"** belongs to Ann and is Donne's elegy
for her. It is, and considerably more besides.

In this lovely and lonely elegy, Donne pays Ann the highest tribute he could have paid: he puts her at the heart of
his poetry. Her death recalls to him the collapsed world
of *The First Anniversary,* loathsome in deformity there,
"Dead and enterr'd" here. Without her, he has been converted into his own angry man of **"Loves Alchymie"**: as
in that bitter poem, love's alchemy is perverse and has produced "A quintessence even from nothingnesse" (**"Nocturnall"**). Ann is metamorphosed into the fantasy woman
of the later love poetry, the weeper of the valedictions, the
private kingdom of **"The Good-morrow"** and **"The Anniversarie"**:

> Oft a flood
> Have wee two wept, and so
> Drownd the whole world, us two; oft did we grow
> To be two Chaosses, when we did show
> Care to ought else; and often absences
> Withdrew our soules, and made us carcasses.
(**"Nocturnall"**)

Her death has brought about what he had flirted with in
"Aire and Angels," complete extinction:

> But I am by her death, (which word wrongs her)
> Of the first nothing, the Elixer grown; . . .
(**"Nocturnall"**)

Grieving, Donne names Ann the genius of his love poetry.
When he took Holy Orders in 1615, he anticipated making
an offer of his poetry as the most suitable abnegation of
the world; this gift he makes to his wife is offered in the
same spirit, the presentation of his creativity.

The poem, however, continues beyond lament into vision;
and Ann becomes the spirit of rebirth following upon annihilation. Borrowing qualities from St. Lucy, she becomes the promise of light. Apparently drawing on the
Roman breviary, Donne presents his wife as a manifestation of St. Lucy, identifies his own dejection with this anniversary of martyrdom, and forecasts a resurrection and re-
uniting. The figure addressed in the closing lines is both
Ann and St. Lucy:

> Since shee enjoyes her long nights festivall,
> Let mee prepare towards her, and let mee call
> This houre her Vigill, and her Eve, since this
> Both the yeares, and the dayes deep midnight is.

Donne's title and certain details point to the nocturns of
the matins service as contained in the traditional Roman
breviary. (pp. 215-16)

In his poem, Donne contrasts the heat of the world with
the coolness of the night, the time of the vigil for St. Lucy.
His sun, his love for Ann, cannot renew (in the second
nocturn, beginning at midnight, the breviary prayer is
rogavi . . . ut ignis iste non dominetur mei). Carnal lovers
will experience the flame of passion:

> You lovers, for whose sake, the lesser Sunne
> At this time to the Goat is runne
> To fetch new lust, and give it you,
> Enjoy your summer all; . . .

Ann, however, is now free from such heats, "she enjoyes
her long nights festivall" (in the first nocturn, St. Lucy is

addressed, *tuae festivitate gaudemus*). In one of the "lectures" of the second nocturn, St. Lucy is venerated in the words *Quia jucundum Deo . . . habitaculum praeparisti,* "you have prepared a joyful dwelling place for the Lord"; now, of Ann, Donne says, "Let mee prepare towards her." By the end of the poem, Ann and St. Lucy have become practically indistinguishable.

The curious fact is that while Ann's office is made to be the same as St. Lucy's, *their* anniversaries are not the same. Ann Donne died in August; Donne certainly did not compose the poem then, for if he had, the central conceit of the poem would have made no sense. Donne wrote the poem on his *natalia,* on December 13, 1617, four months after his wife's death, powerfully interpreting Ann as a hierophant, a concelebrator of the rebirth he had experienced seven years before. **"A Nocturnall upon S. Lucies Day"** keeps the promise that Donne made at the conclusion of **The First Anniversary,** this time a promise kept with Ann:

> As oft as thy feast sees this widowed earth,
> [I] Will yearely celebrate thy second birth,
> That is, thy death.
>
> **(The First Anniversary)**

What Donne had strained for in the sonnets, a sense of temporal and personal resurrection, is nearly achieved in **The First Anniversary.** What needs still to be finished is the total identification of himself with St. Lucy and St. John's epistle, the equation between his own longest night and the anniversary of December 13, the passage from dark to light. All these things occur in **The Second Anniversary.** By 1611 (Donne began **The Second Anniversary,** while still in France, on December 13: the promise kept) Donne's vision is entire: he has sensed his own communal involvement in a perpetual drama of rebirth occurring throughout history. The corroding history of **The Progresse of the Soule** has been opposed by a dimension of light that was from the beginning, that united fourth-century Syracuse and seventeenth-century England, and that knows no time at all.

St. Lucy as the specific virgin-martyr and a *type* of rebirth is not merely repeated in **The Second Anniversary;** her symbolic values are still further expanded to the point where she is not so much an exemplar as she is a microcosm of resurrection. The emphasis in **The Second Anniversary** is not on the long night of decision and death, but on the day of rebirth. As she was a compass, a guide through the world, in **The First Anniversary,** Lucy in this second poem shares an emblem with Seth as Donne described him in the earlier **Progresse of the Soule:** she is an astronomer, a guide through celestial geography. This poem does not re-experience Nicodemus' night, but looks ahead through the icon of St. Lucy to the promised light of St. John's epistle:

> Thinke, then, My soule, that death is but a Groome,
> Which brings a Taper to the outward roome,
> Whence thou spiest first a little glimmering light,
> And after brings it nearer to thy sight: . . .

Lucy's function in **The Second Anniversary** is very like her function in *The Divine Comedy:* she is first a guide out of the Dark Wood, through Inferno and Purgatory, and then the representative of the total light that rests at the end of the progress.

As before, Donne clearly indicates that his poem is a celebration of the feast of December 13 ("my Muse / . . . [whose] chast Ambition is, / Yearely to bring forth such a child as this"), and he is insistent in his use of St. Lucy's emblems. That a death to the world is but a prelude to re-awakening in the spirit is specifically identified with the celebration:

> Thinke that they bury thee, and thinke that rite
> Laies thee to sleepe but a saint Lucies night.

Writing in France, he exempts Lucy from his derision of Catholic hagiolatry:

> Here in a place, where mis-devotion frames
> A thousand praiers to saints, whose very names
> The ancient Church knew not, Heaven knowes not yet,
> And where, what lawes of poetry admit,
> Lawes of religion, have at least the same,
> Immortal Maid, I might invoque thy name.
> Could any Saint provoke that appetite,
> Thou here shouldst make mee a french convertite.

St. Lucy's particular attributes, and especially her allegiance to *light,* account for a most considerable part of the poem's imagery. (pp. 217-20)

But this is not a poem in praise of St. Lucy, and certainly Donne has not abjured the Protestant "rectified devotion" behind a poem like **"A Litanie,"** a devotion where martyrology is decidedly at the outer edges of an evangelical faith. Donne intends all his celebrations of St. Lucy to be read typologically: she is the ideal form of Christian redemption through the Word of the Gospels (particularly the Gospel of St. John). Donne is quite clear on this point: Lucy is the embodiment of a sacred theme and a model of the redeemed spirit. She "could not lacke, what ere this world could give, / Because shee was the forme, that made it live." She is not simply to be venerated, but imitated; in realizing how she typifies the Light, we participate in that Light.

> Onely who have enjoyed
> The sight of God, in fulnesse, can thinke it;
> For it is both the object, and the wit.

Lux, which is Love and Wisdom ("And the light shineth in darkness; and the darkness comprehended it not," John 1:5), is what we recognize in Lucy, and only through Love and Wisdom can man see rightly at all.

> Thou shouldest for life, and death, a patterne bee,
> And that the world should notice have of this,
> The purpose, and th'Autority is his;
> Thou art the Proclamation; and I ame
> The Trumpet, at whose voice the people came.

This sense of Lucy, not as the *Verbum* herself, but as a proclaimed pattern, an incarnate demonstration of the meaning of St. John's Gospel of light and epistle of love, moves not only through the imagery of the poem, but also through its structure. The seven-stage alternation between meditation on the world and eulogy of the vanished virgin pointed out by Professor Martz gains in impact when we realize that the virgin is Lucy, and that the contempt for the world and juxtaposed celebrations of her glory are compressed versions of her legendary scorning of the three temptations. The first passage of *contemptus mundi* compares the world to old clothes, cast off a year ago (i.e., the contemning of the world in **The First Anniversary**), while the eulogy and the refrain respond with recollections of Lucy's eyes, which look beyond "fragmentary rubbidge." The second meditation summons up an awareness of death, voiceless, feverish, and surrounded by ministers of Pride and Lust ("For all that is in the world, the lust of the flesh, and the lust of the eyes, and the pride of life"), and is answered with remembrances of uncorrupted beauty. The cramped and foul body, "A Province Pack'd up in two yards of skinne," is contrasted with the soul quick-threading its way through the spheres to eternity, and such flight is epitomized in the vanished virgin's delicacy and brightness. The silly pedantry of the world is replaced by St. Lucy with her book. The corruption infecting all the affairs of men is renounced for the beadroll of a litany, ending with the virgin martyrs: of the four great virgins of the Latin church (SS. Cecilia, Agatha, Agnes, and Lucy), Lucy is the one representing wisdom, and Donne wittily describes the last virgin as bestowing academic honors on the other three:

> Up to those Virgins, who thought that almost
> They made ioyntenants with the Holy Ghost,
> If they to any should his Temple give.
> Up, up, for in that squadron there doth live
> Shee, who hath carried thether, new degrees
> (As to their number) to their dignitees.

The impermanence of earthly beauty and of everything that man secularly worships is put aside for the permanence of God, to whom Lucy gave her virginity and her life. The vicissitudes of life are balanced against the stability of eternity and of Lucy, who by now has been transformed into her own iconographic book. The seven stages of redemption that Donne later expounds in the sermon at Whitehall in March, 1621/22, are traced out here within the framework of rejection of the world and the search for paradise, typified by St. Lucy's legend. And the final image for Lucy is one that Donne will apply to all mankind in the *Devotions:* she is a book authored by God and translated by death into a better language; she is both book and light to read by, both the object and the wit. (pp. 220-23)

There is a quite spectacular geometry of profound experience between Donne's two progresses of the soul. In 1601, he experienced a metaphorical death; ten years later he is celebrating his own rebirth. The poem of 1601 is a fragment, dealing with a fragmented reality; the poem of 1611 is distinguished by its coherence, order, and totality. The earlier *Progresse* recounts the disruption of God's design in the world; the later *Progres* celebrates the fulfillment of that design. The first poem describes bestiality; the second poem is an affirmation of divine love. *The Progresse of the Soule* was intended to track down the ancestry of Cain and the City of Man, and *Of the Progres of the Soule* reaffirms Seth's generation and the City of God. The earlier poem is a bitter recital of the disunity that flows from rebellion; the later poem is a contemplation of the serenity that follows upon sacrifice and acceptance. *Progresse* is a poem of darkness; *Progres,* of light. The whole sequence of events and the whole cycle of poetry since 1601 peak in the *Anniversary* poems. Donne's own progress is finished in these poems of December 13, and from this point on there is none of that metaphysical ache for a vision of unity in experience that we recognize in the earlier Donne. Doubts, hesitations, and frustrations still scar his career, but they are all transitory, veneer and not substance. Nor

are there are significant developments in his beliefs and insights; what he became by 1611 is what he essentially remained. Donne completes himself by a submersion into a great design controlled by love, enunciated in the Gospels, recurrent through history, forcing itself on his imagination through the winter death of a young girl. The ramifications of his discovery remain to be explored in the great sermons, the *Devotions,* and the few poems yet to be written, but the real progress of John Donne is ended. (pp. 224-25)

> *Richard E. Hughes, in his* The Progress of the Soul: The Interior Career of John Donne, *William Morrow and Company, Inc., 1968, 316 p.*

Brian Vickers   (essay date 1972)

[*In the following excerpt, Vickers discusses Donne's use of hyperbole in his rendering of love and lovers.*]

Anyone who comes to Donne through English love-poetry of the sixteenth century is immediately struck by his novelty. First the language, that confident, brusque immediacy of tone and movement which at first sight appears to have liberated itself from all previous conventions. The power of Donne's language has been the most exciting discovery for the majority of readers in our time, although it is now evident that the critics who did most to promote a new evaluation of it left several gaps in their argument: they ignored the colloquialism of some predecessors (Wyatt and Sidney, in a substantial number of poems); they naïvely equated colloquialism with 'the speaking voice', with 'reality' and so with 'sincerity', they were ignorant of Donne's rich use of traditional rhetoric; they ignored the continued presence of many 'Petrarchan' elements in the poems—reworked, of course, but not always ironically (sighs, tears, groans, broken hearts); and they failed to see Donne's relation to wider classical and European traditions of logic and serious wit. What contemporary criticism and scholarship must do is to fill these gaps, 'place' Donne's inheritance, without, of course, losing our appreciation of his unique energy and impact.

Less often commented on than the language is Donne's treatment of love and the relationship between the sexes. English sixteenth-century love-poetry is characterised by frustration, unfulfilment, loss; the mistress is unavailable, indifferent ('fair cruelty'); she is worshipped with agonised self-abasement on the part of the lover. (pp. 132-33)

Donne broke through this barrier of unattainable desire (in doing so he partly went back to classical models, notably Ovid) and instead of frustration gives us fulfilment, consummation, an extended analysis of a full sexual relationship. The poems are too familiar to need quoting, but we should just recall some of the settings; poems are written on (or in) the lovers' bed, its sheets, their room with its curtains through which the sun disturbs their—sleep?; Donne records the leisure with which they can lie there and watch, for instance, the movements of a flea over their skin; or he argues that, although they spent the night together they did not make love merely because it was dark, and so there is no reason why his mistress should want to get up and go now that it is light; or he imagines himself ('Petrarchan!') having been killed by his mistress's scorn, returning to her bed and watching her in the arms of a new (and 'worse') lover:

> Then thy sicke taper will begin to winke,
> And he, whose thou art then, being tyr'd before,
> Will, if thou stirre, or pinch to wake him, thinke
>   Thou call'st for more,
> And in false sleepe will from thee shrinke,
> And then poor Aspen wretch, neglected thou
> Bath'd in a cold quicksilver sweat wilt lye . . .

                                        ("The Apparition")

In poems such as these—**"The Dreame"**, **"The Flea"**, **"The Good-morrow"**, **"The Sunne Rising"**, **"Breake of Day"**, **"The Exstasie"**—the lover's bed is the focus of the action, and in these and other poems the description of love is frankly physical, either directly or by innuendo. (Learned editors refrain from glossing these passages, and I am never sure whether they have not seen the allusions, or imagine that everyone sees them, or think it indecent to comment on them.) I lack statistics, but I doubt if the bed or the physical celebration of the body had played much part in English love-poetry since *Troilus and Criseyde*. Even the poems of loss are not, like some of his predecessors, those of a fantasy relationship which never materialised: in Donne the loss is (or presents the illusion of) a total physical experience, an overwhelming emptiness.

That, though, is only one way in which he broke with the tradition: I would distinguish three others. First, the masculine assertion. Whereas in the 'Courtly Love' tradition the woman is on a pedestal and the man kneels or grovels before her, Donne often reverses that situation. Man 'gets', 'has', 'casts off' a woman, or picks up again last years 'relict'; the women, some students have complained to me, are hardly ever *there* in Donne's poems: the poems are a description of love from the man's superior position. Secondly, since he can cast her off, and she him, there are poems which invert the whole tradition of loyal, dogged and fruitless dedication to one unattainable mistress by proposing moods of indifference, or a cynicism about male or female faithlessness, a justification, as it were, for having an affair and then moving on. Lastly, and for the purposes of this essay, most important, is the new sense of a relationship between the lovers. They constitute a unit, separated off from the world, not dependent on it, indeed above it. (pp. 135-36)

My argument will be that Donne is remarkable in English Renaissance love-poetry for the way in which he presents the two lovers as a race apart, and that one of the most important ways of creating this separation is by use of the rhetorical figure hyperbole. I mean the type of praise which is exemplified in **"The Sunne Rising"**:

> She' is all States, and all Princes, I,
>   Nothing else is.

                                        (pp. 136-37)

Donne's use of hyperbole is almost point-for-point antithetical: it is a non-ethical, witty, irreverent, at times slightly disreputable figure; it is personal, written from the inside, by the actors themselves, not by a hired (or self-appointed) chronicler; it is not concerned with 'fact' or 'history', indeed almost the main characteristic of the figure is that it is excessive, impossible. (p. 139)

There is no need to argue the case formally for Donne's

knowledge and use of rhetoric—it is evident on almost every page of his prose or poetry. He can hardly not have known about hyperbole. But in any case I do not want to argue for any specific influence on him, rather to show how his own use of hyperbole fulfils all the potential which rhetoricians ascribed to the figure. I would propose two main groups of subjects to which hyperbole is applied: the lovers, and love, considered first as values in themselves; and then considered in relation to the rest of the world.

This first group of poems (which includes many of Donne's most immediate and popular works) makes an assertion of value directly, with no possibility of misunderstanding:

> For love, all love of other sights controules,
>   And makes one little roome, an every where. . . .
> Let us possesse our world, each hath one, and is one.
>   ("The Good-morrow").

> Here upon earth, we'are Kings, and none but wee
> Can be such Kings, nor of such subjects bee;
> Who is so safe as wee? where none can doe
> Treason to us, except one of us two.

                                        ("The Anniversarie")

But the direct assertion can be sustained with wit, as in the boast which opens **"A Valediction: of my Name in the Window"**:

> My name engrav'd herein,
>   Doth contribute my firmnesse to this glasse,
> Which, ever since that charme, hath beene
> As hard, as that which grav'd it, was;

POEMS,

By J. D.

WITH

ELEGIES

ON THE AUTHORS

DEATH.

———————

———————

LONDON.
Printed by *M. F.* for IOHN MARRIOT,
and are to be sold at his shop in St *Dunstans*
Church-yard in *Fleet-street.* 1633.

Title page of Donne's first collection of poetry.

Donne's loyalty is so strong that it has converted glass, one of the most fragile of substances, into the ultimate of hardness, diamond. This tactic of juxtaposing zero and infinity is often used to distinguish their experience of love from other intense experiences:

> But this, all pleasures fancies bee.
> If ever any beauty I did see,
> Which I desir'd, and got, 'twas but a dreame of thee.
>
> **("The Good-morrow")**

> For I had rather owner bee
> Of thee one houre, then all else ever.
>
> **("A Feaver")**

Compared to this, *all* other pleasures are *but* dreams, idle fantasies: it is characteristic of hyperbole that it admits of no intermediate stages between zero and infinity.

If their love is infinite, it can never die: the paradox of constant use and constant growth is one which Donne handles at many levels, from the religious to the physiologically erotic. Since 'all' is one of the words most germane to this type of assertive hyperbole it is no accident that a poem called **"Loves Infiniteness"** should wring every possible significance out of that word and out of the situations which it could describe:

> If yet I have not all thy love,
> Deare, I shall never have it all. . . .

I lack space to trace all the paths of **"Loves riddles"** here, but the opening of the third stanza makes my point most clearly:

> Yet I would not have all yet,
>   Hee that hath all can have no more,
> And since my love doth every day admit
>   New growth, thou shouldst have new rewards in store . . .

That theme is worked out in even more explicitly sexual terms in **"Loves Growth"**. But nowhere is it given greater force than in **"The Anniversarie"**:

> All other things, to their destruction draw,
>   Only our love hath no decay;
> This, no tomorrow hath, nor yesterday,
> Running it never runs from us away,
> But truly keepes his first, last, everlasting day.

Those lines alone would justify all the rhetoricians' claims that hyperbole expresses energy, vehemency, ecstasy, the 'unspeakableness rather than the untruth of the relation'. Particularly illuminating is Priestley's observation that 'in hyperbole the untruth lies in the *affirmation itself,* whereas in most other figures it is concealed in an *epithet'.* Much of the assuredness, the confidence of Donne's hyperboles derives from their being simple present-tense statements, direct affirmations, not indirect description.

If some poems present the infinite, inexhaustible power of their love, others use hyperbole to contemplate unhappiness and suffering in love, illness, death. In **"A Valediction: of Weeping"** the first stanza presents the man—'Let me powre forth / My teares before thy face', his tears being 'Fruits of much griefe'. The stanza ends with the conceit that the beloved's image is reflected, mirror-like, in the tear as it falls, and the reduction of the image to nothingness is related to the way in which the lovers 'are nothing' when separated (again the simplest of verbal

forms is yoked to a statement of ultimate significance). The second stanza takes up again the contrast between zero and infinity: a craftsman pasting maps on to a globe can

> quickly make that, which was nothing, *All,*
>   So doth each teare,
>   Which thee doth weare,
> A globe, yea world by that impression grow,
> Till thy teares mixt with mine doe overflow
> This world, by waters sent from thee, my heaven dissolved
>   so.

Of this stanza Dr Johnson made the caustic remark: 'The tears of lovers are always of great poetical account, but Donne has extended them into worlds. If the lines are not easily understood they may be read again' [see excerpt dated 1779]. He is critical, but has in fact precisely described Donne's method of amplifying an issue, pushing its extremes as far apart as possible. In the last stanza the conceit is taken to its logical conclusion, in cosmic terms: since she controls his world, she can inundate it:

> O more then Moone,
> Draw not up seas to drowne me in thy spheare,
> Weepe me not dead, in thine armes, but forbeare
> To teach the sea, what it may doe too soone. . . .

This continuation of the trope basic to the hyperbole points up one of the characteristics of Donne's extension of *superlatio* over a whole stanza or indeed poem: once we have assented to the initial identification, that non-literal impossibility which this trope embodies, we tend to forget that we are moving along inside a trope; we do not stop to translate it back into 'literal' statement, for we do not have time; Donne has made us his prisoners. We could remember, in this connection, Helen Gardner's admirable definition of a metaphysical conceit [in her *The Metaphysical Poets* (1957)]: 'A conceit is a comparison whose ingenuity is more striking than its justness, or, at least, is more immediately striking. All comparisons discover likeness in things unlike: a comparison becomes a conceit when we are made to concede likeness while being strongly conscious of unlikeness.' So Donne juxtaposes literal and figurative meanings in such a way as to remind us of the identity between the two while stretching it as far as possible.

Some other poems which exploit the cosmic analogy in relation to the theme of 'suffering love' show this trapping process at work. In **"A Feaver"** his mistress is ill, and in the first stanza the poet begs her not to die, for if she did he would hate all women—her included. But the second stanza at once denies even that possibility:

> But yet thou canst not die, I know;
>   To leave this world behinde, is death,
> But when thou from this world wilt goe,
>   The whole world vapors with thy breath.

Again no 'epithet', no circumlocution, a simple direct statement of her absolute value: she is the world. But—since this poem, like many of Donne's lyrics, changes direction at the beginning of a new stanza as if something significant had happened in the interval between them—if her death does not perhaps succeed in extinguishing the whole world, what is left would merely be rubbish. Hence Donne can invent more examples of that gap between zero and infinity which defines her value:

> Or if, when thou, the worlds soule, goest,
> It stay, 'tis but thy carkasse then,
> The fairest woman, but thy ghost,
> But corrupt wormes, the worthyest men.

(Again *tapinosis* cuts the competition down to size.) The next stanza makes a dramatic improvement even on that absolute, by launching an attack on those stoic and Patristic writers who disputed just how the world would be consumed by fire:

> O wrangling schooles, that search what fire
> Shall burne this world, had none the wit
> Unto this knowledge to aspire,
> That this her feaver might be it?

This is indeed a fantastic brag, that she might be the cause of the ultimate conflagration, but once we have conceded the first hyperbole we would feel, somehow, foolish or unimaginative if we dropped out at this stage. We concede the likeness, but the unlikeness is made dramatically apparent. A similar wit, using the same cosmic, if less grandiose analogies for her death can be seen in **"The Dissolution"**, but developed with less cheek. No one could ever forget the intensest expression of this cosmic hyperbole in **"A Nocturnall upon S. Lucies Day"**:

> Oft a flood
> Have wee two wept, and so
> Drownd the whole world, us two; oft did we grow
> To be two Chaosses, when we did show
> Care to ought else; and often absences
> Withdrew our soules, and made us carcasses.

The insistent 'us two' of line 24 seems intended to challenge the reader, to remind him of the trope within which he is moving, to offer him the possibility of escaping from it—if he wishes—by presenting the simple reality which lies behind it, and which justifies this assertion of absolute value.

Finally, in this first group of hyperboles that assert the infinite power of love, I delight in being able to discuss **"The Sunne Rising"**, which uses all the tactics so far distinguished—except, of course, death and cosmic destruction—with unequalled freedom. There is no need to quote the opening stanza's insolent dismissal of the sun, the universal embodiment of order, time, fruition, who is sent about other and less important business, nor its closing use of *tapinosis* (or perhaps *meiosis*—either way, a belittling figure) to affirm the infinity and eternity of love as against 'the rags of time'. The second stanza begins with a non-hyperbolic statement—I could blot out the sun by closing my eyes—and redeems its speciousness by the wit of the motive for not so doing ('But that I would not lose her sight so long'). This point seems to have been established so that Donne can, by violent contrast, move into hyperbole and so invert reality:

> If her eyes have not blinded thine,
> Looke . . .

And when you have made your tour of the globe next, report back, tell me

> Whether both the'India's of spice and Myne
> Be where thou lefst them, or lie here with mee.
> Ask for those Kings whom thou saw'st yesterday,
> And thou shalt heare, All here in one bed lay.

'Boldest of figures' Quintilian called it, yet the supreme confidence with which Donne invests those two boasts must convince all but the unconvincible. We barely need to 'decode' his message: she sums up all symbols of worth. This is undeniable: lovers' values are subjective, relative, and may therefore legitimately represent infinity; since we do not share the love-relationship, it is immune from our criticism. As if realising that point Donne immediately proceeds to develop it to its ultimate pitch, with the same political / national comparisons which ended the preceding verse:

> She'is all States, and all Princes, I,

and again that remarkable juxtaposition of zero and infinity:

> Nothing else is.

The whole of human, animal, vegetable, mineral existence has been annihilated by the comparison.

> Princes doe but play us; compar'd to this,

—the same phrase as in **"The Good-morrow"**—all honour is mere play-acting, all wealth glittering dross. Having diminished all other value-symbols, having drawn a line across experience, put himself and his love above it, everything else at an infinite distance below it, Donne returns to his first target, the sun. He is only 'halfe as happy' as they are (presumably because he can illuminate only half the globe at one time); he is old and needs a rest and finally, most arrogantly of all, having dismissed the sun to less important occupations in the first stanza, Donne changes his mind and recalls him now to his proper 'office':

> since thy duties bee
> To warme the world, that's done in warming us.
> Shine here to us, and thou art every where;
> This bed thy center is, these walls, thy sphaere.

And yet, at this extreme point we see how the hyperbole 'asserts the incredible in order to arrive at the credible': it is, as Sir Thomas Browne might have said, 'not only figuratively, but literally true' that—and by decoding the message I risk a banality which Donne transcended—the universe *does* revolve around them; their bed *is* the centre; nothing else *is;* love *is* 'infinitely delightful . . . infinitely high . . . infinitely great in all extremes'. Who can quarrel with that? (pp. 148-55)

> *Brian Vickers, "The 'Songs and Sonnets' and the Rhetoric of Hyperbole," in John Donne: Essays in Celebration, edited by A. J. Smith, Methuen & Co. Ltd., 1972, pp. 132-74.*

Paul A. Parrish   (essay date 1986)

[*In the following excerpt, Parrish examines the relationship of Donne's "A Funerall Elegie" to its longer companion pieces* The First Anniversarie *and* The Second Anniversarie, *deciding that "A Funerall Elegie" is a unique poem that developed "out of a poet's witty and imaginative use of tradition."*]

Students of Donne have had a difficult time keeping their eyes on **"A Funerall Elegie,"** that modest poem nestled comfortably—one might say obscurely—between the two Anniversary poems. And there are, of course, good reasons for the relative inattention to the **"Elegie."** The Anniversary poems loom large, like two ponderous mountains enclosing a small slope; few adventurers would bother with a knoll when there are awesome peaks to negotiate. Furthermore, the **"Elegie"** intially invites little expectation of anything much beyond itself. It is, simply, **"A Funerall Elegie."** Consider, by contrast, the full title of *The First Anniversary: An Anatomy of the World. Wherein, By occasion of the untimely death of Mistris Elizabeth Drury the frailty and the decay of this whole World is represented,* or that of *The Second Anniversary: Of the Progres of the Soule. Wherein: By occasion of the Religious death of Mistris Elizabeth Drury the incommodities of the Soule in this life and her exaltation in the next, are contemplated.* Readers of the *Anniversaries* have confirmed, in numerous ways and through various methods and insights, the appropriateness of Donne's long titles. The death of Elizabeth Drury is secondary in the poems, and the manner in which that death provides an "occasion" for an extensive and probing meditation on "the frailty and the decay of this whole World" and a contemplation of "the incommodities of the Soule in this life and her exaltation in the next" is acknowledged and amply demonstrated in studies that form a litany of some of the most influential works of the last several decades. . . . (pp. 55-6)

With all of the attention to the two longer and more important poems **"A Funerall Elegie"** has, for the most part, been ignored. We should not, of course, neglect the relationship of the **"Elegie"** to the *Anniversaries.* As the poems have appeared to us since their first printing, we come to the **"Elegie"** after having read the *First Anniversary* and, since the 1612 printing of the three poems, we proceed from the **"Elegie"** to the further perspective of the *Second Anniversary.* I would, nonetheless, like to change the usual emphasis and give greater attention to the short poem, and from that suggest some conclusions to be drawn about the trio of commemorative verses on the "Mistris Elizabeth Drury."

Funeral elegies, as [O. B.] Hardison and others have ably demonstrated, ultimately derive from epideictic oratory and verse: thus, their primary purpose is to offer praise for the dead. Typically, funeral occasions evoke two other prominent responses: lament and consolation. The individual is praised, the death is lamented, the audience is consoled. Because the form of the elegy was so familiar, Renaissance commentators frequently compiled lists of particulars from which a writer might draw for illustrations of actions worth praising or losses worth mourning or beliefs that would be consoling. Consequently, the elegiac tradition is both familiar and detailed, and it yields images and ideas that are commonplace among the writers and audience of Donne's time.

The influence of the elegiac tradition is amply revealed in Donne's **"Funerall Elegie,"** but the proximity of the *Anniversaries,* so obviously and dramatically reaching beyond the tradition, may tempt us to assume too readily that the **"Elegie"** is merely a traditional poem. We know how different the *Anniversaries* are, both from the **"Elegie"** and from the elegiac tradition. It is easy to assume, therefore, that the **"Funerall Elegie"** and the tradition of funeral elegies, are, for the most part, all of a piece. I would suggest that, in fact, the **"Elegie"** moves toward the transforming art of the *Anniversaries* as it moves away from more con-

ventional patterns of the tradition. In the shorter poem Donne does not give his imagination free reign, as he sometimes does in the *Anatomy* and the *Progres,* but he exercises it, distinctly and effectively, in more limited ways. The **"Elegie"** is a poem built solidly on a tradition but, more than that, it is a poem that transforms conventional motifs into poetic experiences unique to Donne and to the *Anniversaries.*

The opening lines of the **"Elegie"** encourage us to view the poem as having been written immediately after the occasion of the death of Elizabeth Drury, as an *epitaphium recens,* for, following tradition, it calls attention to the tomb that houses the dead body. But the argument is also advanced, even in the first two words, that trying to capture, to confine the deceased in a tomb is impossible: "Tis lost, to trust a Tombe with such a ghost, / Or to confine her in a Marble chest."

The effort to confine her is "lost," the poet argues, because her richness outdoes the presumed wealth of the ornate tomb or the riches of the world at large. Compared to her the "two Indies" are as mere glass; compared to "her materials" the equivalent of even ten Spanish Escorials amounts to nothing. Wealth and expansiveness are the attributes most apparent in this "ghest" who cannot be reduced to the occupancy of an enclosing tomb. Although the fact of death does not escape us, images from the opening lines lead us away from it, to valuable jewels, to wealthy lands, to ornate and impressive architecture. The impact of line 9 is thus even more decisive: "Yet shee's demolish'd." That key word "demolish'd" calls up the image of an imposing structure that has been torn down and destroyed, and the concern with physical and material images continues into the next line, with a reiteration of the skepticism apparent throughout this section. But lines 9 and 10 pose a dual question that takes us from one confining structure—the ornate tomb—to another confining structure—the poem: "Can we keepe her then / In workes of hands, or of the wits of men?" The more important question for the poet is not whether the tomb is an appropriate confinement but whether the poem, the structure not of the "workes of hands" but of the "wits of men," can be said to contain her. This greater concern is evident in the lines that follow:

> Can these memorials, ragges of paper, give
> > Life to that name, by which name they must live?
> Sickly, alas, short-liv'd, aborted bee
> > Those Carkas verses, whose soule is not shee.
> And can shee, who no longer would be shee,
> > Being such a Tabernacle, stoope to bee
> In paper wrap't; Or, when she would not lie
> > In such a house, dwell in an Elegie?

These lines engage us primarily through opposition and complement, as they advance relationships between the deceased and the poem, between the poem and life, and between the poem and the tomb. Only because of the girl do the verses of the elegie, the "ragges of paper," exist ("live"), yet "these memorials," properly understood, in turn "give / Life to that name." The paradox is heightened as we understand that death (of the girl) gives life (to the poem) which in turn gives further life (to the "living" memory of the girl). Without this poetic symbiosis, we have only "Carkas verses," "sickly . . . short-liv'd, aborted."

One of the conventions behind these lines, as Manley indicates, is the topos *Exegi monumentum aere perennius.* The poem of Horace that yields the phrase argues for the immortal nature of verse which outlives monuments of bronze. Propertius, Ovid, and countless Renaissance poets similarly portray an art that is able to withstand the ravages of time. Propertius closes one of his poems by asserting that only poetic wit can avoid devouring death. But Donne's poem views it differently, both using and inverting the tradition: in the **"Elegie"** both the tomb (the "workes of hands") and the poem (the "wits of men") are inadequate to house this expansive soul.

Line 19 abruptly dismisses the preceding argument as being largely irrelevant; it does not matter that a tomb is too confining or that an elegie may be short-lived. The world itself, Donne announces, has been mortally wounded with her death: "But 'tis no matter; we may well allow / Verse to live so long as the world will now. / For her death wounded it." The decaying state of the world is, of course, explored most imaginatively and fully in the *First Anniversary,* as Donne extends and transcends the traditional elegiac motif of "nature reversed." In the **"Elegie"** the motif has a more limited, more traditional impact, as the death of an individual is seen to have "wounded," to have made "decrepit," the world. But here, as well, we observe Donne's poetic daring, as he draws on one poetic convention—the immortality of shrine or verse—openly to have its meaning negated by another—the loss of world order. In the **"Elegie"** the functioning of the world is viewed allegorically, as human types—Princes, Counsailors, Lawyers, Divines—are each representative of some part of this world's body. To the girl is given the power to coordinate these parts through the presence of wonder and love:

> But those fine spirits, which doe tune and set
>   This Organ, are those peeces which beget
> Wonder and love; And these were shee; and shee
>   Being spent, the world must needes decrepit bee.

Approaching the **"Elegie"** from the *Anatomy,* we would be reminded of themes and images we encountered in the longer poem. But here, because they are asserted without elaboration and verbal ornamentation, they are more immediately accessible: one who has been a prime image of wonder and love has died, and the world is much the worse for the loss. While elaboration has been reduced from the *First Anniversary,* the **"Elegie"** shows Donne still to be working poetically through hyperbole. The girl is, if not greater than the world, at least its equal, and thus Nature contents itself in knowing that it can experience no worse destruction than what, with the death of the girl, it has just endured.

The two prominent themes of the first third of the **"Elegie"** give credence to Donne's comments about his portrait of Elizabeth Drury, that "it becomes me to say, not what I was sure was just truth, but the best that I could conceive," and to his assertion to Ben Jonson that he "described the Idea of a Woman and not as she was." The greatness of the girl is both assumed and revealed because she cannot be confined by tomb or verse and because her death has such a devastating effect on the world. Proving the girl's worth is not Donne's concern; asserting it is. Praise for the girl and lament for her loss are part of Donne's effort here, as they are traditional elements of ele-

gies generally. But the emphasis is peculiarly Donne's, as he views the girl's image from his perspective as maker of this poem about her and from the perspective of a world that has lost her.

As one would expect from an elegy, praise and lament lead, appropriately, to consolation, and the next segment of the poem, from lines 37 to 54, reveals that aim. As Renaissance commentators frequently noted, one important consolation available to the Christian poet was the consolation of heaven: the deceased has gone on to a better world, a world more deserving of her purity. It is precisely this consolation that Donne explores:

> But must we say shee's dead? May't not be said
>   That as a sundred Clocke is peece-meale laid,
> Not to be lost, but by the makers hand
>   Repolish'd, without error then to stand,
> Or as the Affrique Niger streame enwombs
>   It selfe into the earth, and after comes,
> (Having first made a naturall bridge, to passe
>   For many leagues,) farre greater then it was,
> May't not be said, that her grave shall restore
>   Her, greater, purer, firmer, then before?

The earthly images of the clock and the stream effectively evoke the traditional view of Christian resurrection and lead to an understanding of one form of Christian consolation: that which was "sundred" and "peece-meal" becomes perfection ("without error"); that which was limited in its impact arises "farre greater then it was."

Rather than confirming the importance of this source of consolation, however, Donne minimizes it. "Heaven may say this, and joy in't," but those remaining cannot "here this vantage see." Indeed, this form of consolation is, initially, only a further reminder of the loss. In his recognition of these two perspectives, only one of which brings joy and consolation, Donne draws in miniature a problem central to the longer poems. For one crucial distinction between the two *Anniversaries* is the dominant perspective of each. The *Anatomy* casts an eye downward, toward a decaying and deprived world; the *Progres* casts an eye upward, toward the "progres of the soule" and to a heaven to come. As a particular instance of that distinction, Donne explores in the *Second Anniversary,* especially the final sections of the poem, the differences between the joys and perspective of earth and the joys and perspective of heaven. That important distinction is evident here, and Donne anticipates, in brief form, what he will view more fully in the later poem.

If the essential joy and consolation of heaven are unavailable to the living, they are nonetheless able to find a lesser joy and consolation in their recollection of her presence among them. "The art of salvation," Donne says in a sermon, "is but the art of memory." Memory is here the art of consolation as well: "now the sicke starv'd world must feed upon / This joy, that we had her, who now is gone."

Consolation gained through a memory of her presence in the world leads again to a recognition of her worth, and through that to a repeated praise of her unique position as a representative of all the "force and vigor" of the world. Mind, body and soul are seen to have functioned harmoniously in her, a theme that will be reiterated in the *Second Anniversary.* In the **"Elegie,"** her body ("so pure, and thin, / Because it neede disguise no thought within") is viewed as a virtual extension and revelation of the pure mind and soul. In the *Second Anniversary* we will be told that "her pure and eloquent blood / Spoke in her cheekes, and so distinckly wrought, / That one might almost say, her bodie thought."

The images associated with the girl promote a constant view of her worth; those associated with the living reinforce their deprivation. They are as "aged men" or a "sicke starv'd world." Equally unflattering are the portraits of those who were attentive to her presence but who responded in ways that only confirmed their inability truly to understand her worth. In the *Anatomy* she was a "Magnetique force" with the power to draw the world's disparate parts together; in the **"Elegie"** she is another kind of magnetic force, able to draw out admiration and desire both from those who were nearly incapable of that kind of wonder and from those few who themselves "had worth enough." But admiration and desire lead, not to greater attention to her but to a mistaken kind of competition between her suitors and admirers, though the images Donne chooses, we should note, are not those from secular love:

> As when a Temple's built, Saints emulate
>   To which of them, it shall be consecrate.
> But as when Heav'n lookes on us with new eyes,
>   Those new starres ev'ry Artist exercise,
> What place they should assigne to them they doubt,
>   Argue, and agree not, till those starres go out:
> So the world studied whose this peece should be,
>   Till she can be no bodies else, nor shee.

Like a rare and expensive "Lampe of Balsamum," she revealed her worth but in doing so died early. Donne, like other writers of the genre, converts the early death into a good, for Elizabeth Drury dies still

> Cloath'd in her Virgin white integrity;
>   For mariage, though it doe not staine, doth dye.
> To scape th'infirmities which waite upone
>   Woman, shee went away, before sh'was one.

Typically, Donne cannot resist playing on a word, but he uses that play further to reveal an understanding of the event. Avoiding the sexual "dying" of marriage and the "infirmities which waite upone / Woman," Elizabeth Drury, Donne says, "Tooke so much death, as serv'd for *opium.*" That unflattering reflection on her death immediately gives way to quite a different view. Donne qualifies this previous assertion that she "*tooke* so much death" (emphasis mine) by claiming that "she could not, not could chuse to die," and he views her death now not as an opiate of escape but as a yielding "to too long an Extasie." Elizabeth Drury's death becomes, in this view, both a physical death and a death brought on by religious ecstasy, what Crashaw describes as "a death more mysticall and high."

Throughout this portion of the poem the audience is encouraged to view her death with appropriate ambivalence, and in this ambivalence we are again reminded of both Anniversary poems. The title of the *First Anniversary,* we remember, tells of her "untimely death"; the *Second Anniversary* speaks, instead, of her "Religious death." The **"Elegie"** recalls the one and anticipates the other, as her death is at once untimely and right. On the one hand the story of her life is a "sad History" of one who was "faire, and chast, humble, and high," "Much promis'd, much

perform'd, at not fifteene." Anyone reading the book of her life would find it inexplicably short and conclude that "eyther destiny mistooke, / Or that some leafes were torne out of the booke." On the other hand we are urged to view her death as good and appropriate and fulfilling. It is as an Extasie maintained overlong; it is a death that enables her to retain her "Virgin white integrity." It is an experience in which she participated through easy acceptance, if not through willful choice:

> Her modesty not suffering her to bee
>   Fellow-Commissioner with destinee,
> Shee did no more but die.

This is the final time death is mentioned in the poem; in the lines remaining Donne follows tradition in turning his attention to those left behind. As the girl was earlier a spirit begetting wonder and love and a figure worthy of admiration and desire, so she is also the image of all goodness. Thus those who "dare true good prefer" act, knowingly or not, in emulation of her, and their goodness helps to fill up the blank pages of the abbreviated book of the life of Elizabeth Drury.

One final time Donne recognizes two perspectives, that of earth and that of heaven, but whereas before they reflected a form of opposition, they are at the end of the poem complementary views of the same virtuous action:

> For future vertuous deeds are Legacies,
>   Which from the gift of her example rise.
> And 'tis in heav'n part of spirituall mirth,
>   To see how well, the good play her, on earth.

Heaven's joy is here not wholly separate from that of earth, as it was earlier, but simply superior to it. Before, earth's loss was heaven's gain; earth's lament, heaven's joy. Now virtue leads to joy as a heavenly audience watches while earth's actors, in acting out goodness, "play her." "Playing her" gives her immortality as each of the virtuous accomplishes "that which should have beene her fate." Two forms of immortality are thus apparent: her immortality in verse, realized in the face of the skepticism and unconcern expressed early in the poem, and her immortality in the deeds of others. So long as this poem exists, so long as there is virtue, they "give / Life to that name."

There is no certain evidence as to whether the **"Funerall Elegie"** or the *Anatomy* was written first. It is usually agreed, however, that the shorter and more restrained poem was the earlier creation, with the *First Anniversary* drawing from and reaching beyond the modest and more traditional beginning of the original. That view is sensible though, if true, it raises a question about the placement of the **"Elegie"** between the two longer poems, in spite of its likely priority to either, suggests its particular value there. Closely related to the *Anniversaries* and, as I have suggested, both drawing from the First and anticipating the Second, the **"Elegie"** also allows a pause after the heady imaginative flight of the *Anatomy* and before that of the *Progres.* It might have been introductory to each but, as better placed, it is a bridge between them or, to use my earlier image, a gentle slope comfortably negotiated both after and before challenging climbs. The **"Funerall Elegie"** serves, as well, as a useful reminder that these commemorative poems on Elizabeth Drury have a long and vital tradition behind them. The **"Elegie"** is different from the longer poems, of course, and in some quite fundamental ways. But it is also in important ways a poem that modulates between the two longer works and between those works and poetic convention. And it is closer to them, at times, than it is to the ubiquitous tradition. If the **"Elegie"** was written first it provided a significant basis for the expansion and extension of the *Anniversaries,* not just in its attention to familiar themes and motifs but in its distinctive adoption and adaptation of those motifs. Evidence from the longer poems supports the view that Donne used the **"Elegie"** as an important mediation between the two, as its position quite certainly suggests. But the proximity is more than typographical and more than mere convenience for the printer. The art of the **"Elegie"** is closer to the art of the *Anniversaries* than we have generally acknowledged. Developing out of a poet's witty and imaginative use of tradition, the **"Elegie"** instructively bridges the transforming and symbolic art of the *Anniversaries.* (pp. 56-66)

> *Paul A. Parrish, " 'A Funerall Elegie': Donne's Achievement in Traditional Form," in* Concerning Poetry, *Vol. 19, 1986, pp. 55-66.*

David M. Sullivan   (essay date 1987)

[*In the following excerpt, Sullivan focuses on the death metaphor in Donne's poem "Goodfriday 1613: Riding Westward."*]

East and west are the most important compass points in Donne's symbolic and poetic landscape. Images of maps appear frequently in his work, mostly in his *Divine Poems* and in his sermons. East is consistently associated with Christ and the Resurrection, west with death. These ideas are not unique to him. [In " 'Good-friday, 1613. Riding westward' The Poem and the Tradition," published in *ELH* in 1961,] A. B. Chambers shows in some detail that a long line of Christian geographical symbolism, beginning with Zachariah and extending through the imaginative literature of the Church Fathers into the Renaissance, preceded him in making these same associations.

In the tradition and in Donne's poetry the map metaphor works like this: we are born in the east, and like the sun we are delivered into our grave in the west; but death means resurrection from death, the circle is completed by a kind of fiat, and west automatically becomes its opposite, the east, this time as the eternal joy of heaven. We can watch this symbolism working in one of Donne's finest religious lyrics, the **"Hymne to God my God, in my sicknesse"**:

> Whilst my Physitians by their love are growne
> Cosmographers, and I their Mapp, who lie
> Flat on this bed, that by them may be showne
> That this is my South-west discoverie
> *Per fretum febris,* by these streights to die,
>
> I joy, that in these straits, I see my West;
> For, though theire currants yeeld returne to none,
> What shall my West hurt me? As West and East
> In all flatt Maps (and I am one) are one,
> So death doth touch the Resurrection.

The "South-west discoverie," Clay Hunt says, "refers to the discovery of the navigational passage which the merchant explorers had sought for generations, an ocean passage to the Orient" [see Further Reading list]. He means the Straits of Magellan, the stormy passage the navigator discovered on his way west to the Pacific and the Philippines, where he died. In a similar way, the speaker knows, he must pass "through the strait of fever," as the Latin phrase has it, on his journey west and to death, whose "currants yeeld returne to none." But he joys to see his west because touching death he touches its opposite. "Take a flat Map," says Donne, "a Globe *in plano,* and here is East, and there is West, as far asunder as two points can be put: but reduce this flat Map to roundnesse, which is the true form, and then East and West touch one another, and are all one. . . ." As Hunt puts it nicely,

> He does not regret that the currents will allow him no return from his passage, and he is not afraid to face the hardship and danger which he may expect as he goes farther into the West that now opens before him. . . . He thinks of the West (death) simply as the region that he must pass through to arrive at the East (resurrection and the joy of eternal life in heaven), the goal which all men have dreamed of and which truly adventurous men have actually sought.

It is in this general sense that the symbolism of **"Goodfriday, 1613. Riding Westward"** has traditionally, and rightly, been understood. So far so good. But "Riding Westward" was a colloquialism of Donne's time that meant literally "going to Tyburn"—going to hang on the Middlesex gallows, sometimes called Tyburn tree, located in the west end of London on the west bank of the Tyburn tributary. The speaker of this poem is a man condemned to die, and riding out, in no uncertain terms, to be executed. To appreciate the drama of this poem we must read it as it was understood by Donne's contemporaries, who would have recognized in it the elaborate conceit so highly dated that it has become lost since, and with it part of the poem's coherence and wit. (pp. 1-2)

I wish to cite this passage from the sermon . . . that Donne preached upon Easter Day 1619, on this text from Psalms 89:48: "What man is he that liveth, and shall not see death?"

> Wee are all conceived in close Prison; in our Mothers wombes, we are close Prisoners all; when we are borne, we are borne but to the liberty of the house; Prisoners still, though within larger walls; and then all our life is but a going out to the place of Execution, to death. Now was there ever any man seen to sleep in the Cart, between New-gate, and Tyborne? between the Prison, and the place of Execution, does any man sleep? And we sleep all the way; from the womb to the grave we are never throughly awake; but passe on with such dreames, and imaginations as these, I may live as well, as another, and why should I dye, rather then another? but awake, and tell me, sayes this Text, *Quis homo?* who is that other that thou talkest of ? *What man is he that liveth, and shall not see death?*

It pleased Donne to think of death as an execution. This idea is not necessarily a conceit: insofar as to be a Christian means to imitate Christ, it has an historical justification in the Crucifixion; and some correspondence, actual or symbolic, in the manner of dying, was, for Donne, both inevitable and good. Such a view of death, I am arguing, is the controlling metaphor of **"Goodfriday, 1613. Riding Westward"** and a key to understanding it.

"Goodfriday" falls into two parts, and in each the meaning of death is different. It is first of all a dramatic poem: it records a change of mind, as the Holy Sonnets do frequently. The first part, which constitutes the bulk of the poem, ends with a series of rhetorical questions. While they are being asked, a change of heart occurs and the rider resolves to embrace the kind of death, literally or symbolically, that his religion and faith require.

As the poem opens, the rider betrays that he is dying a kind of spiritual death. Pleasure and business have taken over from devotion and the proper rule of his soul and are whirling him away from the risen Christ of the east, on whom the rider's attention is fixed, and toward the west, distancing him, as he perceives it, from his true faith. . . . Chambers shows that Donne has reversed his cosmology. The primum mobile, in a tradition stretching far back into antiquity, was always westward in motion. Its influence on the spheres, whose motions were naturally recalcitrant and desired to turn eastward, forced them to whirl westward with it. It was the same with the soul. The rational faculties of the soul were also, like the primum mobile, naturally "westward" in motion. They compelled the irrational faculties of the soul to whirl with them against the inclinations of their own baser nature. Whereas, in the traditional cosmology, it was natural for the rider to be carried toward the west, here Donne makes the motion of the first mover naturally eastward in direction in order to emphasize that death is the consequence of the rider's betrayal. Behind and above him in the east, the risen Christ hangs bloody, ragged, and torn. The speaker's predicament is that he cannot, or will not, turn his face to the east: he is afraid to die. . . .

Though my interpretation of this poem, emphasizing the nature of punishment and expiation, is fundamentally different from that of Chambers, who analyzes it in terms of the nature of the soul, I agree fully with his observation that at this point the "westward journey . . . becomes not a rational movement but a departure from the Christian path, a turning from light to enter the ways of darkness." I agree, too, that the rider, at once both Donne and Everyman, "must be pierced, must assume the 'rag'd and torn' apparel of God, and must then be scourged of the deformity thus put on"

The journey westward is both right and wrong. I am assuming that for Donne it is right because, as a follower of Christ, he is naturally, ineluctably, pursuing the path which Christ took as a mortal man—westward to death and execution. Of the inevitability of his end the rider is painfully aware. The journey is wrong, on the other hand, because he is at this moment afraid to meet his fate. Again, we must interpret the essential ambiguity of the poem in terms of Crucifixion. For the rider, the Crucifixion—his Tyburn, if you will—means both the agony of his physical death and his death to the pleasure and business of the world which have usurped the operation of his soul. For Donne and the poets of his time, the word "sun" could hardly pass from pen to paper without a thought that the reader would immediately check for a play on the well-worn tradition that associated sun with Son, by an effective cosmological analogy, as the two rulers of the heavens. When meditating on the agony of the Crucifixion, the speaker acknowledging that it made "the Sunne winke," he is only too conscious of the physical and spiritual pain

he himself must undergo in order to die fully into his faith. Being able to behold the east means being able to make this leap, and he finds the thought of it excruciating:

> Could I behold those hands which span the Poles,
> And tune all spheares at once, peirc'd with those holes?
> Could I behold that endlesse height which is
> Zenith to us, and to'our Antipodes,
> Humble below us? or that blood which is
> The seat of all our Soules, if not of his,
> Made durt of dust, or that flesh which was worne
> By God, for his apparell, rag'd, and torne?
> If on these things I durst not looke, durst I
> Upon his miserable mother cast mine eye,
> Who was Gods partner here, and furnish'd thus
> Halfe of that Sacrifice, which ransom'd us?

In posing these questions, however, he becomes able to answer them. He finds that he can meet his religion on its own terms, for we find that in the next few lines, the second and concluding part of the poem, the speaker is anticipating his punishment with resolution and even eagerness:

> Though these things, as I ride, be from mine eyes,.
> They'are present yet unto my memory,
> For that looks towards them; and thou look'st towards mee,
> O Saviour, as thou hang'st upon the tree;
> I turne my backe to thee, but to receive
> Corrections, till thy mercies bid thee leave.
> O thinke mee worth thine anger, punish mee,
> Burne off my rusts, and my deformity,
> Restore thine Image, so much, by thy grace,
> That thou may'st know mee, and I'll turne my face.

When the speaker recognizes that his westward journey is good—"I turne my backe to thee, but to receive / Corrections"—he accepts the destiny of Christ as man; and in this acceptance and awareness of it he becomes, as it were, fully awake: "was there ever any man seen to sleep in the Cart, between New-gate, and Tyborne? between the Prison, and the place of Execution, does any man sleep? And we sleep all the way; from the womb to the grave we are never thoroughly awake. . . . " The rider is now "conscious." He now sees his death, physical and spiritual, as a punishment which redeems.

Christ is a military figure in this poem, at least inasmuch as Nature is "his owne Lieutenant." And Christ himself, of course, was the victim of a state execution, crucifixion being the punishment commonly reserved for traitors and slaves. He was a traitor by Roman law and paid with his life for the crime. In this sense, the rider is like Christ: for he also is, or was, a traitor, by virtue of his weakness to pleasure and business which he admitted at the outset. Hence his desire for punishment: to be redeemed from fire by fire. By a kind of irony it is Christ, however, who will become his executioner. The moment of his freedom becomes the moment of his ultimate captivity. The speaker resolves the dilemma of his western movement like this: he accepts the consequences of proceeding westward as necessary, even though they mean spiritual and eventually physical death. He accepts them because the punishment which is consequent upon his spiritual death will reform him, just as the fact of his physical death will mean eventually his resurrection. I believe that, for Donne, to turn one's face to the east is possible only after death; for it is presumably only on Resurrection Day that Christ will reappear to the eyes. In making his plea for dissolution, the speaker finds some solace in what Chambers calls his "devotional memory." By this means, as a guide to repentance, the Christian can contemplate the spectacle of the Crucifixion by such imperfect means as are available to him.

When Donne rode westward on the day he composed this poem, as seems fairly certain, he was meditating on several important matters. He was about to enter holy orders—a step he had delayed until he could be sure his mind was set wholly on heavenly things. He was about to die, he must have felt, to a whole way of life. Perhaps it struck him as a strange coincidence, even as a kind of fate, that the eve of his conversion was Good Friday. The speaker of this poem, whether Donne or not, is a man sentenced to die. "That [Christ] was crucified with his face towards the West," says Sir Thomas Browne, "we will not contend with tradition and probable account . . . " This is the significance of the subtitle and such phrases as "carryed towards the West," "as I ride," and "punish mee." I do not believe that the poem dramatizes the meditations of a man actually being carted off to Tyburn, only symbolically, insofar as he is Everyman, and inasmuch as he is, in a minor key, by imitation, Christ himself, as I have tried to show. This poem records a crucial moment in the man's moral life when he becomes fully conscious of his dying, yet manages to meet it with humility and acceptance, though not without fear and trembling. He accepts that to ride westward is not only inevitable but finally more good than bad, since that was the path Christ himself took, who suffered a real death, both before and during the execution, and who yet knew, paradoxically, that in his case, as in the case of all those who, like the rider, imitate Christ, death means life. (pp. 3-7)

> *David M. Sullivan, "Riders to the West: 'Goodfriday, 1613',"* in John Donne Journal: Studies in the Age of Donne, *Vol. 6, No. 1, 1987, pp. 1-8.*

FURTHER READING

Alexander, Henry. "John Donne, Poet and Divine." *Queen's Quarterly* XLII, No. 4 (Winter 1935): 471-81.
 Traces Donne's development as a poet from his youthful conceits to his mature religious poetry.

Bald, R. C. *John Donne: A Life.* New York and Oxford: Oxford University Press, 1970, 627 p.
 Detailed, highly esteemed biography.

Baumlim, James S. "Donne's 'Satyre IV': The Failure of Language and Genre." *Texas Studies in Literature and Language* 30, No. 3 (Fall 1988): 363-87.
 Argues that Donne's "Satyre IV" is an unsuccessful imitation of the works of Archilochus, a Greek precursor of Latin satire.

Bedford, R. D. "Donne's Holy Sonnet, 'Batter My Heart',"
Notes and Queries n.s. 29, No. 1 (February 1982): 15-19.
 Considers various interpretations of Donne's holy sonnet "Batter My Heart" and explicates the poem.

Bennett, Joan. "Donne's Technical Originality." In her *Five Metaphysical Poets: Donne, Herbert, Vaughan, Crashaw, Marvell,* pp. 30-48. Cambridge: Cambridge at the University Press, 1964.
 Identifies Donne's scientific interests as evidenced in his poetry. Bennett offers an explication of what she considers Donne's unique poetic technique.

Bewley, Marius. "Religious Cynicism in Donne's Poetry."
The Kenyon Review 14, No. 4 (Autumn 1952): 619-46.
 Holds that the *Songs and Sonets* "in their inculcation of an outrageous cynicism, in their abuse of religious imagery, in their distortion of scholastic philosophical concepts, in their cavalier employment of logic, represent many years in Donne's private guerrilla warfare against the dispositions of faith."

———. "The Mask of John Donne." In his *Masks & Mirrors: Essays in Criticism,* pp. 3-49. New York: Atheneum, 1970.
 Traces Donne's critical reputation and discusses in depth the poet's religious conversion from Catholicism to Anglicanism.

Bradford, Gamaliel. "The Poetry of Donne." In his *A Naturalist of Souls: Studies in Psychography,* pp. 27-59. New York: Dodd, Mead and Co., 1917.
 Examines the history of critical opinion concerning Donne's poetry and compares his work with that of his contemporaries and literary descendants.

Buckley, Vincent. "John Donne's Passion." In his *Poetry and the Sacred,* pp. 99-116. London: Chatto & Windus, 1968.
 Discerns remarkable poetic passion in Donne's writing.

Cathcart, Dwight. *Doubting Conscience: Donne and the Poetry of Moral Argument.* Ann Arbor: University of Michigan Press, 1975, 199 p.
 Explores the questions of conscience evident in Donne's poetry.

Cox, R. G. "The Poems of John Donne." In *From Donne to Marvell,* edited by Boris Ford, pp. 98-115. Middlesex, Eng.: Penguin Books, 1956.
 Explication of Donne's poetic canon.

Crum, Ralph B. "Poetry and the New Science." In his *Scientific Thought in Poetry,* pp. 40-60. 1931. Reprint. New York: AMC Press, 1966.
 Acknowledges Donne's professed resistance to the evolving scientific thought of the early seventeenth century, but offers evidence that Donne was nonetheless influenced by the new science.

Dowden, Edward. "The Poetry of John Donne." In his *New Studies in Literature,* pp. 90-120. London: Kegan Paul, Trench, Trubner & Co., 1895.
 A biographically based discussion of Donne's major poems.

Dryden, John. "A Discourse concerning the Original and Progress of Satire." In his *Essays of John Dryden,* Vol. II, edited by W. P. Ker, pp. 15-114. Oxford: Oxford at the Clarendon Press, 1900.
 1693 essay labeling Donne a clever craftsman but not an artist. Dryden's commentary marked the beginning of over a century of negative criticism of Donne's poetry.

Duncan, Edgar Hill. "Donne's Alchemical Figures." *ELH* 9, No. 1 (March 1942): 257-85.
 Analyzes "alchemical figures in Donne's poetry against

a background of the theories and practices of alchemy as recorded in the compendious literature of the science current in the late sixteenth and early seventeenth centuries."

Eaton, Horace Ainsworth. " 'The Songs and Sonnets' of John Donne." *The Sewanee Review* XXII, No. 1 (January 1914): 50-72.
Considers the *Songs and Sonets* Donne's most important poetic contribution to modern literature.

Eliot, T. S. "The Metaphysical Poets." In his *Selected Essays,* pp. 241-50. New York: Harcourt, Brace & World, 1950.
Considered one of the signal works of twentieth-century poetry criticism, this study was markedly influential in stirring interest in Donne and his school. Eliot's essay, originally published in 1921 as a review of H. J. C. Grierson's *Metaphysical Lyrics and Poems of the Seventeenth Century,* reveals to contemporary readers the value of metaphysical poetry.

Fausset, Hugh I'Anson. *John Donne: A Study in Discord.* New York: Harcourt, Brace & Co., 1924, 318 p.
Critical biography of Donne in which Fausset concludes that the poet "reflects and condenses the long labour of the man to outgrow the beast and approach the divine."

Fiore, Peter Amadeus, ed. *Just So Much Honor: Essays Commemorating the Four-Hundredth Anniversary of the Birth of John Donne.* University Park and London: Pennsylvania State University Press, 1972, 291 p.
Critical studies by such scholars as David Daiches, John T. Shawcross, Roger Sharrock, and William Empson.

Gosse, Edmund. *The Life and Letters of John Donne,* 2 vols. New York: Dodd, Mead and Co., 1899.
First complete and accurate critical biography of Donne's life and work. Gosse's study did much to dispel many of the myths concerning Donne's life.

Grant, Patrick. "John Donne's 'Anniversaries': New Philosophy and the Act of the Heart." In his *Literature and the Discovery of the Method in the English Renaissance,* pp. 77-101. London: Macmillan, 1985.
Close reading of the *Anniversaries.*

Hunt, Clay. *Donne's Poetry: Essay in Literary Analysis.* New Haven and London: Yale University Press, 1954, 253 p.
Scrutinizes several poems and draws general conclusions about Donne's life and work.

John Donne Journal: Studies in the Age of Donne I— (1982—).
Biannual periodical edited by Donne scholar M. Thomas Hester. Each issue carries scholarly essays on Donne's canon and on the works of such contemporaries as William Shakespeare, Ben Jonson, Inigo Jones, and George Herbert, as well as recent books on the age of Donne.

Johnson, Beatrice. "Classical Allusions in the Poetry of John Donne." *PMLA* XLIII (1928): 1098-1109.
Refutes critics who claim that Donne's poetry contains no classical allusions, asserting that Donne referred to Greek mythology in his works with independence and originality.

Jonson, Ben. "To John Donne." In his *The Works of Ben Jonson, Vol. III,* edited by Francis Cunningham, p. 229. London: John Camden Hotten, 1875.
Verses written in 1610 extolling Donne.

Kermode, Frank. Introduction to *The Poems of John Donne,* by John Donne, edited by Frank Kermode, pp. xi-xxi. New York: Heritage Press, 1970.
General biographical and critical overview.

Lewalski, Barbara Kiefer. *Donne's "Anniversaries" and the Poetry of Praise: The Creation of a Symbolic Mode.* Princeton: Princeton University Press, 1973, 386 p.
Attempts to identify habits and traditions that "gave rise to the *Anniversary* poems and their distinct symbolic mode."

Lewis, C. S. "Donne and Love Poetry in the Seventeenth Century." In *Seventeenth Century Studies Presented to Sir Herbert Grierson,* 1938. Reprint by Octagon Books, 1967, pp. 64-84.
Description and negative assessment of Donne's love poetry.

————. *English Literature in the Sixteenth Century, Excluding Drama,* pp. 469 ff. Oxford: Oxford University Press, Clarendon Press, 1954.
Harsh criticism of Donne's *Satyres, Elegies,* and verse *Letters,* but high praise for the *Songs and Sonets.*

Louthan, Doniphan. *The Poetry of John Donne: A Study in Explication.* 1951. Reprint. Westport, Conn.: Greenwood Press, 1976, 193 p.
General reading of Donne's poetry in which Louthan distinguishes Donne's literary endeavors from his personal life and religious convictions.

Lynd, Robert. "John Donne." *The London Mercury* 1, No. 4 (February 1920): 435-447.
Critical survey of Donne's poetry in which Lynd likens Donne to a "poet-geographer" who travelled far in his art.

Manlove, C. N. "Donne and Marvell." In his *Literature and Reality: 1600-1800,* pp. 3-15. New York: St. Martin's Press, 1978.
Highlights Donne's poetry, arguing that the poet refuses "the awkwardness and the multiple truth of the real world for the singleness of a mental one in his poetry."

Mégroz, R. L. "The Wit and Fantasy of Donne." *The Dublin Magazine* 1, No. 2 (April-June 1926): 47-51.
Argues that Donne's poetry is mystical rather than metaphysical.

Mitchell, Charles. "Donne's 'The Extasie': Love's Sublime Knot." *Studies in English Literature* VIII, No. 1 (Winter 1968): 91-101.
Explication of "The Extasie" studying how the relationship of man and woman influences that of the soul and body within the individual.

Nye, Robert. "The Body in His Book: The Poetry of John Donne." *Critical Quarterly* 14, No. 4 (Winter 1972): 345-60.
Refutes critical charges that Donne's secular and religious poems reveal inconsistent patterns of thought and development in his life and work.

Pearson, Lu Emily. "Anti-Petrarchism: John Donne's Love Lyrics." In her *Elizabethan Love Conventions,* pp. 223-30. Berkeley: University of California Press, 1933.
Examination of Donne's treatment of love and relationships in his poetry as well as his handling of the traditional Petrarchan model.

Pebworth, Ted-Larry. "John Donne, Coterie Poetry, and the

Text as Performance." *Studies in English Literature, 1500-1900* 29, No. 1 (Winter 1989): 61-75.

Investigates Donne's motivation for writing poetry, claiming that Donne participated in a coterie that affected his attitude toward poetry and the manner in which he composed it.

Richards, I. A. "The Interactions of Words." In *The Language of Poetry,* pp. 65-87. Princeton: Princeton University Press, 1942.

Examines Donne's *Anniversaries* and "A Valediction: forbidding mourning" to elucidate the way "through which words, by uniting, bring new beings into the world, or new worlds into being." Richards compares Donne's poems to selected poems by John Dryden, W. B. Yeats, and T. S. Eliot.

Rissanen, Paavo. "The Background of Experience Behind Donne's Secular and Religious Poetry." *Neuphilologische Mitteilungen* LXXVI, No. 2 (1975): 282-98.

Demonstrates that the two apparently divergent personalities of Donne—Jack Donne and Dr. John Donne—successfully coexist in one man.

Roberts, John, ed. *Essential Articles for the Study of John Donne's Poetry.* Hamden, Conn.: Archon Books, 1975, 558 p.

Valuable collection of critical essays by numerous Donne scholars that provides a comprehensive explication and interpretation of Donne's poetry.

Roston, Murray. *The Soul of Wit: A Study of John Donne.* Oxford: Oxford at the Clarendon Press, 1974, 236 p.

Textual analysis of Donne's poetry in which Roston reconciles the seemingly paradoxical natures of Donne's secular and religious poetry.

Saintsbury, George. Introduction to *Poems of John Donne,* Vol. I, by John Donne, edited by E. K. Chambers, pp. xi-xxxiii. London: George Routledge & Sons, 1896.

Selective survey and appraisal of Donne's poetry.

Sanders, Wilbur. *John Donne's Poetry.* Cambridge: Cambridge University Press, 1971, 160 p.

Insightful interpretation of the poems and discussion of Donne's critical heritage.

Scott, W. S. "John Donne." In his *The Fantasticks: Donne, Herbert, Crashaw, Vaughan,* pp. 10-18. London: John Westhouse, 1945.

Suggests reasons for difficulties in understanding Donne's poetry, exploring as well the poet's perspective and motivation for writing.

Smith, A. J., ed. *John Donne: Essays in Celebration.* London: Methuen & Co., 1972, 470 p.

Collection of critical essays commemorating the tercentary of Donne's birth.

Southey, Robert. Preface to his *Specimens of the Later English Poets,* Vol. I, pp. iii-xxxii. London: Longman, Hurst, Rees and Orme, 1807.

Brief entry in which Southey recognizes Donne's intellect but discerns no real poetic talent.

Sprott, S. Ernest. "The Legend of Jack Donne the Libertine." *The University of Toronto Quarterly* XIX, No. 4 (July 1950): 335-53.

Examines and refutes many of the legends surrounding the duality of Donne's temperament.

Stampfer, Judah. *John Donne and the Metaphysical Gesture.* New York: Funk & Wagnalls, 1970, 298 p.

Explication of Donne's poetry, seeking to apprehend its "peculiar personal poignance, one not of unfolding imagination, but in [Donne's] pinched immediate situation, in the poet's grasp for salvation, love, order, sexual fulfillment, against a crumbling universe of reference."

Stein, Arnold. "Meter and Meaning in Donne's Verse." *The Sewanee Review* 52, No. 2 (April-June 1944): 288-301.

Examines various critical interpretations of Donne's metrical technique in his verses and seeks to uncover the authentic voice of the poet.

————. *John Donne's Lyrics: The Eloquence of Action.* Minneapolis: University of Minnesota Press, 1962, 244 p.

Studies questions of style, wit, intent, and content in Donne's poetry in an attempt to gain insight "into the integrity of Donne's poetic mind."

Tuve, Rosemund. *Elizabethan and Metaphysical Imagery: Renaissance Poetic and Twentieth-Century Critics.* Chicago and London: University of Chicago Press, 1947, 436 p.

Study of imagery in the nondramatic poetry of the English Renaissance, with numerous references to Donne's poetry.

Wells, Henry W. "The Radical Image." In his *Poetic Imagery Illustrated from Elizabethan Literature,* pp. 121-37. New York: Russell & Russell, 1961.

Suggests that radical imagery appears in several of Donne's poems and that in his verse, the "Radical metaphor reached its crest."

Whitby, Charles. "The Genius of Donne." *The Poetry Review* XIV, No. 2 (March-April 1923): 67-81.

Offers a favorable assessment of Donne's poetic canon, concluding that passion, power, and originality are the outstanding characteristics in Donne's poetry.

Williamson, George. "The Nature of the Donne Tradition." In his *The Donne Tradition: A Study in English Poetry from Donne to the Death of Cowley,* pp. 20-57. 1930. Reprint. New York: Noonday Press, 1958.

Seeks to identify characteristics of Donne's poetry, examining Thomas Carew's elegiac poem [see excerpt dated 1633] as a key to understanding it.

Lawrence Ferlinghetti

1919?-

(Full name: Lawrence Monsanto Ferlinghetti) American poet, novelist, dramatist, essayist, editor, and publisher.

Ferlinghetti was at the forefront of the Beat Movement, a literary phenomenon of the 1950s which began and was centered in San Francisco. Along with other Beat writers, Ferlinghetti attempted to expand the appreciation and accessibility of poetry by removing it from the exclusivity of the academic sphere. Although he has described himself as a "street poet" and is noted for his antipathy to institutions of higher learning, Ferlinghetti himself received a thorough education, earning a doctorate from the Sorbonne. Ferlinghetti's most important contribution to the Beat Movement may have been his creation of a forum for counterculture writers. In 1953, he established City Lights Books, the country's first exclusively paperback bookstore, which carried works by writers that were, for the most part, unavailable elsewhere. Two years later, Ferlinghetti began publishing the City Lights Pocket Series, which included titles by fellow Beat writers Jack Kerouac, Michael McClure, Gregory Corso, and Allen Ginsberg.

The unorthodox quality of Ferlinghetti's lifestyle can be traced to his earliest years. Born Lawrence Ferling in Yonkers, New York, he spent several years in France with a relative, Emily Mendes-Monsanto, who had assumed responsibility for him after his father's death and his mother's admission to a mental hospital. When Monsanto and Ferlinghetti returned to the United States, they lived with a family for whom Monsanto worked as a governess. It was with this family that Ferlinghetti spent the remainder of his childhood. After attending the University of North Carolina, he served in the United States Naval Reserve. During World War II he was stationed in France, participating as a lieutenant commander in the Normandy invasion. At war's end, he resumed his studies, earning a master's degree at Columbia University before returning to France to study at the Sorbonne, where he achieved his doctorate with a dissertation on the city as a symbol in poetry. After a brief stay in New York, Ferlinghetti settled in San Francisco, where he began his book-selling and publishing endeavors.

In 1957, Ferlinghetti's publication of Ginsberg's *Howl* led to an obscenity trial which attracted wide-spread attention and gained the book's publisher and the Beat Movement national notoriety. His successful defense in this landmark trial is another of Ferlinghetti's significant contributions to contemporary literature. Throughout his career, Ferlinghetti has consistently asserted that such engagement with current social and political issues must remain a primary element of a poet's life and work. In accordance with this view, he has contended that the role of a poet is to provide a dissenting voice that is autonomous of both the political Left and Right. Therefore, he insists, the poet must diligently maintain integrity and guard the independence of his or her expression. In his poems, Ferlinghetti has treated these subjects with an intense commitment, but

also with a wit and irreverent humor that render them accessible to a wide audience.

Ferlinghetti's writing has brought him popular success but a lukewarm critical reception. Like that of other Beat writers, his poetry, which reflects the influence of American idiom and jazz, stresses the oral aspects of literature and is written with performance in mind. Some critics have remarked that his verse is undisciplined and sentimental; others praise what they see as his honest energy. General critical assessment of Ferlinghetti's writing seems to be that it contributed to the open, vibrant sensibility of the Beat Movement, but that unlike the work of Ginsberg or Kerouac, it was not particularly innovative. Nevertheless, *A Coney Island of the Mind*, Ferlinghetti's second book, ranks along with Ginsberg's *Howl* as one of the most widely known volumes of American poetry published after 1950.

Clearly exhibited in Ferlinghetti's most recent works are both the consistency and evolution of his convictions. The pieces in the retrospective collection *Endless Life: Selected Poems*, reflect the abiding concern throughout Ferlinghetti's career with not only political matters but with the nature of beauty and the poetic imagination. This book has prompted a reappraisal of the writer by some critics, who have increasingly come to regard him an important figure among contemporary poets. In his latest collection of verse, *Wild Dreams of a New Beginning,* Ferlinghetti continues to demonstrate, as Diane Wakoski notes, "an immense belief in the power and life of imagination. Belief that it can transform the world, even change it."

(For further information on Ferlinghetti's life and career, see *Contemporary Literary Criticism,* Vols. 2, 6, 10, 27; *Contemporary Authors,* Vols. 5-8 rev. ed.; *Contemporary Authors New Revision Series,* Vol. 3; *Dictionary of Literary Biography,* Vols. 5, 16; and *Concise Dictionary of American Literary Biography: The New Consciousness, 1941-1968.*)

PRINCIPAL WORKS

POETRY

Pictures of the Gone World   1955
*A Coney Island of the Mind   1958
Starting From San Francisco   1961; revised and enlarged, 1967
Penguin Modern Poets 5   1963 [with Gregory Corso and Allen Ginsberg]
An Eye on the World: Selected Poems   1967
The Secret Meaning of Things   1969
Tyrannus Nix?   1969; revised 1973
Back Roads to Far Places   1971
Open Eye, Open Heart   1973
Who are We Now?   1976
Northwest Ecolog   1978
Landscapes of Living & Dying   1979
Endless Life: Selected Poems   1981
A Trip to Italy and France   1981
Over All the Obscene Boundaries: European Poems & Transitions   1984
Wild Dreams of a New Beginning   1988

OTHER MAJOR WORKS

Her   (novel)   1960
Unfair Arguments with Existence: Seven Plays for a New Theatre   (drama)   1963
Routines   (drama)   [includes thirteen short works] 1964
The Mexican Night   (travel essay)   1970
Seven Days in Nicaragua Libre   (prose)   1984

*This work includes "Oral Messages" and selections from *Pictures of the Gone World.*

Harvey Shapiro   (essay date 1958)

[*In the following excerpt, Shapiro offers a favorable review of* A Coney Island of the Mind, *judging it "highly readable and often very funny."*]

Lawrence Ferlinghetti has been a leader in all that jazz about poetry on the West Coast. He now appears with some verse of his own [*A Coney Island of the Mind*], which I find highly readable and often very funny:

    Don't let that horse

        eat that violin
    cried Chagall's mother
            —But he
        kept right on
            painting

His program (as quoted on the back of his book) is "to get poetry out of the inner esthetic sanctum and out of the classroom into the street." He puts it more honestly in his verse: "I am a social climber / climbing downward / And the descent is difficult." For like many writers who keep pointing to their bare feet, Ferlinghetti is a very bookish boy: his hipster verse frequently hangs on a literary reference. His book is a grab bag of undergraduate musings about love and art, much hackneyed satire of American life and some real and wry perceptions of it: "I am in line / for a top job. / I may be moving on / to Detroit. / I am only temporarily / a tie salesman."

> *Harvey Shapiro, "Five Voices in Verse," in* The New York Times Book Review, *September 7, 1958, p. 10.*

M. L. Rosenthal   (essay date 1958)

[*Rosenthal is an American poet, critic, and editor. Among his most influential studies are* The Modern Poets *(1960) and* The New Poets *(1967), which analyze the verse of some of the most important poets of the twentieth century. Rosenthal's critical method is marked by its independence from any particular school of criticism and by its emphasis on individual poems, which the critic attempts to place within the general context of modern literature. In the excerpt below, Rosenthal notes the influence of William Carlos William's poetic techniques on the works in* A Coney Island of the Mind *but considers such modernist devices a "straight jacket" on Ferlinghetti's talent.*]

Lawrence Ferlinghetti is certainly one of [the] advocates of universal nakedness . . . , but he differs from most of the others in his high-flying joyousness of spirit and in his stylistic sophistication. He knows he is not the first man to take a peek at Darien and he has learned some useful things, and gladly, from various European and American experimenters. The religion of sex-and-anarchy, like other religions and creeds, starts off with certain simplicities but does not require its communicants to reiterate them monotonously and mechanically. Ferlinghetti can preach a little tiresomely; he proves he can in the seven "Oral Messages" [in *A Coney Island of the Mind*], written "specifically for jazz accompaniment," in which he tries to rival the worst of Ginsberg, Corso, et al. He doesn't quite succeed, for he is too bright and literate and many of his wisecracks and sideswipes are worth hearing, but finally he does become dull. The "great audiences" Whitman called for are not the improvised audiences of night clubs who must have their poetry ranting and obvious if they are to "get" anything at all.

Apart from the "Oral Messages," however, and from a few other preachy pieces, Ferlinghetti is a deft, rapid-placed, whirling performer. He has a wonderful eye for meaning in the commonplace, as in the lovely, sensual snapshot of a woman hanging clothes on a San Francisco rooftop, or in the memory of a New York candy store where

Jellybeans glowed in the semi-gloom
of that september afternoon
A cat upon the counter moved among
      the licorice sticks
      and tootsie rolls
    and Oh Boy Gum

He has a fine imaginative eye, too, as the bawdy description of a contest with "the widder Fogliani" painting mustaches on the statues in the Borghese gardens shows. Even better—far better, because here he conquers his almost indomitable over-whimsicality—is the contrasting picture of laborers putting up a statue of Saint Francis ("no birds sang" despite the presence of a priest, reporters, and many onlookers) while, unnoticed in the crowd, there passes to and fro

a very tall and very purely naked
            young virgin
with very long and very straight
          straw hair
and wearing only a very small
           bird's nest
in a very existential place. . . .

These quotations will indicate Ferlinghetti's obvious debt to the stanzaic and rhythmic technique of William Carlos Williams and the other "modernist" masters, and his equally obvious independence of idiom. I have mentioned his whimsy and his tendentiousness—I think they are related to his failure as yet to find a really adequate form for the intellectual and idiomatic range of which he gives such encouraging glimpses. There are poems in this volume (for instance, **"The wounded wilderness of Morris Graves"** and **"In Paris in a loud dark winter"**) which demand something more than the light music into which Ferlinghetti's characteristic line virtually forces him. The nakedness-symbolism is another kind of strait jacket. "Take it off !"—or even *"Vive la différence!"*—is a fine old war-cry. But Ferlinghetti is far too gifted to let himself be mesmerized by it, or by his somewhat too-easy mastery of one kind of metrical pyrotechnics. (p. 215)

> *M. L. Rosenthal, "The Naked and the Clad,"*
> *in* The Nation, *New York, Vol. 187, No. 11,*
> *October 11, 1958, pp. 214-15.*

Hayden Carruth   (essay date 1958)

[*An American poet, novelist, and critic, Carruth has won several important prizes for his lyrical and controlled poems. He is most often praised for his sustained meditations, of which* Journey to a Known Place *(1961) is a notable example. In the excerpt below, Carruth attacks Ferlinghetti's claim that* A Coney Island of the Mind *is "street poetry," maintaining that these poems are too "abstract," "long-winded," and "tuneless" to appeal to popular tastes.*]

Lawrence Ferlinghetti, quite properly and recognizably is to be identified among the members of the so-called San Francisco group. He is the proprietor of the City Lights Bookshop, a center of the group's activities, and as such has had a good deal to do with organizing the sort of fraternated arts program which has been so much admired during recent years in the San Francisco area; and he has published much of the group's output in his series of City Lights pamphlets. Moreover, his own work as a poet has

been prominently acclaimed by various members of the coterie as well as others. His new book, *A Coney Island of the Mind,* contains both old and new work, and presumably represents Mr. Ferlinghetti's own selection of the poems he considers his best.

Mr. Ferlinghetti's intention is clearly announced on the cover of his book. "I have been working," he writes, "toward a kind of *street poetry* . . . to get poetry out of the inner esthetic sanctum and out of the classroom into the street. The poet has been contemplating his navel too long, while the world walks by. And the printing press has made poetry so silent that we've forgotten the power of poetry as 'oral messages'. The sound of the streetsinger and the Salvation Army speaker is not to be scorned. . . ." The voice of Vachel Lindsay sounds through these words, and many others' as well. Once I read an excellent paper on the same subject by John Masefield.

One means by which Mr. Ferlinghetti has attempted to ingratiate his "oral messages" with a popular audience is to write them for accompaniment by a jazz band, and a section of his book has been devoted to poems produced in this way. Let me offer a few excerpts from one of them, **"Junkman's Obbligato:"**

> Let us arise and go now
> to where dogs do it
> Over the Hill
> where they keep the earthquakes
> behind the city dumps
> lost among gasmains and garbage.
> Let us see the City Dumps
> for what they are.
> My country tears of thee.
> Let us disappear
> in automobile graveyards
> and reappear years later
> picking rags and newspapers
> drying our drawers
> on garbage fires
> patches on our ass.
> Do not bother
> to say goodbye
> to anyone. . . .

and so on and on for six pages. It must be wonderful to be able to be satisfied with such easy stuff.

First, what is this as poetry? Mr. Ferlinghetti may not like printing presses, but he has consigned his work to the printed page, to be read in silence, and consequently I suppose we may judge it as we would any other verse. The temptation is to let [such excerpts] . . . damn themselves, and say no more about it. But so much has already been said by the avid and, I fear, the uninformed that probably something explicit, something from a contrary view, is needed here. I want to introduce one more quotation by way of comparison, the opening lines of Miss Levertov's *Beyond the End.* This is a poem which Mr. Ferlinghetti presumably tolerates since he himself was its publisher.

> In 'nature' there's no choice—
>   flowers
> swing their heads in the wind, sun & moon
>   are as they are. But we seem
> almost to have it (not just
>   available death)

It's energy: a spider's thread: not to
'go on living' but to quicken, to activate: extend . . .

It's a pity to chop Miss Levertov's poem off in this way,
but perhaps my point is made. Granting these are two very
different poems—and very different poets—does this comparison of works which have been composed in the same
tradition of unmetered verse show that Mr. Ferlinghetti
has any awareness at all of English as a medium of sounds,
motions, accents? Or does it simply show what can happen
to a great style—Eliot's—when it has percolated through
forty years of mediocre sensibilities? Mr. Ferlinghetti
claims to write for the street, in the language of the street,
yet you can hear on any street in the country language
more beautifully and meaningfully and vigorously cadenced than this, even if you take into account the porcine
discontinuity of most American discourse. **"Junkman's
Obbligato"** is as flaccid and nerveless as putty. The first
requirement of any poetry is a respect for the capacities,
of language, the negative capacities, too, if you like, and
a sensitivity to its sounds and speeds. I detect no trace of
these in Mr. Ferlinghetti's verse. And what shall we say
about this unformed cynicism, this blatant, squashy irony?
Or about this look-what-I'm-doing-now degradation of
works and emblems which, in spite of it all, remain untouched? A child would probably know better. What
about this easy glorification of depravity? The point is that
the proof of glory is in the poem, in the wresting of it from
image and word. You don't get it from slovenly verse. And
besides, we have been through Mr. Ferlinghetti's world already, long, long ago, or so it now seems. Sentimentality,
fakery, prop cardboard slums on a Hollywood lot. It was
chicanery then, and it is now, too. I don't say much of our
reality isn't there for the writer who can deal with it truly,
but the junkman himself would be laughing if he knew
what Mr. Ferlinghetti was up to.

Second, what about street poetry, what about poetry and
jazz? I have listened to some of the recordings made by
Mr. Ferlinghetti and Mr. Rexroth with jazz groups, and
I find them no better than previous experiments with poetry and music. Edith Sitwell's, for instance. William Walton's music for *Façade* at least supported the verse; still,
one could not follow the reading without a text, and Dame
Edith's performances minus music were at least equally effective. In the case of the San Francisco experiments, there
are clearly two autonomous activities occurring simultaneously so that the hearer's attention is jerked from one
to the other in a perplexity of indecision: when the poetry
is good the jazz interferes with it; when the jazz is good
the poetry, though it can be partly shut out, remains a nuisance. The arts are separate, thank heaven; and if they
weren't it would be desirable to separate them. Which is
not to say that words and music may not be combined in
song. This is another case altogether, one that involves
special, now largely forgotten rules of procedure.

As for street poetry, it seems to me that a few truisms may
clear the air. (1) Popular poetry must be lively, musical,
rhythmical, iterative, the broadside ballad and today's advertising jingle being two obviously successful types. Mr.
Ferlinghetti's poetry, on the contrary, is, as I have said,
mostly tuneless, mostly arhythmic, and mostly, I imagine,
hard to remember. (2) Popular poetry, except for some
kinds of erotic verse, should possess a strong narrative
content. Mr. Ferlinghetti's has none at all. (3) Popular po-

etry must be as short as is consistent with the active development of the theme. Mr. Ferlinghetti is often rather long-
winded. (4) Popular poetry must be concrete. Mr. Ferlinghetti, though not abstruse by any means, is usually abstract; here he is far from his Objectivist associates. And
(5) popular poetry must contribute, at least supportively,
to the national, racial, or at any rate undifferentiatedly social myth. Mr. Ferlinghetti might argue with me about the
value of his poetry in this connection, but I find his attitudes so generally negative, in spite of his interspersed affirmations of poverty, sex, freedom, etc., that I don't see
how they could attract anything but a fringe audience of
sick souls and pseudo-sophisticates.

Finally, has "street poetry" ever been created by self-
conscious poets? Has it ever had anything at all to do with
literature or the literary world, as we use these terms? And
what conditions must be satisfied before the educated poet
can *honestly* undertake to write for an illiterate audience?

Probably I have said too much on this subject. Let me end
by agreeing wholly with those who deplore the hardening
of our literary tastes, the institutionalization of our literary life. We do indeed need new things in our poetry, we
need them desperately. But I wonder if we can be helped
appreciably by poets whose idea of the new is merely a re-
suscitation of squabbles that died thirty years ago. The
issue is a continuing one, they will say, the battle against
academicism is never won. True, but the avant-garde must
wage its fight in terms that are currently moving and significant. It must offer us a coherently revised image of ourselves in forms that derive rationally from the immediate
complex of art and experience. Above all, it must propose
a renewal of our contact with the permanent verities, not
a further estrangement. The ultimate weapon of the avant-
garde is common sense. (pp. 111-16)

> *Hayden Carruth, in a review of "A Coney Is-
> land of the Mind," in* Poetry, *Vol. XCIII, No.
> 2, November, 1958, pp. 111-16.*

Alan Dugan   (essay date 1962)

[*In the following excerpt, Dugan praises Ferlinghetti's
social and political insight as it is expressed in* Starting
from San Francisco.]

Mr. Ferlinghetti documents his claim to being an oral poet
by including, flapped in the back cover of his new book
[***Starting from San Francisco***], a 7" LP record of himself
reading his poems. . . . Oral poetry has to fit the speaker's voice. At its best it can be true of the poet, his audience, and their common situation. At its worst it can be
flashy or empty, since the poet can jazz up nonsense by
means of vivid performance and not tell, from his local audience's reaction, whether or not he is saying anything
worth repeating except as a party piece. Mr. Ferlinghetti's
verse is perfectly suited to his style of delivery, and his
style of delivery is effective and engaging. Free verse such
as his needs plenty of room for its organizational necessities: repetition, listings, a long looping flow that goes back
to its beginnings so as to make a rounded form. Take the
beginning of **"Hidden Door"** for example:

> Hidden door dead secret
>   which is Mother,
> Hidden door dead secret

which is Father
Hidden door dead secret
    of our buried life
Hidden door behind which man carries
    his footprints along the streets

The poem is too long to quote in full, but it does come
around to a revelation and a conclusion. He has the usual
American obsession, asking, "What is going on in America and how does one survive it?" His answer might be: By
being half a committed outsider and half an innocent Fool.
He makes jokes and chants seriously with equal gusto and
surreal inventiveness, using spoken American in a romantic, flamboyant manner. It is difficult for a guilty child to
grow up to be an innocent adult in this culture, so that
sometimes Mr. Ferlinghetti writes adolescently: **"Big Fat
Hairy Vision of Evil"** is one of his titles. It is equally difficult to follow Walt Whitman after a hundred years of industrialization in America, but when he combines his two
predilections the result, as in a long poem entitled **"Overpopulation,"** the result is new and fine. He treats this political problem with wit, insight, and frankness, and reads it
well on the record. . . .

Mr. Ferlinghetti is fascinated by politics, as his broadsides
prove. (There are four of them in the book, including
**"Tentative Description of a Dinner to Promote the Im-
peachment of President Eisenhower."** A fifth, **"Berlin,"**
is published as a separate pamphlet.) But he is interested
in politics while having an anti-political point of view, so
that the tension between these two attitudes produces a
new, third form. Political verse must be topical, bravely
stated, forceful, and built to last beyond the moment it
deals with. Mr. Ferlinghetti does this, but at the same time
he mocks politics, mocks the form, and asserts the prima-
cy of the anarchic individual as exemplified by himself as
speaker. In the broadside **"Berlin,"** for example, he deals
with the objective political crises of that city in terms of
the poet looking in Woolworth's for the right poem to
make about it and himself in time. (pp. 314-16)

*Alan Dugan, "Three Books, a Pamphlet, and
a Broadside," in* Poetry *Vol. C, No. 5, August
1962, pp. 310-19.*

John William Corrington   (essay date 1965)

[*In the excerpt below, Corrington compares Ferlinghetti's poetry to the work of such artists as Picasso and Ce-
zanne.*]

With the gradual ebb of publicity concerning "The Beat
Generation," it has become possible, in the last year or so,
to read the poetry of Lawrence Ferlinghetti as literature
rather than as a portion of an attenuated and faintly ludicrous social documentary. The "Beat" tag, so long an active element, arousing a surprising degree of partisanship
among otherwise astute readers, has lapsed at last into the
same kind of literary irrelevance as have such relatively
meaningless terms as "The Auden Circle" and "The Imagistes." Having survived the onslaughts of *Life* and the
Saturday Review, the praise of Kenneth Rexroth and the
blame of J. Donald Adams, this most recent of literary
phenomena and the figures connected with it have become
the proper matter of literary criticism. One can, with some
hope of objectivity, attempt to discover what meaningful

sound may persist in certain "Beat" writing, now that the
fury has subsided.

It becomes apparent, I think, to even the most casual reader, that those writers lumped together by news media and
popular reviewers under the "Beat" label are, in fact, as
distinct from one another as was Baudelaire from Rimbaud, Verlaine from Mallarmé. In the case of Ferlinghetti,
one finds it difficult to understand why he has been considered of a kind with his more celebrated contemporaries,
Allen Ginsberg and Gregory Corso. While there are
marked differences between Ginsberg's poetry and that of
Corso, a veritable chasm separates their work from Ferlinghetti's. If Ginsberg can be said to possess form, it is a
form based on rhetorical repetition—a form reminiscent
of Sears catalogues. Corso's shorter poems are loosely unified even considered as lyrics, and his long poems, for the
most part, make use of the same Whitmanesque periods
common to Ginsberg's "Howl." But in Ferlinghetti's poetry, one finds a consistent and subtly developed sense of
form based not upon rhetorical devices or repetition, but
on the analogies between poetry and painting; on the correspondences between written and graphic style; on the
metaphorical and actual unity between major art forms.

In some thirteen poems scattered through *Pictures of the
Gone World* and *A Coney Island of the Mind,* Ferlinghetti
makes constant reference to painters and sculptors, both
ancient and modern. Moreover, even in poems not specifically dealing with or mentioning art and artists, Ferlinghetti betrays his own post-war education in painting and
his dependence upon that background by an overwhelming reliance on visual imagery and by creating a series of
essentially graphic events which contain little of the ideational and narrative matter expected of a literary work.
An example of this nonconceptual poetry is **"poem 1"**
from *Pictures*. . . . Such a poem, when set against the
work of a poet like Dylan Thomas, whose whole artistic
orientation was essentially verbal, who clearly did not
move from image to language but rather conceived in
terms of language itself, becomes readily identifiable as a
work moving from a visual conception into the matrix of
poetic language. Perhaps a concurrent reading of **"poem
1"** from *Pictures* and Thomas's "Altarwise by owl-light"
will illustrate the profound distinction between visually
and verbally conceived writing.

Ferlinghetti, in his exploitation of the image almost bereft
of "idea" as such, follows rather closely upon modern theory developed by major painters. "Subject"—that which
a picture is *about*—is of far less significance than composition—what, in fact, because of the painter's shaping genius, the picture *is.* In a sense, the "subject," whether it
be a horse, a landscape or a human figure is essentially an
excuse for painting, and is hardly to be considered in valu-
ing the picture as a work of art. Speaking of Cézanne, Picasso and the other fathers of Modern Art, Maurice
Grosser says [in *The Painter's Eye*], " . . . their subject
was art itself—how pictures are built. Their aim was to
isolate the essential qualities of character and structure in
a picture which make it a work of art." (pp. 107-09)

By analogy, those poems of Ferlinghetti's which we are
discussing—like many of Mallarmé's, Pound's, Lorca's,
and Rimbaud's—are not concerned with ideas, themes,
narrations, conceptualizations, but rather with the representation of events and entities in such a way as to evoke

a response or a series of responses in the reader. After reading **"poem 1"** from *Pictures* it would seem difficult to explicate the poem except in terms of its graphic significance. It is a paean to woman, to unconscious sexuality, to the art of artlessness—but as a vehicle of idea (in the sense, say, that "Dover Beach" is a vehicle for Matthew Arnold's concepts) the poem would appear insignificant.

In **"poem 5"** from *Pictures,* Ferlinghetti speaks of

> . . . this man who was all eyes
> had no mouth
>   All he could do was show people
> what he meant
>   And it turned out
>   he claimed to be
>   a painter
>   But anyway
> this painter
>   who couldn't talk or tell anything
>   about what he
>   meant
>   looked like just about the happiest painter
>   in all the world
> standing there
>   taking it all "in"
>   and reflecting
> Everything
>   in his great big
>   Hungry Eye. . . .

Departing from the "pure poetry" we have been discussing, Ferlinghetti turns his hand to theoretical matters. This figure who has no mouth, who cannot tell, but must show his meaning, is representative of the painter—and, by logical extension, of the poet as well—who chooses to work outside the limitations of "subject" ordinarily expected and traditionally called for. I suspect the absence of a mouth in Ferlinghetti's "happiest painter" refers not to the muteness of painting, but rather to its refusal to limit its dealings to the logical and narrative, to the merely anecdotal. In this sense, the modern poet, like the painter, frequently has no mouth. Both take in the world through their "Hungry Eyes." But neither limits himself to phenomena: what is taken in is not simply reproduced on canvas or framed in words. The artist's eye is not, in Grosser's phrase, "the innocent eye of the camera." Rather, the world is dissected, sorted, manipulated, and recreated in terms of the artist's vision—which, a Hungry Eye indeed, devours in order to create.

It should be noted that . . . there are numerous figures antedating Ferlinghetti whose work, whether based in the same theory or not, bears considerable resemblance to the "pure poetry" found in *Pictures* and *Coney Island.* (pp. 109-11)

On this question of Ferlinghetti's antecedents among poets whose work was conceived and executed within the frame of modern painting's theory, [there is the example of Pablo Picasso]. . . . It would be difficult to find a piece of modern poetry more completely visual than this:

> fandango of shivering owls souse of evil-omended polyps scouring brush of hairs from priest's tonsures standing naked in the middle of the frying pan—placed upon ice cream cone of codfish fried in the scabs of his lead-ox heart—his mouth full of cinch-bug jelly of his words—sleighbells of the plate of snails braiding guts—little finger in erec-

tion neither grape nor fig—commedia dell'arte of poor weaving and dyeing of clouds—beauty creams from the garbage wagon—rape of maids in tears and in snivels—on his shoulder the shroud stuffed with sausages and mouths—rage distorting the outline of the shadow which flogs his teeth driven in the sand and the horse open wide to the sun which reads it to the flies that stitch to the knots of the net full of anchovies the sky-rocket of lilies. . . .

It is to be expected that a prose-poem by Pablo Picasso would be a flood of imagery. The poem was written during the Spanish Civil War as Picasso prepared a set of sketches to be called "The Dreams and Lies of Franco." It illustrates, with considerable power, a kind of reversal, a feedback from artist to poetry. As Ferlinghetti and his predecessors have drawn both method and conception from the graphic arts, so the most distinguished of modern painters makes use of poetry in order to sketch, as it were, a schema for drawings which he plans.

Perhaps none of Ferlinghetti's poems so fully exploits the method and the shape of a modern painting—and at the same time the form of Picasso's poem and subsequent drawings—as does his **"poem 6"** in *Pictures*. . . . It would seem clear that in Ferlinghetti's mind—and perhaps in Picasso's, too—there is no real or substantive distinction between the act of painting and that of making poetry. Technical differences are simply problems to be overcome—but the modern poem, like the modern painting, must be conceived in terms of composition, not in terms of subject matter. The poem is shaped by what Roger Fry [in his translation of Stephane Mallarmé's *Poems*] calls "poetical necessity"—the poem's form shapes its own requirements. The same holds true of painting. "I have never made trials or experiments," Picasso has said. "Whenever I had something to say, I have said it in the manner in which I felt it ought to be said." Thus we have a poet who calls his poems "Pictures," and a painter who "says" things with his brush.

Insofar as prose statement may be required, Ferlinghetti has not stinted in its use. Indeed, his most recent work has suffered from an almost journalistic flatness, a regrettable lack of the brilliant imagery found in *Pictures* and in much of *Coney Island.* But if the poetry of "reportage," in E. M. Forster's phrase, should fail to match his vision, Ferlinghetti has had at his command the further resources of the painter's eye and the painter's wide-ranging, inclusive theory. . . . If Marc Chagall, in **"poem 14"** from *Coney Island,* serves as an epitome of the painter (as does Picasso in [**"poem 24"**] in *Pictures:* "but that night I dreamt of Picasso / opening doors and closing exits / opening doors and closing exits in the world . . . "), then Lawrence Ferlinghetti may well stand as an epitome of the modern poet. Ferlinghetti, like Kenneth Patchen's "impatient explorer who invents a box in which all journeys may be kept," has ranged into the deep space beyond limiting canons of literature and has created a provocative and significant body of poetry which, while based in the tradition extending from the Symbolistes through Lorca, manipulating theory and technique born with modern painting, is nevertheless still experimental and tentative. Ferlinghetti has produced a poetry in which handling of object attempts to replace "subject" in significance, a poetry which must be apprehended and experienced as cultural event rather than as subject-verb-object reportage of "reality."

Perhaps Ferlinghetti himself has best described the sort of thing he has attempted. In **"poem 13"** from *Coney Island,* he tells how he would "paint" . . . "a different kind / of Paradise,"

> . . . there would be no anxious angels telling them
> how heaven is
> the perfect picture of
> a monarchy
> and there would be no fires burning
> in the hellish   holes below
> in which   I might have stepped
> nor any altars in the sky except
> fountains of imagination
> (pp. 113-16)

John William Corrington, "Lawrence Ferlinghetti and the Painter's Eye," in Nine Essays in Modern Literature, *edited by Donald E. Stanford, Louisiana State University Press, 1965, pp. 107-16.*

James A. Butler (essay date 1966)

[*In the following excerpt, Butler explores the artistry of Ferlinghetti's poetic devices, deeming such complexity incompatible with the writer's claim to be a "street poet."*]

The public first began to suspect Lawrence Ferlinghetti was a dirty old man in 1955, when he published through his own City Lights Press his poetic *Pictures of the Gone World.* This first volume identified Ferlinghetti with the "Beat Generation Poets"—Allen Ginsberg, Jack Kerouac, Gregory Corso, and others—none of whom a girl could comfortably bring home to meet the family. The public's dirty-old-man suspicions were heightened when Ferlinghetti was tried in a 1957 obscenity case for publishing Ginsberg's "Howl." Finally, Ferlinghetti's fame for filthiness was assured by a 1965 *Time* article describing a "happening" at the American Students and Artists Center in Montparnasse: "Beat Poet Lawrence Ferlinghetti intoned his latest work while a naked couple made love vertically in a burlap bag, black light playing on their shoulders."

It is tempting to merely categorize Ferlinghetti as a bush-league sick poet of a sick poetic movement, but several factors make this poet worthy of consideration. His major work, *A Coney Island of the Mind* (1958), is now in its twelfth printing and has sold 130,000 copies to rank near the top of contemporary poetic best-sellers. In addition, *Coney Island* was received as "highly readable and often very funny" by *The New York Times* and as having "something of the importance *The Waste Land* had in 1922," (*Library Journal*). Finally, if a man may be known by the company he keeps, it is significant that the 1965 Spoleto Festival of Two Worlds presented poetry readings by Russia's Yevgeny Yevtushenko, Stephen Spender, Ezra Pound, and Lawrence Ferlinghetti.

In the light of Ferlinghetti's popularity, it is necessary for the critic to determine whether the poet is a best-selling one because of his somewhat scandalous vocabulary and somewhat more scandalous activities, or whether there is intrinsic value in the poetry. The method of this paper is to first develop an evolving understanding of the poetic de-

vices of Ferlinghetti by examining selected instances. The poet's philosophy of a "street poetry" will next be discussed to determine whether Ferlinghetti accomplishes his end. After the above considerations, an attempt will be made to reconcile the dirty old man and the poet.

The first Ferlinghetti poem to be analyzed is from *Coney Island* ["Poem 25"]:

> Cast up
> the heart flops over
> gasping 'Love'
> a foolish fish which tries to draw
> its breath from flesh of air
>
> And no one there to hear its death
> among the sad bushes
> where the world rushes by
> in a blather of asphalt and delay

Perhaps the first thing that strikes the reader in the above poem by Ferlinghetti is the absence of traditional poetic devices: rhyme, meter, uniform left-hand margin. Ferlinghetti's free verse is, of course, indebted to such prosodic pioneers as Walt Whitman and especially William Carlos Williams. . . . In addition to being influenced by Williams' free verse, Ferlinghetti also shows in other poems that he has absorbed some of the visual effects of Williams; e.g., the line visually accentuating the meaning:

> And the way the bell-hop runs downstairs:
> ta tuck a
> ta tuck a
> ta tuck a
> ta tuck a
> ta tuck a
>
> (*Paterson*—W. C. Williams)
>
> like
> a
> ball
> bounced
> down steps
>
> (*Coney Island,* ["Poem 22"])

But these influences on Ferlinghetti's prosody, although important, are not dominant; it is rather the "Projective Verse" of Charles Olson that has not only influenced Ferlinghetti, but has become the new poetics of the new poetry.

Charles Olson's "Projective Verse" first appeared in *Poetry New York* of November 3, 1950. Summary of this complex essay is difficult, but basically Olson says that "form is never more than an extension of content." The syllable, not the foot or meter, is the building block of poetry. The syllables thus do not combine into a foot, but into a line. The length of this line comes only from "the *breathing* of the man who writes at the moment he writes." Meter and rhyme are therefore unimportant in the line length; the line is determined by those places in which the poet takes, and wants the reader to take, a breath. Ferlinghetti has much the same philosophy of sound. . . . (pp. 115-17)

The application of the "projective verse" theory is evident in the first poem selected for analysis. The breathing stops are so placed as to emphasize various lines. The first line, for example, "Cast up," receives very strong stress from the breath taken both before and after. Other short lines also receive stress through breathing: "gasping 'Love'", and "among the sad bushes." On the other hand, the longer lines pound quickly, partly because of the strong, regular, iambic rhythm and partly because of the harsh, spitting *t*'s, *b*'s, *d*'s, *and f*'s:

> a *f*oolish *f*ish which *t*ries *to d*raw
> i*t*s *b*reath *f*rom *f*lesh o*f* air

Throughout the poem, the line length and breathing are not used randomly as may first appear, but to accentuate the meaning.

Ferlinghetti does not, in spite of unconventional metrics, operate independently of poetic tradition. His entire poem is, of course, a metaphor comparing a fish out of water with a heart in love. The lines quoted immediately above represent a highly sophisticated use of metaphor: a heart in love that tries to exist from flesh is as helpless as a fish gasping for air. On the audio level, Ferlinghetti in this poem shows his competence at matching sound and meaning. One example of this skill is the explosive sounds (*t*'s, *b*'s, *d*'s, and *f*'s) used in the line above which through the explosion of sound, then unstressed syllable, then another explosion suggest breathlessness and gasping for air. "Gasping" in 1.3 is in itself onomatopoetic. The only true rhyme in the poem, the feminine rhyme of bushes (1.7) and rushes (1.8), draws our attention to the pun on the meaning of rushes as plants. Finally, the last line plays with the *a* sound in a manner reminiscent of the slant rhymes of Yeats, Auden, Thomas, and Owen. The *a*'s are all short vowels and move quickly to suggest the speed of which the poet speaks until the last, long *a* of "delay" slows the tempo:

> in *a* bl*a*ther of *a*sph*a*lt *a*nd del*a*y.

We have seen in this poem how Ferlinghetti works with a modern prosody based on Whitman, Williams, and Olson. The poet is, in addition, a master of audio effects and in matching sound and meaning. Ferlinghetti also seems to delight in the pun by deliberately drawing attention to it. [**"Poem 14"**] (*Coney Island*) should reinforce those conclusions and add others:

> Don't let that horse
>   eat that violin
> cried Chagall's mother
>   But he
>   kept right on
>   painting
>
> And became famous
> And kept on painting
>   The Horse With Violin In Mouth
> And when he finally finished it
> he jumped up upon the horse
>   and rode away
>   waving the violin
>
> And then with a low bow gave it
> to the first naked nude he ran across
>
> And there were no strings
>   attached

Here Ferlinghetti is seen in a more playful vein than in the previous selection. The projective verse is again used for startling emphasis; e.g. "painting" in 1. 6 and "attached" in 1. 17. But the onomatopoetic use of syllable is not as prominent in this more humorous offering. The lines are kept quick-moving—in accordance with the light tone of the poem—by a majority of short vowels and short lines.

The reference by Ferlinghetti to something such as Chagall's "The Horse With Violin in Mouth" is typical of the poet. Much of Ferlinghetti's work is predicated on the reader's familiarity with culture, both past and present. In the twenty-nine short poems of *Coney Island of the Mind,* the poet refers, directly or indirectly, to Goya, Cervantes, Thoreau, Keats, T. S. Eliot, Hieronymous Bosch, Dante, Kafka, Longfellow, Stockton ("The Lady or the Tiger?"), Cellini, Picasso, Hemingway, Shakespeare, Proust, Lorca, Nichols (*Abie's Irish Rose*), Tolstoy, Freud, and Joyce. Sometimes the entire meaning of a Ferlinghetti poem is based on the reader's ability to recognize a famous line out of context, e.g., Keats' "silent upon a peak in Darien." Obviously, this heavy reliance on cultural allusions somewhat limits Ferlinghetti's audience and will have major implications in regard to his "street poetry."

Ferlinghetti has a strong sense of humor as is evident both in this poem and in several others, notably one which describes the secular excitement of the erecting of a Saint Francis statue, with all the reporters and workers and Italians, "while no birds sang." In the Chagall poem, Ferlinghetti relies on the pun for humorous effect: "bow" meaning both a violin's bow and a bending of the body; "ran across" meaning both run under the horse's hooves and met in passing; and, "no strings attached" referring to the violin and to a gift. The linking of two synonymous words to create an enhanced meaning is also a favorite Ferlinghetti trick. In this poem, he uses "naked nude" for double emphasis; elsewhere he employs such figures as "sperm seed." By such puns and double emphases, Ferlinghetti is clearly trying to combat American semiliteracy, where all read but few stop to understand. Another method this poet uses to stop the reader in his tracks and make him go back to think is the twisting of a familiar saying so that it sounds much the same but means far more. Of several dozen examples, representative effects of this kind include the following: drugged store cowboys; cinemad matrons; unroman senators; conscientious non-objectors; [Christ hanging on the cross] looking real Petered out; My country tears of thee; I hear America singing / in the yellow pages; televised Wise Men / praised the Lord Calvert Whiskey; [Santa Claus] bearing sacks of Humble Gifts from Saks Fifth Avenue.

This second poem thus clearly reveals two more characteristics of Ferlinghetti's work: 1) The poet is heavily dependent on cultural allusions; and, 2) the poet attempts his humorous effects through puns, double emphasis, and changed clichés. (pp. 117-19)

With some idea of Ferlinghetti's characteristics in mind, the philosophy of the poet will now be considered in order to determine whether he reaches his personally-set goals. This philosophy was quoted in *Poetry* of November, 1958 [see Carruth's excerpt above]:

> I have been working toward a kind of *street poetry* . . . to get poetry out of the inner esthetic sanctum and out of the classroom into the street. The poet has been contemplating his navel too long, while the world walks by. The printing press has made poetry so silent that we've forgotten the power of poetry as oral messages. The sound of the

street-singer and the Salvation Army speaker is not to be scorned. . . .

In evaluating Ferlinghetti's success, or lack of it, with poetry for all, three characteristics of "street poetry" should be considered. First, poetry for all the people should be *lively, rhythmic,* and *iterative.* The advertising jingle would be an example of those traits, as would Vachel Lindsay's successful "popular poetry":

> Booth led boldly with his big bass drum—
> (Are you washed in the blood of the Lamb?)
> The Saints smiled gravely and they said: "He's come."
> (Are you washed in the blood of the Lamb?)

Second, popular poetry should be *narrative* as in the ballad or in Lindsay's poem narrating General Booth entering heaven. Third, poetry for all should contain allusions *familiar* to nearly all.

Consideration of Ferlinghetti's poetry in regard to those three points shows definitely that his lines are not "street poetry." In the first place, Ferlinghetti's poetry is mostly tuneless, arhythmic, and hard to remember. Without the printing press, the heavy beat, repetitiveness, and alliteration of Lindsay's lines would make them easy to remember. In contrast, the following lines by Ferlinghetti offer

Ferlinghetti during a reading of Coney Island of the Mind, *October 1959.*

little aid to memorization and are hardly likely to be on the tip of everyone's tongue:

> We squat upon the beach of love
>   among Picasso mandolins struck full of sand
>   and buried catspaws that know no sphinx
>   and picnic papers
>   dead crabs' claws
>   and starfish prints
>
>   (*Coney Island*—["poem 24"])

Secondly, few of Ferlinghetti's poems have a narrative content, as the representative poems selected for analysis show. In regard to the third requirement—familiar allusions—the twenty literary and artistic references mentioned above of this paper are allusions generally specialized to the more widely-read of the populace. Indeed, if an entire poem hangs on a line from Keats or a reference to Kafka, it is not a "street poem."

There is one other trait sometimes found in popular poetry—the erotic—that leads to the consideration of Ferlinghetti as a dirty old man. As might be expected of a dirty old man, Ferlinghetti places prominently last in *Coney Island* a poem that maintains, in a style and vocabulary similar to the conclusion of *Ulysses,* that all is sex and sex is all. Nevertheless, the reputation of Ferlinghetti as an erotic poet is exaggerated—only five of the twenty-nine poems of *Coney Island* have sexual themes. In spite of such description of himself as "the poet obscenely seeing," Ferlinghetti's poems do not show as a dominant trait the ribaldness that to many seems to characterize his personal life. (pp. 121-22)

Thus Ferlinghetti is both dirty old man *and* poet. But the poet is far too gifted to let himself be dominated or destroyed by the dirty old man. The time has come for Ferlinghetti to abandon his "beat" themes and his "beat" vocabulary: "square-type, cool, king-cat," etc. *A Coney Island of the Mind* should be remembered as the early work of an excellent and universal poet and not as the best work of a "beat poet." The poet once wrote:

> I am a social climber
> climbing downward
> and the descent is difficult

The *ascent* into excellence is too near for Ferlinghetti to climb downward into that morass populated by dirty old men and "beat poets." (pp. 122-23)

> *James A. Butler, "Ferlinghetti: Dirty Old Man?" in* Renascence, *Vol. XVIII, No. 3, Spring, 1966, pp. 115-123.*

Jonathan Williams   (essay date 1968)

[*Williams is an American poet, essayist, and publisher. In the excerpt below, he expresses dissatisfaction with* Starting from San Francisco, *suggesting that Ferlinghetti too readily falls into "easy vulgarity" in this work and thus fails to realize his full poetic potential.*]

I remember reviewing Lawrence Ferlinghetti's first book [*Pictures of a Gone World*] back in 1956. I liked it, a kind of zany Prévert-Poulenc sort of book, and I said it was full of "garrulous, light pleasures." Which I still say. His course has been the very opposite of my own. One of his

books [*A Coney Island of the Mind*] has sold 300,000 copies and mine usually sell 537, so, again perhaps I am in no
position to argue, except to note an increasing dissatisfaction with the too easy vulgarity into which he has led himself and his witless readers. Real jivy, real groovy, all
that—but ultimately kind of stupid. Like those bloody
Russians, you fill ball fields with rabid poetry lovers and
you got to come on like both Billy Graham and Rabbi
Chancre. . . .

Ferlinghetti, who is a bright, bright, bright man insisting
on sounding stupid, wows the college girls and boys with
that sneaky line from Tom Wolfe (like the only one they
know, etc..), the two lines from Dylan Thomas, one from
Yeats, a grab from Ginsberg for kicks—it is an amalgam
that makes me very gloomy since he knows so much better. Maybe it only seems worse now because people like
Paul McCartney, [Bob] Dylan, Simon & Garfunkel, and
Leonard Cohen write such very good lyrics and know everything.

"The situation in the West Followed by a Holy Proposal"
is the only poem in *Starting From San Francisco* that
finds the poet up to what he was, and what he was was,
one hopes, only the start. On the jacket he notes he finds
the poems just "stumbling thru the underbrush toward
what I hope will be some higher form of poetry." I wish
him well, not just as some petulant competitor and odd-
sounding friend, but as a poet also trying to light up the
language. He can do many things, which means he has to
climb the mountain and wave goodbye to the Bennington
girls. I may be coming on deaf, dumb and blind, but that
is what I find here.

> *Jonathan Williams, "Stumbling through the
> Underbrush," in* The New York Times Book
> Review, *July 21, 1968, p. 4.*

Walter Sutton   (essay date 1973)

[*In the excerpt below, Sutton makes a connection between Ferlinghetti's poetry and Surrealist painting, noting as well the influence of hallucinogenic drugs on the
poet's writing.*]

Strongly influenced by painting and music, Ferlinghetti
combines in his verse fragmented discontinuous imagery
reminiscent of Dada and Surrealism and a syncopated
jazzlike rhythm achieved largely through an interaction of
grammatical parallelism and interrupted broken lines. His
short staggered lines often suggest a debt to [William Car-
los] Williams, while the longer parallel verses of his later
"visionary" poems reveal his identification with the tradition of Whitman—though with a difference.

The best known of Ferlinghetti's early books are *Pictures
of the Gone World* (1955) and *A Coney Island of the Mind*
(1958). Art and artists provide the subjects of many of the
poems. The first in *A Coney Island* describes Goya's vision
of humanity and asserts its validity for the present as well
as the past:

> In Goya's greatest scenes we seem to see
>   the people of the world
>   exactly at the moment when
>   they first attained the title of
>   'suffering humanity'

> They writhe upon the page
>   in a veritable rage
>   of adversity

>   Heaped up
>   groaning with babies and bayonets
>   under cement skies
>   . . . .
>   it is as if they really still existed
> And they do. . . .

In ["poem 5"] of *Pictures of the Gone World,* Ferlinghetti
makes much the same point, on a different subject, when
he comments on Joaquín Sarolla's paintings of women "in
their picture hats / stretched upon his canvas beaches" as
beguiling the Spanish Impressionists. "And were they
fraudulent pictures / of the world / the way the light
played on them / creating illusions of love?" No, the
speaker answers: their "reality" is almost as real as his
own memory of "today."

In these appeals to art, Ferlinghetti does not make use of
the paintings of an earlier time as a resource for his own
poetic technique. Instead, he extracts "meanings" that
square with his own outlook and uses his characterizations of the paintings to enforce statements that are essentially didactic.

Ferlinghetti explains that his title *A Coney Island of the
Mind,* taken from Henry Miller, expresses the way he felt
about the poems when he wrote them—"as if they were,
taken together, a kind of Coney Island of the mind, a kind
of circus of the soul." The general effect is of a kaleidoscopic view of the world and of life as an absurd carnival
of discontinuous sensory impressions and conscious reflections, each with a ragged shape of its own but without
any underlying thematic unity or interrelationship. To
this extent the collection suggests a Surrealistic vision. But
it differs in that meanings and easily definable themes can
be found in most of the individual poems, even when the
idea of meaninglessness is the central concern.

In ["poem 23"] of *Pictures,* the emphasis is on the *unreality* of art and experience (in contrast to the theme of the
poems on Goya and Sarolla):

> Dada would have liked a day like this
>   with its various very realistic
>   unrealities

The poem ends with an impression of the funeral of a
dancer which gives the poet the opportunity to play on the
word *Dada* in ways that suggest associations with the aesthetic movement of that name, with a child's prattle, and
with Hemingway's nihilistic *Nada:*

>   and her last lover lost
>   in the unlonely crowd
>   and its dancer's darling baby
>   about to say Dada
>   and its passing priest
>   about to pray
>   Dada. . . .

The idea of this poem is more consistent with Ferlinghetti's basic viewpoint than those on Goya and Sarolla, since
its appeal to Dada implies the failure of communication
and meaning in both social forms and language. In ["poem
10"] of *Pictures,* Ferlinghetti comments on the failure of
language to approximate reality and gives his opinion that

the correspondence of word and thing is an impossibility—an attitude in keeping with the premises of his later "visionary" poetry.

Ferlinghetti is a lively and often interesting but uneven poet. He has a weakness for puns that sometimes leads to a cuteness like that of Cummings's less successful poems. Ferlinghetti also has difficulty in maintaining intensity. Some of his more prosaic verse has a Sandburgian flatness, as when, in poem five of *A Coney Island,* he writes about Jesus in hip slang.

In the more recent poems of *Starting from San Francisco* (1961; revised, 1967) and *The Secret Meaning of Things* (1969), there is a deepening sense of social and political disillusionment, in keeping with the mood of the decade, and a compensatory impulse toward drug-induced visionary experience.

The Secret Meaning of Things begins with **"Assassination Raga,"** inspired by the horror of the political murders of the 1960s, and proceeds through five other long poems often marked by a disillusioned treatment of a number of Whitman's visionary themes. In **"Through the Looking Glass,"** Whitman's "Passage to India" becomes a flight on "LSD Airlines" into a realm of "ecstatic insanity." **"After the Cries of the Birds"** combines the judgment of the bankruptcy of the progressive American dream with the observation that when the "Westward march of civilization" comes to a dead stop on the shores of the Pacific, there is "no place to go but In." The idea of an enforced introversion points to what Ferlinghetti seems to regard as a necessary connection between an unendurable social and political reality and an escapist art focused on an inner world of psychedelic vision. Though not generally shared by contemporary poets, this view is typical of the Beat writers and their followers. It is perhaps the most completely pessimistic modern expression of the Romantic visionary tradition, because the inner world of psychedelic hallucination, in contrast to that of the earlier Romantic vision, is essentially meaningless and solipsistic. (pp. 184-87)

> *Walter Sutton, "The Revolution Renewed: Contemporary Poetry," in his* American Free Verse: The Modern Revolution in Poetry, *New Directions Books, 1973, pp. 168-212.*

Crale D. Hopkins   (essay date 1974)

[*In the following excerpt, Hopkins first endeavors to disentangle Ferlinghetti from "the Beat-poet stereotype" and then offers a laudatory appraisal of the poet's overall body of work.*]

In the middle 1950s there were some experimental movements in poetry which soon got caught up in the publicity and subsequent reaction surrounding the discovery of the Beat Generation. Spreads in *Life* magazine, San Francisco, Venice West, movies such as *The Wild Ones,* Jack Kerouac's novels, marijuana, and jazz were all thrown together in the general characterization of Beat, and the whole thing became a subject of much discussion until matters of greater concern on even closer fronts forced themselves into view in the early 1960s. Vietnam, Free Speech, Free Love, Hippies, Yippies, and Heroin all made

it seem surprising that anyone had been much startled by bearded bongo players and shouting poets. (p. 59)

During the period when the Beats were being greatly debated, any new poetry that appeared to be in that camp was often dismissed immediately on that basis; and since the question is no longer vital, it no longer receives much attention. Some poets have escaped the stigma to a degree, such as Brother Antoninus and Gary Snyder, and others have become culture heroes, such as Allen Ginsberg. Lawrence Ferlinghetti has done neither of these things, yet he does deserve further disentanglement from the old Beat-poet characterization. His poetry cannot be dismissed either as protest polemic or as incoherently personalized lyric. His craftsmanship, thematics, and awareness of the tradition justify a further consideration. (pp. 59-60)

The subject of the doctoral thesis Ferlinghetti wrote at the University of Paris was "The Symbolic City in Modern Literature." His poetry reflects this acquaintance with modern European and American literature, and this constitutes the first point at which Ferlinghetti departs from the Beat stereotype. In an article in [*Partisan Review,* Spring, 1958] Norman Podhoretz attacks Beat literature on several grounds, one being that the "primitivism of the Beat Generation serves first of all as a cover for an anti-intellectualism so bitter that it makes the average American's hatred of eggheads seem positively benign. There may have been some degree of truth to this in many instances, but the poetry of Ferlinghetti is not one. In his first collection, *Pictures of The Gone World,* there are references to Praxiteles, Dante, Yeats, Holderlin, and suggestions of Shakespeare and Rimbaud. In *A Coney Island Of The Mind* many of the poems turn upon the recognition of a literary allusion: **"Poem 2"** ends, "with mild surprise / silent upon a peak / in Darien." A second allusion to Keats (a less than typical poet of the post-Eliot/Pound world) is in **"Poem 6,"** when the installation of a statue of St. Francis is being contrasted with the absence of any animal life, and the phrase "where no birds sing" is used as a refrain, echoing "And no birds sing" of "La Belle Dame Sans Merci." Keats comes to mind again in **"Poem 10,"** "a thing of beauty is a joy." The structure of **"Junkman's Obligate"** is built around references to "The Lovesong of J. Alfred Prufrock" and there are additional allusions in the collection to the works of Shakespeare, Wordsworth, A. E. Housman, Yeats, Joyce, Beckett, Gertrude Stein and others. These references and allusions are not used with the intent of satirizing the authors; anti-academic or literary satire in Ferlinghetti is limited and of the mildest tone. . . . Clearly, then, in Ferlinghetti's poetry there is no bitter anti-intellectualism but rather a knowledge and appreciation of traditional literary materials which are integrated into his own verse.

A second generalization has it that all Beat literature is either crippled by disengagement and a poverty of feeling (as Podhoretz charges) or, at the opposite pole, by being limited to "a cry of rage and despair" as Charles Glicksberg charges in a "post mortem" assessment in [*Southwest Review,* Autumn 1960]. Ferlinghetti, however, wrote some of the most sensitive lyrics of the last twenty years. In *A Coney Island Of The Mind,* **"Poem 19"** is in part a criticism of the usual Beat stance, bemoaning

> this unshaved today
> > with its derisive rooks

that rise above dry trees
                    and caw and cry
        and question every other
                    spring and thing

["Poem 20" and "Poem 26"] are also fine lyrics. There are certainly poems of "protest" by Ferlinghetti; but they are all characterized by an ironic tone totally devoid of rage and despair. In *Pictures Of The Gone World*, "Poem 25," "The world is a beautiful place / to be born into," is a gently ironic poem which lists a number of flaws in the beautiful world, "segregations / and congressional investigations / and other constipations" but concludes:

Yes the world is the best of all
                        for a lot of such things as
        making the fun scene
                        and making the love scene
                        ***
        Yes
            but then right in the middle of it
                            comes the smiling
                            mortician.

The protest pieces in *A Coney Island Of The Mind* are largely the "Oral Messages" which are quite restrained, particularly in light of the fact that they were being performed in front of live audiences. They are characteristically a blend of quiet satire and tethered hope. (pp. 61-4)

Ferlinghetti's most recent work, written in an era of violent protest, continues to maintain a balanced tone. Even "Assassination Raga" in *The Secret Meaning of Things* (1968), written after the death of Robert Kennedy, and *Tyrannus Nix?* (a prose piece, 1970) are not polemical, abusive, or raging.

It can be seen from this review that Ferlinghetti does not conform to the Beat-poet stereotype. He is neither anti-intellectual, emotionally disengaged (a point he touches upon himself in "Statements on Poetics" at the end of Donald Allen's book [see Further Reading list]), nor is he a mere voice of protest. With Ferlinghetti it has been useful to begin by establishing what he is not; a detailed consideration of the achievement of his poetry will establish what he is.

The first published work, *Pictures Of The Gone World,* is largely composed of poems of lyric observation. The word "gone" in the title implies in its 50s slang sense that they are "hip" or "groovy" visions of the world, but it also suggests the past, the world that is gone. Thus there is one group of poems that deal with novel insights into the world, such as "Poem 13," "It was a face which darkness could kill"; 15, "funny fantasies are never so real as old style romances"; 18, "London"; 22, "crazy / to be alive in such a strange / world"; or 23, "Dada would have liked a day like this." Some of these are satires on various aspects of modern life, such as "Poem 18," about a model who takes off her clothes once and finds that there is literally *nothing* underneath—she only exists by her apparel; so she "gave up modeling / and forever after / slept in her clothes." Others are surrealistic portraits, which can be quite penetrating:

Yes Dada would have died for a day like this
            with its sweet street carnival
        and its too real funeral
            just passing through it

with its real dead dancer
        so beautiful and dumb
    in her shroud
            and her last lover lost
    in the unlonely crowd
            and its dancers darling baby
about to say Dada
        and its passing priest
about to pray
            Dada
            and offer his so transcendental
            apologies
Yes Dada would have loved a day like this
        with its not so accidental analogies

Characteristically, ["Poem 23"] uses the short broken lines alternatingly to slow the eye and produce a detached ironic effect emphasized by the alliteration and internal rhyme. The poem ends tellingly on the dangling word "analogies," beautifully preceded by "apologies" and the completed multiple rhyme of "transcendental-accidental." These devices, and the puns on Dada, are typical of Ferlinghetti's method in presenting an ironic insight into the incongruities of life.

The second group of poems referred to above are those that deal with the past. These are personal lyrics, placed in Brooklyn, Paris, and San Francisco. "Poem 11" pictures a small epiphany of childhood, the firemen hosing down the street in summer. "Poem 4" is set in Paris: "couples going nude into the sad water / in the profound lasciviousness of spring / in an algebra of lyricism / which I am still deciphering." The "algebra of lyricism" proves to be a continuing concern of Ferlinghetti's. (pp. 64-6)

Several other poems in the collection which are not in these general groups deserve consideration because they prefigure elements that are later merged into major themes. The role of art in the question of illusion and and reality is involved in several poems. "Poem 6" contrasts the passing squabble of the world with the timeless, entranced art of the Luxembourg gardens; ["Poem 8" and "Poem 27"] deal with the "reality" of art. The first poem in the collection prefigures the death vision in "He" (*Starting From San Francisco*). It is a description of a woman hanging up sheets on a rooftop clothesline high above a harbor. The sheets are equated with sails in the wind, and "wind" becomes a *double entendre* as they are blown about and cling to her. The poem ends "while in the reachless seascape spaces / between the blown white shrouds / stand out the bright streamers / to kingdom come." These last lines direct the poem as a vision of ultimate death. "Shrouds" have a double meaning here, as well as "kingdom come"; and the ships invoke the traditional voyage image of death.

The poetry of Ferlinghetti's second, and most famous collection, *A Coney Island Of The Mind,* is more surrealistic and has more satiric social observation. The ultimate surrealist vision of the failed American Dream is in "Poem 3":

America
        with its ghost towns and empty Ellis Islands
    and its surrealist landscape of
                    mindless prairies
                    supermarket suburbs

steamheated cemeteries
cinerama holy days
and protesting cathedrals
a kissproof world of plastic toiletseats tampax and taxis
drugged store cowboys and las vegas virgins
disowned indians and cinemad matrons
unroman senators and conscientious non, objectors
and all the other fatal shorn-up fragments
of the immigrant's dream come too true
and mislaid
among the sunbathers

Some might object that this is not really poetry; it is by any definition an effective piece of work in the Dadaist-surrealist tradition, showing considerable craft. The accuracy of the items heaped together is telling; again, the mocking alliteration (toiletseats tampax and taxis) and the multiple rhyme (prairies-cemeteries) underscore the satire. The puns on drugstore, vestal virgin, and cinema underline the pattern of those lines, which name two merely foolish types (drugstore cowboys and vestal virgins) now become disgusting; then two more, one no longer dignified figure and one never dignified character; then two who are the opposite of two desirable types. The last four lines include an allusion to Eliot (shorn-up fragments) using Eliot's method, which Ferlinghetti does frequently in this collection.

A number of poems take up the theme of illusion and reality—of surrealism itself—and the role of art in that scheme. In **"Poem 15"** the poet is described as balancing on a high-wire: "he's the super realist / who must perforce perceive / taut truth / before the taking of each stance or step." The goal of the high-wire walk is "that still higher perch" where Beauty resides. In **"Poem 16"** beauty, "heavenly weather" becomes identified with the "Mystery of Existence," the "Kafka's Castle" above the world with "labyrinthine wires" radiating from it. "Its blind approach baffles / . . . Yet away around on the far side / like the stage door of a circus tent / is a wide rent in the battlements where even elephants / waltz thru." The ultimate beauty, the Mystery of Existence, can only be reached by the proper approach. Only the super realist who perceives the taut truth of the wire, the path, has any chance of reaching the mystery, the "imagined mystery." The way to this sort of route is mentioned in **"Poem 11"**: "a land that Buddha came upon / from a different direction / It is a wild white next / in the true mad north of introspection." If a "different direction" is required, if true north is "mad," then the super realist must be the *surrealist.*

Ferlinghetti's last poems on this theme are in *Starting From San Francisco.* "Flying Out Of It" is a vision of spinning past heaven among the galaxies: "Death swings / its dumb bell / I'll catch it? . . . Ah there's a slit / to slither through / into eternity / . . . cannot make it / Pied Piper's cave / clangs shut." The abstract diction, cold tone, and short, three or four word triple-spaced lines combine to suggest that the failure to pierce through is due to a lack of that super realism, that mad north of introspection. . . . The final poem on this theme is **"He,"** a portrait of a prophet of the ultimate reality, the surrealist who has achieved "the mad eye of the fourth person singular." The "fourth person singular" is the position above reality, seeing you, him, and himself also.

For he has come at the end of the world

and he is the flippy flesh made word
and he speaks the word he hears in his flesh
and the word is Death

The word "Death" is then printed twenty-eight times spread variously across the page in groups of one or two. The string of poems dealing with the "Mystery of Existence" terminates with this naturalistic conclusion that only death lies beyond reality.

Related to reality and the fourth person singular is the problem of love. A great deal of Ferlinghetti's poetry deals with that subject in one way or another, and it early involves the question of reality, the ideal versus the actual. *Pictures Of The Gone World,* **["Poem 19"]** and **"Poem 21"** in *A Coney Island Of The Mind* are both about girls whose conceptions of the ideal clash with what they apparently find in reality—and they both withdraw from the world. In these poems the clash of the ideal and the actual is not unavoidable—it emanates from the preconceptions of the characters involved. This theme has been discussed at length in an article on Ferlinghetti's novel *Her* [by L. A. Ianni, in *Wisconsin Studies* in *Contemporary Literature,* Summer, 1967]. This writer argues that in *Her* the story concerns the inability of the central character to achieve the viewpoint of the "fourth person singular," the position above reality that affords insight. The two poems mentioned above illustrate this point—that the man of limited vision will not recognize the importance of love in both its sensual and spiritual qualities.

The person with the viewpoint of the "fourth person singular" realizes that the world is "unreal" because it is not permanent—and there is nothing beyond. The values to be cultivated in this "unreal" world are therefore of paramount importance, love perhaps being the most important. The problem is to realize this and to comprehend love in its fullest sense. (pp. 66-70)

"Poem 24" [of *A Coney Island of the Mind*] depicts a landscape covered with the refuse of love: the beach that is the brink of the ocean of love. Lingering too long on the edge, the effort to float out is disastrous: "it is deeper / and much later / than we think / and all goes down / and our lovebuoys fail us / And we drink and drown." The poem turns on the echo from "The Lovesong of J. Alfred Prufrock," as the people of this poem have lingered in indecision too long and can no longer achieve love.

Ferlinghetti admires D. H. Lawrence and, like Lawrence, the love he envisions is the ultimate fusion of passion and spirituality. In **"Poem 25"** the image of "Cast up / the heart flops over / gasping 'Love' / a foolish fish which tries to draw / its breath from flesh of air" suggests that love divorced from the flesh, the sensual, is futile. The lines in **["Poem 26"]** "breathing breasts / and secret lips / and (ah) / bright eyes" (a possible echo of the last line of Gerard Manley Hopkins' "God's Grandeur") emphasize the eyes, the spiritual reflectors. In his take-off . . . on the end of Joyce's *Ulysses* on love and sex, he utilizes lines from *Four Quartets:* "that's the way it always ends and the fire and the rose are one," the fire suggesting passion and the rose spirituality.

In *Starting From San Francisco* several further notes are struck on the theme of the primitive, earthy, Lawrencian sort of love that Ferlinghetti sees as salvation in the unreal world. **"Overpopulation"** . . . , is a poem that, along with

"Underwear" earned Ferlinghetti his reputation as one of the poets of nakedness. The poem narrates the incredulous reading of a newspaper which seems to be reporting all sort of impossibly good news: "I must have misunderstood something / in this story / there must be a misprint / in this paper / . . . The nations have decided / it says here / to abolish themselves at last / It's been decided at the highest level / and at the lowest level / to return to a primitive society." This new society will be rid of modern civilization's artificial imposition on natural man. Realizing that "Life is intoxicating / but can't go on and on," "Medicine must be abolished / so people can die / when they're supposed to." Along with ceasing the unnatural prolonging of life, the authentic sexual experience will be restored: "We've got to get naked again / it says here / . . . Sex without love wears gay deceivers." The attainment of real love, then, is the only way of cheating death: "None of us will ever die / as long as this goes on."

Other than the occasional poems and a few purely whimsical pieces, most of Ferlinghetti's poetry is concerned with his perceptions of the "unreal," ephemeral world and the kind of love that he sees as the only salvation. **"After the Cries of the Birds"** in *The Secret Meaning Of Things* is in part an apocalyptic vision of the triumph of that true love. The vehicle for these ideas, the poetry itself, must be viewed in the proper perspective. The more lyrical pieces, such as **"Poem 20"** of *A Coney Island Of The Mind* . . ., use the traditional devices of rhyme, metrical arrangement, and harmonious alliteration. Rhyme, particularly multiple rhyme, and exaggerated alliteration are employed often in the satirical pieces for mocking and ironic effect. Other than the utilization of these basic poetic effects, though, Ferlinghetti's poetry departs sharply from conventional verse. In the radically different line arrangements his debt to William Carlos Williams has been noted. These are sometimes designed to imitate the action described, as in **"Poem 22"** of *A Coney Island Of The Mind*

> like
>   a
>   ball
>   bounced
>   down steps

or in **"The Great Chinese Dragon,"** *Starting From San Francisco,* where the poem is printed in continuous single-spaced lines beginning at the middle of the page with every seventh or eighth line capitalized and starting at the far left margin. This represents visually the body and many legs of the canvas dragon, with people walking inside supporting it, used in Chinese celebrations. In most of the poems up through *A Coney Island Of The Mind,* though, the spacing on the page is used to lend an ironic tone to the verse and to isolate and emphasize certain words or phrases. From *Starting From San Francisco* onwards he tends to use more continuously and evenly arranged line lengths.

Ferlinghetti's poetry receives much of its force from its diction. The more lyrical poems avoid conventional poetic language and use common speech arranged to achieve its effect through unique juxtapositions and striking but hauntingly familiar images. The more declamatory poems mingle bizarre words, vulgar colloquialisms and literary tags to create a surrealistic, multi-dimensional quality: "pantomimic parrots pierrots castrate disaster / . . .

while cakewalkers and carnival hustlers / all gassed to the gills / strike playbill poses" (*A Coney Island Of The Mind,* ["Poem 17"]); "He is a cat who creeps at night / and sleeps his buddhahood in the violet hour / and listens for the sound of three hands about to clap / . . . He is a talking asshole on a stick." (**"He"** in *Starting From San Francisco*). Ferlinghetti finally introduces most popular four-letter words into his poetry, carrying Wordsworth's dictum to its logical conclusion. It should be said that they are not used for shock value or cheaply, but as they play a part in the day-to-day speech of many people. Ferling-

---

AUTHOR'S COMMENTARY

I always believe that the poem should have a lot of public surface and it should be based on commonsensual experience. Commonsensual—one word. Experience that everyone has no matter what level of education; it shouldn't be based on a bunch of literary references that only five per cent of the population can understand. And it shouldn't be poetry about poetry like the language poets. It shouldn't be hermetic, it should be open. What it seems to me I've been put down for by a lot of literary critics, and even by some of the beats is for having committed the sin of too much clarity. See, claritas is not the ideal of many modern poets or critics. From the days of the Black Mountain School onward, a certain opacity is required, or a certain ambiguity—don't be too clear; if you're obscured a little, you'll look more profound. So a lot of my poems are completely visual, super clear, as far as I'm concerned. That's what I'm trying to get—super clarity. . . .

[On the other hand] I always think the poem has to have more than one level. I wrote a poem called **"Populist Manifesto"** where I say that. It has to have a public surface, but then it has to operate on some other subversive or subjective levels or else it's just journalism. . . .

But still, I think you have to write both kinds of poetry. And I don't see any of the American poets doing that. I don't see anything important being said right now. It's not cool to write about politics or to make impassioned political statements. But I think a poet has to do that. It's perfectly all right if he doesn't want to do it in his poetry or his art; I can say the same for painters. . . . If they don't want to say it in their art, in their writing or in their painting, they should do it in their personal life and actions. So someone could be a completely personal writer and write about subjective matters, but at the same time he should show up at the demonstrations at the city hall against apartheid, for instance, even though he never writes about it.

(interview date 1986)

hetti's victory over those who arrested him for publishing *Howl* is now complete, in fact, as the strongest words to appear in that poem are now not only being spoken but enacted in the popular cinema.

This poetry is striking, powerful, and convincing. It cannot be judged by conventional literary standards, however. Whether or not it is indeed poetry can only be answered when a comprehensive definition of that word is agreed upon—a situation not yet achieved. Ferlinghetti's work is not "message" writing, that must have your assent to receive your appreciation. Like all good imaginative writing it is its own justification: the interplay between statement, image and metaphor, surface meaning and plurisignation fuse and become, not state, its meaning.

It should also be realized that a considerable amount of his work is social poetry. While I don't feel that Ferlinghetti sees himself as a prophet, he clearly has an immediate sense of audience that many other modern poets do not. Many of the poems—nearly all those that are closest to resembling prose—were designed for and read in public. There is some return here to the ancient oral role of poetry. But with audiences that can read, there is no necessity for the regular rhyme, alliteration, and other mnemonic devices that were earlier required for oral transmission of the poetry.

Ferlinghetti's poetry finally should be seen as a small but significant strain within the contemporary tradition. He shares with the more well-known modern poets a reaction to the "academic" poetry of Eliot and Pound but differs in his radical techniques, language, and social orientation. Many individual poems are valuable and significant achievements and the body of his work as a whole must be recognized for its sincere and sensitive cultural perceptions. (pp. 71-4)

> *Crale D. Hopkins, "The Poetry of Lawrence Ferlinghetti: A Reconsideration," in* Italian Americana, *Vol. 1, No. 1, Autumn, 1974, pp. 59-76.*

C. R. Metzger   (essay date 1974)

[*In the following excerpt, Metzger offers an analysis of Ferlinghetti's "Autobiography" from* A Coney Island of the Mind, *contending that this piece is a "riddle poem" modelled after the works of ancient Celtic minstrels.*]

Up to now no serious critical attention has been given to Lawrence Ferlinghetti's poem **"Autobiography,"** one of seven "oral messages" included in his *A Coney Island of the Mind.* Yet this particular poem is both interesting and important for at least two reasons. In the first place, Ferlinghetti's **"Autobiography"** is a highly and mockingly-learned riddle poem. In the second place, it is a witty testament to Ferlinghetti's seriously held poetic faith.

Evidence in support of what I am suggesting appears, naturally, within the fabric of the **"Autobiography"** itself. But its significance, as evidence, is not readily apparent. One can enjoy the poem or be offended by it without knowing that the evidence is there. But one cannot fully appreciate the poem without knowing that Ferlinghetti has written a "pied" or medley poem after the riddling manner of the ancient Celtic unofficial bards or minstrels, and that it

contains allusions not only to ancient Celtic poetic history, but also to even more ancient pre-Cymric, old-Goidelic, myth. These are suggested by the presence of individual lines in Ferlinghetti's poem which are taken exactly from English translations of three ancient Celtic riddle poems. These three poems are (1) the *Hanes Taliesen* (*The Tale of Taliesin*), 2) *the Câd Goddeu* (*The Battle of the Trees*), and 3) the *Song of Amergin.*

Turning, for example, to the **"Autobiography,"** it is apparent that lines 65 and 66 in Ferlinghetti's poem which read "I have been in Asia / with Noah in the ark." are the same, word-for-word, as line 20 in Lady Charlotte Guest's English translation of the *Hanes Taliesin.* Only the terminal punctuation differs—Ferlinghetti's period in place of Lady Charlotte's comma. Ferlinghetti's line 104 "I have travelled." is the same, except for terminal punctuation, as the first hemistitch of line 224 of D. W. Nash's English translation of the *Câd Goddeu.* Ferlinghetti's lines 111 and 117, "I have slept in a hundred islands" and "I have dwelt in a hundred cities" are the same word-for-word as lines 225 and 226 in Nash's version of the *Câd Goddeau.* Ferlinghetti's lines 135, "It is long since I was a herdsman." is the same, including terminal punctuation, as Nash's line 221. Ferlinghetti's lines 226, 232, and 235, "I am a tear of the sun.", "I am a lake upon a plain.", "I am a hill of poetry." are the same word-for-word as lines 6, 10 and 11 in Professor John Mac Neill's translation of the *Song of Amergin.* Only the terminal punctuation has been changed, Ferlinghetti's periods in place of Mac Neill's commas.

Having identified these word-for-word correspondences between lines in Ferlinghetti's poem and lines specifically from three ancient Welsh poems as translated by Lady Charlotte Guest, D. W. Nash, and Professor John Mac Neill, it becomes necessary for me now, having brought the matter up, to explain what these lines "plagiarized" from translations of three ancient Celtic poems are doing in Ferlinghetti's **"Autobiography,"** a poem presumably, and indeed actually, about Ferlinghetti himself, as person, and as poet. I suggest that the explanation lies in the nature and circumstances of these three ancient poems themselves, more particularly as they relate to the bardic tradition of thirteenth century Wales. . . . (pp. 25-6)

The most ancient of the three Celtic riddle poems, lines of which Ferlinghetti includes in his own pied riddle-poem, is the *Song of Amergin* (or Amorgen). [Robert Graves, in his *White Goddess*] reports that the song is "Said to have been chanted by the chief bard of the Milesian invaders, as he set foot on the soil of Ireland, in the year of the world 2763 (1268 B. C.)." Sung then presumably in Old Goidelic, the earliest surviving version is a fairly recent translation into antique colloquial Irish. A version of the same poem also appears "in a garbled form" in medieval Welsh, "put into the mouth of the child bard Taliesin when narrating his transformations in previous existences." (See the "Tale of Taliesin" in the *Romance of Taliesin.*)

The above, apparently gratuitous, erudition regarding the *Song of Amergin* happens to be fairly important. It not only suggests the great age and enduring venerability of that poem, but leads also to the recognition that the beginning part of the poem, in its various versions, suggests at least three speakers. The first speaker is the poet himself, in this case the historio-mythical, the eponymous, Taliesin speaking a garbled version of the poem in the thirteenth century *Romance of Taliesin.* The second is the Almighty God, who is the announced speaker in the version translated by Professor Mac Neill. . . . This version translated by Professor Mac Neill is accompanied by glosses, provided either by some poet-translator, or by some scribe-scholiast. Not counting the author of the glosses as a speaker, the third speaker, also in the Mac Neill version, is the author or speaker of the *envoi,* apparently a "Druid [who] advises the People of the Sea to invoke the poet of the sacred rath to give them a poem. He himself the [Druid] will supply the poet with the necessary material, and together they will compose an incantation."

It is God as speaker, in the Mac Neill translation, who says "I am a tear of the sun," to which the gloss is added suggesting the significance of the statement—" 'a dew-drop'—for clearness." It is God who says "I am a lake on a plain,"—the gloss indicating—"and knowledge." It is the Druid-speaker of the *envoi* who says, "I, who part combatants, I will approach the rath of the Sidhe to seek a cunning poet that together we may concoct incantations."

As I have suggested, Ferlinghetti's lines appear to come from the Mac Neill translation which contains this *envoi.* . . . Ferlinghetti does not pirate directly from the above-mentioned *envoi* for his own poem, but his reference in it to Joyce's "silence, exile, and cunning" is not only appropriate to a description of a portion of his own life, but also suggestive of the cunning and secretive nature of his own poem, as well as the similar nature of the *Song of Amergin* from which he does pirate.

No matter how you slice it, the *Song of Amergin,* as evidenced by surviving versions of it, begins with what amounts to a summons or challenge, voiced by a person of some considerable authority—whether Taliesin, or God Almighty, or a Druid—amounting to a call for a more cunning, extensive, and learned, yet ultimately lucid, poetry, than currently being produced, which is to say, for an incantatory poetry lucid as dewdrops, but not necessarily so as to any but members of an extensively learned *cognoscenti.* Graves suggests in this connection that it is "unlikely that this poem [the *Song of Amergin*] was allowed to reveal its esoteric meaning to all and sundry; it would have been pied as [the poet] Gwion pied his poems [the *Hanes Taliesin* and the *Câd Goddeu*], for reasons of security." (pp. 27-9)

Both Robert Graves and Thomas Clark Lethbridge [in his *Witches: Investigating an Ancient Religion*] . . . argue that Celtic poems such as those presently under consideration are difficult because they have been deliberately pied by the poets, partly . . . to reveal the deficient learning of other contemporary bards, but also, as Graves suggests, to hide "an ancient religious mystery—a blasphemous one from the [thirteenth century Christian] Church's point of view—under the cloak of buffoonery," under the disguise of apparently incomprehensible, Lewis-Carroll-type, nonsense poetry. To this purpose, Graves adds, the riddle-poet has "not made this secret altogether impossible for a well educated fellow poet to guess."

It so happens that Ferlinghetti's **"Autobiography"** demonstrates this kind of deliberately pied, riddling poetry which

Graves describes. It demonstrates equally the kind of poetry which the Druid in the *envoi* at the beginning of the *Song of Amergin* called for: cunning, incantatory, extensively learned, mocking, and crystal clear to sufficiently well educated fellow poets. The crystal is no less clear, one might add, for having been cut with many facets; it merely reflects more light, more images. It so happens that Ferlinghetti, when reciting his **"Autobiography"** in the cellar during the early 1950's, appeared at the time to be what he waggishly was indeed: an amused, witty, mockingly learned, dedicated poet, somewhat incomprehensibly describing himself, under the cloak of buffoonery, as "a tear of the sun," as "a hill of poetry," as a "still of poetry." It also happens that what he was reciting would have been crystal clear to any listener sufficiently learned in that ancient lore. . . . (p. 30)

I should like to point out now that of the eighteen or more writers that Ferlinghetti either quotes, paraphrases, or alludes to in his 302 line poem (all but three are poets), the one poet that Ferlinghetti refers to most often, although never directly by name, is the thirteenth century Welsh bard whom Graves calls Gwion. It is to this Gwion that Graves ascribes the authorship of the versions of the *Câd Goddeu* and the *Hanes Taliesin* that appear in the *Romance of Taliesin.* And it is this Gwion whose lines, translated into English, appear in Ferlinghetti's poem. (p. 31)

[Graves argues that it is Gwion] or at least poets like him, that Phylip Brydydd (c. 1220-30 A. D.) referred to in describing a controversy between himself and "certain vulgar rymsters". These rymsters, he charged, "had no honor," *i. e.,* (says Graves) "did not belong to the privileged class of Cymric freemen from which the court bards were chosen, but were unendowed minstrels." This Phylip Brydydd (Bryddyd *means* bard) was an official poet, one of the "Court Poets of the Welsh Princes." "In the *Romance of Taliesin,*" says Graves, "we have the story [of this controversy between the official poets such as Brydydd and the unchaired minstrels] told, in this instance, from the side of the minstrel."

This thirteenth century controversy between Graves' Gwion, or poets like him, and Phylip Brydydd, and official poets such as he, is important to readers who would clearly understand Ferlinghetti's **"Autobiography"** because it is one of at least four poetic controversies (or battles) suggested by the lines pirated from ancient Welsh poetry and pied into Ferlinghetti's poem. (p. 32)

The last and most recent of these controversies, I suggest, is that celebrated in Ferlinghetti's own poem, **"Autobiography."** It is the controversy between the author and other true poets like himself, on the one hand, including ancient partially mythical, eponymous poets such as Graves' Gwion . . . not to mention more recent poets such as John Keats, Matthew Arnold, Walt Whitman, T. S. Eliot, Ezra Pound, James Joyce, and Robert Graves—all of these true poets, ancient as well as modern, standing in opposition to craven, sycophantic and ignorant academic, *i. e.,* official poets in general.

These academic poets, I suggest, are represented in ancient times by such officially endowed poets as Phylip Brydydd. . . . They are represented in our own times by the abundant but unnamed "housebroken Ezra Pounds" referred to in line 133 of Ferlinghetti's poem. These "housebroken" bards, Ferlinghetti suggests, "should all be freed."

In order to explain more fully the relationships between these . . . poetic controversies and those protagonist-speakers involved in them with whom Ferlinghetti identifies, it is necessary to return for the moment to the anonymous thirteenth century poet whom Graves calls Gwion, and to the poetic situation in medieval Wales. It was customary during the thirteenth century (as quite probably during a considerable time before that) for Celtic poets to celebrate in their poems ancient controversies by way of referring indirectly to contemporary controversies between themselves and other poets, as well as other adversaries, political and religious. (pp. 33-4)

It was also customary for thirteenth century Celtic poets to speak often in the *personae* of the protagonists of these earlier controversies. Hence the difficulty of separating from this already sufficiently complex literature the historical figures, poets and protagonists, from their legendary, their mythical, and their religious counterparts. Hence the merging of Gwidion ap Dôn, historical sixth century and thereafter legendary, with Gwion of Llanfair, historical sixth century and thereafter legendary, with, among others, Merddin (Merlin), Arthur, Taliesin, as well as with earlier druidic and pre-druidic bard-heroes, along with Jehovah, Christ, Hercules-Apollo, and ultimately with the god of true poetry, who, Graves argues, is at once the son, lover, and victim of the White-Goddess, the mother of inspiration, who as Cerridwen, Artemis, Diana, Demeter, Mary, Achren, is as Protean and eponymous as her sons and lovers.

Graves' Gwion, from whom Ferlinghetti quotes, and in whose voice he speaks part of the time at least, is simply one of the latter-day thirteenth century versions of the bard as priest-hero of poetry. And Ferlinghetti himself, I suggest, is a more recent version of incarnation of this Gwion—he in company with fellow true poets such as Eliot, Williams, Ginsberg, and Graves, among others. (pp. 34-5)

Graves argues that his Gwion, the author of the thirteenth century *Hanes Taliesen* and the *Câd Goddeu,* disguised his own controversy between himself and his opponents, the contemporary "big-bellied," the chaired, or endowed bards, such as Brydydd, by presenting his riddling challenges to these official bards of his own day under the guise of describing controversies that were well over six hundred years older. The confusions regarding the identities of authors and protagonists in these and other such poems, Graves argues, was quite intentional. It is difficult and ultimately not really necessary to distinguish these identities altogether. It is not really necessary, insofar as they are all essentially the same types of the eponymous bard-hero; since each poet, whether or not known for certain as an historical person, serves nonetheless in the role of a poet-hero, and each hero serves correspondingly as a hero-poet, and they all speak apparently in pied, riddling, medley poems, each poem composed of parts from several sometimes very ancient poems, artfully pied together and addressed to the immortal controversy between "true poets" and "official poets."

Each of them, Graves' Gwion, Gwion of Llanfair, Gwidion ap Dôn (and to these we must add Robert Graves and Lawrence Ferlinghetti), is in an important sense merely a different transformation of the same, the universal, the true poet, whether identified or not. Each is a version, often unrecognized because often disguised, of Taliesin, of Jehovah, of Hercules-Apollo. Each is inspired, after his own manner, and each has either already given his name as eponym of the type or would most certainly like to do so. It is for this reason I suggest that Ferlinghetti, hopeful of the only kind of success that counts for true poets, wrote of himself at the end of his **"Autobiography"**:

> I have read somewhere
> the Meaning of Existence
> yet have forgotten [*sic*]
> just exactly where.
> But I am the man
> And I'll be there.
> And I may cause the lips
> of those who are asleep
> to speak.
> And I may make my notebooks
> into sheaves of grass.
> And I may write my own
> eponymous epitaph
> instructing the horsemen
> to pass.

(Lines 288-302)

Ferlinghetti is saying in this passage substantially the same thing as Graves' Gwion said when speaking somewhat more confidently from the mouth of his hero Taliesin, who says:

> I was originally little Gwion,
> And at length I am Taliesin.
> I have been instructed
> In the whole system of the universe:
> I shall be till the day of judgement
> On the face of the earth.

As long as there continue to be mortal men, as long as there are poets, suggests Graves' Gwion, there will be some of them who will be inspired to function as true poets. And just so long will there be contention between these true poets and other, more often than not big-bellied, official, poets. (pp. 36-8)

Graves asserts that the true poets' sole mission in life is to celebrate through inspired and often riddling poetry, the true source of inspiration as well as death, the White Goddess, who according to pre-Christian Celtic religions is at once the mother, the lover, and the layer out of the corpse of true poets. She is the ultimate source of both inspiration and death. She is the night-mare whose nest is strewn with the bones and entrails of poets. She is Cerridwen in the *Tale of Taliesin*. She is at once Diana, Artemis, the Sow Goddess, the Mare Goddess, the three witches in Macbeth; she is at once mother, nymph, and hag. In her more attractive form she is the lady without mercy; she has yellow hair, a chalk-white face, lips like rowan berries.

One might reasonably expect, in view of what I have been arguing heretofore, to find reference to her in Ferlinghetti's **"Autobiography."** And it is there. Ferlinghetti writes:

> I have seen the White Goddess dancing
> in the Rue des Beaux Arts
>
> . . . .
> and the Beautiful Dame Without Mercy
> picking her nose in Chumley's.

She did not speak English. [*sic*]
She had yellow hair
and a hoarse voice
and no birds sang.

(Lines 274-275, 277-282)

One has reason to suspect that Ferlinghetti's references earlier in his poem to the Laughing Woman at Luna Park, to the Venus Aphrodite, to the siren singing at One Fifth Avenue, suggest versions of his muse. It is the White Goddess, I suggest further, who is the "very purely naked / young virgin / with very long and very straight / straw hair" who appears in the Statue of Saint Francis poem in the same collection with **"Autobiography."** It is she, I suggest further, who is the principal object, if not subject, of Ferlinghetti's novel *Her.* (pp. 38-9)

In the **"Autobiography"** Ferlinghetti's assertion of the secret meaning of the poem, of his role as a latter day Gwion-Taliesin, of his avowed worship of the White Goddess, is guarded, hidden, and disguised by the pieing into the poem, along with the lines taken from Graves' Gwion, apparently superficial and gratuitous pirating of lines from, as well as references to, relatively recent writers such as Wordsworth, Keats, Matthew Arnold, Browning, Yeats, Joyce, Thoreau, Hawthorne, Melville, Whitman, Twain, Wolfe, Hart, Crane, Pound, Hemingway, and Eliot, among others.

These writers to whom Ferlinghetti alludes in one way or another have in common with Ferlinghetti and Graves' Gwion-Taliesin one important thing—they have been all, I suggest, during at least part of their careers true poets. To my knowledge Ferlinghetti never alludes to an academician-poet teaching in a university, sitting in an endowed chair. Although Ferlinghetti has a B. A., and M. A., as well as a doctorate from the University of Paris, he has never accepted an academic position and appears positively to hate academicians. (pp. 40-1)

Meanwhile, I should like to suggest that the secret meaning of Ferlinghetti's things is out. Upon checking his later works I have discovered that he has not quite ever given up using Welsh bardic techniques in his poems, plays, and his novel, though never, except in the case of *Her,* in the same high concentration as in his **"Autobiography."** (p. 41)

> *C. R. Metzger, "Lawrence Ferlinghetti as Elphin's Bard," in* The Midwest Quarterly, *Vol. XVI, No. 1, October, 1974, pp. 25-41.*

Robert Creeley   (essay date 1981)

[*Creeley is an American poet, novelist, short story writer, essayist and editor. Best known for his poetry, he has been associated both with the Black Mountain and Beat movements. Among his best known works are* For Love: Poems 1950-1960 *(1962),* Pieces *(1968), and* Mirrors *(1983). In the following excerpt from his appraisal of* Endless Life, *Creeley offers a brief review of Ferlinghetti's career, admiring particularly the poet's "tough, public humor and accessibility."*]

Endless Life: Selected Poems is Lawrence Ferlinghetti's own selection from some 40 years of his work, and I think the result proves a sturdy rehearsal of his virtues: tough,

public humor and accessibility. If J. Edgar Hoover (remember him?) once said of this poet, "it appears Ferlinghetti may possibly be a mental case . . . ," he is surely that person we dearly want the wit of, faced with such "institutions" as Hoover suggests, inside or out:

> The world is a beautiful place
> to be born into
> if you don't mind happiness
> not always being
> so very much fun
> **("The World Is a Beautiful Place")**

From the early poems, with their wry, backhanded literacy and good-natured hope, to the final poem [**"Endless Life"**], a "work-in-progress" in which the insistent repetition of "Endless" is both an ingenuously proposed belief. ("Endless the splendid life of the world / Endless its lovely living and breathing") and a bitterly ironic emphasis ("Endless the waiting for God and Godot / the absurd actions absurd plans and the plays / dilemmas and the delays . . .), one is made to recognize the public consequence of any personal existence. We don't, we cannot, live alone:

> Home to the bed we made
> and must lie in
> with 'whoever'
> Or home to the bed still to be made
> of rags & visions
> the bed whose form is pure light
> (and unheard melodies
> dark despairs & inchoate ecstasies
> longings out of reach)
> Who to decipher them who answer them
> singing each to each?
> **("Home Home Home")**

No doubt this will read nostalgically to some, appropriately enough. (p. 5)

> *Robert Creeley, "Poetry of Commitment," in* Book World—The Washington Post, *August 2, 1981, pp. 5-6.*

Stephen Bett   (essay date 1981)

[*In the excerpt below, Bett execrates* Landscapes of Living & Dying, *especially censuring Felinghetti's reliance on "very conventional rhetorical figures and on cliché diction and imagery."*]

As [**Landscapes of Living & Dying**] demonstrates, Ferlinghetti is a poet who (quite ironically when you consider his aesthetic and political stance) remains frequently enslaved by his own language—a language that functions in a fixed, systematic, absolute way. His poetry relies heavily on the referential devices of metaphor and symbol, on very conventional rhetorical figures and on cliché diction and imagery. Such a language is, by almost any 20th century definition, a "closed" language, one that is not designed for risk-taking or experiment and which must settle always for the descriptive rather than—as the Olsonites put it—re-enactment or direct perception. The irony, it seems to me, of Ferlinghetti's evident willingness to hide behind stock tropes and figures is one that needs to be stressed (I counted, incidentally, at least three poems echoing Eliot in the collection). It's as though this so-called "radical" poet is composing according to the dictates of New Criticism: his work is full of witty conceits and tightly turned metaphors, all that tenor/vehicle stuff which was heralded by I. A. Richards several decades ago and which best suits the conceptions of language current in the 17th century. To continue practising this kind of writing today is considered the height of artifice by most of Ferlinghetti'so contemporaries; in fact, it's even thought dishonest, the language of a man who doesn't mean what he says. But here it is in his new volume, all the old "schemes" and "figures" paraded out in all their tiredness, ready to bore any post-modernist into the most stone-laden ground.

Ferlinghetti is like an institution, the fate of most "popular" poets: he simply doesn't change. He keeps on writing the same poems over and over, using the same pat, mechanical figures of speech (especially his over-labored anaphora, a real signpost of his verse), and the same—often too cutesy—laconic, lilting and halting, syncopated voice where alliteration, assonance, rhyme, pararhyme, and so on, predictably precede the Big Image or insight by which his poems are paced—the instances of each of the above being far too numerous to quote here, except to mention my review copy is solidly marked with them on virtually every page (although I must admit personally I haven't quite yet tired of his—I believe—quite original and effective use of the adverbial "still" to intensify the ironic charage and the heavily syncopated measure of his poetic line). (pp. 76-7)

The narrative poems—always a significant number in any Ferlinghetti volume—are built in a very "painterly" way; that is to say they generate a series of representational images by following a single—highly rational, logical—train of thought. Representationalism (or mimesis) is in itself an appropriate and telling term here. The thematic structures Ferlinghetti is able to incorporate into this method are obviously going to be limited—as writers in a previous generation discovered—to what the line of argument will allow, much like the working of a machine. . . . Suffice to say that "straight" narrative poetry has been bankrupt for years, and Ferlinghetti's constant repetitions of it since his first book date his poetic—and will continue to consolidate his popularity—considerably. The more lyrical poems in this as in previous volumes (another deservedly endangered species) follow, although not in some important details, the do's and don'ts of Imagism. Ferlinghetti continues, in *Landscapes of Living & Dying,* to be a recorder of images, a picture taker. Representationalism—or in its watered down form, impressionism—honed to its finest dimensions. I've always thought of Imagism (as very quickly did Pound and Williams, by the way) as a kind of revisionist, classicist period in modern literary history. All those exquisite, fixed, frozen little moments. This is real cliché stuff, as anyone who looks at the hundreds of volumes of coffee-table verse still published every year knows—all those would-be and not so would-be imitators of Des Imagistes busy capturing their effete impressions, their little still-life palpitations of the heart.

Ferlinghetti's diction makes a large contribution to his problems. When he isn't using his worn-out hip jargon (which frequently was, and remains, a legitimate delight in his 1950's work), his sense of technical craftmanship seems to have forced him more and more in recent books into the kind of trite image-making practised by the Victorian imitators of the Romantics—the kind of images that are fluffed up by a very precious, antiquated language (this being the "don't" I referred to above which isn't obeyed in the present volume—"frill" adjectives abound.) I made a list of some of the more notable phrases in each category. As for the jargon, Ferlinghetti offers us the bald, and evidently hungry, harpsicordist who "copped a piece of Moka"; the "cool couple" in a Mercedes and the "two sweet dudes"—the gay mayor and supervisor recently murdered in San Francisco. . . . [Finally, the] poet succumbs to writing rather insipid pop lyrics: "We steal their lives / to feed our own / and with their lives / our dreams are sown." On the other precious side of the ledger we have the worst of Shelley—the Shelley anthologized for his lovely ("pretty") gerunds and participles by the Victorians: "the darkening air"; "the furled clouds"; "the darkling plain"; "streams of silver air"; "myriad flashing cars"; an angel with "gossamer wings"; "the verdant forest"; and finally (I'm going chronologically), "the lapped light of love." On this note I might add that in a poem where Ferlinghetti mocks, by name, Olson and Creeley's great failure, presumably to anthropomorphize and "Breath / a soul into the sea," we are treated to this soulful mouthful: "And I saw the tide pools gasping / the sea's mouth roaring / polyphoboistrous." Dylan Thomas, anyone?

Ferlinghetti's early seventies confusion remains too. Calling for a greater sense of community in his **"Second Populist Manifesto"** he seems to celebrate the same Me Generation he has elsewhere accused of leading to "psychic authoritarianism": "In two hundred years of freedom / we have invented / the permanent alienation of the subjective / . . . / I signal you from Poets' Land / you poets of the alienated breath / to take back your land again / and the deep sea of the subjective." The Whitmanic/Melvillian vision of the self to which Ferlinghetti alludes is handled somewhat ass-backwardly here (unless he *is* attempting to satirize projective "breathers," which is doubtful from the context); according to more scholarly poet-interpreters of American thought (yep, Olson again) modern man suffers his alienation from the world precisely because of his highly subjective—egocentric—Reason and lack of humility as an object among a world of objects. I suppose it's all a matter of how one "handles the dialectic," but for Ferlinghetti this is always a chancy business at its simplistic best.

But I save my biggest harangue for those cutesy, clever metaphors of Ferlinghetti's, all those Model A vehicles and tenors paraded out in trendy, up-to-date chromatic clothing. One that immediately strikes home is the neatly extended metaphor in his poem on Three Mile Island (a must theme for "occasional" verse these days). In Ferlinghetti's version, radioactive fallout is paced through a linguistic metamorphosis from "white rain" to "snowjob" to "snow-white lies," with a few bars echoing Bob Dylan's "It's a Hard Rain" thrown in to keep the readership up. Or there is the California freeway satire about the commuters going home to their warm beds whose "springs quake / on the San Andreas Fault." Or perhaps worst of all, a metaphor which seriously injured Williams' reputation in *Paterson* thirty years ago—the meandering river-of-life, from a poem that closes the volume, **"Reading Apollinaire by the Rogue River"** (which can also be faulted as a mis-take on the French poet). Here, Ferlinghetti's metaphorical river—likened, of course, to a snake—is

Ferlinghetti (standing third from right) and staff of City Lights Books outside of the San Francisco store, 1975.

eventually swallowed up in "that final black hole," the sea. Let's hope he finally means it. (pp. 77-8)

> *Stephen Bett, in a review of "Landscapes of Living & Dying," in* West Coast Review, *Vol. XV, No. 3, Winter, 1981, pp. 72-8.*

J. Martone   (essay date 1982)

[*In the following excerpt, taken from his review of* Endless Life, *Martone expresses disappointment with Ferlinghetti's lack of progress beyond the "repertoire of devices" which worked well in his early poems but "becomes a bit tedious with repetition."*]

The nostalgia one feels on rereading these poems [in *Endless Life: Selected Poems*] is, I think, a measure of their limited success. More than any of his contemporaries, Ferlinghetti has captured the language of the sixties. He has also been captured by it, though, and that is his weakness as a poet.

Endless Life reflects much of the energy and youthfulness that anyone would associate with Ferlinghetti and the era he speaks for, and poems such as **"The World Is a Beautiful Place"** with its smiling mortician, **"Not Like Dante"** and **"Constantly Risking Absurdity"** still possess a wonderful liveliness and humor. Unfortunately, Ferlinghetti never moves beyond—or outgrows—the techniques of these early poems, and his repertoire of devices (deliberately casual literary allusion, self-mockery, hyperbole) becomes a bit tedious with repetition. Although this selection of poems spans some twenty-six years (from 1955 to 1981), it gives little evidence of a developing idiom or vision. The most successful of his later poems (**"The Old Italians Dying,"** for example, or **"Wild Life Cameo, Early Morn"**) are successful in the manner of the earlier work but cover no substantially new ground. At his best, Ferlinghetti aspires to be an American Apollinaire, but he never fully realizes that aspiration—in large part, one suspects, because he is unwilling to go beyond it. His most

recent work—**"Modern Poetry Is Prose (But It Is Saying Plenty)"** and **"Endless Life"**—still depends very much on the poet's witty allusiveness rather than on a truly childish and independent exploration of the Coney Island of the Mind.

Ferlinghetti is, of course, to be credited with introducing a host of readers to poetry both through his own work and through his City Lights imprint. His contribution to the American poetry of the sixties is no small one in this respect, and one wishes that the vitality and generosity of spirit that he brought (and continues to bring) to the art were more generally in evidence today. *A Coney Island of the Mind* and the poet who wrote it deserve far more gratitude than criticism.

> *J. Martone, in a review of "Endless Life: Selected Poems," in* World Literature Today, *Vol. 56, No. 2, Spring, 1982, p. 348.*

Linda Hamalian   (essay date 1984)

[*In the following excerpt, Hamalian surveys Ferlinghetti's career as it is reflected in* Endless Life, *emphasizing the political and social nature of the poems.*]

Among the adjectives customarily used to describe Lawrence Ferlinghetti's poetry, "autobiographical" and "candid" are the first two that come to my mind after reading *Endless Life: Selected Poems.* Chosen by Ferlinghetti himself from his entire opus stretching over almost thirty years, these are "the peoms that still excite him." If I could buy only one book by Ferlinghetti, this would have to be it. Not only does this admirable anthology lay bare his evolving poetics chapter by chapter, as it were, but it also makes plain how essentially positive his political and social expectations have remained while the world (governments, institut people) has followed (for him) a disappointing course. But instead of becoming cynical, he seems to be telling us that although life endures at the price of considerable pain, at the same time it joyfully perpetuates itself. He has no choice but to affirm it, to celebrate it.

Like many of his contemporaries, Ferlinghetti writes about writing about poetry (a characteristic, of course, of the self-conscious twentieth century artist). On several occasions throughout this volume, we are told just what Ferlinghetti wants to do with his poetry. He refuses to emulate the great Dante because he does not want his readers to think his own vision of life is to be identified with "anxious angels telling them / how heaven is / the perfect picture of / a monarchy" (**"Not Like Dante . . . "**). He prefers to present his readers with the image of an acrobat who assumes, temporarily, a dangerous position of superiority to illustrate the dizzying heights of existential freedom, the most we can hope for. Nearly twenty years later, in **"Populist Manifesto,"** Ferlinghetti claims again that poetry is "the common carrier / for the transportation of the public / to higher places." But now Ferlinghetti urges his fellow poets and audience to give up their private literary, philosophical perspectives—ones he may have adopted and discarded himself—for something he generally classifies as "the subjective." In a second manifesto, **"Adieu à Charlot,"** he reiterates this plea for a poetry of the "pure subjective," which he associates with Whitman,

Chaplin and "the Little Man in each of us." In **"Modern Poetry Is Prose (But It is Saying Plenty),"** he mourns this loss of lyricism, something he blames on "machines and macho nationalisms."

From the beginning, Ferlinghetti has always made his antiestablishment politics clear, holding responsible for the suffering and injustice very much in evidence during our lifetime "Our Name Brand society . . . / with its men of distinction / and its men of extinction / and its priests / and other patrolmen" **("The World Is a Beautiful Place").** He takes his poetry into Santa Rita Prison and into Nourse Auditorium, San Francisco, on the day Robert Kennedy was buried. He is particularly clever at contrasting the haves with the have-nots ("they looked like they might be / related to the Kennedys and / they obviously had no Indian or Eyetalian / blood in them") and depicting the various social inequities that exist in this country (see **"Two Scavengers in a Truck, Two Beautiful People in a Mercedes"; "Baseball Canto"; "Third World Calling"; "The Billboard Painters").** He supports ecological sanity. He is an angry spokesman for human and civil rights. Yet by the time he writes his elegy for Mayor George Moscone and Supervisor Harvey Milk, he converts this energy of opposition into a tentative optimism kept in check by his sense of the enormous obstacles that people of faith must overcome: "Do not sit upon the ground and talk / of the death of things beyond / these sad happenings. / Such men as these do rise above / our worst imaginings." As he declares in **"Endless Life,"** there will be an end "to the dog-faced gods / in wingtip shoes in Gucci slippers / in Texas boots and tin hats / in bunkers pushing buttons" because "there is no end / to the doors of perception still to be opened." He believes in the triumph of the human spirit over authority, mythical or real.

And as far as human nature is concerned, Ferlinghetti is a master at describing the joy, the pathos and the tensions of modern personal relationships, from innocent childhood love (**"Fortune . . . "**), through the games of adult infatuation (**"It Was a Face Which Darkness Could Kill"**), the boredom of a worn-out marriage (**"In Golden Gate Park That Day"**), and the pain and tawdriness of a one-night-stand ("Only the next day / she has bad teeth / and really hates / poetry"), an open marriage ("a little simple arithmetic shows / what a workout he's engaged in / crossing & recrossing the city"), and the bewildering effects of divorce (**"People Getting Divorced"**). In all probability, Ferlinghetti is drawing upon his own experience, yet these poems speak so effectively for many of us that even his short **"Recipe for Happiness in Khaborovsky"** proofs. Throughout these emotional exigencies, Ferlinghetti maintains his sense of humor and sustains his faith in romantic love: "We were two naked / light-headed dandelions / with natural hair blown out / floating high over the landscape / blown by zephyr winds" (**"A Sweet Flying Dream"**). These are honest poems about intimate emotions, no holds barred.

Throughout his career, Ferlinghetti has cultivated a style of writing visibly his own. He often writes his line so that it approximates the rhythm and meaning of the line. He also has William Carlos Williams' gift of turning unlikely subjects into witty poems (see **"Underwear"**). He introduces the unexpected, catching his readers open for his frequently sarcastic yet humorous observations: "I have seen the White Goddess dancing / in the Rue des Beaux Arts / on the Fourteenth of July / and the Beautiful Dame Without Mercy / picking her nost at Chumleys" (**"Autobiography"**). Sometimes it seems that Ferlinghetti's most successful poems are those which transform his observations of the natural and ordinary world into commentary on personal circumstance: watching, for example, in **"Wild Life Cameo, Early Morn,"** deer who drink water and then "one by one / climb up so calm / over the rim of the canyon / and without looking back / disappear forever / Like certain people / in my life." Yet despite this seeming simplicity of language and form, Ferlinghetti requires his readers to be well-versed in modern literature, especially Yeats, Pound, D. H. Lawrence, Dylan Thomas, Cummings, Apollinaire, Ginsberg, Sartre, and Beckett (and of course Whitman and WCW).

In an early poem, Ferlinghetti tells us that he first fell in love with unreality in a candystore. Unreality seems to be made up of innocent love, political freedom, social justice, natural beauty, good sex, and the absence of death. He accepts, I think the harsh fact that he can do nothing about the fragile, doomed aspect of innocent love, and the harsher fact that death is an inevitability—which does not mean that he cannot have his fantasies or seriously transcend physical death with a philosophical, spiritual and artistic belief in resurrection, as a glance at the abundant references to phoenixes and rebirths will indicate. Clearly, Ferlinghetti will never give up the struggle for a just, peaceful, harmonious world. But his lines have become less caustic, not out of compromise or concession, but necessity. **"Retired Ballerinas, Central Park West,"** one of the last and best poems in the book, is a sad, sombre poem, filled with lonely, tired people. But it is sprinkled with images of beauty and energy that belie its winter setting, and make us remember that spring comes next.

> *Linda Hamalian, in a review of "Endless Life: Selected Poems," in* The American Book Review, *Vol. 6, No. 3, March-April, 1984, p. 8.*

John Gill   (essay date 1985)

[*In the excerpt below, Gill reviews* Over All the Obscene Boundaries *in a favorable light, considering it one of Ferlinghetti's "best and most controlled" works.*]

Over All The Obscene Boundaries ("boundaries:" meaning anything that ties people down and cuts them off from one another) fly the lovely riffs of Lawrence Ferlinghetti's new book. These European poems, written about France, Italy, Holland, Germany, and the transitions or hops from one country to another, are a series of nostalgic visits to places the poet loves and remembers fondly. Ferlinghetti is not a private, meditative poet; he is primarily social, recalling personal or historic movements, getting the feel of person, place and situation down just right:

"And that was myself / standing on that far corner / Place Saint-Sulpice / first arrived in Paris— . . . / Paris itself a floating dream / a great stone ship adrift / made of dusk and dawn and darkness— / dumb trauma / of youth!"

His world-pictures of Paris, Rome, Amsterdam, make up the bulk of the book and are done with broad strokes. On one level they are travel poems; on another level the best of them are more than painterly surface.

Although I haven't read all of Ferlinghetti's recent work, I'd be willing to bet this book is one of his best and most controlled if only because the list of successful poems is so impressive: **"Darkness Chez George Whitman," "The Angry God," "The Generals," "The Light," "The Mouth of Truth," "Canti Romani," "At the Gare Bruxelles-Midi," "Two Amsterdams," "Firenze," "A Lifetime Later,"** and others. **"The History of the World: A TV Docu-Drama,"** touted on the back cover as a "powerful concluding poem," is a rambling, catch-all, satirical flop. Ferlinghetti can be too easy at times, settling for the obvious ear-full, his lyric gift running away with him.

But when he's on, he's on. And even at his most relaxed, he's a poet we read for his lightness, his ambiance, and most of all for his good nature and I mean "good nature" in the sense that here is a poet who delights in the world and in people, who sees us in our everyday foolish and fond moments and records it all with a delicacy and wit that is a true pleasure to behold.

Reading Ferlinghetti will make you feel good about poetry and about the world—no matter how mucked-up the world may be.

> *John Gill, in a review of "Over All the Obscene Boundaries: European Poems & Transitions," in* New Pages, *No. 9, Spring-Summer, 1985, p. 16.*

John Martone (essay date 1985)

[*In the excerpt below, Martone expresses disappointment in* Over All the Obscene Boundaries, *Ferlinghetti's collection of poems on his European experiences. Rather than offering a fresh approach to the "well-worn genre" of travel writing, the critic claims, the poet here "has not risked enough: he is looking at something new in his customary way."*]

As the subtitle of [*Over All the Obscene Boundaries: European Poems and Transitions*] tells us, Ferlinghetti's most recent poems belong to that well-worn genre of American writing about the experience of Europe. This is a surprising change in direction for a poet as identified as Ferlinghetti is with the American beat; it is potentially a very daring move. I hoped, as I opened the book, to see Ferlinghetti rewrite the terms of the "venerable genre," to see him write about America's immigrant origins and go someplace both new and very old with his own language.

Despite the interesting language and lineation of a few poems (**"The Rebels"** among them), these were on the whole unfortunately not the right expectations. Ferlinghetti never quite succeeds at crossing the boundary of his own recognizable idiom, and all too often he only shows us just how provincial it can be. Consider these lines from **"On the Beach at Ostia":**

> And on the black beach
> fat ladies leading pasta husbands
> hips and breasts sprung loose
> with promise of pneumatic bliss
> and pudgy bambinos
> bandy-legged and drooling
> on leather leashes tied to mamas
> bawling at the sea

and the sea roars back
its lost answer

Ferlinghetti is hardly an ugly American, but there is no way anyone could tell that from his language. I for one have no idea what his intention is. It cannot be humor (the "bambinos" are too grotesque for that). Despite the allusion, it cannot be Eliotian malaise (there is too much life). It cannot be satire (that is not Ferlinghetti's place). The problem, I think, is that the poet has not risked enough; he is looking at something new in his customary way.

Perhaps my disappointment in *Over All the Obscene Boundaries* only reflects how much I expected of it, especially following the very strong new poems of *Endless Life.* I only wish that Ferlinghetti had brought more of the unself-conscious sensitivity of that collection to this one. Paradoxically, Europe has shown this spontaneous American to be a bit stiff.

> *John Martone, in a review of "Over All the Obscene Boundaries: European Poems and Transitions," in* World Literature Today, *Vol. 59, No. 3, Summer, 1985, p. 430.*

Thomas Parkinson (essay date 1985)

[*In the following excerpt, which was originally published in the Spring 1985 issue of* Poetry: San Francisco, *Parkinson asserts that one can find no better introduction to Ferlinghetti's poetry than* Endless Life.]

At the center of the Beat movement when it began, Lawrence Ferlinghetti provided in City Lights Bookstore a meeting place and mail drop. The store carried modern and very new poetry in English, French, and Spanish. After all, Ferlinghetti held a *Doctorat de l'Université* from the Sorbonne and was fluent in French and Spanish. He founded the publishing house City Lights Books which published work by the Beat writers, including his own translations from Prévert and his own early poetry, very witty and urban (not urbane) in the traditions of modern French poetry. His second book, *A Coney Island of the Mind,* has sold around a million copies, and in many ways it is the most satisfying single book by Ferlinghetti. But the best introduction to his work and the qualities of his sensibility is his selected poems, *Endless Life.*

Ferlinghetti is an engaging writer. He publishes perhaps too much, and though he is invariably interesting, *Endless Life* shows him at his consistent best. The most representative poem is called simply **"Dog,"** and that dog "trots freely in the street" and really does see reality, this sad and serious and above all free dog who investigates everything with his unwavering objectivity and will not be muzzled. The dog is the poet, urban, curious, outspoken with his bark and poetry, democratic, questioning, puzzled by existence, hoping always for some victorious answer to everything. He is hopeful, then, and aware of all aspects of his urbanized world. Ferlinghetti is primarily the poet of cities: his doctoral dissertation was on the city in French poetry of the nineteenth century. His poem **"Autobiography"** begins with

> I am leading a quiet life
> in Mike's Place every day
> watching the champs

of the Dante Billiard Parlor
and the French pinball addicts.
I am leading a quiet life
on lower East Broadway.

The poem continues, for nine very funny pages. The setting is North Beach before it attained its current flashy
commercial tone and was instead a cityscape inhabited by
San Francisco Italians and Bohemians, where Ferlinghetti
was at home.

His youth in New York, his university days there and in
Paris, and his maturity in San Francisco give him urban
settings and tones that he thrived on. When he went on
travels to South America, the book was called *Starting
from San Francisco,* and in the selected poems, the book
is represented by a beginning poem on Machu Picchu but
returns to San Francisco finally with a long hilarious work
on **"The Great Chinese Dragon,"** chief attraction in Chi-
natown's parade on Chinese New Year's Day.

The commitment to the city is evident throughout but perhaps most striking in **"Reading Apollinaire by the Rogue
River."** Ferlinghetti has deep feelings for natural power
and beauty, but he tends to use natural objects and processes for symbolic force rather than for their innate quality. The river becomes a snake that stands for doomed
power, leading to reflections on the passage of time and
ultimate destruction of all things, including the river and
the poet equally. The poem concludes with a citation of
Apollinaire's "Sur le Pont Mirabeau":

> As I sit reading a French poet
>   whose most famous poem is about
>   the river that runs through the city
>   taking time & life & lovers with it
>   And none returning
>   none returning

Some of Ferlinghetti's poems may sound a little like E. E.
Cummings, but that comes from the fact that they write
in traditions established by Apollinaire and his French
successors.

Ferlinghetti returns always to the city, so that when he
sees wild horses in the Pacific Northwest he inevitably
compares them to a watercolor by Ben Shahn. The
strength of his obsession with the city is that it grows from
an impassioned love of humanity that frequently extends
to a love of the entire animal world and of the cosmos. Ferlinghetti is an engaging poet; he is also engaged in the issues of the world. The selected poems make him appear
more purely literary (sometimes too literary in his allusions) than he is. Much of his poetry is topical and satirical. His politics are those of the American libertarian tradition, but he has traveled widely and knows a great deal
about other societies. There is nothing precious, removed,
or pretentious about his attitudes or his poetry.

Ferlinghetti, as poet and literary entrepreneur, is the kind
of person that makes civilization possible. The work that
he has done is well epitomized by this selected poems, and
it reminds us that he and his contemporaries among the
Beat writers have been consistently productive and responsible writers and human beings. The reverence for life
that one sees in Ferlinghetti's poems of the city is present
also in the rurally oriented poems of Snyder and the
comic-cosmic plays of McClure. The final poem in this selected poems is also the title poem of the volume, **"Endless

Life."** This work in progress continues the enterprise, in
its wit, in its inclusiveness, and in its peculiar blend of the
playful with the serious. The endless life here celebrated
is not at all single, loveliness followed by horror, paradise
by inferno.

Ferlinghetti remains absorbed in the processes and events
of the life he sees, like his sad, serious, and funny dog. His
hero is Charlie Chaplin. (pp. 299-301)

[The] Beat Writers have become part of the canon of
American literature, each different, all sharing a certain
sense of sad love for the life we knew. Was it a literary
movement? Not if we accept George Moore's definition of
a literary movement as "A group of people living in the
same city who cordially hate each other." They were always friendly and remain so. What they did in the history
of American poetry was to challenge the stiff ornateness
of the poetry then dominant and bring poetry back to the
realities of experience. They expanded the possibilities of
the medium, by restoring Whitman to greater recognition,
by using the experimental possibilities of William Carlos
Williams and of the French and Spanish writers of this
century. And they served to remind us that life is the origin and purpose of poetry. In that general set of aims, Ferlinghetti was, and remains, an important figure. *Endless
Life* is a good book in itself and a good introduction to his
considerable body of work. (pp. 301-302)

*Thomas Parkinson, "Lawrence Ferlinghetti,"
in his* Poets, Poems, Movements, *UMI Research Press, 1987, pp. 299-302.*

Michael Skau   (essay date 1987)

[*In the excerpt below, Skau censures the "subjectivity"
of Ferlinghetti's poetry, in which the writer "celebrates
his own perception" rather than communicates to readers insights into the nature of existence.*]

Among the radical changes of technique and perspective
in the art of the twentieth century, one that is frequently
overlooked is the sociological fact that the situation of the
artist has been altered by the proliferation of the mass
media. Artists have become public to such an extent that
their roles and reputations may easily become their major
concerns—and their primary themes. The use of the first
person in poetry traditionally becomes a device for univer-
salization: an experience or sensation is employed to speak
to or reveal a generalized point, embodying Lautréamont's tenet that "Whoever considers the life of aman
finds therein the history of the species" [*Maldoror (Les
Chants de Maldoror)*]. However, in much of the poetry of
the Beat Generation writers, the personal and subjective
elements become distressingly autistic: everyday trivia and
personal experiences are described, as is frequently the
case in Lawrence Ferlinghetti's poems, to portray and
congratulate the writer himself. A chief subject of Ferlinghetti's poetry is often Ferlinghetti himself. The subjective
element in the poems seems calculated to reveal the poet
to the reader rather than to illuminate the reader. The success of his subjective poems is compromised when Ferlinghetti focuses self-consciously on his role as poet or on nugatory occasions and indulges in mock self-deprecation,
but more frequently the genuine wit and comfortable pres-

ence of his speakers transform personal observations into significant images of the human condition.

Since World War II, the artist has become as important as—if not at times more important than—the work of art. The artist's personality and image are the most important creations. . . . After initial success the artist no longer need produce quality work (or even any work at all), so long as he remains in full view of the public eye.

This situation arises partially because the arts themselves have begun to closely approach the popular media. As the "popular" arts and the "serious" arts become virtually indistinguishable and interchangeable, the serious artists find themselves in the eminently seduceable roles of popular artists and become common property. As a result, their subsequent work, whether in the verbal, plastic, or performing arts, threatens to conform to the role in which they have been cast. The seemingly inevitable result in a diminution or sullying of the quality of their output through repetition and replication, if only to satisfy their constituency—or, at any rate, to avoid the alienation of that constituency. A viable and frequently occurring alternative is for the artists to offer themselves as substitutes for their works of art. Sometimes they, complicitly or inadvertently, find themselves performers within the world of popular art. . . . Popularity and public attention pose severe threats to artists. The quality of their production and the response of established critics to this work become inconsequential—as long as the response is extreme. Thus, a UPI release about the Surrounded Islands project of the artist Christo reveals that "project spokesmen say that reaction—any kind of reaction—is part of the point of the art work" (8 May 1983). In such a case, the very arbiters of artistic taste may await or attempt to anticipate the public verdict. Values grow eclectic until it is not rare to hear someone express enthusiasm for Beethoven *and* the Beatles, Goya *and* Christo, Shakespeare *and* Vonnegut. The critic finds himself forced either to capitulate or to despair.

The Beat Generation writers have certainly perpetuated this problem, with their primarily subjective criteria. Their supporters have been bulwarks and proselytizers of the "I don't know what's good, but I know what I like" approach to the arts. This attitude, though thoroughly democratic, minimizes the validity of the trained eye of critical evaluation. It preaches that art is not to be understood but to be appreciated as experience. The ultimate criterion is intensity of vision; the truth or falseness of that vision matters less. To a limited degree, this intuitive approach has provided a valuable re-invogoration of the arts, but it has also left them terribly vulnerable to abuse.

Ferlinghetti is one of the most conspicuous practitioners of a new type of poetry designed as an intentional rebuke to what the Beats considered the sterility of academic poetry, what Ferlinghetti has characterized as

> the barren, polished poetry and well-mannered verse which had dominated many of the major poetry publications during the past decade or so, not to mention some of the "fashionable incoherence" which has passed for poetry in many of the smaller, *avant-garde* magazines and little presses.

> ("Horn" 134)

The new poetry demands that the reader engage it, inter-

act with it, rather than study it. . . . Together with the development of a fresh poetics, a new type of subject matter arrives which is intensely personal and which often focuses sharply and clearly on the poet's sensibilities, what Leslie Fiedler [in his *Waiting for the End*] calls "the re-emergence of the 'I' at the center of the poem." However, this poetry is not confessional in the conventional sense. The poet details his everyday actions and reactions so that the poems become a record of his existence.

Ferlinghetti's range here is worth detailing: his subjective poems might well be seen as occasional, but the occasions inspiring them are often nugatory, as though the poet were attempting to illustrate another of Lautréamont's suggestions, that the unusual is to be found in the banal, as he tries "to write out the true poem of my life" [see Ferlinghetti's essay "Genesis of 'After the Cry of the Birds'" in Further Reading list]. His poem **"Truth is not the secret of a few"** seems to have resulted from a minor confrontation with either a librarian or an attendant at a museum. The trivial nature of the complaint is reinforced by the conclusion of the poem, where the poet resorts to off-color humor:

> walking around in museums always makes me
>   want to
>   'sit down'
>   I always feel so
>   constipated
> in those
>   high altitudes.

> (*Pictures of the Gone World* #9)

Similarly, in **"Bickford's Buddha"** (*The Secret Meaning of Things*), he recounts being evicted from Harvard Library by guards because he has no student identification card. He takes this eviction personally rather than considering its obviously general application. In a puerile and devastating diatribe, *The Illustrated Wilfred Funk,* Ferlinghetti employs a barrage of adolescent and scatalogical bile to condemn the character Funk, presumably redeeming such juvenilia by sudden self-condemnations of identification with Funk. This form of self-castigation also occurs in other poems as the poet mockingly and self-consciously deprecates himself and his artistic creations. . . . In **"The Third World,"** Ferlinghetti calls attention to

> old funny face
>   myself
>   the bargain tragedian.

> (*Open Eye, Open Heart*)

Such self-criticism might at first glance seem to suggest that the poet's self-pitying disappointment at his supposed lack of physical beauty manifested itself in an outlook of cheap cynicism—until one recognizes how cleverly the poet has managed to link images of the conventional masks of comedy and tragedy.

Artistically damaging, however, are instances when the persona feels his poetic stature threatened. Ferlinghetti, who has described himself as "a poet against my will" **("Genesis"),** incorporates his consciousness of and concern with his poetic role and reputation into the poems themselves. In **"Bickford's Buddha"** the poet visits the Harvard Co-op and hears a girl ask for "books by Ferlinghetti"; with the rather forced humor of colloquial spelling and grammar, he adds parenthetically, "They dint have none" (**Secret**). Later, he passes the Grolier Bookshop, where photographs hang of the poets who have passed there. Because his own picture is not among them, he whines,

> Where am I
> walking by
> not announcing meself
> Phooey I'm a poet too.

> (*Secret*)

Here again non-standard grammar attempts to mask the wounded pride of the speaker. . . . On such occasions, self-aggrandizement can result in the embarrassment of poetic posturing. In **"Autobiography"** he gushes in celebration of his own creativity:

> I am a hill
> where poets run.
> . . . .
> I am a hill of poetry.
> . . . .
> For I am a still
> of poetry.
> I am a bank of song.

> (*A Coney Island of the Mind*)

Sometimes a single evaluative adjective accounts for the disconcerting impression of the poet's self-applause. In **"Holiday Inn Blues,"** the narrator sits in a bar "making up fantastic fictional histories" (**Landscapes of Living & Dying**) of two of the customers. After a series of sexual-religious puns in **"Mock Confessional,"** the speaker describes his jokes as "bright cocktail chatter" (**Open**). **"The Love Nut"** (**Landscapes**) depends entirely upon inverted self-congratulation: the narrator examines himself in a mirror and in mock castigation derides himself for his healthy, humane values. **"Director of Alienation"** (**Who Are We Now?**), also opening with the speaker's sight of himself in a mirror, employs the very same tactic.

Closely connected with this self-concern are examples of the poet bewailing the demands made of him precisely because he is an artist. The result, of course, is obliquely self-congratulatory: the poet compliments himself by regretting the implications of his talent. Thus, when Ferlinghetti states,

> Some days I'm afflicted
> with Observation Fever
> omnivorous perception of phenomena
> not just visual,

> (**"Bickford's Buddha,"** *Secret*)

The pose is that of the artist saying, "Look at me, a poet, looking at things," and the poetic middleman is not easily dismissed, for he becomes the essence of the poem. Ferlinghetti returns to the observer role often, feeling he is

> really afflicted
> with this observation biz
> It never stops
> on & on & on.

> (**"Bickford's Buddha,"** *Secret*)

In a perceptive essay [in the *Massachusetts Review,* Autumn 1982], Sally M. Gall examines a related tendency in contemporary poetry, "which frequently reduces to 'me talking to you about me—my thoughts, my feelings, my

experiences,' " and in which she discovers a "preoccupation with the trivialities of day-to-day existence" and a "Stevensian 'Watch Me Thinking' air." The stance is one which Ferlinghetti repeatedly adopts. As Wordsworth does in his preface to *Lyrical Ballads,* Ferlinghetti emphasizes the poet's ability to see more clearly than the ordinary man, and, to be sure, observation of the details of the world is artistically crucial. However, the difference between the description of this quality and the self-pluming of a man who claims to possess it is disturbing. Arrogance and effrontery do not contribute to the creation of a persona with whom the reader can feel comfortable. Camping out in the wilderness in **"Reading Apollinaire by the Rogue River,"** Ferlinghetti's narrative voice exclaims, "And I see the Rogue for real / as the Indians saw him" (**Northwest Ecolog**). One is reminded of D. H. Lawrence's *Studies in Classic American Literature* with its criticism of Whitman for this type of encompassing presumption.

Ferlinghetti celebrates his own perception as the mystical third eye vision, his "blue blue eyes / which see as one eye / in the middle of the head" (**"True Confessional,"** **Open**). He smugly disparages a fellow passenger on a boattrain for what he assumes must be insensitivity. . . . The effect is one of aesthetic snobbery, and the preening self-inflation is grating.

In several poems Ferlinghetti clearly adopts a voice intended to express a point of view antithetical to his own. In **"One Thousand Fearful Words for Fidel Castro,"** he employs what Samuel Charters [in his *Some Poems/Poets: Studies in American Underground Poetry Since 1945*] calls the "rhetorical technique . . . of the pretended fool" in order to reveal the shallowness and hypocrisy of an ultra-nationalistic American unsympathetic to Castro. The criticisms are hyperbolic and parodistic, until the conclusion, where the poet finally offers an endorsement of Castro's overthrow of Cuban oppression: "I give you my sprig of laurel"(**Starting from San Francisco**). The complexity of the problem of voice increases when one recognizes the allusions in the last stanza of the poem to Whitman's celebrations of Lincoln and the concluding line as a variant of "I give you my sprig of lilac," from "When Lilacs Last in the Dooryard Bloom'd." Similarly, **"Highway Patrol"** becomes an exercise in impersonation, speaking through the persona of a bigoted, vulgar, and violent "red-neck" California patrolman; the poem concludes with a phrase identifying both the source of the persona's value and the source of Ferlinghetti's stereotyped portrait: "Just like in the movies" (**Who** 38). (pp. 57-65)

Many of Ferlinghetti's poems are verbal photographs, and the presence of a subjective quality, even if it serves only in the capacity of a commenting observer, prevents these poems from becoming flat still lifes and injects an experiential dimension. Often this dimension is necessary to maintain a realistic referent in the midst of surreal poetic fantasy. Thus, **"Overpopulation"** projects a futuristic society which is tempered by the narrator's hesitation, aroused by the hole in the newspaper he is reading: "I must have misunderstood something / in this story" (**Starting**), he suggests, anticipating and disarming the reader's own skepticism. Many of Ferlinghetti's poems, including **"Yes"** (**Pictures** #7), **"The pennycandystore beyond the El"** (**Coney**), **"Starting from San Francisco"** (**Starting**), and **"Overpopulation"** (**Starting**), face the reader with impressionistic and/or surrealistic materials, and the first-person presence provides a solidity and integrity which allow the poems to partake of natural human fantasy rather than to remain formal poetic constructs.

Ferlinghetti's subjective poems are most successful when the speaker is employed as a self-effacing, comfortable presence generating wit and warmth. The poet's preoccupation with his creative role can even be presented capably in these circumstances. (p. 66)

Subjective poems set in specific dramatic situations require a focus on details which enables them to avoid the weaknesses of posturing and self-indulgence. Ferlinghetti's **"Great American Waterfront Poem"** (*Who*) and **"In a Time of Revolution, For Instance"** (*Open*) are particularly effective examples. (p. 67)

The success of these poems resides in the naturalness of the first-person voice, articulate in its depiction and development of specific situations, registering a middle range of life's common disappointments. The poems point no finger at specific villains: all are victims or potential victims. More importantly, the best of the subjective poems owe their mastery to the particular focus of perception, concentrating on the objects of observation rather than on the speaker's act of observation, thus revealing the narrator's character indirectly. In the introduction to his transaction of Jacques Prevert's poems, Ferlinghetti applauds the French poet:

> Still there are many so-called poets around these days who have need of such a seeing-eye dog in the street. Prevert remains a great 'see-er' if not a great seer. He writes as one talks while walking, and 'la poesie est dans la demarche.' His ubiquitous eye enumerates the ordinary world with a 'movement transfigurateur.'

The same praise can be offered to Ferlinghetti in his subjective poems—as long as that ubiquitous eye is not turned in upon itself. The "I" of the best of these poems provides a comfortable companion on those walks, a Virgil-like guide pointing to the familiar and the unfamiliar and discovering something to be marvelled at in everything perceived. (p. 69)

Michael Skau, "The Poet as Poem: Ferlinghetti's Songs of Myself," in Concerning Poetry, *Vol. 20, 1987, pp. 57-69.*

Diane Wakoski   (essay date 1989)

[*Wakoski is an American poet who is often linked with the confessional school. In her work, she explores highly personal experiences, with the themes of pain, loneliness, and lost love recurring frequently in her poetry. Her alternating tones of humor and anger, however, save her work from sentimentality. As a critic, Wakoski has been characterized as an intelligent, sometimes controversial commentator on the literary world. In the following excerpt, Wakoski admires the "exuberance and celebratory joy for life" that Ferlinghetti demonstrates in* Wild Dreams of a New Beginning.]

To this reviewer's eyes, Ferlinghetti is one of the great inheritors of all of the attributes that made Whitman so famous among, and beloved by, nineteenth century European literati. His was a fresh, invigorating voice filled with the beauty of spoken language. And his ideas were fresh and invigorating, too: love that was shared; sex that was not forbidden; racial and gender equality. The poetry of Lawrence Ferlinghetti embodies all of these.

His newest collection, *Wild Dreams of a New Beginning,* epitomizes what [Albert Gelpi in his *A Coherent Splendor*] sees in Modernists, Romantics, and even Symbolistes: an immense belief in the power and life of the imagination. Belief that it can transform the world, even save it. One aspect of Ferlinghetti's personal mythology makes him a comic figure ("Looking in the mirrors at Macy's / and thinking it's a subterranean plot / to make me feel like Chaplin"), but he sees himself as more than one present to make others laugh. He's willing to play the fool if it relieves pain, but not if it makes people forget to love each other or causes them to become hypocrites or liars, and not if it takes them away from the tribal communality of the American heritage he feels from Whitman:

> Chaplin is dead but I'd wear his bowler
> having outlived all our myths but his
> the myth of the pure subjective
> the collectve subjective
> the Little Man in each of us
> waiting with Charlot or Pozzo

("Adieu à Charlot")

That "Little Man in each of us" surely is Whitman's "self," which we all share. . . . Ferlinghetti has had no trouble assuming this self from the beginning of his poetic career, and his messages haven't changed. He has always celebrated beauty, as he does in **"A Sweet Flying Dream,"** with its diaphanous image of a couple floating naked like two dandelions in the sky. He has always called attention to natural beauty as he does in **"Wild Life Cameo, Early Morn"** with its fresh crisp tableau of six white-tail deer grazing and drinking at dawn. Both a painter and a poet, he has always used beautiful imagistic moments or visions, as he does in **"Two Scavengers in a Truck, Two Beautiful People in a Mercedes,"** to contrast with his strident (and often funny) poems of invective and tirade. **"Populist Manifesto"** twinkles and sparkles off the page the way vintage Ferlinghetti always has. My favorite passage is this one:

> Where are Whitman's wild children,
> where the great voices speaking out
> with a sense of sweetness and sublimity,
> where the great new vision,
> the great world-view,
> the high prophetic song
> of the immense earth
> and all that sings in it
> And our relation to it—
> Poets, descend
> to the street of the world once more
> And open your minds & eyes
> with the old visual delight,
> Clear your throat and speak up . . .

Ferlinghetti has long preached that poetry is a means to survival, but in the title poem of this collection he imagines the world of cities coming to a (beautiful) conclusion. (pp. 807-08)

Ferlinghetti paints with a broad Dionysian stroke which encompasses a dream of natural processes restored to their natural cycles, with human beings speaking out in love or in engaged attention to the burlesque of civilized life. But no amount of anger at hypocrisy or absurdity can finally dull his exuberance and celebratory joy for life. (p. 808)

> *Diane Wakoski, "Stalking the Barbaric Yawp," in* The Georgia Review, *Vol. XLIII, No. 4, Winter, 1989, pp. 804-14.*

FURTHER READING

Charters, Samuel. "Lawrence Ferlinghetti." In his *Some Poems / Poets: Studies in American Underground Poetry Since 1945,* pp. 77-83. Berkeley, Calif.: Oyez, 1971.
  In-depth study of Ferlinghetti's "One Thousand Fearful Words for Fidel Castro."

Dana, Robert. "An Interview with Lawrence Ferlinghetti." *The Midwest Quarterly* XXIV, No. 4 (Summer 1983): 413-40.
  Ferlinghetti discusses the philosophy behind his poetry, publishing house, and bookstore.

Ferlinghetti, Lawrence. "Statement on Poetics" and "Biographical Note." In *The New American Poetry,* edited by Donald M. Allen, pp. 412, 436-37. New York: Grove Press, Inc., 1960.
  Includes Ferlinghetti's critique of the Beat poets' "non-commitment," maintaining that "only the dead are disengaged." In the "Biographical Note," the writer propagates several myths about his early life and education.

——. "Genesis of 'After the Cry of the Birds'." In *Poetics of the New American Poetry,* edited by Donald Allen and Warren Tallman, pp. 445-49. New York: Grove Press, Inc., 1973.
  Ferlinghetti's introduction to "After the Cry of the Birds," in which he characterizes the piece as "a poem of prophecy alienated from American Nation."

Meltzer, David. "Lawrence Ferlinghetti." In his *The San Francisco Poets,* pp. 135-71. New York: Ballantine Books, 1971.
  Series of interviews in which Ferlinghetti discusses his artistic and political views as well as his relationship to the San Francisco Poets of the late 1960s.

Oppenheimer, Joel. "Weathered Well." *The New York Times Book Review* LXXXVI, No. 44 (1 November 1981): 40-1.
  Evaluation of *Endless Life: Selected Poems* that includes a general appreciation of Ferlinghetti as "the herald of a new age in poetry."

Schwartz, Stephen. "Escapees in Paradise: Literary Life in San Francisco." *The New Criterion* 4, No. 4 (December 1985): 1-5.
  Discusses several Beat poets, including Ferlinghetti. Schwartz dismisses Ferlinghetti as a poet who has "always preferred clowning to writing."

Trimbur, John. Review of *Endless Life: Selected Poems.* *Western American Literature* XVII, No. 1 (May 1982): 79-80.
  Examines the close relationship between Ferlinghetti's poetry and politics. Trimbur also praises the writer as "a force in American poetry," whose works are "strong and clear and deeply felt."

Whittemore, Reed. "The Two Rooms: Humor in Modern American Verse." *Wisconsin Studies in Contemporary Literature* 5, No. 5 (Autumn 1964): 185-91.
  Comparison of several British and American composers of "light verse." In his consideration of Ferlinghetti, Whittemore argues that despite the presence of "colloquial, jazzy phrases" and "deliberately commonplace details," Ferlinghetti's poetry is serious in its purpose.

Robert Frost

1874-1963

(Full name: Robert Lee Frost) American poet, essayist, and critic.

In his verse, Frost described natural scenes with vivid imagery, celebrated ordinary rural activities, and mused upon mysteries of existence, subtly developing dramatic tension he frequently left unresolved, ambiguous, and open to interpretation. Positing that humanity must constantly struggle against chaos and bewilderment, Frost stated that poetry, like all human-made forms, is a "momentary stay against confusion." His finely-crafted poems reflect this belief through thematic explorations of profound philosophical issues, the beauties and terrors of nature, conflicts between individual desires and social obligations, and the value of labor. Frost is particularly noted for his mastery of form and rhythm, through which his poems evoke distinct New England speech patterns. In order to achieve this quality he termed "sound of sense," Frost structured his verse in strict metrical, rhyme, line, and stanzaic arrangements and experimented with such conventional forms as blank verse, sonnets, lyrics, and masques. While viewed by detractors as a simple farmer-poet, Frost is among the most revered, honored, and popular of American writers. Robert Graves observed: "Frost was the first American who could be honestly reckoned a master-poet by world standards. . . . Frost won the title fairly, not by turning his back on ancient European tradition, nor by imitating its successes, but by developing it in a way that at last matches the American climate and the American language."

Born in San Francisco, Frost was eleven years old when his father died, and his family relocated to Lawrence, Massachusetts, where his paternal grandparents lived. In 1892, Frost graduated from Lawrence High School and shared valedictorian honors with Elinor Wylie, whom he married three years later. After graduation, Frost briefly attended Dartmouth College, taught at grammar schools, worked at a mill, and served as a newspaper reporter. He published a chapbook of poems at his own expense, and contributed the poem "The Birds Do Thus" to the *Independent,* a New York magazine. In 1897, Frost entered Harvard University as a special student, but left before completing degree requirements because of a bout with tuberculosis and the birth of his second child. Three years later, the Frost's eldest child died, an event which led to marital discord and which some critics believe Frost later addressed in his poem "Home Burial."

In 1912, having been unable to interest American publishers in his poems, Frost moved his family to a farm in Buckinghamshire, England, where he wrote prolifically, attempting to perfect his distinct poetic voice. Frost met such literary figures as Ezra Pound, an American expatriate and champion of innovative literary approaches, and Edward Thomas, a young English poet associated with the Georgian school of poetry then popular in Great Britain.

Frost's first major collection of verse, *A Boy's Will,* was published in England in 1913, and Pound wrote the first important review of the volume to appear in an American literary journal. Several recurring motifs in Frost's work are introduced in *A Boy's Will.* In "Into My Own," the opening poem, for example, the speaker yearns to enter a dark forest, a metaphor for the mysteries of self and life. "Storm Fear" presents a man awed and subdued by sublime natural forces, while "Mowing" describes a person cultivating a field and thus imposing a sense of order on the world.

Following the success of *A Boy's Will,* Frost relocated to Gloucestershire, England, and directed publication of his second collection, *North of Boston.* This volume contains several of Frost's most frequently anthologized pieces, including "Mending Wall," a meditation on separateness and community inspired by the annual springtime ritual of repatching walls of rock that divide New England farms; "Death of a Hired Man," a dramatic narrative in which a woman pleads for her husband to show sympathy toward an old, unreliable laborer who has returned to their farm; "After Apple-Picking," one of many Frost poems that promote the value of hard work, in which an apple harvest is recounted in reverie; and "Home Burial," in which a couple experience deep emotional conflict over their different manners of grieving for their dead child. Shortly after *North of Boston* was published in Great Britain, the Frost family returned to the United States, settling in Franconia, New Hampshire. The American editions of Frost's first two volumes won critical acclaim upon publication in the United States, and in 1917 Frost began his affiliations with several American universities as professor in literature and poet-in-residence.

Frost's next two collections, *Mountain Interval,* which contains such famous poems as "Birches" and "The Road Not Taken," and the Pulitzer Prize-winning *New Hampshire,* which includes "Fire and Ice," "Stopping by Woods on a Snowy Evening," and "The Witch of Coös," furthered his reputation as a major poet. The speaker in "Birches" wonders whether a bent birch branch was caused by a child at play or by natural elements and metaphorically links tree-climbing with aspirations for heaven. Ruminations on earthly existence and paradise occur frequently in Frost's verse, which, along with his emphasis on self-reliance and his moral observations inspired by nature, led critics to associate his work with that of Ralph Waldo Emerson and other Transcendentalists. In "Birches," Frost concludes that "Earth's the right place for love: / I don't know where it's likely to go better." "The Road Not Taken" and "Stopping by Woods on a Snowy Evening" are two of many Frost poems in which the speaker faces a dilemma of choosing between the unknown, represented by wild nature, or mundane life, represented by a clearing or town. In the former, the speaker chooses a road "less traveled by," while the latter piece, perhaps Frost's most frequently discussed work, ends inconclusively: "The woods are lovely, dark, and deep, / But I have promises to keep, / And miles to go before I sleep, / And miles to go before I sleep." Critics debate whether the speaker ultimately rejects the unfathomable, remains uncertain, or resolves to further explore the alluring mysteries of life. Typical of Frost's verse, "Stopping by Woods on a Snowy Evening" presents a speaker whose imagination has been activated by nature.

In *West-Running Brook* and *A Further Range,* which also was awarded a Pulitzer Prize, Frost expanded upon his characteristic style and subject matter to comment upon social and political issues, including economic hardships of the Depression and turmoil surrounding the advent of World War II. John T. Oglivie observed: "[With these two collections], Frost becomes the more 'neighborly' poet who chats at length with his readers about the issues of the day, and less the objective dramatist and self-exploring lyricist of the earlier books. He becomes more outspoken about himself and about the world of men. He projects himself into the 'further ranges' of politics, science, philosophy, education, and theology. 'Ideas' as such become more important to him than the individual persons and objects of nature." However, Frost's lyrics on nature continued to receive the most attention and praise. These include "Spring Pools," which focuses on both the revivifying and ephemeral qualities of nature; "Tree at My Window," in which a speaker links his emotional fluctuations with the varying kinds of weather endured by a tree outside the speaker's room; and "Design," in which Frost develops a web of symbolic implications to contrast order and randomness, violence and beauty.

While Frost continued to write prolifically and received numerous literary awards as well as honors from the United States government and American universities, his critical reputation waned during the latter part of his career. His final three collections received less enthusiastic reviews, yet contain several pieces acknowledged as among his greatest achievements. *A Witness Tree,* which won Frost a third Pulitzer Prize, contains many brief nature lyrics as well as "The Gift Outright," a poem about the heritage and individual responsibilities of American citizens that Frost recited at the inauguration of President John. F. Kennedy. *Steeple Bush* includes "Directive," in which the speaker expresses ambivalence toward nature but discovers means for reconciliation while undertaking a metaphorical quest through confusion and decay. "Directive" is generally considered Frost's most significant later poem, displaying his command of form to accomodate and accentuate fantasy elements, symbolism, and varying allusions. In "In Winter in the Woods," Frost's final poem in his final collection, *In the Clearing,* the speaker is once again in a forest contemplating the relationship between nature and self.

Frost's reputation as a major American poet is secure, yet many critics express reservations about his artistry. These commentators usually cite such shortcomings as simplistic philosophy, expression of stock sentiments, failure to delve deeply into thematic concerns, and inability to universalize distinct concerns of rural New England. Malcolm Cowley, in his essay "The Case against Mr. Frost," summarized these views: "[Frost] is concerned chiefly with himself and his near neighbors, or with the Yankees among his neighbors. . . . And Frost does not strive toward greater depth to compensate for what he lacks in breadth; he does not strike far inward into the wilderness of human nature. It is true that he often talks about the need for inwardness. . . . [Yet] still he sets limitations on the exploration of himself, as he sets them on almost every other human activity." Cowley added: "If he does not strike far inward, neither does he follow that other great American tradition . . . of standing on a height to observe the panorama of nature and society." Nevertheless, most critics praise the imagery, rhythmic qualities, dramatic tension, and synecdochical qualities of Frost's verse, and his poems are among the most widely studied and appreciated of American literature. Randall Jarrell stated: "Frost, along with [Wallace] Stevens and [T. S.] Eliot seems to me the greatest of the American poets of this century. Frost's virtues are extraordinary. No other [poet of his time] has written so well about the actions of ordinary men: his wonderful dramatic monologues or dramatic scenes come out of a knowledge of people that few poets have had, and they are written in verse that uses, sometimes with absolute mastery, the rhythms of actual speech." Added Robert Graves: "[Frost] reminds us that poems, like love, begin in surprise, delight, and tears, and end in wisdom. Whereas scholars follow projected lines of logic, [Frost] collects his knowledge undeliberately, he says, like burrs that stick to your legs when you walk through a field."

For further information on Frost's life and career, see *Contemporary Literary Criticism,* Vols. 1, 3, 4, 9, 10, 13, 15, 26, 34, 44; *Contemporary Authors,* Vols. 89-92; *Something about the Author, Vol. 14; Dictionary of Literary Bi-*

ography, Vol. 54; and *Concise Dictionary of Literary Biography: The Twenties, 1917-1929.*)

PRINCIPAL WORKS

POETRY

Twilight 1894
A Boy's Will 1913
North of Boston 1914
Mountain Interval 1916
Selected Poems 1923
New Hampshire 1923
Selected Poems 1928
West-Running Brook 1928
The Cow's in the Corn: A One-Act Irish Play in Rhyme 1929
Collected Poems of Robert Frost 1930
Selected Poems: Third Edition 1934
A Further Range 1936
Collected Poems of Robert Frost 1939
A Witness Tree 1942
Come In and Other Poems 1943 (revised as *The Road Not Taken,* 1951)
A Masque of Reason 1945
The Poems of Robert Frost 1946
A Masque of Mercy 1947
Steeple Bush 1947
Complete Poems of Robert Frost, 1949 1949
Dedication/The Gift Outright/The Inaugural Address 1961
In the Clearing 1962
The Poetry of Robert Frost 1966
Early Poems 1981

OTHER MAJOR WORKS

The Letters of Robert Frost (letters) 1963
Robert Frost and John Barlett: The Record of a Friendship (memoirs) 1963
Selected Letters of Robert Frost (letters) 1964
Selected Prose of Robert Frost (essays) 1966
Family Letters of Robert and Elinor Frost (letters) 1972
Robert Frost on Writing (essays) 1973

Ezra Pound   (essay date 1913)

[*An American poet, translator, essayist, and critic, Pound was "the principal inventor of modern poetry," according to Archibald MacLeish. His importance rests in part on his encouragement and editorial and financial support of such artists as William Butler Yeats, T. S. Eliot, James Joyce, William Carlos Williams, and many other distinguished writers, but he is chiefly renowned for his poetic masterpiece, the* Cantos, *which he revised and enlarged throughout much of his life. In the following review of* A Boy's Will *excerpted below, Pound praises Frost's natural voice and simplistic tone.*]

Mr. Frost's [*A Boy's Will*] is a little raw, and has in it a number of infelicities; underneath them it has the tang of the New Hampshire woods, and it has just this utter sin-

cerity. It is not post-Miltonic or post-Swinburnian or post-Kiplonian. This man has the good sense to speak naturally and to paint the thing, the thing as he sees it. And to do this is a very different matter from gunning about for the circumplectious polysyllable.

It is almost on this account that it is a difficult book to quote from.

> She's glad her simple worsted gray
> Is silver now with clinging mist—

does not catch your attention. The lady is praising the autumn rain, and he ends the poem, letting her talk.

> Not yesterday I learned to know
> The love of bare November days,
> Before the coming of the snow;
> But it were vain to tell her so,
> And they are better for her praise.

(pp. 72-3)

I remember that I was once canoeing and thirsty and I put in to a shanty for water and found a man there who had no water and gave me cold coffee instead. And he didn't understand it, he was from a minor city and he "just set there watchin' the river" and didn't "seem to want to go back," and he didn't much care for anything else. And so I presume he entered into Anunda. And I remember Joseph Campbell telling me of meeting a man on a desolate waste of bogs, and he said to him, "It's rather dull here;" and the man said, "Faith, ye can sit on a middan and dream stars."

And that is the essence of folk poetry with distinction between America and Ireland. And Frost's book reminded me of these things.

There is perhaps as much of Frost's personal tone in the following little catch, which is short enough to quote, as in anything else. It is to his wife, written when his grandfather and his uncle had disinherited him of a comfortable fortune and left him in poverty because he was a useless poet instead of a money-getter.

> **"In Neglect"**
> They leave us so to the way we took,
> As two in whom they were proved mistaken,
> That we sit sometimes in a wayside nook,
> With mischievous, vagrant, seraphic look,
> And *try* if we cannot feel forsaken.

There are graver things, but they suffer too much by making excerpts. One reads the book for the "tone," which is homely, by intent, and pleasing, never doubting that it comes direct from his own life, and that no two lives are the same.

He has now and then such a swift and bold expression as

> The whimper of hawks beside the sun.

He has now and then a beautiful simile, well used, but he is for the most part as simple as the lines I have quoted in opening or as in the poem of mowing. He is without sham and without affectation. (pp. 73-4)

> *Ezra Pound, in a review of "A Boy's Will," in* Poetry, *Vol. II, No. 2, May, 1913, pp. 72-4.*

Amy Lowell   (essay date 1915)

[*Lowell was the leading proponent of Imagism in American poetry. Like the Symbolists before her, some of whom she examined in* Six French Poets *(1915), Lowell experimented with free verse forms. Under the influence of Ezra Pound, Lowell's poetry exhibited the new style of Imagism, consisting of clear and precise rhetoric, exact rendering of images, and greater metrical freedom. In her review of* North of Boston, *excerpted below, Lowell comments on Frost's depictions of the New England farming community in transition.*]

Some six months ago there appeared in London a modest little green-covered book, entitled **North of Boston.** It was by an American living in England, so its publication on the other side of the Atlantic came about quite naturally, and was no reflection on the perspicacity of our publishers at home. To those of us who admire Mr. Frost's book it is no small pleasure to take up this new edition, bearing an American imprint, and feel that the stigma of noncomprehension so often put upon us by expatriated Americans can never be justified in this case.

Indeed, Mr. Frost is only expatriated in a physical sense. Living in England he is, nevertheless, saturated with New England. For not only is his work New England in subject, it is so in technique. No hint of European forms has crept into it. It is certainly the most American volume of poetry which has appeared for some time. I use the word American in the way it is constantly employed by contemporary reviewers, to mean work of a color so local as to be almost photographic. Mr. Frost's book is American in the sense that Whittier is American, and not at all in that subtler sense in which Poe ranks as the greatest American poet.

The thing which makes Mr. Frost's work remarkable is the fact that he has chosen to write it as verse. We have been flooded for twenty years with New England stories in prose. The finest and most discerning are the little masterpieces of Alice Brown. She too is a poet in her descriptions, she too has caught the desolation and "dourness" of lonely New England farms, but unlike Mr. Frost she has a rare sense of humor, and that, too, is of New England, although no hint of it appears in **North of Boston.** And just because of the lack of it, just because its place is taken by an irony, sardonic and grim, Mr. Frost's book reveals a disease which is eating into the vitals of our New England life, at least in its rural communities. . . .

Mr. Frost does not deal with the changed population, with the Canadians and Finns who are taking up the deserted farms. His people are left-overs of the old stock, morbid, pursued by phantoms, slowly sinking to insanity. In **"The Black Cottage"** we have the pathos of the abandoned house after the death of the stern narrow woman who had lived in it. In **"A Servant to Servants"** we have a woman already insane once and drifting there again, with the consciousness that her drab, monotonous life is bringing it upon her. **"Home Burial"** gives the morbidness of death in these remote places; a woman unable to take up her life again when her only child had died. The charming idyll. **"After Apple-picking,"** is dusted over with something uncanny, and **"The Fear"** is a horrible revelation of those undercurrents which go on as much in the country as in the city, and with remorse eating away whatever satisfaction the following of desire might have brought. That is also

the theme of **"The Housekeeper,"** while **"The Generations of Men"** shows that foolish pride in a useless race which is so strange a characteristic of these people. It is all here— the book is the epitome of a decaying New England.

And how deftly it is done! (p. 81)

"The Fear" begins with these lines, and we get not only the picture, but the accompanying noises;

> A lantern light from deeper in the barn
> Shone on a man and woman in the door
> And threw their lurching shadows on a house
> Near by, all dark in every glossy window.
> A horse's hoof pawed once the hollow floor,
> And the back of the gig they stood beside
> Moved in a little.

The creak and shift of the wheels is quite plain, although it is not mentioned.

I have said that Mr. Frost's work is almost photographic. The qualification was unnecessary, it is photographic. The pictures, the characters, are reproduced directly from life, they are burnt into his mind as though it were a sensitive plate. He gives out what has been put in, unchanged by any personal mental process. His imagination is bounded by what he has seen, he is confined within the limits of his experience (or at least what might have been his experience) and bent all one way like the wind-blown trees of New England hillsides.

In America we are always a little late in following artistic leads. "Les Soirées de Médun," and all Zola's long influence, are passing away in Europe. In England, even such a would-be realist as Masefield lights his stories with bursts of a very rare imagination. No such bursts flame over Mr. Frost's work. He tells you what he has seen *exactly* as he has seen it. And in the word *exactly* lies the half of his talent. The other half is a great and beautiful simplicity of phrase, the inheritance of a race brought up on the English Bible. Mr. Frost's work is not in the least objective. He is not writing of people whom he has met in summer vacations who strike him as interesting, and whose life he thinks worthy of perpetuation. Mr. Frost writes as a man under the spell of a fixed idea. He is as racial as his own puppets. One of the great interests of the book is the uncompromising New Englander it reveals. That he could have written half so valuable a book had such not been the case I very much doubt. Art is rooted in the soil, and only the very greatest men can be both cosmopolitan and great. Mr. Frost is as New England as Burns is Scotch, Synge Irish, or Mistral Provençal.

And Mr. Frost has chosen his medium with an unerring sense of fitness. As there is no rare and vivid imaginative force playing over his subjects, so there is no exotic music pulsing through his verse. He has not been seduced into subtleties of expression which would be painfully out of place. His words are simple, straightforward, direct, manly, and there is an elemental quality in all he does which would surely be lost if he chose to pursue niceties of place. He writes in classic metres in a way to set the teeth of all the poets of the older schools on edge; . . . and uses inversions and *clichés* whenever he pleases, those devices so abhorred by the newest generation. He goes his own way, regardless of anyone else's rules, and the result is a book of unusual power and sincerity.

The poems are written for the most part in blank verse, blank verse which does not hesitate to leave out a syllable or put one in, whenever it feels like it. To the classicist such liberties would be unendurable. But the method has its advantages. It suggests the hardness and roughness of New England granite. It is halting and maimed, like the life it portrays, unyielding in substance, and broken in effect.

Mr. Frost has done that remarkable thing, caught a fleeting epoch and stamped it into print. He might have done it as well in prose, but I do not think so, and if [*North of Boston*] is not great poetry, it is nevertheless a remarkable achievement. (pp. 81-2)

> Amy Lowell, "North of Boston," in The New Republic, *Vol. II, No. 16, February 20, 1915,* pp. 81-2.

Louise Townsend Nicholl   (essay date 1924)

[*Nicholl offers a very appreciative review of* New Hampshire.]

Frost is, I believe, the greatest, most truly major, poet in this country, bringing earth and sky closer than any other poet does, seeing sudden startling significance and holding it. Simple things are mysterious suddenly—and mysteries resolve into the natural, and curve about the earth. And man, who stands between the two, who *is* the two, is clothed with wondering wisdom, with loneliness and humor. That sudden shifting of the simple to the mysterious, the mysterious to the simple, is the unconscious mechanism of magic. Suddenly the absolute is brought near, made almost visible. Some new meaning, terrible and lovely and hardly understood, has been glimpsed, a small hitherto unnoticed piece of life has been set apart, distinctly, for all time.

"Poignant" is a word much overused; it will not do. But what is the word for that pageful called **"The Runaway"**— the poem about the little horse frightened in the growing darkness of his first snowstorm? That colt, out in weather he does not understand, in something which he does not even *know* is weather, maddened by it, wildly, frankly terrified. . . . Deliciously and obscurely the unknown is there, and all baffled conscious life running in circles to escape. (pp. 679-80)

And yet Frost was simply writing about that colt, literally enough, telling exactly how it was, knowing only that or some reason the thing gave him the beautiful, unquenchable desire which poets know, to write a poem. When that desire is there strongly enough, the unknown absolute is there, though the poet himself may not know it until afterward, when he reads the poem over and has the ecstatic recognition of something beautiful and meaning more than he had thought.

No, Frost never sets out to be absolute. In **"A Star in a Stoneboat,"** for instance, he plays with the fanciful, exhausts the relative—is there any aspect of a star being picked up for a wallstone on which he doesn't ring the changes? And yet, at the last, we are left with the pathos, the vaguely intent compulsiveness, of human nature, the smallness of man on the earth under the heavens on a starry night. I wish I could quote it all; I will select:

> Never tell me that not one star of all
> That slip from heaven at night and softly fall
> Has been picked up with stones to build a wall.
> Some laborer found one faded and stone cold,
> And saving that its weight suggested gold,
> And tugged it from his first too certain hold,
> He noticed nothing in it to remark.
> He was not used to handling stars thrown dark
> And lifeless from an interrupted arc.

(pp. 680-81)

It isn't all poetry, people say. Great handfuls of it are nothing at all, they say. Well, I know what they mean, of course. Sometimes he doesn't "get going" until the last four lines or so of the poem, as, for instance, in **"The Census-Taker,"** and **"A Fountain, A Bottle, A Donkey's Ears and Some Books."** Personally, I never get dissatisfaction. I do not want him to take those last few lines and begin a lyric with them, as he might so easily do. What he has done he has done because he wanted to, because it was the right way, for him and for the thing he was writing about. It is to me always an adventure to see from what tough rock the flowers were wrested—to know the body of which some few lines are the heart. The two narratives mentioned above are not among the best ones in the book; when his best ones are concerned there can be no dissatisfaction anywhere. For in them he gives a shape to sound, and it is made new to us again that Frost is the poet who pioneered for us, and who is still practically alone, in the field of gathering up the cadences of conversation and letting their music, their sweetness, their inevitable rightness, come forth. Take, for instance, **"The Star-Splitter"** (the Brad McLaughlin poem). Here is the flow of life, the sweet-to-the-taste rhythm of joke and gesture and the hum of quiet existence and country nights. Quoting will not show what I mean. But take the poem and get comfortable for your reading, and then drink it in. It gets to have the sound of small waves coming in. No other sound, as when one sits thus by the sea, can be imagined good. Take also **"Place for a Third,"** which is more like the narratives in an earlier book, *North of Boston,* in its almost unbearable starkness of New England life. Facts and emotions both are sunk deeply in the ground like rocks—ungarnished, there to stay. (p. 681)

Frost's lyrics are among the most perfect being written. **"Stopping by Woods on a Snowy Evening"** is already almost a classic example of the lyric, although others—**"The Aim Was Song," "Nothing Gold Can Stay," "Fire and Ice,"** in this book, are also fit to be. **"Stopping by Woods"** has the inexhaustible quality which makes a poem enduring. . . .

The quality which is strong in all real poets of seeing the invisible, the telescope vision, crops out in Frost in many ways. Mysticism the quality might be called. The things he sees are various, but the way he sees them remains the same. He finds in New England, among other things, that strange efflorescence from harsh soil of the superstitious, the fearful, the hectically imagining—as see his witch studies and the legend of **"Paul's Wife."** He finds all beauty suddenly confronting him in that mysterious contact of human and animal consciousness, as in **"Two Look at Two."** . . .

And he sees that strangeness in the human spirit, that conflict between aspiration and some psychic drowsiness which would always hold it back. Perhaps never before has this been quite said, as it is in **"Misgiving."** (p. 682)

The mystery of a real poet, of any real artist, is insoluble; it comes down to the long vision, which connects. As he says in **"I Will Sing you One-O,"** about lying awake at night and hearing the clock strike one, a single stroke which had all the unified universe in it:

> Their solemn peals
> Were not their own:
> They spoke for the clock
> With whose vast wheels
> Theirs interlock. . . .

I can not feel that anyone who kneels at the well of Frost's poetry, unless he kneels entirely "wrong to the light," will fail to see a treasure shining whitely in the depths. (p. 683)

> *Louise Townsend Nicholl, " 'New Hampshire'," in* American Review, *Vol. 2, No. 6, November-December, 1924, pp. 679-83.*

Harriet Monroe (essay date 1929)

[*Monroe was a central figure in the American "poetry renaissance" that took place in the early twentieth century. As the founder and editor of* Poetry: A Magazine of Verse, *Monroe maintained an editorial policy of printing "the best English verse which is being written today, regardless of where, by whom, or under what theory of art it is written." In the following excerpt, taken from a review of* West-Running Brook *and* Selected Poems, *Monroe calls Frost a "frugal poet" and comments on his realistic portrayal of the people, landscape, and speech of his native region.*]

Mr. Frost is an abstemious poet; he is content with frugal fare at the banquet of the muses. They serve him nuts and berries, salty savory green things, washed down with a home-brew of apple brandy or elderberry wine. And of these he partakes sparingly, bringing out, as the result of such stern nourishment, a thin little volume every five or six years.

West-running Brook, the latest of these, is the most frugal of all. Forty poems, mostly of sonnet length or less—a bare six hundred lines in all—are given thick paper and pictures and blank pages to beguile us into gratitude for a book from this well-beloved hand. And some of those brief entries are marked "very early," or "as of about 1893," as if the poet had looked over forgotten portfolios to fill out the tiny volume and excuse to his conscience what he has himself called his "laziness."

Well, these poems are Frost's own, all right, but none of them may be ranked among Frost's best. They have the tang, the flavor, the keen speech-rhythms, the tart human sympathy—all the curves and angles of style and mood which we have learned to associate with Robert Frost, and which so many other poets have imitated in vain. But there is nothing here to match the tragic beauty of **"The Hired Man,"** the fragile delicacy of **"The Hill Wife,"** the spicy humor of **"The Code"** or **"Brown's Descent,"** or even of a little thing like that spring-drunken **"Cow in Apple Time."** The title-poem dialogue is a slight affair beside **"Snow"** or **"Home Burial,"** though an interesting ad-

dition to the poet's gallery of couples more or less comfortably, or uncomfortably, married.

Did I say none of Frost's best? Well, there may be one or two which could hold their own among those chosen for the ***Selected Poems.*** This sententious brief one, **"Dust in the Eyes,"** is delicious:

> If, as they say, some dust thrown in my eyes
> Will keep my talk from getting overwise,
> I'm not the one for putting off the proof.
> Let it be overwhelming, off a roof
> And round a corner, blizzard snow for dust,
> And blind me to a standstill if it must.

(pp. 333-34)

Turning from this latest volume to the ***Selected Poems,*** one is reminded once more of the richness of this poet's genius and of the high strain of honor in it—its utter truth to his region, his neighbors and himself. There is no need of repeating the tributes of praise we have all offered since the days of ***A Boy's Will*** and ***North of Boston,*** or of re-characterizing a temperament and a literary style which fit together like a fox and his fur, and which, like that famous animal, have a canny shrewdness in them and enough wildness to escape the hounds of civilization which are always trying to track down the elect.

It is a good selection, though this frugal poet is less in need of such reducing than his more voluminous peers. One finds most of one's favorite poems, and misses but few. And it makes a book which will be forever memorable in our literary annals. (pp. 335-36)

> *Harriet Monroe, "A Frugal Master," in* Poetry, *Vol. XXXIII, No. 6, March, 1929, pp. 333-36.*

Merrill Moore (essay date 1937)

[*The following excerpt is taken from a review of* A Further Range.]

Robert Frost is still the New England philosopher-poet in [*A Further Range*], his sixth book. And that is to say that he still retains the distinctive flavor and outlook which have made him, for the past twenty or more years, poetically unique.

Cognizant of the times and the discussion being evoked by them, he retains an unruffled core and is only mildly disturbed while other poets are seeing red. While admitting that "the times seem revolutionary bad", a teasing, semi-humorous Yankee outlook enables him to take the world not too seriously while still being aware of it. The present volume is the most cheerful book he has published. He can measure the present with the past—which quality is always conducive to philosophic calm, in his case not the calm of a Plato but that of the New Englander close to the soil. . . .

> Just now you're off democracy
> (With a polite regret to be),
> And leaning on dictatorship;
> But if you will accept the tip,
> In less than no time, tongue and pen,
> You'll be a democrat again.

So speaks Robert Frost. But his tone is not entirely flippant. He is enough of the staunch New Englander to hold a belief in the individual which he feels to be worthy of defending. Chary of collectivist schemes of living, he clings to the older faith, and bids you "to a one-man revolution—the only revolution that is coming", to "steal away and stay away", and not to "join too many gangs." This is his political philosophy as voiced in the long, rambling **"Build Soil"** which critics might claim comes far from being poetry, but which at least gives the author space for airing his views. (pp. 507-08)

Frost is possibly so completely a part of his New England scene that he is not as aware as some others of the grimness of the forces which encircle it. There is at times a faint, almost pathetic, tinge to his lines suggestive of an order of life which is passing away. To some readers his refusal to become ruffled may smack of complacency, especially when he tells his rather idyllic tale of the lone striker who decides to leave the factory and retreat to the tall trees.

> The factory was very fine;
> He wished it all the modern speed,
> Yet, after all, 'twas not divine,
> That is to say, 'twas not a church . . .

There may be some sufficiently realistic to wonder how many factory hands are in a position to retreat. Some may go even further and question whether the factory may not have destroyed the vision and the very yearning for "tall trees".

But Robert Frost has never been a harsh realist. Nor is he a propagandist. In this book, as always, he is at his best in his lyrics in which he writes of humble things. Outstanding is **"A Blue Ribbon at Amesbury"** which describes with a distinctly Chaucerian flavor a noble prize-winning fowl. There is an abundance of lines full of that quality which has so long delighted Frost enthusiasts. . . . (pp. 508-09)

Although this new volume contains nothing to surpass those poems which have endeared themselves to all and have become American classics, *A Further Range* is a sheaf of poems which is worthy of standing alongside of those others which have come before. It shows Frost still secure in the position he has won, and which he seems likely to retain for all time. (p. 509)

> *Merrill Moore, "Poetic Agrarianism: Old Style," in* The Sewanee Review, *Vol. XLV, No. 4, October-December, 1937, pp. 507-09.*

Robert Hillyer   (essay date 1942)

[*Hillyer was an American educator, critic, novelist, and poet whose* Collected Verse *won the Pulitzer Prize in 1934. In the following excerpt, he briefly discusses Frost's use of symbol in* A Witness Tree.]

A Witness Tree is Robert Frost's seventh volume of poems. He is not prolific, his method is his own secret, and he never explains his poems. The poems are enough. Phrases, figures, and meters are beguilingly natural and yield much on first hearing. But one cannot reread even the early pieces which one has almost by heart without discovering new information.

We are told by the 'Moodie Forester' that the Witness Tree is a great beech which has been deeply wounded by a spike once driven into it to mark a boundary of land amid the wood. It

> Has been impressed as Witness Tree
> And made commit to memory
> My proof of being not unbounded.
> Thus truth's established and borne out,
> Though circumstanced by dark and doubt—
> Though by a world of doubt surrounded.

According to the interpretive mood of modern criticism, we might begin looking for 'symbols' and secondary meanings. We should be wiser to contemplate certain individual words together with their derivations—*impressed* and *circumstanced,* for example. The symbol-hunter would ask what the beech represents. Nothing, I should say, except itself. When Frost names things and tells facts, they are what he means. He lacks the contemporary fad for duplicity. But naturally poetry has a meditative application as well, and when Frost strikes deeper into meaning, he tells us so. The first half of the familiar **"Birches"** is straight exposition and picture; the second half states the philosophical theme unmistakably. The fact remains natural throughout the metaphor. Frost never goes 'sailing to Byzantium.' The only attitude demanded of the reader is companionable attention.

His poems are dialogues. Frost expects a listener and an answer. When he foresees agreements, the tone is grave and intimate; he points out things in Nature when 'we' are together. When he wishes to argue, he spins a glittering web of irony to entrap the unwary. . . .

There is so much to be said about individual poems, and so much that has to be left unsaid. **"The Silken Tent"** floats in air more delicate than the substance of its title. **"The Discovery of the Madeiras"** is a strange narrative— strange in itself and new in its manner. In **"The Wind and the Rain"** we find an important warning of the dangers of invoking misfortune by dramatizing it in an adolescent dream. The poem stands in contrast to Housman's melancholy "Luck's a chance, but trouble's sure" or Hardy's "A Young Man's Epigram upon Existence." . . .

A Witness Tree represents Robert Frost at his best. He has taken a yet further range in his stride. His work develops in his own way, which has been his way from the beginning. He is the experimentalist within the great tradition. He cuts his way through the underbrush of familiar truth, a territory so much more arduous than the imaginary jungles of pure fantasy. He is a master of the unforeseen. Sometimes when he seems to be aiming at us, we hear the explosion in another county. *A Witness Tree* is a wonderful book, for this age—for any age.

> *Robert Hillyer, in a review of "A Witness Tree," in* The Atlantic Bookshelf, *a section of* The Atlantic Monthly, *Vol. 169, No. 6, June, 1942.*

Malcolm Cowley   (essay date 1944)

[*Cowley has made several valuable contributions to contemporary letters with his editions of important American authors—Nathaniel Hawthorne, William Faulk-*

ner, and Ernest Hemingway, among others—his writings as a literary critic for The New Republic, *and, above all, his chronicles and criticism of modern American literature. In the essay excerpted below, Cowley considers Frost a minor poet in relation to his New England predecessors and contends that his popularity among American readers stems from his narrow isolationalist views.*]

In a country where poets go to seed, [Robert Frost] has kept his talent ready to produce perfect blossoms (together with some that are misshapen or overgrown). It is a pleasure to name over the poems of his youth and age that become more vivid in one's memory with each new reading: the dramatic dialogues like **"The Death of the Hired Man"** and **"The Witch of Coös,"** besides half a dozen others almost equally good; the descriptions or narrations that turn imperceptibly into Aesop's fables, like **"The Grindstone"** and **"Cow in Apple Time"**; and, best of all, the short lyrics like **"The Pasture," "Now Close the Windows," "The Sound of the Trees," "Fire and Ice," "Stopping by Woods on a Snowy Evening"** (always a favorite with anthologists), **"To Earthward," "Tree at My Window," "Acquainted with the Night," "Neither out Far Nor in Deep," "Beech," "Willful Homing," "Come In"** . . . and I could easily add to the list. One of his best lyrics was written in 1892, when Frost was a freshman at Dartmouth; three or four others were included in his latest book, *A Witness Tree,* published just fifty years later; and these recent poems show more skill and density of expression than almost anything he had written before. This same volume and the one that preceded it—*A Further Range,* published in 1936—also contain bad poems that have been almost equally admired: long monologues in pedestrian blank verse, spoken as if from a cracker barrel among the clouds, and doggerel anecdotes directed (or rather, indirected) against the New Deal; but a poet has the right to be judged by his best work, and Frost at his best has added to our little store of authentic poetry.

If in spite of this I still say that there is a case against him and room for a dissenting opinion, perhaps I chiefly mean that there is a case against the zealous admirers who are not content to take the poet for what he is, but insist on using him as a sort of banner for their own moral or political crusades.

We have lately been watching the growth in this country of a narrow nationalism that has spread from politics into literature (although its literary adherents are usually not political isolationists). They demand, however, that American literature should be affirmative, optimistic, uncritical and "truly of this nation." They have been looking round for a poet to exalt; and Frost, through no fault of his own (but chiefly through the weaker qualities of his work), has been adopted as their symbol. Some of the honors heaped on him are less poetic than political. He is being praised too often and with too great vehemence by people who don't like poetry. And the result is that his honors shed very little of their luster on other poets, who in turn feel none of the pride in his achievements that a battalion feels, for example, when one of its officers is cited for outstanding services. Instead Frost is depicted by his admirers as a sort of Sunday-school paragon, a saint among miserable sinners. His common sense and strict Americanism are used as an excuse for berating and belit-

tling other poets, who have supposedly fallen into the sins of pessimism, obscurity, obscenity and yielding to foreign influences; we even hear of their treachery to the American dream. Frost, on the other hand, is depicted as loyal, autochthonous and almost aboriginal. We are told not only that he is "the purest classical poet of America today"—and there is some truth in Gorham B. Munson's early judgment—but also that he is "the one great American poet of our time" and "the only living New Englander in the great tradition, fit to be placed beside Emerson, Hawthorne and Thoreau."

But when Frost is so placed and measured, his stature seems greatly diminished; it is almost as if a tough little Morgan horse, the best of its breed, had been judged by the standards that apply to Clydesdales and Percherons. Height, breadth and strength: he falls short in all these qualities of the great New Englanders. And the other quality for which he is often praised, his utter faithfulness to the New England spirit, is not one of the virtues they knowingly cultivated. They realized that the New England spirit, when it stands alone, is inclined to be narrow and arithmetical. It has reached its finest growth only when cross-fertilized with alien philosophies.

Hinduism, Sufism, Fourierism and German Romanticism: each of these doctrines contributed its own share to the New England renaissance of the 1850's. Even Thoreau, who died almost in sight of his birthplace, said that he had traveled much in Concord; he spoke of bathing his intellect "in the stupendous and cosmogonal philosophy of the Bhagvat-Geeta. . . . The pure Walden water," he said, "is mingled with the sacred water of the Ganges." And Hawthorne, who told us that "New England is quite as large a lump of earth as my heart can really take in," was eager for any new ideas that might help to explain the nature of New Englanders as individuals or as members of society. . . . Some of his weaker contemporaries were quite unbalanced by the foreign learning with which they overloaded their minds; but the stronger ones assimilated everything and, in the end, reasserted their own New England natures, which had become immensely richer.

And even Frost, as purely Yankee as his character seems today, was partly formed by his three years abroad. . . . In England he made the reputation that enabled him to continue his career as a poet (and also as a "poet in residence"). In England, too, he had the experience of meeting other poets who understood what he was trying to say: Lascelles Abercrombie, Rupert Brooke, Wilfred Wilson Gibson and Edward Thomas. They were willing to learn from him, and Frost, in a sense, learned even more from them: that is, he learned to abandon the conventional language of the Late Victorians and to use his own speech without embarrassment. It is interesting to compare *A Boy's Will,* published in London but written in New Hampshire before his English journey, with *Mountain Interval,* published after his return to this country in 1915 but written chiefly in England. The poems in *A Boy's Will* gave his own picture of the world, but in the language of the genteel poets; they were full of "maidens pale," "sweet pangs" and "airy dalliance." The poems written in the English countryside used the language that is spoken north of Boston. Once it had been regarded as a mere dialect only to be used in ballads like "Skipper Ireson's Ride" and in satirical comments like "The Biglow Papers"; but Frost in England had done what Hemingway would later do in Paris: he had raised his own idiom to the dignity of a literary language.

It was after his return that he carried the process further. Having learned to write New Hampshire, he also began to think New Hampshire, in the sense of accepting its older customs as immutable laws. But this subject of Frost as a social philosopher and, at his worst, a Calvin Coolidge of poetry is one that I should like to discuss next week. (pp. 312-13)

> *Malcolm Cowley, "Frost: A Dissenting Opinion," in* The New Republic, *Vol. 111, No. 11, September 11, 1944, pp. 312-13.*

Malcolm Cowley   (essay date 1944)

[A continuation of Cowley's essay on Frost excerpted above.]

In spite of his achievements as a narrative and lyric poet—some of which I mentioned last week—there is a case against Robert Frost as a special philosopher in verse and as a representative of the New England tradition. He is too much walled in by the past. Unlike the great Yankees of an earlier age, he is opposed to innovations in art, ethics, science, industry or politics. Thus, in one of his longer blank-verse monologues, he bridles when he hears a "New York alec" discussing Freudian psychology, which Frost dismisses as "the new school of the pseudo-phallic." Elsewhere he objects to researches in animal behavior (which he calls "instituting downward comparisons"), to new inventions (saying that ingenuity should be held in check) and even to the theory of evolution—or at least he ridicules one farmer who speaks of it admiringly, whereas he sympathizes with another who stops him on the road to say:

> The trouble with the Mid-Victorians
> Seems to have been a man named John L. Darwin.

New ideas seem worse to him if they come from abroad, and worst of all if they come from Russia. He is continually declaiming against the Russians of all categories: the pessimistic Russians, the revolutionary Russians, the collectivistic Russians, the five-year-planning Russians: he seems to embrace them all in a global and historical dislike that extends from Dostoevsky to Dnieperstroy. He is horrified by the thought that New England might be exposed to the possibility of adopting any good or bad feature of the Russian program. . . .

Sometimes Frost decides that it would be a relief "To put these people at one stroke out of their pain"—these people being the marginal farmers; then next day he wonders how it would be if someone offered to put an end to his own troubles. The upshot is that he proposes to do nothing whatever, being satisfied with the New England countryside as it is—or rather, as it was in his early manhood—and outraged by anyone who tries to improve it.

Yet there are other poems in which he suggests that his faithfulness to "the ancient way" is more a matter of habit than conviction. In **"The Black Cottage,"** he remembers an old woman who had lost her husband in the Civil War and who used to say (in her "quaint phrase," as Frost calls

it) that all men were created free and equal. The old woman was also an orthodox Christian, and her presence in church kept the minister from changing any phrases in the Creed. The minister says, recalling "her old tremulous bonnet in the pew":

> I'm just as glad she made me keep hands off,
> For, dear me, why abandon a belief
> Merely because it ceases to be true.
> Cling to it long enough, and not a doubt
> It will turn true again.

Although the minister is speaking, he seems to express Frost's attitude toward the old New England standards. The poet is more conventional than convinced, more concerned with prudence than with virtue, and very little concerned with sin or suffering; you might say that he is more Puritan, or even prudish, than he is Christian. All the figures in his poems are decently draped; all the love affairs (except in a very late narrative, **"The Subverted Flower"**) are etherealized or intellectualized; and although he sometimes refers to very old adulteries, it is only after they have been wrapped in brown paper and locked away in cupboards. On the other hand, there is little in his work to suggest Christian charity or universal brotherhood under God. He wants us to understand once and for all that he is not his brother's keeper. . . . There is one of his narratives, **"Two Tramps in Mud Time,"** that has often been praised for the admirable lesson with which it ends; and yet a professor told me not long ago that his classes always seemed vaguely uncomfortable when they heard it read aloud. It was first published in 1934, and it deals with what seems to have been an incident of the depression years. The poet tells us that he was working in his dooryard on an April day between winter and spring; he was splitting great blocks of straight-grained beech with a lively sense of satisfaction. Two tramps came walking down the muddy road. One of them said, "Hit them hard," and then lingered by the roadside, suggesting wordlessly that he might take the poet's job for pay. The poet assumed that they had spent the winter in a lumber camp, that they were now unemployed and that they had slept "God knows where last night." In life the meeting may have had a different sequel. Perhaps the poet explained to the homeless men that he liked to split his own wood, but that he had other work for them to do; or perhaps he invited them into the kitchen for a slab of home-baked bread spread thick with apple butter. In the poem, however, he lets them walk away without a promise or a penny; and perhaps that explains why a college class—west of the Alleghanies, at least—cannot hear it read without feeling uneasy. Instead of helping these men who wanted to work, Frost turns to the reader with a sound but rather sententious sermon on the ethical value of the chopping block. . . . (p. 345)

In some of his poems he faintly suggests Emerson, and yet he is preaching only half the doctrine of self-reliance, which embraced the community as well as the individual. Emerson said, for example, "He only who is able to stand alone is qualified for society," thus implying that the self-reliant individual was to use his energies for social ends. Frost, on the other hand, makes no distinction between separateness and self-centeredness. In his poems, fine as the best of them are, the social passions of the great New Englanders are diverted into narrower channels. One cannot imagine him thundering against the Fugitive Slave

Law, like Emerson; or rising like Thoreau to defend John Brown after the Harper's Ferry raid; or even conducting a quietly persistent campaign against brutality on American ships, as Hawthorne did when he was consul at Liverpool. He is concerned chiefly with himself and his near neighbors, or rather with the Yankees among his neighbors (for although his section of New England is largely inhabited by Poles and French Canadians, there are only two poems in which these foreigners are mentioned). . . .

And Frost does not strive toward greater depth to compensate for what he lacks in breadth; he does not strike far inward into the wilderness of human nature. It is true that he often talks about the need for inwardness. He says, for example, in **"Build Soil,"** which for all its limitations of doctrine is the best of his long philosophical poems and perhaps the only one worth preserving:

> We're always too much out or too much in.
> At present from a cosmical dilation
> We're so much out that the odds are against
> Our ever getting inside in again;

—yet still he sets limits on the exploration of himself, as he sets them on almost every other human activity; here again he displays the sense of measure and decorum that puts him in the classical, or rather the neo-classical, tradition. He is always building defenses against the infinite, walls that stand "Between too much and me." . . .

The woods play a curious part in Frost's poems; they seem to be his symbol for the uncharted country within ourselves, full of possible beauty, but also full of horror. From the woods at dusk, you might hear the hidden music of the brook, "a slender, tinkling fall"; or you might see wood creatures, a buck and a doe, looking at you over the stone fence that marks the limit of the pasture lot. But you don't cross the fence, except in dreams; and then, instead of brook or deer, you are likely to meet a strange Demon rising "from his wallow to laugh." And so, for fear of the Demon, and also because of your moral obligations, you merely stand at the edge of the woods to listen. . . . (p. 346)

But Hawthorne before him, timid and thin and conventional as he was in many of his tales, still plucked up his courage and ventured into the inner wilderness; and Conrad Aiken's poems (to mention one example of New England work today) are written almost wholly from within that haunted mid-region. To explore the real horrors of the mind is a long tradition in American letters, one that goes back to our first professional novelist, Charles Brockden Brown. He said in one of his letters, quoted in a footnote by Van Wyck Brooks, "You, you tell me, are one of those who would rather travel into the mind of a plowman than into the interior of Africa. I confess myself of your way of thinking." The same tendency was continued by Poe and Melville and Henry James, and it extends in an almost unbroken line into the late work of Hemingway and Faulkner. But Frost, even in his finest lyrics, is content to stop outside the woods, either in the thrush-haunted dusk or on a snowy evening:

> The woods are lovely, dark and deep.
> But I have promises to keep,
> And miles to go before I sleep,
> And miles to go before I sleep.

If he does not strike far inward, neither does he follow the other great American tradition (extending from Whitman through Dos Passos) of standing on a height to observe the panorama of nature and society. Let us say that he is a poet neither of the mountains nor of the woods, although he lives among both, but rather of the hill pastures, the intervales, the dooryard in autumn with the leaves swirling, the closed house shaking in the winter storms (and who else has described these scenes more accurately, in more lasting colors?). In the same way, he is not the poet of New England in its great days, or in its late-nineteenth-century decline (except in some of his earlier poems); he is rather a poet who celebrates the diminished but prosperous and self-respecting New England of the tourist home and the

---

AUTHOR'S COMMENTARY

The figure a poem makes. It begins in delight and ends in wisdom. The figure is the same as for love. No one can really hold that the ecstasy should be static and stand still in one place. It begins in delight, it inclines to the impulse, it assumes direction with the first line laid down, it runs a course of lucky events, and ends in a clarification of life— not necessarily a great clarification, such as sects and cults are founded on, but in a momentary stay against confusion. It has denouement. It has an outcome that though unforeseen was predestined from the first image of the original mood—and indeed from the very mood. It is but a trick poem and no poem at all if the best of it was thought of first and saved for the last. It finds its own name as it goes and discovers the best waiting for it in some final phrase at once wise and sad—the happy-sad blend of the drinking song.

No tears in the writer, no tears in the reader. No surprise for the writer, no surprise for the reader. For me the initial delight is in the surprise of remembering something I didn't know I knew. . . .

More than once I should have lost my soul to radicalism if it had been the originality it was mistaken for by its young converts. Originality and initiative are what I ask for my country. For myself the originality need be no more than the freshness of a poem run in the way I have described: from delight to wisdom. The figure is the same as for love. Like a piece of ice on a hot stove the poem must ride on its own melting. A poem may be worked over once it is in being, but may not be worried into being. Its most precious quality will remain its having run itself and carried away the poet with it. Read it a hundred times: it will forever keep its freshness as a metal keeps its fragrance. It can never lose its sense of a meaning that once unfolded by surprise as it went.

(essay date 1939)

antique shop in the abandoned gristmill. And the praise heaped on Frost in recent years is somehow connected in one's mind with the search for ancestors and authentic old furniture. You imagine a saltbox cottage restored to its original lines; outside it a wellsweep preserved for its picturesque quality, even though there is also an electric pump; at the doorway a coach lamp wired and polished; inside the house a set of Hitchcock chairs, a Salem rocker, willowware plates and Sandwich glass; and, on the tip-top table, carefully dusted, a first edition of Robert Frost. (pp. 346-47)

> *Malcolm Cowley, "The Case against Mr. Frost: II," in* The New Republic, *Vol. 111, No. 12, September 18, 1944, pp. 345-47.*

Gladys Campbell   (essay date 1947)

[*In the following excerpted review, Campbell comments on the unity of theme and form in the poems comprising* Steeple Bush.]

Robert Frost has been recognized as an important poet by most important critics for almost thirty years. . . . Through text-books and anthologies some of his poems are so well-known to school-boys that they are amazed to find that Frost is a living poet. He belongs with Tennyson, Wordsworth, Longfellow—all those who are to be read before examinations. The works written about him are extensive, and by thoughtful people. And now comes a thin volume called *Steeple Bush,* dedicated to six grandchildren. One hesitates to say more than "Here is another book of lyrics by Robert Frost." The time is long past for casual contemporary evaluation. But since any book by Frost is likely to have a unity as structurally sound and clear as the form of his lyrics, to look for this unity may be an exploration worth our time.

The title *Steeple Bush* comes not from the first poem but from the second of the seven which comprise the introductory group called "Steeple Bush." The other groups are: "Five Nocturnes"; "A Spire and a Belfry"; "Out and Away"; "Editorials." Each of these parts has a complex of ideas which relate to those of the others: the relationships progress as a series. Since, in spite of simple diction and homely instance, Frost's poetry is highly symbolic and metaphorical, a simple prose statement of this progression would violate its meaning. The book presents nothing so simple as a problem and a solution. Yet certainly its major concern is contemplation of the journey of life in the world of 1947. It suggests possible bad roads, possible good roads, sympathetic insight into fears; and it reports flashes of hope lighting the way, even though they come in fiery fusion of stars or lightning of storm.

Perhaps a few selections will not falsify the structure too much if they are used merely to indicate a characteristic color. In the first group, the first poem has special importance since it precedes the title poem. It is about **"A Young Birch"** that was "once in cutting brush along the wall . . . spared from the number of the slain." (pp. 145-46)

The second poem, **"Something for Hope,"** introduces the steeple bush which gives title to the volume. It is a "lovely blooming" but wasteful, not good to eat, and it crowds out the edible grass. No plow can change the situation, but give nature time and the cycle of weeds, forest, and grass

will move around in about a hundred years. . . . The group ends with **"To an Ancient,"** which points out that immortality was achieved for a prehistoric man by one eolith and his own bone. It ends:

> You made the eolith, you grew the bone,
> The second more peculiarly your own,
> And likely to have been enough alone.
> You make me ask if I would go to time
> Would I gain anything by using rhyme?
> Or aren't the bones enough I live to lime?

The second short group seems in a lighter mood, but the implications are not light. The subjects are: fear of the dark; distant lights that give false comfort; ever imminent danger; a satiric watcher of the void, checking off the stars to see if anything happens. The last poem of the group, with its scene laid in the Arctic regions, is a kind of inverse pastoral. Two friends in an igloo, instead of on the hills of Arcadia, pour oil on their fire, recite to each other, crawl out to look at the Northern Lights, share their fish and oil with visitors. The poem and the group end:

> We can rest assured on eider
> There will come another day.

(pp. 146-47)

The poems in the fourth group on first reading may seem somewhat unrelated, but after rereading we appreciate the ambitious attempt to cast a shadow of ourselves on the cosmic screen. The first directs our attention to consideration of the near and far, the universal and local, the absolute. (pp. 147-48)

The last group is frankly called "Editorials." These poems are more explicit, perhaps, and seem sometimes limited and specific, as in **"U. S. King's X,"** but there is always far-reaching suggestion, if not universal comment. A serpent of sand still rears its head to obliterate the mottoes of the city that took pride in its art of **"Passing Losses On."** The book ends with a poem **"To the Right Person,"** telling of a splendidly situated district school planned for coeducation.

> But there's a tight shut look to either door
> And to the windows of its fenestration,
> As if to say mere learning was the devil
> And this school wasn't keeping any more
> Unless for penitents who took their seat
> Upon its doorstep as at mercy's feet
> To make up for a lack of meditation.

Now it would be foolhardy to take these passages and translate them into a thesis—and it would also misrepresent the book. But perhaps they do indicate that the poetry, after the fashion of poetry, is saying a good deal about the confusion of our world, its illness and its hope, though it talks of stars, rivers, ancient bones, cliff dwellings, igloos, and steeple bush. A few of the poems may seem to go too far toward exposition in their direct literal statements, but the book should be read as a whole. A fundamental sequence in a richly varied pattern begins in the beautiful thing, the ornament of the land, and moves through the good heart, ignorance and fears, natural purification, exaltation of the spirit, to hope in humility and learning if the two are kept together. It has its by-paths that seem insignificant, its plateaus that stretch too far, but the mountains rise, and the total landscape is worthy of its author. (pp. 148-49)

Gladys Campbell, " 'A World Torn Loose Went by Me'," in Poetry, Vol. LXXI, No. 3, December, 1947, pp. 145-49.

Yvor Winters (essay date 1948)

[*Winters was a twentieth-century American poet and critic. He was associated with the New Criticism movement and earned a reputation as one of the most stringently anti-Romantic critics of his era. Maintaining that a critic must be concerned with the moral as well as the aesthetic import of a work of art, he also believed that poetry ought to provide rational comment on the human condition. His critical precepts, usually considered extreme, include an emphasis on order, dignity, restraint, and morality. In the following excerpted essay first published in* The Sewanee Review *in 1948 and reprinted in his* The Function of Criticism *(1957), Winters argues that Frost's work "is both overestimated and misunderstood."*]

Robert Frost is one of the most talented poets of our time, but I believe that his work is both overestimated and misunderstood; and it seems to me of the utmost importance that we should understand him with some accuracy. If we can arrive at a reasonably sound understanding of him, we can profit by his virtues without risk of acquiring his defects; and we may incidentally arrive at a better understanding of our present culture. (p. 159)

Frost has been praised as a classical poet, but he is not classical in any sense which I can understand. Like many of his contemporaries, he is an Emersonian Romantic, although with certain mutings and modifications which I shall mention presently, and he has labeled himself as such with a good deal of care. He is a poet of the minor theme, the casual approach, and the discretely eccentric attitude. When a reader calls Frost a classical poet, he probably means that Frost strikes him as a "natural" poet, a poet who somehow resembles himself and his neighbors; but this is merely another way of saying that the reader feels a kinship to him and likes him easily. Classical literature is said to judge human experience with respect to the norm; but it does so with respect to the norm of what humanity ought to be, not with respect to the norm of what it happens to be in a particular place and time. The human average has never been admirable, and in certain cultures it has departed very far from the admirable; that is why in the great classical periods of literature we are likely to observe great works in tragedy and satire, the works of a Racine and a Molière, of a Shakespeare and a Jonson, works which deal in their respective ways with sharp deviations from the ideal norm; and that is why literature which glorifies the average is sentimental rather than classical.

Frost writes of rural subjects, and the American reader of our time has an affection for rural subjects which is partly the product of the Romantic sentimentalization of "nature," but which is partly also a nostalgic looking back to the rural life which predominated in this nation a generation or two ago; the rural life is somehow regarded as the truly American life. I have no objection to the poet's employing rural settings; but we should remember that it is the poet's business to evaluate human experience, and the rural setting is no more valuable for this purpose than any

other or than no particular setting, and one could argue with some plausibility that an exclusive concentration on it may be limiting.

Frost early began his endeavor to make his style approximate as closely as possible the style of conversation, and this endeavor has added to his reputation: it has helped to make him seem "natural." But poetry is not conversation, and I see no reason why poetry should be called upon to imitate conversation. . . . The two forms of expression are extremes, they are not close to each other. We do not praise a violinist for playing as if he were improvising; we praise him for playing well. And when a man plays well or writes well, his audience must have intelligence, training, and patience in order to appreciate him. We do not understand difficult matters "naturally."

The business of the poet can be stated simply. The poet deals with human experience in words. Words are symbols of concepts, which have acquired connotation of feeling in addition to their denotation of concept. The poet, then, as a result of the very nature of his medium, must make a rational statement about an experience, and as rationality is a part of the medium, the ultimate value of the poem will depend in a fair measure on the soundness of the rationality: it is possible, of course, to reason badly, just as it is possible to reason well. But the poet is deliberately employing the connotative content of language as well as the denotative: so that what he must do is make a rational statement about an experience, at the same time employing his language in such a manner as to communicate the emotion which ought to be communicated by that rational understanding of the particular subject. In so far as he is able to do this, the poem will be good; in so far as the subject itself is important, the poem will be great. That is, a poem which merely describes a stone may be excellent but will certainly be minor; whereas a poem which deals with man's contemplation of death and eternity, or with a formative decision of some kind, may be great. It is possible, of course, that the stone may be treated in such a way that it symbolizes something greater than itself; but if this occurs, the poem is about something greater than the stone. The poet is valuable, therefore, in proportion to his ability to apprehend certain kinds of objective truth; in proportion as he is great, he will not resemble ourselves but will resemble what we ought to be. It becomes our business, then, to endeavor to resemble him, and this endeavor is not easy and for this reason few persons make it. Country conversation and colloquial charm are irrelevant to the real issue. (pp. 159-61)

Frost has said that Emerson is his favorite American poet, and he himself appears to be something of an Emersonian. Emerson was a Romantic pantheist: he identified God with the universe; he taught that impulse comes directly from God and should be obeyed, that through surrender to impulse we become one with God; he taught that reason is man-made and bungling and should be suppressed. In moral and aesthetic doctrine, Emerson was a relativist; his most thorough-going disciples in American literature were Walt Whitman and Hart Crane. In Frost, on the other hand, we find a disciple without Emerson's religious conviction: Frost believes in the rightness of impulse, but does not discuss the pantheistic doctrine which would give authority to impulse; as a result of his belief in impulse, he is of necessity a relativist, but his relativism, apparently since it derives from no intense religious conviction, has resulted mainly in ill-natured eccentricity and in increasing melancholy. He is an Emersonian who has become sceptical and uncertain without having reformed; and the scepticism and uncertainty do not appear to have been so much the result of thought as the result of the impact upon his sensibility of conflicting notions of his own era—they appear to be the result of his having taken the easy way and having drifted with the various currents of his time.

I should like first of all to describe a few poems which deal with what in the hands of a more serious writer one could describe as the theme of moral choice. These poems throw more light on Frost as a whole, perhaps, than do any others, and they may serve as an introduction to his work. I have in mind especially three poems from *Mountain Interval:* the introductory piece entitled **"The Road not Taken,"** the post-scriptive piece entitled **"The Sound of the Trees,"** and the lyrical narrative called **"The Hill-Wife;"** and one poem from *A Further Range:* the poem entitled **"The Bearer of Evil Tidings."** These poems all have a single theme: the whimsical, accidental, and incomprehensible nature of the formative decision; and I should like to point out that if one takes this view of the formative decision, one has cut oneself off from understanding most of human experience, for in these terms there is nothing to be understood—one can write of human experience with sentimental approval or with sentimental melancholy, but with little else.

"The Road not Taken," for example, is the poem of a man whom one might fairly call a spiritual drifter; and a spiritual drifter is unlikely to have either the intelligence or the energy to become a major poet. Yet the poem has definite virtues, and these should not be overlooked. In the first place, spiritual drifters exist, they are real; and although their decisions may not be comprehensible, their predicament is comprehensible. The poem renders the experience of such a person, and renders the uncertain melancholy of his plight. Had Frost been a more intelligent man, he might have seen that the plight of the spiritual drifter was not inevitable, he might have judged it in the light of a more comprehensive wisdom. Had he done this, he might have written a greater poem. But his poem is good as far as it goes; the trouble is that it does not go far enough, it is incomplete, and it puts on the reader a burden of critical intelligence which ought to be borne by the poet. We are confronted with a similar critical problem when the Earl of Rochester writes remarkably beautiful poems to invite us to share in the pleasures of drunkenness. The pleasures of drunkenness are real—let no one delude himself on that score—and the Earl of Rochester is one of the most brilliant masters of English verse. But if the pleasures of drunkenness are regarded in what the sentimental critics are wont to term a true perspective, they are seen to be obstacles to other experiences of far greater value, and then they take on the appearance of temptations to sin. Dante would have dealt with these pleasures truly, placing them where they belong in the hierarchy of values; Rochester was not equal to the task, but Rochester gave us a fine evaluation of the experience of a man in his predicament as he himself sees it. (pp. 162-63)

The comparison of Rochester to Frost is unjust in one respect, for Rochester was a consciously vicious man; whereas Robert Frost would not willingly injure anyone.

Yet the comparison in other ways is just, for Frost, as I shall show, has willfully refrained from careful thinking and so is largely responsible for his own condition; and his condition is less dramatic and more easily shared by large numbers of his contemporaries than was the condition of Rochester, so that he is probably a greater menace to the general intelligence. Rochester knew himself to be a sinner, and he knew that he would be regarded as one. Frost by a process of devious evasions has convinced himself that he is a wise and virtuous man, and he is regarded as a kind of embodiment of human wisdom by hundreds of thousands of Americans from high school age to the brink of senility. He embodies a common delusion regarding human nature, and he is strongly reinforcing that delusion in the minds of his contemporaries.

"The Sound of the Trees" deals with a longing to depart which has never quite been realized. The trees

> are that which talks of going
> But never gets away.

The poem ends as follows:

> I shall make the reckless choice
> Some day when they are in voice
> And tossing so as to scare
> The white clouds over them on.
> I shall have less to say,
> But I shall be gone.

The poem has the same quality of uncertainty and incomprehension as **"The Road not Taken;"** it is written with about the same degree of success, with about the same charm, and with about the same quality of vague melancholy. In considering either of these poems, especially if one compares them even to minor works by sixteenth and seventeenth century masters, one will observe not only the limitations of intelligence which I have mentioned, but a quality, slight though it may be, of imprecision in the rendering of the detail and of the total attitude, which is the result of the limitations. Such a poem as Robert Herrick's *Night-Piece to Julia* is as sharp as a knife in comparison. Herrick knew exactly what he was saying and exactly what it was worth. Frost, on the other hand, is mistaking whimsical impulse for moral choice, and the blunder obscures his understanding and even leaves his mood uncertain with regard to the value of the whole business. He is vaguely afraid that he may be neither wrong nor right.

"The Hill Wife" is a less happy specimen than the poems just mentioned. It deals, not with a personal experience of the author, but with a dramatic situation seen from without; and the dramatic crisis is offered as something incomprehensible. The wife leaves her husband because she is lonely on their back-country farm, but there is no clear understanding of her motive; we are told that she is disturbed when the birds leave in the fall, and frightened by a casual tramp, and that a pine near the window obsesses her thoughts. The last section, characteristically entitled *The Impulse,* describes her final act as a sudden and unpremeditated one. The poem has an eery quality, like that of dream or of neurosis, but it has little else. As a study in human relationships, it amounts to nothing, and one has only to compare it to *Eros Turannos* by Robinson to discern its triviality. **"The Bearer of Evil Tidings"** deals with a similarly casual and sudden decision, although it is a more interesting poem. And one might mention also the poem from *A Witness Tree* entitled **"A Serious Step Lightly Taken":** the serious step in question is merely the buying of a farm; but the title is characteristic, and the title implies approval and not disapproval—it implies that serious steps ought to be lightly taken. But if serious steps are to be lightly taken, then poetry, at least, is impoverished, and the poet can have very little to say. Most of the world's great poetry has had to do with serious steps seriously taken, and when the seriousness goes from life, it goes from poetry.

I shall consider next some of the more clearly didactic poems, which will reinforce what I have been saying. I should perhaps mention briefly as one of these, a short lyric in **West-Running Brook,** a lyric called **"Sand Dunes,"** of which the clearly stated theme is the Emersonian notion that man can think better if he frees himself wholly from the past. The last poem in the same volume, at least as the volume originally appeared, is called **"The Bear."** The poem compares the wild bear to the bear in a cage; the uncaged bear is a creature of free impulse and is compared by implication to man as he would be were he guided by impulse; and the caged bear is compared to rational man as he is. The poem is amusing on first reading, but it wears thin with time. The difficulty is this, that satirical poetry is a branch of didactic poetry, for whereas purely didactic poetry endeavors to convince directly, satirical poetry endeavors to convince indirectly by ridiculing what the poet takes to be a deviation from wisdom; and both forms depend rather obviously upon the soundness of the ideas which they expound or assume. Frost tells us in this poem that reasoning man is ridiculous because he appears to labor and to change his mind; and he implies that impulsive man would be a wiser and a nobler creature. . . . Within relatively recent years, we have had two tragic examples, in Hart Crane and in Ezra Pound, of what a man of genius can do to himself and to his work by energetically living the life of impulse. It is not foolish to change one's mind; one learns by changing one's mind. Life is a process of revision in the interests of greater understanding, and it is by means of this process that men came down from the trees and out of the caves. . . . The uncaged bear, or the unreflective cave-man, is inferior to Thomas Aquinas and to Richard Hooker, to Dante and to Ben Jonson, and to assert the contrary is merely irresponsible foolishness. Frost then is satirizing the intelligent man from the point of view of the unintelligent; and the more often one reads the poem, the more obvious this fact becomes, and the more trivial the poem appears. (pp. 164-67)

Frost has something to say of the relationship of the individual to society. His most extensive poem on this subject is called **"Build Soil—A Political Pastoral,"** and was delivered at Columbia University, May 31, 1932, before the national party conventions of that year. It will be remembered that these were the conventions which led to the first election of Franklin D. Roosevelt, and that the time was one of the darkest periods in the history of the nation. The poem is Frost's most ambitious effort to deal with his social, political, and economic views. As to his economic views, he says that if he were dictator of the country:

> I'd let things take their course
> And then I'd claim the credit for the outcome.

This statement, if it means anything at all, is a statement of belief in an unrestrained laissez-faire system, of the sort that Emerson would have approved; a belief that if things are left alone they must come right. It represents a doctrine of political drifting which corresponds to the doctrine of personal drifting which we have already seen; in practice, it could lead only to the withdrawal from public affairs of the citizen not concerned primarily with personal aggrandizement, and to the surrender of the nation to the unscrupulous go-getter, who, though he may not be a drifter, is not governed by admirable aims. It is similarly an obscurantistic doctrine: it implies that this realm of human activity, like others, cannot be dealt with rationally and is better if not understood. . . . The individual is thus advised against any kind of political activity in a time of national collapse. The difficulties of effective political action are obvious; the English-speaking peoples have been struggling with the problems of constitutional government for centuries. But if the reality of the difficulties results in our stealing away from them, society will be taken over, as I have said, by the efficient scoundrels who are always ready to take over when everyone else abdicates. In a dictatorship by scoundrels, the Frosts and the Thoreaus, the amateur anarchists and village eccentrics, would find life somewhat more difficult than they have found it to date. (pp. 168-70)

The same sentimental dislike for society, for community of interest, can be found in the poem called **"The Egg and the Machine,"** a poem appended in the *Collected Poems* to the group called *West-Running Brook*. The poem tells of a Thoreau-like adventurer who is exasperated to encounter a railroad running through his favorite marsh. After a locomotive passes him, he proceeds to find a nestful of turtle eggs, and Frost writes:

> If there was one egg in it there were nine,
> Torpedo-like, with shell of gritty leather
> All packed in sand to wait the trump together.
> 'You'd better not disturb me any more,'
> He told the distance, 'I am armed for war.
> The next machine that has the power to pass
> Will get this plasm in its goggle-glass.'

Here are several familiar Romantic attitudes: resentment at being unable to achieve the absolute privacy which Frost names as a primary desideratum in **"Build Soil,"** the sentimental regard for the untouched wilderness (the untouched wilderness would provide absolute privacy for the unique Romantic), and the sentimental hatred for the machine. I am willing to admit, in connection with the last matter, that machinery is sometimes far from beautiful, both in itself and in some of its effects, but its benefits have been overwhelmingly great, and the literary farmer in Vermont could scarcely hope to subsist either as farmer or as writer without its help, any more than he could hope to subsist unless a good many people faced moral and political realities; and it is curiously unjust that the locomotive, that patient and innocuous draft horse of civilization, should be selected to symbolize the viciousness of machinery. Frost's real objection to the machine, I suspect, is its social nature; it requires and facilitates cooperation, and Frost is unwilling to recognize its respectability mainly for this reason. (pp. 170-71)

There is a kind of half dramatic, half didactic poem occasionally, of which I shall mention two examples: **"West-Running Brook"** and **"A Masque of Reason."** The first of these is a brief affair in the form of a dialogue between a young husband and wife who apparently have just established themselves on a farm next to a brook which runs west instead of east; they observe a ripple in the brook, in which the water is thrown upward and apparently backward against the current. The husband comments upon the ripple in certain lines which are the chief part of the poem. . . .

> It is this backward motion toward the source
> Against the stream that most we see ourselves in,
> The tribute of the current to the source.
> It is from this in nature we are from.

The theology of this passage, if we may call it theology, is tenuous and incomplete; it is what a certain kind of critic would call suggestive, rather than definitive; there is, in brief, very little to it. Frost seems to have suspected this, for he did not let his meditation on the ripple stand alone on its merits; he framed it in the dialogue I have mentioned and made his young people responsible for it. Yet the people are not depicted as characters, and their remarks lead to no dramatic action; the meditation gives the momentary illusion that the characters are more important than they are; the conversational framework gives the momentary illusion that the meditation is more important than it is. Thus the structure of the poem is actually a piece of deception, and the substance of the poem is negligible.

"A Masque of Reason" is the same kind of poem on a larger scale. The characters are God, the Devil, Job, and Job's wife. The scene is "A fair oasis in the purest desert"; the time is the Day of Judgment. Job and his wife suddenly discover the presence of the Burning Bush. She says:

> Job: There's a strange light on everything today.
> The myrrh tree gives it. Smell the rosin burning?
> The ornaments the Greek artificers
> Made for the Emperor Alexius,
> The Star of Bethlehem, the pomegranates,
> The birds, seem all on fire with Paradise.
> And hark, the gold enameled nightingales
> Are singing. Yes, and look, the Tree is troubled.
> Someone's caught in the branches.
>
> Wife: So there is.
> He can't get out.
>
> Job: He's loose! He's out!
>
> Wife: It's God.
> I'd know him by Blake's picture anywhere.
> Now what's he doing?
>
> Job: Pitching throne, I guess.
> Here by our atoll.
>
> Wife: Something Byzantine.
>
> *(The throne's a ply-wood flat, prefabricated,*
> *That God pulls lightly upright on its hinges*
> *And stands beside, supporting it in place.)*

This brief passage gives a clue to the nature of the whole poem. Job's first speech above is a piece of remarkable rhetoric; there is nothing else in the poem to equal it. It reminds one of Yeats, especially of Yeats's brilliant but whimsical poem called *Sailing to Byzantium.* From that passage onward, through the references to Blake and to

the plywood throne, we have details which are offered merely for the shock of cleverness; the details are irrelevant to any theme discernible in the poem. Frost, the rustic realist of *North of Boston,* appears in his old age as a standard exemplar of irresponsible Romantic irony, of the kind of irony that has degenerated steadily from the moderately low level of Laforgue, through Pound, Eliot, Cummings, and their younger imitators. The method is employed throughout the poem.

The poem falls roughly into three parts. The first of these deals with God's first explanation to Job of the treatment Job had been accorded in life. . . . So far as the ideas in this passage are concerned, the passage belongs to the fideistic tradition of New England Calvinism; the ideas can be found in more than one passage in Jonathan Edwards, as well as elsewhere. The carefully flippant tone, however, is something else; it belongs to the tradition of Romantic irony which I have already mentioned, and is used to make the ideas seem trivial. The ideas and the tone together express the Romantic ennui or disillusionment which is born of spiritual laziness, the laziness which is justified by the Romantic doctrine that one can best apprehend the truth by intuition and without labor. One can find the same ennui, expressed in various ways, in Henry Adams, in Laforgue, in Eliot, and in scores of others.

The second passage of chief importance is the one in which God revises his explanation. Job insists that God's explanation is not the true one, that God is concealing something. . . . The general idea is the same as in the preceding passage, but the debasement of the attitude toward the idea becomes now a matter of explicit statement as well as of stylistic tone. There is no understanding of good and evil in themselves, of the metaphysical questions involved. Good is submission to an anthropomorphic and undignified God and is made to seem preposterous. Evil is made equally preposterous, and for similar reasons. The poem resembles **"The Bear,"** but is on a larger scale. If these concepts of good and evil were the only concepts available, or if they were the best concepts available, then Frost's satire would be justified. But they are not, and in reading the poem one can only be appalled at Frost's willful ignorance, at his smug stupidity.

In spite of the close relationship between the two passages . . . however, the poem is far from unified. These two passages are separated by various outbursts of indignation on the part of Job's wife at the way female witches are treated, in spite of the fact that male prophets have always been received with honor; and there are other minor excursions. The concluding pages are devoted to the appearance of the Devil, who is called up by God, so that Job's wife may photograph the three main actors in the old drama as a memento. . . . In this passage, the satire is aimed at the word *tendency,* but the exact meaning of the word is not clear: it may mean a trivial fashion; it may mean an intellectual movement; it may indicate that Frost is unable to distinguish between a trivial fashion and an intellectual movement, just as he is unable to differentiate among reformers. The mutilated fragment from Herrick serves no purpose, but is merely an aimless effort to be funny. The poem as a whole is at loose ends; no single part of it is intelligent or even tries to be intelligent. It is a curious performance to signalize the seventieth birthday of a poet of so great a reputation. It is matched in triviality and general ineptitude by the collection of short poems entitled *Steeple Bush* and published more recently. (pp. 172-77)

It is worth while to mention one other poem in connection with Frost's retreat from the serious subject. The poem I have in mind is called **"The Times Table."** The poem deals with a farmer who is given to commenting on death and who is reproved by Frost: Frost remarks that such comments should not be made

> Unless our purpose is doing harm,
> And then I know of no better way
> To close a road, abandon a farm,
> Reduce the births of the human race,
> And bring back nature in people's place.

We should remember that Frost is a poet and normally speaks with full consciousness of his role as poet; it is reasonable to assume that this poem applies to the poet as well as to other persons. The poet, then, should not deal with death or with comparably disturbing topics, because these topics distress and discourage people. Yet I wish to point out that all people die, that human life is filled with tragedy, and that commonly the tragedies accumulate all but overwhelmingly toward the end. To ignore the tragic subject is to leave oneself unprepared for the tragic experience; it is likely to lead to disaster and collapse. It is the business of the poet, let me repeat, to understand his subjects, and as far as may be the most difficult and important subjects, in rational terms, and at the same time to communicate the feeling which ought to be communicated by that rational understanding. The great poet judges the tragic subject completely, that is, rationally and emotionally; the nature of the human mind is such that we can enter the poet's mind by way of his poem, if we are willing to make the effort, and share his judgment. In this way we may gain both understanding and strength, for the human mind is so made that it is capable of growth and of growth in part through its own self-directed effort. This is the virtue of poetry; in so far as it is good, and we understand both its goodness and its limitations, it enables us to achieve a more nearly perfect and comprehensive being, to reduce that margin of spiritual privation which is evil. But Frost advises us to turn away from serious topics, and for the greater part he confines himself to minor topics. The major topics impinge upon his personal experience, however, for after all they are unavoidable; but his treatment of them is usually whimsical, sentimental, and evasive; and in his latter years his poetry is more and more pervaded by an obscure melancholy which he can neither control nor understand.

Yet Frost has a genuine gift for writing, as I have pointed out, and this gift emerges more clearly in his later work than in his earlier, though still hesitantly and momentarily. The view of human nature which we have seen Frost to hold is one that must lead of necessity to a feeling that the individual man is small, lost, and unimportant in the midst of a vast and changing universe. This feeling is expressed in the well-known poem entitled **"On Going Unnoticed."** The nostalgic love for the chaotic and the dream-like, which Frost inherits from the Romantic tradition, along with an habitual but unreasoned hesitancy or fear, which is the heritage of the earlier New England, keeps Frost looking two ways, unable to move decisively in either direction. He is neither a truly vigorous Roman-

tic, such as Hart Crane, nor a truly reactionary Classicist, such as E. A. Robinson. He cannot decide whether to go or to stay, and the result is uncertainty and increasing melancholy. One may see the same difficulty in **"Tree at My Window."** Frost sees his own mind as similar to the vague dream-head of the tree, the thing next most diffuse to cloud, and the feeling of the poem is one of a melancholy longing to share the dream-like experience more fully. One can trace the manner in which Frost has arrived at this state of mind, and to that extent the poem is comprehensible. The feeling appears to be rendered more or less truly; that is, it seems to be an acceptable version of the feelings of a man in this predicament. But the poet does not understand the nature or the limitations of the predicament; and to that extent the poem is incomplete and not quite sure of itself. Like **"The Road not Taken"** it puts on the reader a burden of critical intelligence which ought to have been born more fully by the poet; and if the reader is not capable of the necessary intelligence, the poem is likely to draw him into a similar state of mind. (pp. 179-81)

The symbolic lyrics which I have been discussing are all to be found in the volume called *West-Running Brook,* the fifth collection. There is one poem in the volume, the sonnet entitled **"Acquainted with the Night,"** which surpasses any poem thus far mentioned and which seems to me one of the two or three best poems that Frost has written. Superficially, the poem deals with the feeling of loneliness which one has when walking late at night in a strange city; but symbolically it deals with the poet's loneliness in a strange and obscure world, and the clock which tells him that the time is neither wrong nor right is a symbol of the relativism which causes his melancholy. The understanding of his predicament appears to be greater in this poem than in most of the others; he knows, at least, that it is a predicament and realizes the state of mind to which it has brought him. In the seventh volume, *A Witness Tree,* there is an even more impressive piece entitled **"The Most of It."** This poem represents a momentary insight into the vast and brute indifference of nature, the nature toward which Frost has cherished so sentimental a feeling through so many poems. For a moment the poet appears to be appalled. The poem deals with a protagonist who seems to have cultivated solitude, like Frost, and who heard only the echo of his own voice in the wilderness but who longed for a personal reply from nature. The reply, when it came, was not the one he had wanted. One morning he saw a splash on the far side of the lake, and something swimming toward him, and then:

> Instead of proving human when it neared
> And some one else additional to him,
> As a great buck it powerfully appeared,
> Pushing the crumpled water up ahead,
> And landed pouring like a waterfall,
> And stumbled through the rocks with horny tread,
> And forced the underbrush—and that was all.

Frost's buck has much the same kind of symbolic grandeur as the apocryphal beast in *The Second Coming,* by Yeats, and he has the advantage of greater reality; the style combines descriptive precision with great concentration of meaning and at the same time is wholly free from decoration, ineptitude, and other irrelevancy. The poem gives one some idea of how great a poet Frost might conceivably have been, had he been willing to use his mind instead of letting it wither. In this poem especially, and to some extent in **"Acquainted with the Night,"** the poet confronts his condition fairly and sees it for what it is, but the insight is momentary: he neither proceeds from this point to further understanding nor even manages to retain the realization that he has achieved. Much else in *A Witness Tree* is similar to the earlier work, and the next two books, *A Masque of Reason* (which I have described in some detail) and *Steeple Bush* are his feeblest and least serious efforts. (pp. 182-83)

In *A Witness Tree* there is a narrative of considerable interest, **"The Discovery of the Madeiras."** It retells a story from Hackluyt about a pair of lovers who elope from England; the captain of their vessel, who had been a slaver, tells the man a singularly brutal story about the murder of a pair of negroes who were lovers; the man repeats it to his lady, and she withdraws to her cabin, becomes ill, and eventually dies. . . . It is written in eight-syllable lines riming in couplets and has something of the effect of a modern and sophisticated ballad. But the best of the old border ballads differ in one important respect: they deal, commonly, with an important decision consciously made, and with the resultant action, which is frequently violent but which is also important, either for good or for evil; Frost's poem deals with the accidental impingement of a brutal fact upon a morbid sensibility and the collapse of the sensibility. Frost's poem to this extent is the product of a decadent state of mind. Frost runs up against another difficulty in this poem which he encounters in all his narratives: the virtual impossibility of writing a short and purely realistic narrative which shall attain great power. The narrative, if it is to be short, must be symbolical or allegorical, it must be packed with the power of generalization; if it is to be purely realistic, it must be developed and explored fully in its capacity as a particular history. The short story writer in prose meets the same difficulty, but the short story is a longer and freer form and so has a better chance of success; and furthermore it makes a more modest claim upon our expectations, so that we are less likely to trouble ourselves about its limits.

These remarks have been unfair to Frost in certain respects. I have quoted most extensively from his didactic poems, and especially from those in blank verse. Frost is at his worst in didactic writing, in spite of his fondness for it: his ideas are impossible and his style is exceptionally shoddy. Furthermore, although Frost is frequently very skillful in the handling of short rimed forms, he is extremely inept in managing blank verse; in blank verse his theory of conversational style shows itself at its worst— the rhythms are undistinguished and are repetitious to the point of deadly monotony. But it is in these poems that Frost states his ideas most unmistakably, and it is necessary to understand the ideas to form an estimate of him at all. He is at his best, as regards style, in the short rimed lyric, but his short lyrics are less explicit in stating their themes, and unless one comes to them with a clear concept of Frost's principal themes one may overlook the themes or mistake them. Frost is at his best in such poems as **"The Most of It"** and **"Acquainted with the Night,"** in which he seems to be more or less aware of the untenability of his own position and to face his difficulty, or as **"The Vindictives,"** in which as the result of a fortunate accident of some kind he is able simply to ignore his usual themes and write as if he had never heard of them. The greater part of his really memorable work, however, is to be found among the symbolic lyrics, of which **"The Last Mowing"** and **"Spring Pools"** are excellent examples, lyrics in which the descriptive element is beautifully handled, in which the feeling is communicated with a sufficient degree of success to make them unforgettable but with so great a degree of imprecision as to make them curiously unsatisfactory. For the feeling does not arise merely from the contemplation of the natural objects described: if it did so, it would be too strong and too mysteriously elusive for its origins; the feeling arises mainly from the concepts of which the natural objects are the symbolic vehicles, and those concepts, as I have shown, are unacceptable, and when one tries to project them clearly into terms of human action are unimaginable. Frost's instinctualism, his nostalgia for dream and chaos, are merely the symptoms of sentimental obscurantism when, as in Frost's work, they are dealt with lightly and whimsically, but if taken seriously, as in the work of Crane and Pound, they may lead to more serious difficulties. They do not lead toward intelligence, no matter how far the individual devotee may travel in their company; they lead away from intelligence. They lead away from the true comprehension of human experience which makes for great, or even for successful, poetry. (pp. 184-86)

Frost, then, may be described as a good poet in so far as he may be said to exist, but a dangerous influence in so far as his existence is incomplete. He is in no sense a great poet, but he is at times a distinguished and valuable poet. In order to evaluate his work and profit by it, however, we must understand him far better than he understands himself, and this fact indicates a very serious weakness in his talent. If we do not so understand him, his poetry is bound to reinforce some of the most dangerous tendencies of our time; his weakness is commonly mistaken for wisdom, his vague and sentimental feeling for profound emotion, as his reputation and the public honors accorded him plainly testify. He is the nearest thing we have to a poet laureate, a national poet; and this fact is evidence of the community of thought and feeling between Frost and a very large part of the American literary public. The principles which have saved some part of Frost's talent, the principles of Greek and Christian thought, are principles which are seldom openly defended and of which the implications and ramifications are understood by relatively few of our contemporaries, by Frost least of all; they operate upon Frost at a distance, through social inheritance, and he has done his best to adopt principles which are opposed to them. The principles which have hampered Frost's development, the principles of Emersonian and Thoreauistic Romanticism, are the principles which he has openly espoused, and they are widespread in our culture. Until we understand these last and the dangers inherent in them and so abandon them in favor of better, we are unlikely to produce many poets greater than Frost, although a few poets may have intelligence enough to work clear of such influences; and we are likely to deteriorate more or less rapidly both as individuals and as a nation. (p. 187)

Yvor Winters, "Robert Frost, Or the Spiritual Drifter as Poet," in his The Function of Criticism: Problems and Exercises, *Alan Swallow, 1957, pp. 157-87.*

C. M. Bowra   (essay date 1950)

[*Bowra, an English critic and literary historian, was considered among the foremost classical scholars of the first half of the twentieth century. He also wrote extensively on modern literature, particularly modern European poetry, in studies noted for their erudition, lucidity, and straightforward style. In the following excerpt, Bowra examines the themes and techniques inherent in Frost's work.*]

The achievement of the United States in poetry is undeniably paradoxical. This vast country, with its wide variety of landscape and human beings, has seldom found a truly national poet who speaks primarily of American experience from an American point of view. It has given Edgar Allan Poe to Europe and T. S. Eliot to England, but in the nineteenth century its only great national poet was Walt Whitman. . . . He was the poet of pioneers and explorers, of 1848 and the Civil War, but not of established American life, of the farms and villages which created the American people and gave to it some of its most notable characteristics. His more respectable and more respected contemporaries in New England lacked his essentially American outlook. They put too much trust in European standards and models, and their work is American only in a limited sense. In Longfellow and Whittier, even in Emerson, we miss the local accent, the indigenous touch. In their desire to keep abreast of their time and to speak to the word, they fell too often into a standardised view of life which lacks colour and does not always carry conviction. The twentieth century has been more adventurous and more consciously American. If at times it has been too adventurous, it has at least tried to speak of a world that it knows and to make the most of it.

With the possible exception of Virginia, New England is the most individual region of the United States. With a history that goes back to the Pilgrim Fathers, with its old, if uneasy, connections with the British Isles, with its Puritan independence, with its peculiar dialect noted for its nasal inflections and its biblical turns of phrase, it has still in its country districts a homogeneity and an originality which can hardly be found elsewhere in the United States. Its white, wooden villages, with their array of rival church round a village green, have a character unlike anything in the Middle West, with its interminable main streets and its devotion to corrugated iron. Outside the large towns New England is a country of hills and rivers, of agriculture and forestry. . . . Here are a past and background and a richness of colour which we do not always associate with America. Such a society provides material for a special kind of poetry. It has those finer shades which come from long established habits and from local idiosyncrasies. The Puritan tradition is even now not broken and still gives a pattern and a style to village life. Such conditions may well produce a poet, and in Robert Frost, New England has at last come into its own. Through him New Hampshire and Vermont and the outlying parts of Massachusetts have found a voice—a voice not of Boston and its Brahmins but of the fields and the woods.

Frost was actually born in California, but he came of New England stock and has spent most of his life in New England. To it he owes nearly all his subjects, and its marks are clear on everything that he writes. He speaks for it with special knowledge and special authority. Just because

Frost using his homemade writing board, 1915.

he is a New Englander, he was slow to start. Though he was born in 1875, he did not publish his first book of poems, *A Boy's Will,* until 1913, when he was thirty-eight years old, and even then he had not found his essential gifts or his really personal utterance. There is still something conventional and artificial about most of these poems. The language is a little too careful, the tone too sweet, the music too tender, and too regular. But once or twice something unusual makes itself heard, and it is clear that Frost has begun to find his special gifts. (pp. 46-7)

Frost found himself with **North of Boston** and **Mountain Interval**. . . . His poetry is concerned not merely with his own corner of New England but, strictly and accurately, with what he actually knows of it. Since it deals in the first place not with fancies but with facts, it can fairly be called realistic. Its subjects are drawn from country life and often from its most familiar activities, and are presented with an experienced knowledge which proves that the poet is a true countryman. This realism is not a form of display but comes from a pleasure in the manifold aspects of life in farms and fields. Frost dwells on details because he loves them and what they stand for, and likes to honour them with careful sketches of them. He builds his verses on a precise observation of common things and common sights. (pp. 48-9)

Through his loving observation of otherwise unnoticed things Frost secures a special kind of success. Just because he himself is engaged so deeply by what he sees, he makes others feel that even the most modest sight may have a special interest. By the mere act of noticing something and turning his mind to it he suddenly makes it vivid. Everyone knows the familiar sight of broken walls in the country, nor does it usually excite comment. Frost, however, has his own view of the matter:

> Something there is that doesn't love a wall,
> That sends the frozen ground-swell under it,
> And spills the upper boulders in the sun;
> And makes gaps even two can pass abreast.

This is only the start for a poem which raises several original and pertinent questions and touches on several sides of life. But it is an excellent start because it is solidly grounded in fact. Again, many poets have written about the spring, but Frost has his own contribution to make in his precise account of April weather:

> The sun was warm but the wind was chill.
> You know how it is with an April day;
> When the sun is out and the wind is still,
> You're one month on in the middle of May.
> But if you so much as dare to speak,
> A cloud comes over the sunlit arch,
> A wind comes off a frozen peak,
> And you're two months back in the middle of March.

This is admirable, partly because the observation is so keen and sensitive, partly because it has more than observation. The poet not only notices the freakish moods of the sun but gives to each its exact quality and catches the whimsical atmosphere of such a day.

This observation of real things is presented in a gentle and unobtrusive style. Frost deals with familiar objects and does not try to pretend that they are essentially different from what they are to the common man. Frost may see more in them than others do, but they belong to the ordinary world and must not be presented in too grandiose a manner. This style may be a development of the language used by the Georgian poets, but it has more life and distinction than its origins would suggest. It is never flat or dull, and its quiet air is the product of accomplished art. Frost sets his tone at this pitch because he is concerned with real things in the same way as other men are. But his language has many half-concealed virtues. It responds exactly to Frost's moods; it is never lazy or verbose; its occasional flashes of conversational idiom are perfectly timed and produced with unerring tact: it has been severely pruned of literary echoes. Frost brings off his special effects because he operates with a style so natural and straightforward that even the slightest shock or surprise seems almost violent in his level tones. He fulfils Wordsworth's requirements for the language of poetry but without either Wordsworth's reversions to a grand style or the sophisticated simplicity of such poems as "We are Seven". Frost writes as he speaks with complete ease and felicity in the natural language of other men.

This naturalness is guided by a sure sense of the value and force of words in relation to each other. In such a style any word which is at all unusual or unexpected has a redoubled power and draws the whole poem to itself. It may even overweight the poem and spoil its balance. How skillfully Frost avoids this danger can be seen from many places where he uses an unexpected word and makes it do its full work without asserting itself unduly. . . . More often Frost uses a more subtle art and plans his emphasis so well that we hardly notice it. Take, for instance the poem **"Acquainted with the Night."** . . . The charm of this poem largely depends on the slight heightening of tone in the phrase 'acquainted with the night'. Just because it is a little out of the ordinary, it carries a special burden, and its repitition both stresses the main idea of the poem and pulls the whole together.

Frost uses these slight variations to secure surprise. Since he operates in a limited and largely familiar field, they cannot be very violent or impressive, but they give the delightful shock which comes from something seen and enjoyed for the first time. Frost likes to make discoveries, to start from some quite usual situation and then to find in it an unanticipated excitement or paradox or pathos. He is clever at finding such situations. He knows that they need not be very impressive, nor does he wish to make them so. He sees their charm and presents it on its merits. In this poetry the slightest change of direction, the smallest variation of tone, may produce surprise enough, as in **"Stopping by Woods on a Snowy Evening"**:

> Whose woods these are I think I know.
> His house is in the village though;
> He will not see me stopping here
> To watch his woods fill up with snow.
>
> My little horse must think it queer
> To stop without a farmhouse near
> Between the woods and frozen lake
> The darkest evening of the year.
>
> He gives his harness bells a shake
> To ask if there is some mistake.
> The only other sound's the sweep
> Of easy wind and downy flake.
>
> The woods are lovely, dark and deep.
> But I have promises to keep,
> And miles to go before I sleep,
> And miles to go before I sleep.

The last verse is a complete surprise. Most of the poem is taken up with a situation which has its own charm, but this becomes much more interesting because it is the prelude to something else which is the more mysterious because very little is said about it. Frost marks this change in his subject with a slight change of technique in the last verse, where a single rhyme and the repetition of the last line show that something important is afoot. (pp. 49-52)

In Frost's narratives there is always a central point, a theme which appeals by its unexpected character, though it may not be at all sensational. Frost likes the odd, the unforeseen, the paradoxical, but he is quite content that it should be found in small ways and on a small scale. Yet he succeeds in making his subjects significant and in relating them to fundamental issues of human life. Behind the vivid special cases we can see universal rules at work and know that even the oddest behaviour rises from something fundamental in man. For instance, in **"The Code"** Frost illustrates how countrymen have their own kind of honour and feel insulted when they are told how to do something of which they are perfectly capable. In this case a farmer goes too far with one of his hands and patronises him when he makes a hayrick. The hand takes his revenge by smothering the farmer with hay in the barn and leaving him under an enormous pile, not caring what happens to him. The farmer emerges, but is next seen not in the barn picking peas in the garden, and the tale ends with a neat little crisis:

"Weren't you relieved to find he wasn't dead?"

"No! and yet I don't know—it's hard to say.
I went about to kill him fair enough."

"You took an awkward way. Did he discharge you?"

"Discharge me? No! He knew I did just right."

That is all. The question of honour is settled, and the drama which turns on it reaches an appropriate conclusion in the farmer's tacit admission that he has offended against the proprieties of his profession.

This is not to say that Frost avoids exciting and mysterious themes. More than once he assays them. The country has its full share of secrets and horrors and Frost makes a proper use of them. **"The Death of the Hired Man"** is a humble tragedy of a farmworker who is of very little use since he always leaves the farm at the busiest time or tries to cajole the farmer with boasts and promises which he cannot fulfil. Yet he has his own pathos, because he has no home other than the farm, and, despite his poor efforts to better himself, he always comes back to it. Now he comes back for the last time, and, as the farmer's wife sees, he is dying. The farmer resents his presence and refuses to believe that anything is wrong with him, and anyhow why cannot he go to his brother who is quite well off? The wife feels differently and understands the situation, as she says to her husband:

> "Warren," she said, "he has come home to die;
> You needn't be afraid he'll leave you this time."

The husband resists the appeal to his sympathy, feels that anyhow he has done enough, and that anyhow the whole thing is a nuisance. Then he goes to look for the man and comes back quietly to say that he is dead. The poem is about the pathos of men who have no roots and no ties and no firm grip on life. Despite his defects and lack of character the hired man has his own minor tragedy, which emerges through the quite different views which the husband and wife take of him. (pp. 53-5)

New England has its traditions of witches and witchcraft, of which memories and more than memories still linger in the villages. In **"The Witch of Coos"** Frost touches on the subject. A mother and son whom he meets on a farm behind the mountains, talk freely to him. The son is proud of the mother, who, he claims, can do some unusual things:

> Mother can make a common table rear
> And kick with two legs like an army mule.

The mother is more reticent and claims no great powers for herself. She admits that she has spoken with spirits, but she is not very proud of it and thinks "there's something the dead are keeping back". But, none the less, she has her tale to tell. In her attic is a skeleton behind a nailed door. It is that of a man whom her husband killed when he tried to lay hands on her. In the night it can be heard in the attic trying to get back to the cellar where it came from. Then the story comes. The son, who was a baby at the time, gives his account of what happened:

> It left the cellar forty years ago
> And carried itself like a pile of dishes
> Up one flight from the cellar to the kitchen,
> Another from the kitchen to the bedroom,

Another from the bedroom to the attic,
Right past both father and mother and neither stopped it.

The mother confirms the story and adds other details, how she saw the creature coming upstairs, knocked its finger off when it approached her, and with her husband trapped it in the attic and locked it in. She used to keep the finger-bone in her button-box, and, though she cannot at the moment find it, her word is not disputed. It is all circumstantial and convincing, and its reality is the greater because we hear no more than what the mother and son themselves believe. It is not clear that the mother is in any sense a witch. Beyond the mountains such things are quite plausible, and there Frost leaves it.

Frost's lyrical poetry is a different kind of art from these stories. It has the same loving observation and the same quiet surprises; but it has other qualities outside the scope of story-telling. It is in the first place the poetry of Frost's intimate acquaintance with the country. In its traditional activities he finds much that is new and enchanting, and this gives a special quality to his record of it. While he carries out the hum-drum duties of farm life, he notices all manner of small things and so gives himself up to his tasks that everything in them has a special vividness. (pp. 55-6)

Frost's observation is always accompanied by delight in what he sees. He asks no great rewards from nature because it has more than enough to offer. The small surprises of country life are an endless source of pleasure to him. He sees a runaway colt on a mountain pasture. It shies away from him:

> And now he comes again with a clatter of stone,
> And mounts the wall again with whited eyes
> And all his tail that isn't hair up straight.
> He shudders his coat as if to throw off flies.

He sees the countryside covered with snow and thinks of the time when it will thaw:

> Nothing will be left white but here a birch
> And there a clump of houses with a church.
>
> (pp. 57-8)

Frost is much more than a recorder of what he sees. His visual powers are clear and exact, but they start other forces working in him and take him beyond description. In particular they evoke a special kind of fancy. A thing seen suggests something else, and Frost uses this second thing to bring out hidden qualities of the first, to make them clearer and to show what they mean. His fancy forms vivid pictures and no doubt owes much to sensations stored and matured in his memory. Some sight may so excite him that for the moment he believes it to be something else. This is not make-believe or even a momentary suspension of unbelief. It is real belief which transforms phenomena not usually associated with them. Frost seems to have had this faculty in childhood. In San Francisco, with its famous Golden Gate and its glittering atmosphere he heard tales of gold and told what these meant to him:

> Dust always blowing about the town,
> Except when the sea-fog laid it down,
> And I was one of the children told
> Some of the blowing dust was gold.
>
> All the dust the wind blew high
> Appeared like gold in the sunset sky,

But I was one of the children told
Some of the dust was really gold.

Such was the life in the Golden Gate;
Gold dust all we drank and ate,
And I was one of the children told,
"We all must eat our peck of gold."

This is of course a fancy, but a fancy based not only on a child's belief but on a real insight into actual conditions and an imaginative delight in them. This gift plays a large part in Frost's poetry and is responsible for some of its most striking qualities.

This fancy displays itself through the usual instruments of image and simile and always reflects Frost's discriminating insight. But it does more. Whole poems owe their success to it, because it provides them with just the moment that really counts, with the sudden thrill for which Frost prepares the way with sensitive care. (pp. 58-9)

Frost is for many reasons an unusual figure in the contemporary scene. He has hardly been touched by the modern desire to make poetry as intense and as suggestive as possible. His gifts are different. He is quite happy not to hint but to describe, to present not complex states of mind but simple emotions and moments of vivid insight into ordinary things. For his own ends he has evolved a truly adequate technique which secures those quiet and yet delightful effects which are his domain. He is fortunate in having New England behind him; for it gives to his work a background and a unity of character which are lacking to many more travelled and more cosmopolitan poets. But New England too is fortunate in having found an authentic voice in Frost. Perhaps this rural world of which he speaks with such love and knowledge will decay. The trees are already growing again in the clearings which the old colonists made, and ruinous farm-houses, deserted by men who have gone to richer pastures in the West, are the haunt of wild animals. Frost has caught the spirit of this world while it is still alive. He shows no sign of melancholy or fear of decay. This world is good enough for him. He knows its faults and its failures, but he trusts in the wisdom of men and wishes them to be happy. . . . (pp. 63-4)

> *C. M. Bowra, "Re-Assessments," in* The Adelphi, *Vol. 27, No. 1, November, 1950, pp. 46-64.*

Robert Frost [INTERVIEW WITH Richard Poirier]

[*The interview from which this excerpt is taken was originally published in* The Paris Review, *Summer-Fall 1960.*]

[*Poirier*]: *When you started to write poetry, was there any poet that you admired very much?*

[Frost]: I was the enemy of that theory—that idea of Stevenson's that you should play the sedulous ape to anybody. That did more harm to American education than anything ever got out.

Did you ever feel any affinity between your work and any other poet's?

I'll leave that for somebody else to tell me. I wouldn't know.

But when you read Robinson or Stevens, for example, do

you find anything that is familiar to you from your own poetry?

Wallace Stevens? He was years after me.

I mean in your reading of him, whether or not you felt any. . . .

Any affinity, you mean? Oh, you couldn't say that. No.

Once he said to me, "You write on subjects." And I said, "You write on bric-a-brac." And when he sent me his next book, he'd written "S'more bric-a-brac" in it. Just took it good-naturedly.

No, I had no affinity with him. We were friends. Oh, gee, miles away. I don't know who you'd connect me with.

Well, you once said in my hearing that Robert Lowell had tried to connect you with Faulkner, told you you were a lot like Faulkner.

Did I say that?

No, you said that Robert Lowell told you that you were a lot like Faulkner.

Well, you know what Robert Lowell said once? He said, "My uncle's dialect—the New England dialect, *The Bigelow Papers*—was just the same as Burns's, wasn't it?" I said, "Robert! Burns's was not a dialect. Scotch is not a dialect. It's a language." But he'd say anything, Robert, for the hell of it. (pp. 229-30)

I've been asking a lot of questions about the relationship of your poetry to other poetry, but of course there are many other non-literary things that have been equally important. You've been very much interested in science, for example.

Yes, you're influenced by the science of your time, aren't you? Somebody noticed that all through my book there's astronomy.

Like "The Literate Farmer and the Planet Venus"?

Yes, but it's all through the book, all through the book. Many poems—I can name twenty that have astronomy in them. Somebody noticed that the other day: "Why has nobody ever seen how much you're interested in astronomy?" That's a bias, you could say. (p. 231)

Would you agree that there are probably more good prizes for poetry today than there are good poets?

I don't know. I hate to judge that. It's nice for them—it's so nice for them to be interested in us, with their foundations. You don't know what'll come of it. You know the real thing is that the sense of sacrifice and risk is one of the greatest stimuli in the world. And you take that all out of it—take that away from it so that there's no risk in being a poet—I bet you'd lose a lot of the pious spirits. They're in it for the—hell of it. Just the same as these fellows breaking through the sound barrier up there, just the same.

I was once asked in public, in front of four or five hundred women, just how I found leisure to write. I said, "Confidentially—since there's only five hundred of you here, and all women—like a sneak I stole some of it, like a man I seized some of it, and I had a little in my tin cup."

Sounds as if I'd been a beggar, but I've never been consciously a beggar. . . . I've been a beneficiary around colleges and all. And this is one of the advantages to the American way: I've never had to write a word of thanks to anybody I had a cent from. The colleges came between.

Poetry has always been a beggar. Scholars have also been beggars, but they delegate their begging to the president of the college to do for them.

I was suggesting just now that perhaps the number of emoluments for poets greatly exceeds the number of people whose work deserves to be honored. Isn't this a situation in which mediocrity will necessarily be exalted? And won't this make it more rather than less difficult for people to recognize really good achievement when it does occur?

You know, I was once asked that, and I said I never knew how many disadvantages anyone needed to get anywhere in the world. And you don't know how to measure that. No psychology will ever tell you who needs a whip and who needs a spur to win races.

I think the greatest thing about it with me has been this, and I wonder if others think it: I look at a poem as a performance. I look on the poet as a man of prowess, just like an athlete. He's a performer. And the things you can do in a poem are very various. You speak of figures, tones of voice varying all the time.

I'm always interested, you know, when I have three or four stanzas, in the way I *lay* the sentences in them. I'd hate to have the sentences all lie the same in the stanzas. Every poem is like that: some sort of achievement in performance.

Somebody has said that poetry among other things is the marrow of wit. That's probably way back somewhere—marrow of wit. There's got to be wit. And that's very, very much left out of a lot of this labored stuff. It doesn't sparkle at all.

Another thing to say is that every thought—poetical or otherwise—every thought is a feat of association. They tell of old Gibbon; as he was dying he was the same Gibbon at his historical parallels. All thought is a feat of association: having what's in front of you bring up something in your mind that you almost didn't know you knew. Putting this and that together. That click.

Can you give an example of how this feat of association, as you call it, works?

Well, one of my masques turns on one association like that. God says: "I was just showing off to the Devil, Job." Job looks puzzled about it, distressed a little. God says, "Do you mind?" And, "No, no," he says, ("No," in that tone, you know: "No") and so on.

That tone is everything, the way you say that "no." I noticed that—that's what made me write that. Just that one thing made that.

*Did your other masque—**Masque of Mercy**—have a similar impetus?*

I noticed that the first time in the world's history when mercy is entirely the subject is in Jonah. It does say somewhere earlier in the Bible, "If ten can be found in the city, will you spare it? Ten good people?" But in Jonah there is something worse than that. Jonah is told to go and prophesy against the city—and he *knows* God will let him down. He can't trust God to be unmerciful. You can trust God to be anything but unmerciful. So he ran away and—and got into a whale. That's the point of that and nobody notices it. They miss it. (pp. 231-33)

See, the masques are full of good orthodox doctrine. One of them turns on the thought that evil shows off to good and good shows off to evil. I made a couplet out of that for [the rabbis and Jesuits] in Kansas City, just the way I often do, offhand:

> It's from their having stood contrasted
> That good and bad so long have lasted.

Making couplets "off hand" is something like writing on schedule, isn't it? I know a young poet who claims he can write every morning from six to nine, presumably before class.

Well, there's more than one way to skin a cat. I don't know what that would be like, myself. When I get going on something, I don't want to just—you know. . . .

Very first one I wrote I was walking home from school and I began to make it—a March day—and I was making it all afternoon and making it so I was late at my grandmother's for dinner. I finished it, but it burned right up—just burned right up, you know. And what started that? What burned it?

So many talk (I wonder how falsely) about what it costs them, what agony it is to write. I've often been quoted: "No tears in the writer, no tears in the reader. No surprise for the writer, no surprise for the reader" [see Author Commentary]. But another distinction I made is: However sad, no grievance; grief without grievance.

How could I, how could anyone, have a good time with what cost me too much agony? How could they? What do I want to communicate but what a *hell* of a good time I had writing it?

The whole thing is performance and prowess and feats of association. Why don't critics talk about those things: what a feat it was to turn that that way and what a feat it was to remember that—to be reminded of that by this? Why don't they talk about that? Scoring. You've got to *score*. They say not, but you've got to score—in all the realms: theology, politics, astronomy, history, and the country life around you. (pp. 233-34)

Do young poets send you things?

Yes, some—not much, because I don't respond. I don't write letters and all that. But I get a little, and I meet them, talk with them. I get some books.

I wonder what they're at. There's one book that sounded as if it might be good, *Aw Hell.* The book was called *Aw Hell.* Because "aw"—the way you say "aw," you know: "Aw, hell!" That might be something.

Most of the titles are funny. One is called Howl *and another* Gasoline.

Gasoline, eh? I've seen a little of it, kicking round. I saw a bunch of nine of them in a magazine in Chicago when I was through there. They were all San Franciscans. Nothing I could talk about afterwards, though, either way. (pp. 234-35)

When you look at a new poem that might be sent to you, what is it usually that makes you want to read it all or not want to read it?

This thing of performance and prowess and feats of association—that's where it all lies. One of my ways of looking at a poem right away it's sent to me, right off, is to see if it's rhymed. Then I know just when to look at it.

The rhymes come in pairs, don't they? And nine times out of ten with an ordinary writer, one of two of the terms is better than the other. One makeshift will do, and then they get another that's good and then another makeshift and then another one that's good. That is in the realm of performance; that's the deadly test with me. I want to be unable to tell which of those he thought of first. If there's any trick about it—putting the better one first so as to deceive me—I can tell pretty soon.

That's all in the performance realm. They can belong to any school of thought they want to, Spinoza or Schopenhauer, it doesn't matter to me. (p. 235)

You once saw a manuscript of Dylan Thomas's where he'd put all the rhymes down first and then backed into them. That's clearly not what you mean by performance, is it?

See, that's very dreadful. It ought to be that you're thinking forward, with the feeling of strength that you're getting them good all the way, carrying out some intention more felt than thought. It begins. And what it is that guides us—what is it?

Young people wonder about that, don't they? But I tell them it's just the same as when you feel a joke coming. You see somebody coming down the street that you're accustomed to abuse, and you feel it rising in you: something to say as you pass each other. Coming over him the same way.

And where do these thoughts come from? Where does a thought? Something does it to you. It's him coming toward you that gives you the animus, you know.

When they want to know about inspiration, I tell them it's mostly animus. (pp. 235-36)

> *Robert Frost and Richard Poirier, in an interview in* Interviews with Robert Frost, *edited by Edward Connery Latham, Holt, Rinehart and Winston, 1966, pp. 229-36.*

Philip Booth (essay date 1962)

[*Booth is an American critic, editor, and poet. In his review of* In the Clearing, *excerpted below, he perceives incongruities in Frost's poetry.*]

What first comes clear in Robert Frost's new collection of poems [*In the Clearing*], which is being published . . . in celebration of his eighty-eighth birthday, is the telling image of its title. Since Frost has long contended that "Poetry is simply made of metaphor" ("saying one thing and meaning another, saying one thing in terms of another, the pleasure of ulteriority"), then it is clear that he means this image of cleared woodland to be more than a simple image. Condensed from a fine poem called **"A Cabin in the Clearing,"** the title is, by Frost's own definition of metaphor, a metaphor for the sake of clarification, which is his new book's subject. But because he takes double pleasure in "saying one thing in terms of another," he draws from his early poem, **"The Pasture,"** the line he uses to introduce his new poems: "And wait to watch the water clear, I may."

In itself, this epigraph is Frost's ulterior way of implying that *In the Clearing* is perhaps his final book. Taken together, title and epigraph measure between them those "miles to go before I sleep" which the poet has traveled from a clouded pasture spring to the deep and lonely clearing he has cut for himself in the dark woods.

If nothing less than a topographic map of Frost's complete poems can show the tote-road he has taken to reach his present vantage point, *In the Clearing* at least deeds its readers a definitive key to that map, and deeds them the freedom of those woods which he long since staked out as the unknown territory his poetry would explore. New poem after new poem makes clear how deeply each Frost poem bears on all Frost poems, and how surely all are a constant symbol of his life's commitment to making metaphors that clarify the dark paradoxes they contain.

The central paradox is, of course, Robert Frost himself: the darkly ulterior poet who has become confirmed, lightly, as a great public figure. The poet who sees himself plotted as a solo (if summer) Vermonter has come down-country to find himself blinded by the winter sun of a Presidential inauguration; yet he can still write, "persuaded that he will be rather more than less himself for having forsworn the world," as if not now a worldly old New Englander, but still the California boy born under U. S. Grant and christened Robert Lee.

The paradoxes of our civil history are personified in Frost's own history; his own rebellious demands for freedom have earned him that full understanding of America's revolution which he freely deeds to President Kennedy in **"The Gift Outright"**:

> Something we were withholding made us weak
> Until we found out that it was ourselves
> We were withholding from our land of living,
> And forthwith found salvation in surrender.

No poem about America contains a greater sense of the paradox America was and is; no poem demonstrates more clearly the resolution-by-paradox which distinguishes Robert Frost's poetry.

As we became a free nation not in surrender to a parent-state, but by giving ourselves outright to the revolutionary impulse that let us claim and explore "the land vaguely realizing westward," so Frost's saving freedom has been his slow surrender to the dark New England woods in which his metaphors are rooted. For America, "The deed of gift was many deeds of war"; for Frost owns a lifelong "lover's quarrel with the world," the deeds have been those poems through which he has, paradoxically, found salvation in surrendering to the conflicts they define. (p. 1)

Because just such conflicts underlie the best of his new work, it is useful to remember that Frost could not begin to resolve them until he asked in his full maturity "what to make of a diminished thing," until he surrendered himself to the dark woods that were both magnetic and dangerous, both "lovely" and "deep." Outside those woods, Frost has repeatedly played at being **"A Drumlin Woodchuck,"** shrewdly retreating into his well-known "crevice and burrow." But his greatest poems, as he must have instinctively anticipated, are those which confront conflict by exploring the dark woods that repeatedly symbolize the unknown, even as, at their darkest, they contain the final unknown of death.

Ambivalent as Frost's attitude toward those woods has always been, the very title of his new book makes clear how all-encompassing is their importance, and how consciously he has continued to explore them. Old poems like **"The Demiurge's Laugh," "The Road Not Taken," "Stopping by Woods on a Snowy Evening," "On a Tree Fallen Across the Road," "Desert Places," "Come In"** and **"Directive"** map, in sequence, the road Frost took into the dark woods, and record the serial ordeal he survived by surrendering himself to the conflicts such poems dramatize.

Frost has, from first to last, deeded his readers a metaphorical share in his ordeal. Those sunny-day friends who continue to count **"Stopping by Woods on a Snowy Evening"** as a winter lullaby should look at it again in the light cast by its terrifying new companion-piece, **"The Draft Horse."** And those critics who have trilled their recent discovery of how far in the dark Frost has traveled might be reminded, right as they are, that **"Into My Own,"** the first poem in Frost's first book, *A Boy's Will* (1913), from the beginning directed whoever would understand him to follow him into the dark woods. Only in those woods would the world, he said, "not find me changed from him they knew— / Only more sure of all I thought was true." Boyishly willful as this assertion was, it stands in retrospect as a first signpost to the direction of Frost's intent, and as a true beginning of his belief that poetry can and must be "words that have become deeds."

Robert Frost's deeds have been the words of dark poems, narrative and lyric: poems that explore those conflicts which, as they are partially resolved by definition, allow a man to range further and further into the unknown. The last poem from *In the Clearing,* as it distantly echoes **"Into My Own,"** and consciously completes the dark-woods sequence, is Frost's way of deeding to readers his final sense of just such terms of survival. . . . (pp. 1, 44)

It has become fashionable, perhaps under the influence of the newly old New Criticism, to discuss Frost's work as though he were two poets: the privately dark Frost of the great poems, the lightly public Frost of the lesser. That his lesser poems seem stunted in the shade of his great ones is natural; nobody needs be told that what the poet dramatizes in his rough iambics will long outlive the bard's departmentally rhymed didacticisms. But just as "the figure a poem makes . . . begins in delight and ends in wisdom," the poet is a single figure, capable of writing what's wisely light as well as what's darkly wise. Frost's latest platform couplet, "It takes all sorts of in and outdoor schooling / To get adapted to my kind of fooling," should serve as a reminder that Frost's public footnotes repeatedly cast light on how his metaphors should be privately read. . . .

In the Clearing, containing, as it does, new titles like **"One More Brevity," "Ends,"** and the revised **"Closed for**

Good," is wisely and consciously shaped as a deed of great age, and in it Frost has paid private debts by a series of dedications to old friends. Far more than that—as he knows that work begun in delight can end "in a clarification of life . . . in a momentary stay against confusion"— Frost is concerned with deeding to his readers some final clarification of those paradoxes that are his own stay against confusion.

Never is such clarification more open than in those poems that look heavenward from *In the Clearing.* If the dark woods he has weathered seldom permitted looking out far, Frost can now keep long watch on the deep brilliance of winter starts, "to satisfy a lifelong curiosity / About our place among the infinities." Some of the most moving new poems look up (as if **"Accidentally on Purpose"**) to be assured that the universe "must have had the purpose from the first / To produce purpose." . . .

Explicitly autobiographical as **"Kitty Hawk"** surprisingly is, its extensive revision from Frost's 1956 Christmas poem is more than a reseeing of Frost's long fascination with how science can substantiate or subvert spirit . . . . Frost [demonstrates] that poetry is a rational "pass / At the infinite," which is made substantial infinite image and resolving metaphor . . . .

Frost's first material metaphor for that spirit appears in his early *West-Running Brook,* the brook which, like the marriage it symbolizes, "Can trust itself to go by contraries." As the black stream catching on a sunken rock contains a white wave which, "by some strange resistance in itself," is flung counter to the current, Frost says it is this natural paradox "that most we see ourselves in," and he eternally defines it as "The tribute of the current to the source."

It is in this counter-current that we most see Robert Frost. By demonstrating, poem after poem, that just such images as a brook or a star sustain implicit metaphors, Frost has paid lifelong tribute to the margin of cosmic order which makes poems possible. By trusting himself to go by the contraries of paradox, he has surrendered in the dark woods to that strange resistance to downfall which is his poetry's strongest current. Asking of America no less resistance, **"The Gift Outright"** stands in itself as a symbol of the tribute Frost has deeded "our land of living," the source of those paradoxes to which men must surrender in order to survive.

What unknown conflicts a poet must survive, in order to find his own terms of survival, no one knows better than Robert Frost. Lost as he once was in the dark woods, he has by his own **"Directive"** fully found himself *In the Clearing,* and has earned every right to "wait to watch the water clear." As "a figure of the will braving alien entanglements," he has written and lived by his own paradox: "Strongly spent is synonymous with kept," and he has spent himself strongly in deeding us poems to keep. (p. 44)

Philip Booth, "Journey Out of a Dark Forest," in The New York Times Book Review, *March 25, 1962, pp. 1, 44.*

W. W. Robson   (essay date 1966)

[In the following essay excerpted below, Robson delineates Frost's achievements in American literature.]

An English critic (A. Alvarez in The Shaping Spirit) has this to say about Frost's present reputation in England: "Perhaps the only modern American poet who really is concerned with manners is Robert Frost. . . . I think this is why Frost has been so readily accepted in England; he is peculiarly congenial; we are easy with the tradition of country poetry, simple language and simple wisdom. American cosmopolitanism, even Eliot's, has always seemed a suspicious virtue, whereas Frost seems assured, he does not have to strive; he has New England behind him. . . . " Alvarez, perhaps unwittingly, gives the impression (which I do not share) that Frost's poetry is widely read in England. But otherwise this implicit placing of Frost ("country poetry, simple language and simple wisdom") in a familiar minor niche, does, I think, convey a true account of Frost's actual standing here. His reputation is based, it would seem, on a handful of well-known anthology pieces. "Everyone" knows **"Stopping by Woods on a Snowy Evening,"** just as "everyone" knows Masefield's "Cargoes," but that is not enough to put either poet in a context of active discussion. My own impression, for what it is worth, is that if Frost is mentioned at all, it is as a worthy but dull poet of about the rank of Masefield. And if this patronizing attitude is accompanied by a more sympathetic note, that may derive from the memory of America's unofficial poet laureate as a white-haired old man pathetically inaudible at Kennedy's inauguration. (pp. 735-36)

One of the chief problems for poets at the end of the nineteenth century was how to emancipate themselves from the coarse measures, the emphatic movement, so prevalent in Victorian poetry. Vers libre was one seemingly unavoidable consequence of the reaction against the often overemphatic meters of Tennyson or Swinburne or Meredith. But vers libre, in the hands of its inferior practitioners, became an excuse for carelessness, or exposed them as lacking the conviction that poetry is an art. Such an attitude was unthinkable in a poetic craftsman like Frost. His solution to the technical problem was to retain meter, but to incorporate into it the cadences of speech. It is the speech of New England speakers; its staple, the talk of an educated man at the point just before it crystallizes into formal prose. We do not speak prose; Moliere's M. Jourdain was wrong; we evolve it from the movement and syntax and cadence of educated speech. The artistic achievement of Frost was to evolve verse from these. Locutions like "admittedly," "to do that to," "of course," he brought into impassioned poems. Yet he did so in a manner which does not disturb our sense that we are reading poetry, something with its origins in song. His versification can always go back to the cantabile, yet it includes little that does not belong to modern (if sometimes a little old-fashioned) educated speech. (pp. 739-40)

Frost's colloquialism is famous. It is also notorious, for in his anecdotal poems he can sometimes sink to an unparralleled flatness. But critics have sometimes misrepresented this quality of his work by overstatement, seeing in it the whole of his innovation. This does not do him justice. The most casual reader sees that Frost is colloquial; reading which is more than casual brings out how much of the "ar-chaic" and "literary" language of traditional poetry he has retained. Thus no one familiar with Frost's work will find [**"The Silken Tent"**] uncharacteristic; yet to call it "colloquial" misdescribes it. So far from being the anecdotal jotting down of some incident of New England rural life, or a piece of gnarled rustic wisdom or country sentiment, it is a gracefully sustained literary fancy which (one might be inclined to say) could have come from an accomplished traditional poet. . . . [At first the poem] seems to belong with "literary" poetry; in its diction, syntactical organization, and structure—the careful and explicit working out of the central idea—it is obviously a "thing made," not a "happening," like a jewel, not like a pebble or a snowflake, as so many of Frost's typical poems seem to be. But "going slightly taut"—that is one's feeling about the poem: it is the reminder of the poet's formal control which here brings into unusual prominence Frost's usual firm grip on the sensory facts which provide the notation for his graceful compliment and comment; so that this delicate, consciously elaborated sonnet is, after all, of a piece with the most rugged of his poems. Frost's is a manner which can accommodate the literary and the artificial as well as other modes. (pp. 740-41)

Frost's technical innovation is a notable one, guaranteeing him a place in the history of poetry. A question that naturally arises is how far it was solely his innovation; and a related question, whether it should be regarded primarily as an American contribution to the poetry of the common language, or seen more in the terms of English poetic history. It would be ludicrous to deny that Frost's poetry is American poetry, not only in its manifest subject matter, but in more impalpable qualities. But, as often, the definition of "English" as opposed to "American," in literary matters, is not simple. Notwithstanding the debt which American readers may perceive Frost to owe to Edwin Arlington Robinson, it seems clear that the development we note between the bulk of the poems in **A Boy's Will,** and the poems in **North of Boston,** has a vital connection with the work and study in which Frost joined with English poets in England. It was in the course of this association that Frost acquired a knowledge of other poetic experimenting, and a confidence in his own discovered "voice" in poetry, which enabled him in the long run to exert an influence and attain a status denied to the isolated poet of Gardiner, Maine. What seems unquestionable is that Frost, in whatever other ways American critics may want to describe him, cannot be considered altogether apart from the Georgian phase of English literary history. (pp. 742-73)

"Georgian" was once an honorific description. . . . But it has now become the reverse, being generally used to stigmatize all the weakness and spuriousness of the writers brought together in Georgian Poetry by Edward Marsh. Their work is associated with facile weekend garden sentiment and a false affectation of simplicity. Schoolboys and undergraduates know that they were feeble escapists whom Modern Poetry consigned to the rubbish heap. What is sometimes forgotten, even by more mature students, is that Georgian poetry in its day was modern poetry. At least some of these poets thought of themselves as managing a revolt against established and popular traditionalists like Sir Henry Newbolt and Alfred Noyes. What they thought they were doing is doubtless irrelevant. And there is no need to have a very high opinion, or to weigh seriously the "modernity" or otherwise of that terrain of Georgianism in which Rupert Brooke is the dominant figure and his *Grantchester* the representative poem. The more relevant consideration is that some gifted writers, as well as some less gifted, do seem in retrospect to have enough in common for some characterizing adjective without a contemptuous overtone. The poets with whom Frost worked (Gibson, Abercrombie, Edward Thomas), Frost's own poetry, the short stories of A. E. Coppard, the early work of D. H. Lawrence—the period of English literature which contains these things reveals enough continuity between them and the work of weaker representative writers of the time, to need a historical description; and the word "Georgian," notwithstanding its unfortunate associations, is the only one currently available.

What these writers have in common is a preoccupation, amounting in some cases to a positive obsession, with personal freedom. No reader of Frost will need to be reminded of his obsessive concern with it. This plays a large part, clearly, in that sanctification of whim and impulse for which Yvor Winters, his severest critic, has castigated him [see excerpt dated 1948]; many of the poems quoted for adverse comment by Winters show that this attitude of "let me alone," a stubborn refusal to be pushed around by powers spiritual or temporal, is by no means confined to poems of playful whimsicality; a piece like **"The Objection to Being Stepped On"** is itself trifling enough, but the protest it epitomizes is the expression of something fundamental in Frost's work. No doubt in Frost it has to be related to the history of New England, and of the United States for that matter, as well as to his personal life and character. But it found a congenial environment, an echo of sympathy, in the Georgianism of "old" England also.

This passion for privacy can be the foundation of a distinguished and strong personal art. But it can also come out in attitudes and mannerisms and tones of voice that have in them something tiresomely complacent and limited. In Frost we see the tiresome side of his cult of freedom in a certain cranky obscurantism in politics and a grumpiness in personal relations (see his letters). In the English Georgians we have something worse (at least from a literary point of view): the attempt to invest with spiritual distinction a self-congratulatory sensitiveness about country walks, garden suburbs, and afternoon tea. That poem by Brooke which begins "Safe in the magic of my woods" . . . is a good example. The individual private responsiveness to nature on which the speaker in this poem congratulates himself, may be called the mysticism of the *rentier;* and mysticism in this context is apt to be the spiritual correlate of a vagueness about the sources of one's income. (pp. 743-44)

Frost, like Lawrence, seems to have brought refreshment from outside into this somewhat stuffy atmosphere. That there was harshness and bleakness in what he brought was no disadvantage. But these are not the qualities to stress here. The distinction that Frost brought to Georgianism, the moral and emotional stimulus he gave to a poet like Edward Thomas (we think of poems of Thomas such as "Bob's Lane") were due to a positive, attractive quality in his way of writing, a quality that distinguishes him not only from the Georgians but from almost any English poet since Chaucer. For this quality of feeling there is no satisfactory name. If, in default of better, we have to fall back

on "democracy," it must be in the full recognition that this word has little descriptive meaning, has become vapid; it belongs to political rhetoric, and—what in the present context is much worse—it suggests a backslapping *faux-bonhomme,* pretending friendliness which is utterly alien to the spirit of Frost's best work. And if we substitute "fellow-feeling," it must again be without any suggestion of the easy gush of egalitarian emotion. There is, it is true, a trace of friendliness in some of Frost's invitations to his reader ("I sha'n't be gone long.—You come too"). But his manner of warm geniality frequently covers something much colder. No one can suppose that the fellow feeling which is the subject of the poet of **"Snow"** (in *Mountain Interval*) or **"The Axe-Helve"** (in *New Hampshire*) is a feeling which springs easily into the hearts of the hard, sometimes curmudgeonly, caste conscious people Frost is writing about. No one can doubt that for Frost himself the impulse to "let go" emotionally is not one that is easily yielded to, or that there is much of his own voice in the speaker of **"Wild Grapes"**:

> I had not learned to let go with the hands,
> As still I have not learned to with the heart,
> And have no wish to with the heart—nor need,
> That I can see. The mind—is not the heart.
> I may yet live, as I know others live,
> To wish in vain to let go with the mind—
> Of cares, at night, to sleep; but nothing tells me
> That I need learn to let go with the heart.

Yet the capacity to express fellow feeling with a deep and complete sincerity seems truly typical of Frost; and to describe it adequately is to give full weight to the importance for criticism of Frost's being an American.

There is, of course, a danger here of oversimplification. We must not sentimentalize away the realities of caste or class consciousness in American life, either in the present or the recent past. The recognition of them is obvious in Frost's poetry itself, and has clearly played an important part in his perception of his subject matter. The situation in **"A Hundred Collars,"** when a professor has to share a room for the night with a traveling salesman, is just as uncomfortable as if they had been Englishmen. But it is uncomfortable in a different way; and to decide just what the difference is, is to bring out something essential in Frost's poetry. The difference is in the poet's attitude. We may imagine the situation treated by a liberal English writer of Frost's generation, like E. M. Forster. The vein might well be lightly ironical; the English writer, in the person of the professor, would have been ashamed of himself, would have known what he ought to feel, and would have done his best to feel it. Frost's attitude also includes an element of irony. But whereas the English writer would know what the professor felt, but would have to guess at what the salesman felt, Frost knows both. That is the difference. The conditions of American society and American life here give the American writer an advantage over his English counterpart.

Such an observation, however, could be made about a novelist or short story writer. In speaking of a poet we should be more closely concerned with technical considerations. What Frost brought home to some English poets in the early twentieth century was the truth in [Wordsworth's] famous description of a poet as a man speaking to men. (pp. 745-46)

But when we have granted the value of Frost's technical innovation, have we said anything more than that he achieved a style which (in Auden's words) is "quiet and sensible"? Whether one agrees with Winters' essay or not, it is surely its virtue to insist that criticism—as distinct from "appreciation"—*begins* here. Frost may have developed an all-purpose style which he could go on using for the rest of his life, and which other poets could learn from—English as well as American poets: for if some present-day English poetry (as is often said) has gone back to Georgianism, it is a Georgianism which has learned the lesson of Frost, unpretentiousness, plainness, lightness; that "pinch of salt," not taking everything seriously that is said solemnly, which William James is said to have brought back into philosophy, Frost brought back into poetry. But what is to be *done* with that style? And what did Frost himself do with it?

In considering the last question, an English critic's disadvantages are obvious. He has to consider Frost's New England, Frost's America, purely as a country of the mind. And he has to remember the warning conveyed by the answer a Frenchman gave when Matthew Arnold asked why the French thought Lamartine a great poet: "He is a great poet *for us.*" But there may be one or two compensating advantages. The American critic appraising Frost is in danger of other disturbances of judgment, as examples have shown. He cannot but be concerned with politics in the widest sense of that word. It is his critical duty, for example, to consider whether or not Frost has been rated beyond his merits as a poet because of an idealization of the older, rural America for which his work, and his supposed personal qualities, have been used as a sanction and a symbol. And it is his duty to consider how far Frost's work really does warrant this use. He must consider the issue, mentioned by Alvarez, of "cosmopolitanism" against "rootedness"; he must consider what conclusions for American criticism and American literature should be drawn from the fact—if it is a fact—that, as an American poet, Frost is the antithesis of Pound. (pp. 748-49)

The question he cannot avoid is whether Frost has ever written a really considerable poem. This is not very different from the question whether he is a great poet; but a critic might be discouraged from asking that question, partly no doubt because of the vagueness of the category, but in the main because of Eliot's authoritative insistence, over the years, on the relative unimportance of surmises about "greatness" in comparison with considerations of "goodness" or "genuineness." Yet it seems a reasonable condition even of the good and genuine poet that he shall have a poem to offer us. The search for it surely takes precedence over the historical inquiry (in itself of some interest) how the "Georgian" poet of 1914 developed into the candidate for the status of American national poet—vacant since Whitman—which was urged for him when it began to be felt that Carl Sandburg somehow would not do. No amount of national appeal, country charm, regional flavor, or anecdotal personality can be a substitute for a poem; it is only in the world of the higher publicity and literary fashions that "poems," "poetry," a general poetical atmosphere, appear to compensate for the absence of a "Sailing to Byzantium," a "Cimetière Marin," a *Four Quartets.*

But it may be objected that Frost is not the kind of poet who invites description in terms of single masterpieces: that his claim to distinction is the impressive level maintained in a large body of work. In that case the question may be put in a different form, while remaining in essence much the same: what has he to say? what is the substance of his poetic achievement? And when we turn our attention to that question the frequent embarrassment of Frost's commentators is ominous. . . . But what is troubling, as we explore their commentaries, is the thinness which he and other writers on Frost seem to sense in their subject matter, and their apparent need to import some density into it by paraphrasing Frost's thought and considering Emerson, Thoreau, and a cultural tradition and habit of sensibility deriving from them. Of course this embarrassment of the commentators may reflect no more than the unsuitability of modern critical techniques, influenced by modern poetic fashions, to get hold of so traditional and unfashionable a poet. The kind of ironies, ambiguities, or "polysemy" to which those techniques are adapted—and which indeed, in some poets of academic provenance, they may have actually inspired—are not there. Nor is Frost the kind of poet congenial to erudite exegetes; he has not constructed an esoteric world system, or a scheme of private allusions; there is no code to be broken. To be an adequate critic, it would seem, all you need is a heart and feelings and a capacity for independent thoughts about your life and your world; ingenuity and tenacious industry are not only not enough, they are irrelevant and distracting. Hence the plight of the commentator. But to take this line is to come dangerously near the position of those admirers who have institutionalized our poet, removed him from the talons of criticism, by insisting (in effect) that the scope of his achievement is no more open to rational discussion than the goodness of maple syrup. This kind of protectiveness really insults him. Frost's work may well require a different critical approach or procedure from that appropriate to discussion of Yeats's, Eliot's, or Valéry's; but the same final considerations of value, substance, and interest are as relevant in appraising it as to theirs.

If we do find a certain thinness in Frost's poetry, it is not because he has omitted to bolster it up with anything equivalent to Yeats's *A Vision* or Eliot's arcane allusiveness. . . . Frost has left us no poem of the quality of *Resolution and Independence,* a particular vision of man's life with its natural setting and tragic destiny. To avoid the charge of unfairness, we should at once turn to a poem of Frost which may come to mind as a counterexample, **"The Death of the Hired Man."** This is one of Frost's best known and finest poems, and no better illustration could be given of the poignancy he can achieve in spare allusive dialogue. Yet something forbids us to call **"The Death of the Hired Man"** great poetry, and what this is may come out when we place it beside Wordsworth's "Michael." What strikes the reader of Frost's poem in comparison with Wordsworth's is the *absence* of something. There is nothing in it corresponding to the poetic intensity with which Wordsworth invests the Dalesman's feeling about his ownership of his bit of land, a man's elementary desire to have something to hand on to his children. This inner lack may be pointed out locally, when we consider those passages of **"The Death of the Hired Man"** in which we are most aware that we are reading poetry:

Part of a moon was falling down the west,
Dragging the whole sky with it to the hills.
Its light poured softly in her lap. She saw it
And spread her apron to it. She put out her hand
Among the harp-like morning-glory strings,
Taut with the dew from garden bed to eaves,
As if she played unheard some tenderness
That wrought on him beside her in the night.
'Warren,' she said, 'he has come home to die:
You needn't be afraid he'll leave you this time.'

'Home,' he mocked gently.
                         'Yes, what else but home?
It all depends on what you mean by home.
Of course he's nothing to us, any more
Than was the hound that came a stranger to us
Out of the woods, worn out upon the trail.'

'Home is the place where, when you have to go
    there,
They have to take you in.'
                       'I should have called it
Something you somehow haven't to deserve.'

This is the emotional center of the poem, what the poem is "about." But, moving and tender as it is, the effect of the "background" passage about the moonlight is curiously extraneous. Indeed, the pathos of what is said in the poem about the life and death of Silas depends largely on the *absence* from the dialogue of anything like this capacity to give a universal representation of human sympathy; Frost's art, that is, is more akin to that of the short story writer than the poet. The passages about the moon seem something added to the story to make it poetry. Wordsworth contemplates the mode of life of the Dalesman with the same poetic vision as he does the mountain landscape:

> Among the rocks
> He went, and still looked up to sun and cloud,
> And listened to the wind; and, as before,
> Performed all kinds of labour for his sheep,
> And for the land, his small inheritance.

The significant difference between the poems—the difference in spiritual value—lies in the pastoral quality with which Wordsworth invests his simple story. He uses pastoral—normally a mode of irony for Frost—with complete seriousness; and the result is that generalizing effect which we look for in poetry of the highest order. By including this pastoral element Wordsworth has got further away from his characters than Frost; but he has also given a greater universality to his theme. (pp. 749-53)

The characteristic difficulty readers have with Frost is not "What does he mean?" but "What is the *point* of it?" Why has he chosen to crystallize *this* perception, rather than countless others? This kind of difficulty, it will be remembered, presented itself strongly—perhaps it still does—to Wordsworth's readers. But Wordsworth's little anecdotes, even if they do not always carry the charge of significance Wordsworth himself found in them, can be better understood in the context of Wordsworth's whole work—in the poems (by far the greater number) in which the poet speaks directly, not dramatically, sets out to communicate explicitly his thought or "message." Now Frost too speaks directly in the greater part of his poetry. And it will hardly be disputed that the quintessence of his work—his rarest and finest achievement—lies in the lyrical-reflective pieces in which he speaks with his own personal voice. But it is in that "personal" work also that we are most conscious, not only of limitations, but of weaknesses.

His principal weakness—the one that makes for the most doubt about his claim to high poetic rank—is monotony. This may be attributed in part to the very nature of his gift. What is represented by **North of Boston,** the achievement praised so warmly by Thomas and Pound, is of a kind that could be represented in comparatively few poems. How much of Frost's whole corpus (we cannot help asking) do we really need? His work calls out for anthologizing, as Wordsworth's, I think, does not. No one will doubt that Wordsworth wrote a great many mediocre poems, or worse, but we have to have *The Prelude,* and much else, before we can form a fair estimate of him. Frost's distinction seems only notably present in a few poems. His average—to speak bluntly—is rather dull. Johnson observes of Dryden that "he that writes much cannot escape a manner"; but "Dryden is always *another and the same.*" This could hardly be said of Frost, at least of the later volumes.

For there are dangerous temptations in a colloquial style, and Frost has often succumbed to them. The chief danger is self-indulgence. So far from making an effort to "escape a manner," he rather cultivates it. Old age can be the extenuation of much of the writing in **Steeple Bush,** where he seems at times to be maundering. But the same tendency can be observed in earlier work; Frost, like Hardy, seems to be a poet who, once he had formed his manner, stuck to it: there is no such technical (or personal) development as we find in a Rilke or an Eliot or a Yeats. This is both his strength and his weakness. (pp. 754-55)

In Frost's least satisfactory work, all that we tend to remember is the manner. **"Build Soil,"** the "political pastoral," is a case in point. No poet deserves to be judged on the basis of his political ideas in a narrow sense. And **"Build Soil"** itself shows that Frost is well aware of the warning conveyed in the words of Yeats: "We have no gift to set a statesman right." But as he adopts it in this poem the ironical plain-man manner comes to sound like a form of conceit. Frost has no "public" voice; so that when, as is apparently the case, he is recommending unrestricted laissez-faire (in 1932, a singularly inopportune moment one would think) it sounds like an attempt to elevate personal selfishness into a lofty principle. Undoubtedly the basis of this attitude is that passion for personal freedom, that need to feel self-sufficient, which permeates Frost's best work. But the manner of this poem makes it seem unattractive and smug. Less injurious, perhaps, is the playful manner of Frost's excursions into "astrometaphysics," though one understands the irritation of Malcolm Cowley at the "cracker-barrel-in-the-clouds" effect of much of this writing [see Cowley's excerpts dated 1944]. Frost's "metaphysics," it is true, are saved by the playfulness from sounding quite so hollow as those portentous reverberations, in cadences reminiscent of the later Eliot, which we hear in Wallace Stevens' philosophical poetry. His paraphrasable content is less empty; the poetry is less pretentious. But unless we find Frost's manner so congenial that we are critically disarmed, we must be tempted to ask why, if the poet himself (apparently) cannot take his ideas seriously, anyone else should be expected to do so.

A worse incongruity results when Frost brings the same manner into the field of tragic experience. In things like **"A Masque of Reason"** he is plainly out of his depth. The manner of that "masque," contriving as it does to be both smart and naïve, would be an affront if we were to bring it seriously into comparison with the tragic poetry of the Book of Job. No doubt in its characteristic weakness, as in the weakness of some of Frost's political poetry, we may see that tendency to blur the edges of Job's terrible problem in an optimistic transcendentalism where "evil tendencies cancel," and the waywardness, uncanniness, and utter incomprehensibility of the universe become somehow tokens of ultimate good. But optimism and reassurance are not qualities of Frost's deepest genius, which rests upon something hard and cold. Although a generalized geniality and a weak whimsicality are unfortunately common in Frost's work, they do not represent its strength. When he is a poet he is not genial: his true power, his peculiar sensitiveness, is closely bound up with those landscapes in which the season is always late autumn or winter, with flurries of snow, and a feeling of loneliness and danger impending; when a stranger is not a potential friend, but an object of suspicion. In his quasi-homiletic poetry Frost seems to be offering some vague theological equivalent of a friendliness and cosmic optimism which are antipathetic to his own creative powers. (pp. 755-56)

[It] is time now to draw to a conclusion about Frost's real strength, his personal poetry. This is not to be found in the most characteristic part of that poetry: the pithy observations, the wry gnarled apothegms, engaging and quotable as many of them are; but in more elusive poems, where the personality, or persona, of the poet is not strongly felt at all; where what we are given is the aperçu, the glimpse, the perception crystallized, where the poet seems to be beside the reader, sharing his vision, not gesturing in front. In such poems Frost has affinities with Hardy, the Hardy of poems like "The Wound":

> I climbed to the crest,
> And, fog-festooned,
> The sun lay west
> Like a crimson wound:
>
> Like that wound of mine
> Of which none knew,
> For I'd given no sign
> That it pierced me through.

We may compare Frost's **"Dust of Snow"**:

> The way a crow
> Shook down on me
> The dust of snow
> From a hemlock tree
>
> Has given my heart
> A change of mood
> And saved some part
> Of a day I had rued.

In the nature of the case such poems are delicate achievements, and it must be a matter of critical controversy whether some of them succeed or fail. **"The Lockless Door,"** for example, seems to me to fail. . . . The reader is asked to do too much; to keep pondering over a poem so slight and so imperfectly formulated until he has convinced himself of a significance which the poet may or may not have put there. On the other hand, **"Gathering Leaves"** seems perfect. (Its method may be usefully contrasted with the beautiful earlier poem **"The Quest of the Purple-Fringed."**) That the tone of voice is utterly unpre-

tentious, the rhythm light, even gay, far from detracting from the essential poignancy, actually increases it. . . . The subject of the whole poem is the same as that of Tennyson's "Tears, idle tears," but how much Frost gains from not *saying* anything like "O Death in Life, the days that are no more." Doing without sonority, doing without any play for a full-volumed response, Frost makes us live through (as we imaginatively participate in the simple actions he describes) the paradox of memory, real and unreal, intangible but substantial.

The obvious way of describing **"Gathering Leaves"** is to say that it is symbolic. But this suggests another observation about Frost's poetic gift. Too many poets seem to imagine that they have made a thing symbolic by saying so—sometimes in so many words. They expect us to read profound meanings into what they have created, without having created anything. Here Frost's strength is apparent. He can make real to us, as freshly felt, objects, places, processes. His snow is truly cold, his hills barren, his woods impenetrably deep. This solidity, due to the poet's power to convince us that his image or fancy is based on a true and strong perception of a real world outside him, is felt even when, in a poem like **"Sand Dunes,"** the explicit topic is the human mind or spirit's independence of nature. (pp. 756-58)

A preoccupation of these short poems is human transience, the poet's deep sense of flux and movement, and the brevity of "the span of life." For this immemorial subject of lyrical poetry Frost finds a note that is peculiarly his own. His strength here, as is customary with him, lies not in any very original formulation, or piece of consecutive thought or argument—the metaphysical passages in [**"West-Running Brook"**] are not particularly convincing—but in the transmission of a sense of transience as a process which is at one and the same time experienced, lived through, and steadily contemplated. The emotional tone of this contemplation, as often in Frost, has to be described by remarking on an element that is missing. There is no wistfulness. (p. 759)

To say that Frost avoids nostalgia is not to say that his poetry lacks the note of longing. But it seems to have more affinity with what we find in Wallace Stevens' poetry. This poet of grey lives and grey landscapes suffers from "the malady of the quotidian," is hungry for color, radiance, everything that is unexpected, brilliant, spectacular.

> 'Oh, that's the Paradise-in-bloom,' I said;
> And truly it was fair enough for flowers
>
> Had we but in us to assume in March
> Such white luxuriance of May for ours.
>
> We stood a moment so in a strange world,
> Myself as one his own pretense deceives . . .
> **("A Boundless Moment")**

(pp. 759-60)

But most typical of Frost's finest work is **"Neither Out Far Nor In Deep."** . . . The poem represents in metaphorical form men's constant awareness that they must die; and it does this without appealing to pity or horror or any mode of evasion: we are invited to contemplate the fact within the metaphor quite steadily. Yet there is an emotional tone, however hard to describe; the "they" of the poem are "we" and "I"; this fellow feeling prevents the

The Frost family in Bridgewater, New Hampshire, 1915.

poem from sounding dry or abstract, or gnomic in the manner of Emerson. Poems like these are perhaps marginal in Frost's work; marginal perhaps in comparison with other poets' more ambitious statements. They offer no easy comfort, are never likely to be popular; they are as remote as they could be from the whimsical or crusty persona of the farmer-poet. Yet it seems to me that in their combination of apparent slightness with extraordinary depth Frost achieves something highly distinctive, and indeed unique. (pp. 760-61)

> *W. W. Robson, "The Achievement of Robert Frost," in* The Southern Review, *Louisiana State University, Vol. 2, No. 4, Autumn, 1966, pp. 735-61.*

Allen Tate   (lecture date 1974)

[*Tate was an important critic, editor, and poet who is closely associated with two critical movements, the Agrarians and the New Criticism. The Agrarians were concerned with political and social issues as well as literature, and were dedicated to preserving traditional Southern values. The New Critics, one of the most influential critical movements of the mid-twentieth century, did not subscribe to a single set of principles but agreed that a work of literature should be examined as an object in itself through close textual analysis and could not be evaluated in the general terms of any nonliterary discipline. Tate, however, believed that literature is the principal form of knowledge and revelation which restores human beings to a proper relationship with nature*

and the spiritual realm. The following excerpt is taken from a transcript of a lecture Tate delivered at a symposium sponsored by the Library of Congress held on March 26, 1974.]

Robert Frost, "like other poets who have written with narrow views, and paid court to temporary prejudices, has been at one time too much praised, and too much neglected at another." I have substituted Robert Frost for Abraham Cowley in this quotation from Samuel Johnson's *Life of Cowley;* the sentence introduces the critical discussion of Cowley's poems and of certain other poets whom Johnson mistakenly called "metaphysical," as mistakenly as I have called Frost a metaphysical poet. Everybody knows that Johnson meant by "metaphysical" something like abstruse, complex, difficult. But so is Robert Frost difficult, in his own way. What looks like simplicity will turn out to be—or so my reading of him tells me—mere simplicity at the surface, below which lies a *selva oscura* that I shall be able to point to without quite getting inside it. And I must say here at the outset that I am not alluding to Mr. Lionel Trilling's famous 85th-birthday speech, even though I agree with it [see Further Reading list]. It was the first critical effort to break through the Chinese Wall of Frostian adulation. Although I am aware that I am beginning with the negative side of my observations on Robert Frost, I must go a little further and confess that Frost was not, when I was a young man, my kind of poet; nor is he now that I am an old man; and yet I am convinced that he wrote some of the finest poems of our time, or of any time. The Earl of Rochester wrote some of the best short poems in the language, but he is not my kind of poet. I am not linking Rochester and Frost; I am merely saying that one may admire what is not entirely sympathetic, and by not sympathetic I could mean that perhaps the poet wouldn't unreservedly like me.

Now, 11 years after his death, Frost is in partial eclipse. And nine years after his death, T. S. Eliot is equally in the penumbra of a declining reputation. One expects this immediately after the death of a famous writer. One wonders whether an occasion, such as this centenary celebration, will restore some of the popularity that Robert Frost enjoyed for almost 50 years. Is the living voice, back of the printed line, necessary? During his lifetime his readers could see, synesthetically, back of the poems they were reading, the handsome, massive face of the master and the dramatic changes of expression. Without the living presence one attends more closely to what is said and how Frost says it. For Johnson's phrase "narrow views" I would substitute monotonous metrics and a monotony of tone which results from a narrowly calculated vocabulary. In this he resembles Housman or even John Clare, but the resemblance is only superficial. I don't want the old gentleman to turn over in his grave; and yet I must risk it when I agree with Herbert Howarth that Frost was a reformer of poetic diction, contemporaneous with Ford Madox Ford, Pound, and Eliot, and that the necessity of reform was as plain to him, even if the result was different, as it was to his younger contemporaries. (pp. 57-8)

In more than 50 years of writing he published about 560 poems, some long, others no more than a few lines. How many did he discard, unpublished? No poet so prolific as Robert Frost could expect to write more good poems than he wrote. Those that I shall comment on may seem to the

Frost devotée an ungenerous, even perverse selection. Are not all the works of the master sacrosanct? If he has written one great poem, even a very short one, all the others must be considered. To my way of looking at poetry, he wrote more than one great—I shall not say lyric—more than one great short poem, and perhaps a dozen longer pieces. I don't know what else to call the longer poems. They are either meditations or short stories in verse, usually in iambic pentameter and always, whatever the meter and foot, metrical: there is always the tennis net. As to the shorter pieces, he never wrote anything as bad as Shakespeare's Sonnet LXXXV or as great as Sonnet LXXIII; not a bad rating, for those interested in ratings, for any poet since 1616. And although his scene is almost always "country things," I cannot see him with Mr. John F. Lynen as a pastoral poet. . . . I can find neither prelapsarian shepherds nor abstract sheep. There is nothing resembling either the *Idyls* of Theocritus or the *Eclogues* of Vergil. We know that Frost's Latin was fluent, and his Greek adequate, and his command of both languages probably better than Ezra Pound's more ostentatious exhibits. But Frost seems to me to have been too canny to write eclogues and idyls, even though his dialogs may have been suggested by his early reading of Vergil and Theocritus.

Before we pass on from this phase of Frost I should like to look rather closely at what I consider his finest longer—not very long or longest—poem: **"The Witch of Coös."** A month ago, or a few months hence, I might prefer the shorter **"The Wood-Pile"** or **"West-Running Brook"**; for with a poet who wrote so many fine poems, choice becomes uncertain and difficult. I am thinking of **"The Witch of Coös"** because it is typical of Frost's whimsical preference for the shocking circumstance that lies hidden beneath a conventional human situation. Like every first-rate work of art—poem, picture, sculpture, film—it invites endlessly varied interpretations, and all of them may be "right." I wish to look at **"The Witch of Coös"** through the eyes of Henry James—if I may commit a double presumption, even impertinence. To the question of what makes the skeleton in the poem fictionally real, there may be several answers. I assume that everybody knows the plot, but I shall have to repeat it in outline. The scene is set in the three opening lines:

> I stayed the night for shelter at a farm
> Behind the mountain, with a mother and son,
> Two old-believers. They did all the talking.

This is not quite plausible. Why should the mother tell her dreadful secret to a stranger, whom the poet makes no effort to establish as a character? Why did Henry James let the governess in *The Turn of the Screw* write her horrid story for nobody in particular, although in the prologue James explains how her manuscript got into the hands of his host at an English country house? A fiction must be told to somebody, if it aims at the highest plausibility; otherwise, as in the primitive novel, the novelist is merely listening to the sound of his own voice, as Thackeray, a sophisticated Londoner, is doing in his unsophisticated novel *Vanity Fair*. In **"The Witch of Coös,"** the wayfaring stranger, in the three lines that I have quoted, not only sets the scene in a remote place—"behind the mountain"—he tells us that both mother and son are "old-believers"—hindsight some time after the action to prepare us for something, an incident, an unusual natural phenomenon,

or some discredited superstition, to which he will be the witness. I say "witness" because he not only hears, he *sees* up to the limit that language will permit us to see, and it is not fictionally necessary to know whether this shadowy reporter actually believes what he hears and sees.

But let me dispose at once of the single flaw that I can find in an otherwise almost perfect work; I say almost because no work of art is perfect. It was not at all necessary to make the mother a spirit-medium, a table-rapper who can make the table kick "like an army mule." The action begins when the son asks his mother

> You wouldn't want to tell him what we have
> Up in the attic . . . ?

And she replies:

> Bones—a skeleton.

This "dreadfully" complex poem is, amusingly enough, a marvelous development of the common saying that we all have a skeleton in the closet. What appears to have happened is this: the mother had committed adultery with a man whom her husband killed, she says, "instead of me." They bury the corpse in the cellar. Her relation to her husband is frigid. . . . The bones come up the cellar stairs, "two footsteps for each step." Her curiosity is so great that she waits for him to see "how they were mounted for this walk." The skeleton stretched out its hand and she struck it, breaking it off, and she keeps a finger in her "button box." The common details by which the bones are made credible are the selection of a master; we are not allowed to see too much, or even very much. Frost instinctively found himself among the masters of credibility for the supernatural—Henry James and W. W. Jacobs. Whether the supernatural be hallucinatory or what it purports to be, need not concern us here. Let us glance at the way the woman sees the bones (as she always speaks of them), for that is the way Frost will let us see them. The "bones" emerge from the cellar; she envisions "them put together / Not like a man, but like a chandelier." And then:

> Still going every which way in the joints, though,
> So that it looked like lightning or a scribble,
> From the slap I had just now given its hand.

She calls upstairs to her husband to get up, and she follows the bones to their bedroom, where she admits to her husband, whose curious name is Toffile, that she can't see the bones, but insists that they want to go up to the attic, which they do without being seen by her husband, or seen a second time by her. Toffile is ordered by his wife to get nails and nail up the door to the attic where the bones have presumably fled; and Toffile pushed the headboard of their bed against the attic door. . . . The wayfaring stranger has the last word:

> She hadn't found the finger-bone she wanted
> Among the buttons poured out in her lap.
> I verified the name next morning: Toffile.
> The rural letter box said Toffile Lajway.

James would not have let her find it; nor would Jacobs in his masterpiece "The Monkey's Paw." (pp. 60-3)

Is the widow a witch because she alone, *when alone,* could see the bones and snatch a finger? There is no indication that she saw them again. Are they merely the "dry rattling of a shutter?" We shall never know, and I submit that

Frost's little masterpiece would be ruined if we could know. Canny old Robert might himself have told us that he didn't know. At any rate, what James said in the preface to *The Aspern Papers* is a rule that Frost's genius knew without James' help. Apparitions, said James, should do as little as is consistent with their consenting to appear at all.

Frost's most popular poems are little short stories in verse, a feature observed by many critics, preeminently by W. W. Robson, whose essay in the autumn 1966 issue of *The Southern Review* seems to me the best short study of Frost that we have [see Robson's excerpt dated 1966]. I would amend Robson's perception: short story to anecdote. I would cite a few famous poems that seem to me to be brilliant anecdotes. An anecdote differs from a short story in having a simple plot, or a single incident, in which there is no change of character. Even **"The Witch of Coös"** is an elaborated anecdote. The most obvious of Robert Frost's anecdotes is **"The Death of the Hired Man"** (it is not only obvious; it is one of the best of its genre). The old man comes back to work, and he is a skilled hay-pitcher. Warren, the farmer-employer, doesn't want to take him back, but his wife insists. So Warren goes back to the old man, returns to his wife to report him dead, and the poem ends. The anecdote is "used," the old, dying hired man is "used," to create a quasi-dramatic situation for two opposing epigrams about the nature of a home. Warren's:

> Home is the place where, when you have to go there,
> They have to take you in.

Mary's:

> I should have called it
> Something you somehow haven't to deserve.

There is always with us the famous **"Birches,"** a poem that I am fond of with the least possible admiration—the way we sometimes feel about certain old friends. Not that it isn't beautifully written. I don't remember ever mentioning it in print, but I must have long ago, for Mr. Radcliffe Squires says that I consider it an allegory of the poet. . . . Poets are like swingers of birches, for they too are engaged upon a profitless enterprise. "That would be good both going and coming back": it is good to write the poem (this is the upswing), and it is good to see it finished (this is the downswing). I have felt for a long time that "Marse Robert" might have spared us the sententious meiosis of the last line. Do I need to quote it? I will quote it: "One could do worse than be a swinger of birches." Yes, of course; but unless they are symbolic birches (in an Emersonian direction), if they are just plain birches, one could talk back and say that one could do a lot better than be a swinger of birches. The birches seem too frail to bear such a portentous allegory.

And now the famous wall that has a fine, domestic, and civic effect upon the people it divides. Either wall or fence. Alas, *something* can neither like nor dislike a wall—unless Frost is saying that mystery shrouds the human resistance to confinement, or perimeters, of any kind; and he observes nature's harsh treatment of walls and fences; the stones must be put up again, year after year, as the two characters in the poem are doing. This is the action to which their dialog about fences is the accompaniment. Nobody likes walls or fences, but if we are going to live near one another, if we are going to have even the first bare rudiment of a civilized society, we had better do something to preserve the privacy of the family, like putting up a fence or a wall; otherwise we will find ourselves living atavistically in a tribal society. I hope my rather feckless paraphrase of this poem is at least as tiresome as the poem itself. I have a little more to say about it. Good neighbors are good to have, but good fences do not make them good neighbors. Here we have Frost's perilous teetering upon the brink of sentimentality. Fences good or bad make nothing; but upon the rhetorical trick that attributes causation to them the poem depends. I could wish that this fine poet had drawn upon his classical learning and had alluded to the first thing the Romans did when they were making a settlement: they built a low wall that would enclose a forum and in the middle set up an altar. The wall around the altar shut out the Infinite, . . . as if they might have foreseen the disorderly love of infinity that Walt Whitman would bring into the world. May I suggest that Frost's limited perspective in this poem is due to what I have called (after Samuel Johnson) his "narrow views." The views are not only opinions but the deliberate restriction of his language to the range possible to that ghostly, hypothetical person, the "literate farmer." Short range of consciousness means limited diction. (pp. 63-5)

I cannot do much about a list of very fine poems which there is no time to discuss in detail. **"The White-Tailed Hornet," "Place for a Third," "A Star in a Stone Boat," "Two Tramps in Mud Time," "Fear," "Once by the Pacific," "After Apple-Picking."** One tires of making lists. Tomorrow I might make another list equally distinguished, attaching to it a list of neutral poems that exhibit the defect of Frost's quality. So I shall now indulge in what will look like a digression, and may actually be a digression, which was suggested by Mr. Howarth's valuable essay in the Frost symposium in the autumn 1966 issue of *The Southern Review*. He is, I believe, the only critic to see in Frost's restricted diction a revolutionary reform contemporaneous with the experiments in poetic diction of Pound and Eliot. Pound, in England, was Frost's first champion, but Frost would not follow Pound into an international, eclectic, and "learned" style. (Is this the meaning of Frost's **"The Road Not Taken"**? Perhaps.) At any rate Frost must have believed that in order to break new stylistic ground he had to *locate it literally*. It was inevitable that he would locate it in New England. Half Scottish, half New Englander, he was taken by his widowed mother from San Francisco to New England when he was 11. He had the ideal upbringing for a poet, and it is irrelevant that he disliked it. He was half in and half out, and he could take nothing for granted. Thus his powers of observation, which were great, led to equally great gifts for discovery: he saw New England nature and the nature of New England man as his own, but both natures had to be discovered. He therefore invented a language for this double imaginative activity. He was much more the conscious technician than some of his critics have thought. Did he not write to his friend John Bartlett that he was one of the great craftsmen? There is nothing reprehensible in this kind of boasting if it is true; and this was.

For many years I have argued with skeptics that the Eliot-Pound revolution was as radical as that brought about by two other young men in 1798—or rather by one of them, William Wordsworth. In the famous Preface to the 1800 edition of *Lyrical Ballads,* Wordsworth said that he wanted to write in the "real language of men." Which men? Rural men was the answer, and he wrote a masterpiece called "Michael." But Frost's "literate farmer" never gave utterance to such absurdities as "Peter Bell" and "The Idiot Boy"; nor did he ever, as Mr. Robson points out, achieve the grandeur of "Resolution and Independence." Wordsworth broke out of his early mould; Robert Frost did not. Yet in certain respects Frost was subtler and a more sensitive listener to the sounds of poetry. He anticipated by many years T. S. Eliot's discovery of the "auditory imagination." Frost called it the audile (or audial) imagination, and he described it as the "sound of the meaning"—a very different effect from that which Pope had in mind when he wrote that "The sound must seem to echo in the sense." I take it that Frost would have said that there is no meaning to be sounded in a line like "The Hounds of Spring are on winter's traces," etc.

As I approach the end of these scattered observations I allude to three or four poems that seem to me Robert Frost's best: **"The Wood-Pile,"** which ends with the great line "With the slow smokeless burning of decay"; **"After Apple-Picking"**; **"The Onset"**; and **"The Oven Bird."** But where is **"Stopping by Woods on a Snowy Evening?"** Had Frost written this one short masterpiece, and no others, his name would last as long as poetry itself will last. . . . It has the rhyme scheme of Fitzgerald's *Rubaiyat* stanza: *a a b a.* But the meter is tetrameter, not, as in the *Rubaiyat,* pentameter. The four stanzas are "linked" in much the same way as Dante's *terzine* are linked. The unrhymed "here" in the first stanza is rhymed with the two first lines and with the fourth of the second, and so on, until we get to the last stanza, in which the third line rhymes with two and four; in short, one rhyme only in that stanza, as one will repeat a phrase, or see oneself walking in a dream, or as one drifts off into sleep. These formalistic external features of the poem have scarcely been noticed; they contribute to the overwhelming, if quiet, effect. Here our literate farmer is, in the very first line, highly sophisticated. It contains both a question and the answer to the question: "Whose woods are these?" And in the same grammatical sequence: "I think I know." But the owner is in town, and he will not see me observe the recurrent mystery of winter, which is snow. We are not told that the man watching the snowfall is in a sleigh. The horse knows that something unusual is happening, though not to the eye, his or his master's. There is no house nearby; the man is isolated in the "darkest evening," his own darkness. The "harness bells" add a dimension of sound to the sibilance of the blowing snow. The lake is frozen; the usually beneficent water is obdurate, and nature has withdrawn her protection. The fourth stanza has all the appearance of the calculation of genius. But Frost told a friend that the entire poem came to him in a flash, or rather phrase by phrase, rhyme scheme and meter, without a pause. There is every reason to believe him. The external pattern reflects perfectly what we are told; instead of the third unrhymed line, as in the three other stanzas, there is, as I have said, one rhyme: deep-keep-sleep-sleep. As one falls asleep it takes too much effort to find a rhyme; so sleep echoes sleep. We may see here what Mr. Cleanth Brooks formerly saw as a paradox: the poet falls asleep as he tells us that he will not. But the most brilliant single word in the poem is that common word "lovely." Years ago I almost dismissed the poem because "lovely" struck me as a lazy evasion of the precise word. But it *is* the precise word. The woods are a

lovely woman, but a woman cold, mysterious (dark), and unfathomable, and he must not succumb to this temptress, who is both life and death. Frost thought of the poem as a "death poem." As I see it, it has as much of life in it as any poem of the same length in the language. It could hold its own with the great lyric of the 19th century, "Tears, Idle Tears."

In the spring of 1961 Robert Frost came to Minneapolis to give a reading at the University of Minnesota. I was asked to introduce him, which I took great pleasure in doing, to a packed auditorium of 5,000 persons. He was the houseguest of a colleague of mine, Charles Foster, a former student of Frost's at Amherst. Frost was with us almost a week. I had two parties for him. At the second party, at about two in the morning, after all the guests except the Fosters had gone home, he asked for another brandy. I brought it to him, though I could hardly stand up, not from intoxication but from fatigue. He was then 87.

On January 5, 1963, I was at Yale, in the library, as a member of the jury for the Bollingen Prize of 1962. Up to that time the Bollingen juries tacitly assumed that to award Robert Frost the prize would carry coals to Newcastle. But in 1963 we knew he was dying in a Boston hospital. There was no time left for him to get the Nobel Prize. The jury—composed of Robert Lowell, John Hall Wheelock, Richard Eberhart, the late Louise Bogan, and myself—voted unanimously to award him the prize. Would he accept it? I was appointed to telephone him and ask. I did; his feeble voice came through distinctly. "Is this Allen?" he said. I said, "Yes, and we hope you will accept the Bollingen Prize for 1962." After a brief silence he said, "I've wondered where you fellows stood." (pp. 65-8)

> *Allen Tate, " 'Inner Weather': Robert Frost as a Metaphysical Poet," in* Robert Frost: Lectures on the Centennial of His Birth *by Helen Bacon and others, Library of Congress, 1975, pp. 57-68.*

A. Zverev   (essay date 1976)

[*Zverev is a Soviet literary historian and critic who has published numerous reviews and essays on such American writers as James Baldwin, John Gardner, William Carlos Williams, and Denise Levertov. He is also the editor of* Contemporary American Poetry *(1975). In his essay on Frost, excerpted below, Zverev analyzes some of Frost's major themes.*]

To picture American poetry of the 20th century without Robert Frost would be as difficult as picturing 19th century poetry without Edgar Allan Poe or Walt Whitman. Poe, Whitman and Frost represent the three high-points in American poetry. The significance of each has long since been acknowledged unanimously and universally. Even people who have no interest whatsoever in verse know these names. . . .

Frost's visit to the USSR in the autumn of 1962 was a memorable event for many. The eighty-eight-year-old poet astonished everyone not only with his youthful heart, his avid interest in the country he was shown and the people whose acquaintance he made, but also because here, as rarely happens, the real man coincided with the image of the poet conveyed in his verses. (p. 241)

A superficial reading of Frost's poetry may give the impression that he is an artist who has delved deeply into the law of eternal return: birth, flowering, death, new birth. Or an artist whose works are all authentic and autobiographical. Or an escapist philosopher, a Thoreau of the 20th century who has retreated from the soulless and cruel reality of the megalopolis and found refuge under the forest canopy of New England.

Each of these impressions is true and reveals some facet of Frost's poetic world. But let us try to read Frost not only as a poet who has given us marvellous examples of lyrical and dramatic poetry, but also as one who has left us with an uncommonly authentic artistic testimony of *our epoch.* In the stream of books on Frost issuing from his native land the poet's work is rarely viewed from such an angle. Yet such an approach might prove both important and useful. The fact is that Frost, like many other eminent writers, became a sort of legend in his lifetime, and his "public image", created by numerous critics, from the Georgians on down to the critics represented in Richard Thornton's anthology *Recognition of Robert Frost,* proved, it seems, to be rather distant from the essence of Frost as poet. (p. 244)

It is one thing to recognize an artist, but to understand his work is something far more difficult. Frost's earliest verses made it clear that here was a completely independent poet unlike any other. Frost was like an island, situated, it is true, not all that far from the mainland of American poetry, but separated from it by a sufficiently broad strait. It was necessary to understand what exactly distinguished Frost from his contemporaries. And the explanation was quickly found. Too quickly, in fact, for though it was based on actual features of Frost's poetic conceptions, it overlooked others, as a result of which Frost's creative temper was distorted. The explanation ran as follows: Frost in principle did not want to be a contemporary poet, did not want to respond to the "spirit of the times".

The situation in which American poetry found itself in the nineteen tens was complex, and it would be too perilous to outline this situation in a few words. Nonetheless one must observe that this was a period of decisive thematic and artistic renewal. Reality was saturated with sharp social conflicts. Life was changing at a headlong, abnormal pace. The tentacles of sprawling cities were sweeping aside the sleepy provinces. America was becoming a land of "smoke and steel", to quote the title of one of Sandburg's collections. The first harbingers of the "jazz age" were making their appearance.

The feverish tempo of life infected poetry, and its canons, which had only recently appeared unassailable, were now collapsing.

Looking for support to the discoveries made by Whitman, who had not been understood by his contemporaries, young poets strove to convey the dynamism of their stormy age. Industrial America found its voice in Sandburg. Lindsay expressed the confusion of the young as they faced a civilization of material wealth and spiritual poverty; later F. Scott Fitzgerald and John Dos Passos would write on the same theme. Anderson's *Winesburg,*

Ohio and Lewis' *Gopher Prairie* traced their lineage back to [Masters'] *Spoon River.*

In another camp—this one headed by Ezra Pound—mind-boggling experiments with verse were taking place, and such avant-garde schools as Imagism, "Amygism" and Vorticism appeared and disappeared in rapid succession.

And what about Frost? He seemed to stand on the sidelines of these poetic movements, remaining a "conservative", an "archaist". He was not attracted by new themes or by *vers libre,* which was rapidly and decisively crowding out metrical verse. He learned far more from the English and American romantics than from *Leaves of Grass.* In many ways taking after Thoreau, Emerson and Keats, Frost reworked their favorite themes: he described nature, the farmer's labors, native scenes of rural New England. Among his favorite genres were those very ones which the "interim" poets had succeeded in hopelessly compromising—all those epigones in the Riley mold imitating the Victorians with their syrupy voices. Frost loved the ballad, the song, the landscape, the pastoral.

When the public, which had begun to take an interest in *A Boy's Will* and **North of Boston,** discovered that the author had spent his boyhood in the country, that he had devoted his life to farming and found time to write poetry only in the evening, they formed a permanent image of Frost in their minds as a "peasant poet" far removed from the distemper of his times, one who strove consciously to speak not of the transient, but of the eternal.

So it seemed that the "national American poet" was indifferent to the drama and conflicts which agitated the America of his times.

Thus already at the onset of Frost's literary career there arose the myth of "the quietest of poets", the "stubborn optimist" with a profound faith in the eternal spiritual values of the toiling farmer, the poet who had retreated from the "madding crowd" to the canopied shelter of the eternally lovely New England woods, and urged his readers to follow his example. Thus arose the widespread and still prevailing notion of Frost as a custodian of the traditions of lyrical poetry, singing of the "simple life". (pp. 245-47)

Such judgements of Frost are not, of course, without foundation—he really was a "peasant poet", a bard of patriarchal New England. His quest for a harmonious and integrated perception of the world was undoubtedly inherent to his artistic thought. His "Horatian serenity" was a unique phenomenon for an epoch in which poets "ran wild in the quest of new ways to be new", an epoch governed by the spirit of reckless poetic experimentation. [In his preface to Edwin Arlington Robinson's *King Jasper,* Frost wrote:] "Poetry, for example, was tried without punctuation. It was tried without capital letters. . . . It was tried without any images but those to the eye. . . . It was tried without content under the trade name of poesie pure. . . . It was tried without ability."

All these extremes of experimentation . . . were always in the poet's field of vision; in opposition to the coquettish "difference" of many of his contemporaries, he chose "the old-fashioned way to be new" and felt a keen responsibility for the poetic word. The "archaic" quality of Frost, who clung stubbornly to traditional forms and vocabulary and felt himself to be a direct heir of the New England poets—Thoreau and Emerson, was called to life in part by the fact that American poetry at the time needed someone who would preserve the great romantic tradition, in some ways related to social utopianism. Frost realized it was his calling to guard this tradition, to develop it, and to oppose tendencies which "sorely strained" the "limits of poetry". (pp. 247-48)

Frost called poetry "an effort to explain life", by which, of course, he meant contemporary life. He did not write free verse and said that he would rather play tennis without a net than employ *vers libre,* but this does not in the least imply that Frost's metrical verse was the same as Longfellow's. He did not strive along with his contemporaries "to include a larger material", for often as a result of such efforts the poet "gets lost in his material without a gathering metaphor to throw it into shape and order". In comparison to T. S. Eliot or Carl Sandburg Frost was a poet of "narrow", local and always traditional material. But does that mean that Frost's "metaphor", in other words his poetic image, is equivalent to James Russell Lowell's "metaphors" or those of Edwin Arlington Robinson, a poet incomparably closer to Frost? Does this mean that Frost's "narrow" material does not reveal some absolutely new artistic qualities to the reader, or appear in an absolutely new artistic dimension?

Frost is too strikingly different from his New England predecessors for us to explain away these differences simply in terms of the creative individuality or uniqueness which nature bestows on any outstanding talent. It would be difficult to solve the "riddle" of Frost by examining his poetics from the inside, as a closed system. In the first decades of the 20th century the American poetic tradition was being rejuvenated, and here Frost had a decisive role to play. The American literature of those years was realistic, and Frost belonged to the aesthetic movement of his times, regardless of how traditional and "timeless" he may have appeared to be.

Here we approach the very essence of the problem. A realistic artistic system does not, of course, presuppose photographic fidelity in its reflection of the surrounding world. It presupposes above all an attempt to grasp the true laws of life, to penetrate the essence of life processes—social and individual, spiritual and psychological. It demands an objective view of the world. It entails not only a new aggregate of expressive means, but also a reconsideration of various aesthetic and philosophical categories which have determined the specific features of poetry in earlier periods, in particular romantic poetry.

For Frost the most important of these categories was understanding the people and the life of the people.

The romantic tradition lay at the foundation of his art, but as an artist of realistic bent he gave new meaning to a principal aspect of this tradition—the way it reflected the people's life. For the romantics "the people" was an abstract and static spiritual substance. For Frost "the people" emerges as a category of historical existence. This was a great shift. Having apparently exhausted all its possibilities and now compromised in the "twilight interval", the romantic tradition received a powerful stimulus. Facing new aesthetic demands, the tradition proved its vitality, and the continuity of poetry was preserved.

In place of the mythologized and decorative "folk style" of the romantics Frost brought a peculiar artistic concept of "autochthony", to borrow the term from Mircea Eliade's *Myth, Dreams and Mysteries.* Speaking of "autochthony", Eliade implies a profound and frequently unconscious sense of belonging to the place: "men feel that they are *people of the place,* and this is a feeling of cosmic relatedness deeper than that of familial and ancestral solidarity".

This seems to be a relevant and true description of Frost's outlook too. In the context of literary history this "autochthonic" sense which is conveyed in his poetry is possibly Frost's greatest achievement. (pp. 248-50)

When I speak of Frost as the most "autochthonic" American poet of the 20th century, I have in mind not only such poems as **"The Gift Outright"** (which, however, are certainly worth rereading particularly at this point, when books like Gore Vidal's *Burr* are so astonishingly popular). Rather, I have in mind those poems which contain no outright declarations, poems which recreate with unique breadth and objectivity a picture of the people's life in all its diversity, its normal course, which for the poet is inseparable from the course of his own life; poems like the ones you find in Frost's two best collections—**North of Boston** and **New Hampshire.**

> I touch my tongue to the shoes now,
> And unless my sense is at fault,
> On one I can taste Atlantic,
> On the other Pacific, salt.

Here is a precisely formulated poetic motif, one which is repeated at various stages in Frost's artistic development. Though a "New England" poet, he often returned to this theme of the great American expanses, moving far beyond the immediate horizons of New England. When he was a child Frost crossed the American continent twice over, and as a poet he was keenly aware that this was his world, his universe; in his verses the most varied facets of the image of America are explored. But Frost's America is always a country that belongs to people capable of preserving the vital link that binds them to nature and to each other, of filling their lives with high ethical meaning, for this is an active, creative, morally pure and healthy life. And the major lyrical principle in all of Frost's books— from *A Boy's Will* to the last collection *In the Clearing*— is the feeling that the poet and his world are indivisible, that all men are brothers working together on this earth . . . , that nature and man and all men are united:

> I had for my winter evening walk—
> No one at all with whom to talk,
> But I had the cottages in a row
> Up to their shining eyes in snow.
>
> And I thought I had the folk within:
> I had the sound of a violin;
> I had a glimpse through curtain laces
> Of youthful forms and youthful faces.
>
> I had such company outward bound . . .

(pp. 250-51)

In his time Malcolm Cowley severely rebuked Frost for his unwillingness to speak of life definitively and clearly, for the vagueness of his poetic judgements [see excerpts dated 1944]. . . . It would be hard to find a more unjust statement regarding the poet. In his brilliant essay "The Figure a Poem Makes" Frost asserts, "The possibilities for tune from the dramatic tones of meaning struck across the rigidity of a limited meter are endless." The poet's own experience led him to this conviction; a poem by Frost is always the most subtle interweaving of "dramatic tones of meaning", whereas graphic precision of line and clarity of meaning would only destroy the entire artistic structure of Frost's poetry.

Cowley's mistake consists in the fact that he immediately identifies the poetic device with the content of the lyric. But the content itself was never ambiguous or vague. Edward Thomas, a member of the Georgian circle, wrote that **North of Boston** was "one of the most revolutionary books of the time", and though Frost was never a revolutionary in his social views, one could nonetheless concur completely with this statement. Frost's epic canvas with its profound fidelity to life was very much a revolutionary event in American poetry. Frost's objective view on the life of the people, his effort to merge totally with the people and assume their view on life's fundamental problems—all these things were in fact revolutionary for the poetry of the time. (pp. 251-52)

"I had a lover's quarrel with the world," Frost said of himself, and he could not have expressed himself more exactly, for his truly was a lover's quarrel, a recognition of life's drama which did not lead to a rejection of this life in the name of some ideal, nor to the setting up of his own, isolated world in contrast to the life around him. Yes, Frost belonged to this world, but he never looked at it through the rose-colored glasses of superficially understood patriotism. He saw this world in its true light and linked himself irrevocably to it. Otherwise he would have proved incapable of that organic understanding of the world's anxieties which so astonishes us in Frost's lyrics. The call of the city, luring us with its tawdry splendors, the lost harmony of man and the earth on which he toils, the growing mistrust and alienation between people who were once united by common cares, and the poet's unflagging feeling of belonging to that great body known as the People—all this we find in Frost and his remarkably, profoundly realistic panorama of the people's life.

Frost's comments on "two types of realist" are well known: "There are two types of realist—the one who offers a good deal of dirt with his potato to show that it is a real one; and the one who is satisfied with the potato brushed clean. I am inclined to be the second kind. To me, the thing that art does for life is to clean it, to strip it to form." Another of his statements on the same subject is less well known: "Instead of a realist—if I must be classified—I think I might better be called a Synecdochist; for I am fond of the synecdoche in poetry—that figure of speech in which we use a part for the whole."

It is this "synecdochism" which constitutes the basis for Frost's realistic poetics. The situations described in his dramatic verses sometimes come close to being casual, and in any case very commonplace. But they are imbued with genuinely poetic content, for behind the "individual" there is always the "general", the "autochthonic". In **"Mending Wall"** Frost talks about a most commonplace occurrence: the wall separating a farmer's land from that of his neighbor has crumbled and must be repaired. For the romantic poet this would serve as an occasion to em-

bark on a poetical meditation on the passage of time; such a possibility is also hinted at in **"Mending Wall"**:

> Something there is that doesn't love a wall,
> That wants it down. I could say "Elves" to him,
> But it's not elves exactly . . .

But Frost is a poet with a realistic bent; he discovers a completely different aspect in the motif "Something there is that doesn't love a wall", a rich image which serves to convey notions of true and false in the mind of the people. The "autochthonic" sense in this poem is not, of course, conveyed by the simple, peasant-like, practical considerations which Frost imputes to his hero ("My apple trees will never get across / And eat the cones under his pines"), nor by the abundance of folkish expressions. The poet, as it were, set himself the task of reproducing in detail the thought processes of an ordinary farmer, and every trifle is important for him—the fact that there is no livestock on the farm, and therefore that the wall serves no purpose, and the fact that in lifting up the stones he and his neighbor scrape their fingers raw: "The work of hunters is another thing: / I have come after them and made repair." Frost's realism is based in large measure on his exact knowledge of the material at hand; but this is not the realism of the "particular", not the realism of details, but of the "universal", the people's point of view. The desire to fence oneself off from others, to shut oneself off in one's own little world, is a notion quite alien to the people. . . . (pp. 253-55)

The fact that a nearby farmer with such a motto as "Good fences make good neighbors" appears in Frost's poem is not mere coincidence. Even though for Frost's hero he is "like an old-stone savage armed", Frost himself realized that such neighbors on nearby farms were increasing in number. The tragic spirit that informs so many of Frost's poems consists in the fact that his attraction to the people clashes with his realization of the growing differentiation, particularly social differentiation, among the people. As an artist and realist Frost could not ignore this process. Throughout his works one can find images that speak of the passing of the village, that cradle of unity and "plebeian" democracy which was so dear to Frost, images telling us how this world has collapsed under the pressures of the 20th century, that it is undergoing a period of crisis and decline. (p. 255)

But Frost's importance consists, of course, not only in the fact that he recognized the "seeds of degeneration" which had fallen on New England soil. Perhaps he was even mistaken in defending the view that the village, despite all its internal conflicts (of which Frost was well aware), nonetheless remained the only firm foundation for democratic world order. But having accepted the "autochthonic" view of the state of things (even sometimes equating it with the viewpoint of the ordinary farmer—granted that to a certain degree he was a conventional figure), and having come to a realistic perception of life, Frost was able to grasp genuinely and subtly the changes taking place in his native rural America, and to defend, convincingly but without pretention, ideals shared by the people. Without this indivisibility of the poet and the people, Frost's artistic vision would lack that real originality which draws us in such masterpieces as **"The Pasture"**, **"October"**, **"Blueberries"**, **"Birches"**, or **"Stopping by Woods on a Snowy Evening"**. Amazing in their intensity of lyrical feeling and their musicality, all these verses are born of a perception of nature which would be impossible for a man who had not come into daily contact with it—like a farmer or laborer.

The feeling of distress over the changes taking place in his native region is sometimes expressed with surprising forcefulness in Frost's verses. His images are artless, but they are animated by an elevated sense of tragedy, as for example in **"The Woodpile"**, where a stack of firewood left lying outdoors becomes a symbol for neglect, for a land that is wasted, for disintegration. . . . (pp. 255-56)

Nonetheless it would hardly be accurate to describe Frost's poetry as "saturnine terror that creeps up unnoticed" (as Ivan Kashkin once described it). Yes, Frost felt deeply the tragedy of the land, how it had been reclaimed from the swamps and salinas and had flowered, and now, against the will of those who had made it bear fruit, it was once again reverting to a state of wildness and desolation. The poet felt himself a part of the drama of that disintegrating world out of which America had grown. But regardless of how distressing were the consequences of the onset of the "machine age" in world so dear to Frost, the poet saw that democratic ideals had not died, and his faith in the imperishability of the people's moral health lent even greater cogency to his work.

His poetry is imbued with this faith. Sometimes, immersed in his love for his native land, Frost seems not to notice that enormous world, replete with its own concerns, which extends beyond the horizons of New England. At times he resembles the hero of his poem **"The Mountain"**, who tries to fence himself off from the universe, to withdraw into the shell of his own monotonous existence, to limit himself to the confines of his own village. . . . (pp. 256-57)

But Frost had good reason to call his *North of Boston* a "Book of People". The character of this collection, like that of all of Frost's works, is defined by those poems in which the poet gazes intently on the people's life without taking "shelter from a wind", penetrating its drama and playing the role of an active participant. This distinguishing trait of Frost's poetry emerges with particular clarity in his dramatic works. Sometimes they are called "narrative", which is inaccurate. It is precisely the dramatic element which Frost valued so highly in poetry. He wrote, "Everything written is as good as it is dramatic." The form and subject of these stories and scenes written in blank verse, were for the most part taken directly from folk ballads. The folkloric base also makes itself felt in the devices Frost uses to develop character, and even in the choice of character (for example, the tight-fisted boss and the sharp farm-hand in the poem **"The Code"**). Perhaps the best known of all of Frost's dramatic works is **"The Death of a Hired Man"**. It is one of Frost's most brilliant poems. Here, perhaps, more than anywhere else, we find the fullest treatment of Frost's major themes—the disintegration of the once unified world of New England, and the search for what is undyingly human. (pp. 257-58)

In his books this world was examined in a unique and profound manner, and the ideals to which Silas [in **"The Death of a Hired Man"**] adhered and which were so dear to Frost himself were far from being reactionary ("back to patriarchal simplicity") but rather democratic in char-

acter. Frost's realism and sincere democratic impulses made him the greatest American poet of the 20th century.

And a broad range of readers (not only in the poet's homeland) have long since acknowledged Frost, the real Frost—not as an intellectual dressed in home-spun farmers' clothes, not as a conformist, not as an unthinking composer of idylls and pastorals, but as an artist who expressed the people's view on the complex, sharply contradictory world of America in the 20th century, one who believed in the people and shared their hopes, their democratic traditions and ideals. This is how he appears if we approach his work without prejudice. (pp. 259-60)

> A. Zverev, "A Lover's Quarrel with the World: Robert Frost," in *20th Century American Literature: A Soviet View, translated by Ronald Vroon, Progress Publishers, 1976, pp. 241-60.*

Patricia Wallace (essay date 1984)

[*Wallace examines the theme of solitude and isolation in Frost's verse.*]

"His poems make me so mad," confesses a colleague of mine about Robert Frost. She has read the poems for years, with attention and thought, yet her anger comes from the feeling that they elude her or, more accurately, exclude her. I think she is right about something central in Frost—the way the poems push away, peel off, walk out into the swamp away from the town. They are often poems of a solitary figure, and their cramped geography and harsh climates are the terms and limits of a life which Frost acknowledges, swings away from, returns to. His region can be, and often is, cramped, impoverished, silent, deserted, full of ruins, and without easy beauty. Think of the cold swamps, the burned-out houses, the snowy fields, the cellar holes "closing like a dent in dough." His landscape with its stoney walls forbids us from merely wishing away the barriers between ourselves and a larger social world, ourselves and nature and even ourselves and each other. Frost does not even allow us the comfort of an illu-

Frost at John F. Kennedy's inauguration with the President and Dwight D. Eisenhower, January, 1961.

sionary community born of a sentimental response to loneliness, a response which in Frost takes the form of a sigh, an imprecise lament, but he will playfully show us the actual pleasures of our solitude in a poem like **"Birches."** Frost's skepticism toward community often extends to his own poetic audience, and the speaker of a Frost poem, whether it is the poetic "I" or the voice of one of his dramatic characters, is a person talking to him or her self often knowing that no one listens.

But in all of Frost's adherence to boundaries, his recognition of our individual separateness from the world of society, nature, things, and even each other, there is an underlying sense of what is risked or "dared" when walls are down or remade, when encounter takes place. Genuine reciprocity in Frost is awesome, capable of reordering the self and its world, a powerful transgression that often remains a matter of "as if." If we come into a Frost poem with unexamined assumptions of community, with the belief that the poet speaks to "us" (whoever "we" may be) as one of "us," then we miss the self-awareness which gives life to Frost's work. We become an anonymous audience which Frost dismisses, or manipulates. But when we hear how the poet listens to himself, when we notice the playful turnings of his own voice, then we are the single, genuine listener Frost demands, and we share with him the landscape of privacy he so often insists upon.

That landscape has its fair share of walls, each of them part of an unresolved question put best by Stanley Cavell: "whether human knowledge and human community require the recognizing or dismantling of limits." In **"Mending Wall,"** which James M. Cox calls one of Frost's self-defining poems, Frost defines separateness and community for himself. Frost knows that the teasing speaker's declaration, "Something there is that doesn't love a wall / That wants it down" is only the beginning of the story (or the poem). Because he writes insisting on his separateness through the very particularity of his poetic voice, Frost knows as well how radical and difficult it is to "take in" another, and yet maintains a sense of one's own and the other's distinctness. Many a "something" or someone wants a wall down with no acknowledgement of distinctness and no real courage in the act. And clearly Frost's teasing speaker is not sure in his own mind what he thinks. When, in the poem's central moment, he drops his teasing tone, he has come to some insight which makes his playful dispute of barriers something else again:

> I see him there
> Bringing a stone grasped firmly by the top
> In each hand, like an old-stone savage armed.
> He moves in darkness as it seems to me
> Not of woods only and the shade of trees.

This is the poem's central moment, and our response to it is dictated in part by the way the voice shifts. That shift in voice, a slowing down and steadying of rhythm, a contemplativeness previously absent, does not simply mime the slow actions of the neighbor. It reflects a revision in the speaker as he imagines the neighbor, and acknowledges how far from him—how *other* from him—the neighbor is, a distance which is metaphorical and rendered here temporally through "like an old stone savage." He realizes that *it seems to him* the neighbor is surrounded and enclosed by something opaque, something like darkness, a darkness perceptible to the speaker who must take ac-

count of it, and also must know his own separateness more fully. As he confronts that darkness and distance, he can consider what barriers, if any, he would *want* down, what barriers he simply cannot cross, and what such an act might take.

Whatever doesn't love a wall must take account of such ignorance, as the speaker must also take account of the way his own teasing is as much a form of darkness, of hiding "behind," as the neighbor's repetition. Does the poem settle the question in favor of barriers or not? The point is not to settle a question. The poem explores the meaning and difficulty of Frost's sense of separateness, the difficulty of community. (pp. 1-2)

Much of the time in Frost's work the separateness of individual life implies a sharply limited relation to the natural or social world. The end of **"Out, Out—"** has always seemed to me hard to bear. The matter-of-fact summation, "And they, since they / Were not the ones dead, turned to their affairs" is a truth so cold one wonders Frost can speak it. The chill comes from the isolation of the dead boy, not only from the tranquil natural scene which opens the poem, or from the world of things, like the saw, which turn on him, but the way in which the poem denies the family as a given community. In the poem that community, which for some of us promises hope of comfort and consolation, is an indistinct "they"—the general pronoun emphasized by repetition and line break. It is as if, at the end, Frost himself turned from both the boy and the family he created, turned because of the poem's understanding of barriers, and the absoluteness which is death in Frost's poems. He turns out of a conviction that—whether we are family, friends, lovers, or parents—we do not go hand in hand the whole stretch of the way. In **"Out, Out—"** Frost takes separateness right to the edge and explores it at its worst. This doesn't mean that **"Out, Out—"** resolves Frost's position or summarizes it. It is the imagination of what the worst in Frost's sense of human separateness might mean.

There are other poems written out of a similar spirit, among them **"Neither Out Far nor In Deep," "Design"** and **"Provide, Provide."** . . . Reading them we remember that the strand of separateness which Frost carries out in American literature does not belong to him alone. It also belongs to the traditions of Thoreau, Melville, Crane, and Dickinson. Frost is the strain in our literature which seems most easily Whitman's antithesis; he is not large, he does not contain multitudes. He is a single, sharply defined self, but one on guard and given to teasing and hiding. In his emphatic individualism he resembles Thoreau, but unlike Thoreau he is not willing to be representative. He is the skeptic both of the Whitmanian impulse to merge and the Thoreauvian impulse to find in a single life an emblem of all lives. Hence Frost's poems make almost no concession to autobiography, the genre of the representative, individual life. Like Whitman's, Frost's are often road poems, though the journey is always shorter. But unlike Whitman's, Frost's road does not open into and embrace others. It is not the open road but the closed, the ladder road which **"Directive"** instructs us to pull in behind us "And put a sign up CLOSED to all but me." American writers who share Frost's sense of lonely individualism often don't share his resistance to the sentimentality of that position, or, like Crane or Melville, are writers of novels and stories in which the larger, social world has *some* place, whereas in Frost its place is seriously in question. (pp. 3-4)

At his best Frost is a critic of a culture of false connection. He sees the barriers between the single self and the larger social world. His skepticism makes for the absoluteness of a poem like **"Neither Out Far nor In Deep"** where what stands out is the distance of the poet from what he sees, from all those "people along the strand" who "All turn and look one way." Frost uses the noun "people" in contrast to the way a poet like Sandburg uses it; he uses it with a chill for its anonymity. He gives us an undiscriminating mass. And he wants as little to do with that "people" as possible, for they are exactly the group against which he asserts his distinctive voice. Yet the coldness and uncharacteristic flatness of the poem contain his knowledge that his own distance from them repeats their gesture of turning their backs on the land. They are as anonymous to him as everything else is to them, and he looks no farther out nor deeper into them than they look along the strand. This feeling for a culture which turns its back, which replaces community with abstraction, and in which no one looks too deeply, provides some of the propositions which also appear in **"Provide, Provide,"** whose ostensible subject is a strategy for uselessness and decay:

> The witch that came (the withered hag)
> To wash the steps with pail and rag
> Was once the beauty Abishag,
>
> The picture pride of Hollywood
> Too many fall from great and good
> For you to doubt the likelihood.

Like many *things* in Frost (broken dishes, burned-out houses, forgotten flowers, dried-up pumps) Abishag is a castoff in a culture always turning to new tasks. But there is absolutely no nostalgia in the poem for her, no imagined sense of her lost beauty, no feeling. Frost isn't moved by Abishag, and we aren't meant to be either; the tight form and witty rhymes of his stanzas cut short any sympathetic response. The vision of society in the poem, of a culture where friendship is "boughten" and the purchase of the stock exchange *might* assure "regard" is the poem's center, the center Frost resists and confronts, and both acts are part of his coming to terms. The acknowledgement Frost rehearses for himself in **"Provide, Provide"** is compelling (and literary fame may be the implicit equivalent of Hollywood). It is as if he instructed himself in the terms dictated by his sense of a world which affirms that *nothing* "Atones for later disregard / Or keeps the end from being hard." Not love, not fame, not family or friends, not beauty or art, not even the sense of one's own exceptional nature. There is a matter-of-factness frightening in its implications in the poem, but even as Frost says all this to himself, his own poem presses against a common fate with all of its wit and distinctiveness, as if by virtue of that wit and control he might just exempt himself.

Abishag is one of Frost's versions of how society absorbs people, uses them up and leaves them isolated, something he treats with unrestrained feeling in **"The Death of the Hired Man"** or **"A Servant to Servants."** But here Frost doesn't focus on the human figure. In the society he imagines in the poem, Abishag is simply one fact of uselessness in a culture of use, the far limit of American pragmatism. Like **"Neither Out Far nor In Deep"** or the well-known

"Design," this poem thinks about and feels out the hard side of Frost's sense of barriers and separateness, and his lack of conviction in community. This hard side is not all there is to the question in Frost, but we ought not to be surprised by it, or to doubt its likelihood.

But when we weary of such considerations, Frost offers us poems written in the spirit of solitude, with all of her delights. Solitude is separateness seen upside down, or from the other side, where what are sometimes felt as limits are not barriers at all. Therefore the popularity of **"Birches"** isn't at all incidental to Frost's central concerns. **"Birches"** truly is representative Frost, but in it privacy is choice, and the sweetness of the poem is genuine, the sweetness of solitude. Because Frost's intelligence is always part of feeling in his best poems, **"Birches"** fills us with the recognizable delight of a world inhabited only by the self, a world made by the self, at the same time that it recognizes the limits and temptations of that satisfaction. **"Birches"** makes a grove of privacy, creates the place where the poet imagines the poem's central figure:

> Some boy too far from town to learn baseball
> Whose only play was what he found himself,
> Summer or winter, and could play alone.

We never feel the boy's loneliness as deprivation, but as pleasure. The imagined grove of trees becomes the scene, in the poet's mind, for a boy's playing out of his impulses, subduing and bending the world to his own shape as only solitude permits us. In this privacy there is the wide space of freedom. **"Birches"** is characteristic Frost because in it he confirms his own connection both to a landscape of solitude and to a solitary figure. And what we love about the poem, no matter how long we have read or studied Frost, is what first drew us to it and draws us back again: the image of the trees, at one with our memory and longing for the child's world which is the self, where everything bends to the self, and our whole being seems to spill out of us, and yet is contained, like a cup filled "even above the brim." (pp. 4-6)

We are at home with solitude in Frost; the poems make us so. What other poet could begin a poem, as Frost does **"The Wood-Pile,"** with the decision to walk farther into a frozen swamp on a grey day and yet make us feel a pleasure in it? One of the things Frost does in **"The Wood-Pile"** is explore a form of solitude distinct from the pure delight which is **"Birches."** He explores solitude where the world doesn't bend to the self, but seems to stand apart from it. And he is seeing just how far he can maintain his sense of his own distinctness as he tests out the reaches of the self. In this exploration the thing which stops him in his tracks, the image which the poem seems genuinely to discover at its center, is the wood-pile.

A number of Frost's so-called nature poems have been read as testimony of his sense of the clear barriers between man and nature and the separateness of man from the natural world. But those barriers, and that separateness, are as much under question and under exploration in Frost as are those between ourselves and the social world. For the main thing which stops Frost in his poetic tracks is the way the wood-pile is evidence of someone else who has been there before him.

> I thought that only
> Someone who lived in turning to fresh tasks

Could so forget his handiwork on which
He spent himself, the labour of his ax,
And leave it there far from a useful fireplace
To warm the frozen swamp as best it could
With the slow smokeless burning of decay.

Frost gives us the speech of a man turning something over in himself, listening to himself as he thinks. When he imagines the maker as someone who leaves things behind him, someone "always turning to new tasks," he implicitly recognizes his own capacity to forget, to turn aside. The wood-pile itself is an embodiment of the presence of another in the landscape of solitude, much of whose being the poet must leave in ignorance. And his tone yields to the woodpile as an image where he sees the natural and human worlds without a clear line of distinction. Like the strings of clematis on the wood-pile, they overlap. Finally, the poem gives us the poet's pause, embodied in the wood-pile which halts him on his walk, between the necessity to turn aside, and the inevitable claims our experience makes within us not to turn aside.

While many Frost poems explore the barriers and relations between a man and the social world, between a man and the natural world, or the world of things as in **"The Need of Being Versed in Country Things,"** some of his finest and most indispensable poems are explorations of both the barriers and connections between individuals. Sometimes he gives us the finality of the barriers. This is the case in **"Home Burial,"** a dialogue poem about the failure of dialogue. While there are two distinct voices in the poem, the man's and the woman's, the two cannot hear each other. The woman's grief (and it is the poem's triumph to make us understand this) is a wall. It is like the place where no one can follow because others, like the birds in **"Country Things,"** will (as the woman tells us) "make the best of their way back to life." Her grief is like the unshared and isolated snowfield in Frost's **"Desert Places."** And Frost's woman lives in that grief, even as she cries out she won't "have grief so." We hear it in her voice, and there isn't any way to get through it, for the grief is as palpable and enclosing as the darkness surrounding the farmer neighbor in **"Mending Wall."** The husband speaks separately as one who has already made the best of a way back to life, one whose speech tries to convert the woman back to life as if he thought she could hear him. It is as if the two stood on opposite banks of a river, each speaking genuinely to him or her self, but not with a speech the other can hear. That's why when the woman repeats in anger the man's words as he dug the child's grave ("Three foggy mornings and one rainy day / Will rot the best birch fence a man can build") she has no idea of what he was saying. And the husband, from his side, hears so little the power of her grief, its enclosure, that he can believe talking will make her feel better. Nothing in the poem convinces us the barriers will fall. (pp. 6-7)

While **"Home Burial"** confirms an isolating separateness, **"The Death of the Hired Man"** does not. There is no question that in **"Hired Man"** Frost creates two voices, each of which listens to, and takes in, something of the other. Mary and Warren form a little community; in their marriage, in their capacity to be "home" for Silas. These qualities in **"The Death of the Hired Man"** set it apart from many Frost poems, even though its rural characters, homely language, and country details have made it seem characteristic Frost. The poem explores questions of home, and of separateness, but the exploration has different results from those of most of Frost's poems. Mary and Warren share what Virginia Woolf once called "the crepuscular wall" of intimacy, the wall which maintains their distinctness yet is not the barrier Frost so often creates or discovers. They form a reciprocity in a poetic canon where singularity is more often the rule. They are home in a poetry most often written "a little far from home." **"The Death of the Hired Man"** is a powerful exception to the consistency of the largest number of Frost poems, and it is in just such necessary exceptions that poems insist on their autonomy from themes, critical arguments, and categories.

The power of Silas within the poem has a good deal to do with Frost's questions of separateness and solitude as I have been discussing them here. Silas is the castoff; he is the human equivalent to the pump in **"The Need of Being Versed in Country Things"** which throws up an awkward arm, and he is the element of decay in the poem. Mary tells us he has "nothing to look backward to with pride / And nothing to look forward to with hope." Mary also tells us that Silas is "broken," so broken that at first his sleeping shape was unrecognizable to her. In her description of that moment ("Huddled against the barn-door fast asleep") Silas resembles a corpse. He is like the sack which William Carlos Williams sees on the bridge into Mexico in "Desert Music." For Williams that sack is both corpse and embryo, decay and new beginning, and that is why from the desert he makes music. But for Frost, even within the community this poem makes and believes in, Silas's shape has no such ambiguity. The structure of the poem enforces a finality built into Silas's figure. In the ending of the poem Mary and Warren are side by side, but that image does not push forward into the future. Not that we lose faith in Mary and Warren, we don't because Frost doesn't, but our attention shifts from the community of marriage to the breaking off of community, the separateness which is death. The last line, a half line really, is spoken by Warren in answer to Mary's question "Warren?": " 'Dead,' was all he answered." It is possible to see one version of Frost's career in the outline of this poem: once the solitary castoff, Silas, enters the world of "home," something changes. For to truly "take in" Silas means that the nature of home as it was defined before must change: the risks of such change are a part of any "taking in" for Frost. The figure of Silas lays some claim to the place of Mary and Warren, to the dialogue of marriage and home, and it deepens and stretches itself out in later poems like **"The Hill Wife"** with its knowledge of finalities / Besides the grave" or in **"Out, Out—"** with its harsh sense of how, even in "home," everyone turns away.

But a version of Frost's career which restricted itself to poems of finalities would not accommodate the full range of his best work. In the language of his poems and lectures, Frost always insisted on the importance of "as if," and nowhere is that "as if " more central than when he asks the questions of reciprocity and the return of love. Frost will always leave true reciprocity a matter of "as if " because he recognizes how powerful a transgression love is. Any remaking of barriers in Frost has powerful implications, even (or especially) when, as in **"Mending Wall,"** the poem is also playful. The crossing of barriers in Frost is always a remaking, a revision of both the self and its world. These implications are especially clear in his poem **"Two Look at Two,"** whose very title counters the consistent solitary figure in Frost. The poem contains two sets of two, the first of which is the lovers who are "sighers." The poem begins as they stop their journey up the mountain, sighing, "This is all" and "Good-night to woods." They are like us, and like Frost, when we romanticize the call to come in and lament, or when we cast our experience in melodramatic terms, as Frost does playfully in the conclusion of **"The Road Not Taken."** The lovers' sigh has a sentimental sense of ending, and it creates a melodrama of farewell. Their sigh, "This is all" (with minor variations) makes one of the poem's refrains. (pp. 7-9)

The journey the lovers are making is a journey of solitude much like that of Frost's solitary walkers. The lovers are moved by an "onward impulse"; their walk has taken them into a landscape increasingly rough, and empty of others ("where, if a stone / Or earth slide moved at night, it moved itself; / No footstep moved it.") And Frost understands in the poem that the lovers, like the rest of us, move in a world that is often "unsafe." But since they are lovers, and Frost names them simply as that, they make a little universe with one another and imagine a world where everything bends to their love, even though the poem witnesses a landscape far more resistant. In these ways they resemble the boy of **"Birches,"** for as lovers their own reciprocity makes a form of solitude; their absorption in one another is a kind of enclosure. Therefore they *read* the appearance of the two deer as earth's "unlooked-for favor" which, in the poem's final line, "Had made them certain earth returned their love."

But Frost has an understanding which the lovers' solitude does not encompass, and his understanding is the life of the poem. That is why he creates a moment which sets a limit to the onward impulse of "Love and forgetting"— which sets a limit to solitude like the wood-pile. When the doe appears in the poem Frost tells himself, "She saw them in their field, they her in hers." This is just the kind of recognition true seeing must make in Frost. It must make the distinction of fields, but that distinction is not absolute. It can be remade, but only after it has been acknowledged. When the buck also appears, and views the lovers from his field, Frost recognizes in the lovers (and in himself as he identifies with the lovers) the temptation to overcome barriers, to mingle the two fields. So his lovers feel an impulse to gesture toward the buck: "Thus till he had them *almost* feeling dared / To stretch a proffering hand—and a spell-breaking" (my emphasis). The "almost" in this poem is as crucial as it is in **"Come In."** The moment of encounter tempts the lovers to will away the wall, to imagine they want to cross it. Frost does not tell himself that such transgression is impossible, or that we can only know the worlds of man and nature as two distinct fields. Rather he tells himself that the lovers almost dare, but do *not* dare—and the verb is crucial. Part of what Frost understands in the poem is the way the lovers resist enlarging their world, the way the solitude they make together holds them back from breaking out of their enclosure. He does not disassociate himself from the lovers' withheld gesture. He does not mock them for it, for he knows how much is dared when a hand stretches forth; he knows what is at stake when a spell is "broken." He earns such knowledge over and over again in his poems. Two have seen two—and that for Frost, and for the lovers, is enough. It respects the truth of what happens. When the lovers (and the poet) sigh at the end of the poem "This

must be all," the poet also speaks without the sigh, "It was all." Recognizing the lovers' solitude in himself, Frost understands it and gives it sympathy, but he also discriminates between their certainty, born of a solitude where their love bends the world to them, and his uncertainty. In the world of this poem favor *might* be accident, or it *might* be that a proffered hand would or would not drive away the deer, but Frost leaves us in ignorance of that. He puts the question of the meeting before us, the question of its boundaries, the distinctions of its fields, and puts forth the risk of transgression as well, though his own language always insists on grounding those questions in less lofty terms, in a particular drama as generous and as restrained as is **"Birches."**

Frost's feeling for the meaning and responsibilities of reciprocity is all there in the great poem **"The Most of It."** That poem stands at the center of Frost's explorations of the recognition and dismantling of boundaries, and puts it within the context of the longing for "counter-love." Frost keeps his man crying out indistinct and unspecified, while at the same time making the voice of his own poem, in its initial forthrightness and grounding of tone, fully and even assertively Frost: "He thought he kept the universe alone." When the man calls out with the familiar longing for "counter-love, original response" Frost gives that longing sharpness because he both recognizes the man in himself, and also writes with an awareness larger than the man crying out. The poem comes to an understanding of what "original response" asks, for such response, original with another, can never be a simple counterpart to our own desires. Instead it will compel the recognition of another's distinctness, with all that it might ask of us. As in **"Come In,"** the invitation in the man's call across the cliff asks something from the one who offers it. Response is often unexpected in Frost country. Far more likely is the situation the man finds, where "nothing ever came of what he cried." But here Frost does not leave it so simply; he qualifies the nothing with a crucial "unless": "Unless it was the embodiment that crashed / In the cliff's talus on the other side."

Frost leaves this "embodiment" mysterious. He leaves a certain ignorance about it within the poem. But most important to my sense of Frost is the power of it, a power as great as that of a "great buck." The power is all there in the verbs "crashed," "Pushing," "forced," in that verb-turned-adjective in the remarkable "Pushing the crumpled water up ahead," and in the enormous push of the lines, sustained by the repeated "and." The rhythm of the last third of the poem just keeps pushing forward. In this rhythm and this image is the power of "original response," one equal to, and more than, the longing which calls it forth unknowing of how astonishing, and even overwhelming, it might be. The man who cries out for love is like a person unhappy in his loneliness who cries out for response without any idea of what it would ask of him, of how it could trample and push through his idea of a universe where "someone else" is simply "*additional* to him" (my emphasis). In these ways Frost's indistinct man very much resembles Narcissus, who also believed that original response could be simple addition, the addition of another self just like his own. Frost knows Narcissus in himself but he also knows that any call for response is a remaking of boundaries with the potential force of a buck, a force which will not leave the self unchanged. By the end of the poem he acknowledges both this tremendous power, and its status as simple "fact"—therefore the understated closing which so resembles **"Two Look at Two"**:—"and that was all." For all the awareness Frost comes to in the poem, it remains important that he hears the man's voice in his own. He encompasses in his poem that recognition even while he distinguishes himself from the man. **"The Most of It"** does not resolve the question of transgression, or boundaries, but it gives us Frost's strength in imagining what a call for original response might summon (including the possibility of no answer), and what, potentially, it could ask of the caller. In all of Frost's adherence to boundaries, and his understanding of solitude, he also carried with him the sense of what is risked or "dared" when walls are down, or remade, when genuine encounter takes place.

Frost's willingness to acknowledge the ignorance in which we experience both our separateness and our longing for community, and his willingness to acknowledge barriers rather than wish them away, earns him not only his great poems of human separateness and solitude but also his recognition about the power of reciprocity. All the solitary walkers who walk out and turn back, all the walls which dot the landscape, are the context for poems like **"The Need of Being Versed in Country Things"** or **"The Most of It"** or **"Never Again Would Birds' Song Be the Same"** where something dares to wish the walls down, while recognizing that they exist. Therefore in his role as the poet of our separateness, and the critic of our false connections, Frost is also a witness to the enormity of what we fall short of, to a rigorous ideal of human community and an awe before the power of original response. He is even honest enough to write poems in which he explores his own fear and timidity of both that ideal and that response, and at times to write poems in which, for the moment of the poem, he can no longer believe in the possibility.

And as a poet of a culture full of disconnection, and equally full of the longing for connection, a longing so deep that we are often willing to invent community where we have not earned it and to imagine love where we have not risked anything, Frost helps us to confront the voice of our own solitude and separateness. He reminds us of the powerfully exclusionary gestures of the self, and he admonishes us not to pretend that others pay much attention to us at all. . . . His terrain with its stoney walls forbids us from merely wishing away the barriers between one self and another, between ourselves and the natural world, between ourselves and the world of things. He is a poet on the side of limits, unwilling to romanticize either himself (in his best poems), or human vanity, or the culture of forgetting in which he lives. Therefore his poems will not let us make sentimental communities of lamentation and will not let us believe that counter-love and original response can be delight without fear, or addition without revision. If we live in a culture where community is cheap, where drinking the same soft drink promises to bring us all together, where dialing the phone rebuilds families, Frost's poems crumple that easy sense of community. Sometimes they fail to replace it with another, and leave us looking at the worst our separateness can take us to, and sometimes they remind us of a community or a reciprocity far more difficult, earned, and genuine. In the spirit of **"Provide, Provide"** Frost would tell us you don't get something for nothing. You don't get the joys of solitude, the sweetness

of it, without the responsibility of return. You don't take someone or something in without changing yourself in ways you can't know ahead of time. Out of that unknowing, that ignorance, he writes his best poems. And if we read them listening as critically as he listens to himself, willing to double back on our own assumptions, to be honest about our own vanities, fears and longings, then he can be one of our necessary poets, both asking of us and giving to us far more than the Robert Frost of public performance; the Frost we only imagine confirms our unearned assumptions of togetherness. (pp. 9-12)

> *Patricia Wallace, "Separateness and Solitude in Frost," in* The Kenyon Review, *n.s. Vol. 6, No. 1, Winter, 1984, pp. 1-12.*

FURTHER READING

Adams, J. Donald. "Speaking of Books." *The New York Times Book Review* (12 April 1959): 2.
  Refutes Lionel Trilling's description of Frost as a "terrifying poet" [see below], in a speech Trilling delivered at Henry Holt and Company's dinner in honor of Frost's eighty-fifth birthday.

Burnshaw, Stanley. *Robert Frost Himself.* New York: George Braziller, 1986, 342 p.
  Biographical and critical study.

Chamberlain, William. "The Emersonianism of Robert Frost." *ESQ: Emerson Society Quarterly Journal of American Renaissance.* No. 57, (1969): 61-6.
  Discusses the influence of Ralph Waldo Emerson on Frost's philosophy of poetry through an examination of Frost's poems "West-Running Brook" and "Directive."

Dabbs, J. McBride. "Robert Frost and the Dark Woods." *The Yale Review* XXIII, No. 3, (March 1934): 514-20.
  Examines Frost's treatment of nature and its relation to humanity.

Dendinger, Lloyd N. "Robert Frost: The Popular and the Central Poetic Images." *American Quarterly* XXI, No. 4 (Winter 1969): 792-804.
  Explores Frost's reputation among popular audiences and critical scholars and discusses the literary community's reactions to the Lionel Trilling-J. Donald Adams debate.

Donoghue, Dennis. "The Limitations of Robert Frost." *The Twentieth Century* 166, No. 989 (July 1959): 13-22.
  Discusses Frost's style and contends that the poet lacks concentration and economy.

Eberhart, Richard. "Robert Frost: His Personality." *The Southern Review* 2, No. 4 (Autumn 1966): 762-88.
  Asserts that Frost was a poet with a personality totally integrated with the life of his times, his country, and with nature.

Frost, Robert. *Robert Frost and His World: An Elder Wise Man Describes His Life and Poetry.* Center for Cassette Studies 3116, 1975 [audio cassette], 27 minutes.
  Frost discusses his life as a New England farmer, his

early poetry and themes, and gives his thoughts on a variety of topics. He also reads from his works.

Gerber, Philip L. *Robert Frost*. Rev. ed. Boston: Twayne Publishers, 1982, 203 p.
> Biographical and critical study.

Greiner, Donald J. "The Use of Irony in Robert Frost." *South Atlantic Bulletin* XXXVIII, No. 2 (May 1973): 52-60.
> Suggests that Frost's ironic tone stems from his "suspicion of three human comforts, God, communion with nature, and human companionship."

Huston, J. Dennis. " 'The Wonder of Unexpected Supply': Robert Frost and a Poetry Beyond Confusion." *The Centennial Review* XIII, No. 3 (1969): 317-29.
> Explores the theme of uncertainty and terror in several of Frost's poems and suggests that Frost shares certain affinities with filmmaker Alfred Hitchcock.

Lindner, Carl M. "Robert Frost: Dark Romantic." *Arizona Quarterly* 29, No. 3 (Autumn 1973): 235-45.
> Describes Frost's verse as dark parables of the human condition and relates such poems as "Design," "Storm Fear," and "Desert Places" to Herman Melville's classic novel *Moby Dick*.

Morrison, Theodore. "Frost: Country Poet and Cosmopolitan Poet." *The Yale Review* LIX, No. 2 (December 1969): 179-96.
> Brief survey of Frost's rural and urban poetry.

Napier, John T. "A Momentary Stay Against Confusion." *The Virginia Quarterly Review* 33, No. 3, (Summer 1957): 378-94.
> Examines two of Frost's prefatory essays, "The Constant Symbol" and "The Figure a Poem Makes" [see Author's Commentary in entry], which delineate Frost's views on the poetic process.

Paz, Octavio. "Robert Frost: Visit to a Poet." In his *On Poets and Others,* translated by Michael Schmidt, pp. 1-7. New York: Seaver Books, 1986.
> Recounts a visit Paz made to Frost while attending the Bread Loaf Writers' Conference in the summer of 1945.

Pritchard, William H. *Frost: A Literary Life Reconsidered.* New York: Oxford University Press, 1984, 286 p.
> A biographical and critical study in which Pritchard attempts to dispel the portrait of Frost by his authorized biographer, Lawrance Thompson [see below].

Stanlis, Peter J. "Robert Frost: The Individual and Society." *The Intercollegiate Review* 8, No. 5 (Summer 1973): 211-34.
> Interpretive essay on Frost's vision of modern humanity.

Thompson, Lawrance. *Robert Frost: The Early Years, 1874-1915.* New York: Holt, Rinehart and Winston, 1966, 641 p.

————. *Robert Frost: The Years of Triumph, 1915-1938.* New York: Holt, Rinehart and Winston, 1970, 743 p.

Thompson, Lawrance and Winnick, R. H. *Robert Frost: The Later Years, 1938-1963.* New York: Holt, Rinehart and Winston, 1976, 468 p.
> This three-volume work is regarded by many as the definitive biography of Frost, yet the author's less than flattering portrait of Frost's personality has spawned much debate among Frost's defenders and detractors within the literary community.

Tharpe, Jac, ed. *Frost: Centennial Essays I.* Jackson: University Press of Mississippi, 1976, 322 p.
> Contains over twenty critical and biographical essays written by such critics as Joseph Kau, Walton Beacham, and Dorothy Tyler.

Trilling, Lionel. "A Speech on Robert Frost: A Cultural Episode." *Partisan Review* XXVI, No. 3 (Summer 1959): 445-52.
> A transcript of a controversial speech Trilling delivered at the eighty-fifth birthday dinner in honor of Frost given by his publishers, Henry Holt and Company, on March 26, 1959. In the speech, Trilling attempts to challenge the generally accepted depiction of Frost as a poet of contentment by exploring his journeys into the darker realms of humanity. Includes a brief prefatory essay.

Van Doren, Mark. "The Permanence of Robert Frost." *The American Scholar* 5, No. 2 (Spring 1936): 190-98.
> Discusses the durability of Frost's verse. Contends that his direct, unadorned style, subject matter, and avoidance of poetical extremities will garner him a permanent place in American letters.

Watkins, Floyd C. "The Poetry of the Unsaid—Robert Frost's Narrative and Dramatic Poems." *The Texas Quarterly* XV, No. 4 (Winter 1972): 85-98.
> Evaluates several of Frost's dramatic and narrative poems published between 1914 and 1923.

Langston Hughes

1902-1967

(Full name: James Mercer Langston Hughes) American poet, short story writer, novelist, dramatist, autobiographer, editor, translator, and author of children's books.

A seminal figure of the Harlem Renaissance, an era of unprecedented excellence in African-American art and literature that took place during the 1920s and 1930s, Hughes devoted his versatile and prolific career to portraying the urban experience of working-class blacks. Called "the Poet Laureate of Harlem" by Carl Van Vechten, Hughes integrated the rhythm and mood of jazz and blues music into his work and employed colloquial language to reflect the essence of black American culture. Hughes's gentle humor and wry irony often belie the magnitude of his themes. Having been a victim of poverty and discrimination, Hughes wrote of the frustration of being seduced by the American Dream of freedom and equality only to be denied its realization due to racism. Unlike the works of many African-American writers, Hughes's poetry and prose are devoid of bitterness; as Theodore R. Hudson has stated: "Dipping his pen in ink, not acid, [Hughes's] method was to expose rather than excoriate, to reveal rather than revile."

Hughes was born in Joplin, Missouri to James Nathaniel and Carrie Mercer Langston Hughes, who separated shortly after Hughes's birth. His father left the United States for Cuba and later settled in Mexico, where he lived the remainder of his life as a prosperous attorney and landowner. In contrast, Hughes's mother lived a transitory life, often leaving him in the care of his maternal grandmother while searching for permanent employment in Missouri and in Kansas. Hughes spent most of his childhood living with his maternal grandmother in Lawrence, Kansas. Following his grandmother's death in 1910, Hughes lived with family friends and various relatives, and in 1914, joined his mother and new stepfather in Cleveland, Ohio. Hughes attended Central High School, where he excelled academically and in sports. He also wrote poetry and short fiction for the *Belfry Owl,* the high school literary magazine, and edited the school yearbook. In the summer of 1919 Hughes visited his father in Mexico for the first time, but soon became disillusioned with his father's materialistic values and his contempt for blacks, Mexicans, and Indians, whom he believed were lazy and ignorant. Upon graduating from high school in 1920, Hughes returned to Mexico, where he taught English for a year and submitted several poems and prose pieces for publication to the *Crisis,* the magazine of the National Association for the Advancement of Colored People. With the assistance of his father, who had originally urged him to study engineering in Switzerland or Germany, Hughes enrolled at Columbia University in New York City in 1921. Subjected to bigotry on campus and in the dormitory where he lived, Hughes often missed classes in order to attend shows, lectures, and readings sponsored by the American Socialist Society. Following his freshman year, Hughes dropped out of Columbia and worked a series of menial jobs while supporting his mother, who had recently moved to Harlem. Hughes also published several poems in the *Crisis* during this period. In 1923, he signed on as a cabin boy on a merchant freighter en route to West Africa.

Hughes spent the majority of the following year overseas. After resigning his position on the *S. S. McKeesport* in the Netherlands, Hughes lived in virtual poverty in France and Italy. Returning to the United States in 1925, Hughes resettled with his mother and half brother in Washington, D. C. He continued writing poetry while working menial jobs, experimenting with language, form, and rhythms reminiscent of the blues and jazz compositions he had heard in Parisian nightclubs. In May and August of 1925, Hughes's verse garnered him literary prizes from both *Opportunity* magazine and the *Crisis.* In December, Hughes, now a busboy at a Washington D.C. hotel, attracted the attention of poet Vachel Lindsay by placing three of his poems on Lindsay's dinner table. Later that evening, Lindsay read Hughes's poems to an audience and announced his discovery of a "Negro busboy poet," garnering national attention. Hughes returned to New York City shortly afterward and, with the assistance of Carl Van Vechten, a writer and supporter of African-American art and literature, published his first book of poetry, *The Weary Blues,* in 1926.

The poems collected in *The Weary Blues* reflect a variety of themes and personal experiences. Most of the selections in this volume approximate the phrasing and meter of blues music, a musical genre popularized in the early 1920s by rural and urban blacks. In such pieces as "Jazzonia," "Cabaret," and "The Weary Blues," Hughes evokes the frenzied, hedonistic atmosphere of Harlem's famous nightclubs and speakeasies, while "The Jester" and "Mother to Son" comment upon racial conflict. Hughes also included several pieces relating his travels to Africa, as well as "The Negro Speaks of Rivers," a much-anthologized poem Hughes wrote during his second visit to Mexico in 1920. The lines "I bathed in the Euphrates when dawns were young / I built my hut near the Congo and it lulled me to sleep," foreshadow the nationalist writings later popularized by the New Negro writers of the Harlem Renaissance and anticipate the work of young militant poets of the Civil Rights era four decades later. *The Weary Blues* received largely mixed reviews due to its blues and jazz verse centering on Harlem life. Countee Cullen wrote: "I regard these jazz poems as interlopers in the company of the truly beautiful poems. . . . There is too much emphasis here on strictly Negro themes."

Shortly before the publication of *The Weary Blues,* Hughes enrolled at Lincoln University in Pennsylvania, and during the summer of 1926 he became active in the Harlem Renaissance, publishing new poetry, short stories, and essays in mainstream and black-oriented periodicals. In 1927, together with Zora Neale Hurston and other writers, Hughes founded *Fire!,* a literary journal devoted to African-American culture that ceased publication after its premiere issue as a result of financial difficulties and a fire that destroyed the editorial offices. In the spring of 1927, Hughes published his second collection of verse, *Fine Clothes to the Jew.* In this volume, he included several ballads and chose Harlem's lower class as his principle subject. This approach dismayed several leading black intellectuals and critics, who felt that Hughes's depictions of crap games, street brawls, and other unsavory activities were detrimental to the cause of improving race relations. Alain Locke, however, held an opposing view: "[*Fine Clothes to the Jew*] is notable as an achievement in poetic realism in addition to its particular value as a folk study in verse of Negro life."

In *Shakespeare in Harlem* and *Fields of Wonder,* Hughes's next two major volumes of verse, the carefree hedonism of the 1920s is replaced by the reality of the Depression. Hughes writes of economic chaos and its effects on Harlem residents in both collections, which include such pieces as "Cabaret Girl Dies on Welfare Island" and "Trumpet Player: 52nd Street." Most critics comment on a lack of thematic progression or maturity in Hughes's poems, and Owen Dodson charged in a review of *Shakespeare in Harlem* that Hughes was "backing into the future looking at the past." A subsequent volume, *One-Way Ticket,* evinces Hughes's growing disenchantment with America's treatment of blacks following World War II. This collection is highlighted by a cycle of poems revolving around Alberta K. Johnson, an "Everywoman" whose daily encounters with racism reflect the aspirations and disappointments of many African-Americans during this period.

Hughes's first book-length poem, *Montage of a Dream Deferred,* contrasts the drastically deteriorated state of Harlem in the 1950s to the Harlem he had known in the 1920s. Employing dramatic dialogue and colloquialisms, Hughes laments that the exuberance of nightclub life and the vitality of cultural renaissance have been superseded by a ghetto plagued by poverty, drugs, and crime. Paralleling the change in tone is a change in rhythm; the smooth patterns and gentle melancholy of blues music were replaced by the abrupt, fragmented structure of postwar jazz, particularly bebop, which many commentators view as symbolic of urban society in transition. John W. Parker commented: "[*Montage of a Dream Deferred*] is a fast-moving story of a people who, despite their own imperfections and the bitter and corroding circumstances they face from day to day, have never relinquished their dream of a tomorrow that will be better. But it is a dream born out of heartache, a dream much like life in dark Harlem."

Ask Your Mama: 12 Moods for Jazz consists of twelve irreverent poems that comment on the political turbulence of the early 1960s. Intended to be read aloud with musical accompaniment, Hughes's verse offers acerbic solutions to segregation and the disenfranchisement of Southern blacks. He also renders an imaginary South in which civil rights leader Martin Luther King, Jr. is elected governor of the state of Georgia, and Orval Faubus, the Arkansas governor who defied federal court orders to desegregate public schools, becomes a mammy in charge of rearing black children. Hughes's final collection of verse, *The Panther and the Lash,* was published posthumously in 1967. The aggressive tone in such pieces as "Black Panther" and "The Backlash Blues" is indicative of protest literature written during this period. Hughes also chronicles African colonies on the verge of independence in "Angola's Question Mark" and "Lumumba's Grave." This volume received scant critical attention upon its publication; some reviewers viewed the work as a polemical effort, surrendering to political fashion. W. Edward Farrison, however, considered *The Panther and the Lash* an appropriate conclusion to Hughes's career: "From the beginning of his career as an author, Hughes was articulate in the Negro's struggle for first-class citizenship. It is indeed fitting that this volume with which his career ended is a vital contribution to that struggle as well as to American poetry."

Throughout his career, Hughes encountered mixed reactions to his work. Many black intellectuals denounced him for portraying unsophisticated aspects of lower-class life, claiming that his focus furthered an unfavorable image of African-Americans. Hughes, however, believed not only in the inherent worth of the black masses but in the need to present the truth as he perceived it: "I didn't know the upper class Negroes well enough to write much about them. I knew only the people I had grown up with, and they weren't people whose shoes were always shined, who had been to Harvard, or who had heard of Bach. But they seemed to me good people, too." As the struggle for civil rights became increasingly widespread in America toward the end of his career, Hughes was also faulted by militant artists and leaders for what they perceived as a failure to address controversial issues. Nevertheless, Hughes's reputation has remained consistently strong, largely due to his accessible portraits of urban life.

(For further information on Hughes's life and career, see *Contemporary Literary Criticism*, Vols. 1, 5, 10, 15, 35, 44; *Short Story Criticism*, Vol. 6; *Children's Literature Review*, Vol. 17; *Contemporary Authors*, Vols. 1-4, rev. ed., Vols. 25-28, rev. ed. [obituary]; *Contemporary Authors New Revision Series*, Vol, 1; *Something about the Author*, Vols. 4, 33; *Dictionary of Literary Biography*, Vols. 4, 7, 48, 51; and *Concise Dictionary of American Literary Biography: The Age of Maturity, 1929-1941*.)

PRINCIPAL WORKS

POETRY

The Weary Blues   1926
Fine Clothes to the Jew   1927
The Negro Mother and Other Dramatic Recitations   1931
Dear Lovely Death   1931
The Dream Keeper and Other Poems   1932
Scottsboro Limited: Four Poems and a Play in Verse   1932
Shakespeare in Harlem   1942
Freedom's Plow   1943
Jim Crow's Last Stand   1943
Lament for Dark Peoples and Other Poems   1944
Fields of Wonder   1947
One-Way Ticket   1949
Montage of a Dream Deferred   1951
Selected Poems of Langston Hughes   1959
Ask Your Mama: 12 Moods for Jazz   1961
The Panther and the Lash: Poems of Our Times   1967

OTHER MAJOR WORKS

Not without Laughter   (novel)   1930
The Ways of White Folks   (short stories)   1934
Little Ham   (drama)   1935
Mulatto   (drama)   1935
Don't You Want to be Free?   (drama)   1937
Soul Gone Home   (drama)   1937
The Big Sea   (autobiography)   1940
Simple Speaks His Mind   (short stories)   1950
Laughing to Keep from Crying   (short stories)   1952
Simple Takes a Wife   (short stories)   1953
The Sweet Flypaper of Life, with Roy De Carava   (nonfiction)   1955
I Wonder as I Wander: An Autobiographical Journey (autobiography)   1956
Simple Stakes a Claim   (short stories)   1957
Simply Heavenly   (drama)   1957
Tambourines to Glory   (novel)   1958
The Best of Simple   (short stories)   1961
Five Plays by Langston Hughes, edited by Webster Smalley (drama)   1963
Something in Common and Other Stories   (short stories) 1963
Simple's Uncle Sam   (short stories)   1965

Carl Van Vechten   (essay date 1925)

[*An American critic and novelist, Van Vechten was one of the first established white authors to take a serious and active role in reviewing and promoting the works of African-American writers, musicians, and artists during the Harlem Renaissance. Through his literary contacts Van Vechten aided many young black writers, including Langston Hughes, whose first book of poetry,* The Weary Blues, *was published by Van Vechten's own publisher, Alfred A. Knopf. In the following excerpted introduction to* The Weary Blues, *Van Vechten extols Hughes's ability to evoke different moods in his verse and proclaims him a poet of great promise.*]

At the moment I cannot recall the name of any other person whatever who, at the age of twenty-three, has enjoyed so picturesque and rambling an existence as Langston Hughes. Indeed, a complete account of his disorderly and delightfully fantastic career would make a fascinating picaresque romance which I hope this young Negro will write before so much more befalls him that he may find it difficult to capture all the salient episodes within the limits of a single volume. (p. 9)

[Hughes's poems] are by no means limited to an exclusive mood; he writes caressingly of little black prostitutes in Harlem; his cabaret songs throb with the true jazz rhythm; his sea-pieces ache with a clam, melancholy lyricism; he cries bitterly from the heart of his race in **"Cross"** and **"The Jester"**; he sighs, in one of the most successful of his fragile poems, over the loss of a loved friend. Always, however, his stanzas are subjective, personal. They are the (I had almost said informal, for they have a highly deceptive air of spontaneous improvisation) expression of an essentially sensitive and subtly illusive nature, seeking always to break through the veil that obscures for him, at least in some degree, the ultimate needs of that nature.

To the Negro race in America, since the day when Phillis Wheatley indited lines to General George Washington and other aristocratic figures (for Phillis Wheatley never sang "My way's cloudy," or "By an' by, I'm goin' to lay down dis heavy load") there have been born many poets. Paul Laurence Dunbar, James Weldon Johnson, Claude McKay, Jean Toomer, Georgia Douglas Johnson, Countée Cullen, are a few of the more memorable names. Not the least of these names, I think, is that of Langston Hughes, and perhaps his adventures and personality offer the promise of as rich a fulfillment as has been the lot of any of the others. (p. 13)

> *Carl Van Vechten, in an introduction to* The Weary Blues *by Langston Hughes, Alfred A. Knopf, 1926, pp. 9-13.*

Countee Cullen   (essay date 1926)

[*Cullen, an American poet and novelist, was one of the outstanding poets of the Harlem Renaissance and one of the first black poets after Paul Laurence Dunbar to achieve national recognition, particularly for such volumes of verse as* Color *(1925) and* The Ballad of the Brown Girl *(1927). In the following review of* The Weary Blues, *excerpted below, Cullen praises Hughes's spontaneity and energy yet faults his limited subject matter.*]

Here is a poet with whom to reckon, to experience, and here and there, with that apologetic feeling of presumption that should companion all criticism, to quarrel.

What has always struck me most forcibly in reading Mr. Hughes' poems has been their utter spontaneity and expression of a unique personality. This feeling is intensified with the appearance of his work in concert between the covers of a book [*The Weary Blues*]. It must be acknowledged at the outset that these poems are peculiarly Mr. Hughes' and no one's else. I cannot imagine his work as that of any other poet, not even of any poet of that particular group of which Mr. Hughes is a member. Of course, a microscopic assiduity might reveal derivation and influences, but these are weak undercurrents in the flow of Mr. Hughes' own talent. This poet represents a transcendently emancipated spirit among a class of young writers whose particular battle-cry is freedom. With the enthusiasm of a zealot, he pursues his way, scornful, in subject matter, in photography, and rhythmical treatment, of whatever obstructions time and tradition have placed before him. To him it is essential that he be himself. Essential and commendable surely; yet the thought persists that some of these poems would have been better had Mr. Hughes held himself a bit in check. In his admirable introduction to the book, Carl Van Vechten says the poems have a *highly deceptive air of spontaneous improvisation* [see excerpt dated 1925]. I do not feel that the air is deceptive.

If I have the least powers of prediction, the first section of . . . *The Weary Blues* will be most admired, even if less from intrinsic poetical worth than because of its dissociation from the traditionally poetic. Never having been one to think all subjects and forms proper for poetic consideration, I regard these jazz poems as interlopers in the company of the truly beautiful poems in other sections of the book. They move along with the frenzy and electric heat of a Methodist or Baptist revival meeting, and affect me in much the same manner. The revival meeting excites me, cooling and flushing me with alternate chills and fevers of emotion; so do these poems. But when the storm is over, I wonder if the quiet way of communing is not more spiritual for the God-seeking heart; and in the light of reflection I wonder if jazz poems really belong to that dignified company, that select and austere circle of high literary expression which we call poetry. Surely, when in **"Negro Dancers"** Mr. Hughes says

Me an' ma baby's
Got two mo' ways,
Two mo' ways to do de buck!

he voices, in lyrical, thumb-at-nose fashion the happy careless attitude, akin to poetry, that is found in certain types. And certainly he achieves one of his loveliest lyrics in **"Young Singer"**. Thus I find myself straddling a fence. It needs only **"The Cat and The Saxaphone,"** however, to knock me over completely on the side of bewilderment, and incredulity. This creation is a *tour de force* of its kind, but is it a poem:

EVERYBODY

Half-pint,—
Gin?
No, make it

LOVES MY BABY

corn. You like
don't you, honey?
BUT MY BABY ....

In the face of accomplished fact, I cannot say *This will never do,* but I feel that it ought never to have been done.

But Mr. Hughes can be as fine and as polished as you like, etching his work in calm, quiet lyrics that linger and repeat themselves. Witness **"Sea Calm"**:

How still,
How strangely still
The water is today.
It is not good
For water
To be so still that way.

Or take **"Suicide's Note"**:

The Calm,
Cool face of the river
Asked me for a kiss.

(p. 73)

Mr. Hughes is a remarkable poet of the colorful; through all his verses the rainbow riots and dazzles, yet never wearies the eye, although at times it intrigues the brain into astonishment and exaggerated admiration when reading, say something like **"Caribbean Sunset"**:

God having a hemorrhage,
Blood coughed across the sky,
Staining the dark sea red:
That is sunset in the Caribbean.

Taken as a group the selections in this book seem one-sided to me. They tend to hurl this poet into the gaping pit that lies before all Negro writers, in the confines of which they become racial artists instead of artists pure and simple. There is too much emphasis here on strictly Negro themes; and this is probably an added reason for my coldness toward the jazz poems—they seem to set a too definite limit upon an already limited field.

Dull books cause no schisms, raise no dissensions, create no parties. Much will be said of *The Weary Blues* because it is a definite achievement, and because Mr. Hughes, in his own way, with a first book that cannot be dismissed as merely *promising,* has arrived. (pp. 73-4)

> *Countee Cullen, "Poet on Poet," in* Opportunity, *Vol. IV, No. 38, February, 1926, pp. 73-4.*

Du Bose Heyward (essay date 1926)

[*Heyward, an American dramatist and novelist, was best known for his novels* Porgy *(1925) and* Mamba's Daughters *(1927), both of which depict the lives of the Gullah blacks of South Carolina and the Sea Islands. The former work was later adapted for the stage and served as the basis for George and Ira Gershwin's opera,* Porgy and Bess. *In the following excerpt, Heyward praises Hughes's jazz motifs and use of other indigenous African-American musical forms in* The Weary Blues.]

The Weary Blues challenges more serious consideration than that generally accorded a "first book." Langston Hughes, although only twenty-four years old, is already conspicuous in the group of Negro intellectuals who are dignifying Harlem with a genuine art life. And, too, his use of syncopation in his prize poem [**"The Weary Blues"**] suggested the possibility of a conflict in the rhythms of poetry paralleling that which is taking place between the spiritual and jazz exponents of Negro music.

Let it be said at once then that this author has done nothing particularly revolutionary in the field of rhythm. He is endowed with too subtle a musical sense to employ the banjo music of Vachel Lindsay, but he is close kin to Carl Sandburg in his use of freer, subtler syncopation. In fact, he has wisely refused to be fettered by a theory and has allowed his mood to select its own music. Several of the short free verse poems might have been written by Amy Lowell.

But if he derives little that is new in rhythm from his "Blues" he has managed to capture the mood of his type of Negro song, and thereby has caught its very essence. When he is able to create a minor, devil-may-care music, and through it to release a throb of pain, he is doing what the Negroes have done for generations, whether in the "Blues" of the Mississippi region or a song like "I Can't Help from Cryin' Sometimes," as sung by the black folk of the Carolina low country.

As he says in his **"Cabaret"**:

Does a jazz band ever sob?
They say a jazz band's gay.
Yet as the vulgar dancers whirled
And the wan night wore away,
One said she heard the jazz band sob
When the little dawn was gray.

That Langston Hughes has not altogether escaped an inevitable pitfall of the Negro intellectual is to be regretted. In one or two places in [*The Weary Blues*] the artist is obscured by the propagandist. Pegasus has been made a pack-horse. It is natural that the Negro writer should feel keenly the lack of sympathy in the South. That the South is a great loser thereby brings him small comfort. In the soul of a poet, a revolt so born may be transmutted through the alchemy of art into poetry that, while it stings the eyes with tears, causes the reader to wonder. (pp. 4-5)

But far more often in the volume the artist is victor:

We have to-morrow
Bright before us
Like a flame.

Yesterday
A night-gone thing,
A sun-down name.

And dawn to-day
Bread arch above the road we came.

It is, however, as an individual poet, not as a member of a new and interesting literary group, or as spokesman for a race, that Langston Hughes must stand or fall, and in the numerous poems in *The Weary Blues* that give poignant moods and vivid glimpses of seas and lands caught by the young poet in his wanderings I find an exceptional endowment. Always intensely subjective, passionate, keenly sensitive to beauty and possessed of an unfaltering musical sense, Langston Hughes has give us a "first book" that marks the opening of a career well worth watching. (p. 5)

Du Bose Heyward, "The Jazz Band's Sob," in New York Herald Tribune Books, *August 1, 1926, pp. 4-5.*

Babette Deutsch   (essay date 1927)

[*An American poet, critic, and editor, Deutsch was known for her study of modern poetry,* Poetry in Our Time *(1952), and for her translations of Russian, German, and French verse. In the review excerpted below, Deutsch offers a negative assessment of* Fine Clothes to the Jew.]

Messrs. Pound, Ransom, and Van Doren are all three learned and, for the most part, urbane gentlemen, whose poetry is fed in almost equal streams by literature and life. The verses of Langston Hughes [in *Fine Clothes to the Jew*] are completely unliterary, often wilfully illiterate, and as naively vital as any old ballad or folk song. The dialect pieces fairly sing themselves when read aloud, and the others show craftsmanship of a high order. Poems like **"Railroad Avenue"** and **"Magnolia Flower"** echo in the memory. Typical of the poet's feeling for symmetry is the manner in which the last lyric in the book balances the first.

Babette Deutsch, in a review of "Fine Clothes to the Jew," in The Bookman, *New York, Vol. LXV, No. 2, April, 1927, p. 221.*

Alain Locke   (essay date 1927)

[*Locke was an American critic, essayist, and editor whose writings and activities made a significant impact upon the Harlem Renaissance movement. His major work,* The New Negro: An Interpretation *(1925) helped introduce a new literary and cultural aesthetic which espoused African-American nationalism while advocating a new social order based on equal opportunity for all Americans. In the following appreciative review of* Fine Clothes to the Jew, *Locke commends Hughes's use of folk idioms to portray the lives of ordinary black Harlemites.*]

Fine clothes may not make either the poet or the gentleman, but they certainly help; and it is a rare genius that can strip life to the buff and still poetize it. This, however, Langston Hughes has done [in *Fine Clothes to the Jew*], a volume that is even more starkly realistic and colloquial than his first. . . . It is a current ambition in American poetry to take the common clay of life and fashion it to living beauty, but very few have succeeded, even Masters and Sandburg not invariably. They get their effects, but often at the expense of poetry. Here, on the contrary, there is scarcely a prosaic note or a spiritual sag in spite of the fact that never has cruder colloquialism or more sordid life been put into the substance of poetry. The book is, therefore, notable as an achievement in poetic realism in addition to its particular value as a folk study in verse of Negro life.

The success of these poems owes much to the clever and apt device of taking folk-song forms and idioms as the mold into which the life of the plain people is descriptively poured. This gives not only an authentic background and the impression that it is the people themselves speaking, but the sordidness of common life is caught up in the lilt of its own poetry and without any sentimental propping attains something of the necessary elevation of art. Many of the poems are modelled in the exact metrical form of the Negro "Blues," now so suddenly popular, and in thought and style of expression are so close as scarcely to be distinguishable from the popular variety. But these poems are not transcriptions, every now and then one catches sight of the deft poetic touch that unostentatiously transforms them into folk portraits. . . . The author apparently loves the plain people in every aspect of their lives, their gin-drinking carousals, their street brawls, their tenement publicity, and their slum matings and partings, and reveals this segment of Negro life as it has never been shown before. Its open frankness will be a shock and a snare for the critic and moralist who cannot distinguish clay from mire. The poet has himself said elsewhere,— "The 'low-down' Negroes furnish a wealth of colorful, distinctive material for any artist, because they hold their individuality in the face of American standardizations. And perhaps these common people will give to the world its truly great Negro artist, the one who is not afraid to be himself." And as one watches Langston Hughes's own career, one wonders. . . .

However, there are poems of other than the folk character in the book,—none more notable than **"The Mulatto,"**— too long to quote, even though it is a lyric condensation of the deepest tragedy of the race problem. One that is just as pregnant with social as well as individual tragedy [is **"Song for a Dark Girl,"**] a brief sample of this side of younger Negro genius for tragic vision and utterance:

Way Down South in Dixie
(Break the heart of me)
They hung my black young lover
To a cross roads tree.

Way Down South in Dixie
(Bruised body high in air)
I asked the white Lord Jesus
What was the use of prayer.

Way Down South in Dixie
(Break the heart of me)
Love is a naked shadow
On a gnarled and naked tree.

After this there is nothing to be said about the finest tragedy having always to be Greek.

Alain Locke, "Common Clay and Poetry," in The Saturday Review of Literature, *Vol. III, No. 37, April 9, 1927, p. 712.*

Abbe Niles   (essay date 1927)

[*In the following excerpt, Niles analyzes the blues rhythms in* Fine Clothes to the Jew.]

To this reviewer, the most interesting portion of Mr. Langston Hughes' [*Fine Clothes to the Jew*] is his dialect verse, and especially the seventeen poems in the manner of the Negro folk-blues, of which he offers far the best concise description in print:

The *Blues,* unlike the *Spirituals,* have a strict poetic pattern: one long line repeated and a third line to rhyme with the other two. Sometimes the second line in repetition is slightly changed and sometimes, but very seldom, it is omitted. The mood of the *Blues* is almost always despondency, but when they are sung people laugh.

The last sentence is remarkable for what it leaves unsaid,

for commentators on the blues, including the reviewer, have expressed overdefinite conclusions on the state of mind they represent. Their psychology, or their philosophy, if any, is in fact too complex to fit into any single pigeon-hole such as that of bravery, humility, optimism, "making the best of things," or, since they presuppose no audience, exhibitionism or appeal to sympathy. Although the gusto in their best phrases is unmistakable, even the comfort of having well stated one's grievance will not invariably explain them. For one thing, the singer has quite frequently disguised a real trouble and built his blues on one which is quite fictitious. For another, there has been a curious phenomenon of sympathetic coöperation, which is implied in Mr. Hughes' **"Misery"**: a honky-tonk pianist has been approached by a woman with the request: "My man's lef' me—gimme a blues," and straightway her obscure need has been supplied on such material as she has furnished:

Oh, Sis Kate's lost her rider, so she got de blues . . .

The long and short of the matter is that the spirit of the blues, which, unlike their "pattern," is not peculiar to them in American Negro folk-song, can be defined only in terms of their creators themselves: unlettered people who know an inner necessity to sing of their contacts with life, and whose stream of thought takes characteristic jumps and turns, sometimes diverting to others and sometimes, pleasantly, to themselves.

Mr. Hughes' thought need not follow the channel which in those instinctive singers produces such jumps and turns, but at his pleasure it is able to do so. It is still his thought, not theirs, so that he expresses the feelings of the porters, elevator boys, Harlem prostitutes and Memphis bad men into whose shoes he momentarily steps, with an explicitness and coherence which would be beyond most of them; and the resulting absence, in his work, of the streakiness which has been mentioned above, at once takes it out of the category of mere pastiche. It is apparently out of the same ability, and consequent desire, to be explicit, that he resorts to the anomaly of a blues *sequence* forming a single poem. Yet the reviewer finds in this volume but a single line which—since he has never, in his experience, encountered in folk-song a similar assertion that "A *is* B," instead of "A is like B"—he ventures to believe incongruous:

De railroad bridge's a sad song in de air.

These experiments derive both from spirituals and from secular song, but from only a limited class of the latter. There is none corresponding to the pure fancy of the folk-dance:

Popped ma whip—*Sangaree!*
Popped it loud—*Sangaree!*
Whip got tangled—*Sangaree!*
Behind a cloud—*Sangaree!*

Popped ma whip—*Sangaree!*
Popped it strong—*Sangaree!*
Whip got tangled—*Sangaree!*
In de wagon-tongue—*Sangaree!*

and there is little to suggest the faint ambiguous melancholy of the folk-blues. . . . [But] one does find Hughes' vein in another anonymous verse:

You don't love me, honey—you don' need to lie . . .

But de day you leaves me, dat's de day you die

His people are immediately conscious of specific and personal wants, inconveniences and designs, and it is from the depths that they raise their various voices:

. . . I hates dem rinney yaller gals
An' I wants my Albert back. . . .

Verse of this character should be made complete and its rhythms brought out by music such as the author must have had in mind as he wrote, and it is pleasant to record that there is actually a "Golden Brown Blues" by Hughes and [W. C.] Handy, containing the verse, reminiscent of Van Vechten's Harlem novel [*Nigger Heaven*]:

If I hits the numbers, I'm tellin' you the fac's . . .
Gonna get a Golden Brown with my income tax.

Mr. Hughes' range is broader than the scope of this review has indicated; quotations could be multiplied so as to bring out, among other things, his quick sensitiveness to any manifestation of beauty or ugliness, or the exceeding bitterness of some of his reflections. But he has much left to say, he is consistently saying it to better effect, and the variety of his considerable qualities is unlikely to want for critics to number them. (p. 77)

*Abbe Niles, "Real and Artificial Folk-Song,"
in* The New Republic, *Vol. LI, No. 653, June 8, 1927, pp. 76-7.*

Eda Lou Walton   (essay date 1942)

[*Walton suggests that Hughes's themes in* Shakespeare in Harlem *are dated and not indicative of the impact of World War II and racial conflicts upon American society.*]

If a poet needs a history, a culture, something implicit and of some duration to communicate, the Negro poet has this. His problem is old, his cause just. The culture out of which he writes is more or less homogeneous. The symbols of race suffering and oppression are well understood.

This new collection of Langston Hughes' "blues songs" [*Shakespeare in Harlem*] is not unlike his earlier collections. These are the known lonely songs and rhythms of his people, their love songs too. Back of the simple rhythms lies suffering. The poems are close to folk song. It may be said, however, that they probably had been in preparation for some time. They indicate no awareness of the changed war world, they are not even profoundly class or race-conscious. I think on the whole they are a little too easily composed. Folk poetry is always the picture of a people. But a poet like Langston Hughes should have something more to say than is said in these strummed out "blues songs" which can too easily be listened to and do not call forth enough thought.

Eda Lou Walton, "Nothing New under the Sun," in New Masses, *Vol. XLIII, No. 11, June 16, 1942, p. 23.*

Owen Dodson   (essay date 1942)

[*In the following excerpted review of* Shakespeare in Harlem, *Dodson considers the collection inferior to*

Hughes's earlier work and contends that the poet's portrayal of African-American life is one-dimensional.]

This Shakespeare still rolls dice in Harlem, grabs a wishbone, makes a wish for his sweet mamma, long gone, long lost; still lies in bed in the noon of the day. This Shakespeare is lazy, unpoetic, common and vulgar. In short Mr. Langston Shakespeare Hughes is still holding his mirror up to a gold-toothed, flashy nature. It is the same mirror he has held up before but somehow the glass is cracked and his deep insight and discipline has dimmed. There is no getting away from the fact that this book, superior in format, is a careless surface job and unworthy of the author Mr. Van Vechten calls the "Negro Poet Laureate," who loves his race and reports and interprets it feelingly and understandingly to itself and other races. His verse resounds with the exultant throb of Negro pain and gladness.

Once Mr. Hughes wrote

Because my mouth
Is wide with laughter
You do not hear
My inner cry;
Because my feet
Are gay with dancing
You do not know
I die.

In [*Shakespeare in Harlem*] we merely hear the laughter: loud, lewd, unwholesome and degenerate. We see and hear a cartoon doing a black-face, white-lip number, trying terribly to please the populace. None of the inner struggle is revealed, no bitter cries, no protests, no gentleness, no ladders of hope being climbed. These things are hard to say about a poet I very much admire. But they must be said.

Mr. Hughes states at the beginning of the book that this is "light verse. Afro-Americana in the blues mood. Poems syncopated and variegated in the colors of Harlem, Beale Street, West Dallas, and Chicago's South Side. Blues, ballads and reels to be read aloud, crooned, shouted, recited and sung. Some with gestures, some not—as you like. None with a far-away voice." This statement screens a thousand sins. Because verse is "light" it doesn't therefore follow that anything goes. The technique of light verse is as exacting as that of serious verse, almost more so.

If this were Mr. Hughes' first book we would say, here is some promise but in a few years he will deepen this stream, he will broaden this stream. But as this is his fourth volume of verse all I can say is that he is "backing into the future looking at the past" to say nothing of the present.

Eight sections make up the book: "Seven Moments of Love", "Declarations", "Blues for Men", "Death in Harlem", "Mammy Songs", "Ballads", "Blues for Ladies", "Lenox Avenue". (pp. 337-38)

The real "nitty gritty" is a poem in the "Lenox Avenue" section called **"Shakespeare in Harlem"**

Hey ninny neigh!
And a hey nonny no!
Where, oh, where
Did my sweet mama go?

Hey ninny neigh!
With a tra-la-la-la!

They say your sweet mama
Went home to her ma.

But the "cup" is poems like **"Hey-Hey Blues"**, and **"Little Lyric"**. Whoever drinks will choke on these. (p. 338)

Owen Dodson, *"Shakespeare in Harlem,"* in PHYLON: The Atlanta University Review of Race and Culture, *Vol. III, No. 3, third quarter (June, 1942), pp. 337-38.*

AUTHOR'S COMMENTARY

Most of my . . . poems are racial in theme and treatment, derived from the life I know. In many of them I try to grasp and hold some of the meanings and rhythms of jazz. I am sincere as I know how to be in these poems and yet after every reading I answer questions like these from my own people: Do you think Negroes should always write about Negroes? I wish you wouldn't read some of your poems to white folks. How do you find anything interesting in a place like a cabaret? Why do you write about black people? You aren't black. What makes you do so many jazz poems?

But jazz to me is one of the inherent expressions of Negro life in America: the eternal tom-tom beating in the Negro soul—the tom-tom of revolt against weariness in a white world, a world of subway trains, and work, work, work; the tom-tom of joy and laughter, and pain swallowed in a smile. Yet the Philadelphia clubwoman is ashamed to say that her race created it and she does not like me to write about it. The old subconscious "white is best" runs through her mind. . . .

We younger Negro artists who create now intend to express our individual dark-skinned selves without fear or shame. If white people are pleased we are glad. If they are not, it doesn't matter. We know we are beautiful. And ugly too. The tom-tom cries and the tom-tom laughs. If colored people are pleased we are glad. If they are not, their displeasure doesn't matter either. We build our temples for tomorrow, strong as we know how, and we stand on top of the mountain, free within ourselves.

(essay date 1926)

Bertram L. Woodruff   (essay date 1947)

[*Woodruff discusses Hughes's use of imagery and metaphor in* Fields of Wonder.]

Fields of Wonder charms with its simplicity. A far cry from the complex significance of Cullen, the poetry of Mr. Hughes matches the symbolic canvases of Horace Pippin in the release of the evocative power of personal and traditional metaphors. Mr. Hughes apostrophizes the "fields of wonder" which give birth to the stars and the poet with his cosmic destiny.

To distinguish between the beauty of poetic matter and poetry itself is to hear a word and a tone in silence, Langston Hughes avers. He offers the beauty of poetic matter in such lines as

In times of silver rain
The butterflies
Lift silken wings
To catch a rainbow cry.

But, although pictorial and musical beauties are poetic, they do not constitute poetry itself. Explicit description or onomatopoeia must be refracted and reflected obliquely by metaphor in order to acquire intensity of poetic feeling. Mr. Hughes therefore succeeds with the personal symbols that awaken for the reader old memories and reflections:

Rocks and the firm roots of trees.
The rising shafts of mountains.
Something strong to put my hands on.

Empathy is aroused in the reader by the exquisite speculation on the little snail on a rose "drinking the dew drop's mystery," and by the loneliness of a likker bottle on a table "All by itself." The use of sexual imagery deepens from adumbrations in **"Sleep"** and **"Desire"** to the seething surge of the waves in **"Moonlight Night: Carmel."** To reinforce kinesthetic sensations by aural recollections, folk speech is used. Langston Hughes calls the graveyard a "no stretching place" and "that-never-get-up-no-more Place." Also, when he becomes cryptic, all the stops of mystery and suspense sound in such poems as **"Night, Four Songs," "Poppy Flower,"** and **"End."**

This body of poetry is not without deep social implications. Mr. Hughes drops a given symbol like a pebble in the reader's consciousness to spread widening ripples of emotional agitation. The circles thus set in vibration have power to limn suggestfully the economic and political nightmares of our times. For example, **"Dust Bowl"** conjures up the curse on American agriculture and the baffled love for the land at the same time that it reaffirms man's harmony with nature. Like Cullen, Langston Hughes is deeply religious. In **"Prayer"** he asks for pity for

All the scum
Of our weary city

and he trusts that divine love will gather up those who expect no love. (pp. 199-200)

Bertram L. Woodruff, *"Of Myth and Symbol,"* in PHYLON: The Atlanta University Review of Race and Culture, *Vol. VIII, No. 2, second quarter (June, 1947), pp. 198-200.*

Hubert Creekmore   (essay date 1947)

[*The following is excerpted from a review of* Fields of Wonder.]

[**Fields of Wonder**] is notable for the brevity and leanness of its lyrics. Many are only four to six lines long, and others would be, if the regular lines were not broken up. For instance, the last stanza of **"Snail"**:

Weather and rose
Is all you see,
Drinking
The dewdrop's
Mystery.

However, the physical appearance of a poem has little to do with its effect or its value. In most cases, the effect here is of a sudden, sensitive gasp of feeling. Often the poems project a sketchiness of image, a questionable logic (as in the lines quoted above), or a suspicion in the reader that the emotional climate has not been rendered fully.

Since the poems are so stripped, so direct, except in the abundance of repetition and abstract or general terms, their brevity allows for little expansion within the reader. Among the successful ones, **"Snake," "Songs"** and **"Personal"** have the hardness of Greek epigrams. But others—poems of nature, longing, love or **"Dreamdust,"** as one is called—are frugally romantic in treatment. Little in the book is regionally or racially inspired, and much of the latter seems strained and lacking in the easy power of Mr. Hughes' earlier poems. However, after a trite beginning, **"Trumpet Player: 52nd Street"** shows fine penetration in its last page.

For all its variety of subject matter, the collection seems monotonous in treatment. In spite of a certain individuality in Mr. Hughes' approach, there are such strong echoes of other poets that the names of Emily Dickinson, Stephen Crane, and a whisper of E. A. Robinson and Ernest Dowson (there are even two Pierrots and a Pierrette) keep coming to mind. . . .

This matter of influences or resemblances is, of course, unavoidable and no censure of Mr. Hughes' work. His poems have their own qualities of delicate lyricism and honesty of vision, and undoubtedly many of them will appeal to the great audience now crying for verse that appeals to their emotions without being stereotypes of the Victorian models.

> *Hubert Creekmore, "Poems by Langston Hughes," in* The New York Times Book Review, *May 4, 1947, p. 10.*

Rolfe Humphries   (essay date 1949)

[*In the following excerpted review of* One-Way Ticket, *Humphries comments on Hughes's unadorned style and suggests that such understatement may be unsatisfying to readers.*]

The virtues of Mr. Hughes's poetry are, mainly, those of forbearance. Given the single theme [in **One Way Ticket**] he treats his data with great restraint: basic vocabulary, simple rhymes, short line; no violence, no hyperbole, no verbalizing. The rhetoric, such as there is, is that of understatement; this kind of rhetoric is easier to slide over than that of exaggeration, but it contains, no less, the contrived element, and in the long run Mr. Hughes's use of these devices induces in the reader an effect opposite, I feel sure, to that which he intends. The studied artlessness pretty soon puts the reader too off guard, makes him condescending, patronizing. "How simple the Negro is," he will be saying to himself if he doesn't watch out, and, in a few minutes, "How quaint!" I for one should like to see what Mr. Hughes could do if he would try his hand on work more elaborate, involved, complex. . . .

> *Rolfe Humphries, in a review of "One-Way Ticket," in* The Nation, *New York, Vol. 168, No. 3, January 15, 1949, p. 80.*

G. Lewis Chandler   (essay date 1949)

[*Chandler offers a positive assessment of* One-Way Ticket.]

Beginning brilliantly in 1921 with his **"The Negro Speaks of Rivers,"** Hughes has consistently entertained, stimulated, and shared experiences with his public. . . . Chaucerian sly humor and realism, Wordsworthian simplicity, Shakespearean blending of comedy and tragedy, Emersonian individualism and precision, Whitmanesque earthiness and cosmopolitanism—all of these flow throughout Hughes' prose and poetry, with every now and then a note struck reminding us of the dramatic monologues of Browning and Dunbar, the bohemian vagabondia of Bliss Carman and Richard Hovey, the puzzling irony of Frost and Emily Dickinson, and the spiritual exploration of Edwin Arlington Robinson.

One Way Ticket is indeed a legitimate and normal member of Hughes' family of works. All the basic family traits (humor, irony, tragedy, folksiness, earthiness, brevity, subtlety, puckishness, hope) are in it. And, as a whole, it is neither stronger nor weaker than the rest. It is not new in look nor different in manner. The blues are here—note particularly **"Bad Morning"**; the spirit of **"Brass Spittoons"** comes to life in the section entitled "Madam to You"; racial themes ironically expressed are in such poems as **"The Ballad of Margie Polite," "Roland Hayes Beaten," "Who But the Lord,"** and **"Lynching Song."** The features of the well known **"I Too Sing America"** and of **"Mother to Son"** are found in the countenance of **"Man into Men"** and in **"Democracy."**

Besides expressing typical family themes, **One Way Ticket,** in voice and manner, also resembles the other members of Hughes' literary siblings. Prevalent in the work is that first person singular pronoun "I," which is not personal, the way Hughes employs it, but is universal and all inclusive—something like the "I" in Whitman. For this reason and for his treatment of an individual or racial experience as a universal, human one, Hughes is a synchdochist, as most good poets are. Moreover, Hughes, through the medium of informal talk (like that of Frost—only, of course, in a different rhythm and on a somewhat different linguistic level) time and time again effectively places before us solid common sense and truths—the one way ticket to real living—under the disguise of nonsense, or frustration, or ignorance, or depravity, or protest. (pp. 189-90)

It seems clear that although **One Way Ticket**—replete with Hughesian dirges, soliloquies, ballads, blues, love songs, vagabondia—adds nothing new to its family, the work is certainly not an albino or a black sheep. What is really important is an artist is not so much that he adds but that he digs. In digging he might find something new, something different—and then he might not. If he does not, he is still an artist despite our protest: "Old stuff!" (p. 190)

G. Lewis Chandler, "Selfsameness and a Promise," in PHYLON: The Atlanta University Review of Race and Culture, *Vol. X, No. 2, second quarter (June, 1949), pp. 189-91.*

John W. Parker   (essay date 1949)

[*Parker surveys Hughes's career up to the publication of* Fields of Wonder.]

Carl Van Vechten once referred to Langston Hughes as the "Negro Poet Laureate," and in his introduction to the young poet's first book of poems, **The Weary Blues,** confessed that he could recall no other person whatsoever who, at the age of twenty-three, had enjoyed so picturesque and so rambling an experience [see Dodson's excerpt dated 1925]. Hughes's facility in interpreting feelingly and understandingly to themselves and to others the emotional heights and depths of the Negro people has increasingly lengthened his shadow as a man of letters and fastened him unmistakably upon the popular imagination of the American people. Since the publication in 1921 of the poem **"The Negro Speaks of Rivers,"** his first selection to attract wide attention, Hughes has succeeded as poet, fictionist, essayist, dramatist, and lecturer; and many of his poems and some of his articles and stories have been translated into German, French, Spanish, Russian, Chinese, Japanese, and Dutch. (pp. 438-39)

Three themes have for the most part engaged Hughes's attention: the primitivistic naturalism of the Harlem dweller, the propagandistic left-wing writing in support of a more articulate proletarian group, and the literature of protest against the social and economic maladjustments of the Negro people. That Harlem should have been the basis of much that Hughes wrote may be explained by the fact that, far more than any other single spot, here were the foreign-born blacks, the carefree Negro from the South, the disappointed Negro veteran back from the war, in fact, the "melting pot" of Negro culture. Life, at least much of it, was characterized by a spirit of abandon, and it was this emphasis upon the hectic, the coarse, and the sensational that brought Hughes in for many a critical lashing. When in his **Shakespeare in Harlem,** Hughes returned to the Harlem theme, Owen Dodson charged,that he was "backing into the future looking at the past" [see Dodson's excerpt dated 1942].

The emphasis of the Negro renaissance came to an end with the change of the decade, and during the years immediately following Hughes devoted much of his effort to a rapidly expanding proletarian movement as is evidenced by such selections as *The Way of White Folks* (1934), *A New Song* (1938), and *Front Porch* (1939). Likewise, the selfconscious revolt against the American scheme of things is a theme to which the poet recurs. Color prejudice, segregation and discrimination, in fact, the totality of the black man's marginal existence in American life is implied in four lines from **Fields of Wonder**:

Four walls can shelter
So much sorrow,
Garnered from yesterday
And held for tomorrow!

The events of the past two decades have been accompanied by a depressing sense of futility and a loss of faith. Security has seemed nowhere. Today's youth have seen more struggle and chaos and groping in the darkness than any generation of youth in the entire span of our national history. Nor has Hughes escaped the impact of this upheaval; but, while he has been pre-eminently a man of the present, he has maintained a healthful view of the future. The night and the gloom and the darkness have offered a challenge, but never disillusionment.

Being walkers with the dawn and morning,
Walkers with the sun and morning,
We are not afraid of the night,
Nor days of gloom,
Nor darkness—
Being walkers with the sun and morning.

But Hughes's view of a new day for his people, somehow inevitable in the nature and in the trend of things, is not always a clear one; frequently it is beclouded by a "weariness that bows me down," a "dream that is vague and all confused." Recalling the injured pride and the pent-up emotions of the porter at the railroad station, Hughes asks defiantly,

Must I say
Yes, Sir
To you all the time.
Yes, Sir!
Yes, Sir!
All my days?

(pp. 439-40)

Loss of faith, however, is a temporary condition. Before long the poet regains perspective and sees, if but imperfectly, the new order being carved out of the old. In **"Park Bench,"** as in **"Porter,"** he continues in the vein of the "Crusader," as Verna Anery once labeled him [see Further Reading list]; for here he makes a savage thrust at the wealthy class on Park Avenue and offers a sober warning that the new awakening which is settling upon the Negro people may subsequently find expression in a change of the mores:

But I'm wakin' up!
Say ain't you afraid
That I might, just maybe,
In a year or two
Move on over
To Park Avenue?

Although he writes mainly concerning his own people, Hughes has proceeded on the sound assumption that the so-called Negro problem is not an isolated one but a single segment of a complex American culture. Color prejudice moves hand in hand with race prejudice and religious prejudice, and, despite the artificial line that divides them, humble folk of all races face a common lot; their children in the swamps of Mississippi as in the orange groves of California, weary and disillusioned, march toward a common destiny. **"The Kids Who Die,"** to which a Darwinian note attaches, is disarmingly forthright:

> But the day will come—
> You are sure yourself that it is coming—
> When the marching feet of the masses
> Will raise for a monument of love,
> And joy, and laughter,
> And black hands and white hands clasped as one
> And a song that reaches the sky—
> The song of the new life triumphant
> Through the Kids that die!
>
> (p. 440)

Although increasingly, as *Fields of Wonder* reveals, Langston Hughes has written on a variety of topics, it is true that in the main he has followed the course of the "social poet"; he has been concerned not so much with moonlight and roses, sweetness and light, as with "whole groups of people's problems"—poverty, the ghetto, trade-unions, color lines, and Georgia lynchings. But, like Chesnutt, Hughes has stored no hate in his soul, nor has he descended to the level of the propagandist. His healthy view of the tomorrows yet to be is an outgrowth of his faith in the essential goodness of the human heart and hence the ultimate flowering of the democratic way of life in America. (p. 441)

> *John W. Parker, " 'Tomorrow' in the Writings of Langston Hughes," in* College English, *Vol. 10, No. 8, May, 1949, pp. 438-41.*

Harvey Curtis Webster   (essay date 1950)

[*In the review excerpted below, Webster offers a general appraisal of* One-Way Ticket *but finds Hughes's subject matter repetitive.*]

Because the poetry of Langston Hughes is so uneven and so far removed—even at its very good best—from the formal traditions the dominant school of criticism respects, it has been neglected unduly. Much of Hughes' poetry, of course, deserves this neglect—more, I should say, than is usual for a writer of talent who publishes many poems. As one can see by looking at the selections he himself has made for *The Poetry of the Negro,* his range of subject matter is limited and he tends to write almost the same poems many times: long, loosely phrased and constructed poems about what the Negro needs (and I think deserves); short, over-cute verses about the lighter aspects of Negro experience. Still, as one reads such excellent poems as **"Song for a Dark Girl"** and **"Cross"** in the same anthology, he realizes that Hughes' talent must be treated with respect and that there may be pleasure of a high order in each new book he publishes.

There is great pleasure for the reader of *One-Way Ticket,* Langston Hughes' most recent volume of verse. Almost all of the poems read well the first time; about a dozen re-read well: **"Madam and the Wrong Visitor," "Madam and Her Might-Have Been"** (the saga of Madam Johnson, Alberta K, is almost consistently pleasurable), **"Juice Joint: Northern City"** (which is more ambitious and most of the way more successful than the others before it relapses into carelessness), **"The Ballad of Margie Polite," "Man into Men," "Roland Hayes Beaten," "Late Last Night," "Little Old Letter," "Too Blue," "Little Green Tree"** (which

I like better than any of Hughes' earlier blues), **"Request for Requiems."** As these titles indicate, Hughes writes of a variety of experiences; as the poems indicate, he writes of them in a variety of tones despite the fact that he usually uses the form he made popular in his early modifications of the blues. Compare, for example, the skillful lightness with which Hughes manipulates the blues form in **"Madam and the Wrong Visitor"** and the restrained seriousness with which he uses it in **"Roland Hayes Beaten"**:

> A man knocked three times.
> I never seen him before.
> He said, Are you Madam?
> I said, What's the score?
>
> He said, I reckon
> You don't know my name,
> But I've come to call
> On you just the same.
>
> I stepped back
> Like he had a charm.
> He said, I really
> Don't mean no harm.
>
> I'm just Old Death
> And I thought I might
> Pay you a visit
> Before night.
>
> He said, You're Johnson—
> Madame Alberta K?
> I said, Yes—but Alberta
> Ain't goin' with you today!
>
> No sooner had I told him
> Than I awoke.
> The doctor said, Madam,
> Your fever's broke—
>
> Nurse put her on a diet,
> And buy her some chicken.
> I said, Better buy *two*—
> Cause I'm still here kickin'!
>
> . . . .
>
> Negroes,
> Sweet and docile,
> Meek, humble, and kind:
> Beware the day
> They change their minds!
>
> Wind
> In the cotton fields,
> Gentle breeze:
> Beware the hour
> It uproots trees!

In these two poems and in many of the others in which he skillfully varies the rhythm and the rhyme of the simple blues form, Hughes is as distinguished a craftsman as, say, W. H. Auden in his manipulation of the couplet.

But the comparison brings one up short by its suggestion of limitation. Auden is almost always careful, even when he writes badly; Auden knows and experiments with and has mastered dozens of forms; Auden writes of an infinite variety of subjects, has extensity and intensity, breadth and depth. Hughes is careless when he strays from the one form he has chosen to master. . . . And Hughes, though he is an inspired reporter of the surface of things and of those upper layers of emotions that concern an individual as a member of a group rather than as a singular human being, never moves one deeply. Perhaps this limitation in depth is as much a product of second-class citizenship as is his restriction of substance to the American Negro and what he does and faces. Without trying to exonerate myself or my society of a social blame that, at least, contributes to aesthetic demerit, I hope that Hughes, like Robert Hayden, Gwendolyn Brooks and a few others, will move in new directions and to new depths in the many volumes of his poetry I still hope to have the pleasure of reading. (pp. 300-02)

Harvey Curtis Webster, "One-Way Poetry," in Poetry, *Vol. LXXV, No. V, February, 1950, pp. 300-02.*

Saunders Redding   (essay date 1951)

[*Redding, a distinguished critic, historian, and novelist, is best remembered as the author of* To Make a Poet Black *(1939), a seminal study of African-American poetry. As one of the first anthologies of its type to be written by a black critic, this book is considered a landmark in African-American literary criticism. In his discussion of* Montage of a Dream Deferred, *excerpted below, Redding expresses regret over Hughes's adherence to tradition and reluctance to experiment with different poetic styles.*]

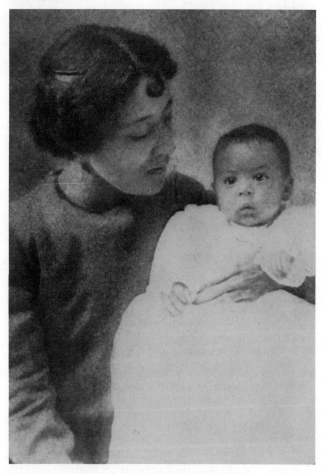

Hughes with his mother, Carrie, 1902.

In *Montage of a Dream Deferred,* Langston Hughes again proves himself the provocative folk singer who enchanted and sometimes distressed readers of *The Weary Blues, Fine Clothes to the Jew* and *Fields of Wonder.* In the interval between the publication of *One-Way Ticket* (1949) and this new book, he seems to have made a spiritually rewarding return to the heritage that was distinctly his in the days of the Negro renaissance. His images are again quick, vibrant and probing, but they no longer educate. They probe into old emotions and experiences with fine sensitiveness—

> Into the laps
> of black celebrities
> white girls fall
> like pale plums from a tree
> beyond a high tension wall
> wired for killing
> which makes it
> more thrilling—

but they reveal nothing new. He still views his function as being useful to social reform and (though it is no fault in itself) such a view tends to date him in the same way that a poet like Byron is dated. . . .

The idiom, like the heritage to which he returns, is also distinctly Hughes'. In earlier work, however, it was adapted to the smooth and relatively simple rhythm of jazz. In *Montage of a Dream Deferred* it is fitted to the jarring dissonances and broken rhythms of be-bop. The result is a bold and frequently shocking distortion of tempo and tone, and this will fret and repel some readers. But Hughes has always required of his readers a sophisticated ear. It is the price of admission into the meanings of his experiences, and when he is at his best, it is not too high a price. In some of the pieces in *Montage,* he is at his best, in **"Island,"** for instance, and **"Freedom Train"** and **"Tell Me."**

Yet it seems to me that Hughes does have a too great concern for perpetuating his reputation as an "experimenter." That he was this cannot be denied. Few present-day poets have been so impatient of tradition and so zealous in seeking new and more flexible forms. But experimentation is for something: it leads to or produces a result. One would think that after twenty-five years of writing Hughes has long since found his form, his idiom and his proper, particular tone. If he has, let him be content with the apparatus he has fashioned, and let him go on now to say the things which many readers believe he, alone of American poets, was born to say.

Saunders Redding, "Langston Hughes in an Old Vein With New Rhythms," in New York Herald Tribune Book Review, *March 11, 1951, p. 5.*

Babette Deutsch   (essay date 1951)

[*In this excerpt taken from a review of* Montage of a Dream Deferred, *Deutsch praises Hughes's use of rhythm yet faults his unwillingness to develop and execute new themes and techniques.*]

The title of this little book of verse [*Montage of a Dream Deferred*] tells a good deal about it. The language is that of the work-a-day urban world whose pleasures are sometimes drearier than its pains. The scene is the particular part of the Waste Land that belongs to Harlem. The singer is steeped in the bitter knowledge that fills the blues. Sometimes his verse invites approval, but again it lapses into a facile sentimentality that stifles real feeling as with cheap scent. As he bandies about the word "dream," he introduces a whiff of the nineteenth century that casts a slight mustiness on the liveliest context.

Langston Hughes can write pages that throb with the abrupt rhythms of popular music. He can draw thumbnail sketches of Harlem lives and deaths that etch themselves harshly in the memory. Yet the book as a whole leaves one less responsive to the poet's achievement than conscious of the limitations of folk art. . . . His verse suffers from a kind of contrived naïveté, or from a will to shock the reader, who is apt to respond coldly to such obvious devices.

It is a pity that a poet of undeniable gifts has not been more rigorous in his use of them. There are several contemporaries, especially among the French, whose subject matter and whose method are not too different from his, but who, being more sensitive artists, are also more powerful. Mr. Hughes would do well to emulate them.

> Babette Deutsch, "Waste Land of Harlem," in The New York Times Book Review, *May 6, 1951, p. 23.*

John W. Parker   (essay date 1951)

[*An appreciative assessment of* Montage of a Dream Deferred.]

With the recent publication of **Montage of a Dream Deferred,** his second book on the contemporary Harlem scene to appear within a year, Langston Hughes has rejuvenated the Harlem theme of the Mid-Twenties, and reasserted his faith in popular verse, particularly that which draws upon popular Negro folk music. Implicit throughout the volume is a seriousness of purpose and a sense of awareness of times transhifting. And, like such previous studies as **The Weary Blues** (1926), *The Street* (1946), and even *Simple Speaks His Mind* (1950), **Montage of a Dream Deferred** runs the gamut of the ups and downs that constitute the way of life for present-day Harlem; unlike them, however, it betrays the inner conflict of Harlem's Brown Americans, and a consciousness of the steady pull exerted by this urban community in transition. It is a fast-moving story of a people who, despite their own imperfections and the bitter and corroding circumstances they face from day to day, have never relinquished their dream of a tomorrow that will be better. But it is a dream born out of a heartache, a dream much like life in dark Harlem—"all mixed up." (p. 195)

Scattered generously throughout the volume are poems written after the style of Negro folk songs known as boogie-woogie and be-bop. Of the manner in which he has appropriated popular Negro folk music to heighten the effectiveness of poetry that is equally popular, Hughes writes in the introductory statement: "In terms of current Afro-American popular music and the sources from which it has progressed—jazz, ragtime, swing, blues, boogie-woogie, and be-bop—this poem on contemporary Harlem, like be-bop, is marked by conflicting changes, sudden nuances, sharp and imprudent interjections, broken

rhythms, and passages sometimes in the manner of a jam session." Thus the reader is prepared for innovations as he may find them—the occasional omission of the latter part of a line, the excessive employment of the dash for a sudden and sometimes unwarranted break in thought, the insertion of such otherwise meaningless expressions as "oop-pop-a-da," and, of course, **"Figurine,"** a one-line poem that is limited to an even two words. By and large the measures throughout the book are cut to absolute simplicity, and the language, the imagery, and the easy flow of syllables enhance one of the collection's strong features—its popular appeal. Unlike the position taken by James Joyce a few years back, Hughes is convinced that comprehensibility in poetic expression is a virtue, not a vice.

The goings-on in Harlem as disclosed by **Montage of a Dream Deferred** leave much to be desired. The "bad nigger," who can out Herod Herod, proceeds from joint to joint; wide-eyed newcomers from the South encounter "bars at each gate"; the low and the high look, not across, but up and down at one another; pimps make the rounds at Lenox Avenue ginmills while hustlers wait in dark doorways; and in the effort to get along on a "dime and a prayer," many sicken and die. It is the same old story of "dig and be dug" and of "trying to forget to remember the taste of day."

The nine-line poem, **"Jam Session,"** which appears in the section, "Early Bright," defines a situation that is fraught with tragedy and comedy, hope and despair, faith and disillusionment, but one that reveals the black man's struggle to salt his dreams away:

> Letting midnight
> out of jail
>
>   pop-a-da
> having been
> detained in jail
>
>   oop-pop-a-da
> for sprinkling salt
> on a dreamer's tail
>
>   pop-a-da

First and last, **Montage of a Dream Deferred** . . . suggests the manner in which Mr. Hughes has gone on loving life and writing upon those aspects of it that have stirred his emotion deeply—"Negro life, and its relations to the problems of Democracy." Convinced that the writing of poetry about Brown Americans is serious business in these times of transition, he has remained indifferent to criticism sometimes levelled at his "predominantly-Negro themes," and at the extreme popular aspect of his poetic output. Likewise, he has shied away from the recent tendency on the part of some Negro writers in the direction of a "return to form" and of international and global perspective.

But that is Langston Hughes. And it is perhaps one of the reasons that his name has become synonymous with popular Negro poetry. With its freshness of approach, its powerful rhythm, and its moving quality, **Montage of a Dream Deferred** further justifies its author's claim to the title by which he is frequently designated in literary circles, "The Negro Poet Laureate." (pp. 195-97)

> John W. Parker, *"Poetry of Harlem in Transi-*

tion," in PHYLON: The Atlanta University Review of Race and Culture, *Vol. XII, No. 2, second quarter (June, 1951), pp. 195-97.*

Arthur P. Davis   (essay date 1952)

[*Davis is the author of* From the Dark Tower *(1974), an important survey of modern black American literature. In his critical study of Hughes excerpted below, Davis analyzes Hughes's portrayal of Harlemites as symbolic of the aspirations and disappointments of blacks throughout urban America.*]

In a very real sense, Langston Hughes is the poet-laureate of Harlem. From his first publication down to his latest, Mr. Hughes has been concerned with the black metropolis. Returning to the theme again and again, he has written about Harlem oftener and more fully than any other poet. (p. 276)

When Mr. Hughes' first publication, *The Weary Blues* (1926), appeared, the New Negro Movement was in full swing; and Harlem, as the intellectual center of the movement, had become the Mecca of all aspiring young Negro writers and artists. This so-called Renaissance not only encouraged and inspired the black creative artist, but it served also to focus as never before the attention of America upon the Negro artist and scholar. As a result of this new interest, Harlem became a gathering place for downtown intellectuals and Bohemians—many of them honestly seeking a knowledge of Negro art and culture, others merely looking for exotic thrills in the black community. Naturally, the latter group was much the larger of the two; and Harlem, capitalizing on this new demand for "primitive" thrills, opened a series of spectacular cabarets. For a period of about ten years, the most obvious and the most sensational aspect of the New Negro Movement for downtown New York was the night life of Harlem. The 1925 Renaissance, of course, was not just a cabaret boom, and it would be decidedly unfair to give that impression. But the Harlem cabaret life of the period was definitely an important by-product of the new interest in the Negro created by the movement, and this life strongly influenced the early poetry of Langston Hughes.

Coming to Harlem, as he did, a twenty-two-year-old adventurer who had knocked around the world as sailor and beachcomber, it was only natural that Hughes should be attracted to the most exotic part of that city—its night life. The Harlem of *The Weary Blues* became therefore for him "Jazzonia," a new world of escape and release, an exciting never-never land in which "sleek black boys" blew their hearts out on silver trumpets in a "whirling cabaret." It was a place where the bold eyes of white girls called to black men, and "dark brown girls" were found "in blond men's arms." It was a city where "shameless gals" strutted and wiggled, and the "night dark girl of the swaying hips" danced beneath a papier-mâché jungle moon. The most important inhabitants of this magic city are a **"Nude Young Dancer," "Midnight Nan at Leroy's,"** a **"Young Singer"** of *chansons vulgaires,* and a **"Black Dancer in the Little Savoy."**

This cabaret Harlem, this Jazzonia is a joyous city, but the joyousness is not unmixed; it has a certain strident and hectic quality, and there are overtones of weariness and despair. "The long-headed jazzers" and whirling dancing girls are desperately trying to find some new delight, and some new escape. They seem obsessed with the idea of seizing the present moment as though afraid of the future: "Tomorrow . . . is darkness / Joy today!" "The rhythm of life / Is a jazz rhythm" for them, but it brings only "The broken heart of love / The weary, weary heart of pain." It is this weariness and this intensity that one hears above the laughter and even above the blare of the jazz bands.

There is no daytime in Jazzonia, no getting up and going to work. It is wholly a sundown city, illuminated by soft lights, spotlights, jewel-eyed sparklers, and synthetic stars in the scenery. Daylight is the one great enemy here, and when "the new dawn / Wan and pale / Descends like a white mist," it brings only an "aching emptiness," and out of this emptiness there often comes in the clear cool light of morning the disturbing thought that the jazz band may not be an escape, it may not be gay after all. . . . (pp. 276-77)

In this respect, the figure of the black piano player in ["**The Weary Blues**"] is highly symbolic. Trying beneath "the pale dull pallor of an old gas light" to rid his soul of the blues that bedeviled it, he played all night, but when the dawn approached:

> The singer stopped playing and went to bed
> While the Weary Blues echoed through his head.
> He slept like a rock or a man that's dead.

It is hard to fool oneself in the honest light of dawn, but sleep, like dancing and singing and wild hilarity, is another means of escape. Unfortunately, it too is only a temporary evasion. One has to wake up sometime and face the harsh reality of daylight and everyday living.

And in the final pages of *The Weary Blues,* the poet begins to sense this fact; he realizes that a "jazz-tuned" way of life is not the answer to the Negro's search for escape. The last poem on the Harlem theme in this work has the suggestive title **"Disillusionment"** and the even more suggestive lines:

> I would be simple again,
> Simple and clean . . .
> Nor ever know,
> Dark Harlem,
> The wild laughter
> Of your mirth . . .
> Be kind to me,
> Oh, great dark city.
> Let me forget.
> I will not come
> To you again.

Evidently Hughes did want to forget, at least temporarily, the dark city, for there is no mention of Harlem in his next work, *Fine Clothes to the Jew.* . . . Although several of the other themes treated in the first volume are continued in this the second, it is the only major production in which the name Harlem does not appear. (pp. 277-78)

The picture of Harlem presented in *Shakespeare in Harlem* (1942) has very little in common with that found in *The Weary Blues.* By 1942 the black metropolis was a disillusioned city. The Depression of 1929, having struck the ghetto harder than any other section of New York, showed Harlem just how basically "marginal" and precarious its economic foundations were. Embittered by this knowledge, the black community had struck back blindly at things in general in the 1935 riot. The riot brought an end to the New Negro era; the Cotton Club, the most lavish of the uptown cabarets, closed its doors and moved to Broadway; and the black city settled down to the drab existence of WPA and relief living.

In the two groups of poems labeled "Death in Harlem" and "Lenox Avenue," Hughes has given us a few glimpses of this new Harlem. There are no bright colors in the scene, only the sombre and realistic shades appropriate to the depiction of a community that has somehow lost its grip on things. The inhabitants of this new Harlem impress one as a beaten people. A man loses his job because, "awake all night with loving," he cannot get to work on time. When he is discharged, his only comment is "So I went on back to bed . . ." and to the "sweetest dreams" **("Fired")**. In another poem, a man and his wife wrangle over the family's last dime which he had thrown away gambling **("Early Evening Quarrel")**. Harlem love has lost its former joyous abandon, and the playboy of the cabaret era has become a calculating pimp who wants to "share your bed / And your money too" **("50-50")**. In fact all of the lovers in this section—men and women alike—are an aggrieved lot, whining perpetually about being "done wrong." Even the night spots have lost their jungle magic, and like Dixie's joint have become earthy and sordid places. . . . All of the fun, all of the illusion have gone from this new and brutal night life world; and as a fitting symbol of the change which has come about, we find a little cabaret girl dying forlornly as a ward of the city **("Cabaret Girl Dies on Welfare Island")**.

There is seemingly only one bright spot in this new Harlem—the spectrum-colored beauty of the girls on Sugar Hill **("Harlem Sweeties")**; but this is only a momentary lightening of the mood. The prevailing tone is one of depression and futility:

> Down on the Harlem River
> Two A.M.
> Midnight
> By yourself!
> Lawd, I wish I could die—
> But who would miss me if I left?

We see here the spectacle of a city feeling sorry for itself, the most dismal and depressing of all spectacles. Hughes has given us a whining Harlem. It is not yet the belligerent Harlem of the 1943 riot, but it is a city acquiring the mood from which this riot will inevitably spring.

The Harlem poems in *Fields of Wonder* (1947) are grouped under the title "Stars Over Harlem," but they do not speak out as clearly and as definitely as former pieces on the theme have done. The mood, however, continues in the sombre vein of *Shakespeare in Harlem,* and the idea of escape is stated or implied in each of the poems. In the first of the group, **"Trumpet Player: 52nd Street,"** we find a curious shift in the African imagery used. Practically all former pieces having an African background tended to stress either the white-mooned loveliness of jungle nights or the pulse-stirring rhythm of the tom-tom. But from the weary eyes of the 52nd Street musician there blazes forth only "the smoldering memory of slave ships." In this new Harlem even the jazz players are infected with the sectional melancholy, and this performer finds only a vague release and escape in the golden tones he creates.

In **"Harlem Dance Hall"** there is again an interesting use of the escape motif. The poet describes the hall as having no dignity at all until the band began to play and then: "Suddenly the earth was there, / And flowers, / Trees, / And air." In short, this new dignity was achieved by an imaginative escape from the close and unnatural life of the dance hall (and of Harlem) into the freedom and wholesomeness of nature and normal living. (pp. 278-80)

One Way Ticket (1949) and *Montage of a Dream Deferred* (1951), especially the latter work, bring to a full cycle the turning away from the Harlem of *The Weary Blues.* The Harlem depicted in these two works has come through World War II, but has discovered that a global victory for democracy does not necessarily have too much pertinence at home. Although the Harlem of the 1949-51 period has far more opportunity than the 1926 Harlem ever dreamed of, it is still not free; and the modern city having caught the vision of total freedom and total integration will not be satisfied with anything less than the ideal. It is therefore a critical, a demanding, a sensitive, and utterly cynical city.

In *One Way Ticket,* for example, Harlem remembers "the old lies," "the old kicks in the back," the jobs it never could have and still cannot get because of color:

> So we stand here
> On the edge of hell
> In Harlem
> And look out on the world
> And wonder
> What we're gonna do
> In the face of
> What we remember.

But even though Harlem is the "edge of hell," it still can be a refuge for the black servant who works downtown all day bowing and scraping to white folks **("Negro Servant")**. Dark Harlem becomes for him a "sweet relief from faces that are white." The earlier Harlem was a place to be shared with fun-seeking whites from below 125th Street; the new city is a sanctuary from them. (p. 280)

The longest and most revealing Harlem poem in *One Way Ticket* is the thumping **"Ballad of Margie Polite,"** the Negro girl who "cussed" a cop in the lobby of the Braddock Hotel and caused a riot when a Negro soldier taking her part was shot in the back by a white cop. In these thirteen short stanzas, Langston Hughes has distilled, as it were, all of the trigger-sensitiveness to injustice—real or imagined; all of the pent-up anti-white bitterness; and all of the sick-and-tired-of-being-kicked-around feelings which characterize the masses of present-day Harlem. It is indeed a provocative analysis of the frictions and the tensions in the black ghetto, this narrative of Margie Polite, who

> Kept the Mayor
> And Walter White
> And everybody
> Up all night!

In *Montage of a Dream Deferred* . . . the Harlem theme receives its fullest and most comprehensive statement. Devoting the whole volume to the subject, he has touched on many aspects of the city unnoticed before. His understanding is now deep and sure, his handling of the theme defter and more mature than in any of the previous works. (p. 281)

[We] are to consider the whole book of ninety-odd pieces as really one long poem, marked by the conflicting changes, broken rhythms, and sudden interjections characteristic of a jam session. This "jam session" technique is highly effective because, tying together as it does fragmentary and otherwise unrelated segments in the work, it allows the poet, without being monotonous, to return again and again to his overall-theme, that of Harlem's frustration. Like the deep and persistent rolling of a boogie bass—now loud and raucous, now soft and pathetic—this theme of Harlem's dream deferred marches relentlessly throughout the poem. Hughes knows that Harlem is neither a gay nor healthy but basically a tragic and frustrated city, and he beats that message home. Because of the fugue-like structure of the poem, it is impossible for the reader to miss the theme or to forget it.

This 1951 Harlem is a full and many-sided community. Here one finds the pathos of night funerals and fraternal parades: "A chance to let / the whole world see / old black me!"; or the grim realism of slum-dwellers who like war because it means prosperity; or the humor of a wife playing via a dream book the number suggested by her husband's dying words. This is the Harlem of black celebrities and their white girl admirers, the Harlem of vice squad detectives "spotting fairies" in night spots, the Harlem of bitter anti-Semitism, and the Harlem of churches and street corner orators, of college formals at the Renaissance Casino and of Negro students writing themes at CCNY. It is now definitely a class-conscious Harlem, a community of dicties and nobodies; and the Cadillac-riding professional dicties feel that they are let down by the nobodies who "talk too loud / cuss too loud / and look too black." It is a Harlem of some gaiety and of much sardonic laughter; but above all else, it is Harlem of a dream long deferred; and a people's deferred dream can "fester like a sore" or "sag like a heavy load."

Whatever else it may or may not believe, this Harlem has no illusion about the all-inclusiveness of American democracy. Even the children know that there is still a Jim Crow coach on the Freedom Train.

> What don't bug
> them white kids
> sure bugs me;
> We knows everybody
> ain't free.

Perhaps the dominant over-all impression that one gets from *Montage of a Dream Deferred* is that of a vague unrest. Tense and moody, the inhabitants of this 1951 Harlem seem to be seeking feverishly and forlornly for some simple yet apparently unattainable satisfaction in life: "one more bottle of gin"; "my furniture paid for"; "I always did want to study French"; "that white enamel stove"; "a wife who will work with me and not against me." The book begins and ends on this note of dissatisfaction and unrest. There is "a certain amount of nothing in a dream deferred."

These then are the scenes that make up the Harlem of Langston Hughes' poetry. The picture, one must remember, is that of a poet and not a sociologist; it naturally lacks the logic and the statistical accuracy of a scientific study,

but in its way the picture is just as revealing and truthful as an academic study. As one looks at this series of Harlems he is impressed by the growing sense of frustration which characterizes each of them. Whether it is in the dream fantasy world of *The Weary Blues* or in the realistic city of *Montage of a Dream Deferred,* one sees a people searching—and searching in vain—for a way to make Harlem a part of the American dream. And one must bear in mind that with Langston Hughes Harlem is both place and symbol. When he depicts the hopes, the aspirations, the frustrations, and the deep-seated discontent of the New York ghetto, he is expressing the feelings of Negroes in black ghettos throughout America. (pp. 282-83)

> *Arthur P. Davis, "The Harlem of Langston Hughes' Poetry," in* PHYLON: The Atlanta University Review of Race and Culture, *Vol. XIII, No. 4, forth quarter (December, 1952), pp. 276-83.*

James Baldwin (essay date 1959)

[*Best known as the author of* Go Tell It on the Mountain *(1953), Baldwin was an influential American novelist, essayist, and dramatist whose writings exposed the racial and sexual polarization of modern American society. In his review of Hughes's* Selected Poems, *excerpted below, Baldwin cites Hughes's failure to explore new themes and formats in his verse.*]

Every time I read Langston Hughes I am amazed all over again by his genuine gifts—and depressed that he has done so little with them. A real discussion of his work demands more space than I have here, but this book [*Selected Poems of Langston Hughes*] contains a great deal which a more disciplined poet would have thrown into the waste-basket. . . .

There are the poems which almost succeed but which do not succeed, poems which take refuge, finally, in a fake simplicity in order to avoid the very difficult simplicity of the experience! And one sometimes has the impression, as in a poem like **"Third Degree"**—which is about the beating up of a Negro boy in a police station—that Hughes has had to hold the experience outside him in order to be able to write at all. And certainly this is understandable. Nevertheless, the poetic trick, so to speak, is to be within the experience and outside it at the same time—and the poem fails.

Mr. Hughes is at his best in brief, sardonic asides, or in lyrics like **"Mother to Son,"** and **"The Negro Speaks of Rivers."** Or **"Dream Variations."**

I do not like all of **"The Weary Blues,"** which copies, rather than exploits, the cadence of the blues, but it comes to a remarkable end. And I am also very fond of **"Island,"** which begins "Wave of sorrow / Do not drown me now."

Hughes, in his sermons, blues and prayers, has working for him the power and the beat of Negro speech and Negro music. Negro speech is vivid largely because it is private. It is a kind of emotional shorthand—or sleight-of-hand—by means of which Negroes express, not only their relationship to each other, but their judgment of the white world. And, as the white world takes over this vocabulary—without the faintest notion of what it really means—the vocabulary is forced to change. The same thing is true of Negro music, which has had to become more and more complex in order to continue to express any of the private or collective experience.

Hughes knows the bitter truth behind these hieroglyphics: what they are designed to protect, what they are designed to convey. But he has not forced them into the realm of art where their meaning would become clear and overwhelming. . . .

Hughes is an American Negro poet and has no choice but to be acutely aware of it. He is not the first American Negro to find the war between his social and artistic responsibilities all but irreconcilable.

> *James Baldwin, "Sermons and Blues," in* The New York Times Book Review, *March 29, 1959, p. 6.*

Henry F. Winslow   (essay date 1959)

[*Winslow offers an appreciative review of* Selected Poems.]

It is somewhat difficult to accept the fact that Langston Hughes has for thirty-eight years been before the public as a poet, because there is throughout his works, in whatever form, an enduring exuberance of spirit such as one usually finds and expects only in the young. (p. 512)

His poetry comes to us from within—it is easy to come from within, provided one ever gets there; ay, there's the rub. And because he is humble enough to live within the experience of his people, one finds more authenticity in those twenty lines of, for example, **"Mother and Son,"** than in the imposing cultural histories:

> Well, son, I'll tell you:
> Life for me ain't been no crystal stair.
> It's had tacks in it,
> And splinters,
> And boards torn up,
> And places with no carpet on the floor—
> Bare. . . .

In this poetry words serve the mood and convey the feeling: they are words of wisdom rather than a wisdom with words. He has a way with words which brings the sense all the way home, as in the concluding lines of **"Trumpet Player"**:

> But softly
> As the tune comes from his throat
> Trouble
> Mellows to a golden note.

Speaking of life through people, he points to **"Ruby Brown"** whom Mayville offered no "fuel for the clean flame of joy / That tried to burn within her soul," so she changed occupational traps, leaving the white woman's kitchen for the sinister shuttered house where white men paid her more money.

In general, his subjects (they are never his objects) are those people with whom he lives and who like him have made the journey from rural to urban setting—from the scorching sun of corn and cotton fields to hovels in Harlem; his overall theme is how they fare with dreams deferred; his big sea is their restless hopes and hearts; his poetry the songs of their experience.

One wishes that these magnificently bound poems were dated so as to provide for some chronological approach to Hughes as a writer. One wonders how he would sound if he treated the church-centered, spiritual aspect of Negro life as faithfully as he deals with the secular problems; or the evil-natured with unsparing truth. But this perhaps asks him to be what he is not. For certainly, as they are, these poems are worthy of having and handing down to unborn generations. (pp. 512-13)

> *Henry F. Winslow, "Enduring Exuberance," in* The Crisis, *Vol. 66, No. 8, October, 1959, pp. 512-13.*

Dudley Fitts   (essay date 1961)

[*An American poet, critic, educator, and translator of classical Greek literature, Fitts is best known for his modern colloquial translations of Aristophanes's plays, particularly* The Birds. *Here, Fitts briefly discusses the musical qualities of* Ask Your Mama.]

Langston Hughes' twelve jazz pieces [in **Ask Your Mama: 12 Moods for Jazz**] cannot be evaluated by any canon dealing with literary right or wrong. They are nonliterary—oral, vocal, compositions to be spoken, or shouted, to the accompaniment of drum and flute and bass. For that matter, they speak from the page, the verses being set in capitals throughout; and there is a running gloss of dynamic signs and indications for the proper instrument to use at the moment. (One of these signs, used repeatedly, is "TACIT," which I find as obscure as Mr. Ciardi's "dust like darks howing," unless indeed it stands for the orchestral indication *tacet*.)

In this respect, **Ask Your Mama** goes back to Vachel Lindsay and his *Congo*; and I suppose it is fair to say that this is stunt poetry, a nightclub turn. The fury of indignation and the wild comedy, however, are very far from Lindsay. The voice is comparable to that of Nicolás Guillén, the Cuban poet, or of the Puerto Rican Luis Palés Matos—comparable, not imitative; insistent and strong in what is clearly a parallel development. (pp. 16-17)

> *Dudley Fitts, "A Trio of Singers in Varied Keys," in* The New York Times Book Review, *October 29, 1961, pp. 16-17.*

Ulysses Lee   (essay date 1963)

[*Lee delineates Hughes's political and social verse in* Ask Your Mama.]

Anyone who is still unconvinced that Langston Hughes occupies a major position in the stream of American literary humorists and experimental poets should find convincing proofs in **Ask Your Mama.** This volume is a series of twelve connected poems intended to be read aloud to musical accompaniment, much of it jazz variations and improvisations on the traditional "Hesitation Blues" spiked with fragments of "Shave and a Haircut," German lieder, spirituals, gospels, calypsos, Hebraic chants, "Dixie," and "The Battle Hymn of the Republic." These, in turn, are to be performed by a piano, a flute, bongo drums, guitar, maracas, and a full Dixieland band playing in blues, mambo, bop, and cha-cha rhythms, sometimes alone and sometimes in chorus. Appropriately, the whole is dedicated to Louis Armstrong. . . . (p. 225)

The twelve poems are allusive comments on the present situation, especially as it affects American Negroes. They impudently combine the leading cultural heroes of the day with images of plantation quarters and slum inequities. In some ways, the whole set of poems is an extension of the old insult word-game, the dozens, from which the title comes. As in the dozens, the satirical tone is incisive; the biting humor is always clever and funny even when it borders upon the shocking. Hughes' targets are always the right ones:

> And they asked me right at Christmas
> If my blackness, would it rub off?
> I said, Ask your mama.

But the more significant lines in the poems bring together unexpected images and lists of the currently well-known in the manner of the dadaists and expressionists of the European 1920's. In the opening poem, **"Cultural Exchange,"** an African diplomat is sent by the State Department

> . . . Among the shacks to meet the blacks:
> Leontyne Sammy Harry Poitier
> Lovely Lena Marian Louis Pearlie Mae . . .
> Where the railroad and the river
> Have doors that face each way
> And the entrance to the movie's
> Up an alley up the side.

(pp. 225-26)

Whether a poem evokes a dream world where Negroes have voted out the Dixiecrats, Martin Luther King is governor of Georgia with Rufus Clement as advisor, and Negro children have white mammies (Mammy Faubus / Mammy Eastland / Mammy Patterson. / Dear, *dear* darling old white mammies— / sometimes even buried with our family! / *Dear* old / Mammy Faubus!) or whether a poem alludes to the tangle in the Congo, it always conveys the frenetic disorders of our time. The blend of politics, economics, and the entertainment world spread against a jazz background must make fascinating sounds when read aloud as intended; it also makes fascinating sense in any case. (p. 226)

> *Ulysses Lee, in a review of "Ask You Mama: 12 Moods for Jazz," in* CLA Journal, *Vol. VI, No. 3, March, 1963, pp. 225-26.*

James Presley   (essay date 1963)

[*In the following excerpted essay, Presley analyzes Hughes's vision of the American Dream as an often unattainable goal for many black Americans.*]

One summer in Chicago when he was a teen-ager Langston Hughes felt the American Dream explode in his face; a gang of white youths beat him up so badly that he went home with blacked eyes and a swollen jaw.

He had been punished for cutting through a white neighborhood in the South Side on his way home from work. That night as he tended his injuries young Hughes must have mused disturbed thoughts about fulfilment of his American dream of freedom, justice, and opportunity for all.

A few years after that traumatic Chicago afternoon Hughes inaugurated a prolific and versatile writing career. Over the four decades separating then and now, his reaction to the American Dream has been one of his most frequently recurring themes. For many years Hughes, often hailed as "the poet laureate of the Negro people," has been recognized by white critics as an author-poet of the protest genre. Others, more conservative and denunciatory, have assailed Hughes as radical and leftist, to mention the more polite language. In both instances the critics referred to Hughes's treatment of imperfections in the American Dream that we, as a nation, hold so dear.

The American Dream may have come dramatically true for many, Hughes says, but for the Negro (and other assorted poor people) the American Dream is merely that—a dream. If the critics and would-be censors had read further they would have noted that for Hughes the American Dream has even greater meaning: it is the *raison d'être* of this nation. Nevertheless, Hughes was still a regular target for right-wing barbs as recently as the 1960's, having been anathema to the right wing for decades. (p. 380)

As might be expected Hughes has written most frequently, though not exclusively, of Negro characters. Consequently the importance of the color line in America is frequently reflected in his work. The effect of the color line on the American Dream is therefore an integral part of his protest. In one of his biographies for young people, *Famous Negro Music Makers* (1961), Hughes quotes musician Bert Williams as saying: "It is no disgrace to be a Negro, but it is very inconvenient." In viewing the string of "inconveniences" vitally affecting the dignity of black Americans Hughes voices his reactions to shriveled freedom, dwarfed equality, and shrunken opportunity—blemishes on the essential ingredients of the American Dream. His poetry and prose echo protest and, usually, hope.

Two poems especially reflect his theme of protest and hope. **"Let America Be America Again,"** published in *Esquire* and in the International Worker Order pamphlet *A New Song* (1938), pleads for fulfilment of the Dream that never was. It speaks of the freedom and equality which America boasts, but never had. It looks forward to a day when "Liberty is crowned with no false patriotic wreath" and America is "that great strong land of love." Hughes, though, is not limiting his plea to the downtrodden Negro; he includes, as well, the poor white, the Indian, the immigrant—farmer, worker, "the people" share the Dream that has not been. The Dream still beckons. In **"Freedom's Plow"** he points out that "America is a dream" and the product of the seed of freedom is not only for all Americans but for all the world. The American Dream of brotherhood, freedom, and democracy must come to all peoples and all races of the world, he insists.

Almost invariably Hughes reflects hope, for that is part of his American Dream. However, some of his poems, apparently written in angry protest, are content to catch the emotion of sorrow in the face of hopelessness and gross injustice. One of his most biting is a verse in *Jim Crow's Last Stand* (1943). Aimed at southern lynch law which had just taken the lives of two fourteen-year-old Negro boys in Mississippi, and dedicated to their memory, the poem cried that **"The Bitter River"** has

> . . . strangled my dream:
> The book studied—but useless,
> Tools handled—but unused,
> Knowledge acquired but thrown away,
> Ambition battered and bruised.

In one of his children's poems, **"As I Grow Older,"** the poet looks at the Dream again. He had almost forgotten his dream; then it reappeared to him. But a wall rose—a high, sky-high wall. A shadow: he was black. The wall and the shadow blotted out the dream, chasing the brightness away. But the poet's dark hands sustain him. (p. 382)

In *Montage of a Dream Deferred* (1951) Hughes might have been thinking of the wall which blackness had erected in the child's poem. *Montage's* background is Harlem. There is a wall about Harlem, and the American Dream, as a reality, exists outside Harlem. Harlem (and, one can just as well add, the world of the American Negro) is a walled-in reality where dreams are deferred. The faded Dream pierces black New Yorkers to their hearts. Things which "don't bug . . . white kids" bother Harlemites profoundly. White boys cling to the stimulating dream that any American may grow up to be President of the United States. The Negro boy knows better. He also knows that the liberty and justice of the Pledge to the Flag are inherent rights only of white folks. Even in Harlem, the capital of the North which Hughes once described in a novel as "mighty magnet of the colored race," the American Dream is frayed and ragged.

Probably the greatest portion of Hughes's poetry does not refer specifically to the American Dream, despite the habit of many critics' labeling him a protest writer primarily. But in *Ask Your Mama: 12 Moods for Jazz* (1961) he returns to the Dream, in jazz tempo with barbs appropriate for a dream too long deferred. With an impish introduction of the melody "Dixie" in the background, the poet combines dreams and nightmares to produce a mural of black power in the South; he dreams the Negroes have voted the Dixiecrats out of office. As a result Martin Luther King becomes governor of Georgia and high posts go to other Negro patriots. The remainder of the passage reflects the opposite of the southern power structure for the past hundred years or so. Negroes relax on the verandas of their mansions while their white sharecroppers sweat on the plantations. The reverse pattern of historical reality is carried out even to the extent of Negro children having white mammies. . . . The patronizing air of the plantation white bourbon is reproduced as the poet notes that the "*dear* darling old white mammies" are sometimes even buried with the family!

But the grandiose dream sequence, itself reflecting how one-sided the American Dream has been in the South, is short-lived. The poet returns to the pessimistic here and now. The Negro can't keep from losing, even when he's winning, he moans in blues tempo. *Ask Your Mama* relates to the vast spectrum of the American Dream, as it affects Negroes. There are the hardships of blockbusting, or integrating a white residential area, the bitterness of Negro artists, the stereotyped attitudes of whites toward Negroes, the hope of a better material world for ambitious Negroes, and the eternal suspicions cast upon any Negro who does anything worthwhile or, often, anything that is ordinary for white folks to do. (pp. 383-84)

Throughout Hughes's life—and his literary expression—the American Dream has appeared as a ragged, uneven, splotched, and often unattainable goal which often became a nightmare, but there is always hope of the fulfilled dream even in the darkest moments. . . . The American Dream is bruised and often made a travesty for Negroes and other underdogs, Hughes keeps saying, but the American Dream does exist. And the Dream *must* be fulfilled. In one of his verses he put it more plainly. He might have been speaking to his harshest political critics or to the white youths who beat him up on that long-ago summer day in Chicago.

> Listen, America—
> I live here, too.
> I want freedom
> Just as you.

(p. 386)

James Presley, "The American Dream of Langston Hughes," in Southwest Review, *Vol. XLVIII, No. 4, Autumn, 1963, pp. 380-86.*

W. Edward Farrison   (essay date 1968)

[*Farrison discusses the aggressive tone and subject matter in* The Panther and the Lash.]

This collection of poems [*The Panther and the Lash: Poems of Our Times*] was prepared for publication by the author himself and was in press when he died. Its title was derived from two recent outgrowths of matters racial in America—the Black Panthers and the white backlash. The work is dedicated to Mrs. Rosa Parks of Montgomery, Alabama, who refused to move to the back of a bus, "thus setting off in 1955 the boycotts, the sit-ins, the Freedom Rides, the petitions, the marches, the voter registration drives, and *I Shall Not Be Moved*." Twenty-six of the seventy poems in the collection were selected from Hughes's previously published volumes of verse. The other forty-four are herein first published in one volume, seventeen of them having formerly appeared in periodicals, and twenty-seven now appearing in print for the first time. All of them are indeed poems of our times, for all of them pertain directly or indirectly to the Negro's continuing struggle to achieve first-class citizenship in America. The poems are written in short-line free verse or in occasional rhymes, by both of which Hughes's poetic work has long been distinguished.

The selections are grouped under seven headings, the first of these being "Words on Fire." In this group is **"The Backlash Blues."** . . . Not only is this one of the new poems but also it has been said to have been the last poem that Hughes submitted for publication before he died. It is an emphatic expression of determined aggressiveness against the opponents of civil rights for Negroes. Also in the first group and new is **"Black Panther."** . . . Avowedly militant, like Claude McKay's "If We Must Die," this poem has for its theme the determination of black men to give no further ground to oppressors but to stand and fight back desperately, like a panther when cornered.

More ironical than militant is the group called "American

Heartbreak," in whose initial poem with the same title a Negro declares generically that "I am the American heartbreak— / The rock on which Freedom / Stumped its toe—" Still more ironical as a whole is the group called "The Bible Belt"—a group in which life principally in Alabama and Mississippi is portrayed at its non-Biblical worst. Singularly memorable as well as new is the poem in this group entitled **"Birmingham Sunday,"** which consists of reflections on the deaths of four little Negro Sunday-school girls who were victims of the bombing of a church in Birmingham on September 15, 1963.

Especially noteworthy at present because of prevailing international affairs is the small group entitled "The Face of War." Two provocative poems in this group are **"Mother in Wartime"** and **"Without Benefit of Declaration,"** both of which deal with the common failure to understand the wherefores and the futility of war. The mother, "Believing everything she read / In the daily news," was quite unaware that both sides "Might lose." Meanwhile the draftee must go "Out there where / The rain is lead," but is told "Don't ask me why. / Just go ahead and die." What simple, convincing explanatory declaration is there to give him? Alas one is reminded of John Dewey's all but forgotten observations that "The more horrible a depersonalized scientific mass war becomes, the more necessary it is to find universal ideal motives to justify it"; and "The more prosaic the actual causes, the more necessary is it to find glowingly sublime motives."

The group puckishly entitled "Dinner Guest: Me" satirizes a variety of things. . . . **"Un-American Investigators"** coarsely twits a Congressional committee for its arbitrary methods of dealing with persons summoned before it. **"Cultural Exchange,"** the longest poem in the volume, envisions a radical change in Southern culture in the sociological sense—an inversion of the positions of Negroes and white people in the South with Negroes living "In white pillared mansions," white sharecroppers working on black plantations, and Negro children attended by "white mammies." The *bouleversement* imagined in this poem, which was published in *Ask Your Mama* in 1961, is more ingeniously recounted in "Rude Awakening" in *Simple's Uncle Sam,* which was published in 1965.

Finally there is the group called "Daybreak in Alabama"—a title in which there is a ray of hope for the optimistic, among whom Hughes belonged. As should now be evident, two of the poems in this group rang with prophetic tones when they were published in *One-way Ticket* in 1949. Observing that first-class citizenship would never come "Through compromise and fear," **"Democracy,"** now entitled **"Freedom,"** left no doubt that other means of achieving it must be employed. And admonishing America to "Beware the day" when Negroes, "Meek, humble, and kind," changed their minds, **"Roland Hayes Beaten,"** now entitled **"Warning,"** foreshadowed at least implicitly the various freedom movements mentioned in the dedication of *The Panther and the Lash.* From the beginning of his career as an author, Hughes was articulate in the Negro's struggle for first-class citizenship. It is indeed fitting that this volume with which his career ended is a vital contribution to that struggle as well as to American poetry. (pp. 259-61)

> *W. Edward Farrison, in a review of "The Panther and the Lash: Poems of Our Times," in*

CLA Journal, *Vol. XI, No. 3, March, 1968, pp. 259-61.*

Laurence Lieberman (essay date 1968)

[*An American poet and critic, Lieberman praises Hughes's technical assertiveness in the new poems featured in* The Panther and the Lash *but contends that many of them suffer from didacticism which undermines Hughes's poetics.*]

[*The Panther and the Lash* catches] fire from the Negro American's changing face. To a degree I would never have expected from his earlier work, his sensibility has kept pace with the times, and the intensity of his new concerns—helping him to shake loose old crippling mannerisms, the trade marks of his art—comes to fruition in many of the best poems of his career: **"Northern Liberal," "Dinner Guest: Me," "Crowns and Garlands,"** to name a few.

Regrettably, in different poems, he is fatally prone to sympathize with starkly antithetical politics of race. A reader can appreciate his catholicity, his tolerance of all the rival—and mutually hostile—views of his outspoken compatriots, from Martin Luther King to Stokely Carmichael, but we are tempted to ask, what are Hughes's politics? And if he has none, why not? The age demands intellectual commitment from its spokesmen. A poetry whose chief claim on our attention is moral, rather than aesthetic, must take sides politically. His impartiality is supportable in **"Black Panther,"** a central thematic poem of *The Panther and the Lash.* The panther, a symbol of the new Negro militancy, dramatizes the shift in politics from nonviolence to Black Power, from a defensive to an offensive stance: Hughes stresses the essential underlying will to survival—against brutal odds—of either position. He is less concerned with approving or disapproving of Black Power than with demonstrating the necessity and inevitability of the shift, in today's racial crisis.

"Justice," an early poem that teaches the aesthetic value of rage, exhibits Hughes's knack for investing metaphor with a fierce potency that is as satisfying poetically as it is politically tumultuous:

> That justice is a blind goddess
> Is a thing to which we black are wise:
> Her bandage hides two festering sores
> That once perhaps were eyes.

But this skill is all but asphyxiated in many of the new poems by an ungovernable weakness for essayistic polemicizing that distracts the poet from the more serious demands of his art, and frequently undermines his poetics. Another technique that Hughes often employs successfully in the new poems is the chanting of names of key figures in the Negro Revolution. This primitive device has often been employed as a staple ingredient in good political poetry, as in Yeats's "Easter 1916." But when the poem relies too exclusively on this heroic cataloguing—whether of persons or events—for its structural mainstay, as in **"Final Call,"** it sinks under the freight of self-conscious historicity. (pp. 339-40)

> *Laurence Lieberman, in a review of "The Pan-*

ther and the Lash," in Poetry, *Vol. CXII, No. 5, August, 1968, pp. 339-40.*

James Presley   (essay date 1969)

[*The following excerpt is a personal tribute to Hughes's life and career.*]

Clarence Darrow said it and I remembered it when I learned in May, 1967, that Langston Hughes was dead at sixty-five: "I know that no man who ever wrote a line that I read failed to influence me to some extent. I know that every life I ever touched influenced me, and I influenced it." I had known Langston Hughes for the last seven years of his life. I recall vividly that dark winter's afternoon in San Antonio where I met him. I do not mean I met him in person, but I met him personally, in the pages of his autobiographical *I Wonder As I Wander* that I took from the public library. Through the years we corresponded and I read most of what he had published in books, and I wrote of his work. He had touched my life, me, a white man almost three decades his junior, across the light years separating my Texas from his Harlem.

Because he had touched my life, because we were friends by correspondence, it hurt to hear at his death, as I had heard through the years, that he was considered old-fashioned by a younger, very angry generation of Negroes. I had always thought of him as, most of all, honest, a man who could eat watermelon, if he wished to, without feeling embarrassed. His career had stretched from Ernest Hemingway and William Faulkner to Richard Wright and John Steinbeck to James Baldwin and Norman Mailer. He had, it seemed clear to me, been relevant to every decade he had worked in. Antiquated? Clinging to old customs, old ideas?

Langston Hughes?

But there was no doubt about it, he somehow hadn't touched the hearts of the black militant generation who had called him old-fashioned. The man who was "the poet laureate of the Negro people" by the nineteen-twenties wasn't fiery, polemical, and gut-burning enough to please them. Wasn't that it? To them, he was left over from the past, a man like Countee Cullen, also from the twenties, signifying another generation.

It is strange that in this time when folk music is being discovered and elevated, a man who devoted more than forty years of his life to writing stories, poems, plays and books of the Negro folk, rural and urban, is thought to be out-of-date. . . . Perhaps one day a renaissance will rediscover Langston Hughes and, especially, his poetry, for his poems came from the working-class Negroes, to whom he spoke in a language they—and I—understood, a talent that poets do not always exhibit. The folks back home understood Langston Hughes because his poetry was simple and powerful. He communicated with a folk poetry that outlives the elaborate and the gorgeous. Whether it was in children's gentle verses or blues or "protest" lines, he remained the poet of the people. This was his greatest strength. (pp. 79-80)

[He] made the best of a bad situation, possibly the worst situation: a black man in America writing for a living, most of the time when a man, because he was black, had a small and fickle public, if one at all. "I'm trying to conduct a major career on a minor income," Hughes told one recent interviewer who called him, accurately enough, a literary jack-of-all-trades. Depending on grants, fellowships, ten cross-country lecture tours, recordings, teaching . . . , his columns in the *Chicago Defender,* and his royalties, he lived long enough to practice almost every literary form known to man: novels, autobiographies, poetry, plays, juveniles, anthologies, musicals, short stories, humor, journalism, histories, songs, and essays—adding up to thirty or forty books.

To be sure, his work at times was uneven and much of it less than his best. But who expects all of one's work to be uniformly fine? Even Balzac omitted some of his books from the *Comédie Humaine.* No man who had well over a dozen different publishers, as Hughes did, can have had an easy time of it as a professional writer, yet he did leave enough that was very good to earn his own niche in American letters. His poetry is almost always good, from *The Weary Blues* (1926) to *Jim Crow's Last Stand* (1943) to *Montage of a Dream Deferred* (1951) to *Ask Your Mama: 12 Moods for Jazz* (1961). (pp. 80-1)

Throughout his long career he wrote of life as he saw it. *Not Without Laughter* reflected his growing up in Kansas on the dark side of the color line. He moved easily into the mainstream of the protest literature of the thirties. *A New Song* (1938) was filled with poems of protest, among which his Whitmanesque **"Let America Be America Again"** is a classic pleading for the poor white, the Negro, the worker, the hungry—those underdogs who made this country with their hands.

> From those who live like leeches on the people's lives,
> We must take back our land again,
> America!

The class struggle, or the writing of it anyway, may appear old hat now. Yet one wonders how a later generation would respond if in the poet's warning to "all Nazis, Fascists, and Klansmen" in *Jim Crow's Last Stand* (1943) they substituted "racists," or Stokely Carmichael's "honkies." (pp. 81-2)

Ask Your Mama: 12 Moods for Jazz (1961), written to be read to jazz accompaniment, is a kaleidoscope of Negro names and Negro problems. Dreams follow nightmares. The poet dreams the Negroes of the South have voted out the Dixiecrats, made Martin Luther King governor of Georgia. Negroes sit on comfortable verandahs of pillared mansions, served by whites, their plantations worked by white sharecroppers, their colored children cared for by white mammies. "Culture," the poet quotes, "is a two-way street," and he admonishes the mammy to make haste with his mint julep. The jazz mood runs international, bringing in [Gamal] Nasser, [Fidel] Castro, [Sékou] Touré, [Jomo] Kenyatta, [Kwame] Nkrumah. In one mood, a Negro moves out to Long Island, where he is the only colored man, and becomes famous—"the hard way"—known downtown and across the world. For all the irritating questions that whites have for him about Negroes, he has one question-stopping reply, the theme, *Ask your mama.*

> THEY ASKED ME AT THANKSGIVING
> DID I VOTE FOR NIXON?

> I SAID, VOTED FOR YOUR MAMA.
>
> (p. 82)

Hughes had his critics, white and black. One Negro reviewer called *Fine Clothes to the Jew* (1927) "trash," and the Negro press in general concurred. Bourgeois Negroes, proving that brown Babbits are no different from white Babbits, wanted Negro artists to depict educated, cultured Negroes—not the kind of people Hughes knew and loved and wrote about. A few, more perceptive, like James Weldon Johnson, praised the poems.

White critics frequently downgraded all of his work by labeling him a "protest" writer, the old technique of dismissing a Negro artist, and to a generation or two of *bigotis americanis* he was the radical agitator who went to Russia with a Negro company to film *Porgy and Bess* under the auspices of the Soviet Union. The movie was never made, but Hughes saw Russia. If that weren't enough, *A New Song* was published by the International Workers Order, since designated as a Communist-front organization by the U.S. Attorney General and the House Un-American Activities Committee. When McCarthyism swept this country, self-anointed textbook and library purgers found these facts to be powerful ammunition against his work.

Now, ironically, it seems he did not protest enough.

It is possible that it is the textbook Hughes, the writer of the twenties and the thirties now enshrined in anthologies, that obscures the view of the younger Negro. Each generation seeks its own image, from its own ranks. If that is so, I hope they will reread him, and read his later work. (p. 83)

Come what may, Langston Hughes, in the quarter of the Negroes, in the world of us all: a man should get credit for what he is, and what he has been, and what he does, and what he has done. Come what may, my friend.

> WHEN THEY ASKED ME IN MID-SUMMER
> IN THE QUARTER OF THE NEGROES,
> IS LANGSTON HUGHES OLD-FASHIONED?
> I SAID, ASK YOUR MAMA!
>
> (pp. 83-4)

James Presley, "Langston Hughes: A Personal Farewell," in Southwest Review, *Vol. LIV, No. 1, Winter, 1969, pp. 79-84.*

Edward E. Waldron (essay date 1971)

[*Waldron is an American author and critic whose articles have appeared in* CLA Journal, Phylon, Negro American Literature Forum, *and other periodicals. In the following excerpted essay, he explores three themes indicative of Hughes's blues poetry: love, bad luck, and flight.*]

As a form of folk expression, the blues has come to occupy a justly revered spot in American music; at long last, recognition is being given to the artists—and the audience—that were instrumental in creating this art form. At the same time, many writers/poets have attempted for years to incorporate the essence of the blues into works outside the reference of music—i.e., into stories and poetry. One of the most successful poets in this endeavor was Langston

Hughes, the "Poet Laureate" of Black America. In his blues poetry Langston Hughes captures the mood, the feel, and the spirit of the blues; his poems have the rhythm and the impact of the musical form they incorporate. Indeed, the blues poems of Langston Hughes *are* blues as well as poetry. . . .

[The] blues reflects the trials and tribulations of the Negro in America on a secular level, much as the spirituals do on the religious level. Both expressions are, certainly, necessary releases. In one of his "Blues for Men" poems in *Shakespeare in Harlem,* Hughes dramatizes the necessity for this release. Lamenting the dirty treatment he has received from his woman, the singer of **"In a Troubled Key"** (the narrator of a blues poem *is* a singer, in effect) sings:

> Still I can't help lovin' you,
> Even though you do me wrong.
> Says I can't help lovin' you
> Though you do me wrong—
> But my love might turn into a knife
> Instead of to a song.

Here we see the blues maker turning his despair into song instead of into murder; and, one has the feeling that the mood of the blues is often one step away from death—either murder or suicide—and that the presence of the blues form makes it possible for the anguished one to direct his sorrow inward into song and find happiness in the release. (p. 140)

The blues, as any art form, has definite patterns which are adhered to in its composition. In [an] introductory "Note on Blues," . . . in *Fine Clothes to the Jew,* Hughes gives us the most common pattern:

> The *Blues,* unlike the *Spirituals,* have a strict poetic pattern: one long line repeated and a third line to rhyme with the first two. Sometimes the second line in repetition is slightly changed and sometimes, but very seldom, it is omitted.

In order to maintain a closer semblance to poetic form, Hughes breaks the first two lines into two lines each and also divides the final line, creating a six-line stanza. A typical stanza is this one from **"Po' Boy Blues"**:

> When I was home de
> Sunshine seemed like gold.
> When I was home de
> Sunshine seemed like gold.
> Since I come up North de
> Whole damn world's turned cold.

The second stanza of the poem illustrates the change that often occurs in the repeated line(s):

> I was a good boy,
> Never done no wrong.
> Yes, I was a good boy,
> Never done no wrong.
> But this world is weary
> An' de road is hard an' long.

In the case of a line changed in repetition, sometimes a word of exclamation, such as the "Yes" of this example, is added, and sometimes a word or two might be omitted, if not the whole line. For example, consider this stanza from **"Bound No'th Blues"**:

> Goin' down de road, Lawd,
> Goin' down de road.

Down de road, Lawd,
Way, way, down de road.
Got to find somebody
To help me carry dis load.

Here we see both kinds of change taking place; the repeated first line has dropped a word, and the repeated second line has changed by dropping one word and adding others in its place. This changing of lines helps keep the flow of the poem going, without ruining the effectiveness of the repetition. (pp. 141-42)

As with any poetic style, the blues' form is directly related to its content. Although what a particular blues is about may vary from blues to blues, the basic content of the blues usually has to do with some form of disappointment, most commonly in love, but also in other areas of life—or maybe in just plain living. [E. Simms] Campbell may be going a little overboard when he states that the blues ". . . are songs of sorrow charged with satire, with that potent quality of ironic verse clothed in the raiment of the buffoon." Yet, he is close to the same concept of the blues that Hughes voiced in the "Note on Blues" in *Fine Clothes to the Jew*:

> The mood of the *Blues* is almost always despondency, but when they are sung people laugh.

This seemingly paradoxical statement reflects an essence that is found in almost every facet of Black American expression: the duality of laughing and crying at the same time or, as Hughes says it, "laughing to keep from crying." Laughing at trouble is a concept we may all try to adopt at one time or another, but Black American writers have wrought this fine ability into a grand motif that consistently runs through their works; and Langston Hughes is certainly qualified as an artist in weaving this quality into his poetry and other works. (p. 142)

An extensive treatment of the man's side of the lost-love blues is found in the "Seven Moments of Love" section of *Shakespeare in Harlem,* which Hughes subtitled "An Un-Sonnet Sequence in Blues." This is a progressive series of seven poems dealing with a man's state of mind after his woman has left him. At first **("Twilight Reverie")** he wants to shoot her, but his loneliness begins to take away that mood. By **"Supper Time"** his despair has advanced to the point where he can hear his "heartbeats trying to think" and his "footprints walking on the floor." **"Bed Time"** is even worse; he wants to go out and have fun, but his habits of being with his woman won't let him go: "A human gets lonesome if there ain't two." He wakes up the next day **("Daybreak")**, miserable, and wonders "if white folks ever feels bad / Getting up in the morning lonesome and sad?" **"Sunday"** finds him thinking again about how "glad" he is to be "free"—"But this house is mighty quiet!" On **"Pay Day"** he recalls how he used to have to give his woman all the money, but now he is free to spend it all by himself. He is going to give up the furniture and things and go back to renting "a cubby-hole with a single bed." His dismay at his woman has the sound of frustrated humanity in it:

Women's abominations! Just like a
curse!
You was the best—but you *the worst!*

Finally, he hears from Cassie and writes her a "Letter" telling her to come back: "I can't get along with you, I can't get along without." With this last echoing thought, a thought that permeates the blues of love, Hughes closes one of his more ambitious blues poetry experiments. Throughout this series of poems Hughes manages to maintain a sense of identity in the singer of the blues and keeps at work a progression that ties together all seven poems very neatly. (p. 143)

While men do get to sing some of the blues written by Langston Hughes, the women seem to find favor with the poet more frequently, and their reactions often are more severe. Two poems from *Fine Clothes to the Jew* state explicitly the blues singer's desire to kill herself. The first stanza in **"Suicide,"** as well as the title itself, makes the singer's intent quite clear:

Ma sweet good man has
Packed his trunk and left.
Ma sweet good man has
Packed his trunk and left.
Nobody to love me:
I'm gonna kill ma self.

The river usually serves as the focal point for the suicide's thoughts of self-murder, although this woman does consider using a knife first. She rejects the blade, though, in favor of the water. . . . Of course, no one expects the blues singer to go out and commit suicide; after all, singing the blues is supposed to help relieve the hurt and act to channel the emotions away from self-directed or other-directed murder (see **"In a Troubled Key"** mentioned earlier).

In another woman's blues, **"Midnight Chippie's Lament"** (*Shakespeare in Harlem*), Hughes presents us with a blues person who seeks out the blues instead of death for her release:

I looked down 31st Street,
Not a soul but Lonesome Blue.
Down on 31st Street,
Nobody but Lonesome Blue.
I said come here, Lonesome,
And I will love you, too.

But "Lonesome Blue" rejects her offer, saying:

Woman, listen! Hey!
Buy you two for a quarter
On State Street any day.

Although Hughes ends this blues with a bit of sardonic humor ("Cry to yourself, girls, / So nobody can't low-rate you"), it still remains obvious that the woman singing this blues has reached a desperate level; she'd rather have the lonesome blues than *nothing* at all. (pp. 143-44)

[Love] is not the only subject of the blues, even though it does dominate as the main concern of the blues. Another common theme of the blues is bad luck. **"Hard Luck"** in *Fine Clothes to the Jew* is a good example of this kind of blues and gives the source of the title of that collection:

When hard luck overtakes you
Nothin' for you to do.
When hard luck overtakes you
Nothin' for you to do.
Gather up yo' fine clothes
An' sell 'em to de Jew.

"De Jew" here is, of course, the local pawnbroker, the

man to whom the desperate must turn in order to scrape up a few pennies with the last of their possessions. That the amount given for the goods received is rarely considered equitable is reflected in the second stanza:

Jew takes yo' fine clothes,
Gives you a dollar an' a half.
Jew takes yo' fine clothes,
Gives you a dollar an' a half.
Go to de bootleg's
Git some cheap gin to make you laugh.

(p. 145)

A final dominant theme in blues poetry is the idea of moving, of traveling, of getting away. **"Six-Bit Blues,"** an early poem which appeared originally in *Opportunity* (February, 1939), has this idea as its central theme:

Gimme six-bits' worth o' ticket
On a train that runs somewhere.
I say six-bits' worth o' ticket
On a train that runs somewhere.
I don't care where it's goin'
Just so it goes away from here.

The urgent need to move and to escape does not precede the need for love, but it makes that need somehow less binding:

Make it short and sweet, your lovin',
So I can roll along.

I got to roll along!

The final "tag" line, italicized for emphasis, reinforces the singer's urgent desire to get away. No explanation is given about why he wants to leave, but an explanation really is not necessary. In fact, given the nature of the blues, the question is probably irrelevant. (pp. 146-47)

Humor dominates in a few of the blues poems of Langston Hughes. **"Crowing-Hen Blues"** (*Poetry*, September, 1943) is a blues that is also pure folk humor. The singer, after a rough night of drinking, swears he hears his cat talking:

I had a cat, I called him
Battling Tom Mc Cann.
Had a big black cat, I called him
Battling Tom Mc Cann.
Last night that cat riz up and
Started talking like a man.

Waking up his "baby" to tell her the news, he gets a skeptical reaction: "I don't hear nothin' / But your drunken snorin', dear." Undaunted, the singer stands up for his right to drink and hallucinate all he wants. . . . (p. 147)

Another humorous blues poem by Hughes is **"Morning After,"** from the "Blues for Men" section of *Shakespeare in Harlem.* The subject of this blues, again a hangover and its effect on the singer, seems more the subject of a standup comedian than a blues maker, but the blues form does suit this particular poem. The first stanza establishes the man's problem:

I was so sick last night I
Didn't hardly know my mind.
So sick last night I
Didn't know my mind.
I drunk some bad licker that
Almost made me blind.

Hughes employed as a busboy at a Washington, D.C. hotel, 1925.

The humor gets very heavy-handed in the last two stanzas, as the man laments that his baby's "mouth was open like a well" and made enough noise for "a great big crowd." While this type of blues may not be as common as other blues, it does illustrate the wide possibilities of the blues form. Clearly, the mood of this blues poem is *not* despondency.

In addition to the more common subjects for blues that Hughes makes use of in his poetry, he also uses other, less common, subjects. A natural disaster would most likely find its way into a blues or a folk ballad, and Hughes took a terrible flooding of the Mississippi as the subject for his **"Mississippi Levee."** In the poem the singer cries out in anguish as the flood-waters keep coming in spite of his efforts to stop them. . . . A sense of hopelessness dominates this poem and is made clear in the final stanza:

Levee, Levee,
How high have you got to be?
Levee, Levee,
How high have you got to be?
To keep them cold muddy waters
From washin' over me?

Folk material has always made use of local natural disorders as subject matter, and this poem is in keeping with that tradition.

Finally, the blues themselves serve as the subject for some of the blues written by Langston Hughes, and the best single example of this type of poem is the title poem from *The Weary Blues.* In this poem, Hughes sets up a "frame" wherein he recalls the performance of a blues singer-pianist "on Lenox Avenue the other night":

> With his ebony hands on each ivory key He made
> that poor piano moan with melody—
>
>   . . .
>
>   Sweet Blues!
> Coming from a black man's soul.

After an exhausting performance, one that both drains and relaxes the blues man as only a creative act can, he quits his playing and goes to bed:

> While the Weary Blues echoed through his head.
> He slept like a rock or a man that's dead.

This form proves quite effective, since in it the reader receives not only the blues of the singer, but also a look at the creation of this blues from an outside source—the poet. In this way we become totally involved in the creative blues process.

The blues poetry of Langston Hughes, then, has a great deal to offer. Within this limited source of Hughes's creativity alone, we confront many of the themes that he develops more fully in other works. Loneliness, despair, frustration, and a nameless sense of longing are all represented in the blues poetry; and, these themes dominate not only the works of Hughes but also those of most Black American writers.

What direction Hughes's poetry of the blues might have taken thematically were he writing today is hinted at in the one traditional-form blues included in his last collection of verse, *The Panther and The Lash:* **"The Backlash Blues."** Once again Hughes underscores his concern with the social plight of the Black man in America in this poem, which also warns—

> I'm gonna leave you, Mister Backlash,
> Singing your mean old backlash blues.
>
> You're the one,
> Yes, you're the one
> Will have the blues.

While the blues traditionally have not concerned themselves *directly* with sociopolitical problems, and while Hughes follows this tradition fairly closely in his blues poetry, one sees in this, his final published blues poem the potential that Hughes might have developed in light of today's Black Power movement. Whether he would have gone in this direction or not is, of course, mere speculation, but his concern with the common man throughout his blues poetry—and other works—could have led him in this direction.

At any rate the blues poems we *do* have from this gifted poet illustrate quite well the effectiveness of this great American art form—even though his blues are read and not sung. Indeed, Hughes's sensitive reproduction of the language of the blues, which is the language of the common man/blues maker, and his ability to recreate the rhythmic effect of a sung blues make it difficult *not* to sing,

however softly, the blues of Langston Hughes. (pp. 147-49)

Edward E. Waldron, "The Blues Poetry of Langston Hughes," in Negro American Literature Forum, *Vol. 5, No. 4, Winter, 1971, pp. 140-49.*

"I am ashamed for the black poet who says, 'I want to be a poet, not a Negro poet,' as though his own racial world were not as interesting as any other world."
—Langston Hughes, 1926

Donald B. Gibson   (essay date 1971)

[*In the following excerpt taken from an essay in* Langston Hughes: Black Genius, *Gibson discusses the similarities and differences in the poetry of Hughes and Walt Whitman.*]

A direct link between Langston Hughes and Walt Whitman is established by Hughes himself in a tribute to the poet called **"Old Walt."** . . . If we were to substitute "Old Lang" for **"Old Walt"** throughout, we would have a poem as applicable to the one poet as to the other. The easiness of such a substitution is a clue to the relation between the two poets. The meaning of Hughes's poem is in its tone, its spirit rather than its correctness and specificity. It conveys an attitude rather than precise meaning. The relation between the two consists in their sharing common attitudes, certain feelings about what is worthwhile and valuable. Hughes, then, is not a direct descendant of Whitman; he was probably more directly influenced by Carl Sandburg and Vachel Lindsay and hence in regard to influence is at one remove. And Hughes is in some very important ways unlike Whitman—the comparison I am making should not obscure this fact. Yet, had Whitman not written, Hughes could not have been the same poet.

Both reveal in their poems certain rather obvious similarities. Hughes and Whitman are firm believers in the possibilities of realization of the American ideal; both see the American nation as in process of becoming. Both are more cheerful than not. Both approached the writing of their poems in generally non-traditional fashion, though Hughes uses rhyme and traditional metrics more than Whitman. Both are free in their choice of subject, writing about matters (especially sexual matters) traditionally considered unsuitable for poetry. Both adopt personae, preferring to speak in voices other than their own. They are social poets in the sense that they rarely write about private, subjective matters, about the workings of the inner recesses of their own minds. . . . And both have a remarkably similar notion of the nature and function of poetry. (pp. 65-6)

Whitman is most commonly known as the poet of American democracy and his most widely known poems have been such poems as "I Hear America Singing," "For You O Democracy," "O Captain! My Captain!" and others which reflect in various ways his commitment to democracy. Convinced of the essential unity of mankind, Whitman found democracy so appealing because of its promise to do away with social distinctions. Democracy was compatible with Whitman's philosophical notions about the ultimate unity of all things. Indeed the thrust of a good deal of his poetry is toward the doing away with distinctions between things.

Hughes also wanted to break down distinctions. His desire to break down the kinds of distinctions which make racism possible is not unrelated to a yearning to break down distinctions of all kinds. His **"I, Too," "Low To High,"** and **"High To Low," "In Explanation of Our Times," "Freedom's Plow,"** and **"Democracy"** all express Hughes's desire to see unity among people, social equality, economic equality, and cultural equality among the people not only of America, but of the world. The forms of many of his poems indicate his desire to break down, as did Whitman, the traditionally rigid distinctions between poetry and prose; though he did not go as far as Whitman in his desire to see all things as related, his tendencies were in that direction. He valued flexibility and abhorred rigidity. His temperament was such that he was much more inclined to see the unity of experience than its disparateness. Hence the title of one of his books of short stories, *Something in Common.* (pp. 66-7)

Hughes's commitment to the American ideal was deep felt and abiding. He held on to it despite his acute awareness of the inequities of democracy, and he seemed to feel that in time justice would prevail, that the promises of the dream would be fulfilled. His early poem, **"I, Too"** (*The Weary Blues,* 1926), is testimony to his faith.

> I, too, sing America.
>
> I am the darker brother.
> They send me to eat in the kitchen
> When company comes,
> But I laugh,
> And eat well,
> And grow strong.
>
> Tomorrow,
> I'll be at the table
> When company comes.
> Nobody'll dare
> Say to me,
> "Eat in the kitchen,"
> Then.

In an essay titled "My America" (included in *The Langston Hughes Reader*) Hughes attempted to express his complex feelings about the United States. The essay begins, "This is my land America. Naturally, I love it—it is home—and I am vitally concerned about its mores, its democracy, and its well-being." The piece concludes with another testament of faith: ". . . we know . . . that America is a land in transition. And we know it is within our (black people's) power to help in its further change toward a finer and better democracy than any citizen has known before. The American Negro believes in democracy. We want to make it real, complete, workable, not only for ourselves—the fifteen million dark ones—but for all Americans all over the land."

As optimists generally do, Langston Hughes and Walt Whitman lacked a sense of evil. This (and all it implies) puts Hughes in a tradition with other American writers. He stands with Whitman, Emerson, Thoreau, and later Sandburg, Lindsay, and Steinbeck, as opposed to Hawthorne, Poe, Melville, James, Faulkner, and Eliot. This is not to say that he did not recognize the existence of evil, but, as Yeats says of Emerson and Whitman, he lacked the "Vision of Evil." He did not see evil as inherent in the character of nature and man, hence he felt that the evil (small *e*) about which he wrote so frequently in his poems (lynchings, segregation, discrimination of all kinds) would be eradicated with the passage of time. Of course the Hughes of *The Panther and the Lash* (1967) is not as easily optimistic as the poet was twenty or twenty-five years before. Hughes could not have written **"I, Too"** or even **"The Negro Speaks of Rivers"** in the sixties. But the evidence as I see it has it that though he does not speak so readily about the fulfillment of the American ideal for black people, and though something of the spirit of having waited too long prevails, still the optimism remains. This is evidenced by his choosing to include the poems with an optimistic bias in his last two volumes of verse, *Selected Poems* and *The Panther and the Lash.*

Montage of a Dream Deferred (1951), included in *Selected Poems,* describes the dream as deferred, not dead nor incapable of fulfillment. There is a certain grimness in the poem, for example in its most famous section "Harlem" which begins, "What happens to a dream deferred? / Does it dry up / like a raisin in the sun?" but the grimness is by no means unrelieved. There is, as a matter of fact, a lightness of tone throughout the poem which could not exist did the poet see the ravages of racial discrimination as manifestations of Evil. . . . The whole tone of *Montage of a Dream Deferred* is characterized by the well-known **"Ballad of the Landlord."** There the bitter-sweet quality of Hughes's attitude toward his subject is clear.

The Panther and the Lash is the least cheerful, the least optimistic of Hughes's volumes of poetry. Even this book, however, is not devoid of hope.

> Quick sunrise, come!
> Sunrise out of Africa,
> Quick, come!
> Sunrise, please come!
> Come! Come!
>
>   Four little girls
> Might be awakened someday soon
> By songs upon the breeze
> As yet unfelt among magnolia trees.

It must be said in all truth that though Hughes's optimism remains, his faith is not so much in democracy, nor America, nor, for that matter, in any specifically stated program or system. *The Panther and the Lash* reveals a generalized hope and optimism very much dimmed, comparatively. There is in respect to optimism no poem the least bit like **"I, Too."**

Whitman and Hughes share a similar attitude toward the relation of the poet to poetic tradition. Neither looked to the past for the sake of discovering suitable or acceptable forms or subject matter. Both poets were thoroughly engaged in their time, were men of the present and the future and not primarily of the past. I say "primarily" because both used to some extent the methods of traditional poetry—rhyme, regular metrical structures, poetic diction. But their work gives the impression on the whole that they were more reliant on their own sense of what constitutes poetry, were more inclined to look inward than outward in creating poems. Both found free verse to be more compatible with their aims than more structured verse though Hughes probably relied more than did Whitman on traditional form. Even so, neither poet looked backwards for poetic examples—at least not as a common practice. Whitman, of course, is our most original poet even though he was influenced by others. Hughes looked to other poets, but to his contemporaries. (pp. 67-72)

Whitman and Hughes were as unconventional in their subject matter as in thier form, and both were attacked for their lack of delicacy, especially in matters related to sex. . . . Hughes's **Fine Clothes to the Jew** was called "trash" by *The Pittsburgh Courier* in 1927. In a defense of his poems, published in the same newspaper, he wrote the following:

> My poems are indelicate. But so is life.
>
> I write about "harlots and gin-bibers." But they are human. Solomon, Homer, Shakespeare, and Walt Whitman were not afraid or ashamed to include them.

Such attitudes as these are not inconsistent with the poets' general stance against the *status quo*. Both seek change in the American society, and both welcome change. Hence they are less bound than many others to institutional ways of perceiving and responding. "A Woman Waits for Me" must have been even more shocking to genteel readers in the nineteenth century than Hughes's "indelicacies" have been in the twentieth. But the salient point is that the two poets shared the same impulse: to write honestly and truly about what they saw around them, and not to allow considerations of propriety to obfuscate their vision.

Another similarity between them is their choosing to speak through a mask, a persona, Whitman more consistently than Hughes. The observation that the poet who speaks in *Leaves of Grass* and Walt Whitman the man are not one and the same is by now common knowledge. (pp. 72-3)

Whitman's reasons for projecting into the poem a kind of mythical, larger-than-life hero are multifarious, but clearly enough he wished to convey the impression of a figure who in spirit would contain the essence of the American nation and, ultimately, of humankind. Hughes's use of the persona is somewhat different though not always entirely dissimilar. The speaker, for example, of **"I, Too"** is obviously not an individual; his is a collective "I," the same representative figure who says, "I've known rivers" in **"The Negro Speaks of Rivers."** Whereas Whitman's persona is a single, fairly consistent, developing consciousness, Hughes assumes a multitude of personae. At one time he is the spirit of the race who represents Negro or Black Man. Then he is a shoeshine boy, a black mother, a black woman quarreling with her husband, a black man without a job or money, a prostitute, a slum tenant. Sometimes he is a consciousness whose role is incapable of determination. And sometimes he speaks, though comparatively rarely, as the poet.

In those poems about black life, thought, and character we could say that the persona is the same. It may well be that we are expected to see a commonality among the various experiences set forth in Hughes's poems of this type. If so,

then we could say that a consistent persona speaks in a great number of Hughes's poems.

Most of the poems of Hughes and Whitman have an end beyond themselves, and they differ, therefore, from the poems of poets who seek to write poems beautiful in themselves and void of ideas. In writing poetry Hughes and Whitman felt they were performing a function beyond mere entertainment. Both intended to influence the thinking and actions of men; both intended to change the world through their poetry. Whitman's poetry is suffused with poems whose intention is to instill in men's minds the basic tenets of democracy. . . . Hughes likewise wished to encourage men to know and love democracy. One of many such poems about democracy and the value of freedom and equality is Hughes's **"I Dream a World,"** an aria in the opera, *Troubled Island,* by William Grant Still; libretto by Langston Hughes. (pp. 73-5)

There are undoubtedly more parallels than I have pointed out between Whitman and Hughes, but it should also be noted that there are many, many differences as well. For one thing Hughes was not a mystic nor does his poetry . . . indicate any kind of supernatural belief. He was a naturalist and a humanist, and his attention was toward the world. This seems to me to relate to Hughes's little poem, **"Personal."**

> In an envelope marked:
> *Personal*
> God addressed me a letter.
> In an envelope marked:
> *Personal*
> I have given my answer.

The poem, written by a naturalist, a disbeliever, is ironic, and the irony and mild humor consist in the fact that the poet equates himself with God and tells Him, man to man, what he thinks of Him.

Much of his poetry, unlike Whitman's, was written to be read aloud. Hughes must have read to more people than any other twentieth-century poet. Some of his most apparently mundane and lifeless poems sparkled to life in his reading of them. Unlike Whitman's, many of his poems depend upon the reader's familiarity with black expressions, both urban and rural. Some readers simply cannot respond to much of his poetry because they do not understand the rhythms, pronunciations, and meaning of his language. In this regard, though Whitman often forced the language to his own purposes, Hughes is the less formal poet. Of course these observations do not apply to Hughes's more formal poems which are usually quite conventional.

Though Hughes was a great admirer of Whitman, it is doubtful that he knew how Whitman the man really felt about black people. Asselineau points out in detail Whitman's strong personal aversion to black people in the chapter, "Democracy and Racialism—Slavery," in his book, *The Evolution of Walt Whitman.* . . . Asselineau reports that Whitman found it "curious to see Lincoln 'standing with his hat off' to a regiment of black troops 'just the same as the rest' as they passed by" and that Whitman "in 1872, in the course of a visit to his sister's home in Vermont, rejoiced at not seeing a single Negro." (pp. 78-9)

These feelings were for the most part personally expressed and did not enter directly into *Leaves of Grass.* On the contrary Whitman must have recognized the grave contradiction between his personal feelings and his notions about liberty and equality and certainly did not wish the poet of the poems to appear to be a bigot. There is, however, no poem on the Emancipation Proclamation and only one allusion to emancipation in *Leaves of Grass.* It should be pointed out, in all fairness, that Whitman was not *simply* a bigot. He abhorred the fugitive slave law; he felt slavery to be degrading to slave and slave owner; and he several times depicts the horrors of slavery in *Leaves of Grass.* It is this latter aspect of Whitman's character which Hughes knew from *Leaves of Grass* and admired. Hence Hughes might have felt the same (or similarly) toward Whitman had he known of the good gray poet's personal repugnance toward black people. Walt Whitman the man might have been a bigot, but Walt Whitman the poet was a thorough-going equalitarian.

There are many more differences that might be pointed out. But suffice it to say that in Whitman the poet, Hughes found a compatible spirit, a man of large sympathy, of broad vision, and great faith in the potential of America and Americans. Hughes and Whitman would have disagreed on many things had they known and talked with each other, but on most basic issues, on matters basic to the sustaining of life, on matters having to do with the well-being of the majority of people, they would have found many points of agreement. And it is for this reason, it seems to me, that the two poets want comparison. (pp. 79-80)

> Donald B. Gibson, "The Good Black Poet and the Good Gray Poet: The Poetry of Hughes and Whitman," in Langston Hughes, Black Genius: A Critical Evaluation, *edited by Therman B. O'Daniel, William Morrow & Company, Inc., 1971, pp. 65-80.*

Arthur P. Davis   (essay date 1974)

[*In this excerpt taken from his book* From the Dark Tower, *Davis surveys Hughes's literary career.*]

Poet, fiction writer, dramatist, newspaper columnist, writer of autobiography, anthologist, compiler of children's works, and translator, Langston Hughes was by far the most experimental and versatile author of the Renaissance—and time may find him the greatest.

A man of good will who believed that all races and groups are essentially the same in things that really count, Hughes fought the blackman's fight for dignity and equality with rare insight, great tolerance, and a vast amount of humor. Always a protester, he was seldom if ever bitter; always a race author, he was never a racist. Keenly aware of the Negro's position in America, he never espoused separatism or black nationalism. "I too sing America" was not merely a verse of poetry to him, it was part of his credo.

Negro writing owes much to Hughes: he showed by example and experiment the importance of the folk contribution to black writing through his use of the blues, spirituals, ballads, jazz, and folk speech; he gave Negro drama a shot in the arm when it needed it most; he exemplified

the kind of freedom, the breaking away from stereotypes which many New Negro authors preached but did not always practice; and he preserved, in the face of an increasing seriousness on the part of militant young black writers, a much-needed sense of tolerance and old-fashioned humor. (p. 61)

The bulk of Hughes's poetry is found in ten major publications, ranging from 1926 to 1967, the year of his death. During this span of over forty years he touched on many subjects and experimented with various techniques, but he never quite gave up any of the old approaches he used in the earliest works. One notes that in his last volume of poems, *The Panther and the Lash,* he has examples of works from all the previous volumes. With regard to subject matter, he was equally consistent. As a matter of fact, he really had but one theme during his entire poetic career, and that was to delineate the wrongs, the sorrows, the humor, and the enduring quality of the Negro. There are, of course, brief excursions into nonracial themes, but these are very rare.

His works may be divided into the following major categories: poems of protest and social commentary; Harlem poems; poems influenced by folk material; poems on African and negritude themes; and miscellaneous poems. . . . Naturally, there is some overlapping among these categories, but in the main they are valid. If there is one quality which characterized all Hughes's poetry—in fact all his works—it is simplicity: the plain acts of everyday people written in the uncomplicated language of their speech.

The protest-and-social-commentary theme runs through the whole body of Hughes's poetry. He freely acknowledged that he was a propagandist. One notes, however, that in his first two works, *The Weary Blues* and *Fine Clothes to the Jew,* there are very few protest poems. By the time of *One Way Ticket* (1949) the stream is flowing freely, and from this work on down to his last, social protest and commentary become increasingly important. Like other New Negro poets, Hughes used lynching as the supreme symbol of American injustice, and in *One Way Ticket* devotes a whole section of the work ("Silhouette") to lynch poems. His protest-and-social-commentary poems are usually topical, and if a reader were to put them all together, he would have a dramatic and revealing account of the many glaring instances of injustice perpetrated by America on the black citizen—an account that would include the Harlem Riot of 1935 and the trials and tribulations of Stokely Carmichael and other recent Black Power leaders; an account which would perhaps give as much insight, if not more, than a library of sociological works.

Langston Hughes, like other young Negroes of the thirties and forties, saw hope for the oppressed in the Marxist position. Although he never became a Communist, many of his social poems during this period show leftist influence. But nothing could disturb for long Hughes's innate "coolness," his ability to see both sides of an issue. Characteristic of him is a late poem called **"Impasse"** in which he cleverly gets at the heart of the racial dilemma in America:

> I could tell you,
> If I wanted to,
> What makes me
> What I am.

But I don't
Really want to,
And you don't
Give a damn.

It is revealing to contrast Hughes's attitude toward racial protest poetry with that of Countee Cullen. During most of his career Cullen used to complain about being a *Negro poet*. "To make a poet black and bid him sing" was considered a peculiar kind of malevolence on the part of God. Hughes, on the other hand, seemed to glory in his mission as a black propagandist, looking upon his protest poems as a weapon in the arsenal of democracy.

Called the poet laureate of Harlem, Hughes retained all his life a deep love for that colorful city within a city, and he never tired of delineating the changing moods of that ghetto. Except for one, there are specific poems on Harlem in every major poetical work. To Hughes, Harlem was place, symbol, and on occasion protagonist. It is a city of rapid transformation: the Harlem of the first two works is a gay, joyous city of cabaret life, the Harlem that jaded downtown whites seeking the exotic and the primitive flocked uptown to see. This Harlem of **"Jazzonia"** was never the *real* Harlem; that begins to appear in *One Way Ticket* (1949) after a riot and a depression have made the ghetto into an "edge of hell" for its discouraged and frustrated inhabitants, though still a refuge from the white man's world.

The fullest and best treatment of Harlem (and Hughes's best volume of poetry) is found in *Montage of a Dream Deferred* (1951). Actually one long poem of 75 pages, it employs a "jam-session technique" to give every possible shade and nuance of Harlem life. Very few cities have received such a swinging and comprehensive poetic coverage. The key poem of the work is prophetic in its implications:

What happens to a dream deferred?
Does it dry up
like a raisin in the sun?
Or fester like a sore—
And then run?
Does it stink like a rotten meat?
Or crust and sugar over—
like a syrupy sweet?
Maybe it just sags
like a heavy load.
Or *does it explode?*

Although Dunbar and Chesnutt had tapped the reservoir of Negro folk material during the late nineteenth century, the New Negro writers were the first to make broad use of this important body of songs and literature. No longer interested in the dialect tradition, they fashioned new forms of expression based on the spirituals, the blues, the ballads, the work and dance songs, and the folk sermon. The most important and the most dedicated experimenter with these forms was Langston Hughes.

In his first works he emphasized the blues form, a form for which he had a special fondness probably because it was congenial to his style and to his temperament. The title poem of his first volume [**"The Weary Blues"**] has a bluestype form; seventeen of the poems in his second work are blues; and his first novel, *Not Without Laughter* and two of his best-known plays, "Don't You Want to Be Free?" and *Tambourines to Glory*, lean heavily on folk in-

fluence and folk blues and spirituals for artistic support. Hughes also employed ballad forms and on occasion dance rhythms, as in:

Me and ma baby's
Got two mo' ways,
Two mo' ways to do de Charleston!
Da,Da,
Da,Da,Da!
Two mo' ways to do de Charleston!

The experimentation with folk forms and rhythms reached brilliant heights in two later works: *Montage of a Dream Deferred* and *Ask Your Mama: 12 Moods for Jazz.* In the first work Langston Hughes seeks to capture "the conflicting changes, sudden nuances, sharp and impudent interjections, broken rhythms, and passages some times in the manner of the jam session. . . ." In short, he blends light and shadow, serious and comic, harmony and dissonance after the manner of jazz music to give the reader a unified picture of many-faceted Harlem. *Ask Your Mama* is a different type of jazz experiment, and though not quite as impressive as *Montage,* it is still a successful work. For this volume the poet uses the traditional folk melody of "The Hesitation Blues" as a leitmotif. "In and around it," he tells us, "along with the other recognizable melodies employed, there is room for spontaneous jazz improvisation. . . ." Printed in the margins beside each of the poems one finds elaborate directions for the musical accompaniment to the verse. It should be noted that Hughes, if not the first, as some critics claim, was among the pioneers of the poetry-read-to-jazz movement.

Langston Hughes's treatment of the African-negritude theme changed and deepened over the years. Like other New Negro poets, he featured in his earlier poems the alien-and-exile theme. . . . This early treatment of Africa was little more than a literary pose, a kind of literary Garveyism, and neither the New Negro poets nor their readers took it seriously. Hughes's later African poems, however, are not conventional when he writes of a real and embittered Africa battling its way into freedom:

Lumumba was black
And he didn't trust
The whores all powdered
With uranium dust. . . .

Lumumba was black.
His blood was red—
And for being a man
They killed him dead. . . .

This concern with Africa brings to mind Langston Hughes's role in the negritude movement. Space will not permit a discussion of this question, but it should be noted that the poetry of Langston Hughes greatly influenced West African and West Indian negritude. He is counted among the fathers of that movement. Hughes was always deeply interested in Africa, but he never considered changing his name or metaphorically donning a dashiki. He never renounced his American citizenship—literary or otherwise. (pp. 62-6)

Arthur P. Davis, "First Fruits: Langston Hughes," in his From the Dark Tower: Afro-American Writers 1900-1960, *Howard University Press, 1974, pp. 61-73.*

Cary D. Wintz (essay date 1975)

[*Wintz traces Hughes's portrayal of the black working class from the Depression to the Civil Rights era.*]

The Harlem Renaissance of the 1920's was the first major literary movement in the Negro's experience in America. As such it provides an important and well-developed statement of the Negro's attempt to come to terms with his experience in America. The Renaissance occurred at a critical moment in the history of the American Negro. On the one hand, during the 1920's the urban ghetto was rapidly replacing the rural South as the principal environment of blacks in this country. At the same time blacks were re-evaluating their approach to racial problems. The death of Booker T. Washington, the rise of the National Association for the Advancement of Colored People, and the postwar race riots signaled an increasing impatience with accommodation and the growth of racial pride. The black writers of the Harlem Renaissance gave expression to these feelings of social and political unrest, and they attempted to define the Negro experience in a manner which would integrate the Negro's rural heritage with his new urban existence.

Ironically, most of the black writers who participated in the Harlem Renaissance came from backgrounds that were far removed from the harsh but colorful life of the black ghetto. Langston Hughes, one of the most gifted writers of the period, spent his formative years in Topeka and Lawrence, Kansas, more than a thousand miles from the sidewalks and tenements of Harlem. Nevertheless, Hughes emerged as the most brilliant of Harlem's Renaissance poets, and as the one who created the most vibrant portrait of the Negro's urban experience.

The road from Lawrence, Kansas, to Harlem was a long one, and it would not have been unusual if Hughes had ignored his small-town background as he became a spokesman for the black metropolis. At first glance, Hughes's Renaissance poetry, with its emphasis on urban themes, seems to support this premise. However, at least during the 1920's he never completely severed his ties with the heritage of his childhood. Many of his values, particularly his interest in the common man and his racial pride, much of his intellectual curiosity, and his fascination with literature were born during his years in Kansas. And before he withdrew from involvement with the Harlem Renaissance, Hughes focused his literary talents on the experiences of his youth, and produced a rare picture of black life in Kansas. (p. 58)

In 1926 Hughes had published his first volume of poetry, *The Weary Blues.* This book, published with the assistance of novelist Carl Van Vechten, contained a sampling of much of the material he had written up to this point. The most outstanding feature in this volume was the use of Negro music as a model for a number of poems. The blues and jazz, the distinctive music of Negro life, provided the form for the title poem and several others. This stylistic experimentation was one of the major elements in Hughes's work. In this first volume the young poet also introduced the two major themes that would characterize his poetry throughout his long career. First, he expressed a deep commitment to the Negro masses. Years earlier he had learned from his grandmother the dignity and drama of the oppressed's struggle against injustice, and he had observed first hand the lives of the ordinary Negro working people. It is not surprising, then, that as a poet he consistently sang the song of the people. Most of his work focused on the men and women he saw around him—elevator operators, workers, cabaret dancers, prostitutes, and ordinary people walking down the street. His verses reflected a keen insight into the life of the Negro masses, including a vivid picture of the poverty and deprivation of their life. The poignant advice in **"Mother to Son"** captured this element in Hughes's work:

> Well, son, I'll tell you:
> Life for me ain't been no crystal stair.
> It's had tacks in it,
> And splinters,
> And boards torn up,
> And places with no carpet on the floor—
> Bare.

The second theme that Hughes introduced in his first volume of poetry was Harlem. Although he depicted Negro life in the rural South, and occasionally in his native Midwest, Hughes was essentially an urban poet, and life in the Negro metropolis was a basic element in his work throughout his career. As Arthur P. Davis observed, "either stated or implied, used as subject or background or protagonist, and on occasion even as a symbol for Negroes everywhere, Harlem has been a constantly recurring theme in Langston Hughes' poetry." In every book except one, beginning with *The Weary Blues* and ending with *The Panther and the Lash* in 1967, Hughes examined life in Harlem.

In 1926 Hughes's Harlem was the Renaissance metropolis with the sounds of jazz floating down the streets and a club on every corner where "sleek black boys" and "shameless girls" found joy in a "whirling cabaret." Hughes, however, was also a realist. More clearly than most other Renaissance writers he saw that beneath Harlem's glitter was an oppressive, melancholy slum; the excitement of jazz contrasted sharply with the weary blues. . . . (pp. 60-1)

Hughes published his second volume of poetry, *Fine Clothes for the Jew,* in 1927. In this collection he continued to develop the themes that he introduced in the first volume. He felt that this book was better than *The Weary Blues* because "it was more impersonal, more about other people than myself, and because it made use of the Negro folk-song forms, and included poems about work and the problems of finding work, that are always so pressing with the Negro people." However, a number of black critics did not share this conviction. Many Negro intellectuals and much of the Negro press condemned Hughes for his preoccupation with the lower classes, and viewed his jazz and blues poems as a disgrace to the race and a return to the dialect tradition of Paul Dunbar. Most white critics liked the book, although a number of Jews were offended by the title. With his second volume of poetry Hughes established himself as one of the better young black poets, and as one of the most controversial. He had won the reputation of a talented but radical poet who flirted with the leftist political doctrines and opened his pages to the Negro proletariat. (p. 61)

Throughout the Renaissance Hughes continued to be preoccupied with the themes he had introduced in *The Weary Blues.* As he matured as a poet in the late 1920's he turned his attention more and more on the Negro lower classes, examining all aspects of their lives—joy, sorrow, pleasure, and poverty. In later years Hughes would refer to himself as a "social poet," and note that he often focused his attention on the proletariat. However, as deep as his commitment was to the lower classes, he never lost touch with the individual, and his poetry remained on a personal level. During the Renaissance, at least, he always addressed himself to the problems of living, breathing individuals, not to the abstraction of a faceless social class. In an article written several years after the Renaissance Hughes looked back on his career and explained why he so often directed his art toward the life and social problems of the lower classes:

> Beauty and lyricism are really related to another world, to ivory towers, to your head in the clouds, feet floating off the earth. Unfortunately, having been born poor—and also colored—in Missouri, I was stuck in the mud from the beginning. Try as I might to float off into the clouds, poverty and Jim Crow would grab me by the heels, and right back to earth I would land.

In addition Hughes believed that there was more vitality among the lower classes, and that this made them better material for literature. . . . (p. 62)

In *The Weary Blues* and especially in *Fine Clothes for the Jew,* Hughes's poetry reflected this preoccupation with the working class. In **"Elevator Boy,"** for example, he examined one of the menial jobs that many blacks drifted into and then quickly out of. Jobs, he observed, were closely related to luck—occasionally he would find a good one, but frequently he would hit a string of bad luck and drift from one poor job to another, earning barely enough to provide the necessities of life. . . . In **"Brass Spittoons"** Hughes exposed the oppressive nature of much of the work set aside for blacks. In this case the job was not only menial, it was also demeaning. . . . Like the elevator operator, the spittoon boy worked for the basic necessities of life—house rent, shoes for the baby, and gin on Saturday. For this he endured a distasteful job which was meaningful only in his fantasies. Always, though, his dreams evaporated with the rude snarl of his boss.

The life of the poor was not all work. Hughes also examined the ghetto night clubs and cabarets where he found blacks at play. . . . Unlike other black poets who often depicted only the glamorous side of the ghetto existence, Hughes never lost sight of the uncertainties of poverty. The pleasures and joy of the cabaret were at best only temporary rays of sunshine which brightened an otherwise bleak landscape. There were, of course, some pleasures that were less transitory:

> When Susanna Jones wears red
> Her face is like an ancient cameo
> Turned brown by the ages.
> Come with a blast of trumpets, Jesus!

These poems, and much of what Hughes wrote during this period, reflected his second major concern, life in Harlem. The bars, streets, and tenements of the Negro metropolis formed a constant background for much of Hughes's work. This element in his poetry culminated in 1951 in a book-length epic discourse on Harlem, *Montage of a Dream Deferred.* During the Renaissance he carefully laid the foundations for this work with numerous poetic sketches of ghetto life.

As Hughes developed his portrayal of the black lower classes and their ghetto environment, he became more and more preoccupied with the question of the Negro's racial identity. Hughes had begun his search for the meaning of the racial experience in America shortly after he graduated from high school. In his first mature poem, **"A Negro Speaks of Rivers,"** he found an analogy between the river that flowed through his native Midwest and the ancient rivers that watered the lands where his race was born:

> I've known rivers:
> I've known rivers ancient as the world and older than the
>   flow of human blood in human veins.
> My soul has grown deep like the rivers

Hughes continued this investigation in several directions. First, like many of his contemporaries, he looked to Africa, where he found few answers but a great many questions. In 1923 he had visited Africa while working on an American freighter. At first he saw his ancient homeland as an exotic land of black, beautiful people, sensual women, and strong men laboring on the docks. Then, he found to his amazement that the Africans considered him white because of his light skin and straight hair. Finally he saw that the principal feature of Africa in the 1920's was its domination by Western imperialism. Even his own ship had come to carry away the wealth of the continent. In his poetry Africa became a symbol of lost roots, of a distant past that could never be retrieved. (pp. 62-4)

Except in his very early poetry Hughes did not devote as much attention to African roots as did several other Renaissance poets. As one who had grown up in America's heartland he seemed content with his conclusion that American blacks were Americans, not Africans, and consequently he focused his attention on the Negro's identity problems in this country. In particular, on several occasions he looked into the role of the mulatto in American society. In a number of poems, and in a play he wrote in 1935, he investigated the frustrations of those suspended between black and white America. **"Cross,"** which first appeared in the *Crisis* in 1925, was his simplest and most powerful statement of this dilemma:

> My old man's a white old man
> And my old mother's black.
> If ever I cursed my white old man
> I take my curses back.
>
> If ever I cursed my black old mother
> And wished she were in hell,
> I'm sorry for that evil wish
> And now I wish her well.
>
> My old man died in a fine big house.
> My ma died in a shack.
> I wonder where I'm gonna die,
> Being neither white nor black?

Very quickly, very directly, Hughes moved beyond anger and resentment to expose the isolation that was the real tragedy of the mulatto in a racist society. He followed this poem with an equally dramatic, but a more bitter examination in **"Mulatto."** Here he wove together two themes, an angry confrontation between an illegitimate youth and his white relatives, and a taunting description of the violent act of miscegenation. . . . Here were all the themes of racial sex exploitation. A black woman raped in the southern night, an angry mulatto disowned and mocked

Hughes with Mikhail Koltzov, Ernest Hemingway, and Nicolás Guillén in Madrid, 1937.

by his white father and half-brothers. The situation was both universal and highly personal. Hughes, however, carefully avoided the usual stereotypes which depicted the mulatto as the victim of a divided heritage, with intellectual ambitions contrasted with tendencies toward savagery. Instead he described him as an individual of divided heritage, unable to relate to either race in America.

Given Hughes's interest in the problems of the lower classes and his attempt to uncover the difficulties of being black in the United States, it is not surprising that he occasionally turned his pen against racial and social injustice. Fortunately his protest poetry did not succumb to bitterness. Perhaps because he had grown up in the Midwest where lynching and the other more violent expressions of racism were not common occurrences, his poems never seemed dogmatic or excessively propagandistic (at least during the Renaissance period). Instead, he approached the subject of racial oppression through satire, understatement, or wry, sardonic humor. The poem **"Cross"** was a clear example of his ability to expose an extremely controversial subject in a cool, matter-of-fact fashion. In **"Mulatto"** his language was angry and even inflammatory, but the impact of the poem remained controlled and powerful. This was also true of his most controversial protest poem, **"Christ in Alabama,"** which he wrote at the height of the Scottsboro case. . . .

Christ is a Nigger
Beaten and black—
O, bare your back.

Mary is His Mother—
Mammy of the South,
Silence your mouth.

God's His Father—
White Master above,
Grant us your love.

Most holy bastard
Of the bleeding mouth:
Nigger Christ
On the Cross of the South.

Hughes described this piece as "an ironic poem inspired by the thought of how Christ, with no human father, would be accepted if he were born in the South of a Negro mother." Its power, like that of most of his poetry, came through using inflammatory images to produce a cool, controlled anger.

Perhaps the most interesting feature of Hughes's poetry was his innovative style. Throughout his literary career he experimented with adapting black musical forms to his work. It is not particularly surprising, given his commitment to the black masses, that he would use their art form, music, in his poetry. Beginning with *The Weary Blues* he experimented with blues, jazz, and folk forms in his writing. As a result, he emerged as one of the few truly innovative writers to come out of the Harlem Renaissance, and in the process he uncovered a poetic style that was adaptable to a variety of circumstances. The blues form, for example, with its repetitive reinforcement, was a very effective technique to impart a subtle sense of suffering and despondency:

When I was home de
Sunshine seemed like gold.
When I was home de
Sunshine seemed like gold.
Since I came up North de
Whole damn world's turned cold.

(pp. 64-5)

Hughes used jazz rhythms and the tempo of black work music to achieve different effects. In **"Brass Spittoons,"** for example, work rhythms set the pace of the poem and captured the feeling of menial, methodical labor. In jazz he found a particularly fertile area for experimentation. Early in his career he observed that "jazz . . . is one of the inherent expressions of Negro life in America: the eternal tom-tom beating in the Negro soul—the tom-tom of revolt against weariness in a white world, a world of subway trains, and work, work, work; the tom-tom of joy and laughter, and pain swallowed in a smile." Hughes took this music with its choppy, breathless, almost chaotic tempo and recreated the bustling rhythms of city life and the boisterous atmosphere of the ghetto at night. An early example of this technique appeared in **"Lenox Avenue: Midnight"**:

The rhythm of life
Is a jazz rhythm,
Honey.

The gods are laughing at us.

The broken heart of love
The weary, weary heart of pain—
Overtones,
Undertones,
To the rumble of street cars,
To the swish of rain.

Lenox Avenue,
Honey.
Midnight,
And the gods are laughing at us.

This was not one of Hughes's better pieces, but it demonstrated the possibilities of applying jazz structures in poetry about urban life. He refined this technique in his post-Renaissance poetry and applied it most successfully in his Harlem epic, *Montage of a Dream Deferred,* where he used jazz models to capture the full essence of Harlem life. (p. 66)

Here he examined the black metropolis that had become a slum, and concluded with the question:

What happens to a dream deferred?

Does it dry up
like a raisin in the sun?
Or fester like a sore—
And then run?

Does it stink like rotten meat?

Or crust and sugar over—
like a syrupy sweet?

Maybe it just sags
like a heavy load.

Or does it explode?

Hughes's poetry also shifted to the left during the 1930's. Although he always had been concerned with the problems of blacks and of the poor, during the depression years he moved closer to Communism in his personal beliefs, and his poetry became angrier and more inclined toward propaganda. Unfortunately, as Hughes became more political, the quality of his work declined.

In spite of his various shortcomings Missouri-born, Kansas-raised Langston Hughes was one of the most successful writers of the Harlem Renaissance. He was, for example, the only one who supported himself entirely through the income of his writing. Also, his literary career, which stretched into the 1960's, lasted long after his Renaissance colleagues had become silent. In fact, Hughes continued to write until his death in 1967. Finally, Hughes was the best known of all the Renaissance writers. For many who had never heard of the Harlem Renaissance, Hughes was the premier Negro poet in America. (pp. 68-9)

> *Cary D. Wintz, "Langston Hughes: A Kansas Poet in the Harlem Renaissance," in* Kansas Quarterly, *Vol. 7, No. 3, Summer, 1975, pp. 58-69.*

Walter C. Farrell, Jr. and Patricia A. Johnson (essay date 1981)

[*Farrell and Johnson examine Hughes's fusion of jazz rhythms and social protest in delineating "the unrest and anxiety" of post-World War II Black America.*]

During the early 1940s, a revolutionary new movement in black music was underway that would change the shape and direction of jazz history for an entire decade. Bebop, as the new music was called, was first introduced to the public at Minton's Playhouse, a small nightclub on 52nd Street in Harlem. In the late hours of the night, a group of avant garde black musicians would gather at this unpretentious location to perform their history-making new sounds. Charlie Parker and Dizzy Gillespie are listed by most jazz historians as the chief innovators of this new style of music. (p. 57)

The bebop revolution grew out of a period that brought America out of the depression and into another world war. Black Americans fought valiantly in that war, only to discover that heroism could not save them from racial injustice. Under threat of a massive march on Washington, war-time industry opened its doors to prospective black employees. But once the war was over, massive unemployment once again became a redefining characteristic of black life.

The "bebop era" was also one of unrest, anxiety, and massive discontent in the urban ghetto. Harlem, for example, was the scene of a bloody race riot in 1943. The just indignation of Afro-American people had finally surfaced in the form of massive violence. But the injustice of racism and poverty was only compounded by the injustices of police brutality. Black urban workers found themselves not only trapped in the ghetto but pinned beneath the heel of police repression as well.

Langston Hughes was among the few black intellectuals of this era to sympathize with justly aggrieved poor people in Harlem. In a 1944 edition of *Negro Digest,* he denounced the snobbery of "Sugar Hill" Negroes who viewed the riot as a deterrent to "Negro advancement." Examining the economic determinants of the disturbance, Hughes compared the lifestyles of Harlem's well-to-do Negroes with that of her working poor. . . . (pp. 58-9)

Hughes's poetic commentary on the unrest and anxiety of post-war Black America was presented in a collection published in 1951 entitled *Montage of a Dream Deferred.* In a prefatory note, Hughes explains that his poems were designed to reflect the mood and tempo of bebop. As Hughes puts it:

> In terms of current Afro-American popular music and the sources from which it has progressed— jazz, ragtime, swing, blues, boogie-woogie, and bebop—this poem on contemporary Harlem, like be-bop, is marked by conflicting changes, sudden nuances, sharp and impudent interjections, broken rhythms, and passages sometimes in the manner of the jam session, sometimes the popular song, punctuated by the riffs, runs, breaks, and distortions of the music of a community in transition.

When *Montage* was published, Hughes regarded bebop as a new type of jazz music that drew its strength and substance from a composite vernacular of black musical forms. In conjunction with this notion Hughes incorporated a variety of music-related poems into this collection. The blues form, for example, appears with slight variations in a poem entitled **"Blues at Dawn"**:

> I don't dare start thinking in the morning.
> I don't dare start thinking in the morning.
>   If I thought thoughts in bed,
>   Them thoughts would bust my head——
> So I don't dare start thinking in the morning.
> I don't dare remember in the morning
> Don't dare remember in the morning.
>   If I recall the day before,
>   I wouldn't get up no more—
> So I don't dare remember in the morning.

"Lady's Boogie" vibrates to the sassy rhythms of boogie-woogie:

> See that lady
> Dressed so fine?
> She ain't got boogie woogie
> On her mind——
>
> But if she was to listen
> I bet she'd hear,
> Way up in the treble
> The tingle of a tear.
>
> BE-BACH!
>
> (pp. 60-1)

In *Montage* Hughes took advantage of the structural characteristics of bebop by drastically reordering the traditional limitations imposed on the poem. By breaking down the barrier between the beginning of one poem and the end of another, Hughes created a new technique in poetry. Perhaps one could more accurately describe *Mon-*

tage as a series of short poems or phrases that contribute to the making of one long poem. Each poem maintains some individual identity as a separate unit while contributing to the composite poetic message. Movement between passages is achieved by thematic or topical congruency or by interior dialogue. **"What? So Soon"** and **"Comment Against the Lamp"**, two poems that appear in succession, provide an excellent example of the latter technique:

> WHAT? SO SOON!
>
> I believe my old lady's
> pregnant again!
>
> Fate must have
> some kind of trickeration
> to populate the
> cullud nation!
>
> COMMENT AGAINST LAMP POST
>
> YOU CALL IT FATE?
>
> (pp. 61-2)

Hughes developed a form of poetry writing which would allow him to compress a wide and complex range of images into one kaleidoscopic impression of life in Harlem during the 1940s. The fact that these images are historically accurate and the fact that they convey something of what it meant to be black in America during this crucial war-torn era are proofs of Hughes's profound understanding of the events and issues that have shaped the contemporary world.

The idea that America has perennially denied her black working masses the right to life, liberty and the pursuit of happiness is the concentric unifying theme of *Montage of a Dream Deferred.* In practical terms, these rights include access to adequate housing, a decent standard of living, and fair and profitable employment. Hughes had developed this theme earlier—on a much more general level— in a poem published in 1926 entitled **"A Dream Deferred."** In *Montage,* Hughes expanded the thematic substance of this poem and injected it with powerful social and political connotations.

Montage is divided topically into six main sections: "Boogie Segue to Bop," "Dig and Be Dug," "Early Bright," "Vice Versa to Bach," "Dream Deferred," and "Lenox Avenue Mural." Each section emphasizes a different aspect of life in Harlem—be it social, political, cultural, or economic—but without excluding any of these aspects.

"Boogie Segue to Bach," for instance, glorifies the fullness and richness of black culture, especially black music, through a cogent analysis of its social and political implications. **"Dream Boogie,"** the first poetic passage in this section, identifies a questionable rumbling in the rhythms of bebop and boogie woogie. And since music has always served as the "heartbeat" of the black community, that rumbling becomes symbolic of an underlying state of anxiety and unrest in the urban ghetto. . . . (pp. 62-3)

In a section entitled "Dig and be Dug" we catch glimpses of an introspective Harlem, a Harlem that exposes the exploiters of the people and simultaneously laughs at itself as the victim of exploitation. A poem entitled **"Movies,"** for example, focuses on the cynical laughter of Harlem movie fans who have been amused by studio-produced caricatures of black life:

> The Roosevelt, Renaissance, Gem, Alhambra
> Harlem laughing in all the wrong places
> at the crocodile art
> that you know
> in your heart
> is crocodile:
>
> > (Hollywood
> > laughs at me,
> > black——
> > So I laugh
> > back).
>
> (p. 66)

"Dig and be Dug" examines a Harlem that is full of cynical self-awareness that is in tune to the political and social conditions that define its existence: there is a belligerent outcry against racist slumlords in **"Ballad of the Landlord,"** the cruel survival value of the black poor's faith in the numbers' racket in **"Numbers,"** a day-to-day awareness of the invigorating effects of war on the American economy in **"Green Memory"**; all these images combine to create a portrait of a Harlem that knows and sees itself as being a part of the larger world scheme, a Harlem that is aware of its strengths and weaknesses. Perhaps the overall theme of this section is best expressed in a poem entitled **"Motto"**:

> I play it cool
> And dig all jive
> That's the reason
> I stay alive.
>
> My motto,
> As I live and learn
>   is:
> DIG AND BE DUG
> IN RETURN

"Vice Versa to Bach" is an interesting section because it reveals Hughes's sensitivity to the development of class differentiations among black people. There is one group that is socially mobile, that moves "to the outskirts of town" and then seeks to sever itself from the inner city ghetto and all it stands for. Then there is the other group—the vast majority—that finds itself hopelessly trapped in poverty. In a set of poems entitled **"High to Low"** and **"Low to High"**, the socially mobile and socially stagnant groups engage in open dialogue. The low accuse the high Negroes of denying their blackness by snubbing their racial kinsmen of the ghetto. . . . The high accuses the low of what might comically be referred to as "conspicuous Negritude." . . . Alain Locke has pointed out that a tendency to deny racial heritage, and a pathological aping of things white are characteristic of the bourgeois segment of any oppressed minority group. The class attitudes revealed in these poems lend credence to Locke's observations. Taken together, these two poems offer an artistically profound analysis of the dynamics of class contradictions among black people.

Some of the poems in *Montage* are significant for the insight they provide into the nuances of urban living after the second World War. The war brought about a second wave of mass migration and placed an even greater number of black people under the onus of ghetto life. Upon their arrival to the urban north, blacks were housed in poorly kept run-down tenement buildings and charged exorbitant rental fees for the privilege of staying there. Hence the landlord-tenant conflict has become a recurrent feature of ghetto life. In **"Ballad of the Landlord"** a justly aggrieved black tenant refuses to pay his rent until the leaking roof and run-down stairway of his ghetto tenement are repaired. . . . (pp. 67-8)

A poignant reminder of the fact that blacks are usually the last hired and the first fired is found in a poem entitled **"Relief."** Following the end of World War II, jobs once again became scarce, and blacks of the urban north were the first to feel the pinch of an unstable peacetime economy. In this poem, a Harlemite hopes that a third world war will come along to bail him out of his impoverishment. . . . (p. 69)

The inhuman and demoralizing conditions of ghetto life caused some black people—especially the young—to turn to drugs as a means of escape. During the forties, drug abuse was not the national problem it is today, for frustrated blacks of the urban north were then the major constituents of the drug market. Drug addiction was most noticeable among bebop musicians who expressed their disenchantment with urban life and American society by assuming a posture of "cool" defiance. . . .

Hughes was aware of the widespread use of drugs among black musicians of the forties. A poem entitled **"Flatted Fifth,"** for example, gives the reader an inside view of the musician's "high" by showing how narcotics have drastically transformed the user's perception of objects around him. . . . The "frantic cullud boys" that participate in this ritual wear the characteristic beard and beret of the bebop musician. . . . (p. 70)

A short poem entitled **"Bebop Boys"** points to another aspect of the bebop movement, the conversion of many musicians to Islam. Despite the alteration of their religious convictions, the musicians' prayers seemed to remain the same. Here the reader is once again reminded of the link between art and economics.

> Imploring Mecca
> to achieve
> six decks
> with Decca.

Beneath their cool detached facade, their unconventional religious affiliations, and eccentric wearing apparel, the bebop generation was haunted by the prevailing national and international disorders of the day. And since this era began with World War II and ended with the Korean War, it comes as no surprise that many beboppers were draft dodgers as well:

> Little cullud boys
>   with fears,
>   frantic,
> Nudge their draftee years.
>   PO A DA!

Arthur P. Davis's description of the images of Harlem reflected in *Montage of a Dream Deferred* adequately expresses our ideas on this subject. Davis observed that the Harlem depicted in *Montage* had

> . . . come through World War II, but [had] discovered that a global victory for democracy [did] not necessarily have too much pertinence at home. Al-

though the Harlem of the 1948-1951 period [had] far more opportunity than the 1926 Harlem ever dreamed of, it [was] still not free; and the modern city having caught the vision of total freedom and total integration would not be satisfied with anything less than the idea. It [was] therefore a critical, a demanding, a sensitive, and utterly cynical city" [see excerpt dated 1952].

That cynicism was part of the overall feeling of disenchantment, of frustration, bewilderment and despair that informed the music—the very life impulse—of postwar urban life in America, as Langston Hughes knew. (pp. 71-2)

> Walter C. Farrell, Jr. and Patricia A. Johnson, "Poetic Interpretations of Urban Black Folk Culture: Langston Hughes and the 'Bebop' Era," in MELUS, Vol. 8, No. 3, Fall, 1981, pp. 57-72.

Arnold Rampersad   (essay date 1986)

[*An American educator and writer, Rampersad is the author of the two-volume study* The Life of Langston Hughes, *(1986, 1988), considered by many critics the definitive biography of Hughes. In the following excerpt, Rampersad analyzes* Fine Clothes to the Jew *and concludes that the collection "marked the height of [Hughes's] creative originality as a poet."*]

As prolific as Langston Hughes strove to be in a variety of genres—poetry, fiction, drama, and essays notably—he saw himself from first to last primarily as a poet. Of his many collections of verse, nine must be considered major in his career by almost any accounting: *The Weary Blues* (1926); *Fine Clothes to the Jew* (1927); *Shakespeare in Harlem* (1942); *Fields of Wonder* (1947); *One-Way Ticket* (1949); *Montage of a Dream Deferred* (1951); *Ask Your Mama* (1961); and *The Panther and the Lash* (posthumously in 1967, the year of his death). To these efforts might be added the volume published by the leftist International Workers Order, *A New Song* (1938); although it contained no new poems, the verse in that slender pamphlet was unusually radical and had not been collected previously.

Of these volumes, the least successful both in terms of sales and of critical reception, at least among black reviewers, was unquestionably *Fine Clothes to the Jew.* I would like to argue that, paradoxically, this volume was by far Hughes's greatest collection of verse, that the collection marked the height of his creative originality as a poet, and that it remains one of the most significant single volumes of poetry ever published in the United States. In fact, despite its failure to gain recognition, *Fine Clothes to the Jew* may stand in relationship to black American poetry in a way not unlike Walt Whitman's 1855 edition of *Leaves of Grass* stands in relationship to white American poetry, or to the poetry of the nation as a whole.

Fine Clothes to the Jew appeared almost ten years after Hughes first began to write poetry. While his work in Lincoln, Illinois (where by his own account he wrote his first poem, in 1916), is lost, almost all of his poems written in high school in Cleveland and thereafter are available to scholars. They may be found in the *Central High School Monthly, Crisis, Opportunity,* and other magazines published largely by blacks, as well as in white magazines that cover the broad ideological spectrum from *Vanity Fair,* on one hand, to the communist *New Masses,* on the other. The work of these first years culminated in the appearance from Knopf of Hughes's first book of any kind, *The Weary Blues. Fine Clothes to the Jew,* the next, built on elements found in the previous volume and in the magazines, but with such emphases and revisions that it marked, in effect, an unparalleled rethinking by Hughes about poetry in the context of black America.

Once Hughes shed his most youthful approaches to poetry and felt the stirring influence of Walt Whitman, whose lines he echoed unmistakably in his first published free verse poem, **"A Song of the Soul of Central"** (*Central High School Monthly,* January 1919) and Carl Sandburg ("my guiding star"), his poetry fell almost inevitably into three distinct areas. The first area found Hughes dwelling on isolation, despair, suicide, and the like—conventional themes for a young, romantic poet, to be sure, but notions strongly felt by Hughes personally as he struggled to overcome the effects of his father's desertion and his mother's flighty compromise of her relationship with her son. . . . The second area, also present virtually from the start of Hughes's career as a poet and fiction writer, reveals an aggressive socialist, non-racial intelligence, as for example in the very titles of two poems written later, in 1932: **"Good Morning Revolution"** and **"Goodbye Christ."** The third area, for which Hughes is almost certainly best known, finds him creating in direct response to the needs of black people—epitomized by **"The Negro Speaks of Rivers,"** published in 1921. (pp. 144-45)

Fine Clothes to the Jew falls outside of these categories. Although all of the poems in the various categories naturally involve a poetic concern with the manipulation of form, *Fine Clothes to the Jew* is based in essence on what one might acknowledge as a separate aesthetic, a different approach to poetic art. In the other work, Hughes writes—in spite of his concern with race—as a poet impelled by the literary tradition as defined by certain major poets of the language—in particular, Walt Whitman and his epigones, notably Carl Sandburg and Vachel Lindsay. But in *Fine Clothes* Hughes attempted to work in a way no black or white poet had ever attempted to work: deliberately defining poetic tradition according to the standards of a group often seen as sub-poetic—the black masses. (p. 145)

While *The Weary Blues* was in press and in the months following its appearance, Hughes went through certain experiences that revolutionized his aesthetic. First was his sojourn . . . among the black poor in Washington. Second was his entry into black Lincon University a few days after *The Weary Blues* appeared, when for the first time since he was nine or ten, Hughes went to school with a majority of blacks (and all male)—an experience of incalculable effect on his sense of race. Third was the impact of the brilliant circle of young stars—the key members of the Harlem Renaissance—in Harlem at the same time: Aaron Douglass, Arna Bontemps, Wallace Thurman, Bruce Nugent, and Zora Neale Hurston, for whom Hughes's *Nation* essay of June 1926, "The Negro Artist and the Racial Mountain," [see *Author's Commentary* above] was manifesto; to these should be added the names of musicians

Hall Johnson, Paul Robeson, Clarence Cameron White, and W. C. Handy (often called the father of the blues), with whom Hughes either worked or consulted in the summer of 1926, especially in connection with a musical, to star Robeson, called "O Blues!" (from **"The Weary Blues"**). The fourth experience was the reaction of the black press to Carl Van Vechten's Harlem novel, *Nigger Heaven,* and to the appearance of *Fire!!* magazine.

The younger writers in general enthusiastically approved of *Nigger Heaven* ("Colored people can't help but like it," Hughes had predicted; the novel read as if it were written by "an N.A.A.C.P. official or Jessie Fauset. But it's good"). To almost all the young black writers, Van Vechten's troubles were their own. The attack on him was an attack on what they themselves, or most of them, stood for—artistic and sexual freedom, a love of the black masses, a refusal to idealize black life, and a revolt against bourgeois hypocrisy. They decided to publish their own magizine, instead of relying on the staid *Crisis* and the like. For their pains, *Fire!!* received a withering reception in the black press. "I have just tossed the first issue of *Fire* into the fire," the reviewer in the *Baltimore Afro-American* fumed; Aaron Douglass had ruined "three perfectly good pages and a cover" with his drawings, while Langston Hughes displayed "his usual ability to say nothing in many words."

These experiences prompted Hughes to go where no poet had gone before; in the summer of 1926 he wrote poems that differed sharply from the spirit of **The Weary Blues** and that contested the right of the middle class to criticize the mores and manners of the black masses. (The rebellious campaign continued into the fall, when Hughes wrote his first short stories since high school, the "West Illana" sequence of stories set on a ship much like the one on which he had sailed to Africa in 1923. Hughes's fiction navigated more sensual waters than ever before; whatever their limitations as art, the stories that resulted steam suggestively of miscegenation, adultery, promiscuity, and the turmoil of sexual repression—subjects all taboo to the critics who hated *Fire!!.*) During the summer he wrote almost feverishly; back in Lincoln for the fall term, he soon gathered his new poems into what he hoped would be his second book.

On Sunday, October 3, he visited New York and delivered the manuscript to Carl Van Vechten, to whom the collection was dedicated. As with Hughes's first book, they went over each of the poems; exactly what part Van Vechten played now is unclear. Three weeks later, Langston presented the revised collection to him to take to Knopf. By this time it had a name: "Fine Clothes to the Jew," after a line from Hughes's **"Hard Luck"**:

> When hard luck overtakes you
> Nothin' for you to do
> Gather up yo' fine clothes
> An' sell 'em to de Jew . . .

Knopf accepted "Fine Clothes to the Jew," but not without balking at the title (the firm had published *Nigger Heaven* apparently without difficulty). After Van Vechten personally defended the name, as he recorded in his journal, it was allowed to stand. Van Vechten perhaps had also chosen it, as he had chosen "The Weary Blues." Certainly, Hughes had been thinking of using "Brass Spitoons,"

from one of his poems. The choice was unfortunate. Apparently no one alerted Hughes to the effect his title would have on sales, which proved to be opposite to the result of Van Vechten's own crudeness. But he later regarded the title as one of the main reasons for the failure of the book: it was "a bad title, because it was confusing and many Jewish people did not like it."

By mid-January, 1927, Hughes had copies of **Fine Clothes to the Jew.** The first reports were encouraging. Far from objecting to the title, his friend and supporter, Amy Spingarn, liked the book even more than **The Weary Blues,** because it seemed "more out of the core of life." Her brother-in-law, Arthur Spingarn, who was also Jewish, noted the title but found the book a "splendid" work, in which "Jacob and the Negro come into their own." The black conservative George Schuyler praised Hughes as "the poet of the modern Negro proletariat." But after the attacks on *Nigger Heaven* and *Fire!!,* Hughes was nervous. "It's harder and more cynical," he explained defensively to Dewey Jones of the Chicago *Defender,* and "limited to an interpretation of the 'lower classes,' the ones to whom life is least kind. I try to catch the hurt of their lives, the monotony of their 'jobs,' and the veiled weariness of their songs. They are the people I know best."

On February 5, just as he prepared to set out on a tour for Negro History Week, the black critics opened fire. Under a headline proclaiming Hughes a "SEWER DWELLER," William M. Kelley of the New York *Amsterdam News,* denounced **Fine Clothes to the Jew** as "about 100 pages of trash. . . . It reeks of the gutter and sewer." The regular reviewer of the *Philadelphia Tribune* adamantly refused to publicize it; Eustance Gay confessed that **Fine Clothes to the Jew** "disgusts me." In the *Pittsburgh Courier,* historian J. A. Rogers called it "piffling trash" that left him "positively sick." The Chicago *Whip* sneered at the dedication to Van Vechten, "a literary gutter-tat" who perhaps alone "will revel in the lecherous, lust-reeking characters that Hughes finds time to poeticize about. . . . These poems are unsanitary, insipid and repulsing." Hughes was the "poet 'low-rate' of Harlem." The following week, refining its position, the *Tribune* lamented Hughes's "obsession for the more degenerate elements" of black life; the book was "a study in the perversions of the Negro." It is questionable whether any book of American poetry, other than *Leaves of Grass,* had ever been greeted so contemptuously.

To these and other black critics, Hughes had allowed the "secret" shame of their culture, especially its apparently unspeakable or unprintable sexual mores, to be bruited by thick-lipped black whores and roustabouts. How could he have dared to publish **"Red Silk Stockings"**?

> Put on yo' red silk stockings,
> Black gal.
> Go out an' let de white boys
> Look at yo' legs.
>
> Ain't nothin' to do for you, nohow,
> Round this town,—
> You's too pretty.
> Put on yo' red silk stockings, gal,
> An' tomorrow's chile'll
> Be a high yaller.
> Go out an' let de white boys
> Look at yo' legs.

Or **"Beale Street Love"**?

Love
Is a brown man's fist
With hard knuckles
Crushing the lips,
Blackening the eyes,—
Hit me again
Says Clorinda.

By pandering to the taste of whites for the sensational (the critics ignored their own sensationalism, demonstrable in the scandal-ridden sheets of most black weeklies), Hughes had betrayed his race.

In spite of this hostility, *Fine Clothes to the Jew* marked Hughes's maturity as a poet after a decade of writing, and his most radical achievement in language. While *The Weary Blues* had opened with references to the blues and poems written in dialect, before presenting the sweeter, more traditional lyrics, a prefatory note ("the mood of the *Blues* is almost always despondency, but when they are sung people laugh") now indicated the far greater extent to which *Fine Clothes to the Jew* falls deliberately within the range of authentic blues emotion and blues culture. Gone are the conventional lyrics about nature and loneliness, or poems in which the experience of the common black folk is framed by conventional poetic language and a superior, sometimes ironic poetic diction. Here few poems are beyond range of utterance of common black folk, except in so far as any formal poetry by definition belongs to a more privileged world. *Fine Clothes to the Jew* was the perfect companion piece to Hughes's manifesto, "The Negro Artist and the Racial Mountain."

As a measure of his deeper penetration of the culture and his increased confidence as a poet, three kinds of poems are barely present in *Fine Clothes to the Jew*—those that praise black people and culture directly, those that directly protest their condition, and those that reflect his own personal sense of desolation. For example: **"Laughters,"** which celebrates blacks as "Loud laughers in the hands of Fate," is also probably the earliest piece in the book, having been published first as **"My People"** in June, 1922. **"Mulatto"** lodges perhaps the strongest protest, but is staged dramatically:

. . . The Southern night is full of stars,
Great big yellow stars.
  O, sweet as earth,
  Dusk dark bodies
  Give sweet birth
To little yellow bastard boys.

  Git on back there in the night.
  You aint white.

The bright stars scatter everywhere.
Pine wood scent in the evening air.
  A nigger night,
  A nigger joy.

I am your son, white man!

  A little yellow
  Bastard boy.

Only one poem, **"Sport,"** proposes life as an empty nothingness—as "the shivering of a great drum / Beaten with swift sticks."

Sorrow and despair dominate *Fine Clothes to the Jew,* but mainly through the expressive medium of the blues and its place in the lives of poor black men and women. In **"Hey!"** the blues is mysterious: "I feels de blues a comin', / Wonder what de blues'll bring?" It is also, as in **"Misery,"** soothing, or even cathartic. . . . (pp. 149-52)

In *Fine Clothes to the Jew,* the singers and mourners are mainly women. By comparison, men are almost shallow; one man (**"Bad Man"**) beats his wife and "ma side gal too": "Don't know why I do it but / It keeps me from feelin' blue." Men may be hurt in love, like the fellow in **"Po' Boy Blues"** who met "a gal I thought was kind. / She made me lose ma money / An' almost lose ma mind." But the blues are sung most often, and most brilliantly, by black women. Sometimes they sing to warn their sisters (**"Listen Here Blues"**). . . . Women lament being cheated, for having been done wrong by "a yellow papa," who "took ma last thin dime" (**"Gypsy Man"**); or, as in **"Hard Daddy,"** they grieve over male coldness:

I cried on his shoulder but
He turned his back on me.
Cried on his shoulder but
He turned his back on me.
He said a woman's cryin's
Never gonna bother me.

But the blues can reflect great joy as well as sorrow, as in **"Ma Man,"** where a black woman's emotional and sexual ecstasy is so overpowering it drives her into song. . . . The last stanza of this poem, the second to last in the book (as if Hughes tried to hide it), was among the most sexually teasing in American poetry—to those who understood that "eagle-rocking" was possibly more than a popular dance step. (pp. 153-55)

When the *Pittsburgh Courier* invited Hughes to defend himself against his critics, he did not hesitate. In "These Bad New Negros: A Critique on Critics," he identified four reasons for the attacks: the low self-esteem of the "best" blacks; their obsession with white opinion; their *nouveau riche* snobbery; and their lack of artistic and cultural training "from which to view either their own or the white man's books or pictures." As for the "ill-mannered onslaught" on Van Vechten: the man's "sincere, friendly, and helpful interest in things Negro" should have brought "serious, rather than vulgar, reviews of his book." A nine-point defense of his own views and practices ended in praise of the young writers, including Toomer, Fisher, Thurman, Cullen, Hurston, and the Lincoln poet Edward Silvera. And Hughes himself: "My poems are indelicate. But so is life," he pointed out. He wrote about "harlots and gin-bibers. But they are human. Solomon, Homer, Shakespeare, and Walt Whitman were not afraid or ashamed to include them." (Van Vechten thought the situation easy to explain; "you and I," he joked to Hughes while making an important distinction, "are the only colored people who really love *niggers.*"

Hughes was not without friends in the black press. The *New York Age* found the book evocative of the joy and pathos, beauty and ugliness of black Americans, if of the more primitive type. The poet Alice Dunbar-Nelson, once married to Paul Laurence Dunbar, compared the book to Wordsworth and Coleridge's once maligned yet celebrated venture, *Lyrical Ballads,* which used the lives and speech of the common people; Hughes was "a rare poet." Theophilus Lewis praised the book in the *Messenger,* and in the *Saturday Review of Literature* Alain Locke was deft about *Fine Clothes to the Jew:* "Its open frankness will be a shock and a snare for the critic and moralist who cannot distinguish clay from mire" [see Locke's excerpt dated 1927]. And Claude McKay wrote privately to congratulate Hughes on having written a book superior to his first.

Among white reviewers, perhaps the most perceptive evaluation came from the young cultural historian Howard Mumford Jones [in The *Chicago Daily News*]. Using black dialect austerely, Hughes had scraped the blues form down to the bone, and raised the folk form to literary art. "In a sense," Jones concluded, "He has contributed a really new verse form to the English language." Although, like Wordsworth, he sometimes lapsed into "vapid simplicity." But if Hughes continued to grow, he was "dangerously near becoming a major American poet." (pp. 155-56)

The ignorant blasts of the black press were nicely offset when Hughes accepted an invitation ("a great honor for me") from the Walt Whitman foundation to speak at the poet's home on Mickle Street in Camden, New Jersey. Stressing Whitman's humane depictions of blacks in his poetry, Hughes when on to claim that modern free verse, and his own work, descended from Whitman's great example. "I believe," Langston told the little gathering, "that poetry should be direct, comprehensible and the epitome of simplicity." Suspicious of theory, Hughes had nevertheless identified one of the main ideas behind his theory of composition—the notion of an aesthetic of simplicity, sanctioned finally by democratic culture but having a discipline and standards just as the baroque or the rococo, for example, had their own. That simplicity had its dangers both extended its challenge and increased its rewards. The visit to Whitman's home left Hughes elated; to Van Vechten he mailed a postcard imprinted with an excerpt from Whitman's "Song of the Open Road": "All seems beautiful to me."

Although Hughes would place the emphasis in his poetry in a different direction in the 1930s, when he wrote his most politically radical verse, he continued to write the blues even during this period. After the Depression, when Knopf published his *Shakespeare in Harlem,* the blues dominated the volume. When in the late 1940s and 1950s he allowed first be-bop (as in *Montage of a Dream Deferred*) and then increasingly "progressive" jazz (as in *Ask Your Mama*) also to shape his poetry, he was applying a basic principle he had first learned in the context of the blues. He never abandoned the form, because the blues continued as perhaps the most fertile form of black expressivity; *Ask Your Mama,* for example, is explicitly based on the "Hesitation Blues."

His initiative in the blues remains the only genuinely original achievement in form by any black American poet—notwithstanding the excellence of much of the work of writers such as Countee Cullen, Melvin Tolson, Gwendolyn Brooks, Robert Hayden, and even the rebel Amiri Baraka (surely the greatest names in modern black poetry). Their art is largely derivative by comparison. Afro-American poets did not rush to build on Hughes's foundation; most remained black poets who wished to be known simply as poets. But some poets followed the lead. Sterling Brown's *Southern Roads,* the most distinguished book of verse by an Afro-American in the 1930s, was certainly indebted to Hughes. . . . Richard Wright, initially a poet,

tried to write the blues, and even published one poem in collaboration with Hughes. Among whites, Elizabeth Bishop tried her hand at the form, with results certainly no worse than Wright's—the blues, they learned, is not as simple as it seems.

Black poetry, however, had to wait until the late 1960s and 1970s, with the emergence of writers such as Sherley Anne Williams, Michael S. Harper, and Raymond Patterson, to capitalize fully on Hughes's historic achievement. Ironically, because of the obscurity in which *Fine Clothes to the Jew* remains, and because the full extent of Hughes's artistic revolution has not been appreciated, many young black poets are unaware of the history of the form that they nevertheless understand as providing the only indisputably honorable link between their literary and cultural ambitions as blacks and the language compelled on them by history. (pp. 156-57)

> *Arnold Rampersad, "Langston Hughes's 'Fine Clothes to the Jew',"* in Callaloo, *Vol. 9, No. 1, Winter, 1986, pp. 144-58.*

FURTHER READING

Ako, Edward O. "Langston Hughes and the Négritude Movement: A Study in Literary Influences." *CLA Journal* XXVIII, No. 1 (September 1984): 46-56.
  Discusses Hughes's influence in the works of Francophone poets Léopold Sédar Senghor, Leon Damas, and Aime Césaire.

Arvey, Verna. "Langston Hughes: Crusader." *Opportunity* XVIII, No. 12 (December 1940): 363-64.
  Brief laudatory tribute to Hughes.

Barksdale, Richard K. *Langston Hughes: The Poet and His Critics.* Chicago: American Library Association, 1977, 155p.
  Surveys the critical reception of Hughes's works throughout his career.

Bontemps, Arna. "Langston Hughes: He Spoke of Rivers." *Freedomways* 8, No. 2 (Second Quarter 1968): 140-43.
  Brief account of the author's first meeting with Hughes during the Harlem Renaissance.

Brooks, Gwendolyn. "Langston Hughes." *The Nation* 205, No. 1 (3 July 1967): 7.
  Tribute to Hughes shortly after his death.

Davis, Arthur P. "The Tragic Mulatto Theme in Six Works of Langston Hughes." *Phylon* XVI, No. 2 (Second Quarter 1955): 195-204.
  Analyzes Hughes's portrayal of racially-mixed individuals in his poetry, short fiction, and drama.

Emanuel, James A. *Langston Hughes.* New Haven, Conn.: College and University Press, 1967, 192p.
  Literary biography of Hughes.

———. "Christ in Alabama: Religion in the Poetry of Langston Hughes." In *Modern Black Poets: A Collection of Critical Essays.* Edited by Donald B. Gibson, pp. 57-68. Englewood Cliffs, N.J.: Prentice-Hall, Inc., 1973.

Examines Hughes's use of Christian doctrine in the poems "Brass Spitoons," "Negro Mother," and "Christ in Alabama." Contends that "Hughes writes with most emotional strength and aptness of form when he records cynicism about religion in America, compares Black experience with the fate of Christ, or writes the religious impulse with his race's determination to survive."

Embree, Edwin R. "Langston Hughes: Shakespeare in Harlem." In his *13 Against the Odds,* pp. 117-38. New York: The Viking Press, 1944.
    Biographical-critical study, covering Hughes's life up to the publication of *Shakespeare in Harlem.*

Farrison, W. Edward. "Langston Hughes: Poet of the Negro Renaissance." *CLA Journal* XV, No. 4 (June 1972): 401-10.
    Overview of Hughes's career, emphasizing his prominent role in the Harlem Renaissance.

Fauset, Jessie. Review of *The Weary Blues* by Langston Hughes. *The Crisis* 31, No. 5 (March 1926): 239.
    Brief critical assessment of Hughes's first collection of poetry with references to the poet's early work submitted to *The Crisis* for publication.

Hughes, Langston. "My Adventures as a Social Poet." *Phylon* VIII, No. (Third Quarter 1947): 205-12.
    A brief account of Hughes's experiences with censorship and public protest over his poetry.

Jemie, Onwuchekwa. *Langston Hughes: An Introduction to the Poetry.* New York: Columbia University Press, 1973, 234p.
    Critical survey.

Johnson, Lemuel A. "Langston Hughes and United States Negro Folklore." In his *The Devil, the Gargoyle, and the Buffoon,* pp. 107-35. Port Washington, N.Y.: National University Publications, Kennikat Press, 1969.
    Explores Hughes's blues motif in *The Weary Blues.*

Kramer, Aaron. "Robert Burns and Langston Hughes." *Freedomways* 8, No. 2 (Spring 1968): 159-66.
    Discusses the similarities and differences in the poetry of Robert Burns and Hughes, stressing in particular their affinities with the working class.

Martin, Dellita L. "The 'Madam Poems' as Dramatic Monologue." *Black American Literature Forum* 15, No. 3 (Fall 1981): 97-9.
    Appreciative essay on Hughes's verse revolving around Alberta K. Johnson, who "encompasses the heroic, comic, and tragic dimensions immortalized by Hughes' dramatic presentation of archetypal woman."

Rampersad, Arnold. "The Origins of Poetry in Langston Hughes." *The Southern Review* 21, No. 3 (Summer 1985): 695-705.
    Contends that many of Hughes's poems evolved from several traumatic incidents in his early adulthood.

——. *The Life of Langston Hughes: I, Too, Sing America, Volume I, 1902-1941.* New York: Oxford University Press, 1986, 468p.
    Literary biography of Hughes up to the publication of his autobiography *The Big Sea.*

——. *The Life of Langston Hughes: I Dream a World, Volume II, 1941-1967.* New York: Oxford University Press, 1988, 512p.
    Continues discussion of Hughes's life and career.

Randall, Dudley. "The Black Aesthetic in the Thirties, Forties, and Fifties." In *The Black Aesthetic.* Edited by Addison Gayle, Jr., pp. 224-34. Garden City, N.Y.: Doubleday and Company, Inc., 1971.
    Examines black nationalism in Hughes's poetry and prose.

Redding, J. Saunders. *To Make a Poet Black.* Ithaca, N.Y.: Cornell University Press, 1988, 142p.
    Critical survey.

Taylor, Patricia A. "Langston Hughes and the Harlem Renaissance, 1921-1931: Major Events and Publications." In *The Harlem Renaissance Remembered.* Edited by Arna Bontemps, pp. 90-102. New York: Dodd, Mead, & Company, 1972.
    Brief social history of Harlem during the 1920s and its influence on Hughes's poetry.

John Keats

1795-1821

English poet and dramatist.

Keats is recognized as a major poet and, particularly, as a key figure in the English Romantic movement. The writers associated with this literary trend placed the individual at the core of all experience, valued imagination and beauty, and looked to nature for revelation of truth. Although his literary career spanned only four years, Keats achieved remarkable intellectual and artistic development. His poems, especially the later works published in *Lamia, Isabella, The Eve of St. Agnes, and Other Poems,* are praised not only for their sensuous imagery and passionate tone, but also for the insight they provide into aesthetic and human concerns, particularly the transiency of beauty and happiness. The artistic philosophy delineated in Keats's poetry in such famous words as those from the "Ode on a Grecian Urn"—"beauty is truth, truth beauty"—are clarified in his correspondence with his family and friends. In these letters it is possible to trace the evolution of Keats's poetic thought and technique as he matured and refined his ideas and beliefs regarding literature. In his correspondence, Keats set down poetic theories that have become standards of literary criticism, such as his theory of *Negative Capability*, "that is when man is capable of being in uncertainties, mysteries, doubts, without any irritable reaching after fact and reason." As Wolf Z. Hirst has noted: "Negative capability is the . . . quality to which Keats aspires throughout his creative life. Negative capability frees a thinking man from the weary weight of the unintelligible world by raising mystery to the province of the imagination, and it permits a poet to submerge his identity in that of others whenever he composes or meditates on poetry. Keats's repeated suppressions of self in his works reinforce a native susceptibility to new experience and a capacity for growth; whereas, in turn, his evolving soul is the best guarantee for his talent to forget his own self in the subject of a new poem."

Despite Keats's present high status, recognition of his genius was slow in coming. His fervent tone and sensual imagery appeared shockingly effusive to early nineteenth-century critics schooled in the more formal neoclassical poetics of the eighteenth century. In addition, Keats's early affiliation with Leigh Hunt, the liberal Whig poet and editor, inadvertently associated him with the so-called "Cockney School of Poetry" led by Hunt. This friendship incited conservative Tory reviewers to malign Keats's works, sometimes viciously. Thus, in spite of the efforts of a loyal group of supporters, Keats's poems were virtually unknown during his lifetime and for twenty years after his death. It was not until the mid-nineteenth century that his writings began to draw a significant readership and to attract serious critical consideration. By the turn of the century, Keats was widely acknowledged as a poet of the first rank; frequent comparisons between Keats and Shakespeare were made due to their similar poetic styles, subject matter, and use of sensuous imagery.

Scholars often note that Keats's childhood provides no

hint of the genius who was to emerge. The oldest of four children of a stable-keeper, he was raised in Moorfields, London. His father died from injuries sustained in a fall from a horse when Keats was seven. In 1803, Keats enrolled at the Clarke school in nearby Enfield, where he was distinguished only by his small stature (he was barely over five feet tall as an adult) and somewhat pugnacious disposition. At the Clarke school, Keats first encountered the works that influenced his early poetry, including Edmund Spenser's *The Faerie Queen* and Lemprière's *Classical Dictionary,* on which he based his knowledge of Greek mythology. The vivid imagery and the use of allegory and romance in Keats's poetry reflect the lasting impression made on the young poet by these works. Keats's mother died of tuberculosis in 1810, and the Keats children were placed in the care of a guardian, Richard Abbey. At fifteen, Keats was apprenticed to an apothecary; four years later he entered Guy's and St. Thomas's Hospitals in London, where he completed medical courses and in 1816 passed the examinations to become an apothecary. Keats had begun to compose poetry as early as 1812, however, and secretly decided to support himself on his small inheritance after graduation and devote himself to writing. In order to avoid a confrontation with his guardian, Keats continued his studies to become a surgeon, carefully concealing his decision from Abbey until he had reached the age of majority and was free of his guardian's jurisdiction.

Keats's meeting in 1816 with Leigh Hunt influenced his decision to pursue a career as a poet, and Hunt published Keats's early poems in his liberal journal, the *Examiner.* Keats was drawn readily into Hunt's circle, which included the poet John Hamilton Reynolds, the critic William Hazlitt, and the painter Benjamin Robert Haydon. *Poems,* an early collection, was published two years later, but received little attention. His next work, *Endymion: A Poetic Romance,* a full-length allegory based on Greek mythology, was published the following year to mixed reviews. Soon after the appearance of *Endymion,* Keats began to experience the first symptoms of tuberculosis, the disease that had killed his mother and in 1818 took his brother, Tom. Following Tom's death, Keats lived with his close friend Charles Armitage Brown in Hampstead. He continued writing and spent a considerable amount of time reading the works of William Wordsworth, John Milton, and Shakespeare. Here Keats also fell in love with Fanny Brawne, a neighbor's daughter. The rigors of work, poor health, and constant financial difficulties prevented the two from fulfilling their desire to be married. Keats's final publication, *Lamia, Isabella, The Eve of St. Agnes, and Other Poems,* included, in addition to the noted title poems, Keats's famous odes and *Hyperion: A Fragment,* an unfinished narrative based on Greek mythology that stylistically owed much to Milton's *Paradise Lost. The Fall of Hyperion* was a later, unsuccessful attempted completion and revision of *Hyperion.* This work remained unpublished until 1856. Other uncollected writings, including the humorous verse "Cap and Bells; or, The Jealousies" and Keats's final sonnet, "Bright Star," were first published in 1848 in *The Life, Letters, and Literary Remains of John Keats,* compiled in 1848 by Richard Monckton Milnes. In a final effort to regain his health, Keats sailed to Italy in September 1820; he died in Rome in February of the following year. He was buried there beneath a gravestone which bore an epitaph that he himself composed: "Here lies one whose name was writ on water."

The history of Keats's early reputation is dominated by two hostile, unsigned reviews of *Endymion,* one credited to John Gibson Lockhart in *Blackwood's Edinburgh Magazine* and the other to John Wilson Croker in the *Quarterly Review.* Lockhart, a vociferous detractor of what he termed "The Cockney School," named for its members's ties to London and their alleged lack of refinement, attacked not only Keats's poem, which he denigrated on artistic and moral grounds, but on what he perceived as the poet's lack of taste, education, and upbringing. While Croker was neither as vitriolic nor personally degrading as Lockhart—critics acknowledge, in fact, the legitimacy of several of his complaints—his essay was singled out as damaging and unjust by Keats's supporters, who rushed to the poet's defense. While Keats was apparently disturbed only temporarily by these attacks, the story circulated after his death that his demise had been caused, or at least hastened, by these two reviews. A chief perpetrator of this notion was Percy Bysshe Shelley, who composed and published his famous *Adonais: An Elegy on the Death of the Poet John Keats* shortly after Keats's death. The preface to this work implicated Croker as Keats's murderer. *Adonais,* in conjunction with the writings of Keats's well-meaning friends, effectively created a legend of the poet as a sickly and unnaturally delicate man so fragile that a magazine article was capable of killing him. Lord Byron commented wryly on this image of Keats in a famous couplet in his poem *Don Juan:* " 'Tis strange the mind, that very fiery particle / Should let itself be snuffed out by an article."

The *Adonais* image of Keats lent credence to the view that he was merely a poet of the senses, capable only of evoking pleasurable sensations, an assumption that dominated Keats scholarship for forty years after his death and lingered into the twentieth century. The critic responsible for initially establishing Keats as a poet of ideas worthy of serious critical consideration was Milnes, whose landmark biography, *Life, Letters, and Literary Remains of John Keats,* presented Keats's own letters and poems as evidence of his intellectual maturity and artistic worth. The 1880 publication of Matthew Arnold's essay identifying Keats as "standing with Shakespeare" marked the beginning of Keats's critical reputation as an intellectual poet. At the same time, however, such Pre-Raphaelite artists as William Morris, Dante Gabriel Rossetti, and William Holman Hunt sustained the old image of Keats by championing him as their artistic forebear because of his richly pictorial descriptions and lush imagery. Similarly, Arthur Symons admired Keats's poems for the "art for art's sake" quality they evinced. By the early twentieth century, however, such respected critics as Ernest de Selincourt, A. C. Bradley, and Robert Bridges had confirmed Keats's status as an intellectual as well as an emotive or pictorial poet, and full-length works by Clarence DeWitt Thorpe and John Middleton Murry, among others, echoed their beliefs. Contemporary critics continue to find much to explore in Keats's complex intellectual nuances as well as in the beauties of his poetic technique.

While early nineteenth-century critics focused on *Endymion* in their discussions of the poet of sensations, and later Victorian scholars often chose *Hyperion* as a subject of study, contemporary commentators frequently concentrate on the odes. Considered by many the most mature and highest expression of Keats's genius, the odes are also considered his most intellectually challenging works. The themes of the transience of beauty, the "eternal quality of art," and the desire to transcend the human world unite such poems as "Ode to a Nightingale," "Ode on a Grecian Urn," and "Ode on Melancholy." Contemporary critics often associate Keats's narrative poetry with his odes because of their similar maturity of expression. Miriam Allott writes that " 'The Eve of St. Agnes' . . . celebrates the warmth of a requited passion but, characteristically, cannot forget its attendant hazards or its vulnerability to time." She also claims that "La Belle Dame Sans Merci" presents this theme in a more decisive way: "the destructiveness of passion is expressed as keenly as its delight, the emotion is still more ambivalent and the presence of death yet more haunting." The approaches employed by twentieth-century critics in interpreting these works are varied, however, and encompass such subjects as Keats's affiliation with other artists, including Shelley and Wordsworth, and the writers who influenced his literary style, such as Spenser and Shakespeare. Also of interest are the evolution of Keats's aesthetic theory and his use of various poetic images, such as metamorphosis and biological and nature imagery.

While his provocative intellect and stunning artistic ability form the basis of Keats's reputation, critics acknowledge the fact that, to many, the poet himself is as compelling as his work. The astonishing use Keats made of his brief creative life continues to awe readers. But above all, the singlemindedness with which he pursued his goal of becoming a successful poet has won the sympathy and imaginations of his readers. As Douglas Bush wrote: "No other English poet of the century had his poetic endowment, and no other strove so intensely. . . . However high one's estimate of what he wrote, one may really think—to use an often meaningless cliche—that Keats was greater than his poems."

(For further information on Keats's life and career, see *Nineteenth-Century Literature Criticism*, Vol. 8.)

PRINCIPAL WORKS

POETRY

Poems   1817
Endymion: A Poetic Romance   1818
Lamia, Isabella, The Eve of St. Agnes, and Other Poems   1820
Life, Letters, and Literary Remains of John Keats   1848
Another Version of Keats's "Hyperion"   1856
The Complete Poetical Works and Letters of John Keats   1899

OTHER MAJOR WORKS

Letters of John Keats to Fanny Brawne   (letters)   1878
Letters of John Keats to His Family and Friends   (letters)   1891

Richard Woodhouse   (letter date 1818)

[*Woodhouse was an English literary critic. In the following excerpt from a letter to his cousin, Mary Frogley, that was not published until April 16, 1914, in* The Times Literary Supplement, *he praises the work of Keats and prophesies that the poet will reach a greatness that will only be recognized after his death.*]

I returned from Hounslow late last night, and your mother desired me to forward to you the enclosed letter. I brought **Endymion** back, thinking you might like to have it in Town whilst with your friends.

You were so flattering as to say the other day, you wished I had been in a company where you were, to defend Keats.—In all places, and at all times, and before all persons, I would express and as far as I am able, support, my high opinion of his poetical merits—such a genius, I verily believe, has not appeared since Shakespeare and Milton: and I may assert without fear of contradiction from any one competent to Judge, that if his **Endymion** be compared with Shakespeare's earliest work (his *Venus and Adonis*) written about the same age, Keats's poem will be found to contain more beauties, more poetry (and that of a higher order) less conceit and bad taste and in a word much more promise of excellence than are to be found in Shakespeare's work,—This is a deliberate opinion; nor is it merely my own. The justice of which, however, can only be demonstrated to another upon a full review of the parts and of the whole of each work. I should not shrink from the task of doing it to one whose candour I was acquainted with, and whose judgment I respected.

But in our common conversation upon his merits, we should always bear in mind that his fame may be more hurt by indiscriminate praise than by wholesale censure. I would at once admit that he has great faults—enough indeed to sink another writer. But they are more than counterbalanced by his beauties: and this is the proper mode of appreciating an original genius. His faulte will wear away—his fire will be chastened—and then eyes will do homage to his brilliancy. But genius is wayward, trembling, easily daunted. And shall we not excuse the errors, the luxuriancy of youth? Are we to expect that poets are to be given to the world, as our first parents were, in a state of maturity? Are they to have no season of childhood? are they to have no room to try their wings before the steadiness and strength of their flight are to be finally judged of ? So says Mr. Gifford of the *Quarterly*—But the world meted out a far different measure to his youthful Infirmities,—though he forgets it. So said the Edinburgh Reviewer of Lord Byron—So said the *Monthly* of Kirke White—So said Horace Walpole of Chatterton. And how are such critics now execrated for their cruel injustice.—I see the daily papers teem with remonstrances against Gifford's arbitrary decision. An appeal to the Country is lodged against it. Perhaps this age, certainly posterity,—will judge rightly—However the decision be, the competence of a poet to write, and of a critic to judge of poetry are involved in the dispute, and *one* reputation must suffer deeply. Had I any literary reputation I would stake it on the result. You know the side I should espouse As it is,—I can only prophecy. And now, while Keats is unknown, unheeded, despised of one of our arch-critics, neglected by the rest—in the teeth of the world, and in the face of "these curious days," I express my conviction, that Keats, during his life (if it please God to spare him to the usual age of man, and the critics not to drive him from the free air of the Poetic heaven before his Wings are fully fledged) will rank on a level with the best of the last or of the present generation: and after his death will take his place at their head. But, while I think thus, I would make persons respect my judgment by the discrimination of my praise, and by the freedom of my censure where his writings are open to it. These are the Elements of true criticism. It is easy, like Momus, to find fault with the clattering of the slipper worn by the Goddess of beauty; but "the serious Gods" found better employment in admiration of her unapproachable loveliness. A Poet ought to write for Posterity. But a critic should do so, too. Those of our times write for the day, or rather the hour. Their thoughts and Judgments are fashionable garbs, such as they imagine a skin-wise world would like to array itself in at second hand.

Richard Woodhouse, in a letter to Mary Frogley in Autumn, 1818, in The Times Literary Supplement, *No. 639, April 16, 1914, pp. 181-82.*

The Edinburgh Review (essay date 1820)

[*In the following excerpt from an unsigned review of Keats's* Endymion: A Poetic Romance *and* Lamia, Isabella, The Eve of St. Agnes, and other Poems *in* The Edinburgh Review, *the critic praises the literary style of Keats, while commenting on his "extravagance and irregularity."*]

We had never happened to see either [*Endymion: A Poetic Romance* or *Lamia, Isabella, The Eve of St Agnes, and other Poems*] till very lately—and have been exceedingly struck with the genius they display, and the spirit of poetry which breathes through all their extravagance. That imitation of our older writers, and especially of our older dramatists, to which we cannot help flattering ourselves that we have somewhat contributed, has brought on, as it were, a second spring in our poetry;—and few of its blossoms are either more profuse of sweetness or richer in promise, than this which is now before us. Mr Keats, we understand, is still a very young man; and his whole works, indeed, bear evidence enough of the fact. They are full of extravagance and irregularity, rash attempts at originality, interminable wanderings, and excessive obscurity. They manifestly require, therefore, all the indulgence that can be claimed for a first attempt:—but we think it no less plain that they deserve it; for they are flushed all over with the rich lights of fancy, and so coloured and bestrewn with the flowers of poetry, that even while perplexed and bewildered in their labyrinths, it is impossible to resist the intoxication of their sweetness, or to shut our hearts to the enchantments they so lavishly present. The models upon which he has formed himself, in the *Endymion,* the earliest and by much the most considerable of his poems, are obviously the *Faithful Shepherdess* of Fletcher, and the *Sad Shepherd* of Ben Jonson;—the exquisite metres and inspired diction of which he has copied with great boldness and fidelity—and, like his great originals, has also contrived to impart to the whole piece that true rural and poetical air which breathes only in them and in Theocritus—which is at once homely and majestic, luxurious and rude, and sets before us the genuine sights and sounds and smells of the country, with all the magic and grace of Elysium. His subject has the disadvantage of being mythological; and in this respect, as well as on account of the raised and rapturous tone it consequently assumes, his poetry may be better compared perhaps to the *Comus* and the *Arcades* of Milton, of which, also, there are many traces of imitation. The great distinction, however, between him and these divine authors, is, that imagination in them is subordinate to reason and judgment, while, with him, it is paramount and supreme—that their ornaments and images are employed to embellish and recommend just sentiments, engaging incidents, and natural characters, while his are poured out without measure or restraint, and with no apparent design but to unburden the breast of the author, and give vent to the overflowing vein of his fancy. The thin and scanty tissue of his story is merely the light frame work on which his florid wreaths are suspended; and while his imaginations go rambling and entangling themselves everywhere, like wild honeysuckles, all idea of sober reason, and plan, and consistency, is utterly forgotten, and are 'strangled in their waste fertility.' A great part of the work indeed, is written in the strangest and most fantastical manner that can be imagined. It seems as if the author had ventured everything that occurred to him in the shape of a glittering image or striking expression—taken the first word that presented itself to make up a rhyme, and then made that word the germ of a new cluster of images—a hint for a new excursion of the fancy—and so wandered on, equally forgetful whence he came, and heedless whither he was going, till he had covered his pages with an interminable arabesque of connected and incongruous figures, that multiplied as they extended, and were only harmonized by the brightness of their tints, and the graces of their forms. In this rash and headlong career he has of course many lapses and failures. There is no work, accordingly, from which a malicious critic could cull more matter for ridicule, or select more obscure, unnatural, or absurd passages. But we do not take *that* to be our office;—and just beg leave, on the contrary, to say, that any one who, on this account, would represent the whole poem as despicable, must either have no notion of poetry, or no regard to truth.

It is, in truth, at least as full of genius as of absurdity; and he who does not find a great deal in it to admire and to give delight, cannot in his heart see much beauty in the two exquisite dramas to which we have already alluded, or find any great pleasure in some of the finest creations of Milton and Shakespeare. (pp. 203-05)

> *A review of "Endymion: A Poetic Romance" and "Lamia, Isabella, The Eve of St. Agnes, and other Poems," in* The Edinburgh Review, *Vol. XXXIV, No. LXVII, August, 1820, pp. 203-13.*

Matthew Arnold (essay date 1880)

[*Arnold is considered one of the most influential authors of the later Victorian period in England. His forceful literary criticism, which is based on his humanistic belief in the value of balance and clarity in literature, significantly shaped modern theory. Arnold's essay, first published in 1880, opens with an attack on Keats's letters to Fanny Brawne that many consider to be the most vilifying criticism he ever wrote. The body of his essay, however, is keenly appreciative of Keats and was influential in gaining him wide acceptance as more than a poet of sensation alone. Arnold ultimately concludes that "'the yearning passion for the Beautiful,' which was with Keats, as he himself truly says, the master passion. . . is not a passion of the sensuous or sentimental poet. It is an intellectual and spiritual passion."*]

Keats as a poet is abundantly and enchantingly sensuous; the question with some people will be, whether he is anything else. Many things may be brought forward which seem to show him as under the fascination and sole dominion of sense, and desiring nothing better. There is the exclamation in one of his letters: 'O for a life of sensations rather than of thoughts!' There is the thesis, in another, 'that with a great Poet the sense of Beauty overcomes every other consideration, or rather obliterates all consideration.' There is Haydon's story of him, how 'he once covered his tongue and throat as far as he could reach with Cayenne pepper, in order to appreciate the delicious coldness of claret in all its glory—his own expression.' (pp. 100-01)

Character and self-control, . . . so necessary for every

kind of greatness, and for the great artist, too, indispensable, appear to be wanting, certainly, to this Keats of Haydon's portraiture. They are wanting also to the Keats of the *Letters to Fanny Brawne*. . . . [The publication of the letters] appears to me, I confess, inexcusable; they ought never to have been published. But published they are, and we have to take notice of them. Letters written when Keats was near his end, under the throttling and unmanning grasp of mortal disease, we will not judge. But here is a letter written some months before he was taken ill. It is printed just as Keats wrote it.

> You have absorb'd me. I have a sensation at the present moment as though I was dissolving—I should be exquisitely miserable without the hope of soon seeing you. I should be afraid to separate myself far from you. My sweet Fanny, will your heart never change? My love, will it? I have no limit now to my love. . . . Your note came in just here. I cannot be happier away from you. 'Tis richer than an Argosy of Pearles. Do not threat me even in jest. I have been astonished that Men could die Martyrs for religion—I have shuddered at it. I shudder no more—I could be martyred for my Religion—Love is my religion—I could die for that. I could die for you. My Creed is Love and you are its only tenet. You have ravished me away by a Power I cannot resist; and yet I could resist till I saw you; and even since I have seen you I have endeavoured often "to reason against the reasons of my Love." I can do that no more—the pain would be too great. My love is selfish. I cannot breathe without you.

A man who writes love-letters in this strain is probably predestined, one may observe, to misfortune in his love-affairs; but that is nothing. The complete enervation of the writer is the real point for remark. We have the tone, or rather the entire want of tone, the abandonment of all reticence and all dignity, of the merely sensuous man, of the man who 'is passion's slave.' Nay, we have them in such wise that one is tempted to speak even as *Blackwood* or the *Quarterly* were in the old days wont to speak; one is tempted to say that Keats's love-letter is the love-letter of a surgeon's apprentice. It has in its relaxed self-abandonment something underbred and ignoble, as of a youth ill brought up, without the training which teaches us that we must put some constraint upon our feelings and upon the expression of them. It is the sort of love-letter of a surgeon's apprentice which one might hear read out in a breach of promise case, or in the Divorce Court. The sensuous man speaks in it, and the sensuous man of a badly bred and badly trained sort. . . . [The] sensuous strain Keats had, and a man of his poetic powers could not, whatever his strain, but show his talent in it. But he has something more, and something better. We who believe Keats to have been by his promise, at any rate, if not fully by his performance, one of the very greatest of English poets, and who believe also that a merely sensuous man cannot either by promise or by performance be a very great poet, because poetry interprets life, and so large and noble a part of life is outside of such a man's ken,—we cannot but look for signs in him of something more than sensuousness, for signs of character and virtue. And indeed the elements of high character Keats undoubtedly has, and the effort to develop them; the effort is frustrated and cut short by misfortune, and disease, and time, but for the due understanding of Keats's worth the recognition of this effort, and of the elements on which it worked, is necessary.

Lord Houghton, who praises very discriminatingly the poetry of Keats, has on his character also a remark full of discrimination. He says: 'The faults of Keats's disposition were precisely the contrary of those attributed to him by common opinion.' And he gives a letter written after the death of Keats by his brother George, in which the writer, speaking of the fantastic *Johnny Keats* invented for common opinion by Lord Byron and by the reviewers, declares indignantly: 'John was the very soul of manliness and courage, and as much like the Holy Ghost as *Johnny Keats*.' It is important to note this testimony, and to look well for whatever illustrates and confirms it. (pp. 101-06)

Signs of virtue, in the true and large sense of the word, the instinct for virtue passing into the life of Keats and strengthening it, I find in the admirable wisdom and temper of what he says to his friend Bailey on the occasion of a quarrel between Reynolds and Haydon:—

> Things have happened lately of great perplexity; you must have heard of them; Reynolds and Haydon retorting and recriminating, and parting for ever. The same thing has happened between Haydon and Hunt. It is unfortunate; men should bear with each other; there lives not the man who may not be cut up, aye, lashed to pieces, on his weakest side. The best of men have but a portion of good in them. . . . The sure way, Bailey, is first to know a man's faults, and then be passive. If, after that, he insensibly draws you towards him, then you have no power to break the link. Before I felt interested in either Reynolds or Haydon, I was well read in their faults; yet, knowing them, I have been cementing gradually with both. I have an affection for them both, for reasons almost opposite; and to both must I of necessity cling, supported always by the hope that when a little time, a few years, shall have tried me more fully in their esteem, I may be able to bring them together.

Butler has well said that 'endeavouring to enforce upon our own minds a practical sense of virtue, or to beget in others that practical sense of it which a man really has himself, is a virtuous *act*.' And such an 'endeavouring' is that of Keats in those words written to Bailey. It is more than mere words; so justly thought and so discreetly urged as it is, it rises to the height of a virtuous *act*. It is proof of character. (pp. 106-08)

What character, again, what strength and clearness of judgment, in his criticism of his own productions, of the public, and of 'the literary circles'! His words after the severe reviews of **Endymion** have often been quoted; they cannot be quoted too often. . . . (p. 109)

Young poets almost inevitably over-rate what they call 'the might of poesy,' and its power over the world which now is. Keats is not a dupe on this matter any more than he is a dupe about the merit of his own performances:—

> I have no trust whatever in poetry. I don't wonder at it; the marvel is to me how people read so much of it.

His attitude towards the public is that of a strong man, not of a weakling avid of praise, and made to 'be snuff'd out by an article':—

> I shall ever consider the public as debtors to me for verses, not myself to them for admiration, which I can do without.

[The] thing to be seized is, that Keats had flint and iron in him, that he had character; that he was, as his brother George says, 'as much like the Holy Ghost as *Johnny Keats,*'—as that imagined sensuous weakling, the delight of the literary circles of Hampstead. (p. 112)

[Nothing] is more remarkable in Keats than his clear-sightedness, his lucidity; and lucidity is in itself akin to character and to high and severe work. In spite, therefore, of his overpowering feeling for beauty, in spite of his sensuousness, in spite of his facility, in spite of his gift of expression, Keats could say resolutely:—

> I know nothing, I have read nothing; and I mean to follow Solomon's directions: "Get learning, get understanding." There is but one way for me. The road lies through application, study, and thought. I will pursue it.

And of Milton, instead of resting in Milton's incomparable phrases, Keats could say, although indeed all the while 'looking upon fine phrases,' as he himself tells us, 'like a lover'—

> Milton had an exquisite passion for what is properly, in the sense of ease and pleasure, poetical luxury; and with that, it appears to me, he would fain have been content, if he could, so doing, preserve his self-respect and feeling of duty performed; but there was working in him, as it were, that same sort of thing which operates in the great world to the end of a prophecy's being accomplished. Therefore he devoted himself rather to the ardours than the pleasures of song, solacing himself at intervals with cups of old wine.

In his own poetry, too, Keats felt that place must be found for 'the ardours rather than the pleasures of song,' although he was aware that he was not yet ripe for it—

> But my flag is not unfurl'd
> On the Admiral-staff, and to philosophise
> I dare not yet.

Even in his pursuit of 'the pleasures of song,' however, there is that stamp of high work which is akin to character, which is character passing into intellectual production. '*The best sort of poetry*—that,' he truly says, 'is all I care for, all I live for.' It is curious to observe how this severe addiction of his to the best sort of poetry affects him with a certain coldness, as if the addiction had been to mathematics, towards those prime objects of a sensuous and passionate poet's regard, love and women. He speaks of 'the opinion I have formed of the generality of women, who appear to me as children to whom I would rather give a sugar-plum than my time.' He confesses 'a tendency to class women in my books with roses and sweet-meats—they never see themselves dominant'; and he can understand how the unpopularity of his poems may be in part due to 'the offence which the ladies,' not unnaturally 'take at him' from this cause. (pp. 113-15)

The truth is that 'the yearning passion for the Beautiful,' which was with Keats, as he himself truly says, the master-passion, is not a passion of the sensuous or sentimental man, is not a passion of the sensuous or sentimental poet. It is an intellectual and spiritual passion. It is 'connected and made one,' as Keats declares that in his case it was, 'with the ambition of the intellect.' It is, as he again says, 'the mighty *abstract idea* of Beauty in all things.' And in his last days Keats wrote: 'If I should die, I have left no immortal work behind me—nothing to make my friends proud of my memory; *but I have loved the principle of beauty in all things,* and if I had had time I would have made myself remembered.' He *has* made himself remembered. . . . (pp. 115-16)

For to see things in their beauty is to see things in their truth, and Keats knew it. 'What the Imagination seizes as Beauty must be Truth,' he says in prose; and in immortal verse he has said the same thing—

> Beauty is truth, truth beauty,—that is all
> Ye know on earth, and all ye need to know.

No, it is not all; but it is true, deeply true, and we have deep need to know it. And with beauty goes not only truth, joy goes with her also; and this too Keats saw and said, as in the famous first line of his *Endymion* it stands written—

> A thing of beauty is a joy for ever.

It is no small thing to have so loved the principle of beauty as to perceive the necessary relation of beauty with truth, and of both with joy. Keats was a great spirit, and counts for far more than many even of his admirers suppose, because this just and high perception made itself clear to him. Therefore a dignity and a glory shed gleams over his life. . . . (pp. 116-17)

[By] virtue of his feeling for beauty and of his perception of the vital connection of beauty with truth, Keats accomplished so much in poetry, that in one of the two great modes by which poetry interprets, in the faculty of naturalistic interpretation, in what we call natural magic, he ranks with Shakespeare. 'The tongue of Kean,' he says in an admirable criticism of that great actor and of his enchanting elocution, 'the tongue of Kean must seem to have robbed the Hybla bees and left them honeyless. There is an indescribable *gusto* in his voice.' . . . This magic, this 'indescribable *gusto* in the voice,' Keats himself, too, exhibits in his poetic expression. No one else in English poetry, save Shakespeare, has in expression quite the fascinating felicity of Keats, his perfection of loveliness. 'I think,' he said humbly, 'I shall be among the English poets after my death.' He is; he is with Shakespeare.

For the second great half of poetic interpretation, for that faculty of moral interpretation which is in Shakespeare, and is informed by him with the same power of beauty as his naturalistic interpretation, Keats was not ripe. For the architectonics of poetry . . . he was not ripe. His *Endymion,* as he himself well saw, is a failure, and his *Hyperion,* fine things as it contains, is not a success. But in shorter things, where the matured power of moral interpretation, and the high architectonics which go with complete poetic development, are not required, he is perfect. [His poems] prove it,—prove it far better by themselves than anything which can be said about them will prove it. Therefore I have chiefly spoken here of the man, and of the elements in him which explain the production of such work. Shakespearian work it is; not imitative, indeed, of Shakespeare, but Shakespearian, because its expression has that rounded perfection and felicity of loveliness of which Shakespeare is the great master. To show such work is to praise it. (pp. 119-21)

Matthew Arnold, *"John Keats," in his* Essays in Criticism, second series, *The Macmillan Company, 1924, pp. 100-21.*

T. Hall Caine   (essay date 1882)

[*In the excerpt below, Caine comments on the stylistic maturation of Keats's poetry from 1818 until his death in 1821.*]

The lack of proportion, which was the distinctive characteristic of Keats's early artistic method, had almost disappeared before the close of the four years that covered his active literary career. Perhaps his genius would ever have hovered over such an exquisite sense of the luxurious in animated imagery as would have made the chaste shapeliness of a balanced creation a difficult thing to him. But the tissues of his sensuous fantasy were being rapidly separated by keen experience. His earliest works sparkled with the many-coloured brightness of a prism; his latest works began to glow with the steady presence of a purer light. Scheme, in his first efforts, was often subordinated to incident, incident to image, image to phrase. . . . But signs are not wanting that even before the completion of *Endymion* judgment was doing its work with Keats. The fulness of fantasy became greater, and yet the disposition unduly to yield to it became less. Then each after each of the few poems that followed—*Hyperion, Lamia,* "Isabella," the "Eve of St. Agnes"—revealed Keats's strengthening power over the fixed laws of proportion, and his increasing command over the universal sensuousness that ran wild in the days that had gone by.

We cannot see more clearly to what perfectness the artistic method of Keats had attained than by glancing at a poem which, though little known and less talked of, was one of the last and the loveliest he gave us. The ballad, **"La Belle Dame sans Merci,"** is wholly simple and direct, and informed throughout by reposeful strength. In all the qualities that rule and shape poetry into unity of form, this little work strides, perhaps, leagues in advance of *Endymion.* That more ambitious work was in full sense poetic—soft and rich and sweetly linked. This harmonious gem is higher than poetic—it is a poem. As a tale of midday witchery, it is, though slight, as flawless as the first part of 'Christabel,' and immeasurably in advance of its own author's *Lamia.* As a work of complete beauty, there are few poems to match it:

> O, what can ail thee, knight-at-arms,
> Alone and palely loitering?
> The sedge has withered from the lake,
> And no birds sing.

>   • • • • •

> I see a lily on thy brow,
> With anguish moist and fever dew,
> And on thy cheeks a fading rose
> Fast withereth too.
>   . . .

The ballad is simple and direct, but not of a simplicity and directness proper to prose. In this poem the poet moves through an atmosphere peculiar to poetry, lacing and interlacing his combinations of thought and measure, incorporating his meaning with his music, thinking to the melody of his song, and listening to the beat of rhythm echoing

always ahead of him. The beautiful fragment, the **"Eve of St. Mark,"** will furnish the necessary supplement to these remarks; and if it be objected to what is here advanced that the Ariosto-like *Cap and Bells,* and the loosely-knit *Otho the Great,* do not prove that Keats's method was maturing, it must be replied that the structural imperfections of the latter should not be charged against him, and that the poor babble of the former shows only that Keats, like every lesser man, was subject to hours of inequality such as may not fairly be measured against his best and happiest moments.

The sonnets evidence his progress. The fine one on Chapman's *Homer* came early, it is true, as also did the fanciful one on the "Flower and Leaf;" but these came leashed with many a sorry draft, such as no judicious lover of Keats would grieve much to see suppressed. Later came **"The Day is gone," "As Hermes once," "On the Elgin Marbles," "Why did I laugh to-night?"** and **"To Homer,"** a sonnet containing that, perhaps, finest single line in Keats:

> There is a budding morrow in midnight;

and lastly came **"Bright Star."**

If, then, it is allowed that Keats was advancing in all that constituted his glory as an artist, and that, had he lived to the average age of man, he would have perfected his hold on that direct simplicity of method which is a treasure no true artist may forego, what shall we say of his progress and his prospect in all that constituted his value as a teacher? The word may startle some to whom Keats has seemed simply an imaginative youth, sometimes ecstatically inspired, moving forward in the world in moods intellectually and sensuously vacillating, and scarcely known to himself. And, indeed, it is easy to waste words in digging beneath the surface of his poetry for ethical meanings that were never hidden there; but it is quite as easy to undervalue his sense of what was due from him as a man. 'True,' he said, 'we hate poetry that has a palpable design upon us, and, if we do not agree, seems to put its hands into its breeches-pocket'. . . . ' Indications are not wanting that Keats, at one period, did, indeed, turn all his heart to the love of philosophy. He was never a weakling; his earliest prose quite clearly proves that the romantic boy, who seemed to live in a world of naïads and sirens, might have reached distinction in any—the most austere—literary walk. Year after year feeling and experience did their work with him. . . . Perhaps, too, at the beginning, and, indeed, even until the end, he overrated the Paradise of Sensation in contrast with the Paradise of Mind:

> Beauty is truth, truth beauty—that is all
> Ye know on earth, and all ye need to know.

(pp. 197-99)

Perhaps, as Keats himself hinted, the chance of leaving the world suddenly impressed a sense of his duties upon him. We may sometimes see what self-reproaches were wrung from him at but too opportune moments. How soon Keats would have risen above the bias of his own nature to the heights of a great purpose, we may not know. Already in the fragment *Hyperion* (of which, forsooth, the *Edinburgh* could not advise the completion) we see him sitting at the feet of Milton, than whom no man held his fantasy under stronger command. Keats was a true heir of Shakespeare's early fancy: would he have inherited something of Shakespeare's maturer imagination? We know that he was learning to know and love the early Italian poets: would he at length have put by his fretful restlessness and stood where Dante sat, and laved his tired forehead in the same river of resignation? We may not know; but at least we see him, before the completion of his twenty-third year, already conscious that the 'Infant Chamber of Sensation,' wherein he at first thought to delay for ever, must very soon be abandoned. This at least is certain, and it is much: 'I take poetry to be the chief, yet there is something else wanting. . . . I find earlier days are gone by. . . . I find there is no worthy pursuit but the idea of doing some good to the world. . . . There is but one way for me. . . . I will pursue it.' (p. 200)

T. Hall Caine, "That Keats was Maturing," in Tinsley's Magazine, *Vol. XXI, August, 1882, pp. 197-200.*

Arthur Symons   (essay date 1901)

[*Symons was a Welsh-born English literary critic and poet. He is respected for his explicative criticism on a variety of literary topics. In the following excerpt from an article in the October, 1901 edition of* The Monthly Review, *he comments upon the role of imagination in Keats's poetry.*]

The poetry of Keats is an aspiration towards happiness, towards the deliciousness of life, towards the restfulness of beauty, towards the delightful sharpness of sensations not too sharp to be painful. He accepted life in the spirit of art, asking only the simple pleasures, which he seemed to be among the few who could not share, of physical health, the capacity to enjoy sensation without being overcome by it. He was not troubled about his soul, the meaning of the universe, or any other metaphysical questions, to which he shows a happy indifference, or rather, a placid unconsciousness. "I scarcely remember counting upon any happiness," he notes. "I look not for it if it be not in the present hour. Nothing startles me beyond the moment. The setting sun will always set me to rights, or if a sparrow were before my window, I take part in its existence, and pick about the gravel." It is here, perhaps, that he is what people choose to call pagan; though it would be both simpler and truer to say that he is the natural animal, to whom the sense of sin has never whispered itself. Only a cloud makes him uneasy in the sunshine. "Happy days, or else to die," he asks for, not aware of any reason why he should not easily be happy under flawless weather. He knows that

> All charms fly
> At the mere touch of cold philosophy,

and he is not cursed with that spirit of analysis which tears our pleasures to pieces, as in a child's hands, to find out, what can never be found out, the secret of their making. In a profound passage on Shakespeare he notes how

> Several things dove-tailed in my mind, and at once it struck me what quality went to form a man of achievement, especially in literature, and which Shakespeare possessed so enormously—I mean *negative capability,* that is, when a man is capable of being in uncertainties, mysteries, doubts, without any irritable reaching after fact and reason.

Coleridge, for instance, would let go by a fine isolated verisimilitude, caught from the penetralium of Mystery, from being incapable of remaining content with half measures.

And so he is willing to linger among imaginative happinesses, satisfyingly, rather than to wander in uneasy search after perhaps troubling certainties. He had a nature to which happiness was natural, until nerves and disease came to disturb it. And so his poetry has only a sort of accidental sadness, reflected back upon it from our consciousness of the shortness of the time he himself had had to enjoy delight.

> And they shall be accounted poet-kings
> Who simply tell the most heart-easing things,

he says in **"Sleep and Poetry,"** and, while he notes with admiration that Milton "devoted himself rather to the ardours than the pleasures of song, solacing himself at intervals with cups of old wine," he adds that "those are, with some exceptions, the finest parts of the poem." To him, poetry was always those "cups of old wine," a rest in some "leafy luxury" by the way. (pp. 144-45)

Keats, at a time when the phrase had not yet been invented, practised the theory of art for art's sake. He is the type, not of the poet, but of the artist. He was not a great personality; his work comes to us as a greater thing than his personality. When we read his verse, we think of the verse, not of John Keats. When we read the verse of Byron, of Coleridge, of Shelley, of Wordsworth, we are conscious, in different degrees, of the work being a personal utterance, and it obtains much of its power over us by our consciousness of that fact. But when we read the verse of Keats, we are conscious only of an enchantment which seems to have invented itself. If we think of the writer, we think of him as of a flattering mirror, in which the face of beauty becomes more beautiful; not as of the creator of beauty. We cannot distinguish him from that which he reflects.

Keats has a firm common sense of the imagination, seeming to be at home in it, as if it were literally this world, and not the dream of another. Thus, in his most serious moments, he can jest with it, as men do with those they live with and love most. (p. 150)

"Man should not dispute or assert, but whisper results to his neighbour," he affirms; "let us open our leaves like a flower, and be passive and receptive, budding patiently under the eye of Apollo, and taking hints from every noble insect that favours us with a visit." That passive and receptive mood was always his own attitude towards the visitings of the imagination; he was always "looking on the sun, the moon, the stars, the earth and its contents, as materials to form greater things"; always waiting, now "all of a tremble from not having written anything of late," now vainly longing to "compose without fever," now reminding a friend: "If you should have any reason to regret this state of excitement in me, I will turn the tide of your feelings in the right channel by mentioning that it is the only state for the best kind of poetry—that is all I care for, all I live for." Perhaps it is this waiting mood, a kind of electrically charged expectancy which draws its own desire to itself out of the universe, that Mr. Bridges means when he speaks of Keats' "unbroken and unflagging earnestness, which is so utterly unconscious and unobservant of itself as to be almost unmatched." In its dependence on a kind of direct inspiration, the fidelity to first thoughts, it accounts, perhaps, for much of what is technically deficient in his poetry.

When Keats gave his famous counsel to Shelley, urging him to "load every rift with ore," he expressed a significant criticism, both of his own and of Shelley's work. With Shelley, even though he may at times seem to become vague in thought, there is always an intellectual structure; Keats, definite in every word, in every image, lacks intellectual structure. He saw words as things, and he saw them one at a time. "I look upon fine phrases like a lover," he confessed, but with him the fine phrase was but the translation of a thing actually seen by the imagination. He was conscious of the need there is for the poet to be something more than a creature of sensations, but even his consciousness of this necessity is that of one to whom knowledge is merely an aid to flight. "The difference," he says, in a splendid sentence, "of high sensations, with and without knowledge, appears to me this: in the latter case we are continually falling ten thousand fathoms deep, and being blown up again, without wings, and with all the horror of a bare-shouldered creature; in the former case our shoulders are fledged, and we go through the same air and space without fear." When Keats wrote poetry he knew that he was writing poetry; naturally as it came to him, he never fancied that he was but expressing himself, or putting down something which his own mind had realised for its own sake. "The imagination," he tells us, in a phrase which has become famous, "may be compared to Adam's dream—he awoke and found it truth." Only Keats, unlike most other poets, never slept, or, it may be, never awoke. Poetry was literally almost everything to him; and he could deal with it so objectively, as with a thing outside himself, precisely because it was an almost bodily part of him, like the hand he wrote with. "If poetry," he said, in an axiom sent to his publisher, "comes not as naturally as the leaves to a tree, it had better not come at all." (pp. 150-52)

"To load every rift with ore": that, to Keats, was the essential thing; and it meant to pack the verse with poetry, with the stuff of the imagination, so that every line should be heavy with it. For the rest, the poem is to come as best it may; only once, in *Lamia,* with any real skill in narrative, or any care for that skill. There, doubtless, it was the passing influence of Dryden which set him upon a kind of experiment, which he may have done largely for the experiment's sake; doing it, of course, consummately. *Hyperion* was another kind of experiment; and this time, for all its splendour, less personal to his own style, or way of feeling. "I have given up *Hyperion,*" he writes; "there were too many Miltonic inversions in it—Miltonic verse cannot be written but in an artful, or, rather, artist's humour. I wish to give myself up to other sensations." . . . It was just because Keats was so much, so exclusively, possessed by his own imagination, so exclusively concerned with the shaping of it into poetry, that all his poems seem to have been written for the sake of something else than their story, or thought, or indeed emotion. Even the odes are mental picture added to mental picture, separate stanza added to separate stanza, rather than the development of a thought which must express itself, creating its own form. Meditation brings to him no inner vision, no rapture of the soul;

but seems to germinate upon the page in actual flowers and corn and fruit.

Keats' sense of form, if by form is meant perfection rather of outline than of detail, was by no means certain. Most poets work only in outline: Keats worked on every inch of his surface. Perhaps no poet has ever packed so much poetic detail into so small a space, or been so satisfied with having done so. Metrically, he is often slipshod; with all his genius for words, he often uses them incorrectly, or with but a vague sense of their meaning; even in the **"Ode to a Nightingale"** he will leave lines in which the inspiration seems suddenly to flag; such lines as

Though the dull brain perplexes and retards,

which is nerveless; or

In ancient days by emperor and clown,

where the antithesis, logically justifiable, has the sound of an antithesis brought in for the sake of rhyme. In the **"Ode on a Grecian Urn,"** two lines near the end seem to halt by the way, are not firm and direct in movement:

Thou shalt remain, in midst of other woe
Than ours, a friend to man, to whom thou say'st.

That is slipshod writing, both as intellectual and as metrical structure; and it occurs in a poem which is one of the greatest lyrical poems in the language. We have only to look closely enough to see numberless faults of this kind in Keats; and yet, if we do not look very closely, we shall not see them; and, however closely we may look, and however many faults we may find, we shall end, as we began, by realising that they do not essentially matter. Why is this?

Wordsworth, who at his best may seem to be the supreme master of poetical style, is often out of key; Shelley, who at his best may seem to be almost the supreme singer, is often prosaic: Keats is never prosaic and never out of key. To read Wordsworth or Shelley, you must get in touch with their ideas, at least apprehend them; to read Keats you have only to surrender your senses to their natural happiness. You have to get at Shelley's or Wordsworth's point of view; but Keats has only the point of view of the sunlight. He cannot write without making pictures with his words, and every picture has its own atmosphere. Tennyson, who learnt so much from Keats, learnt from him something of his skill in making pictures; but Tennyson's pictures are chill, conscious of themselves, almost colourless. The pictures of Keats are all aglow with colour, not always very accurate painter's colour, but colour which captivates or overwhelms the senses. . . . That is why he can call up atmosphere by the mere bewitchment of a verse which seems to make a casual statement; because nothing, with him, can be a casual statement, nothing can be prosaic, or conceived of coldly, apart from that "principle of beauty in all things" which he tells us that he had always loved, and which to him was the principle of life itself. (pp. 152-55)

Arthur Symons, "John Keats," in The Monthly Review, *Vol. V, No. 13, October, 1901, pp. 139-55.*

Mary de Reyes (essay date 1913)

[*In the following excerpt, de Reyes comments on the influences upon and literary style of Keats's poetry.*]

No poet at the age of twenty-four has produced work comparable with the 1820 volume in depth of thought, in beauty of imagery and in easy mastery of technique. The reason for Keats's early maturity lies in his high conception of his art. He knew that if poetry was to be his vocation it must correspond to his whole being and demanded nothing less than his whole life.

That he must bring to it, not only knowledge of lyric technique, but also a deep understanding of the mind of man, in its conflicts with and in its ultimate harmony in nature. It was thus to the two great masters of Life and Nature—Shakespeare and Wordsworth—that the young poet turned. He went to them—not for inspiration—for that was already his—but rather for direction of his intellect. From them he brought away that philosophic view of all creation as a whole, wherewith to interpret his thought. Much of Wordsworth's poetry may have seemed to him a studied expression of a definite philosophy rather than a great spontaneous emotion which by its strength and directness enters straightly into the soul, nevertheless, Keats saw truly in Wordsworth a poet who had first drawn his inspiration from Nature through the great contemplation of her mysteries, and had so obtained that height of philosophy in which "thought and feeling are one."

It has been said that Keats luxuriated in emotions, and his famous ejaculation "Oh for a life of sensations rather than of thoughts" has often been used to denounce him. But Keats was no mere luxuriator in emotions. He realized how the poet uses all sense beauty and purifies it through the high purpose of his vision into intellectual flame. Intuition expresses his attitude, rather than sensation. "One does well to trust imagination's light when reason's fails" he wrote. There is much in his 1817 volume which has not been so intellectualized, but in his later work, the greatest restraining influence—that of Greek thought—had come upon him. It was through the lectures of Haydon on the Elgin marbles that Keats was first brought into knowledge of the Greek world. Much of Greek thought appealed to him as an expression of truth in forms essentially beautiful. From it, he learnt that the most ideal representations of life are not incompatible with the minutest detail, and thus the vagueness of his earlier poems gave place to definite poetic shapes. We may trace the growth of this influence in the great advance from *Endymion* to *Hyperion.* The lesson of artistic concentration has been learnt, the limp and effeminate verbiage has been replaced by a stern compression of all superfluity. The work is possessed with something "of the large utterance of the early gods." (pp. 77-9)

But Keats was not a poet of ancient Greece alone. He was also an interpreter of the Romance world. **"Isabella," "The Eve of St Agnes," "La Belle Dame sans Merci"** are all exquisite renderings of the glamour of the mediaeval world, deepened by the all pervading spirit of Nature. We have only to contrast **"Isabella"** with the original in the tale of Boccaccio to see what this means. Boccaccio gives us the story in all its horror of detail to arouse in us a sense of genuine tragedy and awful exultancy. With Keats, the tragedy of the story lies wholly in the depth of passion.

This is given not by acts of violence but by interpretation of the human heart through nature. The tender susceptibility of the lovers in each other's presence, the complete absorption of Isabella in her basil, oblivious of the changing loveliness of the world.

> And she forgot the sun and moon and stars
> And she forgot the wind above the trees
> She had no knowledge when the day was done
> And she forgot the chilly autumn breeze.

While the tragic loneliness of the murdered man is revealed through the dim, ghostlike perception of sounds.

> Alone I chant the holy Mass
> While little sounds of life are round me knelling.
> And glossy bees at noon do fieldward pass
> And many a chapel bell the hour is telling,
> Paining me through: those sounds grow strange to me
> And thou art distant in Humanity.

The dream-like atmosphere of mediaevalism hangs over the **"Eve of St Agnes."** The shifting moonlight, the buttresses black against it, are alike creations of an enchanted world. The wonderful felicity of word and phrase, the wealth of imagery and vivid colouring give it an intensely Spenserian effect.

In contrast to this picture of love, satisfying and victorious, is that of the fascination and doom of **"La Belle Dame sans Merci."**

In the magical touch of this picture of desolation and gloom, there is much of the spirit of Coleridge. There is no full description. The poem is lyrical rather than narrative. The wonderful slight suggestion of the landscape,

> The sedge is withered from the lake,
> And no birds sing.

gives the very spirit of the old romance world. And in the intense lyrical feeling we have the climax of passion. (pp. 79-80)

Keats is at his greatest in his odes. Though it may be true that he lacks the glowing intensity of Shelley, the spontaneity of the Elizabethans to whom they were simply outbursts of song, they are nevertheless free from phraseology and over elaboration of form. They are instinct with beauty of thought and rhythm, and in them, all the different elements of his genius are harmonized.

Such are the odes to **"Autumn"** and to the **"Nightingale"** where the effect is produced by the simplest forms, by such wonderful lines as these:—

> Where youth grows pale, and spectre-thin and dies.
> The self same song that found a path
> Through the sad heart of Ruth, when, sick for home,
> She stood in tears amid the alien corn.

The long drawn out lines brood over their own sweetness, and in them is a fine excess which is yet never exaggeration.

The poetry of Keats is throughout that of a mind which has loved beauty and which seeks amid the ruin of the transitory the one thing permanent.

This is the message of the **"Ode on a Grecian Urn."** Here the mutability of life is contrasted with the immortality of the principle of beauty which in its completeness stands "all breathing human passion far above." So too in the **"Ode to Autumn"** all is serenity of mind. Vain questioning is laid aside, reason is wrapt in faith. This high ennobling thought is significant of the end of Keats's work where, like Shakespeare, he rises to the supreme acceptance of all life, and sees it in its entirety, permeated with the one divine purposefulness. The quiet and peace of the whole spirit of autumn passes into the figure of the reaper, the gleaner, the maiden at the cider press, giving them a grace other than their own. "The season of mists and mellow fruitfulness" has its beauty also, a beauty no less than that of the songs of spring.

The greatness of Keats's poetry lies in the extreme sensitiveness of his mind to impression, and in his power of interpreting and translating this emotion in the terms of common life.

The gorgeous Oriental pageant of Bacchus is for him as for the Indian maiden, a passing splendour. What the poet gives must be transcripts of his actual experience, and his sympathy with Nature must always depend upon his sympathy with humanity. Feeling for Nature may only find voice in language applicable to human emotion, and so also beauty of nature is his unfailing resource for the expression of the subtlest soul emotions.

In this lies the secret of the Greek spell, and this is how Keats realized the spirit in which the Greek legends had been created. When the poet tells how the dead lovers lift their heads at the passing of Endymion "as doth a flower at Apollo's touch" he gives no idle personification but the embodiment of his belief in the healing power of a radiant presence in an image of perfect simplicity and truth.

Yet great as was his affinity with the Greek world, he was also in closest sympathy with the thought of his own day. It is he who by the spirit of Wordsworth is able to interpret the moods of nature. Whatever his imagination touched thrills with a sense of the mystery and awe underlying common things. In all nature he saw a high romance answering to the infinite longing of the soul, and alone capable of satisfying it. He does not therefore desire us to read lessons from Nature or to learn of her. He calls us not to reason but rather to watch and to adore. The message of the thrush in the yellow glory of a February morning gives the truth of this:—

> O fret not after knowledge! I have none
> And yet my song comes native with the warmth.
> O fret not after knowledge! I have none
> And yet the evening listens!

Such are the moments of a poet's ecstasy when his heart beats in unison with the mighty heart of the universe, and his own individuality is but a medium through which to express the universal. In this lies complete self-realization and utter poesy of life and thought. (pp. 80-2)

> *Mary de Reyes, "John Keats," in* Poetry Review, *Vol. III, No. 2, August, 1913, pp. 72-82.*

Martha Hale Shackford (essay date 1924)

[*Shackford was an American literary critic and educator. In the excerpt below, she examines the impact of Keats's personal misfortune on his poetry, concluding that while he recognized the "unescapable suffering and*

struggle in human life," he also maintained a belief in humankind to overcome these obstacles and view them as "having a meaning greater than individual pain or grief."]

Keats, at the height of his physical strength, was under the most intense emotional and intellectual stress. His reveries are marked by a deep melancholy, culminating in the **"Ode to a Nightingale,"** but prepared for by several poems of brooding sadness. This ode has a power over readers that seems to illustrate something of the Aristotelian doctrine of purification and refinement of feeling through an imaginative sharing of the tragic experiences of others. So profound is the emotion awakened in reading it, so deep is the sense of sympathy given and received, that the poem is one of the most beloved lyrics in the English language. It has the distinction, too, of being the most perfect expression of that meditative melancholy characteristic of some of the poets of Romanticism. The mournful egotism of Chateaubriand, the pessimism of Schopenhauer, the dull sadness of Blair's *Grave,* Young's *Night Thoughts,* and even the stately beauty of Gray's *Elegy Written in a Country Churchyard* express moods that are intellectual and that have a certain pleasure in their consciousness of their power of analyzing this melancholy. But the **"Ode to a Nightingale"** has none of the quality of curious, pleased self-observation, none of the reasoned sadness arising from non-partisan contemplation of man's eternal fate. It is a poem of intense feeling, cadenced with the accents of doubt and sorrow keenly felt by an individual; it is the direct result of individual experience which has given the poet insight into the griefs of all mankind. Personal as it is, it has an entire aloofness from the egotistical vanity of Byron's recitals of woe, or from the cold, ghoulish self-analysis of De Quincey.

Weary and dejected, the poet listened to the song of the nightingale and was, for a moment, exalted by the full-throated music of the bird whose very existence is inwrought with summer shadows and the unthinking joy of mere existence. Keats longed vehemently for some magic potion, a draught that would help the poetic imagination to escape from the brooding sorrows of the world of men, the world of mind and suffering. Poverty and grinding toil in youth, accompanied by starvation, fever, and exhaustion; palsy and miserable old age, are the lot of the mortal. The pleasure man finds in nature, in beauty, in love, fluctuates and passes swiftly. Death seems the only release from a world where loneliness and disappointment are made even more keen by sharp contrast with the radiant joy of the bird. Man's life—so brief, so transitory, so full of beauty desired but not attained—is sad and defeated, while the nightingale's is the very voice of triumphant happiness. The melody, the beauty, to which struggling Keats wished so intensely to attain in his art, are the birthright of a mere nightingale, whose song has outlived many generations, bringing swift, lovely fancies to far-away, solitary dreamers. Men indeed, as a race, survive, but the individual, with all his hopes, his aspirations, his 'identity', his potential power of creation, passes, becoming again an integral part of nature,—a sod.

Keats suggests here both the bane and the antidote of life. Doubtless everyone who cares for the ode feels that in suggesting this perpetual interrelation between man and nature, the very sentiment of despair and dejection is by implication soothed by the unconscious ministry of nature's beauty. Interwoven with allusions to mortal grief, are descriptions of beechen green, the forst dim, the flowers whose fragrances proclaim through the darkness their identity. Not wholly uncomforted was the man who could so perfectly perceive the path of life passing through "verdurous glooms and winding mossy ways." (pp. 478-80)

Keats had few illusions,—he knew that the whole principle of life was one of varying suffering for man and beast. He saw man often vain, selfish, frivolous, cruel by intent as well as through sheer stupidity. Yet he could say: "Scenery is fine—but human nature is finer." (p. 482)

Keats acted instinctively, upon a faith which he later brought to verbal expression. His ethical theory was based upon sound foundations of experience. He seems not to have shared the early views of Wordsworth and of Shelley, who accepted the Godwinian doctrine that evil is the result of what man has made of man. The *Lyrical Ballads* are full of protest against selfishness, greed, cruelty. Goody Blake, poor, shivering with cold as she toiled unceasingly in her miserable broken old age, is pictured as the victim of man's arrogant inhumanity Heal the heart of man and life will be sweet, was the doctrine of young Wordsworth. Later, when he became more acquainted with bodily suffering and the calamities of life not chargeable to man's cruelty, he voiced his belief in an overruling Power in whom man must have faith:—

> One adequate support
> For the calamities of mortal life
> Exists—one only; an assured belief
> That the procession of our fate, howe'er
> Sad or disturbed, is ordered by a Being
> Of infinite benevolence and power;
> Whose everlasting purposes embrace
> All accidents, converting them to good.

Shelley saw men as victims of human tyranny and selfishness, and believed that they might be wholly happy if wholly free from laws. He ignored the physical ills of man, regarding them apparently as the result of poverty and oppression. He never grasped the fact that rich and poor alike are almost as much victims of nature as of man's tyranny, he said little of the tragic law of spiritual causality which makes man pay the penalty for his own weakness and ill-will.

Byron, in *Cain* and elsewhere, upbraids the Deity for wanton cruelty to man. His philosophy of life was crude, for he absolved man more or less in order to place the burden upon God. The idea that man must atone for his own sins, must discipline himself, did not enter very definitely into Byron's scheme of lordly existence.

Keats avoided both these extremes. He did not see mankind divided into two clearly separated classes—oppressed and oppressors. While he had few illusions about man's nature, seeing him lacking in "disinterestedness", Keats recognized the fact that men are of mixed impulses and ideals,—neither wholly good nor wholly bad. As regards God, however, Keats certainly did not believe in a Being bestowing good and evil according to his caprice, or for the pleasure of seeing human beings suffer, or through impotence to control evil, or through any antagonism towards man. The God of Hebrew literature and of Calvinism was not his. He accepted the existence of a Power, supremely great and irrevocably identified with the inner life of every creature. He believed that God had from the beginning endowed men with power to think and to judge, with freedom of will and of action. (pp. 483-84)

Evidently Keats was profoundly conscious of the fact that human destiny is not yet complete; that the universe itself is still in evolution. He seems to have regarded the world as the work of a supreme creative artist, but, since all art is tentative, the Great Artist did not win immediate outward perfection. Much still remains to be accomplished before Ultimate Beauty is realized. Although he had little to say about the nature of God, Keats everywhere seems to assume a process that works constantly for perfection. Evil is not a definitely planned arrangement for rewarding the wicked or chastening the good. We call evil the experiences which we judge by a limited conception of the tremendous destiny of life. In our puny way we see experiences that cause anguish to our bodies and to our souls, and because of our human frailty we shrink from them. But the strong, intelligent soul knows that the bitterness is temporal; inherent in it is wisdom of the greatest depth and dynamic power. Humanity must consider spiritual, not physical, truth if life is to be clearly understood and rightly lived. We should—

> . . . . see as a god sees, and take the depth
> Of things as nimbly as the outward eye
> Can size and shape pervade.

The sheltered life careful of itself is as unstable and insignificant as the moth's. The adventurous life with all its mistakes and sufferings is vital and self-justifying.

> Not till this moment did I ever feel
> My spirit's faculties.

The individual must accept his existence as part of a great organic relationship, involving the whole order of life. And so John Keats, knowing that "axioms of philosophy are not axioms until they are proved upon our pulses", believed that he must regard his personal sufferings as having a meaning greater than individual pain or grief. The agony of his last year of life often expressed itself in bitter outcries against fate, he endured a desperate dispute with "impassioned clay", with physical prostration that dragged down the struggling spirit, but we must recognize the fact that he remained always—

> At war with all the frailty of grief.

Hyperion, more than any other of Keats's poems, express-

The Enfield School, where Keats studied as a boy.

es the poet's mature judgment regarding the presence of unescapable suffering and struggle in human life; gives us Keats's faith in the ceaseless onward movement of life "to fresh perfection" through the power of beauty; and shows us his conception of the inexhaustible resources of the individual will. (pp. 486-87)

Martha Hale Shackford, "Keats and Adversity," in The Sewanee Review, *Vol. XXXII, No. 4, October, 1924, pp. 474-87.*

Amy Lowell   (essay date 1925)

[*Lowell was the leading proponent of Imagism in American poetry. Like the Symbolists before her, whose works she examined in* Six French Poets *(1915), Lowell experimented with free verse forms. Under the influence of Ezra Pound, Lowell's poetry exhibits the style of Imagism, consisting of clear and precise rhetoric, exact rendering of images, and metrical freedom. Although her poetry garnered critical notice in her time, modern evaluations of Lowell accord her more importance as a poet in her own right. In the following excerpt from her exhaustive biography of Keats, she discusses the source and literary style of "The Eve of St. Agnes."*]

The **"Eve of St. Agnes"** is one of those poems, often among the most beautiful, which spring out of reading. It is written in the Spenserian stanza, and contains more than one reference to Spenser. Here are bits of Cary's *Dante;* suggestions of the Elizabethans; chips of Chatterton; a fragment of Burton; a little flash from Shakespeare. For all these strands of reminiscence I must refer my readers to Buxton Forman's and Professor de Sélincourt's editions. Extraordinarily interesting as these things are, I cannot dwell too long upon them here. It is high time that we returned to the poem itself, and to its subject, which is its one indisputable source—the legend of St. Agnes' Eve.

Leigh Hunt adduces Brand's *Popular Antiquities* as a convenient book in which to read of the legend. This work, first published in 1813 in an edition of two quarto volumes edited by Sir Henry Ellis after Brand's manuscript notes, was probably well known to Keats. In it is given a brief sketch of the legend proper, and a much longer commentary on the popular superstitions and ceremonies which had grown up about it. St. Agnes was a Roman virgin, a convert to Christianity, who was sentenced to suffer martyrdom in the tenth persecution under the Emperor Diocletian, A.D. 306. According to the legend, "She was condemned to be debauched in the public stews before her execution, but her virginity was miraculously preserved by thunder and lightning. Not long after her death, her parents, going to pray at her tomb, saw in a vision a host of angels with their dead daughter in the midst, and a lamb standing beside her as white as snow, an emblem of her spotless purity. With the centuries, St. Agnes assumed in the popular mind a special tenderness toward pure young girls, and took them under her protection to the extent of according them the power of seeing their future husbands in a dream on one night of the year, the eve of the day sacred to her. Certain rites had to be performed preparatory to the receiving of this boon, of which the principal seems to have been that the girl who courted St. Agnes' favour must fast all day and go to bed fasting, and must not kiss man, woman, or child until her dream lover broke the fast with her. This was called "fasting St. Agnes' fast." The young girl must lie on her back with her arms clasped beneath her head, and falling asleep in this position she will dream that a man is standing beside her bed, and that man she will marry. These rites differ somewhat in different places, and Brand gives one or two variants of them, but as the one I have given was the one followed by Keats we need not concern ourselves with the others. Among many quotations which show the prevalence of the custom, Brand prints some lines from Ben Jonson's *Satyr,* which were probably familiar to Keats. They are:

And on sweet St. Anna's night
Please you with the promis'd sight,
Some of husbands, some of lovers,
Which an empty dream discovers.

To see one's love in a dream, and know that however many ups and downs the waking course of true love is obliged to undergo the desired end will certainly be accomplished eventually, must have been a very sympathetic idea to Keats, enduring his first separation from Fanny Brawne. His whole soul was in **"St. Agnes' Eve;"** his humanity and his genius sublimating themselves through the longing of separation into a finely tempered whole. This is Keats's first completely successful long poem, and the first of his narratives not disfigured by glaring immaturities. Perhaps Hunt is not far wrong when he says: "Among his finished productions, however, of any length, the **"Eve of St. Agnes"** still appears to me the most delightful and complete specimen of his genius." And he goes on to: "It is young, but full-grown poetry of the rarest description; graceful as the beardless Apollo; glowing and gorgeous with the colours of romance." Hunt's expression here is a little florid, but has he not gone to the core of the matter? And Hunt knew what he was talking about, no man better. Here is what he has to say of Keats's technique: "Let the student of poetry observe, that in all the luxury of the **"Eve of St. Agnes"** there is nothing of the conventional craft of artificial writers; no heaping up of words or similes for their own sakes or for the rhyme's sake; no gaudy common-places; no borrowed airs of earnestness; no tricks of inversion; no substitution of reading or of ingenious thoughts for feeling or spontaneity: no irrelevancy or unfitness of any sort. All flows out of sincerity and passion. The writer is as much in love with the heroine as the hero is; his description of the painted window, however gorgeous, has not an untrue or superfluous word; and the only speck of a fault in the whole poem arises from an excess of emotion."

An excess of emotion there certainly is in the **"Eve of St. Agnes,"** but however much of a fault that may be in certain types of poetry—and unquestionably controlled emotion is generally far more effective than that which is over-expressed—in this particular poem I cannot regard it as a fault. The poem is singularly homogeneous in texture. It is all one long sensuous utterance. Not sensual—it is never that—but lyrical. It is an expression of lyrical emotion presented in the form of a tale. In it, Keats writes as poet and astounding craftsman. Every scrap of effectual knowledge which he knew he wrought into it; his feeling for colour, his sensitiveness to verbal music, his power of condensed suggestion, these are all here. His very profusion is a part of his effect. No one of Keats's manuscripts which I have seen is so carefully worked over as this. A glance at the reproduction of two of the pages of the first draft will show how shrewdly and carefully he shaped and reshaped his material, always with the object of increasing some splendour, making clearer some manner of feeling, adding some brighter lustre to an image, captivating the ear with some stranger, more unexpected, harmony of sound. This was Keats following his own advice tendered to Shelley a year and a half later to "load every rift with ore." His mood was the antithesis of astringent. His prime care was to give his emotion full rein, only endeavoring to keep the expression of it to the level of his best achievement, and in this he signally succeeded. To those people who are forever condemning the sensuous aspect of Keats's conception of love, there is but one answer. That sensuous beauty of this kind is its own perfect excuse, and we already know that natural beauty of all sorts stood to Keats as a religion, or, at least, as the sole possible way of expressing the truths which were religion to him. "St. Agnes' Eve" was a great choral hymn written to celebrate his love for Fanny Brawne. To say that he had to be separated from her to bring it into existence, is merely to state a truism of the functioning of the creative faculty. Poetry is seldom written in the midst of an action or a state of being; reflection is its essence. It is the perfume of something which has been, but is not; a remembrance and a hope, but a fact no longer.

I suppose that few poems in the English language are so well known and so much loved as the "Eve of St. Agnes." It stands as a personal efflorescence to generation after generation of young people. This is a poem for youth, and youth alone is capable of appraising it. As we grow older, we may come to prefer others of Keats's poems to it, but to the age to which it appeals it is completely satisfying, and little more praise can be given to any poem than this. Browning has spoken of "the last of life for which the first was made," a consoling idea to those who see life constantly shortening in front of them; but was he right? I fear not. Youth is more than age, energy worth more than meditation. The "Eve of St. Agnes" is a pæan of youth, a great masterpiece and epitome of one of the principal ages of man.

I call the "Eve of St. Agnes" a "choral hymn" and I do so advisedly, for its effect is not single and melodic, but massed and contrapuntal, and this double effect is kept up throughout. In the first place, there is the environment and the time set with the extreme of clarity in the opening stanzas of the poem: the freezing Winter night, outside the castle; inside, the chill chapel with the monuments of dead knights and ladies who seem to "ache in icy hoods and mails." The cold night is made none the less bitter by the draughty gusts of loud music which sweep along the corridors, and this metallic music, this piercing sound of "silver, snarling trumpets," gains an added touch of magnificence and chill from its juxtaposition to the sculptured architraves from which

> The carved angels, ever eager-eyed,
> Star'd, where upon their heads the cornice rests,
> With hair blown back, and wings put cross-wise on their
> breasts.

This, which we may call the motif of night, and cold, and heartless splendour, is never allowed to sink out of consciousness for very long; even when the love motif itself

is in full swing, in the scene between Porphyro and Madeline in Madeline's chamber, suddenly across the silence

> The boisterous, midnight, festive clarion,
> The kettle-drum, and far-heard clarinet,
> Affray his ears, though but in dying tone:—
> The hall door shuts again, and all the noise is gone.

And it follows through to the end of the poem, in the description of the arras which lines the passages along which the lovers flee,

> Flutter'd in the besieging wind's uproar,

in the drunken Porter asleep "in uneasy sprawl," in the "wakeful blood-hound," in the "foot-worn stones" of the hall, and the door groaning upon its hinges.

The second theme of the poem is the story of Porphyro and Madeline, with its symbols of the fast and the subsequent supper, as lightly and delicately tinted as the great hall is grey with sculptured stone and garish with plumes and flashing armour. Throughout the poem, Keats plays two sets of impressions, of emotions, against each other. To the sound of the kettle-drums and metallic wind instruments, he opposes strings, the strings of a lute. Against the

> . . . argent revelry
> With plume, tiara, and all rich array,

in the "thronged resort" of the great hall, he sets the "pallid moonshine" of the little still chamber, and the faint, beautiful colours thrown by the moonlit window. Never was riot more skilfully made to enhance silence. The world, and the soul; the life of outward seeming and inward fruition—no allegory, but a provable and proven fact.

But the "Eve of St. Agnes" is more than simply choral, it is antiphonal as well. For Keats, even in the heyday of his love experience, could not quite shake off his natural morbidness. Sinister, cynical, the mutter of death shudders always just beneath the surface of the tale. The lovers are happy, but beside them in the castle death sweeps upon its prey. Angela, the Beadsman, both die; the storm which protects the flight of the lovers howls round the castle suddenly become a tomb. It is the old story of the cruelty of nature. For two who are happy, life demands the insatiable toll of death. It is no mere charming tale of love which Keats has written here, but a profoundly dramatic study of an unplumbed mystery. And it is on this note that Keats ends his poem.

"St. Agnes' Eve" is so familiar to all readers of poetry that any detailed description of it seems unnecessary. Nevertheless, there are a few little points which I wish to touch upon before we finish with it for the moment. One thing which should be carefully noted is the extraordinary way in which Keats was able to stay the movement of composition in order to correct his impulse. This is a very difficult thing to do, and yet, in this instance, much alteration, and several false starts, do not seem to have lessened the vigour, the *élan*, of his creative power in the slightest degree. A careful study . . . will teach a student more of the marvellous way in which Keats was capable of holding to the thread of his unconscious creation, while at the same time consciously employing his critical faculty, than pages of explanation could do. All these variations and changes are reproduced by Buxton Forman, but only by seeing them set down as Keats, in the hurry of composition, wrote them, can we really comprehend how, and why, they came to his mind.

The stanzas about the window are in many ways the finest in the poem. What if Keats did make the mistake of supposing that moonlight was strong enough to transmit the colour values of stained glass, does it matter a jot? Would any one wish these stanzas away because they are false to fact? The truth of art is not necessarily the truth of nature. Where a poet has made undeniable beauty, the critic does well who refrains from applying a rule of thumb.

Hunt has pointed out what appears a distinct weakness in Stanza xxv, where Keats says that Porphyro, looking at Madeline kneeling beneath the moonlit window, "grew faint" at the sight of her purity and loveliness. Hunt did not apparently know that this faintness was part and parcel of romance narrative, and that Keats was merely following a very old model in introducing it, but, leaving that aside, what Hunt has to say on this subject is absolute truth, and should be taken into consideration by every reader:

> He had, at the time of his writing this poem, the seeds of a mortal illness in him, and he, doubtless, wrote as he had felt, for he was also deeply in love; and extreme sensibility struggled in him with a great understanding.

The last clause might be taken as a motto for Keats's life. (pp. 165-73)

One more thing I wish my readers to notice. The gradual increasing and brightening of the colours as the love-scene continues, and the marvellous way in which these colours are managed. From the lights of the window, the symbol is continued through the banquet; but the window tints are stated, the hues of the fruits merely implied, it would have marred both effects to have duplicated the technique employed in them. The window colours and the colour of the table-cloth are "flat," given simply as themselves; the fruits are heightened by inference, they are full, rounded, literary, if you like, and this change in the method of presentation sets them before us in the most excellent relief. From this moment, the room becomes warm with "perfume light." It is a beautiful conceit to have Porphyro think of these colours—the "lustrous salvers" gleaming in the moonlight, the "golden fringe" of the table-cover lying upon the carpet—as almost noisy in their effect, as though so much brilliance must wake Madeline.

It has been the fashion to condemn Keats's "carpets." Unnecessary preciosity! Carpets were known in Europe even before the assumed period of Keats's poem. They seem to have been chiefly used for ladies' bowers, so that the presence of one in Madeline's chamber was entirely according to custom. As to those in the corridors, there is no absolute reason to condemn them, but it is quite possible to conclude that Keats here used the word "carpet" in its sense of "covering," and meant to imply woven rushes rather than woven stuffs.

The colour symbols having served their turn, Keats quenches them with the setting of St. Agnes' moon and the beginning of the elfin storm. Admirable indeed is Keats's manipulation of his various themes and meanings in the last five stanzas of the poem. Even at the very moment

when we are told of Porphyro that "into her dream he melted," at that very instant come the words:

> . . . meantime the frost-wind blows
> Like Love's alarum pattering the sharp sleet
> Against the window-panes; St. Agnes' moon hath set.

The dream is over, reality has begun. Past death, misunderstanding, the imprisonment of personality, the lovers escape toward life together, not into a live-happy-ever-after kind of existence, but into the stress and storm of a future which at least they face side by side. (pp. 174-75)

> *Amy Lowell, in her* John Keats, Vol. II, *Houghton Mifflin Company, 1925, 662 p.*

AUTHOR'S COMMENTARY

It is a sorry thing for me that any one should have to overcome Prejudices in reading my Verses—that affects me more than any hyper-criticism on any particular Passage. In *Endymion* I have most likely but moved into the Go-cart from the leading strings. In Poetry I have a few Axioms, and you will see how far I am from their Centre. 1st. I think Poetry should surprise by a fine excess and not by Singularity—it should strike the Reader as a wording of his own highest thoughts, and appear almost a Remembrance—2nd. Its touches of Beauty should never be half way thereby making the reader breathless instead of content: the rise, the progress, the setting of imagery should like the sun come natural to him—shine over him and set soberly although in magnificence leaving him in the Luxury of twilight—but it is easier to think what Poetry should be than to write it—and this leads me to another axiom. That if Poetry comes not as naturally as the Leaves to a tree it had better not come at all. However it may be with me I cannot help looking into new countries with 'O for a Muse of fire to ascend!'

(letter date 1818)

John Middleton Murry   (essay date 1926)

[*Murry was an eminent English literary critic. His book-length critical works are noted for their impassioned tone and startling discoveries; biographically centered critical studies such as his* Keats and Shakespeare: A Study of Keats' Poetic Life from 1816-1820 *(1925), contain controversial conclusions that have angered scholars who favor more traditional approaches. In the following excerpt from that study, Murry examines the Keatsian concept of "beauty in all things," especially in relation to* Hyperion.]

The greatest of all Keats' long poems is to me undoubtedly *Hyperion,* whether we consider it in its original and familiar form, as it appeared in the 1820 volume, or in the revised form as *The Fall of Hyperion: a Dream.* But in neither form is *Hyperion* as perfect as the Odes. They have the same deep sufficiency of inspiration and the same wealth of profound experience as *Hyperion,* and they have a perfection of form which *Hyperion* has not. Still, *Hyperion* is the greater achievement. It was begun in the autumn of this year 1818, when Keats had returned ill from his Scottish tour and was spending painful days at the bedside of his dying brother, dying of the same disease of which Keats' obstinate sore-throat was a premonitory symptom.

Hyperion differs from all Keats' other poems in one important respect. Its composition was frequently interrupted and abandoned and resumed. *Endymion,* "Isabella," "The Eve of St. Agnes," *Lamia* were all written in one piece. But *Hyperion* was composed quite differently. It is impossible to say with the certainty of external evidence when many parts of it were written. We know that it was begun in the September of 1818, that it was taken up again in January and the early spring of 1819, that a complete recast of the poem was begun in the summer, and finally that the poem was abandoned altogether in both forms in September 1819. In this book the attempt is made to prove by internal evidence that the first two books of *Hyperion* were written before the end of 1819; but that the main portion of the third book belongs to a different and later period of Keats' development.

A consideration of the causes why *Hyperion* was abandoned does not belong to this year 1818, but only a consideration of the causes why it was begun. We may say that Keats had fallen under the spell of Milton: and, if we remember the nature of the man of whom we are speaking, the phrase will pass. But few of those who use the phrase do remember the nature of the man of whom they use it, and therefore they forget that the kind of spell which Milton had for Keats was in the nature of things limited and circumscribed. We need only to remember the letter to Reynolds, in which Keats compares Milton with Wordsworth, and decides that Wordsworth 'thinks deeper into the human heart' to see that Milton could not finally satisfy Keats, and to understand the nature of the spell which Milton exerted upon him. It was the spell of a great technique and a prodigious art; and, more potent than this, it was the spell of a verse which could be constructed by a man of genius in abstraction from the torment of experience. Milton held for Keats the promise of a release from the pain of life, of a world of abstractions into which he could enter and be free, where his poetic genius would be nobly occupied and his overstrained nerves relaxed. (pp. 69-75)

Hyperion and Miltonics were a refuge of abstractions that Keats was building for himself to shut out the concrete world. But the hiding place which an architect of genius builds for himself is a palace. I am not, as I hope to prove abundantly, trying to diminish by a single scruple the sublime beauty of *Hyperion.* For me, taken together with its recast induction, it is the pinnacle of Keats' actual achievement; but because I wish to show that Keats was greater, far greater, than his actual achievement, because I wish to present him as the perfect type of the great poet, as a poetic genius second only to Shakespeare in our literature, and of the same pattern as Shakespeare, I am concerned at this moment to show that *Hyperion* was not central to Keats' poetic purposes. Those purposes were persis-

tent, and I have tried to show their inward nature. They had a definite outward embodiment also. Keats' purpose was not to write epics, or even odes, but to write plays; all the poems he wrote from *Endymion* onwards were but a step towards his 'chief attempt in the drama'; he desired to reveal the truth of human life, not through abstractions, but in a mirrored reflection of life itself. The drama as the supreme height of literature was a necessary part of Keats' 'vast idea'; it was in the hierarchy of literary forms that alone which permitted the identification of the poet with every manifestation of the human universe, which as he had told Woodhouse in a letter of this time (27th October) was fundamental to the poetical character:

> As to the poetical character itself (he wrote)—I mean that sort, of which, if I am anything, I am a member; that sort distinguished from the Wordsworthian or egotistical Sublime— . . . it is not itself—it has no self.—It is everything and nothing.—It has no character—it enjoys light and shade; it lives in gusto, be it foul or fair, high or low, rich or poor, mean or elevated. It has as much delight in conceiving an Iago as an Imogen. What shocks the virtuous philosopher delights the chameleon poet . . . A poet is the most unpoetical of any thing in existence, because he has no Identity—he is continually in for and filling some other body.

Keats saw truly into the nature of his own genius. It was, as we say nowadays, objective; it was concrete; it moved not in a world of philosophic thought and abstraction, but in a world of imaginative realizations. It was purely and truly poetic; and it turned towards the drama as the form which offered the most complete fulfilment of its own nature. (pp. 70-1)

The drama, then, as the necessary form of 'the vast idea', was already an essential part of Keats' intention; and perhaps we have gained some perception of what was to be embodied in it—the apprehension of Beauty as Truth, the high reason which brings with it 'the love of good and ill,' the acceptance of the burden of the mystery as a thing not to be dissipated by some trick of the intellect, or by some self-delusion imposed by 'an irritable reaching after fact and reason.' But we shall find no deeper, nor any more transparent, phrase for the content of Keats' ideal poetry than his own familiar words: 'the principle of beauty in all things.' (p. 71)

The meaning of the words 'I have loved the principle of beauty in all things' is not obvious. Of course, if they are taken vaguely as meaning 'I have loved beauty,' there is no difficulty; and since I have never seen an admission that a difficulty exists, I suppose that this vague sense is the one that is usually given to them. It seems clear to me that they mean more than this; but when we try to extract the further meaning from them, by giving each word its full weight the difficulty begins. For we can read them in two ways, thus: 'I have loved the principle of beauty—in all things,' or, 'I have loved the principle—of beauty in all things.' Between these two interpretations there is a vital difference. In the first case 'principle' means 'element': it is the old *principium* of the scholastic philosophers which survives in such a phrase as 'the vital principle': and Keats' sentence will run 'I have loved the element of beauty—in all things.' And, again, even this is not quite clear: he may be saying that he has loved this element of beauty, in whatsoever things he has found it, or he may be saying that he has loved this element of beauty, and he has found it in all things. Even there the difference is important: but whichever of these interpretations we choose, the underlying thought is the famous thought of Plato: that there is an ideal and perfect Beauty which is partially manifested, as a shadow is a manifestation of the object which casts it, in the beautiful things of earth. 'This ideal beauty,' Keats will then be saying, 'I have loved'; and there is no means of telling whether he is saying further that he has loved it in whatsoever thing he has found it, or that he has found it in everything.

This may appear a singularly abstruse sort of quibbling. I ask those who shrink from it to remember that we are dealing with Keats' central thought, and that the central thought of a poetic genius such as his is not likely to be simple to understand; I ask them also to realize that there is all the difference in the world between the statement 'I have loved beauty, and beauty is in all things' and the statement 'I have loved all beautiful things.' The one implies acceptance, the other, rejection. With a sense of that difference in our minds, and a sense also of the importance of deciding which was Keats' belief, let us read the sentence as I believe it should be read, not as 'I have loved the principle of beauty—in all things,' but as 'I have loved the principle—of beauty in all things.' 'Principle' now does not mean 'element,' it means 'idea'; and Keats is saying 'I have loved the idea, that there is beauty in all things.' Now, I admit that if I had that single sentence alone to interpret: 'I have loved the principle of beauty in all things,' I should hesistate to read it 'I have loved the principle—of beauty in all things,' even though I am convinced that Keats meant by his sentence not that he had loved all beautiful things; but that he had loved beauty and beauty is in all things.

But the sentence does not stand alone. The phrase 'the principle of Beauty' occurs elsewhere in Keats' letters; so does the phrase 'Beauty in all things.' In the spring of this year, 1818, he had written to Reynolds (9th April): 'I have not the slightest feel of humility towards the public—or to anything in existence—but the eternal Being, the principle of Beauty, and the Memory of great Men.' That absolute use of the phrase would settle the question, were it not that six months later (October 1818) we find him writing to his brother George, then in America: 'The mighty abstract Idea I have of Beauty in all things stifles the more divided and minute domestic happiness.'

Those two sentences, in their sequence, the first in the spring, the second in the autumn of this year of 'purgatory blind,' are of cardinal importance. They establish the real meaning of 'I have loved the principle—of Beauty in all things': that love is essentially the same as 'the love of good and ill' for which he had striven. They reveal the intimate connection between 'the principle—of Beauty in all things' and 'the vast idea' which came to Keats in **"Sleep and Poetry"**; it was 'the mighty abstract idea of Beauty in all things.' And above all they reveal, in the history of a single phrase, the secret movement of Keats' mind. The 'vast idea' of **"Sleep and Poetry"** had involved the poet's passing beyond 'the realm of Flora and old Pan,' that is away from the realm of beautiful things. He had asked

And can I ever bid these joys farewell?

And he had answered:

Yes, I must pass them for a nobler life
Where I may find the agonies, the strife
Of human hearts.

He had thus, in that prophetic poem, seen beyond the principle of beauty to the principle of beauty in all things. But in **Endymion,** for all his efforts, he had remained almost wholly within 'the realm of Flora and old Pan.' The principle of beauty had triumphed over the principle of beauty in all things. For many reasons, but for one in chief: Keats was a truly natural poet who could not write save out of that which he had proved upon his pulses: 'The agonies, the strife of human hearts' had not yet touched him directly. Ecstatic contemplation of beauty, the being thrown 'into a sort of oneness'—that he knew by direct experience; but the pain of life he did not know. He knew that he had to triumph over pain, but the pain had not yet come, and he was not one to invoke it intellectually. A merely intellectual reality was no reality at all to him; even 'a proverb was no proverb to him until his life had illustrated it.' And so in April 1818, when he is writing to Reynolds with **Endymion** in his mind, regarding the preface to **Endymion,** it is simply 'the principle of beauty' of which he speaks. He has just been putting his loyalty to the principle again to the proof by writing **"Isabella,"** which is preeminently a romantic tale in the sense of being devoid of all substance of actual life-experience. (pp. 72-4)

The exquisite sense of the luxurious is the homage to the principle of beauty; philosophy is to Keats the apprehension of the principle of beauty in *all* things. Now he is caught midway between the two: he has lost hold of the one, he has not laid hold of the other. This is the condition he describes in the **"Epistle to Reynolds"**:

Or is it that Imagination brought
Beyond its proper bound, yet still confin'd,
Lost in a sort of Purgatory blind
Cannot refer to any standard law
Of either earth or heaven? It is a flaw
In happiness to see beyond our bourn.

This 'purgatory blind' is the condition which lies between allegiance to the principle of beauty and discovery of the principle of beauty in all things. This year 1818 had been a year of such a purgatory. After **"Isabella"** Keats wrote nothing until he began **Hyperion,** and in that poem the principle of beauty changes to the principle of beauty in all things. It is, as he tells his brother George, still a mighty *abstract* idea; he speaks, as ever, truly, for in **Hyperion** the 'vast idea' is abstract; but it is there—and the remainder of Keats' life was to be burned away in the process of its becoming concrete in and through him.

'Beauty in all things.' This was Keats' great poetic intuition, and the revelation of this beauty the great human purpose to which he dedicated himself and for which he was prepared to die. It sounds simple; it is tremendous. It involves a profound acceptance of life as it is, a passing beyond all rebellion, not into the apathy of stoic resignation, but into a condition of soul to which the sum of things— 'foul or fair, high or low, rich or poor'—is revealed as necessary and true and beautiful: and for the creative genius of the poet it means not only to have this vision, not only to have attained 'high reason, and the love of good and ill,' but to have the purpose and the power to reveal to men that good and ill are to be loved; not only the faculty to see that the sum of things is supremely beautiful, but the faculty to show to other men that it is supremely beautiful.

Such an achievement, Keats knew, was possible only in the form in which Shakespeare had achieved it, in the drama, in the poetry or representation, which in the hands of great genius, does perform this manifest miracle or revealing the secret harmony and high design which lie behind all human discomfiture. This consummate poetry which represents and reveals was, as Keats had already confessed to Taylor, and as he was to confess to him more fully hereafter, his poetic goal: it was one which he never attained. It was in the despairing vision of this unattained ideal that, when he wrote to Fanny Brawne, all his glorious poetic achievement dissolved away and he said that he had left no immortal work behind him, but if he had had time he would have made himself remembered. He is remembered; he will never be forgotten: but he is remembered, too often, and even by those who have devoted themselves to his memory, as something of a weakling, as a boy of genius in whose soul there was an element of sickness and sickliness, as someone who can be patronized, and be told that he was wrong to love with a passion so devouring, misguided to reject the influence of Milton, peevish and morbid to spoil his beautiful *Hyperion* by adding to it an opening in a different tone and manner.

That Keats should be remembered in this way fills me with passionate indignation. It is wrong, utterly wrong. There is no man living, and no man has lived, who has the right to pass judgement upon Keats. It is an act of terrible presumption. When I read in a Life of Keats that 'there was a great spiritual flaw in his nature,' I am first amazed, then indignant. By what standard, by what right is Keats thus judged? What spiritual flaw was in him that was not in Shakespeare? And if we do not dare to say that Shakespeare was morbid and sickly, let us have at least the generosity to hold our peace about Keats. With the genius of the pure poet, as Keats' was, you cannot make conditions: you cannot say you will accept this and reject that, approve of this and disapprove of that. You must accept the whole; you must understand that the elements of which you disapprove are the foundation of the achievement which you do approve, and therefore in addition to rank ingratitude you lay yourself open to the charge of not truly understanding what you profess to admire. (pp. 74-6)

> *John Middleton Murry, in his* Keats and Shakespeare: A Study of Keats' Poetic Life from 1816 to 1820, *Oxford University Press, London, 1926, 248 p.*

Solomon F. Gingerich   (essay date 1932)

[*In the following excerpt, Gingerich examines the development of Keats's concept of beauty in his poetry.*]

Keats approached beauty from a direction diametrically opposite to that of Shelley. He started by absorbing sense impressions of natural surroundings and building a theory of beauty thereon. Shelley's approach to beauty was from the beginning abstruse and highly sophisticated; that of Keats was simple and unsophisticated. Shelley found this "dull dense world" now and then lighted up as by the rays of some alien Power of Beauty; Keats found beauty as a constituent part of the earth itself, and of all the objects of the earth. "A thing of beauty is a joy," he said. He stressed things—small, large, common, unusual—all kinds of things, such as, he says, "the sun, the moon, trees old and young," sheep on a hillside, daffodils, streams, lovely tales, heroic deeds, "the grandeur of the dooms we have imagined for the mighty dead,"

> An endless fountain of immortal drink,
> Pouring unto us from the heaven's brink.

Everywhere around us Keats discovered a plenitude of beauty to feed the eyes and ears and other senses. (pp. 177-78)

This was the foundation and beginning of Keats' devotion to beauty; but no more. His famous saying, "O for a life of Sensations rather than Thoughts!" is true only as applied to his earliest literary years, for he soon began to rationalize his love of the beautiful. The first step in this rationalization lay in his discovery of a principle of permanency in beauty. Sensations were always a joy—sensations and sense-imagery are basic in poetry, and their importance must not be minimized—but the discovery that there is something lasting in beauty was an advance to a higher level of perception. This is the special significance of the famous opening lines of *Endymion:*

> A thing of beauty is a joy forever;
> Its loveliness increases; it will never
> Pass into nothingness.

This everlastingness in a thing of beauty, rather than the idea that beauty is truth, or the idea of the worship of beauty in itself, is the theme of the great **"Ode on a Grecian Urn."** . . . Not "truth" but "forever" is the key word; this poem is one of the superb examples in all literature for its expression in every image and every stanza of an abstract truth by imaginative suggestion, without overt assertion. The emotional reaction is also completely integrated with the idea of the poem.

The idea of the permanency of beauty leads directly to "the worship of the principle of beauty in all things," which is the central position with Keats. He clung to "things" in order that beauty as he conceived it should not become too impalpable; but it is the "principle" that is more and more the object of devotion as he develops toward fullness of power; the principle itself also becomes more austere as the poet grows toward maturity. It is this that saves Keats, on the one hand, from being a worshiper of impalpable abstractions, and, on the other, from being a mere reveler in sensuous beauty. In short, Keats has put himself on the highroad, I believe, to a very healthy and sound aesthetics.

For the principle of beauty, as Keats conceived it, is a principle inherent in the very constitution of creation itself. Take, for instance, proportion, harmony, order—technical, but fundamental, elements of beauty. An organism exists by virtue of the relation of its parts to each other, and of all the parts to the whole; if some parts are displaced, or irregular, there is a lack of harmony. In the larger sense order runs throughout created existence. The destruction of order and harmony in the universe would throw the universe back into chaos. Beauty, which includes order and harmony, is thus as essential to creation and existing things as is truth; it stands side by side with truth as necessary to life and reality. Keats had a far deeper realization than most men of the vitality and significance of beauty in this sense, and it is in this sense that he thought of it as truth.

It was this phase of beauty that Keats essayed in *Hyperion.* As the fallen Saturn and his followers had ruled over a Heaven and an Earth that were fairer far than Chaos and blank Darkness, so the new race of gods represents a higher harmony and beauty:

> So on our heels a fresh perfection treads,
> A power more strong in beauty, born of us
> And fated to excel us, as we pass
> In glory that old Darkness: nor are we
> Thereby more conquer'd, than by us the rule
> Of shapeless Chaos.

Oceanus, who speaks these words, asserts that he had found the "one avenue" that leads to "eternal truth," and the truth is that the excellencies of existing things and the order to which they belong is basically determined by the law of beauty—beauty is eternal truth. This is "Nature's law." The proud forest is more comely than the dull soil from which it has sprung. The golden-feathered eagles tower in their greater beauty above the forest. Keats makes Oceanus not only assert the eternal law of beauty on the basis of a higher and more powerful order of creation than that which formerly existed, but also suggest, daringly, cycles of orders of still higher perfection and beauty:

> 'T is the eternal law
> That first in beauty should be first in might:
> Yea, by that law, another race may drive
> Our conquerors to mourn as we do now.

The level to which a thing belongs, or to which it may attain, is determined by the quality and order of beauty it possesses. Unquestionably Keats identified beauty not only with truth, but also with might and with power. It represents Keats' fundamental way of approach to the meaning of life.

Thus far Keats pursued the principle of beauty, but no further. He progressed rapidly from the idea of beauty as Sensation to beauty as Truth and Power, in several steps. The phrase in *Endymion* about the everlastingness of beauty became the theme, a little later, of the **"Ode on a Grecian Urn."** The phrase at the close of this Ode, which identified beauty with truth, was later amplified and illustrated in *Hyperion.* A developing theory of beauty was thus worked out in Keats' writings. But its evolution in poetic practice was far from complete; the possibilities that inhere in the theory were far from being exhausted by Keats: the poet's life was too short for that.

Keats' theorizing in his poetry on beauty distinctly influences the poetry itself. His early poems, such as **"I Stood on Tiptoe," "Sleep and Poetry,"** and large portions of *Endymion,* are remarkable mainly for their sensuous beauty, a certain naturalistic atmosphere, and for felicitous expressions. They are "simple, sensuous," if not passionate. Here Keats indulges in sense-imagery, with but little restraint, piling up sensations indiscriminately and with unflagging delight:

> I was light-hearted,

> And many pleasures to my vision started:
> So I straightway began to pluck a posey

> Of luxuries bright, milky, soft and rosy.

He feels, to the point of cloying, "overwhelming sweets"—"a breathless honey-feel of bliss" from

> Dew-drops, and dewy buds, and leaves, and flowers.

The sensuous luxury is as marked as in Shakespeare's early *Venus and Adonis,* both poets having at their disposal in youth a wealth of raw material, a richness of sensuous content from which they could draw in unlimited measure. This, and the verbal and stylistic felicities abounding in both poets at an early age, indicate important likenesses, and suggest that, after Shakespeare, Keats was the most richly endowed poetic nature in English literature. Luxurious sense-imagery is to be found here and there throughout Shakespeare's works, and not least in some of his later plays, such as *The Winter's Tale.* In his early poems Keats copiously "heaped with glowing hand" image upon image, producing a "purple riot" of varied effects, in language of "voluptuous accents."

From these somewhat formless and sometimes top-heavy poems Keats progressed rapidly to that period in which he exercised restraint and showed selective ability, wherein he singled out individual objects—Elgin Marbles, a Grecian Urn, a Nightingale—and formed shapely poems, meaningful, close-knit, organically unified, making the principle of beauty stand out clearly, either by the theme or by the poem itself as a concrete example. Here the poet's practice kept pace with his theory. Instead of the former riot of luxuriousness we now have sensuous richness toned down to the purpose of strict unity. The ideas and feelings are perfectly integrated with the rich texture of the poems. On the level on which these poems move—it must be noted that they do not create human characters or deal with personality in moral conflict, or with ultimate human destiny—Keats has rendered the principle of beauty in forms as rich and lovely and perfect as poetry is able to achieve.

But in *Hyperion,* where he essayed a much wider formula for the principle of beauty, namely, truth and power, he was only partially successful, not alone in integrating the statement of the theory with the poetry itself, but in illustrating it in the incidents and events and, most of all, in the characters of the poem. As a matter of fact, this purpose of revealing the principle of beauty with all high seriousness in action and character calls for a kind of breadth and wisdom of experience which we have no right to expect from any man under the age of twenty-four in any period of literary history. Attacked by mortal illness at the age of twenty-four, and dying at the age of twenty-five, Keats left his theories and their application incomplete. The five years' advantage that Shelley had over Keats, and the fifteen years' advantage that Poe had make an immense difference with regard to the growth of their concepts to maturity. There are many signs that, had not his health failed, Keats would have succeeded in applying his principle of beauty to far wider experiences of life. His letters reveal the fact that he was aiming to reach out to the possession of wider knowledge and the grasp of deeper philosophic wisdom. "There is but one way for me," he said. "The road lies through application, study, and thought. . . . I will pursue it." He said he would study philosophy, by which he undoubtedly did not mean, primarily, technical philosophy, but a broad study of human experience and human truth. The restlessness accompanying this purpose of widening his knowledge and experience was not, as Mr. G. R. Elliott has asserted (in *The Cycle of Modern Poetry*), an indication of an intellectual and spiritual tragedy in him preceding the pathos of his early death. This restlessness was literally no more nor less than the pains of growth accompanying the rapid development of a normal but extraordinary youth of twenty-three who could proudly declare that he saved his feeling of humility for "the Eternal Being, the Principle of Beauty, and the Memory of Great Men." (pp. 178-83)

As has been noted, Keats perceived the principle of beauty as inhering in and being integrally a part of the very constitution of things—as being primarily essential to their existence. The vitality with which this principle is seized, and the penetration with which it is expressed, give it significance and render possible its application not only to things, objects and organisms, but to the whole round of life—to human conduct under all the conditions of actual life, to the poise and balance of human character evolved from human suffering and moral conflict, to the moral and religious experience of mankind, and to the ultimate destiny of humanity. But there is relatively little of these high matters in the extant poetry of Keats. He did say, to be sure, in **"Sleep and Poetry,"** when speaking of sensuous joys:

> And can I ever bid these joys farewell?
> Yes, I must pass them for a nobler life,
> Where I may find the agonies, the strife
> Of human hearts.

And he said similar things at other times. Yet it is a hope and a promise rather than an achievement; nor have we a right to expect that it should be otherwise. The years of Keats' life were too few to provide him with the experience necessary to realize and embody these high matters within the compass of his principle of beauty. A slow growth, the maturing of all a poet's powers, and many actual experiences of life are necessary in order to reach such a level of experience and achievement. It was not a tragedy, but a triumph, that at the age of twenty-three Keats was able to see as clearly as he did the way in which he must go.

The things which Keats actually did reflect sufficient glory upon him to make it unnecessary to ascribe to him things which he did not do. He did not produce a *Divine Comedy*, or a *Macbeth*, or a *Paradise Lost*. But he did seize with exceptional strength the principle of beauty in things, and he put his theory of beauty with extraordinary vigor, with "astonishing strength," into practice. He pursued his vision of beauty with clear-eyed sanity in a perfect balance of theory and practice, so far as his youth and experience permitted. His is the glory of having reached as high a level of achievement at the age of twenty-five as any poet on record, and of having consistently and everlastingly traveled the right road toward high achievement. (pp. 183-85)

> *Solomon F. Gingerich, "The Conception of Beauty in the Works of Shelley, Keats, and Poe," in* Essays and Studies, *Vol. VIII, 1932, pp. 169-94.*

Cleanth Brooks, Jr. (essay date 1944)

[*Brooks is the most prominent of the New Critics, an influential movement in American criticism that also included Allen Tate, John Crowe Ransom, and Robert Penn Warren. Although the New Critics did not subscribe to a single set of principles, they believed that a work of literature had to be examined as an object in itself through a process of close analysis of symbol, image, and metaphor. For Brooks, metaphor was the primary element of literary art, and the effect of that metaphor of primary importance. In the following excerpt, he analyzes "Ode on a Grecian Urn" to determine the relationship of the final two lines to the poem's total context.*]

[Our] specific question [regarding **"Ode on a Grecian Urn"**] is not what did Keats the man probably want to assert here about the relation of beauty and truth; it is rather: was Keats the poet able to exemplify that relation in this particular poem. Middleton Murry is right: the relation of the final statement in the poem to the total context is all-important.

Indeed, Eliot, in [a] passage in which he attacks the **"Ode,"** has indicated the general line which we are to take in its defense. In that passage, Eliot goes on to contrast the closing lines of the **"Ode"** with a line from *King Lear*, "Ripeness is all." Keats' lines strike him as false; Shakespeare's, on the other hand, as not clearly false, and as possibly quite true. Shakespeare's generalization, in other words, avoids raising the question of truth. But is it really a question of truth and falsity? One is tempted to account for the difference of effect which Eliot feels in this way: "Ripeness is all" is a statement put in the mouth of a dramatic character and a statement which is governed and qualified by the whole context of the play. It does not directly challenge an examination into its truth because its relevance is pointed up and modified by the dramatic context.

Now, suppose that one could show that Keats' lines, *in quite the same way*, constitute a speech, a consciously riddling paradox, put in the mouth of a particular character, and modified by the total context of the poem. If we could demonstrate that the speech was "in character," was dramatically appropriate, was properly prepared for, then would not the lines have all the justification of "Ripeness is all"? (p. 91)

The silence of the urn is stressed—it is a "bride of quietness;" it is the "foster-child of silence," but the urn is a "historian" too. Historians tell the truth, or are at least expected to tell the truth. What is a "sylvan historian?" A historian who is like the forest rustic, a woodlander? Or, a historian who writes histories of the forest? Presumably, the urn is sylvan in both senses. True, the latter meaning is uppermost; the urn can "express / A flowery tale more sweetly than our ryme," and what the urn goes on to express are tales of Tempe and the dales of Arcady. But the urn, like the "leaf-fring'd legend" which it tells, is covered with emblems of the fields and forests: "Overwrought / With forest branches and the trodden weed." When we consider the way in which the urn utters its history, the fact that it must be sylvan in both senses is seen as inevitable. Perhaps, too, the fact that it is a rural historian, a rustic, a peasant historian, qualifies in our minds the dignity and the "truth" of the histories which it recites. Its histories, Keats has already conceded, may be characterized as "tales"—not formal history at all.

The sylvan historian certainly supplies no names and dates—"What men or gods are these?" the poet asks. What it does give is action—of men *or* gods, of godlike men or of super-human (though not daemonic) gods—action, which is not the less intense for all that the urn is cool marble. The words "mad" and "ecstasy" occur, but it is the quiet, rigid urn which gives the dynamic picture. And the paradox goes further: the scene is one of violent love-making, a Bacchanalian scene, but the urn itself is like a "still unravished bride," or like a child, a child "of silence and slow time." It is not merely like a child, but like a "foster-child." The exactness of the term can be defended. "Silence and slow time," it is suggested, are not the true parents, but foster-parents. They are too old, one feels, to have borne the child themselves. Moreover, they dote upon the "child" as grandparents do. The urn is fresh and unblemished; it is still young, for all its antiquity and time which destroys so much has "fostered" it.

With Stanza II we move into the world presented by the urn, into an examination, not of the urn as a whole—as an entity with its own form—but of the details which overlay it. But as we enter that world, the paradox of silent speech is carried on, this time in terms of the objects portrayed on the vase.

The first lines of the stanza state a rather bold paradox—even the dulling effect of many readings has hardly blunted it. At least we can easily revive its sharpness. Attended to with care, it is a statement which is preposterous, and yet true—true on the same level on which the original metaphor of the speaking urn is true. The unheard music is sweeter than any audible music. The poet has rather cunningly enforced his conceit by using the phrase, "Ye soft pipes." Actually, we might accept the poet's metaphor without being forced to accept the adjective "soft." The pipes might, although unheard, be shrill, just as the action which is frozen in the figures on the urn can be violent and ecstatic as in Stanza I and slow and dignified as in Stanza IV (the procession to the sacrifice). Yet, by characterizing the pipes as "soft," the poet provides a sort of realistic basis for his metaphor: the pipes, it is suggested, are playing very softly; if we listen carefully, we can hear them; their music is just below the threshold of normal sound.

This general paradox runs through the stanza: action goes on though the actors are motionless; the song will not cease; the lover cannot leave his song; the maiden, always to be kissed, never actually kissed, will remain changelessly beautiful. The maiden is, indeed, like the urn itself, a "still unravished bride of quietness"—not even ravished by a kiss; and it is implied, perhaps, that her changeless beauty, like that of the urn, springs from this fact.

The poet is obviously stressing the fresh, unwearied charm of the scene itself which can defy time and is deathless. But, at the same time, the poet is being perfectly fair to the terms of his metaphor. The beauty portrayed is deathless because it is lifeless. And it would be possible to shift the tone easily and ever so slightly by insisting more heavily on some of the phrasing so as to give them a darker implication. Thus, in the case of "thou canst not leave / Thy song," one could interpret: he cannot leave the song even

if he would: he is fettered to it, a prisoner. In the same way, one could enlarge on the hint that the lover is not wholly satisfied and content: "never canst thou kiss, / . . . yet do not grieve." These items are mentioned here, not because one wishes to maintain that the poet is bitterly ironical, but because it is important for us to see that even here the paradox is being used fairly, particularly in view of the shift in tone which comes in the next stanza.

This third stanza represents, as various critics have pointed out, a recapitulation of earlier motifs. The boughs which cannot shed their leaves, the unwearied melodist, and the ever-ardent lover reappear. Indeed, I am not sure that this stanza can altogether be defended against the charge that it represents a falling-off from the delicate but firm precision of the earlier stanzas. There is a tendency to linger over the scene sentimentally: the repetition of the word "happy" is perhaps symptomatic of what is occurring. Here, if anywhere, in my opinion, is to be found the blemish on the ode—not in the last two lines. (pp. 92-5)

But though the poet has developed and extended his metaphors furthest here in this third stanza, the ironic counterpoise is developed furthest too. The love which a line earlier was "warm" and "panting" becomes suddenly in the next line, "All breathing human passion far above." But if it is *above* all breathing passion, it is, after all, outside the realm of breathing passion, and therefore, not human passion at all.

(If one argues that we are to take "All breathing human passion" as qualified by "That leaves a heart high-sorrowful and cloy'd"—that is, if one argues that Keats is saying that the love depicted on the urn is above only that human passion which leaves one cloyed and not above human passion in general, he misses the point. For Keats in the **"Ode"** is stressing the ironic fact that all human passion *does* leave one cloyed; hence the superiority of art.)

The purpose in emphasizing the ironic undercurrent in the foregoing lines is not at all to disparage Keats—to point up implications of his poem of which he was himself unaware. Far from it: the poet knows precisely what he is doing. The point is to be made simply in order to make sure that we are completely aware of what he *is* doing. Garrod, sensing this ironic undercurrent, seems to interpret it as an element over which Keats was not able to exercise full control. He says: "Truth to his main theme [the fixity given by art to forms which in life are impermanent] has taken Keats farther than he meant to go. The pure and ideal art of this 'cold Pastoral,' this 'silent form,' *has* a cold silentness which in some degree saddens him. In the last lines of the fourth stanza, especially the last three lines . . . every reader is conscious, I should suppose, of an undertone of sadness, of disappointment." The undertone is there, but Keats has not been taken "farther than he meant to go." Keats' attitude, even in the early stanzas, is more complex than Garrod would allow: it is more complex and more ironic, and a recognition of this is important if we are to be able to relate the last stanza to the rest of the **"Ode."** Keats is perfectly aware that the frozen moment of loveliness is more dynamic than is the fluid world of reality only because it *is* frozen. The love depicted on the urn remains warm and young because it is not human flesh at all but cold, ancient marble.

With Stanza IV, we are still within the world depicted by the urn, but the scene presented in this stanza forms a contrast to the earlier scenes. It emphasizes, not individual aspiration and desire, but communal life. It constitutes another chapter in the history that the "sylvan historian" has to tell. And again, names and dates have been omitted. We are not told to what god's altar the procession moves, nor the occasion of the sacrifice. (pp. 95-7)

The stanza has been justly admired. Its magic of effect defies reduction to any formula. Yet, without pretending to "account" for the effect in any mechanical fashion, one can point to some of the elements active in securing the effect: there is the suggestiveness of the word "green" in green altar—something natural, spontaneous, living; there is the suggestion that the little town is caught in a curve of the seashore, or nestled in a fold of the mountains—at any rate, is something secluded and something naturally related to its terrain; there is the effect of the phrase "peaceful citadel," a phrase which involves a clash between the ideas of war and peace and resolves it in the sense of stability and independence without imperialistic ambition—the sense of stable repose.

But to return to the larger pattern of the poem: Keats does something in this fourth stanza which is highly interesting in itself and thoroughly relevant to the sense in which the urn is a historian. One of the most moving passages in the poem is that in which the poet speculates on the strange emptiness of the little town which, of course, has not been pictured on the urn at all.

The little town which has been merely implied by the procession portrayed on the urn is endowed with a poignance beyond anything else in the poem. Its streets will "for evermore be silent," its desolation forever shrouded in a mystery. No one in the figured procession will ever be able to go back to the town to break the silence there, not even one to tell the stranger there why the town remains desolate.

If one attends closely to what Keats is doing here, he may easily come to feel that the poet is indulging himself in an ingenious fancy, an indulgence, however, which is gratuitous and finally silly; that is, the poet has created in his own imagination the town implied by the procession of worshippers, has given it a special character of desolation and loneliness, and then has gone on to treat it as if it were a real town to which a stranger might actually come and be puzzled by its emptiness. (I can see no other interpretation of the line, "and not a soul to tell / Why thou art desolate can ere return.") But, actually, of course, no one will ever discover the town except by the very same process by which Keats discovers it: namely, through the figured urn, and then, of course, he will not need to ask why it is empty. One can well imagine what a typical eighteenth-century critic would have made of this flaw in logic.

It will not be too difficult, however, to show that Keats' extension of the fancy is not irrelevant to the poem as a whole. The "reality" of the little town has a very close relation to the urn's character as a historian. If the earlier stanzas have been concerned with such paradoxes as the ability of static carving to convey dynamic action, of the soundless pipes to play music sweeter than that of the heard melody, of the figured lover to have a love more warm and panting than that of breathing flesh and blood,

so in the same way the town implied by the urn comes to have a richer and more important history than that of actual cities. Indeed, the imagined town is to the figured procession as the unheard melody is to the carved pipes of the unwearied melodist. And the poet, by pretending to take the town as real—so real that he can imagine the effect of its silent streets upon the stranger who chances to come into it—has suggested in the most powerful way that he can its essential reality for him—and for us. It is a case of the doctor's taking his own medicine: the poet is prepared to stand by the illusion of his own making.

With Stanza V we move out of the enchanted world portrayed by the urn to consider the urn itself once more as a whole, as an object. The shift in point of view is marked with the first line of the stanza by the apostrophe, "O Attic shape. . . . " It is the urn itself as a formed thing, as an autonomous world, to which the poet addresses these last words. And the rich, almost breathing world which the poet has conjured up for us contracts and hardens into the decorated motifs on the urn itself: "with brede / Of marble men and maidens over-wrought." The beings who have a life above life—"All breathing human passion far above"—are marble, after all.

This last is a matter which, of course, the poet has never denied. The recognition that the men and maidens are frozen, fixed, arrested, has, as we have already seen, run through the second, third, and fourth stanzas as an ironic undercurrent. The central paradox of the poem, thus, comes to conclusion in the phrase, "cold Pastoral." The word "pastoral" suggests warmth, spontaneity, the natural, and the informal as well as the idyllic, the simple, and the informally charming. What the urn tells is a "flowery tale," a "leaf-fring'd legend," but the "sylvan historian" works in terms of marble. The urn itself is cold, and the life beyond life which it expresses is life which has been formed, arranged. The urn itself is a "silent form," and it speaks, not by means of statement, but by "teasing us out of thought." It is as enigmatic as eternity is, for, like eternity, its history is beyond time, outside time, and for this very reason bewilders our time-ridden minds: it teases us. (pp. 97-9)

The urn is beautiful, and yet its beauty is based—what else is the poem concerned with?—on an imaginative perception of essentials. Such a vision is beautiful but it is also true. / The Sylvan historian presents us with beautiful histories, but they are true histories, and it is a good historian.

Moreover, the "truth" which the sylvan historian gives is the only kind of truth which we are likely to get on this earth, and, furthermore, it is the only kind that we *have* to have. The names, dates, and special circumstances, the wealth of data—these the sylvan historian quietly ignores. But we shall never get all the facts anyway—there is no end to the accumulation of facts. Moreover, mere accumulations of facts—a point our own generation is beginning to realize—are meaningless. The sylvan historian does better than that: it takes a few details and so orders them that we have not only beauty but insight into essential truth. Its "history," in short, is a history without footnotes. It has the validity of myth—not myth as a pretty but irrelevant make-belief, an idle fancy, but myth as a valid perception into reality. (p. 100)

And now, what of the objection that the final lines break

the tone of the poem with a display of misplaced sententiousness? One can summarize the answer already implied thus: throughout the poem the poet has stressed the paradox of the speaking urn. First, the urn itself can tell a story, can give a history. Then, the various figures depicted upon the urn play music or speak or sing. If we have been alive to these items, we shall not, perhaps be too much surprised to have the urn speak once more, not in the sense in which it tells a story—a metaphor which is rather easy to accept—but, to have it speak on a higher level, to have it make a commentary on its own nature. If the urn has been properly dramatized, if we have followed the development of the metaphors, if we have been alive to the paradoxes which work thoughout the poem, perhaps then, we shall be prepared for the enigmatic, final paradox which the "silent form" utters. But in that case, we shall not feel that the generalization, unqualified and to be taken literally, is meant to march out of its context to compete with the scientific and philosophical generalizations which dominate our world.

"Truth is beauty, beauty truth" has precisely the same status, and the same justification as Shakespeare's "Ripeness is all." It is a speech "in character" and supported by a dramatic context. (pp. 100-01)

> *Cleanth Brooks, Jr., "History without Footnotes: An Account of Keats' Urn," in* The Sewanee Review, *Vol. LII, No. 1, Winter, 1944, pp. 89-101.*

Allen Tate   (essay date 1946)

[*Tate was an important critic, editor, and poet who is closely associated with two critical movements, the Agrarians and the New Criticism. The Agrarians were concerned with political and social issues as well as literature, and were dedicated to preserving traditional Southern values. The New Critics, one of the most influential critical movements of the mid-twentieth century, did not subscribe to a single set of principals but agreed that a work of literature should be examined as an object in itself and could not be evaluated in the general terms of any nonliterary discipline. Tate, however, believed that literature is the principal form of knowledge and revelation which restores human beings to a proper relationship with nature and the spiritual realm. In the excerpt below, he discusses Keats's pictorial technique, focusing on "Ode to a Nightingale" and "Ode on a Grecian Urn."*]

When Keats adds to "things as perceived," what does he add? That, it seems to me, is the special problem of Keats. In the simplest language it is the problem of adding movement to a static picture, of putting into motion the "languor which lingers in the main design" (Robert Bridges) of even the later work.

Of the eight stanzas of **"Ode to a Nightingale"** six are distinctly pictorial in method; a seventh, stanza three, in which Keats expresses his complaint of common life, develops as a meditation out of the second stanza, the picture of Provence. The only stanza which does not give us or in some way pertain to a definite scene is number seven; for though the method there is pictorial, the effect is allusive. The permanence of the nightingale's song is established in

a rapid series of vignettes, ending with the famous "faery lands forlorn." It is the only stanza, as some critic has remarked, which contains a statement contradictory of our sense of common reality.

> Thou wast not born for death, immortal Bird,

he says to the nightingale, and we cannot agree. The assertion is out of form in an obvious sense, for the poem is an accumulation of pictorial situations, and the claim of immortality for the bird is dramatic and lyrical.

I am raising the question whether the metonymy which attributes to the literal nightingale the asserted immortality of the song is convincing enough to carry the whole imaginative insight of the poem. I think it is, given the limits of Keats's art, but I am still nagged by a difficulty. . . . It seems to me that the ambivalence of the nightingale symbol contains almost the whole substance of the poem: the bird, as bird, shares the mortality of the world; as symbol, it purports to transcend it. And I feel that the pictorial technique has not been quite dramatic enough to give the transcendence of the symbol life in some visibly presented experience. The far more implausible, even far-fetched metaphor of the draughtsman's compasses, in Donne, comes out a little better because through a series of dialectical transformations, from the dying man to the Ptolemaic spheres, and then through the malleable gold to the compasses, there is a series of connected analogies, given us step by step. We acknowledge the identity of compasses and lovers as imaginatively possible. Keats merely *asserts:* song equals immortality; and I feel there is some disparity between the symbol and what it is expected to convey—not an inherent disparity, for such is not imaginatively conceivable, but a disparity such as we should get in the simple equation A = B, if we found that the assigned values of A and B were respectively I and 3.

This disparity of symbol and visible object we shall find in **"Ode on a Grecian Urn,"** but not in **"Ode to Psyche."** I confess that I do not know what to do about this anomalous poem, except to admire it. There appears to me to be very little genuine *sensation* in Keats (rather what Arnold and his contemporaries mistook for sensation), but there is more of it in **"Ode to Psyche"** than anywhere else in the great odes. Mr. T. S. Eliot puts it first among the odes, possibly because most of its detail is genuinely experienced and because it contains no developed attitude towards life. The other odes do, and it is an attitude less mature than that which Mr. Eliot finds in the *Letters.* With this part of his view of Keats one must agree. (pp. 189-90)

At any rate, the disparity to which I have referred is doubtless connected with the common prejudice that romantic art tends not only to be pictorial but "off center" and lacking in the mastery of logical structure which we ordinarily associate with the maturity of Donne and Dryden or even Pope. I do not want to get into this classical-and-romantic affair, for the usual reasons, and for a reason of my own, which is that it has a way of backfiring. Mr. Eliot has said that Coleridge and Wordsworth on one side are "as eighteenth century as anybody." So is Keats. The apostrophe to the nightingale, which I have been at some pains to try to understand, is quite "eighteenth century." But it is not nearly so eighteenth century as the entire third stanza, which I shall now try to understand, assuming that what it says has a close connection with that literal part of the nightingale, the physical bird, which Keats seemed not to know what to do with (except to make it, in the last stanza, fly away). Here it is:

> Fade far away, dissolve, and quite forget
> What thou among the leaves hast never known,
> The weariness, the fever, and the fret
> Here where men sit and hear each other groan;
> Where palsy shakes a few, sad, last gray hairs,
> Where youth grows pale, and spectre-thin, and dies;
> Where but to think is to be full of sorrow
> And leaden-eyed despairs,
> Where beauty cannot keep her lustrous eyes,
> Or new Love pine at them beyond tomorrow.

Looked at from any point of view, this stanza is bad; the best that one ought to say of it perhaps is that there are worse things in Shelley and Wordsworth, and in Keats himself. It is bad in the same way that the passages in Shelley's "Adonaïs" which exhibit the troops of mourners are bad. Keats here is relapsing into weakened eighteenth-century rhetoric. Blake could have put into the personifications imaginative power, and Pope genuine feeling—or at any rate an elegance and vigor which would have carried them. (pp. 190-91)

What I wish to indicate, for the consideration of more thorough readers, is that stanza three may be of the utmost significance in any attempt to understand the structure of Keats's poetry. It gives us a "picture" of common reality, in which the life of man is all mutability and frustration. But here, if anywhere in the poem, the necessity to dramatize time or the pressure of actuality is paramount. *Keats has no language of his own for this realm of experience.* That is the capital point. He either falls into the poetic language of the preceding age, or, if he writes spontaneously, he commits his notorious errors of taste. In either case the language is not adequate to the object— or, to put it "cognitively," he lacks a dynamic symbolism through which he may *know* the common and the ideal reality in a single imaginative act. (pp. 191-92)

The consciousness of change and decay, which can, and did in Keats, inform one of the great modes of poetry, is deeply involved with his special attitude towards sexual love. He never presents love directly and dramatically; it is in terms of Renaissance tapestry, as in **"The Eve of St. Agnes"**; in a fable of Italian violence, as in **"Isabella"**; or, most interesting of all, in terms of a little myth, Lamia the snake-woman—a symbol which permits Keats to objectify the mingled attraction and repulsion which his treatment of love usually contains. I sometimes think that for this reason **Lamia** is his best long poem: the symbol inherently contains the repulsive element, but keeps it at a distance, so that he does not have to face it in terms of common experience, his own, or as he was aware of it in his age. Is it saying too much to suppose that Keats's acceptance of the pictorial method is to a large extent connected with his unwillingness to deal with passion dramatically? (There is sensuous detail, but no sensation as direct experience, such as we find in Baudelaire.) (p. 192)

Messrs. Brooks and Warren, in their excellent if somewhat confident analysis of the Nightingale ode in *Understanding Poetry,* argue with much conviction that the dramatic frame of the poem, the painful accession to the trance in the opening lines and the return to immediate reality ("Do I wake or sleep?") at the end, provides a sufficient form.

I confess that I am not sure. I am not certain of the meaning of what happens inside the frame, but at times I am not certain that it is necessary to understand it. There is no perfection in poetry. All criticism must in the end be comparative (this does not mean critical relativity); it must constantly refer to what poetry has accomplished in order to estimate what it can accomplish, not what it ought to accomplish: we must heed Mr. Ransom's warning that perfect unity or integration in a work of art is a critical delusion. **"Ode to a Nightingale"** is by any standard one of the great poems of the world. Our philosophical difficulties with it are not the same as Keats's imaginative difficulties, which pertain to the order of experience and not of reason. The poem is an emblem of one limit of our experience: the impossibility of synthesizing, in the order of experience, the antinomy of the ideal and the real. And although that antinomy strikes the human mind with a different force in different ages (Donne's dualism is not Keats's), it is sufficiently common to all men in all times to be understood.

If we glance at **"Ode on a Grecian Urn,"** we shall see Keats trying to unify his pictorial effects by means of direct philosophical statement. "Do I wake or sleep?" at the end of the Nightingale ode asks the question: Which is reality, the symbolic nightingale, or the common world? The famous Truth-Beauty synthesis at the end of the **"Grecian Urn"** contains the same question, but this time it is answered. As Mr. Kenneth Burke sees it, Truth is the practical scientific world and Beauty is the ideal world above change. The "frozen" figures on the urn, being both alive and dead, constitute a scene which is at once perceptible and fixed. "This transcendent scene," says Mr. Burke, "is the level at which the earthly laws of contradiction no longer prevail." The one and the many, the eternal and the passing, the sculpturesque and the dramatic, become synthesized in a higher truth. (pp. 193-94)

I would point to a particular feature, in the last six lines of stanza four, which I feel that neither Mr. Brooks nor Mr. Burke has taken into a certain important kind of consideration. Here Keats tells us that in the background of this world of eternal youth there is another, from which it came, and that this second world has thus been emptied and is indeed a dead world:

> What little town by river or sea-shore,
> Or mountain-built with peaceful citadel,
> Is emptied of this folk, this pious morn?
> And, little town, thy streets for evermore
> Will silent be; and not a soul to tell
> Why thou art desolate, can e'er return.

Mr. Burke quite rightly sees in this passage the key to the symbolism of the entire poem. It is properly the "constatation" of the tensions of the imagery. What is the meaning of this perpetual youth on the urn? One of its meanings is that it is perpetually anti-youth and anti-life; it is in fact dead, and "can ne'er return." Are we not faced again with the same paradox we had in the Nightingale ode, that the intensest life is achieved in death? Mr. Burke brings out with great skill the erotic equivalents of the life-death symbols, and for his analysis of the developing imagery throughout we owe him a great debt. Yet I feel that Mr. Burke's own dialectical skill leads him to consider the poem, when he is through with it, a philosophical discourse. But it is, if it is anything (and it is a great deal) what is ordinarily known as a work of art. Mr. Burke's elucidation of the Truth-Beauty proposition in the last stanza is the most convincing dialectically that I have seen; but Keats did not write Mr. Burke's elucidation, and I feel that the entire last stanza, except the phrase "Cold Pastoral" (which probably ought to be somewhere else in the poem) is an illicit commentary added by the poet to a "meaning" which was symbolically complete at the end of the preceding stanza, number four. Or perhaps it may be said that Keats did to some extent write Mr. Burke's elucidation; that may be why I feel that the final stanza (though magnificently written) is redundant and out of form.

To the degree that I am guilty with Mr. Burke of a prepossession which may blind me to the whole value of this poem (as his seems to limit his perception of possible defects), I am not qualified to criticize it. Here, towards the end of this [discussion], I glance back at the confession, which I made earlier, of the distance and detachment of my warmest admiration for Keats. It is now time that I tried to state the reasons for this a little more summarily—in brief, a comparison of the two fine odes that we have been considering.

Both odes are constructed pictorially in spatial blocks, for the eye to take in serially. Though to my mind this method is better suited to the subject of the **"Grecian Urn,"** which is itself a plastic object, than to the Nightingale ode, I take the latter, in spite of the blemishes of detail (only some of which we have looked at),, to be the finer poem. If there is not as much in it as in the **"Grecian Urn"** for the elucidation of verbal complexity, there is nowhere the radical violation of its set limits that one finds in the last stanza of the **"Grecian Urn"**:

> Thou shalt remain, in midst of other woes
> Than ours, a friend to man, to whom thou say'st,
> Beauty is truth, truth beauty,—that is all
> Ye know on earth, and all ye need to know.

It is here that the poem gets out of form, that the break in "point of view" occurs; and if it is a return to Samuel Johnson's dislike of "Lycidas" (I don't think it is) to ask how an urn can say anything, I shall have to suffer the consequences of that view. It is Keats himself, of course, who says it; but "Keats" is here not implicit in the structure of the poem, as he is in **"Ode to a Nightingale."** What he says is what the mathematicians call an extrapolation, an intrusion of matter from another field of discourse, so that even if it be "true" philosophically, it is not a visible function of what the poem says. With the "dead" mountain citadel in mind, could we not phrase the message of the urn equally well as follows: Truth is *not* beauty, since even art itself cannot do more with death than preserve it, and the beauty frozen on the urn is also dead since it cannot move. This "pessimism" may be found as easily in the poem as Keats's comforting paradox. So I should return to the Nightingale ode for its superior *dramatic* credibility, even though the death-life antinomy is not more satisfactorily resolved than in the **"Grecian Urn."** The fall of the "I" of the poem into the trance-like meditation in the first stanza, and the shocked coming-to at the end, *ground* the poem in imaginable action, so that the dialectics of the nightingale symbol do not press for resolution. So I confess a reserved agreement with Brooks and Warren.

The outlines of the conflicting claims of the ideal and the actual, in Keats's mind, I have set down in this portion of my [discussion]. I have been immediately concerned with the technical exemplification of Keats's art, yet the technical limits of an art must always if only negatively point towards the *kind* of experience which a poet is able to bring to order. That Keats's mind was "larger" than any single poem he wrote has long been a critical intuition. It has been one of the purposes of this [discussion] to set forth a possible meaning for that intuition. I hope that other writers will give us their "meanings," and that in this way the poetry of Keats will continue to prove itself alive. (pp. 195-97)

> *Allen Tate, "A Reading of Keats (II)," in* The American Scholar, *Vol. 15, No. 2, Spring, 1946, pp. 189-97.*

Richard H. Fogle   (essay date 1947)

[*In the excerpt below, Fogle refutes literary critic and historian Douglas Bush's contention that "Ode to a Nightingale" and "Ode on a Grecian Urn" express "the very acme of melancholy."*]

Douglas Bush remarks of Keats's poetry in general, "From first to last Keats's important poems are related to, or grow directly out of . . . inner conflicts," and of the "Odes" he says

> At first sight Keats's theme in the **"Ode to a Nightingale"** and the **"Ode on a Grecian Urn"** . . . is the belief that whereas the momentary experience of beauty is fleeting, the ideal embodiment of that moment in art, in song, or in marble, is an imperishable source of joy. If that were all, these odes should be hymns of triumph, and they are not. It is the very acme of melancholy that the joy he celebrates is joy in beauty that must die.

This comment is valuable, but misleading in emphasis. There are indeed conflicts in Keats's poetry, but in the odes cited by Professor Bush these conflicts are reconciled. The "Odes" do not express "the very acme of melancholy" any more than they express the very acme of joy. They express an exquisite awareness of the existence of joy and melancholy, pleasure and pain, and art and life. They express a feeling that these are inseparable, although not identical, and they express acceptance of this inseparability of the elements of human experience. In the **"Ode to a Nightingale"** Keats portrays a state of intense aesthetic and imaginative feeling, too poignant for long duration, which arises with the song of a bird and vanishes when the song is done. The poet records his emotion and its passing without comment.

The impossibility of maintaining this mood of exaltation is the condition of its existence, for it is relative, and describable only by comparing it with more commonplace states of mind. No mood, furthermore, is simple and unalloyed by other feelings. Keats begins,

> My heart aches, and a drowsy numbness pains
> My sense, as though of hemlock I had drunk. . . .

This is not from grief, or envy of the nightingale, but from

> . . . being too happy in thine happiness.

As in the **"Ode on Melancholy"** he declares that intense pleasure is almost indistinguishable from numbing pain.

The **"Nightingale"** moves as a whole with the same steady advance and withdrawal as does the **"Grecian Urn."** Stanzas II and III, however, represent as it were a false start, after the mood has been established in I. The "draught of vintage" by whose magic power Keats would escape "the weariness, the fever, and the fret" of life is rejected. If the last five lines of stanza III are drawn from Keats's own suffering, that suffering is here sublimated.

> Where Beauty cannot keep her lustrous eyes,
> Or new Love pine at them beyond tomorrow

has a serenity and ironic undertone not to be found in the poet's relations with Fanny Brawne.

The true beginning comes in Stanza IV. Keats flies to the nightingale—

> Not charioted by Bacchus and his pards,
> But on the viewless wings of Poesy.

The poem reaches its full intensity in this stanza and the three following. This outpouring of imaginative exaltation contrasts with the melancholy of the low-pitched stanza III, by itself unremarkable but functioning as an integral part of the poetic whole. As in the **"Eve of St. Agnes"** Keats uses life at its most unpromising as a point of departure. Only by being aware of sorrow can the poet devote himself wholeheartedly to joy, conscious the while that his respite will be brief. The soft and heavy texture of the imagery in IV and V reflects a spontaneous luxuriance of feeling and perception, a self-abandonment which is merely another aspect of his previous depression.

Stanza VI commences

> Darkling I listen; and, for many a time
> I have been half in love with easeful Death, . . .

The vivid sensuousness of the two preceding stanzas has been leading toward this. Death itself may offer the fullest sense of life:

> Now more than ever seems it *rich* to die.

If the **"Nightingale"** is a lament for the brevity of life and joy, as Professor Bush has said, these are sentiments difficult to explain; but if the poem is simply an imaginative reflection of the complexity and intensity of human experience, Death may quite reasonably be viewed as its culmination.

The spell is deepest in stanza VII, of which M. R. Ridley has said that it "would, I suppose, by common consent be taken along with 'Kubla Khan,' as offering us the distilled sorceries of Romanticism." In these lines the apparent contrast between the immortality of the Bird and the fugitive temporality of its hearers is strongly insisted upon:

> No hungry generations tread thee down;
> The voice I hear this passing night was heard
> In ancient days by emperor and clown:
> Perhaps the self-same song that found a path
> Through the sad heart of Ruth, when, sick for home
> She stood in tears amid the alien corn. . . .

Yet this opposition is not real. The "sad heart of Ruth" is as enduring as the nightingale, and after the same fashion. The temporal Ruth died long ago, the eternal Ruth lives on in poetry. Nor can one separate the temporal from the eternal, for it is by virtue of her grief, her exposure to accidental circumstance long since passed away, that she remains alive. So with the "magic casements" which follow, but with a difference. Paradoxically, these are immortal because they have long since vanished, or alternatively because they never in cold fact existed. This paradox is the essence of their charm and their reality; viewed faintly down long vistas of time, or created consciously by imagination from diverse materials seized from the actual world, they have a unique being of their own. They exist as fully as the stubbornest, most intractable actuality, but they arise from actuality and cannot live apart from it. In this stanza the notions of temporality and timelessness do not conflict, but are brought together in harmonious relationship.

It is not mere accident that Keats breaks off here, at the peak of imaginative intensity, on the word "forlorn," which has its feet in two worlds. For the value of the imaginative experience depends upon its transience; it is only one mode, albeit the highest, among many. With consummate irony and psychological truth "forlorn" breaks in like the tolling of a bell to signal the end of the poet's emotional exaltation. The "faery lands" were "forlorn" because remote and strange; the word itself is enchanted. The second "forlorn" is homely and familiar, with a half-humorous ruefulness. It dwells upon the common earth, to which the poet now returns.

The final stanza fills out the perfect rondure of the poem in a slow withdrawal, symbolized by the retreat of the bird itself so that objective description and subjective emotion are fused. The fading-away is slow and regular,

> Past the near meadows, over the still stream,
> Up the hill-side; and now 'tis buried deep
> In the next valley-glades . . .

and in the last two verses the process of withdrawal, now solely within the poet, comes to a smooth and quiet end:

> Was it a vision or a waking dream?
> Fled is that music:—Do I wake or sleep?

Keats does not moralize after the event, nor utter lyric cries of pain, as he might be expected to if he were writing, for example, about the sadness of mutability. He has been writing about a full and rich experience, and having described that experience he stops. (pp. 81-4)

> *Richard H. Fogle, "A Note on Keats's 'Ode to a Nightingale',"* in Modern Language Quarterly, *Vol. 8, No. 1, March, 1947, pp. 81-4.*

Leonard Unger   (essay date 1950)

[*Unger was an American educator and literary critic. In the excerpt below, he examines the theme, imagery, and artistic achievement of "To Autumn." He also provides succinct comparisons to the other "great Odes."*]

It seems generally agreed that **"To Autumn"** is a rich and vivid description of nature, expertly achieved within a fairly intricate stanzaic pattern. The words are successfully descriptive (or evocative) in their phonetic qualities and rhythmical arrangement, as well as in their imagistic references. If we are familiar with Keats' other work, however, we can discover that the poem is not only rich in pictorial and sensuous details, but that it has a depth of meaning and a characteristic complexity of structure. **"To Autumn"** is allied especially to the odes on Melancholy, on a Grecian Urn, and to a Nightingale. The four poems are various treatments presenting differing aspects of a single theme.

In so far as the theme is "stated" in any of the poems, it is most clearly stated in the **"Ode on Melancholy."** In fact, if we want a general formulation of the theme, we need only quote the last stanza—especially these lines:

> Ay, in the very temple of Delight
> Veil'd Melancholy has her sovran shrine,
> Though seen of none save him whose strenuous tongue
> Can burst Joy's grape against his palate fine.

Keats was obviously preoccupied with the consideration that beauty and melancholy are closely related: true melancholy is to be found only in the fullness of living, in beauty, joy and delight, for these experiences make most poignant the passage of time, through which such experiences and then life itself must come to an end.

All this is clear enough in the **"Ode on Melancholy."** There is, however, the implication that the relationship between beauty and melancholy works both ways. That is, either joy or sadness is most intensely felt when it is attended by a consciousness of the experience which is opposite and yet so closely related to it. The theme, then, is more complex and subtle than the aspect of it which appears on the surface in **"Ode on Melancholy."** Other implications of the theme may be found throughout the four poems, which illuminate and clarify each other. This is not to say that the poems are merely repetitions of the same theme, which Keats had in mind before he wrote any of them. When we understand the poems we might find it more accurate to say that each is the exploration of a certain theme.

With so much of its context in mind, let us examine closely **"To Autumn."** The poem opens with an apostrophe to the season, and with a description of natural objects at their richest and ripest stage.

> Season of mists and mellow fruitfulness,
> Close bosom-friend of the maturing sun;
> Conspiring with him how to load and bless
> With fruit the vines that round the thatch-eaves run;
> To bend with apples the moss'd cottage-trees,
> And fill all fruit with ripeness to the core;
> To swell the gourd, and plump the hazel shells
> With a sweet kernel; to set budding more,
> And still more, later flowers for the bees,
> Until they think warm days will never cease,
> For Summer has o'er-brimm'd their clammy cells.

The details about the fruit, the flowers and the bees constitute a lush and colorful picture of autumn and the effects of the "maturing sun." In the final lines of the first stanza, however, slight implications about the passage of time begin to operate. The flowers are called "later," the bees are assumed to think that "warm days will never cease," and there is a reference to the summer which has already past.

In the second stanza, an imaginative element enters the description, and we get a personification of the season in several appropriate postures and settings.

> Who hath not seen thee oft amid thy store?
> Sometimes whoever seeks abroad may find
> Thee sitting careless on a granary floor,
> Thy hair soft-lifted by the winnowing wind;
> Or on a half-reap'd furrow sound asleep,
> Drows'd with the fume of poppies, while thy hook
> Spares the next swath and all its twined flowers:
> And sometimes like a gleaner thou dost keep
> Steady thy laden head across a brook;
> Or by a cyder-press, with patient look,
> Thou watchest the last oozings hours by hours.

As this stanza proceeds, the implications of the descriptive details become increasingly strong. For example, autumn is now seen, not as setting the flowers to budding, but as already bringing some of them to an end, although it "Spares the next swath." Autumn has become a "gleaner." The whole stanza presents the paradoxical qualities of autumn, its aspects both of lingering and passing. This is especially true of the final image. Autumn is the season of dying as well as of fulfilling. Hence it is with "*patient* look" that she (or he?) watches "the last oozings hours by hours." Oozing, or a steady dripping, is, of course, not unfamiliar as a symbol of the passage of time.

It is in the last stanza that the theme emerges most conspicuously.

> Where are the songs of Spring? Ay, where are they?
> Think not of them, thou hast thy music too,—
> While barred clouds bloom the soft-dying day,
> And touch the stubble-plains with rosy hue;
> Then in a wailful choir the small gnats mourn
> Among the river sallows, borne aloft
> Or sinking as the light wind lives or dies;
> And full-grown lambs loud bleat from hilly bourn;
> Hedge-crickets sing; and now with treble soft
> The red-breast whistles from a garden-croft;
> And gathering swallows twitter in the skies.

The opening question implies that the season of youth and rebirth, with its beauties of sight and sound, has passed, and that the season of autumn is passing. But autumn, too, *while* it lasts—"While barred clouds bloom the soft-dying day"—has its beauties, its music, as Keats' poem demonstrates. The imagery of the last stanza contrasts significantly with that of the first, and the final development of the poem adds meaning to its earlier portions. The slight implications are confirmed. We may recall that "maturing" means aging and ending as well as ripening. The earlier imagery is, of course, that of ripeness. But the final imagery is more truly autumnal. The first words used to describe the music of autumn are "wailful" and "mourn." The opening stanza suggests the height of day, when the sun is strong and the bees are gathering honey from the open flowers. But in the last stanza, after the passing of "hours and hours," we have "the soft-dying day," the imagery of sunset and deepening twilight, when the clouds impart their glow to the day and the plains. The transitive, somewhat rare use of the verb *bloom,* with its springlike associations, is perhaps surprising, and certainly appropriate and effective in suggesting the tensions of the theme, in picturing a beauty that is lingering, but *only* lingering. The conjunction of "rosy hue" and "stubble-plains" has the same significant incongruity, although the image is wholly convincing and actual in its reference. While the poem is more descriptive and suggestive than dramatic, its latent theme of transitoriness and mortality is symbolically dramatized by the passing course of the day. All these characteristics of the poem are to be found in its final image: "And gathering swallows twitter in the skies." Here we have the music of autumn. And our attention is directed toward the darkening skies. Birds habitually gather in flocks toward nightfall, particularly when they are preparing to fly south at the approach of winter. But they are still gathering. The day, the season, are "soft-dying" and are both the reality and the symbol of life as most intensely and poignantly beautiful when viewed from this melancholy perspective.

This reading of **"To Autumn"** is obviously slanted in the direction of a theme which is also found in the other odes. The theme is, of course, only a part of the poem, a kind of dimension, or extension, which is almost concealed by other features of the poem, particularly by the wealth of concrete descriptive detail. Whereas in **"Ode on Melancholy"** the theme, in one of its aspects, is the immediate subject, in **"To Autumn"** the season is the subject and the details which describe and thus present the subject are also the medium by which the theme is explored. (pp. 20-4)

The poem has an obvious structure in so far as it is a coherent description. Its structure, however, is not simple in the sense of being merely continuous. For example, the course of the day parallels the development of the poem. And an awareness of the theme gives even greater significance to the structure, for the theme merges with increasing clarity and fullness throughout the poem until the very last line. Because the theme is always in the process of emerging without ever shaking off the medium in which it is developed, the several parts of the poem have a relationship to each other beyond their progression in a single direction. The gathering swallows return some borrowed meaning to the soft-dying day with substantial interest, and the whole last stanza negotiates with the first in a similar relationship. (If we had a special word for this kind of structure in poetry, we should be less inclined to discuss it figuratively. The words *organic* and *dynamic* have been used, as well as the word *dramatic*. Particularly in regard to Keats' poetry has *spatial* been used as a critical term (by Tate). For example, we might say that the structure of **"To Autumn"** is *spatial,* not only because of the quality of the imagery, but because the structural elements exist, or co-exist, in a relationship with each other which is different from the temporal progression that constitutes, on one level, all descriptive, narrative, and discursive writing. This *spatial* metaphor is applicable in more or less degree to any piece of writing in so far as it fulfills the formal conditions of art. It is by such considerations that we move in an ever widening circle away from the particular poem or experience, and the expressions which were initially metaphors thus tend to become abstract critical terms. **"To Autumn"** itself, as we have seen, has implications about space and time, but because it scarcely takes the first step into metaphor, which is also a step toward statement, it is of all the odes at the farthest extreme from abstraction.)

We have observed the descriptive, temporal (course of day), and thematic aspects of the structure. Another aspect of structure appears when, once more, we consider the poem within the context of Keats' work. **"To Autumn"** shares a feature of development with the odes on the Nightingale and the Grecian Urn. Each of these poems begins with presentation of realistic circumstances, then

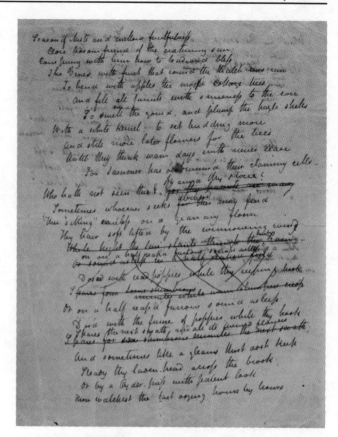

A portion of the handwritten manuscript of "To Autumn."

moves into an imagined realm, and ends with a return to the realistic. In **"Ode to a Nightingale,"** the most clearly dramatic of the poems, the speaker, hearing the song of the nightingale, wishes to fade with it "into the forest dim" and to forget the painful realities of life. This wish is fulfilled in the fourth stanza—the speaker exclaims, "Already with thee!" As the poem proceeds and while the imagined realm is maintained, the unpleasant realities come back into view. From the transition that begins with the desire for "easeful Death" and through the references to "hungry generations" and "the sad heart of Ruth," the imagined and the real, the beautiful and the melancholy, are held balanced against each other. Then, on the word "forlorn," the speaker turns away from the imagined, back to the real and his "sole self."

"Ode on a Grecian Urn" opens with an apostrophe to the actual urn. In the second stanza the imagined realm, the "ditties of no tone," is invoked, and the "leaf-fringed legend" comes to life. And here, too, the imagined life and real life are set in contrast against each other—the imagined is the negation of the real. It is in the fourth stanza that the imagined life is most fully developed and at the same time collapses into the real. The urn is left behind and the people are considered as not only in the scenes depicted on the urn, but as having left some little town. With the image of the town, desolate and silent, the imagination has completed its course. The people can never return to the town. In the final stanza they are again "marble men and maidens" and the urn is a "Cold Pastoral." The statement about truth and beauty with which the poem ends is famous and much debated. It is conceivable that Keats is saying here what he has said elsewhere and in another way—in the Ode that begins

> Bards of Passion and of Mirth,
> Ye have left your souls on earth!
> Have ye souls in heaven too,
> Double-lived in regions new?

Toward the end of the poem there are these lines:

> Here, your earth-born souls still speak
> To mortals, of their little week;
> Of their sorrows and delights;
> Of their passions and their spites;
> Of their glory and their shame;
> What doth strengthen and what maim.
> Thus ye teach us, every day
> Wisdom, though fled far away.

Keats is not didactic here, nor does he claim didacticism for the bards. Their earth-born souls, their works, teach wisdom in speaking of the lives of men, and in bringing to men, generation after generation, an intensified awareness and thrill of being alive. It is the same wisdom which the urn will continue to teach "in midst of other woe." Keats believed that man's life, though rounded by a little sleep, is the stuff of which "a thing of beauty" is made. Art takes its truth from life, and then returns it to life as beauty. The paradox that "teases us out of thought" is that in a work of art there is a kind of life which is both dead and immortal. But, a melancholy truth, *only* the dead are immortal. If there is a heaven, Keats wanted it to be very much like earth, with a Mermaid Tavern where poets could bowse "with contented smack." Delight is inseparable from melancholy because it is not conceivable apart from the mortal predicament. The answer to the question at the end of **"Ode to a Nightingale"**—"Do I wake or sleep?"—is, Both. In the structural imaginative arc of the poem, the speaker is returned to the "drowsy numbness" wherein he is awake to his own mortal lot and no longer awake to the vision of beauty. Yet he knows that it is the same human melancholy which is in the beauty of the bird's "plaintive anthem" and in the truth of his renewed depression. His way of stating this knowledge is to ask the question. Such considerations may clarify the truth-beauty passage. Whether they justify artistically Keats' use of these clichés of Platonic speculation is another matter. Keats was no Platonist, and if he had avoided those terms or if he had indicated more obviously, within the poem, that he was using the word *truth* in a sense close to the materialism of his own times, **"Ode on a Grecian Urn"** would have had a different career in the history of literary criticism. It is unlikely that any amount of exegesis can rescue those last lines of the poem from associations with Platonic pietism, for Keats was not enough of a witty and conscious ironist to exploit successfully the philosophical ambiguities of *truth*. His romanticism was neither reactionary nor modernist in that way, and he may not even have been clearly aware of the ambiguity involved. If it could be proved that he was innocent of the ambiguity, and wanted only the philosophical prestige of the Platonic associations, then from his point of view the poem would not suffer from the difficulties which the merest sophistication can ascribe to it. Whether such ignorance of the law would be too outrageous to merit critical exoneration is a nice problem for critical theory.

In considering the arc of imagination as an aspect of structure, we have noticed that **"Ode to a Nightingale"** approaches general statement and that **"Ode on Grecian Urn"** arrives at it. **"To Autumn"** is obviously less explicit, although it shows the same structural aspect. The lush and realistic description of the first stanza is followed by the imagined picture of autumn as a person who, while a lovely part of a lively scene, is also intent upon destroying it. The personification is dropped in the final stanza, and there is again a realistic description, still beautiful but no longer lush, and suggesting an approaching bleakness.

The imaginative aspect of structure which the three odes have in common illustrates opinions which are in accord with the thought of Keats' times and which he occasionally expressed in his poetry. The romantic poets' preoccupation with nature is proverbial, and there are a number of studies (e.g., Caldwell's on Keats) relating their work and thought to the associationist psychology which was current in their times. According to this psychology, all complex ideas and all products of the imagination were, by the association of remembered sensations, evolved from sensory experiences. Keats found this doctrine interesting and important not because it led back to the mechanical functioning of the brain and the nervous system, but because sensations led to the imagination and finally to myth and poetry, and because the beauty of nature was thus allied with the beauty of art. In the early poem which begins, "I stood tip-toe upon a little hill," Keats suggests that the legends of classical mythology were created by poets responding to the beauties of nature:

> For what has made the sage or poet write
> But the fair paradise of Nature's light?
> In the calm grandeur of a sober line,
> We see the waving of the mountain pine;
> And when a tale is beautifully staid,
> We feel the safety of a hawthorn glade:
> • • • • • • • • • • • • • • •
> While at our feet, the voice of crystal bubbles
> Charms us at once away from all our troubles:
> So that we feel uplifted from the world,
> Walking upon the white clouds wreathed and curled.
> So felt he, who first told, how Psyche went
> On the smooth wind to realms of wonderment.
> • • • • • • • • • • • • • • •
> What first inspired a bard of old to sing
> Narcissus pining o'er the untainted spring?
> In some delicious ramble, he had found
> A little space with boughs all woven round;
> And in the midst of all, a clearer pool . . .

In the **"Ode to Psyche,"** which was written during the same year as the other odes (1819), Keats claims a similar experience for himself and contrasts it with those of the "bards of old." He has come upon Cupid and Psyche while he "wandered in a forest thoughtlessly." Although the times are "too late for antique vows" and the "fond believing lyre," he is still by his "own eyes inspired." If he cannot celebrate this symbolic deity with rites and shrine, then he proposes to do so with the service of the imagination, with "the wreath'd trellis of a working brain, . . . all the gardener Fancy e'er could feign" and with all that "shadowy thought can win." Conspicuous throughout Keats' work, blended and adjusted according to his own temperament and for his own purposes, are these *donnèes* of his time: a theory of the imagination, the Romantic preoccupation with nature, and the refreshed literary tradition of classical mythology. These are reflected by the structure of his most successful poems, and are an element in their interrelatedness.

"To Autumn" is shorter than the other odes, and simpler on the surface in several respects. The nightingale sings of summer "in full-throated ease," and the boughs in the flowery tale on the urn cannot shed their leaves "nor ever bid the Spring adieu." The world in which the longer odes have their setting is either young or in its prime, spring or summer. Consequently, in these poems some directness of statement and a greater complexity are necessary in order to develop the paradoxical theme, in order to penetrate deeply enough the temple of Delight and arrive at the sovran shrine of Melancholy. The urn's "happy melodist" plays a song of spring, and the "self-same song" of the nightingale is of summer. One of these songs has "no tone," and the other is in either "a vision or a waking dream," for the voice of the "immortal Bird" is finally symbolized beyond the "sensual ear." But the music of autumn, the twittering of the swallows, remains realistic and literal, because the tensions of Keats' theme are implicit in the actual conditions of autumn, when beauty and melancholy are merging on the very surface of reality. Keats' genius was away from statement and toward description, and in autumn he had the natural symbol for his meanings. If **"To Autumn"** is shorter than the other odes and less complex in its materials, it has the peculiar distinction of great compression achieved in simple terms. (pp. 24-9)

> Leonard Unger, "Keats and the Music of Autumn," in his The Man in the Name: Essays on the Experience of Poetry, *University of Minnesota Press, Minneapolis, 1956, pp. 18-29.*

Graham Hough (essay date 1953)

[*Hough is an English poet and literary critic. Hough rejects the New Criticism movement, preferring "the kind of biographical criticism that can see a work in relation to the whole mental and spiritual life of its author." In the following excerpt, he explains Keats's theory of negative capability, using excerpts from Keats's correspondence and poetry for clarification.*]

For Keats, the necessary precondition of poetry is submission to things as they are, without trying to intellectualize them into something else, submission to people as they are, without trying to indoctrinate or improve them. (We meet all this again, developed into a whole poetical creed, in Yeats's early essays.) Keats found this quality at its fullest in Shakespeare.

> It struck me what quality went to form a man of achievement, especially in literature—I mean *Negative Capability*, that is, when a man is capable of being in uncertainties, mysteries, doubts, without any irritable reaching after fact and reason.

This way of feeling grows naturally into a strong active and dramatic tendency, a wish to participate in the life of others, and an understanding of other people that is everywhere evident in the letters. Often Keats feels that this participation in the life of others, "the agony and strife of human hearts", ought to be the mainspring of his poetry. But it is not. The dealings with character and emotion are not the most memorable things in Keats's poetry. There are natures whose passion for life includes, but goes beyond, personality. D. H. Lawrence was perhaps one of these, and there is something of it in Keats. The total impression of the moment, the fusion of his own subjective emotion with sensations from the outside world is the ultimate reality for him; and the most typical and individual remarks in the letters seem to be in passages like the following:

> I scarcely remember counting upon any Happiness—I look not for it if it be not in the present hour—nothing startles me beyond the Moment. The setting sun will always set me to rights—or if a sparrow comes before my window I take part in its existence and pick about the Gravel.

Such a nature is not likely to find its best expression in a narrative of character and events, (or, as Keats hoped, in drama). It is at its height in moments of impassioned contemplation, when the life of the spirit is closely bound up with the objects of immediate sensuous experience. It was in some such mood that the **"Ode on Indolence"** was written. It is the first of the great Odes, written in March 1819; and all of them were written in this year. In the **"Ode on Indolence"** not Love, nor Ambition, nor Poetry makes it worth while to give up the luxurious enjoyment of the moment: none of them is

> so sweet as drowsy noons
> And evenings steep'd in honied indolence;
> O, for an age so sheltered from annoy,
> That I may never know how change the moons,
> Or hear the voice of busy common-sense!

Lines which might have served Matthew Arnold as the text for his sermon on Keats, the relaxed and sensuous man. "But what shocks the virtuous philosopher delights the camelion Poet."

> My soul had been a lawn besprinkled o'er
> With flowers, and stirring shades, and baffled beams:
> The morn was clouded, but no shower fell,
> Tho' in her lids hung the sweet tears of May;
> The open casement pressed a new-leaved vine,
> Let in the budding warmth and throstle's lay;

It is all exquisite and all utterly transitory; and out of the knowledge of this is born a longing for a world in which such moments could become eternal. All the Odes are closely bound up with this theme of transience and permanency. Yeats, on the same theme, wrote simply

> Man is in love, and loves what vanishes.
> What is there more to say?

Keats is not capable of this sort of twentieth-century stoicism; he must attempt to reconcile the contradiction. Perhaps this is one of the differences between classical and romantic poetry. It is the classical poet who accepts with resignation the passing of earthly joys and is, therefore, free to gather his rosebuds while he may (Yeats is writing above in an untypically neo-classic moment); the romantic poet tries desperately to find some permanent and unchanging refuge in a world of flux, longing for an age in which he may never know the moon's changes, or for a shadowy isle of bliss where he can forget the beating of the steely sea. Thus for the romantic there is always the element of conflict, either in the poetry, itself or just outside it; and since he is asking questions to which there is no answer, he is little likely to reach a serene conclusion. The best he can do is to find a way of facing a contradiction whose intensity he refuses to minimize; and this is better than saying you don't believe in ghosts while there is one breathing down your neck. (pp. 170-72)

"Indolence" records a moment when sensuous happiness is complete and sufficient and its own justification. The trouble with such experiences, as the poem implicitly recognizes, is that they are only momentary. To Keats, with his appetite for the immediately experienced, they are the most real and important things in life. "We become intoxicated with the light and the atmosphere" of such moments: but among the effects they give rise to is that "of convincing one's nerves that the world is full of Misery and Heartbreak, Pain, Sickness and Oppression". At the time he wrote the **"Ode to a Nightingale,"** Keats needed little reminding of this. It was only a few months after the death of his brother Tom from a painful and distressing illness, and the memory of this is in the third stanza. The poem is not, as is sometimes said, a contrast between his own despondency and the happiness of the bird. It is about the contrast between his own immediately experienced happiness in the bird's song, his imaginative participation in an untroubled natural life, and a less immediate but more enduring knowledge of sorrow. Happiness is momentary and transient: the only thing certain is

> The weariness, the fever and the fret
> Here, where men sit and hear each other groan;
> Where palsy shakes a few, sad, last grey hairs,
> Where youth grows pale, and spectre-thin, and dies,
> Where but to think is to be full of sorrow
> And leaden-eyed despairs.

The heart-ache and the drowsy numbness of the opening lines do not describe mere dejection, but a sort of drugged state, which can only be maintained by further intoxication (Stanza 2). Wine is the traditional soother of men's cares, the traditional means of prolonging a drowsy sensuous enjoyment; and Keats sometimes said he enjoyed claret. But though he had his Anacreontic intervals, they are no real answer for him, and in the fourth stanza he realizes that the only way of escaping to share the happiness of the bird is "on the viewless wings of Poesy". Poetry means first of all imagination—imaginative participation in the bird's life: secondly, it means the actual poetry he is writing—the incantatory loveliness of the fourth and fifth stanzas does make this moment permanent, in a sense: but not in the sense that Keats the living and suffering human being really desires. The only way in which it can really be made eternal is to die at the moment of greatest sensuous happiness. "I have been half in love with easeful death." Much ink has been spilt on the romantic poets' pursuit of death. "Keats's longing for death and his mother has become a by-word among the learned." . . . Maybe it has; but like the Freudian death-wish which has also become a by-word, it does not mean what is most obvious on the surface. The Freudian death-wish is the desire of the cell to resist the encroachments of outside experience, to remain enclosed in its own kind of contentment. So the romantic poet's desire for death is not a longing for extinction, it is the desire to make a happiness that he knows to be transient last for ever. And Keats is only half in love with easeful death—the other half of his consciousness knows well enough that this answer is only the negation of any possible answer. But art offers a type of perma-

nence; and by a startling transformation in the seventh stanza the nightingale becomes a symbol of the artist and its song a symbol of art.

It has often been said that this is an audacious paradox, that the nightingale, so far from being immortal, has a considerably shorter life than man, and that its song is only immortal in the sense that through history there have always been nightingales' songs and that they have always had the same power of enchantment. But it is only in this sense that immortality can be predicated of poets; in fact, the poet's position is stronger, for his individual song endures. There is, therefore, no breach in the poetic logic. But the argument is a casuistry none the less, because the special case of poetic immortality is used, or is on the point of being used, as if it offered the kind of enduring happiness that Keats seeks as a man. But it does not, and cannot do so. . . . So the last word of the seventh stanza, "forlorn", recalls Keats the poet who creates, foreseeing a poetic immortality, to Keats the man who suffers, foreseeing only sickness and sorrow and an early death. The song of the nightingale fades, and Keats finishes where, unlike Shelley, he generally finishes, with his feet on the ground. On the level of ordinary human experience there is no solution to the conflict. The poet who creates can offer little consolation to the man who suffers: but on the level of poetic creation the conflict disappears. Transitory human happiness is given permanence in a different sense by being embodied in art.

The **"Ode on a Grecian Urn"** takes up the thought of the seventh stanza of the **"Ode to a Nightingale."** De Selincourt suggests as its motto a phrase of Leonardo's: *Cosa bella mortal passa e non d'arte*—Mortal beauties pass away, but not those of art. It is a much more objective and descriptive poem than the **"Nightingale."** It is too often forgotten that Keats's imaginative glimpse of Greece was derived not only from translated literary sources, but also from actual Greek plastic art, and that he had had more chance of experiencing it at first hand than earlier and more learned neo-classical connoisseurs; for the Elgin marbles had been recently acquired by the British Museum, and Keats had been profoundly impressed by them. Indeed the imagery of the ode seems to have been suggested more by these sculptures than by any individual vase-painting. The urn is taken as a type of enduring beauty; and again the immortality of art is only a quasi-immortality; for though ceramics last longer than most things they are not in any metaphysical sense more indestructible than mere human clay. There is no real analogy between the loves and pastoral felicities on the urn and "breathing human passion"; the contrast between the permanence of the one and the transience of the other is another poetic casuistry. But this time it is directed to a different end. The poet's momentary emotional state enters less into the poem. He is concerned to establish at least one enduring value below the sphere of the moon, and he finds it in the existence of the beauty of art. It is the only way in which human feeling and natural loveliness can be given lasting significance. The happy boughs that cannot shed their leaves and the lover who can never kiss, but whose love can never fade, are types of the only earthly paradise that exists; and the fact that it is not quite of the kind that men are looking for is not now in the foreground of consciousness.

The last two lines of the poem have been much discussed. That beauty is truth, truth beauty is not all that we know on earth, and certainly not all that we need to know. In the days when it was the custom to take romantic modes of expression simply at their face value these lines were often read as the expression of a profound philosophy. Dr. Richards has taught his disciples to laugh at this reading of them, that the statement is conceptually meaningless and is only there for its value in communicating and organizing emotion. Neither of these views is particularly helpful. The lines must be read in their context, and in the context of the other odes. They are of course in the first place the expression of a moment of rapturous recognition of a beautiful object, and so far are equivalent to an exclamation of joy and reverence. But the sensuous resources of Keats's verse are so rich that he has no need to disguise his emotions of this kind as philosophical statements, unless he also means them in some sense to be so. And he says the same thing in prose: "I never can feel certain of any truth, but from a clear perception of its Beauty". In this context, where transience and permanence are the two poles of the argument, "truth" means "that which has lasting value". (The truth is great *and shall prevail.* What is true all the week is "truer" than what is true only on Monday morning.) Keats is saying that beauty is "truer" than love, pleasure and other forms of value, because they pass away while beauty can be embodied in a lasting quasi-permanent form. When poets say "ye" they are often addressing themselves or other poets. That beauty is truth and truth beauty is all that the artist, as artist, knows, and all he needs to know for the practice of his art.

> Tout passe: l'art robuste
> Seule à l'éternité.

Again, Keats finds a solution to his conflict valid for the artist, but leaving the suffering and experiencing man exactly where he was. (pp. 173-77)

It would be idle to try to turn the Odes into great philosophical poems. They come to no conclusion and make no synthesis. Keats does not wholly avoid confusion between *permanent value* and *value permanently accessible to the individual.* His temperament, with its eager love of life, would have been satisfied with a speculative solution like Yeats's belief in reincarnation: but he would surely have dismissed it as too fantastic: or like that of Mr. Dunne, whose New Immortality, if I have not misunderstood it, suggests that after death a kind of consciousness persists, that is in permanent possession of its past experience.

> These metaphysics of magicians
> And necromantic books are heavenly.

But theirs was not the kind of speculation to which Keats was prone. Yet the Odes are not merely decorative and descriptive poems, as parts of them appear to be; nor yet poems of luxurious self-abandonment; nor yet mere manipulations of feeling. The deep conflict from which they spring is both emotional and intellectual; yet they proceed solely by the methods peculiar to poetry, not by the aid of the speculative intelligence. They are in fact supreme examples of Negative Capability, "when a man is capable of being in uncertainties, mysteries, doubts, without any irritable reaching after fact and reason". (p. 179)

Graham Hough, "Keats," in his The Roman-
tic Poets, *Hutchinson's University Library, 1953, pp. 156-94.*

Kenneth Muir   (essay date 1958)

[*Muir is an English literary critic who has written extensively on Shakespeare. In the excerpt below, he discusses the influence of Keats's confusion over aspects of his personal life on several of his odes and sonnets.*]

Between the middle of February 1819, when he laid aside **"The Eve of St. Mark,"** and the end of April, when he copied out the first of the Odes, Keats wrote very little verse; and it is apparent from several remarks in his letters that he did not fully realise that his indolence was a necessary pause before another period of creation. It was closely linked with the Negative Capability he felt to be a characteristic of the best poets, alternating moods of activity and indolence being, in fact, the rhythm of the mind necessary for the exercise of Negative Capability. It is arguable, indeed, that since during the act of creation the poet must organize, choose, and reject, he can exercise Negative Capability only during his moods of receptive indolence— what Wordsworth called 'a wise passiveness'.

We can see from a passage in the long letter to George and Georgiana that, by overcoming the feverish desire for poetic fame and by ceasing to be obsessed with his love, Keats managed to see life more steadily:

> Neither Poetry, nor Ambition, nor Love have any alertness of countenance as they pass by me: they seem rather like figures on a Greek vase—A Man and two women whom no one but myself could distinguish in their disguisement.

This passage is clearly the germ of the **"Ode on Indolence"**, though the poem may not have been written until a month or two later. Keats was wise to exclude this ode from the 1820 volume, because it is less highly wrought than the others, because the satirical tone of certain lines is out of key with the remainder of the poem, and because he had used some of its imagery elsewhere. He told Miss Jeffrey that the thing he had 'most enjoyed this year had been writing an ode to Indolence'. 'The throstle's lay' links this ode to his own lines 'What the thrush said' and to Wordsworth's declaration that the blithe throstle was 'no mean preacher'. But the ode, like the letter, combines the praise of indolence with a repudiation of Love, Ambition and Poetry. Keats included in the same letter two sonnets in which he had attacked the desire for fame, and there were times when he seemed anxious to escape from the bondage of love—that is the apparent meaning of **"La Belle Dame Sans Merci"**. In the **"Ode on a Grecian Urn"**, earthly passion is said to leave a cloyed heart, 'a burning forehead and a parching tongue'. In the **"Ode on Indolence"** Keats seems to repudiate love altogether. But he was able to reject love, ambition and poetry only by satirizing them:

> For I would not be dieted with praise,
> A pet-lamb in a sentimental farce.

The uncertainty of tone is the result of his personal situation. He could acquire the means to marry only by earning fame as a poet. The praise of a wise passiveness is spoilt by the juxtaposition of the irritable attack on vulgarity. Keats should have written two separate poems.

In the same letter to George and Georgiana, Keats wrote his parable of the world as a vale of soul-making—an idea which was implicit in the third book of **Hyperion.** Near the end of the same letter he copied out **"La Belle Dame Sans Merci"** and the sonnet on Paolo and Francesca, both based on the fifth canto of the *Inferno,* and both related, we may suppose, to his love for Fanny Brawne. Another sonnet, **"Why did I laugh tonight"**, concludes with the thought that death is 'intenser' than life, that it is 'Life's high meed'—a thought which was to recur in the **"Ode to a Nightingale"**.

In the weeks before the writing of the Odes we find that Keats was gradually realizing the creative function of indolence, he was anxious to achieve a state of non-attachment, and he was filled with a desire to find a meaning in human suffering so that his own and that of others could in some way be justified. He was torn between his continuing passion for Fanny and a wish to escape from the toils of ambition and love.

For an understanding of the Odes, however, it is necessary to go back a year, to the **"Epistle to Reynolds"**, written in March 1818. In the course of this poem Keats gives examples of the coherent and creative dreams—the waking dreams—enjoyed by the poet and the painter. One of these is the picture of the sacrifice, which was later to find a place on the Grecian Urn:

> Some Titian colours touch'd into real life,—
> The sacrifice goes on; the pontiff knife
> Gleams in the Sun, the milk-white heifer lows,
> The pipes go shrilly, the libation flows:
> A white sail shows above the green-head cliff,
> Moves round the point, and throws her anchor stiff;
> The mariners join hymn with those on land.

Another picture, based on Claude's 'Enchanted Castle', with 'windows as if latch'd by Fays and Elves' perhaps contributed to the 'magic casements' of the Nightingale ode. Keats goes on to express a wish that all our dreams might take their colours

> From something of material sublime,
> Rather than shadow our own soul's day-time
> In the dark void of night

that is, that they should mirror objective reality rather than the frustrations and inner conflicts of the dreamer. He confesses that he dare not yet philosophize, and doubts whether he will ever attain to the prize:

> High reason, and the love of good and ill.

Whether we read *love* or *lore* (words easily confused in Keats's handwriting) Mr. Murry is probably right in thinking that the poet meant not the knowledge of good and evil, but rather a recognition that particular evil is universal good, an ability to see 'the balance of good and evil'. But Keats could not then make his experience of life fit a philosophical theory. Things—the problems of life— 'tease us out of thought', as the Urn, and Eternity, were to do. When the poet turns from the imaginary world of his creating to the actual world, his imagination is

> Lost in a sort of Purgatory blind.

He is dissatisfied with escapist poetry, and not strong enough to cope with the problems of good and evil. He convinces his

> nerves that the world is full of Misery and Heart-
> break, Pain, Sickness and Oppression.

The 'Chamber of Maiden Thought becomes gradually darken'd' and he feels the 'burden of the Mystery'. Such speculations inevitably interfere with the enjoyment of the present, so that in the **"Epistle"** Keats declares that

> It is a flaw
> In happiness, to see beyond our bourn,—
> It forces us in summer skies to mourn,
> It spoils the singing of the Nightingale.

At the end of the Nightingale ode the real world breaks in on the ecstasy of the bird's song.

In the concluding section of the **"Epistle"** we learn that the particular problem which was agitating Keats at this time was the struggle for survival in the animal kingdom—'an eternal fierce destruction' symbolized not merely by shark and hawk, but by the Robin, 'Ravening a worm'. When he came to write the Odes a year later the death of Tom had become for Keats the prime example of nature's cruelty. But we can see in the careless and disconnected thoughts of the **"Epistle"** that many of the themes treated in the Odes were already in his mind.

The first of the great Odes, **"To Psyche"**,—the first poem with which Keats had taken 'even moderate pains'—is, as Wordsworth said of another poem, 'a pretty piece of paganism'. Keats was apparently looking for a surrogate for religion. He speaks nostalgically of 'the fond believing lyre', and looks back to a pantheistic world when air, water and fire were holy. He is mainly concerned with the relationship between Psyche and Cupid. In becoming her priest he builds a fane where she can receive her lover— not as formerly in darkness, but with a bright torch. In other words Keats is proposing love as a substitute for religion; but, as Psyche is the soul, the poem may also be linked with his conception of the world as a vale of soul-making and with the deification of Apollo in **Hyperion.**

The **"Ode to a Nightingale"** begins with a description of a man falling into a drugged sleep, so that it comes as something of a shock when we learn in the sixth line that the poet is 'too happy' in the happiness of the bird. This paradox is resolved in the sixth stanza in which Keats tells us that he has often 'been half in love with easeful death', and that in listening to the nightingale,

> Now more than ever seems it rich to die.

> (pp. 63-7)

Keats, then, too happy in the happiness of the bird, dreams of escaping from the miseries of the world, first by a 'draught of vintage', and then 'on the viewless wings of Poesy'. The drink is to act, like the bird's song, as an opiate, allowing him to 'leave the world unseen'; and even in the richly sensuous evocation of the surrounding darkness we are reminded again of death in the phrase 'embalmed darkness'—an echo of the sonnet to sleep, death's counterfeit, the 'soft embalmer of the still midnight'. Now Keats toys with the idea of dying:

> To cease upon the midnight with no pain

with the bird singing his requiem.

Bridges complained of the illogicality of Stanza 7, since the nightingale, like man, is born for death. But the bird, unlike man, is not conscious of the hungry generations; and it is no more illogical for Keats to pretend that he is listening to the same bird as the one that sang to Ruth, than it was for Wordsworth to imagine he was listening to the same cuckoo he had heard in childhood, or for Rousseau to cry out when he saw the periwinkle. Hazlitt, indeed, referred in the peroration of one of his lectures to Wordsworth's lines to the Cuckoo, to Rousseau, and to Philomel; Wordsworth's poem, like Keats's stanza, ends with a reference to faeryland; and it is significant that the reading of the draft 'perhaps the self-same voice' is nearer than that of the published text to Wordsworth's 'wandering voice . . . A voice . . . The same'. Another of Wordsworth's poems, "The Solitary Reaper", may, as Mr. Garrod has suggested, 'by some obscure process of association', have contributed to the same stanza of Keats's ode. The 'solitary Highland Lass', reaping the corn and singing 'a melancholy strain', recalled Ruth standing 'in tears amid the alien corn'. Wordsworth mentions the nightingale and the cuckoo; like Keats he uses the epithet 'plaintive'; and in both poems the song fades away at the end.

But in any case the apparent illogicality of the stanza is transcended when the underlying symbolism is understood: the song of the bird is the song of the poet. Keats is contrasting the immortality of poetry with the mortality of the poet. He is saying with Horace, *Non omnis moriar.* This is the climax of the poem and the point where the different themes are harmonized—the beauty of the nightingale's song, the loveliness of the Spring night, the miseries of the world, the desire to escape from those miseries by death, by wine, or by poetry. Whereas when Keats wrote the **"Epistle to Reynolds"** the problems of life spoiled the singing of the nightingale, the song now acquired a greater poignancy from the miseries of the world.

The ode is not the expression of a single mood, but of a succession of moods. From being too happy in the happiness of the bird's song, Keats becomes aware of the contrast between the bird's apparent joy and the misery of the human condition, from the thought of which he can only momentarily escape by wine, by poetry, by the beauty of nature, or by the thought of death. In the seventh stanza the contrast is sharpened: the immortal bird, representing natural beauty as well as poetry, is set against the 'hungry generations' of mankind. The contrast is followed back into history and legend with Ruth in tears and the 'magic casements opening on the foam of perilous seas'—which, as in the **"Epistle to Reynolds,"** conceal a bitter struggle for survival. Even the faery lands are forlorn. Reality breaks in on the poetic dream and *tolls* the poet back to his self. Fancy, the muse of escape poetry, is a deceiving elf. Keats expresses with a maximum of intensity the desire to escape from reality, and yet he recognizes that no escape is possible.

One kind of mastery displayed by Keats in this ode is worth noting—the continuous shifting of view-point. We are transported from the poet in the garden to the bird in the trees; in the second stanza we have glimpses of Flora and Provence, followed by one of the poet drinking the wine; in the fourth stanza we are taken up into the starlit skies, and in the next we are back again in the flower-scented darkness. In the seventh stanza we range furthest in time and place, as we have seen; and in the last stanza we start again from the Hampstead garden, and then follow the nightingale as it disappears in the distance. (pp. 67-9)

The **"Ode on Melancholy"** has links with several of the other odes. Keats had proposed to honour Psyche by making 'a moan upon the midnight hours', and his fane would have 'thoughts, new grown with pleasant pain'. The song of the nightingale had made him too happy, his heart aching, and his senses pained by a drowsy numbness. . . . Melancholy is to be sought in beauty and joy—in a rose, a rainbow, or the anger of a mistress. Because beauty is transient, because love and joy fade, enjoyment must be accompanied with melancholy. Beauty is lovely because it dies and impermanence is the essence of joy; so that only those who are exquisitely sensuous and able to relish the finest joys can behold the 'Veil'd Melancholy'. (pp. 71-2)

Keats is really writing about the poetical character. The fine sensitivity necessary for the writing of poetry makes the poet vulnerable both to joy and sorrow. The realization that love and beauty are subject to time intensifies his joy in them, as we can see from Keats's own poems or Shakespeare's *Sonnets.*

This ode is not quite perfect. The last three lines of the second stanza exhibit both the awkwardness that is apt to beset Keats when he is writing of women and also the lapses he is led into by the need to find a rhyme. It is difficult otherwise to explain 'let her rave'. The beautiful image at the beginning of the same stanza has been criticized for its irrelevance. The 'weeping cloud' and the 'April shroud' are admirable; but the information that the rain 'fosters the droop-headed flowers all' suggests, what Keats presumably did not intend, that the melancholy fit is creative. (p. 72)

> *Kenneth Muir, "The Meaning of the Odes," in* John Keats: A Reassessment, *edited by Kenneth Muir, Liverpool University Press, 1958, pp. 63-73.*

James D. Boulger (essay date 1961)

[*In the following excerpt, Boulger discusses the symbolism contained within "Ode to a Nightingale," "The Eve of St. Agnes," and* Lamia, *arguing that "in these symbolic experiences the poet projects on the highest imaginative level man's dream of permanence for his more hopeful psychological states of being."*]

In Keats' poetry there is a tension between spirit and matter, between vision and existence, which has not gone unnoticed by critics who refuse to view Keats only as the mindless esthete, the cultivator of "Romantic" sensibility. It is true that Keats longed to shape existence into the permanent form of beauty, but he could never forget the sense of anguish and limitation in his individual self. The tension arising from this dualism caused him to search for symbols which might unite in permanent and meaningful form the play between the transient anguish of life and the world of his imagination. For Keats it was a quest of a special kind to create a symbolic world in which the qualities of the spirit modify harsh facts of nature, yet where the colors, sounds and attitudes of the natural world are the

realities of the poetic vision. When successful this romantic vision achieves permanence in the world of art equal
to that of a grecian urn. In moments of failure the existential anxiety of the unsatisfied individual breaks through to
destroy the symbol.

This quest for the perfect medium of poetic vision Keats
followed into all areas of human experience. His perception of the natural world creates the bird symbol in **"Ode
to a Nightingale,"** intensely refined passion the religious
symbolism surrounding the lovers in **"The Eve of St.
Agnes,"** and a semi-divine force operating in the world the
myth symbolism of *Lamia.* In these symbolic experiences
the poet projects on the highest imaginative level man's
dream of permanence for his more hopeful psychological
states of being.

Lacking successful symbolic projection, Keats believed,
man exists in an unrelieved world of pain, boredom and
sensuality, condemned by his nature to view with despair
the gap between the actual and the ideal. There are various
symbols in Keats' poetry by means of which the imagination attempts to bridge this gap. Drink is the most realistic
and the most common, but in both **"Ode to a Nightingale"**
and *Lamia* this coarse physical way is practiced by the ordinary sensual breed, not by the poet or his hero. The
more successful symbols, taken from the world of nature,
mythology, love and art, appear in **"Ode to a Nightingale,"** *Lamia,* **"The Eve of St. Agnes,"** and **"Ode on a Grecian Urn,"** respectively. The structure of these symbols,
and the degree to which each succeeds in representing the
unified state of real and ideal desired by the imagination,
differ widely. (pp. 244-45)

In the **"Ode to a Nightingale"** the dominant symbol, taken
from the natural world, is the bird, by the manipulation
of which the poet hopes to achieve the identification of
man with nature, temporal with eternal. But there is also,
in counterpoint as it were, a struggle between the poet and
the nightingale which fragments finally into a dichotomy
of ideal being for the bird and despair for the poet. While
the Nightingale soars upward as some kind of concrete
universal, the "forlorn" poet becomes a "sod." The very
structure of the symbol prevents the kind of interpenetra-
tion between subject and object which Keats desired, and
leads rather to the alienation he feared.

In the first stanza we assume that Keats is speaking of an
individual nightingale. By stanza seven this individual has
become something quite different, perhaps the species
nightingale. This view would satisfy biological and prosaic
truth, but does not account for the complexity of the symbol, or lead the reader to anticipate the sudden failure of
communication between the poet and the bird which follows. The nightingale is not merely a complex "metaphysical" image, nor is it a simple abstraction such as are Love,
Ambition and Poesy in the **"Ode on Indolence."** The symbolic nightingale is a kind of concrete universal.

In the first stanza the nightingale is an individual with a
symbolic meaning, the symbol and meaning being identical to that of the grape in the climax of the **"Ode on Melancholy."** The bird has replaced the grape as the quintessence of earthly pleasure:

> 'Tis not through envy of thy happy lot,
> But being too happy in thine happiness.

At this point the poet is experiencing a more ordinary kind
of pain and human discomfort. The tale of human misery,
prominent in stanzas three and six, is in sharp contrast to
the upward surge of the theme embodied in the bird itself.
The shift from an individual nightingale to something
quite higher in the ontological order occurs in stanza
three. The bird no longer represents mere human joy or
sorrow of the most intense degree. The lines:

> Fade far away, dissolve, and quite forget
> What thou among the leaves hast never known,

seem to remove the bird from the order of individual existence, and also cancel its validity as a symbol of human
pain and joy. The nightingale has stepped into the immaterial world, the world of universals, which is paradoxically
both more and less permanent or real than the actual
world. In this new world the essence of pleasure is extract-
able and indestructible; the bird as universal is everywhere
and nowhere, everything and nothing, as is supported by
the words of the **"Ode"**:

> Thou wast not born for death, immortal Bird!
> No hungry generations tread thee down.

Such a view of a universal bird symbol is not exactly Platonic. It does not imply an ideal world behind the real
world, yet something akin to that is what has taken place.
The universal bird, permanent and eternal symbol of concrete beauty, has been freed from the dross of individual
existence. Yet it remains a conception dependent upon the
mind of man. Does this new bird symbol attain a higher
order of being, that is, in line with Keats' theory of disinterestedness, existence as a universal independent of the
conception of it in the mind of man, in other words as a
concrete "real" universal in the Platonic sense? Possibly
so. Stanza seven might support this view. The "real" universal would be the bird song rather than the bird, the
song heard by Ruth, by emperor and clown. It is another
"ditty of no tone." This universal has attained independent existence of some "real" kind, since it is no longer dependent upon individuals in the actual order for its reality.
(pp. 245-47)

Death then becomes the logical progression from alienation to annihilation, a fairly negative thing, "easeful," a
luxury, "To cease upon the midnight with no pain." It
means identification with nature in the sense of becoming
inanimate in an eternity of silence and nothingness. Death
is the supreme moment, the last sensation, which would
agonize the soul with sense of loss unless it can be made
easeful, unconscious. The nature imagery in the poem
takes on its importance in terms of this attitude toward
death. Natural things are gross, palpable, individual gratifications to each of the five senses. The poet lingers over
the names and sensuous impressions which each possesses:

> The grass, the thicket, and the fruit-tree wild;
> White hawthorne, and the pastoral eglantine;
> Fast fading violets cover'd up in leaves.

Awareness of the existence of such beauty becomes excruciating torture in the presence of death, unless death itself
be transformed into the most sensuous experience of all.
It is agony for the poet suddenly caught up in the egocentric predicament again to view the beauties of the world
which he, and not the universal, eternal nightingale, in nature, must leave. The paradox is too poignant not to make

the poet forlorn; in order to become a part of nature, to be with the bird in any real sense, the poet must relinquish his distinctive feature, consciousness, which is the source of agony and beauty, pain and perception. The poem ends in a mood of sadness, and on a revival of the essential paradox of human existence, the duality of human experience. The symbolic victory over the duality was both partial and transitory.

In *Lamia* Keats' moment of symbolic vision is longer, glimpsed in the world of Greek mythology, while dull philosophy, which makes man aware of his human limitations, enlarges the death-wish theme of **"Ode to a Nightingale."** In the poem this philosophy, meaning in particular the scientific spirit, has with its tools for quantitative measurement destroyed the rainbow. Motion and dimension have been reduced to law. The qualitative items in experience, formerly embodied in mythology, are ignored, and this produces the terror of a "dead universe" for ordinary people and poets. Whereas the dialectic of the narrator reluctantly destroyed his own vision in **"Ode to a Nightingale,"** the method in *Lamia* is intensely dramatic. Apollonius represents the scientific point of view and performs the function of destroyer in regard to Greek mythology. In *Lamia* Crete is the natural home of the symbolic imagination, of mythology, while Corinth holds sensuality, materialism, and the philosopher. Lycius, the poet's hero, is caught between the two. This is a dramatic representation of the opposition between the imagination and life, and human awareness of limitation, leading to death.

Lycius was trained in the rational philosophy of his time, but was unhappy with it. He is occupied with the quest of all Keats' heroes, to bridge the gap between the world of sense and understanding, and that of the imaginative ideal (in this poem, by means of a kind of love which symbolizes the imaginative way). Mythology is the comprehensive symbol in the poem, and provides the frame for the clash between the logical, quantitative world of Apollonius and the symbolic mode of man's myth-making power. The frequently discussed love relationships function as a part of this greater contrast. Love is the focus for the major incidents in the poem, and these incidents are ordered and made meaningful by the mythological structure. That is to say, the kinds of love present varying degrees of insight into the mythological vision of the world.

On the lowest level, there is the sensuality at Corinth, the center of rationalism and sensism in philosophy. Next there is "love in a hut," common everyday love between average men and women, representing the "common sense" philosophy. These loves cannot symbolize aspiration toward the higher level of the imaginative mode, and cannot satisfy a man such as Lycius, whose philosophical studies have not quenched a yearning for the ineffable. For him there had to be human love on an ideal level, with the Lamia, as there had to be love of a divine being for Keats' other hero, Endymion. But he could never rise to the level of divine love between immortals, as do Cupid and Psyche in the **"Ode to Psyche,"** or perhaps Hermes and the Nymph in this poem. In relation to divine love, the two possibilities open to mortals were destined to prove unsatisfying, one because magic is necessary to preserve it, the other because the very human limitations of the participants make it impossible to sustain. The corresponding

comment on the fate of man's mythological structures in the modern, scientific world is equally grim.

Thus it follows that, in terms of the love symbolism itself, it is not only the logic in the discursive mind of Apollonius which opposes the love between Lamia and Lycius; logic is really a latent factor in Lycius' mortal nature which serves to destroy his vision. Love as a symbol of the imagination is exposed in its inherent weakness. And at the center of the conflict remain the logic of the philosopher and the mythological structures of the poet. That the solution has unpleasant implications for mythology as the embodiment of the symbolic mode, no less than for human love, is not an indication that the poet permanently despairs. It does indicate his ability to criticize his early attempt at transcendence in *Endymion* and also his awareness of the impossibilities inherent in his own system of mythology, created in the **"Ode to Psyche," "Ode on Indolence"** and other poems. It led him finally to view a kind of religious love and art as the most valid modes of transcending the human condition.

An examination of the "ideal" love between Hermes and the Nymph, the foil against which to judge the preternatural love of Lamia and Lycius, shows how the mythological: logical contrast subsumes the love relationships in the poem. Critics have often noted the importance of the following famous lines:

> Real are the dreams of Gods, and smoothly pass
> Their pleasures in a long immortal dream.

This is certainly divine love in the particular Keatsian sense that the pleasure of love exists without the pain, and for an indefinite period. In this sense it can be contrasted to that of Lamia and Lycius, which can achieve the effect only by magic, by cheating human nature. But is this relationship between Hermes and the Nymph intended primarily as an example of ideal love? If so, why Hermes, the rake of the gods, and a mere nymph? Thomas Burton, whose *Anatomy of Melancholy* was Keats' source for the Lamia episode, does not provide a basis for the earlier part of the story. Had Keats desired to make this a portrait of ideal love, he was free to choose a more dignified pair, such as Cupid and Psyche, or Endymion and Cynthia. (pp. 247-50)

Lamia is not an "ideal" mythological figure, as is Cynthia in *Endymion.* Without some outside preconception for the Hermes–Nymph relationship as the foil of ideal love, against which to judge Lycius and Lamia, their relationship would never strike a reader as the ideal of earthly love, as does that of Porphyro and Madeline in **"The Eve of St. Agnes."** The reader sees that the relationship between Lycius and Lamia is created by magic, by deception, in short, by a witch. The relationship emphasizes physical, sexual, yet not entirely sensual, love. It avoids love melancholy and pain, but fails as the perfect vehicle for presenting the ideal through love symbolism. This love fails from its inherent weakness, and Apollonius deals with it to prepare himself for more important tasks. (pp. 250-51)

The physical, intensely human aspect of the relationship is important for several reasons. For one, it helps to explain the miraculous transformation of the snake into a beautiful woman. The horror, the agony of her transformation is the price which had to be paid for cheating human nature. "Nothing but pain and ugliness were left" is the termination of a process in which the good and beautiful in the love relationship are separated from the evil and ugly. By paying a price, she was able to give "unperplexed bliss," to remove the points of contact between beauty and ugliness, and good and evil. She could defy temporarily the experience of the worshipper in the **"Ode on Melancholy,"** who found:

> Ay, in the very temple of Delight
> Veil'd Melancholy has her sovran shrine,
> Though seen of none save him whose strenuous tongue
> Can burst Joy's grape against his palate fine;
> His soul shall taste the sadness of her might,
> And be among her cloudy trophies hung.

Stress on the defiance of nature in her relationship with Lycius is made many times. She wants physical love, and she gives it, yet the cloying consequences are always avoided. Distraction is prevented by the secret palace, tedium by the dreamy trance in which Lycius is placed, and thought excluded by seclusion from the normal life of Corinth. Through her it is possible temporarily to cheat life; she is a virgin with the experience of a harlot. The lovers have it all their own way.

Of course the instrument of delusion is magic. At no point in the experience does the poet forget the impact of **"Ode to a Nightingale."** The ruse is carried by the common myth in literature, that of a beautiful woman with rotten interior, who can separate seeming good from evil. There are obvious similarities between Lamia and Spenser's Duessa and False Florimel in *The Fairy Queen*. In both poems the evil and futility of magic is noticed, but in *The Fairy Queen* there is also a moral commitment, based on both Christian and Platonic sanctions. But in *Lamia* the emotional commitment is not entirely at one with the intellectual. Lycius, and presumably Keats, raise a cry of frustrated feeling even while the intellect relentlessly destroys the illusion of the erotic dream. Lycius helps destroy his own Lamia, his own dream world, through use of the laws of his own understanding. All the magic at Lamia's disposal could not prevent him from musing beyond her, or from hearing the trumpets of the outside world, from finally feeling the ennui of love in a palace, from desiring other emotional outlets, such as pride in display, and excitement in festival. Thus the communion through sexual passion with symbolic modes of being destroys itself by its very nature and rhythm. The inevitability of stimulus—climax—triste could not be avoided by magic or self-delusion. And with the aftermath came desire for other goods.

When Lycius met Lamia he was prepared for a symbolic flight of some kind. His training in philosophy had not satisfied him. Recently having sacrificed to Jove for some unmentioned boon, and "Perhaps grown wearied of their Corinth talk," he had allowed his reason to fade into the twilight of the dream world. In other words he bore some secret, perhaps unrecognized, grudge against his educational training with Apollonius. Lamia offered a way out of the dreary sensible world and he took it. He himself and the magical element made its failure inevitable, yet it was reserved for Apollonius to administer the *coup de grace*. This was necessary for two reasons, to point out Apollonius' method of proceeding by the understanding, and to reveal his true purpose and real enemy. The climax is intensely dramatic. The eye of discursive logic, "Keen, cruel, perceant, stinging," pierces Lamia's secret, and by *naming* her species, "a serpent," reduces at once the dream to nothing. Lycius' arms were empty of delight. But he, in a moment of terror, reveals the poet's view of the secret intention of the philosopher, which is to empty all such creations of the human spirit of their substance, to destroy the productive life of Hermes, and leave mankind's symbolic yearnings in a winding sheet with Lycius:

> Shut, shut those juggling eyes, thou ruthless man!
> Turn them aside, wretch! or the righteous ban
> Of all the Gods, whose dreadful images
> Here represent their shadowy presences,
> May pierce them on a sudden with the thorn
> Of painful blindness; leaving thee forlorn,
> In trembling dotage to the feeblest fright
> Of conscience, for their long offended might,
> For all thine impious proud-heart sophistries,
> Unlawful magic, and enticing lies.

What Apollonius had done to Lycius through the destruction of the Lamia, discursive thought in general would do to the rainbow, to mythology, and to experiences of a qualitative kind in general. Science denudes the woods of all life, and despairing man remains in a dead universe.

The poem ends on a shriek because the poet is trying to save his vision of the world. But Keats cannot save his vision with this symbolism. His attempts to revitalize classical mythology in this poem, in *Endymion,* the **"Ode to Psyche,"** and in *Hyperion,* were too late and too *precieux* to be successful. In *Lamia* its lamented decline and fall is poignantly illustrated. The final dichotomy between desire and reality becomes exactly that of **"Ode to a Nightingale."** The poet finds in the collective mythology of the past, as in his own bird symbol, no respite from the agony and despair of consciousness in the blankness of the modern world. But the poem *Lamia* is neither confused nor unsatisfactory. In it there is an honest inspection of the meaning and value of symbols, and recognition that new forms must be found to represent the vision of the artist in the modern world.

In **"The Eve of St. Agnes"** Keats again explores man's dualism through the medium of love symbols. In this poem the love symbolism is successful, because the poet discards his unsuccessful and complicated eternal: temporal, human: divine dichotomies, and invests his love symbolism in a quasi-religious formal unity.

The obvious dichotomy between the world of the lovers and that of the other groups in the poem is quickly observed. The contrast corresponds to similar ones in *Lamia*; for example, the sensualists at Corinth to the revelers in Madeline's castle, "Love in a hut" to the common sense of Angela, and so forth. But there is a more important contrast in **"The Eve of St. Agnes,"** set up by the presence of the Beadsman, which did not appear in the other poems. There are some obvious contrasts, as, for instance, the Beadsman's denial of sensuous experience, and his attempt to reach spirituality in a manner which was unfruitful in Keats' mode of symbolization. The lovers flee to a world of bliss; the Beadsman is left cold and unsought for among his thousand Aves. But there is a more important level on which the relationship between the Beadsman and the lovers ought to be taken, on which the contrast becomes its opposite, a powerful force for the fusion of the religious with the sensual ideal in the poem.

In terms of the general Christian tradition which lies behind the poem, the actions of the Beadsman are commendatory, while those of the lovers are in a sense a sacrilege. But in the values which the poem itself generates the Beadsman's activity is a waste, a delusion, while the lovers perform the sacred rites, the "mysteries" which lead to the "miracle." This is not to assert that values from outside Keats' own thinking intrude to destroy the meanings set up within the framework of his poem, but rather that knowledge of the outside values makes the framework of the poem more meaningful. We have to know the meaning of mystery and miracle in the Christian tradition, and the usual rites which symbolize them in the activity of the Beadsman, in order to appreciate the full significance of the Beadsman's actions in relation to those of the lovers. The actions of the juxtaposed groups comment upon each other in a profound way. Through this commentary the values in the poem are balanced in delicate equipoise with those which press from without.

In the Christian framework the Beadsman's entire life is a preparation for complete union with Christ. This is the goal of all Christian mystics and the purpose of the asceticism in their lives. . . . In the poem the Beadsman's prayers are directed toward the Virgin, and carry this usual significance. The entire direction of love has been changed from the ordinary ends of human activity, but the same emotions and drives are present. Thus it is that religious devotion and poetry will often assume the external appearance of a love rite, while love rites likewise usurp the form of religious exercises. The Beadsman enjoys his love and devotions, which are aimed at promoting the same union with essence enjoyed by the lovers. But in the poem his purposes are frustrated; for him, in terms of the symbolic relationship, there is no fruition, no union. This is because the love relationship, usually on a lower level, has usurped the powers of sacramental efficacy. Sacrilegious as it might appear to be in a sense, Love has become a sacrament, and the performance of its rites assures the unfolding of the mystery, and finally the miracle. The way of Thomas a Kempis is replaced by that of early pagan cults. In these rites the mysteries become associated with a religion of fertility, and gods of both sexes replace the Uniate God of Christianity. Also the idea of the immortal soul as an immaterial essence gives way to a notion that the concrete individual existence is universalized and eternalized, so that the sensations of this life can be repeated in a "finer tone."

The revolution is accomplished in a bold fashion, since outward terms and rites of the Christian tradition are not replaced by pagan symbols, but are merely altered to serve the new purpose. The Beadsman is the foil for this sacred parody, and his observances of the penances preparatory to union with Christ run in counterpoint to the penances of Porphyro and Madeline. Words and gestures of Christian ritual are approximated by the mystery and miracle of the lovers' union. The Beadsman's presence as representative of the Christian tradition sets the tone in which the actions of the lovers are to be construed. Let us see how daring this approximation is.

Madeline's room is the scene for the performance of the mysteries and the miracle. It is a fit repository for such a sacred action, "silken, hush'd, and chaste." She enters it "like a mission'd spirit" with a taper in her hand. Thus the preparation for the sacrifice begins. Madeline is a child of St. Agnes, a lamb, "so pure a thing, so free from mortal taint," preparing herself for the consummation. In the love-mystery she is the *Agnus Dei,* the Lamb of God. Her movements and observances are a kind of Offertory service. What she is offering is herself, a pure and spotless victim, to love, and what is consecrated is her vision, the "miracle" which allows communion with the ideal and real Porphyro.

First she kneels and offers herself as the love victim, "As down she knelt for heaven's grace and boon." Next, she prepares her body for the love rite,

> her vespers done,
> Of all its wreathed pearls her hair she frees;
> . . .
> Her rich attire creeps rustling to her knees.

The altar in this love sacrifice is, of course, the bed, where she, a sacred victim, is placed, and before which the worshipper, in this case Porphyro, will kneel. She is also fasting, in order to be worthy of the vision, an observance obviously related to rules for the worthy reception of the sacrament in the Christian tradition. When Madeline enters the bed her function as active participant in the dual sacramental mystery is taken over by Porphyro.

This act roughly corresponds to the point of Consecration when the role of the priest as primary in the preparation of the Sacrament is taken over by the worshippers in the congregation. Madeline fades into her soft and chilly nest, her "soul fatigued away; / Flown, like a thought, until the morrow-day," in a manner similar to the recession of the priest, whose role to this point she has approximated. Of course in **"St. Agnes,"** the situation is somewhat different. The receding Madeline is the girl of the realistic mode, who has prepared herself for an ascension into that of ideal vision. The miracle is not complete at this point in the love rite for the same reason that Porphyro in this service is much more important than are the worshippers in Christian services. The emphasis is always on the duality of the religious rite in the love-service, even though the externals are similar to the Christian rite. The real miracle is not the achievement of one of its members, but the union of both. In the Sacrament the Consecration is the key mystery and miracle; the reception of it by the worshippers is also quite marvellous, but of secondary interest. Madeline's achievement of the Vision is in a sense a Transubstantiation, but it is only through union and communion with Porphyro that the mystery attains the status of a miracle.

Porphyro's worship of Madeline corresponds to the adoration offered by the congregation, but it is much more intense, because his participation in the miracle must be earned in an active way. Not only must he show adoration of the miraculous gift, and prepare himself by passive steps for its worthy reception, as would the congregation or the Beadsman, but he must actively participate in the mysteries in order to obtain the miracle. It is at this point that the essential difference between the Keatsian and Christian ritual is made manifest, even though the symbolic acts of each have similarities. The Keatsian priest is always an active worshipper, whose own exertions are necessary for the consummation.

The food offerings of Porphyro are obviously ritualistic in intention. Porphyro has a sacrifice table, an altar cloth of crimson, gold, and jet, but of course his offering is not symbolic of a Christian mode of participation in the Divine. The stainless white host of the Christian ascetic sacrifice has been replaced by the deluge of oriental sensuality. This, as has been pointed out, indicates the levels of sensuous experience through which Porphyro must pass in order to be ready for the transformation into the spiritual mode. His offerings, on golden dishes, are the counterpart of the Aves, just as the perfumed light sent up by them parallels the gloom and ashes of the hermit's cell. Porphyro's anguish, generated by the tension between basic physical desire and the aspiration to reach a more perfect mode of sensuous experience, stems from the same attitude of reproach which gives rise to the feeling of sinfulness in the souls of Communicants during the adoration period. Both Porphyro and the worshippers are offering unworthy sacrifices to an *Agnus Dei,* and the feeling of complete absorption in the worshipped object, although for different reasons, is no less complete in one instance than in the other. Porphyro says:

> Thou art my heaven, and I thine eremite:
> Open thine eyes, for meek St. Agnes' sake,
> Or I shall drowse beside thee, so my soul doth ache.

Through devout consumption of the Host, the communicants are united with Christ, and achieve to the extent that it is possible in this world, a feeling of spirituality, a glimpse of an existence possible above the world of flesh, space, and time. This is exactly what Porphyro achieves by performing the sacred rites, the banquet and the lute playing, a consummation with his *Agnus Dei.* His absorption into the dream is a symbolic equivalent of the consumption of the Sacrament. (pp. 251-58)

Keats has subsumed the conventional religious symbolism of Christian ritual for a very special purpose in this poem. The exact nature of the relationship between Porphyro and Madeline could be expressed only through mysteries, and achieved by miracle. Love has replaced the Eucharist as the sacrament in his system. Without this transferred mystery and miracle symbolism from the Christian tradition, his attempts to attain a vision of the eternal through love and nature fragmented into dichotomies, as we have seen. By borrowing and reworking for his own purpose the central mystery of the Christian ritual, clearly removed from its original sacred context, he was able to use the Beadsman as a foil to develop successfully, in this poem at least, the *mysterium fidei* of his own sacramental universe. (pp. 258-59)

James D. Boulger, "Keats' Symbolism," in ELH, *Vol. 28, No. 3, September, 1961, pp. 244-59.*

Martin Halpern   (essay date 1966)

[Halpern is an American playwright and literary critic. In the excerpt below, he comments upon humorous aspects of several of Keats's poems following Endymion.*]*

The completion of *Endymion* marked an important turning point in Keats's career, and one indication of his search for new directions after his long and often discouraging labor on the youthful *magnum opus* was a sudden increase during the early months of 1818 in his output of humorous verse, which had hitherto been sparse and sporadic. For all of its thematic concern with a unification of the ideal and the real, as represented by the final identity of the moon-goddess and the Indian maid, the world of *Endymion* was a very unreal one, and its atmosphere rarefied to the point of uninhabitability. Now, perhaps in reaction against that atmosphere, we find Keats experimenting in several of his occasional poems with a quality of broad realistic humor—with, most notably, playful bawdiness in lyrics like **"Sharing Eve's Apple,"** the **"Daisy's Song"** in *Extracts from an Opera,* **"The Devon Maid,"** and **"Dawlish Fair"**; and skeptical anti-romantic irony in such a poem as **"Modern Love"** and the section of *Extracts from an Opera* which begins:

> Oh, I am frighten'd with most hateful thoughts!
> Perhaps her voice is not a nightingale's,
> Perhaps her teeth are not the fairest pearl;
> Her eye-lashes may be, for aught I know,
> Not longer than the May-fly's small fan-horns; . . .

For the most part, however, poems like these, as well as the several comic pieces which Keats included in his letters during his walking tour in the summer of the same year, seem to have been tossed off casually in moods of emotional relaxation. Even the most skillful seem little more than exercises in the whimsical mode. Taken by themselves, such pieces could be cited in support of James Caldwell's view that the function of laughter in Keats's verse is generally limited to the occasional relieving of "inner tensions"; and that once the relief was effected, he felt no further need for wit and humor in their profounder applications to "the anomalies, the discrepancies, the contradictions in supposedly ordered life" which are "the very sources of comedy." Indeed, though the anti-romantic strain was later to gain intensity in poems like *Lamia* and *The Cap and Bells,* its occurrences in the 1818 poems seem more self-therapeutic than seriously critical. . . . (pp. 69-70)

There are, however, a number of other poems in the 1818 group which point to a weightier concern on Keats's part to understand, exalt, and assimilate into his serious poetic vision his own strong sense of laughter—a concern that was to call forth a considerable expenditure of "psychic labor" during the rest of his writing career. One such poem . . . is the little song Keats wrote on a blank page of Beaumont and Fletcher's *Works,* and which, though undated, has traditionally and with good reason been ascribed to 1818. It is not a humorous poem in the narrower sense, nor is it as skillful a song as some of those previously cited; but what it has to say about laughter is important to an understanding of the general direction in which Keats's work was tending at this time:

I.

> Spirit here that reignest!
> Spirit here that painest!
> Spirit here that burnest!
> Spirit here that mournest!
> Spirit, I bow
> My forehead low,
> Enshaded with thy pinions!

Spirit, I look
All passion-struck
Into thy pale dominions.

II.

Spirit here that laughest!
Spirit here that quaffest!
Spirit here that dancest!
Noble soul that prancest!
Spirit, with thee
I join in the glee,
A-nudging the elbow of Momus.
Spirit, I flush
With a Bacchanal blush
Just fresh from the Banquet of Comus.

The song is, in a small way, Keats's *L'Allegro-Il Penseroso,*
but with a difference. Whereas in Milton's poems the spirit
of *L'Allegro* must begin by banishing that of *Il Penseroso*
and vice versa, in Keats's song the stanza division implies
no such idea of mutual exclusiveness. The very point of the
song is, in fact, that the spirits of the first and second stanzas are not antithetical but complementary, and that the
poet's allegiance is to both equally and both together. The
same may be said of that other and more famous 1818
poem which Keats wrote on another blank page of the
Beaumont and Fletcher volume, where he celebrated its
authors as, simultaneously and inseparably, **"Bards of
Passion *and* of Mirth."** And in yet another of the 1818 lyrics, the **"Song of Opposites,"** we find still more explicit expression of the essential oneness of the two spirits invoked
in the quoted song:

Welcome joy, and welcome sorrow,
Lethe's weed and Hermes' feather;
Come to-day, and come to-morrow,
I do love you both together!
I love to mark sad faces in fair weather;
And hear a merry laugh amid the thunder;
Fair and foul I love together.
Meadows sweet where flames are under,
And a giggle at a wonder; . . .

Several critics, particularly Murry, have pointed out the
rather Blakean tendency in Keats to view moral questions
in terms of reconcilable "contraries" rather than absolute
mutual "negations." These 1818 lyrics, besides resembling
some of Blake's lyrics stylistically, also reflect a comparably Blakean tendency to reconcile emotional contraries by
breaking down the barriers between the human sense of
the solemn and sublime, and the human impulse toward
gaiety and laughter. In an age when prominent poets and
critics were declaring the spirit of laughter incompatible
with the higher aims of poetry and the higher aspirations
of the human spirit (Hazlitt, for instance, remarked,
". . . we laugh at what only disappoints our expectations
in trifles," and "There is nothing more troublesome than
what are called laughing people"; and Shelley announced,
"I am convinced that there can be no entire regeneration
of mankind until laughter is put down") Keats insisted,
as had Blake in his own way, that to see life whole was to
see it under the aspects of both passion *and* mirth at once;
for these were not eternally opposed states of the spirit but
rather complementary states whose fusion was part of the
special achievement of the true poet's vision. (pp. 71-3)

That the **"Ode on Melancholy"** is a poem about the unity
of contraries is obvious enough; what is perhaps less obvi-

ous, or at least less generally recognized by critics, is the
way the poem's thematic content is reinforced, and in
large measure created, by Keats's management of tone
and mood in the language itself.

Critics have been quite unanimous in applauding Keats's
omission of the poem's original first stanza, and some, notably Douglas Bush, have carried over their condemnation
of that stanza's "macabre extravagance" into the present
first stanza. Yet, though one may agree that the original
beginning was inferior in quality to the rest of the poem,
one may also argue that, as far as its tone and mood were
concerned, the stanza was entirely in harmony with the
poem as we now have it:

Though you should build a bark of dead men's bones,
And rear a phantom gibbet for a mast,
Stitch shrouds together for a sail, with groans
To fill it out, blood-stained and aghast;
Although your rudder be a dragon's tail
Long sever'd, yet still hard with agony,
Your cordage large uprootings from the skull
Of bald Medusa, certes you would fail
To find the Melancholy—whether she
Dreameth in any isle of Lethe dull. . . .

The images out of which the ship in quest of "the Melancholy" is built rise in a crescendo of absurdity to the final
rejection. It is evident that Keats is attempting to exorcise
his attraction to the "Lethean" way by deriding it as extravagantly as he can; and even without the last three
lines, the stanza would make its point solely through the
comic grotesqueries of its images and the tone of jocular
irony in which they are presented. But this tone, and the
humorously macabre mood which it reflects, serve a purpose beyond that of simply ridiculing a rejected escapism.
The very excessiveness of the catalogue, and the obvious
pleasure which the poet takes in his own verbal excesses,
lend to the stanza a quality of high farce, a somewhat Rabelaisian indulgence in the extravagantly ludicrous for its
own sake. And much the same may be said of the present
first stanza, with its comparable effect of absurdity created
by the sheer piling up of images and allusions associated
with the desire for escape into oblivion. Again, the absurdity serves to deride a mental state which the poet is concerned to reject; but again, the sense of his own gratuitous
delight in his verbal high-jinks is as central to the stanza's
effect as the sense of corrective ridicule. . . . (pp. 73-6)

When Keats turns in the last stanza, then, to a direct and
high-serious statement of his paradoxical theme, we have
been prepared for that statement by the language of the
preceding stanzas—including even the rejected one. Solemn truths and serious emotions—the desire for oblivion,
the "weeping cloud" of melancholy, the anguished knowledge of mutability, a mistress' anger—have been presented
in a mood of jocularity and a tone of high comic irony; and
the union of laughter and sorrow in the mood and tone
parallels the thematic union of Joy and Melancholy. Just
as the goddess Melancholy inhabits the same temple as the
Goddess of Delight, so the "Spirit that mournest" has
been shown to inhabit the same heart as the "Spirit that
laughest"; and just as Melancholy is perceived in her truest essence by him who can "burst Joy's grape against his
palate fine," so the gravest emotions have been shown as
experienced at their fullest by a sensibility richly capable
of laughter. The performance of the poem itself has pro-

vided the dramatic embodiment of its abstract theme. (p. 78)

Martin Halpern, "Keats and the 'Spirit That Laughest'," in Keats-Shelley Journal, *Vol. XV, Winter, 1966, pp. 69-86.*

Helen Vendler   (lecture date 1984)

[*Vendler is an American literary critic and educator. She is the author of the critically acclaimed* The Odes of John Keats *(1983). In the following excerpt from an essay delivered in 1984 at The Eleventh Alabama Symposium on English and American Literature, she examines Keats's conception of the social functions of art and poetry.*]

Keats, in his early poetry, enumerates four social functions of poetry: a historical one, as epic poetry recorded history of an exalted sort, written by "bards, that erst sublimely told heroic deeds"; a representational (if allegorical) one, as Shakespeare gave, in his dramatic poetry, an incarnation of the passions; a didactic one, as in Spenser's "hymn in praise of spotless Chastity" (**"Ode to Apollo"**); and a linguistically preservative one, which can "revive" for our day "the dying tones of minstrelsy" (**"Specimen of an Induction to a Poem"**). And yet, Keats perhaps sensed that these functions—historical, allegorically representational, didactic, and linguistically preservative—were not to be his own: these claims for the social functions of poetry are, in his early work, asserted merely, not enacted. (p. 68)

While the emphasis on social service always brings in, for Keats, the relief of pain, the emphasis in descriptions of art itself, in early Keats, dwells always on the pleasure principle, so that even woe must be, in literature, "pleasing woe" (**"To Lord Byron"**), and poetry must make "pleasing music, and not wild uproar" (**"How Many Bards"**) full of glorious tones and delicious endings (**"On Leaving Some Friends"**). In these early poems, Keats expresses the characteristic view of the youthful poet, to whom the aesthetic can be found only in the beautiful.

Keats's first attempt to reconcile his philosophical emphasis on social service and his instinctive commitment to those aesthetic interests proper to composition appears in **"I stood tiptoe,"** where he proposes an ingenious reconciliation by suggesting that form allegorically represents content:

In the calm grandeur of a sober line,
We see the waving of the mountain pine;
And when a tale is beautifully staid,
We feel the safety of a hawthorn glade.

The myths of the gods are said, in **"I stood tiptoe,"** to be formally allegorical renditions of man's life in nature: a poet seeing a flower bending over a pool invents the myth of Narcissus. This is a promising solution for Keats—that form, being an allegory for content, bears not a mimetic but an algebraic relation to life. But in **"I stood tiptoe,"** this solution is conceptualized rather than formally enacted.

In his next manifesto, **"Sleep and Poetry,"** Keats makes an advance on the thematic level, realizing that his former advocacy of a consoling thematic happiness to cure

human sorrow cannot survive as a poetic program. Rather, he says, he must "pass the realm of Flora and old Pan" for a "nobler life" where he may encounter "the agonies, the strife / Of human hearts." With the thematic admission of tragic material, formal notions of power and strength can at last enter into Keats's aesthetic and fortify his former aesthetic values—beauty and mildness—with a new sculptural majesty:

A drainless shower
Of light is Poesy; 'tis the supreme power;
'Tis might half-slumbering on its own right arm.

Nonetheless, Keats is still critical of a poetry that "feeds upon the burrs, / And thorns of life," arguing rather for the therapeutic function of poetry, "that it should be a friend / To soothe the cares, and lift the thoughts of man"—an end still envisaged in the later **"Ode on a Grecian Urn."** The poet is simply to "to tell the most hearteasing things"; and the poetry of earth ranges only from the grasshopper's delight to the cricket's song "in warmth increasing ever." (pp. 69-71)

The long romance **Endymion** marks Keats's first success in finding poetic embodiments for the principles he had so far been able merely to assert. The tale of Endymion is not socially mimetic, but rather, allegorical of human experiences; however, it is still a "pleasing tale," a pastoral, not a tragedy. Even so, Keats admits in **Endymion** two tragic principles that he will later eleborate: that in contrast to warm and moving nature, art must seem cold and carved or inscribed (a marble altar garlanded with a tress of flowers [90-91], the inscribed cloak of Glaucus); and that the action demanded of their devotees by Apollo and Pan is a sacrifice of the fruits of the earth. Art is admitted for the first time to be effortful: Pan is implored to be "the unimaginable lodge / For solitary thinkings; such as a dodge / Conception to the very bourne of heaven, / Then leave the naked brain." These daring and difficult solitary thinkings and new concepts will become, says Keats, "the leaven, / That spreading in this dull and clodded earth / Gives it a touch ethereal—a new birth."

In one sense, this passage represents the end of Keats's theoretical thinking about the nature and social value of poetry. But he could not yet describe how solitary original thinkings become a leaven to resurrect society. The poem **Endymion,** as it journeys between the transcendent Cynthia and the Indian maid, may be seen as a journeying to and from between the two elements of solitude and society, as Keats looks for a place where he can stand. He would like to avert his gaze from the misery of solitude, where those solitary thinkings take place, but he summons up the courage to confront the necessities of his own writing. Eventually, he arrives at two embodying symbols. The first is the cloak of Glaucus, "o'erwrought with symbols by . . . ambitious magic," wherein everything in the world is symbolized, not directly or mimetically, but in emblems and in miniaturizations. Gazed at, however, these printed reductions swell into mimetic reality:

The gulfing whale was like a dot in the spell.
Yet look upon it, and 'twould size and swell
To its huge self, and the minutest fish
Would pass the very hardest gazer's wish,
And show his little eye's anatomy.

Keats faces up, here, to the symbolic nature of art. Art

cannot, he sees, be directly mimetic; it must always bear an allegorical or emblematic relation to reality. Also, art is not a picture (he is speaking here of his own art of writing), but a hieroglyph much smaller than its original. However, by the cooperation of the gazer (and only by that cooperation), the hieroglyph "swells into reality." Without "the very hardest gazer's wish" the little fish could not manifest himself.

In this way, as later in the **"Ode on a Grecian Urn,"** Keats declares that art requires a social cooperation between the encoder-artist and the decoder-beholder. The prescriptions written on the scroll carried by Glaucus announce Keats's new program for poetic immortality; the poet must "explore all forms and substances / Straight homeward to their symbol-essences": he must "pursue this task of joy and grief"; and enshrine all dead lovers. In the allegory that follows, all dead lovers are resurrected by having pieces of Glaucus's scroll sprinkled on them by Endymion. Endymion goes "onward . . . upon his high employ, / Showering those powerful fragments on the dead."

This allegory suggests that one of the social functions of poetry is to revive the erotic past of the race so that it lives again. But in the fourth book of *Endymion,* as Keats admits to the poem the human maiden Phoebe and her companion Sorrow, the poem begins to refuse its own erotic idealizations and resurrections. At the allegorical center of Book IV, the narrator of *Endymion* finds at last his second major symbol of art, the solitary and desolate Cave of Quietude, a "dark Paradise" where "silence dreariest is most articulate; . . . / Where those eyes are the brightest far that keep / Their lids shut longest in a dreamless sleep." This is the place of deepest content, even though "a grievous feud" is said to have led Endymion to the Cave of Quietude.

Keats thought that this discovery of the tragic, hieroglyphic, and solitary center of art meant that he must bid farewell to creative imagination, to "cloudy phantasms . . . / And air of vision, and the monstrous swell / Of visionary seas":

> No, never more
> Shall airy voices cheat me to the shore
> Of tangled wonder, breathless and aghast.

This farewall to "airy" imagination displays the choice that Keats at first felt compelled to make in deciding on a tragic and human art. He could not yet see a relation between the airy voices of visionary shores and human truth; and he felt obliged to choose truth. "I deem," says the narrator of *Endymion,* "Truth the best music." *Endymion,* uneasily balancing the visionary, the symbolic, and the truthful, had nonetheless brought Keats to his view of art as necessarily related, though in symbolic terms, to human reality; as necessarily hieroglyphic; as the locus of social cooperation by which the symbol regained mimetic force; and as a social resurrective power.

Shortly afterward, in a sudden leap of insight, Keats came upon his final symbol for the social function of art, a symbol not to find its ultimate elaboration, however, until Keats was able to write the ode **"To Autumn."** In his sonnet **"When I have fears that I may cease to be,"** Keats summons up a rich gestalt:

> When I have fears that I may cease to be,

> Before my pen has glean'd my teeming brain,
> Before high-piled books, in charact'ry,
> Hold like rich garners the full-ripen'd grain. . . .

The poet's "teeming brain" is the field gleaned by his pen; the produce of his brain, "full-ripened grain," is then stored in the hieroglyphic charactery of books, which are like rich garners. Organic nature, after its transmutation into charactery (like that of Glaucus's magic symbols) becomes edible grain. By means of this gestalt, Keats asserts that the material sublime, the teeming fields of earth, can enter the brain and be hieroglyphically processed into print. Keats's aim is now to see the whole world with godlike range and power, with the seeing of Diana, "Queen of Earth, and Heaven, and Hell" (**"To Homer"**) or that of Minos, the judge of all things (**"On Visiting the Tomb of Burns"**).

Still, Keats has not yet enacted very far his convictions about the social function of art. The audience has been suggested as the consumer of the gleaned wheat that the poet had processed into grain; and the audience has been mentioned as the necessary cooperator in the reading of Glaucus's symbols, and as the resurrected beneficiaries of Glaucus's distributed scroll fragments. Now, in his greatest performative invention, Keats decides to play, in his own poetry, the role of audience and interpreter of symbols, not (as he so far had tended to do) the role of artist. This seems to me Keats's most successful aesthetic decision, one that distances him from his own investments (therapeutic and pleasurable alike) in creating. By playing the audience, he approaches his own art as one of its auditors, who may well want to know of what use this art will be to him.

In the odes on **"Indolence"** and to **"Psyche,"** Keats had played the role of the creating artist; but in the **"Ode to a Nightingale"** and the **"Ode on a Grecian Urn"** he is respectively the listener to music and the beholder of sculpture. Each of these odes inquires what the recipient of art stands to receive from art. Keats here represents the audience for art as a single individual, rather than as a collective social group such as his Greek worshippers on the urn. In the absence of ideational content (**"Nightingale"**), no social collective audience can be postulated; and a modern beholder does not belong to the society that produced the urn. Keats seems to suggest that the social audience is, in the case of art, an aggregate of individual recipients, since the aesthetic experience is primarily a personal one; but what the individual receives, society, as a multiplication of individuals, also receives, as we conclude from the enumeration of listeners to the nightingale through the ages.

In the two "aesthetic odes" proper to the senses of hearing and sight, Keats begins to enact the theories of the social function of art that he had previously only asserted. As the listener to the nightingale, Keats enters a realm of wordless and nonconceptual, nonrepresentational song. He leaves behind the human pageant of sorrow and the griefs of consciousness; he forsakes the conceptual faculty, the perplexing and retarding brain. He offers himself up to beauty in the form of Sensation, as he becomes a blind ear, ravished by the consolations of sweet sounds articulated together by the composer-singer, the nightingale.

In the **"Ode on a Grecian Urn,"** by contrast, Keats as audience opens his eyes to representational (if allegorical) art and readmits his brain, with all its perplexities and interrogations, to aesthetic experience. In this fiction, one function of art is still, as in the case of the **"Nightingale"** ode, to offer a delight of an aesthetic and sensuous sort—this time a delight to the eye rather than to the ear. But no longer does art, with consolatory intent, ravish its audience away from the human scene; instead, it draws its audience into its truthful representational and representative pictures carved in stone. The fiction of artistic creation as a spontaneous outpouring to an invisible audience—the fiction of the **"Nightingale"** ode—is jettisoned in favor of admitting the laborious nature of art, as sculpted artifice. And Keats, in the **"Urn,"** establishes the fact that appreciation need not be coincident with creation; he is appreciating the urn now, even though it was sculpted centuries ago. The freshness and perpetuity of art is insisted on, as is its social service to many generations, each of whom brings its woe to the urn, each of whom finds itself solaced by the urn, a friend to man. The social function of art, Keats discovers here, is to remind its audience, by means of recognizable representative figures, of emotions and events common to all human life—here, lust, love, and sacrifice. (pp. 71-5)

In **"Autumn,"** in his final understanding of the social function of art, Keats chooses nature and culture as the two poles of his symbolic system. He sees the work of the artist as the transformation of nature into culture, the transmutation of the teeming fields into garnered grain (the gleaning of the natural into books, as his earlier sonnet had described it). Since civilization itself arose from man's dominion over nature, the processing of nature by agriculture became the symbol in Greece of the most sacred mysteries. The vegetation goddess Demeter, with her sheaf of corn and her poppies, was honored in the Eleusinian rituals. And the two symbolic harvests, bread and wine, food and drink, remain transmuted even to this day in the Christian Eucharist.

Keats's **"Autumn"** ode takes as its allegory for art the making of nature into nurture. The artist, with reaping hook, gleaning basket, and cider press, denudes nature, we may say, but creates food. We cannot, so to speak, drink apples or eat wheat; we can only consume processed nature, apple juice and grain. Since the artist is his own teeming field, art, in this allegory, is a process of self-immolation. As life is processed into art by the gleaning pen or threshing flail, the artist's own life substance disappears, and where wheat was, only a stubble plain can be seen; but over the plain there rises a song. Song is produced by the steady rhythm of nature transmuted by self-sacrifice into culture. Art does not mimetically resemble nature, any more than cider mimetically resembles apples. But without apples there would be no cider; without life there would be no hieroglyphs of life. In this way, Keats insists again on the radically nonmimetic nature of art but yet argues for its intelligible relation to life in its representative symbolic order. (pp. 76-7)

Helen Vendler, "Keats and the Use of Poetry," in What Is a Poet? Essays from the Eleventh Alabama Symposium on English and American Literature, *edited by Hank Lazer, The University of Alabama Press, 1987, pp. 66-83.*

FURTHER READING

Allott, Miriam. *John Keats.* Writers and Their Works, edited by Ian Scott-Kilvert. Essex: Longman Group, 1976, 62 p.
　　Concise overview in which Allott traces the evolution of Keats's thought. Allott's essay succeeds Edmund Blunden's contribution to the same series (see annotation below).

Baker, John. "Dialectics and Reduction: Keats Criticism and the 'Ode to a Nightingale'." *Studies in Romanticism* 27, No. 1 (Spring 1988): 109-28.
　　Discusses various critical views of Keats's poetry. These methods of interpretation are then used to explicate "Ode to a Nightingale."

Balslev, Thora. *Keats and Wordsworth: A Comparative Study.* Munskaard: Norwegian Universities Press, 1962, 192 p.
　　Traces William Wordsworth's influence upon Keats's poetry and analyzes the relationship between various aspects of the two poets' art, including symbol and imagery.

Barnard, John. "Keats's Tactile Vision: 'Ode to Psyche' and the Early Poetry." In *Keats-Shelley Memorial Bulletin, Rome,* No. XXXIII, edited by Timothy Webb, pp. 1-24. Heslington, York: Keats-Shelley Memorial Association, 1982.
　　Examines the synesthetic tendency of the sensual imagery of Keats's poetry.

Bate, Walter Jackson. *The Stylistic Development of Keats.* New York: Humanities Press, 1962, 214 p.
　　Largely prosodic study in which Bate seeks "to give a precise description of the unfolding and development of a great poet's stylistic craftmanship, and to ally this technical progression with the changing bents of mind which gave it rise and direction."

———. *John Keats.* Cambridge, Mass.: Harvard University Press, Belknap Press, 1963, 732 p.
　　Detailed biography that is considered the most reliable and comprehensive modern source. Bate incorporates the biographical information that came to light subsequent to World War II, particularly the material included in Hyder Edward Rollins's *The Keats Circle: Letters and Papers, 1816-1878* [see annotation below].

Bernbaum, Ernest. "John Keats." In his *Guide through the Romantic Movement,* 2d. ed., pp. 86-110. New York: Ronald Press, 1972.
　　An introductory guide to the history of Keats criticism.

Blackstone, Bernard. *The Consecrated Urn: An Interpretation of Keats in Terms of Growth and Form.* London: Longmans, Green, 1959, 426 p.
　　A provocative study of Keats's poetic and philosophical growth based on his use of biological images. As Blackstone states in his preface, he approaches his subject from a "botanico-physiologico-cosmogonical" slant.

Bloom, Harold. "Keats and the Embarrassments of Poetic Tradition." In *From Sensibility to Romanticism: Essays Presented to Frederick A. Pottle,* edited by Frederick W. Hilles and Harold Bloom, pp. 513-26. New York: Oxford University Press, 1965.

Discusses Keats's break from the Miltonic tradition that dominated English poetry into the nineteenth century.

Blunden, Edmund. *John Keats.* Rev. ed. Writers and Their Works, edited by Geoffrey Bullough, no. 6. London: Longmans, Green, 1966, 40 p.
Excellent biographical and critical introduction.

Boulger, James D. "Keats' Symbolism." *English Literary History* 28, No. 3 (September 1961): 244-59.
Discusses several recurring symbols and themes found in Keats's poetry.

Bromwich, David. "Keats's Radicalism." *Studies in Romanticism* 25, No. 2 (Summer 1986): 197-210.
Suggests that several of Keats's poems contain political undertones, providing supporting documentation from Keats's correspondence and poetry.

Bush, Douglas. *John Keats: His Life and Writings.* Masters of World Literature Series, edited by Louis Kronenberger. New York: Macmillan, 1966, 224 p.
Concise and readable biography.

————. *Mythology and the Romantic Tradition in English Poetry.* Cambridge, Mass.: Harvard University Press, 1937, 647 p.
Discusses the influence of mythology on the works of the English Romantic poets.

Colvin, Sidney. *Keats.* London: Macmillan & Co., 1964, 240 p.
A biography, first published in 1887, that helped to expose a broader audience to Keats's life and works. Colvin expanded on this book in a later, more detailed study (see annotation below).

————. *John Keats: His Life and Poetry, His Friends, Critics, and After-Fame.* New York: Octagon Books, 1970, 598 p.
Standard biographical source based on Colvin's earlier biography (see annotation above).

Courthope, W. J. "Romanticism in English Poetry: Keats." In his *A History of English Poetry: The Romantic Movement in English Poetry, Effects of the French Revolution, Vol. VI,* pp. 320-56. London: Macmillan and Co., 1910.
Somewhat cursory critical overview notable because Courthope upholds the view that Keats is a merely pictorial and therefore inferior poet. Courthope was one of the most influential critics—indeed, one of the only critics—of his day to maintain this stance.

D'Avanzo, Mario. *Keats's Metaphors for the Poetic.* Durham, N. C.: Duke University Press, 1967, 232 p.
Examines within the context of Keats's entire œuvre recurring metaphors for imagination and poetic creativity. Among the metaphors D'Avanzo examines are sleep and dreams, the bower, and images of reality. D'Avanzo notes as particularly important Keats's use of all forms of art, such as painting, poetry, sculpture, and architecture, as subjects for his poems.

Dickstein, Morris. *Keats and His Poetry: A Study in Development.* Chicago: University of Chicago Press, 1971, 270 p.
A chronological reading of Keats's development in terms, according to the critic, "of his changing attitude toward 'consciousness,' what Keats calls 'the thinking principle,' by which he means not pure intellection so much as self-awareness. . . ." Dickstein's study is representative of recent academic criticism.

Empson, William. *Seven Types of Ambiguity.* Rev. ed. London: Chatto & Windus, 1949, 258 p.
Landmark modernist work that includes in chapter seven a brief discussion of "Ode to Melancholy." The ode, which Empson says "pounds together the sensations of joy and sorrow until they combine into sexuality," is cited as exhibiting what Empson defines as a "seventh type ambiguity," or that which is "full of contradiction, marking a division in the author's mind."

Finney, Claude Lee. *The Evolution of Keats's Poetry.* 2 vols. New York: Russell & Russell, 1963.
Detailed biographical criticism. The critic related only those facts of Keats's life that relate to his poetry in an attempt "to reconstruct the environment in which Keats lived and to present and explain the personal, social, and practical forces which inspired and influenced his poems."

Fogle, Richard Harter. *The Imagery of Keats and Shelley: A Comparative Study.* Hamden, Conn.: Archon Books, 1962, 296 p.
A comparison of the imagery of Keats and Percy Bysshe Shelley focusing on imagery of sensation in addition to synesthetic, empathetic, concrete, and abstract imagery.

Ford, Newell F. *The Prefigurative Imagination of John Keats: A Study of the Beauty-Time Identification and Its Implications.* Hamden, Conn.: Archon Books, 1966, 168 p.
Analysis of Keats's identification of beauty and truth based primarily on a concordance of the occurrence of the word "truth" throughout his writings. After Ford discusses his study, he reinterprets many of Keats's major writings in light of his findings.

Gittings, Robert. *John Keats: The Living Year, 21 September 1818 to 21 September 1819.* Cambridge, Mass.: Harvard University Press, 1954, 247 p.
Account of the single year of Keats's life during which, according to the critic, he wrote "nearly all" his greatest poetry. Gittings focuses on the events and sources that provided Keats's inspiration; the prologue and epilogue provide the details of the other periods of Keats's life.

————. *John Keats.* London: Heinemann, 1968, 469 p.
Scholarly biography that is considered the most factually accurate account of Keats's life. The book contains extensive illustrations and illuminating footnotes.

Goldberg, M. A. *The Poetics of Romanticism.* Yellow Springs, Ohio: Antioch Press, 1969, 186 p.
Examines Keats's poetic theory as delineated in his poems and letters and attempts to place it in literary history from Plato to Sigmund Freud, James Joyce, and T. S. Eliot.

Green, David Bonnell, and Wilson, Edwin Graves, eds. *Keats, Shelley, Byron, Hunt, and Their Circles: A Bibliography, July 1, 1950-June 30, 1962.* Lincoln: University of Nebraska Press, 1964, 323 p.
A collection of bibliographies originally published in volumes I-XII of the *Keats-Shelley Journal.* The collection lists all books and articles dealing with Keats, Percy Bysshe Shelley, Lord Byron, Leigh Hunt, and their circles, and the editors frequently supply helpful brief descriptions of the material. See annotation below by Robert A. Hartley for the continuation of the bibliography.

Haber, Tom Burns. "The Unifying Influence of Love in

Keats's Poetry." *Philological Quarterly* XVI, No. 2 (April 1937): 192-209.

Traces the development of the theme of love in Keats's poetry, correlating it with the poet's own experiences.

Hartley, Robert A., ed. *Keats, Shelley, Byron, Hunt, and Their Circles: A Bibliography, July 1, 1962-December 31, 1974.* Lincoln: University of Nebraska Press, 1978, 487 p.

A continuation of the earlier work edited by David Bonnell Green and Edwin Graves Wilson (see annotation above).

Herford, C. H. "The Shelley Group." In his *The Age of Wordsworth,* rev. ed., pp. 216-84. London: George Bell & Sons, 1909.

Provides a succinct overview of Keats's life and career.

Jack, Ian. "Keats." In his *English Literature: 1815-1832,* pp. 105-29. The Oxford History of English Literature, edited by F. P. Wilson and Bonamy Dobrée, Vol. X. Oxford: Clarendon Press, 1963.

Surveys Keats's poetry, providing information regarding manner of composition, literary style, and critical reception.

Jones, Leonidas M. "The 'Ode to Psyche': An Allegorical Introduction to Keats's Great Odes." In *Keats-Shelley Memorial Bulletin, Rome,* No. IX, edited by Dorothy Hewlett, pp. 22-6. Richmond, Surrey: Keats-Shelley Memorial Association, 1958.

Provides a brief allegorical reading of "Ode to Psyche," succeeded by an explication of how the theme of the importance of imagination is introduced in this poem and further developed in the great Odes.

Kauvar, Gerald B. *The Other Poetry of Keats.* Rutherford, N. J.: Fairleigh Dickinson University Press, 1969, 238 p.

Focuses on Keats's lesser known and less frequently studied works, particularly the early and late poems, for their intrinsic artistic value as well as for the light they shed on Keats's development.

The Keats House Committee. *The John Keats Memorial Volume.* London: John Lane, the Bodley Head, 1921, 276 p.

A centenary compilation of critical essays and biographical articles on Keats and his circle as well as a bibliography of Keats's writings and several translations of his poems into various languages. The volume includes contributions, in both English and foreign languages, from ninety British, American, European, and Oriental critics and scholars, including George Santsbury, Amy Lowell, Clement Shorter, A. C. Bradley, and Robert Bridges.

Lyon, Harvey T. *Keats' Well-Read Urn: An Introduction to Literary Method.* New York: Henry Holt and Co., 1958, 118 p.

A superb introduction to Keats's "Ode on a Grecian Urn." In an attempt "to introduce the student to poetry through criticism, and to criticism through poetry," Lyon offers excerpts from significant textual, scholarly, and critical commentary on the odes by eight writers, from Keats's contemporaries to modern scholars.

MacGillivray, J. R. *Keats: A Bibliography and Reference Guide with an Essay on Keats' Reputation.* University of Toronto Department of English, Studies and Texts, no. 3. Toronto: University of Toronto Press, 1949, 210 p.

A bibliography through 1946 of primary sources, including first editions and later editions of Keats's poetry, letters, and prose, translations, and creative writings inspired by Keats's life and works, as well as criticism from periodicals and books. MacGillivray also provides a lengthy, useful overview of the rise of Keats's reputation through 1946.

Matthews, G. M., ed. *Keats: The Critical Heritage.* The Critical Heritage Series, edited by B. C. Southam. New York: Barnes & Noble, 1971, 430 p.

An anthology of Keats criticism drawn from books, magazines, letters, and journal entries from the first reviews through 1863. Informative annotations preface each critical piece, and the editor has contributed a helpful introductory overview of Keats's reputation.

Muir, Kenneth, ed. *John Keats: A Reassessment.* Liverpool English Texts and Studies, no. 5. Liverpool: Liverpool University Press, 1958, 182 p.

Significant collection of ten essays by such noted scholars as Kenneth Muir, Miriam Allott, R. T. Davies, and David I. Masson. Topics explored include Keats's debt to the Elizabethans and his relationship with William Hazlitt, but the majority of the essays are on single poems.

Murry, John Middleton. *Keats.* New York: Noonday Press, 1955, 322 p.

Important essays in which Murry discusses various biographical and critical concerns, including Keats's relationship to John Milton, William Blake, and William Wordsworth, his ideas on friendship, and his various poetic theories. This collection was originally published in 1930 as *Studies in Keats* and appeared in revised and enlarged editions as *Studies in Keats: New and Old* in 1939 and *The Mystery of Keats* in 1949. *Keats,* the final incarnation, is intended, as are the earlier volumes, as a companion to Murry's *Keats and Shakespeare: A Study of Keats' Poetic Life from 1816 to 1820.*

Pettet, E. C. *On the Poetry of Keats.* 1957. Reprint. Cambridge: Cambridge at the University Press, 1970, 395 p.

An examination of Keats's poetry from various viewpoints. While most of Keats's poetry is discussed, the ode "To Autumn" and *The Fall of Hyperion* are considered only briefly. The greatest attention is reserved for *Endymion,* particularly in an effort to discourage its interpretation as evidence that Keats was a metaphysical writer.

Reiman, Donald H. "John Keats." In his *English Romantic Poetry, 1800-1835: A Guide to Information Sources,* pp. 167-83. American Literature, English Literature, and World Literatures in English Information Guide Series, vol. 27. Detroit: Gale Research Co., 1979.

A concise bibliography of collected, selected, and translated editions of Keats's works as well as key textual and critical material. Reiman includes useful descriptive annotations.

Rollins, Hyder Edward. *Keats's Reputation in America to 1848.* Cambridge, Mass.: Harvard University Press, 1946, 147 p.

An exhaustive study of a somewhat limited subject: Keats's reception and reputation in America before 1850.

Smallwood, R. L. "The Occasion of Keats's 'Ode to a Nightingale'." *Durham University Journal* LXVII, No. 1 (December 1974): 49-56.

Discusses the conflicting critical views regarding the date and manner of Keats's "Ode to a Nightingale."

Tate, Allen. "A Reading of Keats." In his *The Hovering Fly and Other Essays,* pp. 52-70. 1949. Reprint. Freeport, N. Y.: Books for Libraries Press, 1968.
Analyzes Keats's use of the pictorial method in "Ode to a Nightingale." Tate integrates a discussion of late nineteenth and early twentieth-century Keats criticism into his study.

Thorpe, Clarence De Witt. *The Mind of John Keats.* New York: Russell & Russell, 1964, 209 p.
The first and most significant arguments that Keats was an intellectual poet as well as one of sensations.

Unger, Leonard. "Keats and the Music of Autumn." In his *The Man in the Name: Essays on the Experience of Poetry,* pp. 18-29. Minneapolis: University of Minnesota Press, 1956.
Examines the theme, imagery, and artistic achievement of "To Autumn." Unger also compares this poem to the other odes on several stylistic and critical points.

Van Ghent, Dorothy. *Keats: The Myth of the Hero.* Rev. ed. Edited by Jeffrey Cane Robinson. Princeton, N.J.: Princeton University Press, 1983, 277 p.
Traces the myth of the hero archetype through Keats's works. The study is an edited and revised edition of an unfinished manuscript left by Van Ghent at her death in 1967.

Ward, Aileen. *John Keats: The Making of a Poet.* New York: Viking Press, 1964, 450 p.
Considered among the best modern biographies. Ward's study is a critical account written from a subtly psychological perspective.

Wasserman, Earl R. *The Finer Tone: Keats' Major Poems.* Baltimore: Johns Hopkins Press, 1953, 228 p.
Influential analysis of Keats's philosophic tendencies and his poetic technique. Wasserman discusses five poems: "Ode on a Grecian Urn," "La Belle Dame sans Merci," "The Eve of St. Agnes," "Lamia," and "Ode to a Nightingale."

Wilson, Katharine M. *The Nightingale and the Hawk: A Psychological Study of Keats' Ode.* London: George Allen and Unwin, 1964, 157 p.
Jungian interpretation of Keats's poetic imagery in "Ode to a Nightingale."

Zillman, Lawrence John. *John Keats and the Sonnet Tradition: A Critical and Comparative Study.* Los Angeles: Lyman House, 1939, 209 p.
Explores the formal and technical aspects of Keats's sonnets in relation to the English sonnet tradition from Sir Thomas Wyatt and Henry Howard.

Edgar Lee Masters

1868-1950

(Also wrote under the pseudonyms Dexter Wallace, Webster Ford, Harley Prowler, Elmer Chubb, Lute Puckett, and Lucius Atherton) American poet, novelist, dramatist, biographer, autobiographer, and essayist.

Masters is considered an important figure in American poetry. He is best remembered for the *Spoon River Anthology,* a collection of poems highly acclaimed for their brevity in depicting startling realities of small-town life. The *Spoon River Anthology* is said to have helped revolutionize American poetry during the early twentieth century, for in these free verse poems, which take the form of epitaphs for the long-dead and recently deceased citizens of a Midwestern town, the characters spoke more freely about their lives in death than they might otherwise have revealed. The *Anthology* was the first popular work to explode the myth of traditional American values, and for this reason Masters is closely associated with Sinclair Lewis and Sherwood Anderson. Although nearly all critics extol the *Anthology* as Masters's greatest literary achievement, he was prolific throughout his life, writing numerous volumes of poetry and works in other genres.

Masters was born in Garnett, Kansas, though he soon moved with his family to Illinois. He spent his childhood and early adult life in several rural Illinois communities, including Petersburg and Lewistown, which provided him with models for Spoon River. Masters's mother was a devout Methodist interested in the fine arts, while his father was devoted to his legal career and political activities and had very little interest in religion. Masters seemed to have taken on the value systems of both parents, but was more positively influenced by his father and paternal grandparents. Critics often note that "Lucinda Matlock," an epitaph from the *Spoon River Anthology* based on his grandmother Lucinda Masters, is, an affirmation of pioneer strength.

While Masters had only one year of university education, he was a voracious reader and became well-versed in history, philosophy, and classical studies. Upon his father's urging he read law for the Illinois bar, which he passed in 1891. After practicing law with his father for a year, Masters moved to Chicago in 1892, where he established a successful legal career marked by his partnership with acclaimed criminal defense attorney Clarence Darrow. Masters married Helen Jenkins in 1898, the year his first volume of poetry, *A Book of Verses,* appeared to very little recognition. While establishing his legal reputation in Chicago, Masters continued to write poetry and began associating with other writers of the Chicago Renaissance, most notably Theodore Dreiser and Carl Sandburg. In 1907 Masters met William Marion Reedy, editor of the St. Louis weekly *Reedy's Mirror.* Masters's association with Reedy provided both a life-long friendship and an important literary influence. Reedy published some of Masters's earliest verse, but more importantly, he introduced Masters to *Epigrams from the Greek Anthology,* a work that provided the structural inspiration for the *Spoon River An-*

thology. Masters's epitaphs began appearing in the *Mirror* in 1914, and at the age of forty-five he finally achieved status as a respected poet. Masters continued to write until 1942 when health problems prevented him from working. He died in a convalescent home in 1950.

Masters had originally considered writing the Spoon River poems in novel form. As early as 1906, he had planned to write a long fictional work in which he would display sensibilities of a small town as a microcosm of American society. Not until his introduction to the *Greek Anthology* in 1913 and a conversation with his mother in 1914 in which they reminisced about his boyhood, however, did Masters decide to depict his idea in verse. Masters sent eight poems to Reedy who enthusiastically published them in the *Mirror* under the pseudonym Webster Ford. Within a year, Reedy had revealed Masters as the actual author, and the poems were gathered and published as the *Spoon River Anthology.* Considered a *succès de scandale,* the poems generated popular acclaim and critical controversy. In contrast to the expanding industrialization in most American cities prior to World War I, Robert Naverson wrote that "the small town was still the official haven of innocence and virtue." Masters shattered this image with his ironic epigrams in which upstanding citizens of Spoon River revealed dark, often sinister sides to their personalities. For example, a vigilant prohibitionist discloses in his epitaph that he died of cirrhosis of the liver. The acknowledged villain of the *Anthology,* Thomas Rhodes, victimizes innocent people of Spoon River, despite his status as a successful businessman, deacon, and influential citizen. The complete story of the characters is not always told in a single epitaph; many of the tales are exposed through several poems so that different epitaphs unveil the interrelated lives of characters from varying perspectives. An often cited example of this technique is the Pantier epitaphs. Benjamin Pantier's epitaph and the subsequent reply from his wife give both sides to their failed marriage, and additional epitaphs from various people reflect repercussions of the discord between the Pantiers. Critics maintain that each individual story contributes to the whole narrative and its universality.

Not only did Masters's satiric criticism of American society shock readers, but his use of free verse, poetry characterized by short lines of irregular length and meter lacking rhythm, aroused controversy as well. Reviewers often turned their discussion of the *Anthology* into heated debates on whether to consider the work poetry or prose. Ezra Pound defended the work as poetry and extolled Masters as an authentic American poet, while other critics vehemently denounced his work. Amy Lowell noted: "[*Vers libre* poems] gave him the clue to just what he needed—freedom from the too patterned effects of rhyme and metre, brevity, and conciseness. Such a form seemed absolutely made for his purpose." Lowell hailed Masters as a poet who embodied the American spirit but faulted him for stressing sexual issues, although only twelve of the 214 poems employ sex as subject matter. The characters in the *Anthology* represent nearly all social and economic classes. Masters delineated psychological rather than sociological character studies and many reviewers noted a pessimistic outlook in his authentic character portrayals. John T. Flanagan has stated that Masters was both an iconoclast and an idealist, ascribing a truthful but still hopeful outlook to Masters's vision. Masters himself stated that he arranged the *Anthology* in a three-part progression: "the fools, the drunkards, and the failures came first, the people of one-birth minds got second place, and the heroes and the enlightened spirits came last, a sort of *Divine Comedy.* . . . "

In the years immediately following the *Anthology,* Masters published four volumes of poetry in rapid succession, all of which garnered a marginal critical reception. *Songs and Satires,* a collection of traditional verse, is noted, not often favorably, for a heightened sense of romantic idealism. Some critics have speculated that many of the poems in *Songs and Satires* actually may have been written prior to the *Anthology.* The next three volumes all return to the Illinois countryside for setting and subject matter. *The Great Valley* is composed of nostalgic poems lamenting the agrarian past and angry attacks on the corruptions of cities and religion. Masters's next collection, *Toward the Gulf,* is described by Herb Russell as "a record of losses." Although reviewers note that some of the poems in *Toward the Gulf* reflect Masters's idealism and a mature outlook, the majority of the portraits show characters who are frustrated in their quest for an ideal, and the tone of this work is considered overly subjective. In his analysis of *Starved Rock,* Masters's subsequent volume, Russell de-

scribed the work as a "vehicle for the poet to revenge himself on his enemies," contending that with this volume Masters revealed himself as a bitter, defeated poet. Russell asserts that Masters's "death" as an artist parallels these poems that retell the legend of the Illini Indians who, in the eighteenth century, were driven to a cliff at Starved Rock where they died of hunger and thirst. More favorable reviews of the work acknowledge an intensity and sincerity to the poems even though Masters is faulted for being overtly philosophical on occasion.

Masters considered *Domesday Book,* a long narrative poem composed in blank verse, his best work. This book-length piece details the life and death of Elenor Murray, a free-spirited woman whose body is found by a riverbank. Through flashbacks, her private life is imparted by testimonies from all the people who had known her. *Domesday Book,* with its complexities of the interrelated lives of the characters, did not receive much critical attention, further subordinating Masters's efforts to write a work as successful as the *Anthology.* In 1924, Masters published *The New Spoon River,* intended as a sequel to the *Spoon River Anthology.* According to Willis Barnstone in his introduction to the *New Spoon River,* Masters employs colloquial language to reiterate such themes as the invasion of urban and industrial values, the city as both liberator and destroyer, and the restructuring of small-town values. Because the shocking themes and style of the *Anthology* had long dissipated, *The New Spoon River* garnered only cursory reviews. Several critics assert that Master's objective point of view in the original *Anthology* is lost to a subjective perspective in the sequel, which at times detracts from the universality of the work.

Despite Masters's prolific efforts to write a work as popular and as critically acclaimed as the *Spoon River Anthology,* he never equalled the notoriety and success of his chief work. Though Masters remains an enigmatic figure in American literature, his contribution to American poetry is firmly established with the *Spoon River Anthology.* The *Anthology* remains a brilliantly original representation of an archetypal American small town, and many of the individual poems from the collection are considered among the finest works of modern American poetry.

(For further information on Masters's life and career, see *Twentieth-Century Literary Criticism,* Vols. 2, 25; *Contemporary Authors,* Vol. 104; *Dictionary of Literary Biography,* Vol. 54; and *Concise Dictionary of American Literary Biography: Realism, Naturalism, and Local Color, 1865-1917.*)

PRINCIPAL WORKS

POETRY

A Book of Verses   1898
The Blood of the Prophets [as Dexter Wallace]   1905
Songs and Sonnets [as Webster Ford]   1910
Songs and Sonnets, Second Series [as Webster Ford]   1912
Spoon River Anthology   1915; revised edition, 1916
The Great Valley   1916
Songs and Satires   1916
Toward the Gulf   1918
Starved Rock   1919

Domesday Book   1920
The Open Sea   1921
The New Spoon River   1924
Selected Poems   1925
Lee: A Dramatic Poem   1926
Jack Kelso: A Dramatic Poem   1928
The Fate of the Jury: An Epilogue to Domesday Book
      1929
Lichee Nuts   1930
Godbey: A Dramatic Poem   1931
The Serpent in the Wilderness   1933
Richmond: A Dramatic Poem   1934
Invisible Landscapes   1935
The Golden Fleece of California   1936
Poems of People   1936
The New World   1937
More People   1939
Illinois Poems   1941
Along the Illinois   1942
The Harmony of Deeper Music: Posthumous Poems of
      Edgar Lee Masters   1976

OTHER MAJOR WORKS

Maximilian   (drama)   1902
The New Star Chamber, and Other Essays   (essays)
      1904
Althea   (drama)   1907
The Trifler   (drama)   1908
The Leaves of the Tree   (drama)   1909
Eileen   (drama)   1910
The Locket   (drama)   1910
The Bread of Idleness   (drama)   1911
Mitch Miller   (novel)   1920
Children of the Market Place   (novel)   1922
The Nuptial Flight   (novel)   1923
Skeeters Kirby   (novel)   1923
Mirage   (novel)   1924
Kit O'Brien   (novel)   1927
Levy Mayer and the New Industrial Era   (biography)
      1927
Gettysburg, Manila, Acoma [first publication date]
      (drama)   1930
Lincoln: The Man   (biography)   1931
The Tale of Chicago   (nonfiction)   1933
Dramatic Duologues: Four Short Plays in Verse [first publi-
      cation date]   (drama)   1934
Vachel Lindsay: A Poet in America   (biography)   1935
Across Spoon River   (autobiography)   1936
The Tide of Time   (novel)   1937
Whitman   (biography)   1937
Mark Twain: A Portrait   (biography)   1938
The Sangamon   (nonfiction)   1942

Ezra Pound   (essay date 1915)

[*An American poet and critic, Pound was "the principal
inventor of modern poetry," according to Archibald
MacLeish. He is chiefly renowned for his ambitious poetry cycle, the* Cantos, *which he revised and enlarged
throughout much of his life. These poems are noted for
their lyrical intensity, metrical experimentation, literary*
allusions, varied subject matter and verse forms. Pound
is also noted for his instrumental role in encouraging
other authors as he obtained editorial and financial assistance for T. S. Eliot, William Butler Yeats, and many
other distinguished writers. In the excerpt below, Pound
enthusiastically hails "Webster Ford" (the pseudonym
under which Masters first wrote the* Spoon River Anthology) *as the first American poet since Walt Whitman
to treat American themes realistically.*]

At last! At last America has discovered a poet. Do not
mistake me, America, that great land of hypothetical fu-
tures, has had various poets born within her borders, but
since Whitman they have invariably had to come abroad
for their recognition. . . .

At last the American West has produced a poet strong
enough to weather the climate, capable of dealing with life
directly, without circumlocution, without resonant meaningless phrases. Ready to say what he has to say, and to
shut up when he has said it. Able to treat Spoon River as
Villon treated Paris in 1460. The essence of this treatment
consists in looking at things unaffectedly. Villon did not
pretend that fifteenth-century Paris was Rome of the first
century B.C. Webster Ford does not pretend that Spoon
River of 1914 is Paris of 1460.

The quality of this treatment is that it can treat actual details without being interested in them, without in the least
depending upon them. The bore, the demnition bore of
pseudo-modernity, is that the avowed modernist thinks he
can make a poem out of a steam shovel more easily and
more effectively than out of the traditional sow's ear. The
accidents and detail are made to stand for the core.

Good poetry is always the same; the changes are superficial. We have the real poem in nature. The real poet thinking the real poem absorbs the *decor* almost unconsciously.
(p. 11)

I have before me an early book by Webster Ford, [***Songs
and Sonnets, Second Series***], printed in 1912. . . . Nine-
teen-twelve was a bad year, we all ran about like puppies
with ten tin cans tied to our tails. The tin cans of Swinburnian rhyming, of Browningisms, even, in Mr. Ford's
case, of Kiplingisms, a resonant pendant, magniloquent,
Miltonic, sonorous.

The fine thing about Mr. Ford's ***Songs and Sonnets*** is that
in spite of the trappings one gets the conviction of a real
author, determined to speak the truth despite the sec-
tionised state of his medium. And despite cliches of phrase
and of rhythm one receives emotions, of various strength,
some tragic and violent. There is moral reflection, etc., but
what is the use discussing faults which a man has already
discarded.

In the ***Spoon River Anthology*** we find the straight writing,
language unaffected. No longer the murmurous derivative, but:—

   "My wife hated me, my son went to the dogs."

That is to say the speech of a man in process of getting
something said, not merely in quest of polysyllabic decoration.

It is a great and significant thing that America should contain an editor (of the *St. Louis Mirror*) with sense enough

to print such straight writing, and a critic sane enough to find such work in a "common newspaper" and quote it in an American review (i.e. *Poetry*).

The silly will tell you that: "It isn't poetry." The decrepit will tell you it isn't poetry. There are even loathsome atavisms, creatures of my own generation who are so steeped in the abysmal ignorance of generations, now, thank heaven, fading from the world, who will tell you: "It isn't poetry." By which they mean: "It isn't ornament. It is an integral part of an emotion. It is a statement, a bare statement of something which is part of the mood, something which contributes to the mood, not merely a bit of chiffon attached." (pp. 11-12)

I have read a reasonable amount of bad American magazine verse, pseudo-Masefieldian false pastoral and so on. Not one of the writers had had the sense, which Mr. Ford shows here, in calling up the reality of the Middle West by the very simple device of names. . . . (p. 12)

> *Ezra Pound, "Webster Ford," in* The Egoist, *Vol. II, No. 1, January 1, 1915, pp. 11-12.*

Lawrence Gilman   (essay date 1915)

[*In the following excerpt, Gilman terms* Spoon River Anthology *a work of "cinematographic verse," noting the universality and originality of Masters's work.*]

It is apparently not yet agreed what Mr. Masters' book [***Spoon River Anthology***] is,—except that it is "free verse." Convinced that it is certainly not poetry, and horrified by its content and structure, the æsthetic Calvinists have exhorted Mr. Masters to be still, in the spirit of the command of the immortal ship-captain to his mate: "What I wants of you, Mr. Coffin, is SILENCE, and damn little of that." But Mr. Masters is unlikely to oblige. It is extremely doubtful if silence is his long suit. Certainly it is not a conspicuous characteristic of his ***Spoon River Anthology,*** which is nothing if not articulate and alive and what we have a fancy to call psychically reverberatory. In this village *comédie humaine* are assembled the life histories of the inhabitants of Spoon River, and the overtones of the jangling music of these spent lives reverberate from page to page, clash and re-echo, attaining at times a poignancy which we do not quite know how to regard or appraise.

They speak to us from their graves, these Spoon River people:

> Where are Elmer, Herman, Bert, Tom and Charley,
> The weak of will, the strong of arm, the clown, the boozer,
>   the fighter?
> All, all, are sleeping on the hill.

And when, through Mr. Masters, they have spoken, we know them beyond the power of forgetting; their actuality is amazing. . . . (pp. 271-72)

Throughout two hundred and fifty pages this unique human comedy unfolds itself—the life of Spoon River and its men and women, its girls and boys. The *Anthology* has a microcosmic completeness. We hear, told by themselves, the life-histories of village belles and grocer's clerks, farmers and farmer's wives, travelling salesmen, lawyers, blacksmiths, school-girls, politicians, tramps, doctors, bank-presidents, druggists, the village poetess, the village dandy, deacons, school-teachers, saloon-keepers, preachers, adulteresses and Sunday-school superintendents, hired girls and circuit-judges, newspaper editors, whores, bullys, grafters, crooks, murderers, gamblers, wantons, drunkards, ne'er-do-wells, dreamers, idealists, wastrels and paupers and prudes. Here are tragedies, sordid or touching, horrible or grim; pitiful romances, scandals, little histories of violence and tenderness, of patient waiting and rebellious enduring; grotesque comedies, preposterous melodramas; a humanity that is universal. (pp. 272-73)

What Mr. Masters has accomplished is the cinematographing of narrative-verse. He has reversed the practice of the moving-picture people,—who give us stories in picture-form,—and offers us a kind of moving-picture in the form of fictional verse. The ***Spoon River Anthology*** is a series of vivid, concentrated, rapidly shifting visualizations, related and interwoven, and employing that favorite device of the screen-play: a single event exhibited from different dramatic angles. You get, for example, Aner Clute's story of how she happened to "lead the life": well, it was a silk dress, and a promise of marriage from a rich man (Lucius Atherton); and because they gave her the name for it, why, that made her what she was. You get, then, Lucius Atherton's picture flashed on the screen: the former town dandy,—"an excellent knave of hearts who took many a trick,"—now old and shabby, living at the village restaurant; "a gray, untidy, toothless, discarded, rural Don Juan." But this is not all: Homer Clapp is put before you, begging of Aner Clute a parting kiss at the gate—a kiss that she refused, "saying we should be engaged before that"; but no sooner had he gone (so he learned afterward) than Lucius Atherton stole in at her window. So he died cursing himself for one of Life's fools, "whom only death would treat as the equal of other men."

Just what relation Mr. Masters' cinematographic verse bears to poetry it is not easy to declare with confidence. We have said somewhat of the substance of his book, nothing of its form. Here is a fair sample of it at its most characteristic—it is Deacon Taylor speaking:

> I belonged to the church,
> And to the party of prohibition;
> And the villagers thought I had died of eating watermel-
>   on.
> In truth I had cirrhosis of the liver,
> For every noon for thirty years,
> I slipped behind the prescription partition
> In Trainor's drug store
> And poured a generous drink
> From the bottle marked
> *"Spiritus frumenti."*

Clearly this is as remote from poetry—the poetry of Whitman no less than the poetry of Swinburne—as the music of young Mr. Leo Ornstein is remote from the music of Chopin. It is perfectly easy to conclude that it is not poetry at all. To call it "free verse" is as idle as it would be to call it blank verse, or a sonnet. Nine-tenths of the ***Spoon River Anthology*** is, as verse, equally bald, flat, and uncouth. Occasionally it attains a measure of grave eloquence, an exaltation of speech that is seen at its best in the picture of Isaiah Beethoven, with but three months to live, brooding in the darkness by the mill-stream, where

The flame of the moon ran under my eyes
Amid a forest stillness broken
By a flute in a hut on the hill.

But there is little in the book that is of this fibre. Most of it is of a piece with the **"Deacon Taylor"** passage. So, reading about the trial of Dr. Duval for the murder of Zora Clemens, we come back to the question that disturbs us throughout most of the *Anthology:* If this is poetry:

Alas, that love, so gentle in his view,
Should be so tyrannous and rough in proof!

what, then, is this?—

It was clear he had got her in a family way;
And to let the child be born
Would not do.

When, in Whitman, we weary of reading that

The President holding a cabinet council is surrounded
by the great Secretaries,

we can turn a few pages and find this:

I am he that walks with the tender and growing night.
. . . .
Smile, O voluptuous cool-breath'd earth!
Earth of the slumbering and liquid trees!

There are no such compensations in Mr. Masters' verse. You will seek there in vain for what Stevenson called the "unexcelled imaginative justness of language" that is in Whitman. The *Spoon River Anthology* prevails—seizes you, engrosses you, haunts you—not because of its verse, but in spite of it. It is often as rank and as candid as the records of a police-court; but it is ineluctably detaining, at times extraordinarily moving. It is a miracle of veracious characterization; fiction of an unexampled kind; a new thing under the sun. But why drag in poetry? (pp. 274-76)

> *Lawrence Gilman, "Moving-Picture Poetry,"*
> *in* The North American Review, *Vol. CCII,*
> *No. 717, August, 1915, pp. 271-76.*

Willard Huntington Wright   (essay date 1916)

[*Wright was an American critic, editor, and author who is regarded as the inaugurator of the Golden Age in American detective fiction. In the following excerpt, he negatively appraises* Spoon River Anthology *in terms of aesthetic form and "minor literary appurtenances."*]

The only true basis of artistic judgment is æsthetic form. All other methods are necessarily superficial and dependent on prejudice, taste, preference and a whole suite of irrelevant "appeals" which emanate from the individual and do not touch on the *inherent* merit or demerit of the work criticized. Deny this, and you deny psychology, chemistry, heliotropism and biology—all of which sciences are the bases of æsthetic apperception. . . . [In] literature, the most laggard of all the arts, the cultured world still clings to the shallow, abecedary methods of judgment—methods which even the illiterate would scorn to apply to music: that is, we still judge literature and its chlorotic offspring, poetry, by their documentary, illustrative, atmospheric, meteorological or mimetic accretions. A book or a poem we pronounce good or bad according to its ability to give us a realistic picture, to stir up our as-sociative processes, or to inspire in us specific sentiments such as joy, sorrow, pity, revenge, longing, etc. We even evade important qualities of art so far as to talk of the teachings or philosophy of a literary work.

No better example of this inadequate and irrelevant system of judgment can be found than in the recent babble set in motion by Mr. Edgar Lee Masters' book of *vers libre,* **Spoon River Anthology.** Not even the author, I warrant, would claim for his efforts any strictly æsthetic merit, namely, that they follow the empathical form and rhythmic organization which accord with the emotional reactions as analyzed and recorded. . . . If he should make such a claim it would be to confess his total ignorance of the science of æsthetics. For the æstetician, the man who is deeply concerned with the larger and fundamental issues of art, Mr. Masters' book is of no more interest or importance than a newspaper obituary. As art, in the true sense, it is non-existent.

But let us, on the other hand, consider the book from the customary points of approach—realism, lyricism, document, photography, philosophy, psychology (in the sense of trait-probing), poetic diction, atmosphere, and originality. What has Mr. Masters to offer to the lovers of such minor literary appurtenances?

As realism the book obviously will not stand. It is too deficient in details, too crowded with speculation and omniscient assumptions. To use a man's or a woman's real name, in place of "he" and "she," is only a spurious method of provoking a pseudo-realism. (pp. 109-10)

Lyricism, that precise and musical form of writing, Mr. Masters has frankly avoided. The melodious care of a Swinburne or a Shelley is, by implication, to him anathema. His lines repudiate scansion, as he himself repudiates rhyme. (p. 110)

As a document the **Spoon River Anthology** is unvital and cutaneous. It treats exclusively of the aspects and effects of human actions and reactions: never of the underlying causes, of impulses or desires to which one could apply, even casually, such an adjective as cosmic, basic or protoplasmic. Motives are not advanced, only reasons, such as religion, breeding, failure, love, desire, lust, hatred, maternalism, and the like. Each one of these emotions is, in itself, the surface effect of a subterranean cause. Even motherhood, the deepest of Mr. Masters' actuating impulses, is only a manifestation of a greater and more cryptic impulse in human nature. But these profounder motivations are not once suggested: the biological or chemical imperative, for Mr. Masters, does not exist. As document, therefore, his book is the sheerest reportorialism.

In illustration—the most insignificant of all literary considerations—Mr. Masters makes his strongest appeal. He gives us pictures. But ask yourself if these pictures are one-tenth as powerful as many of the stories of the better-class war-correspondent. Are they as complete and powerful, in fact, as the pictures of such second-rate novelists as Jack London, Rex Beach and Henry Milner Rideout? Are they as comprehensive in their depiction of the social life of a small city as a dozen novels you can name, which specialize in localized characterizations? (pp. 110-11)

Philosophically Mr. Masters has nothing to offer, unless we are to accept the lesson of human tolerance. Such a preachment is not new; it is a platitude, and many eminent thinkers have questioned its worth, tracing it to decadent and weakened organisms. We find it in nearly every issue of the popular magazines; and even were it an established truth, it would be scarcely enough to give viability to a nearly defunct literary effort.

In the matter of "psychology"—as that word is loosely used in connection with fiction—the *Spoon River Anthology* is unable to qualify beyond the most superficial empiricism. There is no observation in the book which could not be made by any shrewd reporter who had served an apprenticeship in the police courts. "A grasp of human nature"—as the phrase goes—is all Mr. Masters possesses; but this gift is so common, even among serious second-rate writers, that one cannot assume it to be a distinguishing trait.

Consider, next, the book's diction. You may search in vain for Pater's "gypsy phrase," for any inevitable juxtaposition of words, for any moving figures of speech, for any striking expressions which lift bald prose into the realm of beauty. (pp. 111-12)

Has the *Spoon River Anthology* atmosphere? Suppose the point is admitted: does that give its author any claim to greatness? As any literary craftsman knows, atmosphere is a trick—a thing to be found in hundreds of books which no one pretends to take seriously. It is, in fact, almost impossible for an experienced author to write of a locality with which he is intimate without "creating an atmosphere." The trick is to a great extent unconscious. Oblivion is peopled with makers of "atmosphere." The lesser painters and musicians are full of it. It is perhaps the meagrest of all artistic appeals.

We come now to the subject of Mr. Masters' originality—a quality for which he has been widely acclaimed. But here again we must deny him admittance. Turn back to Edwin Arlington Robinson's *Children of the Night,* copyright in 1896 and 1897, and published in 1905, and you will find the undeniable source of this new author's ideas and inspiration—not only in his broad scheme, but down to the smallest general details. Mr. Robinson, nearly twenty years ago, did almost exactly what Mr. Masters has done this year, only the former did it beautifully, skilfully and poetically. Read such poems of Mr. Robinson's as "John Everaldown," "Richard Cory," "Cliff Klingenhagen," "Fleming Helphenstine," "Reuben Bright" and "The Tavern": then read Mr. Masters' **"Eugene Carman," "Richard Bone," "Chase Henry," " 'Butch' Weldy," "Tom Merritt"** and **"Barry Holden."** The parallels between these two writers is too close, too self-evident, to be denied. Mr. Masters comes direct from Mr. Robinson; just as Mr. Robinson grew out of George Crabbe. The "originality" of the *Spoon River Anthology* is its smallest claim to our attention.

If the book, then, fails consistently in all these tests, what is left? . . . Nothing. But why should it have created so extensive a sensation, and gained for its author so pleasant a reputation? The answer lies in the very faults and shortcomings of the book. The Anglo-Saxon is a lover of superficial speciousness, of quasi-materialism, of cheap novelty. He also takes a secret delight in boldness of expression and morbid sexual details—the hypocritical Freudian reaction to a zymotic puritanism. These things are all summed up and emphasized in the *Spoon River Anthology.* (pp. 112-13)

Willard Huntington Wright, "Mr. Masters' 'Spoon River Anthology': A Criticism," in Forum, *Vol. LV, January, 1916, pp. 109-13.*

Shaemas O'Sheel   (essay date 1916)

[*O'Sheel was an American poet who wrote in the tradition of Irish Renaissance poets. In the following excerpt, he classifies* Spoon River Anthology *an epic in which Masters has created "a stirring tale of souls and destiny."*]

If poetry be the inspired revelation of the great mysterious forces that shape the flow of life, and the noble telling of the struggles of passion and hope to shape these forces, regardless of form, then assuredly *Spoon River Anthology* is poetry. It is no longer necessary, of course, to argue that regular metre and rhyme are not essential to poetry; but I am not ready to abandon the idea that rhythm is the indispensable characteristic which, without prejudice to other forms of literature, distinguishes poetry from them all. Rhythm Whitman for the most part had, and rhythm Mr. Masters' creations for the most part have not. Therefore I do not call *Spoon River Anthology* a book of poems.

It has been called a novel, but this seems to me a weak subterfuge. A novel is the development of a plot with continuity, coherence and logic. Mr. Masters' work will not be squeezed into those limits. (p. 121)

What then is *Spoon River Anthology*? Let me humbly suggest that it is an epic. Humbly, because the epic is much out of fashion now—supposed to be dead, I believe. And yet life is never unepical; it is we that have not the vision to see it epically. Where great vision is, there is the epic. Let us call an epic that which is seen greatly and told greatly, that vision in which the soul battling with the Fates is seen behind the man battling with petty things, and which is told with a high passion. Such vision is possessed by, and such a book has been written by this Middle West lawyer, so suddenly flashing like a sun through the sickly clouds of our tawdry literature.

It is a stirring tale of souls and destiny. Life is an eternal struggle—did it ever begin?—can it ever end?—between a godlike, gleaming, fiery element in man, flashing and burning upward, seeking its kindred fire in God; and a vast and terrible dark chaos, hideous with beasts and demons, choking and smothering the fire and the flame under its inexorable deadweight. Time after time the inwardness of this tragedy is flashed upon our apprehensions in these clairvoyant pages. Sometimes the flame conquers—burns through the demoniac element triumphantly; but generally it is tragedy—tragedy sometimes seen by the world, oftener borne secretly, unguessed, or only sneered at as mere bestial, tawdry sin and failure. To Masters, the soul is always visible. His understanding is uncanny; his pity beyond words; his irony godlike. Only in the hypocrite he sees no gleam of divinity. The unjust judge, the callous lawyer, the capitalist "who ran the church as well as the store and the bank" and wrecked the lives of a score of fellow-beings, these and all the "whited sepulchres" are spewed from his mouth with the loathing of Christ.

The epitaphs "Lucinda Matlock" and "Davis Matlock" were based upon Masters's paternal grandparents, Lucinda and Squire Davis Masters, pictured above.

The words that come to mind most persistently in reading these stories are "grim," "tragic" and "horrible." They make no attempt to present a balanced picture of life, for while life in Spoon River and elsewhere has its large proportion of happiness and content, these are the norm, and only the aberrations from that norm call for the irony, the pity, the vision of the artist. There is no need to add to the flattery which we are wont to offer ourselves and our institutions. But look at these pictures, drawn by an inexorable master-hand, each bearing the signature of Truth Terribly in Earnest. Remember that this is civilization; Christian civilization of the Nineteenth and Twentieth Centuries, among the superior white people of Northern European stock, in the Great Republic of Freedom and Opportunity. Read of these girls betrayed and hounded to hell on earth; these wives and husbands consuming each other's souls through lingering years of hatred; these men and women made mad by loneliness and slander; these hypocrites exalted and these joyous souls pushed down by the black hand of puritanism into drunkenness and despair; these churches arrayed against beauty and joy, and these political institutions bought and sold amid riot and arson. It is not a pretty picture, but it is one we have known all along to be true; and it is a picture we like to ignore. Now comes a man capable of bearing the pain of gazing steadily on this tragic welter of life, capable of drawing it in stark reality, touching it with irony, touching it with pity. For my part, I think that this is one of the works that deserve to be called a Book; the only Human Book, as distinguished

from cloudy books, and pattern books, and fashion books, and demon books, that we have had in—let Clio say how long a time!

And among these perfect tragedies which compose this perfect epic of the burning soul battling alone, in the gloom of the humble body and the banality of Spoon River, against the Fates and Furies, there are gleams of philosophical wisdom comparable, in sense and imagery, to anything from Plato to Goethe. . . . (pp. 121-23)

It should be added, even in so brief a note as this, that the art of Edgar Lee Masters, be it poetry or what, is in its kind perfect. It would be easy, with these subjects and this manner, to become banal, redundant, tiresome, gaunt, repulsive and ludicrous; but *Spoon River Anthology* has infinite variety, crystal clarity, unfailing grip, emotional power, and the dignity of a great work of art. It demands re-reading; it is one of those books which, once understood, become a part of one's life. (p. 123)

Shaemas O'Sheel, "Where Great Vision Is," in
Forum, *Vol. LV, January, 1916, pp. 121-23.*

Harriet Monroe   (essay date 1916)

[*As the founder and editor of* Poetry: A Magazine of Verse, *Monroe was a key figure in the American poetry renaissance that took place in the early twentieth century.* Poetry *was the first periodical devoted primarily to the works of new poets and to poetry criticism, and from 1912 until her death in 1936 Monroe maintained an editorial policy of printing "the best English verse which is being written today, regardless of where, by whom, or under what theory of art it is written." In the following excerpt, she extols Masters's idealistic and satiric bent for revealing "the divinity and absurdity of man."*]

If *Spoon River* was [Mr. Masters'] speech to the jury in the great court-room of life, this new book [*Songs and Satires*] is informal talking and story-swapping after the court has adjourned. The excited galleries would like to have the speech go on, but there is a time for all things: another masterpiece tomorrow maybe—meantime let's talk about Helen of Troy, or Saint Peter, or the way God makes atoms and worlds, or Jim's rather plodding love affair, or my best beloved uncle, or any old queerness of this antic-loving planet. And talk he does—"very near singing," sometimes; and more entertainingly and with more variety than any other poet in seven counties—I mean countries.

Thus the new book is all kinds for all men—good, bad or indifferent, just as it happens. But if **"Helen of Troy"** is almost the worst poem which that long-suffering lady has ever had to endure, **"So We Grew Together,"** and **"Silence,"** and **"Simon Surnamed Peter,"** and **"The Cocked Hat"** and **"William Marion Reedy,"** are fascinating, intriguing poems of beauty and passion; yes, and also, quite surprisingly, those three on legendary subjects—the two Lancelot ballads, which throw Tennyson's expurgated version into the discard by giving us the real Malory; and the finely intuitive **"Saint Francis and Lady Clare,"** which strips bare the impassioned soul of a nun, revealing her quaintly mediaeval, ecstatic religiosity.

Here, in short, is a big, all-round, profoundly imaginative poet. Not one of fine shades and nice selections, an exact student of his own art; but a real man and a generous lover of life, who is kindled to a singing flame by the mysterious harmonies and discords of the world. He lights up for us not only wide open spaces, but all sorts of odd tricks and dark corners; sometimes with a white fire of truth, and again, with smoky, earth-smelling, loud-crackling laughter. And he speaks in our idiom. He is modern in our time just as Dante was in his, or Molière in his; like them at heart a haughty idealist, he also is bent upon pulling down the hollow shells of outworn systems which have thickened and darkened around the souls of men, and showing us how to build the new more democratic city toward which our steps are stumbling.

The absurdity and divinity of that morsel of dust and fire which we call a human being—what modern poet, what modern writer, expresses this with such uncanny intimacy as Mr. Masters? Was satire ever more searching than in **"A Cocked Hat"**—or, in a certain sense, more loving, as the best satire must be? Mr. Bryan's portrait—the majestic failure of his career—is painted for all time; and incidentally the facile ideals and weaknesses of the "typical American" are held up for his own sober second thought. And the same theme—the divinity and absurdity of man—is treated in a mood of serious sympathy in **"So We Grew Together"** and **"All Life in a Life,"** and in a mood of exaltation in **"The Cry," "The Conversation"** and **"The Star."**

There are those, strangely enough, who find in *Spoon River* a "shriveling of life," failing to see the fierce, white-hot idealism which vitalizes its bitter knowledge. Perhaps they may find it in this new volume. (pp. 148-50)

> *Harriet Monroe, "Mr. Masters' New Book," in* Poetry, *Vol. VIII, No. 3, June, 1916, pp. 148-51.*

Amy Lowell (essay date 1917)

[*Lowell was the leading proponent of Imagism in American poetry. Like the Symbolists before her, whose works she examined in* Six French Poets *(1915), Lowell experimented with free verse forms. Under the influence of Ezra Pound, Lowell's poetry exhibits the style of Imagism, consisting of clear and precise rhetoric, exact rendering of images, and metrical freedom. Although her poetry garnered critical notice in her time, modern evaluations of Lowell accord her more importance as a promoter of new artistic ideas than as a poet in her own right. In her analysis of Masters's work, excerpted below, Lowell discusses the superior quality of the* Anthology *over* Songs and Satires *and* The Great Valley, *placing Masters at the head of the "middle era" of a three-part movement toward a native school of purely American poetry.*]

I think it is not too much to say that no book, in the memory of the present generation, has had such a general effect upon the reading community as has [*Spoon River Anthology*]. Every one who reads at all has read it. Its admirers are not confined to those who like poetry, people who have never cared for a poem before are enthusiastic over *Spoon River,* while professed poetry lovers stand, some aghast and some delighted, but all interested and amazed. Even its enemies admit it to be extraordinary. It has been char-

acterized as an American "Comédie Humaine," [see Gilman's excerpt dated 1915], but I think Dostoevsky in *vers libre* would be more accurate. Mr. Masters' habit of thought is more akin to the Russian than to the French. In fact, Mr. Masters is in some ways closer to the Swede, August Strindberg, than to any other modern writer.

Of course, analogies of this kind must not be pushed too far. If Mr. Masters resembles Balzac in the fecundity he shows in inventing characters and lives to fit them, he is also like Strindberg in showing only a narrow stratum of society. If he is like Balzac in confining his *mise en scène* in a small compass, he is again like Strindberg in being primarily interested in one important phase of life—that of sex. Balzac was no poet, but he realized that man is impelled by many motives; in Strindberg, the actions of the characters are all dependent upon their sex impulses. (pp. 139-40)

Mr. Robinson and Mr. Frost represent various things in the "new movement"—Realism, Direct Speech, Simplicity, and the like. They represent also the first stage of the progression I have been analyzing. Mr. Masters, who also stands for other things as well, embodies the second stage. I have put him and Mr. Sandburg together principally for that reason, although they have other points of contact besides this one. We may regard the work of these two poets as being the most revolutionary that America has yet produced. (p. 142)

Poetry published many *vers libre* poems during the first years of its existence, and Mr. Masters has often said that it was these poems which opened for him the way to *Spoon River.* In fact, they gave him the clue to just what he needed—freedom from the too patterned effects of rhyme and metre, brevity, and conciseness. Such a form seemed absolutely made for his purpose. Substance he had never lacked, fitting his substance to these short, sharp lines gave him a perfect instrument.

What suggested the idea of the anthology, I do not know, possibly he took it from the *Greek Anthology.* . . . The idea of epitaphs grew naturally out of the succinct brevity of the form, much in little, and in this very brevity Mr. Masters has found his happiest expression. Of course, a *vers libre* poem is not necessarily short, it may or may not be, as the author chooses. But the first poems in this form published by *Poetry* happened to be so, and that was fortunate for Mr. Masters. Had he attempted long poems in this medium in the beginning, I fear he would have wrecked *Spoon River* at the start. He has written many long *vers libre* poems since, but none of them has attained the rounded strength of the shorter, earlier pieces. (pp. 160-61)

Spoon River purports to be a small town in the Middle West. It is said that Hanover, Illinois, served as its prototype. The poems are supposed to be the epitaphs in the cemetery of this town. Or rather, it is as if its dead denizens arose, and each speaking the truth, perforce, revealed his own life exactly as it had been, and the real cause of his death. When I add that there are two hundred and fourteen of these people, we can see what a colossal study of character the book is. The mere inventing of two hundred and fourteen names is a staggering feat. How many names Balzac invented, or Scott, or Shakespeare, or Molière, I have not an idea, but the work of these men extended over a lifetime; Mr. Masters' two hundred and fourteen were all collected in one year.

The quality of the book already stands revealed in these names. They are uncompromising in their realism; hard, crude, completely local. Mr. Masters permits himself no subterfuges with fact. He throws no glamour over his creations. We hear of no Flammondes, no Bokardos, instead are Hannah Armstrong, Archibald Higbie, Bert Killion, Faith Matheny, Jennie M'Grew, Reuben Pantier, Albert Schirding, George Trimble, Oaks Tutt, Zenas Witt, and a host of others. What are these names? Some are Anglo-Saxon, some are clearly German; one, **"Russian Sonia,"** tells of an origin, if not distinctly national, at least distinctly cosmopolitan; another, **"Yee Bow,"** is as obviously Chinese.

We do not find German, French, Chinese names in Mr. Frost's books. Here, therefore, at once, in the table of contents, we are confronted with the piquant realism of locality. The highest art is undeniably that which compromises the farthest flights of imagination, but next to that, the most satisfying is the one which holds within it the pungency of place, undiluted. (pp. 162-63)

[The] difference between Mr. Frost and Mr. Masters is not only that they write about different parts of the country, it is a profound divergence of points of view. Mr. Frost . . . belongs to the first stage of the "new movement"; Mr. Masters to the second. Mr. Frost records with quiet sympathy; Mr. Masters is mordant and denunciatory. Mr. Frost is resigned, smilingly thinking resistance futile; Mr. Masters resists with every fibre of his being. Mr. Frost's work gives us the effect of a constant withdrawal; Mr. Masters' of a constant pushing forward.

Spoon River is a volume which should be read from the first page to the last. (Always excepting the final poem, **"The Spooniad,"** a dreary effusion, which fits but slightly into the general scheme, and should never have been included.) No idea of its breadth and variety can be gained from fragmentary quotations. Each poem is a character, and as the characters multiply, the whole town is gradually built up before us. Other authors have given us characters, other authors have given us cross-sections of a community. But in most books we have a set of primary characters, and the others are forced more or less into the background by the exigencies of the case. We see the life from this or that angle, we do not get it entire.

In *Spoon River,* there are no primary characters, no secondary characters. We have only a town and the people who inhabit it. The Chinese laundry-man is as important to himself as the State's Attorney is to himself. None are forced back to give others prominence, but all together make the town. (pp. 163-64)

It is true, as has been said, that Mr. Masters sees life from the standpoint of a novelist. The material which the novelist spreads out and amplifies is condensed to its essence in these vignettes of a few lines. In them, Mr. Masters gives us background, character, and the inevitable approach of inexorable Fate. . . . (p. 169)

Mr. Masters has humour of a kind, a robust and rather brutal kind, it must be admitted, but still the quality is there. (p. 170)

Mr. Masters, with all his sociological tendencies, does not deify the working-man as Mr. Sandburg and many other sociological poets do. He sees life in too rounded a compass for that. (p. 173)

It cannot be denied even by Mr. Masters' most convinced admirers that, with all his vitality and courage, with all his wealth of experience and vividness of presentation, his point of view is often tortured and needlessly sensual and cruel.

Undoubtedly this element added to the immediate notoriety of *Spoon River.* But the book would not be worth commenting upon, and Mr. Masters would in no sense rank as the poet he does, if its sensuality were not counteracted by other and great qualities. (p. 176)

Spoon River undoubtedly errs on the side of a too great preoccupation with crime and disease. But it would be unfair to its author not to remark the occasional bursts of tenderness throughout the book. One [is] **"Emily Sparks."** . . . But there is another which is to me the most beautiful and most tragic poem in the volume. [**"Doc Hill"**] is real tragedy, not the tragedy of sordid giving way to inclination, but the tragedy of circumstance nobly faced, the tragedy of success out of failure, of joy denied and yet abundantly received. . . . (p. 178)

[It] had been stated that Mr. Masters was indebted to Mr. Robinson for his idea of these short sketches of men's lives [see Wright's excerpt dated 1916]. As a matter of fact, I know it to be true that, at the time he wrote *Spoon River,* Mr. Masters had not read a line of Mr. Robinson's poetry. It is only the most superficial observer who could ever have supposed one to be derived from the other. The whole scheme upon which the two poets work is utterly different. Mr. Robinson analyzes the psychology of his characters to the minutest fraction, he splits emotions and subsplits them. His people are interesting to him because of their thought-processes, or as psychic reactions to environment. Indeed, the environment is frequently misty, except where it impinges upon personality. Mr. Masters reveals the character of his *dramatis personæ* chiefly through their actions. What they do is, of course, the outcome of what they think, but it is usually the doing which the poet has set down on paper. His people are elementary and crude, carved on broad, flat planes.

The Tilbury Town of Mr. Robinson's books belongs more to the realm of mental phenomena than to actual fact. It is a symbol of certain states of mind. We feel it, but we do not see it. Spoon River, on the other hand, is indubitably and geographically a place. We know it even better than we do its inhabitants. Just as a person is a whole to us although made up of parts—eyes, ears, hands, nose, hair, etc.—so Spoon River is a whole, although constructed out of the life-histories of two hundred and fourteen of its citizens. We can see the cemetery, the Court House, the various churches, the shops, the railroad station, almost with our physical eyes.

It is not only that Mr. Robinson and Mr. Masters employ a different method of approach, an absolutely different technique; it is that fundamentally their ideas, not only of art, but of life, differ. To one, fact is the vague essence through which the soul of man wanders; to the other, man is a part, usually a tortured part, of a huge, hard, unyielding substance, the unalterable actuality of the world he inhabits.

If Mr. Masters has a prototype, that prototype can best be found in some of the poems in the *Greek Anthology.* (pp. 180-82)

Indeed, humanity varies very little throughout the ages. It is just this which makes *Spoon River* so remarkable—its humanity. These are not artificial personages, these two hundred men and women, they are real flesh and blood, with beating hearts and throbbing brains, revealing themselves to us with all their foibles and weaknesses, and their occasional grandeur. If, heaped one upon another, this monument of mid-Western American life errs on the side of over-sordidness, over-bitterness, over-sensuality, taken each one for itself, we have a true picture. It is never the individual characters who are false to type; it is only in the aggregate that the balance is lost by a too great preponderance of one sort of person.

It has been insisted over and over again, since the publication of *Spoon River,* that here was the great American poet, this verse was at last absolutely of America, that not since Whitman had anything so national appeared in print. The importance of *Spoon River* can hardly be overstated, and its dominant Americanism is without doubt a prime factor in that importance; but, because Mr. Masters' work is thoroughly local, is not to deny the same quality to work of quite a different kind. Was Poe less American than Whitman?—is a question which may very pertinently be asked here. Was Shakespeare less English because he wrote *Hamlet?* Was that arch-Englishman, Matthew Arnold, false to his birthright because he published "Empedocles on Etna"? How foolish this point of view is when so stated, is apparent at a glance. Nationality is so subtle a thing that it permeates all a man says and does. He cannot escape it, no matter what subjects stimulate his imagination. (pp. 183-84)

Mr. Masters is a thoroughly American poet, but not because he deals exclusively with American subjects. Truth to tell, he does not, as we shall see when, in a moment, we consider his later books. No, Mr. Masters is American because he is of the bones, and blood, and spirit of America. His thought is American; his reactions are as national as our clear blue skies.

The poets of the New Movement are all intensely national; they are not, as I have already pointed out, what the older generation were, followers of an English tradition. . . . When Mr. Masters is intensely moved, he becomes blatant. He keeps nothing to himself, out it comes on a swirl of passion. So this Americanism of his is a very obvious thing. It is a sort of *leitmotif* appearing again and again, and preferably on the trumpets. The symbol of this Americanism is the figure of Lincoln.

Washington and Lincoln are the two great symbols of American life. But to deal adequately with Washington needs a historical sense, a knowledge of the eighteenth century, which few of our poets yet possess. . . . It is therefore to Lincoln that our poets turn as an embodiment of the highest form of the typical American, the fine flower and culmination of our life as a separate nation. (pp. 184-85)

[With] Mr. Masters, Lincoln is a man first of all, but a man

who, in his actual life, typifies a national aspiration. He is conceived as boldly, as surely, as any other of Mr. Masters' characters, and although venerated and loved with unchanging ardour, it is always as a man, neither conventionalized by tradition, nor flung by a powerful imagination into the realm of legend.

There is one little touch of Lincoln in *Spoon River,* a very beautiful touch, although only a collateral one. It is the epitaph of Ann Rutledge, the girl whom Lincoln loved, but who died before they could be married. (p. 186)

Just one year after the publication of the *Spoon River Anthology,* appeared another book from Mr. Masters' pen, a new volume of poems, *Songs and Satires.*

It has been hinted that many of the poems in this volume are reprinted from those earlier books which have slipt into oblivion. One would prefer to hope so, for it seems inconceivable that the author of the stark, vigorous *Spoon River* poems could afterwards perpetrate such a banality as ["When Under the Icy Eaves."] (p. 187)

Here are all the old *clichés:* doves grieving for their lost mates, young lambs at play, swallows who *herald* the sun, winds that *bluster,* snows which *pass* over *tawny* hills, even the *spirit of life* awaking by a *lake* bordered with *flags.* . . . It reads like a parody; yet it is not intended as a parody, but as a serious and beautiful lyric. It gives us more than an insight into the reasons for Mr. Masters' early failures.

It would be unfair to the volume, however, to give the impression that all the poems are as bad as this. There are a number of weak lyrics scattered through the book, however, which no admirer of Mr. Masters can do other than deplore. And there are narrative poems on such hackneyed subjects as **"Helen of Troy"** and **"Launcelot and Elaine,"** in which the treatment does nothing to add freshness to the themes. (pp. 187-88)

There are ghastly attempts at an old English diction in ["**The Ballad of Launcelot and Elaine"**]. We have "trees of spicery," "morn's underne," "spake with a dreary steven."

That Mr. Masters should have written these poems among his early four hundred is not strange, what is strange is that he should have considered them worth resurrecting after he had written *Spoon River.*

Mr. Masters is seldom original when he writes in regular forms. It seems as though some obscure instinct of relation set his mind echoing with old tunes, old words, old pictures. Sometimes the result is a parody of the verse of the past; sometimes only a copy, quite beautiful, were it only his own. (p. 189)

What makes the book such a jumble is that these ancient ditties are interspersed with perfectly modern poems like **"The Cocked Hat," " 'So We Grew Together,' " "All Life in a Life,"** and the underworld studies: **"Arabel,"** and **"Jim and Arabel's Sister."** But, in these modern poems, Mr. Masters has deserted the brevity of the *Spoon River* pieces, and his doing so has lost him much and won him nothing. When he allows himself a free hand, he does not know when to stop. In **" 'So We Grew Together,' "** he takes nine pages where in *Spoon River* one would have sufficed. **"Arabel"** is six pages in length, **"The Cocked**

Hat" is seven, and none of these poems gains anything, either in vigour or analysis, by the change.

"The Loop" is a descriptive sketch of the heart of Chicago. But there is no quick flash of vision here, no unforgettable picture imposed upon the mind in a few words. Instead, the poem enumerates long catalogues of objects, one after the other. They have neither form, colour, nor relation. They are not presented poetically, pictorially, not even musically (as the older verse counted music), for the poem is marred by such false rhymes as "current" and "torrent." They are just lists, as dreary as an advertisement from a department store. (pp. 189-90)

There is one poem in the book which shows Mr. Masters assuming a new rôle or rather an old rôle in a new manner. **"In Michigan"** has a lyric quality very unusual to the poet's work. Most of his lyrics are couched in regular metres, and, for some strange reason, Mr. Masters does not seem able to think his own thoughts in conventional verse. Not only his expressions, his very ideas, run merrily back into the old moulds. On the other hand, Mr. Masters' free verse poems are singularly devoid of the lyricism of either sound or vision. So much so, indeed, that certain critics have declared him to be a novelist rather than a poet. **"In Michigan"** proves this verdict to be but partially true. . . . (p. 192)

If **"The Loop"** is without poetical images, **"In Michigan"** shows that the poet is really sensitive to beauty, and at times possesses the power to catch that beauty in a phrase:

> . . . a quiet land
> A lotus place of farms and meadows

gives the sleepy, lost quality of the landscape excellently well. (p. 193)

He speaks of the "misty eyelids" of "drowsy lamps," of a moon sinking "like a red bomb," of a land-spit running out into the lake until

> . . . it seemed to dive under,
> Or waste away in a sudden depth of water.

But even in this free-verse lyric, echoes of the older poets haunt him, and not to his advantage:

> . . . a star that shows like a match which lights
> To a blue intenseness amid the glow of a hearth

challenges a comparison, which proves Browning's

> blue spurt of a lighted match

to be infinitely finer.

The haste with which Mr. Masters has followed up the success of *Spoon River* has undoubtedly been his undoing. Temporary, let us hope, but for the time, a fact. Eight months after the publication of *Songs and Satires,* his third book, *The Great Valley,* made its appearance.

The Great Valley is of course that flat stretch of continent between the Alleghany Mountains and the Rockies. It is a paraphrase for what we commonly call the Middle West. In other words, these are again poems of a locality. The book is a sort of extended *Spoon River.* The place is no more a little provincial town, but Chicago and the country adjacent. The horizon of place and character is wider than *Spoon River,* the poems are longer and more detailed; but,

as in the long poems in *Songs and Satires,* the stretching out of his stories has not worked to the poet's advantage. Had *Spoon River* never been written, *The Great Valley* would have been a remarkable book. Unfortunately, it is still surpassed by the earlier volume. One of the most interesting traits of *Spoon River* was its homogeneity; the volume was a whole, as closely related within itself as is a novel, or a volume of essays grouped about a central theme. I have called *Songs and Satires* a jumble, Mr. Masters' taste again fails him in *The Great Valley.* What have such classical subjects as **"Marsyas,"** **"The Furies,"** **"Apollo at Pheræ,"** to do with the shouting Americanism of the rest of the book?

The truth is that in the back of the poet's heart, he still longs for that atmosphere of poesy which . . . [was] the unappeased desire of his adolescence. These poems represent the nostalgia of beauty. It eludes him still. He is the poet of the real, the absolute. He cannot break his bonds. Co-ordination is an integral part of beauty; in art, we call this co-ordination—taste, and of this particular kind of taste Mr. Masters has not a particle. The classic poems are thrown pell-mell among the others so carelessly that one wonders if Mr. Masters really arranged the book at all. One of the most unpleasant of the author's modern sex-tragedies is printed immediately after **"Apollo at Pheræ."**

There is one new note in the volume, a sort of tinkling sneer. As though a funeral march were to be played on the *glockenspiel.* This kitchen lyric is excellent in technique, but whether the sort of thing is worthy of a man who could produce some of the *Spoon River* poems is another question. (pp. 194-96)

Yes, Mr. Masters is the chief poet of our middle era. . . . Mr. Masters stands up rugged, solid, energetic, clearing his way by stern force of will. Much passes him by, there are notes in our national life too high or too low for him to catch. He cannot always give back those he does catch. But what he does give back is resonant with the overtones of personality, with the truth of heart, body, and mind. Whatever America is to become, *Spoon River* will always stand in her libraries, a work of genius and a record of what was. Already it vanishes, even as it is being written down. Mr. Masters himself feels this, in **"Come, Republic,"** he exhorts his country to step forward boldly into the new time. He sees it glimmering on the horizon, but too far still for him quite to focus. (p. 200)

> *Amy Lowell, "Edgar Lee Masters and Carl Sandburg," in her* Tendencies in Modern American Poetry, *The Macmillan Company, 1917, pp. 139-232.*

Dorothy Dudley (essay date 1918)

[*In a review of* Toward the Gulf, *excerpted below, Dudley commends Masters's verse in the volume, noting the bold and authentic quality of his poems.*]

Prosody at best provides the poet with but a set of diagrams more or less diverting, of which certainly a work of art, intact, complete, like the *Spoon River Anthology,* bears no trace. Its right to an official metric-term is well enough, but less relevant than the fact that the short, fluid, fateful lines invade the ear with the terseness of the grave; that in a new fabric of words, the limbs of life, the face, the voice, the hands, appear once more to manifest themselves. *The Great Valley,* and this new volume *Toward the Gulf,* which, to quote from the preface, "continue the attempts of *Spoon River* to mirror the age and country in which we live," often afford delight keen and painful as the *Anthology,* but not, I think, so unbrokenly. This new book at least mingles a sprinkling of verse, wherein prosody does usurp the lines, with poems authentic as daylight, and, like the *Anthology,* freighted with the presence of reality—the cargo of great art.

To read certain of them—**"Johnny Appleseed", "The Lake Boats," "Sir Galahad"**—is to touch the soil of Illinois and the states south, to get the very voices of the midwestern country—their slight flatness of tone in contrast to the fragrance of land and water. . . . (pp. 150-51)

Then there are poems less sleepy than these that scarcely detach themselves from the landscape they celebrate. **"The Eighth Crusade,"** for one, lifts its characters for a minute from their rocking-chairs in Pleasant Plains into the midst of plump Swiss life; the Orient glimmers on the horizon, and faintly about the tale hangs the ancient raillery of Venus—so deftly are these people made to take their places under the sun.

One hears too the nervous voices of the city; the prostitute and the editor at Perko's; the sound and look of beggars and venders in "the granite ways of mad Chicago." And there is the sharp sketch of an Indian runner and his voice saying:

> It was under a sky as blue as the cup of a harebell,
> It was by a red and yellow mountain,
> It was by a great river
> That we ran.

Besides these bas-reliefs is larger modelling—extravagant ineffectual figures emerging more dramatically from the background—their divergence and abortive return. With the enterprise and at times the elegance of a Velasquez, Mr. Masters shapes these images—the dream-ridden, the paranoiac, the spendthrift, the nymphomaniac, the dogmatist, the fanatic. Root and branch he evolves them. (pp. 151-52)

As if to bring such lives into scale, three studies—Voltaire, Napoleon, Thomas Paine—rear themselves handsomely above the horizon. And a number of poems—**"Grand River Marshes," "Poor Pierrot," "Song of Women"** among them—mirror with a most caressing music the beauties of flesh and flowers, earth, air and water. One of them, **"Widow La Rue,"** has grim terror veiled in a very skilful ballad, soft and wanton like a scarf.

Notwithstanding, there are holes, I think, in the weave of the book. Some of these very poems, for the most part green beneath the bark, contain dry twigs, dead branches. And over a number of them rhetoric reigns. Possibly Mr. Masters is a poet who looks sometimes with too dissective a mind, and losing the sense of mystery in vainly seeking the cause, now and then forsakes poetry for speculation and analysis. Not always content to witness, select and mirror the image, he seems to try going about it, back of it, into it even; till it withers and is broken and no longer is able to communicate its sap and bloom to his words. The language then becomes clever, toneless, literary, and even rattles a little at times.

Also one feels that in strange contradiction to his patrician quality of mind that directs an unflinching gaze, this book shows now and then a slight strain of idealism—the "cream tart of the bourgeois," according to Rodin. Like the Friar Yves of his own poem he weeps because

> Nothing is left but life indeed.
> I have burned heaven! I have quenched hell.

then, as if to console himself, he fashions sometimes utopian heavens, dreams of wholesale liberty, democracy, nobility, made almost from the butterick-patterns of poetry, and wearing a false glad air, among the strange, proud, authentic, wistful cadences of the book.

But if cleverness tarnishes these pages somewhat, as indeed it did with Byron and Browning, or sentimentality blunts them sometimes, as in the case of Whitman even, one thing is clear and refreshing: Mr. Masters never writes from a sense of chic; is afraid of no detail that happens to belong in the picture—no inelegance as of rubber heels or Christian Science. Striking almost at random, *Toward the Gulf* evokes a wealth of shapes and casts exciting shadows, which, though varied, seem held together by the mad idea of unity. As in the last poem, **"Botanical Gardens"**—a review of all life—a flower, a tree, a man, a woman, stand side by side in the landscape moved or warped by the same impulse of seed, root and branch. About them in this book falls frequently the relentless light of a gray day, but sometimes the brilliance of the sun or the ease of rain. In a manner more formal than is usual with Mr. Masters, and equally poignant, **"Poor Pierrot"** seems to reach the soul of rain. (pp. 152-54)

> *Dorothy Dudley, "Large Measures," in* Poetry, *Vol. XI, No. 3, June, 1918, pp. 150-54.*

Edmund Gosse   (essay date 1923)

[*Gosse was a distinguished British literary historian, critic, poet, and biographer who was one of the most important English translators and critics of Scandinavian literature. Among his works are studies of John Donne, Thomas Gray, Sir Thomas Browne, and important early articles on nineteenth century literature. In the following excerpt, Gosse analyzes* Domesday Book, *remarking that Masters addresses the "horror of private life" in a cynical and vivid manner.*]

Domesday Book, which is as long as *Paradise Lost,* and much longer than *The Excursion,* is a modern story of American provincial life, told in blank verse. That it should be hailed as one of "the masterpieces of the world" is an example of the hysterical tendency of the hour to exaggerate the value of anything which is startling or unusual, and especially of anything which is ugly and depressing. It is also an instance of the inability of current criticism to express itself in terms of moderation. **Domesday Book** is a curious and interesting production; by the side of great imperfections, it presents some sterling merits. It is very readable, and it indulges to the full the fashionable pessimism and preference for squalor. It demands careful attention, but it is no more "one of the masterpieces of the world" than is some very handsome system of public sewage.

In 1915, Mr. Edgar Lee Masters, who is an American

writer resident, I believe, in Chicago, created a certain sensation by publishing a strange book called *Spoon River Anthology*. . . . Mr. Masters has repeated his experiment in slightly different form, and whereas the *Anthology* had no other plan than the arrangement of long epitaphs side by side, we have in *Domesday Book* a systematic construction.

Mr. Masters has a passion for naked reality, and a great power of dissecting that *"pauvre et triste humanité"* which it is most people's instinct to cover up and protect. He tears away not merely the clothes but the bandages, and spares us no horror of the soul. His manner has, very foolishly, been compared with that of Walt Whitman; no two authors are more diametrically contrasted. Whitman is an optimist, full of aspiration and indulgence; if he strips away the raiment of humanity, it is to show the world how beautiful is the body beneath. Everything pleases Whitman, and he exults in his vitality. The author of *Spoon River* and *Domesday Book* is a pessimist of the darkest dye, for whom there is, in that provincial American scene which *Leaves of Grass* so radiantly described, nothing but dullness and concealed wretchedness. The most striking feature of Mr. Master's pictures of life is their extraordinary desolation and mediocrity. One is inclined to ask, if existence in Illinois and Ohio is really like this, why do these poor millions of Americans take the trouble to live at all?

The nearest parallel to the tone of *Domesday Book* may be found in certain of the poems of Crabbe, especially in *The Parish Register* and in *The Borough.* In 1812, in a remarkable preface, Crabbe refused to "adopt the notions of a pastoral simplicity" among the peasants of Suffolk, and undertook, in harsh and sombre verse, to describe them, type after type, as they really were. This is exactly what Mr. Masters does, and with even more acrimony and contempt, in violent reaction against the sentimentality of the American literature of the nineteenth century, as exemplified by Howells and Mark Twain.

His gallery of tragic portraits is impressive and surprising. In telling us the secret history of some fifty persons, all living in one country community, he hesitates to offer us a single gleam of light. All the characters were failures, most of them were criminals, while all, or almost all, preserved a veneer of respectability until the grim hour when the death of Elinor Murray led, mechanically, to a general revelation of their shortcomings. All of them, the poet says:—

> "Are gone to dust, now, like the garden things
> That sprout up, fall and rot. At times it seems
> All waste to me."

There is no sense of a higher life; all is saturnine and cynical. It is only fair to say that, like other dreadful spectacles, the picture is often extremely vivid.

As in *The Ring and the Book,* of which *Domesday Book* faintly but frequently reminds us, the subject is the death of Pompilia, and how it moulded the lives of a large number of persons, so in Mr. Masters' new poem the subject is the finding of the body of Elinor Murray, and the effect of that discovery on the hidden existence of a whole chain of her acquaintances. First we have an account of the childhood of the heroine, and then, abruptly, the conditions in which her dead body, with no sign upon it of violence or disease, was found on the shore of a river. The remainder of the poem is occupied by the affidavits of various witnesses at or in connection with the inquest held by Coroner Merival.

Mr. Masters is fascinated by the phenomenon which Lord Haldane describes in his *Reign of Relativity,* the fact that "in the plane of our lives as human beings in the world of nature, physical and social, we belong to the stream of the events which we experience." The corpse of Elinor Murray is suddenly arrested and exposed, and at once becomes a snag on which the reputations of half a hundred persons are caught and wrecked. . . . His theme is the horror of private life, and he penetrates its selfishness and secrecy with a gusto that is almost shocking.

If there is a moral to be found in *Domesday Book* it is that lives are wasted from lack of sympathy and imagination. There is no reason why any of the characters should have been wretched if they could have spoken frankly and their idiosyncrasies have been openly accepted. The horror is due to a system of universal misunderstanding and hypocritical concealment, acting in a narrow society which is defaced by poverty and mediocrity. Elinor Murray, who is the type of the self-emancipated victim of this bondage, is the daughter of a druggist in the village of Le Roy. Husband and wife have kept up the show of decent relations, but secretly hate one another; the woman is a sort of vampire. Elinor is clever, earns her own education, leaves her parents' house and disappears, a teacher in a Western state. At the end of three years she comes back. . . . Elinor becomes more cultivated in mind and delicate in taste, and the druggist's store grows intolerable to her. Nevertheless she strives to be kind and filial, but when the war breaks out, she takes occasion to go over to France, and disappears again. At the armistice she reappears in New York, but instead of returning to her parents, pays a visit to an aunt "to rest and get the country air." During this visit she goes out for a walk, and is found dead by the river. We are led to suppose that she was walking alone, until near the close of the poem, when we learn that a lover, hitherto unmentioned, one Barrett Bays of Chicago, was with her when she had a fainting fit, and holding her up, when he ought to have laid her down, had the embarrassment of finding that she died in his arms, at which, in a paroxysm of terror, he left her on the river bank and fled away to Chicago until conscience forced him to confess.

The multitude of Elinor Murray's lovers, not one of whom had in her lifetime been more than faintly suspected of flirtation, is so great as to be almost ludicrous. They have to turn up one after another, from all sorts of unlikely places, to fill Mr. Masters' canvas. One of them says, more pointedly than poetically,

> "She had more life than she knew how to use,
> And had not learned her own machine."

The result of this abundance of lovers is to lower our estimate of the character of Elinor Murray, with which Mr. Masters desires that we should sympathise. We do sympathise; her restlessness and longings, her ups and downs of ecstasy and dejection, the hopelessness of her emancipation, and the mess that she makes of her whole conquered independence, appeal to our pity and interest. Her useless culture, her vague aspirations, her characteristic revolt against any species of family restraint are intelligible, and the stern picture of them timely. But we cannot help regretting that she had secret affairs with such a very large number of men. They all come, one after another, and confess with great prolixity to Coroner Merival; but how about poor Elinor Murray? Her polyandry, when every excuse has been made for it, continues to seem rather grotesque. (pp. 353-58)

[*Domesday Book*] is what is called "outspoken"; in plainer language, it is very coarse. I find no fault with Mr. Masters on this account, since his purpose is serious, and he would doubtless reply that nature is entirely indelicate. . . .

With regard to the purely literary aspect of *Domesday Book,* it may be a salutary lesson to compare the account which the State Governor gives his wife of the effect of the murder evidence on his mind with the Pope's soliliquy in *The Ring and the Book.* The parallel is often quite close, and might be used to explain why Browning is a poet and Mr. Masters is not. But the American satirist is a keen thinker and a powerful writer, with an unfortunate tendency (*Spoon River Anthology* betrayed it) to prolixity. His blank verse is plain and unaffected, but such lines as

"His duties ended, he sat at a window,"

or,

"By angina pectoris, let it drop,"

or,

"Gregory Wenner's brother married the mother"

are too frequent. To sum up, this curious volume is a disquisition on a theme which has been commonly ignored or evaded in Anglo-Saxon literature, namely, that the happiness of youth is undermined by having to conceal the tortures and risks of sexual instinct. (p. 358)

> Edmund Gosse, "Domesday Book," in his More Books on the Table, *Charles Scribner's Sons,* 1923, pp. 351-58.

Harriet Monroe   (essay date 1924)

[*In the following excerpt, Monroe examines several of Masters's poetry collections to assert his stature as a modern epic poet.*]

Edgar Lee Masters, whatever else one may say of him, has size. He bulks large, and it may be that in that "next age," to which we accord the ultimate accounting, he will make a number of other figures now conspicuous look small. He has, not unnaturally, the faults that go with size—careless technique, uncritical sanctionings, indelicacies of emotional excess, far-sightedness which misses obvious imperfections of detail. The world will sift out and throw away many poems in his numerous books of verse, and much of his prose—not all—will go into the discard. But when hurrying time has done its worst, enough will remain to prove a giant's stature and other attributes of power in this Illinois lawyer-poet of a changing age. (p. 204)

A Book of Verses, published under the author's own name in 1898, was about as mild an affair as Byron's *Hours of Idleness*—indeed, these two poets offer many proofs of kinship. But Masters developed more slowly; already thir-

ty years old when this first book appeared, he had reached thirty-four, with his sense of humor still in abeyance, when he put out a solemn blank-verse tragedy on the subject of that be-whiskered busy-body of pitiable history, Maximilian, so-called emperor of Mexico.

Of course there was a drama in Mexico at that moment, but it did not follow academic lines. One would have expected a modern mind to find it, but Masters' theories of poetic art were intensely academic, and even eight years later, in 1912, when he issued *Songs and Sonnets* under the pseudonym of Webster Ford, we find him writing such things as an **"Ode to Fame"** in the most approved all-hail-to-thee style. This book also fell flat, of course; and its author, at forty-four a failure as a poet, was in danger of becoming embittered when even his friend Bill Reedy sent back his classic poems; for he could contrast the silence around him with the réclame which was beginning to salute the imagists and other free-versifiers during 1913.

One can almost see the satiric smile with which he said to himself, "If that's what they want, I'll give it to them!" But *Spoon River,* begun as a more or less satirical challenge to "the new movement," soon caught him up and carried him out to the depths. For the first time he found a theme which drew upon his humor as well as his knowledge and fervor and sympathy; and a form which made him forget old-fashioned prejudices and thereby freed his art. By the time the world found him he had found himself. And it was a big discovery.

It is hardly necessary to repeat certain things that were said of this book in the first flush of its success. It fulfilled the old time-honored principle: present a local group completely, in its heights and depths and averages, and you present the race as it is in every time and clime. *Spoon River,* with its humors and tragedies and commonplaces, its strange interweavings of destiny, is precisely central Illinois, the very heart of Middle-west America; yet Lucretius or Omar or Li Po would recognize its types and incidents, and probably the poets of the twenty-fifth century will still pronounce it true. And not only true but beautiful, for the form of those terse little epitaphs is not only a perfect fit but that triumphant completion and fulfilment which marks the masterpieces of all the arts.

Spoon River classed its author as essentially an epic poet—that is, a poet whose chief urge is to tell the tale of the tribe. And although Mr. Masters has written fine lyrics, most of his best poems emphasize the epic quality of his vision. There be critics who aver that he has done nothing since *Spoon River,* but such a myopic verdict can come only from minds groping for details and blind to mass effects. Since *Spoon River* the very titles of his books have spread a large canvas; he has travelled down the Mississippi in *The Great Valley, Toward the Gulf, Starved Rock* and *The Open Sea,* with *Domesday Book* crossing the Atlantic and accepting the immensities of the World War. And although each of these volumes needs weeding out, each of them, except perhaps *The Open Sea,* contains a few essential and memorable poems which help to symmetrize and complete this poet's record of our time and place.

Throughout one is swept along by the man's impassioned quest of truth. In this quest he is absolutely sincere and uncompromising; yet, though he admits humanity's crimes, and lashes our smug and faulty civilization with laughter or even fury, one feels always the warmth of a big-hearted wistful sympathy with all God's sorely tried and tempted creatures as they move about among illusions and are ignorantly stirred by appearances and dreams. He is the attorney for the defense before the bar of ultimate justice, admitting the strong case against his client but pleading the sadness and bitter irony of man's endless struggle between beauty and sordidness.

If he plies the whip on Thomas Rhodes and Editor Whedon, and stings with laughter Bryan and Mrs. Purkapile and the Reverend Percy Ferguson, he has a sympathetic smile for Daisy Frazer and Roscoe Purkapile and "dear old Dick," a wrench of the heart for Doc Hill and the pair at Perko's, and a splendid burning candle-flare of beauty for Anne Rutledge and Lucinda Matlock . . . and a few other simple and loyal souls. And always one feels these more or less imperfect creatures cast into their true perspective by the poet's ever-present, clear-sighted sense of humor. It is a humor enormous, like Swift's, in its satirical sweep and power, but more genial than that of the Queen Anne cynic. It permeates all his work, of course, and helps to make his portraits so intensely and sympathetically alive. But his sense of pity is just as keen, and the two in perfect unison sometimes combine to produce a masterpiece of portraiture as marvellous as Velasquez, like **"Slipshoe Lovey," "Archibald Higbie"** or **"Fiddler Jones."**

Indeed, the human tenderness of this often harsh poet, in his handling of such a battered bit of flesh and blood as Elinor Murray of the **Domesday Book,** cannot be too highly praised: in spite of her manifest and numerous slips and sins, he reveals her as nobody's slave—a free and generous spirit capable of heights as well as depths, and escaping vulgarity by a certain inner flare of something like a hidden and hunted love of truth. The poet turns more lights on her than Browning on Pompilia in *The Ring and the Book,* indulging too far his lawyer's love of presenting the complete and voluminous testimony of many witnesses. But, however over-laden, the book is a powerful modern epic of democratic human averages; an episode of the eternal struggle of the race to save its soul, like Browning's and every other epic that ever was written. To complain that much of it is prose masquerading as bad blank verse, and that even its best passages are guilty of excruciating banalities of style and technique, is as idle as criticism of a mountain. The mountain is there, imperfect in line, rough and craggy in detail; but massive and mighty as it rests broadly on the solid earth and lifts its austere brow into the clouds.

But if Masters is fundamentally epic in the sweep of his vision, his prolific art indulges also other moods. Certain fine poems of more or less cosmic motive are epic corollaries, no doubt—such things as **"The World's Desire," "The Loom," "The Star," "Silence," "Worlds."** And many poems about real or typical characters— **"Autochthon," "William Marion Reedy," "Cato Braden," "Widow La Rue," "Emily Brosseau," "Sir Galahad"** and others—as well as out-door poems like **"Grand River Marshes," "The Landscape,"** and the supremely joyous **"Lake Boats,"** may be classed as details of the story of his place and people which is this poet's chief legacy to art.

Sometimes his prolific genius is tempted by the past, and

we have monologues from Shakespeare, Byron, Voltaire, and others. These are always interesting, whether one agrees or not with the poet's analyses of motives. But such excursions are tangents from the main curve of his orbit, and when they are pursued too deliberately, as in certain dialogues in **The Open Sea,** which elaborate the Brutus theme through the centuries, they become the most ineffective chapter of Mr. Masters' artistic history. Occasionally, however, one finds an intensely vivid study of remote and alien character, as in that rather early lyrical ballad **"Saint Francis and Lady Clare,"** which has all the emotion of a personal song.

Now and then the poet utters a real lyric cry. Poems like **"I Shall Never See You Again," "Song of Women," "Poor Pierrot," "Recessional," "My Light with Yours," "Sounds Out of Sorrow," "The Sign,"** make a strong bid for remembrance because their intense rhapsodic passion burns away all imperfections and sweeps the reader along in its flame of beauty unstudied and sincere. Even the poet's technique, so often slipshod, has nobilities of its own at ecstatic moments. Perhaps the great thing about him is that he is *capable* of ecstasy, that he lives hard and deep, and knows the extremes, the agonies. Thus his art is sincere, convincing; one never doubts the emotion behind it. And to a poet who believes much may be forgiven. (pp. 205-10)

Harriet Monroe, "Edgar Lee Masters," in Poetry, *Vol. XXIV, No. 4, July, 1924, pp. 204-10.*

Harriet Monroe   (essay date 1925)

[*In the following excerpt, Monroe praises* The New Spoon River, *stressing a deepened maturity in Masters's philosophy since the* Spoon River Anthology.]

One opens [**The New Spoon River**] with some misgivings, wondering whether the thrill of the first **Spoon River** can be repeated. But no thrill is ever repeated—each experience has its own place and value, differing from every other. It was adventurous, no doubt, for the poet to return to that unmapped Illinois town and ravel out for the second time its tangled human destinies. He risked the disappointment of readers who expect the impossible renewal, and so underestimate what they receive. (p. 273)

At least there is no repetition—this poet sees each person as an individual, with marvellous insight for the perplexities which environed him, with pity for his sufferings, laughter for his absurdities, or scorn for his hypocrisies. Underlying the whole spiritual pageant is the same passion for life, the same deep tragic love and pity for men and women caught in the toils of fate, the same high outreaching toward infinite beauty, which were the central inspiration of the earlier book; and all enriched by the eight or ten more years of deep living and thinking which have passed between the two series.

His capacity for fierce living and hard thinking is what gives size and depth to this poet's work. One pictures his imagination as a battle-ground of ecstasies and agonies— more completely than with most poets his puppets' feelings become his own. His philosophy therefore is built on human examples—abstract reasoning apart from life is impossible to him. It is an epicurean philosophy, no doubt, one which follows earthly paths and finds happiness a sufficient aim; but beyond this immediate goal lies the remote horizon of mystery. Mr. Masters may be a realist, but we are constantly reminded that his realism transcends mere fact, that the finite and the infinite are equally real to him and equally of the tenuous stuff of dreams. (pp. 273-74)

Again and again he chants the praise of life—this splendid garment of happiness which is offered so often in vain, and which most of us, at the best, wear so clumsily. . . .

The desecration of life—that is the unpardonable sin which he lashes in countless epitaphs. The magnificence of the opportunity and the insignificance of our response to it—that is the gods' food for laughter, and the poet's stuff of satire. Mr. Masters does not predict, though he does not deny, that some future life may give us another chance; in his mind that is irrelevant to the immediate and important issue—our unworthy and inadequate use of the life we have. (p. 275)

[It] is the narrow and self-righteous patterns of respectability whom Masters lashes with his sharpest satire, the static immovable human clods who obstruct the path of the adventurers, of the free and open-minded children of light. The book's tragedies are mostly of this order. **"Claud Antle"** is

> A deer compelled to live with the hounds.

"Heine La Salle" suffers

> Persecution, because society fears
> Always the genius soul.

"Cowley Rider," slaving all his life for a thankless family, finds at the end that

> The wages of goodness is Death.

"Kay Rutledge" says:

> I loved fiddlers and dancers
> And the tellers of stories . . .
> And you saw me as the victim of unrighteousness,
> And passed me by.

(pp. 275-76)

We may be stressing too hard Mr. Masters' philosophy—though indeed he stresses it more in this book than the earlier one. I feel this emphasis more strongly than the motive he speaks of on the jacket—the "encroachment of the city," the "standardized community," the "foreign stocks holding office," etc. *The New Spoon River* seems not much more metropolitan than the old, but its poet is perhaps more inclined to associate present details with ultimate immensities. Is the keen edge of observation dulled by this more philosophical attitude? I cannot find the evidence of it in these soul-searching epitaphs. None of them, I think, attains the sheer lyric beauty of **"Anne Rutledge,"** nor is the **"Stephen A. Douglas"** so convincing a revelation of historic character as the side-lights on Lincoln in **"William H. Herndon"** and other poems of the earlier book. Nor is there anything so funny as **"Daisy Frazer."** But with these exceptions the new series seems as powerful and varied as the old, and possibly more far-reaching. (p. 277)

> *Harriet Monroe, "Spoon River Again," in Po-*
> *etry, Vol. XXV, No. 5, February, 1925, pp.*
> *273-78.*

AUTHOR'S COMMENTARY

Twenty years ago poets were busy writing masses on Lincoln and sonnets on Shakespeare. It was book poetry, second-hand stuff. A few daring spirits there were, indeed, who wrote about the familiar things, the homely things, but most of their stuff was tainted with sweetness and sentimentality. . . . I am not criticizing them adversely; I like a good deal they have written, but the fact remains that a poet thought it his craft and his vocation in life to write only of the virtuous and noble. Life is not made up of such things alone. Walt Whitman, of course, took a new and bold stride. But he stands apart by himself. He is not typical. I was no better than the rest. For a long time I wrote book poetry. It was pretty bad stuff. It took a long time for me to wake up to the fact that the poetry I sought was not in fancies in my brain but in the life about me. . . . And here was I living in a community rife with gossip and tradition and story. Here was poetry. I knew it all; I had grown up with it, lived with it, was part of it. I wrote it and woke up to find the *Anthology* a best seller. It was as startling to me as my publishers. But what's the answer to it? The public responded to something that was real, something that they understood, something that was as much a part of them as it was a part of me. [Robert] Burns's mother, it is said, never could understand why he ranked as a poet. The things he wrote were things that were common gossip in the neighborhood. They weren't deep, or soulful, or noble, not to her at any rate. She couldn't understand the kinship of the world to the stuff out of which he spun his poetry. My mother still cannot understand how it is that my book was a success. She's known these things of which I write for many years; to her there's nothing remarkable about them. Yet these ordinary stories, these incidents talked over in the kitchen, in the parlor, at the corner drug store, these make the poetical well into which my mind dips. The poems are accepted as honest revealment of the lives of men who live in small towns and . . . the small town is a microcosm of the large city. It gives the note of America.

(interview date 1924)

Llewellyn Jones (essay date 1925)

[In the following excerpt, Jones provides an overview of Masters's poetry in which he emphasizes the totality of Masters's work and his "real faith in life."]

Matthew Arnold is credited—unjustly—with defining poetry as a criticism of life, which, taken, as it is, without his qualifications, applies as much to suicide as it does to poetry. But whether or no poetry ought to be a criticism of life, Edgar Lee Masters' poetry is that—and sometimes it is only that.

Among the tories, of course, Mr. Masters has the reputation of being a sort of literary bolshevik, and his *Spoon River* was hailed as something new and strange in form as well as something ugly and materialistic in substance. It was neither. So far from being a radical in form Masters may be said to be the most literary of our contemporary poets. As a lad he studied Greek in college and read Shelley: his first poetry, published obscurely and not widely read, owed much to his reading of Shelley's poetic dramas. His *Spoon River Anthology* was regarded as something new and radical in form because so few of his readers recognized in it the form of Book VII of the *Greek Anthology,* the general form, that is, and also a few direct translations. In his later books he has put the sharp vintages of his Middle Western vineyards into the old but convenient wine-skins of the Browning dramatic soliloquy. (pp. 69-70)

This does not mean that Masters is imitative. Rather the literary form he chooses enables him to get the very maximum out of his theme. And it certainly gives a dignity to his treatment of his theme which might otherwise be lacking. For Masters has led a double life, one his literary and philosophic life, giving him both background and dignity; the other a life as a Chicago lawyer in which dignity gave way to the fighting instinct, a life which accustomed him, although it did not inure him, to seeing injustice done, a life which brought out passionate resentments and which gave him a coarse and effective vocabulary, an urban vocabulary one might call it, with which to criticize judges, lawyers and law-breakers. (p. 70)

[As] a general rule, we shall find that Mr. Masters, condemned by the nature of his profession to live with these people, seeks his own high spaces, and speaks in his poetic as opposed to his denunciatory voice, through literary forms that have tradition and dignity and that automatically guard him against the contagion of the mob which he rightly despises.

And this working through an old form was uniquely successful in the *Spoon River Anthology.* That book is so well known that one hardly need quote from it at this day. It is an undoubtedly veridical picture of a small town rotten because it is out of touch with the currents of modern life. Its people either live parasitic lives on their poorer neighbors, escape, by fair means or foul, or else they die, the victims of their surroundings. But the people who regarded the story, truly told after death, by each member of the community, as in sum a black and sordid chronicle did not read to the end of the book, or read none of it understandingly. For Mr. Masters did see good as well as bad; where a soul, by some inner force or by freedom from the outer influences of the place grew in beauty and health, Mr. Masters saw as clearly as he saw the evils of the place, and he recorded it. (pp. 72-3)

And there are not only some portraits beautiful in themselves but some that indicate what is, in fact, one of Masters' own strong bents—that toward mysticism. Here, for example, is the portrait of **"The Village Atheist"**:

> Ye young debaters over the doctrine
> Of the soul's immortality,
> I who lie here was the village atheist,
> Talkative, contentious, versed in the arguments
> Of the infidels.
> But through a long sickness
> Coughing myself to death

> I read the *Upanishads* and the poetry of Jesus.
> And they lighted a torch of hope and intuition
> And desire which the Shadow,
> Leading me swiftly through the caverns of darkness,
> Could not extinguish.
> Listen to me, ye who live in the senses
> And think through the senses only:
> Immortality is not a gift,
> Immortality is an achievement;
> And only those who strive mightily
> Shall possess it.

Indeed, in a later edition of the book, published two years after its first appearance—which was in 1914—Mr. Masters has an epilogue which itself ends, not on a note of disillusion or despair but on a note of pantheistic assertion of the unending reign of infinite life and infinite law.

Spoon River was followed at short intervals by *Songs and Satires, Toward the Gulf, Starved Rock, Domesday Book* and *The Open Sea* in verse, while in 1920 Masters published his first work of prose fiction, *Mitch Miller. . . .* (pp. 73-4)

To return to the poetry. We find, besides the poems directly denunciatory of present day civilization in America, a number of historical portraits, the most interesting of them being, perhaps, of early American heroes and later. In *Toward the Gulf,* for instance, we have a striking portrait of Thomas Paine, as seen through the eyes of a London dramatist who revered him and would fain writing a play with Paine as a hero. (p. 75)

And from these American portraits he proceeds to others: that of Voltaire—for Masters' hero is always the liberator—being a particularly fine one (**"Front the Ages with a Smile"**) ending:

> So you smiled till the lines of your mouth
> A crescent became with dimples for horns, so expressing
> To centuries after who see you in marble: behold me,
> I lived, I loved, I laughed, I toiled without ceasing
> Through eighty-four years for realities—O let them pass,
> Let life go by. Would you rise over death like a god?
> Front the ages with a smile.

From Voltaire, Napoleon—whom Mr. Masters sees as the great democrat thwarted by Tory England—and Shakespeare, Mr. Masters goes further back and gives us a series of Biblical studies in which his satire appears and in which it is left for something nearer to pure poetry. Some of them express not so much satire as a sort of humorous recognition of the twosideness of those episodes in the New Testament which we use on one side only—for edification. Mr. Masters asks, for example, what were the feelings of the owner of the Gadarene swine, or of the accursed fig tree? What ought to be the culminating poem in this kind was one of the first to be published, **"All Life in a Life,"** a portrait of Jesus in most realistic terms and with the atmosphere of his day and city denoted in terms of our own day. For instance the story of the Temptation is put in these terms:

> But there was a certain sinister
> Fellow who came to him hearing of his renown
> And said "You can be mayor of this city,
> We need a man like you for mayor."

The total effect of the poem is not, perhaps, altogether happy.

In the volumes mentioned, there is, besides the groups—though they are not arranged in groups—already mentioned, a bewildering variety of poems on problematical subjects. Poetry may be, as Wordsworth says, the finer spirit of all knowledge but it is not very likely to be the essential distillate of that which is not knowledge but problem. And hence many of these poems on such subjects as heredity and the relation of mind and brain will date: they are poetic journalism rather than poetry. And scattered among them are other poems which bear the earmarks of being left over from the poet's juvenilia. But among these works *Domesday Book* stands out as an impressive achievement. It impresses by its strength rather than by beauty of workmanship, but it is strong enough to win praise, though grudging praise, from no less prejudiced a critic than Edmund Gosse [see excerpt dated 1923]—prejudiced because he is an Englishman evaluating an American's work and because he is a classicist in taste and with an ear more attuned to the rhythms of Milton than to those of the coroner and jury at a Middle Western American inquest. But, like Wordsworth in certain moods, Mr. Masters has not been afraid to squeeze inquest proceedings, legal phraseology and even the evidence of a coroner's physician into the form of blank verse, and we forgive the plateaus of pedestrian versifying for the occasional risings to a climax. (pp. 76-9)

The poet . . . sets out to show us how every move in [Elenor Murray's] life and the fact of her death, had its reverberations in other lives, and would, if its influences were traced far enough, give

> . . . a census spiritual
> Taken of our America . . .

And the terms of this census are achievement and waste. Merivale, the coroner, does not hold a merely perfunctory inquest but tries through the evidence here, as he has done in other inquests, to collect not only the immediate but the ramifying evidence, so that from his inquests he will gain data toward the solution of the great question of human waste in our civilization. He is a philosopher, a man of means, who took the coroner's office indeed with this quest in view. And so, in the death of Elenor Murray he traces every separate riffle, going into the implications of the facts as well as the facts. And the book is made up of each witness's contribution to the unraveling of the riddle of Elenor's death, not only as physically caused but as the final act in a life which was achievement in part—the question is in what part? and which in part was waste—the question is in what degree and why?

As witness after witness testifies, we not only have a growing revelation of the complex strands of Elenor Murray's life but pictures of the lives that she affected. And at length Elenor Murray herself becomes a symbol of the blindness, the struggle, the complexity, of our national life. (pp. 79-80)

Taking it in the mass this is as impressive a piece of work as Masters has done since *The Spoon River Anthology.* Like that work, it is, if not—to use the title of a poem already referred to—"All Life in a Life" at least a great deal of life in one life. And other personages as well as Elenor Murray stand forth and live in its pages. But [*Domesday Book*] must be read for its totality and not for the sensuous satisfaction of perfect heroic lines. For when Masters is building his poems he never stops to reject imperfect bricks nor does he always trim his cement. It is not that he is incompetent—for as a matter of fact he is not. Indeed no poet could be incompetent enough—to take examples from other poems—to rhyme "wakened" and "unshakened" and it hardly reads like a typographical error, or to write the word "upborned"—no, it is not incompetence, It is a desperate hurry. It is the trick of a man so anxious to make his notes on life that he cares not for the elegance of his writing.

And indeed impatience, impatience with the stupidity, the cruelty, and the short-sightedness of those around him must have been the mood in which much of Masters' work was written. But we must not assume that that impatience has driven him into cynicism or pessimism. Behind his anger at our fumbling with life there is a real faith in life. It is not a faith that can be formulated in any way, because life, as Masters sees it, transcends good and evil—but if life transcends not only good but evil, one cannot logically be a pessimist. And Masters has written at least one poem which already dissociates his point of view from that of the pessimist. It is "Nature" at the end of *The Open Sea.* . . . (pp. 81-2)

[It] would be unfair to Masters to regard him only as the poet of broad effects, of satire, of disillusionment expressed on a semi-epical scale. For at times he is none of these but is for a moment content to be only a poet. To show him in this aspect I could quote the two simple but very beautiful lyrics written to and given the names of his daughters Marcia and Madeline when they were small children (in *Songs and Satires*) but instead here is a line or two from an even more poetic—because, in a manner more disinterested, study of a little servant girl, "Slip Shoe Lovey"—and what tenderness there is under the raillery:

> You're the cook's understudy,
> A gentle idiot body.
> You are slender like a broom
> Weaving up and down the room,
> With your dirt hair in a twist
> And your left eye in a mist.
> Never thinkin', never hopin'
> With your wet mouth open.
> So bewildered and so busy
> As you scrape the dirty kettles,
> O Slip Shoe Lizzie
> As you rattle with the pans.
> There's a clatter of old metals,
> O Slip Shoe Lovey,
> As you clean the milk cans.
> You're a greasy little dovey,
> A laughing scullery daughter,
> As you slop the dish water,
> So abstracted and so dizzy,
> O Slip Shoe Lizzie! . . .

(pp. 83-4)

[Masters] has been accused and with some show of justice of a deficiency in the faculty of self-criticism. But that faculty may simply have been unexercised as yet. Undoubtedly when in the course of time he collects his poems he will discard many of the more ephemeral and those that deal with problems—such a heredity—whose very terms and symbols are changing. But even when he does that, a respectable canon of significant poetry will remain. (p. 84)

Llewellyn Jones, "Edgar Lee Masters," in his

First Impressions: Essays on Poetry, Criticism, and Prosody, *Alfred A. Knopf, 1925, pp. 69-84.*

John Cowper Powys   (essay date 1929)

[*Powys was an English novelist, poet, and critic who is perhaps best known for his novels set in Wessex county, though he is also highly regarded for such nonfiction books as* The Complex Vision (*1920*) *and* The Enjoyment of Literature (*1929*). *Powys's early favorable reviews of* Spoon River Anthology *helped establish Masters's reputation as a modern poet. In the following excerpt, he offers a positive appraisal of Masters's poetry, stressing the unique characteristics of Masters's work among his contemporaries of modern poetry.*]

Spoon River Anthology remains, in the face of all detractions, the most original work—with the exception of Theodore Dreiser's novels—that American genius has produced since the death of Henry James. Nor could it have become what it is if its author had not in his own nature combined a deep Rabelaisian zest for the freer aspects of this gross village life with an infinite loathing of its cramped limitations. In the contrasted intensity of his love and his hate for this America of his, Mr. Masters's mind is an almost perfect medium for the precise enterprise that blind chance or his good tutelary genius set him upon undertaking. (p. 650)

There is a purely philosophical reason why the real importance of Masters's achievement is likely to be rated more highly by posterity than by his contemporaries. This is the fact that his philosophy of life, like that of the great neglected poets in his library, is neither optimistic nor pessimistic; but full of a stoical resignation that influences you indirectly and sideways, like an unseen "black" frost permeating the atmosphere.

For even the most disillusioned and antinomian writers of our time, whose chief rôle is an ego-centric solipsism, make of their contempt for the older systems a sort of Pyrrhonean "credo" which, in its brilliant, flippant dogmatism, hits you like a catapult. But Masters has nothing of this sensational cynicism. There is something almost Confucian in the obstinate rigor of his sublimated common sense. And it is just because of such an indomitable vein of antique aplomb in this modern American that the earthy loam of his genius breeds such sad humorous pity for human fate as it universalizes itself by the banks of a little Illinois creek. (p. 651)

Indigenous or not to the land he writes of, there certainly hover now and then over the level movement of his verse strange, mystical intimations. As it happens with Wordsworth, who also in his less inspired hours has such a lack of porousness, the very solidity of Mr. Masters's mind, his grim pot-house humor, his massive quizzical passivity, give a vibrant convincingness to these rarer visions. When such wild hawk wings do sweep across the heavy ploughlands of his steady furrowing their reality is like the reality of life itself. One of the most striking of these interludes is that queer poem entitled **"The Star"**; a poem the mere existence of which, in a later volume, proves that he is not in any sense the poet of one single book. There is something about this poem that seems, to my mind at least, to carry an imaginative suggestiveness unequalled in modern American poetry.

And it is real *imagination*—not just a clever fancy, not just a picturesque image, or a startling recondite *tour de force.* What I mean is that this strange poem reveals a floating intangible whisper from the earth-consciousness itself, penetrating the thickest human skulls as they go to and fro about their affairs. There are perturbations of sudden approach, "fallings from us, vanishings", disquietudes and tremors, produced by the tap of a dead leaf, the rustle of a branch in the wind, a footstep in the silence of dawn, the trotting of a horse "beyond the creek" which touch now and again the most sodden brains, the most hard-boiled nerves, with an uneasy sense of mystery. And what one feels that Mr. Masters has caught just here is that deep withdrawn vein of secretive *insanity* lurking under so many weather-beaten foreheads in these places, under so many high cheek-bones, hollow eye-sockets, and lean ribs!

And he is profoundly original in his manner of conjuring up this insane element from beneath the mask of bully-boy *bonhomie* in American small-town life. Compare the "mad Frederick" of this extraordinary poem with the idiot-boy of Wordsworth's verse, or the idiot-girl in Dostoievski's *The Possessed.* The English and Russian idiots are just tragic personalities, among the rest. But "mad Frederick" is a myth, a symbol, the incarnated "eidolon" of a widespread uncanny tendency among such by-products of the "growth of the soil". (pp. 652-53)

In Masters's most characteristic work, as you ponder upon it in the first ***Anthology,*** the poetic element is deliberately suppressed for the sake of the pitiful and the human. But when at rare moments this element *is* permitted full play—the milieu still remaining that of the small rural community—a unique effect is produced! This is noticeable in the poem called **"The Sign"**, another fine poem in a later volume, where that peculiar voice of the inanimate which is always projecting itself like a goblinish commentary upon our futile proceedings, in doorways, in chimneys, in floor-boards, in gate-hinges, in clock-tickings, rises to the pitch of a wistful malediction. . . . (p 653)

It is a great mistake to assume that Mr. Masters's genius has not remained fully alive; now that thirteen years have

Masters's home on Kenwood Avenue in Chicago, where he lived from 1909 until 1925. He composed most of the Spoon River Anthology *here.*

passed since the publication of *Spoon River.* A poem like "Tirzah Potter", published recently in the *Century Magazine,* is sufficient proof of this. But the quality diffused through all his work did surely condense its rare essence in that disconcerting volume to a degree never since surpassed. And nowhere else but in America, nowhere else but in the Middle West, could all these outraged, thwarted, frustrated, poisoned human spirits, drawing their lineage from every race in Europe, whirl up out of the dust as they do here with a sound like that sound that made Dante tremble and even Virgil turn pale, on the brink of the Inferno.

And the way they play into each other's hands, the way they turn and rend each other, the horrible irony of their partial angles of vision, their furious stupidity, their crazed greed, their nauseating self-humiliations,—all these things, as one gives oneself up to them, gradually evoke an attitude towards life upon earth which—whether "philosophical" or not—is free from all affectation of esthetic or moral superiority. For where *Spoon River* is so great, where it overtops all recent American work—unless, as I have hinted, you throw the weight of Dreiser's writings into the scale—is in its extraordinary indulgence for what is called "sin". With the exception of some half-dozen cold-blooded exploiters of the people, not a ghost among these wraiths but is understood, condoned, allowed for, and forgiven. In the rank mephitic arena of all this squalor the poet preserves his grand, equal, unmitigated equilibrium, as he had learned it from his classic models.

It is noticeable that Mr. Masters, once again rather in the manner of Chinese than of European sages, finds the dominant element in life to be pure Chance. Moralists love to talk of "character" being fate; but what could "character" do to save half these poor doddypolls from their miserable destinies? Accident here, accident there—and the battle not to the strong, neither the race to the swift; but time and chance waiting for all men!

Mr. Masters ought to have been made Poet Laureate of America for thus touching "the real and true"—those dogs "that must to kennel"!—with the transmuting fingers of genius. Not all perhaps have ears to catch the subtle cadences, evoked from the common speech of men, that lend to these immortal monodies their woebegone charm. (pp. 653-54)

I cannot feel that we have yet done justice to this completely new form of poetry. The clarified objectivity and austere condensation of the *Greek Anthology* gave Masters his cue; but the form he uses seems to have grown between his hands out of the earth itself—an organic plant of American soil—as was Walt Whitman's *Leaves of Grass.* It is in fact a reply to *Leaves of Grass* from the viewpoint of those Children of Adam whose engendering has been blighted and whose days gangrened by their "democratic" environment.

There is one human subject, however, that both as a realist and a classicist Masters can treat after his own heart to the furthest limit and the result be only noble and beautiful! Am I not on sure ground when I say that the essential greatness of a poet can be judged better by what he writes of Death than by anything else? I doubt if any modern poet, either in England or America, has written of death more nobly than in ["Howard Lamson."] . . . (p. 654)

I think it is in the rugged naturalness of a soul whose powers of love and hate are equal, that now and then Mr. Masters touches a chord of emotional intensity such as, just because we have acquired a certain clever shame at feeling directly and simply, has become rare among us. An excellent example of what I mean occurs in a poem of his entitled, "I shall never see you again". Possibly we might even discover here, in the poet's forgetfulness of "art" and "reader" and "philosophy" and all overtones and undertones, a justification for the authentic human affections in the Middle West! (p. 655)

Edgar Lee Masters is a solitary figure in American letters and he is likely to remain so. Not one of the dominant modern tendencies plays any part in his work. In this respect he is as un-porous as his own *Starved Rock.* The subjective pessimism of our age does not touch him. The modern fashion of reducing all the idiosyncrasies of human character to certain unconscious psychic forces leaves him cold.

In the midst of a generation that turns, jaded and cynical, towards a de-personalized natural magic, where even the very elements themselves—rain and vapor and twilight and drifting clouds—seem to be purged of all human association, he persists in finding his chief poetic interest, just as the great Eighteenth Century humorists did before him, in individual, personal, happy, unhappy human beings! (pp. 655-56)

> *John Cowper Powys, "Edgar Lee Masters," in* The Bookman, *New York, Vol. LXIX, No. 6, August, 1929, pp. 650-56.*

William Rose Benét   (essay date 1930)

[*Benét was an American poet, critic, short story writer, and editor who helped establish the* Saturday Review of Literature *in 1924. In his review of* Lichee Nuts, *excerpted below, Benét praises the new direction Masters takes with this volume.*]

Mr. Masters's new book is of a different flavor. . . . His *Lichee Nuts* create for us a group of Chinese living in the midst of New York City. Their comments are not on life in general . . . but directed ironically against modern America. Some years ago Mr. Masters created the character of Elmer Chubb which he used for the purpose of writing fundamentalist letters to the newspapers in a deeply satiric spirit. In *Lichee Nuts* Elmer comes in contact with the Oriental and is bested in every argument. It seems to us that Mr. Masters conveys very well the Chinese attitude of passivity steeped in deep philosophy. The English used in the book is very slightly pidgin. Its imperfections are not overdone. And even though the separate poems are brief, several definite Chinese character-types are built up for the reader. On laying the book down we are sorry to leave such mellow though trenchant friends. We like this volume better than anything of Mr. Masters's that we have seen for some time.

> *William Rose Benét, "Round About Parnassus," in* The Saturday Review of Literature, *Vol. VII, No. 14, October 25, 1930, p. 290.*

John T. Flanagan   (essay date 1953)

[*Flanagan is an American educator and critic. In the following excerpt, he evaluates Masters's career, focusing on characteristics of* Spoon River Anthology *that mark this work as his greatest poetic achievement.*]

The publication of the **Spoon River Anthology** in the spring of 1915 is a memorable date in the history of American poetry. (p. 226)

Unfortunately Masters did not go on to greater heights. He did not even maintain the level which in one great creative burst he had reached in his forty-fifth year. It was not that he lapsed into silence. He continued to write and publish poetry to the end of his days. And poetry was only one of several literary mediums for his fertile and restless mind. . . . His very prodigality of expression, as with Dreiser and Wolfe, became a liability, and he was certainly not immune from the charge of writing largely to make money which he leveled so frequently and so scornfully at Mark Twain. His vast literary output, all too often slovenly in form and style, had the effect of blinding both readers and critics to many solid gifts, and his frequent attempts to diverge from the rut of satiric epitaphy brought little acclaim. When he died in the spring of 1950 the few metropolitan newspapers that printed extensive obituaries unmistakably emphasized the past. His demise elicited one common observation: the creator of Spoon River was dead, and the rest of his work merited only a speedy oblivion.

Although it is difficult to quarrel with this harsh verdict, not all of Masters' later work is arid and unrewarding. It should be remembered that the poet himself preferred various descriptive lyrics such as **"The Mourner's Bench"** and his ambitious narrative poem **Domesday Book** to the Spoon River portraits. Possibly this preference was the result of a psychological revolt from the obvious, much as Rachmaninoff tired of constantly playing his "Prelude" and Vachel Lindsay wearied of perennial audience demand for "The Congo." Or it may have been one more instance of the creative writer's amazing uncertainty about the true value of his own achievements—Henry James's addiction to playwriting, for example, or Mark Twain's assurance that his life of Joan of Arc was his masterpiece. But even the admiring reader of the **Spoon River Anthology** will benefit from some knowledge of Masters' later career.

As a narrative poet he frequently attempted long and complex stories with only mediocre success. Padraic Colum thought that **The New World,** which depicts America as a land of prophecies, many of them unrealized, and which skilfully integrates many threads of a colorful fabric, was unjustly neglected. But **The New World** has found few readers. Little more can be said for **Godbey** or **Lee** or **Jack Kelso.** But the **Domesday Book** might prove more durable even though in form and substance it is antithetical to the work which brought Masters recognition.

The **Domesday Book** is a narrative poem in blank verse built around the death of Elenor Murray, whose body was found one morning by a rabbit hunter on the shore of the Illinois River near Starved Rock. . . . Masters' method here, obviously similar to that of Browning's *The Ring and the Book* (though he vigorously denied using it as a model), was to sketch the biography of everyone remotely associated with Elenor Murray and then to let each person contribute what he could to the reconstruction through dramatic monologue of the dead girl's life. This plan allowed the poet not only to continue on a somewhat larger scale the psychological analysis of the **Spoon River Anthology** but also to review a large segment of American life. (pp. 226-28)

As a whole, the **Domesday Book** has interest and impact. Masters deftly fits the sections together and skilfully varies the evidence and the witnesses. Flashbacks reveal both Elenor Murray and her period, and the characters who impinge even momentarily on her life epitomize much of America. Nevertheless, Masters' preference for the poem on the score of originality and literary finish seems unwarranted. The monologues are longer than the Spoon River epitaphs and because they are self-confessions they lack incisiveness. Their effect is further weakened because of Masters' tendency to become the trial lawyer cross-examining witnesses rather than the psychologist probing into motives and deeds. Elenor Murray, wishing to burn her candle at both ends and motivated by a craving for self-satisfaction rather than by idealism, is a weak prototype of revolt against social conventions. Moreover, as in much of the poet's later verse, the style is rough and careless. Masters could use blank verse adroitly but here the lines often become turgid, and the scope of the narrative prevents the fine chiseling which won so many partisans for the **Spoon River Anthology.**

In the September, 1915, issue of *Poetry: A Magazine of Verse,* Masters rejected all earlier definitions of poetry, especially those like Poe's which explicitly stated the need of meter and rhythm, and emphasized that poetry was always a question of substance. The complete artist, he avowed, must always accept whatever forms are necessary to achieve the desired effect and should no more refuse to write in free verse than he should hesitate to employ sonnets and villanelles. Poetry to Masters came out of the vibrations of the soul; form was subsidiary to content. It was a matter of supreme unimportance whether a poet was traditional or rebellious in his medium; all that counted was the poet's freedom to choose the form which he felt was most appropriate.

It is conceivable that in his later poetic writing Masters deliberately tried to put this theory into practice, and that his technique was unable to sustain his vision. Occasionally earnestness and sincerity did support his pen in an attempt to encompass a large theme. But the great bulk of Masters' later verse is repetitive and flat, and he was too poor a self-critic to perceive that he was sapping his strength by being wastefully prolific and by monotonously rehandling similar themes. At the end of his creative life he had little to say, and his subordination of form to content deprived him even of a dependable technique in which to express his banality.

Indeed, when Masters at the beginning of his eighth decade returned to the publication of lyric verse, he celebrated the Illinois landscape which he had so loved in youth, and his poems assume that nostalgic idealization familiar in those on whom the years weigh heavily. Without producing any very memorable poetry he managed to convey some of the charm of the streams, copses, and towns which he once knew intimately. . . . One looks in vain here for the Spoon River touch. If Boardman Robinson, the artist who caught so wonderfully the expressions and features of the Spoon River people, had been called to il-lustrate-these poems, he would have needed to soften his lines. For Masters remembered chiefly the physical loveli-ness of the landscape. Corrosive human portraiture had little place in these final affectionate tributes to the land of his boyhood. As he admitted somewhat pathetically, his life had taken him far from the Illinois prairies, but his heart still lay in the little town of Petersburg. (pp. 228-29)

It is indeed easy for the superficial reader of Masters to be deceived by the pessimism which seems to supply the core of the famous anthology. Actually there is much evidence to prove that Masters considered himself a meliorist. (p. 232)

Masters thought of himself as a southern liberal, a Demo-crat in politics, a man who inevitably opposed materialism and the rights of property but who fought instinctively for freedom and progress. Certainly he shared Emerson's dis-dain for a period in which things were in the saddle and rode mankind. And although he could not conscientiously claim a completely southern ancestry and flatly repudiate New England, as his Illinois contemporary Vachel Lind-say could and did, he consistently allied himself with the forces of progressivism. (pp. 232-33)

In his early practice as a lawyer in Chicago Masters was frequently concerned with cases involving the exploitation of labor. Even at the risk of sacrificing his own fees he acted in cases where the plaintiffs were waitresses, dispos-sessed tenants, and the victims of industrial accidents. Equally significant, perhaps, is the fact that the enlight-ened spirits of the *Spoon River Anthology* are those who fought for humanitarianism, the editors who risked mar-tyrdom to present the facts, the religious leaders who sought tolerance, the idealists who were motivated by a passion for truth. (p. 233)

But neither Masters' personality nor his politics explains the *Spoon River Anthology,* and every reader of his work must ultimately return to his one acknowledged master-piece. Prior to 1915 Masters had been a diligent but unsuc-cessful poet treading conventional paths. . . . Masters lavished his talents on these little people of the Spoon River world and as a consequence produced some of his most vivid sketches. The portraits that occupy the central portion of the book are less exciting and less dramatic, al-though Penniwit the photographer and Jonathan Swift Somers the poet are memorably drawn. Here too are the sketches of the bird-hunter Bert Kessler, who died of a rat-tlesnake bite, and of Amelia Garrick (actually Masters' youthful sweetheart Margaret George). Last of all come the heroes and the genuinely enlightened spirits, the char-acters who at once justify and exemplify the poet's faith. Postponed almost to the end but among Masters' finest poems are the sketches of the artist Rutherford McDo-well, of the Village Atheist (a remarkably sensitive por-trait), of Lucinda Matlock, as well as the genuine elegies for Anne Rutledge and William H. Herndon. These merit careful reading if only as a counterbalance to the earlier notoriety. For in his best work Masters was sincere and hopeful; his scorn for the present was matched by his con-viction that a better life could and would be reached. The paradox that iconoclast and idealist are one and the same is not unprecedented.

Masters' fame will never again be as great as it was in the decade following the appearance of the *Spoon River An-thology* in 1915. American verse was then just recovering from the doldrums of the genteel tradition and was slowly responding to the revitalization being provided by Robin-son, Frost, Pound, Sandburg, and Masters himself. Old forms were being renovated or abandoned, vitality count-ed for more than method, and the extension of subject matter proclaimed by Whitman long before was finally being achieved. (pp. 233-36)

Masters with his flouting of tradition, with his scorn for hypocrisy, with his sympathetic appreciation of the eter-nal problems of the artist as well as the eternal frustrations imposed by a materialistic culture, found himself the poet-ic voice of the age to much the same degree that Sinclair Lewis and F. Scott Fitzgerald were the fictional voices. Today we can still admire the skill and finish of the Spoon River portraits even though we turn increasingly to poetry with greater intellectual subtlety and a richer use of lan-guage. Artists are now as eager to return to the village, al-beit a different village, as they were to escape it in 1915. The atomic age has made rural complacency seem superi-or to urban congestion; and with the revolt against the small town having run its course, the artist fights his bat-tles on a larger front. Yet because of Masters' imaginative power Spoon River as a fictional place name is almost as imperishable as Wessex or Barsetshire. (p. 236)

John T. Flanagan, "The Spoon River Poet," in Southwest Review, *Vol. XXXVIII, No. 3, Summer, 1953, pp. 226-37.*

Dylan Thomas   (broadcast date 1955)

[*Thomas was a Welsh poet, prose writer, and critic whose work is noted for its obscurity and mysticism. Thomas was interested in American literature and it has been noted that similarities exist between his play* Under Milk Wood *(1954) and Masters's* Spoon River Anthol-ogy. *The following excerpt is a transcript from his select-ed readings of the* Anthology *that were broadcast post-humously in 1955. Thomas reflects on the popularity of the* Anthology *when it first appeared in 1915 and af-firms its lasting significance.*]

[*Spoon River Anthology*] became the first best seller of the 'poetic Renaissance' which began in the Middle West with Masters, Vachel Lindsay, Carl Sandburg and Harriet Monroe's oddly-named *Poetry: a Magazine of Verse;* and the memories of its sensational success have lasted so long that even today it is regarded, when it is regarded at all, with deep suspicion, though the reasons for the present suspicion are quite different from what they were when the book boomed out first to the hand-lifted horror of the giant parish press, the prairie pulpits, the thin, baffled, sour officials of taste in the literary periodicals, and the in-numerable societies of militant gentility. Now, *Spoon River* is, I suppose, hardly read at all by the thousands of university students who 'take' poetry in such enormous doses. The poetry workshops attached to many universi-ties and private colleges leave him, I should think, un-taught and alone, except as a figure of minor historical in-terest, a cross, rhetorical, old Bohemian lawyer rambling and ranting away in the bad past about the conflict be-tween materialism and idealism: a conflict considered so old-fashioned that many of those in the poetry workshops must imagine it to have been satisfactorily settled long ago. (p. 68)

And the brash, antiseptic, forty-two-toothed, ardent, crewcut collegiates, grimly pursuing the art of poetry with net, notebook, poison bottle, pin and label, may be quite likely to dismiss Edgar Lee Masters altogether because, in his lifetime, he *was* so successful. I've noticed before, in the States, how very many students devotedly read and devour masses of modern poetry and insist, at the same time, that poetry devotedly read and devoured by such numbers of people can't be any good. Ezra Pound—for instance—can be appreciated by only a very few, say armies of culture-vultures every day as they drive through the *Cantos* with apparent ecstacy and understanding. Masters was too successful to be honest, I've heard it said: a rather touching remark, perhaps, to come from an enlightened representative of a people notoriously not averse to success in any way of life. But it was Masters' ironic honesty that made **Spoon River** so popular among its denigrators. Americans seem to enjoy being furious and indignant at being kicked in their most sensitive places—and what more sensitive a place than that great, dry backbone, the Middle West?

People bought and read **Spoon River,** when it first appeared, for many reasons, few of which had anything to do with the undoubted fact that it was poetry. Many people read it in order to deny that it was true; many, discovering that in essence it was, denied it even more loudly. One of the chief reactions to these angry, sardonic, moving poems seemed to be: '*Some* of the inhabitants of small towns in Illinois may indeed be narrow-minded and corrupt, fanatically joyless, respectable to the point of insanity, malevolent and malcontent, but not in the Illinois towns in which *we* live.' "East is East and West is West, but the Middle West is terrible," Louis Untermeyer once wrote, but he was a sophisticated cosmopolitan raconteur and man-of-smart-letters, and his opinion of the *Real America* could be taken as merely ignorant and facetious. . . . Masters, however, was a proper Middle-Westerner; he knew what he was writing about; and his detestation of the bitter and crippling puritanism in which he struggled and simmered up was nothing less than treacherous. 'He knows us too well, the liar,' was a common attitude.

I am very fond, myself, of the writers who came out of the Middle West round about the beginning of the First World War. All the stale literary guidebook phrases aside—the 'honest ruggedness,' the 'pioneering vitality,' the 'earthy humor,' the 'undying folk tradition,' etc.—the hick-town radicals and iconoclasts, the sports journalists, the contributors to *Reedy's Mirror,* the drinking, noisy Chicago preachers and atheists and ballad singers and shabby professional men, did bring something rough and good into a language that was dying on its feet; and not its own feet, either.

There is Vachel Lindsay: the semireligious revivalist; recreator of railroad songs and sagas. . . . And Sherwood Anderson, whose book of stories, *Winesburg, Ohio,* is so near in place and spirit to **Spoon River,** but whose remembered vision of youth in that rich, remote, constricting, Main-Streeted desert is so much more detailed and more gentle, in spite of its terrors. And Carl Sandburg, born of Swedish immigrant parents, who, when he began to write about the packinghouses and factories of Chicago, did not see them as ephemeral features of an industrial nightmare but as living and undeniable facts of concrete, steel, flesh, and blood, who knew that the material of legend and song and ballad can never die so long as there are men working together. And, most of all, Edgar Lee Masters, jaundiced missionary, stubborn tub-thumper with a snarl and a flourish, acute in the particulars of ironic portraiture and lavish with high-blown abstractions, verbose, grotesquely concise, a man with a temper he wouldn't sell for a fortune.

In this sequence of poems, the dead of the town of Spoon River speak, from the graveyard on the Hill, their honest epitaphs. Or, rather, they speak as honestly as they can, having, while on earth, been defeated by their honesty and therefore grown bitter, or by their dishonesty and therefore grown suspicious of the motives of all others. In life, they had failed to make their peace with the world; now, in death, they are trying to make their peace with God in whom they might not even believe.

'Here lies the body of '—and then the name the monumental mason insignificantly engraved. Masters stopped at 'Here lies,' and then engraved his fierce, wounded, compassionate version of the skewball truth. He was never deluded into thinking that the truth is simple and one-sided, that values are clearly defined: he knew that the true motives of men about their business on earth are complex and muddled, that man moves in a mysterious way his blunders to perform, that the heart is not only a bloody pumping muscle but an old ball, too, of wet woolly fluff in the breast, a "foul rag-and-bone shop," in Yeats's phrase, a nest of errors, a terrible compulsion that lives by its hurt. And, what is more, he knew that people had poetry always, even if it wasn't always very good.

He wrote about the war between the sexes. The great gulf between men, that was created by the laws of men. The incompatibility of those who live their short lives together because of economic convenience, loneliness, the cavernous and ever-increasing distance from the first maternal grave, casual physical desire. Not that the reasons of economic convenience, or the assuaging of casual, though none the less urgent, lust are, in themselves, inconductive to a state of tranquility between two people lost; but who wants tranquility? Better burn than marry, if marriage puts the fire out.

He wrote about waste: how man wastes his vitality in the pursuit of cynical irrelevancies; and his aspirations through his allegiance to the bad laws, theologies, social institutions and discriminations, the injustices, greeds and fears, that have constantly and resentfully been reinforced by all those human beings of the past who also have suffered and died of them.

He wrote about the waste of man, but loudly, awkwardly, passionately revered the possibilities of greatness in what there was to waste. (pp. 68-9, 115)

Dylan Thomas, "Dylan Thomas on Edgar Lee Masters," in Harper's Bazaar, *No. 3019, June, 1963, pp. 68-9, 115.*

Herb Russell (essay date 1976)

[*In the following excerpt, Russell examines the four volumes of poetry that followed the* Spoon River Anthology *to trace what he considers Masters's personal and artistic decline. In his analysis of these works written between 1916 and 1919, Russell notes that Masters began this period as a romantic idealist, but "soon descended to rancor and disgust."*]

The years from 1916 to 1919 form an important and interesting segment of Edgar Lee Masters' career, but unfortunately too little is known about this period of his life, and the books published during these years have received almost no attention from scholars. The years that led up to *Spoon River Anthology* (1915) are well documented through Masters' autobiography, *Across Spoon River* (1936), but after he became famous not much is known about the man—except that his writing deteriorated. During this World War I period Masters produced four volumes of poetry. In the first of these, *Songs and Satires* (1916), he published poems which he characterized as "new," but since many of them were simply chosen from among the hundreds of poems he had written earlier, their real interest lies in why Masters printed the particular ones that he did. Three later volumes, *The Great Valley* (1916), *Toward the Gulf* (1918), and *Starved Rock* (1919), also contain poems which are not especially distinguished but which are well worth examining for at least three reasons. First, many of them reflect events which came after 1915, and thus they provide a perspective on Masters' attitudes and interests during the period just after *Spoon River Anthology,* which had made him the most talked-about poet in America. Second, they offer various special insights into Masters' esthetic problems, his struggles and failures as a poet. Third—and perhaps most important—these books, in conjunction with *Songs and Satires,* suggest a solution to the riddle of why Masters never wrote another book equal to *Spoon River.*

The first book to follow *Spoon River* has often puzzled critics because Masters returned to some of the banal themes of an earlier time. Three of the lyrics in *Songs and Satires* had appeared in his first collection of poems, *A Book of Verses* (1898), and several others show (through form and style) evidence of having been composed much earlier—before the free verse movement had gained momentum. However, it is not the quality of the poems which I want to discuss, nor the dates of their composition, but rather the question of why Masters chose to publish these particular poems as the successors to *Spoon River.*

Fourteen of the forty-five lyrics in *Songs and Satires* stress achievement or dedication to a goal, and concern romantic idealists—many of whom undergo major tests on their long marches to success. Implicit in several poems is the suggestion that the individual owes it to himself to follow through with his early ideals. The quest for achievement is often linked to a religious concept and given the quality of a crusade, and a couple of the poems are even based on figures from the Bible: **"Simon Surnamed Peter"** and **"All Life in a Life"** (on Christ). The essentially religious nature of the idealist's quest is also reflected in the title of another poem, **"Soul's Desire,"** and in **"The Star,"** where fulfillment of the ideal leads to spiritual health and peace. . . . (pp. 74-5)

His secular romantics work with much the same zeal. Some look for the ideal in beauty (as in **"Helen of Troy,"** excerpted from the 1898 volume), some in love (as in **"A Study"**), while others yearn for the visionary capacity itself, as in **"The Vision."** Even war, generally excoriated by Masters, is seen as a possible expression of human vision in **"O Glorious France,"** in which he says of the soldiers: "life to these / Prophetic and enraptured souls is vision." He concludes the poem by describing how "the soul of man / May to one greatest purpose make itself / A lens of clearness."

Of the remaining poems in *Songs and Satires* a few show signs of an irascible state of mind, such as **"The Cocked Hat,"** a study of William Jennings Bryan, and **"On a Bust,"** in which the speaker says to the bronze head of an unnamed leader:

> You cannot glorify
> Our dreams, or aspirations, or deep thirst.
> To you the world's a fig tree which is curst.
> You have preached every faith but to betray;
> The artist shows us you have had your day.

But in most of the poems Masters is as congenial as he ever was to be in print. He is especially cordial in **"William Marion Reedy,"** praising the editor whose advice he so respected by comparing him to Buddha (for wisdom) and Rabelais (for humor). All in all, however, there are few satisfying poems in the volume. One other that is at least worth reading is **"Silence,"** which was for many years his most frequently anthologized poem. (p. 75)

Because so many of the poems in *Songs and Satires* repeat the same theme—a dogged devotion to idealistic achievement—the internal evidence suggests that Masters was here giving expression to the personal philosophy which had worked so well for him. He had, after all, achieved his long-sought goal of literary eminence by never giving up and by dint of hard work. The question for the future was how would he react in print when the philosophy he seemed to tout did not result in a continuation of his success.

After the success of *Spoon River Anthology,* and the publication of some earlier poems in *Songs and Satires,* Masters turned back to the Illinois countryside as subject matter for his next three volumes. For several reasons he also gravitated toward the iconoclasm which had worked so successfully in the epitaphs. Implicit in his choice of titles, however, is the ominous suggestion that he began this period of his career with hope and ended it with disgust. *The Great Valley* starts as a panoramic volume about the greatness of Illinois and the Midwest; it concludes with angry enumeration of the country's decline. *Toward the Gulf* continues the anger, but the emphasis is on Masters' personal losses, especially the end of his romantic idealism. *Starved Rock* reveals Masters as an introspective and bitter poet making irate attacks on those whom he blames for his, and the country's, woes.

In the first of these, *The Great Valley,* we see a brief continuation of the romantic side of Masters. The title poem, which opens the volume, has eight sections. In the first, "Fort Dearborn," Masters presents an idealized portrait of the pioneer history of Chicago. . . . Much later, in section eight ("Grant and Logan and Our Tears"), Masters contrasts this early culture with a more recent society which has grown up indifferent to the pioneer past. . . . Throughout the long opening poem, Masters stresses that the present is at variance with what once existed, and he speaks of a degeneracy, especially in politics and religion.

The chief political losses are associated with events which came during and after the Civil War, a war Masters blamed on Lincoln:

> he became a man who broke all law
> To have his law. He killed a million men
> For what he called the Union. . . .

Instead of a stable, rural, and essentially simple culture, Masters saw a new, urban society growing up indifferent to the old values. Instead of strong local governments—extolled by "The Little Giant" in "The Lincoln and Douglas Debates" section—there now seemed to be a loosely federated system of corruption, which the poet describes in "Hanging the Picture" (section five).

Elsewhere in *The Great Valley* Masters asserted that the venality of the modern city had passed to the country. This is especially evident in a trio of poems set in a rural village: **"Cato Braden," "Winston Prairie,"** and **"Will Boyden Lectures."** In the second of these, the poet attacked those who were responsible for this corruption, the "court-house rings and judges in the rings."

This rural-urban duality characterizes much of *The Great Valley.* Often a character reflects favorably on his own agrarian past or on that of the pioneers in the Midwest, as in **"Past and Present," "Memorabilia,"** and **"Worlds Back of Worlds."** In the last of these, the speaker meditates on the past: "The windmills, barns and houses swim / In a sphered ether, wheeling, dim." On the other hand, some of the more lengthy poems are about urban dwellers or urban values, and here we detect Masters' hostility. The subject of **"The Typical American?"** is described as "a cog-wheel in the filthy trade / Of justice courts, police, and graft in wine." (pp. 76-7)

We see a similar hostility and sense of loss when Masters turns to the subject of religion. Christianity had a good beginning in its attempt to achieve spiritual fulfillment, but as time went on, Christians took what they wished from pagan learning and then attempted to stifle or change the remaining elements of paganism—as he points out in **"The Apology of Demetrius."** Thus, in Masters' mind repression and Christianity were always joined. In **"Malachy Deagan"** he speaks of the innocent diversions of a small town "before the Puritan rake / Combed through the city." He elsewhere examines ways in which churches try to force people to act contrary to their own inclinations (**"The Mourner's Bench"** and **"The Church and the Hotel"**). He even shows how a man might lose his life for a minor breach of the moral code (in **"Steam Shovel Cut"**): "They hung him up for a little beer / With a woman on his knees." Masters chose as his champion in this fight against religion "the great agnostic," Robert Ingersoll, one of the most noted—and denounced—residents of turn-of-the-century Illinois. In **"Robert G. Ingersoll"** he labelled him "a general in the war of ideas for freedom."

Why Masters felt free to use his verse in such a vituperative way is partially explained in three other groups of poems from *The Great Valley.* They are important because they foreshadow the direction his later verse would take. These are the poems about the failure of idealists, the success of cynics, and the necessity of national reform. In **"The Search,"** the last poem in the volume, he tells of three romantics (Don Quixote, Hamlet, and Faust) whose idealism has led them to nothing, and all of Masters' other idealists, artists, and aspirant souls in the volume also fail. At one extreme we find a person unjustly punished—in **"The Furies"**—who speaks of "ambition that eludes, love never found" and "the memory of the dream." (pp. 77-8)

Contrasted with these lyrics about fictive idealists who fail are two much more interesting poems about real men—successes, whom Masters saw as cynics: **"Theodore Dreiser"** and **"John Cowper Powys."** Both figures are characterized as shrewd men unafraid to speak openly about society's ills. Their success comes in great part from their pessimism. . . . Given Masters' admiration for these two men, here characterized as scoffers and cynics, one wonders how much Masters' verse was influenced by his friendships.

That he was open to outside literary influences may be seen by his comments on the third area here under scrutiny, national reform. In **"Come Republic,"** one of the better poems in the volume, he sounds like the mature Whitman in his attacks on the depravity of politics, religion, and society:

> Come! United States of America,
> And you one hundred million souls, O Republic,
> Throw out your chests, lift up your heads,
> And walk with a soldier's stride.

Masters seems, however, to have been convinced that the "greater republic" for which he was looking was not coming very fast. He could hardly hope for the nation's betterment when it was obvious that the integrity of his own "great valley" was declining. What he could not know was that he himself was shortly to experience a decline.

His next book, *Toward the Gulf,* was written in 1917 in Michigan, and certain events there had a negative effect on his poetry. Just when it seemed he had established his reputation and could devote his time to writing, his dreams were suddenly dashed. He had hoped for years to retire to a rural place and to write in what he called a writer's "haven." He thought he had found such a place in Spring Lake, Michigan. However, after moving to that tiny community, he feuded with local residents, was plagued with the presence of an old girl-friend, and, as we also learn from the autobiography [*Across Spoon River*], was even considered a suspicious person after the war-hysteria hit. Masters complicated everything in September of 1917 by walking out of what he had long considered an impossible marriage.

His troubles may have been his own fault, but in his mind he was certain he had been driven out by religious fundamentalists and political conservatives. He says exactly this in his poem **"Spring Lake"** (in *Starved Rock*) where the artist-hero, "the God Apollo," is driven out of town by a posse of preachers, teachers, and dullards. Masters suggested that such philistines cost him his farm; there is little doubt that they also helped cost him his art, for he used his poetry (and much of his fiction) to punish them, to expose them, and at times simply to call them names. Put together during these trying circumstances, *Toward the*

Gulf is a record of losses. No fewer than fifteen of the forty-six poems discuss a romantic ideal which has in some way failed, and, significantly, the poems are more visibly subjective than in the previous volume.

All the idealistic people in these poems suffer a loss of hope. . . . Among those who lose the ideal vision, two are left baffled (in **"Mirage of the Desert"** and **"The Room of Mirrors"**), one grows bitter (in **"Black Eagle Returns to St. Joe"**), and one (in **"Heaven is But the Hour"**) mourns its loss: "The tragedy is when Life has made you over / And denied you, and dulled your dreams." Another (in **"The Landscape"**) must rely on memory to return him to the days of his youth, when romance was a possibility: "In the room where the dormer windows look— / There were your knight and the tattered book." It is significant too that the penultimate poem in the volume is **"The End of the Search,"** in which the same three figures found in **"The Search"** in the previous book are frustrated in their quest. One finally "sings a song of Euphorion / To hide his heart's despair." The very title of the poem serves notice that Masters himself is no longer a philosophical traveler with idealists.

His next book, **Starved Rock,** simply became a vehicle for the poet to revenge himself on his enemies. The title poem is an apologia, of sorts, for what follows. In it Masters writes from the vantage point of the Illini Indians who perished on Starved Rock. Like the poet, they perished in what they had thought would be a haven: "And this starved scarp of stone / Is now the emblem of our tribulation."

Unlike the Illini, however, Masters is able to counterattack. In **"Oh You Sabbatarians!"** he denounces the villagers of Spring Lake and ridicules what the town holds sacred. His vituperation is so intense that his lines barely pass for verse:

> Oh you sabbatarians, methodists and puritans;
> You bigots, devotees and ranters;
> You formalists, pietists and fanatics,
> Teetotalers and hydropots. . . .

Elsewhere he attacks simplistic views of God and Christ (in **"Mournin' for Religion"**), refers to divinity students as "crook-nosed psychopaths" and "thick-lipped onanists" (in **"They'd Never Know Me Now"**), shows how politicians dupe the faithful (in **"The Christian Statesman"**), and even invokes the aid of a pagan goddess (in **"Pallas Athene"**) to rid the world of certain strict Protestant sects. . . . (pp. 78-80)

While many of the poems in **Starved Rock** are personal invectives too nasty to pass for verse and are deservedly forgotten, the events which led up to the poems should be remembered: by 1919 the poet was at odds with his wife, was without a real home, and in certain respects, was without a country—for the "old America" he claimed to love was assuredly gone with the war. He was suspicious of the traditional institutions: marital, ecclesiastical, and political. His personal idealism had suffered severe blows, and he had fallen short in his own quest to be an increasingly admired writer and live on a fine estate. In fact, his estate would soon be entirely gone (with his divorce), and his reputation as a writer was in decline.

Thus, while Masters began the period after **Spoon River**

at the height of his fame and with a desire "to memorialize Illinois and the country which had given so many distinguished men to America," he soon descended to rancor and disgust. He began this period by publishing early poems of idealism and by praising Illinois; he ended it by speaking of himself and his enemies. The hatred generated during these years manifested itself so frequently in his writings that it soon came to dominate, and neither the art nor the artist ever recovered. When Masters wrote his autobiography two decades later, he ended it with the year 1917. (p. 80)

> Herb Russell, "After 'Spoon River': Masters' Poetic Development 1916-1919," in The Vision of this Land: Studies of Vachel Lindsay, Edgar Lee Masters, and Carl Sandburg, edited by John E. Hallwas and Dennis J. Reader, Western Illinois University, 1976, pp. 74-81.

James Hurt   (essay date 1980)

[*In the following excerpt, Hurt studies aspects of Masters's personal life derived his reading of* Across Spoon River *and "The Genesis of Spoon River" to analyze the* Anthology *on a psychological level, stating that Masters created a subjective "portrait of the artist as a small town."*]

To regard Spoon River merely as a sociological microcosm, the small town as world, is to leave out a great deal of the book—the highly personal mysticism of many of the epitaphs of the last section, for example, the systematic imagery that runs throughout the collection, and the almost obsessive recurrence through the epitaphs of certain subjective motifs.

To do justice to the complexity of the **Anthology,** the reader must recognize the highly personal nature of the epitaphs, the extent to which they present not just the small town as world but also the poet himself as small town. Masters' constant presence in the book behind the formally "objective," dramatic epitaphs is inescapable, but it is usually dismissed or deplored as distortion, a skewing of "the truth" about Spoon River in the direction of Masters' various prejudices and preconceptions. The book's subjectivity might instead be regarded as its strength, its very reason for being, not as an objective critique of village life but as a sustained piece of self-revelation, a portrait of the artist as a small town. (pp. 403-04)

Masters wrote himself into the **Spoon River Anthology** not only as **"Webster Ford,"** his pseudonym for the magazine publication of the **Anthology,** but in a number of other epitaphs as well. But in 1933, he declared that his "cosmology" was best represented not by any epitaph in the original **Anthology** of 1915 but by the epitaph of **"Clifford Ridell"** in the **New Spoon River** of 1924 [see Master's "The Genesis of Spoon River" in Further Reading list]. This epitaph is significant enough in the interpretation of the **Spoon River Anthology** to merit quotation in full:

> Nothing outside of it,
> Boundless and filling all space.
> At one with itself, being all,
> And bent to no will but its own.
> Changing forever, but never diminishing.
> Every part of it true to the whole of it,

However a part of it wars with a part of it.
Disharmony comes from two, not one.
Friendly with itself, for otherwise
It would perish.
Is it good or evil? But how evil,
Since there is nothing with which to compare it,
And make it a blunder, a mistake?
Without disaster, having no fate, being fate itself.
Unutterable unity,
Eternal creation,
Changing, but never destroying, not even me!

The Ridell epitaph is an extreme example of the cloudy abstraction and pseudo-philosophy which mar much of the *New Spoon River* as well as some of the last-written epitaphs in the original *Anthology.* What is the subject of the speaker's discourse, the referent of "it" in the first line? Is it Life? Reality? The Universe? Creation? There is no way of knowing, and the poem does not make us care very much; it seems as if almost any capitalized abstraction will serve to make the poem an equally meaningful or meaningless piece of vaguely mystical wisdom.

Read philosophically, the poem is insignificant; read psychologically, it is considerably more revealing. The last three words of the poem are a startling plunge from the heights of abstract impersonality into the personal and the dramatic: "not even me." With these words, we are forced to rethink the entire poem, not as a philosophical generalization, but as a dramatic utterance, an expression by a specific person of his perceptions of the world and of himself. The tone of those last three words is a complex combination of self-loathing and defiance. If "it" ever turned to destruction, the first to be destroyed would be "me," a self which is perhaps especially guilty or especially vulnerable. Mingled with this attitude is a suggestion of defiance, as well, a sense of daring "it" to do its worst and determining not to be destroyed.

If we read back from these final words, the entire poem expresses not so much a philosophy or a "cosmology" as a psychological position. The speaker is tormented by conflicts and divisions in which "a part of it wars with a part of it." But he attempts to transcend these divisions by looking beyond them to a vision of seamless unity, "every part of it true to the whole of it," beyond the categories of will, of good and evil, and of fate, endlessly changing but never destroying.

Such a vision seems to have more in it of a wish than of a firm belief. The self-hatred of the last three words gives a retrospective reality to the disharmony, evil, and disaster of the preceding lines, compared to which the perhaps overvehement assertion of an "unutterable unity," an "eternal creation," seems an expression of yearning rather than of faith. The epitaph has in it none of the pithy, anecdotal detail that makes many of the poems in the earlier *Anthology* so memorable. Nevertheless, it conveys a strong sense of the personality of **"Clifford Ridell"** as a man tormented to the point of obsession with disharmonies, perhaps both internal and external, and yearning, almost beyond hope, for integration and unity.

This psychological position is the one that underlies the *Spoon River Anthology;* this is the "cosmology" that governs the "microcosm" of Spoon River, however it may be rationalized into political views, theories of society, and various other doctrines.

Masters himself repeatedly made clear that the composition of the *Spoon River Anthology* coincided with the most important psychological crisis in his life and that the epitaphs were both an expression of that crisis and a means of working through it. He began to write the epitaphs without previous planning and in a style unlike his voluminous earlier work, and as the composition proceeded over a period of about eight months, it became the means and expression of a gradual loss of self, the collapse of strained psychological defenses, a rapid psychological regression, and ultimately a kind of symbolic death. The characters in the *Anthology* were not the products of ordinary memory or nostalgia, but Masters' own ghosts, internalized images of primal conflicts dredged up and confronted through the medium of his art.

Masters left two full and moving accounts of the psychological crisis that produced the *Anthology.* The earliest published account appeared in the *American Mercury* in 1933 in an article called "The Genesis of Spoon River." This account was the basis of the fuller account which appeared in Masters' autobiography *Across Spoon River* (1936).

The book and the crisis began on the weekend of May 20, 1914, when Masters' mother, Emma Masters, visited him in Chicago, and they spent the weekend reminiscing about people and events in Petersburg and Lewistown. Masters describes this as a "truly wonderful" experience, and uses the language of regression to describe his feelings: "Along the way I was reinvested with myself in those incarnations that had long since surrendered their sheaths to the changes of the years." On Sunday, he walked her to the train station and then walked back home, "full of a strange pensiveness." He particularly recalls the sound of a church bell and a feeling of spring in the air. He immediately went to his room and wrote **"The Hill,"** the opening piece in the *Anthology,* and wrote "two or three" of the epitaphs. (pp. 404-07)

Once he had begun, Masters produced the epitaphs very rapidly, despite heavy court commitments which his law practice required. The only block seems to have been Masters' initial uncertainty about the merit of the new work. Actually, one epitaph had been written earlier as an experiment in using the *Greek Anthology* poems as models, that of **"Theodore the Poet,"** a whimsical tribute to Theodore Dreiser. The first submission to William Marion Reedy, the *Mirror's* editor, was **"The Hill," "Fletcher McGee,"** and **"Hod Putt,"** and Masters reported that he had scrawled across the top of the manuscript the title *Spoon River Anthology,* regarding it as "the most preposterous title known to the realm of books," apparently as a friendly jibe at Reedy's tastes. When Reedy immediately accepted the poems, Masters wanted to change the title to the conventionally pretty *Pleasant Plains Anthology,* but Reedy insisted that it remain the *Spoon River Anthology.* Once this initial doubt had been overcome, Masters apparently surrendered to what seemed to him an almost miraculous flooding out of material. He wrote the epitaphs, he said, on Saturday afternoons and Sundays, "on the street car, or in court, or at luncheon, or at night after I had gone to bed." (pp. 407-08)

As the writing proceeded over an eight-month period, Masters began to experience feelings of possession and depersonalization. . . . He also describes himself [in

Across Spoon River] as being in a "hypersensitive" state of "clairvoyance and clairaudience," and describes a recurring feeling of "lightness of body," in which he felt he could "float to the ceiling" or "drift out the window without falling."

Masters himself points out that the progress of his state of mind during this period can be retraced by examining the order of composition of the poems and their publication in Reedy's magazine. (The order in which they appear in the final book is unrelated to the order of composition). This progress seems to have been from comparatively recent memories, treated more or less whimsically or ironically, to earlier, more personal, and more deeply repressed ones. (pp. 408-09)

In [the *Mirror's*] issue of January 15, Masters epitaphed himself as **"Webster Ford,"** the pseudonym under which the poems had appeared. "That was the last. And I was about ready to be laid away and given a stone with these verses." When Reedy revealed the identity of "Webster Ford," against Masters' better judgment, in the issue of November 20, 1915, Masters reported that he read the article announcing him as the author "with a kind of terror, a kind of sickness, such as one might feel who has died and for a moment is permitted to look down upon the body that he has abandoned." Almost immediately after the publication of the **"Webster Ford"** epitaph Masters developed a severe cold which confined him to his home, and ten days later, he contracted pneumonia. The illness was severe, the doctor warned Mrs. Masters that he might not recover, and his father came for a deathbed visit. He reached the crisis of the illness precisely one week after it had begun. . . . [Hallucinatory] sensations are of course not uncommon in cases of high fever, but in association with the recurring feelings of loss of self over the preceding several months, they take on a particular significance. It appears likely that the composition of the *Spoon River Anthology* was intimately linked with a severe ego-crisis on the part of Masters, which began with his mother's visit in May, which stretched through eight months of regressive activity accompanied by increasingly powerful feelings of loss of self and which culminated in this powerful experience, during a high fever and physical collapse, of ultimate regression and symbolic death. (pp. 409-10)

The materials for understanding the background of Masters' collapse, its meaning, and the part the composition of the *Spoon River Anthology* had in it are to be found in *Across Spoon River* itself. The autobiography is a working out of the themes of the Ridell epitaph in terms of a life history. Masters' personal world he sees as locked in a web of desperate conflict, each part of it warring with another part. Every thesis—father, Petersburg, the South, the law—has its antithesis—mother, Lewistown, the North, poetry—and the two stand frozen in perpetual opposition. Nothing is ever forgotten or softened by the passing of time; childhood sibling rivalries are wounds as fresh at the age of sixty-seven as at the age of six. The rare images of fusion or unity, for example his grandparents' home, are presented as almost impossibly remote, more objects of helpless yearning than attainable goals. All these labyrinthine conflicts are, however, externalized, projected onto the outside world. Masters presents himself as assaulted by division, but seldom as divided himself. For the most part, his favorite image of himself suggests a powerful bull,

set about by bulldogs (or more often, stinging insects), but doggedly pushing his way forward. "As always in my life," he writes in a characteristic passage, "my head was down, and I was thrusting my way forward." collapse, of ultimate regression and symbolic death. (pp. 409-10)

As *Across Spoon River* recasts the vision of **"Clifford Ridell"** as an autobiographical narrative, so the *Spoon River Anthology* projects the same vision as an imaginary town. Or rather two towns, for the most fundamental conflict in the *Anthology* is between the worlds of Petersburg and Lewistown. It is part of the plan of the sequence that the towns be melded in a single composite, but the melding is not quite complete, and the careful reader of the *Anthology* can still see the joints. It is not quite accurate to write, as some have done, of Masters' "ambivalence" or his "love-hate relationship" with the small town. The ambivalence is, typically for Masters, translated into radical conflict, with all the love going to Petersburg and all the hate going to Lewistown. He makes the contrast explicit in his article . . . "The Genesis of Spoon River." Petersburg was a "genial neighborhood of fiddlers, dancers and feasters," and it "furnished the purest springs for the *Anthology,* and colored the noblest portraits of the book." Petersburg was heavily Southern in population and spirit; it had "no New England influences of any moment," including Calvinism and such Puritan constraints as Prohibitionism or taboos on dancing. While Petersburg was rural and Southern, Lewistown was urban and Northern; it was "inhabited by a people of tough and muscular minds, where political lines were bitterly drawn by the G.A.R., and competition at the bar was intense, and where New England and Calvinism waged a death struggle on the matter of Prohibition and the church with the Virginians and free livers." "It was this atmosphere of Northern light and cold winds," Masters wrote, "that clarified my mind at last to the beauty of the Petersburg material, and pointed with steel the pen with which I drew the microcosm of the Spoon river country."

Masters himself hints that the distinction between Petersburg and Lewistown survives in the final version of the *Anthology* when he writes that there were "fifty-three poems with names drawn from the Petersburg-New Salem-Concord-Sandridge country; and sixty-five from the Spoon river country." But one does not need to know the origins of the names; the distinction is clear on internal evidence alone. Characters in the *Anthology* tend to fall into two groups, the members of which refer to each other but not to members of the other group. Thus references to the Hatfields, the Sievers, Fiddler Jones, etc. identify epitaphs as "Petersburg" epitaphs, while references to Thomas Rhodes, Editor Whedon, Doctor Meyers, the Reverend Abner Peet, etc. mark the "Lewistown" epitaphs. Internal evidence of this kind allows us to place twenty-eight of Masters' fifty-three epitaphs in Petersburg, and sixty-five of Masters' sixty-six in Lewistown. (pp. 420-21)

These figures are not significant in themselves—certainly the effect the *Anthology* leaves on a casual reader is that there is only one town—but they do demonstrate the way Masters built into his composite "Spoon River" not a vague ambivalence but a precise and well articulated polarity, the one he associated with Petersburg and Lewistown.

Portrait of Masters as a young man.

ters' early literary ambitions and later became a writer herself.

Looked at from a slightly different angle, however, the Pantiers seem to be Masters himself and his wife. Some of the tensions in Masters' first marriage replicated, perhaps not coincidentally, those in his parents' marriage, and certainly we can hear behind Mrs. Pantier's distaste for whiskey, onions, and sex the voice of Helen Jenkins, who made Masters serve a year of church-going and abstinence from whiskey and cigars before she would marry him. (pp. 421-22)

Whatever its models, the Pantier misalliance, and all the other relationships it sets in motion, is a complex tissue of opposing forces which are never reconciled though the multiple points of view temper the bitterness of individual voices. Trainor, the Druggist, has an important part of the truth when he says that Pantier and his wife were "good in themselves, but evil toward each other: / He oxygen, she hydrogen, / Their son, a devastating fire." Pantier himself is full of bitterness and self-pity: "she, who survives me, snared my soul / With a snare which bled me to death." But his wife, when she speaks for herself, is by no means an unsympathetic character, absurd perhaps in her pride at being a "lady" and having "delicate tastes," but as tragic a victim as Pantier in that "law and morality" have trapped her in a marriage with a man with whom having the "marital relation" "fills you with disgust / Everytime you think of it—while you think of it / Everytime you see him."

Dora Williams is the indirect victim of the Pantiers' conflicts. Seduced by Reuben Pantier, their troubled son, and rejected by him, she has, however, managed to turn the tables on men. A series of rich husbands who died quickly left her "versed in the world and rich" until her last husband, an Italian count, poisoned her. She finds in death release from the Pantiers' conflicts as they were transmitted to her: on her tomb in Rome is carved, *"Contessa Navigato / Implora eterna quiete."* (p. 423)

The chief victim of the combination of oxygen and hydrogen that was the Pantiers' marriage, however, is their son Reuben, who has become a "devastating fire" of dissipation and self-destructiveness. It takes Emily Sparks, his former teacher with "the virgin heart," to see that Reuben is torn between "the clay" and "the fire" and that Reuben's fire could be not the fire of self-destruction but the purifying fire of the spirit. "My boy," she calls, "wherever you are, / Work for your soul's sake, / That all the clay of you, all of the dross of you, / May yield to the fire of you, / Till the fire is nothing but light . . . / Nothing but light!"

The story of the Pantiers' marriage and its multiple reverberations may be taken as a paradigm of life in Spoon River. There is always the potentiality—perhaps a memory, perhaps a hope—of a seamless unity, but actual life is a clash of opposites; everywhere "a part of it wars with a part of it." The rift that runs through the Pantier marriage reappears in every aspect of life in Spoon River: religion, politics, art, work. The life-hating Puritanism of the Rev. Abner Peet wars against the tolerant compassion of a Doctor Meyers; Elliott Hawkins' political conservatism wars with John Cabanis' liberal idealism; Petit the Poet's fashionable but trivial verses triumph over the ridiculed but

Fortunately, Masters did not extend this polarity to the individuals in the *Anthology.* Not all the villains come from Lewistown and not all the heroes come from Petersburg. Most of the people in the collection are of "mixed character," complex mixtures of good and bad, strength and weakness. One of the most striking sustained groups of epitaphs is the "Pantier" group, which includes seven epitaphs grouped together—**"Benjamin Pantier," "Mrs. Benjamin Pantier," "Reuben Pantier," "Emily Sparks,"** and **"Trainor the Druggist"**—and two later in the collection: **"Dora Williams"** and **"Mrs. Williams."** The models for the Pantier family are complex and instructive. The chief model would appear to be Masters' own family. The conflict between the earthy, "common" country lawyer Benjamin Pantier and his "delicate," "artistic" wife seems to duplicate fairly exactly the relationship between his parents described in *Across Spoon River.* This would make **"Reuben Pantier,"** their son, Masters himself, and again the identification seems accurate. Reuben, scarred by the conflict between his mother and father and the object of gossip about his sex life in Spoon River, goes out into the world and passes through "every peril known / Of wine and women and the joy of life." The model for his idealistic teacher, **"Emily Sparks,"** is also implicitly identified in *Across Spoon River* as Mary Fisher, who encouraged Mas-

passionate poetry of Minerva Jones, and the self-destructive work ethic of a Cooney Potter clashes with the joyful playfulness of a Fiddler Jones.

This desperate vision of life as ceaseless, radical conflict is not unrelieved by rays of hope, however. Masters' Dantean division of the book into an Inferno of "fools, drunkards, and failures," a Purgatory of "people of one-birth minds," and a Paradise of "heroes and enlightened spirits" has perhaps obscured a more fundamental historical division among past, present, and future. A small group of epitaphs, most notably those of Lucinda and Davis Matlock, are voices out of a past culture that was unified and coherent. In their lives, work, play, marriage, religion, and social relationships were harmonious and fulfilling, welded together by a passionate joy in living. The photographer Rutherford McDowell senses this lost unity in the photographs of the old pioneers and studies their faces to try to understand their secret. . . . (pp. 423-25)

It is not so much that the "third generation," that of the present, are "fools, drunkards, and failures" as that they live in a society at war with itself. There are many heroes even in the first, "Inferno" section of the *Anthology:* Kinsey Keene, Emily Sparks, Doctor Meyers, Doc Hill, Dorcas Gustine. If such people are failures, it is not through any deficiency of their own but because they are caught up and sometimes crushed in the forces clashing around them. . . . Many transformations of Masters' father and of one aspect of Masters himself move through this section in figures forced by their society into a perpetual stance of defiance, figures such as Dorcas Gustine, Jefferson Howard, and Kinsey Keene, who says, with Cambronne at Waterloo, "merde" to the whole Spoon River establishment. Such men are admirable but tragically reduced from the models of the past such as Davis Matlock or Aaron Hatfield. To be involved in such a society is to be involved in eternal warfare.

Many of the "heroes and enlightened spirits" of the last section of the *Anthology,* those who have risen above the conflicts of Spoon River to a vision of integration and unity, are therefore outside the mainstream of Spoon River life, eccentrics, recluses, and dropouts who have rejected the establishment or have been rejected by it and who live in the private world of the imagination where they find the hope of some future redemption of the fallen world of Spoon River. This final section opens with the **"Anne Rutledge"** epitaph and contains most of the idealized pioneer epitaphs as well as those of the visionaries of the future. This juxtaposition of the harmony of the past and the hope of the future enriches the implications of each. The epitaph of Davis Matlock, for example, is immediately followed by that of the contemporary hero Herman Altman, whose very name suggests that in his idealism he is an "old man" like Matlock. And the epitaph of the pioneer Aaron Hatfield is immediately preceded by that of Russell Kincaid, who finds the same unity in the identification with nature that Hatfield found in the communion at Concord Church.

Images of a unity to counter the fragmentation of Spoon River life appear throughout the *Anthology,* though they are concentrated in this last third. The most pervasive and important of these is announced by Emily Sparks (a significant name in itself) when she tells Reuben Pantier to work that his clay may yield to his fire, "Till the fire is

nothing but light! . . . / Nothing but light!" The patron god of the *Spoon River Anthology,* as Masters makes clear in the Webster Ford epitaph, is Apollo, and imagery of fire, light, and the sun appear throughout in connection with the ecstatic achievement of unity. The image is treated comically in the epitaph of Jonathan Swift Somers, the voice along with Webster Ford of Masters as poet, perhaps his satirical, "cyclopean" eye as opposed to the "dreaming," "mystical" eyes of Webster Ford. Somers hopes that when, after he has risen to a total vision of the world, his soul takes fire, life will not "fiddle" as Nero did. (pp. 425-27)

But the earth and the clay are not always images of blindness and the flesh. As in much mystical thought, Masters' images of ecstatic integration tend to be double. Reuben Pantier's fire may be either a "devastating fire" of self-destruction or a purifying fire of self-transcendence. In the same way, the earth may be not the prison of the spirit but the gateway to it. The symbol of Siever's apple orchard moves through the *Anthology* as a means of mystic integration with natural process. Siever himself lies under the roots of a northern-spy apple tree, to "move in the chemic change and circle of life, / Into the soil and into the flesh of the tree, / And into the living epitaphs / Of redder apples!" And the village idiot Willie Metcalf attains to a kind of wisdom denied wiser heads when he has the feeling that he was not "a separate thing from the earth." "I never knew," he says, "whether I was a part of the earth / With flowers growing in me, or whether I walked— / Now I know."

The stars and music similarly stand as images of mystic unity. Alfonso Churchill has an astronomer's vision of the stars, while Elijah Browning has a mystic's apprehension of them. In his strange dream-vision which immediately precedes the final epitaph of Webster Ford, he ascends through levels of life and experience—childhood, commerce, love—to a mountain peak with a solitary star above it. (p. 427)

These various images of harmony and unity are all highly private and mystical; there is not much sense in the concluding sections of the *Anthology* of a political solution to the conflicts in Spoon River, little more than Anne Rutledge's hope that the Republic may "bloom forever" from the dust of her bosom. A strong death wish moves behind these images of transcendent unity. To achieve peace and integration one must move beyond consciousness itself into the "final flame" or the cycles of nature or the high, cold star beyond life.

The movement toward the peace of death culminates in **"Webster Ford,"** the last epitaph in the book and Masters' own literary epitaph. In this extraordinary poem, addressed to the "Delphic Apollo," Masters associates himself with Mickey M'Grew, a minor figure from earlier in the *Anthology.* Mickey M'Grew is one of Masters' many doubles in the *Anthology;* he expresses the familiar Masters attitude that "It was just like everything else in life; / Something outside myself drew me down, / My own strength never failed me." Forced to give up the money to his father that he had saved for an education, he has became a man-of-all-work in Spoon River. Atop the town water-tower, which he is cleaning, he unhooks his safety rope and laughs as he flings his arms over the lip of the tower. But they slip on the "treacherous slime" and he plunges to his death, "down, down, down . . . Through bellowing darkness!"

Masters seems to feel a deep kinship with Mickey M'Grew and his one heroic, defiant gesture followed by a plunge into a "bellowing darkness." This affinity is further explored in **"Webster Ford."** Ford, M'Grew, and the banker's son have seen a vision of Apollo on the river bank at sunset. The banker's son has denied the vision: "It's light / By the flags at the water's edge, you half-witted fools." Ford and M'Grew, as spiritual brothers, acknowledge the vision; M'Grew, though he recognizes the vision only as "a ghost," carries the vision of Apollo with him to his death. Ford's own stewardship of the vision is a sad summary of Masters' own spiritual life. He has hidden the vision, "for fear / Of the son of the banker," and Apollo has avenged himself by turning Ford into a tree, "growing indurant, turning to stone." But as the metamorphosis progresses, from the gradually hardening trunk and branches there burst forth laurel leaves, the pages of the *Spoon River Anthology.* " 'Tis vain, O youth," he cries, "to fly the call of Apollo." (pp. 428-29)

The shadows are gathering fast in the last pages of the *Spoon River Anthology,* and "Webster Ford's" last words are a race against the spreading numbness of death, that goal toward which the entire collection has been increasingly directed, a death which is the only real release from the painful conflicts of life.

Within days after writing this epitaph, Masters actually felt the numbness moving into his limbs and approached the threshold of death. And after a prolonged recovery and the appearance of the *Anthology* in book form, he felt that the book was alien to him, as if it had been written by another person. It seemed, he wrote, to be a "creation which had come from me and now seemed to have no relation to me." And in a sense it had been written by another person. The man who, under the influence of his mother's reminiscences, had begun the *Anthology* in the spring of 1914 had been engaged for years in an exhausting psychological struggle, preserving his own self-image as an invulnerable stoic, head down and pushing his way forward, by denying his own inner conflicts and projecting them into competing figures in the external world. The writing of the *Anthology* functioned both as an attempt to preserve this strategy by dramatizing it and as the signal of its ultimate collapse. The "swarms of powers and beings" Masters sensed hovering over his head as he wrote, both protesting and inspiring him to go on, were the projections of his own conflicts, now assuming an independent existence and taking their leave. The act of writing was an act of undoing, of moving backward through his life, symbolically killing the images of his conflicts, returning to his origins, and attempting to begin again. This act culminated in the symbolic suicide of the Webster Ford epitaph and the final fantasy of his illness, the music, the flame, the "black disk" of annihilation, and the "vast warm tide" of oceanic peace. Perhaps unfortunately, "rebirth" in fantasy is seldom a permanent transformation in real life. After a period of recovery, Masters appears to have gradually reconstructed a similar defense system, and the Masters of 1916 was not markedly different from the Masters of 1914.

The origins of a work of art are not necessarily relevant to its meaning. But in the case of the *Spoon River Anthology,* consideration of the poet in the poems suggests levels of depth and complexity in the poems that have generally been ignored. The collection is on its most fundamental level a spiritual autobiography, an account of "the poet's mind." Only upon this substructure are the microcosm of small-town life and the macrocosm of social criticism of American life constructed. It is largely beside the point to try to determine whether Spoon River presents a true "cross-section" of a real village, whether marriage was really as dreadful in 1900 as it seems to be in the *Anthology,* or whether such war really existed in small-town political life. Spoon River is a highly personal, highly subjective vision of small-town life and the national life, not an objective or scientific account. To ignore the personal dimension in the *Anthology* is to ignore its underlying structure, the significance of its symbolism, the nature of its emotional power and much else that makes it continue to command our interest. (pp. 429-31)

> *James Hurt, "The Sources of the Spoon: Edgar Lee Masters and the 'Spoon River Anthology',"* in The Centennial Review, Vol. XXIV, No. 4, Fall, 1980, pp. 403-31.

FURTHER READING

Alden, Raymond M. "Recent Poetry." *The Dial* LIX, No. 697 (24 June 1915): 26-30.

> Unfavorable essay on Imagism, *vers libre,* and other components of "new poetry" in which Alden denotes the *Spoon River Anthology* the *"reductio ad absurdum"* of modernist poetry.

Barnstone, Willis. Introduction to *The New Spoon River,* by Edgar Lee Masters, pp. xvii-xxvi. New York: Macmillan Co., 1968.

> Studies and compares the structure of the *Spoon River Anthology* and *The New Spoon River* to the *Greek Anthology.*

Burgess, Charles E. "Ancestral Lore in *Spoon River Anthology:* Fact and Fancy." *Papers on Language and Literature* 20, No. 2 (Spring 1984): 185-204.

> Examines ancestral lore that Masters drew upon in writing the Spoon River poems by focusing on the southern branches of Masters's family and his paternal grandmother Lucinda Masters.

Chandran, K. Narayana. "Revolt from the Grave: *Spoon River Anthology* by Edgar Lee Masters." *The Midwest Quarterly* XXIX, No. 4 (Summer 1988): 438-47.

> Discusses the symbolic significance of the rural community Spoon River.

Childs, Herbert Ellsworth. "Agrarianism and Sex: Edgar Lee Masters and the Modern Spirit." *The Sewanee Review* XLI (1933): 331-43.

> An analysis of Masters's poetry and novels that identify his position among writers of the 1920s. Childs focuses on what he considers the modern spirit of that era, placing Masters as a leader in the revolt against accepted codes of morality.

Crawford, John W. "Naturalistic Tendencies in *Spoon River Anthology*." *The CEA Critic* XXX, No. 9 (June 1968): 6, 8.
Characterizes *Spoon River Anthology* as a work that adheres to naturalistic tendencies. [See Ernest Earnest's rebuttal below].

Dell, Floyd. "Spoon River People." *The New Republic* II, No. 24 (17 April 1915): 14-15.
Discusses Masters's treatment of small-town life and his attitude toward American Romanticism.

Derleth, August. "Masters and the Revolt from the Village." *The Colorado Quarterly* VIII, No. 2 (Autumn 1959): 164-67.
Brief interview given in 1940 in which Masters offers his opinions on critics and contradicts the widely accepted "revolt from the village" theme in his work and other American writers of the Chicago Renaissance.

Duffey, Bernard. "Edgar Lee Masters: The Advent of Liberation." In his *The Chicago Renaissance in American Letters: A Critical History,* pp. 143-70. 1954. Reprint. Westport, Conn.: Greenwood Press, 1972.
Focusing on *Spoon River Anthology,* Duffey studies the Chicago Liberation movement during the early twentieth century, as well as Masters's personal life.

Earnest, Ernest. "A One-Eyed View of Spoon River." *The CEA Critic* XXXI, No. 2 (November 1968): 8-9.
Disputes John Crawford's analysis of the *Anthology* in his essay "Naturalistic Tendencies in *Spoon River Anthology*" [see above], citing that Crawford misrepresents the work by isolating only one theme.

Eliot, T. S. "Reflections on *Vers Libre*." *The New Statesman* VIII, No. 204 (3 March 1917): 518-19.
Maintains that *vers libre* does not exist as a verse form. In his brief reference to Masters, Eliot asserts that Masters's poetry suffers from an absence of "a more rigid verse-form."

Firkins, O. W. "The Return to Spoon River." *The Saturday Review of Literature* I, No. 11 (11 October 1924): 178.
Critique of *The New Spoon River.* Firkins discusses this work as Masters's attempt to continue writing unified, concise epitaphs as he did in *Spoon River Anthology.*

Flanagan, John T. *Edgar Lee Masters: The Spoon River Poet and his Critics.* Metuchen, N. J.: Scarecrow Press, 1974, 175 p.
Collection of critical responses to Masters's poetry and prose, including references from William Rose Benét, Amy Lowell, and H. L. Mencken.

Littell, Robert. "The New Spoon River." *The New Republic* XL, No. 514 (8 October 1924): 148.
Review of *The New Spoon River* in which Littell asserts that Masters focuses on his own thoughts and feelings and deemphasizes the individual characters in his poems.

Masters, Edgar Lee. "The Genesis of Spoon River." *The American Mercury* XXVIII, No. 109 (January 1933): 38-55.
Recounts the literary influences of *Spoon River Anthology* and the circumstances under which it was written.

Naverson, Robert. "*Spoon River Anthology:* An Introduction." *MidAmerica* VII (1980): 52-72.
Discusses principal themes and the structure of *Spoon River Anthology.*

"The New Movement in American Poetry." *The New York Times Review of Books* (7 January 1917): 1-2.
Review of *The Great Valley* in which the reviewer, citing a lack of subtleties, expresses disappointment in the volume.

Pavese, Cesare. "The *Spoon River Anthology*" and "The Dead at Spoon River." In his *American Literature: Essays and Opinions,* translated by Edwin Fussell, pp. 42-54; 168-76. Berkeley: University of California Press, 1970.
Explores ways in which *Spoon River Anthology* is a seminal representation of modern American literature.

Pratt, Julius W. "Whitman and Masters: A Contrast." *The South Atlantic Quarterly* XVI, No. 2 (April 1917): 155-58.
Asserts that Masters and Walt Whitman differ greatly in technique and philosophies.

Putzel, Max. "Crossing Spoon River." In his *The Man in the Mirror: William Marion Reedy and his Magazine,* pp. 193-216. Cambridge, Mass.: Harvard University Press, 1963.
Discusses circumstances leading to the publication of *Spoon River Anthology* in the *Mirror,* and summarizes the critical reaction to the *Anthology.*

Swenson, May. Introduction to *Spoon River Anthology,* by Edgar Lee Masters, pp. 5-13. New York: Collier Books, 1962.
Discusses biographical, polemical, and technical points of *Spoon River Anthology.*

Wrenn, John H., and Wrenn, Margaret M. *Edgar Lee Masters.* Boston: Twayne, 1983, 144 p.
Critical biography.

Octavio Paz

1914-

Mexican poet, essayist, critic, nonfiction writer, dramatist, editor, journalist, and translator.

Paz has earned international acclaim for works in which he seeks to reconcile divisive forces in human life. He stresses that language and love can provide means for attaining unity and wholeness, and his works accommodate such antithetical topics as culture and nature, the meditative and the sensuous, and the linear and circular nature of time. In his verse, Paz experiments with form to achieve clarity and directness while expressing a sense of vitality and vivacity. He commented: "Wouldn't it be better to turn life into poetry rather than to make poetry from life? And cannot poetry have as its primary objective, rather than the creation of poems, the creation of poetic moments?" Paz's works also reflect his knowledge of the history, myths, and landscape of Mexico as well as his interest in Surrealism, existentialism, Romanticism, Oriental thought, particularly Buddhism, and diverse political ideologies.

Paz was born in Mexico City. His mother's family had emigrated to Mexico from Spain and his father's ancestors traced their heritage to early Mexican settlers and indigenous peoples. Paz's paternal grandfather was a journalist and political activist, and his father, an attorney, joined Emiliano Zapata's agrarian revolution in the early 1900s. During the Mexican Civil War, Paz's family lost their home and relocated to a nearby suburb of Mexico City where they lived under financially unstable conditions. Nonetheless, Paz received his secondary education at a French school administered by Marist priests and later attended the National University of Mexico. While in his late teens, he began his literary career by founding *Barrandal,* an avant-garde journal, and published his first volume of poems, *Luna silvestre.* In 1937, Paz traveled to Spain and participated in several antifascist movements before moving on to France. In Paris, he became interested in Surrealism, a highly influential literary and artistic movement dedicated to examining the irrational, paranormal, and subconscious aspects of the human mind. After returning to Mexico in 1938, Paz founded and edited several literary and political periodicals and wrote newspaper columns on international affairs. In 1944, he traveled extensively in the United States, where he became influenced by the formal experiments of such modernist poets as William Carlos Williams and Wallace Stevens.

Paz joined the Mexican diplomatic service in 1955 and was assigned to the Mexican embassy in Paris. While in France, he became reacquainted with the aesthetics of Surrealism and the philosophy of existentialism, eventually favoring what he termed "the vital attitude" of Surrealism. During the 1950s, Paz's reputation as a major literary figure was secured with the publication of two nonfiction works and *Piedra de sol* (*Sun Stone*), a long poem generally considered his finest achievement in verse. Paz was named ambassador to India in 1962 and served in this position until 1968, when he resigned in protest following the

killings of student demonstrators in Mexico City by government forces. Since relinquishing his ambassadorship, Paz has traveled extensively while continuing his literary career.

In his early verse, Paz experimented with such diverse forms as the sonnet and free verse, reflecting his desire to renew and clarify Spanish language in order to lyrically evoke images and impressions. In many of these poems, Paz employs the surrealist technique of developing a series of related or unrelated images to emphasize sudden moments of perception, a particular emotional state, or a fusion of such polarities as dream and reality, life and death. According to Paz, Surrealism is a "negation of the contemporary world and at the same time an attempt to substitute other values for those of democratic bourgeois society: eroticism, poetry, imagination, liberty, spiritual adventure, vision." Topics of Paz's formative verse include political and social issues, the brutality of war, and eroticism and love. *Aguila o sol?* (*Eagle or Sun?*), one of his most important early volumes, is a sequence of visionary prose poems concerning the past, present, and future of Mexico. *Selected Poems,* published in 1963, and *Early Poems: 1935-1955,* contain representative compositions in Spanish and in English translation.

Critics frequently note that *Sun Stone,* which adheres to the arrangement of the Aztec calendar, initiates a more radical phase of experimentation in Paz's career. Comprising 584 eleven-syllable lines that form a circular sentence, this poem blends myth, cosmology, social commentary, and personal and historical references in a phantasmagoric presentation of images and allusions to project the psychological processes by which an individual attempts to make sense of existence. Sven Birkerts noted: "*Sun Stone* is, like so many of Paz's longer poems, a lyrically discursive exploration of time and memory, of erotic love, of art and writing, of myth and mysticism." The variety of forms and topics in Paz's later poems mirror his diverse interests. *Blanco,* widely considered his most complex work, consists of three columns of verse arranged in a chapbook format that folds out into a long single page. Each column develops four main themes relating to language, nature, and the means by which an individual analyzes and orders life. In *Ladera este: 1962-1968,* Paz blends simple diction and complicated syntax to create poems that investigate Oriental philosophy, religion, and art. In his long poem *Pasado en claro* (*A Draft of Shadows*), Paz examines selfhood and memory by focusing on poignant personal moments in the manner of William Wordsworth's autobiographical poem *The Prelude. Vuelta* collects topical verse that Paz wrote after resigning from his ambassadorship. *The Collected Poems of Octavio Paz, 1957-1987* reprints poems in Spanish and in English translation from the latter phase of his career. A recent volume, *Arbol adentro,* includes a sequence of highly descriptive poems devoted to such Surrealist painters as Marcel Duchamp and Joan Miró.

(For further information on Paz's life and career, see *Contemporary Literary Criticism,* Vols. 3, 4, 6, 10, 19, 51 and *Contemporary Authors,* Vols. 73-76.)

PRINCIPAL WORKS

POETRY

Luna silvestre   1933
Raiz del hombre   1937
Bajo tu clara sombra   1941
A la orilla del mundo y Primer dia: Bajo tu clara sombra, Raiz del hombre, Noche de resurrecciones   1942
Libertad abjo palabra   1949
Aguila o sol?   1951
   [*Aguila o sol? Eagle or Sun?*]   1970
Semillas para un himno   1954
Piedra de sol   1957
   [*Sun Stone*]   1963
La estación violenta   1958
Agua y viento   1959
Salamandra, 1958-1961   1962
Selected Poems   1963
Blanco   1967
La centana: Poemas, 1935-1968   1969
Ladera este: 1962-1968   1968
Configurations   1971
Renga: Un Poema   1972
Early Poems: 1935-1955   1973
Pasado en claro   1975
Vuelta   1976
Poemas, 1935-1975   1979

Selected Poems   1984
The Collected Poems of Octavio Paz, 1957-1987   1988
Arbol adentro   1988

OTHER MAJOR WORKS

El laberinto de la soledad   (nonfiction)   1950
   [*The Labryrinth of Solitude*]   1961
El arco y la lira: El poema, la revelación poetica, poesia, e historia   (literary criticism)   1956
   [*The Bow and the Lyre: The Poem, the Poetic Revelation, Poetry, and History*]   1973
Corriente alterna   (essays)   1967
   [*Alternating Current*]   1973
Conjunciones y disjunciones   (nonfiction)   1969
   [*Conjunctions and Disjunctions*]   1973
Posdata   (nonfiction)   1970
   [*The Other Mexico: Critique of the Pyramid*]   1972
Le singe grammairien   (nonfiction)   1972
   [published in Mexico as *El mono gramático,* 1974; *The Monkey Grammarian,* 1981]
Los hijos del Limo: Del romanticismo a la vanguardia   (literary criticism)   1974
   [*Children of the Mire: Modern Poetry from Romanticism to the Avant-Garde*]   1974
Tiempo nublado   (essays)   1984
   [*One Earth, Four or Five Worlds: Reflections on Contemporary History*]   1985
On Poets and Others   (essays)   1986
Convergences: Essays on Art and Literature   (essays)   1987

J. M. Cohen   (essay date 1966)

[*In the following excerpt taken from his book* Poetry of This Age *(1966), Cohen surveys Paz's early verse.*]

The first poet to draw together the Spanish and the Náhuatl strands of Mexican poetry has been Octavio Paz who has come to his task by way of a persistent questioning of all reality. 'Paz seems to have set out in search of the most desperate experience in order to emerge from it with at least a grain of hope', wrote the critic Ramón Xirau. Certainly Paz's early poetry is of violence and disbelief. Technically the influences upon him were both social and surrealist; he witnessed the defeat of the Spanish Republic, and shared with Aleixandre and Neruda the emotional rediscovery of man's physical kinship with nature. But unlike them he came through to no positive values. Paz's early poetry is so negative that it questions both the poet's own existence and the validity of the poetic act. But the solitude that he finds at the heart of every activity rouses in him a glimmer of expectation. Paz's search is in essence religious. In one of his few purely social poems, his **"Elegy for a friend killed in the civil war"**, he states that we stand at the opening of a new epoch in the world:

> [You died, comrade,
> at the burning dawn of the world.
> You died when your world
> and ours was scarcely dawning].

This is partially a political statement; Paz has always supposed that a new political organisation was a necessary prelude to the spiritual change that has been the true subject of his poetry. Like Neruda, he was, in his early writing, necessarily on the side of death, but all the time in search of some power with which to counterbalance it. He moved towards participation, but was driven back into solitude by lack of belief in his own existence. . . . (pp. 228-29)

Against this despair only one force could be set, the moment of experience outside time, which is the subject of Eliot's *Four Quartets*. But Paz's escape from his Waste Land was far from complete. Theoretically he had accepted a religious attitude: expectation began to outweigh despair. Yet the experience itself never took clear shape; or rather many experiences masqueraded as the true one; vision and hallucination remained indistinguishable, and Freud, the Marquis de Sade, Rimbaud, André Breton and the Masters of Zen Buddhism were all accepted on a par as prophets of the new certainty that could be born out of utter negation. In the poem **"La poesía"** (**"Poetry"**) the dilemma is stated:

> [Opposing images cloud my eyes,
> and other images
> from a greater depth deny these,
> like a burning babble,
> waters that a more secret and heavier water drowns].

The poet is describing the processes prior to the composition of his poem. This is a situation in which he finds himself unreal; only the poem, rising from a depth at which

> [Tranquillity and movement are the same]. . . .

triumphs over all contradictions and by its existence proves to the poet that he too exists. . . . (p. 229)

Yet in the next verse, the poem too is described as a dream, a dream in which there is both violence and movement. Paz is in fact most in love with the world at the moment when it seems about to slip away into abstraction. The moment of creation is for him a moment of intense living. The parallel is with the harsh imagery of Aleixandre's early poetry. But where Aleixandre moves in a direct line from solitude to participation, Paz, in three most important poems, sets out to reconcile the two opposites, solitude and utterance. The first is the principal piece in the book **Libertad bajo palabra** (**Liberty behind the Words**), a vision set in 1948, and entitled **"Himno entre ruinas"** (**"Hymn among the ruins"**). Here there is an alternation between stanzas of vision and stanzas of comment. The vision is at first abstract, of colour, sea and stone, but it is succeeded by an evocation of contemporary Mexico. Boys are smoking marihuana on top of an Aztec pyramid. Then in the third verse, the vision becomes more sensual; eyes and hands confirm and expand the message of the inner eye. But actuality again breaks in with a 'waste land' picture of Europe in ruins, and the rich consuming the poor. (p. 230)

The poet's thoughts divide, start again and lose motion. 'Must everything end in a spatter of stagnant water?' he asks. But the last stanza triumphantly proclaims that the poem begins where thinking stops; the solitary broodings of the early work are transcended; the minute becomes rich as the commenting mind sinks into peace:

> [Intellect finally incarnates in forms,

the two hostile halves are reconcile,
and the conscience-mirror liquifies,
becomes once more a fountain, a source of stories:
man a tree of images,
words that are flowers, that are fruit, that are deeds].

The title poem of a small collection of lyrics **Semillas para un himno** (**Seeds for a hymn**) which he published five years later, returns to the theme of the moment overflowing with all time in a manner somewhat reminiscent of Eliot. . . . (p. 231)

"Piedra de sol" (**"Sunstone"**), the outstanding poem in his next volume, **La estación violenta** (**The season of violence**) of 1958, is the most sustained piece that Paz has so far attempted. It is a hymn to the planet Venus in her two aspects as morning and evening star and, by Náhuatl symbolism, as sun and water. It is at the same time a hymn to sexual love as the supreme form of communion between creatures who are otherwise no more than shadows with no true experience of their own lives. . . . (pp. 231-32)

With the exception of T. S. Eliot, Octavio Paz is the only contemporary poet capable of feeling his metaphysics, and calling them to life. **"Piedra de sol"** is a closely organised poem, composed of precisely one line for each of the 584 days of the revolution of Venus. It is woven of two strands, that of memory and that of vision. For Paz calls up scenes of the past in which love has made life real—in particular a moment during the siege of Madrid in which two lovers embrace to 'defend their portion of eternity, their ration of time and paradise' in face of the Fascist bombardment. The conclusion of the poem, though philosophically more completely worked out, is similar in feeling to the conclusion of **"Himno entre ruinas"**, an affirmation of birth and light in contrast to the perpetual presence of death and shadow. In time all is dark, out of time lies the moment of communion, the sudden striking of the sun's light on the waters, Eliot's 'still point of the turning world'. One is carried back to the primal imagery of the first chapter of *Genesis*.

> [open your hand
> lady of seeds that are days,
> the day is immortal, it ascends, grows,
> ends by being born and never ends,
> each day is a birth, a birth
> is every dawn and I am rising,
> we all rise,
> the sun rises with its sun face, John rises
> with his John face, with his everyone's face.
> Gateway to being, awake me, dawn,
> and let me see the countenance of this day].

The male principle celebrates the female principle, night hymns day, and the poet performs his magical act in calling up shapes from the inchoate, light out of darkness. This poem of 1957, one of the last important poems to be published in the western world, marks a culminating stage in Paz's development. His next collection, **Salamandra** (1962), continues to explore metaphysical problems of time and reality, but in a more lyrical and traditional manner. Some of the love-poems are as simple as Eluard's; an occasional landscape resolves into the essential lines of a Chinese painting on silk. Yet in his last poem, **Viento entero** (**Intact wind**) of 1965, he once more considers the 'eternal present' of a land—Afghanistan in which he was travelling—and of human history. (pp. 232-33)

J. M. Cohen, "Virgin Soil," in his Poetry of This Age: 1908-1965, revised edition, Hutchinson University Library, 1966, pp. 205-34.

The Times Literary Supplement (essay date 1970)

[In the following excerpt, the anonymous critic offers a positive summation of Ladera este.]

As the title suggests, Octavio Paz's new collection of poetry [Ladera este] records his experience of India, Afghanistan and Ceylon. This does not mean that they are occasional poems, rather they are further explorations of lifelong interests. Even in his earliest writings, he tended to see Western civilization as an aberration, a deforming process. Love (the erotic) and poetry were restoratives, assertions of authenticity in a lying age. Both were subversive activities, alien to a world in which order and reason had become instruments of state. His appointment as Mexican Ambassador to India confronted him with a culture which offered new insights and confirmed his basic assumptions; Ladera este is a diary of this discovery and confirmation.

Taking as their starting point people and places—the antheap of an Indian city, the mausoleum of Humayún, the painter Swaminathan—the poems dissolve into a seeming chaos of impressions and then reform again, in a constant dialectical process between the phenomenal world and the world of the imagination. In one of his critical essays and in the poem "Al pintor Swaminathan", Octavio Paz refers to the words on the page, to the paint on the canvas as "fountains of signs". Certainly comparison could be made with pointilliste technique, for sharply contrasted words are juxtaposed and then fused, in a process akin to "optical mixing", in the eye of the observer. Consider, for instance, a description of Delhi . . . where juxtaposed colours suggest refraction of light, giving new associations and meaning to the word "caído".

The comparison with painting is not irrelevant. In the Swaminathan poem, the poet achieves the difficult feat of conveying the painting of a picture in words. The poem projects the tactile and visual experience of putting paint on canvas and ends on a note of quietude as the painting is finished. . . .

Most of the poems come back, in this way, to the process of creation. And this process is not an end in itself but a step towards self-realization, "the other side" of the "fragile bridge of words." . . . So self-realization and the act of creation are inextricable links in an unending chain.

There must be few living poets able to command such a deep knowledge of Eastern and Western culture as Octavio Paz.

"Assertions of Authenticity," in The Times Literary Supplement, No. 3554, April 9, 1970, p. 379.

Ronald Christ (essay date 1970)

[Christ is an American critic and scholar who specializes in Latin American literature. In his review of Eagle or Sun? excerpted below, Christ considers the collection a

polished introduction to all of Paz's works in translation.]

Octavio Paz is Mexico's greatest living poet. But let's face it: that's like saying William Carlos Williams was Paterson's best writer. For Americans, a better way of indicating Paz's importance will have to be found. Perhaps it would be more suggestive to say that in the universe of Latin American writing, Neruda's poetry is solar: a lavish, Hispanic fulmination—like a Tamayo watermelon—and Paz's poetry lunar: a rarer, Gallic luminosity—like a Magritte moon—; or, to put it another way, to say that while Neruda is directly concerned with the world, its objects and processes (including poetry), Paz is more frequently concerned with poetry, its procedures and words (meaning things).

But let's really face it: Paz is an even better essayist than he is a poet. His 1950 evocation of Mexican character and culture, The Labyrinth of Solitude, is, in fact, devoted to the real world and it produces an astonishing image of a whole nation, truer than the profound truths it reveals for presenting them in a mythos made entirely beautiful. Written in a lucid, rich prose, Labyrinths of Solitude is Paz's poetic masterpiece. (p. 148)

[Eagle or Sun?] is a significant experiment in the career of a significant poet, and its longest piece, "My Life with the Wave" (which tells of a man's falling in love with a wave, his taking her home and the tides of their affair until she freezes in his absence and he sells her to a waiter who chops her up into little pieces to chill bottles) is a breathtaking success. It is a fantasy as delicate as anything by Hans Christian Andersen or Perrault, as magical as anything by André Breton or Dali and as beautiful as anything else by Paz. "My Life with the Wave" alone justifies the experiment and the volume. (pp. 148-49)

Like so much contemporary art, Eagle or Sun? is self-consciously about itself; but, for a change, intelligently, illuminatingly so. Thus it is not a carefree volume, because Paz explains that "Every poem is made at the poet's expense"; and while it sings the pain of creation—the Passion of Poetry, not the passion in poetry is Paz's theme—it also celebrates the poetic opportunity by rejoicing in the "World to populate, blank page," privileging us to witness a poet who can accurately say that "From my body images gush" while he gracefully avoids that modern literary pitfall, "a bramble of allusions, tangled and fatal." Of course everything in Eagle or Sun? is not as good as "My Life with the Wave," but by pointing always in the direction of itself, the book establishes its own elevated norms and provides a fine introduction to all of Paz's work. (p. 149)

Ronald Christ, in a review of "Eagle Or Sun?" in Commonweal, Vol. XCII, No. 6, April 24, 1970, pp. 148-50.

Robert Bly (essay date 1971)

[Bly is a prominent and influential figure in contemporary American poetry whose imagistic verse is distinguished by its unadorned language. He has also translated the work of such Latin American poets as Federico García Lorca and Pablo Neruda. In the following excerpted review of Configurations, Bly argues that Paz is trapped in the current Spanish-American literary tradi-

tion which, "at its worst, . . . leans into soft oceans of romantic mush."]

A powerful river of poetry has come out of South America in this century. Pablo Neruda and Cesar Vallejo are in my opinion the greatest poets born on the American continent since Whitman. Octavio Paz, born in Mexico in 1914, who has had a previous volume of selected poems in English, has become the most highly praised poet of the generation immediately after Vallejo and Neruda. The present book [*Configurations*], containing work since 1957, makes clear certain drawbacks that the Spanish American literary tradition has as well. At its best, as in Vallejo and Neruda, and Vicente Huidobro, the Latin American drives forward into "what has never been named," into states of anguish the Europeans never managed to describe; at its worst, it leans into soft oceans of romantic mush, where all women are fiery and all roses are sacred and all kisses are eternal.

One of the traditions of Spanish-American modernism is that romantic loving can solve a lot of things. In a central passage from Paz's major poem, **Sun Stone,** he says:

> To love is to struggle, and if two people kiss
> the world is transformed, and all desires made flesh
> and intellect is made flesh; great wings put forth
> their shoots from the shoulders of the slave . . . .

The translation, by Muriel Rukeyser, is a bit overblown, but adequate. If the Spaniard Antonio Machado were writing this passage, the word "solitude" would appear: "If a man is in solitude, the world is transformed . . . and wings sprout from the shoulders of the slave." In other words, Paz hopes for as much from kissing as Machado does from solitude. (p. 6)

It is lovely to be able to walk around to the other side of your idea and see it from the back. How marvelous it would be if Paz could say: "Once I kissed a woman and nothing happened." But he can't say that, because in some way he is the property of his own poetic ideas. He is not really thinking. His poems have a lot of flaming ears, and queens of daybreak, and venomous ivy, and nightingales on ramparts, and fallen stars, and solar arrows—I love all these things in poems, yet in Paz they appear as if they meant something in themselves.

When Cesar Vallejo and Antonio Machado throw up translucent roosters and fountains, they want you to see right through them: just behind them are the massive granite shapes of their own lives, anguish humped over, snout to the ground. If you want to reach through the light show and touch that lump you can—Machado's bark of death is there, your fingers feel it, or Vallejo's anguish with its fur clotted. They are real. In a later poem, **"Certainty,"** Octavio Paz talks about his own life, but it's not clear how real it is, even to him:

> If it is real the white
> Light from this lamp, real
> The writing hand, are they
> Real, the eyes looking at what I write?
> From one word to the other
> What I say vanishes.
> I know that I am alive
> Between two parentheses.

I don't like the poem. I must admit that I dislike seeing human life compared to something smaller than itself, making love compared to commas, death to periods. The trouble is that life is not manmade, but grammar is. So the sense of life disappears in the presence of the literary. It's like someone looking at a sunset who says, "Doesn't it look just like a painting?"

I am not presenting this poem as the best of Paz's poems, but merely as an example. In it Paz himself seems to realize that he is stuck in some literary tradition, and can't get out.

American poetry in the fifties became trapped in a different literary garden—not with flaming Peruvian breasts—but in Italian landscapes imagined in graduate school, full of what Rexroth called "little John Donnes with hayseed in their hair." A number of American poets have broken out of that through different gates. Now we are all in danger of being retrapped in the Spanish-American literary stage sets; we should read Octavio Paz and be warned.

I am not saying that Paz is a bad writer: I find his essays excellent—*Labyrinth of Solitude* for example—because in them he is actually thinking his way through a mass of original material. Occasionally a poem of his will have, as his essays have, the weight of a real body. In this collection I like very much **"Duration,"** **"Ustica,"** and the poem for John Cage, **"On Reading John Cage."** . . . I'll quote the strong, final section of ["Duration"]:

> I will speak to you in stone-language
> (Answer with a green syllable)
> I will speak to you in snow-language
> (Answer with a fan of bees)
> I will speak to you in water-language
> (Answer with a canoe of lightning)
> I will speak to you in blood-language
> (Answer with a tower of birds)

Yet Paz oddly fails to outgrow his addiction to poetic Disneylands as he gets older: his long poem, **Blanco,** published five years ago in Spanish and translated here entire, is a disaster. It is one of those rigged-up poems, a monument to ingenuity and lots of time. It has a main text running down the center of the page, and you can read that, or you can read the outrigger poems wired to the sides. The poemlets in the left margin, we are told, refer to the four medieval elements; the poemlets on the right refer to Jung's four "functions"—sensation, perception, imagination, and understanding. Before the poem Paz sets down notes listing many different ways the poems may be read, in case you missed the complexity of it at first glance.

Literary constructions like this don't work, probably because the reader slips into the mood appropriate for intelligence tests, which is not the mood in which you can feel a poem. I like about 20 lines of this poem, in which he suddenly speaks from his gut. Here are four or five. He mentions Mexico and says:

> I am the dust of that mud . . .
>   To speak
> while the others work
> is to polish bones,
>   To sharpen
> Silences
> To the point of
>   transparency. . . .

That almost wins me back to him; it is strong, but a few

minutes later the poem dissolves again into fiery butterflies and a "pilgrimage toward clarities." Paz is a puzzle, a man of great intelligence and feeling, who in a rich poetic tradition has become not deeper, but more shallow.

Why? In **Sun Stone** it's clear that Paz made a decision early to seek his self, not inside himself, but in others. (pp. 6, 20, 22)

Let's see what happened after that decision. The poems of **Ladera Este** (1962-68), well represented here, spring from his experiences as Mexican Ambassador to India. He tries to find his "self" now among the "others" in India. The Indian poems I find hollow and empty—tourist poems; the attempt failed.

The problem in trying to find yourself in others is that eventually you become the property of something outside yourself: in this case, Paz has become the property of the Spanish-American poetic tradition. He is not dragging it behind him, as Vallejo did, it is dragging him. He is not flying with his own frail arms, he is being carried.

If a man feels an emptiness inside, it is better for him to work without elaborate literary properties. Rich literary texture implies that you are rich inside too, and that illusion merely hinders the "bare" man's progress. Robert Creeley feels an absence inside, and he threw away rich literary texture, so as to express the absence better. He took the action Paz could not take.

Machado has a lovely poem:

> It is good knowing that glasses
> are to drink from;
> the bad thing is not to know
> what thirst is for.

If we rewrote that into prose for Paz, it would go: "It is good knowing what rich literary texture is for; the bad thing is not knowing what the absence of literary texture is for." (p. 22)

> Robert Bly, "At Best New Anguish, At Worst Old Mush," in The New York Times Book Review, *April 18, 1971, pp. 6, 20, 22.*

Octavio Paz [INTERVIEW WITH Roberto González Echevarría and Emir Rodríguez Monegal] (interview date 1972)

[*The following excerpt is taken from an interview in which Paz expounds upon his lectures on modern poetry given at Harvard University.*]

[*Roberto González Echevarría*]: *Could we begin by talking about your* **Piedra de sol** *and* The Waste Land?

[*Octavio Paz:*]: I don't see any relationship between them. The form is different, the vocabulary is different, the images, the vision of the world, the structure—everything is different. **Piedra de sol** is a linear poem that ceaselessly turns back upon itself, it is a circle or rather a spiral. *The Waste Land* is much more complex. It has been said that it is a *collage,* but I would say that it is an *assemblage de pièces détachées.* An extraordinary verbal machine that sends forth poetic significations by means of the rotation and the friction of one part against another and of the whole with the reader. No, I prefer *The Waste Land* to

Piedra de sol, frankly. If one wants to compare something of mine with *The Waste Land*—but I see neither the reason nor the necessity for the comparison—it seems to me that one would have to think of **"Homenaje y profanaciones," "Salamandra," "Viento entero"** or **Blanco.** At the same time, all those poems say something very different from what Eliot's poems say. . . .

[*Emir Rodríguez Monegal*]: *Why don't you tell us how you came to know Eliot?*

His poetry. I never knew the man. Eliot's poetry became known very early, relatively speaking, in Mexico. Until the thirties he was a poet almost entirely unknown in Spanish. Juan Ramón Jiménez had published, at the beginning of the thirties, some translations of Eliot's short poems, such as "Marine." They were all in prose, if I remember correctly. The first translation of *The Waste Land* was done by a Mexican poet, Enrique Munjía, and it was published in the magazine *Contemporáneos* in 1931 or 1932. . . . He also did some translations of Valéry. Shortly afterward, Angel Flores' translation came out, one which is very superior to Munjía's, don't you think? At the end of that decade and in the first years of the forties, Eliot was a great influence in Mexico and several translations of his poems were published.

[*RGE*]: *In Cuba, translations also appeared in the magazine* Orígenes, *where you also published some poems.*

They came later. Let me sketch some history. The Mexican poets of the generation preceding mine, like the majority of Latin Americans, were immersed in French poetry. Nevertheless, around 1920 an interest in North American poetry sprang up in Mexico. . . . Salvador Novo published an *Anthology of Young North-American Poetry* in those years. In the following decade, beginning with the Flores translation of *The Waste Land,* Eliot came into vogue in the Spanish-speaking world. In Mexico the poet Ortiz de Montellano translated—and very well—several poems of the intermediate period, such as "Ash-Wednesday." Octavio Barreda also did some excellent translations. And there is a very good one by Rodolfo Usigli of "The Love Song of J. Alfred Prufrock." It's a memorable translation, the product of an affinity. Not because Usigli resembled Eliot but rather Prufrock. All these Mexican translations are a bit earlier than those of *Orígenes.* (p. 35)

[*ERM*]: *I would like to go back to* **Piedra de sol.** *How do you see it, since you say it bears no relationship to* The Waste Land?

No, it has nothing to do with Eliot. It is another world, another vision of the world. The word *pleasure* is one of the axes of **Piedra de sol.** A word that doesn't exist in Eliot's poetry. Even the word *death* has a meaning, a *flavor,* which is very different. And the word *rebellion.*

[*RGE*]: *I hesitate to bring up this topic, but in that very negative review which Bly wrote about* **Configurations,** *he seemed to have in mind a connection between you and Eliot the academic poet [see Bly's excerpt dated 1971].*

I have very little to say about Bly, and even that is negative, so I prefer to say nothing. It is not a problem of intellectual, political, or literary differences, or even one of sensitivity—it is an *affaire* of hygiene. After pronouncing certain names it is necessary to wash out one's mouth. Apart from this reason of an *olfactory* order, as Duchamp would say, it seems to me that Bly does not have the authority to speak about Latin American poetry. And I suspect that he is likewise unqualified to talk about poetry in his own language.

[ERM]: *Bly's note was so absurd because it ignored an entire form of poetry, let's say, from Mallarmé, Pound and Eliot onward.*

Yes, he had previously attacked Pound, Wallace Stevens, Eliot, and how many others . . . Bly's name leads me to touch on another more important topic. Bly speaks of a "Spanish Surrealism," and he thus repeats a widespread error. Stefant Baciu put things in their proper place in the essay which he published some years ago in *Cahiers Dada*. It is necessary to begin by saying that there is only *one* surrealist movement, so that it is absurd to talk about various Surrealisms, be they Spanish, French, Chilean, or Egyptian. Surrealism was an international movement that extended over almost the entire world. Breton always emphasized the international character of Surrealism. It is true that in the field of literature—the case of painting is different—the manifestations of Surrealism were particularly important in the French language, although there were also Surrealist poets in other languages and other countries. . . . All those poets and artists *belonged—in effect—to the Surrealist movement;* they established relations with other Surrealist groups, especially with the French, and carried out a Surrealist program, in the true sense of the word. There was, in addition, a different phenomenon: the existence, in many places and many languages, of poets *influenced* by Surrealism. In our language, Surrealism influenced and branded perhaps the best period of the poetry of García Lorca, Cernuda, Aleixandre, Neruda, and Alberti. But none of them can rightfully claim to be a Surrealist poet. They do not appear in any anthology of the Surrealists and it is possible that they themselves would not be pleased to be so called.

[RGE]: *And so?*

And so it is nonsense to speak of two Surrealisms: one, the French, which would be intellectual, florid, speculative, decadent, literary; and another, the Hispanic, that would be terrestrial—mundane, telluric, virile, sexual . . . . This is comical. It is a literary "machismo"—which, like all machismos, is hardly virile. It is certain that there were poets of the Spanish language who were influenced by the French Surrealists, but the inverse is not true. This does not imply a negation of the contribution of Spaniards or Hispanoamericans to Surrealism. Their contribution was great, and André Breton frequently acknowledged it. . . . Among the Hispano-americans, one would have to cite the painters Matta, Lam y Gerzo, and several poets: the Peruvians César Moro and Adolfo Westphalen; the Chileans Braulio Arenas, Gómez-Correa, and Cáceres; the Argentinians Enrique Molina and Aldo Pellegrini; and one Mexican . . . .

[RGE]: *Octavio Paz?*

Precisely.

[RGE]: *Then you consider yourself a Surrealist?*

I was a Surrealist at a certain moment in my life, as were

Buñuel, Moro, Lam and so many others of our language. I try not to be unfaithful to that moment. In the *Anthology of Surrealist Poetry* of Jean Louis Bedouin—which is, one might say, the "official" anthology of Surrealism—several Hispanic figures appear: Picasso, Picabia, Dali, César Moro, Arrabal and myself. In fact, Bedouin has written a history of the Surrealist movement *after* 1939 that completes Maurice Nadeau's book. Bedouin's book takes apart another critical prejudice, which insists on bringing Surrealism to its conclusion in 1939, with the beginning of the Second World War. That's absurd, isn't it? During the war, and in the Forties, Breton wrote two of his best works: "Arcane 17" and the *Ode à Fourier.* Shortly afterward Benjamin Péret wrote his greatest poem: "Air mexicain." After the war, a great poet entered the surrealist group: Aimé Césaire. Julien Gracq, André Pieyre de Mandiargues, and a poet of Lebanese origin whom Breton admired and whom Saint-John Perse considered to be one of the best contemporary French poets, Georges Schehadé, also joined the movement.

[RGE]: *But wasn't the period of the post-war dominated by existentialism?*

Yes, it is true that the post-war was dominated by existentialism, but that ideological movement was of an extraordinary artistic and poetic indigence. Who today can read the novels or the theater of Sartre? The *littérature engagée* tried to be historical but it grew old before history itself. . . . What remains is Beckett, Genet, some texts of Camus, and especially the work of several poets closely linked with Surrealism: Michaux, Char, Ponge. No, it is not true that Surrealism was dead in 1939. In Latin America it had a great influence after the war. (pp. 36-7)

[RGE]: *I would like to discuss* **"Homenaje y profanaciones,"** *that poem in* **Salamandra** *which is a kind of gloss of the celebrated sonnet of Quevedo, "Amor constante más allá de la muerte." Which of the Baroque poets have influenced you most?*

I think there are three: Góngora, Quevedo, and Sor Juana. When I wrote that poem I was a true believer in the poetry of Quevedo. Now I like him less.

[RGE]: *And that sonnet in particular?*

It is admirable as a perfect rhetorical machine. Although its theme is love, it is not an impassioned poem, but rather a poem whose theme is passion. It is the baroque culmination of Petrarchism, with its affirmation of the eternity of love: love is eternal because the soul is eternal. But bodies aren't eternal. Modern passion is not an eternity in time, but rather in *this* time. It is not *ex*tensive, but *in*tensive. It is corporeal. For that reason, my poem is an homage and a profanation—a mockery in the same vein in which Picasso repainted *Las meninas*—a mockery and a veneration. My poem is a sonnet of sonnets. It is divided into three parts. The first sonnet represents the first quartet, the second, the second quartet, and the third, divided into two parts, represents the tercets. There is in each part, in addition, another sonnet. Just like the image of a mirror in a mirror: sonnets of sonnets of sonnets. But free sonnets and, finally, hardly sonnet-like. Praise and profanation. The whole composition is governed by a numerical proportion that would be very tedious to explain. Suffice it to say that it is the projection of a sonnet and its parts.

[*RGE*]: **Piedra de sol** is also based on a numerical structure, isn't it?

The number of verses of **Piedra de sol** is exactly the number of days in the revolution of the planet Venus. The conjunction of Venus and the sun is realized after a circular course of 584 days, and that of the poem with itself, after 584 verses. Venus is a double planet: Vesper and Lucifer. In pre-Columbian Mexico there was Quetzalcoatl: celestial body, bird, and serpent at the same time. The text unfolds within this mythical-astronomical framework. That is to say, the unique history of one man, who belongs to a generation, a country and an epoch, is inserted into the circular time of the myth.

[*RGE*]: *Unique?*

Time perhaps is cyclical and thus immortal. Such, at least, is the time of myths and poems: it turns back over upon itself, it repeats itself. But man is finite and is not repeated. That which indeed repeats itself is the experience of finiteness: all men know that they are going to die. They know it, they feel it, they dream it, and they die. The same thing happens with the other basic human experiences: love, desire, work. These experiences *are* historical: they happen to us, and they pass. At the same time, they are *not* historical: they are repeated. For that reason, poems can be written about these experiences. Poems are machines that produce time and that continually return to their origin: they are anti-historical mechanisms. On the other hand, poems cannot be made from ideas, opinions and other purely historical experiences of man. That was the error of *engagée* literature several years ago, in its existentialist and Communist branches. That is the paradox of our condition: our fundamental experiences are almost always instantaneous, but they are not historical. Our experiences are not historical, but we are. Each one of us is unique but the experiences of death or love are universal and are repeated. Poetry is born of this contradiction. In fact, it is made out of this contradiction.

[*RGE*]: *Isn't that the central theme of* **Blanco**?

That is the theme of all poems and all poets.

[*RGE*]: *Would you care to tell us, in conclusion, something more specific about* **Blanco**?

Well, it's terrible (and also tempting) to speak about what one has written. But I will allow you that pleasure, as bittersweet as it may be to me. In **Blanco** the combinations are not temporal but rather spatial. The poem is constructed from diverse parts, like a crossword puzzle. The reader can associate or dissociate the parts; there are more than twenty possibilities. Each part is in itself a poem and each association or dissociation yields a text. Thus, unlike a crossword puzzle which has only one solution and one figure, **Blanco** has more than twenty figures, more than twenty texts. Each text is different and they all say the same thing. The extreme flexibility of **Blanco** is resolved in rigidity. Quite the contrary of **Piedra de sol,** which is a linear poem that flows continuously. **Blanco** tends to crystallize, that is, to convert itself into a mere verbal transparency, and then, to dissolve. That's why it's called **Blanco.** It is the negation of **Piedra de sol** since, in a certain way, it negates time; only the present exists. That present is its presence: the feminine body seen, touched, smelled, and felt like a landscape; and both, the earth and the woman, gathered up and read like a text, heard and pronounced like a poem. **Blanco** is a verbal body; a body that reveals itself and, upon doing so, passes out of sight. That, at least, is what I wanted it to be. (pp. 39-40)

Octavio Paz with Roberto González Echevarría and Emir Rodríguez Monegal, in an interview translated by Rolena Adorno in Diacritics, *Vol. II, No. 3, Fall, 1972, pp. 35-40.*

"The poet is not one who names things, but one who dissolves their names, one who discovers that things do not have a name and that the names that we call them are not theirs . . . . Through writing we abolish things, we turn them into meaning; through reading we abolish signs, we extract the meaning from them, and almost immediately thereafter, we dissipate it; the meaning returns to the primordial stuff."
—Octavio Paz, 1972

Gordon Brotherston   (essay date 1975)

[*Brotherston is an English critic who has written and translated numerous scholarly studies on Latin American literature. In the following excerpt, he surveys Paz's poetry up to his return to Mexico in 1968.*]

Paz began publishing in late adolescence, in the 1930s. Since then he has travelled widely in literature and the world, and his writing has passed through several important stages, chapters of an unusually rich intellectual biography. Universalist by inclination, he has been successively affected by different cultures, philosophies and religions, of which he made 'creeds' of his own: ancient Mexican, Surrealist, Hispanic, Oriental, and so on. Of course, these stages of his creeds can seldom be separated cleanly from one another. . . . Moreover, there are undoubted constants in his work, ideas which he comes back to again and again, and which have been well described in criticism: a disrespect for inherited language, which dates from his earliest poems (**"Las palabras", "Destino del poeta"**); his eroticism; his quest for primordial man; his anarchic equation of sexual with social form. However, a progression of particular enthusiasms can be seen in his writing about poetry no less than in the poetry itself. For it is on these twin testimonies that his considerable authority rests, both inside and outside Mexico. As a poet-critic he is unrivalled as an interpreter of the poetry and poetic traditions of his sub-continent. . . . (p. 138)

Paz differs from those 'indigenist' writers who feed on the old lore of their country. Specifically, he parts company from those compatriots of his who believe in the cultural programme of the Mexican Revolution, which in the 1920s had produced murals of paradisiacal Indians, like Orozco's Malinche, the Mexican Eve. All this was false or fond, while the proposition that Mexicans should recover the customs of their American forebears, and their language (which Paz himself displays little knowledge of), seemed to him preposterous or even 'lunatic'. He would himself wish to descend from neither Indian nor Spaniard but to 'deny' them both. In his poetry this is exactly what he has done, encasing Tlaloc and rending Itzpapalotl in two. Very occasionally a phrase of his will catch an Aztec expression: the 'flowered bone' in **"Vaivén"** derives from the Nahuatl lyrics in the *Cantares mexicanos*. But little more. His attitude is perhaps best drawn in his most famous 'Mexican' poem, *Sun Stone, Piedra de sol.*

This title is the name given to a large stone disc prominently displayed in the Anthropological Museum in Mexico City. Its discovery excited much attention but the full meaning of the designs carved on it remains unclear. Sunstone may well prove to be a misnomer; but there can be no doubt that it records facts of the Mesoamerican calendar and possibly correlates the magic *tonalpohualli* of the Aztecs (the divinatory count formed of 20 signs and 13 numbers), with solar and planetary cycles. Paz in fact allots to his poem the same number of lines (584) as there are days in the synodic cycle of Venus, a planet which in turn unquestionably features in many Mesoamerican myths, as the heavenly form of Quetzalcoatl and other heroes. He also makes his poem circular like the stone, by bringing us at the end back to the opening lines:

> A crystal willow, a poplar of water,
> a high jet arched by the wind,
> a tree well planted but dancing,
> a river movement which bends,
> advances, goes back,
> turns round and arrives always:

Within this circular time he sets episodes from his life, his first loves in Mexico, being in Madrid during the Spanish Civil War. His plan is to switch loves and deaths out of their separate histories into a state where 'what happened was not but is being', and in which identity itself becomes plural (like 'personal' names derived from the *tonalpohualli*); or shockingly, even a disgusting illusion:

> When are we really what we are?,
> closely considered we are not, by ourselves
> we never are anything but vertigo and vacuum,
> grimace in the mirror, horror and vomit.

The force of the poem, Paz's first major lyric, is palpable, and due in part to reliance on an arcane sense of time and personality. Yet 'closely considered', in precisely those respects, he proves to be much less an Indian sage than a late Spanish Romantic: 'fate', 'presage', 'omen' are spoken of not in the holistic terms of the *tonalpohualli* but in a nineteenth-century idiom which looks back to the Counter Reformation and the Spanish Golden Age. . . .

While doubtless the formal context of the poem continues to create tension with this very foreign mode within it, the conflicts of such a relationship hardly suggest that the poet is wholly in control of or even very interested in them. For all his desire to collapse linear history into a moment, in a key passage about crime and evil in the world (lines 436-74) we progress through it (and through an immaculately Western version of it at that) in relentless sequence, from Cain and Abel (lines whose atmospheric sentimentality incidentally echoes Manuel Machado and Albert Samain) to the death throes of Trotsky and Madero. Linear movement, from one point to another, is further enforced by the use of such etymologically resonant verbs as *disertar* ('the jackal dissertates among the ruins of Niniveh'). A last

irony is the fact that though Paz would credit the ancient Mexicans with no more than a circular notion of time (into which his own is more or less loosely fitted), their codices show that they were quite aware of the problems implicit in *Sun Stone* and of expressing them formally perhaps more satisfyingly than this poem does.

In the last analysis it would probably be no less delicate a task to trace Paz's Mexican origin in his poetry than it would be to think of Vallejo or Neruda as specifically *South* American poets. . . . At any rate, a Mexico of literature and personal experience was Paz's touchstone in *Labyrinth of Solitude* and *Eagle or Sun?* (pp. 140-42)

In most respects Paz's biggest 'Mexican' poem, *Sun Stone,* in fact belongs more properly to the collection it appeared in: *La estación violenta* (*The Violent Season,* 1958). Complemented by Paz's first major work of criticism, *El arco y la lira* (*The Bow and the Lyre,* 1956), these poems as a whole amount if anything to a certain scepticism about the idea of Mexico. At any event, he openly repudiates the indigenists and the social realists, and all forms of national concern with culture. Against these traditions he would set another, which had come to fascinate him more and more from the late 1940s onwards, that of the Surrealists. In a metaphor fundamental to all his writing, but especially to that of this period, he would break out of his labyrinth of solitude into new utterance. Out of empty constriction, in which man is fragmented socially and erotically, he would join the Surrealists in conjuring that marvellous instant when we truly 'inhabit our names'. (p. 146)

Though these poems abound with epigraphs and submerged quotations from this source, Paz rarely pushes towards those extremes of traumatic distortion or fluidity which mark, say, Dali's paintings, or David Gascoyne's response to them. Nor do his poems often flash with 'absurd' humour. Figures like 'the girl who slips over the shining edge of the guillotine', and the man who descends from the moon with a fragrant bunch of epitaphs (two of the **"Masks of Dawn"**), are rare visitors. It was as though, having heard the Surrealist message a little late, he felt bound to take it very seriously. There is little in *The Violent Season* which does not conform to a set of given *ideas*. For example, the poem just mentioned, **"Masks of Dawn"**, clearly has a lot to do with the Apollinaire of a poem like "Zone". There is the same location in a city (Venice, Paris) at specific times of the day, the same attention to the names and shapes of places in the city, and to the very different types of people who inhabit it. Further, both poets attribute a certain deadness in life to 'this ancient world' of Europe, driven back to Byzantium by the new spirit. But while Apollinaire's footwork is so fast and subtle (beyond the amazing effects of "Zone" being an *ambulatory* poem) that we could hardly identify anything as fixed as a stance or an attitude, Paz makes his closing lines into little less than a manifesto:

> But the light advances in great strides
> squashing yawns and death agonies.
> Jubilant splendours that grab you!
> The dawn throws its first knife.

Faced with enthusiasm of such directness (or 'healthiness' as one critic has put it), we are hardly discouraged from reading the whole poem as a gloss, an earnest working out, of the single line from Apollinaire which forms the epigraph to *The Violent Season*: 'O Soleil c'est le temps de la Raison ardente'. If 'ardent reason' is an oxymoron, then these poems tend more to the second than to the first term.

Setting his experience thus in space and time, Paz effectively compartmentalizes his cosmopolitanism as a citizen of the twentieth century in a way most surrealists made a point of trying to supersede. In his **"Himmno entre ruinas" ("Hymn among Ruins"),** the ruins (like the masks of Venice) retain that near-Parnassian solidity we noted earlier in Paz. A further separation is made into luminous positive odd-numbered stanzas in Roman type and dark negative even ones in italics; all however are subject more or less effortlessly to the 'high yellow shout' of the sun at the end and its 'impartial beneficence'. As before, the poet's psyche does not luxuriate in its own realm but flows in carefully defined stanzas, or into outbursts of unrestricted generality, in a pattern more reminiscent of Darío's "Divagación" than of the French surrealists. The 'Mexican' stanza is the first of the italicized series:

> Night falls on Teotihuacan.
> The Mexican song explodes in an oath,
> star of colours that fades,
> stone which cuts off our doors of contact.
> The land tastes of agèd land.

Here we are back in the labyrinth, the stone unenlivened by sun, with the young men of the state smoking grass and playing Spanish guitars; the old music of the 'canto mexicano' (or the Nahuatl lyric) issues only into foreign blasphemy. The word is too deeply buried and gods can no longer be made at teo-ti-hua-can ('God-making-place' in Nahuatl); as is the case in other dead cities, with their Eliotic rats and 'anaemic' sun (stanza 4). The last epithet is in fact a good clue to the way Paz is operating in this and other poems of his so-called violent season. In its context, 'anaemic' cannot but evoke the solar blood cults of Aztec and other religions, would anticipate some ritual antidote of cosmic proportions of the kind invoked by Apollinaire in "Zone" (the blood of the 'cou coupé' at sunrise), by the Surrealist Artaud in his response to the 'primitive' rites of the Tarahumara, or for that matter by José Emilio Pacheco in his Tlatelolco and other poems. Paz prefers to be less violent than that. The very stanzaic divisions of his poem, act in this sense as safety compartments. More important, he resolves whatever tension there is in it in the 'sweet' and reasonable final image of the orange, segmented yet whole. . . . (pp. 146-48)

It should be emphasized that by the time Paz had his direct knowledge of Surrealism through Breton, that movement was considered dead by most of its former advocates. Certainly Breton himself, however noble in his refusal to accommodate his faith to the politics of, say, the Casablanca Conference and their consequences in Europe and the world, was by then no longer involving himself in primary questions of literature and society with quite the passion of the early manifestos, and publications like *Le Surréalisme au service de la Révolution*. In any case he had moved steadily from that total trust in the subconscious, as the 'automatic' source of writing, painting and politics alike, towards allowing credit to such a concept as 'superior reason'. It is the latter Breton who influenced Paz the more, fostering in him 'ardent reason' sooner than total iconoclasm since that had somehow already been gone through. The way Paz has reacted to that 'revelatory' fifth

chapter of *L'Amour fou* would certainly support this view. For Breton's account in that chapter of his experience with his wife in the gardens of Orotava and their ascent of the peak of Teide, in Tenerife, stands as a document of the Golden Age in the fullest sense. Indeed, inspired by Buñuel and Dali's film *L'Age d'or,* Breton draws out all that he can discover Marx and Freud to have in common, suggesting 'mad' hope for human beings who are both social and in love. These protestations could of course be understood as an attempt to make good the dilemma which had led to his break with the Communist Party and which would estrange him increasingly from the 'committed' Eluard and Aragon. Yet even as such an attempt it vastly enriches his deliberate rewriting of Genesis in *L'Amour fou,* in favour of the natural innocence of man.

Paz picks up very little on this concern. Not that he should for one moment be thought 'a-political'. He began his publishing career in the 1930s with strong Marxist sympathies; and while he did not remain orthodox for long, events like the Spanish Civil War, the US invasion of Santo Domingo, the death of Che Guevara, intrude strongly into his verse. And he repudiated the Tlatelolco massacre of 1968 more boldly than most, and resigned his post as ambassador (to India). Enthused by this and other, less tragic, desecrations of 'the temple of Capitalism', he reported feeling his poetry to be inadequate as a gesture, or even 'infamous'. What ever this ultimately may or may not say about Paz's good faith (given that 'sincerity' can be found in such matters), it is in fact hard to detect in his poems a coherent or sustained feeling for man in society. (pp. 149-50)

As if spiritual alliance with Breton had somehow given him the impetus he needed, Paz emerged from *The Violent Season* ready to explore territory around him neglected hitherto. In the books which followed this one he appropriated regions which previously his ambiguous sense of nationality, and then his strong interest in the Europe of the Surrealists, had encouraged him to skirt around. *Salamandra* (1962), and its complementary book of criticism *Cuadrivio* (1965), might well be called his Hispanic books. They involve him in a series of dialogues with poets of his language, which make clearer his points of difference with the Surrealists and help to define him specifically as a Hispanic poet.

Of course Paz could always be said to have 'belonged here', especially in his earliest collections, where his debt to the 'post-Modernist' tradition in Mexico and Latin America is obvious. But his doubts about the literary traditions of 'arthritic Spanish' had been persistent. And now he was on to something more ambitious, which in the first instance would oblige him to face squarely that other 'Golden Age' of his past: the literature of imperial sixteenth- and seventeenth-century Spain, especially the poets Góngora and Quevedo. . . . A poem like **"Ustica"** (in *Salamandra*) brings out strongly both the covert Mediterranean in Góngora, hinted at already in the epigraph to **"Hymn among Ruins"** ('where foaming the Sicilian sea . . . '); and that poet's neo-Platonic or elemental view of landscape. When Paz speaks of the Sicilian island in question as a 'hard peach', a 'drop of sun petrified', he comes very close indeed to the process of distillation and immobilization at the heart of the *Solitudes*. However, **"Ustica"** would finally be all *against* that kind of solitude and petrification: to the extent that Paz admits Góngora against this wish he is no longer simply ignoring reactionary forces in him (also palpable in his earlier Parnassianism) that run counter to his ostensible poetica of fluidity. This admission had been made already in **"Hymn among Ruins"**, an uncharacteristically structured poem, but one in which, as we have seen, order and sweet reason triumph too easily. The result in **"Ustica"** is a poem of extraordinary power and potential violence not least because of what Góngora taught him about the loneliness of man in nature. Paz's revaluation of Góngora's near contemporary, Quevedo, was more dramatic though it affected his poetry less profoundly. The funereal scatologist depicted in *Labyrinth of Solitude* is made in **Salamandra** into the object of homage as a poet of love. Quevedo's sonnet "Love constant beyond death" is celebrated in an extensive gloss by Paz which, whatever its own merit, declares intentions of rapprochement, especially in the closing **"Lauda".** (pp. 153-54)

The mood of frustrated coherence in **Salamandra** is perhaps best represented in the title poem and **"Ustica"** (which are closely akin to each other). The latter is one of Paz's most powerful poems; it catches especially well that suppressed violence, the extremity of both his passion and of his fears for its meaning matched with death; further, for its survival in a groundswell of incest and ominous telluric myth. The first stanza, verbless, has the pained impatience of **"Augurios",** and leaves us with similarly little hope, in this case in the eventual fate of the sun, its capacity to resist atrophy, a career to 'cooled matter'. The alliterative 's's work like an exasperated hiss ('sol', 'sucesivo', 'solo'). Then comes his view of the 'petrified' island Ustica, mentioned earlier. This initial constriction and contracting of matter makes the plight of surviving life, the sweet water of the cisterns, the more acute:

> At night the sound
> of the cisterns breathing,
> the panting of the sweet water
> perturbed by the sea.
> The hour is high and streaked with green.
> The dark body of the wine
> sleeping in the jars
> is a blacker, fresher sun.

The sea thus becomes the ambient of 'the rose of the depths', a candelabra of pink veins which can survive only down there. On land it becomes as calcareous as López Velarde's skeletons. At this point the poet first introduces himself and his companion into the text:

> Sulphur-coloured rocks,
> tall austere stones.
> You are at my side.
> Your thoughts are black and gold.
> If I were to stretch out my hand,
> I should pluck a bunch of intact truths.

What these truths might be is left unsaid. Could they survive intact in an atmosphere so turbulent and electric, where sulphur threatens gold and the horizontal and the vertical are so violently juxtaposed? He is kept from realizing the expectations of his grasp. We focus now again on the sea, in a salt light of huge intensity, bright yet eerily phosphorescent. The sea is many-armed like its rose, but also an abyss, because its organic chemistry also decom-

poses. As a wholly un-innocent repository of life it recalls Baudelaire's dazzling dream of a sea of ebony:

> Below, among sparkling cliffs,
> the sea comes and goes full of arms.
> Vertigo. The light rushes down.
> I looked at your face,
> I rimmed the abyss:
> mortality is transparence.

Such an insight can hardly be borne. The bold love cadences of the **"Hymn among Ruins"** or **"Broken jar",** the fruit taken that is word and act (and not the hypothetical bunch dependent on a subjunctive verb), yield to the horrific intuition that there may be no transcendence, no escape from matter, *mater-materia,* that in an Eden which is a graveyard only the helpless innocence of incest can endure. . . . Testing his erotic creed against a growing obsession with death and decay, Paz creates a poem of extraordinary tension and issues into a desperate form of love that is (as he is clearly aware) both prior to the first social taboo, and solipsistic the moment he ceases to be god. In this state he was readier for his next encounter: with the Orient.

Paz's acquaintance with the East began in the 1950s when he travelled to India and Japan. In 1962 he became Mexican ambassador to India, and deeply immersed himself in that country before his resignation six years later. It was there also that he got to know his second wife. The fruits of these experiences is the collection of poems which exactly spans this period: *East Slope* (*Ladera Este*). His explorations in geography and philosophy are witnessed in the very titles of the poems: **"Tanghi-Garu Pass"**, **"Madurai"**, **"Vrindaban"**, **"Happiness in Herat",** the trilogy on Himachal Pradesh (the part of the Western Himalayas where the Vedas were reputedly composed); the erotic pair **"Maithuna".** In the first instance the very difference of climate kept him from the devastating introspection of **Salamandra,** and, for example, of Neruda's 'Eastern' poems in *Residence on Earth.* In the bar of the British Club in Madurai he rises even to the jocular, a rare mood for him. Intercalating the phrases (in italics) of a certain Sri K. J. Chidambaram into his own observations, he plays with a contrast between the holy and the commercial India, a game repeated in the second Himachal Pradesh poem. More frequently, the landscape and the lore of country demand of him less divided attention. Indeed the exterior world, in an apparent regress, can acquire the 'objectivity' of much earlier pieces:

> Mountains of mica. Black goats.
> Under the somnambulant
> hooves the slate gleams, rugged.
> Fixed sun, nailed
> on the huge scar of stone.
> Death thinks us.

Scale, rare atmosphere, and the ease with which 'elements' display themselves, permit him simply to reveal them and their message. The same might be said of the forms and concepts of Buddhist and Hindu philosophy, those categories like sunyata, sansara and nirvana which in their uncommon precision can pattern a poem almost of themselves.

Reflecting on his Indian experience in **"Cuento de dos jardines"** (**"Story of Two Gardens"**) and placing it in the story of his own life, Paz makes of it a beginning, of the same order as his own physical origin as a human being. One of the two gardens is in Mixcoac, his Mexican birthplace (now a suburb of the capital); there, as a child already he 'spied the feverish construction of my ruin' and learnt 'to say goodbye' to himself. The other is in India, and he enters it not as a new home but as the beginning of the Beginning, another Eden where before the huge tree, the nim, his sexual ecstasy is consecrated. . . . The Indian garden, with its tree and preternatural colours, becomes an emblem of the country itself, whose vagina is 'soaked with sap, semen, poisonous juices'; the atmosphere of the place is every bit as electric as Breton's Orotava. The remarkable thing, however, in this heavily autobiographical, or better, confessional poem, is the poet's admission that, chronologically, between these two gardens, of childhood and fruition, there were no others ('no hubo jardines'). In other words, we are given a hint why the intense eroticism of **The Violent Season** was not sustained and why *Salamandra* manifested a certain dispeptic dualism. If we are to take Paz at his word, only on the 'East Slope' did he begin to match philosophy with experience, forming of them both a new creed that would be referred to its source only to poetic advantage.

The best poems in *East Slope,* "Viento entero" and "Vrindaban", demonstrate how this might be so. In Vrindaban, the sacred Hindu city, he both questions the sources of his belief and asserts his self in a way hardly precedented in his poetry. From the start the poem is (appropriately) about himself as a poet, writing and pausing, surrounded by a darkness rich in foliage and breath. The momentum of the car he was travelling in a few moments earlier sustains the tracing of a few taut signs, black on white, a tiny garden of letters, and leads him past commonplaces of experience and phrase to the question: 'Do I believe in men or the stars?' He does not answer directly. Belief is at least what is seen: 'I believe / (here, a row of dots) / I see'. But what is seen, the phenomenal world (here, the jasmine and the stench, the brillance and the misery, of India), is too myriad and protean to furnish guarantee. It spreads like fire and leaves him striving to control it like the poor mortal in Buddhist philosophy, 'mountebank, monkey of the Absolute'. At this point he is fixed by *another* eye: a mystic looks at him from the other bank of perfect knowledge ('prajnaparamita'), immobile in his perennial philosophy:

> Crouching,
> covered with pale ashes,
> a sadhu was looking at me and smiling,
> from his bank he was looking at me.

The message from over there is a sacred chant, like the one which closes *The Waste Land,* grotesquely mixed with bowel rumblings. This sadhu may have seen Krishna herself, have been servant to her ravishing blue tree, have touched the cleft in the rock, the ultimate feminine abyss. In any case, his formless vertigo is why he lives in total abjection 'on the quay where they burn the dead'. The experience of being located in this way by another eye finally provokes Paz into one of his frankest admissions:

> Absolutes eternities
> and their purlieus
> are not my theme,
> I have a hunger to live and also to die.
> I know what I believe and what I write.

The startling directness of the statement may be due to the

long time it took him to make it. The past stages of his life are implicitly recognized here, perhaps for the first time, as is a self that is not all. On the East Slope he defines his hunger as a first premise, and articulates a deeply Western need for movement and flow. But of course for such a realization to happen, in order indeed that it can be thinkable, some exterior fixity has to be there. That is why the encounter with the sadhu in Vrindaban was fortunate for more than this poem. It offered the chance of dialogue, a radical challenge to solipsism, as is the hope of the final lines:

> I am never alone.
> I talk always with you. You talk always with me.
> I go in the dark and plant signs.

The high point of *East Slope* is "Viento entero" ("Whole Wind"), probably Paz's finest achievement as a poet. Following the line suggested in "Vrindaban" and elaborating further his crucial experience of India, he subsumes and transmutes the recurrent passions and ambitions of his earlier poetry. As in **Sun Stone,** he would integrate in a continuous present separate moments of time and space (the bazaar at Kabul, Paris, and 'various places and areas in northern India, West Pakistan and Afghanistan', as his notes tell us). As in "Hymn among Ruins", another 'major' poem, these are arranged in sections to produce an intricate pattern of echo and opposition. In this case there are nine (rather than seven) stanzas or strophes, which are not separate but hinge or turn on the refrain 'the present is perpetual'. "Whole Wind" also presents a characteristically Paz-like view of the phenomenal world: his interest in elemental colours and textures (mountains of bone and snow, day of agate, black cloud on a black mountain in a landscape like a petrified ochre storm), and in the four humours: water, fire, earth, and the air of the title. As previously, he strives to discover in a world of such composition objective correlatives for his condition: the internal correspondences of the poem, over its considerable length, are intricate and unusually hard to describe.

However, Paz has told us how his condition was newly defined for him in Vrindaban. From the beginning of "Whole Wind", the phenomenal world is more radically matched with its transcendental opposite, samsara with nirvana. The noise and the light of bazaar at Kabul, thus equivalent, are intercalated into silent spaces which are just as real:

> High glare sculptured
> by hammer blows in the lacunae of silence,
> there burst out
> the shouts of the children.

Later on, by the same dialectic, two or three birds 'invent' a garden out of nothing. Similarly the four humours, essences of phenomena, are made to counteract each other to suggest a reality beyond them. Rather than tie each one to a specific quality, as he had often done before, he sets them in self-cancelling contradiction. The girl who appears in the second strophe is a flame 'if water is fire'; later she is a diaphanous drop of water 'if fire is water'. Together earth and wind create the vortex which moves the poem; air perturbs matter in a persistent whirl which becomes the turning of space itself by the final strophe.

Throughout, the spiral also informs the progress of the poem through pairs of strophes which reciprocate but do not eclipse each other, and which steadily expand the circumference of reality. At first he is simply the observer, of mountains and merchants. . . . By contrast he dominates the second strophe, where in Paris he greets the girl, the 'you' which with him makes the 'we' that traverses with effortless intimacy 'the four spaces the three times (tenses)'. In the third and fourth strophes he and his companion are in a garden: she is naked, on a quilt. He contemplates, but with thoughts of the outside world in his head: by now the outer and the inner are more intricately mixed. A 'great flight of crows' (a line from Darío) reminds him specifically of his Latin American condition: news of the US invasion of Santo Domingo recalls in turn revolutionary spirit in Mexico, and, in an overtly Third World idiom, resistance to the imperial British in Misarag. However, rather than accentuate the opposition implicit here or erect a protective wall around the garden to make the *hortus conclusus* of earlier poems, he boldly associates the woman's bright passion (like 'wine in the glass jar') with the secular world ('el siglo'), which

> has been lit in our lands
> with its glow,
> their hands scorched
> the builders of cathedrals and pyramids
> will erect their transparent houses.

In strophe 4, as if exhausted by this transference, the woman's quilt turns from red to black and the sun sets in her breasts. She may be 'fruit', a 'date', but this old metaphor cannot by itself work for long either, and the dark ghost of solipsism eerily returns in the near homonym Datia, the phantom walled city in Madhya Pradesh, self-enclosing and uninhabited.

This initial exploration of his erotic and social self vastly enhances the climax of strophe 5, which is matched its turn by strophe 6. In the high, ferociously unpeopled landscape around the Salang Gorge human beings are reduced to the rush of water below, the white leap in the river that leaves their bodies 'abandoned'. In primary, elemental solitudes he comes nearer to orgasmic origin that can of itself lead only to dispersion and fragmentation. Yet the turning line of the poem continues. The transition, from strophes 5 to 6, through the alliterative refrain, is one of Paz's most compelling moments. The reverberations of the word 'white' alone are amazing, against black, hot, then phosphorescent, foam, then blank and calm, the beard of the marabout ('morabito') against the mulberry ('moral'), half echoed as 'blanco' in 'flanco' (flank), and so on. . . . The sweet wholeness of the orange in the **"Hymn among Ruins"** is a far cry from here. It is half remembered perhaps in the pomegranate offered to them by the river Amu-Darya (by an adolescent with green eyes, a hallucinatory colour switch): by the grains of the fruit, ashen now for containing those dispersed syllables, the broken alphabet of the Bactrian plain and dust-covered names, he rises to the vow: 'I swear to be earth and wind / vortex / on your bones'.

His being would, then, be constant turbulence, the current instability confessed to at a similar juncture in **"Vrinda-ban"** (**"I am in the unstable hour"**). Here however, the movement is less gratuitous, less dependent on given fixity (the sadhu's eye), and formally even more part of the poem itself, in the spiralling images and the conflict of humours already mentioned, in the persistent end-of-line

twists where verbs both conclude and refer forward, and in the refrain ('the present is perpetual') set as a half line now to the left now to the right of the page. Nowhere does he vindicate the shape of his utterance quite as he does in **"Whole Wind"**. Like an undeniable turbine the poem carries him through the further pre or super human oppositions of strophes 7 and 8, the dark monsoon forests of the 'anima mundi' below the 'peak of the world', Kalaisai in the Himalayas, where Shiva and Parvati caress each other and 'each caress lasts a century for the god and for man'. Neither is denied in the time the poem has by now generated 'between heaven (sky) and earth', kept coherent by perpetual motion between the two. In his poem on **"Reading John Cage"** (also in *East Slope*), Paz translated that writer's ideas of music and silence into what he had made of oriental philosophy, in the neat phrase: 'Nirvana is Samsara, Samsara is not Nirvana'. In his notes he points out that the Buddhist formula is wholly reciprocal, an all-enclosing circle (Nirvana is Samsara, Samsara is Nirvana). Refusing to subjugate self and the phenomenal world in this way he would sustain them in the widening spiral so brilliantly traced in **"Whole Wind"**.

Such is the power of 'the movement in which is moulded and unmade the whole being' that the orbit of the closing strophe encompasses both intimate memories of infancy and open space. The childhood garden half recalls that of Ustica and, by its allusion to the fairy tale "Almendrita", the **"Story of Two Gardens"**:

> It rains on my infancy,
> it rains on the garden of fever,
> flowers of silica trees of smoke,
> on a fig leaf you sail
> through my brow.

But since the world can by now uproot itself, the old tension, the violent vision of the 'buried mother', is released in a final 'launching':

> Space turns,
> the world tears up its roots,
> our bodies weigh no more than the dawn
> outstretched.

Since his return from India Paz's poetry has entered yet another chapter. His friendship with Cage (also acknowledged in Cage's *A Year from Monday*), and a lively involvement with the structuralists, commemorated in his book on Lévi-Strauss, had already been corroborated in the long poem *Blanco* (1967), which Paz advises us ought to be read as a succession of signs on a single page. Further: 'as the reading goes on the page unfolds in a space which in its movement allows the text to appear and which in a certain sense produces it'. His concern to relate 'temporal text to the space surrounding it was taken a step further in *Topoemas* (1968), a neologism from *topos* and *poema*. At the same time his special sense of poetic identity has underlain the experiments of *Renga,* poetry written in immediate collaboration with poets of other nationalities and languages (Charles Tomlinson, Jacques Roubaud and Edoardo Sanguineti). But this chapter of his plural career cannot yet be written about for the simple reason that it itself is still being written. (pp. 158-68)

> *Gordon Brotherston, "The Traditions of Octavio Paz," in his* Latin American Poetry: Ori-

gins and Presence, *Cambridge University Press, 1975, pp. 138-68.*

Jason Wilson   (essay date 1979)

[*In the following excerpt Wilson examines surrealist elements in Paz's verse.*]

[Surrealism] affected Paz mentally, as *ideas.* For Paz, surrealism is an attitude of mind based on the possibility of using poetry to transcend life's inherent contradictions; to make man whole again, communing with his fellows, participating and reintegrated in experiences that defy time; a poetics of the timeless moment, the *instante poético.* (p. 22)

[All] that he writes falls within the opposition between attitude and activity. What Paz accepts and rejects follows a clear pattern of values based on that opposition. For Paz, surrealism as a historical movement degenerated into style and convention. All that is tainted with history, all that is subject to time's corrosion, is rejected by Paz.

Paz has lifted surrealism out of time and social context, elevating it into an attitude of mind. This was possible because he arrived late at the surrealists' table. Sifting theory from practice also enabled Paz to view surrealism as eternal, a universal constant impervious to time and change. Circumstantial involvement did not blur these clear distinctions. . . . (p.23)

Paz was relatively indifferent to surrealism's explorations of madness, or of black humour, and he did not hold *'chance'* in Breton's high (early) esteem; Paz did not share the passion for coincidences, chance meetings, *trouvailles.* Yet, because he was so close to Breton, he did hold that erotic love was regenerative; that woman was the answer to the riddle or mediatrix, and poetry was the key to life's problems. He prized surrealism's explorations of 'inspiration', related to the concept of the 'other' as against the dominant ego, the false persona and its various roles. He singled out the notions of utopia, of analogy and the *instante poético* as the constants that universalised surrealism beyond mere literary style. (p. 24)

Poetry as self-defence, as exorcism, as life-enhancing in a moment when life had been cheapened; this is the centre of Paz's Bretonian surrealism, and it echoes an earlier epoch when Breton also defined poetry as 'self-defence'. That Paz played down his actual activity only strengthens the claim of his 'principles'. But Paz did not start from ideas, but experiences.

"Mariposa de obsidiana", Paz's first surrealist contribution, reiterates on another level Paz's family ties with Breton. The prose poem's surface is 'decorative' Mexican precolumbian *exotica* . . . and the poem functions both as a gloss on Paz's researches into the mythic substrata of Mexican culture in his *El laberinto de la soledad,* and as (another) poetics involving the fertile 'eternal feminine' where the ancient goddess Itzpapálotl ('our mother') is transformed into Tonantzin and the Virgin of Guadalupe (thus defying historical change). . . . (p. 26)

Paz turned to surrealism as part of his rejection of post-revolutionary Mexican nationalism, Stalinism, or official ideologies of any sort. . . . He seeks a critical stance, hos-

tile to and free from official, repressive culture. This is where surrealism, first within the Mexican context, then more universally, offered him a way out. . . . (p. 28)

Surrealist poetics is an answer to the enigma and stigma of death. After the failure of the sciences, the collapse of organised religions and philosophy and metaphysics, twentieth-century man . . . ['will seek a Poetics']. This *'poetics'* (surrealist lived poetry, utopian dream) is the new wisdom. (pp. 28-9)

Paz correctly intuited surrealism's quasi-religious function. According to him, modern poetry is the 'new sacred'. . . . (p. 29)

Paz consciously separated attitude from activity, raising surrealism to the category of *idea,* thought, spiritual orientation; but only because he could reject the historical and anecdotal side: he had lived it with Breton in Paris and not through 'books', and so he transcended it. Surrealism answered many of Paz's problems; it was a . . . ['desperate attempt to find the way out']. Surrealism was, then, the new *wisdom* based on a system of values personified and embodied in Péret's and Breton's moral examples. It was an extra-religious religion that answered the question in the poem **"¿No hay salida?" ("Is there no way out?").** Yes, there is—through poetry. . . . It is a poetry that is both written and lived. Surrealism is thus a quest for the 'true life' so desperately sought by Breton and still sought by Paz. (pp. 32-3)

[The poem **"El prisionero" ("The prisoner")**] perfectly formulates his adhesion to surrealist concerns. . . . [It is a] poetics dealing with a reputation [the Marquis de Sade's]. (p. 34)

Paz suggests that Sade, who was against the world, has become a 'name', a 'leader' and a 'flag' for a whole group of people, from erudites to madmen and poets, who . . . ['fight like dogs over the scraps of your work']. Paz separates himself from these 'dogs'.

Those who particularly invoked Sade were the surrealists; Sade's position in their hierarchy was unequivocal. . . . However, the surrealists' relationship with Sade was ambiguous, especially in Breton's case; and this is what Paz siezes on.

The surrealists find little interest in Sade's literary style or his aesthetics; he is not a literary influence. He is not a 'pornographer' for them either—they do not evoke his mathematical combinations; nor do they explore the political aspect of his work. (pp. 34-5)

Octavio Paz clearly sensed this paradox. He was puzzled by Breton's admiration for Sade, feeling that Rousseau was closer. (p. 35)

In his uncollected prose piece on Sade (1961), Paz repeats the surrealist case. Sade's originality is seen as a breaking down of taboos concerning our natural instincts, for morality has nothing to do with passion; erotic acts are . . . ['extra-vagancies', 'disorders']. Sade's philosophical rigour is praised; his destruction of limits, of the modes in which words distort the reality of sensations; pain and pleasure melt together. . . . For Paz, Sade opened sealed doors, for Breton he made a breach. Up to this point in his piece, Paz is 'orthodox'. Then his reading of Blanchot allows him to diverge from Breton's 'blind' admiration.

Paz with Peruvian novelist Mario Vargas Llosa, 1978.

Sade's negation of God, morality, man, and nature lead to a negation of self. Thus Sade's thinking is circular. Further, by elevating the libertine as his only model of conduct, Sade condemns himself to total isolation, for people are but objects; there is no communication and Sade cannot escape himself.

This leads to Paz's poem, which conveys a similar 'reading', but imagistically and passionately; the intention is identical. The title **"El prisionero"** . . . relates to this divergence; it conjures up not just the physical prison of history (Sade spent some twenty-seven years in eleven prisons), but a 'mental' prison, the ego-prison, the libertine prisoner in himself, imprisoned by his system. (p. 37)

Paz is a humanist in a godless world where relationships are what humanise; the human voice fills the silence; poetry relates, links and unites. For Paz there is a way out, a breach:

> Only in my fellow do I transcend myself, only
> his blood bears witness to another existence.

Self-transcendence through awareness of the 'other'; passionate, erotic love solves the problem of solitude, for love is a relationship. It would not be forcing the metaphor to include writing and reading as an act of communication made out of emptiness and loneliness.

The final stanza passionately enlarges upon this ethic; it is a surrealist manifesto defending poetry as the answer to life's limitations. Behind the 'seeming' chaos and heat, the fusions of lava and sperm, nature and man continue to function and dictate their tensions. Imagination, desire and boredom, death, pleasure, flooding, vomit—all overflow their categories and melt into each other; desire, madness and dreams soften the rigidities which fence life in. Paz's list ends on the word 'desmesuras' (excesses): that excess that Sade exploited, that surrealism preached in order to become human again. . . . (p. 41)

Paz dares the reader (and himself ?) to follow Sade and the surrealists. Only through risk can liberty be won, that . . . ['liberty the colour of man'] that Breton sought. Liberty is the choice of necessity; liberty is not accepting destiny but fighting; it is a necessity because man is the only free being. . . . (p. 42)

Read this way, Paz's poem affirms a poetic by proposing an alternative. Paz diverges from surrealist orthodoxy in favour of a hidden Bretonian vein that leads back to Rousseau, utopia and love. Sade ignored poetry; and poetry is communion, an erotic relationship that results in the *ay* of self-transcendence. Paz yokes poetry to intention. (p. 43)

Spiritual liberty is the name for the celestial vision at the centre of Paz's poetics. . . . ['The celestial image is a vision of liberty; levitation, dissolution of the ego. Light confronts stone']. The antinomy of light and stone expresses that of liberty and its limitations; light and life against insensitivity, gravity and death. All of Paz's poetry spreads out in waves from this tension; for 'spirit' only exists in terms of its repression, as a relationship. Any other word, like 'being' or 'desire' (for the same area) would also imply this dynamic concept of truth.

In the relationship between liberty and poetry, the perception and experience of the spirit is liberty, is language purged and washed of its fixed associations, freed from dead metaphor. (p. 45)

[The] quest for intensified life never ends, is never satisfied. Man finds nothing, there is no gold (only fool's gold?). For Paz, life is not static, and we live in time. He emphasises the open, the flowing.

With the notion of quest, we also articulate that of journey; poetry is a process of discovery, an adventure, an exploration. (pp. 46-7)

Because the journey-quest is an inner one, undertaken by the imagination in symbols and exteriorised into poems, the poet does not see, but *invents*. To 'in-vent' (with distant associations of wind, breath and inspiration) is not to coin neologisms but to drag up to light; to restore language's original purity through the critical, selective and surgical act of writing where language is released from the 'chains' of convention, its *karma,* and allowed to be. . . . Poetry, which is freed language, speaks the real 'me'. Words, made autonomous, living beings freed by the poet, create the poet by releasing his being, dulled and made opaque by cliché and culture. (pp. 49-50)

At the same time, Paz doubts the value of merely writing poetry. He asks the crucial question . . . ['Wouldn't it be better to transform life into poetry than to make poetry with life?']; and he reiterates the vision of a universal, live poetry with man freed of gods and masters. . . . This ideal, frustrated by actuality, is based on the inner organisation of the poem in relation to the 'communing' reader. This is surrealism. Breton's 'comportement lyrique' heralds the end of the poem, where the reader is transformed into the poet, and where the dream is of opening the door out of the poet's shaky house to find oneself 'on his feet in life'. For Paz this dream too is surrealism . . . ['surrealism is poetry's desperate attempt to incarnate itself in history. That is why its lot is tied to that of man himself']. Paz's disillusion with politics only temporarily blurred his vision; his contact with the surrealists, that brotherhood who lived a utopia of open friendship, enabled him to 'believe' again. (pp. 53-4)

Paz the poet sees beyond what man has earmarked as reality; but this is done only through desire, liberating the self from this marking, the deformation. Poetry helps because it 'cleans the doors of perception' by stripping language of its dead, dirty 'skins'. That sight is the prime sense in Paz is clear; from his interest in the visual arts to his visionary poetics, his aim is to *see*. His intention is to 'dream again with his eyes closed' and, living that dream, to become himself. (p. 64)

The open mind, the surrealists' 'disponibilité', always open to chance and arbitrary experiences, responding to whatever stimuli it received without imposing any deforming schema or grid; this corresponds to Paz's poetics, to his dialectic of 'loneliness' and 'communion'. . . .

Soledad (*Loneliness*) shows that the root of man is his essential loneliness; the fact that only he himself can die and that his profoundest experiences are solitary and incommunicable. On another level, meditating, thinking, reading and writing are solitary acts. Each poem begins in an act of *soledad* and only from this inner laboratory of loneliness will the new poetry spring. . . . It is this real *soledad* that forces man to communicate, talk, write, make love and transcend his solitary self.

The poet suffers this *soledad* more intensely because of his values, his insights, his lucidities, that isolate him from the mass of society and place him to one side of the time-sanctioned securities. (p. 65)

[The] central symbol of 'unity' in Paz's poetics [is] . . . *light*. Paz is a poet who *looks,* lucidly seeking enlightenment. Light bathes his concerns; it is the light of creativity as well as mental light, and as well as the sun or the dawn revealing the world as it really is. (p. 76)

Paz is rooted in this tradition of poets who give evidence of the sovereignty of light. He has his eyes open and sees the light that reveals, destroys, creates and gilds a world indifferent to man. . . .

Paz's *Semillas para un himno* (1954) is a series of poems about the paradisal world before man, inundated with light; it explores a dual theme, linking this dawn of prehistory and myth with the creative act itself in the form of the *birth* of the solar, luminous world—word. Light leads the world out of the darkness of chaos, and the word out of the dark mass of language. Here light fuses inner and outer, poet and paradise. . . . (p. 77)

The dawn of light is the dawn of the word in poetry, and the result is language perceived sensuously. Real man, buried under a civilised mask, is a fragment of this cosmic light. Through woman this light can be recovered in the *instante* of erotic love which leaves the poet dazzled. . . . (p. 78)

Paz's claim is that man has severed himself from nature culturally, through excessive reliance on his intellect or his analytical reason, placing them above the voice of his feelings and experience. (p. 81)

> *Jason Wilson, in his* Octavio Paz: A Study of His Poetics, *Cambridge University Press, 1979, 192 p.*

"We often confuse eloquence with poetry."
—Octavio Paz, 1973

Claude Esteban   (essay date 1980)

[*The essay excerpted below is a translation of "De la poésie comme insurrection," Esteban's introduction to* Versant est *(1978), the French edition of Paz's* Ladera este.]

On the verge of each poem by Octavio Paz, in the first breath which gives birth to it, there is less the desire for an affirmation than the sudden awakening, as in the morning—the individual, mind and body, in an almost uncontrollable flight towards what is undefined, outside; towards what has neither place nor form nor figure; and will gain all this from a man and from his glance. What claims our attention, even beyond the magnificence of a word— from the first lines of **Luna silvestre** to the feverish overture of **"Petrificada petrificante,"** written some forty years later—is this refusal of the inevitable, this rebellion incited without end against the certainties already gained—yesterday's knowledge—and facing that knowledge, the dark wall, as if unbroached, of the world.

> I open my eyes
> > I am
> Still alive
> > At the center
> Of a wound still fresh

Others—and so near us—have invested the poetic enterprise with the value only of "restricted action," abandoning the world of the senses to its enigmas, to its wanderings, in order to save in the end, the joy of a few words set side by side. Octavio Paz has not heard these invitations—or, fervent reader of Mallarmé, he has not believed that the destiny of modern poetry should be wholly identified with the dark descent towards the tomb of Midnight in which Igitur's will was buried, and with his will the ambition of a word which could sustain Being. Isn't it still the poet's task to fight off the menacing hegemony of Signs, to keep the distance from growing too great between the vocables that summon reality and the little reality which remains to us? . . . It is true that the gods have left; that our symbols have grown old; that things have lost their native force, their substance; and those who question them, with their gestures, their words, have lost the power to restore their weight, their place, their presence at the heart of a universe which slips through their hands and where they themselves are at a loss for a footing. This ontological failure, pushed at times to the edge of the intolerable, is the only foundation on which Octavio Paz will build those "wandering republics of sound and meaning" which constitute his poems. (pp. 83-4)

The word of poetry is made in the image of this earth, of this history which we live: sparse, ruined with emptiness, incomplete. If in so many poems by Octavio Paz we confront landscapes of flint and ash, shouldn't we hesitate to identify these landscapes with memories of a life and its travels? These high plateaus of broken stone, these deserts from the Orient or Mexico, represent in their cruel evidence something like the crystallization, at once metaphorical and tangible, of another abandonment that grips us at the edge of a world in so many ways *deserted*—a dead world, as we would say of a dead language, and one which offers our mental vision only "the signs of an alphabet in ruins." This is the birthplace of a poetry which knew itself from the beginning to be the approach, perhaps the sad apprehension of absence.

But that is also the end, for Octavio Paz, of what I will call the fascination with Mallarmé, if not of the discomfort which this fascination provokes. For the apprehension— even lucid—of a "default" in the world's being, the discovery of a metaphysical solitude lends itself to a nostalgia anchored in the deep memory, which we must relinquish each morning. (p. 84)

We know the significance which his meeting with that "important passerby" of our century, André Breton, held for Octavio Paz. Paz himself has confirmed all that his own questioning, his poetic and even his political choices, owed during those years to the healthy mutiny of the word rising against the artifices and conventions of the concept. I do not mean to minimize the importance of this rebellion; but I think it necessary to define the ways in which Paz's attitude differs from a poetics with which he sympathized, but which he did not embrace. Where surrealism finds a second certainty—the discursive capacity of the unconscious—and builds on this certainty a system of perception and representation of the psychic universe, Octavio Paz sees an ambiguous return to rationality, a new law of the relations between consciousness and appearance, in short a reassuring logic which he cannot fully accept. To define the *surreal* and to set its limits, to find a touchstone within oneself—wasn't this, for Western thought, yet another return to the old mandate of the *logos,* wasn't this to push farther from us what fails and fades before speech? Surrealism did not question the authenticity of the deep self, still less its seemingly innocent epiphany in the word. Descending step by step, venturing in the dark of himself, Octavio Paz did not find this kind, ceaseless murmur, but only more darkness, more silence and more danger than in the space of the visible. "There is nothing in me but a great wound." A wound through which the sap escapes, the substance of the world and of the self—and which it would be futile to disguise, resorting to some turning in on oneself. The *space within* has not yielded all its monsters. . . . And not everyone can force them up from the depths and, like Henri Michaux, seize and conjure them.

If the poetry of our time, as Paz has said, cannot on its own escape its isolation, poets owe it to themselves to fight, with all their strength, against a condition of moral isolation which compromises their desire for communication, which diminishes them, and which walls them into their own monologue. Throughout his great meditation on the poetic act, *El arco y la lira,* Octavio Paz reaffirms that "To be oneself, is to condemn oneself to mutilation, for humankind is the perpetual desire to be other." And still more explicitly in these phrases which question a certain egomania of contemporary poetry: "I aspire to Being, to the Being which changes, not to the salvation of the self." How far from this or that concern for individual salvation, the salvation which orients so many experiments today— intellectual, poetic, pictorial—experiments guided by an extravagant love of self. . . . And what a horizon stretches before the poem, what progress is promised to one who is no longer afraid to lose himself! I spoke earlier of the first impulse in Octavio Paz's writing, consubstantial with the poem's ascent, and which continues to set its direction. I will not distort the meaning of this impulse if I say that it represents a purgation—in the ascetic sense—of the passions, the subjective drives; the writer placing himself outside himself for the sake of what will be written through him. Octavio Paz has said again and again that poets are the ones who work "outside themselves." It is not that he exalts a delirium, or yields to the famous "derangement" (*dérèglement*) more or less concerted of all the senses which certain fragile disciples of Rimbaud have practiced, not to deliver themselves from this unhappy self, but to amplify it beyond measure and to better possess it. To wish himself "outside himself" is for Octavio Paz to refuse the limits which consciousness imposes, and more, to abandon all the refuges which our subjectivity, jealous of its quiet, does not cease to propose. It is finally and above all to respond to this vocation of *otherness* inherent in humankind, the prestige of its power which our fear disguises. (pp. 85-6)

Poetry—Octavio Paz tells us—is a movement *towards,* never a preestablished itinerary which could award itself the reassuring perspective of an *as far as.* And if the unappeased *I* of the poet aspires to become that *other* which Rimbaud dreamt, he cannot attain his dream except by that abandon of self and by the loss even of the memory of loss. Poetry is a bow aimed towards the improbable, but if it is not now for us to reach the target, still the arrow is new in our hands.

It is the presence of death which we find at the threshold of this journey undertaken by the thought and poetry of Octavio Paz. Moving and unmoving, solemn and furtive, death enters—as, always alive, it enters the flesh—the heart of the words which refuse it. Octavio Paz does not believe in the god who came with the ships from Europe, who claims to redeem, and complete what's left undone, save Being from its wound or from its blasphemy. But Paz reveres a dark force which rules us and which we must not oppose, but accept with open eyes. "The dead do not exist, only Death, our mother." We can feel sure that it is not a taste for the archaeological restoration of a culture, its religious imagery and its rituals which has led Paz to give the Aztecs' cosmology and their anthropological vision a privileged place in his thought and, from early in his career, in his poems. Christianity could not vanquish the old mysteries in Mexico any more than it could in Asia; unable to convert them, it could only give a name to the great terror of things. Octavio Paz has rejected the too simple assurances of Christianity in order to hear the lessons of the sacred Serpent. Quetzalcóatl does not fear death or despise it; death is not a place of despair or the physical sign of a punishment. He passes through death—in order to join the two aspects of being and to fuse them. He gives himself to secret liturgies of the sun; he offers life, in the guise of death. Octavio Paz has long contemplated this demiurge of astral and terrestrial revolutions: *Piedra de sol,* among other poems, bears the sign of the crowned and rampant god. Paz has done more than adhere to this highest figure among Mexican deities, figure which has in fact nourished his experience and his writing. I will leave it to the commentators to verify certain correspondences which seem obvious to me and which, moreover, Paz has discussed. I believe his return to the great drama of pre-Columbian consciousness has confirmed and comforted a feeling in him, an intimate experience of death, experience which has escaped the imperatives of a Christian ethic—as it has abandoned the form and the spirit of those Hispanic models which influenced the poet for a time. (pp. 87-8)

The poetry of Octavio Paz does not forsake the sensible world; nor does Paz take refuge in an imaginary or unreal world, evasions which so often represent the last subterfuge of a poetics chafing at its limits. It is the "creatures" nearest us, in the universe which surrounds us—a tree, an instant of rain, this insect crying in the underbrush—that claim Paz's attention and a keenness of perception more speculative than visual. For Paz, to see and to retain these few images is already to raise them beyond a purely spatial and temporal vision, to discern their tangible presence and at the same time to feel that they may change. "Things are the same, and other."

We can certainly hear an echo of Buddhist doctrine and something of the great teaching of the Tao. But what is in Oriental thought an ascent beyond the body, silence and plenitude beyond gestures and words, regains an active dimension in Paz's writing, which seems to generate energy—a dimension which the Orient has nearly always refused. Not that I wish to minimize their enterprise or claim that it is easy to attain the transcendence of contradictions which alone permits one, according to the Upanishads, to experience the beatific state of *ananda,* delight of the spirit in the breast of the One. But I think it as much of an adventure, for a consciousness which operates in the ambiguous space of language—and our Latin idioms more than others, with their play of mental mirrors . . . —yes, I judge that the adventure is at least as perilous for a Western poet to escape the dualist idea of the world and to reunite in words what remains separated in things. For me, this is Paz's essential ambition, and the surprisingly modern grandeur of his poetry. The critique of writing to which he has devoted himself does not lead, as so often in our poetry, to an ethics of suspicion, to the decor of signs which seek only to be persuaded of their futility and to deconstruct. Octavio Paz orients his search towards a less desolate horizon. If he distrusts the certainties of language, it is in order to reassert another power of which language has let itself be stripped—not to represent but to express the live flesh of things, to be of one substance with things, to rediscover itself, as in the first sun-filled morning, both word and presence. "Names seek a body." Words will no longer stay behind the glittering bars of abstractions. A world waits for them—only a mortal world, our world, but where a heart will beat again, where "We feel our lost unity beyond the invisible walls, the rotten masks which separate us from each other." Names seek a body—and the body, in its turn, seeks a name which will free it from the old fears of the self, from its silence.

It is love which allows us this glimpse of our lost unity—and which may restore it to us, if we consent. Not the love which sanctifies itself in its difference, but that which is incarnate in the embrace of two bodies. The poetry of Octavio Paz seeks to become a passionate celebration, a fervor and even at times a furor of Eros. Since the eclipse of the natural myths, we have too often confused erotic poetry with a licentious confession, with a verbal exaltation whose only motivation seemed the private satisfaction of a sensuality. Octavio Paz has returned to eroticism some of its panicked seriousness, the signs of its truth. For him, love is more than the desire which carries individuals outside themselves—and withdraws them briefly from their solitude; it is a rebirth of the other, and through the intermediary of these bodies joining, the hope of a fusion with the protean substance of the world. Paz's most beautiful erotic poems, **"Maithuna," *Blanco*,** are also those in which the cosmic reality is revealed in all its transparence. As if by embracing a bare body, marrying its landscape, quenching its thirst, the reality of the world would become more tangible, its firmament fill with light above us, the conjunction of male and female stars endure in a single flash of light. The distance which subsisted between the self and the other, between things and words, will now be effaced in the act of love—mingling and fusion of You and Me in We who are created indivisible. . . .

The world is visible now in your body,
Transparent in your transparence

In the new mythology generated by the poet, Eros is no longer the futile god of the legends, blind and blinding. He is once more the dazzled walker, the pilgrim hungering for the absolute—and in his steps, as once for Orpheus, the dark fails and the dead stones come alive. The world has found its center again—not determined by a despotic consciousness but by a will rising in each of us and which transcends us, "an unnamed pronoun" which is Eros' force becoming a poem. (pp. 90-2)

For Octavio Paz, the image is the unquestionable manifestation, at the climax of writing, of that eroticism which sets the entire universe in motion, which carries it off—live matter, heart and spirit—in a whirlwind of metamorphosis. What intrigues Paz's reader from the start, what will always fascinate us, is an explosion, a fertile exchange among forms and figures which seem to give birth to one another, to separate, rejoin, burst into a thousand suns of signs, into constellations of metaphors, into a stardust of metonymies. . . . But the image, as it is practiced here does not depend on an arbitrary proceeding of the intellect, any more than it leads to the caprices of an imaginary world. (p. 93)

Through images, the poetry of Octavio Paz approaches a *reconciliation*—the hope of all unitive philosophies—and not a problematic conciliation of opposites. He escapes in this way, and even at the level of language, the intolerance which has been the pride of Western thought, in which each conscious subject is confined within its domain, and perceives others only in the belligerent relations of supremacy or submission. By affirming that "things are the same and other," Octavio Paz not only blurs the categories we hold to—that was surrealism's objective—he captures the naturant energy of the universe in "cages of light where identity is annulled among likenesses, difference in contradictions." For Octavio Paz, the poem is an insurrection of the word against the conventions and the precarious equilibriums of the concept. More, it is the insurrection of sense against the repressive system of particular meanings. Faced with a rhetoric of reification, with ideologies of the beautiful totality, the poem rediscovers itself as *uprising,* at once rebellion and rebirth. Uprising of the sensible world, towards a transparence which is more than an intelligibility promised to the mind. Uprising of Being towards a *truth,* the truth of which Rimbaud spoke, present at last *in one body and soul.*

Poetry must now free itself, as much as possible, from its fascination with the figure of destruction in whom Mallarmé recognized a guardian angel, his Beatrice. . . . If poets have come to distrust, and not without reason, the capacity of language to recover a real and not a simulated presence, they must also fear that the conscience and conduct of negativity, taken to extremes, may be lost in mutism, or, more perniciously, may end in verbal terrorism, in a didactics of over-abundance or of emptiness. Octavio Paz affirms that if poetry is first of all the cruel ordeal of separation, it must transcend this negative stage of the "Deus absconditus" and force itself, once more, to gather the sparse words of the real in a single phrase—always threatened, always to be born—of certainty. The poet refuses the dispersion of sensible phenomena which others have made a fatality. As Eros reunites the You and the Me

in a single pronoun—a single presence—so the poem is a moment of fervor, an act of faith which will carry the poet "to the other side of night where I am you, where we are others." For words are that much more our own if, in the exchange with others, in their recognition, they can once more belong to everyone. The language of poetry cannot be reduced to an idiolect, to a system of signs which is indecipherable for those who do not hold the key. Poetry is, in the real sense of the term, the creation of a "common place," the affirmation of a shared word, the reassertion of an unbroken history. (pp. 94-5)

> *Claude Esteban, "Poetry as Insurrection," translated by Susanna Lang, in* Octavio Paz: Homage to the Poet, *edited by Kosrof Chantikian, Kosmos, 1980, pp. 83-95.*

José Miguel Oviedo   (essay date 1982)

[*Oviedo examines several autobiographical and historical elements in* Pasado en claro *and* Vuelta.]

When one writes on the work of Octavio Paz, one has two conflicting impressions: that criticism has said it all, and that at the same time everything remains to be said. Thus, in spite of the constant effort not only to examine the new but also to read the preceding work and to evaluate the early texts, this corpus always eludes the siege; it keeps its essential nucleus from examination, and it seems to be moving continuously in an unreachable direction. All of us immediately recognize the voice of Paz, but we are left behind by its nuances. We fail even more in knowing how far his play with resonances, modulations, recurrences and alternations extends, and we fail to know where or how he produces that unique, fertile blend of his own voice with those of other poets. Yet the most elusive aspect of Paz is precisely the "I" that generates the whole mental, intellectual, sensorial, erotic, mystical process which inspires his poetic search. . . . I shall try—somewhat daringly perhaps, since the theme is complex—to consider this "I." (p. 612)

Pasado en claro [1975] (translated as *A Draft of Shadows*) is the most autobiographical, the most confessional poem that Paz has written, quite apart from being the most extensive single poetic text in all his work. One must situate it with the other major poems which Paz has produced, poems which demarcate his poetic vision at different stages of its evolution: *Entre la piedra y la flor* (1937), *Mutra* (1952), *Piedra de sol* (1957), *Salamandra* (1960), *Viento entero* (1965) and *Blanco* (1966). (p. 613)

Like all these great poems, [*Pasado en claro*] is many things—a constellation of themes, a formal exploration in various directions—but above all it is an exploration of origin, a falling within and into the past. The Spanish title itself shows this with its magnificent semantic triangulation: an explanation of the past, but also a version which the "I" edits, and further, nocturnal tribulation. Insofar as it responds to the essential question "Who, really, am I?," the question is an anagnorisis, a vast poem of self-knowledge which reviews the past of the poetic subject with an urgent "originary tension." Paz explores his personal past and intellectual background, his relationship with Mexico, with universal culture, with the poetic act and especially with himself, that evasive image which from the beginning of his work he has arduously tried to reach. The preoccupation is therefore not new, but the intensity and the inclusive impulse of the search are. There is no romantic individualism in this search for memories of the past: the poem does not represent any exaltation of the "I," but rather its dissolution or its incorporation into the flow of the world. In its opening passage *Pasado en claro* develops two opposite but equally true affirmations: "I drift away from myself" and "I travel toward myself." This flight, which is also a persecution, is subtly announced at the close of the first section of the text with a verse split into a movement of opening out, followed by one of falling back: "the sun opens my forehead, / balcony / perched within me."

Within this setting at once closed and open, the "I" begins its passage through a continual shuffling of images. The visual nature of many of these images is not only a trace of surrealism but also a consequence of the affinity of Paz's vision with light, transparency and clarity. Seeing and remembering are analogous experiences: memory is itself an image, the eye its own object; the one which evokes is the evoked subject itself.

> I am inside the eye: the well where,
> from the beginning, a boy is falling,
> the well where I recount the time
> spent falling from the beginning,
> the well of the account of my account,
> where the water rises
> and my shadow falls.

This fall into himself, into the waters of childhood, takes place within the frame of a ritual scene, one perfectly recognizable for the reader, since it constitutes a system of references which guide the searching conscience: elements, places or familial objects which are rearranged in the memory like a magic circle—"Patio, wall, ash tree, well." They will reappear many times, always new, always the same. Time is not time past, but revived time, invented now by memory. In truth, there is no break between yesterday and today; as the poet says, "I am where I was." And this unity makes more precise, in the man who is, the memory of the boy who was.

The games of childhood thus are analogous to the great figures or moments of history: "Abd al-Rahman, Pompeii, Xicontencatl, / battles on the Oxus or on top of the wall / with Ernesto and Guillermo." This image is charged with emotion, for it deals with the incongruity which the child perceives between the models set up by his education and the data of direct experience. . . . In the poem the remembrance of heroes is followed immediately by a long passage on sexual initiation and desire as a form of knowledge, a passage over which presides another magical presence of long-standing significance in Paz's work—"the primordial fig tree, / leafy chapel of . . . rituals"—and which culminates in a recollection of his grandfather. (pp. 613-14)

This figure, General Ireneo Paz, the poet's paternal grandfather, was a writer and a liberal journalist, at first a supporter of Porfirio Díaz and later his enemy. . . . Suppressed by his religious education, Paz's young imagination overflowed into the world of literature opened for him by his grandfather: reality entered through the eyes and through fantasy. After quoting or alluding to those books and authors (Góngora, Homer, Dante, Villaurrutia, Jules

Verne and Apuleius, among others), Paz combines his adventures as a reader with his destiny as a poet, and upon doing so he confirms his vision of the sacred power of the word. (p. 614)

Memory returns to the paternal home and recovers the image of its material decadence and of family life: "The big house, / stranded in a clogged time." Paz has never been as painfully sincere and detailed as he is here. The quarrels in the home and the solitude to which they condemned him are examined with undisguised bitterness. . . . New figures parade through the precipice of memory: his mother ("self-sacrificing, ferocious, stubborn, provident, / titmouse, bitch, ant, wild boar"); an aunt ("a virgin who talked in her sleep"); and, most dramatic of all, his father.

> Between vomit and thirst,
> strapped to the rack of alcohol,
> my father came and went through flames.
> . . . .
> I could never talk to him.
> I meet him now in dreams.

This image is the other face of the memories which Paz has recounted of this paternal figure: "My father took part in the Mexican Revolution and represented Zapata in the United States. He was one of the founders of agrarian reform."

Completing his spiritual autobiography, the poet again invokes "the primordial fig tree" in order to place its sensual lessons ("my body spoke to me, the bodies of my body"); in opposition to the promises of religion and power: "neither power nor gain. Nor sanctity either. Poetry remains the sole instrument of reconciliation with himself. Paz critically examines this last possibility and the experimental forms which poetic creation had to adopt for him: "I wanted to name it / with a solar name, / a word without reverse. / I exhausted the dice box and *ars combinatoria*."

Here the poem reaches its critical point: if the memory of the "I" is only a vacuum that dissipates in the snare of the very language that revives it, what is the nature of the "I" that undertook the journey? What is the ultimate reality of this poetic consciousness that explores itself? A key verse, one that opens the floodgates of personal memories, reappears in the final passage of the text: "I am where I was." Memory's theatre is an empty stage corroded by time. No one person thinks or remembers: the words themselves think or remember, inventing the fiction of the "I," inventing the world, creating a splendid fragile reality—eternity in an instant. There is nothing outside the poem; in other words, there is nothing outside the poetic experience, which the voice shares with the reader. The lights kindled by a consciousness fierce in its intent are put out ceremonially: "I hear the voices that I think, / the voices that think me as I think them. / I am the shadow my words cast." (pp. 614-15)

[**"Nocturno de San Ildefonso"** and **"Vuelta,"** published together in the volume *Vuelta,*] are two of the most important testimonies on the poet's return to [Mexico], about 1971, after long years spent in the Orient and in Europe. This is a particularly conflict-ridden period for Paz: he must readapt himself to a country which, in its burgeoning growth, is now something of an unknown environment for him. . . . A new intellectual generation has grown up in

Mexico for which Paz is a central figure; he has to assume this responsibility. . . . And above all, to return to Mexico is to run up against the reality of politics conceived of as congealed practice, completely inadequate to the demands of society. History dominates Paz's preoccupation as an essayist and poet more than ever.

It is not that history was absent before: the reader of *Piedra de sol* will remember, for example, the burning memory of Madrid in 1937 and of the Spanish Civil War in the middle of that text, which precisely wishes to relive historical time. What has happened is that disillusion and bitterness have grown, and they seem to confine the poet to an all-encompassing dark vision. Both texts from *Vuelta,* although they are different, express a common sensation of sorrow and even of moral revulsion; both are also poems about Mexico City and reflections on the irrationality of its "development"; both are reencounters with urban life as metaphors of the reencounter with oneself—the central theme of *Pasado en claro.* Whereas *Pasado* investigates time, the poems from *Vuelta* also investigate concrete space: the modern city, the native country. **"Nocturno"** opens with a clear reference to the place of meditation: "In my window night / invents another night, / another space." And **"Vuelta"** begins: "Voices at the corner's turn / voices / through the sun's spread hand / almost liquid." But suddenly this localization of **"Nocturno"** breaks loose into vertigo, a spiral through which the contemplating eye is converted into the consciousness that remembers. With it we fall into a past veiled by oppressive ghosts. (p. 615)

In its second part the poem recovers a date, "Mexico, circa 1931." . . . This date generates a specific space in the poem: "the red walls of San Ildefonso," an eighteenth-century construction used for the school. A note to the poem clarifies that the architectural beauty of the edifice suffered the consequences of its public use. San Ildefonso is therefore a symbol of the general decay of the city, trying to adapt itself (poorly) to its new reality.

> Empty streets, squinting lights.
>   On a corner,
> the ghost of a dog
>   . . . .
> Loitering sparrows,
>   a flock of children
> builds a nest
>   of unsold newspapers.
>   . . . .
> These streets were once canals.
>   In the sun,
> the houses were silver:
>   city of mortar and stone,
> moon fallen in the lake.
>
>   (pp. 615-16)

Another illustrious place is named in Paz's text: the Zócalo Plaza, which in turn evokes the presence of History and the private history of which these young Mexicans were protagonists in 1931: "There, / between Alyosha K and Julien S, / we devised bolts of lightning / against the century and its cliques." These allusions to Dostoevsky and Stendhal are not accidental. In a recent article on Dostoevsky, Paz remembers:

> He is (or was) the author preferred by the young: I can still remember the endless conversations which I carried on, upon finishing up the *bachillerato,* with some classmates during walks that

began at twilight in San Ildefonso and ended, past midnight, in Santa María or at Insurgentes Avenue, looking for the last streetcar. Ivan and Dimitri Karamazov fought in each one of us.

The reflection upon Dostoevsky highlights the Russian novelist's analysis of the "psychic split, the divided consciousness" of the modern age, whose model is that of nihilism, the "disease of intellectuals." This temptation of absolute power—remember the double negation "neither power nor gain" in *Pasado en claro*—is opposed, Paz says, by "the supernatural joy of Alyosha," the character cited in **"Nocturno."** These burning discussions of politics and literature are and are not part of the past; they are reproduced identically, with other voices and other more feverish faces, as the decade of the seventies begins, and they will repeat themselves in the future: time is cyclical.

> The boy who walks through this poem,
> between San Ildefonso and the Zócalo,
> is the man who writes it:
>   this page too
> is a ramble through the night.

This is the beginning of the third part of the poem, which is in violent contradiction to the fourth and final part. Paz places two activities of the human spirit in opposition: politics and its ideological absolutism in the face of eroticism and the perception of the Other as a person distinct from and of equal value to ourselves. Rarely has Paz expressed his disenchantment toward history and the language of modern politics with as much mordancy as he does here. Although he only expresses it occasionally, there is an accusing and angry force within the poetry of Paz—a surrealist, specifically Bretonian inheritance—which cannot be ignored. His diatribe against the pride of intellectual dogmatism is a good example.

> Some
> became secretaries to the secretary
> to the General Secretary of the Inferno.
>   Rage
> became philosophy,
>   its drivel has covered the planet.
> Reason came down to earth,
> took the form of a gallows
>   —and is worshiped by millions.

If the truth of history is that "Further than dates, / closer than names, . . . / which history scorns," the poet wants to reach the other bank, where "Truth / is the swell of a breath / and the visions closed eyes see: / the palpable mystery of the person." Contemplating the body of the woman sleeping next to him, who seems to float, reconciled with the world and dispersed into its form, he refuses to see physical space, the grim spectacle of the city, and he listens.

> I close my eyes,
>   I hear in my skull
> the footsteps of my blood,
>   I hear
> time pass through my temples.

The meaning of this culminating passage radiates on multiple levels and is refracted in other texts by Paz. It leaves open a perspective which *Pasado en claro* will take up again, as it begins with a similar movement: "Heard by the soul, footsteps / in the mind more than shadows, / shadows of thought more than footsteps." (p. 616)

The genesis of [*El mono gramático, The Monkey Grammarian*] is relevant for an understanding of the work: it was written especially for a select French collection entitled "Les sentiers de la création," which attempts to explore the integration of verbal and visual language. Paz explains:

> I decided to take the meaning of the title of the collection literally: the paths of creation. I chose a road and began to walk. . . . A road which I walked many times with Marie José, my wife. The road to Galta, which is an abandoned place in ruins near Jaipur, in Rajasthan. Ruins of houses and palaces from the eighteenth and nineteenth centuries, now inhabited by a caste of pariahs . . . and by bands of monkeys. The analogy between the act of writing and that of tracing a road is obvious; just as the act of reading is equivalent to walking the road—except that in reading we dissipate the text we read and in walking we erase the path. As you see, the relationship with **Blanco** is a direct one.

Today we can look back and discover that *El mono gramático* literally opens up the space that **"Nocturno de San Ildefonso"** and **Pasado en claro** will cross: the steps build on one another, back and forth many times, making them deeper and (as the author would say) dissipating them, thereby making the reading even more disquieting. In fact, the metaphor of the road, central to *El mono gramático,* appears at the beginning of **Pasado en claro,** at the close of **"Nocturno"** as we have just seen, and even in **"Vuelta."**

> I walk without moving forward
> We never arrive
>   Never reach where we are
> Not the past
>   the present is untouchable.

I do not have space here to analyze the question of the genre to which this work belongs, much less to give an idea of its enormous complexity. I will only say, in regard to the first matter, that its having been written in prose is decisive. Paz wished to produce a text which would be an intersection of poetry, narrative and essay, thus putting into practice his famous assertion that poetry is always a sort of "critical poetry," a reflection of itself. Paz has written: "It is no accident that modern poetry found expression in the novel before it did in lyric poetry. The novel is the modern genre *par excellence,* and it is the one that has best expressed the poetry of modernity: the poetry of prose." Apart from the aid that this passage in *Los hijos del limo* gives us in understanding Paz's own characterization of *El mono gramático* as a "pseudo-novel that destroys itself," that essay written in June 1972 has a close relationship with the poem: the ideas of *analogical thought* and of *negation of language* are common to both. *El mono gramático* does not belong to any specific genre—although it has a bit of all of them—because it is deliberately written at the edge of genres, in the interstice precisely at which Breton wrote some of his principal works (*Nadja, Les vases communicants, L'amour fou, Arcane 17*). This prose, entirely foreign to any standard genre or convention of literary tradition, can only be classified as a free text, one in which words are associated in accord with the analogical principle and one in which language is exercised to the point of exhaustion.

Apparently, nothing could have been less directly autobiographical than this experiment in which words seem to de-

tach themselves from referential links and to float in abstract weightlessness or to immolate themselves in passionate visions that reduce them to ashes. A more attentive reading reveals not only that this is untrue, but that the text is oriented toward or refers to certain passages which I have already examined in later poems. The poem is based on symmetry—the trip to Galta at four in the afternoon and the act of writing it while contemplating from the window the typically English landscape "on this afternoon in Cambridge," simultaneously walking and writing—and it culminates in dissolution: that of language into the magical presence of Splendor, the goddess of love or, rather, that of the word in eroticism. The road ends and is converted into a bridge, one which leads us everywhere: we are here and there at the same time. In a triumph of analogy language becomes magnetized and achieves the harmony of opposites. (pp. 616-17)

The walking/writing analogy leads to another: hanging vines/lines over the paper. All reality empties out into the text, in the here and now that it continually re-creates. Thus the road to Galta is also a return to the origin by the "I" in order to discover, as in **Pasado en claro,** that reality is nothing more than the sign that represents itself: "Inside myself: from the beginning I have been falling inside myself and I still am falling. From the beginning I am always going to where I already am, yet I never arrive at where I am. I am always myself somewhere else: the same place, the other I." Therefore, the divided "I" sees in the ruins of Galta the ruins of another place and time, evoked by the perpetual present of the poetry.

> The light of three o'clock in the afternoon, a long time ago, on the cobblestones of a narrow street in a town in the Valley of Mexico, the body of a peasant dressed in white cotton work clothes lying in a pool of blood, the dog that is licking at it, the screams of the women in dark skirts and purple shawls running in the direction of the dead man.

Now we are confronting not landscapes, but signs and symbols which attempt to recover them. Now we understand that the "Patio, wall, ash tree, well" of **Pasado en claro** are archetypes, elements in a common search in which memory, imagination and a tireless intellectual and linguistic process have mixed them together indiscernibly. Now we understand why, in the midst of this effort to "travel toward myself," there emerge two tutelary trees: the banyan in its secular assault "on the vertical patience of a wall," the same one whose vines are lines in *El mono gramático,* and "the primordial fig tree," whose split trunk is the image of sex and erotic passion. The fig tree, *ficaria,* is of the same class as the banyan. These trees are also time, time lived but rescued too in the plural dimension of writing where the palace of Galta is the family home in Mixcoac, the English garden in Cambridge, the act of remembering or of inventing them, the boy and the man who writes. The "I" is an invention that retraces biographical time. . . . If poetry is "the convergence of every point," to have reached the end of the road has another meaning: we can begin again. Our origin is before us, and we are free to create it. The voyage is always beginning. (pp. 617-18)

José Miguel Oviedo, "Return to the Beginning: Paz in His Recent Poetry," translated by Mary

Paz receiving the Cervantes Prize from King Juan Carlos of Spain, April, 1982.

E. Davis, in World Literature Today, *Vol. 56, No. 4, Autumn, 1982, pp. 612-18.*

Sven Birkerts (essay date 1988)

[*Birkerts is a respected critic whose first book,* Artificial Wilderness: Essays on Twentieth-Century Literature, *won the National Book Critics Circle Award for criticism in 1986. In the following excerpt he offers a appreciative review of* The Collected Poems of Octavio Paz, 1957-1987.]

The assertion implicit in Weinberger's editing—which will not be contested here—is that Paz first came into his own with the publication of his tour-de-force long poem *Sunstone* (1957), which is the opening selection. He had been writing poems for decades already (an *Early Poems, 1935-1955* was published [in 1973]), but with this performance he is ready to start making his mark on international literature. Indeed, in its ambitiously synthetic momentum, *Sunstone* can be viewed as an important precursor of the innovative work of Carlos Fuentes, Gabriel García-Márquez, Julio Cortazar, and other writers of the celebrated "boom" of the 1960s.

Sunstone is written as a single circular sentence—its end joining its beginning—of 584 11-syllable lines. Its structural basis is the circular Aztec calendar, which measures the synodic period of the planet Venus. (I take this from the helpful "Author's Notes" at the back.) But the reader need not be alarmed by this esoteric correlative design. While it organizes the work, it does not circumscribe its subject. *Sunstone* is, like so many of Paz's longer poems, a lyrically discursive exploration of time and memory, of erotic love, of art and writing, of myth and mysticism. The axis is the urgently ruminating "I"; the links between one flight and the next, often between one line and the next, are forged by the relentless alchemical transformations of metaphor. . . . (p. 36)

Paz's procedure allows him to create a vast and fluid-feeling panorama of the psyche in intensified motion, with all of its dilations and shifts. The hazard is one that threatens all such inclusive (and, yes, baroque) undertakings: that the pressure of necessity will be vitiated by the too-bountiful imaginings, that the progress on the page will at times resemble a free-for-all of competing ideas and images. Stunning as Paz's cadenzas can be, the reader may long at times for a clearer sense of directional development. (Paz's polymorphous tendency is encouraged, I suspect, by the vowel-rich sonorities of the Spanish language; it would be difficult to generate so hypnotic a flow of sounds in our Anglo-Saxon-based tongue.)

Though Paz's reigning structural conceit in *Sunstone* harks back to the indigenous Aztecs, his poetic art strongly reflects the influence of André Breton and the French surrealists, as well as the deep Symbolist heritage running back through Eliot to Rimbaud. . . . Paz is clearly less interested in subject matter than he is in recreating the momentum of psychic—and spiritual—processes. ***Sunstone*** is as much about the porosity of boundaries and the frailty of the ego as it is about the solar mythologies of the Aztecs.

One does not have to read far to discover a rather striking artistic split at the core of Paz's endeavor. Throughout the compendium, long, all-embracing poems of the ***Sunstone*** variety alternate with short, stripped-down lyrics. The latter are often lyrically superior—cleaner, more mysterious, less didactic—but they bear no freight of ideas. It is almost as if these were the two warring sides of the poet's nature—a will to proliferation and a will to asceticism. (pp. 36-7)

In 1962, when he was 48, Paz was appointed to the post of Mexican ambassador to India. Out of the 6-year period that he served—the key years of poetic maturity—came the collection ***Ladera Este,*** or ***Eastern Slope.*** The impact of Indian religious creeds on a sensibility avid for spiritual syntheses was, predictably, immense. Paz already suspected the fortified boundaries of the ego. Now, for a time, he would seek to tear asunder the veil of Maya (or "illusion"). Here, for instance, are some lines from **"Reading John Cage,"** a remarkable fusion of Paz's avant-garde inclinations and his more mystical probings:

> It is not the same,
> hearing the footsteps of the afternoon
> among the trees and houses,
>   and
> seeing this same afternoon
> among the same trees and
>   houses now
>   after reading
> *Silence:*
>   Nirvana is Samsara,
>   silence is music.

Even more ethereally pitched is Paz's long fugal poem ***Blanco,*** which reads in places like some Eastern holy text. . . . (p. 37)

Paz is not the first Occidental poet to have embraced Oriental ways. The great Swedish poet Gunnar Ekelöf put himself through a similar sea-change; and both Gary Snyder and Allen Ginsberg have, for periods, brought their aesthetics in line with the practice of Eastern religious disciplines. The marriage of strains has often resulted, as it did in some of Paz's poetry of the time, in a haunting, if peculiar, music.

But the Indian period was not to last. The 1968 massacre of student demonstrators by government troops at the Mexico City Olympiad stunned Paz. He resigned his post in protest and returned home. Though he had long since broken with the leftist orthodoxy of the Latin American intelligentsia, he had no tolerance for the repressions of the state's pretend democracy, either. His gesture marked him as a radical without an ideological portfolio—a status that continues to irk many of his countrymen.

The poetry from this turbulent epoch (1969-1975) was collected in ***Vuelta,*** or ***Return.*** (***Vuelta*** is also the name of the cultural journal that Paz began to edit at this time.) The poet appeared to be turning away from the quietistic meditations of his India years. A poem like the title-piece, **"Return,"** reveals a preoccupation with the crises of the day,

and sequences of sharply surrealistic imagery expose a distinctly non-transcendental point of vantage:

> We have dug up Rage
> The amphitheater of the genital sun is a dungheap
> The fountain of lunar water is a dungheap
> The lovers' park is a dungheap
> The library is a nest of killer rats
> The university is a muck full of frogs
> The altar is Chanfalla's swindle
> The eggheads are stained with ink
> The doctors dispute in a den of thieves

Once again, Ginsberg comes to mind, this time the Ginsberg of "Howl" (1956). We see the same effort in both writers to find a declamatory idiom adequate to the outrageous character of contemporary events.

Rage is not the only thing that Paz disinterred upon his return. He also became fascinated with the myth of the self and of the past (a fascination that might have signalled the return of the repressed ego). In 1974 Paz published his long poem ***A Draft of Shadows.*** The epigraph is drawn from Wordsworth's *Prelude:* "A Fair seed-time had my soul, and I grew up / Fostered alike by beauty and by fear." Throughout the poem, Paz attempts through repeated elisions of memory to come to terms with his family history, his own emotional and spiritual experience, and his poetic vocation. He begins with an Eliotic evocation of the mysteries of memory . . . carries on through hundreds of lines figuring phrases in his autobiography . . . and finally concludes with these enigmatically Symbolist lines:

> I am where I was:
> I walk behind the murmur,
> footsteps within me, heard with my eyes,
> the murmur is in the mind, I am my footsteps,
> I hear the voices that I think,
> the voices that think me as I think them.
> I am the shadow my words cast.

If Paz had earlier, in ***Blanco,*** opposed the reality of the world to that of the word, he appears here to have cast his lot with the latter. He is hardly the first poet to have looked to language as the seat of the real—Rimbaud, Mallarmé, Eliot, and Stevens all did—but few poets have subjected their readers at such length to the to-and-fro of the preliminary meditations. Indeed, this might well be the main complaint against this grand *oeuvre:* that it asks us to track what are often just the reflex actions of a soul bent on transcending the here and now. When Paz is at his best, we can feel the struggle pressurizing the verse. But there are too many instances of the mind milling abstract nouns, and too many patches of "sublime" musing that come across more as a conjuring with verbal counters than as a pitched battle with necessity. This unevenness keeps Paz from being a poet of the very first order—the ore keeps disappearing inside the bedrock. (pp. 37-8)

[***The Collected Poems of Octavio Paz, 1957-1987***] concludes with the hitherto uncollected poems of ***Arbol Adentro*** (***A Tree Within,*** 1976-1987). Paz's spiritual battles continue unabated. It may be tempting to read the more recent poems as episodes in an elderly poet's confrontation with mortality. And the evidence can be found for such a tack. In the long poem **"Preparatory Exercise (Diptych with votive tablet),"** for instance, the speaker laments: "The Buddha did not teach me how to die." But an open-eyed assessment shows a contrary development as well. Many of these poems give us Paz at his most celebratory— and most youthful. He sounded older at 40 when he was tormenting himself with metaphysics. Now, in places, we need a sprightlier voice, a vision that looks to the earthly as well as to the ineffable. . . . Paz's career may yet have room for a poetry of earth. (p. 39)

> Sven Birkerts, "Rage and Return," in The New Republic, Vol. 198, No. 11, March 14, 1988, pp. 36-9.

J. D. McClatchy   (essay date 1989)

[*McClatchy is a prominent critic and editor whose essays and reviews have appeared in such periodicals as* Poetry, the New Republic, *and* the Yale Review. *While praising Paz as* "one of the truly imposing figures in the cultural life of the New World," *McClatchy contends in his review of* The Collected Poems of Octavio Paz, 1957-1987 *excerpted below, that much of Paz's verse is one-dimensional in tone and structure.*]

In the prologue to his magisterial study of Sor Juana, [*Sor Juana: Her Life and Her World*], as part of a meditation on "the system of implicit authorizations and prohibitions" in modern culture, Octavio Paz speculates that the democratic and progressivist societies dominant in the West since the late eighteenth century are constitutionally hostile to certain literary genres. Bourgeois rationalism and poetry, for instance, are oil and water. The methods and attitudes, the very nature of poetry has grown hostile to the dogmas of the day and the cult of the future, to the moral pieties of modern society. Poetry is a violation. Baudelaire and the Symbolists, the pioneers of Modernism, the Surrealists—these were enemies within the walls, and remain the champions of all those forces opposed to the relentless progress of twentieth-century life.

There is more than a little truth in Paz's view of history, and more than a little self-justification. Certainly those champions have been his masters, and his career has been devoted to the idea that as "an operation capable of changing the world, poetic activity is revolutionary by nature; a spiritual exercise, it is a means of interior liberation." Though it reveals the world and its *correspondances,* it denies history. It is simultaneously the voice of the people, the language of the elect, and the word of the solitary. Like those of his Modernist masters, Paz's poems have preferred the fragmentary and ecstatic, the discoveries of chance and dream, the infernal landscape of the city, nostalgic glimpses of paradisal literature from the past, the unredeemable self *in extremis.* Such views derive largely from European models, and have put Paz in one camp (along with Borges, he has been a sort of major general) of a continuing battle that rages (or used to) in Latin America as in its northern neighbor. He himself tells the story of meeting, decades ago, Gabriela Mistral. She had just won the Nobel Prize, and asked the young, unknown Paz to show her his poems. He sent a slim volume. A few days later, she greeted him at a party with that slightly too formal politeness one understands to be a reproof: "I like your poems," she said, "though they are not at all what I feel. You could well be a European poet; for my taste, you are not *telluric* enough." What she meant by the peculiar term is that Paz was airborne rather than deeply root-

ed, a cosmopolite rather than a native. Any Latin American writer, he would counter, is actually both, working between the traditions of European civilization and the realities of American culture. The convergence appears even, or first, in the language itself. The Spanish of Spain is pure, solid, substantialist; the Spanish of Latin America is a hybrid, "sometimes a mask, sometimes a passion—never a habit."

Masks and passions would likewise describe the surface, the *sound,* of this new **Collected Poems.** The book picks up where **Early Poems: 1935-1955,** published fifteen years ago by New Directions, leaves off, and with these two volumes the reader will have most of Paz's poems, attractively presented and fluently translated. The past three decades have taken Paz far afield, most notably during his years as the Mexican Ambassador to India, and resulted in some of his strongest work. But I'll confess I have always preferred Paz's essays to his poems. Only in prose does the full range of his extraordinary mind stand revealed, its breadth of reference and brilliance of analogy. The poems, oddly, seem more one-dimensional. They are nearly always lyrics; there is no narrative, little portraiture or evocation of specific places, not much variety of tone. He is a poet of phrases, what he calls "a succession of signs," as if sustained argument would somehow handicap a poem's spontaneity. Surrealist gestures, "the apple of fire on the tree of syntax," electrify by moments, but are often merely scintillant sparks. Other rhetorical gestures are more grandiose, but hollow:

> The things were buried deep in themselves
> and my eyes of flesh saw them
> weary of being, realities
> stripped of their names. My two eyes
> were souls grieving for the world.
> On the empty street the presence
> passed without passing, vanishing
> into the forms, fixed in its changes,
> and turned now into houses, oaks, snow, time.
> Life and death flowed on, blurred together.

There are worse examples of this same sort of vatic mannerism throughout the new collection, though it is fair to say it sounds flatter in English than in Spanish.

What here seems a fault is elsewhere a virtue of Paz's restless search for the world behind the world. "Poetry is not truth," he says in **"San Ildefonso Nocturne,"** "it is the resurrection of presences." The best poems here are rites. What we get is an invocation of powers, a litany of images, the ascent to vision, and the ritualistic struggle of opposing psychic and mythic forces. If Paz sometimes seems impatient to get beyond language, at other times he celebrates the textuality of the self. (pp. 29-31)

This new collection falls into three parts. At the heart of the earlier work here is the long poem that first brought Paz to the attention of an international audience, **Sunstone** (1957). Reading it is rather like listening to Messiaen's *Turangalila:* you're overwhelmed, but don't want to repeat it very often. Memory's "swimming flame"—at once sensuous and metaphysical—flickers in corners of his life, and on the faces of women he has loved. And it's right that this poem be placed first in a volume that is obsessed with women: with real women, like his wife and mother; with the idea of woman, fertile and mysterious, Mother India or the *anima mundi* or "the feminine void"; and finally with woman as the type of the muse, the lyric, the imagination, *la palabra,* the word itself, "stainless / promiscuous / speechless / nameless."

With *Ladera Este* (*East Slope,* 1968) we move with Paz to India, and to material congenial to his mystical temperament but also exotic enough to be transcribed into poems much denser, richer than before. Like India itself, these poems are a collage of details both elemental and quotidian. The waking dream of Orientalism calls forth from Paz some of his most sharply observed and powerful lines. (pp. 31-2)

In 1968 Paz resigned his post in New Delhi to protest the massacre by government troops of student demonstrators in Mexico City. After a stay in England and the United States, where he taught at Harvard and Texas, he returned to Mexico in 1971, and the title of his next book, *Vuelta* (*Return,* 1975), indicates his spiritual turn back towards Mexican themes. The title poem itself is a stinging jeremiad that scans from the hilltop of indignation the city which has swallowed up his native village:

> On corners and in plazas
> on the wide pedestals of the public squares
> the Fathers of the Civic Church
> a silent conclave of puppet buffoons
> neither eagles nor jaguars
>   buzzard lawyers
> locusts
>   wings of ink   sawing mandibles
> ventriloquist coyotes
>   peddlers of shadows
> beneficent satraps
>   the cacomistle   thief of hens
> the monument to the Rattle and its snake
> the altar to the mauser and the machete
> the mausoleum of the epauletted cayman
> rhetoric sculpted in phrases of cement.

Paz's most recent work, *Arbol Adentro* (*A Tree Within,* 1988) is the last section of this book, but as a courtesy to readers who have all the earlier books it has also been published simultaneously and separately by New Directions. Though it contains a remarkable poem, **"Preparatory Exercise,"** which speculates about his own death, this generous group is hardly valedictory; it includes some of Paz's most vigorous work. There is a suite of poems addressed to painters—among them, Balthus, Miró, Duchamp, Rauschenberg, Matta, and Alechinsky—that set out to recreate the surfaces and moods of their paintings. In other poems too, the economy of the visionary and the descriptive, the prophetic and the panegyric, is wonderfully balanced. I finished this book convinced that Paz stands out like a ziggurat in the literary landscape of Mexico. And though to North American tastes much of his poetry will seem like a rather inflated throwback, Paz remains, at seventy-five, one of the truly imposing figures in the cultural life of the New World. (pp. 33-4)

> *J. D. McClatchy, "Masks and Passions," in* Poetry, *Vol. CLIV, No. 1, April, 1989, pp. 29-48.*

> **"I find the word 'boom' repulsive. There can be a 'boom' in petroleum or wheat, but there can't be a boom in the novel and less still in poetry. . . . What I am opposed to is that criticism should be supplanted by propaganda and an attempt made to reduce Latin American literature to the novel alone, for commercial or publishing reasons. A mutilation amputating half its body: poetry."**
> **—Octavio Paz, 1973**

Arthur Terry   (essay date 1989)

[*In the following excerpt, Terry offers a positive assessment of* The Collected Poems of Octavio Paz, 1957-1987, *yet considers the quality of many of the translations marginal.*]

Octavio Paz is unquestionably one of the finest poets writing in any language, a fact which [*Collected Poems, 1957-1987*] should make abundantly clear to English readers. Though earlier selections have done much to convey the quality of his poetry, only a thorough reading of his work of the past three decades can bring out the often subtle relations between individual poems and an overall structure of great ambition and integrity. At the same time, as readers of his prose can confirm, the integrity of Paz's vision is not purely a poetical matter: his continuing reflections on a multiplicity of themes, from art and anthropology to the contingencies of world politics and the society of his native Mexico, bear witness to an intelligence which both feeds off, and feeds into, his activity as a poet.

Something of the nature of this relationship emerges from one of Paz's best-known statements: "Poetry is the *other* voice. Not the voice of history or of anti-history, but the voice which, in history, is always saying something different". What this means in practice is that any poem involves a "breaking of silence" or, as he puts it in his note to *Blanco* (1966), "the passage of the word from silence before speech to silence after it". This already suggests Paz's affinities with both Mallarmé and the Surrealists: where Breton, for instance, rejects the notion of an "external theme" in poetry, Paz sees the poem not as a means of representing the world but as a way of reproducing it through the behaviour of language itself. Thus each of his major poems, from *Piedra de sol* (1957) to **"Carta de creencia"** (1987), forms a kind of "itinerary" in which the composition of the poem is made to reflect the actual experience of reading a poem. This is not to say that external reality is excluded from the poem, but rather that such references as there are—to outside events or to moments in the poet's own experience—tend to lead back into the verbal structure of the text. As for the anture of the "itinerary", this more often than not takes the form of a movement towards a particular moment which remains fixed in the poem, where it acts as a mirror for the poet's own consciousness.

What prevents this from being merely narcissistic is Paz's sense of "the Other": in poem after poem, the individual consciousness is made to confront that which is not itself in an attempt to reach the unity which, in Paz's view of things, lies beyond this essential duality. In the course of the process, Otherness assumes a number of forms—language, the human body, the world itself—each of which is interchangeable with the others. Hence the eroticism which is central to Paz's poetry is never an isolated force: its subversiveness owes something to Surrealism, but sexual love is both a way of escaping from the constrictions of the self and a metaphor for a kind of fusion which language itself can only hint at. The line which occurs near the beginning of *Piedra de sol*—"the world is now visible through your body"—is both the starting-point of the poem and the axis around which the whole complex sequence of images revolves. Similarly, *Blanco*—Paz's most "experimental" poem, in which a single poem breaks up into a constellation of shorter sequences, each self-sufficient yet complementary to the others—may be read simultaneously as a love poem and as a meditation on knowledge and on the nature of poetic language.

Paz's achievement as a poet rests ultimately on his power to create a kind of poetry which both exemplifies, and at the same time questions, the ability of language to come to terms with the world it claims to know. The kind of transaction this implies, he would argue, can never be more than provisional; as he says in *El mono gramático*, probably his finest prose text, "fixity can only be momentary", and the final poem in his most recent volume ends, simply and movingly, with a sense of new beginnings:

> Perhaps to love is to learn
> to walk through this world.
> To learn to be silent
> like the oak and the linden of the fable.
> To learn to see,
> Your glance scatters seeds.
> It planted a tree.
>   I talk
> because you shake its leaves.

The collection from which this comes, *Árbol adentro (A Tree Within)*, forms the last section of Eliot Weinberger's massive and beautifully produced bilingual edition, which contains virtually all of Paz's poetry from his first major poem, *Piedra de sol (Sunstone)*, to the present. The quality of the translations, it has to be said, is variable: though Weinberger has sensibly included a number of fine versions by Elizabeth Bishop, Denise Levertov, Charles Tomlinson and others, the greater part of the book is his own work, and it is here that most of the mistakes occur. Sometimes these twist what Paz is actually saying: "hasta los mexicanos somos felices" ("even we Mexicans are happy") comes out as "till all Mexicans are happy", and "me descubrió la muerte" ("death discovered me") as "I discovered death". . . . More often than not, however, it is a question of elementary errors which a glance at a dictionary would have avoided: "Ródano" is the Spanish for the River Rhône; "anochece" means "it is getting dark", not "last night", "el vértigo de la dicha" is "the vertigo of happiness", not "the vertigo of speech". . . . Such lapses—there are quite a few more—are all the more strange since for long stretches of the book Weinberger

shows himself to be a reliable and often resourceful translator.

Whatever its faults, however, this book deserves to be widely read, and one must applaud the efforts of both editor and publisher in making available a body of work which engages so lucidly and on so many levels with the possibilities and limitations of modern poetry.

> *Arthur Terry, "Back to the Other," in* The Times Literary Supplement, *No. 4489, April 14-20, 1989, p. 402.*

FURTHER READING

Chiles, Frances. *Octavio Paz: The Mythic Dimension.* American University Studies, Series II, Romance Languages and Literature, Vol. 6. New York: Peter Lang, 1987, 224 p.
    Examines Paz's conception of myth and its relation to his poetry.

Fein, John M. *Toward Octavio Paz: A Reading of His Major Poems, 1957-1976.* Lexington, Ky.: University of Kentucky Press, 1986, 189 p.
    Scholarly analysis of such collections as *Piedra de sol, Blanco,* and *Vuelta.*

Guibert, Rita. "Octavio Paz." In her *Seven Voices: Seven Latin American Writers Talk to Rita Guibert,* pp. 183-275. Translated by Frances Partridge. New York: Alfred A. Knopf, 1973.
    An in-depth conversation with Paz on his life and career.

Nugent, Robert. "Structure and Meaning in Octavio Paz's 'Piedra de sol'." *Kentucky Foreign Language Quarterly* XIII, No. III (1966): 138-46.
    Approaches the thematic content and technical construction of Paz's *Piedra de sol* through an examination of his use of imagery, language, and awareness of myth.

Phillips, Rachel. *The Poetic Modes of Octavio Paz.* London: Oxford University Press, 1972, 168 p.
    Critical overview.

Rodman, Selden. "Octavio Paz." In his *Tongues of Fallen Angels,* pp. 135-61. New York: New Directions Books, 1972.
    Interview with the author.

Schmidt, Michael. "Octavio Paz: The Dream Set Free." *PN Review* 141, No. 57 (1987): 37-40.
    Brief biocritical tribute.

"Homage to Octavio Paz, Our 1982 Neustadt Laureate." *World Literature Today* 56, No. 4 (Autumn 1982): 589-643.
    Contains encomiums and critical essays on Paz, including pieces by Manuel Durán, Jorge Guillén, Ivar Ivask, and José Miguel Ortega.

Sylvia Plath

1932-1963

(Also wrote under the pseudonym Victoria Lucas) American poet, novelist, short story writer, essayist, memoirist, and scriptwriter.

Considered an important poet of the post-World War II era, Plath became widely known following her suicide in 1963 and the posthumous publication of *Ariel,* a collection containing her most startling and acclaimed verse. Through bold metaphors and stark, often violent and unsettling imagery, Plath's works evoke mythic qualities in nature and humanity. Her vivid, intense poems explore such topics as personal and feminine identity, individual suffering and oppression, and the inevitability of death. Deeply informed by autobiographical elements, Plath's writings poignantly reflect her struggles with despair and mental illness. Her efforts to assert a strong female identity and to balance familial, marital, and career aspirations have established her as a representative voice for feminist concerns. While Plath is frequently linked with confessional poets Robert Lowell, Anne Sexton, and John Berryman, all of whom directly express personal torments and anguish in their work, critics have noted that many of Plath's poems are dramatic monologues voiced by a character who is not necessarily autobiographical. Although sometimes faulted as indulgent and preoccupied with death and psychological suffering, Plath's work continues to be read widely and has generated numerous scholarly studies.

Born in Boston, Massachusetts, Plath enjoyed an idyllic early childhood near the sea. Her father, a German immigrant, was a professor of entomology at Boston College who maintained a special interest in the study of bees. His sudden death from diabetes mellitus in 1940 devastated the eight-year-old Plath, and many critics note the significance of this traumatic experience in interpreting her poetry, which frequently contains both brutal and reverential images of her father, as well as sea imagery and allusions to bees. Plath began publishing poetry at an early age in such publications as *Seventeen* magazine and the *Christian Science Monitor,* and in 1950 she earned a scholarship to Smith College in Northampton, Massachusetts. After spending a month during the summer of her junior year in New York City as a guest editor for *Mademoiselle* magazine, Plath suffered a mental collapse that resulted in a suicide attempt and her subsequent institutionalization. Plath later chronicled the circumstances and consequences of this breakdown in her best-selling novel, *The Bell Jar.* Following her recovery, Plath returned to Smith and graduated summa cum laude in 1955. After winning a Fulbright fellowship to study at Cambridge University, Plath met and married English poet Ted Hughes in 1956. The eventual breakdown of their marriage during the early 1960s and the ensuing struggles with severe depression that led to her suicide are considered crucial elements of Plath's most critically acclaimed poetry.

Plath's verse is represented in several volumes. *The Colossus,* the only book of her poems published during her life-

time, collects pieces dating from the mid- to late 1950s; *Ariel* contains poems selected by Hughes from among the many works Plath composed during the final months before her death; *Winter Trees* collects several more of the *Ariel* poems and reflects Hughes's plan to publish Plath's later works in intervals; *Crossing the Water: Transitional Poems* reprints most of her post-*Colossus* and pre-*Ariel* verse; and *The Collected Poems,* which won a Pulitzer Prize in 1982, features all of her verse, including juvenilia and several previously unpublished pieces in order of composition. Critics often maintain that during her brief career, Plath's verse evolved from a somewhat derivative early style to that of a unique and accomplished poetic voice. Katha Pollitt commented: "Plath's was one of those rare poetic careers—Keats's was another—that moved consistently and with gathering rapidity and assurance to an ever greater daring and individuality."

Plath's early verse reflects various poetic influences, evoking the mythic qualities of the works of William Butler Yeats and Ted Hughes, the diverse experiments with form and language of Gerard Manley Hopkins and W. H. Auden, and the focus on personal concerns that dominates the verse of Robert Lowell and Theodore Roethke. Most of her early poems are formal, meticulously crafted, and feature elaborate syntax and well-developed metaphors, as Plath employed such forms as the ode, the villanelle, and the pastoral lyric to examine art, love, nature, and personal themes. These pieces are more subdued than the later work for which she would become renowned. Critics generally believe that some of the later poems in *The Colossus* heralded a new phase in Plath's career. Marjorie Perloff commented: "[When], in the last two years of her life, [Plath] finally came into her own, the adopted voices merely evaporated, and a new harsh, demonic, devastating self, only partially prefigured in such poems as 'The Thin People' (1957) and 'The Stones' (1959), came into being."

Plath's later work evidences the increasing frustration of her desires. Her ambitions of finding happiness through work, marriage, and family were thwarted by such events as hospital stays for a miscarriage and an appendectomy, the breakup of her marriage, and fluctuating moods in which she felt vulnerable to male domination and threatening natural forces, particularly death. Following the dissolution of her marriage, Plath moved with her two children from the Devon countryside to a London flat, where Irish poet William Butler Yeats once resided, and wrote feverishly from the summer of 1962 until her death in February of the following year. Many of her best-known poems, including "Daddy," "Lady Lazarus," "Lesbos," "Purdah," and "Edge," were composed during this period and form the nucleus of the *Ariel* collection. These pieces, which reflect her increasing anger, bitterness, and despair toward life, feature intense, rhythmic language that blends terse statements, sing-song passages, repetitive phrasing, and sudden violent images, metaphors, and declarations. For example, in "Daddy," perhaps her most frequently discussed and anthologized work, Plath denounces her father's dominance over her life and, among other allusions, associates him with nazism and herself with Jewish victims of the Holocaust: "I have always been scared of *you* / With your Luftwaffe, your gobbledygoo. / And your neat moustache / And your Aryan eye, bright blue. / Panzer-man, panzer-man, O You—." Plath explained in a radio broadcast that the poem's narrator is "a girl with an Electra complex. Her father died while she thought he was God." Response to "Daddy" reflects the general opinion of much of her later work. Some critics contend that Plath's jarring effects are extravagant, and many object to her equation of personal sufferings with such horrors as those experienced by victims of Nazi genocide. Others, however, praise the passion and formal structure of her later poems, through which she confronts her tensions and conflicts. Stanley Plumly stated that "behind the separate masks, all the masks of [Plath's] good poems, there is a unity, an integrity, and an integrating of imagination— that whatever the hammer-splittings of the self, behind the sad mask of the woman is the mind and heart of someone making transcendent poems."

(For further information on Plath's life and career, see *Contemporary Literary Criticism,* Vols. 1, 2, 3, 5, 9, 11, 14, 17, 50, 51; *Contemporary Authors,* Vols. 19-20; *Contemporary Authors Permanent Series,* Vol. 2; *Dictionary of Literary Biography,* Vols. 5, 6; and *Concise Dictionary of American Literary Biography: The New Consciousness, 1941-1968.*)

PRINCIPAL WORKS

POETRY

*The Colossus   1960
*Ariel   1965
*Crossing the Water   1971
*Winter Trees   1971
The Collected Poems   1981

OTHER MAJOR WORKS

The Bell Jar [as Victoria Lucas]   (novel)   1963; also published as *The Bell Jar* [as Sylvia Plath], 1966
Letters Home: Correspondence, 1960-1963 (letters) 1975
Johnny Panic and the Bible of Dreams, and Other Prose Writings (prose) 1977; also published as *Johnny Panic and the Bible of Dreams: Short Stories, Prose and Diary Excerpts* [enlarged edition], 1979
The Journals of Sylvia Plath (journals) 1982

*Each of these volumes, which were originally published in England, were published in the United States with an alternate selection of poems as *The Colossus, and Other Poems* (1962), *Ariel* (1966), *Crossing the Water: Transitional Poems* (1971), and *Winter Trees* (1972).

Robert Lowell   (essay date 1966)

[*A central figure in American poetry during the mid-twentieth century, Lowell was a significant contributor to the development of "confessional poetry," the characteristics of which are perhaps best exemplified in his volume* Life Studies *(1959). In these poems, Lowell abandoned the formal concerns of his earlier work, turned to free verse, and created a poetic voice of intense personal concern. Plath acknowledged the influence of this volume on her work, and many critics have associated Plath's poetry with Lowell's. In the following excerpt from the foreword to the American edition of Plath's collection* Ariel, *Lowell ardently characterizes Plath as a mythic figure "driven foreward [in her poetry] by the pounding pistons of her heart."*]

In these poems [in *Ariel*], written in the last months of her life and often rushed out at the rate of two or three a day, Sylvia Plath becomes herself, becomes something imaginary, newly, wildly and subtly created—hardly a person at all, or a woman, certainly not another "poetess," but one of those super-real, hypnotic, great classical heroines. This character is feminine, rather than female, though almost everything we customarily think of as feminine is turned on its head. The voice is now coolly amused, witty, now sour, now fanciful, girlish, charming, now sinking to the strident rasp of the vampire—a Dido, Phaedra, or Medea, who can laugh at herself as "cow-heavy and floral in my Victorian nightgown." Though lines get repeated, and sometimes the plot is lost, language never dies in her mouth.

Everything in these poems is personal, confessional, felt, but the manner of feeling is controlled hallucination, the autobiography of a fever. She burns to be on the move, a walk, a ride, a journey, the flight of the queen bee. She is driven forward by the pounding pistons of her heart. The title *Ariel* summons up Shakespeare's lovely, though slightly chilling and androgenous spirit, but the truth is that this *Ariel* is the author's horse. Dangerous, more powerful than man, machinelike from hard training, she herself is a little like a racehorse, galloping relentlessly with risked, outstretched neck, death hurdle after death hurdle topped. She cries out for that rapid life of starting pistols, snapping tapes, and new world records broken. What is most heroic in her, though, is not her force, but the desperate practicality of her control, her hand of metal with its modest, womanish touch. Almost pure motion, she can endure "God, the great stasis in his vacuous night," hospitals, fever, paralysis, the iron lung, being stripped like a girl in the booth of a circus sideshow, dressed like a mannequin, tied down like Gulliver by the Lilliputians . . . apartments, babies, prim English landscapes, beehives, yew trees, gardens, the moon, hooks, the black boot, wounds, flowers with mouths like wounds, Belsen's lampshades made of human skin, Hitler's homicidal iron tanks clanking over Russia. Suicide, father-hatred, self-loathing—nothing is too much for the macabre gaiety of her control. Yet it is too much; her art's immortality is life's disintegration. The surprise, the shimmering, unwrapped birthday present, the transcendence "into the red eye, the cauldron of morning," and the lover, who are always waiting for her, are Death, her own abrupt and defiant death.

> He tells me how badly I photograph.
> He tells me how sweet
> The babies look in their hospital
> Icebox, a simple
>
> Frill at the neck,
> Then the flutings of their Ionian
> Death-gowns,
> Then two little feet.

There is a peculiar, haunting challenge to these poems. Probably many, after reading *Ariel,* will recoil from their first overawed shock, and painfully wonder why so much of it leaves them feeling empty, evasive and inarticulate. In her lines, I often hear the serpent whisper, "Come, if only you had the courage, you too could have my rightness, audacity and ease of inspiration." But most of us will turn back. These poems are playing Russian roulette with six cartridges in the cylinder, a game of "chicken," the wheels of both cars locked and unable to swerve. Oh, for that heaven of the humble copyist, those millennia of Egyptian artists repeating their lofty set patterns! And yet Sylvia Plath's poems are not the celebration of some savage and debauched existence, that of the "damned" poet, glad to burn out his body for a few years of continuous intensity. This poetry and life are not a career; they tell that life, even when disciplined, is simply not worth it.

It is poignant, looking back, to realize that the secret of Sylvia Plath's last irresistible blaze lies lost somewhere in the checks and courtesies of her early laborious shyness. She was never a student of mine, but for a couple of months seven years ago, she used to drop in on my poetry seminar at Boston University. I see her dim against the bright sky of a high window, viewless unless one cared to look down on the city outskirts' defeated yellow brick and

square concrete pillbox filling stations. She was willowy, long-waisted, sharp-elbowed, nervous, giggly, gracious—a brilliant tense presence embarrassed by restraint. Her humility and willingness to accept what was admired seemed at times to give her an air of maddening docility that hid her unfashionable patience and boldness. She showed us poems that later, more or less unchanged, went into her first book, *The Colossus.* They were somber, formidably expert in stanza structure, and had a flair for alliteration and Massachusetts' low-tide dolor.

> A mongrel working his legs to a gallop
> Hustles the gull flock to flap off the sand-spit.

Other lines showed her wit and directness.

> The pears fatten like little Buddhas.

Somehow none of it sank very deep into my awareness. I sensed her abashment and distinction, and never guessed her later appalling and triumphant fulfillment. (pp. vii-ix)

> *Robert Lowell, in a foreword to* Ariel *by Sylvia Plath, Harper & Row, Publishers, 1966, pp. vii-ix.*

A. Alvarez   (essay date 1966)

[*Alvarez is a prominent British critic, editor, poet, and novelist. In his writings of the early 1960s, Alvarez campaigned against what he viewed as the excessive gentility of British poetry since World War II, advocating instead poetry of extreme personal, emotional, and political import. His controversial* The Savage God: A Study of Suicide *(1971) includes a lengthy portrait of his working and personal relationship with Plath during her time in England, as well as commentary on her verse. In the following excerpt from the text of a memorial broadcast on British radio that aired shortly after Plath's death, Alvarez summarizes the development of Plath's poetry from* The Colossus *to* Ariel.*]

What follows was originally written as a memorial broadcast which went out on the BBC Third Programme very shortly after Sylvia Plath's death in 1963. It was designed partly as a tribute and partly as an attempt to show how those strange last poems might be read. Clearly, their newness made some kind of explanation, or hints, seem necessary. The British Council had interviewed her and taped her reading some of the last poems not long before she died. I based my broadcast on these tapes, and planned it as little more than a running commentary. So inevitably it lacks the formal poise of a proper essay. And because it was written so close to her death—a time of great turmoil and confusion—it is far rougher than anything I would do today. But perhaps that roughness is a genuine part of the thing; it seems impossible now, without entirely recasting it, to polish it up much or amplify the many points that are made too briefly. I don't even believe that more elegance would be appropriate.

At the time, it seemed more important to try to define the extraordinary originality of her later poems—what they were doing and how they were doing it—than to dwell on the tragic circumstances of her death. I still believe that that is the right priority.

The broadcast was later published in The Review *and*

seemed, as a result, to acquire some kind of underground critical currency. But in the process, some of the closing remarks have been misunderstood. So I have added a final note to try to get the emphasis right.

She was a tall, spindly girl with waist-length sandy hair, which she usually wore in a bun, and that curious, advertisement-trained, transatlantic air of anxious pleasantness. But this was merely a nervous social manner; under it, she was ruthless about her perceptions, wary and very individual. (p. 65)

Her first poem came out in the *Boston Traveller,* when she was eight-and-a-half. I have no idea what these earliest poems were like, though their subject-matter appears to have been conventional enough: 'Birds, bees, spring, fall', she said in an interview.

> —all those subjects which are absolute gifts to the person who doesn't have any interior experience to write about.

Clearly the poems were very precocious, like everything she did in her school and college days. She seemed effortlessly good at things: she was a prize scholar as well as a prize poet; and later, when she married, she was good at having children and keeping a house clean, cooking, making honey, even at riding horses. There was a ruthless efficiency in all she did which left no room for mistakes or uncertainties.

Poetry, however, is not made by efficiency—least of all Sylvia Plath's poetry. Instead, her extraordinary general competence was, I think, made necessary by what made her write: an underlying sense of violent unease. It took a great deal of efficiency to cope with that, to keep it in check. And when the efficiency finally failed, her world collapsed.

But she was disciplined in art, as in everything else. For a first volume, by someone still in her twenties, *The Colossus* is exceptionally accomplished. A poem like **"The Ghost's Leave-taking"** is fairly typical. It exhibits her broad and flexible range of language, in which the unexpected, right word comes so easily:

> . . . the waking head rubbishes out of the draggled lot
> Of sulphurous landscapes and obscure lunar conundrums

and her ability to make startling images out of humdrum objects:

> The oracular ghost who dwindles on pin-legs
> To a knot of laundry, with a classic bunch of sheets
> Upraised, as a hand, emblematic of farewell.

But that last line is also typical of the book's weakness: certainly it's beautiful; but it is also peculiarly careful, held in check, a bit ornate and rhetorical. Throughout *The Colossus* she is using her art to keep the disturbance, out of which she made her verse, at a distance. It is as though she had not yet come to grips with her subject as an artist. She has Style, but not properly her own style. You can trace the influence of Ted Hughes, and there are also poems which sound like Theodore Roethke's—including the long **"Poem for a Birthday"**, which stands last in the book and attempts, I think, to deal with a subject which later possessed her: her nervous breakdown and near suicide at the age of nineteen. It was this which also made the climax and main subject of her novel.

Most of the poems in *The Colossus* were written during the first three years of her marriage, from 1956 to 1959. The *real* poems began in 1960, after the birth of her daughter, Frieda. It is as though the child were a proof of her identity, as though it liberated her into her real self. I think this guess is borne out by the fact that her most creative period followed the birth of her son, two years later. This triggered off an extraordinary outburst: for two or three months, right up to her death, she was writing one, or two, sometimes three, poems a day, seven days a week. She said, in a note written for the BBC:

> These new poems of mine have one thing in common. They were all written at about four in the morning—that still blue, almost eternal hour before the baby's cry, before the glassy music of the milkman, settling his bottles.

A poem like **"Poppies in October"** is simpler, much more direct, than those in *The Colossus.* The unexpectedness is still there, both in the language—

> a sky palely and flamily igniting its carbon monoxide

and the images—

> the woman in the ambulance whose red heart blooms
> through her coat so astoundingly.

But that leaping, arching imagination is no longer baroque, no longer a gesture on the surface of the poem. It is part of what she is actually saying. The poem is about the unexpectedness of the poppies, their gratuitous beauty in her own frozen life.

This change of tone and access of strength is partly, as she said herself, a technical development:

> May I say this: that the ones I've read are very recent, and I have found myself having to read them aloud to myself. Now this is something I didn't do. For example, my first book, *The Colossus*—I can't read any of the poems aloud now. I didn't write them to be read aloud. In fact, they quite privately bore me. Now these very recent ones—I've got to say them. I speak them to myself. Whatever lucidity they may have comes from the fact that I say them aloud.

The difference, in short, is between finger-count and ear-count; one measures the rhythm by rules, the other catches the movement by the inner disturbance it creates. And she could only 'write poems out loud' when she had discovered her own speaking voice; that is, her own identity.

The second main difference between this and her earlier verse is in the direct relevance of the experience. In **"The Ghost's Leave-taking"** the subject is nominally very personal—it's about the way dreams stay with you when you first wake up—but the effect is predominantly of very brilliant scene-setting. In **"Poppies in October"**, on the other hand, what starts as a description finishes as a way of defining her own state of mind. This, I think, is the key to the later poems; the more vivid and imaginative the details are, the more resolutely she turns them inwards. The more objective they seem, the more subjective they, in fact, become. Take, for example, a poem about her favourite horse, **"Ariel"**. . . . The difficulty with this poem lies in separating one element from another. And yet that is also its theme; the rider is one with the horse, the horse is one with the furrowed earth, and the dew on the furrow is one with the rider. The movement of the imagery, like that of the perceptions, is circular. There is also another peculiarity: although the poem is nominally about riding a horse, it is curiously 'substanceless'—to use her own word. You are made to *feel* the horse's physical presence, but not to see it. The detail is all inward. It is as though the horse itself were an emotional state. So the poem is not about 'Ariel'; it is about what happens when the 'stasis in darkness' ceases to be static, when the potential violence of the animal is unleashed. And also the violence of the rider.

In a way, most of her later poems are about just that: about the unleashing of power, about tapping the roots of her own inner violence. There is, of course, nothing so very extraordinary about that. I think that this, in general, is the direction all the best contemporary poetry is taking. She, certainly, did not claim to be original in the kind of writing she was doing, [citing Robert Lowell and Anne Sexton as influences]. . . . (pp. 66-9)

[But] I think Sylvia Plath took further than either of them her analysis of the intolerable and the 'taboo.' And she did it in a wholly original way. For example, her poem **"Fever 103°"**, which she described in this way:

> This poem is about two kinds of fire—the fires of hell, which merely agonize, and the fires of heaven, which purify. During the poem, the first sort of fire suffers itself into the second.

Reading it for the first time, it sounds as though it were just free association on a theme: the theme that illness and pain are cumbersome and intolerable, but that if they go on long enough they cancel themselves out and the purity of death takes over. But the progress is not in fact haphazard. Death is there from the start: 'dull, fat Cerberus . . . wheezes at the gate' right from the beginning. What the poem does is to work away at this idea of a heavy, mundane death until it is purified of all extraneous matter and only the essential bodilessness remains. At the same time this movement is also that of a personal catharsis. She is clarifying not only an abstract death but also her feelings about it, from the cluttered and insufferable to the pure and acceptable. Her method is to let image breed image until, in some curious way, they also breed statements, conclusions. . . . (pp. 69-70)

Now, the movement is complicated. Often in these last poems it seems unnecessarily so. The images came so easily to her that sometimes they confuse each other until the poems choke in the obscurity of their own inventiveness. But they never suffer from the final insoluble obscurity of private references—as, say, Pound's do in the *Pisan Cantos*. The reasons for Sylvia Plath's images are always there, though sometimes you have to work hard to find them. She is, in short, always in intelligent control of her feelings. . . . It seems to me that it was only by her determination both to face her most inward and terrifying experiences and to use her intelligence in doing so—so as not to be overwhelmed by them—that she managed to write these extraordinary last poems, which are at once deeply autobiographical and yet detached, generally relevant.

"Lady Lazarus" is a stage further on from **"Fever 103°"**; its subject is the total purification of achieved death. It is also far more intimately concerned with the drift of Sylvia Plath's life. The deaths of Lady Lazarus correspond to her own crises: the first just after her father died, the second

when she had her nervous breakdown, the third perhaps a presentiment of the death that was shortly to come. Maybe this closeness of the subject helped make the poem so direct. The details don't clog each other: they are swept forward by the current of immediate feeling, marshalled by it and ordered. But what is remarkable about the poem is the objectivity with which she handles such personal material. She is not just talking about her own private suffering. Instead, it is the very closeness of her pain which gives it a general meaning; through it she assumes the suffering of all the modern victims. Above all, she becomes an imaginary Jew. I think this is a vitally important element in her work. For two reasons. First, because anyone whose subject is suffering has a ready-made modern example of hell on earth in the concentration camps. And what matters in them is not so much the physical torture—since sadism is general and perennial—but the way modern, as it were industrial, techniques can be used to destroy utterly the human identity. Individual suffering can be heroic provided it leaves the person who suffers a sense of his own individuality—provided, that is, there is an illusion of choice remaining to him. But when suffering is mass-produced, men and women become as equal and identity-less as objects on an assembly line, and nothing remains—certainly no values, no humanity. This anonymity of pain, which makes all dignity impossible, was Sylvia Plath's subject. Second, she seemed convinced, in these last poems, that the root of her suffering was the death of her father, whom she loved, who abandoned her and who dragged her after him into death. And her father was pure German, pure Aryan, pure anti-semite.

It all comes together in the most powerful of her last poems, **"Daddy"**, about which she wrote the following bleak note:

> The poem is spoken by a girl with an Electra complex. Her father died while she thought he was God. Her case is complicated by the fact that her father was also a Nazi and her mother very possibly part Jewish. In the daughter the two strains marry and paralyze each other—she has to act out the awful little allegory before she is free of it.

"Lady Lazarus" ends with a final, defensive, desperate assertion of omnipotence. . . . Not even that defence is left her in **"Daddy"**; instead, she goes right down to the deep spring of her sickness and describes it purely. What comes through most powerfully, I think, is the terrible *unforgivingness* of her verse, the continual sense not so much of violence—although there is a good deal of that—as of violent resentment that this should have been done to *her*. What she does in the poem is, with a weird detachment, to turn the violence against herself so as to show that she can equal her oppressors with her self-inflicted oppression. And this is the strategy of the concentration camps. When suffering is there whatever you do, by inflicting it upon yourself you achieve your identity, you set yourself free.

Yet the tone of the poem, like its psychological mechanism, is not single or simple, and she uses a great deal of skill to keep it complex. Basically, her trick is to tell this horror story in a verse form as insistently jaunty and ritualistic as a nursery rhyme. And this helps her to maintain towards all the protagonists—her father, her husband and herself—a note of hard and sardonic anger, as though she were almost amused that her own suffering should be so extreme, so grotesque. The technical psychoanalytic term for this kind of insistent gaiety to protect you from what, if faced nakedly, would be insufferable, is 'manic defence.' But what, in a neurotic, is a means of avoiding reality can become, for an artist, a source of creative strength, a way of handling the unhandleable, and presenting the situation in all its fullness. When she first read me the poem a few days after she wrote it, she called it a piece of 'light verse.' It obviously isn't, yet equally obviously it also isn't the racking personal confession that a mere description or précis of it might make it sound.

Yet neither is it unchangingly vindictive or angry. The whole poem works on one single, returning note and rhyme, echoing from start to finish:

> You do not do, you do not do . . .
> . . . I used to pray to recover you.
> Ach, du . . .

There is a kind of cooing tenderness in this which complicates the other, more savage note of resentment. It brings in an element of pity, less for herself and her own suffering than for the person who made her suffer. Despite everything, **"Daddy"** is a love poem.

When Sylvia Plath died I wrote an epitaph on her in *The Observer*, at the end of which I said 'The loss to literature is inestimable.' But someone pointed out to me that this wasn't quite true. The achievement of her final style is to make poetry and death inseparable. The one could not exist without the other. And this is right. In a curious way, the poems read as though they were written posthumously. It needed not only great intelligence and insight to handle the material of them, it also took a kind of bravery. Poetry of this order is a murderous art.

Postscript, 1966.

These final remarks seem to have caused some confusion. I was not *in any sense meaning to imply that breakdown or suicide is a validation of what I now call Extremist poetry. No amount of personal horror will make a good poet out of a bad one. Rather, the opposite: to know from evidence outside the poetry that a man has suffered a great deal will throw into high relief just how much he lacks as an artist.*

I was also not *in any sense meaning to imply that a breakdown or suicide is the necessary corollary or result of Extremist work. Obviously, the poet is not obliged to prove in his life that what he writes about is genuine. After all, he is a poet by virtue of his ability to create an imaginative world which has an objective existence apart from him. The poetry is its own proof. Indeed, the chances are that the more hip the art, the squarer the life of the artist who creates it. A genuinely hip life leaves little time for art.*

But I did mean to imply that this kind of writing involves an element of risk. The Extremist artist sets out deliberately to explore the roots of his emotions, the obscurest springs of his personality, maybe even the sickness he feels himself to be prey to, 'giving himself over to it,' as I have written elsewhere, 'for the sake of the range and intensity of his art.' It is precisely here that the risk lies. I do not personally believe in the classical Freudian argument that art is therapeutic, that the artist is relieved of his fantasies by expressing them. On the contrary, the weird logic of art seems to be that the act of formal expression merely makes the dredged-up material more readily available to the artist. So

the result of handling it in his art may well be that he finds himself living it out. Keats is the prime example of this devious mechanism: the poems of his great period—from the second Hyperion *onwards—are all about death. Apparently, this great creative outburst was triggered off by nursing his brother Tom through his final illness. But if Tom's death were the cause, Keats' own may have been the ultimate effect. He had, that is, pushed death so much to the foreground of his consciousness that it became unavoidable; having written the poems there was nothing left for him to do except die.*

I think much the same happened with Sylvia Plath. The very source of her creative energy was, it turned out, her self-destructiveness. But it was, precisely, a source of living energy, of her imaginative, creative power. So, though death itself may have been a side-issue, it was also an unavoidable risk in writing her kind of poem. My own impression of the circumstances surrounding her eventual death is that she gambled, not much caring whether she won or lost; and she lost. Had she won, the power of those last poems would have been in no way altered or falsified, and she would have been free to go on to other work. That she didn't is the real tragedy. (pp. 70-4)

A. Alvarez, "Sylvia Plath," in TriQuarterly, No. 7, Fall, 1966, pp. 65-74.

Robert Boyers   (essay date 1969)

[*Boyers is a prolific American critic and editor who is the founder and editor-in-chief of the literary journal* Salmagundi. *In his writings, many of which are contained in* Excursions: Selected Literary Essays of Robert Boyers *(1977), Boyers often views literature from a psychological perspective. In the following excerpt, he asserts that Plath's poetry is subversive, calling it art at the expense of life, intended not to resolve conflict but to heighten it.*]

The poetry of Sylvia Plath's *Ariel* is a poetry of surrender, surrender to an imagination that destroys life instead of enhancing it. Nowhere in our literature has a finely wrought art proven so subversive as hers, so utterly at odds with those designs, those structures within which we customarily enclose ourselves to hold experience off at a distance. Emerging from encounter with her poems, as from the murky, subterranean depths of a well, one feels not so much emotionally raped as simply breathless with weariness and confusion. It is as though we had been flung into hideous contact with another order of being, suffocated by a presence too driven and hungry to be supported by the thinness of the air we breathe, a presence thrashing about, taking no notice of us, poor mortal creatures, a presence, finally, reaching, touching, shrieking on a scale that dwarfs into insignificance the familiar scale of our activities. It is with caution and humility that we must approach her art, for it is vaporous with potions that do not intoxicate, but depress and confound. If we listen humbly, there are insistent voices trembling beneath the surface of the poetry, voices which beckon to us, suggesting that we lift our heads from the page and answer the poet in kind, assenting to manipulation by that imagination which has taken everything around it for its own, wringing experience to satisfy its hungers.

In spite of the voices, in spite perhaps even of his own sympathies, the reader will relate to Sylvia Plath's poetry largely in aesthetic terms. The poetic surfaces are bristling with the energy and design of a craftsman, and one will frequently be tempted to remark the virtuosity of the phrasing, or the subtle variations of rhyme, or the arrangements of words in lines which permit her perceptions to come upon us in sharp thrusts, rather than as a flood of continuities which surround and finally drown the reader. There is a rush of associations, but they are somehow detached one from the other, though firmly contained and related by the context which gives them life and meaning. It is all a matter of phrasing and syntax. Units of meaning are at once self-contained and yet open to the influence of other units. They are never arbitrary, but the sequence of correspondences is not always clear. This absence of apparent sequence serves as a goad and a challenge to the reader, drawing him into the dense networks of the poet's imagination, tempting him somehow to understand the principles of selection operant in that sensibility, and thereby to acquiesce in those principles. This is a poetry fraught with implicit dangers.

How little present were the luminous qualities that distinguish her *Ariel* in the pages of her first collection, entitled *The Colossus* (1960). Here and there, of course, a line, a phrase, something grotesque, a weird juxtaposition, a flash of wit or self-parody, would perhaps suggest a mostly latent propensity that might spring to fruition under appropriate circumstances. One may be permitted to smile—how appropriate the final years of that horribly brief life, how propitious the suicidal hysteria and absence of all defenses. She has left us a legacy.

Ariel points an implicit accusatory finger at the critical language we habitually employ to describe the poetry we love. Indeed it is doubtful that one ought even to assay an explanation of his strange love of these poems, with their repellent details and anguished evocation of insufficiency and dread. Perhaps one can be content merely to locate the major sources of our fascination, wherever possible refusing to dilute the tensions which constitute the very fiber of the poetry. The late R. P. Blackmur has described literary criticism as the resolute creation of "a fiction to school the urgency of reading." It is possible to take issue with the word "fiction," which in application to criticism may evoke pejorative connotations. It should not. Clearly, any attempt to generalize, to abstract patterns from a veritable maelstrom of seething particulars, will involve the reader in falsification. To comment is in its nature to falsify, to give less than the thing in itself. And if this is true for criticism of any poetry, how much more applicable must it be for a poetry which is the very embodiment of that divine preternatural madness which has ever been the bane of critics who would mediate between the inspired and the anxiously normal.

The notion of pervasive victimization is a convenient "fiction," if you will, a skeletal structure around which a reader may weave a varied tissue of lesser fictions, all related, and which may finally constitute an organism of sufficient complexity to convey some impression of the poetry. The victimization, of course, entails a fundamental opposition, in Plath's case an opposition between life and art, between reality and the imagination that appropriates it. Almost always in Plath's work it is the imagination that wins. The

poetry is generated at the expense of life, as the rigors of selection overwhelm the comforts of a more benign pluralism. The poet selects in such a way that the diverse aspects of her experience are fixed into immutable categories. Locked within these relatively static structures they participate in mythic interaction with elements of a different order, an order deriving from broader cultural perspectives, which function similarly as categories holding their peculiar elements in recurrent patterns. Always in Plath's poetry we are aware of the functional paradox, in which the most literal transcriptions of painful reality, down to gross particulars, only serve to point to a level of experience which is defiantly abstract, mythic, "fictional." The subject of these poems is not a woman, not a life, but the way in which one woman consents to participate in the transformation of the particulars of her life by an imagination which cares nothing for life except as it provides materials for the play of metamorphic virtuosity. In *Ariel*, art is not a means for resolving conflicts, but for heightening them to a degree of glowing intensity in which all extraneous superficies are burned away, until finally nothing is left but that dreadful image of ash which litters the surface of several poems in the volume.

To close in, as it were, on individual poems, is to see how willful Plath's imagination can be, how it insists, sometimes petulantly, on what it knows it should not want. Conflict is intermittently apparent in a poem like **"Poppies In July,"** in which the poet struggles to see natural phenomena in such a way that they will validate her despairing perception of violence and suffering everywhere. The opening four lines of this brief poem are instructive:

Plath with her children, Frieda and Nicholas, in 1962.

Little poppies, little hell flames,
Do you do no harm?
You flicker, I cannot touch you.
I put my hands among the flames. Nothing burns.

In these lines the speaker is surprised to find that the objects of her attention are at least neutral in their effect upon her. "Do you do no harm?" she asks, as though the poppy were some noxious weed or ghastly augur which might be expected to injure or frighten. But the poet will not be satisfied by a perception of neutrality, and strains her imagination to appropriate the poppies as symbolic validations of the violence that smolders within her. The more ugly and menacing they grow, the more the poet wishes to identify with them, to become the thing she watches and poetically imitates. From the image of "a mouth just bloodied," which she forces the flowers to evoke, it is but a brief step to "If I could bleed, or sleep!—If my mouth could marry a hurt like that!" Such yearnings are, of course, suicidal, for they indicate the gradual dissolution of those barriers which separate the ego from the objects of its concern. Time and again in these poems, Plath becomes the thing or person imagined and described, so that cumulatively the poems evolve an image not of a single human victim, but of a monstrous, abstract victim whose condition is general and unavoidable.

Plath's most ambitious and successful poems are those in which she effects a conjugation between the concretely personal and the specifically cultural. Such a poem is **"Cut."** . . . It is in every respect a remarkable poem, which works out its meanings on a level that wholly transcends simple logic. No principle can be said to order the progression of associations which issue from the poet's obsessive focus on her injured finger, but one is never disposed to question the essential structure of the poem. Perhaps this acquiescence in the idiosyncracy of her progression is attributable to the thin sequential principle which dictates the extremities of the poem, that is, the beginning and the end. Clearly, the poem begins with the moment of incision, followed by the inevitable flow of blood, and proceeding finally to the dressing and bandaging of the wound. These inevitable steps define the contours of the poem and lend to it an aura of order and unity which is responsible for guiding and controlling the diverse impressions evoked by particular lines or images.

Plath is always aware of herself as a spectacle, aware also of the morbid curiosity that so frequently attracts people to the outcast, the freak and the mad. She does not cringe before the glare of attention, but performs, forcing herself into the most macabre postures, chastising in the extremity of her gestures the voyeuristic exploitations of her life and work. This component of performance and spectacle is largely subdued in **"Cut,"** but it is an element of the poem's opening line, which is a giddy exclamation, almost light-hearted and playful. The poet savors the pained sensation which sends a thrill coursing through her veins, alerting the nervous system to an impending release of energy. She anticipates the prospect of working her virtuosic variations on a theme. In this poem, as in so many others, a sharp sense impression provides the necessary occasion for a devastating display, in the course of which the poet locates the sources of her convulsive anxieties. The poet employs the word "celebration," and it is well taken, for poems like these are celebrations of the creative imagination and the urgencies of the poet's vision. All is colored

and transformed by the context, so that the "bottle / Of pink fizz" functions naturally on two levels, simultaneously mercurochrome and champagne. In creating such identities, the poet destroys all separation between the literal and the visionary, for neither can exist fruitfully without the other in this poetry. Jarring juxtapositions fail to jar, and we are left to wonder at the more permanent and serious effects these juxtapositions conspire to produce.

The poem is in itself so strange, the occasion for a comprehensive cultural statement so unorthodox and unexpected, that one may not notice the nature of the cultural references Plath makes. For the most part it is an accumulation of clichéd references which in themselves might call forth nothing more than a show of lassitude or irritation. Set alongside the vivid reality of the bleeding thumb, however, and the stricken sensibility which is able to collect and unite such material, the references assume a relevance and insistence that may chill the reader. What the succession of cultural references calls forth are notions of constant violence and persecution, from America's genocidal destruction of the Indians to white America's more recent brutalization of the Negro. The various examples of institutionalized violence, violence which is manifested in modes of behavior and policies practiced by an entire culture, are not identified merely as counterparts of the more intimate varieties of aggression we can find in our own private lives. Plath is locating sources for her malaise in the history of western culture, drawing on particular moments in time to have them stand for pervasive tendencies which are apparent to those who will have eyes to see and read. The history of the West as it appears in Plath's poetry can with little difficulty be accommodated within the rigid framework of violence, injustice and betrayal, within a single category, that is.

Such knowledge is debilitating in the extreme, necessarily making for a relativity of values. Brutality is indivisible. "Whose side are they on?" Plath asks, contemplating the line of soldiers advancing like the blood cells pouring from her finger. Alliances will be formed not by mutual commitments to an informing value system, but will be dictated by the exigencies of the cultural moment. Suffering and retreat are normative under such conditions, and there is no need any longer to wonder why the spectre of victimization haunts these pages. In the poem, of course, there is pleasure in following the trajectory of Plath's projections, a pleasure which in no way diminishes the effect of what she is saying. The effect is, after all, achieved by the mode of saying, and in Plath we can never properly extricate our awareness of content from awareness of form and expressive language, for it is the processes of her imagination that lure us, beyond the materials it employs. And so we are fascinated by the rapid metamorphoses the thumb undergoes. But more gripping still is the poet's shifting of allegiances and identifications in response to these stereotyped purveyors of violence. By the middle of the poem, she has accepted her victimization at the hands of these agents of darkness, and she turns to "a pill to kill / The thin / Papery feeling." The thumb with all its metamorphic propensities has become her enemy, her tormentor. But in Plath, hatred and resentment are never very far removed from their opposites, and the poet can as well project one potential as another. Ultimately the bandage stain strikes the poet as a kind of head-wound sustained by the enemy-thumb, and the personified finger becomes nothing less than an equal, a fellow sufferer. The final three lines are not description, but total identification. They are united, the "trepanned" veterans of the world, the put upon, the feeble, left alone to contemplate, perhaps, the "Hiroshima ash" and murderous "radiation" evoked in **"Fever 103°."**

The extraordinary transformation of the thumb from oppressor to victimized comrade in retreat from the world is explicable in terms of the archetypal oppressor-figure which dominates Plath's imagination. Sylvia Plath was born in Boston, but her parents were of German descent, both of them teachers. Her father was the dominant figure, though he died in 1941 when his daughter was only nine. He is remembered as an impressively powerful man, a supporter of the Nazi cause, and a confirmed anti-Semite. There is reason to believe that Plath's mother was partially Jewish, retrospectively providing the mature poet with a familial pattern that perfectly parallels and enforces the basic dichotomy which controls her thought, in which men are conceived either as victims or persecutors. As a child, of course, Plath could not have understood the cultural parallel implicit in daily confrontations between an anti-Semitic father and a Jewish mother. She loved her father when he was alive, but always tended to see him as a god-figure, sublimely authoritarian and efficient. This family background, taken together with the poet's need to see everything in terms of symbols and peculiar connotations, quite effectively accounts for Plath's compulsive practice of moving rapidly between contrary sensations, between love and hate, between weakness and manic strength. The strange love-hate relationship which she carried on with the memory of her father became a pattern which she imposed on practically every aspect of her experience as it was expressed in the poetry.

The major symbolic identities around which several of her better poems revolve include the Jew as victim, and the German as Nazi or oppressor. Frequently the cultural setting within which such identities are appropriate is lightly sketched, suggested by no more than a word or phrase. A poem like **"Lady Lazarus"** raises interesting questions about the legitimacy of certain stereotypes as literary symbols. After all, much has been made of Pound's and Eliot's use of the Jew as Shylock, a stock figure who has been a source of great resentment among many literary intellectuals. Since World War II, however, the Jew as victim has been a far more characteristic figure in western literature, though frequently the identity has been deliberately ambiguous. One thinks of a novel like Saul Bellow's *The Victim,* in which the Jew serves as symbolic victim and potential avenger of his own malignant destiny. Bellow's victim cannot wholly dispel even from his own mind the ancient blight, the heritage of the Shylock out for his pound of flesh. What distinguishes his novel from others on similar conflicts is precisely that Bellow's stereotypes work to enforce ambiguities, rather than to suggest that there are absolute distinctions among men which are permanently irreconcilable. Plath's racial stereotypes are in this tradition and confirm our impression that what is chiefly important is how the stereotypes are managed. The stereotypes are neither good nor bad in themselves. In Plath, they are successfully employed because their juxtaposition within the context of other themes and a variety of concrete details permits the reader to tie together apparently diverse, even unrelated elements. By the time **"Lady Lazarus"** moves towards its apocalyptic climax, we are prepared for Plath's reference to her tormentor as "Herr Doktor," "Herr Enemy." In the course of the poem it has become acceptable to view any victim as a Jew and any enemy as a German. This does not represent a political judgment but a commitment to particular expedient categories which are functional within the poem alone. They are acceptable and functional because the poet needs to see her suffering as emblematic of a more widespread affliction, and because she is able to draw upon a wealth of concrete details from the Nazi debacle, details which for the moment at least are capable of releasing tremendous rage and pity in most of us.

"Lady Lazarus" presents the poet in the midst of her final, successful suicide attempt. She marvels at her ability to stay alive: "A sort of walking miracle, my skin / Bright as a Nazi lampshade." Right away, the strategy is clear, though one feels that for Sylvia Plath it was more a habitual mode of confronting her life than a temporary strategy. The details which permit her identifications continually to exert effect include: "A cake of soap, / A wedding ring, / A gold filling," all summoning concrete images associated with the great holocaust. When she howls such lines, summons such visions, we know she speaks as the Jewess, and who would tell her to be rational, to respond normally, to get hold of herself? Who would tell her that there is no need to call upon "Herr God," that the manifestly various authorities before which she has cowered all her life have not been such as to evoke terror? And finally, who will tell her that madness is not the most authentic response to the human condition as we now see it?

The ambiguity of Plath's identifications is nowhere more evident than in **"Daddy,"** a thoroughly devastating performance which A. Alvarez calls a love poem [see excerpt dated 1966], and it just might be possible that he is right. M. L. Rosenthal reports the poet's description of it as a poem about a girl with an Electra complex, whose father died while she thought he was God. In this poem, Plath becomes an absolute victim, the Jew confined by barbed wire in the concentration camp, unable to explain to herself the reasons for her persecution at the hands of faceless, omnipresent authorities. But there is nothing pathetic about the spectacle, for here the poet has refused to be merely the victim. In desperation, and with hatred for the role she has consented for too long to play, she forces herself simultaneously to assume the contrary role of the avenger, fierce and unyielding. An incredible tension is established, in which the associations dredged up by the poet are at odds with the passionate defiance that rings in the poet's rhythms and language. While the image of the inexorable "roller / Of wars, wars, wars" stalks her consciousness, she defies any power that would roll over her life, trampling her right to be what she would be. The bruising "You" which falls like a sentence of execution at the end of so many lines in **"Daddy"** points up the tension and ambiguity which is the very life of the poem. It is at once an accusation, a challenge flung in the teeth of tormentors everywhere, and an admission of weakness and subordination. "Ich, ich, ich, ich" the poet cries, struggling to assert that she exists, an "I," a subject in fundamental opposition to that "other" which is the world and its multiple embodiments in diverse authority-figures.

"Daddy" confronts, as no other poem has, the problem of

retaining one's individuality, that is, humanity, in the face of a repression that threatens literally to obliterate all distinctions among men. In exploring with deadly precision the manifestations of this problem, the poet creates a fluid language which permits her to pass back and forth from the level of personal experience to vast cultural moments, so that finally it is impossible to extricate one from the other. The internal repression which prevented her from communicating meaningfully with her father becomes simultaneously the more general barriers to communication which traditionally have kept victims and oppressors apart: "I never could talk to you. / The tongue stuck in my jaw. / It stuck in a barb wire snare." So completely do the two levels of repression fuse in this poem that there is no possibility of the speaker's personal problems diminishing the obvious magnitude of the political situation. In the course of establishing these identities, the poet suggests the peculiarly modern aspects inherent in such repression. The barriers to communication are not simply superficial obstacles imposed at various points upon the flow of discourse, obstacles which can be removed at will. Rather, they must be understood as permanent features of conventional discourse which one cannot hope to evade, totalitarian language structures which render genuine communication virtually impossible. George Steiner has written at length on the obscene corruptions of language which lay at the heart of the totalitarian prose employed in Germany during Hitler's ascendancy. I do not know for a fact that Sylvia Plath was familiar with Steiner's work, especially his controversial essay, "The Hollow Miracle," originally published in 1959, but in **"Daddy"** she gives poetic expression to a perception which no one has articulated with greater understanding and concern than Steiner:

> A language shows that it has in it the germ of dissolution in several ways. Actions of the mind that were once spontaneous become mechanical, frozen habits (dead metaphors, mock similes, slogans). Words grow longer and more ambiguous. Instead of style there is rhetoric. Instead of precise common usage, there is jargon . . . the language no longer sharpens thought but blurs it . . . it loosens and disperses the intensity of feeling.

With normal modes of expression helpless to convey feeling, there is an inclination to scream for attention, to indulge the extreme gesture in an effort to transcend the clotted verbal matrix. And such impulses are not limited to inhabitants of totalitarian dictatorships. They represent a frustration of which citizens in the western democracies must be more and more aware.

For one who has screamed and stamped and pointed to no avail, whose extreme gestures have been chastised or ignored, there are few available options for maintaining contact with the world. There is a feeling of smallness, of that utter psychic alienation from which there is rarely any return. In **"Daddy,"** the poet feels that the common language is simply inadequate for any reasonable communication of her needs. Her infrequent attempts at regaining her foothold in the world are easily repulsed. Always she feels she has been disposed of, a mere nuisance who can but barely be tolerated. And finally she develops the language of the permanently *aliéné,* the madman, the Jew forever denied grace:

> And the language obscene
> An engine, an engine
> Chuffing me off like a Jew.
> A Jew to Dachau, Auschwitz, Belsen.
> I began to talk like a Jew.
> I think I may well be a Jew.

The language of the hopelessly victimized is not without its expressive richness, but it is a dangerously narrowing instrument. It perpetually justifies its myopic determinacy by taking relish in its own peculiar dynamics, by tending to turn more and more in on itself, ultimately, and most disastrously, with neither reference nor recourse to anything beyond its own defiantly detached and self-sufficient matrix. **"Daddy"** does not open onto visions of experience, but engulfs fragments of experience and inflates them into wholes, forcing them to stand as general statements rather than as indications of merely contingent necessities. As Sylvia Plath speaks of adopting at least the accoutrements of Jewish discourse, with its built-in defense mechanisms and pervasive negativism, one thinks inevitably of Kafka and his unforgettable aggregations of victim-characters. One thinks of the imaginary Siberian self-exile of George Bendemann in "The Judgment," of his pathetic self-sentencing and execution.

Both Kafka and Plath demonstrate a psychotic attraction to forms of brute power that tend towards extermination of their victims, inducing paroxysms of self-contempt and complicity in their own destruction. *Ariel* presents the poet in the final throes of a heroic but doomed effort to preserve that self through the assertion of its own violence and desires, an assertion Kafka was never able even to attempt. The magnitude and strain of Plath's effort is evident in the pervasive hysteria of these poems, some of them containing the hysteria beneath the surface in latent though potentially explosive forms. In **"Daddy,"** the poet attempts to purge the violence which threatens to tear her and everyone around her to pieces, to purge it by allowing it expression in that sublimation which is the poem. The poet conjures up an image of herself as a group of villagers, enacting some primitive ceremony which in its ritualistic order and communally sanctioned mode of unfolding can cleanse the soul and satisfy:

> There's a stake in your fat black heart
> And the villagers never liked you.
> They are dancing and stamping on you.
> They always *knew* it was you.
> Daddy, daddy, you bastard, I'm through.

In so many of Plath's poems, the cyclical recurrence of words and phrases, and the hammering, static regularity of syntactical arrangements help to provide a ceremonial atmosphere, evoking images of a hideous black sacrament in continual progress. But nowhere in her poetry are such intimations given explicit sanction as they are in **"Daddy."** The symbolic murder is, of course, nothing more than that—symbolic. But the poet's concluding "I'm through" may suggest either an acknowledgment of failure or a determinedly unrealistic wish-fulfillment. Needless to say, as long as she lived, she could not be "through." The word is best taken to refer to her imminent death, towards which perhaps she could look more hopefully, having at least imaginatively settled the score once and for all.

Clearly though, the father-figure who is stamped upon in **"Daddy"** is no more than a convenient and intimate representative of something so general and powerful that it cannot be abolished or forgotten, except in the moment of our death. Unless, of course, we consent to be permanently drugged, to settle for "the black amnesias of heaven" which the poet is unable to retreat into in **"The Night Dances."** Remarkably, Sylvia Plath demonstrates a positive contempt for those who have not eyes to see and delight in the beauties of the created universe, despite the admixture, even the predominance of suffering that is certain to dilute or extinguish pleasure. As she stares with pleasure in **"Poppies In October,"** she notices around her "eyes / Dulled to a halt under bowlers," and she exclaims in wonder that beauty should persist, beset as it is by indifference or malignity. Always she projects the familiar imagery of destruction and creeping numbness, the "forest of frost," the "slow / Horse the colour of rust," the "dolorous bells." We are grateful for her sake at least that those final months were not wholly grim, that once, perhaps, the light of stars, "these lamps," fell "like blessings." (pp. 138-53)

> *Robert Boyers, "Sylvia Plath: The Trepanned Veteran," in* The Centennial Review, *Vol. XIII, No. 2, Spring, 1969, pp. 138-53.*

Ted Hughes   (essay date 1970)

[*Hughes was named Poet Laureate of England in 1984. His poetry is characterized by bold metaphors, striking imagery, and an elemental power deeply rooted in nature and myth. His influence on Plath's poetry has been noted by many critics. Hughes met and married Plath in 1956, although the two were living separately at the time of Plath's death. In the following excerpt, Hughes provides a chronology of composition for Plath's poems in* The Colossus *and* Ariel.]

In a poet whose development was as phenomenal as hers, the chronological order of the poems is an important help to understanding them. Most readers will perceive pretty readily the single centre of power and light which her poems all share, but I think it will be a service if I point out just how little of her poetry is 'occasional', and how faithfully her separate poems build up into one long poem. She faced a task in herself, and her poetry is the record of her progress in the task. The poems are chapters in a mythology where the plot, seen as a whole and in retrospect, is strong and clear—even if the origins of it and the *dramatis personae,* are at bottom enigmatic. The world of her poetry is one of emblematic visionary events, mathematical symmetries, clairvoyance and metamorphoses. Her poetry escapes ordinary analysis in the way clairvoyance and mediumship do: her psychic gifts, at almost any time, were strong enough to make her frequently wish to be rid of them.

As will be shown by the sequence of her poems, and of her preoccupations right from the start, her initiation into this spiritual world was inevitable, and nothing very sudden. In her, as with perhaps few poets ever, the nature, the poetic genius and the active self, were the same. Maybe we don't need psychological explanations to understand what a difficult and peculiar destiny that means. She had none of the usual guards and remote controls to protect herself from her own reality. She lived right in it, especially during the last two years of her life. Perhaps that is one of the privileges, or prices, of being a woman and at the same time an initiate into the poetic order of events. Though the brains, the strength, the abundance and vivacity of spirits, the artistic virtuosity, the thousand incidental gifts that can turn it into such poetry as hers are another matter.

Before her first book, *The Colossus,* she had written great quantities of verse, all of it characteristic and unique, with a dense crop of inspired phrases that a poet of any age would have been glad to have secured. But she never saved lines or phrases. She wrote her early poems very slowly, Thesaurus open on her knee, in her large, strange handwriting, like a mosaic, where every letter stands separate within the work, a hieroglyph to itself. If she didn't like a poem, she scrapped it entire. She rescued nothing of it. Every poem grew complete from its own root, in that laborious inching way, as if she were working out a mathematical problem, chewing her lips, putting a thick dark ring of ink around each word that stirred for her on the page of the Thesaurus.

"The Faun" was one of the earliest poems she saved. This dates from spring, 1956, while she was an undergraduate at Cambridge, in England.

"Strumpet Song": dates from about the same time.

"Spinster": dates from this time. The opposition of a prickly, fastidious defence and an imminent volcano is, one way or another, an element in all her early poems. A variant on the theme is the dreary meaninglessness and exhaustion of those times when for some reason or another the volcano is inactive or under a flood.

"All The Dead Dears": belongs here.

"Watercolor Of Grantchester Meadows": belongs here.

"Departure": is a memory of the summer of 1956, which we spent renting a house in Benidorm, a Spanish fishing village, not much spoiled at that time.

"Hardcastle Crags": is a deep narrow valley in the Pennines in West Yorks, and makes the southern boundary of the moorland made famous by Emily Brontë in *Wuthering Heights.* The village she describes, which is on a hilltop overlooking this valley, is very ancient.

"Sow": commemorates a great sow that lived near this village.

Between these and the next poems we moved to the United States, where she took up a teaching post on the English faculty at Smith College.

"Mussel Hunter At Rock Harbour": she wrote this in the summer, on Cape Cod, before she started teaching. This was one of her first poems in syllabics, which were her first step, technically, in her self-exploration. She was a lucky fisherman.

The next group of poems belongs to the time she was teaching. They all share a likeness—and there were others of the same family, as good and as chilling. **"The Thin People," "Lorelei," "Full Fathom Five," "Frog Autumn," "The Disquieting Muses," "Snakecharmer," "The Ghost's Leavetaking," "Sculptor," "Night Shift,"** are the ones she saved.

In **"The Disquieting Muses,"** as in **"Snakecharmer," "The Ghost's Leavetaking"** and several poems not collected, she shows clearly how native she was to the world of the Primitive Painters. Her vision, particularly in its aspect—strong at this time—of the deathly paradise, belongs with theirs perhaps more readily than with anything in poetry, but these poems are, ultimately, about her world, not theirs, and it is not a world of merely visual effects. **"Snakecharmer,"** after a picture by Rousseau, is what she did not know, a specific vision revealed to yogis at a certain advanced stage, to take just one instance.

"Sculptor": Leonard Baskin's work struck her very hard, as well it might, since some of the gods he was carving at the time were also part of her pantheon—namely, the huge bald angels, the mutilated dead men, the person with the owl growing out of his shoulder.

"Lorelei" and **"Full Fathom Five":** she was prompted to these by reading one of Cousteau's accounts of his diving and underwater explorations. At this distance of time, one can see that in these poems for the first time she accepts the invitation of her inner world. These poems coincided with a decision, made with great difficulty and against great tactical opposition from individuals she regarded as her benefactors, to leave teaching and throw herself on writing for a few years.

Between these last and the next group of poems is a gap of some months. From late summer 1958 to mid-1959, we lived in Boston. It was a difficult time for her: a lifetime's training, and fierce and highly successful effort to prepare herself to teach in a University, with many other deep compulsions to the same end, were not surrendered so easily. From this year there was not much poetry, but it was a decisive time.

"The Eye-Mote" dates from this period. The mention of Oedipus, and the Greek Tragedians' figures elsewhere, may seem literary, but if one can take her dream life as evidence, those personalities were deeply involved in her affairs. Her openness to the ambiguous populations of 'the living ether' took its toll. Her reactions to hurts in other people and animals, and even tiny desecrations of plant-life were extremely violent. The chemical poisoning of nature, the pile-up of atomic waste, were horrors that persecuted her like an illness—as her latest poems record. Auschwitz and the rest were merely the open wounds, in her idea of the great civilized crime of intelligence that like the half-imbecile, omnipotent, spoiled brat Nero has turned on its mother.

"The Man In Black" belongs here.

"The Hermit At Outermost House" is a fore-runner of the style that she possessed completely only after her first book was completed. It has the comic goblin, the trickster-ish spirit, the crackling verbal energy, that was the nymph-form—a lot of Caliban in it—of *Ariel.*

"The Beekeeper's Daughter" is one of a group of poems that she wrote at this time about her father. Besides being a general biologist and botanist, he was a specialist in bees, and wrote a book called *Bumblebees and Their Ways.* This poem, one of her chilliest, recounts a key event in her *Vita Nuova.*

"Point Shirley" was a deliberate exercise in Robert Lowell's early style. The setting is the bit of coast off Boston Harbour where she spent her first years.

"Aftermath," "Two Views of a Cadaver Room," and **"Suicide Off Egg Rock"** come clear of the domination of heavy iambic lines, have the casual fluency of her syllabic poems, yet a greater naturalness of tone and a warmer fullness of phrasing than anything she had done before. Also, they steer in quite masterfully towards some point in her life that had been painful. For the first time, she tried deliberately to locate just what it was that hurt.

In the Autumn of 1959, after touring around the States, we were invited to Yaddo [a retreat for artists and writers in Saratoga Springs, New York]. The weeks spent at Yaddo—with only three or four other residents—completed the poems in *The Colossus.* It was, in several ways, the culmination of the first part of her life. For three months, while seeing the States, she had not touched verse. Her first child would be born six months later. We had decided to live in Europe, and were to go there straight from Yaddo. It was an end and a new beginning. She took childbearing in a deeply symbolic way. Maybe it is truer to say that she accepted the symbolic consequences of an event. In those weeks, she changed at great speed and with steady effort.

"Blue Moles" records two dead moles we found in the grounds at Yaddo.

"Flute Notes From A Reedy Pond": like most of the pieces she wrote at this time, it is an elegy for an old order, the promise of a new. The sudden enrichment of the texture of her verse, and the nimble shifting of focus, were something new and surprised her. At this time she was concentratedly trying to break down the tyranny, the fixed focus and public persona which descriptive or discoursive poems take as a norm. We devised exercises of meditation and invocation.

"The Winter Ship" belongs here.

"Mushrooms": this developed from an invocation.

"The Burnt-Out Spa": records an old spa near Yaddo.

"The Manor Garden": This is about the last of the old order, and the new birth is requisitioning all nature to its delivery. The new style is just under the surface. **"You're,"** in *Ariel,* is another poem, written some months later, with a similar combination of elements, which shows how close natural kin she was, at this point in her development, with Emily Dickinson.

"The Stones" was the last poem she wrote at Yaddo, and the last in America. The immediate source of it was a series of poems she began as a deliberate exercise in experimental improvisation on set themes. She had never in her life improvised. The powers that compelled her to write so slowly had always been stronger than she was. But quite suddenly she found herself free to let herself drop, rather than inch over bridges of concepts.

She was reading Paul Radin's collection of African folk-tales with great excitement. In these, she found the underworld of her worst nightmares throwing up intensely beautiful adventures, where the most unsuspected voices thrived under the pressures of a reality that made most accepted fiction seem artificial and spurious. At the same time she was reading—closely and sympathetically for the first time—Roethke's poems. The result was a series of pieces, each a monologue of some character in an underground, primitive drama. **"Stones"** was the last of them, and the only one not obviously influenced by Roethke. It is full of specific details of her experience in a mental hospital, and is clearly enough the first eruption of the voice that produced *Ariel*. It is the poem where the self, shattered in 1953, suddenly finds itself whole. The series was called **"Poem For A Birthday."**

That was the end of the first phase of her development. When she consolidated her hold on the second phase, two years later, she dismissed everything prior to **"The Stones"** as Juvenilia, produced in the days before she became herself. In England, she wrote one more poem, **"You're,"** which I have already mentioned, before her first child was born, at home, without anaesthetic, with great ease and speed, at exactly sunrise, on the first day of April, the day she regularly marked as the first day of Spring.

Once she had arrived so surely at her own centre of gravity, everything that happened to her or that she undertook, enriching and enlarging herself, also enriched and enlarged her poetry. With the birth of her first child she received herself, and was able to turn to her advantage all the forces of a highly-disciplined, highly intellectual style of education which had, up to this point, worked mainly against her, but without which she could hardly have gone so coolly into the regions she now entered. The birth of her second child, in January of 1962, completed the preparation.

The two years between 1960 and 1962 had produced some beautiful poems, but only three that she selected for *Ariel*. She had heard what her real voice sounded like, and now had new standard for herself. The poem called **"Tulips,"** was the first sign of what was on its way. She wrote this poem without her usual studies over the Thesaurus, and at top speed, as one might write an urgent letter. From then on, all her poems were written in this way.

"Tulips" belongs to March 1961, and records some tulips she had in the hospital where she was recovering from an appendectomy. Another poem, written at the same time and in almost identical form, published in *The London Magazine,* but not collected, the weaker twin of this one, was the monologue of a body completely, impatiently, enclosed in a plaster cast—which was the actual condition of a patient in a bed near her.

"Morning Song," a poem about her daughter Frieda, dates from this time, and from later in the year comes **"Little Fugue."** Her interest in music was average. As a young girl she had played the viola, and could play on the piano any number of popular hits from the early 1950s. But suddenly now she became absorbed by the late quartet music of Beethoven, particularly the Grosse Fugue.

The first poem of the final phase was **"Elm."** This particular tree, enormous, stands over our yard in England. The poems dates from April 1962.

"The Moon And The Yew Tree" came soon after. Opposite the front of our house stands a church. Early one morning, in the dark, I saw the full moon setting on to a large yew that grows in the churchyard, and I suggested she make a poem of it. By midday, she had written it. It depressed me greatly. It's my suspicion that no poem can be a poem that is not a statement from the powers in control of our life, the ultimate suffering and decision in us. It seems to me that this is poetry's only real distinction from the literary forms that we call 'not poetry'. And I had no doubt that this was a poem, and perhaps a great poem. She insisted that it was an exercise on the theme.

"The Rival" is a poem left over from a series specifically about that woman in the moon, the disquieting muse.

"Berck-Plage": In June, 1961, we had visited Berck-Plage, a long beach and resort on the coast of France north of Rouen. Some sort of hospital or convalescent home for the disabled fronts the beach. It was one of her nightmares stepped into the real world. A year later—almost to the day—our next door neighbour, an old man, died after a short grim illness during which time his wife repeatedly needed our help. In this poem that visit to the beach and the death and funeral of our neighbour are combined. It belongs to July 1962.

The next group of poems, including everything in *Ariel* up to the end of the Bee sequence, arrived in October and November of 1962. There were a few others not collected. She occasionally wrote two or three in the same day. The Bee poems came first.

"Nick And The Candlestick": Nicholas is the name of the little boy, her second child.

"The Night Dances": This records Nicholas' dancing in his cot. He devised an eerie set of joyful, slow prancing movements which must be called a dance, and which he used to go through when he woke up at night.

Ariel was the name of the horse on which she went riding weekly. Long before, while she was a student at Cambridge (England), she went riding with an American friend out towards Grantchester. Her horse bolted, the stirrups fell off, and she came all the way home to the stables, about two miles, at full gallop, hanging around the horse's neck.

The final group of poems dates from mid-January 1963.

AUTHOR'S COMMENTARY

I think my poems immediately come out of the sensuous and emotional experiences I have, but I must say I cannot sympathize with these cries from the heart that are informed by nothing except a needle or a knife, or whatever it is. I believe that one should be able to control and manipulate experiences, even the most terrifying, like madness, being tortured, this sort of experience, and one should be able to manipulate these experiences with an informed and an intelligent mind. I think that personal experience is very important, but certainly it shouldn't be a kind of shut-box and mirror-looking, narcissistic experience. I believe it should be *relevant,* and relevant to the larger things, the bigger things such as Hiroshima and Dachau and so on.

(interview date 1962)

"The Munich Mannequins" and **"Totem"** were composed over the same two days.

"Paralytic" soon after.

"Balloons," "Contusion," "Kindness," "Edge" and **"Words"** belong to the last week of her life.

Surveyed as a whole, with attention to the order of composition, I think the unity of her opus is clear. Once the unity shows itself, the logic and inevitability of the language, which controls and contains such conflagrations and collisions within itself, becomes more obviously what it is—direct, and even plain, speech. (pp. 187-94)

> Ted Hughes, "Notes on the Chronological Order of Sylvia Plath's Poems," in The Art of Sylvia Plath: A Symposium, *edited by Charles Newman, Indiana University Press, 1970, pp. 187-95.*

Irving Howe   (essay date 1972)

[*A longtime editor of the leftist magazine* Dissent *and a regular contributor to the* New Republic, *Howe is one of America's most highly respected literary critics and social historians. He has been a socialist since the 1930s, and his criticism is frequently informed by a liberal social viewpoint. Howe is widely praised for what F. R. Dulles has termed his "knowledgeable understanding, critical acumen and forthright candor." In the following excerpt, Howe offers a balanced critique of Plath's poetry in which he observes a "mixture of strong phrasing and structural incoherence," and reveals reservations concerning Plath's use of Nazi death camp imagery in her poem "Daddy." Howe considers those of Plath's poems most striking that are least confessional and concludes that "Plath will be regarded as an interesting minor poet whose personal story was deeply poignant."*]

In dissenting a little from the Plath celebration, one has the sense not so much of disagreeing about the merits of certain poems but of plunging into a harsh *kulturkampf.* For one party in this struggle Sylvia Plath has become an icon, and the dangers for those in the other party are also considerable, since it would be unjust to allow one's irritation with her devotees to spill over into one's response to her work. So let us move quickly to the facts about her career and then to the poems she wrote toward the end of her life, crucial for any judgment of her work.

Her father, a professor of biology and (it's important to note) a man of German descent, died when she was nine. The reverberations of this event are heavy in the poems, though its precise significance for Sylvia Plath as either person or poet is very hard to grasp. She then lived with her mother in Wellesley, Massachusetts; she went to Smith, an ardent student who swept up all the prizes; she suffered from psychic disorders; she won a Fulbright at Cambridge University, then met and married a gifted English poet, Ted Hughes. In 1960 she published her first book of poems, **The Colossus**—it rings with distinguished echoes, proclaims unripe gifts, contains more quotable passages than successful poems (true for all her work.) She had two children, in 1960 and 1962, to whom she seems to have been fiercely attached and about whom she wrote

some of her better poems. She was separated from her husband, lived one freezing winter in London with her children, and, experiencing an onslaught of energy at once overwhelming and frightening, wrote her best-known poems during the last weeks of her life. On February 11, 1963, she killed herself.

Crossing the Water, recently issued, contains some of the poems she wrote between the early work of **The Colossus** and the final outburst that would posthumously appear in 1965 as **Ariel.** Her gifts can be seen in **Crossing the Water;** her failings too. There are graphic lines, but few poems fully achieved. "The desert is white as a blind man's eye, / Comfortless as salt . . . " we read in a poem not otherwise notable. The drive to self-destruction that would tyrannize the last poems is already at work in these "middle" ones:

> If I pay the roots of the heather
> Too close attention, they will invite me
> To whiten my bones among them.

The poems in **Crossing the Water** are, nevertheless, more open in voice and variable in theme than those for which Sylvia Plath has become famous; there is less power but also less pathology. She writes well, in snatches and stanzas, about the impersonal moments of personal experience, when the sense of everything beyond one's selfhood dominates the mind. She writes well, that is, precisely about the portion of human experience that is most absent in the **Ariel** poems; such poems as **"Parliament Hill Fields," "Small Hours,"** and a few others in **Crossing the Water,** unheroic in temper and unforced in pitch, can yield conventional pleasures. The flaws in her work she describes charmingly in **"Stillborn,"** though it's characteristic that, after the vivid opening stanza, the poem itself should seem stillborn. . . . (p. 88)

At a crucial point in her career Sylvia Plath came under the influence of Robert Lowell's *Life Studies,* and it is this relationship that has led many admirers to speak of her late work as "confessional poetry." The category is interesting but dubious, both in general and when applied to Sylvia Plath. (p. 89)

At times Sylvia Plath . . . wrote confessional poetry, as in the much-praised **"Lady Lazarus,"** a poem about her recurrent suicide attempts. Its opening lines, like almost all her opening lines, come at one with the force of a driven hammer:

> I have done it again.
> One year in every ten
> I manage it—
>
> A sort of walking miracle, my skin
> Bright as a Nazi lampshade,
> My right foot
>
> A paperweight,
> My face a featureless, fine
> Jew linen.

The tone is jeeringly tough, but at least partly directed against herself. There is a strain of self-irony ("a sort of walking miracle") such as poetry of this kind can never have enough of. But one must be infatuated with the Plath legend to ignore the poet's need for enlarging the magnitude of her act through illegitimate comparisons with the

Jewish-Nazi holocaust (a point to which I will return later).

Sylvia Plath's most notable gift as a writer—a gift for the single, isolate image—comes through later in the poem when, recalling an earlier suicide attempt, she writes that they had to "pick the worms off me like sticky pearls." But then, after patching together some fragments of recollection, she collapses into an archness about her suicide attempts that is shocking in a way she could not have intended:

> I do it so it feels like hell.
> I do it so it feels real.
> I guess you could say I've a call.
>
> It's easy enough to do it in a cell,
> It's easy enough to do it and stay put.

As if uneasy about the tone of such lines, she then drives toward what I can only see as a willed hysteric tone, the forcing of language to make up for an inability to develop the matter. The result is sentimental violence:

> A cake of soap,
> A wedding ring,
> A gold filling. . . .
>
> Out of the ash
> I rise with my red hair
> And I eat men like air.

In the end, the several remarkable lines in this poem serve only to intensify its badness, for in their isolation, without the support of a rational structure, they leave the author with no possibility of development other than violent wrenchings in tone. And this is a kind of badness that seems a constant temptation in confessional poetry, the temptation to reveal all while one eye measures the effect of the revelation.

There's another famous poem by Sylvia Plath entitled, **"Cut,"** in which she shows the same mixture of strong phrasing and structural incoherence. **"Cut"** opens on a sensational note, or touch:

> What a thrill—
> My thumb instead of an onion.
> The top quite gone
> Except for a sort of hinge
>
> Of skin,
> A flap like a hat,
> Dead white,
> Then that red plush.

This is vivid, no denying it. Morbid too. The question is whether the morbidity is an experience the writer struggles with or yields to, examines dispassionately or caresses indulgently.

There is a saving wit in the opening lines ("My thumb instead of an onion") and this provides some necessary distance between invoked experience and invoking speaker. But the poem collapses through Sylvia Plath's inability to do more with her theme than thrust it against our eyes, displaying her wound in all its red plushy woundedness.

> The stain on your
> Gauze Ku Klux Klan
> Babushka
> Darkens and tarnishes . . .

The bandage is seen as a babushka, an old lady's scarf. All right. But the Ku Klux Klan? And still more dubious, the "Ku Klux Klan Babushka"? One supposes the KKK is being used here because it is repressive, the Babushka-bandage is "repressing" the blood, and in the poem's graphic pathology, the flow of blood from the cut is attractive, fruitful, perhaps healthy ("a celebration, this is," runs one line). But even if my reading is accurate, does that help us very much with the stanza? Isn't this stanza an example of weakness through excess?

Sylvia Plath's most famous poem, adored, it seems, by many sons and daughters, is **"Daddy."** It is a poem that deals with an affecting theme, the feelings of the speaker as she regathers the pain of her father's premature death and her persuasion that he has betrayed her by dying:

> I was ten when they buried you.
> At twenty I tried to die
> And get back, back, back to you.

In the poem Sylvia Plath identifies the father (we recall his German birth) with the Nazis ("Panzer-man, panzer-man, O You") and flares out with assaults for which nothing in the poem (nor, so far as we know, in Sylvia Plath's own life) offers any warrant: "A cleft in your chin instead of your foot / But no less a devil for that . . . " Nor does anything in the poem offer warrant, other than the free-flowing hysteria of the speaker, for the assault of such lines as, "There's a stake in your fat black heart / And the villagers never liked you." Or for the snappy violence of.

> Every woman adores a Fascist,
> The boot in the face, the brute
> Brute heart of a brute like you.

What we have here is a revenge fantasy feeding upon filial love-hatred, and thereby mostly of clinical interest. But seemingly aware that the merely clinical can't provide the materials for a satisfying poem. Sylvia Plath tries to enlarge upon the personal plight, give meaning to the personal outcry, by fancying the girl as victim of a Nazi father:

> An engine, an engine
> Chuffing me off like a Jew.
> A Jew to Dachau, Auschwitz,
>   Belsen.
> I began to talk like a Jew,
> I think I may well be a Jew.

The more sophisticated admirers of this poem may say that I fail to see it as a dramatic presentation, a monologue spoken by a disturbed girl not necessarily to be identified with Sylvia Plath herself, despite the many similarities of detail between the events of the poem and the events of her life. I cannot accept this view, for the following reasons: the personal-confessional element, strident and undisciplined, is simply too obtrusive to suppose the poem no more than a dramatic picture of a certain style of disturbance. If, however, we do accept such a reading of **"Daddy,"** we fatally narrow its claims to emotional or moral significance, for we then confine it to a mere vivid imaging of a pathological state. That, surely, is not how its admirers really take the poem.

It is clearly not how the critic George Steiner takes the poem when he calls it "the *Guernica* of modern poetry." But then, in an astonishing turn, he asks: "In what sense does anyone, himself uninvolved and long after the event, commit a subtle larceny when he invokes the echoes and trappings of Auschwitz and appropriates an enormity of ready emotion to his own private design?" The question is devastating and makes nonsense of his earlier comparison to *Guernica.* Picasso's painting objectifies the horrors of Guernica, through the distancing of art; no one can suppose that he shares or participates in them. Plath's poem aggrandizes on the "enormity of ready emotion" invoked by references to the concentration camps, in behalf of an ill-controlled if occasionally brilliant outburst. There is something monstrous when tangled emotions about one's father are deliberately compared with the historical fate of the European Jews; something sad, if the comparison is made spontaneously. **"Daddy"** persuades one again, through the force of negative example, of how accurate T. S. Eliot was in saying, "The more perfect the artist, the more completely separate in him will be the man who suffers and the mind which creates."

The most interesting poems in **Ariel** are not confessional at all. A confessional poem would seem to be one in which the writer speaks *to* the reader, telling him, without the mediating presence of imagined events or *persona,* something about his life: I had a nervous breakdown, my wife and I sometimes lie in bed, sterile of heart, through sterile nights. The sense of direct speech addressed to an audience is central to confessional writing. But the most striking poems Sylvia Plath wrote are quite different. They are poems written out of an extreme condition, a state of being in which the speaker, for all practical purposes Sylvia Plath herself, has abandoned the sense of audience and cares nothing about—indeed, is hardly aware of—the presence of anyone but herself. She writes with a hallucinatory, self-contained fervor. She addresses herself to the air, to the walls. She speaks not as a daylight self, with its familiar internal struggles and doubts, its familiar hesitations before the needs and pressures of others. There is something utterly monolithic, fixated about the voice that emerges in these poems, a voice unmodulated and asocial.

It's as if we are overhearing the rasps of a mind that has found its own habitation and need not measure its distance from, even consider its relation to, other minds. And the stakes are far higher than can ever be involved in mere confession. She exists in some mediate province between living and dying, and she appears to be balancing coolly the claims of the two, drawn almost equally to both yet oddly comfortable with the perils of where she is. This is not the by-now worn romanticism of *Liebestod.* It is something very strange, very fearful: a different kind of existence, at ease at the gate of dying. I don't believe that the poems Sylvia Plath wrote in this state of being are "great" poems, but I can hardly doubt that they are remarkable. For they do bring into poetry an element of experience that, so far as I know, is new, and thereby they do advance the thrust of literary modernism by another inch or so. A poem like **"Kindness"** is set squarely in what I have called the mediate province between living and dying. . . . (pp. 89-91)

The poems written out of this strange equilibrium— **"Fever 103," "Totem," "Edge"**—are notable, and the best of them seems to me **"Edge."** . . .

The vision of death as composure, a work done well, is beautifully realized in the first four stanzas. The next sev-

eral, with "Each dead child coiled, a white serpent," seem to me to drop into a kind of sensationalism—not the kind one finds in the confessional poems, with their alternating archness and violence, but one that invokes the completion that may come once death is done and finished. The penultimate stanza is very fine; the last lines again seem forced.

Even in this kind of poetry, which does strike an original note, there are many limitations. The poems often shock; they seldom surprise. They are deficient in plasticity of feeling, that modulation of voice that a poet writing out of a controlled maturity of consciousness can muster. Even the best of Sylvia Plath's poems, as her admirer Stephen Spender admits, "have little principle of beginning or ending, but seem fragments, not so much of one long poem, as of an outpouring which could not stop with the lapsing of the poet's hysteria." For, as Elizabeth Hardwick has written, "the elements of pathology" are "deeply rooted" and "little resisted" in both Sylvia Plath's work and her life.

Perhaps the hardest critical question remains, and in a short essay I won't pretend to answer it. Given the fact that in a few poems Sylvia Plath illustrates an extreme state of existence, one at the very boundary of nonexistence, what illumination—moral, psychological, social— can be provided of either this state or the general human condition by a writer so deeply rooted in the extremity of her plight? Suicide is an eternal possibility of our life and therefore always interesting; but what is the relation between a sensibility so deeply captive to the idea of suicide and the claims and possibilities of human existence in general? That her story is intensely moving, that her talent was notable, that her final breakthrough rouses admiration—of course! Yet in none of the essays devoted to praising Sylvia Plath have I found a coherent statement as to the nature, let alone the value, of her vision. Perhaps it is assumed that to enter the state of mind in which she found herself at the end of her life is its own ground for high valuation; but what will her admirers say to those who reply that precisely this assumption is what needs to be questioned?

After the noise abates and judgment returns, Sylvia Plath will be regarded as an interesting minor poet whose personal story was deeply poignant. A few of her poems will find a place in anthologies—and when you consider the common fate of talent, that, after all, will not be a small acknowledgment. (p. 91)

> *Irving Howe, "Sylvia Plath: A Partial Disagreement," in* Harper's Magazine, *Vol. 244, No. 1460, January, 1972, pp. 88-91.*

Anita Rapone   (essay date 1972)

[*In the excerpt below, Rapone explores the theme of the alienated woman in Plath's verse, asserting that in her work Plath both reflects and rebels against social values that have prescribed the role of women.*]

Sylvia Plath's poetry, particularly the collection **Ariel,** is the articulation of female pain in a world which denies a woman full value as a human being. The poetry constructs the coherent world-view of a single passive persona, and as such, in the voice of one woman, speaks to all women.

In the world which emerges from her work, the female is reduced to biological and social functions which she can neither reject nor transcend. These roles conspire to lock her into a mere physical presence. Thus limited to her body, she is especially threatened by decay and destruction. And she is subject to physical and psychological control by others. Her body is her vulnerability. This absence of self-determination and autonomy results in self-hatred and alienation from both herself and others.

Sylvia Plath has written three volumes of poetry which show a progressive concentration on the particularities of being female. The first volume, *Colossus,* has occasional signs of sex-role tension and polarization. In *Crossing the Water: Transitional Poems,* she begins to treat the female situation more directly. By using a persona—a single voice—she focuses on the alienating experience of being female, especially physically female. In **"Face Lift,"** for instance, there is self-objectification in the persona imagining her discarded face, "the dewlapped lady / . . . trapped . . . in some laboratory jar." In other poems, the persona describes her sense of occupying a body, of internal struggle. In **"Witch Burning"** she says: "I inhabit / The wax image of myself, a doll's body. / Sickness begins here." To save itself, the ego is forced to flee from the body.

In *Ariel,* the last volume before her death, Sylvia Plath describes the biological predicament as a social predicament. Here she treats a fuller range of experience with the added dimension of social consciousness. Caught between reflecting social values and rebelling against them, the persona has conflicting attitudes toward the female biological role of reproduction. This conflict and preoccupation is displayed through her choice of recurrent images. A few poems connect worth with fertility through the image of the moon. In **"Munich Mannequins,"** for example, the round complete, self-sufficient moon is associated with menstruation, a lost opportunity for reproduction. . . . In **"Elm,"** the moon is described as "Diminished and flat, as after radical surgery." Flatness, the result of mastectomy, lessens her value. In other poems, flatness itself means superficiality, removal from life, deadness.

Rebellion against the reproductive role is articulated in poems whose central image is the bee colony. This image makes connections between the reproductive function and its social enforcement. On the most simple literal level, **"The Bee Meeting"** is about a group of villagers who are removing the virgin bees from an old hive in order to start new hives. This activity becomes, on another level, a ceremony preparing the persona for marriage and motherhood. The villagers—the rector, the midwife, and sexton, among others—first dress her in a white smock and straw hat with a significantly black veil. As they walk through the bean field, she notices flowers, "blood clots . . . that will one day be edible." The image connects the phases of the reproductive process.

As the poem develops, the tension of the persona increases. She becomes aware of the possibility for rebellion, which she is incapable of choosing, even though ceremonial acquiescence means self-destruction. . . . The sexual references throughout the poem create the sense of the oppressiveness of the reproductive role. The hive, a "virgin" who has sealed "off her brood cells," is being raped.

A similar theme is developed in **"Stings,"** a poem which describes the removing of honey from the hive. The persona identifies herself with the queen bee, whose life and value is determined by her biological function in the hive. Although in **"The Bee Meeting"** she was unable to defend herself, here she threatens a retaliatory return. . . . (pp. 407-09)

The conflicting attitudes of the persona toward the biological role depends upon whether she is considering it for other women or herself. While she makes accusations against others who do not fulfill their reproductive function, the persona senses the inherent threat to herself in this definition. She identifies with the prodded queen and virgin bees.

The reproductive role is only half of the definition externally imposed upon the persona. She is also assigned the role of wife. She sees this role as one in which her needs as a human being are secondary to her husband's. She must be constantly adapting to his varying needs, be they sexual, physical or emotional. This role is bitterly satirized in **"The Applicant,"** where a fast talker is selling a living doll that not only cooks and sews, but talks.

While **"The Applicant"** is a functional description of the wife role, the pain of the lived experience comes through when the persona speaks directly, in poems such as **"Lesbos."** In this poem, the male-female relationship is so destructive to her that it affects all other relationships. Husbands are parasites on the emotional and sexual energies of their wives. The opening description of traditionally female territory, the kitchen, uses the metaphor of a Hollywood stage set, the appropriate home for a "living doll." The mood is repressed rebellion. The male-female relationship is presented in the image of female sexuality and male impotency. His needs and dependencies are such that they exhaust and limit her. Everyday, she must "fill him with soul-stuff, like a pitcher." This self-denial for the needs of the husband turns into self-hatred.

The ultimate destructiveness of this role system is dramatized by the inability of the persona in **"Lesbos"** to establish a meaningful relationship with the woman to whom she is speaking. Locked in their respective kitchens, they are kept apart by their own self-hatred. The poem conveys the feeling that they can change neither themselves nor the situation. Instead, they perpetuate the cycle by projecting their own self-hatred onto the girl-child. She is described as an "unstrung puppet, kicking to disappear," a girl who will "cut her throat at ten if she's mad at two." She indicates a special female insanity that comes from accepting an unacceptably limiting situation.

These poems, then, present a world in which the female is defined by two overlapping functions that focus her meaning in her body. When the definition of self is limited to the body in this way, it leads to an obsessive emphasis on physical vulnerability. The body is threatened by natural elements, such as the sun which gives ulcers, or the wind which gives T.B. It is subject to decay from within, such as in **"Contusion,"** where a bruise is the first step to death. Fumes threaten to choke the body like Isadora's scarves. The body can be hurt by man-made implements such as axes and knives. The awareness of the body's vulnerability can become so heightened that ordinarily neutral or life-affirming things can threaten annihilation. In

"Tulips," the red flowers watch her, use up her oxygen, and become "red lead sinkers round (her) neck."

The body is also the means through which she is controlled by others. One frequent image for this theme is the health care/patient relationship. In the poem "Tulips" the persona is hospitalized. She is merely an object in the bureaucratic mechanics of the hospital, "a pebble to them." Reducing her body to an object for tending, the hospital staff affects her psyche as well. She says, "They have swabbed me clear of my loving associations." In this situation her defense is passive withdrawal. (pp. 409-11)

In "Tulips" the situation is impersonal and functional; but, in poems such as "Lady Lazarus," she imputes malevolent motivation to the health deliverers. The doctor becomes "Herr Doktor, . . . Herr Enemy." She is his "opus," his "valuable, / The pure gold baby." The poem is a cry of hatred, ending in a threat to return as something terrible which will "eat men like air." However, even in those few poems where she personalizes the situation, thus focusing her anger on a particular target, she cannot overcome her passivity. She can only go as far as threatening a menacing comeback, the "red scar in the sky." But the future does not materially change the present, and the battle on the physical plane is lost.

The experience of being controlled by another person and the hatred it creates overflows in "Daddy." The persona and her father move through a series of images in which their identities change, but the relationship between them remains constant. In this way, the poem explores several dimensions of the dominance-submission dynamic. In the first image she is a white foot totally contained by a black shoe. The black shoe grows into the Nazi, and the persona becomes first the Jew, then the gypsy, then the masochistic woman. The image then changes to the teacher-child, the teacher cleft-chinned, a devil, who then becomes the vampire finally killed by a stake in his heart.

Ariel is the presentation of a persona caught in a world which denies her humanity by defining her sexually. As a female, she has no substantial freedom or self-definition. The poems are studies of the resulting states of mind; we experience how she feels. Descriptions of scenery, for example, tell us not so much how the world looks, as how the world symbolizes her feelings. Not surprisingly, images concerned with the body recur throughout *Ariel.* On one level, the body can be directly affected by others, as in the doctor-patient images. Control is so complete that a doctor can obstruct her desire to die; he can force her to live. On another level, psychological and emotional oppression are physically rooted. The photograph of her husband and child are "smiles that catch onto my skin, little smiling hooks." Hooks, vampires, blood-suckers are images that recur throughout the poems.

Because the world gets to her by attacking her body, she has strong desires for self-dissolvement into amorphism. Escape into death becomes rarefaction into air, or dissolution into water. The call of the elements is the release from painful solidity. As the body unlocks, the spirit is released.

Finally, *Ariel* gives us the world in which destructive feelings and pain are grounded in real causes. As the poetry develops, the treatment of these themes becomes explicit, and is rooted in women's place in a woman-hostile world. The biological prison, the preoccupation with physical pain and deadness, are intimate consequences of a preeminently social ordeal. Inexorably trapped, the persona sharpens, narrows. Her defensive passivity, her search for dissolution into primordial sea and air, lead her forward to a single answer, a single way out. (pp. 411-12)

Anita Rapone, "The Body Is the Role: Sylvia Plath," in Radical Feminism, *Anne Koedt, Ellen Levine, Anita Rapone, eds., Quadrangle Books, 1973, pp. 407-12.*

"The autobiographical details in Sylvia Plath's poetry work differently. She sets them out like masks, which are then lifted up by dramatis personae of nearly supernatural qualities."
—Ted Hughes, 1966

John Romano   (essay date 1974)

[*In the following excerpt, Romano decries what he calls the "intense and apparently irresponsible collation of (Plath's) suicide and her poetry," concluding that "Plath's failure as an artist is not rooted in a failure to apprehend herself, it is rooted in a failure to apprehend the self in others."*]

Sylvia Plath, martyr and archetype in the imagination of many, dangerously courted some portion of the blame for these irrelevant labels in more than one aspect of her poetry. Admiring critics in the decade since she committed suicide at the age of thirty have tried assiduously to dissociate her from the death-happy exultation of her cult. Yet this very ghoulishness has marked, often enough, their own accounts of her talent. It was A. Alvarez who, shortly after Sylvia Plath's own solemnizing gesture, established the orthodox tone of her praise [see excerpt dated 1966]:

> When Sylvia Plath died I wrote an epitaph on her in *The Observer,* at the end of which I said, "The loss to literature is inestimable." But someone pointed out to me that this wasn't quite true. The achievement of her final style is to make poetry and death inseparable. The one could not exist without the other. And this is right. In a curious way, the poems read as though they were written posthumously. It needed not only great intelligence and insight to handle the material of them, it also took a kind of bravery. Poetry of this order is a murderous art.

Murderous, that is, rather than suicidal: Sylvia Plath is a martyr in this view to the demands of her art. It follows that to appreciate her poetry we must recognize the rightness, even the value, of her self-destruction.

The aesthetic that underlies this claim is not only confused but disastrous; though Alvarez's sympathy for the poet is incontrovertible, what he urges is ultimately unfeeling and inhumane. And though not all subsequent appreciation of Plath has struck his peculiar and abyss-dwelling note, it has been decisive for the conventional understanding of her poetry until now, and may be heard even in the more responsible views of Stephen Spender. Of the crisis of the spirit from which Plath produced "these disconcerting, terrifying poems," Spender has written: "The guarantees of the authenticity of the situation are insanity (or near-insanity) and death." Her poetry is the proof that she meant what she said. One inspired disciple of this view has gone so far as to sneer at Kafka for lacking Plath's "final courage," though he shared her vision of life's meaninglessness. A special case is her canonization by the New Feminists, several of whom have suggested that if there had been a movement for Women's Liberation in 1963, her suicide might not have been necessary. Alvarez has done much—very nearly everything—to influence our way of receiving the poems, and some of it has been useful; for example, his sketch of the poet's last, dismal weeks, alone with two children in a cold and depressingly Victorian flat in London, the phone out, the muse violent. But his disservice may be more enduring still.

What is most suspicious and disconcerting, however, about this intense and apparently irresponsible collation of her suicide and her poetry is the ease with which the case may be supported by citation from the poems themselves:

> The blood jet is poetry,
> There is no stopping it.

Equally troubling are those moments, for example in **"Lady Lazarus,"** when Plath envisions suicide attempts, quite as the cult of Plath does, as fundamentally performances, pieces of art, like poetry itself:

> The peanut-crunching crowd
> Shoves in to see
>
> Them unwrap me hand and foot—
> The big strip tease.
> Gentlemen, ladies,
>
> These are my hands,
> My knees.

The notion of theatrical suicide is satirized, of course, but it is also relished, even sexually relished: "The big strip tease." (It may be said that the analogy between suicide and strip tease is not obscene only in the complicated sense in which Fellini is not obscene.) The poem records a series of three unsuccessful suicide attempts, each of which the lady is proud of having performed, proud of having survived:

> I have done it again.
> One year in every ten
> I manage it—
>
> A sort of walking miracle . . .

The tone is weirdly masochistic and show-offy. ("I guess you could say I've a call") and remarkably free of dread. But it's not the private and discreet suicide that appeals to her, nor, indeed, the successful one. Rather,

> It's the theatrical
>
> Comeback in broad day
> To the same place, the same face,
>   the same brute
> Amused shout:
>
> "A miracle!"
> That knocks me out.

I do not mean to say of such a poem that, having written

it, Sylvia Plath had invited the "peanut-crunching crowd" to a celebration of her own, real suicide, though come they did. Nor does she imply that a performance of this kind could be painlessly observed: "There is a charge / For the eyeing of my scars." But even in this detail, self-importance mixes with self-loathing: a decidedly public self-immolation.

The most suitable defense against the charge I have just made is that the "I" of Sylvia Plath's poetry is an artificial construct, and not Sylvia herself—in spite of the avowed "confessional" models, such as Robert Lowell and Anne Sexton, in spite of the unmistakable and direct autobiographical inspirations, in spite of the fact that more than a few of her poems, and among them the most important, are partially or wholly unintelligible without autobiographical gloss. It is not Sylvia Plath, but the *persona* of **"Lady Lazarus,"** who is self-aggrandizing, the *persona* of **"Daddy"** who is vindictive, etc. I am not convinced by this defense, though it has New Critical good sense behind it, because in the case of Plath it leaves too much excepted, too much in awkward doubt. I suspect that when it is rigorously prosecuted, and it rarely is, it would end in a preference for the earliest Plath, the poems of *Colossus* (1960), a technically sure but derivative and generally bland first book. Plath's achievement, whatever its merits, rests on the posthumous collections, *Ariel* (1966), *Crossing the Water* (1971), and *Winter Trees* (1971), where indisputable originality of voice and subject matter abounds. One has the feeling, in turning from *Colossus* to these, that a mask has been dropped, and any understanding of her poetry which depends upon the assumption of a mask must stop where these begin. Her husband, Ted Hughes, said of the horrific **"Last Words"** ("I do not want a plain box, I want a sarcophagus / With tigery stripes, and a face on it / Round as the moon . . . ") that it "would have been safer said by a *persona* in some kind of play," but implicit in his words is the concession that the speaker is Sylvia Plath.

Moreover, it is not the autobiographical nature of the poems that wants defending. To find the occasions of poetry in the events of one's life is, after all, the rule and not the exception. But where the poet chooses a method especially "confessional" and direct, as in Plath's poetry, or as in Robert Lowell's *Life Studies,* there are two contingencies. First, the poet runs the risk, more openly than ever, of sheer self-absorption. He is granted unusual privileges of egotism, and his art may fall victim to the pleasures of performance. Secondly, the obligation to be shrewd and knowing about the self becomes especially keen: a lack of self-knowledge can have dire aesthetic consequences. By self-knowledge I mean not some tidy, amateur delineation of psychic cause and psychic effect, but a sensitive, probative apprehension of root contradiction, root ambivalence in the self, without which the poetry, however "felt" or strident, must be shallow, unsponsored from within. The poem **"Lady Lazarus"** is, in the end, not autobiographical enough: it tells us something about how much she suffers, and less about how, and nothing about why. And that is true of Sylvia Plath's presentation of the other themes of her poetry: death, and bearing children, and hating one's father, and going without love. (pp. 47-8)

At the time when Sylvia Plath ended her career, she was producing poems at the rate of several a day. That the poems of her final weeks and days are her bleakest will surprise no one, but it is characteristic of her art that they are among her most controlled and precise. The mood to which she finally succumbed was something other than rage. As she had explained in **"Death & Co.,"** the attraction of death is twofold. On one hand, it is calmness, silence, and cold perfection. On the other, it is a violent, if "substanceless," apotheosis. "The piston in motion" and "the hooves of horses, / Their merciless churn." From the vantage point of her suicide, it is easy enough to conclude that the choice was never one between life and death, but between these two versions of death's condition. There had been rearguard actions: for example, in the poem **"For a Fatherless Son,"** where the nostalgia for her father's love is a source of tenderness for her own child, rather than a source of violent and radical despair. It was love for her children, no doubt, that provided whatever resistance the invitation to death encountered at the very end. At that time, she wrote of her son:

> You are the one
> Solid the spaces lean on, envious.
> You are the baby in the barn.

With such evidence of her capacity to feel love for what is alive and well and living in the world, it is maudlin and depraved to speak of her death as if it were inevitable, or of her suicide as if it were murder. This, finally, is what Alvarez does, suggesting that the poet was (and is) a victim not in the sense in which we all are, but in some elect and especially stricken way. Plath herself goes further, and identifies suicide not only with murder but even with genocide:

>   my skin
> Bright as a Nazi lampshade,
> My right foot
>
> A paperweight,
> My face is a featureless, fine
> Jew linen.

It is an image of herself she returns to often, as in **"Daddy,"** where her father is a German "with a Meinkampf look" and the German language is an engine

> Chuffing me off like a Jew.
> A Jew to Dachau, Auschwitz, Belsen.
> I began to talk like a Jew.
> I think I may well be a Jew.

Her comparison of her suffering to the suffering of the six million has been, of course, one of the most controversial features of her poems, as it is one of their most striking. I have seen it defended on the grounds that the concentration camps offer a "ready-made modern example of hell on earth," though I think its ready-madeness one of the chief things to be said against the analogy. Sylvia Plath addressed the matter in an interview in 1962. "Personal experience," she said, "shouldn't be a kind of shut-box and mirror-looking, narcissistic experience. I believe it should be . . . relevant to the larger things, the bigger things such as Hiroshima and Dachau and so on."

But what relevance do her poems establish? In **"Lady Lazarus,"** the Belsen allusions tell us that she is oppressed, now by the "brute amused" crowd, now by "Herr Doktor" and "Herr God, Herr Lucifer." We know that she takes over from her oppressors the act of her own persecution, perhaps to win their approval, or to give to herself the sense of identity and self-command. We know also that such reversals were common in the concentration camps. The allusion has intensified her suffering in our imagination, and lent to it an air of cultural and historical importance. But where is there even a pretense of its legitimacy, a shred of support for such claims? There is none; and granted this, can the Holocaust allusions be other than the "larceny" that George Steiner has called them? Moreover, what can Plath's claims for the "relevance" of her personal suffering mean? Despite the account of suffering it contains, and the larger amount that it invokes, **"Lady Lazarus"** conspicuously fails to tell us anything about the nature of suffering itself.

Plath's commitment to death was obscure—obscure to herself, we can only assume, because obscure in her art—and in her failure of insight, she left herself only the choice between a cold, still death and a "bed of fire." The sardonic triumph of the former is recorded in **"Edge."** . . . In earlier poems she has been offended by this condition: "Perfection is terrible, it cannot have children." Now she sees only its desirability. Having achieved it, the woman wears "the smile of accomplishment." What precisely has she accomplished? The tidiest possible death. In what ought to be, but is not, a satire of maternal care, she has "folded" the children at her breasts. She does not disturb her clothing. But "the smile of accomplishment" has other, and subtly more terrible, associations, with Sylvia Plath's "fifteen years of straight A's": the implication is that all accomplishment, all the earnest endeavor of our lives, tends toward this final perfection. It is a perfection that is achieved, moreover, with "the illusion of a Greek necessity," that is, as if our state were naturally and necessarily so perfect, which it is not. Instead, we must accomplish death: we die by art. Her poem itself is the penultimate gesture, the cutting **"Edge."** The garden "Stiffens," the serpent is an infant child, and the myth of man's perfectibility has taken its grimmest turn.

Having given the poem this reading, very much on its own terms, it remains for me to say how mean a poem it is, how fundamentally coldhearted and unkind. One may take as an example its very simplest unkindness: the image of the dead children "coiled" at the woman's breast. Their own deaths are, of course, irrelevant to the poem; they exist only as props. As such, they are examples of what the poet has called "flat," "cardboard" people, meaning "the other": ultimately, anyone but herself. The failure to imagine the other as having what George Eliot called an "equivalent center of self " is, of course, a moral lapse, but it is also an aesthetic one. Where Sylvia Plath's failure as an artist is not rooted in a failure to apprehend herself, it is rooted in a failure to apprehend the self in others.

Such judgments are possible—I would say, necessary—when we have wiped from our minds, "like chalk from a blackboard," the myth of Sylvia Plath's martyrdom. Her death, they say, begs all questions of sincerity in her poems. It may be so. It is impossible to read her poetry without being convinced of the pain in which it had its origin. It is impossible not to be moved. But in the end we must make judgments based upon our allegiance to life. (pp. 50-2)

John Romano, "Sylvia Plath Reconsidered,"

in Commentary, *Vol. 57, No. 4, April, 1974, pp. 47-52.*

M. D. Uroff (essay date 1977)

[*Uroff is an American critic who served as editor of* New England Review *from 1961-63. She is also the author of* Sylvia Plath and Ted Hughes (1979), *a study of these poets' influence on each other's work. In the following excerpt, Uroff re-examines Plath's assigned position as a confessional poet.*]

When M. L. Rosenthal first used the term, confessional poetry [in his *The New Poets*], he had in mind a phase in Robert Lowell's career when Lowell turned to themes of sexual guilt, alcoholism, confinement in a mental hospital, and developed them in the first person in a way that intended, in Rosenthal's view, to point to the poet himself. Rosenthal was careful to limit the possibilities of the mode but he did name Sylvia Plath a confessional poet as well because, he said, she put the speaker herself at the center of her poems in such a way as to make her psychological vulnerability and shame an embodiment of her civilization. Rosenthal's widely accepted estimation was challenged first by Ted Hughes who pointed out that Plath uses autobiographical details in her poetry in a more emblematic way than Lowell, and more recently by Marjorie Perloff who claims that Plath's poetry lacks the realistic detail of Lowell's work. If Hughes and Perloff are right, and I think they are, then we should reconsider the nature of the speaker in Plath's poems, her relationship to the poet, and the extent to which the poems are confessional.

What distinguishes Plath's poems from Lowell's is precisely the kind of person in the poem. With Lowell, according to Rosenthal, it is the literal self. Lowell himself has said that while he invented some of his autobiography, he nonetheless wants the reader to feel it is true, that he is getting the real Robert Lowell. The literal self in Lowell's poetry is to be sure a literary self, but fairly consistently developed as a self-deprecating, modest, comic figure with identifiable parents, summer homes, experiences at particular addresses. When he discloses under these circumstances his weaknesses, his ineptitude, his misery, his inflicting of pain on others, he is in fact revealing information that is humiliating or prejudicial to himself. In this sense, the person in the poem is making an act of confession, and, although we as readers have no power to forgive, Lowell's self-accusatory manner makes it impossible to judge. We are not outraged but chastened by such revelations. With Plath, it is otherwise. The person in her poem calls certain people father or mother but her characters lack the particularity of Commander and Mrs. Lowell. They are generalized figures not real-life people, types that Plath manipulates dramatically in order to reveal their limitations. Precisely because they are such types, the information that Plath reveals about them is necessarily prejudicial and has consequently misled some readers who react with hostility to what she has to reveal. Elizabeth Hardwick calls her lacerating and claims that Plath has the distinction of never being in her poems a nice person. While niceness is not a perfect standard for judging a person in a poem, Hardwick's reaction and that of many other critics who follow her reveal the particular way in which Plath's revelations are prejudicial to her. Plath's

outraged speakers do not confess their misery so much as they vent it, and this attitude, unlike that of Lowell's characters, makes them susceptible to rather severe critical judgments. However, if we look at the strategy of the poems, we might arrive at a more accurate estimate of the person in them and of her relationship to the poet. (pp. 104-05)

[Lowell] says that when he started writing the poems in *Life Studies* he had been doing a number of readings on the West Coast and found that he was simplifying his poems, breaking the meter, making impromptu changes as he read. He claimed that poets had become proficient in forms and needed to make a "breakthrough back into life." *Life Studies* may be read as that repossession of his own life, and its mode is properly confessional because both in the poems and the prose of that volume the suffering and victimizing speaker searches through his own pain in order to perceive some truth about the nature of his experience. Plath's speakers make no such search. They are anxious to contain rather than to understand their situation. When Lowell's speaker in "Skunk Hour" says, "My mind's not right," he expresses some kind of desolate self-knowledge. By contrast, Plath calls the maddened woman in **"Miss Drake Proceeds to Supper,"** "No novice / In those elaborate rituals / Which allay the malice / Of knotted table and crooked chair." Both characters may be mad but their strategies differ. Where Lowell's character confesses his weakness, Plath's character employs all her energies in maintaining a ritualistic defense against her situation. She seems in a perverse way to act out the program of the poet whose informed and intelligent mind must manipulate its terrifying experiences. There is in fact a strange correspondence between Miss Drake's methods and those of her creator. Miss Drake is superbly sensitive, wildly inventive in objectifying her fears, and skilled at controlling them. But there is also a vast distance between Miss Drake and the poet, a distance that may be measured by the techniques of parody, caricature, hyperbole that Plath employs in characterizing her. There is something perversely comical about Miss Drake who "can see in the nick of time / How perilous needles grain the floorboards." If Miss Drake's rigid efforts are not quite ridiculed, it is fair to say that she does not engage our sympathies in the way that Lowell's speaker in "Skunk Hour" (who may also be ridiculous) does. She has been distanced from us by the poet who sees her as a grotesque reflection of herself, employing the manipulative strategies of the uninformed mind against an undefined terror, channeling what might have been creative energy into pointless rituals.

"Miss Drake Proceeds to Supper" is an early poem but it reveals the way in which Plath controlled her own terrifying experiences in her poetry. She did so by creating characters and later speakers who demonstrate the way in which the embattled mind operates. Far from speaking for the poet, they stage crazy performances which are parodic versions of the imaginative act. Through them, Plath shows how terror may grip the mind and render it rigid. Through her speaker's projective fantasies, she projects her own understanding of hysterical control and the darker knowledge of its perilous subversion of the imagination. While Miss Drake's elaborate rituals are designed to hold off her fears, the poet who created her is handling in the act of the poem, however indirectly, her own frightening knowledge of madness. What for the mad woman is a means of avoiding experience becomes for the poet a means of controlling it. The poems, unlike the speakers in them, reveal Plath's terrifying self-knowledge.

In her poems, Plath is not concerned with the nature of her experience, rather she is engaged in demonstrating the way in which the mind deals with extreme circumstances or circumstances to which it responds with excessive sensitivity. The typical strategy of her speakers is to heighten or exaggerate ordinary experience and at the same time to intensify the mind's manipulative skills so that fathers become Fascists and the mind that must deal with the image it has conjured up becomes rigidly ritualistic. In her early poems, Plath stands outside and judges her characters, drawing caricatures not only of madness but of its counterpart, hysterical sanity. As she continued to write however, she began to let the characters speak for themselves in caricature, parody, and hyperbole which they use not as vehicles of judgment but as inevitable methods of their performances. When the mind that must deal with terror stiffens and rigidifies, parody will become its natural means of expression.

Between **"Miss Drake Proceeds to Supper"** and her late poems, however, Plath explored another way in which the mind responds to its terrors. In what has been called her middle period, Plath became interested in a kind of character who had been exhausted by her fears and could not control experience. For example, the insomniac of **"Zoo Keeper's Wife"** lies awake at night thinking over her grievances and the particular horrors of her husband's zoo full of "wolf-headed fruit bats" and the "bird-eating spider." Her response to her husband is as hyperbolic as the hysterical spinster's disdain for love's slovenliness in an early Plath poem but she has no rituals with which to deal with it nor barricades to hide behind. Rather, she says, "I can't get it out of my mind." All she can do is "flog apes owls bears sheep / Over their iron stile" and still she can't sleep. Again, in **"Insomniac,"** the mind cannot handle memories that "jostle each other for face-room like obsolete film stars." The speaker's "head is a little interior of grey mirrors. / Each gesture flees immediately down an alley / Of diminishing perspectives, and its significance / Drains like water out the hole at the far end." It is in these poems and others like them of this period that Plath's speakers sound most like Lowell's in his more exhausted and despairing moods yet even here Plath focuses on the function or nonfunction of the mind rather than on the meaning of the experience.

As Plath turned into her later period in a poem such as **"Tulips"** the speaker of her poem seems to welcome the loss of control that had harried the insomniacs. As she goes into the hospital in this poem, she claims to be learning peacefulness, and she hands herself over to the hospital attendants to be propped up and tended to. The nurses bring her numbness in "bright needles," and, as she succumbs to the anethesia, she claims that she only wanted to be utterly empty. However, she does not rest in that attitude very long before she comes out of the operating room and its anesthetized state and begins reluctantly to confront her pain. Her first response is to complain that the tulips hurt her, watch her, that they eat up her oxygen. But, when the speaker claims a correspondence between the tulips' redness and her own wound, her manipulative

mind begins to function again, first in negative ways, tormenting itself by objectifying its pain. Then, in a brief but alarming reversal, the speaker associates the tulips not only with the pain but with the heart so that the outside threat and power are not only overcome but subsumed. Because the speaker here has so exaggerated her own emptiness and the tulips' violence and vitality, she must then accept in herself the attributes she has cast onto the tulips which now return to her. The heart blooms. Here, for once, the manipulative mind works its own cure. If the supersensitive mind can turn tulips into explosions, it can also reverse the process and turn dangerous animals into blooming hearts. What it cannot do, despite the speaker's claim, is accept utter emptiness. It cannot refuse to be excited by the flowers that it does not want.

"Tulips" is an unusual poem in Plath's work not because it demonstrates how the mind may generate hyperboles to torture itself (which is a common strategy of Plath's poems) but because it shows how this generative faculty may have a positive as well as a negative function. **"Tulips"** is not a cheerful poem, but it does move from cold to warmth, from numbness to love, from empty whiteness to vivid redness, a process manipulated by the associative imagination. The speaker herself seems surprised by her own gifts and ends the poem on a tentative note, moving toward the faraway country of health. Despite this possibly hopeful ending, however, the body of the poem demonstrates the way in which the mind may intensify its pain by objectifying it.

What takes place in **"Tulips"** in a private meditation (and perhaps the privacy accounts for the mind's pliancy) is given a much more ferocious treatment in the public performances of Plath's late poems. It is in fact the sense of being on public display that calls forth the rage of the speakers in these late poems. Forced to perform, they develop elaborate rituals. Their manipulative powers become a curse not a cure. In **"The Tour,"** the speaker, caught "in slippers and housedress with no lipstick," greets with mock hospitality her maiden aunt who wants "to be shown about": "Do step into the hall," "Yes, yes, this is my address. / Not a patch on *your* place, I guess." Instead of refusing to become a victim of the aunt's meddlesome curiosity, the speaker readily assents to it. After apologizing for the mess, she leads her aunt right into it, showing her the frost-box that bites, the furnace that exploded, the sink that ate "seven maids and a plumber." With mock concern, she warns the aunt, "O I shouldn't put my finger on *that*," "O I shouldn't dip my hankie in, it *hurts!*" "I am bitter? I'm averse?" she asks, dropping for a second her polite mask but resuming it immediately in her refrain, "Toddle on home to tea now." The speaker manipulates the aunt's curiosity, turning it back on itself by maintaining a tone of insistent courtesy and forced intimacy that is designed to jeeringly protect the aunt from the brazen exhibition of the open house of horrors. She appears to contrast her own dreary domestic appliances to her aunt's exotic possessions (the gecko she wears a costume jewelry, her Javanese geese and monkey trees); but actually her machines are "wild," she says, and in a different way unlike her aunt's tamed decorations. However, when she calls herself "creepy-creepy," she seems to have assumed her aunt's gecko-like qualities. The staginess of this speaker, her insistent rhyming, exclamatory sentences, italicized words, all provide not only a grotesque reflection of the aunt's alarm, but also suggest a kind of hysterical control. The speaker's ability to manipulate the aunt is matched by a more sinister ability to manipulate her own horrors, to locate them in furnace and stove, and there to give them a separate identity. Her mind, like Miss Drake's, is extremely skilled at objectifying her fears. The poet who felt that the intelligent mind must manipulate its most terrifying experiences also knew that the deranged mind could operate in such a way as to hold off its terror, separate itself from the agony it suffered, and the speaker here exemplifies that process. When at the end she warns the aunt not to trip over the nurse-midwife who "can bring the dead to life," she points to the source of her misery, the creative principle that has itself assumed an objective identity and become part of the mess. The midwife, like a poet, delivers life with "wiggly fingers," and she has in fact been very active in endowing dead household appliances with a lively if destructive energy; but now she too has been cast out.

In this speaker who can not only caricature her aunt with the "specs" and "flat hat" but also her own creepiness as well as her "awfully nice" creative faculties, Plath presents a damning portrait of the too inventive mind that exults in self-laceration. It is not quite accurate to say that this speaker is unaware of her own strategies because she is supremely self-conscious; but she is trapped by them. Where others have been devoured or repelled, she lives on, neither despairing nor shocked but charged with a hysterical energy that she deploys finally against herself. Her nurse-midwife is eyeless. She too can only see herself now as others see her. Her ability to manipulate her own suffering is a subversion of the poet's creative powers; it becomes a means of holding off rather than exploring her situation.

A quite different manipulator is the speaker in **"The Applicant"** who appears to be a comic figure, reveling in her machinations. Unlike the woman in **"The Tour,"** she seems to speak for others not for herself. She starts out with the characteristic question of the convention-loving woman, "First, are you our sort of person?" What interests her, she reveals, is not what we might expect from someone who would ask that question, the social qualities of her marriage applicant, but rather her physical parts. "Our sort of person" has no glass eyes, false teeth, rubber breasts, stitches to show something's missing. Once having assured herself on that score, she presents her applicant's hand in marriage, promising not only the traditional services that it will "bring teacups and roll away headaches" but that at the end it will even "dissolve of sorrow." Then, as if this "guaranteed" emotion might be too much for the man, she confides, "We make new stock from the salt." Such economy, such efficiency, this marriage broker seems to cluck. The woman "willing" "to do whatever you tell it" can be easily recycled. Next the speaker turns to the man who like the woman is "stark naked." Instead of putting him through the same examination of parts, she quickly offers him a wedding suit, "Black and stiff," that he can reuse as a funeral shroud. She adopts the familiar tone of the tailor ("How about this suit—" "Believe me, they'll bury you in it.") that shades into that of the mortician. Suddenly the suit, the girl, the deadly convention of marriage are all one, like a tomb, equally "waterproof, shatterproof, proof / Against fire and bombs through the roof." The subversive excess of her promises here is hastily passed over as her sales pitch con-

tinues: "Now your head, excuse me, is empty. / I have the ticket for that. / Come here, sweetie, out of the closet." What she presents is "A living doll" whose value will increase with each anniversary, paper at first but silver in 25 years and gold at 50 years.

It might be argued that **"The Applicant"** does not properly belong to those poems in which Plath exposes the mind's manipulation of terrifying experiences. After all, marriage—and especially the marriage contracted here—is a conventional arrangement which should not affect the fears or passions or emotions of either the man or the woman. In addition, the speaker here appears safely removed from the situation she directs. These facts, however, do not explain the tone of the poem which comes through in the insistent refrain, "Will you marry it?" This speaker who has "the ticket" for everything seems, despite her all-knowing and consoling comic pose, very anxious to have her question answered. Again, as in the other poems we have discussed, the nature of the speaker in **"The Applicant"** deserves more attention than it has received. What she says is obvious enough but why does she say it? I have called her a woman although her sex is nowhere identified partly because of her language (she calls the woman "sweetie" and the man "My boy") and partly because of her claim that her applicant can sew, cook and "talk, talk, talk" (no man, I believe would have considered that last feature a selling point) but chiefly because she seems to be extremely concerned for the successful outcome of her applicant. She is like the applicant herself willing to make any claim and to accede to any demands in order to strike a bargain. Hers is a pose of course, but it is the pose of the compliant woman. Like the patient in **"Tulips"** who accepts the gift of flowers that torment her and the niece in **"The Tour"** who responds to her aunt's detested visit, the speaker here insists on participating in a situation the demands of which she finds abhorrent. Her only recourse for dealing with it is a mode at which she is particularly skilled, burlesque. Yet behind the scorn and the scoffing is another feeling, something like hysteria, that expresses itself in her repeated question. She seems trapped by the sexual stereotypes she parodies. The ventriloquism of this poem hides the fact that this is an internal debate. The sexual fear that has driven the "sweetie" into the closet and the boy to his last resort also propels the manipulations of this shrewd if too agreeable woman. Here again is the controlling mind using its powers to compartmentalize rather than explore its situation.

"The Applicant" has been given serious consideration as Plath's statement on marriage yet it does not point to the poet herself in the same way that, for example, Robert Lowell's "Man and Wife" does. Its characters are unparticularized and unconnected to any specific event in Plath's experience. Its sexual stereotypes (the girl willing to do anything in order to be married and the boy only willing to marry if he can be convinced that he will get a worthwhile product) are manipulated by a speaker whose tension-filled control reveals not only their power over her but the terror that informs them. This speaker can manage, but she cannot escape her situation.

The relationship between poet and speaker in two other late poems, **"Lady Lazarus"** and **"Daddy,"** is somewhat more complicated because these poems do call upon specific incidents in Plath's biography, her suicide attempts and her father's death. Yet to associate the poet with the speaker directly, as many critics have done, does not account for the fact that Plath employs here as before the techniques of caricature, hyperbole, and parody that serve both to distance the speaker from the poet and at the same time to project onto the speaker a subversive variety of the poet's own strategies. In **"Lady Lazarus,"** the nature of the speaker is peculiar and defies our ordinary notions of someone prone to attempt suicide. Suicide is not a joyous act, and yet there is something of triumph in the speaker's assertion that she has done it again. The person recovering from a suicide attempt, as this speaker says she is, cannot possibly be so confident at the very moment of her recovery that her sour breath will vanish in a day and that she will soon be a smiling woman. Nor could she have the presence of mind to characterize those who surround her as a "peanut-crunching crowd" and her rescuers as enemies. And finally it seems psychologically impossible for the suicide victim to have the energy to rise at all against other people, much less to threaten to "eat men like air." The person who speaks here does so not to explore her situation but to control it. She is first of all a performer, and, although she adopts many different roles, she is chiefly remarkable for her control not only of herself but of the effects she wishes to work on those who surround her. She speaks of herself in hyperboles, calling herself a "walking miracle," boasting that she has "nine times to die," exclaiming that dying is an art she does "exceptionally well," asserting that "the theatrical / Comeback in broad day" knocks her out. Her treatment of suicide in such buoyant terms amounts to a parody of her own act. When she compares her suicide to the victimization of the Jews and later on when she claims there is a charge for a piece of her hair or clothes and thus compares her rescued self to the crucified Christ or martyred saint, she is engaging in self-parody. She employs these techniques partly to defy the crowd with its "brute / Amused shout: / 'A miracle!' " and partly to taunt her rescuers, "Herr Doktor" "Herr Enemy," who regard her as their "opus." She is neither a miracle nor an opus, and she fends off those who would regard her in this way. But the techniques have another function as well; they display the extent to which she can objectify herself, ritualize her fears, manipulate her own terror. Her extreme control in fact is intimately entwined with her suicidal tendencies. The suicide is her own victim, can control her own fate. If she is not to succumb to this desire, she must engage in the elaborate ritual which goes on all the time in the mind of the would-be suicide by which she allays her persistent wish to destroy herself. Her act is the only means of dealing with a situation she cannot face. Her control is not sane but hysterical. When the speaker assures the crowd that she is "the same, identical woman" after her rescue, she is in fact telling them her inmost fear that she could and probably will do it again. What the crowd takes for a return to health, the speaker sees as a return to the perilous conditions that have driven her three times to suicide. By making a spectacle out of herself and by locating the victimizer outside herself in the doctor and the crowd, she is casting out her terrors so that she can control them. When she says at the end that she will rise and eat men like air, she is projecting (and again perhaps she is only boasting) her destruction outward. That last stanza of defiance is in fact an effort of the mind to triumph over terror, to rise and not to succumb to its own victimization.

The speaker's tone is hysterical, triumphant, defiant. Only once does she drop this tone to admit the despair that underlies it when she says, "What a trash / To annihilate each decade." Otherwise she maintains her rigid self-control in accents that range from frenzied gaiety to spiteful threats. Although her situation is much more extreme than those social occasions of **"Tulips," "The Tour," "The Applicant,"** it is like them not of her own making. She has been rescued when she wanted to die. Her response is perverse. She does not welcome her rescuers, nor does she examine the condition that forced her death wish; instead she accepts her fate and presents herself as in complete control. The effort of her act which comes through in her tone is intense yet necessary because without it she would have to face the fact that she is not in control. Her performance is a defense against utter desolation. Here again is the mind manipulating its own terrors. Plath was no stranger to this method, as we have said before, but while she works here with a parallel between hysterical control and creative control she presents the first as a mad reflection of the second. The speaker like Miss Drake is "No novice / In those elaborate rituals" that allay her terror yet her tremendous energies are so absorbed in maintaining them that she has no reserve with which to understand why she performs as she does. When she sees herself as a victimized Jew or Christ, she may be engaging in self-parody but the extremity of her circumstances does not allow her to realize it. The poet behind the poem is not caricaturing Lady Lazarus as she had Miss Drake; she is rather allowing Lady Lazarus to caricature herself and thus demonstrating the way in which the mind turns ritualistic against horror. Despite the fact that "Lady Lazarus" draws on Plath's own suicide attempt, the poem tells us little more than a newspaper account of the actual event. It is not a personal confession. What it does reveal is Plath's understanding of the way the suicidal person thinks.

"Daddy" is an even more complicated treatment of the same process. The poem opens with the daughter's assertion that "You do not do, you do not do." But if Daddy will not do, neither will he not not do, and we find this speaker in the characteristic Plath trap, forcing herself to deal with a situation she finds unacceptable. **"Daddy"** is not so much an account of a true-life situation as a demonstration of the mind confronting its own suffering and trying to control that by which it feels controlled. The simplistic, insistent rhythm is one form of control, the obsessive rhyming and repeated short phrases are others, means by which she attempts to charm and hold off the evil spirits. But the speaker is even more crafty than this technical expertise demonstrates. She is skilled at image-making like a poet and she can manipulate her images with extreme facility. The images themselves are important for what they tell us of her sense of being victimized and victimizer but more significant than the actual image is the swift ease with which she can turn it to various uses. For example, she starts out imagining herself as a prisoner living like a foot in the black shoe of her father. Then she casts her father in her own role and he becomes "one grey toe / Big as a Frisco seal" and then quickly she is looking for his foot, his root. Next he reverts to his original boot identity, and she is the one with "The boot in the face." And immediately he returns with "A cleft in your chin instead of your foot." At the end, she sees the villagers stamping on

Pen drawing by Plath of the village Benidorm, where she and her husband Ted Hughes stayed while visiting Spain in 1956.

him. Thus she moves from booted to booter as her father reverses the direction. The mind that works in this way is neither logical nor psychologically penetrating; it is simply extremely adept at juggling images. In fact, the speaker is caught in her own strategies. She can control her terrors by forcing them into images, but she seems to have no understanding of the confusion her wild image-making betrays. When she identifies herself as a foot, she suggests that she is trapped, but when she calls her father a foot the associations break down. In the same way, when she caricatures her father as a Fascist and herself as a Jew, she develops associations of torture which are not exactly reversed when she reverses the identification and calls herself the killer of her vampire-father. The speaker here can categorize and manipulate her feelings in name-calling, in rituals, in images, but these are only techniques, and her frenzied use of them suggests that they are methods she employs in the absence of any other. When she says, "Daddy, I have had to kill you," she seems to realize the necessity of the exorcism and to understand the ritual she performs, but the frantic pitch of the language and the swift switches of images do not confirm any self-understanding. The pace of the poem reveals its speaker as one driven by a hysterical need for complete control, a need that stems from the fear that without such control she will be destroyed. Her simple, incantatory monologue is the perfect vehicle of expression for the orderly disordered mind.

In talking to A. Alvarez, Plath called these poems "light verse." **"Daddy"** does not seem to fall easily into that category despite its nonsense rhymes and rhythms, its quickly flicking images. It is neither decorous nor playful. On the other hand, given its subject, neither is it ponderous or solemn. Above all it offers no insight into the speaker, no mitigating evidence, no justification. Plath's classification is clear perhaps only if we consider her speaker a parodic version of the poet. The speaker manipulates her terror in singsong language and thus delivers herself in "light verse" that employs its craft in holding off its subject. For all the frankness of this poem, the name-calling and blaming, the dark feeling that pervades it is undefined, held back rather than revealed by the technique. The poet who has created this speaker knows the speaker's strategies because they are a perverted version of her own, and that is the distinction between the speaker's "light verse" and the poet's serious poem.

From her earliest madwomen and hysterical virgins to the late suicides and father-killers, Plath portrays characters whose stagey performances are subversions of the creative act. Absorbed in their rituals, they confess nothing. They are not anxious to make a breakthrough back into life. In fact, their energies are engaged in erecting a barricade against self-revelation. Plath's fascination with this parodic image of the creative artist stems from a deep knowledge of the machinations of the mind. If she reveals herself in these poems, she does so in the grotesque mirror of parody. If these poems come out of her own emotional experiences, as she said they did, they are not uninformed cries from the heart. Rather, she chose to deal with her experience by creating characters who could not deal with theirs and through their rituals demonstrate their failure. These poems, like the speakers in them, are superbly controlled; but the poet behind the poem uses her immense technical control to manipulate the tone, the rhythm, the rhyme, the pace of the speakers' language in order to reveal truths about the speakers that their obsessive assertions deny. (pp. 105-15)

M. D. Uroff, "Sylvia Plath and Confessional Poetry: A Reconsideration," in The Iowa Review, *Vol. 8, No. 1, Winter, 1977, pp. 104-15.*

David Shapiro   (essay date 1979)

[*Shapiro is an American poet and critic of art and literature. The following excerpt is taken from an essay that appeared in* Sylvia Plath: New Views on the Poetry, *a collection of specially commissioned critical appraisals of Plath that includes pieces by Hugh Kenner and Marjorie Perloff. In the following excerpt, Shapiro provides what he terms a "demystifying" of Plath criticism. Shapiro finds fault with Plath's poetry itself as overwritten and melodramatic, stating: "The whole tendency is to a diction-dominated formlessness punctuated by hyperbole appealing to the emotions."*]

There is no doubt that [Plath's] poetry is part of the history of sensibility, as it were, rather than centrally involved in the history of our poetry. She had the advantages and disadvantages of a sequestered education at Smith; note the continuous tissue of clichés from the letters of those days to her mother. She had also, of course, as she understood it, the outrageous difficulty of laboring for "women's magazines," and *toward* a largely male literary scene. She had, finally, an embodiment of that scene in her husband; I take it that the peculiar form of the late melodramatic works now so celebrated was largely induced by the all too vivid pseudo-masculine tone of Hughes, a poet notoriously overrated but particularly overrated in relation, as Alvarez never stops telling us, to the bland others of English poetry. (p. 46)

This might account for the sense in much of Plath's later poetry that there is less a constructivist bias than a "destructivist" one. The early strenuous attempts to gain money from potboilers lead to a constant melancholy tone of the overwritten and the aspirational in metaphor. She is not one for "the art of sinking." She never properly learned to humiliate her diction, and works constantly in a species of expensive materials. Her mythological tone is what Hughes appropriated from the worst of Lawrence. Her humor, which saves so much of the novel and letters, is a right she largely abrogates in a mode of rigor mortis. One must be necessarily harsh here.

The harshness of my critique is part of the unpleasant task of demystifying (a notion that always involves, as Hartman has said, a slight form of contempt) her critics in their constant enchantments. Alvarez has compared the last year with the marvelous 1819 of Keats [see Alvarez's excerpt dated 1966]; Kroll has contributed a lugubrious study of her mythology, as if moon imagery and rebirth configurations would save the poems; Newman very early contributed a volume decent only in hagiography, whose bibliography of early reviews bristled with vindictive comment by Mary Kinzie against anyone so unfortunate as to have made practical complaints concerning the poetry. It is Sexton who has said somewhere that suicide is the opposite of poetry. Certainly stupidity is the opposite of poetry, and I am going to take to task silently those who have been entranced by the false glamors of biography, glamors Alvarez himself deposes while contributing to them, glamors that unfortunately are part of the weakest poems. As the Russian formalists have pointed out, the diction of the biographies, the life itself, and the poems coincide in much *byronisme* and elsewhere. Here, in the latest of our late romantics, critics and poet have ensnared themselves. Possibly the most interesting work that one might achieve as regards Plath is merely a "deconstruction" of her critics, by now industrialized and more than itching. One doesn't want to become like that don she insults so wittily in the letters, the one who criticizes by comparisons to Donne.

It is not a criticism by comparison alone that operates here, but certainly her work through its notoriety, and her critics by their notorious superlatives, now deserve no less than the severest standards. For example, those who compare her work to that of Georg Trakl should be reminded that Trakl completed his magnificent revision of Rimbaud by the First World War, and it is an expressionism that is controlled and more than controlled in the largest canvasses of his large poems. The small poems brood with a sensuous concreteness and hallucinatory mode that Plath merely parodies in her late poems. If one wants to understand what a real revaluation of Trakl and Rilke might be, one might look at O'Hara's transformations of German expressionism in his most conscious and self-conscious, self-reflexive works of the 1950s. Plath's work is about as

jejeune an imitation as her illustrationy drawings and her taste in the visual arts, Baskin, for example, among contemporaries. Trakl proceeds constantly in contrast and balance and his work, adequately meditated upon by Heidegger, needs no mediation here. But I am thrilled negatively by the absence of any criticism that would depose Plath as a parody of German expressionism. The organization of the late poems is so close to Trakl that it seems she may have known them in the Hamburger translations or from the German-English versions extant in the 1960s. I suggest, however, to adopt unwillingly a stern and Leavisite tone, that any practical survey of the specimen texts will show the first intensity in the work of Trakl. Near these texts, Plath is student and imitator.

Alvarez in his study speaks too easily of the "prissy, pausing flourish in the manner of Wallace Stevens." He is constantly searching for depths and deposing the poetry of so-called surface, but one wonders whether he is differentiating at all between the elegances of Stevens and the refinements of a Wilbur or Hecht. He seems unwilling to believe in a methodology that might digest the philosophical kinetics of Stevens rather than diverge to an explicit poetry along the lines of the all too discursive Lawrence (not that Lawrence did not contribute sometimes our finest Whitmanesque bestiaries and *bateaux ivres*). In other words, Alvarez and so many others see the glory of Plath in early "mastering the craft" and later letting the disturbances rise to a newly opened view. This is the royal lie as concerns Ginsberg, Lowell, Plath, Berryman, and so many others, and I presume that we are beginning to find in the work of Ashbery, for instance, other methodologies that have never involved the empurpled confessionals. All poetry, of course, is a matter of reticence and confession; but it is distasteful to recall a period in which poetry was called upon to deny itself, as it were, in a new form of naturalism. The best of Plath goes beyond this naturalism of occasions. But, as with the novel, it is always an almost Zola- if not Salinger-esque possibility. A whimsical naturalism modulated to a hysterical melodrama was part of her recipe in youth for successful "heartbreaking" potboilers. Like Dickens and Dostoevsky, she of course was involved in sublimating and transforming low genres, but the formula remains and seriously disturbs.

The late work is involved not only with the breakdown of the trope of *reticentia*, but is involved in a desublimation that Lionel Trilling so nobly analyses in his last two studies. One does not want to set too simply *Civilization and Its Discontents* as a "lion in the path" of the bolting horse of Plath. But it is impossible not to sense in her apotheosis and that of the late poems a flight from construction and self-regulating wholes praised by that magnificent structuralist Piaget. Her work is part of an age of the shattered narrative, but what I lament is not the shatter but the lack of any fruitful flatness, of any holding to the picture plane, by analogy here, of composition. In other words, she took to *utterance* and her poetry, which she loved to utter, is exactly deficient in the consciousness of writing itself. This may or may not be attributed to the era of Laing and Brown and Ginsberg. Lowell was always involved in the most devious way with a rapprochement between utterance, anecdote, and the difficulties of writing without mere voice. It does not take a Derrida of negative theology to see what is merely positive in the explicit utterances of the poetry of Plath. It is what now stands revealed in the work of Dylan Thomas as mere performance (called thirteenth rate for good reason by Pound). The flight into performance is like the flight into illness. In an age of Jasper Johns and the rarest forms of self-reflexiveness in American art, Plath's poetry becomes a mere theatre, somewhat akin to the sterile forms of happenings of Kaprow, but even less *dadaist* and *collagiste* than these. Her chants are the insipid corollaries of a notion of poetry as voice and cadence. It infects the Black Mountain School and is part of the detritus of Williams.

Again, let us remember that poetry is not voice or utterance but is structure. Emptiness is not a pretense in poetry anymore than space is in architecture. What is wanted is a well—a *vide*—and not a well-made urn. The works of Plath are overdetermined, largely and with remarkable vengeance jejunely referential. Like her drawings and her sentimental taste for the whimsical in Klee, she uses language as a pencil and does not permit language to speak through her. Thus, one feels in the poems a constant program of the referential in an age of degraded public realisms. While many of her critics have lamented her prose for women's magazines, few have noted the relative ease in which that realism and hyperbolic Grubean prose modulates to the poetry of hyperbole. Alvarez gives us some late poignant scenes in which he remonstrated about the exaggeration in the lines "The nude / Verdigris of the condor." Her response was not even to deal with this as device, but to suggest to her interlocutor that she take him to the zoo, where he might see for himself the factualness of her proposition. Thus, she was twisted upon the poles of a hyperbolic melodramatic masquerading as a realism. Like Bly and Ginsberg, she was quickly attaining the status of prophet for herself and losing the whole delicious sense of the nondiscursive in poetry. Her dream of a perfect language and her hypostasized notion of speech leads inevitably to a horrifying impasse. Poetry as pencil, as voice, and as magic failed her.

Practical criticism of Plath's poetry must fasten upon the overwriting and the aspirational quality of her devices. It is not simply in evidence in the late poems, but is part of the very initiation of her career in *The Colossus:* "Incense of death." Here we have neither the incense nor the concreteness of death but a literary abstraction, refusing both. Nor does she refuse the cliché: "Hours of blankness." Repetition is not used as a beautiful persistence, as in Gertrude Stein, but for copiousness and the haunting voice of the Gothic romance: "The small birds converge, converge." I emphasize this, because the shrill repetition in the late poems has been praised, and as a lover of repetition I would point out that she never employs this favorite device of American pragmatics for the sake of difference, but for the sake of copiousness and abundance. She thus uses and abuses the device of repetition, in much the way Bly and Wright abuse certain functions of hallucinatory repetition found in Spanish and French surrealism. Plath is *harping* upon a word here, rather than giving us through repetition the playful poetics of its new position. Her delicacies, learnt explicitly from Auden at times, are all too seldom this *imitatio* of "Musée des Beaux Arts": "Yet desolation, stalled in paint, spares the little country / Foolish, delicate, in the lower right hand corner." Rarely did she permit herself the luxury of spareness. She was always too poetical and lacked the prosiness of Elizabeth Bishop or the constant linguistic research of Laura Riding.

Often the modifiers are dismayingly clotted. This is doubtless part of the heritage of Lawrence and Thomas and of Hughes in his animal poems. In **"Sow"** the adjectives pile up to inverse effect, as in the ending: "The seven troughed seas and every earthquaking continent." She colors in with her adjectives the way that she colors in in her black and white illustrations. The adjectives have no presence, they are merely stippling for the sake of stippling but always in relation to an object or emotion, never abstract enough to make a fundamental dislocation, as in Rimbaud's floating glimmers. Nor does she control the mock heroic: "Unhorsed and shredded in the grove of combat / By a grislybristled / Boar." This is the species of overwriting that is recapitulated in the phylogenies of *Crow.*

The best poem in **Colossus,** it seems to me, succeeds in a Roethke-like vein of accepting smallness for what it is, with a negative capability that does not need the hypostasizing tone. In **"Mushrooms,"** Path holds herself in, as it were, to present the very quiet voice of the fungus, a parable of *petitesse* and big sensations. She becomes not just an Other, but a nice schizy mass. She ends with the commonplace, "Our foot's in the door," with a Bishop-like smile. As a matter of fact, one thinks of Bishop's "Snail." The little tercets are woven discretely and are concerned with discretions. But there is no mere self-contempt and there is a cry and aggression. While it is still a ghost story of a Gothic forest encroaching, its intimacy is musical and unfaltering.

Everywhere, there is the usual furniture of the Gothic romance and the thriller, for example in the transitional poems, so-called, of *Crossing the Water.* As a matter of fact, speaking of this word "transitional," it is about time to lacerate the Darwinian notion of this young poet. She did not necessarily evolve in her last year to some sudden organic complexity. If anything, as we might see with less dogmatic eyes, the late utterances are simplified and archaic in their explicitness. Yes, they are not drab and academic, but compare the late poems with "Fresh Air" of Kenneth Koch, for instance, a poem also explicitly against the academic strictures of the 1950s, the age of the lean quarterly and the missus and the midterms and myths. Koch has exuberantly given one a whole palette of possibilities, a labyrinth of homages and parodies, an exuberant cadenza with a proper sense of endlessness to its closure. Plath's poems click like boxes in Housman's sense of strict closure. Compared to some of the early and middle work, she sacrificed a great deal to get the histrionic condensations of the late ejaculatory style. It is a pity if this last season is to be judged merely chronologically as the crown. It is as if we called Keats' "To Fanny" the harbinger of a new period and the crown of the balanced odes. Paul de Man comes close to doing this as an homage to consciousness in Keats, but still in both poets we do a disservice by searching for a crown in chronos, which is as we know *not* history.

Many instances of overwriting might be collected; **"Finisterre"** will be paradigmatic. This is the country of "Black admonitory cliffs, and the sea exploding." The sea in thrilling fashion can do nothing less, one presumes, than explode here, as the surf creamed in earlier poems. All is orgasmic. All is terrifying. Compare this sea, by the way, with the well-excavated grave of Marianne Moore and its terrifyingly prosey acceptances. It is Moore who once said the poet must be as clear as natural reticence permits. The animations amid the pathos of Plath, as with Hughes, permitted no such reticence: "Other rocks hide their grudges under the water." "Souls, rolled in the doom-noise of the sea." One cannot help suspecting that the fashion of the occult, as noticed by Alvarez in Hughes and Plath, infects these lines with the same dreary and lugubrious lack of convincingness that we hear in the worst imitators of Yeats. This is the academic occult, and one mustn't forget that Ginsberg and his continental analogues were as academic as ever in their antiacademic escape into homemade theodicies. Eliot has said that we must get a religion for fear of having unconsciously a bad one; in Plath, we see "Our Lady of the Shipwrecked . . . striding toward the horizon." While Plath speaks of being "in love with the beautiful formlessness of the sea," her much-vaunted forms are mediocre and enclosed in poor thought; they do not uncover new thought, in Heidegger's sense of *aletheia.* Here all is covered in too much speech. Like Eliot's Othello, she is trying to cheer herself up.

"Stillborn" is an almost successful attempt at a more self-reflexive and self-comprehending text. The poem begins with a self-lacerating humor that is reminiscent of the best in *The Bell Jar:* "These poems do not live: it's a sad diagnosis." In too many of her poems, one might say she overvitalizes her texts. Eliot once said the best religious poems are not necessarily those done by mystics celebrating union; too often overpiety mars our religious poetry as overimpiety and the vividly negative mar Plath's and Hughes's work. Here in **"Stillborn,"** she makes her dilemma a type of celebration. The single trope of birth is clumsy but kept up; how congruent with the very *topos* of clumsy death is its style and stylelessness. The poem becomes a criticism in the simplest way, and yet the whole "bulge[s] with concentration." The repetition is bizarrely flat and persistent and concerned with persistence: "They smile and smile and smile and smile at me. . . . They are not pigs, they are not even fish, / Though they have a piggy and fishy air." Here the jauntiness is more successful than the later sacrifice of all gentilities. . . . It is a poem of deletion by a poet elsewhere loading too many rifts with ore. Still, the topic is the uncanny horror of a death before life, an emblem of her father.

Many of her critics assail formalism and speak of Plath's work as the triumph of an antiformal way. But there is no escape from form. Too many critics, like Malkoff on the Projectivists, think of the two roads of American poetry as that of the urn or the tree. But poetry is neither a well-wrought urn nor an esemplasticity of Coleridge's dream. Hölderlin said: To live is to defend a form. The forms of Plath are rarely whole. The letters are as genial as Keats's but marred by constant cliché. She lived indeed in the prisonhouse of language, and one senses the terrible pressure that these clichés—clichés of the college, clichés of education, clichés of the mother, still in her bowdlerizing and her notes—exerted upon her. In *Ariel* and elsewhere she exerted pressure against these clichés, but I sense more pathos and defeat than victory. Thus the expressionism, which Borges has called the refuge of the young person. Like randomness in a later day, Plath used expressionism and a quasi-allegorical mode to heroize her own attempts. She never lets anything alone. In comparison to the great masters of the colloquial, Gertrude Stein, Riding, and Bishop, and with her great precursor Dickinson in mind,

she refused to be domestic but in the end seems falsest in her very flights:

> And I
> Am the arrow,
>
> The dew that flies
> Suicidal, at one with the drive
> Into the red
>
> Eye, the cauldron of morning.

Her best poems, like **"Tulips,"** are relaxations from this Mayakovsky-like bolting toward death.

In **"Tulips"** she is permitted a wider structure and a tone that is comfortable with still life, even with the insidious, still Gothic sense of *natura morte.* The verbs that were purple and melodramatic have quietly passed to verbs of being, as in the strong beginning that concerns weakness: "The tulips are too excitable, it is winter here." Look, says the poem, and one recalls Heidegger asking us to "Take a look at being." A difficult prescription, but one made even more difficult by the constant unwillingness of Plath to let things alone and, finally, to let language alone. Is this what suicide may also mean, a murder that is unwilling to accept the central lack of explanation? One feels a certain wisdom in Alvarez's confession that he was perplexed to find nothing proposed as explanation by his own suicide. Possibly poetry, as opposed to philosophy of a certain kind, takes pleasure in the unanswerable problem and must not pad itself with too much explanation. Instead of playacting at a constant malevolent drama of self-annihilation, Plath is best when she attempts to give up all theater. Of course, she is always theatrical, and **"Tulips,"** too, is a presentation of the theme: "la vie est un hôpital." It is a constricting topic, it is by now an outworn and *symboliste* convention, and it leads her to a rhetoric never consistently deflated or transformed. Her charm is in certain relaxed poems and in the letters, but her mythical, manic, troubling, late poems charm her critics. (pp. 46-53)

If Aristotle is correct in defining structure as that which dominates diction in tragic drama, then we might define melodrama as that in which diction and spectacle threaten the life of structure. The Oxford English Dictionary's sense of melodrama is that sensational drama in which songs interspersed with incidents gained appeal by violence and sudden happy endings. One also thinks of the orchestral accompaniment of melodramatic action as part of the degradation here. How does this permit us analogue in poetry? Let us call dramatic those poems whose structure dominates diction; those poems melodramatic in which the whole tendency is to a diction-dominated formlessness punctuated by hyperbole appealing to the emotions. Interestingly, the happy ending in Plath is usually one of revenge in murder or self-murder. My definitions are purposely vague: exactness in some matters, Whitehead said, was a fake. But tragedy is not a snark, nor is melodrama. Too often, in the texts of Plath, we bump into stubborn, irreducible melodrama. (p. 53)

David Shapiro, "Sylvia Plath: Drama and Melodrama," in Sylvia Plath: New Views on the Poetry, *edited by Gary Lane, The Johns Hopkins University Press, 1979, pp. 45-53.*

Stanley Plumly   (essay date 1985)

[*Plumly is an American poet, critic, and editor whose narrative poems focus on the psychological dramas that develop around personal experience. His collections include* In the Outer Dark *(1970) and* Summer Celestial *(1983). In the following excerpt, Plumly explores Plath's use of and experiments with form in her verse.*]

"Her attitude to her verse was artisan-like: if she couldn't get a table out of the material, she was quite happy to get a chair, or even a toy. The end product for her was not so much a successful poem, as something that had temporarily exhausted her ingenuity." This comment by Ted Hughes, in 1981, in his well-known introduction to *The Collected Poems* [see Further Reading list], must have come as a surprise to many of Sylvia Plath's readers. Still nearly twenty years after her death, the notion that the poet of suicidal imperatives might be as committed to form, right up to the end of her career, as she appeared to be committed to content must have seemed secondary or at least beside the point. . . . Yet until the last year of Plath's life, March to February, her poems have none of the cold confessional, frenetic, lean, somebody's-done-for, apocalyptic drive of that sad time. Instead, they reveal a poetry preoccupied with the inventions of rhythm, pattern, and an emphatic, sometimes excessive aural sense of the way words bond within the line or sentence. They reveal a poetry in constant preparation for the next move, the next place to be—whether it meant slanting the rhyme, divesting the stanza of a scheme, or opening the poem to the indictment of immediate experience. (p. 13)

Elaborations of the labor of poetry tend to be the rule before 1959, the labor of apprenticing, so much so that John Frederick Nims could speak, in his review of *Ariel,* of the "drudgery" of the first book. What distinguishes Plath, though, from other budding formalists of the time is that she worked to invent forms rather than fill them. Aside from the obligatory school-girl sonnets and villanelles and sestinas, there are very few traditional forms in her career. She was always inventing, contriving, conjuring. Form was something she could create, even repeat; it could mean passage to the next poem, and to the future. Those who found *Ariel* profoundly different from the work that preceded it could have looked back, for formal guidance and anticipation, to **"Mushrooms,"** the last poem written for the first book—

> Overnight, very
> Whitely, discreetly,
> Very quietly
>
> Our toes, our noses
> Take hold on the loam,
> Acquire the air.

And before that to **"Moonrise"** ("Death whitens in the egg and out of it. / I can see no color for this whiteness. / White: it is a complexion of the mind."). And before that to **"The Thin People"** ("Empty of complaint, forever / Drinking vinegar from tin cups: they wore / The insufferable nimbus of the lot-drawn / Scapegoat. . . . "). And before that to a small piece of a poem entitled **"Resolve"**—

> Day of mist: day of tarnish
>
> with hands
> unserviceable, I wait

> for the milk van
> the one-eared cat
> laps its gray paw—

of which these are the first few lines, written in 1956. Cat's paws, thin people, and mushrooms are obviously not the issue here. The predominant mode of *Ariel* is couplets and triplets, and the short line, stanzas of psychological shorthand, of the quick take, the hook. Whatever the difference on the scale of pain the poems of the last year represent, they had models for their making, antecedents for their craft.

If *Ariel* was, and has been since, worshiped for its perceived confessional content, its doom images, its words-torn-from-the-death-flesh heart of experience, worshiped for poems, in Lowell's phrase, that "play Russian roulette with six cartridges in the cylinder," it is also a book justly celebrated for its powerful and poignant testimony—at the nerve end and at the cutting edge—of a life that became simply too vulnerable. At its best it survives the "O-gape of complete despair" by the sheer discipline of its art. But we need accept neither the cynicism of Hugh Kenner, who maintains that "all Plath's life, a reader had been someone to manipulate," nor the anxiety of A. Alvarez, who speculates that "it is as though she had decided that, for her poetry to be valid, it must tackle head-on nothing less than her own death," to question assumptions about the nature of Plath's achievement and the position her most famous book holds within the perspective of her *Collected Poems.* What concerns me, as it has concerned others, is that the biography and autobiography, *The Bell Jar* and the letters, the rumor and the psychoanalysis not displace the beauty and triumph of the range of her art. Whatever "confessional" means to the poetry to which it is too often ill-ascribed, it is first of all a kind of journalism, a reductive label intended to *get at* something in the work, something of publicity value. It is about the news in a poem, its gossip. With the names and the dates in place, it would paraphrase, extrapolate the projected psychological content, not unlike the theme-mongering sometimes promoted in the academy. Except that it would not be looking for ideas but intimacy, the dream-data, the midnight or dawn compulsions. It would turn poetry into the prose of therapy. And it would fantasize the poet as victim and the domestic and daily terrors of the world as villain, chief of which is the paradigm of the lost or bad parent. "We suggest that a pattern of guilt over imagined incest informs all of Plath's prose and poetry. When Otto Plath died of natural causes in a hospital on November 2, 1940, he might just as well have been a lover jilting his beloved." Whether the critic here is right or wrong is not the issue; the issue is that Plath's guilt is irrelevant to the good reading of her poems. Not that we need to see her poetry in isolation or in a vacuum, but independent of tabloid vagaries and mythic pretentions. The life in her poetry is a transformation, not an imitation. Its terms and its struggles are acted out within the form, within the crux and often crisis of form. **"Daddy"** may or may not be light verse, as Plath herself once suggested. It is certainly less confessional than it is personal writing—intoxicating, relentless, allegorical, and, finally, dark. It is patently ironical, and nearly Swiftian in its satire. **"Lady Lazarus"** may or may not be a signature poem, but it is far too close to being a parody of the poet as suicide and the publicity of suicide to be confessional. Taken straight, beware, beware, it is only funny, or worse, bald angry. The fact that these poems too have antecedents in earlier work (**"Daddy"** as far back as the rhythms of **"The Disquieting Muses"**—"I learned, I learned, I learned elsewhere, / From muses unhired by you, dear mother"; **"Lady Lazarus"** as far back as the gothicism of **"All the Dead Dears"**—"This lady here's no kin / Of mine, yet kin she is: she'll suck / Blood and whistle my marrow clean") implies that even angst requires strategy and preparation in order to be effective, especially under the pressures of the extreme. They are both crafty poems, with histories to their craft. Nazi lampshades and Meinkampf looks, vampirism and witchery are part of the planning, among the buttons pushed. Path did not suddenly become a poet with such poems or with the publication of *Ariel,* nor did she become a success at the moment of her death. She worked hard at a craft for which she had the gift for a good ten years.

We can run a search for the Medusan imagery or plead a case for Yeatsian cosmology, we can concentrate on the "Sivvy" poems (mother) or on the beekeeper poems (father), we can read her as a romantic or as a precipitant expressionist, we can locate influences as different as Theodore Roethke and Wallace Stevens. We can, in the long postmortem, see her as Esther Greenwood or as Lady Lazarus, daughter or mother, supplicant or applicant, sinned against or sinning. We can place her in history or alone with her ambitions. We can test Plath's work, in other words, in any number of ways alternate to the trials and errors of confessionalism. And we have. But where is there room, in the various critical/biographical approaches, for the unforced visual quality of **"Departure,"** written in 1956 and included in *The Colossus,* where is there room for the aural power and density of **"Blackberrying,"** written in the early fall of 1961 and excluded from *Ariel*—among the assumptions about her content and the "staticky / Noise of the new," among the attractions of violence, both sentimental and rhetorical, where is the notice, in Keats's word, of Plath's capacity for *disinterestedness,* her ability to be at one with or disappear into the richness of the text?

At one level, **"Departure"** looks to be not much more than a sharply focused study, in brilliant painter's terms, of a fishing village, Benidorm, along the Spanish coast: table and chair work, even though the concretion of images generates especial energy.

> The figs on the fig tree in the yard are green;
> Green, also, the grapes on the green vine
> Shading the brickred porch tiles.
> The money's run out.
>
> How nature, sensing this, compounds her bitters.
> Ungifted, ungrieved, our leavetaking.
> The sun shines on unripe corn.
> Cats play in the stalks.
>
> Retrospect shall not soften such penury—
> Sun's brass, the moon's steely patinas,
> The leaden slag of the world—
> But always expose
>
> The scraggy rock spit shielding the town's blue bay
> Against which the brunt of outer sea
> Beats, is brutal endlessly.
> Gull-fouled, a stone hut
>
> Bares its low lintel to corroding weathers:

> Across the jut of ochreous rock
> Goats shamble, morose, rank-haired,
> To lick the sea-salt.

The sea, the coastal territory, "water striving to reestablish its mirror / Over the rock," will become central and stock figures in Plath's work right to the end. In this poem, perhaps the first purely realized of her early pieces, a poem fairly free of the self-conscious and compacting busyness of a great deal of the writing at this time, the sea and environs represent the antagonist, the life principle. They make it possible for the object world itself to become the subject, because unlike the majority of the popular writing starring the first-person singular Plath, this piece mutes the position of the speaker to simple motivational status—resignation. "The money's run out. / Ungifted, ungrieved, our leavetaking." What shines in the real eye is correlative nature. True, in its own small way, it is a natural world that could hardly be called neutral—what is not kinetic is vitally colorful—but neither is it parceled into the raw examples of what become, later, psychic fractures. This "quick" study reads whole, it pays attention, directly, to detail—the green figs and grapes, the cats in the unripe corn—and without editorial help allows the details to develop and complicate the moment on their own. The halfserious line "Retrospect shall not soften such penury" permits the poet her chance to project: from that line the images go up in volume and increase in intensity. The simple fact of penury and the need to move on, the poem's motivation, force a growth in strategy—the eye can no longer just see, it must interpret.

This is the way in which, in the logic and psychologic of the structure, brass and steely patinas, nature compounds her bitters. The corroding weathers of the rest of the poem are consequences of powers within the poem, leading all the way back to the flat report that the money's run out. Nothing in this poem, therefore, is imposed from outside its world. Its lines of clear delineation and projection come from within what is immediately established, as in any good story. Compare the longer, softer rhythms of the first three lines to the same length of work in the last two stanzas; once the money's gone (penury), the rhythms turn tighter, much more consonantal, and abrupt. Thus we know, in the plot of things, why the prosody has changed, and we know, by the time the sea is brutal endlessly, that something serious is at stake without the speaker having to promote her cause. Later, of course, by 1962, what is at stake will take on absolute proportions. By then the poems will have acquired so much external life, such an autobiographic force-field, that it will seem difficult to judge whether a particular poem has created sufficient self-reference not to depend on the author's prose therapies.

"Departure" represents a psychological landscape (seascape). It is as well an accurate rendering: it begins and ends *inside* the picture, within the framing warmth of the fig trees and the harshness of the sea-salt. Its otherness is the object, and objective, world, but also natural, chronological, alive. A few years into the future, Plath will write, along with **"Mussel Hunter at Rock Harbor," "Tulips,"** and **"Last Words,"** one of her finest poems of that narrative, objective category in which the line-into-sentence is extended in time, and connects and continues fully enough to fill the white space—her "wide" poems, as one observer puts it. **"Blackberrying"** rests somewhere between the beating of the outer sea of **"Departure"** and the Devon coast of **"Sheep in Fog,"** where the "hills step off " into whiteness. It certainly rests between them "stylistically," between the clearly delineated shapes and solids of the older poem and the spare, poetry-as-absence surrealism of one of her last. (pp. 14-19)

Eliot is fond of referring to the "aural imagination," the ability of the language to transform the image in the process of its pronouncement. Valéry speaks, in his notebooks, of the language within language. And Rilke says that "if a thing is to speak to you, you must regard it for a certain time as *the only one that exists.*" **"Blackberrying,"** it seems to me, brings together the best vocal and most effective visual impulses in Plath's poetry. It gives the speaker her role without sacrificing the poem's purchase on the actual impinging natural world. It enlarges rather than reduces. Its ceremony comes from one of the poet's most disguised sources, the small moment, the domestic life. (**"Mushrooms,"** the poems for her children, the poppy poems all share, for example, a sense of size, even though they derive from objects and experiences small and diurnal in scale.) **"Blackberrying"** likewise isolates the action to the job at hand, and to the story line. But unlike the sound and image effects of poems better known, this one is not driving nails, sawing on one Orphic string, or ritualizing an extreme psychological state. No question that at the point of entry the reader is tested: either accept the muscular terms of the poem or stay out. Timed in the present progressive, it opens in motion, in saturation, incantatory. We are led, immediately, in hooks, down a blackberry alley, where a sea, somewhere at the end of it, is heaving. The impression is one of tunneling, of being drawn into and through narrow, yet thick space. All the senses are crowded, even exchanged ("Blackberries / Big as the ball of my thumb, and dumb as eyes / Ebon in the hedges, fat . . . "). What is remarkable is the way Plath, in shifting the context of the blackberries from container (alley) to contained (milkbottle), intensifies the feel of claustrophobia. Once the berries are in the bottle—"they squander on my fingers . . . they must love me"—they flatten their sides in order to accommodate; they, in effect, choke on the space. It is a brilliant telescoping and projecting and resolving of the speaker's "going down in hooks," and is prepared by a stanzaic pattern of free verse that allows the middle lines to fill before breaking at emphatic (sea/Blackberries/eyes/fat) hooks in the sentence. The credibility and vitality of the movement of the full stanza, however, are validated by what will carry the rest of the poem—Plath's skill at creating aural equivalents, images that gain their first power from their hearing. The first line, for instance, though one of the least apparent "imaged" in the poem, still manages to effect a strong visual pull by letting "nobody in the lane" be picked up and quickly reinforced by "nothing, nothing" only to bump, abruptly, into "but blackberries." It is a line of wonderful subtraction by addition, the content filling the needs of the form. This same sense of abutment structures the remaining stanza. By repeating and paralleling the word "blackberries" three strategic times, Plath makes, in effect, a single alley-and-hook sentence down to the last two and a half lines. Then, like a stepping-off of periods, she shuts off with three full stops, each a little longer in coming than the one before. This vertical rhythm is what pacing in a poem, and music in poetry, is all about.

If the enclosures of the alley and milkbottle help organize the experience in the beginning stanza, the plan of the whole poem becomes obvious by the second. The cloister opens to the overarching sky, and by the third stanza to the open sea. This Devon landscape-to-seascape is right out of Hardy—nobody in the lane, far from the madding crowd. In just the time it takes to get from the blackout, blackberry close of the alley, where we can hear the great source "heaving," to the "high, green meadows," over which go birds that are "bits of burnt paper wheeling in a blown sky," we realize the speaker is being pulled along, compelled. The mimetic language is becoming denser, a little waxy—"the choughs in black, cacophonous flocks." The first three lines of the second stanza, in fact, press their vocalization, their repetitions of sounds—"protesting, protesting"—about as far as they dare, leading the poet to counter the buildup, as she does everywhere in the poem, with a flat, declarative notice, in this case, that "I do not think the sea will appear at all." Two of the longest lines Plath ever wrote appear at the end of this stanza. They make a kind of couplet, coming out of one of the poem's best balanced lines:

> I come to one bush of berries so ripe it is a bush of flies,
> Hanging their bluegreen bellies and their wing panes in a Chinese screen.
> The honey-feast of the berries has stunned them; they believe in heaven.

Looking ahead to the denials in the forms of the later work, we can appreciate the fecundity here, not simply in the fullness of the image of the berries, but in the progression of the idea of the berries—berries, flies, bellies, wing panes, honey-feast, heaven. And the berries that have been blue-red juices so squandered on fingers they must love me are now the honey-feast of flies that believe in heaven. This is the countryside of health; the speaker's senses are sated. There is uncharacteristic generosity in this writing *sans* the sometimes characteristic rhetoric. There is giving-over to the world, to the natural world, to the life outside, beyond the nerve ends of the self. Giving over, however, does not mean giving up. "The only thing to come now is the sea," announces the speaker at the start of the last stanza. She emerges, as into a sense of light, from the winding sheep path, from the high meadows, from the blackberry alley, with the wind, the open wind, suddenly blowing its phantom laundry in her face. The close, interior dimensions of where she has come from in order to get here, having been called by the clues of the heaving of wind on water and overhead, having picked her way—of all tests— through blackberries, have brought her, one last hook, to the edge, the north face.

Plath's position at the end of **"Blackberrying"** is a reading of her position for the remainder of her life leading up to the "edge" of her last poem. "We have come so far, it is over." Here, however, at this full and apparently open moment, looking toward the complementary, fantasy coast of Brittany (another "Finisterre"), it is not over. The sea may be "beating an intractable metal" and the speaker may be looking out at "a great space," but this climactic image, as psychologically as it is actually audible, underscores the rich, insulating presence of the whole of this writing. Nearly every line risks the heavy hand that has marked too many of her narrative-nature poems: the clogged consonance, the alliterative tattoo, the aureate weight of the diction. Yet the insistent winding path of its structure (the movement from the blind and sensual alley to the meadow sighting of bird flocks and flies to the vulnerability of the dissociative mind confronting the intractable) and the absorption of the speaker into the flow of the action (though she is the actor, she is led) help keep the language of **"Blackberrying"** on the line and insures that the incantatory effects result from the inwardness of the experience, from even the threat of the experience. The images of the Chinese screen and the metal of silversmiths, as opposed to the homely milkbottle, may seem extracurricular to the landscape of the poem, but they are as much a part of the transformation as are the choral features of nothing, nothing, protesting, protesting, beating, beating. These images are projections; their dimensions get their measure within the text. If the speaker, ontologically, is as cut off by the white and pewter lights and the din of the silversmiths as she has been by the opacity of the blackberries and the bush of flies, perhaps we have come back to the "nothing" in the last stanza for a reason. Her condition, throughout the poem, is static, in a dark that is blind and in a light that is blinding. It is the blackberrying itself that is the motion, the active principle. But it is more than a motive: it is the act of the lyric form answering itself at every turning, every *ing,* making of the emotion an enclosure.

"Blackberrying" is high rhetorical style compared to the great majority of poems that finally made it into the posthumous *Ariel.* Only **"The Moon and the Yew Tree"** and **"Tulips"** suggest its density of texture, though in tone they both better approximate the "light of the mind" of what became a very strange and luminous book. If Valéry is right, that form in poetry is the voice in action, then Plath was obviously in some debate as to what her true voice was: the poet of riches or the poet of austerity, the poet of connection or the poet of the quick cut. It is a formal debate inherent in her career, declaration or denial. To her credit, she allowed the debate to become a dialectic, allowed the energy of the argument to produce rather than paralyze the work at hand. Nevertheless, by the end of her life—the last year, year and a half—it is clear that the poetry of absence, "words dry and riderless," is the rule. So much so that almost every good poem in the manner of

> Axes
> After whose stroke the wood rings,
> And the echoes!
> Echoes traveling
> Off from the center like horses
>
> **("Words")**

turns into an *ars poetica,* an address of and to her art. Which is to say that concomitant with the struggle for life is her struggle with the form her passion wished to take. Poems as superficially variant in subject as **"Words"** and **"Sheep in Fog"** and the incomparable **"Ariel"** share this interest in a self-reflexive, self-defining purity of purpose, and each chooses the expressive terms of "indefatigable hoof-taps" (**"Words"**) and "hooves, dolorous bells" (**"Sheep in Fog"**) to enact the purification. **"Ariel"** is, of course, Plath's singular and famous example of the form completely at one with its substance, the language exactly the speedy act of its text. The point for the poet is obvious: "How one we grow, / Pivot of heels and knees." The speaker thus becomes as much Ariel as the horse, and together they become the one thing, the poem itself, "the arrow, / The dew that flies / Suicidal, at one with the drive." The run from stasis in darkness into the red eye

of morning is a miraculous inhabiting, in which the natural and referential world dissembles, blurs into absence, to the point that the transformation of the horse and rider can become absolute. "Something else / Hauls me through air . . . " In seconds, she is a white Godiva, unpeeling dead hands and stringencies, then, almost simultaneously, she is foam to wheat, and at that freeing instant, in terror or in ecstasy, the child's cry melts in the wall. **"Ariel"** is as close to a poetry of pure, self-generating, associative action as we could hope for, as if the spirit, at last, had found its correlative, had transcended, in the moment, memory. Mallarmé once speculated that the ideal poem would be "a reasonable number of words stretched beneath our mastering glance, arranged in enduring figures, and followed by silence." This is generic enough to account for a lot of symbolist writing. It certainly accounts for the nigger-eye berries that cast dark hooks.

Plath did not live long enough to sort out a form that could negotiate between the enclosing rhetoric of a **"Blackberrying"** and the absolute, open language of an **"Ariel."** Likely she would have never needed to. Likely this "third" form is a wished-for integration of personality, the healing of fracture. For me, though, the writing near the end is not up to the discipline of **"Ariel,"** and feels instead a little starved, anorectic. Such writing may be accurate of the state of her soul, but it is beyond the perfection of her art, the perfection that **"Blackberrying,"** in September of 1961, and **"Ariel,"** in October of 1962, individually represent. Here is a poet who could either project into the landscape or internalize it so as to disappear; she could both narrate and configure experience. In either case, she was committed to the transforming powers of the art, emblems of a life outside her own. Putting the "blood sisterhood" of **"Blackberrying"** beside the red-eyed cauldron sunrise of **"Ariel,"** we can begin to see that behind the separate masks, all the masks of her good poems, there

---

AUTHOR'S COMMENTARY

I much prefer doctors, midwives, lawyers, anything but writers. I think writers and artists are the most narcissistic people. I mustn't say this, I like many of them, in fact a great many of my friends happen to be writers and artists. But I must say what I admire most is the person who masters an area of practical experience, and can teach me something. I mean, my local midwife has taught me how to keep bees. Well, she can't understand anything I write. And I find myself liking her, may I say, more than most poets. And among my friends I find people who know all about boats or know all about certain sports, or how to cut somebody open and remove an organ. I'm fascinated by this mastery of the practical. As a poet, one lives a bit on air. I always like someone who can teach me something practical.

(interview date 1962)

is a unity, an integrity, and an integrating of imagination—that whatever the hammer-splittings of the self, behind the sad mask of the woman is the mind and heart of someone making transcendent poems. To the extent that Plath is "artisan-like" is the extent to which she is whole. Beginning in the fall of 1961, she will have written the truest symbolist poetry we have had since Hart Crane, and before him since Dickinson. (pp. 20-5)

> Stanley Plumly, "What Ceremony of Words," in Ariel Ascending: Writings about Sylvia Plath, *edited by Paul Alexander, Harper & Row, Publishers, 1985, pp. 13-25.*

Pamela J. Annas   (essay date 1988)

[*In the following excerpt from a chapter in her book-length study* A Disturbance in Mirrors: The Poetry of Sylvia Plath, *Annas examines Plath's use of bee imagery and metaphors in her five bee poems in* Ariel, *describing these works as "a vision of a female community with mutual work and survival interests."*]

Plath's most promising attempt in *Ariel* at resolving the conflict between stasis and process, purity and rebirth, is her image of the beehive. The five bee poems in *Ariel*—"The Bee Meeting," "The Arrival of the Bee Box," "Stings," "The Swarm," and "Wintering"—written, in that order, between October 3 and October 9, 1962, contain one of Sylvia Plath's more complex statements of the tension between self-image and image of the world, Apollo and Dionysus, dying and living, the alienation or the integration of the individual into her society. They move beyond the retaliatory anger of "Daddy" to a vision of a female community with mutual work and survival interests.

The beehive is a complex image cluster which goes beyond itself to draw together a number of Plath's other major images: the moon, the tree, the stone. The image of the beehive makes a distinction between the functioning world of the hive, the female worker bees centered around their queen, and the essentially alien drones. Plath was familiar with Erich Neumann's *The Great Mother,* published in 1955, and her word choice in the bee poems in *Ariel* often echoes Neumann's. Kroll's *Chapters in a Mythology* includes a fascinating, lengthy, and specific discussion of Plath's use of Neumann and elements of the White Goddess myth in her poetry as moon/goddess/witch. My own interest in these poems is in Plath's political use of mythical material. For, though the derivation of the bee imagery is mythical, Plath is careful to place the image of the beehive within a social context. She does this most systematically through the stages she traces in these poems of the relationship between the poet, the beehive, and the beekeeper. She moves from her father as beekeeper in the three pre-*Ariel* bee poems to an image of the village midwife as beekeeper and finally to herself as beekeeper in *Ariel.* Thus a complex set of identifications between the bees and herself and a complex set of oppositions between the bees and herself and a complex set of oppositions between the bees and an essentially patriarchal human world is set up; also suggested are a number of ways in which the metaphor of the beehive relates to the larger context of a capitalist society.

Sylvia Plath's father, Otto Plath, a professor of biology at Boston University and a recognized authority on bees, published *Bumblebees and Their Ways* in 1934, two years after Sylvia was born. In three early poems—"Lament" (1951-52), "Electra on Azalea Path" (1959), and "The Beekeeper's Daughter" (1959)—Plath directs the symbolic significance of the bees and the beehive toward her relationship with her father. In "Lament," an awkward early poem, her father is described as a god-like figure oblivious to storm, sea and lightning, who was nevertheless and ludicrously struck down by a swarm of bees. "A scowl of sun struck down my mother, / tolling her grave with golden gongs, / but the sting of bees took away my father." By the time she writes the two 1959 poems, Plath has begun to identify herself with the bees and thus somehow to assign herself guilt for her father's death, even though she says, in the opening stanza of "Electra on Azalea Path," "I had nothing to do with guilt or anything." "Electra on Azalea Path" begins by identifying the speaker of the poem with a hive of wintering bees. "The day you died I went into the dirt / . . . Where bees, striped black and gold, sleep out the blizzard / Like hieratic stones," she says, and, "It was good for twenty years, that wintering—." Somehow, she implies in this poem, it was her birth that presaged her father's death, and her love which finally killed him. Her assumption of guilt is clear in the poem's end: "O pardon the one who knocks for pardon at / Your gate, father—your hound-bitch, daughter, friend. / It was my love that did us both to death."

Plath built up a mythical temporal schema into which she fit what she saw as the significant events in her life. Thus she says in "Lady Lazarus" of her suicide attempts, "I have done it again. / One year in every ten / I manage it—." Her first suicide attempt was at age twenty, during the summer of 1953, and she worked backward and forward from this center. She sometimes says she was ten when her father died, but actually she had just turned eight years old when he died on November 2, 1940. Her birthday is October 27, and her father was dying then, so it is not strange that an eight-year-old would connect the two events and feel a certain guilt. Especially since, as Plath suggests in a number of places, including "Electra on Azalea Path," her mother quite naturally tried to soften the loss to her children: "My mother said; you died like any man. / How shall I age into that state of mind?" To an eight-year-old child, who felt the loss of her father but didn't quite understand it, his disappearance followed by what might have seemed a conspiracy of silence would have been both strange and suspicious. Why was no one saying anything to her about her father? Was it because his death was somehow her fault? In any case, Plath makes her father's death fall a third of the way through her life, and her own first suicide attempt marks the second third. That her final and successful suicide attempt came at age thirty does suggest that to some extent she became caught up in her own systematizing. Of course, the actual reasons for seeing suicide as a solution go far beyond what some readers of Plath's poetry have been tempted to call a need to reenact in life what one has structured in art.

"The Beekeeper's Daughter" (*The Colossus*) is a description of a lush, symbolically female scene of open flowers, dense scented air, and "many-breasted hives." As a natural by-product of their food gathering, the bees are cross-fertilizing the flowers, and the entire poem has an intensely sexual atmosphere. The man, the beekeeper, moves through this rich, lush landscape, spare, vertical, and essentially alien to it. The one line in the poem that describes him is: "Hieratical in your frock coat, maestro of the bees." Her father, the beekeeper, is designated as priest-like; he both controls and sanctifies the riot of fertilization going on around him while remaining aloof from it himself. . . . The speaker of this poem, the beekeeper's daughter, is, one might imagine, following along through the garden behind her father; her response to what is emotionally taking place is three lines, one of which follows each of the three stanzas: "My heart under your foot, sister of a stone"; "A fruit that's death to taste: dark flesh, dark parings"; and "The queen bee marries the winter of your year." The speaker of the poem functions primarily as an observer, watching both her father and the bees in the garden, but there are already the beginnings of an identification of the poet with the bees, especially with the queen bee, which characterizes the later bee poems in *Ariel.* Certainly the speaker of **"The Beekeeper's Daughter"** sympathizes with the fertile atmosphere and activity of the garden and wants to convert to this type of response to the universe the one figure which is out of place: the beekeeper, frock-coated, probably in black, upright walking, and priest-like or celibate. It is also a way of sanctioning and mediating sexual desire for her long-dead father or for what he represents. Plath is quite aware of this as the title of the contemporaneous **"Electra on Azalea Path"** indicates.

The question of where the poet herself stands, in relation to the beekeeper's separation from the garden and in relation to the bees' natural functioning within it, is considered in great detail in the bee poems in *Ariel.* These five poems form a cycle of the stages of the hive and also a cycle of the relationship of the beekeeper to the hive and of the poet to the metaphor of the beehive. From the summer of 1961 through December 1962, while Sylvia Plath and Ted Hughes lived in a country house in Devon, Plath became an enthusiastic beekeeper. Given the impulse toward rebirth in Plath's poetry, it is significant for the bee poems in *Ariel* that the person who introduced her to beekeeping was the local midwife, who had assisted at the birth of Plath's second child.

What characterizes **"The Bee Meeting"** is its atmosphere of ritual. **"The Beekeeper's Daughter"** also had ritual elements, but the center of the poem was her father as beekeeper and outside herself, except insofar as the poem as a whole was a ritual. In **"The Bee Meeting,"** the poet herself has taken over her father's role, has become the beekeeper, or is in the process of so doing. The poem is a rite of investiture. As a rite, it can be seen in at least three ways in this poem. First, she is being made a priest and dressed in priestly robes. Her relationship to the beehive in this sense is not so much as an actor or participant, but as a conductor of the action. She is also being initiated into a group of "priests," others robed as she is. Second, when they give her the "fashionable white straw Italian hat / And a black veil that moulds to my face," they are not only making her one of them, they are also to some extent setting her apart from them in their own "veils tacked to ancient hats," their "square black" heads. In some sense, she is being crowned, foreshadowing her fascination and finally identification with the queen bee, the still center of the hive. Third, the white crown the speaker of the poem receives is possibly a scapegoat's crown as well; that is, because of her quite understandable fear of the bees, she

partly sees herself in the role of victim to them, a kind of living sacrifice in a pagan religion. So the investiture going on in the poem is simultaneously that of priest, god/queen, and sacrifice.

The last stanza of **"The Bee Meeting,"** brings all of these possibilities together and begins Plath's identification with the bees. . . . The white straw Italian hat and the white hive earlier in the poem, the magician's girl and the knife thrower's assistant who is a white pillar, and the white box in the last line which is both the beehive and the speaker's coffin, pull together the set of identifications within the poem. The exhaustion, the fear of death in the knife throwing image, and the coffin/hive equation also connect the bee poems to the theme of rebirth in *Ariel.* It is necessary to die to be reborn. The crucial question in *Ariel* is whether these symbolic deaths, these imaginative transformations of self, will ever lead to a rebirth into a transformed and positive world. The bee poems, taken as a whole, seem to be the only extended imaginative structure in Sylvia Plath's poetry which suggest that a transformation of self and world might occur together. (pp. 144-49)

The possibility of a qualitatively different rebirth is central to the bee poems. In **"The Arrival of the Bee Box,"** the hive is also conditionally and initially compared to a coffin. The crate full of bees is an intrusion, though she ordered it; it frightens her, though she reminds herself that she is the owner. Like death, the crate of bees repels and attracts her at the same time. "The box is locked, it is dangerous. / I have to live with it overnight / And I can't keep away from it." The poem is a series of fantasies based on the question: what shall I do with them? She can send them back; she can let them stay in the box and starve. Then she thinks, what if I let them out? What would happen? . . . The speaker of the poem imagines herself, like Daphne, turning into a tree to escape a threat. A follower of Artemis, goddess of the moon and of purity and chastity, Daphne was the unwilling object of Apollo's infatuation. Her allegiance to Artemis in danger, she appealed to her father, a minor river god, for help, and he turned her into a tree. Plath's use of this fable is revealing, and it suggests a number of possibilities for transformation. Apollo, the sun god, the oracle, and a patron of poetry and philosophy, represented to the Greeks who created him an intellectual, rational approach to life. Experience could be understood and controlled to some extent in language. Dionysus, the god of wine and fecundity, was the other side of classical Greek religion and philosophy. Also associated with poetry, Dionysus represented divine inspiration or creative frenzy and a sensual, organic approach to experience. With the Apollonian we associate intellectuality, the sun, and, as noted previously in Plath's poetry, depersonalization and sterility. Apollo is seen as representing an essentially patriarchal approach, the god of the ruling class. Dionysus or Bacchus, with his entourage of maddened women, represented sensuality, frenzy, darkness, fertility, and imagination; he was the god of a conquered culture. The latter is a combination which opens the individual to more danger because it requires commitment and involvement rather than separation. However, Dionysus also represents a loss of control and in that sense a loss of self. The captive bees in **"The Arrival of the Bee Box"** are described in Dionysian terms; they are "black on black," noisy, unintelligible, angry. The two alternatives the poet feels herself faced with are to identify with the bees or to identify with her father the beekeeper, thereby making the Apollonian choice of separation and intellectuality. In this poem, and perhaps finally in her poetry as a whole, Plath sidesteps this particular choice, or rather redefines it by choosing an allegiance to Artemis, by accepting the moon as her muse instead of either the rationality of Apollo or the uncontrolled frenzy of Dionysus. (pp. 150-51)

The search of Sylvia Plath's poetry for a transformed self reborn into a transformed world can be seen as a search for an androgynous self and world. The two extremes of Apollo and Dionysus are finally unsatisfactory for a woman poet precisely because both are male defined. Artemis, goddess of the moon and the forests, Artemis the huntress, protector of pregnant women and virgin goddess, is an androgynous choice, if only because of her essential self-sufficiency and transcendence of sexually based behavior patterns. Artemis represents androgyny defined from a female rather than a male perspective. However, Cynthia Secor, in "Androgyny: An Early Reappraisal," suggests that the image of the androgyne is less useful for women than the image of the strong woman—for example, the witch or the Amazon—because while the latter suggest energy, power, and movement, the androgyne is an image of "static completion." Static completion is one pole of the possibilities for self Plath works with in the late poems; she uses it most directly in poems like **"Edge,"** where the moon invokes dormancy and sense deprivation, and the self is removed from passion and process.

Sylvia Plath's vacillation between Dionysian and Apollian modes of perception, her fascination with the moon, the tree, the stone, and the beehive, all traditionally connected mythic symbols for the original, undifferentiated primal Feminine which she places against traditional male-oriented symbols, reflect a need, on the part of the creative artist who is a woman, to transcend at the least the limiting manifestations of sex role differentiations and to reach some androgynous moment of aesthetic and mystical completion. Judith Kroll points out Plath's familiarity with Robert Graves's 1961 *Oxford Addresses on Poetry;* in "The Dedicated Poet," Artemisian and Dionysian qualities come together into what Graves calls the Muse. . . . For the poet to turn into a tree, like Daphne, or to put on her "moon suit and funeral veil," as she does in **"The Arrival of the Bee Box,"** is to make a mediating choice, for though Artemis is not identical to Graves's Muse, she is kin to her; Artemis is like Dionysus in her passion and wildness, and like Apollo in her austerity. And indeed, Plath's poetry combines a highly emotional, intense tone with a tightly controlled form. However, as the association of funeral veil with moon suit suggests, the possibility of an allegiance to Artemis is finally ambivalent as well, since her remoteness also implies, for Plath, not only invulnerability but separation, nonfertility, and death. The speaker of **"The Arrival of the Bee Box"** says at last, "I am no source of honey / So why should they turn on me?"

There is a connection between this fear of her own possible sterility in **"The Arrival of the Bee Box"** and the central theme of **"The Swarm"** (which she wrote a day after **"Stings,"** but **"Stings"** and **"Wintering"** will be discussed together). One of Plath's war poems, like **"Totem"** and **"Getting There," "The Swarm"** describes the negative historical and economic context in which the positive myth

of the beehive exists. **"The Swarm"** is perhaps the least successful poetically of the bee poems, perhaps because it is too cluttered; it tries to make too many connections that are not fully worked out within the poem. What is both interesting and clear about this poem, however, is the identification of Napoleon—and the beginning of modern warfare on a large and impersonal scale—with "the man with gray hands." Literally the bee seller, the man with gray hands represents competitive capitalism and the spirit of the modern industrial West. . . . What the man of business does is to disrupt the cycle of nature for practical and mercenary ends. The poet, in her sympathy with the bees, sees them metaphorically as victims of war, their flight halted, "the honeycomb / Of their dream" shot down, defeated. As one who stands to profit from this interruption of nature's cycle, though, the speaker of the poem feels complicity. She is caught between the bees and the beeseller, between the victims of war and the warmakers. She is caught somewhere between the present system and some alternative, between forces that sustain the status quo and forces that question it.

The relationship between the poet and the bees is complex, ambivalent and deliberately ambiguous throughout the bee poems. She is somewhere in between the efficient humans like the beeseller who see in the bees only profit, and therefore remain separate from them as had her father in **"The Beekeeper's Daughter,"** and the bees themselves with whose essentially feminine and cyclic world she gradually begins to identify within these five poems. Because of her very ambivalence, she feels vulnerable to the bees. She feels at times that she must turn into a tree or something in nature in order to be safe from them. In contrast, the beeseller and those like him are invulnerable, their hands asbestos; they are invulnerable precisely because they do not identify with the bees. They see the bees solely as items of profit, as producers of a commodity which they can sell as well as the bees themselves. And along with their invulnerability goes a certain insensitivity and numbness. They are like the cardboard men in the office in *Three Women,* like the business partners in **"Death & Co."**

There is an analogy between the way these men of business see the beehive as a commodity and the poem as commodity. The capitalist world view, which trains us to see processes as products, also transforms art into a commodity, to be marketed and sold and inventoried in the same way that the beehive and the honey are not a mystery but simply a commodity to the men with gray hands. (pp. 151-54)

Beekeeping seems in these five poems to be as well a metaphor for the act of making poems, for the work of a poet, especially if one keeps in mind Robert Graves's distinction between Apollonian poetry and Muse poetry. The bees' conversion of pollen to honey is essentially a mystery, as is the Muse poet's channel to the unconscious and its powerful images and emotions. Beekeeping itself is analogous to the application of poetic craft and discipline toward the shaping of raw material, though in another sense the poet/beekeeper is a midwife, like the woman who introduced Plath to beekeeping and helped deliver her second child. As midwife, the beekeeper/poet is primarily witness to and facilitator of a process of creation outside her conscious control. Whether to remain in control or to give up control is paralleled in these poems by the speaker's choice of whether to ally with the gray men with asbestos hands or with the bees themselves. A mediating choice is for the poet to gain control through giving up control, through accepting that the creative process itself, though in her, is outside her conscious control, though she can shape through craft what she is given to work with. In **"Stings,"** it is her identification with the hive, her resolution at last of where her loyalties lie, that finally allows her to say: "I am in control. / Here is my honey-machine, / It will work without thinking."

Plath's closest identification of herself with the bees as woman and as poet is in **"Wintering"** and **"Stings,"** which are concerned with the life cycle or stages of the hive. In **"Wintering"** the speaker of the poem feels guilty; she has "whirled the midwife's extractor" and taken their honey and now the bees must live through the winter on an artificial substitute. In her role as beekeeper, she feels as though she has exploited them. The fear which had been directed at the bees themselves in **"The Arrival of the Bee Box"** is in **"Wintering"** directed rather at the dark cellar she has put them in and in which she herself feels suffocated. She begins the poem as beekeeper presumably in control of the bees and their product, her six jars of honey, but by the fourth stanza the dynamic has reached its own conclusion and reversed: "Possession. / It is they who own me." With this giving up of ownership and control and her position as a woman of business, her fear also seems to disappear as her identification with the bees takes its place. In **"Wintering,"** this identification remains generic rather than specific.

> The bees are all women,
> Maids and the long royal lady.
> They have got rid of the men,
>
> The blunt, clumsy stumblers, the boors.
> Winter is for women—
> The woman, still at her knitting,
> At the cradle of Spanish walnut

Endurance, waiting, a capacity to reduce life down to its essentials in order to survive are the qualities of the bees Plath focuses on in **"Wintering."** Plath ends **"Wintering"** with the spring flight of the bees and in **"Stings,"** which marks the closest identification of the poet with the bees, she discusses characteristics of the hive which are corollaries to those in **"Wintering"**: movement instead of stasis, rebirth instead of waiting, vengeance instead of endurance.

The hive exists as a colony, a society which can be seen from the outside as a single entity. In **"The Bee Meeting,"** the poet sees the hive as a virgin, sealed off and inwardly brooding. But the hive has a center: the queen. Normally, the queen is the unmoving center of a vortex of activity of the worker bees, neutered females. She does not move unless the hive swarms. In the society of the beehive, the queen alone is capable of creativity and, though she will eventually be destroyed by a new queen, the hive itself has the potential for immortality. Neumann's discussion of the symbol of the beehive in *The Great Mother* is particularly helpful to a reading of **"Stings."**

> The "virginity" of the Great Mother, i.e., her independence of the male, becomes particularly evident in the Amazonian bee state, where only the queen is fecundated by the male, and she only once. For this reason, and because of the food she eats, the bee is pure; Demeter must, like the Vestals and many other priestesses of the Great Mother, be virgins. And among the bees, as so often among beasts and men, matriarchal womanhood assumes a character of the "terrible" in its relation to the males; for after mating, the drone mate and all other drones are slain like aliens by the female group inhabiting the hive.
>
> The beehive is an attribute of the Great Goddess as Demeter-Ceres-Spes. But the bee is also associated with the moon: the priestesses of the moon goddess were called "bees," and it was believed that all honey came from the moon, the hive whose bees were the stars.

The association of the bee with the moon, the use of and then independence from the male, the related concept of purity, and the "terrible" (a word Plath echoes in **"Stings"**) vengeance of the bees, all are part of the complex of associations which adhere to Plath's image of the beehive. In **"Stings,"** the poet has moved from a generic identification of the beehive as a female society to a specific exploration of her own identity in her differentiation of the queen bee and the worker bees.

There are three separate distinctions in the speaker's self-image in **"Stings."** The first, and perhaps least important for this poem, is the distinction between the bees and herself as beekeeper, though it is important to note that here, for the first time, she is not afraid of the bees: "Bare-handed, I hand the combs." The second distinction is between herself (both as beekeeper and therefore observer, and as the bees and therefore participant) and the third person whom the bees attack: "The bees found him out, / Molding onto his lips like lies, / Complicating his features." Finally, and most important to this poem, there is the distinction between herself as worker bee and herself as queen bee. The first image is centered on the old queen and she asks of the hive: "Is there any queen at all in it?" . . . The two roles Plath has been playing—as wife, mother, hostess, and secretary on the one hand and as poet on the other—correspond in many ways to these two images of the workers and the queen bee. (pp. 155-58)

The last two stanzas of **"Stings,"** after the worker bees have turned on the third person, exposed him and sent him away, are of the flight of the queen, reborn into solitude and creativity. . . . These two images, of the old and reborn queen, correspond to the two self-images of **"Lady Lazarus,"** a poem which is also about the relation between the poet and a society which consistently defines her in a way she feels to be false. Like the arrow into the red eye of morning in **"Ariel,"** like Lady Lazarus, who rises out of the ash with her red hair, the queen is reborn. Her flight is an escape, a defiance, and an act of creation all at once, since this is literally the beginning of a new cycle and a new hive. In general, Plath is more interested in the beginnings and endings, the crisis points, of the cycle, than in its quiescent periods. She is interested in potential transformations of self.

However, what works against transformation of self are the internalized conflicts of identity within the poet. There are two separate conflicts of identity within the bee poems and they finally work against each other. First is the conflict between bee and beekeeper. The self-image as bee, with its associations of periodic rebirth and the sense of being an integral part of a community, of purity and wholeness, of a connection not only with one's immediate society but with a larger, transcendent world, moves the poet toward an androgynous moment of completion, union, and dialectical cyclical alternation of stasis and process. On the other hand is her self-image as beekeeper, modeled on the intellectuality of her father, an exploiter of the bees, manipulator of them, interrupter and interpreter of their cycle but separate from them, like the man of business with asbestos hands. This particular conflict occurs in various forms throughout Plath's late poetry—in the conflict between poet and audience in **"Lady Lazarus,"** in **"Daddy"** in the conflict between a patriarchal authority structure and the woman who speaks the poem, in **"Tulips"** between health and illness, presence and absence.

The second conflict of identity becomes explicit in **"Stings"** in the two images of herself as worker and as queen. . . . This need to set the creative part of herself, the poet, off from the drudge who does "women's work," and to see her poetic self as both strange and dangerous, is one way of resolving a central dilemma of the woman artist. Which of the two women am I: the one who feels driven by the need to create, who can say "the blood jet is poetry, / There is no stopping it," or the woman who does work which no one takes seriously, least of all herself? What this conflict can lead to is a contempt for other women and for that aspect of herself which she sees as "drudge."

In fact, Sylvia Plath had little real contact with other women. Esther Greenwood's rejection of one unsatisfactory female role model after another—from Doreen to J. C. to her mother—in *The Bell Jar* is indicative. In particular, Plath had very little contact with other women writers. Though she got to know Anne Sexton slightly when they both sat in on Robert Lowell's poetry class one summer, though she writes in a letter to her brother how excited she is finally to have met Adrienne Rich, describing her as "the girl whose poetry I've followed from her first publication," Plath seemed to have very little sense of a community among women writers based on similar interests and themes. Like most of the handful of women poets successful in the first two-thirds of the twentieth century, Sylvia Plath aligned herself primarily with male poets. To identify oneself as a woman poet, a poetess, was to admit that you did not expect to be taken seriously. Even the most cursory survey of American literary criticism yields examples of negative and patronizing pronouncements based on the poet or novelist's sex. Yet the themes of Plath's strongest poetry are clearly based on her experience as a woman poet trying to do creative work in a field which had been overwhelmingly male-dominated and in a world which did not take women's creativity seriously. The lack of community among women writers in the 1950s and early 1960s had, for Plath, the result of isolating her within her own psyche. If any one thing leads to Sylvia Plath's anger and her sense, finally, that there was no place to get to, it is this experience of isolation: temporally, from history, in that she could not find a tradition from which she did not feel alienated; spatially, in that she could not find a community that shared her language, images, assumptions.

This experience of isolation is connected, for a woman writer, to ambivalence about self-image, image of the world, and relationship between self and world: an ambivalence that arises from being defined not by oneself, but by some other, and from being defined in a way that provides little support for creative and committed action on the part of the individual so defined. Sylvia Plath's attempt, from *The Colossus* poems on, to redefine herself through a medium, language, of which she is suspicious, her uneasiness that language is based on social expectations and assumptions shaped by an economic base and a cultural superstructure inimical to her own growth, create an ambivalence that leads to a kind of existential paralysis, a sense that one is enclosed in a circumscribed and solitary place where no real choice is possible.

Even the metaphor of the beehive, Plath's most positive image of the possibility of community, is finally ambivalent. The self is both bee and beekeeper, worker and queen, on the boundary between commitment and alienation, trapped within her culture but refusing to accept her assigned place in it. Sylvia Plath's poetry images and narrates the various forms that the conflict of self and world within the self can take. To see yourself trapped between sets of mutually exclusive alternatives, neither of which fits no matter how many reconciling images you generate, is to live in a circus hall of mirrors, where the self is distorted, disguised, or shattered into slivers of reflection. But it is the struggle to be whole that engages the poet and empowers the poems. (pp. 158-61)

> *Pamela J. Annas, in her* A Disturbance in Mirrors: The Poetry of Sylvia Plath, *Greenwood Press, 1988, 186 p.*

FURTHER READING

Alvarez, A. "Sylvia Plath: A Memoir." *New American Review,* No. 12 (1971): 9-40.

> Controversial personal and critical portrait of Plath in which, among other assertions, Alvarez contends that Plath's suicide was a calculated risk that was not intended to succeed. Alvarez describes Plath's action alternately as a risk she took while in a depression, "not much caring whether she won or lost"; as a " 'cry for help' which fatally misfired"; and as "a last, desperate attempt to exorcise the death she had summoned up in her poems." This piece subsequently appeared as part of Alvarez's book *The Savage God: A Study of Suicide* (1971).

Broe, Mary Lynn. *Protean Poetic: The Poetry of Sylvia Plath.* Columbia & London: University of Missouri Press, 1980, 226 p.

> Chronological approach to Plath's career that attempts to "demythologize Sivvy [a nickname Plath often used in reference to herself], to describe her 'theatrical comeback in broad day' to the art of poemmaking—the changing nature of her imaginative vision, her developing poetic, the growth of her creative sensibility, the singular daring achievement of her voice and tone."

Butscher, Edward. *Sylvia Plath: Method and Madness.* New York: Seabury Press, 1976, 378 p.
Psychologically based study of Plath's life and work.

Butscher, Edward, ed. *Sylvia Plath: The Woman and the Work.* New York: Dodd, Mead & Co., 1977, 242 p.
Anthology of biographical and critical essays, including pieces by Richard Wilbur, Marjorie G. Perloff, Robert Phillips, and Joyce Carol Oates.

Dutta, Ujjal. "Poetry As Performance: A Reading of Sylvia Plath." *The Literary Criterion* XVI, No. 3 (1981): 1-11.
Interpretation of Plath's poetry in which the critic concludes: "Plath's poetry matters not because of its confessional pressures but because, at her best, she could organize such pressures into an independent experience, into a poetic action, at once personal and impersonal."

Gordon, Jan B. " 'Who Is Sylvia?' The Art of Sylvia Plath." *Modern Poetry Studies* I, No. 1 (1970): 6-34.
Psychological explication of Plath's life and poetry.

Hardy, Barbara. "The Poetry of Sylvia Plath," in *Women Reading Women's Writing,* edited by Sue Roe, pp. 207-25. Brighton, England: Harvester Press, 1987.
Consideration of Plath's "transformation of the themes, structures and language of sexuality" in her poetry.

Holbrook, David. *Sylvia Plath: Poetry and Existence.* London: Athlone Press, University of London, 1976, 308 p.
Examination of Plath's life and poetry from a psychological perspective.

Hoyle, James F. "Sylvia Plath: A Poetry of Suicidal Mania." *Literature and Psychology* XVIII, No. 4 (1968): 187-203.
Deeply psychological approach to Plath's poetry. Views Plath as a manic-depressive and states that the "coherence of her work is that of an excited artist working at both the production of lyric poems and the death of herself."

Hughes, Ted. "Commentary." *The Times Literary Supplement* No. 3638 (19 November 1971): 1448.
Letter to the editor in which Hughes discredits the memoir of Plath written by A. Alvarez which was published in the *New American Review* (see above in Further Reading list) and included in his book *The Savage God: A Study of Suicide* (1971).

King, P. R. " 'Dying Is an Art': The Poetry of Sylvia Plath," in his *Nine Contemporary Poets,* pp. 152-89. London and New York: Methuen, 1979.
Overview of Plath's poetry in which the critic states: "These poems express a collapse of identity, and yet their language, imagery and rhythm have a paradoxical zest and energy of life. The affirmation of meaning that the poet seems denied is bequeathed to the reader in his response to the power of the style of the poetry."

Kroll, Judith. *Chapters in a Mythology: The Poetry of Sylvia Plath.* New York: Harper & Row Publishers, 1976, 303 p.
Systematic approach to the "thematic meaning of Plath's late poems" through interpretation of Plath's symbols. Also focuses on the effects of Plath's reading on her own writing.

Lane, Gary, ed. *Sylvia Plath: New Views on the Poetry.* Baltimore and London: Johns Hopkins University Press, 1979, 264 p.
Compilation of criticism commissioned for this book, in-cluding essays by Calvin Bedient, Hugh Kenner, Marjorie Perloff, and Carole Ferrier, among others.

Lane, Gary, and Stevens, Maria, eds. *Sylvia Plath: A Bibliography.* The Scarecrow Author Bibliographies, No. 36. Metuchen, N. J.: Scarecrow Press, 1978, 144 p.
Book-length bibliography, divided into sections of works by and works about Plath. Also includes appendices on the chronology of Plath's publications, differences between British and American editions of her books, forthcoming works by and about Plath, and selected anthologies in which Plath's poems appear.

Newman, Charles, ed. *The Art of Sylvia Plath: A Symposium.* Bloomington and London: Indiana University Press, 1970, 319 p.
Collection of both previously published and commissioned criticism. Includes A. Alvarez on Plath's later poems, a memoir by Anne Sexton, reviews by Stephen Spender and George Steiner, and an appendix of some of Plath's previously unpublished poetry.

Perloff, Marjorie. "The Two *Ariels:* The (Re)Making of the Sylvia Plath Canon," in *Poems in Their Place: The Intertextuality and Order of Poetic Collections,* edited by Neil Fraistat, pp. 308-33. Chapel Hill and London: University of North Carolina Press, 1986.
Contends that the published and popularly known version of *Ariel* that was edited by Ted Hughes differs radically from Plath's intended book.

Rosenblatt, Jon. *Sylvia Plath: Poetry of Initiation.* Chapel Hill: University of North Carolina Press, 1979, 180 p.
A concerted attempt to detach Plath's poetry from her life and study the relationship between the "powerful images and rhythms" of her work and its "ritual or quasi-ritual patterns,"

Sigmund, Elizabeth. "Sylvia, 1962: A Memoir." *The New Review* 3, No. 26 (May 1976): 63-5.
Reminiscence of Plath during her last year of life by a friend and neighbor in Devon, England.

Smith, Dave. "Some Recent American Poetry: Come All Ye Fair and Tender Ladies—Part III: Sylvia Plath, The Electric Horse." *The American Poetry Review* II, No. 1 (January-February 1982): 43-6.
Review of *The Collected Poems* in which Smith describes the volume as "the record of [Plath's] struggle to know herself, which was the struggle finally to accept the self she was."

Steiner, Nancy Hunter. *A Closer Look at Ariel: A Memory of Sylvia Plath.* New York: Harper's Magazine Press, 1973, 83 p.
Memoir by a friend and roommate of Plath's at Smith College during 1953 and 1954. Includes an informative introduction by George Stade.

Stevenson, Anne. *Bitter Fame: A Life of Sylvia Plath.* Boston: Houghton Mifflin Co., 1989, 413 p.
Highly regarded and dispassionate treatment of Plath's life and work.

Uroff, Margaret Dickie. *Sylvia Plath and Ted Hughes.* Urbana: University of Illinois Press, 1979, 235 p.
Book-length study of the "poetic collaboration" between Plath and Hughes "in order to see how it influenced their development."

Wagner, Linda W. *Critical Essays on Sylvia Plath.* Critical Essays on American Literature, edited by James Nagel. Boston: G. K. Hall & Co., 1984, 231 p.

Anthology of previously published criticism on Plath's poetry and prose. Includes a section each of reviews and essays.

Edgar Allan Poe

1809-1849

American poet, short story writer, critic, editor, essayist, and novelist.

Poe's stature as a major figure in world literature is primarily based on his ingenious and profound poems, short stories, and critical theories, which established a highly influential rationale for the short form in both poetry and fiction. Poe's poetry and short stories greatly influenced the French Symbolists of the late nineteenth century, who in turn altered the direction of modern literature, and it is this philosophical and artistic transaction that accounts for much of his importance in literary history. Poe's first love as a writer was poetry; he demonstrated an inspired, original imagination as well as a brilliant command of language unique in American poetry for its haunting, musical quality.

Poe's father and mother were professional actors who at the time of his birth were members of a repertory company in Boston. Before Poe was three years old both of his parents died, and he was raised in the home of John Allan, a prosperous exporter from Richmond, Virginia, who never legally adopted his foster son. As a boy, Poe attended the best schools available, and was admitted to the University of Virginia at Charlottesville in 1825. While there he distinguished himself academically but was forced to leave after less than a year because of bad debts and inadequate financial support from Allan. Poe's relationship with Allan disintegrated upon his return to Richmond in 1827, and soon after Poe left for Boston, where he enlisted in the army and also published his first collection, *Tamerlane, and Other Poems, "By A Bostonian."* The volume went unnoticed by readers and reviewers, and a second collection, *Al Aaraaf, Tamerlane, and Minor Poems,* received only slightly more attention when it appeared in 1829. That same year Poe was honorably discharged from the army, having attained the rank of regimental sergeant major, and was then admitted to the United States Military Academy at West Point. However, because Allan would neither provide his foster son with sufficient funds to maintain himself as a cadet nor give the consent necessary to resign from the Academy, Poe was court-martialed and dismissed for ignoring his duties and violating regulations. He subsequently went to New York City, where *Poems,* his third collection of verse, was published in 1831, and then to Baltimore, where he lived at the home of his aunt, Mrs. Maria Clemm.

Over the next few years Poe's first short stories appeared in the Philadelphia *Saturday Courier* and his "MS. Found in a Bottle" won a cash prize for best story in the Baltimore *Saturday Visitor.* Nevertheless, Poe was still not earning enough to live independently, nor did Allan's death in 1834 provide him with a legacy. The following year, however, his financial problems were temporarily alleviated when he accepted an editor position at *The Southern Literary Messenger* in Richmond, bringing with him his aunt and his twelve-year-old cousin Virginia, whom he married in 1836. *The Southern Literary Messenger* was the

first of several journals Poe would direct over the next ten years and through which he rose to prominence as a leading man of letters in America. Poe made himself known not only as a superlative author of poetry and fiction, but also as a literary critic whose level of imagination and insight had hitherto been unapproached in American literature. While Poe's writings gained attention in the late 1830s and early 1840s, the profits from his work remained meager, and he thus supported himself by editing *Burton's Gentleman's Magazine* and *Graham's Magazine* in Philadelphia and the *Broadway Journal* in New York City. After his wife's death from tuberculosis in 1847, Poe became involved in a number of romantic affairs. It was while he prepared for his second marriage that Poe, for reasons unknown, arrived in Baltimore in late September of 1849. On October 3, he was discovered in a state of semi-consciousness; he died four days later without regaining the necessary lucidity to explain what had happened during the last days of his life.

Poe's most conspicuous contribution to world literature derives from the analytical method he practiced. His self-declared intention was to formulate strictly artistic ideals in a milieu he thought overly concerned with the utilitarian value of literature. While Poe's position includes the chief requisites of pure aestheticism, his emphasis on literary formalism was directly linked to his philosophical ideals: through the calculated use of language a writer may express, though always imperfectly, a vision of truth and the essential condition of human existence. Poe's theory of literary creation is noted for two central points: first, a work must create a unity of effect on the reader to be considered successful; second, the production of this single effect should not be left to the hazards of accident or inspiration, but should be—to the minutest detail of style and subject—the result of rational deliberation on the part of the author. In poetry, this single effect must arouse a reader's sense of beauty, an ideal that Poe closely associated with sadness, strangeness, and loss. Discussing "The Raven" in his seminal essay "Philosophy of Composition" (1846), Poe noted: "[The] death . . . of a beautiful woman is, unquestionably, the most poetical topic in the world—and equally it is beyond doubt that the lips best suited for such topic are those of a bereaved lover."

Poe began writing poetry while in his adolescence. His early verse reflects the influence of such English romantics as Lord Byron, John Keats, and Percy Bysshe Shelley, yet foreshadows his later poetry which illuminates his subjective outlook and surreal, mystic vision. "Tamerlane" and "Al Aaraaf," for example, reveal Poe's evolution from portraying Byronic heroes to journeys within his own imagination and subconscious. The former piece, reminiscent of Byron's "Childe Harold's Pilgrimage," recounts the life and adventures of a fourteenth-century Mongol conqueror; the latter poem portrays a dreamworld where neither the good nor evil permanently reside and where absolute beauty can be directly discerned. In other poems—"To Helen," "Lenore," and "The Raven" in particular—Poe investigates the loss of ideal beauty and the difficulty in regaining it. These pieces are usually narrated by a young man who laments the untimely death of his beloved. "To Helen" is a three stanza lyric that has been called one of the most beautiful love poems in the English language. The subject of the work is a woman who becomes, in the eyes of the narrator, a personification of the classical beauty of ancient Greece and Rome. "Lenore" presents ways in which the dead is best remembered, either by mourning or celebrating life beyond earthly boundaries. In "The Raven," Poe successfully unites his philosophical and aesthetic ideals. In this psychological piece, a young scholar is tormented with doubt by the frightening answer of a raven to his question of whether he will see his deceased lover in another life. The emotional intensity of the narrator's fateful interpretation and his resulting unhappiness are heightened by the raven's ominous repetition of "Nevermore." In his introduction to the French edition of "The Raven," Charles Baudelaire noted: "It is indeed the poem of the sleeplessness of despair; it lacks nothing: neither the fever of ideas, nor the violence of colors, nor sickly reasoning, nor drivelling terror, nor even the bizarre gaiety of suffering which makes it more terrible." Poe also wrote poems that were intended to be read aloud. Experimenting with combinations of sound and rhythm, he employed such technical devices as repetition, parallelism, internal rhyme, alliteration, and assonance. In "The Bells," for example, the repetition of the word "bells" in various structures accentuates the unique tonality of the different types of bells described in the poem.

While his works were not conspicuously acclaimed during his lifetime, Poe did earn respect as a gifted poet, fiction writer, and essayist, occasionally achieving a measure of popular success with the appearance of such poems as "The Raven." After his death, however, the history of his critical reception reflects dramatically uneven judgments and interpretations. This state of affairs was initiated by Poe's one-time friend and literary executor R. W. Griswold, who, in a libelous obituary notice bearing the byline "Ludwig" in the *New York Tribune,* attributed the depravity and psychological aberrations of many of the characters in Poe's fiction to Poe himself. In retrospect, Griswold's vilifications seem ultimately to have elicited as much sympathy as censure with respect to Poe and his work, leading subsequent biographers of the late nineteenth century to defend, sometimes too zealously, Poe's reputation. It was not until A. H. Quinn's 1941 biography that an objective portrait was provided of Poe, his work, and the relationship between the author's life and his imagination. Nevertheless, the identification of Poe with the murderers and madmen of his works survived and flourished in the twentieth century, most prominently in the form of psychoanalytical studies such as those of Marie Bonaparte and Joseph Wood Krutch. In addition to the controversy over the sanity or maturity of Poe was the question of the value of Poe's works as serious literature. At the forefront of his detractors were such eminent figures as Henry James, Aldous Huxley, and T. S. Eliot, who dismissed Poe's poetry and short stories as juvenile, vulgar, and artistically debased; in contrast, these same works have been judged of the highest literary merit by such writers as Bernard Shaw and William Carlos Williams. Complementing Poe's erratic reputation among English and American commentators is the more stable, and generally more elevated opinion of critics elsewhere in the world, especially in France. Following the extensive translations and commentaries of Charles Baudelaire in the 1850s, Poe's works were received with a peculiar esteem by French writers, particularly concerning his transcendent aspirations as a poet; the twentieth-century movement of Surrealism, which valued Poe's bizarre and apparently unruled imagination; and such figures as Paul Valéry, who found in Poe's theories and thought an ideal of supreme rationalism. Poe's poetry has enjoyed a similar regard in other countries, and numerous studies have been written tracing Poe's influence on international literature, especially in the Soviet Union, Japan, Scandinavia, and Latin America.

Today, Poe is recognized as one of the foremost progenitors of modern American literature, both in its popular forms and in its more complex and self-conscious forms, which represent the essential artistic manner of the twentieth century. In contrast to earlier critics who considered the man and his works as one, criticism of the past twenty-five years has developed a view of Poe as a detached artist who was more concerned with displaying his virtuosity than with expressing his "soul," and who maintained an ironic rather that an autobiographical relationship to his writings. While at one time such scholars as Yvor Winters aspired to remove Poe from literary history, his works remain integral to any conception of modernism in world literature. Joseph Auslander wrote in an essay entitled "The

Poet of Ravens and Lost Ladies": "We know in some degree the hell that was in [Poe's] heart. . . . Even his wild hallucinations, grotesque lamps and waving arras, dim cities and leaden seas, rouse a familiarity in us. Poe, the high priest of despair, has suffered darker contradictions in his soul than most of us have known, but they are, after all, human contradictions."

(For further information on Poe's life and career, see *Nineteenth-Century Literature Criticism,* Vols. 1, 16; *Short Story Criticism,* Vol. 1; *Something about the Author,* Vol. 23; *Dictionary of Literary Biography,* Vols. 3, 59, 73, 74; and *Concise Dictionary of American Literary Biography: Colonization to the American Renaissance, 1640-1865.*)

PRINCIPAL WORKS

POETRY

Tamerlane, and Other Poems, "By A Bostonian"   1827
Al Aaraaf, Tamerlane, and Minor Poems   1829
Poems   1831
The Raven, and Other Poems   1845
Eureka: A Prose Poem   1848

OTHER MAJOR WORKS

The Narrative of Arthur Gordon Pym [*pseud.*] *of Nantucket, North America: Comprising the Details of a Mutiny, Famine, and Shipwreck, During a Voyage to the South Seas; Resulting in Various Extraordinary Adventures and Discoveries in the Eighty-fourth Parallel of South Latitude*   (novel)   1838
Tales of the Grotesque and Arabesque   (short stories) 1840
Tales by Edgar A. Poe   (short stories)   1845
The Literati: Some Honest Opinions about Authorial Merits and Demerits, with Occasional Words of Personality   (criticism)   1850

James Russell Lowell   (essay date 1845)

[*Lowell was a celebrated American poet and essayist, and an editor of two leading journals, the* Atlantic Monthly *and the* North American Review. *He is noted for his satirical and critical writings, including* A Fable for Critics (1848), *a book-length poem featuring witty critical portraits of his contemporaries. Commentators generally agree that Lowell displayed a judicious critical sense—despite the fact that he sometimes relied upon impressions rather than critical precepts in his writings—and rank him among the major nineteenth-century American scholars. In the following excerpt, Lowell deems Poe a genius whose works do not fully reflect his intellectual brilliance.*]

Mr. Poe's early productions show that he could see through the verse to the spirit beneath, and that he already had a feeling that all the life and grace of the one must depend on and be modulated by the will of the other. We call them the most remarkable boyish poems that we have ever read. We know of none that can compare with them for maturity of purpose, and a nice understanding of the ef-

AUTHOR'S COMMENTARY

[In **"The Raven,"** I had] the conception of a Raven—the bird of ill omen—monotonously repeating the one word, "Nevermore," at the conclusion of each stanza, in a poem of melancholy tone, and in length about one hundred lines. Now, never losing sight of the object *supremeness,* or perfection, at all points, I asked myself—"Of all melancholy topics, what, according to the *universal* understanding of mankind, is the *most* melancholy?" Death—was the obvious reply. "And when," I said, "is this most melancholy of topics most poetical?" From what I have already explained at some length, the answer, here also, is obvious—"When it most closely allies itself to *Beauty:* the death, then, of a beautiful woman is, unquestionably, the most poetical topic in the world—and equally is it beyond doubt that the lips best suited for such topic are those of a bereaved lover."

I had now to combine the two ideas, of a lover lamenting his deceased mistress and a Raven continuously repeating the word "Nevermore"—I had to combine these bearing in mind my design of varying, at every turn, the *application* of the word repeated; but the only intelligible mode of such combination is that of imagining the Raven employing the word in answer to the queries of the lover. And here it was that I saw at once the opportunity afforded for the effect on which I had been depending—that is to say, the effect of the *variation of application.* I saw that I could make the first query propounded by the lover—the first query to which the Raven should reply "Nevermore"—that I could make this first query a commonplace one—the second less so—the third still less, and so on—until at length the lover, startled from his original *nonchalance* by the melancholy character of the word itself . . . is at length excited to superstition, and wildly propounds queries of a far different character—queries whose solution he has passionately at heart—propounds them half in superstition and half in that species of despair which delights in self-torture—propounds them not altogether because he believes in the prophetic or demoniac character of the bird (which, reason assures him, is merely repeating a lesson learned by rote) but because he experiences a phrenzied pleasure in so modeling his questions as to receive from the *expected* "Nevermore" the most delicious because the most intolerable of sorrow.

(essay date 1846)

fects of language and metre. Such pieces are only valuable when they display what we can only express by the contradictory phrase of *innate experience*. [In **"To Helen"** there] is a little dimness in the filling up, but the grace and symmetry of the outline are such as few poets ever attain. There is a smack of ambrosia about it. . . . It is the *tendency* of the young poet that impresses us. Here is no "withering scorn," no heart "blighted" ere it has safely got into its teens, none of the drawing-room sansculottism which Byron had brought into vogue. All is limpid and serene, with a pleasant dash of the Greek Helicon in it. The melody of the whole too, is remarkable. It is not of that kind which can be demonstrated arithmetically upon the tips of the fingers. It is of that finer sort which the inner ear alone can estimate. It seems simple, like a Greek column, because of its perfection. (pp. 50-1)

Mr. Poe has that indescribable something which men have agreed to call *genius*. No man could ever tell us precisely what it is, and yet there is none who is not inevitably aware of its presence and its power. Let talent writhe and contort itself as it may, it has no such magnetism. Larger of bone and sinew it may be, but the wings are wanting. Talent sticks fast to earth, and its most perfect works have still one foot of clay. Genius claims kindred with the very workings of Nature herself, so that a sunset shall seem like a quotation from Dante or Milton, and if Shakespeare be read in the very presence of the sea itself, his verses shall but seem nobler for the sublime criticism of ocean. Talent may make friends for itself, but only genius can give to its creations the divine power of winning love and veneration. Enthusiasm cannot cling to what itself is unenthusiastic, nor will he ever have disciples who has not himself impulsive zeal enough to be a disciple. Great wits are allied to madness only inasmuch as they are possessed and carried away by their demon, while talent keeps him, as Paracelsus did, securely prisoned in the pommel of its sword. To the eye of genius, the veil of the spiritual world is ever rent asunder, that it may perceive the ministers of good and evil who throng continually around it. No man of mere talent ever flung his inkstand at the devil.

When we say that Mr. Poe has genius, we do not mean to say that he has produced evidence of the highest. But to say that he possesses it at all is to say that he needs only zeal, industry, and a reverence for the trust reposed in him, to achieve the proudest triumphs and the greenest laurels. (p. 51)

James Russell Lowell, "Edgar Allen Poe," in Graham's Magazine, *Vol. XXVII, No. 2, February, 1845, pp. 49-53.*

Charles Baudelaire   (essay date 1859)

[A French poet and critic, Baudelaire is best known for his famous collection of poems Les fleurs du mal, *which is ranked among the most influential works of French poetry. Baudelaire was an ardent early supporter of Poe; as a result of the French writer's translations and extensive critical commentaries on Poe's works, Poe exerted a profound influence on French literature during the second half of the nineteenth century. In the following excerpt from the preface to his French translation of "The Raven," Baudelaire conveys his impressions of the dark intensity of the poem.]*

It has been said that poetics is derived and developed from the study of poems. [Poe] is a poet who claims that his poem [**"The Raven"**] was composed in accordance with his poetics. He certainly had great genius and more inspiration than anyone else, if by inspiration is understood energy, intellectual enthusiasm, and the ability to keep one's faculties alert. But he also loved work more than anyone else; he was fond of repeating, he who had a mature originality, that originality is a matter of apprenticeship, which does not mean something that can be transmitted by instruction. The accidental and the unintelligible were his two great enemies. Did he make himself, by a strange and amusing vanity, much less inspired than he naturally was? Did he diminish the spontaneous faculty in himself in order to give will a larger share? I should be rather inclined to think so; although at the same time it must not be forgotten that his genius, however ardent and supple it may have been, was passionately fond of analysis, combinations and calculations. Still another of his favorite axioms was this one: "Everything in a poem or a novel, as in a sonnet or a short story, should lead to the conclusion. A good writer already has his last line in mind when he writes the first one." Thanks to this admirable method, the artist can begin his composition at the end, and work on any part whenever it is convenient. The lovers of a *fine frenzy* will perhaps be revolted by these *cynical* maxims; but everyone may take what he wishes from them. It will always be useful to show them what profit art can draw from deliberation, and to make worldly people realize how much labor is required by that object of luxury called Poetry.

After all, a little charlatanism is always permitted to genius, and is even proper to it. It is, like rouge on the cheeks of a naturally beautiful woman, an additional stimulus to the mind.

[**"The Raven"** is] strange above all others. It revolves on a profound and mysterious word, as terrible as infinity, that thousands of contorted lips have repeated since the beginning of time, and that in an idle gesture of despair more than one dreamer has written on the corner of his table in order to try out his pen: *Nevermore!* Immensity, made fruitful by destruction, is filled from top to bottom with this idea, and Humanity, still not brutalized, gladly accepts Hell in order to escape the helpless despair contained in that word.

In casting poetry in the form of prose, there is necessarily a dreadful imperfection; but the result would be even worse in a rimed aping of the original. The reader will understand that it is impossible for me to give him an exact idea of the profound and lugubrious sonority, of the powerful monotony of these verses, whose broad and tripled rimes sound like the tolling of melancholy. It is indeed the poem of the sleeplessness of despair; it lacks nothing: neither the fever of ideas, nor the violence of colors, nor sickly reasoning, nor drivelling terror, nor even the bizarre gaiety of suffering which makes it more terrible. Listen to Lamartine's most plaintive stanzas singing in your memory, the most complicated and the most magnificent rhythms of Victor Hugo; mingle with them the recollection of Théophile Gautier's most subtle and most comprehensive tercets,—from *Ténèbres,* for instance, that garland of formidable conceits on death and nothingness, in which the tripled rime adapts itself so well to the obsessive melancholy,—and you will perhaps get an approximate idea of Poe's talents as a versifier; I say as versifier, for it is superflous, I believe, to speak of his imagination. (pp. 155-57)

Charles Baudelaire, "Critical Miscellany: Preface to 'The Raven'," in his Baudelaire on Poe: Critical Papers, *edited and translated by Lois Hyslop and Francis E. Hyslop, Jr., Bald Eagle Press, 1952, pp. 155-57.*

Walt Whitman   (essay date 1882)

[*An American poet, essayist, novelist, short story writer, journalist, and editor. Whitman is regarded as an exceptional poet and a great literary innovator. His* Leaves of Grass *(1855), in which he celebrated the "divine average," democracy, and sexuality, was a major influence on modern free verse. In the following essay, Whitman declares that Poe's verses "belong among the electric lights of imaginative literature, brilliant and dazzling, but with no heat," yet also admits that Poe's works have a magnetism that deserves special recognition.*]

In diagnosing this disease called Humanity—to assume for the nonce what seems a chief mood of the personality and writings of my subject—I have thought that poets, somewhere or other on the list, present the most marked indications. Comprehending artists in a mass, musicians, painters, actors, and so on, and considering each and all of them as radiations or flanges of that furious whirling wheel, poetry, the centre and axis of the whole, where else indeed may we so well investigate the causes, growths, tally marks of the time—the age's matter and malady?

By common consent there is nothing better for man or woman than a perfect and noble life, morally without flaw, happily balanced in activity, physically sound and pure, giving its due proportion, and no more, to the sympathetic, the human emotional element—a life in all these, unhasting, unresting, untiring to the end. And yet there is another shape of personality dearer far to the artist-sense (which likes the lambent play of strongest lights and shades), where the perfect character, the good, the heroic, although never attained, is never lost sight of, but through failures, sorrows, temporary downfalls, is returned to again and again, and while often violated is passionately adhered to as long as mind, muscles, voice, obey the wondrous power we call volition. This sort of personality we see more or less in Burns, Byron, Schiller and George Sand. But we do not see it in Edgar Poe. While to the character first outlined the service Poe renders is certainly that entire contrast and contradiction which is next best to fully exemplifying it.

Almost without the first sign of moral principle, or of the concrete or its heroisms, or the simpler affections of the heart, Poe's verses illustrate an intense faculty for technical and abstract beauty, with the rhyming art to excess, an incorrigible propensity toward nocturnal themes, a demoniac undertone behind every page, and, by final judgment, probably belong among the electric lights of imaginative literature, brilliant and dazzling, but with no heat. There is an indescribable magnetism about the poet's life and reminiscences as well as the poems. To one who could work out their subtle retracing and retrospect, the latter would make a close tally no doubt between the author's birth and antecedents, his childhood and youth, his physique, his so-called education, his studies and associates, the literary and social Baltimore, Richmond, Philadelphia and New York of those times—not only the places and circumstances in themselves, but often, very often, in a strange spurning of, and reaction from them all.

The following from a report in the Washington *Star* of November 16, 1875, may afford those who care for it something further of my point of view toward this interesting figure and influence of our era. There occurred about that date in Baltimore a public re-burial of Poe's remains, and dedication of a monument over the grave:

Being in Washington on a visit at the time, "the old gray" went over to Baltimore, and though ill from paralysis, consented to hobble up and silently take a seat on the platform, but refused to make any speech, saying, "I have felt a strong impulse to come over and be here to-day myself in memory of Poe, which I have obeyed, but not the slightest impulse to make a speech, which, my dear friends, must also be obeyed."

In an informal circle, however, in conversation after the ceremonies, [I] said: "For a long while, and until lately, I had a distaste for Poe's writings. I wanted, and still want for poetry, the clear sun shining, and fresh air blowing—the strength and power of health, not of delirium, even amid the stormiest passions—with always the background of the eternal moralities. Non-complying with these requirements, Poe's genius has yet conquered a special recognition for itself, and I too have come to fully admit it, and appreciate it and him. Even my own objections draw me to him at last, and those very points, with his sad fate, will doubtless always make him dearer to young and fervid minds.

"In a dream I once had, I saw a vessel on the sea, at midnight, in a storm. It was no great full-rigged ship, nor majestic steamer, steering firmly through the gale, but seemed one of those superb little schooner yachts I had often seen lying anchored, rocking so jauntily, in the waters around New York, or up Long Island Sound; now flying uncontrolled with torn sails and broken spars through the wild sleet and winds and waves of the night. On deck was a slender, slight, beautiful figure, a dim man, apparently enjoying all the terror, the murk, and the dislocation of which he was the centre and the victim. That figure of my lurid dream might stand for Edgar Poe, his spirit, his fortunes, and his poems—themselves all lurid dreams."

Much more may be said, with considerations I have not touched upon. I most desired to exploit the idea put at the beginning. By its popular poets the calibres of an age, the weak spots of its embankments, its sub-currents (often more significant than the biggest surface ones,) are unerringly indicated. The lush and the weird that have taken such extraordinary possession of Nineteenth Century verse-lovers—what mean they? The inevitable tendency of poetic culture to morbidity, abnormal beauty—the sickliness of all technical thought or refinement in itself—the abnegation of the perennial and democratic concretes at first hand, the body, the earth and sea, sex, and the like—and the substitution of something for them at second or third hand—what bearings have they on current pathological study?

Walt Whitman, *"Edgar Poe's Significance,"* in The Critic, *New York, Vol. II, No. 37, June 3, 1882, p. 147.*

Paul Valéry (essay date 1924)

[*A prominent French poet and critic, Valéry is one of the leading practitioners of nineteenth-century Symbolist aestheticism. Valéry's work reflects his desire for total control of his creation; his absorption with the creative process also forms the method of his criticism. In his prose, Valéry displays what is perhaps his most fundamental talent: the ability to apply a well-disciplined mind to a diversity of subjects including art, politics, science, dance, and aesthetics. His critical writings are collected in the five volumes of* Variété *(1924-44;* Variety*) and his personal notebooks, the* Cahiers *(1894-1945). In the following excerpt from an essay originally published in* Variété *in 1924, Valéry considers Poe's prose poem* Eureka *a unification of science and literature—"one of the rare modern specimens of a total explanation of material and spiritual nature."*]

I was twenty years old and I believed in the power of thought. I suffered strangely from being and not being. Sometimes I sensed infinite powers in myself; they collapsed in the face of problems, and the feebleness of my real powers drove me to desperation. I was somber, flighty, apparently pliant but hard underneath, extreme in scorn, absolute in admiration, easy to impress, impossible to convince. I had faith in a few ideas that had come to me, mistaking their conformity with my being, which had given them birth, for a sure sign of their universal value: what presented itself so clearly to my mind seemed invincible; what desire engenders is always clearest.

I protected these shadows of ideas like state secrets. I was ashamed of their oddity. I was afraid they were absurd; I knew that they were, and were not. They were futile in themselves but potent because their singular strength gave me the confidence I had. Vigilance of this frail mystery filled me with a certain vigor.

I had ceased writing poetry, and scarcely read any longer. Novels and poetry seemed no more than the special, impure and half-unconscious applications of some of the properties of those great secrets I believed I had found one day through the single unyielding assurance that they must necessarily exist. As for the philosophers, I had cultivated them little and that little only irritated me, for they never answered any of the questions that tormented me. They gave me nothing but boredom—never the feeling that they communicated an authentic power. And besides, it seemed useless to speculate on abstractions one had not first defined. But is it possible to do otherwise? The only hope, for a philosophy, is to become impersonal. We may expect that great step at the end of the World.

I had dipped into some mysticism. It's impossible to speak ill of that, since we find whatever we bring to it.

At this point I happened on *Eureka.*

My schooling, under dull and sorry masters, had made me believe that science is not love; its fruits are useful, perhaps, but its foliage is very thorny and its bark frightfully rough. Mathematics I reserved for distressingly precise minds, incompatible with mine.

Literature, on the other hand, had often scandalized me by its lack of rigor, sequence and inevitability in ideas. Its object is often trivial. Our poetry is ignorant of everything epic and tragic in the intellect, or else is afraid of it. The few times when our poetry has ventured into the mind it became at once dull and unbearable. Neither Lucretius nor Dante is French; we have no epics of knowledge. Perhaps we have such a decided feeling about the separation of genres, that is to say, the independence of the various movements of the mind, that we cannot endure works that combine them. We do not know how to make song of stuff that can do without song. But for the past hundred years, our poetry has shown such rich resources and such a rare power of renewal that the future may soon give us a few of those works in the grand style and of a noble austerity—works that have power over the sensibility and the intellect.

In a few moments *Eureka* taught me Newton's law, Laplace's name, the hypothesis he proposed and the very existence of investigation and speculation which people never mention to adolescents for fear of their becoming interested, I suppose, instead of measuring the astonishing length of the hour in dreams and yawns. The things that most excite the mind's appetite were in those days relegated to the arcana. That was a time when big heavy books on physics did not breathe a word about gravitation, or the conservation of energy or Carnot's principle; they were fond of three-way watertaps, Magdeburg's hemisphere and the laborious and fragile reasoning inspired by the problem of the siphon.

Yet, would it be a waste of their school days to give young minds some slight sense of the origin, the high destination and the living quality of the dry calculations and propositions inflicted on them in no order, in fact in quite remarkable incoherence? These frigidly taught sciences were founded and developed by men who gave them passionate attention. *Eureka* made me feel something of that passion.

I confess that the enormity of the author's pretensions and ambitions and the solemn tone of his preamble—the strange discussion on method that opens the book—only partly amazed and seduced me. Nevertheless, a master-idea was declared in those first pages, although wrapped in a mystery which suggested not only a certain impotence but also a will to hold back and the enthusiastic mind's distaste for exposing its most precious discovery. . . . And none of that was likely to displease me.

To attain what he calls *truth,* Poe invokes what he calls *consistency.* It is not easy to give an exact definition of that consistency; the author, who has everything necessary to give it, has not done so.

According to him, the *truth* that he seeks can be seized only by immediate acceptance of an intuition in which the mutual dependence of the parts and the properties of the system he examines are presented in actuality, as if tangible to the mind. This mutual dependence extends to successive phases of the system; causality is symmetrical. To a gaze that embraced the entire universe, a cause and its effect would be mistaken for one another and would exchange roles.

Two remarks here. I merely point out the premise which would take us far afield, the reader and I. Finalism has an important place in Poe's theory. That doctrine is no longer in style, and I have neither the ability nor the desire to defend it. But we must agree that the notions of cause and adaptation lead to it almost inevitably (and I do not mention the immense difficulties, and thus the temptations, presented by certain facts—the existence of instincts, etc.). The simplest solution is to dismiss the problem. It can be resolved only by means of pure imagination. Let others exercise it.

Now for the other remark. In Poe's system *consistency* is both the means of discovery and the discovery itself. It is an admirable scheme: pattern and practice of the reciprocity of appropriation. The universe is constructed according to a plan whose profound symmetry is somehow present in the inner structure of our minds. The poetic instinct should therefore lead us blindly to the truth.

Very frequently we find similar ideas in mathematicians. It sometimes occurs to them to consider their discoveries not as the "creations" of their powers of synthesis, but rather as their intellectual raid on a treasury of pre-existent and natural forms which are accessible only through a rare conjunction of rigor, sensibility and desire.

The consequences developed in **Eureka** are not always as exactly deduced or as clearly drawn as one might wish. There are shadows and lacunae. There are poorly explained interferences. There is a God.

Nothing is more fascinating to the lover of intellectual dramas and comedies than the ingenuity, the insistence, the sleight of hand, the anxiety of the inventor in the grip of his own invention, whose vices he knows perfectly. Naturally, he wants to display all its beauties, exploit all its advantages and conceal its poverty. At all costs he wants to make it correspond to what he wills. The merchant sets off his wares. Women are transformed before the mirror. The priest, the philosopher, the politician and, in general, everyone who is committed to proposing dubious things to us, always mingle sincerity with silence (to put it gently). They do not intend us to see what they do not like to consider. . . .

Yet Poe's fundamental idea is profound and sovereign.

It would be no exaggeration of its reach to recognize the theory of consistency as a very precise attempt to define the universe by its *intrinsic properties.* This proposition is found in the eighth chapter of **Eureka**: *Each law of nature depends at every point on all other laws.* If this is not a formula, it is at least the expression of a will toward generalized relativity.

Its kinship with recent concepts is revealed when we discover in this *poem* the affirmation of *symmetrical* and reciprocal relationships among matter, time, space, gravitation and light. I have underlined the word *symmetrical; in fact, a formal symmetry is the essential characteristic of Einstein's representation of the universe.* Symmetry gives it the beauty it has.

But Poe does not limit himself to the physical elements of phenomena; he includes life and consciousness in his design. How many things come to mind here! The time has passed when people readily made distinctions between the material and the spiritual. The entire argument depended on final knowledge of "matter," which they thought they had dispossessed and, in short, on *appearance.*

The appearance of matter is of a dead substance with *potentiality* that passes into *action* only by an exterior intervention entirely foreign to its nature. In the past, people drew invincible conclusions from this definition, but matter now has another face. Experiment has made us conceive the opposite of what pure observation made us see. All of modern physics, which has in some way created *relays* for our senses, has persuaded us that our ancient definition had no absolute or speculative value. It teaches us that matter is strangely various and indefinitely surprising; that it is a mass or collection of transformations that graduate and are lost in smallness; that perpetual motion perhaps occurs. Bodies have an eternal fever.

At this moment we no longer know what a fragment of any body whatsoever can or cannot contain or produce in a moment or in a series of events. The very idea of matter is nearly indistinguishable from that of energy. Everything deepens in motion, in rotation, in exchange, in radiation. Our very eyes, our hands, our nerves are made of it. The first appearance of death or sleep that matter presents, its passivity, its abandon to external actions, is constructed in our senses, like the darkness which is made by certain superimpositions of light.

All this can be summarized by stating that the properties of matter seem to depend only on the scale on which we observe them. But then the classic qualities—continuity or homogeneity of texture—can no longer be absolutely opposed to the concepts of life, sensibility and thought, since these simple characteristics are purely superficial. On this side of the scale—crude observation—all the old definitions miss the mark. We know that unknown properties and forces function in the *infra-world,* for we have disclosed some properties that our senses were not constructed to perceive. But we cannot enumerate them nor even assign a finite number to the growing multiplicity of the chapters on physics. We do not even know whether or not our concepts are illusory when we take them into realms bordering upon our own. To speak of iron or hydrogen is to presuppose entities whose existence and permanence are proved to us only by our very restricted and brief experience. Moreover, there is no reason to think that our space, our time, our causality, have any meaning whatever out there where our bodies cannot exist. And, unquestionably, the man who tries to imagine essence can do no more than adapt the ordinary categories of his mind to it. The more he advances in his research, and the more he increases his powers of categorizing, the more he departs from what one might call the *optimum* of knowledge. Determinism becomes lost in hopelessly tangled systems with millions of variables in which the mind's eye can no longer follow laws and fix upon something that lasts. When discontinuity becomes the rule, imagination, which once strove to attain the truth that perception had suspected and reason had woven, must declare itself impotent. When *means* are the object of our judgments, we give up considering facts themselves. Our knowledge tends toward power and avoids a coordinated contemplation of things. Miracles of mathematical subtility are necessary in order to restore any unity. We no longer speak of first principles, for laws are no more than constantly perfectible tools.

They no longer rule the world, but have put on the infirmity of our minds. We can no longer rest in their simplicity; like a persistent pinprick, there is always some unsatisfied decimal that calls us back to unease and to the sense of the inexhaustible.

We see, by these remarks, that Poe's intuitions about the composition of the total universe—physical, moral and metaphysical—are neither validated nor invalidated by the many important discoveries made since 1847. Some of his views can even be related, without much strain, to quite recent conceptions. When Edgar Poe measures the duration of his Cosmos by the time necessary for all of the possible combinations to be completed we think of the ideas of Boltzmann and his calculation of probability applied to the kinetic theory of gases. In *Eureka* there is a foreshadowing of Carnot's principle and of the representation of this principle by the mechanism of diffusion; the author seems to have anticipated the bold spirits who snatched the universe from its fated death by means of an infinitely brief passage through an infinitely improbable state. (pp. 233-38)

> *Paul Valéry, "On 'Eureka'," in* Affidavits of Genius: Edgar Allan Poe and the French Critics, 1847-1924, *edited by Jean Alexander, Kennikat Press, 1971, pp. 233-43.*

George Saintsbury (essay date 1927)

[*Saintsbury has been called the most influential English literary historian and critic of the late nineteenth and early twentieth centuries. His numerous literary histories and studies of European literature have established him as a leading critical authority. Saintsbury adhered to two distinct sets of critical standards: one for the novel and the other for poetry and drama. As a critic of poetry and drama, he was a radical formalist who frequently asserted that subject is of little importance and that "the so-called 'formal' part is of the essence." René Wellek has praised Saintsbury's critical qualities: his "enormous reading, the almost universal scope of his subject matter, the zest and zeal of his exposition," and "the audacity with which he handles the most ambitious and unattempted arguments." In the following excerpt from an essay that originally appeared in the* Dial *in 1927, Saintsbury lauds Poe as among "the first order of poets."*]

When Lowell, or whoever it was, wrote "Mr. Poe *the poet*", the catch-sound of the words was no doubt, though not ill-naturedly, intentionally the object of the conjunction. But one might, without extravagance, take it seriously. To say that if Poe was not a poet he was nothing, would of course be extravagant. He is something more than a squadron-leader in the story-telling army: and I have myself, in books specially on the subject, done my little best to vindicate for him a higher place than has sometimes been allowed him, both in general and in metrical criticism. But his extreme inequality, arising in the main from insufficient education, injures his work in both respects; and, except in the points where it touches his poetry nearest, his tale-telling is at most "prime amid peers". As a poet he is absolutely alone. . . . Nothing, I think, is a better specimen passage of "Mr. Poe the poet's" poetry, on the smallest scale and neglecting the cumulative effect of

his best pieces as a whole, than the famous couplet in **"The Haunted Palace"**:

> Banners, yellow, glorious, golden
> On its roof did float and flow.

I have said of this in its strictly technical aspect that the trochees themselves "float and flow and settle with the soft slowness of snowflakes". But there is a great deal more than this to be said. In the first place there is the extraordinary manipulation of the vowel-music—the contrast of the prominent sounds *a* and *e* once each and then a whole cascade of *o* in different forms of its sound, with the minor detail of the trisyllabic "glorious" ("gloryous" may be left to whosoever likes it) and its subtle connection with the monosyllabic ending "flow". All that is "music" in a way no doubt: and the additional effect given by the pause at each word of the first line may be such perhaps. But then there is appeal to a quite new sense—the sense of *eyes* of the mind, which insists for itself on the banners, the roof they float from, their colour, and their motion as they flow. You don't want—unless you are the kind of creature for whom "movies" were made and whom they satisfy— any "illustration"; the words make you see the things as they make you hear the music accompanying. And then there comes the tug-of-war between the two critical views of Poe and even between the two sections of his admirers. There is something more which is not music nor picture, but is begotten in some uncanny, though by no means unholy, way by each of the other—the poetic effluence—the charm only perceptible to that *sense* of poetry which merciful nature has not withheld from myriads though it has only granted the power of production which satisfies it to a few.

Of course there is a certain kind of criticism which can amuse itself by shooting its arrows at the moon. For instance, I think I have seen objections taken to the pacification of Psyche in **"Ulalume"** by kissing her, on the ground that Psyche means soul and you can't kiss your—or any—soul. I am not myself so sure of the impossibility. Moreover, Poe addressed this Psyche as his "sister" and you certainly *can* kiss your own sister. Also, I should myself say that this classification of body and soul as brother and sister was not exactly an unpoetical one in itself. But criticism of this sort is better nonsuited than put to its trial on points. It is evidently a case of trying to light the blunt end of a match when chemical contact is required.

A few more short instances may be demanded. One might perhaps make a touchstone of the conclusion of **"To Helen"** (the first) by asking, "Is it as it stands—

> Ah! Psyche, from the regions which
> Are Holy Land—

the same as if it were written in continuous Alexandrine:

> Ah! Psyche, from the regions which are Holy Land?"

But that sample-item of what people are pleased, in this curious century of jargon, to call a *questionnaire* might be rather treacherous. It is better perhaps not to take any example from **"The Raven"**: and **"The Bells"** have always disappointed me. The piece does not seem as if Poe had ever heard real *old* bells, which indeed is possible: and if the excellent Mrs. Shew is to be believed, the subject was suggested to, not imagined by him, and started with rather childish stuff about "little silver bells" and "heavy iron bells". Poe in some of his moods would have been much more likely to shift the adjectives and might have made something of the shifting.

But the three summits of his range—actually it would seem the latest as well as the highest of his exploits of climbing—**"For Annie," "Ulalume,"** and **"Annabel Lee"**—are simply compact of "specimens", besides showing at its best what has not yet been dwelt on—his wonderful power of working "out and up", of *crescendo* and of producing an explosion after which there *must* be silence—a deliverance following which "there is namore to syn". Although instances of the same method, they are not in the slightest degree replicas; each is entirely independent of the others.

Which of the three is "the best" it is unnecessary and probably unwise to inquire; perhaps there is not, except in mere quantity, any "better" or "best" in poetry: a thing is either poetry or it is not. It may be asked, "Is there no difference in intensity?" and perhaps there is: but all these are much on a par there. **"For Annie"** might, though one is loth to say it would, be improved by curtailment. You know, if you possess the faculty of knowing, that the thing is working up to some point and that point may seem to be unduly—at least unkindly—delayed. This delay, too, gives chance to the danger which proverbially attends the sublime. The line

> I am better at length

and indeed the whole stanza which it concludes offer "the sons of Belial" one of those "glorious times" which they seldom miss enjoying. But the magnificence of the first with its concluding couplet—

> And the fever called living
> Is conquered at last—

should carry you over the second triumphantly to the first line of the third—

> And I rest so composedly—

where the adverb is one of those single-word successes of which, considering the small bulk of his whole work in verse, Poe is so astonishingly full.

If the next half-dozen stanzas appeared alone one would certainly not care so much for them as at present: in a ferociously judicial mood you might even lift the blue pencil. But you have to put that down again very soon, with never the least subsequent temptation to take it up, some time before you come to those famous "Puritan pansies" which might induce the stoutest Cavalier to make a name-truce at least with Puritanism. And then after this gracious overture comes the main and never thenceforward failing *rise* of the piece—the introduction of Annie, and as it were the saturation of the poem with her presence and her actions and her name more and more to the end.

Observe, too, how the fellow, having got as it seemed the utmost out of word-fitness with "composedly", audaciously "does it again" in the same stanza with a repetition of that by the substitution of "contentedly"!

I suppose—indeed I may have already hinted at the proposition—that **"Ulalume"** is the prearranged and never-to-be-wholly-done-away-with battle-ground—the Belgium as it were of the Europe and not the Europe only of Poeian criticism. When Lang said fifty years ago that "it might require some moral courage to assert one's belief that the poem has an excuse for its existence", he was by no means speaking in mere irony and still less convicting that curious thing of imagination, "Victorianism", of one of its criminal follies. There were, at least in England, plenty of people who thought **"Ulalume"** quite deserving of existence: and I have seen within the last few months an expression of opinion already referred to, if not in the exact words, that she is not. For my own part, critical or not as the gods or the demons have made me, I cannot find speck or flaw in it, except that the name, capital for a poem, does not seem to me capital for a girl, and one other possible superfluity, of which presently. All the names, including Ulalume itself with the gloss I have given, and allowing the specialisation in rhyme to Auber, suit: there ought to be a Mount Yaanek, if there is not. The singular motion, as of a heavy-laden charger strongly bitted, which he has put on his anapaestic metre; the streak of charm introduced into the dreariness by the presence of Psyche, the "sisterly" Psyche; the amazing stanza which concludes with what is a sort of motto-distich for Poe—

> Astarte's bediamonded crescent
> Distinct with its duplicate horn;

and any number of his marvellous single words, the most marvellous of which is the "immemorial" at the very heart and centre of the first stanza—all these things are there and a great deal more. If anybody says that it would be better without the last stanza, I don't know that I care to argue the point.

But if a critic need not be exactly a Zoilus to suggest thinning in **"For Annie"** and lopping in **"Ulalume,"** he is lost if he even thinks of the shears in connection with **"Annabel Lee."** I can imagine a very *very* poor creature saying, no doubt with perfect truth, that the verb "to covet" will only take an accusative after it and not like "grudge" or "envy" a sort of ablative in the literal sense of that word or dative in the technical as well. One would pat his head and say, "Yes! Yes!" It was perhaps a whim that made Poe wrench the metre a little, without any need or profit, by putting "chilling" at the end of a line. But these are almost beauty-spots—if in the miraculous rush and blaze of the whole thing they are anything at all—the rush that takes one's breath away and the blaze that dazzles one's sight. I am happy enough to have read a not inconsiderable proportion of the poetry which has been vouchsafed to the world in the two great ancient and a few modern languages, with a large amount of sometimes tolerable verse. Of the latter we need say no more, while giving it its own honour in the degree in which it may deserve it. Of the poetry there are many kinds: and in each kind there are degrees of glory. But in its own kind I know nothing that can beat, if I know anything that can equal, **"Annabel Lee."** It begins quite quietly but with a motion of gathering speed and a sort of flicker of light and glow of heat: and these things quicken and brighten and grow till they finish in the last stanza, that incomparable explosion of rapturous regret that towers to the stars and sinks to the sea.

This, however, is no doubt terribly like fine writing, which is not my trade. Let us therefore conclude with perfectly plain prose. Some fifty years ago I was not allowed in England to call Poe "of the first order of poets"; fifty years after that I am able by kind permission of *The Dial* to call him so in his own country.

By what arguments this position was originally supported I cannot exactly say, for except the passage which Lang quoted I do not know what became of my rejected address. If I could not say with Landor that God is the only person of whom I would ask a thing twice, I certainly should not like to offer the same thing a second time, even to the most different person, after it had been once rejected. But I can sum up what has been here said shortly enough. A poet of the first order must be able to satisfy both the ears and the eyes of the mind; and beyond, though through, this satisfaction he must give the indefinable but by the right recipients unmistakable poetic "effluence", "emanation", or whatever you like to call it.

For me and for my house Poe does this. (pp. 316-23)

> *George Saintsbury, "Edgar Allan Poe," in his*
> Prefaces and Essays, *edited by Oliver Elton,*
> *Macmillan and Co., Limited, 1933, pp. 314-*
> *23.*

Aldous Huxley   (essay date 1930)

[*Known primarily for his dystopian novel* Brave New World *(1932), Huxley was a British-American essayist and novelist of ideas. Grandson of noted Darwinist T. H. Huxley and brother of scientist Julian Huxley, Huxley was interested in many fields of knowledge; daring conceptions of science, philosophy, and religion are woven throughout his fiction. In the following essay, Huxley calls Poe's poetry vulgar and questions favorable assessments of the American's works by French critics.*]

Eulalie, Ulalume, Raven and Bells, Conqueror Worm and Haunted Palace. . . . Was Edgar Allan Poe a major poet? It would surely never occur to any English-speaking critic to say so. And yet, in France, from 1850 till the present time, the best poets of each generation—yes, and the best critics, too; for, like most excellent poets, Baudelaire, Mallarmé, Paul Valéry are also admirable critics—have gone out of their way to praise him. Only a year or two ago M. Valéry repeated the now traditional French encomium of Poe, and added at the same time a protest against the faintness of our English praise. We who are speakers of English and not English scholars, who were born into the language and from childhood have been pickled in its literature—we can only say, with all due respect, that Baudelaire, Mallarmé and Valéry are wrong and that Poe is not one of our major poets. A taint of vulgarity spoils, for the English reader, all but two or three of his poems—the marvellous **"City in the Sea"** and **"To Helen,"** for example, whose beauty and crystal perfection make us realize, as we read them, what a very great artist perished on most of the occasions when Poe wrote verse. It is to this perished artist that the French poets pay their tribute. Not being English, they are incapable of appreciating those finer shades of vulgarity that ruin Poe for us, just as we, not being French, are incapable of appreciating those finer shades of lyrical beauty which are, for them, the making of La Fontaine.

The substance of Poe is refined; it is his form that is vulgar. He is, as it were, one of Nature's Gentlemen, unhappily cursed with incorrigible bad taste. To the most sensitive and high-souled man in the world we should find it hard to forgive, shall we say, the wearing of a diamond ring on every finger. Poe does the equivalent of this in his poetry; we notice the solecism and shudder. Foreign observers do not notice it; they detect only the native gentlemanliness in the poetical intention, not the vulgarity in the details of execution. To them, we seem perversely and quite incomprehensibly unjust.

It is when Poe tries to make it too poetical that his poetry takes on its peculiar tinge of badness. Protesting too much that he is a gentleman, and opulent into the bargain, he falls into vulgarity. Diamond rings on every finger proclaim the parvenu.

Consider, for example, the first two stanzas of **"Ulalume."**

> The skies they were ashen and sober;
>   The leaves they were crisped and sere—
>   The leaves they were withering and sere:
> It was night in the lonesome October
>   Of my most immemorial year:
> It was hard by the dim lake of Auber,
>   In the misty mid region of Weir:—
> It was down by the dank tarn of Auber,
>   In the ghoul-haunted woodland of Weir.
>
> Here once, through an alley Titanic,
>   Of cypress, I roamed with my Soul—
>   Of cypress, with Psyche, my Soul.
> These were days when my heart was volcanic
>   As the scoriac rivers that roll—
>   As the lavas that restlessly roll
> Their sulphurous currents down Yaanek,
>   In the ultimate climes of the Pole—
> That groan as they roll down Mount Yaanek,
>   In the realms of the Boreal Pole.

These lines protest too much (and with what a variety of voices!) that they are poetical, and, protesting, are therefore vulgar. To start with, the walloping dactylic metre is all too musical. Poetry ought to be musical, but musical with tact, subtly and variously. Metres whose rhythms, as in this case, are strong, insistent and practically invariable offer the poet a kind of short cut to musicality. They provide him (my subject calls for a mixture of metaphors) with a ready-made, reach-me-down music. He does not have to create a music appropriately modulated to his meaning; all he has to do is to shovel the meaning into the moving stream of the metre and allow the current to carry it along on waves that, like those of the best hairdressers, are guaranteed permanent. Many nineteenth century poets used these metrical short cuts to music, with artistically fatal results.

> Then when nature around me is smiling
>   The last smile which answers to mine,
> I do not believe it beguiling,
>   Because it reminds me of thine.

How can one take even Byron seriously, when he protests his musicalness in such loud and vulgar accents? It is only by luck or an almost super-human poetical skill that these all too musical metres can be made to sound, through their insistent barrel-organ rhythms, the intricate, personal music of the poet's own meaning. Byron occasionally, for a line or two, takes the hard kink out of those dactylic permanent waves and appears, so to speak, in his own musical hair; and Hood, by an unparalleled prodigy of technique, turns even the reach-me-down music of "The Bridge of

Sighs" into a personal music, made to the measure of the subject and his own emotion. Moore, on the contrary, is always perfectly content with the permanent wave; and Swinburne, that super-Moore of a later generation, was also content to be a permanent waver—the most accomplished, perhaps, in all the history of literature. The complexity of his ready-made musics and his technical skill in varying the number, shape and contour of his permanent waves are simply astonishing. But, like Poe and the others, he protested too much, he tried to be too poetical. However elaborately devious his short cuts to music may be, they are still short cuts—and short cuts (this is the irony) to poetical vulgarity.

A quotation and a parody will illustrate the difference between ready-made music and music made to measure. I remember (I trust correctly) a simile of Milton's:

> Like that fair field
> Of Enna, where Proserpine gathering flowers,
> Herself a fairer flower, by gloomy Dis
> Was gathered, which cost Ceres all that pain
> To seek her through the world.

Rearranged according to their musical phrasing, these lines would have to be written thus:

> Like that fair field of Enna,
>   where Proserpine gathering flowers,
> Herself a fairer flower,
>   by gloomy Dis was gathered,
> Which cost Ceres all that pain
> To seek her through the world.

The contrast between the lyrical swiftness of the first four phrases, with that row of limping spondees which tells of Ceres' pain, is thrillingly appropriate. Bespoke, the music fits the sense like a glove.

How would Poe have written on the same theme? I have ventured to invent his opening stanza.

> It was noon in the fair field of Enna,
>   When Proserpina gathering flowers—
>   Herself the most fragrant of flowers,
> Was gathered away to Gehenna
>   By the Prince of Plutonian powers;
> Was borne down the windings of Brenner
>   To the gloom of his amorous bowers—
> Down the tortuous highway of Brenner
>   To the God's agapemonous bowers.

The parody is not too outrageous to be critically beside the point; and anyhow the music is genuine Poe. That permanent wave is unquestionably an *ondulation de chez Edgar.* The much too musical metre is (to change the metaphor once more) like a rich chasuble, so stiff with gold and gems that it stands unsupported, a carapace of jewelled sound, into which the sense, like some snotty little seminarist, irrelevantly creeps and is lost. This music of Poe's—how much less really musical it is than that which, out of his nearly neutral decasyllables. Milton fashioned on purpose to fit the slender beauty of Proserpine, the strength and swiftness of the ravisher and her mother's heavy, despairing sorrow!

Of the versification of **"The Raven"** Poe says, in his "Philosophy of Composition":

> My first object (as usual) was originality. The extent to which this has been neglected, in versifica-tion, is one of the most unaccountable things in the world. Admitting that there is little possibility of variety in mere *rhythm*, it is still clear that the possible varieties of metre and stanza are absolutely infinite—and yet, *for centuries, no man, in verse, has ever done, or ever seemed to think of doing, an original thing.*

This fact, which Poe hardly exaggerates, speaks volumes for the good sense of the poets. Feeling that almost all strikingly original metres and stanzas were only illegitimate short cuts to a music which, when reached, turned out to be but a poor and vulgar substitute for individual music, they wisely stuck to the less blantantly musical metres of tradition. The ordinary iambic decasyllable, for example, is intrinsically musical enough to be just able, when required, to stand up by itself. But its musical stiffness can easily be taken out of it. It can be now a chasuble, a golden carapace of sound, now, if the poet so desires, a pliant, soft and, musically speaking, almost neutral material, out of which he can fashion a special music of his own to fit his thoughts and feelings in all their incessant transformations. Good landscape painters seldom choose a "picturesque" subject; they want to paint their own picture, not have it imposed on them by nature. In the thoroughly paintable little places of this world you will generally find only bad painters. (It's so easy to paint the thoroughly paintable.) The good ones prefer the unspectacular neutralities of the Home Counties to those Cornish coves and Ligurian fishing villages, whose picturesqueness is the delight of all those who have no pictures of their own to project on to the canvas. It is the same with poetry: good poets avoid what I may call, by analogy, "musicesque" metres, preferring to create their own music out of raw materials as nearly as possible neutral. Only bad poets, or good poets against their better judgment, and by mistake, go to the Musicesque for their material. "For centuries no man, in verse, has ever done, or ever seemed to think of doing, an original thing." It remained for Poe and the other nineteenth century metrists to do it; Procrusteslike, they tortured and amputated significance into fitting the ready-made music of their highly original metres and stanzas. The result was, in most cases, as vulgar as a Royal Academy Sunrise on Ben Nevis (with Highland Cattle) or a genuine hand-painted sketch of Portofino.

How could a judge so fastidious as Baudelaire listen to Poe's music and remain unaware of its vulgarity? A happy ignorance of English versification preserved him, I fancy, from this realization. His own imitations of mediaeval hymns prove how far he was from understanding the first principles of versification in a language where the stresses are not, as in French, equal, but essentially and insistently uneven. In his Latin poems Baudelaire makes the ghost of Bernard of Cluny write as though he had learned his art from Racine. The principles of English versification are much the same as those of mediaeval Latin. If Baudelaire could discover lines composed of equally stressed syllables in Bernard, he must also have discovered them in Poe. Interpreted according to Racinian principles, such verses as

> It was down by the dank tarn of Auber,
> In the ghoul-haunted woodland of Weir

must have taken on, for Baudelaire, heaven knows what exotic subtlety of rhythm. We can never hope to guess what that ghoul-haunted woodland means to a Frenchman possessing only a distant and theoretical knowledge of our language.

Returning now to **"Ulalume,"** we find that its too poetical metre has the effect of vulgarizing by contagion what would be otherwise perfectly harmless and refined technical devices. Thus, even the very mild alliterations in "the ghoul-haunted woodland of Weir" seem to protest too much. And yet an iambic verse beginning "Woodland of Weir, ghoul-haunted," would not sound in the least over-poetical. It is only in the dactylic environment that those two w's strike one as protesting too much.

And then there are the proper names. Well used, proper names can be relied on to produce the most thrilling musical-magical effects. But use them without discretion, and the magic evaporates into abracadabrical absurdity, or becomes its own mocking parody; the over-emphatic music shrills first into vulgarity and finally into ridiculousness. Poe tends to place his proper names in the most conspicuous position in the line (he uses them constantly as rhyme words), showing them off—these magical-musical jewels—as the *rastacouaire* might display the twin cabochon emeralds at his shirt cuffs and the platinum wrist watch, with his monogram in diamonds. These proper-name rhyme-jewels are particularly flashy in Poe's case because they are mostly dissyllabic. Now, the dissyllabic rhyme in English is poetically so precious and so conspicuous by its richness that, if it is not perfect in itself and perfectly used, it emphatically ruins what it was meant emphatically to adorn. Thus, sound and association make of "Thule" a musical-magical proper name of exceptional power. But when Poe writes,

> I have reached these lands but newly
> From an ultimate dim Thule,

he spoils the effect which the word ought to produce by insisting too much, and incompetently, on its musicality. He shows off his jewel as conspicuously as he can, but only reveals thereby the badness of its setting and his own Levantine love of display. For "newly" does not rhyme with "Thule"—or only rhymes on condition that you pronounce the adverb as though you were a Bengali, or the name as though you came from Whitechapel. The paramour of Goethe's king rhymed perfectly with the name of his kingdom; and when Laforgue wrote of that "roi de Thulé, Immaculé" his *rime riche* was entirely above suspicion. Poe's rich rhymes, on the contrary, are seldom above suspicion. That dank tarn of Auber is only very dubiously a fit poetical companion for the tenth month, and though Mount Yaanek is, *ex hypothesi,* a volcano, the rhyme with volcanic is, frankly, impossible. On other occasions Poe's proper names rhyme not only well enough, but actually, in the particular context, much too well. Dead D'Elormie, in **"The Bridal Ballad,"** is prosodically in order, because Poe had brought his ancestors over with the Conqueror (as he also imported the ancestors of that Guy de Vere who wept his tear over Lenore) for the express purpose of providing a richly musical-magical rhyme to "bore me" and "before me." Dead D'Elormie is first cousin to Edward Lear's aged Uncle Arly, sitting on a heap of Barley—ludicrous; but also (unlike dear Uncle Arly) horribly vulgar, because of the too musical lusciousness of his invented name and his display, in all tragical seriousness, of an obviously faked Norman pedigree. Dead D'Elormie is a poetical disaster. (pp. 31-7)

Aldous Huxley, "From 'Vulgarity in Literature'," in Poe: A Collection of Critical Essays, edited by Robert Regan, Prentice-Hall, Inc., 1967, pp. 31-7.

Joseph Auslander (essay date 1938)

[*In the following excerpt, Auslander asserts that Poe's poetry is both brilliant and unnatural, theorizing that these qualities stem from the poet's frustrated, tortured life.*]

In 1827, when only nineteen, [Poe] had published a volume of poems. It contained forty pages of verse, and was called *Tamerlane and Other Poems, by a Bostonian.* Of course, Poe, though born in Boston, usually preferred to call himself a "Virginian." But the book appeared in Boston, and might sell better if advertised as being written by a native son. When it suited Poe, he could juggle localities and loyalties. Probably he got a thrill out of such posturing. He was to show all his life a love for nom de plumage and romantic parades and hoaxes. They gave him a sense of secret superiority, and blended into the growing mythology and masquerade he was to create for his own consolation and deception.

"Tamerlane" was not much of a poem—the kind a number of boys of nineteen have written. A second volume published in Baltimore in 1829 was also of little account. But Poe's *Poems,* brought out in New York in 1831, showed that, in turning from life into his own dreams, he had begun to make a strange and mysterious beauty. He put in this volume the brief lyric **"To Helen,"** with its romantic yearning:

> On desperate seas long wont to roam,
> Thy hyacinth hair, thy classic face,
> Thy Naiad airs have brought me home
> To the glory that was Greece
> And the grandeur that was Rome.

He wrote of Israfel, the angel who sang so wildly well in Heaven that

> Tottering above
> In her highest noon,
> The enamoured Moon
> Blushes with love,
> While, to listen, the red levin
> (With the rapid Pleiads, even
> Which were seven),
> Pauses in Heaven

(pp. 120-21)

There was nothing ordinary in such poetry. These lines showed a poet reaching with startling success into a world of imagination for the magnificence he could not find in the everyday world about him. To some extent, at least, all poets do this. Poe, who was to do it perhaps more than any of them, revealed in these early poems the zest and intensity with which he could abandon the real for unreality. (p. 122)

Poe wrote few poems, and, although his tales are more numerous, not a great amount of prose either. He is a proof of the fact that quality in writing is far more important than quantity, for he has come to have a place both in poetry and prose among the unforgettable creators.

There is something in this that seems puzzling. Poe's poems are many of them imitative and melodramatic. He absorbed the glamour of Coleridge, in reading whose poetry he says he trembled "like one who stands upon a volcano, conscious from the very darkness bursting from the crater, of the fire and light that are weltering below." Though he bitterly assailed Longfellow and others because he thought they had stolen phrases and ideas from him and other writers, he borrowed many himself; and **"The Raven,"** published in 1845, certainly owes a great deal to Mrs. Browning's poem, "Lady Geraldine's Courtship," brought out in the previous year. Mrs. Browning had written:

> With a murmurous stir uncertain, in the air, the purple curtain
> Swelleth in and swelleth out around her motionless pale brows;
> While the gliding of the river sends a rippling noise for ever
> Through the open casement whitened by the moonlight's scant repose.
>
> Said he—"Vision of a lady! stand there silent, stand there steady!
> Now I see it plainly, plainly; now I cannot hope or doubt—
> There, the brows of mild repression—there, the lips of silent passion,
> Curv'd like an archer's bow to send the bitter arrows out."

The similarity in metre and rhyme and even in certain words is easily seen.

Yet, as we read Poe, his debts and his stealings seem a small matter. There is something about his poetry that is wholly original. If we wish to understand this, we have only to remind ourselves of his strange life. As we look on it, we see that he was strangely frustrated in the everyday world. Probably, under the best of circumstances, he would have found it a difficult place, but he lived in a growing, successful country where leisure for art was small; he was brought up by foster parents who taught him pride, could not give him sympathy, and denied him money; he was tragically susceptible to drink; he entered manhood with a series of failures behind him. All this threw him into his haunted dream world as no poet was ever thrown, and because he had been so fully rejected in his experience with reality, he made unreality more real than any other poet!

This is not the explanation Poe gave of his art, but it is harmonious with that explanation. Poe said he wrote as he did because he sought "Art for Beauty's sake." He found his duty in Taste—"Taste waging war upon Vice solely on the ground of her deformity—her disproportion—her animosity to the fitting, to the appropriate, to the harmonious . . . in a word, to Beauty." This was a sufficiently good description of Poe's own poetry, but the poetry came first and the description afterward. And it was because Poe had actually lived and suffered more in the realm of imagination than in his everyday world that he could give such intense and exact images, that his Beauty, freed from reality, could be so severely true to its own eerie and terrible self.

And what shall be said of this beauty? We enter it to walk amid bizarre and terrific towers. We are shadowed by mysterious skies, we stand by dark waters. The poet shuts out the sun. It sifts only through thick leafage or stained glass or heavy arras. Perfume comes to us, but it emanates not from flowers, but censers invisibly agitated; it is stealthy and overpowering. We see light, but of tapers and torches wind-shaken, whose writhing shadows are more important than their flame. Graves yawn, caskets disgorge. Feelings of nameless horror float in the air like mist.

This is very different poetry from the human verse of Shakespeare, the simple but exalted truth of Wordsworth, the rich but quiet beauty of Keats. Poe's lines are unnatural, brilliant, fearful in comparison with the work of these more normal poets.

Yet his poetry has its value. There is a kind of terrible mathematical power in his lurid words. He seems to dissolve the substance of speech and give old syllables a new intensity:

> The skies they were ashen and sober;
> The leaves they were crisped and sere,—
> The leaves they were withering and sere,—
> It was night in the lonesome October
> Of my most immemorial year;
> It was hard by the dim lake of Auber,
> In the misty mid-region of Weir,—
> It was down by the dank tarn of Auber,
> In the ghoul-haunted woodland of Weir.

"Auber," "Weir," what and where are they? The poet says them, and they are. So are his "dank tarn," the "misty mid-region," the unnatural leaves. He has brought up from his brooding a severe distillation of sound and atmosphere, has created out of his tortured dream-experience something that is weirdly superb.

Such poetry seems unnatural to many; certainly it is abnormal, yet Poe, with an iced lucidity, gives it a firm artistic form that we must admire for its almost inhuman magnificence. Writing from among the shadows of his soul, he made a beauty so stringent, so close to perfection that it gives, as the French poet Baudelaire says, a "taste of eternity."

Yet it is human, too. We are all to some degree frustrated. We have all known despair. We get in the music of Poe's suppressed experience magnified echoes of our own troubled souls. We know in some degree the hell that was in his heart, the black fire banked up and threatening to break through. Even his wild hallucinations, grotesque lamps and waving arras, dim cities and leaden seas, rouse a familiarity in us. Poe, the high priest of despair, has suffered darker contradictions in his soul than most of us have known, but they are, after all, human contradictions.

So we accept him, terror and horror and agony. We may like the quietly mournful **"Annabel Lee,"** and lines of simple grief like

> Ah! broken is the golden bowl! the spirit flown forever.

Yet we find his most inspired poetry and his most haunting rhythms in his more "unnatural" moods. In these, striding through a dream of mingled pain and splendour, he uttered lines like

> The viol, the violet and the vine,

and made those refrains that beat the mood of his verse into the depth of our souls. This poetry, with its sound and emotion, intensifies our sense of human experience. It has little obvious meaning, but through its dark and glittering perfection it somehow lifts higher for us the significance of life. (pp. 126-29)

Joseph Auslander, "The Poet of Ravens and Lost Ladies," in Muse Anthology of Modern Poetry, *Poe memorial edition, edited by Dorothy Kissling and Arthur E. Nethercot, Carlyle Straub Publishers, 1938, pp. 116-29.*

Arthur Hobson Quinn   (essay date 1941)

[An early twentieth-century American critic, editor, and biographer, Quinn was a strong proponent of American literature before it gained widespread appreciation and critical acceptance. He taught the first graduate course devoted to American literature and edited the first collection of national drama. In addition, he wrote several comprehensive critical and historical surveys of American literature that are respected for their accurate and original research. In the following excerpt from his critical biography of Poe, Hobson determines the value of the scientific ideas presented in Eureka *in relation to the latest nineteenth-century scientific discoveries.]*

Since **Eureka** was to a certain extent the climax of Poe's creative achievement, to which he had devoted so much time and effort, it is of great importance in his biography. An analysis of it will decide whether Poe's mind was weakening during these last years or whether it was clear, active, and still creative. For the true life of Poe lay in the mind of Poe. (p. 541)

[Poe asked] that the work be considered as a poem, but his modern critics have refused to accept this limitation. They insist upon judging it as a scientific treatise, and with a certain amount of reason in their position. If the scientific ideas in **Eureka** are wild and incoherent, or were written without knowledge of what had been discovered in Poe's own day, the essay may be dismissed as unimportant so far as its thinking is concerned. If, on the other hand, it is based on accurate knowledge of the latest scientific discoveries of its *own time*, then it is entitled from that point of view to respect.

No one would, I fancy, claim that Poe has solved the riddle of the creation and the destiny of the universe. But then no one else, scientist or philosopher, has solved it. It is likewise unwise to claim that he has anticipated the mathematical systems of Einstein and other contemporary scientific philosophers. It is enough and quite enough to note in what respect certain of his ideas resemble the greater discoveries of modern times, and to hear what Emerson called in another connection "the far off gathering of the intuition." (p. 542)

[Poe was not], as has been frequently stated, entering in 1848 upon a period of mental decline. His mind was clear and his imaginative power was still capable of dealing with scientific problems that tax the best of modern thinkers. How far he might have proceeded had he possessed adequate technical training we can only surmise. That **Eureka** produced little effect upon the science of its own day is not surprising. Its concepts were in most cases, unusual, and the hospitality of science to unusual theories, especially those of men of letters, is not large.

And yet, ironically, the general reader must have the help of a scientist in reading the essay, for the ideas are not readily grasped. Even when they are, the mysticism of the essay is forbidding to those who are realistically inclined. Poe's message is not to these, and yet as [Sir Arthur] Eddington says, "It is reasonable to inquire whether in the mystical illusions of man there is not a reflection of an underlying reality."

Certainly as a prose poem **Eureka** rises to a lofty height. Poe's conception of the relations of God and man, of the Creator for the created, is one of the important steps taken during the Nineteenth and Twentieth Centuries in that spiritual succession in which William Vaughn Moody and Eugene O'Neill are other figures. When that spiritual progress is fully understood, then perhaps at last **Eureka** will come into its own. (p.557)

Arthur Hobson Quinn, in his Edgar Allan Poe: A Critical Biography, *D. Appleton-Century Company Incorporated, 1941, 804 p.*

W. H. Auden   (essay date 1950)

[Auden, an Anglo-American essayist, dramatist, critic, editor, and translator, is considered a major twentieth-century poet and an influential literary figure. His early poetry and criticism are informed by the psychological and political theories of Sigmund Freud and Karl Marx; his later work is heavily influenced by his conversion to Christianity. Auden believed that an artist's work is by its nature evolutionary and responsive to the changing moral and ideological climate of the age. Among his best-known critical works are The Enchafed Flood; or, The Romantic Iconography of the Sea *(1950),* The Dyer's Hand, and Other Essays *(1962), and* Forewords and Afterwords *(1973). In the following excerpt originally published as the introduction to* Edgar Allan Poe: Selected Prose, Poetry, and Eureka, *Auden examines Poe's career and writings, concurring with Paul Valéry's critical conclusions concerning* Eureka *(see excerpt dated 1924).]*

What every author hopes to receive from posterity—a hope usually disappointed—is justice. Next to oblivion, the two fates which he most fears are becoming the name attached to two or three famous pieces while the rest of his work is unread and becoming the idol of a small circle which reads every word he wrote with the same uncritical reverence. The first fate is unjust because, even if the pieces known are indeed his best work, the reader has not earned the right to say so; the second fate is embarrassing and ridiculous, for no author believes he is that good.

Poe's shade must be more disappointed than most. Certain pieces—how he must hate these old war horses—are probably more familiar to non-Americans than are any pieces by any other American author. I myself cannot remember hearing any poetry before hearing **"The Raven"** and **"The Bells"**; and *The Pit and the Pendulum* was one of the first short stories I ever read. At the same time, the known works of no other author of comparable rank and productivity are so few and so invariably the same. In preparing to make this selection, for example, I asked a number of persons whom I knew to be widely read, but not specialists in American letters, if they had read *Gordon Pym* and **Eu-**

reka, which seem to me to rank among Poe's most important works; not one of them had. On the other hand, I was informed by everyone that to omit *The Cask of Amontillado,* which for my taste is an inferior story, would be commercial suicide. Poor Poe! At first so forgotten that his grave went without a tombstone twenty-six years—when one was finally erected the only American author to attend the ceremony was Whitman; and today in danger of becoming the life study of a few professors. The professors are, of course, very necessary, for it is through their devoted labors that Poe may finally reach the kind of reader every author hopes for, who will read him all, good-humoredly willing to wade through much which is dull or inferior for the delight of discovering something new and admirable. (pp. 209-10)

Poe's best poems are not his most typical or original. **"To Helen,"** which could have been written by Landor, and **"The City in the Sea,"** which could have been written by Hood, are more successfully realized than a poem like **"Ulalume,"** which could have been written by none but Poe.

His difficulty as a poet was that he was interested in too many poetic problems and experiments at once for the time he had to give to them. To make the result conform to the intention—and the more experimental the intention, the more this is true—a writer has to keep his hand in by continual practice. The prose writer who must earn his living has this advantage, that even the purest hack work is practice in his craft; for the penniless poet there is no corresponding exercise. Without the leisure to write and rewrite he cannot develop to his full stature. When we find fault with Poe's poems we must never forget his own sad preface to them.

> In defence of my own taste, it is incumbent upon me to say that I think nothing in this volume of much value to the public, or very creditable to myself. Events not to be controlled have prevented me from making, at any time, any serious effort in what, under happier circumstances, would have been the field of my choice.

For faulty they must be admitted to be. The trouble with **"The Raven,"** for example, is that the thematic interest and the prosodic interest, both of which are considerable, do not combine and are even often at odds.

In *The Philosophy of Composition* Poe discusses his difficulties in preventing the poem from becoming absurd and artificial. The artificiality of the lover asking the proper series of questions to which the refrain would be appropriate could be solved by making him a self-torturer. The difficulty of the speaker of the refrain, however, remained insoluble until the poet hit on the notion of something nonhuman. But the effect could still be ruined unless the narration of the story, as distinct from the questions and answers, flowed naturally; and the meter Poe chose, with its frequent feminine rhymes, so rare in English, works against this and at times defeats him.

> Not the least obeisance made he; not a minute stopped or stayed he;
> But with mien of lord or lady, perched above my chamber door.

Here it is the meter alone and nothing in the speaker or the situation which is responsible for the redundant alternatives of "stopped or stayed he" and "lord or lady."

Similarly, **"Ulalume"** is an interesting experiment in diction but only an experiment, for the poem is about something which never quite gets said because the sense is sacrificed to the vowel sounds. It is an accident if the sound of a place name corresponds to the emotion the place invokes, and the accidental is a comic quality. Edward Lear, the only poet, apparently, to be directly influenced by Poe, succeeds with such names as "The Hills of the Chankly Bore" because he is frankly writing "nonsense" poetry, but **"Ulalume"** has a serious subject and the comic is out of place. **"The Bells,"** though much less interesting a conception than **"Ulalume,"** is more successful because the subject is nothing but an excuse for onomatopoeic effects.

There remains, however, *Eureka.* The man who had flatly asserted that no poem should much exceed a hundred lines in length—"that music (in its modifications of rhythm and rhyme) is of so vast a moment to Poesy as never to be neglected by him who is truly poetical," that neither Truth, the satisfaction of the Intellect, nor Passion, the excitement of the Heart, are the province of Poetry but only Beauty, and that the most poetical topic in the world is the death of a beautiful woman—this man produces at the end of his life a work which he insists is a poem and commends to posterity as his crowning achievement, though it violates every article in his critical creed. It is many pages in length, it is written in prose, it handles scientific ideas in the truth of which the poet is passionately convinced, and the general subject is the origin and destiny of the universe.

Outside France the poem has been neglected, but I do not think Poe was wrong in the importance he attached to it. In the first place, it was a very daring and original notion to take the oldest of the poetic themes—older even than the story of the epic hero—namely, cosmology, the story of how things came to exist as they do, and treat it in a completely contemporary way, to do in English in the nineteenth century what Hesiod and Lucretius had done in Greek and Latin centuries before. Secondly, it is full of remarkable intuitive guesses that subsequent scientific discoveries have confirmed. As Paul Valéry says [see excerpt dated 1924]:

> It would not be exaggerating its importance to recognize, in his theory of consistency, a fairly definite attempt to describe the universe by its *intrinsic properties.* The following proposition can be found toward the end of *Eureka*: "Each law of nature depends at all points on all the other laws." This might easily be considered, if not as a formula, at least as the expression of a tendency toward generalized relativity.
>
> That its tendency approaches recent conceptions becomes evident when one discovers, in the poem under discussion, an affirmation of the *symmetrical* and reciprocal relationship of matter, time, space, gravity, and light.

Lastly, it combines in one work nearly all of Poe's characteristic obsessions: the passion for merging in union with the one which is at the root of tales like *Ligeia,* the passion for logic which dominates the detective and cryptographic studies, the passion for a final explanation and reconciliation which informs the melancholy of much of his verse—

all are brought together in this poem of which the prose is as lucid, as untheatrical, as the best of his critical prose. (pp. 213-15)

W. H. Auden, "Edgar Allan Poe," in his Forewords and Afterwords, *edited by Edward Mendelson. Random House, Inc., 1973, pp. 209-20.*

Anthony Caputi   (essay date 1953)

[*Caputi is an American essayist and academic. In the following excerpt, he examines Poe's versatile use of the refrain in his poetry, exploring as well the poet's reasons for employing this device.*]

Edgar Allan Poe's use of the refrain constitutes a valuable index to his literary practice and to the relation between his practice and theory. An examination of the refrain in his poetry can be helpful in clarifying the disparity between his merits and the frequent puerility of even his best poems. Before turning to his work, however, it is perhaps necessary to distinguish the refrain as a literary device from such related devices as simple repetition, incremental repetition, and parallel structure by limiting it to thematic, patterned repetition. Poe's poetry abounds in all these devices, and sometimes they seem to blur into one another. But refrain can usually be isolated on the basis of its thematic character, whether it consists of the repetition of a single word or of a unit as large as a stanza.

Poe's most complete discussion of the refrain occurs, unfortunately, in a work which critics have viewed with great suspicion. But whatever "The Philosophy of Composition" (1846) may or may not reveal about the composition of **"The Raven,"** it probably sets forth accurately some of Poe's opinions on aesthetic and technical matters. Certainly there is no reason to question his remarks on the general nature of the refrain, since they clearly describe the theory of the refrain which he practiced in his later poems. (p. 169)

Taken as a whole, Poe's poetry reveals that he used the refrain much more extensively in his later work than in his early work. Only two of the poems published in *Tamerlane and Other Poems* (1827) have refrains. Fourteen poems with refrains were included in Griswold's edition in 1850; and though that number included the two of the 1827 volume and at least one other early poem, **"To One in Paradise,"** the evidence favors the conclusion that the remaining eleven were completed within the last five or six years of the poet's life. Even **"Bridal Ballad,"** the present form of which is ascribed to 1837, reveals that Poe tinkered with its refrain considerably later. His use of the refrain in the final years of his life almost amounted to a dependence.

Traces of the theory of the refrain set forth in "The Philosophy of Composition" can be discerned in the earliest poems using the refrain. These poems might be called experimental, since each represents an attempt at quite different effects. **"The happiest day . . . "** (1827) repeats the initial line, "The happiest day—the happiest hour," in the fourth stanza, but hardly involves any manipulation of it for its multiple meanings. The line is deceptive in its initial occurrence; but the nostalgia which attaches to it in the first stanza, when "the happiest day" is placed in the past,

is rather intensified than qualified by the repetition of the line. The **"Song," "I saw thee on thy bridal day"** (1827), presents the first working out of Poe's theory of the "improved" refrain. Opening with the lines

I saw thee on thy bridal day—
    When a burning blush came o'er thee,
Though happiness around thee lay,
    The world all love before thee:

the poem repeats the last two lines without, and the first two with slight variation in the last stanza. The intermediate stanzas elaborate on the "burning blush," showing that it is not the conventional blush of the bride, but the result of the unlooked-for presence of an admirer. This complication renders ironic the repetition at the end of the poem of the lines

Though happiness around thee lay,
The world all love before thee.

It is even probable that the poet was punning on the word "before," placing emphasis on the notion of futurity in line four, but on the meaning "in front of" in line sixteen. This technique, it is apparent, could be productive of very subtle shadings in emotional complexity. Unfortunately, the repetition of lines one and two, with substitutions and additions which Poe apparently felt necessary for proper emphasis, exemplifies the rhetorical puerility which too often vitiates his most interesting effects.

In addition to the poems of the 1827 edition, at least one other early poem throws light on Poe's developing theory of the refrain. **"To One in Paradise"** (1835) does not use a refrain-line at all, but what might be called a refrain-word, a word, that is, which is repeated in pattern and which is the "nucleus of the poetic utterance." The word which fills this function in **"To One in Paradise"** is "all." In the first stanza it occurs three times, constituting an intense affirmation of the fulness of the speaker's experience during his beloved's lifetime.

Thou wast that all to me, love,
    For which my soul did pine—
A green isle in the sea, love,
    A fountain and a shrine,
All wreathed with fairy fruits and flowers,
    And all the flowers were mine.

With an appropriate shift to the present tense the last stanza repeats "all" twice, turning its initial implications back upon themselves by emphasizing the completeness of the reversal from fulness to emptiness, from joy to joylessness.

Poe's experimentation with the range of effects obtainable through the refrain bore fruit in the poems which hardened into final form between 1844 and 1849. Though most of these poems involve weaknesses of various kinds, behind all of them is discernible the purpose of fashioning simple materials to make them refract complexity. Like **"I saw thee on thy bridal day," "Bridal Ballad"** presents a vignette contrasting the surface bliss of a wedding scene with the inner struggle of the bride. The refrain, "And I am happy now," is repeated with slight variation at the end of each stanza, at first expressing the bride's joy, but gradually, as she reflects on her dead lover and her promises to him, nucleating her doubts and misgivings. It mounts in complexity with each repetition, until in the fourth stanza, where it is repeated twice, it brings the poem to a climax in the lines.

> And, though my faith be broken,
> And, though my heart be broken,
> Here is the ring as token
>   That I am happy now.

However picayune the art involved in the first two of these lines, they should not obscure the fact that the passage achieves a highly effective climax: in the temporary success of the present struggling against the past the poem attains a precarious emotional plateau which is held to the end.

In **"Eldorado"** (1849) and **"The Raven"** (1845) Poe apparently turned to the technique developed in **"To One in Paradise"**; but instead of playing the refrain-word off against itself, he used two refrain-words, playing them off against each other. This is perhaps more applicable to **"Eldorado"** than to **"The Raven."** In **"Eldorado"** the refrain-words "shadow" and **"Eldorado"** both rhyme and contrast through four stanzas. They constitute a kind of duet in which each voice qualifies the other, while the combination of the two embodies the theme. **"The Raven,"** on the other hand, does not represent so much a duet as conjunctive solos. Despite all that Poe has said about his selection of "Nevermore" and the method by which he qualified its meaning in successive stanzas, he failed to mention that "Nevermore" has a complement in "nothing more" in the early part of the poem. Of all the patterns of repetition worked into the poem, only these refrain-words and their interrelations constitute more than an attempt at rhetorical emphasis and phonetic lushness. Enough has been said already by Poe and others about the qualification of "Nevermore" in the last seven stanzas of the poem. It should, however, be noted that "Nevermore" functions primarily to qualify "nothing more." The first seven stanzas create the atmosphere of desolation, and desolation which is primarily spiritual, but which also vaguely includes everything beyond the door past which the speaker cannot see. This sense of desolation centers in the refrain-word in these stanzas, "nothing more." The raven introduces "Nevermore" at the end of stanza eight; and thereafter "Nevermore" serves as a reply to the bereaved questioner, finally becoming emblematic of his subjective state. As the sign of his pessimistic melancholy it is an explanation of "nothing more." Only after the raven has become symbolic, after the full extent of the questioner's loss and the degree of his perversity and self-pity are apparent, do the questioner's isolation and self-limitation to "nothing more" become meaningful.

In view of these remarks on **"The Raven"** Poe's claim that the poet must begin with his "*dénouement* constantly in mind" clarifies another of his ideas on the subject of form. **"The Raven"** suggests, as **"Dreamland"** (1844) and **"Ulalume"** (1847) clearly show, that Poe was interested in the kind of circular form that can be achieved through a judicious use of refrain, a form wherein the latter part of the poem comes back upon the beginning. The first stanza of **"Dreamland"** sets forth in concrete terms, however vague and indefinite, the state of mind to be equated with dreaming.

> By a route obscure and lonely,
>   Haunted by ill-angels only,
> Where an Eidolon, named NIGHT,

> On a black throne reigns upright,
> I have reached these lands but newly
>   From an ultimate dim Thule—
> From a wide weird clime that lieth, sublime,
>   Out of SPACE—out of TIME.

There is no immediate hint beyond that provided by the title that the journey described is wholly subjective. The description proceeds, detailing "bottomless vales" and "boundless floods," "seas that restlessly aspire" and "dismal tarns and pools"; but it does not establish a palpable connection with its tenor, the mind, until the penultimate stanza. By a process of suggestion the speaker gradually makes clear that he is speaking about the mind, not the mind as it becomes while dreaming, but the mind as it always is, and as it reveals itself in the dream-state. Once this connection is established, the speaker draws back at the spectacle:

> But the traveller, travelling through it;
> May not—dare not openly view it;

and the poem concludes with the repetition of the first six lines of the first stanza. The circle of the journey is completed by the substitution of "I have wandered home but newly" for "I have reached these lands but newly," leaving the reader with the impenetrable images with which the poem had begun.

"Ulalume" is ordered on much the same principle. Though **"Ulalume"** makes much more extensive use of incremental repetition in the interests of intensification and the kind of emphasis and intricate rhyme that can be observed in **"The Raven,"** like **"Dreamland,"** its theme is organized by the crucial repetition of a descriptive passage emblematic of a state of mind. The poem opens with a similar description of a place into which the speaker is journeying.

> The skies they were ashen and sober;
>   The leaves they were crisped and sere—
>   The leaves they were withering and sere;
> It was night in the lonesome October
>   Of my most immemorial year;
> It was hard by the dim lake of Auber,
>   In the misty mid region of Weir—
> It was down by the dank tarn of Auber,
>   In the ghoul-haunted woodland of Weir.

Again, there is no immediate hint that the description is wholly subjective. Only gradually, after the debate between body and soul, Psyche and Astarte, has begun and the problem of choice has arisen, does the speaker become conscious of his familiarity with the quality of mind which he is describing. First, he recognizes it as love, for he has been to this place before; and then, almost immediately, he recognizes it as love-melancholy, for the place is associated not only with love, but also with the death of the speaker's beloved. The paradox resulting from the fact that the same place, the same mind, must beget both emotions is, of course, a peculiarity of a mind of pronounced idealistic turn: the idealist can love only once; for him the *grand amour* usurps the mind completely. The poem closes on this paradox and, by a final repetition of the opening descriptive passage, turns in on itself, much as its subject, the mind, turns in on itself. Many things are to be regretted in **"Ulalume,"** but certainly its conception is not among them.

Poe's versatility with the refrain was not exhausted, however, with **"Ulalume"** and **"Dreamland,"** though it probably never took a better direction. In **"For Annie"** (1849) the lines "Now in my bed," "that you fancy me dead," and "the fever called living" rather anticlimactically qualify the theme of peace in death, since the theme is very baldly stated in the lines

> For a man never slept
> In a different bed;
> And, to *sleep*, you must slumber
> In just such a bed.

In **"Annabel Lee"** (1849?) the repetition of "Annabel Lee" and the phrase "In the kingdom by the sea" probably comes closer to purely phonetic repetition than to refrain; but the contrast between the booming-receding onomatopoeia of the latter line and the serenity of the name re-enforces the irony of lying down by the side of Annabel Lee, while she lies by the side of the sea. The poem which represents Poe's most ambitious effort with the refrain and at the same time his most colossal failure is **"The Bells."** **"The Bells"** (1849) furnishes final proof, if such proof is necessary, that ingenious technique never made poetry. Poe's purpose in the poem was apparently to synthesize the ambivalences of experience by underscoring heavily the multifaceted complexity of a single object. To accomplish this purpose, he mustered the most intricate patterns of rhyme, vowel-motives, and refrains to be found in his poetry. Beginning with the sleigh bells, he qualifies "bells" all down the line: first wedding bells, then alarum bells, and finally funeral bells. Each repetition of the "Bells, bells, bells" refrain theoretically folds in another area of experience. Out of the welter the "Bells" refrain emerges in the last stanza in duet with the lines

> Keeping time, time, time,
> In a sort of Runic rhyme,

building to a frenzy in answer to the implicit question: "Who is responsible?" Poe's versatility was never more in evidence than here, and never more ineffectual.

But if **"The Bells"** marks the high tide of Poe's ineffectuality, it also bears testimony to his immense gift for poetic conception and thereby confronts us with the peculiar problem of this poet. Whatever might be said in praise of Poe's gift for poetic conception, there is a discrepancy between it and the means by which he attempted to transmute conception into poetry. Inferior technique might provide part of the answer; but it does not provide all of the answer, as many of the poems thus far reviewed attest. The rest of the answer is probably to be found in Poe's attitude toward technique, a key to which is offered by two poems which use the refrain but which were not well conceived. **"Lenore"** (1844) and **"A Dream Within a Dream"** (1849?) contain the rhetoric of certain passages of **"The Raven"** and **"Ulalume,"** but no sign of a controlling intention. In **"Lenore"** the refrain "died so young" is introduced in the first stanza, qualified in the second, but dropped thereafter. **"A Dream Within a Dream"** fails to move out of the title, which is repeated at the end of each of its two stanzas. These poems almost confirm what the others too frequently suggest: that Poe was not above using the refrain for whatever return it might bring.

Poe believed that Beauty existed in eternity, that terrestrial life was graced by only the most fugitive reflections of it. The best the poet could hope to do was catch as many of these reflected lights in his poetry as possible; and, as Yvor Winters has put it, "Poe had certain definite ideas in regard to which forms of human experience lent themselves best to this proceeding, and also in regard to the rules of procedure." (pp. 171-78)

[There is] every reason to believe that Poe viewed the refrain largely as a device, even a kind of trick, by which to produce emotional excitement. . . . [In "The Philosophy of Composition"] he made reference to the "artistic piquancy" which he hoped to achieve by it and compared it to "*points*, in the theatrical sense." It was, of course, only one of the group of devices which recur in his poetry with such distressing regularity. That he was frequently successful with the refrain suggests that he probably understood it better than he understood the other devices. At his worst his use of the refrain descends to sheer rhetoric. At his best the refrain is integral in his poetic conception, though frequently submerged in rhetoric of other kinds. But even when Poe's art is most in evidence, the art which conceals art is conspicuous by its absence. (p. 178)

> *Anthony Caputi, "The Refrain in Poe's Poetry," in* American Literature, *Vol. XXV, No. 2, May, 1953, pp. 169-78.*

Roy Harvey Pearce   (essay date 1961)

[*Pearce is an American educator, editor, and the author of* Colonial American Writing *(1951) and* The Continuity of American Poetry *(1961). In the following excerpt from the latter work, Pearce disparages what he views as Poe's desperate attempt to escape reality in his poetry.*]

Poe is quite obviously the poet of dream-work. The obviousness makes for a kind of over-insistence which to American readers at least must seem to be no less than vulgar. To recall the gross characteristics of the poems: metrical effects are forced until they become virtually hypnotic, and language is used primarily as it carries exotic, unworldly meaning, or can be made to do so. Thus in the opening lines of **"The Sleeper"**:

> At midnight, in the month of June,
> I stand beneath the mystic moon.
> An opiate vapor, dewy, dim,
> Exhales from out her golden rim,
> And, softly dripping, drop by drop,
> Upon the quiet mountain-top,
>
> Steals drowsily and musically
> Into the universal valley.

Here the effect is of a willed irrelevance to everyday reality. A place is described, but only so as to make locating it impossible, since the locale is set in a manner which cancels out its potential for being a locale. There persists only the fact that something has been done in such a way as immediately to make it a good deal less than something. In short, we sense the willed quality; and we are shocked into attention by it. The effect is everywhere in Poe's poems, even those with ostensibly firmer arguments, **"Annabel Lee"** and **"The City By the Sea,"** for example. The poem exists simply as an attention-getting device, but of an especially demanding sort. Indeed, in some of his more ambitious criticism, Poe was ready to settle on this as the chief aim of poetry. For what else is his inordinately technical criticism—and its corollary compulsion to free the "Imagination" from the toils of both the "Heart" (the emotions) and the "Intellect" (the reason)—but an insistence that the poet mind his business, which was chiefly one of expressive technique?

Expressive of what? one now asks. In Poe's poems the answer would seem to be: Expressive of itself, as "pure" expression. Then we must ask further what it meant for Poe to make poems whose sole strength consists in this extraordinary weakness. We can view him as what he appears to have set out to be—a kind of culture hero of the imagination. His contemporaries would worry much lest life turn out to be an empty dream, and he would show how in dreams there was manifest nothing less than the naked power of the imagination. It was, in point of fact, imaginative experience which Poe's anti-poetic society could make little use of—imaginative experience for its own sake, in belles lettres. Dream-work just happened to be the most obvious, because it was the wildest, form of imaginative experience. Fantasy could be willed away; dream-work could not.

The "official" philosophy of Poe's society, Scottish Common Sense, put such a low valuation on the products of the imagination that they were granted a right to exist only as they could lead to practical, "social" ends. The critics and imaginative writers whom Poe battled were nursed on Blair's *Rhetoric,* or any of a number of versions and imitations of it. He battled them in his criticism, certainly; and in doing so, used whatever philosophical help he could find in his wide-ranging but on the whole superficial reading. His principal weapon was his own genius and his devotion to the creative power, realizable in the supernally beautiful, that he knew to be beyond the ken of common sense and orthodox rhetoric. His work and his fate are wholly characteristic of those of his contemporaries—but pushed to tragic absurdity. "It is the curse of a certain order of mind," he wrote in his *Marginalia,* "that it can never rest satisfied with the consciousness of its ability to do a thing. Still less is it content with doing it. It must both know and show how it is done."

If Poe was a Coleridgean, it was not so much to promulgate Coleridgean doctrine as to verify his own sense of the purely expressive power of poetry. He read Coleridge as, say, Baudelaire read Swedenborg and Poe himself—not so much to learn, as to verify something he already knew. Hence his criticism is a useful guide to nothing but the sort of poems whose mode it rationalizes. Expounding not the name and nature of poetry but Poe's sensibility, it was in the end Poe's means of establishing, in discursive language, a way by which readers in his own time could leave behind their false, anti-poetic (and therefore, he was sure, anti-human) world and move toward his.

Much of the energy which Poe put into his creative work is specifically a product of his fierce resistance to his culture's almost universal claims for the overriding values of common sense. Critics of Poe have too often been taken in by him (as he was taken in by himself) and been brought to grant to his poetics and his poetry the kind of acultural purity with which he strove in vain to endow it. The fact of the matter is that this drive toward purity is so extreme, so neurotic, so lacking in reality principle that it cannot be understood unless it is put into its historical situation. Poe then appears as a man of genius trying desperately to realize himself among men who were sure not only that they had no need for genius of his kind but that they could also prove that such genius was at the very least an aberration from right reason.

Poe had neither the scholarly attainments (in spite of his display of learning) nor the sense of tradition (in spite of his appeals to his background) which might have integrated his creative work and given it a center grounded in the actuality of real life, actually lived-through. Without that center, his creative work could not, and cannot, sustain itself artistically. He seems to have been unable to comprehend, even on his own terms, such substantial workaday reality as his genius directed him to examine. It may well have been that his own terms were such as literally to destroy (not transform) that workaday reality. In any case, his mind and attainments were of the sort to forbid compromise with the anti-poetic world. He could not even use it as material for his poems. Driven to want to leave that world behind for the one he could create, he set himself apart from Emerson and his other major contemporaries. Poe had to grant an absolute disjunction between the world of common sense and the world of the imagination. The others were by and large concerned, in the name of man, to see the two worlds as one. (pp. 141-44)

[Nineteenth-century critics Evart and George Duyckinck concluded of Poe]:

> A certain longing of passion, without hearty animality, marked . . . early the ill-regulated disposition of a man of genius uncontrolled by the restraint of sound principle and profound literary motives. . . . [His] sensitive, spiritual organization, deriving no support from healthy moral powers, became ghostly and unreal. His rude contact with the world, which might have set up a novelist for life with materials of adventure, seems scarcely to have impinged upon his perceptions. His mind, walking in a vain show, was taught nothing by experience or suffering. Altogether wanting in the higher faculty of humor, he could extract nothing from the rough usages of the world but a cold, frivolous mockery of its plans and pursuits. His intellectual enjoyment was in the power of his mind over literature as an art; his skill, in forcing the mere letters of the alphabet, the dry elements of the dictionary, to take forms of beauty and apparent life which would command the admiration of the world. . . . He could afford to trust nothing to the things themselves, since [his writings] had no root in realities.

Such, then, was Poe's literary world and his manifest place in its life; and such was the larger world which, in creating that smaller literary world, had created him too. It was to move against that world, while perforce moving in it, that Poe came to feel his deepest and truest need, his vocation. And out of his vocation came his poems, such as they are.

Viewed thus, the poems can be seen to be of a piece with his detective stories and his fantasies. If the poems are only a little short of the hysterical in their assertion of the absolute power of the creative imagination, the detective stories are almost droll in their demonstration that common sense is itself powerless unless pushed to apparently ridiculous extremes—extremes, indeed, of the imagination. (p. 147)

In his poetry, Poe worked assiduously away from a sense of the figure toward a sense of the summoning-up. The movement is away from a **"Tamerlane"** (1827) and an **"Al Aaraaf"** (1829) toward a **"Raven"** (1845) and a **"Ulalume"** (1847): from poems which attempt to define, in allegorized autobiography, the situation of the poet, to poems which take that situation as a given and drawn forth from it the implication that the poetic must be disengaged from the "real" world if it is to survive and reveal "ultimate" meaning. That meaning is never discovered. Poe could speak *about* it in his critical writing and could describe the conditions for its realization in his fiction, but in his poems he wanted to do more than this, and failed inevitably. The ultimate meaning he sought could come only if it were possible to manage an absolute disjunction between the real world and the imagined. Strictly speaking, such meaning could not be put into words, since words were ineradicably tainted by the reality of the things and states to which they referred. All that Poe can do in his later poems is manipulate the sensibility in such a way as to indicate that something is about to be revealed—or has been, only we have been incapable of knowing it. But at least we know that we do not know, and now can grant the "real" existence of that borderland of consciousness into which Poe took Arthur Gordon Pym.

If we attend to the poems themselves and not to the hypotheses which derive from them in Poe's critical theorizing, all emphasis must necessarily be on the poem as self-assertive act. The early **"Dreams"** (1827) ends:

> I *have been* happy, though in a dream.
> I have been happy—and I love the theme—
> Dreams! in their vivid coloring of life,
> As in that fleeting, shadowy, misty strife
> Of semblance with reality, which brings
> To the delirious eye more lovely things
> Of Paradise and Love—and all our own—
> Than young Hope in his sunniest hour hath known.

This is to locate in the real world a place, or a state, in which one can conceive of the possibility of going beyond and above it. The poem is, again, about the situation of the poet and his involvement with semblances of reality. But, caught as he is in semblances, the poet is not yet able to create absolutely. To do so, he must free himself from them. When he does so, he will have made a world of words released from its obligation to take note of such semblances. That world will be significant only by virtue of what is created out of words, not at all by virtue of what those words have "really" meant. This is what we can make out of a late poem on the same subject, **"Dreamland"** (1844), which significantly ends almost as it has begun:

> By a route obscure and lonely,
> Haunted by ill angels only,
> Where an Eidolon, named Night,
> On a black throne reigns upright,
> I have wandered home but newly
> From this ultimate dim Thule.

Dream-land is no longer understood as a place, or even as a process related to a place. It is a state—an utterly disengaged creative act which would assert the purity of its creativity by being, as the poem tells us, "Out of SPACE— out of TIME." Ending as it has begun, it encapsulates the chaotic world of disengaged creativity for which the logic of Poe's poetics forced him to strive.

No wonder, then, that the poet in **"Ulalume,"** despite the warnings of his "Psyche," must make one last attempt to bring back his beloved from the dead, and do it by going on that creative journey of the self which is the argument of the poem. For he is, actually, trying to learn just how far imagination will carry him beyond common-sense reality. He fails, of course, since death is above all an aspect of that reality—for Poe its one absolutely valid aspect. All that the poet can do is interpret the sign as the clearest indication that it is his vocation solely to make poems celebrating the disjunction of the creative spirit from reality. The fact is that Poe wrote little poetry after **"Ulalume,"** even as he tried steadily in his criticism to create a rationale for the sort of poetry he would have written if he could have. Perhaps it was this creative impasse of which he wrote in **"To——— ——— —————"** of 1848:

> Not long ago the writer of these lines,
> In the mad pride of intellectuality,
> Maintained "the power of words"—denied that ever
> A thought arose within the human brain
> Beyond the utterance of the human tongue . . .

Now, he continues in this surprisingly discursive poem, he knows that this is not so; for he cannot conceive of putting into words his feeling for his beloved, his sense of *"thee only."* But the poem says more than just this. It expresses Poe's sense, on practical grounds, of the impossibility of his creative quest, even if hypothetically that quest *had* to be possible. His whole career as artist was grounded on that hypothesis, so that his poetry came to be in the end a series of manic oxymorons: expressive of nothing more than the fact that they would express the inexpressible.

It is tragic that the value of Poe's poems lies primarily in their over-insistent exhibitions of an imagination trying in vain to demonstrate its power to reach beyond itself. But it is this fact, apparently, that helped French poets, not so sensitive to the vulgarities of that over-insistence as Americans can now be, to write poems of a seriousness which Poe could not attain. Moreover, it is the fact of Poe's poetic gift which set the pattern of his fiction—with its concern to explore the delicately harrowing relations between the world of common sense and that of the dream. Because his fiction has pattern, it is greater than his poetry, which has only force. Nonetheless, the life of the fiction seems to have been released by powers which could have been discovered only in the process of making poems. The poems take Poe's anti-poetic world as a given and strain to expose the mysterious poetic power which he feels informs it. That such a world exists is a prime assumption without which the poems would have little or no meaning. They depend for their force upon a dialectic of simple opposition to the world for which they are written. Yet they make little or no contact with that world. They exist, as it were, to remind their readers of a possibility, "Out of SPACE—out of TIME," which by definition is never actualizable in a "real," common-sense situation.

The authentic poet is Israfel, whose world is the simple negative of this one. Poe must strive to be Israfel, so to escape the very world in which even Israfel would "not sing so wildly well / A mortal melody. . . ." The poems project disembodied creativity, so to speak—the force of an imagination driven to be true to itself at all costs. (In his long prose treatise *Eureka,* Poe tried to construct a rationale for such disembodied creativity; the net effect of the world is at the least one of helpless megalomania, at the most one of wilful demonism.) The egocentrism of Poe's poems achieves its greatest value by being finally, in its very agonizingly self-indulgent lyricism, an unsharable egocentrism. The poet is freed to be true to his sense of his self and his vocation, but only at the cost of cutting himself off from his vulgarly substantial world. He shares the burden of the creative act with his readers and so would force them into releasing whatever potential for creativity is in them. In this he tends to be one with his major contemporaries. He is unlike his contemporaries, however, in that he wilfully pushes this conception of poetry to its extremest limits. For him the poetic act in the end signifies absolutely nothing but itself. Thus, from the perspective of those who can be only his readers, what that act means is considerably more than what it is. This perhaps is the inevitable fate of the work of a man who is more of a culture hero than an artist. (pp. 149-53)

> *Roy Harvey Pearce, "American Renaissance (1): The Poet as Simple, Separate Person," in his* The Continuity of American Poetry, *Princeton University Press, 1961, pp. 137-91.*

Vincent Buranelli   (essay date 1961)

[*In the following excerpt from his critical biography of Poe, Buranelli surveys Poe's lyric poetry.*]

[Poe] was a poet at heart. His first three volumes were of verse—*Tamerlane and Other Poems* (1827), *Al Aaraaf, Tamerlane, and Minor Poems* (1829), and *Poems* (1831). The last two volumes include reprints and revisions, and these are the first witnesses to his characteristic and life-long habit of taking pains to improve his work from edition to edition.

As he began with poetry, he ended with it. His last year brought from him individual pieces as permanently popular as **"For Annie"** and **"Annabel Lee."** Between the beginning and the end he did not let his lyric inspiration die, but turned to poetry as often as he could. Four years before his death he published *The Raven and Other Poems* (1845). To this technical verse should be added prose like "The Colloquy of Monos and Una," which is very close to poetry. Poe's stories are sometimes similar to his poems in tone, mood, and even events; and in some cases he introduces his poetry into his stories to add to the effect: **"The Conqueror Worm"** appears in "Ligeia"; **"To One in Paradise"** in "The Assignation"; and, the most powerful example, **"The Haunted Palace"** in "The Fall of the House of Usher." (pp. 87-8)

Poe's poetry is less dependent than his prose on outside sources. So much is doubtless true of all writers who have worked in both fields, poetry being by its nature a much more *personal* thing than prose, catching nuances of temperament, feeling, and mood that escape the coarser technique of expression. But with Poe the difference is wider than with most of the others. He could learn from his predecessors basic methods of achieving the effects of horror and terror, however much he might contribute from his personal experience and artistic genius. He could not learn in the same way how to present in verse his intuitive in-

sights into Platonic beauty—his hypnagogic experiences on the threshold of sleep.

His poetry has little room for outside influences. True, he begins as a romantic poet who has avidly studied Byron and Moore, imitating their subjects, styles, rhythms, lines; nor did he ever cease to read the poets of his time or to profit from his reading. The salient fact is that Poe quickly moves on from romanticism to new forms of poetry welling up from deep inside his own personality. He probes his subconscious by way of dreams and the dreamlike states during which he hovered between sleep and wakefulness, ravished by beauties never present to him at any other time. Catching sight of strange visions and hearing strange harmonies, he is able to suggest them in words—and that is why he can write astounding poems the likes of which had never before been known.

Poe's leap from romanticism to symbolism, impressionism, even surrealism, may be seen by comparing his first two long poems, **"Tamerlane"** and **"Al Aaraaf."** **"Tamerlane"** rings Byronically throughout. Its hero is one of the world's great conquerors, a chieftain of the marauding Mongol hordes—Tamerlane, whose armies spread death and devastation across Central Asia during the fourteenth century. The place, time, and character are colorful enough to satisfy the most demanding devotee of romanticism. The hero speaks in the romantic idiom of sated ambition, blighted love, and a determination not to submit to fate. There are great lines in **"Tamerlane."**

> I have not always been as now:
> The fever'd diadem on my brow
>   I claim'd and won usurpingly—
> Hath not the same fierce heirdom given
>   Rome to the Caesar—this to me?
>   The heritage of a kingly mind,
> And a proud spirit which hath striven
>   Triumphantly with human kind.

To read **"Tamerlane"** requires no more mental effort than to read Byron. **"Al Aaraaf "** is something entirely different. Poe moves onto a terrain, the various parts of which he will explore and map more carefully in subsequent poems. His imagination has begun to flower, his intuition to reach farther. The defect of **"Al Aaraaf "** is that the poet has not learned how to control his imaginative flights; he has not mastered the discipline of his craft, the laborious art of rethinking and refining and rewriting. He has broken through the limits of the romantic imagination without being able to exploit his breakthrough effectively. The poem is unorganized, confused, and in places seems close to meaningless.

"Al Aaraaf " is the first example of Poe's mingling science with poetry. Taking the title from the Mohammedan name for limbo, a place in the hereafter where dwell neither the wholly good nor the wholly bad, Poe locates it on a star discovered by the Danish astronomer, Tycho Brahe, in the sixteenth century. This prosaic scientific reference would seem somewhat out of place in such a poem if we did not know of Poe's interest in the romance of astronomy. The science in **"Al Aaraaf "** is the more unusual because, in the same volume with it, Poe published a typical romantic protest against the havoc wrought in poetry by the discoveries of factual science. This is his admirable sonnet **"To Science."**

Science! true daughter of Old Time thou art!
  Who alterest all things with thy peering eyes.
Why preyest thou thus upon the poet's heart,
  Vulture, whose wings are dull realities?
How should he love thee? or how deem thee wise,
  Who wouldst not leave him in his wandering
To seek for treasure in the jewelled skies,
  Albeit he soared with an undaunted wing?
Hast thou not dragged Diana from her car,
  And driven the Hamadryad from the wood
To seek a shelter in some happier star?
  Hast thou not torn the Naiad from her flood,
The Elfin from the green grass, and from me
The summer dream beneath the tamarind tree?

The author of this sonnet was on the surface a romantic poet ready to drink confusion to mathematics. **"Al Aaraaf,"** refusing to pursue the thought, recognizes the worth of astronomy even to the poet. From there Poe will go on to the prose poetry of "The Colloquy of Monos and Una" and *Eureka,* and to his conclusion that the science of the stars is more poetic than anything the poet can imagine.

The locale of **"Al Aaraaf "** is a dream world full of ravishing sights, the spiritual home of the poet:

  Oh, nothing of the dross of ours—
  Yet all the beauty—all the flowers
  That list our Love, and deck our bowers—
  Adorn yon world afar, afar—
  The wandering star.

Al Aaraaf is a place where the Platonic Idea of absolute beauty can be known directly instead of through the imperfect things on the earth. Poe's poem is a hymn to the perfection that lies behind and explains the beautiful objects that we see around us:

  Now happiest, loveliest in yon lovely Earth
  Whence sprang the "Idea of Beauty" into birth
  (Falling in wreaths thro' many a startled star,
  Like woman's hair 'mid pearls, until, afar,
  It lit on hills Achaian, and there dwelt),
  She look'd into Infinity—and knelt.

The "She" mentioned here is one of Poe's strange ethereal women, in this case an astral goddess clothed in perfect beauty; but she nonetheless foreshadows the venerated mortal women with whom Poe will populate his later work. Nesace may live on a star, but something of her nature will reappear in Lenore and Annie. At one point **"Al Aaraaf "** becomes less cosmic by referring to the woman who will be the leading figure of one of Poe's best short stories:

  "Ligeia! wherever
    Thy image may be,
  No magic shall sever
    Thy music from thee.

Poe mourns his earth-bound existence—his exile from the Platonic universe of pure beauty—in **"Israfel,"** where he again speaks of Mohammedan legend, this time of its heaven and of its lyrical angel. The poet would change places with the angel if only he could, for he feels hampered only by his human condition, not by his genius.

  If I could dwell
  Where Israfel
    Hath dwelt, and he where I,
  He might not sing so wildly well

  A mortal melody,
  While a bolder note than this might swell
    From my lyre within the sky.

When Poe repeated the dream-world theme in poems like **"The City in the Sea," "The Valley of Unrest,"** and **"Dream Land,"** he made the uncanny more prominent; for he could use poetically as well as prosaically the dreams that are nightmares. The first stanza of **"Dream Land"** reads:

  By a route obscure and lonely,
  Haunted by ill angels only,
  Where an Eidolon, named NIGHT,
  On a black throne reigns upright,
  I have reached these lands but newly
  From an ultimate dim Thule—
  From a wild weird clime that lieth, sublime,
    Out of SPACE—out of TIME.

The note of melancholy, which is simply the fashionable romantic pessimism in **"Tamerlane,"** becomes a cry of deepseated, constitutional depression of the spirit in some of Poe's later works. **"The Haunted Palace"** is central to "The Fall of the House of Usher" because it parallels Roderick Usher's incipient madness. Poe laments the inevitable extinction that will surely engulf all of us in **"The Conqueror Worm,"** the meaning of which is summarized in the poem's concluding judgment on life,

  That the play is the tragedy, "Man,"
  And its hero, the Conqueror Worm.

Poe's theory of poetry makes the death of a beautiful woman the most poetic of themes. His theory is undoubtedly defective; but he certainly acted on a sound instinct when he allowed it to guide his pen in writing **"Annabel Lee," "The Raven," "Lenore,"** and the other poems like them. It is almost mandatory to quote **"Annabel Lee"** at this point in a discussion of Poe's poetry.

  It was many and many a year ago,
    In a kingdom by the sea,
  That a maiden there lived whom you may know
    By the name of Annabel Lee;—
  And this maiden she lived with no other thought
    Than to love and be loved by me.

A much better set of verses on the death of a beautiful woman is **"Lenore,"** the opening lines of which are superior to **"Annabel Lee"** in every way:

  Ah, broken is the golden bowl—the spirit flown forever!
  Let the bell toll!—a saintly soul floats on the Stygian
    river:—
  And, Guy de Vere, hast *thou* no tear?—weep now or nevermore!
  See! on yon drear and rigid bier low lies thy love, Lenore!

Poe's union of beauty and melancholy, not invented, but most forcefully stated and illustrated, by him, was one reason for the practice of the decadent school of literature. Even Oscar Wilde reflected the influence of Poe when he wrote *Salome.*

The poem often considered to be Poe's best, his first **"To Helen,"** departs from his principle about joining beauty, love and death. **"To Helen"** is a love poem, one of the many he wrote for the women he knew. Its most familiar reference, however, has been taken out of context and used as the best comment ever made in two lines on the ancient civilization upon which the culture of the West is founded. Here is all of **"To Helen"**:

> Helen, thy beauty is to me
>   Like those Nicean barks of yore,
> That gently, o'er a perfumed sea,
>   The weary, way-worn wanderer bore
> To his own native shore.
>
> On desperate seas long wont to roam,
>   Thy hyacinth hair, thy classic face,
> Thy Naiad airs have brought me home
>   To the glory that was Greece
> And the grandeur that was Rome.
>
> Lo! in yon brilliant window-niche
>   How statue-like I see thee stand,
>   The agate lamp within thy hand!
> Ah, Psyche, from the regions which
>   Are holy land!

This poem—with its low key, reasoned argument, controlled imagination, and classical restraint matching its classical allusion—was instrumental in the rise of neo-classical poetry. The French Parnassians made it their ideal to write just so.

As in his stories, Poe never let the melancholy or the uncanny monopolize his poems. **"The Coliseum,"** again touching a classical subject, follows **"To Helen."** It is the poem that might have won a prize from the Baltimore *Saturday Visiter* except that the editors, having already awarded Poe their fiction prize for "MS. Found in a Bottle," decided that their poetry prize ought to go to someone else. Poe's pleasing sonnet **"To My Mother"** comes toward the end of his career, and so do the rhythmic triumphs, **"The Bells"** and **"Eldorado."**

The deeper element in Poe emerges in his symbolism which begins with **"Al Aaraaf "** and ends with **"Ulalume."** The first of these poems lays the ground for a universal poetry of symbols, allegories, and metaphors by postulating that

> All Nature speaks, and ev'n ideal things
> Flap shadowy sounds form visionary wings . . .

Symbolical connections, even when natural, are not necessarily easily identifiable. Where the symbols are artificial, the problem is much more complicated. This is the fundamental problem of all symbolism, the best of which is subtle and profound without losing its meaning. Poe objected to allegory and used it little because he thought it too obvious. His tendency is to work with symbols that are not allegories; and his vice is to be, not too obvious, but too abstract: The symbolism of **"Al Aaraaf "** is a subject of much dispute among Poe experts, and the poem will never be interpreted to everybody's satisfaction. Poe introduces symbols private to himself, so that in default of any explanation by the poet, the significance of the poem must remain dubious.

When Poe came to the most celebrated of his poems, he chose to explain his method of operation. His "Philosophy of Composition" deals not only with the genesis of **"The Raven"** but also with the meaning of its symbols. The poem, of course, has a melancholy atmosphere which derives from what Poe's theory considers to be the most poetic of subjects—the death of a beautiful woman. Poe, who is fond of repeating feminine names, gives to this deceased

woman the name Lenore. The poem turns on the questioning of the raven by the bereaved lover, and the answer to every question is "Nevermore." The climax of the poem comes when the raven responds with "Nevermore" to the question of whether the lover and his mistress may ever, in some future life, be reunited.

This meaning is on the surface. There is a second meaning that has to be interpreted through the symbols of the poem, through suggestive signs standing for ideas hidden below the surface. The raven is the principal symbol. By the common consent of mankind, the raven, with its jet black feathers and harsh croak, represents fate: It is, as Poe says, a "bird of ill omen." Therefore he found it pertinent to his poem. He then added a symbolical interpretation of his own. He tells us that *his* raven is "emblematical of *Mournful and Neverending Remembrance,*" which means that the bereaved lover, who is trying "to borrow / From my books surcease of sorrow—sorrow for the lost Lenore," will now have his sorrow brought home to him in the most acute way by this creature that precisely stands for memory. The symbolism reveals itself in the last stanza, which Poe wrote first since it is the culmination of the effect he wants to achieve:

> And the Raven, never flitting, still is sitting, *still*
>   is sitting
> On the pallid bust of Pallas just above my
>   chamber door;
> And his eyes have all the seeming of a demon's
>   that is dreaming,
> And the lamp-light o'er him streaming throws
>   his shadow on the floor;
> And my soul from out that shadow that lies
>   floating on the floor
>   Shall be lifted—nevermore!

The "bust of Pallas" is itself a symbol. Representing the Greek goddess of wisdom, it also represents the life of learning into which the narrator of the poem has plunged in order to drown his sorrow. At the same time, the sculpture contrasts with the raven perched on it—the one white and the other black, the one silent and the other croaking a single dismal word, the one symbolizing serene wisdom and the other crushing fate. The word "Nevermore" is also a symbol. As the poem progresses, the word sounds more and more like the booming of a gong; it begins to take on overtones of universal tragedy, reminding the reader that the tramp of death can be heard by us all, and not just by one individual asking about one dead woman.

The symbolism of **"The Raven"** is not difficult, and has not attracted the amount of critical commentary that surrounds **"Ulalume,"** where Poe is suggestive in his most typical way. Even in his own time readers were baffled by **"Ulalume,"** and he himself jokingly refused to explain the meaning. Poe scholars having performed this function for him, we know it signifies the impossibility of a new love replacing an old one. Words like "Auber" and "Weir" have been cleared up, although "Yaanek" remains bothersome, and "Ulalume" is only hesitatingly defined as "light in sorrow."

But this poem did not have to await and *explication de texte* to be appreciated. It has been generally admired ever since it appeared. The reason is that it, like **"The Raven"** and so many other poems of the same weird type that Poe wrote, is infused with the music that no one but Poe could

And the Raven, never flitting, still is sitting — *still* is sitting
 On the pallid bust of Pallas just above my chamber door,
And his eyes have all the seeming of a demon that is dreaming,
 And the lamp-light o'er him streaming throws his shadow on
                                        { the floor,
 And my soul from out that shadow that lies floating on the floor
     Shall be lifted — nevermore.

Edgar A Poe

Handwritten final stanza of "The Raven."

have put into words. At bottom it is his music that gives him a claim to the title of America's foremost poet. His ear for verbal sounds, verse forms, rhythm and rhyme permitted him to achieve the indefiniteness he wanted, to be suggestive where statement was impossible, to imply those vague fancies and half-dreams that escaped direct description. You do not have to be able to set down a coherent précis of **"Ulalume"** to be affected by such stanzas as:

> The skies they were ashen and sober;
> The leaves they were crisped and sere—
> The leaves they were withering and sere:
> It was night, in the lonesome October
> Of my most immemorial year:
> It was hard by the dim lake of Auber,
> In the misty mid region of Weir—
> It was down by the dank tarn of Auber,
> In the ghoul-haunted woodland of Weir.

It is interesting to know just what a "most immemorial year" is, and why Poe selected the names "Auber" and "Weir." It is vital that the words *sound* exactly right in context, provoking in the reader a mood resonant with dim memories and hoary time and uncanny places; and that is why this poem produces the effect Poe was after even in those who have never bothered to look up the references in a critical edition.

"The Raven" is full of musical lines like these:

> And the silken, sad, uncertain rustling of each
> purple curtain . . .
> . . . .
> But the silence was unbroken, and the stillness
> gave no token,
> And the only word there spoken was the

whispered word "Lenore!"
 . . . .
Then, methought, the air grew denser, perfumed
 from an unseen censer,
Swung by seraphim whose foot-falls tinkled
 on the tufted floor.

Poe's music moves even readers who point out that it is impossible for anything to tinkle on a tufted floor, let alone footfalls. The image does not have to be physically true to be set forth in beautiful verse.

Later poets have not been able to do much with Poe's music (although Vachel Lindsay echoes it). Many of them have done a great deal with his symbolism. One broad current of Western poetry is beholden to him, the current that runs, in Matthiessen's phrase, "from Poe through the symbolists to Eliot."

As Poe's fiction has the vices of its virtues, so does his poetry. His poorer stories show up the tricks of his trade—the melodrama, the deliberate exaggerations, the stiff mechanical outer shell. His poorer poems do the same, for they expose in a cruel light the weakness that can betray the poet of melancholy, symbolism, and word music. In his first book of poetry he was capable of writing **"Fairy Land,"** which opens thus:

> Dim vales—and shadowy floods—
> And cloudy-looking woods,
> Whose forms we can't discover
> For the tears that drip all over:
>
> Huge moons there wax and wane—
> Again—again—again—
> Every moment of the night—

Forever changing places—
And they put out the star-light
With the breath from their pale faces.

Poe might be forgiven this youthful indiscretion were it not that he compounded the crime when he wrote **"Eulalie"** some fifteen years later. **"Eulalie"** begins well enough in Poe's customary vein: "I dwelt alone / In a world of moan / and my soul was a stagnant tide . . . " Poe then goes on to commit this atrocity in his last stanza:

Now Doubt—now Pain
Come never again,
For her soul gives me sigh for sigh,
And all day long
Shines bright and strong,
Astarte within the sky,
While ever to her dear Eulalie upturns her matron eye—
While ever to her young Eulalie upturns her violet eye.

Even later, not long before his death, Poe began his second poem called **"To Helen"** in this fashion: "I saw thee once—once only—years ago: / I must not say *how* many—but *not* many." It is useless to ask how the poet of the first **"To Helen"** could have written such stuff. Poe simply had Wordsworth's talent for writing heroically bad verse. (pp. 95-105)

Vincent Buranelli, in his Edgar Allan Poe, *Twayne Publishers, Inc., 1961, 157 p.*

Floyd Stovall   (essay date 1965)

[*In the following excerpt from his introduction to* The Poems of Edgar Allan Poe, *Stovall discusses Poe's poetic achievement.*]

Poe's poems, like his tales, are notable for their original conceptions and for the technical perfection of their execution. His ear was excellent; such irregularities of meter and discordant collocations as may be found in the late poems were intentional and served a purpose more important, at the moment, than pleasing the senses. But Poe could write mellifluous verse in his later as well as in his early years, as witness **"The Bells"** and **"Annabel Lee."** Like Coleridge, he found music essential to poetry, and in the "Letter to B——," the prefatory essay to *Poems,* 1831, which was his earliest venture in prose criticism, he defined poetry as music combined with a pleasurable idea. There is no question as to the musical quality of his poetry. Some critics, however, have complained of the absence of ideas. In 1909 W. C. Brownell said [in his *American Prose Masters*] of all Poe's writings: "They lack substance. Literature is more than an art." In our time, T. S. Eliot [in his *From Poe to Valéry* (1948)] has called Poe a gifted adolescent, and Allen Tate has said [in his *The Forlorn Demon* (1953)] that his perceptual powers remained undeveloped. There is a certain amount of truth in all of these opinions; but the faults they adduce, if they exist, should be seen in the proper perspective. This perspective is provided by Poe's theory of the nature of poetry and of the function of the poet. The poet's truth is an intuition, an excitement of the soul that he called the Poetic Sentiment, and it is the product not of rational thought but of the contemplation of beauty. The only substance of beauty is form. A rational construction, such as his prose poem *Eureka* or his tales of ratiocination, may have beauty, but that beauty subsists in the consistency, the harmonious relationship, of the ideas, not in the ideas themselves.

Poe's poems can be said to lack substance only if the theory which they exemplify is wrong. If his theory is right, or if we accept that part of it which concerns the relation of beauty and truth, we must admit that his poems have the true substance of art in their power of inducing intuitions of truth in the responsive reader. Such truths are untranslatable—they cannot be expressed in terms of the intellect or of the moral sense—but they are nonetheless real to all who accept truth and beauty as of one essence. Although exponents of the doctrine of "art for art" cannot rightly claim Poe as their prophet, they may well find comfort in his poetry as in his poetic theory. Some modern poets might, in all candor, confess a greater indebtedness to Poe than they have been inclined to do. Poe was surely among the first theorists to affirm that a poem's primary value is in itself, not in what it tells us about something, whether that something be a moral or intellectual truth or some revelation of the poet himself. A poem is not a document, but a total creation; it is not a part of a world only, but a world in itself. When these matters are better understood, Poe's poetry may be more highly estimated.

Of all American writers, critics have found Poe the most difficult to categorize in a phrase. Longfellow has been depreciated as a genial sentimentalist, Emerson tolerated as a hopeful idealist, Hawthorne appreciated as a physician of souls, and Whitman hailed as a prophet of the new Eden. But Poe was neither genial nor hopeful, and he grew to look skeptically on Edens here or hereafter. In his high regard for art he was akin to Hawthorne, and in his speculative intellect he had something in common with Melville; but where in nineteenth-century America will one meet with the equal of his critical acumen, his disciplined narrative skill, or his sure feeling for verbal sounds and rhythms? On the other hand, no other American writer of the first rank lent his talent to weaker performances than some of his carping book reviews or his more grotesque attempts at humor. Three or four of his poems addressed to literary ladies do but slight credit to their author. His late poems, with their ingenious and complicated structure, have been said to "smell of the lamp." But Poe should be judged objectively on positive, not negative, evidence; in the final reckoning, his weaknesses should not be charged against his strength. One does not arrive at the true worth of a literary artist by taking an average of his work.

Perhaps Poe's greatest single literary virtue is his originality. Each of his best poems and tales, as I have said, is unique in its kind. He was not an assembly-line creator. And though his critical ideas may be largely derivative, he made them his own, enlarged them, and used them well to his own purposes. He wrote a dozen poems and nearly as many tales that approach artistic perfection. His tales, however contrived, are vivid, and the strange beauty of his poems is inimitable. Wherein lies his true genius? That would be hard to say with conviction. Any just estimate of his work must take into account his total achievement in the three fields of criticism, fiction, and poetry. In his own mind, and in the minds of a good many, though probably a minority, of his critics, he was a poet first of all and above all else. It is possible that he made his most enduring contribution to literature in the creation of a few unforgettable poems. (pp. xxxvi-xxxvii)

Floyd Stovall, in an introduction to The Poems of Edgar Allan Poe *by Edgar Allan Poe, edited by Floyd Stovall, The University Press of Virginia, 1965, pp. xv-xxxvii.*

Allen Tate   (essay date 1968)

[*An American poet and critic, Tate is closely associated with two critical movements, the Agrarians and the New Critics. A conservative thinker and convert to Catholicism, Tate attacked the tradition of Western philosophy which he felt alienates people from themselves, one another, and nature by divorcing intellectual from natural functions in human life. For Tate, literature is the principal form of knowledge and revelation that restores human beings to a proper relationship between nature and the spiritual realm. In the following excerpt, Tate claims that Poe's poetry contains only one theme—"the demon (Poe) tells us he saw take shape in a cloud" in his early poem "Alone."*]

Eureka is the only piece of adolescent reading in popular astronomy to which I have returned in age; and I still take it seriously. I have wondered why the modern proponents of the Big Bang hypothesis of the creation have not condescended to acknowledge Poe as a forerunner. Big Bang presupposes an agent to set off the explosion of the primordial atom; and that is what Poe presupposed in his fundamental thesis for *Eureka:* "In the original unity of the first thing lies the secondary cause of all things, with the germ of their inevitable annihilation." But the concluding phrase presupposes something else, which is characteristic of Poe in all phases of his work: "inevitable annihilation". The cosmos will shrink back into spatial nothingness, taking man along with it; and hence man, having returned to the original nothing, which is God, will *be* God. The last twenty or so pages of *Eureka* have a lurid, rhetorical magnificence unmatched by anything else that Poe wrote. For *Eureka* is Poe's elaborate, pseudo-systematic attempt to give his compulsive theme of annihilation scientific and philosophical sanctions.

The theme of annihilation is always attractive to young persons: from about twelve to sixteen, annihilation or simply romantic death at the end of sentimental love—an adolescent posture of disorder set against the imposed order of the family or of adult society into which the child resists entrance. This posture of disorder is never quite rejected in maturity, and it is the psychological and moral basis of what today is called Existentialism. One reason why Americans may be a little bored with French Existentialism is that we have always been Existentialists, or have been since the time of Poe, who discovered it in us. For Existentialism assumes—among other things—that man has no relation to a metaphysical reality, a kind of reality that he cannot know even if it existed; he is therefore trapped in a consciousness which cannot be conscious of anything outside itself. He must sink into the non-self. Poe sinks into the vortex, the maelstrom, suffocation of premature burial or of being walled up alive; or he sinks into the sea. We know Coleridge's influence on Poe. How apt for Poe's purposes was the "lifeless ocean" of Coleridge! And the death of a beautiful woman was, for Poe, the most "poetical" subject for poetry—or, as we should say today, the

archetypal subject. One of his best lyrics begins, "Thou wast that all to me, Love, / For which my soul did pine . . . " His love is dead, of course, and he is left *alone*, ready for loss of breath, loss of consciousness, loss of identity—*never more* anything outside himself. I shall have something to say presently about the Raven's "Nevermore". I must end these preliminary observations with some attention to the word *alone*.

Among the poems attributed to Poe, the authorship of which cannot be proved, is a piece entitled **"Alone"**; yet what the scholars call "internal evidence" is so obvious that I do not hesitate to use it as a key to some of his compulsive symbols which are ultimately, as I have indicated, a single symbolic matrix: the vortex, the grave, the pit. Here I quote the significant lines:

> From childhood's hour I have not been
> As others were— . . .
> . . . I could not awaken
> My heart to joy at the same tone;
> And all I lov'd *I* lov'd alone.
> *Then*—in my childhood—in the dawn
> Of a most stormy life—was drawn
> From ev'ry depth of good and ill
> The mystery which binds me still . . .
> From the thunder and the storm,
> And the cloud that took the form
> (When the rest of Heaven was blue)
> Of a demon in my view.

The poem, first published in 1875, was found in an autograph album belonging to a lady in Baltimore; it was the opinion of the late Killis Campbell that the poem was written as early as 1829 or 1830, when Poe was not older than twenty-one. (I pause to observe that four-fifths of Poe's poems, however many times he reprinted them, often in versions revised almost beyond recognition, were written by the time he was twenty-two.) Yet one might guess from the tone of the poem that it was written in retrospect, towards the end of a long life. At twenty-one his childhood was not in the remote past. What kind of demon was it that Poe saw in his childhood—or saw when he was writing the poem, which comes to the same thing? Elsewhere I have called Poe a forlorn demon gazing at himself in a glass; thus could William Wilson be described, and likewise most of Poe's fictional heroes. I suggest that Poe's poetry, which consists of only some sixty-odd authenticated poems, most of them very short, were all written by Poe as his own fictional projection; by Poe as the demon he tells us he saw take shape in a cloud.

There is nothing very shocking about this. A non-theological view of demonology would tell us that a demon is simply a person who cannot develop—a fierce determinism has arrested the rounded growth of his faculties; so that the evil he does other persons is not a positive malice but an insistence that they remain as emotionally and intellectually deprived as he himself must remain. Poe's poems, from first to last, from **"Tamerlane"** to **"Ulalume"**, show almost no change, certainly no acquisition of range and depth that might justly be described as development. All of his poems might have been written in any one year of his life, at age fifteen or age forty (his age when he died); that most of them were written before 1831 was probably due to the later financial necessity of making a living out of literary journalism. (He was the first committed and perhaps still the greatest American literary journalist on the high French model: a critical tradition represented today by Edmund Wilson and Malcolm Cowley.) In the short introduction to *Eureka* he said that poetry with him had been a "passion", leaving the implication that he had had no time to write much of it. One may reasonably doubt the validity of this explanation, though one may not doubt Poe's sincerity in thinking it valid. He had enough time from 1831 to his death in 1849 to rewrite most of the poems, some of them many times. I think it is fair to infer from all the evidence that he had very little, or rather one thing, to say in poetry; in the revisions he was trying to say it better or was trying, by means of deletions and additions, to make old poems look like new poems—for what reason one may only guess: perhaps to sell the same but disguised poem several times, perhaps to keep his "image" as a poet before the public, or perhaps, as I have indicated, to improve the poems. (pp. 215-19)

More than any other romantic poet, here or in England, either of the preceding generation of Coleridge, Wordsworth, and Bryant, or of his own, [Poe] became the *type,* not the greatest but the most representative: that is to say, he became the *type* of the alienated poet, the outcast, the *poète maudit*—the poet accursed. I hope I am not pushing this matter too far if I see in **"Alone"** his early awareness of his plight. The demon-cloud had early uttered its malediction. N. Bryllion Fagin tells us about the "histrionic Mr. Poe", and quite justly; yet the self-conscious dramatization of doom, fully developed towards the end of his life in **"The Raven"** and **"Ulalume"**, was not consciously assumed, as a pose; it came from the inside, out of his early life; and I can think of no other writer of the nineteenth century who was more entitled to a conviction of his doom (if anybody ever is) than Edgar Allan Poe. The doom, then, was sincere, if consciously exploited. (p. 219)

The pure romantic poet, either through choice (Shelley) or through circumstance (Poe), or partly one, partly the other (Keats), must isolate himself, or be isolated, or simply find himself isolated for the deeply felt but not consciously known purposes of his genius. He must, in short, be *alone.*

A poet may have many subjects, but few poets since the time of Blake have had more than one theme; such poets must try again and again to give the theme, in successive poems, new and if possible fuller expression. One might see the relation of theme to subject as a relation of potency to actualization. The romantic poet is trying to write one poem all his life, out of an interior compulsion; each poem is an approximation of the Perfect Romantic Poem. I do not wish to be understood as saying that the Romantic Poet is the polar opposite of the Classical Poet, or that there are generic differences which point to distinct categories of poetry. A poet like Ben Jonson has many themes but only one style; Poe has one theme and many styles, or many approximations of one style, none of them perfect, and some very bad, as we shall presently see.

There are four poems by Poe that I believe everybody can join in admiring: **"The City in the Sea"**, **"The Sleeper"**, **"To Helen"** (the shorter and earlier poem of that title), and **"The Raven"**; one might include **"Ulalume"**, but less as distinguished poetry than as Poe's last and most ambitious attempt to actualize in language his *aloneness.*

"To Helen" is somewhat more complex than the critics have found it to be, or found it necessary to point out. However, the similarity to Landor has been frequently remarked, but nobody knows whether the influence was direct. (Whether the poem was addressed to an older lady who was kind to Poe when he was a boy is irrelevant.) The direct address is to "Helen", inevitably Helen of Troy whether or not Poe had her in mind; and the tact with which she is described is Homeric. She is not *described* at all; she is presented in a long simile of action, in which her beauty is conveyed to the reader through its effect on the speaker of the poem. There is nothing else in Poe's work quite so well done as this. In the second stanza one might detect a small blemish (the poem is so nearly perfect that it invites close scrutiny): the phrase "thy Naiad airs" might be better if the noun were in the singular—"thy Naiad *air*", meaning that her demeanor or bearing is that of a Naiad; the plural has a slight connotation of the colloquial "putting on airs". Helen brings the wanderer home to his native shore, which is the ancient world: the Landoresque perfection of the two last lines of the second stanza has not been surpassed. But the complexity of feeling, unusual in Poe, comes in the last stanza with the image of Helen as a statue in a niche, perhaps at the end of a hall, or on a landing of a stairway. She has all along been both the disturbing Helen and, as a marble, a Vestal Virgin holding her lamp: she is inaccessible. The restrained exclamation "Ah, Psyche" is one of the most brilliant effects in romantic poetry. "Ah" has the force of "alas": alas, that Helen is now in a lost, if holy land, as inaccessible and pure as she herself is. But who is Psyche? She is usually identified with Helen, and she may be Helen, but at the same time she is the Psyche of Eros and Psyche; and Poe must have known the little myth in Apuleius: she could be an archetype of suprasensual love by means of which the classical, sensual Helen is sublimated. (In **"Ulalume"** Psyche appears again, as the sister of the poet.) Poe wrote the poem when he was not more than twenty-one; he pretended to Lowell that he had written it when he was fourteen; but whenever he wrote it he never before nor afterwards had such mastery of diction and rhythm. I need not point out that the theme of the poem is isolation of the poet after great loss. (pp. 220-22)

It has not been pointed out by the biographers and critics that, although Poe attacked the genteel preaching of Longfellow and Lowell as the "heresy of the didactic", he was himself paradoxically a didactic poet, a grim and powerful one at that. He is constantly telling us that we are all alone, that beauty is evanescent, that the only immortality may be a vampirish return from the grave, into which we must sink again through eternity. In **"The Haunted Palace"** we are taught that the intellect cannot know either nature or other persons. In **"The Conqueror Worm"** we are taught that life is a "drama" in which we think we are the protagonists; but the actual hero is death in the guise of a gigantic Worm. This is the human "plot". If, as Poe says in *Eureka,* "the universe is a plot of God," and man participates in the plot as a conscious actor, then the purposeless activity of man has as its goal the horror of death and bodily corruption.

It is no wonder, then, that Poe wrote so few poems. There are not many ways to deliver his message of spiritual solipsism and physical decay if the poet limits himself to romantic expressionism. The "rhythmical creation of Beauty" means very little, if anything, as a general aesthetic principle; it means in Poe's poetry the expression of a Pure Emotion which creates in the reader a pure emotional effect, about which we must not think, and about which we must do nothing.

Of the poems which I have mentioned as being among his best, there is no need to discuss at length **"The Sleeper"**, which many critics consider a masterpiece. There is bad writing in it—"The lily lolls upon the wave"; "And this all solemn silentness"—yet it remains Poe's best treatment of the beautiful female corpse. The "lady" will be taken to a vault where her ancestors lie, against which she had "thrown, In childhood, many an idle stone". This is the only poem in which the dead lady has any life before her appearance on the bier or in the tomb. We can almost believe that she was at some remote time a human being; yet why at the end we are told that she was a "child of sin" I cannot discover.

If Poe wrote any "great" poems they are surely **"The City in the Sea"** and **"The Raven"**.

"The City in the Sea" was first published in 1831 as "The Doomed City"; revised and republished in 1836 as "The City of Sin"; **"The City in the Sea"** is the title in the 1845 edition of the poems. The recurrent symbolism of the vortex that one finds everywhere in the prose tales appears infrequently and incompletely in the poems; but here it receives its most powerful expression in verse. The nineteenth-century critics—Edmund Clarence Stedman, for example—thought the poem a masterpiece; Edwin Markham put it beside "Kubla Khan". But there is nowhere in the poem evidence of Coleridge's magisterial certainty and control. In the first five lines there is a doggerel movement—"Where the good and the bad and the worst and the best / Have gone to their eternal rest." I have written elsewhere that "everything in Poe is dead"; in this poem everything is dead; for the poem might be entitled "The City of Death". Here we go beyond the lovely dead woman to dead humanity; and all nature, as well, is dead. When this dead city slides into the sea we, presumably, go down with it into the vortex: into oblivion. This archetype of life after death is as old as recorded humanity. In Dante the sea to which we return is the will of God; in Poe it is a dire apocalyptic vision in which we suffer "inevitable annihilation". Except for **"To Helen"** the poem contains the best lines Poe ever wrote:

> But light from out the lurid sea
> Streams up the turrets silently—
> . . . .
> Up many and many a marvellous shrine
> Whose wreathèd friezes intertwine
> The viol, the violet, and the vine.

(pp. 223-24)

I can add very little to the criticism of **"The Raven"**, a poem so badly, even vulgarly written in many passages that one wonders how it can be a great poem, which I believe it to be. We have here the two necessary elements— the beautiful, dead, "lost Lenore" and the *poète maudit* who with perfect literary tact is confronted with, I dare to say, the demon of the youthful poem **"Alone"**. It is the same demon, this time come down from the clouds and taking the form of a bird that imitates human speech without knowing what the speech means:

> And his eyes have all the seeming of a demon's that is

dreaming . . .

This poem—a late poem, written in 1844—is the one poem by Poe which is not direct lyrical, or romantic, expressionism. It has dramatic form and progression: the poet conducts a dialogue with his demon; it is the only poem by Poe which leads the reader through an action. In classical terms, the plot is simple, not complex; it is a simple plot of Recognition in which the poet, examining all the implications of the bird's "Nevermore", recognizes his doom.

Henry James said that admiration of Poe represented a "primitive stage of reflection". One agrees; but one must add that without primitive reflection, however one defines it, one cannot move on. (p. 225)

> Allen Tate, "The Poetry of Edgar Allan Poe," in The Sewanee Review, *Vol. LXXXVI, No. 2, Spring, 1968, pp. 214-25.*

Haldeen Braddy (essay date 1973)

[*Braddy is an American author and academic who has published studies on Geoffrey, Chaucer and Poe. In the following excerpt from his* Three Dimensional Poe, *Braddy argues that Poe composed poetry from a predominantly feminine perspective.*]

> Thou wast that all to me, love,
>   For which my soul did pine—
> A green isle in the sea, love,
>   A fountain and a shrine,
> All wreathed with fairy fruits and flowers,
>   And all the flowers were mine.

["To One in Paradise"]

There often occurs in Poe's poetry, not only an overlay of spirituality, but an undercurrent of depth and warmth which can be distinguished only as the product of human passion. Before alcohol deadened his senses, he responded to females naturally; therefore his early poems and what one knows of his erotic youth-time testify that these sentimental emotions sprang from genuine experiences. The later Poe became a victim of disease and overindulgence; therefore it could be contended that impotence, at least a waning of virility, may have plagued his lovelife and etherealized his verses. Recognition of physical love, however, surfaces in poems as early as **"Tamerlane"** (1827):

> We grew in age—and love—together—
>   Roaming the forest, and the wild;
> My breast her shield in wintry weather—
>   And, when the friendly sunshine smil'd,
> And she would mark the opening skies,
>   I saw no Heaven—but in her eyes.

and as late as **"For Annie"** (1849):

> She tenderly kissed me,
>   She fondly caressed me,
> And then I fell gently
>   To sleep on her breast—
> Deeply to sleep
> From the heaven of her breast.

But Poe's references to love can hardly be interpreted as generally echoing traditional masculine affection. Often the earthy quality linked with strong masculinity is absent, as is also the expression of the forthright and gusty passion of man. The more dominant image in Poe's emotional reaction associates itself with the moon and stars, with gardens and flowers, with rare perfumes and impossible heavens. The emotionalism is authentic, but it is femininely so. Even when his description includes anatomical details of the physical body, he is not masculinely contented with the flesh and the world but must reach for the spiritual and hold converse with Heaven. At its best, love transports men and women alike, but few men have dealt so repeatedly with the spiritual effects of human passion as Poe.

The principal element in the psychology of Poe can always be identified as a form of religion; to him love ultimately was a mystical experience; and his poetry vibrates again and again with echoes of spirituality. This amorous verse is permeated to its core with an aura of spiritual emotionalism, and his sentimental references to women are everywhere haloed with the dominant image of the religiosity of love. Moreover, that the actual love-experiences of Poe in real life were markedly tinctured with the chimerical quality of religious thought is evident in the almost identical statements in his letters: he wants, first, Mrs. Whitman in a "divine trance" to be his "hereafter and *forever, in the* Heavens," and, secondly, Mrs. Richmond, as *"wife of my soul—to be mine hereafter & forever in the Heavens . . ."* Sentimental Poe adopts the language of religion to express the agony of his loneliness. (pp. 22-3)

In his prose tales Poe usually alludes to men, as the Rev. Bransby in "William Wilson" and Mr. Allan in "The Business Man," whereas in his poems he addresses women, as Mrs. Richmond in **"For Annie"** and Mrs. Clemm in **"Sonnett—To My Mother."** One should not forget that a most effective poem of his, **"Bridal Ballad"** (1837), beginning "The ring is on my hand," represents itself as written from the point of view of a female:

> The ring is on my hand,
> And the wreath is on my brow;
> Satins and jewels grand
> Are all at my command
> And I am happy now.
>
> And my lord he loves me well;
> But, when first he breathed his vow,
> I felt my bosom swell—
> For the words rang as a knell,
> And the voice seemed his who fell
> In the battle down the dell,
> And who is happy now.

Finally, one must weigh the important datum that of some sixty poems, no fewer than thirty have to do with his regard for women. The facts that half the total number of his verses concern women and that he once even wrote from a bride's point of view combine to form strong evidence for naming Poe the most sensitive male lyricist produced by America on subjects varying from coldly inaccessible heroines to intimate, warm-blooded liaisons.

In making this claim, one draws support from the striking fact that by far the largest number of his verses belong to the category. His rhymes utter little, if anything, about such traditional poetic topics as honor, patriotism, and nature; he reports practically everything about the longing for, the enjoyment of, as well as the loss of love. All familiar arrangements of the lyric—the simple quatrain, the short song, the sentimental sonnet—reappear time after

time to reiterate some variation of the theme of human passion. Of course he occasionally attempted other forms as well, in particular the verse narrative and the metrical ballad; yet it arrests one to see that even in these two other types Poe usually returns to the theme of love. Such long narrative pieces as **"Tamerlane"** and **"Lenore"** have for their main idea the deeply moving theme of love lost beyond regaining, as indeed do also the well-known ballads **"Ulalume," "Bridal Ballad,"** and **"Annabel Lee."** Similarly, his experiments in blank verse include the amorous theme, as is seen in the poem addressed to Mrs. Mary Louise Shew under the title **"To — — —."** So far, then, as the forms of his poetry figure, he wrote about love in the four principal media which he practiced—blank verse, the ballad, the narrative, and especially the ubiquitous lyric.

Poe's fondness for the lyric connects his poetry with the feminine quality. The lyric has long been recognized as the form most successfully cultivated by female writers. Women, however, have had little success with the poetic drama or the poetic epic. In like manner, Poe's attempt at drama in *Politian* was a failure, and his attempt at the epic form in **"Al Aaraaf"** is at best unorganized and incomplete. Secondly, female writers often have experimented boldly with form and language; and this feminine trend towards originality is certainly evident in the work of Poe, who in **"The City in the Sea"** describes in matchless words those "wreathed friezes" which intertwine "The viol, the violet, and the vine." His failure in the drama and the epic, together with his achievement of immortality within the narrow scope of the short poem, thus indissolubly links Poe's poetry with the history of feminine contributions to literature. According to Andrew Jackson Davis, whom the poet visited on January 19, 1846, Poe's "remarkable face bore traces of feminine mental characteristics."

The clearest connections between Poe and the feminine vogue are seen in his occasional poetry. Poe's long poem in blank verse, entitled **"To Helen,"** was composed in response to a composition read by Mrs. Whitman at a Valentine party in New York City on February 14, 1848. At the home of Miss Anne Lynch in New York City on February 14, 1846, Poe had previously read a poem entitled **"A Valentine,"** the first and then succeeding letter of the lines spelling out the name of Frances Sargent Osgood.

> For her these lines are penned, whose luminous eyes,
> B*R*ightly expressive as the twins of Loeda,
> Sh*A*ll find her own sweet name that, nestling, lies
> Upo*N* this page, enwrapped from every reader,
> Sear*C*h narrowly this rhyme, which holds a treasure
> Divin*E*—a talisman—an amulet
> That mu*S*t be worn at heart. Search well the measure;
> The word*S*—the letters themselves. Do not forget
> The trivi*A*lest point, or you may lose your labor.
> And yet the*R*e is in this no Gordian knot
> Which one mi*G*ht not undo without a sabre,
> If one could m*E*rely understand the plot.
> Enwritten upo*N* this page whereon are peering
> Such eager eyes, *T*here lies, I say, *perdu,*
> A well-known name, *O*ft uttered in the hearing
> Of poets, by poets: a*S* the name is a poet's, too.
> Its letters, althou*G*h naturally lying—
> Like the knight Pint*O* (Mendez Ferdinando)—
> Still form a synonym f*O*r truth. Cease trying!
> You will not read the ri*D*dle though you do the best you
> *can* do.
> [Editorial italic capitals]

Three other poems employ the same device of disguised spelling: **"An Acrostic,"** designed according to the arrangement of the initial letters of each succeeding word for Elizabeth, probably Miss Herring, Poe's cousin; the poem **"Elizabeth,"** identical in dedication with the former; and **"An Enigma,"** destined for Sarah Anna Lewis, a poetess of Baltimore and later of Brooklyn and a close friend of Poe in his last years.

On February 14, 1848, sixteen days after Virginia's death, he addressed a valentine to a young school girl named Louise Olivia Hunter.

> Though I turn, I fly not—
>   I cannot depart;
> I would try, but try not
>   To release my heart.
> And my hopes are dying
> While, on dreams relying,
>   I am spelled by art.
>
> Thus the bright snake coiling
>   Neath the forest tree
> Wins the bird, beguiling,
>   To come down and see:
> Like that bird the lover
> Round his fate will hover
> Till the blow is over
>   And he sinks—like me (1849).

These six poems—the three valentines and the three acrostics—most closely associate the poet with the outward manifestations, the literary exercises and social verse competitions, of the new female school of writers.

Amour, then, dominates the lyrical outbursts of love-famished Poe. Most of the passages cherished by his devotees center on variations of the subject. As a masterly writer on this theme of the tenderest and most sublime of human emotions, Poe in his work was inspired in a three-fold way: love of God, love of parents and friends, and love of a beautiful woman. Accordingly, one finds, first, that the poet's **"Hymn"** (1835) is fired with a fervent religious passion for "Maria" (Mrs. Clemm or the Mother of God or both).

> At morn—at noon—at twilight dim—
> Maria! thou hast heard my hymn!
> In joy and woe—in good and ill—
> Mother of God, be with me still!
> When the Hours flew brightly by,
> And not a cloud obscured the sky,
> My soul, lest it should truant be,
> Thy grace did guide to thine and thee;
> Now, when storms of Fate o'ercast
> Darkly my Present and my Past,
> Let my Future radiant shine
> With sweet hopes of thee and thine.

Secondly, one discovers in **"Sonnet—To My Mother"** (1849) an exceptional selection since it is a tribute, not to his own mother, but to Mrs. Clemm, the parent of his beloved Virginia.

> Because I feel that, in the Heavens above,
>   The angels, whispering to one another,
> Can find, among their burning terms of love,
>   None so devotional as that of "Mother,"
> Therefore by that sweet name I long have called you—
>   You who are more than mother unto me,
> And fill my heart of hearts, where Death installed you

> In setting my Virginia's spirit free,
> My mother—my own mother, who died early
>   Was but the mother of myself, but you
> Are mother to the one I loved so dearly,
>   And thus are dearer than the mother I knew
> By that infinity with which my wife
>   Was dearer to my soul than its soul-life.

Thirdly, although dedicating many of his poems to women, his truly heavy reliance upon and need for feminine affection fully divulges itself in **"To One in Paradise,"** where T. O. Mabbott saw "flowers" indicating Platonic and "fruits," carnal love. Of the two, Poe chose the second, "And all the flowers were mine." The more one studies his poetry, the more one becomes persuaded that however he be ranked as a story-teller and critic, Poe in his verses ranks primarily as an amorous poet, and that as such he is in scope and intensity unsurpassed in American literature.

Tragic as was Poe's life from the point of view of his weakness for drinking, borrowing, and gambling, he was fortunate in experiencing the love and affection of several women. His own mother died too early for him to be influenced by her tender regard except as a memory; but both Frances Allan, his foster mother, and Nancy Valentine, his foster aunt, lavished upon him almost every affectionate attention. While he was yet a youngster, he won the sentimental approval of Mrs. Stanard. Known in childhood and early youth as "the little boy," Poe in an unusual degree seems to have inspired women to love him. His youthful attachments with Catherine Poitiaux, Mary Devereaux, and others led, perhaps, to nothing significant; but his esteem for Elizabeth Herring, his own cousin, moved him to versify about her, while his serious affair with Sarah Elmira Royster, though consummating unhappily for him in her marriage to Mr. Shelton, exercised a profound influence upon his literary career and at an impressionable age introduced him to one of the severest human tragedies of man's experience, that of permanently losing, to another, one's beloved. Miss Royster was not his first *princesse perdue,* for death by this date had already claimed Mrs. Stanard, the Helen of his famous first poem so entitled, and was soon to encompass Mrs. Allan, the foster mother who favored him in difficulties arising in the Allan household. All of this was by way of preparation for the greatest sorrow Poe ever experienced, the death of his wife Virginia, whose loss in 1847 almost unhinged the poet's mind though at the same time affording him by a kind of compensation the central theme for his finest love lyrics. The memorable poems about Mrs. Stanard, Miss Royster, and his own Virginia are artistic monuments of impassioned verse on the subject treated most effectively by Poe—namely, sublime love for the *princesse perdue,* the princess of long ago.

After the death of his wife, Poe collapsed. How could he recover the past? Only the medium of his art remained. Thus it is that in his final poems Poe in undying terms began to limn a portrait of his princess of long ago. The portrait was drawn from the human features that for a time throbbed in his fevered memory. But the experience called memory eventually involves in its psychology the process of decay. In fortunate instances of human love, in those where the heart wholly figures, one forgets the unpleasant recollections and remembers the good; the bad dissolves as the good fructifies—and the mind begins to substitute for details now unremembered fresh images unconnected with stimulation from the past.

Poe's description of the *princesse perdue* tends in later poems to have less and less in common with a human woman encased by flesh and blood. The picture which unfolds is that of an idealized heroine, an enchanted princess. In **"To Helen"** (1831) her features are not modern: she has the "classic face"; her coloring is not of human shade—her hair is "hyacinth hair"; and even her body is molded in terms suggesting, not living movement, but stony rigidity—"How statue-like I see thee stand." In the later **"Bridal Ballad"** (1837) one finds, not the animated countenance, but the "pallid brow." In the yet later **"Ulalume"** (1847) the princess has further dissolved, for now she is "Psyche" and his "sweet sister." In **"For Annie"** (1849), written in the same year that he died, he has cured his thirst "For the napthaline river / Of Passions accurst": he breathes "A rosemary odor"; and he sleeps upon "the heaven of her breast." Finally, in **"Annabel Lee"** (1849), the last of these poems, Poe in his poetic flights has returned to his little lost princess.

> And neither the angels in Heaven above
>   Nor the demons down under the sea,
> Can ever dissever my soul from the soul
>   Of the beautiful Annabel Lee.

In analyzing **"The Raven"** in "The Philosophy of Composition," Poe held that "the death of a beautiful woman is, unquestionably, the most poetical topic in the world." A lasting impression one receives in reading his poetry is, then, that he championed beauty and love. Possibly as the result of excessive reliance on alcohol or drugs, he lost his appetite, if he really ever had a strong one, for the gratifications of sexual experience. The most persistent and haunting thought that one carries away from a study of his major writings is that the poet buried himself in the past, in memories of the princess of long ago. Poe brought the tremendous idea of the far-away princess, *la princesse lointaine,* to its final, its logical terminus. Poe's princess dwells farther than far away; she is irretrievably lost, irrevocably dead. (pp. 24-30)

> *Haldeen Braddy, in his* Three Dimensional
> Poe, *Texas Western Press, 1973, 86 p.*

Richard Wilbur   (lecture date 1981)

[*Wilbur is an American poet, translator, critic, and editor who is respected for the craftsmanship and elegance of his verse. As a response to disorder and chaos in modern life, he employs formal poetic structures and smoothly flowing language. Wendy Salinger commented: "Wilbur mistrusts the imagination that would be a world to itself—it is in this sense that he has described his work as a continuing quarrel with the aesthetics of Edgar Allan Poe, who extolled the transcendent escape into the otherworld of the imagination." In the following excerpt from a lecture delivered to the Poe Studies Association in 1981, Wilbur discerns subtle meanings in Poe's poetry conveyed through allegory, imagery, and symbolism.*]

We all know how slow a work of Poe's may be to release its meaning. I have been reading **"Israfel,"** on and off, for most of my life, and I have always regarded it as a simple, flawed, and occasionally felicitous piece in which an earthly poet, while not apologizing for his own limited efforts, applauds the superior lyric powers of an angel. I still read the poem in the same general way, but not long ago I was made suddenly aware that the poem is subtler and more argumentative than I had thought, and that it may be taken, from beginning to end, as a treatise on the place of passion in poetry. Poe's poetic theory, which reached its full development in "The Poetic Principle," distinguishes as we know three primary divisions of the "world of mind": the intellect, which pursues truth; taste, which has for its object beauty; and the moral sense, which concerns itself with duty. Poetry being a wild effort to capture supernal beauty, it is the province of taste alone. The intellect, and the moral sense with its mundane didacticism, are inimical to poetry, and are admissible in a poem only if utterly subjected to the purposes of taste. Since poetry aims at "an elevating excitement of the soul," a spiritual or Uranian kind of love may be the truest of poetic themes; but as for passion, which is "an intoxication of the heart," Poe agrees with Coleridge that it degrades the soul and is discordant with poetry.

And yet, in **"Israfel"**, we meet an angel whose very instrument is the heart, and whose song is all fire, fervor, and "burning measures." He causes the stars to be giddy, the enamored moon to totter and blush, the lightning to be red, and all of his celestial hearers to be mute with rapture. Why is Israfel's song not a degrading performance? We know that it cannot be, since the stars suspend their hymns to God in order to hear it. Most of the answers, however, are given by condensed and muffled implication in the fourth stanza:

> But the skies that angel trod,
>   Where deep thoughts are a duty—
> Where Love's a grown-up God—
>   Where the Houri glances are
> Imbued with all the beauty
>   Which we worship in a star.

Israfel's condition in heaven is here described in terms of the triad of faculties which I have just mentioned. *Deep thoughts* have to do with the intellect, *duty* pertains to the moral sense, and *beauty* to the aesthetic sense, or taste. An angelic soul, it seems, has the same constituents as a human soul, but the difference is that Israfel is an inhabitant of the skies. Throughout his early work, from **"Al Aaraaf "** onward, Poe argues that intellectual knowledge is not fit for man in the earthly condition of his soul, and that it wars with that sense of beauty which is our sole means of approaching the divine; but for the angel Israfel, who dwells "in the high Heaven of pure knowledge," there is no conflict between intellect and taste, and these faculties are in turn perfectly attuned to the moral sense. Israfel has an intact and harmonious soul, as the poet of Earth does not.

Often, when Poe wishes to evoke supernal beauty, he will do so by combining erotic words or images with inhibitory ideas. When Nesace, the spirit of Beauty, arrives at her palace in the second part of **"Al Aaraaf,"** we are given this picture: "From the wild energy of wanton haste / Her cheeks were flushing and her lips apart; / The zone that clung about her gentle waist / Had burst beneath the heaving of her heart." Wantonness, flushing, parted lips and a burst zone are all very libidinous, but these effects are countered by the fact that she is a heavenly spirit whom we have just seen praying to God, and that she is here frozen into immobility like a statue—a statue perhaps by Canova, that sculptor whom Mario Praz once aptly dubbed "The Erotic Refrigerator." The same effect of chastened passion is achieved in two words in the poem **"Evening Star,"** where Poe extols the "distant fire" of Venus. The dark-eyed Houri glances in "Israfel" may for a moment suggest mere voluptuousness, but then we are told that they are "Imbued with all the beauty / Which we worship in a star"—that they are objects of distanced and spiritual devotion. Having chastened his Houris, Poe can then proceed in his following lines to Q.E.D.: "Therefore, thou are not wrong, / Israfeli, who despisest / An unimpassioned song. . . ." Owing to his psychic wholeness and his heavenly environment, Israfel's song can be both passionate and pure; he can handle the erotic; he can intoxicate his heart without risking his spiritual balance; whereas the poet of Earth, a divided soul in a degraded environment, must forever by wary of falling into "The napthalene river of passion accurst."

The first version of **"Israfel"** is even more concentrated on the theme of passion in poetry than the later and more familiar one, but the second contains a parenthetical addition which once seemed to me decorative at best, but now strikes me as thoroughly pertinent. I refer to the lines in which we are told how "the red levin / (With the rapid Pleiads even, / Which were seven,) / Pauses in Heaven." The Pleiades are rapid because, when they were nymphs on Earth, they were pursued by theenamored hunter Orion; translated to Heaven by Zeus, they are safe from Orion's lust, but are still in an attitude of flight from him. As for the reduction of their number from seven to six, one of the Pleiades (named Merope) forsook the skies, according to Ovid, because of her passion for a mortal. Poe's evocation of the Pleiades is thus a double proof that, in Israfel's poetic preserve, unruly earthly passion is not allowed. The fall of Merope resembles, of course, the fall of Angelo and Ianthe in **"Al Aaraaf,"** and means exactly the same thing. Let me add, incidentally, that Merope's fall is a felicitous touch because it affords a counter-movement to the upward yearning of the speaker of the poem.

Assuming that all these things are in **"Israfel,"** why did it take me so long to see them? For one thing, Poe is theoretically opposed to *thinking* in poetry, and there are very few of his poems—the sonnet to Mrs. Clemm would be one of them—which are forthrightly argumentative in nature. One does not therefore feel encouraged to read **"Israfel"** as an implicit discourse on the facultative and emotional basis of poetry in Heaven and Earth. On the contrary, a poem which offers the rhymes *wrong, song, belong* and *long* within a six-line stanza, and gives us *levin, even, seven* and *Heaven* in successive lines, seems chiefly musical rather than verbal in intention—a melodic tribute to the angel's song. The impression that music has priority is strengthened when one notes that, in a present-tense poem, the verb *tread* has been wrenched into the past tense so as to rhyme with *God.* Though there are handsome passages in **"Israfel,"** some of the language seems thoughtless or casual. When Poe seeks to broaden the range of Israfel's passion by speaking of "Thy grief, thy joy, thy hate, thy love," he slips into nonsense; and angel who dwells in "perfect bliss" does not sing of grief and hate. To describe the instrumental use of heart-strings as "unusual" is ba-

thetic, to say the least. In what I take to be the crucial stanza, the expression "deep thoughts" may sound too banal to be taken seriously, while "duty" and "beauty," though they intend to say a great deal, may in so musical a poem be passed over as mere facile rhyming. Finally, although Poe the critic contended that "every work of art should contain within itself all that is requisite for its own comprehension," **"Israfel"** does not, in my experience, yield all of its suggested ideas unless one brings a general familiarity with Poe to bear on it.

Some time ago, at a funeral, I heard a familiar passage from St. Paul and had a delayed insight into **"Annabel Lee."** I had meant to electrify you with the quotation tonight, but in preparing to write this paper I found that the passage is already cited in Professor Mabbott's notes to the poem. This gave me mixed feelings of disappointment and comfort; as Allen Tate once remarked, in interpreting Poe we often fear that we are mad, and it can be reassuring to find that one is not being wholly original. So far as I know, the implications of the passage in question have not been explored, and so I shall state them briefly. Poe's poem says that Annabel Lee and her lover are children, and are therefore close to heaven and unsullied by the world. Their love is "more than love"; it is not merely a strong affection but a kind of blessed communion which the very angels might wish to enjoy. Thus far, what we have is a restatement, in one of Poe's last poems, of some lines from **"Tamerlane":** "Love—as in infancy was mine— / 'Twas such as angel minds above / Might envy. . . ." But now Poe turns that hyperbole into narrative, and most improbably has the envious angels cause the death of Annabel Lee; with whom, nonetheless, the lover continues somehow to be in unbroken communion: "And neither the angels in Heaven above / Nor the demons down under the sea / Can ever dissever my soul from the soul / Of the beautiful ANNABEL LEE. . . ." One of the lessons in the Episcopal *Order for the Burial of the Dead* is taken from the eighth chapter of St. Paul's *Epistle to the Romans.* I shall read to you only the words which are applicable here: "For I am persuaded, that neither death, nor life, nor angels, nor principalities, nor powers, nor things present, nor things to come, nor height, nor depth, nor any other creature, shall be able to separate us from the love of God. . . ." It seems clear to me that St. Paul has emboldened Poe to imagine his angels as seeking to separate love from love and man from God, and that Poe's adaptation of the passage from *Romans* has the inescapable effect of identifying Annabel Lee with "the love of God." Within the burial rite, St. Paul's words are a promise that the dead are safely united with their Maker; but the passage as used by Poe asserts that the soul of Annabel's lover shall never be severed from hers, or from the divine love and beauty which her soul communicates. Annabel Lee, then, is not only a kinswoman of the angels, but a mediatory spirit like Nesace or the Lady Ligeia. Her story, in fact, is the Ligeia-story without Rowena. In **"Annabel Lee,"** the angelic mediatrix is physically lost, but never is she lost to her lover's spirit, which nightly communes with her soul and its message through the glory of the moon and the divine beauty and order of the stars. (pp. 2-6)

Richard Wilbur, "Poe and the Art of Suggestion," in The University of Mississippi Studies in English, *n.s. Vol. III, 1982, pp. 1-13.*

AUTHOR'S COMMENTARY

It has been my purpose to suggest that, while [the Poetic Principle] itself is, strictly and simply, the Human Aspiration for Supernal Beauty, the manifestation of the Principle is always found in *an elevating excitement of the Soul*—quite independent of that passion which is the intoxication of the Heart—or of that Truth which is the satisfaction of the Reason. For, in regard to Passion, alas! its tendency is to degrade, rather than to elevate the Soul. Love, on the contrary—Love—the true, the divine Eros—the Uranian, as distinguished from the Dionæan Venus—is unquestionably the purest and truest of all poetical themes. And in regard to Truth—if, to be sure, through the attainment of a truth, we are led to perceive a harmony where none was apparent before, we experience, at once, the true poetical effect—but this effect is referable to the harmony alone, and not in the least degree to the truth which merely served to render the harmony manifest.

(essay date 1850)

Bettina L. Knapp (essay date 1984)

[*In the following excerpt from her critical study of Poe, Knapp investigates Poe's poetic theory as expressed in his essay "The Poetic Principle" and demonstrated throughout his poetic canon.*]

"I am young—not yet twenty—*am* a poet—if deep worship of beauty can make me one," Poe wrote. "I would give the world to embody one half the ideas afloat in my imagination." Already he was the author of **Tamerlane and Other Poems** (1827) and **Al Aaraaf, Tamerlane, and Minor Poems** (1829) and the future creator of *Poems* (1831) and **The Raven and Other Poems** (1845), works which Poe was to revise many times in his perpetual search to perfect idea, form, and tonal music.

Poe began writing poetry while still a schoolboy. **"O, Tempora! O Mores!"** written in 1825, for example, is redolent with the gusto and fervor of youth. Poetry was to remain a passion with him always, a raison d'être, a means of expressing his innermost feelings as well as a way of satisfying his own aesthetic needs. Influenced by such British romantics as Coleridge, Byron, Shelley, Keats, and Thomas Moore, Poe added his own subjective outlook and poetic style, his own very distinctive brand of mystical vision. Nevertheless, as we have already mentioned, he was also in many ways very much a late eighteenth-century man, benefiting from the scientific disciplines of the Enlightenment. Inspiration, he felt, was not enough for any poet who seeks to create a work of lasting value. Discipline and control are a requisite part of the poetic process. A poem must be thought out; it must be sequentially organized, with each emotion and idea logically proceeding from its predecessor, the whole forming an intricate network of unified construction like the Parthenon in its architectural form, remaining indelibly in the memory. Poetry must be shaped, fashioned, and polished like an organic substance. Poe leaned in his aesthetics toward classical concepts that emphasized symmetry, simplicity, and harmony. This was the goal of the Parnassian poets, those practitioners of art for art's sake: Théophile Gautier, Leconte de Lisle, and later in England Walter Pater. They believed that art and aesthetics were in themselves creative acts, one of the goals of life, and suggested that order, discipline, restraint, and craftsmanship were vital factors in all such endeavors. A work of art must be simple, objective, and impersonal so that it may become the common property of all humanity. The French symbolist poets—Baudelaire, who translated so much of Poe into French, and Mallarmé, who dedicated poems and prose works to this "renegade" American—were drawn to him because of the refinement of his verbal feasts and the hermeticism of his thought. Poe both practiced and advocated a poetics devoid of political and moral connotations, based rather on aesthetic considerations, on cool, distanced observations of the subject, using nuanced and glittering tonal modulations.

Intuitive by nature, Poe discovered and explored realms that lie beyond the visible sphere, beyond the dimensions of time and space. In these supernal spheres he experienced an exaltation of the senses that enabled him to penetrate the very heart of mystery. There he probed and questioned, glimpsed visions sparkling with gentle or iridescent luminosity, strange and elusive outlines, shifting opalescent and crystalline light. He perceived both sonorous and inaudible voices, long moments of silences followed by the emergence of outer-worldly harmonies. The writing of poetry excited and tantalized Poe.

It also satisfied an emotional need in him, allowing him to explore the pain of his isolation and loneliness, the feelings of alienation with which his orphaned childhood had left him: "I have many occasional dealings with Adversity—but the want of parental affection has been the heaviest of my trials." Yet in good Parnassian and symbolist tradition, he never directly portrayed his sense of bereavement and affliction in a personal way, expressing his feelings always by means of symbols, analogies, metaphors, and other indirect stylistic means and methods. His inner emotions were encompassed in the mood he created, in the music of the words, the imagery in which he couched his Platonic essences, his visions of ideality and beauty. Poe's verses were depersonalized, filtered through the poetic process, rid of the dross of the outside world, the imperfections that cling to matter. Like the alchemist of old, Poe bathed his images in supernal waters, cleansing and triturating them until they gleamed in inner and outer resplendence, their unvitiated luminosity concentrated in one singularly magnetic unity. (pp. 43-6)

The concept of ideal beauty was basic to Poe's *ars poetica*. Beauty is the core and essence of the poem, its universality, and its meaning. "I designate beauty as the province of the poem," he wrote in his essay "The Philosophy of Composition," published in 1846. "The *tone* of its highest manifestation" is one of "sadness." As beauty evolves in the written work, it "excites the sensitive soul to tears," thereby ushering into the poem a mood of melancholy, a whole emotional dimension. For Poe, melancholy "is the most legitimate of all poetical tones"; soundings of melancholy reverberating around death, the grief he had known as an orphan and when he lost his "ideal" love, Mrs. Stanard, his "mother" figure, Mrs. Allan, and of course, grief over his wife, Virginia, who was so soon to die.

> Of all the melancholy topics, what, according to the Universal understanding of mankind, is the *most* melancholy? Death which is also the most poetical: "When it most closely allies itself to beauty; the death, then, of a beautiful woman" is the most poetical theme.

Although death, implicit in the temporal world, is equated in Poe's poetic universe with the idea of metempsychosis (passing of a soul into another body after death), it also entails change, disruption, chaos, severing of the ties between loved one and lover, the agonizing, wrenching separation that rends every fiber of being: "Death is the painful metamorphosis. The worm becomes the butterfly—but the butterfly is still material—of a matter, however, which cannot be recognized by our rudimental organs."

Such a view as Poe's is timeless; it is Platonic and Apollonian, not Dionysian, in character. It consists in "the excitement, or pleasurable elevation of the soul," in the delectation of the purest of pleasures life can offer: "the contemplation of the beautiful." Such an appreciation of beauty or of the sense of the beautiful exists "deep within the spirit of man" and is considered by Poe as "an immortal instinct," experienced at its most acute and refined state in the creative artist, the poet.

Poe defines beauty as a transpersonal or archetypal entity that exists over and beyond the chronological, personal, mortal sphere in that fourth dimension of the mystic that no longer bears the impress of the living person grounded in earthly needs. As envisaged by Poe, beauty is divorced from human wants and needs. Like the work of art, it exists in eternal domains.

> It is no mere appreciation of the beauty before us—but wild effort to reach the beauty above. Inspired by an ecstatic prescience of the glories beyond the grave, we struggle, by multiform combinations among the things and thoughts of Time, to attain a portion of that loveliness whose very elements, perhaps, appertain to eternity alone.

Supernal beauty can be grasped during instances of ecstatic intuition, when the poet glimpses the pleasures that come with spiritual ascent and his whole being is infused with rapture. During these glimmerings, in some inexplicable way, the unconscious seems to become open to cosmic vibrations; it grasps, mixes, blends, sorts, and rearranges images, feelings, and sounds—conglomerates of infinite particles—into a new awareness.

Intuition for Poe was the great unifying principle that not only nourished but also reoriented the psyche. The poet, Poe suggests in his prose poem *Eureka,* must be both a Kepler and a Newton. "Kepler *guessed*—that is to say, he *imagined*" [intuited] the laws of gravitation. Later, Newton proved them logically and reasonably. It is during and after experiencing this very special condition of heightened awareness, Poe argues, that the poet is in a position to acquire direct knowledge. Expressed in mystical terms, the intellect knows, taste feels, and the moral notions oblige. Both rational and intuitive faculties function together. One does not block the other; on the contrary, each flows into and interrelates with the other in a most positive and satisfactory way. The mind therefore functions according to its own laws and logical processes—inductive, deductive, and reductive; taste operates through association of ideas and plays on both imagination and fancy. The great poet, Poe suggested, is endowed with vast intuitive powers, acute intellectual faculties, and a high order of taste. When these function at their best, the apprehension of beauty is possible.

The pleasurable feelings engendered by beauty, as Poe views them, are vastly different from the rapturous passion described by the romantic poets. Passion of an earthly kind, Poe believed, "degrades"; it hampers the poet's ascent to ethereal realms, impedes his visionary moments, distracts him from his obligations, "the contemplation of the Beautiful." Earthly passion undermines the serenity needed for the creation of pure beauty in the poems, the true and real love that is noble and altruistic.

In the search for supernal beauty, the poet must abandon reliance on the logic of overly rational processes, which only bog down the visionary zeal, limit the discovery of extraterrestrial realms, and obstruct the paths leading to unknown heights, those limitless vistas the poet must make his own if his voyage is to extend outside the three-dimensional sphere. Only in the world beyond the known can the poet experience this pure, giddying enchantment.

Portrait of Virginia Clemm, Poe's wife.

Paradoxically, once the vision of ethereal essences is grasped firmly in the mind's eye, the poet can return to the mundane world and concretize the vistas opened to him, embedding his new feelings and fresh sensations into multiple rhythms and tonal harmonies. Ideal beauty then can be translated into a language comprehensible to others, with the poet imbuing the symbols and analogies, metaphors, and onomatopeias (words imitating natural sounds) into apocalyptic phantasms.

In each of Poe's poems he sought to express the ideality of his vision; although he realized, as did Coleridge, whom he admired and by whom he was greatly influenced, that the mind is unable to know any realm beyond that of its own understanding or realization. Yet Poe wrote, the poet must endow his work with "the Faculty of Ideality," which "is the sentiment of Poesy." (pp. 47-50)

Ideality for Poe is linked closely to imagination and intuition. It implies a kind of vision that titilates the senses and excites the mind's desire to know, to become a source of ideas, to enhance its power to communicate so that it may apprehend relationships, forms, feelings, and ideas. The road leading to ideality, which calls imagination and intuition into play, is disorganized, a confused mass. To reach such a goal, poetic or otherwise, implies for the mystic the destruction and re-creation of old but worn forms. When, for example, the poet seeks to pierce through the world of matter into a realm beyond, into supernal spheres, he must do away with all earthly, pedestrian, and well-worn paths. Visual and auditory images must take on fresh meanings and tonalities.

The ascension or descent—for the mystic they are the same—of the soul into the Platonic world of ideality allows the poet to appreciate life in both its transpersonal and its personal aspects, resulting in the unification of the universal and the particular. But the fire of inspiration that is known during the moments of poetic creation is not to be sustained, Poe maintained, for long periods of time.

For this reason, a poem must of necessity be brief. One should be able to read it at a "single sitting." If it is longer, intensity flags, interest falters, and the sublime realm is reduced to the paltry and banal. Even such great epics as *Paradise Lost* and the *Iliad,* Poe suggests, are made up of a "succession of brief" poems connected by prose passages. Everything existing in the temporal human sphere is transient and finite, including the creative process. The poet who is unaware that he is destined to fail—in the sense that he cannot know all—is doomed to "sorrow" and to "tears" because his desire will never be assuaged, his imagination being insatiable.

Imagination, Poe maintained, knows no bounds; it energizes the soul's power of ascent and is basic to the poetic process.

> The pure Imagination chooses, from either *beauty* or *deformity,* only the most combinable things hitherto uncombined;—the compound as a general rule, partaking in character, of sublimity or beauty, in the ratio of the respective sublimity of the things combined—which are themselves still to be considered as atomic—that is to say, as previous combinations. But as often analogously happens in physical chemistry, so not unfrequently does it occur in this chemistry of the intellect, that the admixture of two elements will result in a something that shall have

nothing of the quality of one of them—or even nothing of the qualities of either. The range of the Imagination is therefore, unlimited. Its materials extend throughout the Universe. Even out of deformities it fabricates that *Beauty* which is at once its sole object and its inevitable test.

"Music," Poe wrote, "is the perfection of the soul, or idea, of Poetry" and is an essential factor in the creative process. Music, like poetry, is endowed with meter and rhythm, accented and unaccented beat. Both music and sound are mathematically connected. Poe's understanding of music may be likened to that of Pythagoras, the Greek mathematician and metaphysician.

For Pythagoras and for Poe sounds are based on numbers, with a correspondence existing between them since they are physical phenomena as well as abstract concepts. The harmonies inhabiting the cosmos, which Pythagoras called the music of the spheres, endow numbers with intelligible and sensible plenitude. Both heavenly bodies moving about in our earthly orbit and those in distant galaxies produce sounds, Pythagoras suggested. The musical consonances emanating from the various speeds of these bodies cannot always be heard by the human ear simply because of its physical limitations. They are perceptible, however, to other forms of life—and so is silence. Poe added:

> The sentiments deducible from the conception of sweet sound simply are out of reach of analysis— although referable, possibly, in their last result, to that merely mathematical recognition of equality which seems to be the root of all beauty.

Poe frequently used mathematical analogies when defining his aesthetic and philosophical concepts. "It is *Music,* perhaps, that the soul most nearly attains the great end for which, when inspired by the poetic Sentiment, it struggles—the creation of supernal beauty." The sounds of the harp, which Virginia played, or the flute, on which Poe enjoyed practicing, reverberate through increasingly rarefied matter, and only at certain frequencies can they be perceived by the human ear. As sonorities rise through the infinite particles filling the atmosphere, they are carried through space and light by electromagnetic waves until they reach that "unparticled matter permeating and impelling, all things" which Poe defined as God, Unity, One.

When the poet brings forth his work, inculcating it with beauty and sublimity, he is reflecting God's design in His created universe. The tonalities of the words, rhythms, silences, and pauses in the verse are experienced by nature as a whole, not only by the human ear but by flowers, grasses, valleys, rivers, forests, celestial gleamings and forms, each apprehended and mysteriously influenced by the poet's multiple ideographic exhalations and inhalations.

The poet is visionary and musician, a craftsman and a master of verbal incantations, a spiritual and aesthetic guide—a prophet. For the poet, patience and perseverance are not only necessities but obligations if ideality of the vision is to emerge with any sort of brilliance and clarity. Although "ecstatic intuition" and "a species of fine frenzy" are requirements during the stage of initial inspiration, afterward work must proceed "step by step, to its completion with the precision and rigid consequences of a mathematical problem."

The poet must work long hours to enforce the truth of his intuitive images, to express what he wants "in severity rather than efflorescence of language." A poet must be "cool, calm, unimpassioned," analytical, in control of idea, logic, grammar, syntax, and form. He must be ever vigilant that each word, thought, and image be depersonalized and universalized divested of those subjective and personal aspects that particularize, stultify, and mortalize what must be endowed with the eternal.

A poem should never be didactic or moralize; it must be simple and precise, an aspiration in all senses of the word, reminiscent in vision of Shelley's "Hymn to Intellectual Beauty" and his quest for the absolute meaning of life. It must be lyrical and pure in its imaginative course, like the work of Tennyson, whom Poe considered "the noblest poet that ever lived." He continued:

> I call him, and *think* him the noblest of poets—*not* because the impressions he produces are, at *all* times, the most profound—*not* because the poetical excitement which he induces is, at *all* times, the most intense—but because it *is,* at all times, the most ethereal—in other words, the most elevating and the most pure.

Poetry should be lyrical, as Shelley's "If ever poet sang (as a bird sings)—impulsively—earnestly—with utter abandonment—to himself solely—and for the mere joy of his own song—that poet [wrote Poe] was the author of 'The Sensitive Plant.' " Keats is the "sole British poet who has never erred in his themes. Beauty is always his aim," Poe added.

Poetry likewise must not be overburdened with aesthetic and metaphysical theories; it was this flaw that did so much to limit Coleridge's poetic élan, although Poe nevertheless admired him deeply. "Of Coleridge I cannot speak but with reverence. His towering intellect! His gigantic power!" When reading poetry, Poe wrote, "I tremble like one who stands upon a volcano, conscious, from the very darkness bursting from the crater, of the fire and the light that are weltering below." Veracity, not realism, is important. The "willing suspension of disbelief," as Coleridge termed it, must absorb the reader as the poet pours forth his music, having distilled his words, whittled away his emotions, and made manifest his reasoned constructs with their glimmering emanations in keeping with the preestablished design ordered by supernal beauty. Poe's poetry is mystery incarnate. (pp. 50-5)

> Bettina L. Knapp, in her *Edgar Allan Poe,*
> *Frederick Ungar Publishing Co., 1984, 226 p.*

John Heath-Stubbs   (lecture date 1986)

[*An English poet and critic, Heath-Stubbs has written studies on John Dryden, Charles Williams, and, in his* The Darkling Plain *(1950), a number of neglected Victorian authors. In the following excerpt from a lecture delivered at the first annual Poets' Corner Lecture in 1986, he claims that Poe owes his international reputation to the mythology constructed by American writers of their country's literary history.*]

[From] the point of view of the English-speaking reader, Poe's verse, with the exception of only a very few lyrics, must be approached with reserve. Its metrical skill too often seems mechanical, its imagery too narrow, too repetitive, too divorced from actual waking life. To some extent, these deficiencies disappear in translation. It is noteworthy, for example, that the French poet, Stéphane Mallarmé, chose to render Poe's poem **"The Raven"** in prose. There are two, or possibly three, poets of the English-speaking world whose continental European reputation may sometimes seem to the English-speaking reader to be perversely exaggerated. The first of these poets is Lord Byron. The second is Poe, and the third, a rather more doubtful case, I think, is Oscar Wilde. All three of them, with all their brilliance, do show these deficiencies of taste, which I suggest may well get overlooked in translation. All three are in some respects derivative poets. Byron and Wilde were both victims of persecution by their societies, on account of the scandal of their private lives, and the European reader may well consider them to be martyrs to that well-known phenomenon, English—might I say Anglo-Saxon?—hypocrisy. Poe likewise was in some respects an outcast from his society. His life was a kind of nightmare and so was his death: that his body was found on a park bench where he had been abandoned by an election mob who had used him as a dummy voter, had, one is tempted to say, a kind of symbolic quality. It was Byron who became, as it were, the godfather of the first phase of European romanticism. That was the phase which saw the poet as a splendid individualist, a heroic rebel, a flouter of conventions. And Poe is the godfather of the later phase of the same movement, when the poet is thought of as an arcane craftsman, a master of magical incantation, and an interpreter of marginal and shadowy experience.

But Poe is an American poet, and he would not, I venture to state, have attained to international importance had he not been American. (p. 29)

American writers, unlike those of Britain or other European countries, have had to construct their own mythology, to raise a pantheon of symbolic figures from their past, and to this pantheon Poe belongs. But it is the dark side of the American imagination, the nightmare which underlies the American dream, which he represents. 'Why do I always meet you here / Your eyes like agate lanterns?' So wrote Hart Crane, when in his great poem *The Bridge* he encounters the ghost of Poe in a New York subway. In the pattern of Crane's poem the subway is an image of inferno, and that encounter belongs to a poetic tradition of similar encounters in or near the underworld. The origins of this tradition can be traced to Virgil's *Aeneid* and to Homer's *Odyssey* and even further back to the ancient Babylonian epic of Gilgamesh. It leads on to Dante's encounter with the spirit of Virgil in the dark wood, and to that of those two poets and the spirit of Dante's dead master Brunetto Latini in the *Inferno;* the tradition is continued later in Eliot's encounter with the 'familiar compound ghost' (I think mainly W. B. Yeats, but Poe is also indicated) in the fire storm of the London blitz, over Bloomsbury. (p. 30)

James Russell Lowell wrote of ' . . . Poe with his raven, like Barnaby Rudge, / Three-fifths of him genius, and two-fifths sheer fudge'. **"The Raven"** is a paradoxical poem. It goes along with Poe's essay, "The Philosophy of Composition". In that document Poe claims to have constructed the poem step by step in order to achieve the maximum effect of beauty—according to him the only true aim of poetry and to be separated from moral or scientific truth. The most beautiful emotion, Poe claims, is that of sorrow, the most intense sorrow, grief for the death of a beautiful woman. The word 'nevermore' is taken for its musical quality as much as for its meaning and has to serve as a refrain. Therefore something has to repeat it again and again, and what but a talking bird, a raven. In totally severing the link between truth and beauty, Poe goes beyond his romantic masters, beyond Shelley, Coleridge, and even beyond Keats, though their thought seems to have been evolving precisely in this direction. But a far more radical break is made by the assumption that a poem is something to be constructed, coldly, and calculated, as one solves a mathematical problem, instead of being a product of inspiration or afflatus. To Wordsworth the poet was 'a man speaking to men in the language of men', for Shelley the 'unacknowledged legislator of mankind', but the archetype of the poet for Poe is a purely spiritual being: 'The angel Israfel, whose heartstrings are a lute.' The idea that a poem is a deliberate verbal construct was to bear fruit in the twentieth century, notably in Paul Valéry, and even in Yeat's 'fascination with what's difficult'. Similarly, the idea that there is no such thing as a long poem was to be developed by the aesthetic philosopher Benedetto Croce and by the Anglo-American Imagist school. But the poem itself denies the very theory on which it purports to have been constructed. In the first place, we may question whether it is the masterpiece which its early readers, and probably Poe himself, took it to be. The remorselessly trochaic metre—a metre very effective in some other languages—is, at least to my ear, generally mechanical and dead when used in English. Part of the trouble is that as each line must start with a stressed syllable, it is impossible to begin a line in the most usual way of constructing an English sentence, i.e. with a noun preceded by the definite or indefinite article or by a verb preceded by a pronoun. In so far as **"The Raven"** does work as a poem, it works not by virtue of Poe's theory, but as yet another statement of the theme which haunts all Poe's work. The raven is a messenger from the world of the dead, from the lost Lenore—yet another of Poe's buried women whose presence continues to haunt their lovers in this waiting world. It has been suggested to me, in fact, that it is precisely because of the horror of this situation—the situation stemming from the childhood trauma of his mother's death and entombment—that Poe is obliged to deceive himself and his readers into taking the poem as a deliberate intellectual construct.

In Poe, as in the Symbolists, and (in English poetry) in Swinburne, who along with Dante Gabriel Rossetti owed much to Poe, poetry aspires to the condition of music. The words are of course chosen for their musical incantory power as much as for their meaning, and so are the names of Poe's heroines, in which the liquid consonants *l* and *r,* and the nasals, *m* and *n,* predominate. Such names are Lenore, Eulalie, Ligeia, Morella, the Lady Madeline, Annabel Lee. But these are recognisable names. What of the last in the series, **"Ulalume"**? That is not a name at all: it is a primitive infantile wail. The poem that is entitled **"Ulalume"** is in logical terms almost meaningless, although it is of course yet another statement of the continuing theme of the sepulchred beloved. Again, one may question whether it is a very good poem in objective terms,

yet to read it frightens me. It is almost as if we heard the last cry of a soul desperately clutching at articulation before it falls into the abyss.

I said it is as if we heard the voice of a lost soul, but God forbid that I should be thought to be standing in judgement on the man, Edgar Allan Poe. It is true that he was in some ways weak and self-indulgent (I am thinking of his alcohol and opium addiction). Such weakness and such indulgence was all too common in his, as it is in our own, society. In regard to opium one must remember that it was freely used in the early nineteenth century as a painkiller, almost as we use aspirin. It was not only Coleridge and De Quincey who were addicted to it, and to some extent wrecked their lives by this addiction. It was also used by other writers of a different kind, by George Crabbe, and by Wilkie Collins, both of whom managed to organize their lives rather well. Poe was able to survive as long as he did through sheer industry as a writer and a journalist. This is not the mark of a basically weak character; in the artist there is always a kind of inner strength and will to survive. Such a life as Poe's is in its own way a kind of martyrdom. I use the word martyrdom advisedly, bearing in mind the original meaning of the word martyr—a witness. But speaking of a very different writer, the modern Greek poet Constantine P. Cavafy, W. H. Auden spoke of his being 'a witness to the truth', defining this as the prime duty of the poet. Poe in his own way was also a witness. Those who were closest to him seem to have found him gentle and affectionate, but the necrophile, the torturer, the untamed beast, lurked in his psyche as they lurk within each one of us. It was precisely because he had the strength to confront these monsters that his work has its universal appeal, that he was thus driven to explore the dark labyrinths within tells something about the society in which he lived. If a society rejects its poets and its prophets, they may be driven underground, not necessarily as political subversives, but as in Poe's case, psychological subversives. There is a tendency in some quarters today—I am thinking particularly of the European political left—to stress the duty of the artist to be politically committed. This can too easily be a way of bullying the artist. The very rejection of overt political values or social criticism is itself a kind of political statement, and if a poet rejects the world of normal human relationships and experience to explore a dark underworld of fantasies, he should not be regarded as an escapist. He is saying something about the health of his society which that society should take very much to heart. (pp. 32-3)

John Heath-Stubbs, "The Nightmare of Edgar Allan Poe," in PN REVIEW 61, *Vol. 14, No. 5, 1988, pp. 29-33.*

FURTHER READING

Alexander, Jean. *Affidavits of Genius: Edgar Allan Poe and the French Critics, 1847-1924.* Port Washington, N. Y.: Kennikat Press, 1971, 246 p.

Lengthy introduction discussing the reception of Poe's works among French writers of the late nineteenth and early twentieth centuries. A selection of translated studies and statements includes criticism by Charles Baudelaire, J. Barbey d'Aurevilly, Joris Karl Huysmans, Stéphane Mallarmé, Remy de Gourmont, and Paul Valéry.

Assenlineau, Roger. *Edgar Allan Poe.* Minneapolis: University of Minnesota Press, 1970, 48 p.
Introductory study of Poe's major works.

Belgion, Montgomery. "The Mystery of Poe's Poetry." *Essays in Criticism* I, No. 1 (January 1951): 51-66.
Ascertains reasons for the continued popularity of Poe's verse.

Benton, Richard P. "Platonic Allegory in Poe's 'Eleonora'." *Nineteenth-Century Fiction* 22, No. 3 (December 1967): 293-97.
Suggests that in "Eleonora," Poe modified a Platonic model of a love allegory in which the heroines of the poem, Eleonora and Ermengarde, are surrogates for Plato's Twin Venuses.

Bloom, Harold, ed. *Edgar Allan Poe: Modern Critical Views.* New York: Chelsea House Publisher, 1985, 155 p.
Collects major critical essays, including studies by Paul Valéry, D. H. Lawrence, Allen Tate, and Richard Wilbur.

Bowra, C. M. "Edgar Allan Poe." *The Romantic Imagination,* pp. 174-96. Cambridge, Mass.: Harvard University Press, 1949.
Illuminates Poe's theory of poetry to determine whether his verses exemplify the poetic ideals he espoused in "The Poetic Principle." Bowra shows how Poe organized certain characteristically Romantic themes into a "constant dogma."

Braddy, Haldeen. "Poe's Flight from Reality." *Texas Studies in Literature and Language* 1, No. 3 (Autumn 1959): 394-400.
Chronicles Poe's personal escape from reality and depiction in his poetry of a world outside space and time.

Campbell, Killis. *The Mind of Poe and Other Studies.* Cambridge, Mass.: Harvard University Press, 1933, 240 p.
Scholarly essays dealing with the range of Poe's knowledge in the arts and sciences, his literary backgrounds, biographical references in the poetry and fiction, the Griswold controversy, and contemporary evaluation of his work.

Carlson, Eric W., ed. *The Recognition of Edgar Allan Poe: Selected Criticism Since 1829.* Ann Arbor: The University of Michigan Press, 1970, 316 p.
Selected criticism organized into three periods: 1829-1899, 1900-1948, and 1949 to present. These seminal writings on Poe include commentary by Fyodor Dostoevski, A. C. Swinburne, Henry James, T. S. Eliot, and W. H. Auden.

———. *Critical Essays on Edgar Allan Poe.* Boston: G. K. Hall & Co., 1987, 223 p.
Collection of thirty reviews and essays that chronicle Poe's critical reputation.

Carter, H. Holland. "Some Aspects of Poe's Poetry." *The Arena* XXXVII, No. 208 (March 1907): 281-85.
Conveys personal impressions of Poe's poetry, concluding that while his verses fail to provide "great soul upliftment," they are nevertheless enjoyable.

Claudel, Alice Moser. "Poe as Voyager in 'To Helen'." *ESQ,* No. 60 (Fall 1970): 33-37.
Examines symbolism and identifies literary references in Poe's "To Helen."

Clough, Wilson O. "Poe's 'The City in the Sea' Revisited." In *Essays on American Literature in Honor of Jay B. Hubbell,* edited by Clarence Gohdes, pp. 77-89. Durham, N.C.: Duke University Press, 1967.
Attempts to explicate Poe's creative intent in the poem "The City in the Sea" by tracing sources and comparing versions of the poem.

Davidson, Edward. *Poe: A Critical Study.* Cambridge, Mass.: The Belknap Press, 1957, 296 p.
Assumes the viewpoint that "Poe was a 'crisis' in the Romantic and the symbolic imagination. He came near the end . . . of the idealist or Romantic expression and mind. Occupying such a place in the history of art, Poe dramatized the whole problem of what the creative imagination does when it is seeking ways of communicating those ideas lying beyond the common denotive discourse of men."

Davidson, Gustav. "Poe's 'Israfel'." *The Literary Review (Farleigh Dickinson University)* XII, No. 1 (Fall 1968): 86-91.
Discusses Poe's mistaken accreditation of a quoted line in his poem "Israfel" to the Koran.

Du Bois, Arthur E. "The Jazz Bells of Poe." *College English* 2, No. 3 (December 1940): 230-44.
Argues that the sounds and tempos of the words in Poe's "The Bells" are more important than their literal meaning.

Fletcher, Richard M. *The Stylistic Development of Edgar Allan Poe.* De Pro Prietatibus Litterarum, Series Practica 55, edited by C. H. van Schooneveld. The Hague: Mouton, 1973, 192 p.
Explores the evolution of Poe's style in both his poetry and fiction, focusing on such topics as his vocabulary, major themes, and use of symbols.

Fruit, John Phelps. *The Mind and Art of Poe's Poetry.* New York: AMS Press, 1966, 144 p.
Critical study that seeks to examine "not what Poe's poetry is in kind, but what it is in itself."

Gale, Robert L. *Plots and Characters in the Fiction and Poetry of Edgar Allan Poe.* Hamden, Conn.: Archon Books, 1970, 190 p.
Research source for locating plots and characters in Poe's works.

Hearn, Lafcadio. "Poe's Verse." *Interpretations of Literature,* edited by John Erskine, pp. 150-66. New York: Dodd, Mead and Co., 1915.
Discusses Poe's extensive use of repetends, or the repetition of lines and phrases with melodic modifications.

Jones, Buford and Ljungquist, Kent. "Poe, Mrs. Osgood, and 'Annabel Lee'." In *Studies in the American Renaissance,* edited by Joel Myerson, pp. 275-80. Charlottesville, Va.: The University Press of Virginia, 1983.
Examines possible literary sources for the poem "Annabel Lee" and searches for the woman who might have inspired Poe to write the poem.

Keefer, Frederick T. " 'The City in the Sea': A Re-examination." *College English* 25, No. 6 (March 1964): 436-39.
> Interprets "The City in the Sea" as "a word picture of a dead city" and refutes critical interpretations by Louise Pound and Killis Campbell.

Kiehl, James M. "The Valley of Unrest: A Major Metaphor in the Poetry of Edgar Allan Poe." *Thoth* V, No. 1 (Winter 1964): 42-52.
> Asserts that understanding the "valley of unrest" metaphor in Poe's poetry resolves general ambiguities and provides insight into his private symbolism.

Krutch, Joseph Wood. *Edgar Allan Poe: A Study in Genius.* New York: Alfred A. Knopf, 1926, 244 p.
> Traces "Poe's art to an abnormal condition of the nerves and his critical ideas to a rationalized defense of the limitations of his taste." considering the legend of the author's tormented life in his "supreme artistic achievement."

Levine, Stuart. *Edgar Poe: Seer and Craftsman.* Deland, Fla.: Everett/Edwards, 1972, 282 p.
> Attempts to provide a general critical framework for reading Poe based on his literary aesthetics in both theory and practice, primarily considering him in the context of nineteenth-century intellectual movements, the Gothic tradition, and American journalism.

Lewis, Charles Lee. "Edgar Allan Poe and the Sea." *The Southern Literary Messenger* III, No. 1 (January 1941): 5-10.
> Discusses sea imagery in Poe's poetry.

Ljungquist, Kent. *The Grand and the Fair: Poe's Landscape Aesthetics and Pictorial Techniques.* Potomac, Md.: Scripta Humanistica, 1984, 216 p.
> Studies the thematic significance of landscape and other types of imagery in Poe's work, relating Poe's techniques and theories of pictorialism to aesthetic schools of the eighteenth and nineteenth centuries.

Lubbers, Klaus. "Poe's 'The Conqueror Worm'." *American Literature* 39, No. 3 (November 1967): 375-79.
> Offers a brief explication of "The Conqueror Worm," tracing literary sources utilized by Poe as well as critical reception of this poem.

Lynd, Robert. "The Poetry of Poe." *The New Statesman* XVIII, No. 467 (25 March 1922): 704, 706.
> Compares Poe with Walt Whitman and notes that while Poe's poetry is flawed, his verses reveal "a man of genius in literature."

Maddison, Carol Hopkins. "Poe's 'Eureka'." *Texas Studies in Literature and Language* II, No. 3 (Autumn 1960): 350-67.
> Considers *Eureka* Poe's most impressive, imaginative work and claims that this poem is "the culmination and the end of his lifelong investigations into the nature of created things."

Marder, Daniel. "Poe's Perverse Imp and M. Dupin." *College Literature* VIII, No. 2 (Spring 1981): 175-85.
> Discerns a conflict between "impish passion and idealistic longings" in Poe's life and poetry.

Markham, Edwin. "The Poetry of Poe." *The Arena* XXXII, No. 177 (August 1904): 170-75.
> Generally favorable review of Poe's poetic canon.

Matthiessen, F. O. "Poe." *The Sewanee Review* LIV, No. 2 (April-June 1946): 175-205.
> Biographical essay in which Matthiessen links events in Poe's life with his literary canon.

More, Paul Elmer. "A Note on Poe's Method." In his *Shelburne Essays on American Literature,* edited by Daniel Aaron, pp. 99-106. New York: Harcourt, Brace & World, 1963.
> Considers Poe "the poet of unripe boys and unsound men."

Mulqueen, James E. "The Meaning of Poe's 'Ulalume'." *American Transcendental Quarterly,* No. 1 (1969): 27-30.
> Interprets Poe's poem "Ulalume" as a poetic extension of the ideas expressed in his prose poem *Eureka.*

Olivero, Frederico. "Symbolism in Poe's Poetry." *The Westminster Review* CLXXX (August 1913): 201-07.
> Postulates that the landscape symbolism in Poe's poetry reveals the pathos of his soul.

Pittman, Diana. "Key to the Mystery of Edgar Allan Poe: 'To Helen'—To the Ship Hellas." *The Southern Literary Messenger* III, Nos. 10-11 (October-November 1941): 499-501.
> Asserts Poe's poem "To Helen" was written about a Greek ship Poe had seen launched in 1826.

Pollin, Burton R. *Dictionary of Names and Titles in Poe's Collected Works.* New York: Da Capo Press, 1968, 212 p.
> Guide to the location of characters, work titles, and names in Poe's collected works.

———. *Discoveries in Poe.* Notre Dame, Ind.: University of Notre Dame Press, 1970, 303 p.
> Scholarly essays on Poe's literary sources and influences.

Ramakrishna, D. "Poe's 'Eureka' and Hindu Philosophy." *Emerson Society Quarterly,* No. 47 (1967): 28-32.
> Studies Poe's concept of the universe and God as presented in *Eureka,* noting that Poe's theories are strikingly similar to Hindu philosophical thought.

Ransome, Arthur. *Edgar Allan Poe: A Critical Study.* New York: Haskell House Publishers, 1972, 237 p.
> Critical biography of Poe in which Ransome attempts to trace Poe's thought and lifelong attempt to discover a philosophy of beauty.

Renaud, Armand. "Edgar Poe According to his Poetry." In *Affidavits of Genius: Edgar Allan Poe and the French Critics, 1847-1924,* edited by Jean Alexander, pp. 167-79. Port Washington, N.Y.: Kennikat Press, 1971.
> 1846 review of Poe's poetry in which Renaud admires Poe's evocative descriptions and ability to inspire strong emotions.

Smith, C. Alphonso. "Edgar Allan Poe." *The Mentor* 10, No. 8 (September 1922): 3-8.
> Suggests ways in which Poe has influenced world literature.

The Southern Literary Messenger XXV, No. 5 (November 1857): 331-35.
> Early review of "The Raven" in which the anonymous critic praises Poe's unique style and deems the poem unsurpassed in technique.

Stockton, Eric W. "Celestial Inferno: Poe's 'The City in the Sea'." *Tennessee Studies in Literature* VIII (1963): 99-106.

Explicates Poe's "The City in the Sea," deeming it strongly indicative of Poe's artistic nature.

Stovall, Floyd. *Edgar Poe the Poet: Essays New and Old on the Man and His Work.* Charlottesville: University Press of Virginia, 1969, 273 p.
    Collection of biographical, scholarly, and critical essays.

Warfel, Harry R. "The Mathematics of Poe's Poetry." *The CEA Critic* XXI, No. 5 (May 1959): 1, 5-6.
    Theorizes that Poe understood "the mathematical principle of functionality," which allowed him to achieve new heights in syntax.

Williams, Paul O. "A Reading of Poe's 'The Bells'." *Poe Newsletter* I, No. 2 (October 1968): 24-5.
    Asserts that "The Bells" enforces Poe's overriding theme that discord and death alone are triumphant.

Woodberry, George E. *Edgar Allan Poe.* 1885. Reprint. New York: AMS Press, 1968, 354 p.
    One of the earliest full-length examinations of Poe and his work.

Zayed, Georges. *The Genius of Edgar Allan Poe.* Cambridge, Mass.: Schenkman Publishing Co., 1985, 223 p.
    Critical study divided into two parts, the first tracing the development of Poe's reputation in France and the second examining his achievements as a critic, short story writer, poet, and philosopher.

Edwin Arlington Robinson

1869-1935

American poet and dramatist.

Robinson achieved a hard-won prominence in American literature during the early twentieth century. During a period of intense experimentation in verse, he adhered to the terse diction, careful metrical forms, and philosophical themes of his predecessors Robert Browning and Matthew Arnold in his work. Nonetheless, Robinson's poetic style signaled an end to the baroque sentimentality of nineteenth-century American poetry. While he is best known for his powerful narrative poems that dramatize the tribulations of small-town individuals, Robinson was not a systematic philosopher. His works, despite their sad, ironic tone and often tragic conclusions, are considered to be life-affirming, revealing a transcendental belief in God and in the value of human existence. Robinson stated: "I prefer men and women who live, breathe, talk, fight, make love, or go to the devil after the manner of human beings. Art is only valuable to me when it reflects humanity or at least human emotions."

A descendent of the colonial poet Anne Bradstreet, Robinson was born in Head Tide, Maine, and grew up in the nearby town of Gardiner, his model for the fictitious Tilbury Town which figures prominently in his early verse. Fascinated by the sounds and rhythms of words, he began to write poetry at an early age. Robinson attended Harvard University for two years, but a decline in the family's circumstances forced him to return home. Because of his elder brothers's bad financial investments, alcoholism, and drug addiction, Robinson's family was left nearly penniless, and he subsequently rejected a business career in favor of writing poetry. Unable to aid his family financially and dependent on friends for money, Robinson developed a sense of personal failure and guilt which haunted him for the remainder of his life. Robinson's portraits of nonconformists, derelicts, alcoholics, and suicides, as well as his preoccupation with human failure, are attributed by many commentators to his personal experiences with poverty and alienation.

Early in his career, Robinson mastered the poetic form for which he became well known: the dramatic lyric marked by firm stanzaic structure, deft rhyming patterns, and colloquial speech. His first book of poems, *The Torrent and the Night Before,* is a forty-four page pamphlet which Robinson had printed and distributed to numerous critics at his own expense. In addition to dramatic lyrics, this work offers myriad styles: blank and rhymed verse, villanelles and ballades, as well as traditional sonnets and quatrains. While *The Torrent and the Night Before* received a few positive reviews for its stark portraits of Tilbury Town, it was generally ignored by both critics and readers. Robinson's next volume of verse, *The Children of the Night,* consists of psychological portraits of such odd characters as Aaron Stark, a vindictive miser, and Luke Havergal, a deprived lover. "Richard Cory" is a frequently anthologized poem about a seemingly fortuitous gentleman who earned the respect of the townspeople yet " . . .

one calm summer night / Went home and put a bullet through his head." *The Children of the Night* attracted the attention of President Theodore Roosevelt after his son sent him a copy of the book from school. Roosevelt was impressed with Robinson's work and gave it lavish praise, and in the summer of 1905 he helped arrange employment for Robinson at the New York City Custom House so that he could write without financial worry. Robinson's finances, however, remained less than solvent until the late 1920s. The title poem of *Captain Craig,* Robinson's fourth volume, is a dramatic narrative of approximately 2,000 lines about a derelict whose bombastic yet erudite observations of humanity serve as a source of fascination for the unnamed narrator. Although the shorter poems in the collection received scant praise, most reviewers found "Captain Craig" obscure and difficult. William Morton Payne, however, held a dissenting opinion: "['Captain Craig'] displays shrewdness in getting at the heart of life's problems, irony in his treatment of them, and zeal in his warfare upon their adjuncts of insincerity or hypocrisy."

Beginning with *The Town down the River,* Robinson began composing poems centering on historical and public personages, yet the theme of personal ruin remained constant.

"The Island," for example, is a dramatic monologue spoken by French dictator Napoleon Bonaparte in which he recalls events leading to his defeat at Waterloo and his exile on the British island Saint Helena. A companion volume, *The Three Taverns,* features such individuals as abolitionist John Brown, the biblical figure Lazarus, and the early American statesmen Alexander Hamilton and Aaron Burr. *The Man against the Sky* is generally considered Robinson's most successful single volume of verse and received the second of three Pulitzer Prizes awarded to Robinson. Containing the deft psychological portraits which marked his earlier efforts, this collection reflects Robinson's belief in the moral superiority of seemingly worthless characters over their more materially successful neighbors.

In 1922, Robinson earned the Pulitzer Prize for his *Collected Poems.* In addition to reprinting his earlier verse, this volume also includes new poems that are now considered essential to Robinson's canon: "Mr. Flood's Party," "The Tree in Pamela's Garden," and "Rembrandt to Rembrandt." Of Robinson's achievements in this collection, Louis Untermeyer asserted: "When most of the preceding generation were poeticizing in ornate and artificial numbers, Robinson was the first to express himself in that hard and clear utterance which became part of our present manner. . . . Unperturbed by the battles over new forms and metrical innovations, he has gone on, like every first-rate artist, making old forms distinctive and definitely his own." Around the time of *Collected Poems*'s publication, Robinson produced *Lancelot,* which was preceded by *Merlin* and followed by *Tristram.* Commonly referred to as his Arthurian trilogy, these book-length works are composed in blank verse and were well received, but are no longer thought to be as important as Robinson's earlier verse. Despite brief passages of substantial lyric beauty, the poems are generally faulted for their length and monotonous tone. *Tristram,* however, became a best-seller, a rare distinction for a book of poetry, and earned Robinson his third Pulitzer Prize in 1928.

Avon's Harvest is the first of several book-length dramatic dialogues in which Robinson further delineates the theme of guilt and dereliction. The work is a psychological piece featuring a man who is haunted by the spirit of a schoolmate who died on the *Titanic.* For most critics, *The Man Who Died Twice* best represents Robinson's preoccupation with personal ruin. Fernando Nash, the poem's central character, is a talented musician and composer who succumbs to alcohol and debauchery for many years before redeeming himself by playing drums in a Salvation Army band. *The Man Who Died Twice* was one of Robinson's most accessible books and earned him his second Pulitzer Prize. "In *The Man Who Died Twice,*" commented Hoyt C. Franchere, "we see Robinson's finest development of the failure-redeemed theme, not only because of its well-framed structure but also because of the poet's masterful use of the language of music. . . . The poetic imagery sings in a more melodious key than we hear pitched in most of Robinson's blank-verse narratives." Robinson's other book-length poems include *Roman Bartholow* and *Cavender's House,* domestic tragedies depicting betrayal, unrequited love, and adultery.

Robinson's final poems explore the subjects found in his earlier verse. *Nicodemus* is a collection of medium-length pieces which center on biblical themes, the inhabitants of Tilbury Town, and the New England landscape. *Talifer,* another book-length effort, deviates from Robinson's previous domestic tragedies in his rather light-hearted tale of two couples who decide to exchange partners. *Amaranth* is an allegory concerning a disillusioned painter who enters an alternate world populated by other artists whose dreams were thwarted. Robinson's last work, *King Jasper,* was published posthumously in 1935. While favoring his Arthurian trilogy in tone and structure, *King Jasper* consummates Robinson's aesthetic principles and thematic concerns. Although the work was not successful because of its ambitious scope, most commentators agree that its examination of humanity in a transitory world best concludes Robinson's career. "Robinson's poems, the best of them and those that will last," stated Radcliffe Squires, "emerge from an awareness that life is continuously menaced: that innocence and experience alike are threatened by the bland modular construction of society and the soulless press of industrialism."

(For further information on Robinson's life and career, see *Twentieth-Century Literary Criticism,* Vol. 5; *Contemporary Authors,* Vol. 104; *Dictionary of Literary Biography,* Vol. 54; and *Concise Dictionary of Literary Biography: Realism, Naturalism, and Local Color: 1865-1917.*)

PRINCIPAL WORKS

POETRY

The Torrent and the Night Before   1896
The Children of the Night   1897
Captain Craig   1902
The Town Down the River   1910
The Man against the Sky   1916
Merlin   1917
Lancelot   1920
The Three Taverns   1920
Avon's Harvest   1921
Collected Poems   1921
Roman Bartholow   1923
The Man Who Died Twice   1924
Dionysus in Doubt   1925
Tristram   1927
Sonnets, 1889-1927   1928
Cavender's House   1929
The Glory of the Nightingales   1930
Matthias at the Door   1931
Poems   1931
Nicodemus   1932
Talifer   1933
Amaranth   1934
King Jasper   1935
Tilbury Town   1953
Selected Poems   1965

OTHER MAJOR WORKS

Van Zorn (drama) 1914
The Porcupine (drama) 1915
Selected Letters of Edwin Arlington Robinson (letters) 1940
Untriangulated Stars: Letters of Edwin Arlington Robinson to Harry de Forest Smith, 1890-1905 (letters) 1947

William P. Trent   (essay date 1897)

[*An American educator and critic, Trent was the founder and editor of the* Sewanee Review, *an important literary journal featuring the work of Southern writers. Throughout his career, Trent specialized in histories and criticism of American literature, his most notable work being the* Cambridge History of American Literature *(1917-20). In the following excerpted review of* The Torrent and the Night Before, *Trent considers Robinson to be a writer of great promise.*]

Mr. Edwin Arlington Robinson, of Gardiner, Maine has sent us a tiny volume of verse [entitled *The Torrent and the Night Before*]. . . . We wish we could praise . . . the independence shown in the short dedication which runs as follows: "This book is dedicated to any man, woman, or critic who will cut the edges of it.—I have done the top." Independence is all very well—but Mr. Robinson's has an unnecessary note of flippancy about it.

We have, however, made ourselves one of his dedicatees, for we have cut the edges of his book and we are glad to have done so. Mr. Robinson has one important quality of the poet—one that is a sufficient excuse for his having published his verses—to-wit, a knowledge of the technique of his art and an obvious love for it. We fancy that he is young, for we detect the influences of other poets in his work, and if he is, we have decided hopes of him—nay, we not only have hopes of him, which is what almost any kindly critic may say of any fledgling poet, but we have a positive desire to see his next volume. The maturity which years will bring and the love and respect for his art which he already has will surely enable him to take longer and higher flights away from the common-place level of mere versifying around which so many contemporary poets keep hovering.

Mr. Robinson has, of course, a good deal to learn in the coming years. . . . He must learn that the impressionist effect produced in **"The House on the Hill"** is not worth striving after, and that the chaotic effect produced in **"A Poem for Max Nordau"** is distinctly to be avoided. He must learn to put a little more concreteness into such poems as **"Her Eyes,"** and **"An Old Story,"** if he wishes to be loved and "understood" of the people. But it is always easy enough to shower advice good or bad on a young poet, so let us rather give him some ungrudging praise.

We think that he handles the sonnet very well indeed—especially when he writes of his favorite authors. Take for example the close of one to Matthew Arnold:—

> Still does a cry through sad Valhalla go
> For Balder, pierced with Lok's unhappy spray—
> For Balder, all but spared by Frea's charms;
> And still does art's imperial vista show,
> On the hushed sands of Oxus, far away,
> Young Sohrab dying in his father's arms.

Almost if not quite equally as good are the sonnets on Crabbe, Hood, Thomas Hardy, and Verlaine. The verses on Whitman are also excellent, although some may not agree with their note of praise. (pp. 243-45)

But our poet does good work in those commoner measures, which, as Goethe remarked long since, go more swiftly to the heart than the elaborate verse-forms that find so much favor to-day. Here, for example, are [two] strong stanzas from a poem entitled **"The Children of the Night"**:

> And if there be no other life,
> And if there be no other chance
> To weigh their sorrow and their strife
> Than in the scales of circumstance,
>
> 'Twere better, ere the sun go down
> Upon the first day we embark,
> In life's embittered sea to drown
> Than sail forever in the dark.

(p. 245)

The thought expressed in the above verses is not new or profound, the feeling is and has been experienced as intensely by many men, but it is impossible to deny that Mr. Robinson has transmuted them into that indefinable something called poetry.

There are other things to praise in Mr. Robinson's book, the Browning-like verve of the last poem, the felicity of the **"Horace to Leuconoë"** (though surely Mr. Robinson must feel that the sonnet form is a lame one in which to render Horace in spite of the example of a distinguished living poet), the homely patriotism of the sonnet in praise of Boston. There are also other things to condemn such as the lack of restraint in the poem entitled **"The Wilderness."** Our space, however, is limited and we do not wish our readers to suspect us as posing as a "poet-finder." . . . The true poet sooner or later finds his public and his public finds him—often without the intervention of the critic, sometimes in spite of the latter's denunciations. Our purpose is a more modest one—viz. to encourage Mr. Robinson with the thought that he has had at least one interested reader. . . . Certainly the copy that found its way to our table was not bought—but we have bought many worse books. (p. 246)

> *William P. Trent, "A New Poetic Venture," in* The Sewanee Review, *Vol. V, No. 2, April, 1897, pp. 243-46.*

The Nation, NEW YORK   (essay date 1898)

[*In the following excerpt, the anonymous critic offers a favorable review of* The Children of the Night.]

The poet Tennyson, pointing a quarter of a century ago to a copy of Miller's early poems that stood on a shelf of his library, said briefly to an American visitor: "There's power there, but crude." Among all the new American poems which have lately passed across the critic's desk, there is no question which is entitled to just this praise so far as it goes. It is *The Children of the Night,* by Edwin Arlington Robinson. Nay, one can go farther than this, for, while the variety of Mr. Robinson's measure is as yet small, he does his work deftly and thoroughly within that plot of ground, and packs even his sonnets with such vigor and such creative imagination that the whole story is told. He writes of men and women, not of external nature, and uses the latter only as the Greeks did, for a setting, not a theme, which is the better way. When he deals of books, there is the same power of characterization. We expect young poets to have their say about Verlaine and Whitman, but we hardly expect them to have heard of Crabbe; and yet what prose critic ever summed up Crabbe and placed him in his niche so completely as this young American? . . .

And when the young poet, looking away from his bookshelves, turns his lens upon the village street which he knows so well, the result shows the same power of putting a whole life, or a whole generation of lives, into the same narrow compass of fourteen lines:

"The Clerks"

I did not think that I should find them there
When I came back again; but there they stood,
As in the days they dreamed of when young blood
Was in their cheeks and women called them fair.
Be sure, they met me with an ancient air,—
And yes, there was a shopworn brotherhood
About them; but the men were just as good,
And just as human as they ever were.

And you that ache so much to be sublime,
And you that feed yourselves with your descent,
What comes of all your visions and your fears?
Poets and kings are but the clerks of Time,
Tiering the same dull webs of discontent,
Clipping the same sad alnage of the years.

Mr. Robinson is not afraid of odd words where they give just what he needs.

> *A review of "The Children of the Night," in*
> The Nation, *New York, Vol. LXVI, No. 1718,*
> *June 2, 1898, p. 426.*

May Sinclair   (essay date 1906)

[*An English novelist, Sinclair was one of the first authors to incorporate the theories of modern psychology into fiction. In such novels as* The Divine Fire *(1904)* and The Three Sisters *(1914), she utilized the psychoanalytic concepts of Sigmund Freud to explore the subtle consequences of sexual sublimation while rebelling against Victorian sexual and social values. In the following excerpt, Sinclair comments on the spiritual and philosophical aspects of* Captain Craig.]

Mr. Robinson is a poet of another world and another spirit. His poems fall into three groups: lyrics,—including ballads and old ballade forms,—character sketches, and psychological dramas, poems dramatic in everything except form. It is, in fact, difficult to name these dramas that cannot be played, these songs that cannot possibly be sung. But the point of view is dramatic, the emotion lyric. In his songs (since songs they must be called) he has reduced simplicity to its last expression. (p. 330)

He has given us characters drawn to the life in the fourteen lines of [**"Aaron Stark"**]:

Withal a meagre man was Aaron Stark,—
Cursed and unkempt, shrewd, shrivelled, and morose.
A miser was he, with a miser's nose,
And eyes like little dollars in the dark.
His thin, pinched mouth was nothing but a mark,
And when he spoke there came like sullen blows
Through scattered fangs a few snarled words and close,
As if a cur were chary of its bark.

Glad for the murmur of his hard renown,
Year after year he shambled through the town,—
A loveless exile moving with a staff;
And oftentimes there crept into his ears
A sound of alien pity, touched with tears,—
And then (and only then) did Aaron laugh.

(p. 331)

In some of his shorter poems (**"Sainte-Nitouche"** and **"As a World would have It"**) he has pressed allusiveness and simplicity to the verge of vagueness. In his longer psychological dramas—for they are dramas in all save form—he is a little too analytically diffuse. In all he has rendered human thought and human emotion with a force and delicacy which proves him a master of this form. For imaginative insight, subtlety, and emotional volume, **"The Night Before"** may stand beside Browning's "A Soul's Tragedy" and Meredith's "Modern Love;" and **"The Book of Annandale"** will stand alone, though in a lower place, in its burning analysis of the conflict between scruple and desire. Quotation would give no idea of the spirit of this poem. It is woven all of one piece, and its strength lies in its profound human quality rather than in the force of single passages. Mr. Robinson has few purple patches; he works solidly and sombrely, often in gray on gray.

He has the great gift of spiritual imagination, and an unerring skill in disentangling the slender threads of thought and motive and emotion. All these qualities are conspicuous in the long blank-verse poem **"Captain Craig."** . . . At a first glance there is little charm about this severely undecorated poem, written in unmusical and often monotonous blank verse, shot with darts of intellectual brilliance, but unrelieved by any sensuous coloring. The charm grows in the reading. **"Captain Craig"** is a philosophy of life, taught through the humorous lips of a social derelict, a beggared Socrates, disreputable as the world counts reputation. It is a drama of the Unapparent, revealing the divine soul hidden in the starved body of that "sequestered parasite;" a soul that had the courage to be itself, abiding in its dream, facing the world as a superb failure. . . . (pp. 331-32)

Captain Craig is portrayed in all the shining paraphernalia of the inner life. His sustained flight of philosophy is broken by scraps of literary reminiscence, scriptural and classic, fragments, as it were, of gold or marble, showing in what quarries his brilliant youth once dug. There is an immense pathos in the closing scene. The Captain, having made so good a fight, desired to be buried with military honors, and requested that trombones should be played at his funeral, as a tribute to the triumph and majesty of the inner life. . . .

The message of this poet is: Be true to the truth that lies nearest to you; true to God, if you have found him; true to man; true to yourself; true, if you know no better truth, to your primal instincts; but at any cost, be true. **"Captain Craig"** is one prolonged and glorious wantoning and wallowing in truth.

What Mr. Robinson's work will be in the future it is as yet impossible to say. What he has done speaks for itself. His genius has no sense of action, brutal and direct; but he has it in him to write a great human drama, a drama of the soul from which all action proceeds and to which its results return. (p. 333)

May Sinclair, "Three American Poets of To-day," in The Atlantic Monthly, *Vol. 98, No. 3, September, 1906, pp. 325-35.*

Joyce Kilmer (essay date 1912)

[*An appreciative survey of Robinson's poetry.*]

The motives of poets are, as a rule, not hard to find. Thus George Herbert wrote for the glory of God, Walt Whitman for the glory of Man, and Baudelaire for the glory of the Devil. There are few books of verse in which there is not evident a definite purpose to edify, to amuse, to corrupt, to shock, to influence in some way the prospective reader. The most enthusiastic disciples of "Art for Art's Sake" were . . . preachers, whole-heartedly intent on spreading their special gospel of Beauty. Even when the poet's aim is not directly to teach or to persuade, there is frequently a conscious effort at self-advertisement—self-revelation is perhaps a more courteous phrase. The poet is striving to tell the world about his love, or his hate, about his lady or his enemy, about his spiritual or physical emotions or sensations. So even the most personal lyrist becomes didactic from his desire to teach the public to be interested in his affairs.

This statement is not made in a spirit of hostile criticism. From the vine-crowned scop chanting his sage of blood and fire among the warriors in the banquet hall to the modern versemaker typewriting his quatrain for the magazine, the poet has had in mind his audience. This is just; this is, in fact, inevitable. But it is, nevertheless, true that the reader of verse grows weary of the constant repetition of direct and obvious appeals, and seeks often in vain for the poem which shall not force its message upon him, for the poet who shall write neither to persuade nor to exhibit, but in response to the creative urge.

This phenomenon, poetry with no purpose, with no cause save its own demand to be, with no justification save its own beauty, distinguishes the work of Edwin Arlington Robinson from that of most of his contemporaries. It is a fact that Miss May Sinclair, writing in *The Atlantic Monthly* six years ago, stated that this poet had a message, and that it was "Be true to the truth that lies nearest to you, true to God, if you have found him; true to man, true to yourself; true if you know no better truth to your primal instincts; but at any rate be true" [see excerpt dated 1912]. But this teaching is not definitely stated in any of Robinson's poems. If it can be derived from them as a whole, it must be by a reader of the most philosophic type, who sees in every simple statement a premise of some large conclusion.

No, Robinson does not preach, nor does he argue. He states, he describes, he narrates, not, it seems, so much for the sake of his audience as for his own relief. Yet he is by no means remote or unworldly. There are few poets who are so invariably human. In fact, humanity is an obsession with him. He is a realist in the proper meaning of the word; not a nominalist, not a morbid chronicler of sordid detail, but a student of life. He writes of the present, knowing that it is an aspect of eternity; of man, knowing that he is immortal and incomprehensible. There is in his verse a surprising lack of classical allusion and scholarly decoration. His lyrics are austere expressions of simple emotions,

his character sketches are impartial portrayals of subjects rich in actuality, his narratives are economical statements of tremendous and real events. Nothing is added, nothing taken away; the words set forth the fact in all its beautiful and terrible clarity.

One characteristic of his sternly simple method is evident in his treatment of the fixed forms of versification. Usually the poet who prides himself on his strength takes particular delight in breaking the laws of his craft, in showing contempt of rhyme and rhythm. To such a writer the word "sonnet" smells of the prison. The suggestion that he should write a ballade or a rondeau would seem to him a wanton insult. But this is not Robinson's attitude. The forms of poetry exist; they are established; he accepts them. But the forms are made for the poet, not the poet for the forms. So, for example, in **"The Growth of Lorraine"** he makes two sonnets, faultless in construction, tells a story of love and death which, expanded, might fill a volume. This is not the use to which sonnets are generally put, but what does it matter? The sonnet form is a difficult instrument, and the player who has mastered it has won the right to play on it any tune he wishes.

Equally typical is Robinson's treatment of that highly artificial form, the villanelle. What thoughts of delicate splendor that word calls up! Troubadours and lutes and laughter, painted fans and painted ladies. But Robinson does not think of this. There is something he wants to say, the villanelle seems to be a convenient method, so he uses it. The result is a poem of striking simplicity, of striking effectiveness, but so different in spirit from the traditional villanelle that its form is at first scarcely recognized. For Robinson uses the forms of poetry as boldly as though he had invented them. . . .

Aside from **"The Master"** and **"For a Dead Lady,"** Robinson is perhaps best known for his brief sketches in verse, labeled for the most part with unusual proper names, such as Cliff Klingenhagen, Leffingwell, and Miniver Cheevy. Sometimes these are dramas in little, sometimes they are studies of character. It is natural that an isolated poem of this type, seen in the pages of a magazine, should repel rather than attract the casual reader. For, as has been said before, Robinson does not explain or elaborate or even suggest an emotion. The poem arises as the spontaneous expression of a strong impression—it is naked of intent. But when these poems are considered together they develop a congruity and interrelation which make clear the separate meaning of each. **"How Annandale Went Out,"** for example, is mystifying to one who has not read **"The Book of Annandale."** But when it is once seen that there is no lesson to be learned, no hidden meaning to be sought, when the poems are taken at their face value, their power is immediately felt. They are all studies of life. They are tragic, because life is tragic; humorous, because life is humorous; fantastic, because life is fantastic. The rustic amorist, John Evereldown, goes at night through the Maine woods to his assignation in Tilbury Town; Richard Cory, the pattern of wealth and respectability, goes home and puts a bullet through his head; the miser, Aaron Stark, laughs at the sound of unmerited pity; the butcher, Reuben Bright, tears down his slaughter house in grief at his wife's death; Shadrach O'Leary, the erstwhile poet of passion, grows sane and forgets the "small ink-fed Eros of his pen," and Miniver Cheevy keeps on drinking. In these poems men and women do wise, foolish, saintly, and damnable things. For these poems are life; not life as Robinson would wish it to be, or thinks that it was of old, but as it is now, seen clearly and seen whole. He is forced to portray life and to chronicle life. He does not explain, for he cannot understand.

While the thought in Robinson's poems is set down simply and without rhetorical elaboration, it is done with no disregard of technique. In fact, the almost Greek lucidity of his work comes from a scrupulous care for words, a precision which would have delighted Pater. . . .

Not as a prophet, not as a teacher, but as a student of mankind does Robinson hold his place among poets. Always he looks at humanity, patiently, earnestly, searchingly. His poems spring from his contemplation of the fact of life, they are compounded of sympathy and wonder.

> *Joyce Kilmer, "A Classic Poet," in* The New York Times Book Review, *September 8, 1912, p. 487.*

Harriet Monroe   (essay date 1916)

[*Monroe was a central figure in the American "poetry renaissance" that took place in the early twentieth century. As the founder and editor of* Poetry: A Magazine of Verse, *Monroe maintained an editorial policy of printing "the best English verse which is being written today, regardless of where, by whom, or under what theory of art it is written." In the following excerpt taken from a review of* The Man against the Sky, *Monroe praises Robinson's deft character portraits in "Flammonde," "Ben Jonson Entertains a Man from Stratford," and "John Gorham."*]

Certain zealous admirers of Mr. Robinson insist that he was the beginning of the "new movement." In the stern stript austerities of **Captain Craig** they find the heredity of Robert Frost, Edgar Lee Masters, and other poets of modern life. In a certain sense this may be true, even though Mr. Masters, at least, never read a line of Robinson until a year after *Spoon River* was written. Before the heavily scented 'nineties were over, Mr. Robinson was writing, in a grave bare style, simple and direct poems about his neighbors, and since then, in **The Children of the Night** and **The Town Down the River,** he has gone his own way among them with complete independence. If he does not move us so deeply as the other two poets, if his work is less rich, his revelation of life less complete, this may be because of a slower, colder temperament. We do not feel him so much in the midst of things. He seems to stand aloof, like a scientist, analyzing each human being curiously, as a specimen. Perhaps, as Anders Zorn once said of a certain painter, "He does not love enough."

But in my opinion Mr. Robinson has never done better work than in [*The Man against the Sky*]. "Flammonde" is a portrait as deftly drawn as **"Miniver Cheevy,"** and more subtle in its type, that of a whimsically blighted nobility. **"The Gift of God"** presents the almost grotesque exaltation of motherhood, **"John Gorham"** is a complete little tragedy of disillusionment, and in such poems as **"Old Trails"** and **"Llewellyn and the Tree"** we observe certain odd and unexpected tricks by which fate keeps a relentless control over human lives. Only in the final and titular

poem [**"The Man against the Sky"**] does the poet seem to reflect about life in his own person, putting a bitter question to his soul in such lines as these:

> If, after all that we have lived and thought,
> All comes to Naught—
> If there be nothing after Now,
> And we be nothing anyhow,
> And we know that—why live?—
>
> (pp. 46-7)

The portrait of Shakespeare is a masterpiece. Everyone has written about Shakespeare, but no one, so far as I can remember, has got beneath his skin with such devilish ingenuity and angelic divination as Mr. Robinson when, as he puts it in the title, **"Ben Jonson Entertains a Man from Stratford."** The poet cleverly shifts all responsibility by making Rare Ben do the talking, and Ben, with a neighbor's frankness, a friend's humorous affection, and a fellow-poet's admiration, tells what seems the truth about that enigmatic figure as no one has ever told it before. I cannot quote from the poem—it is too compact. Go read it—in this tercentenary month. (pp. 47-8)

> *Harriet Monroe, "A Pioneer," in* Poetry, *Vol. VIII, No. 1, April, 1916, pp. 46-8.*

The New York Times Book Review   (essay date 1917)

[*In the following excerpted review of* Merlin, *the anonymous critic considers Robinson's version of the Arthurian legend to be less than substantial.*]

In choosing to play a variation on an Arthurian theme, Mr. Robinson has most successfully fallen between two stools. On the one hand, the "new" school scorns him for taking what one critic calls the "overworked, overpoetized Camelot crowd" for his subject, while, on the other, the dyed-in-the-wool lover of old Malory is indignant that a mere pigmy of these degenerate days should attempt to wield the staff of a giant.

One criticism is as ill-founded as the other. Any man's right to a subject is measured only by his ability to handle it—very likely there were fastidious persons in Shakespeare's time who shuddered at his presumption in revamping the classical tales of Denmark and Verona. And to choose an "overworked, overpoetized crowd" to write about, or a current one, is largely a matter of taste. The bones of all dramatic poetry, old and new, are the same; only one poet likes his cleansed by time and the kindly earth, and another prefers green corpses. One chooses to be a sexton, another an undertaker.

In **Merlin** Mr. Robinson chooses to be the sexton. It is not a great poem, though its failure is not intrinsic in its subject. The subject simply betrays more openly than a modern one certain defects in the author. Mr. Robinson has been widely praised, and he has praiseworthy qualities, but we have never been able, personally, to feel his greatness to the extent to which it has been lauded. The seriousness with which he takes himself has imposed a like gravity in the minds of many of his critics, but the fact is that he has neither the singing magic of the old school nor the swift, egotistic vitality of the new. He is a respectable poet, but he is heavy.

Yet no man may escape the qualities of his defects, more

than he may the defects of his qualities. Along with Mr. Robinson's weight goes a certain admirable courage. We like him for the fine spirit in which he has attempted *Merlin;* we like him for many a brave line in it—for the "far, nostalgic hauntboys blown from nowhere," for Vivien's eyes "that made a fuel of the night," and the "wild harmony" of blood and olive in her face, and we must admire him for the irony which made of Merlin's stone, under which it was fated that "for all his crafts he should be put in the earth quick," nothing more nor less than domestic bliss with the lady of his choice. As for the lady, the symbolism is less clear. We are told that

> the torch
> Of woman and the light that Galahad found
> Are some day to illuminate the world,

and we are left to infer that Vivien is only waiting in her "golden shell of exile" for the psychological moment to come when she shall sally forth with her torch, and shine, if not exactly like a good deed in a naughty world, at least more noticeably than one. If Mr. Robinson wishes to indulge in cloudy prophecy of this sort, he is wise to set his scene in a legendary hinterland. For in this day and age of the world, the Viviens would seem all to have flown their golden shells—and yet the North River still runs uninflamed.

> *A review of "Merlin: A Poem," in* The New York Times Book Review, *August 26, 1917, p. 313.*

Edwin Arlington Robinson [INTERVIEW WITH Joyce Kilmer] (interview date 1917)

At no time in the history of literature have the critics been able to agree upon a definition of poetry. And the recent popularity of vers libre *and* imagisme *has made the definer's task harder than ever before. Is rhyme essential to poetry? Is rhythm essential to poetry? Can a mere reflection of life justly be called poetry, or must imagination be present?*

I put some of these questions to Edwin Arlington Robinson, who wrote **Captain Craig, The Children of the Night, The Town Down the River, The Man Against the Sky** *and* **Merlin: A Poem.** *And this man, whom William Stanley Braithwaite and other authoritative critics have called the foremost of American poets . . . rewarded my questioning with a new definition of poetry. (pp. 265-66)*

[Robinson]: Poetry is a language that tells us, through a more or less emotional reaction, something that cannot be said.

All real poetry, great or small, does this. . . . And it seems to me that poetry has two characteristics. One is that it is, after all, undefinable. The other is that it is eventually unmistakable.

[Kilmer]: *Eventually. . . . Then you think that poetry is not always appreciated in the lifetime of its maker? . . .*

I never use words enough. . . . It is not unmistakable as soon as it is published, but sooner or later it is unmistakable.

And in the poet's lifetime there are always some people who will understand and appreciate his work. I really

think that it is impossible for a real poet permanently to escape appreciation. And I can't imagine anything sillier for a man to do than to worry about poetry that has once been decently published. The rest is in the hands of Time, and Time has more than often a way of making a pretty thorough job of it. (p. 266)

[*But why is it*] *that a great poet so often is without honor in his own generation, where mediocrity is immediately famous?*

It's hard to say. . . . Many causes prevent poetry from being correctly appraised in its own time. Any poetry that is marked by violence, that is conspicuous in color, that is sensationally odd, makes an immediate appeal. On the other hand, poetry that is not noticeably eccentric sometimes fails for years to attract any attention.

I think that this is why so many of Kipling's worst poems are greatly overpraised, while some of his best poems are not appreciated. *Gunga Din,* which is, of course, a good thing in its way, has been praised far more than it deserves, because of its oddity. And the poem beginning 'There's a whisper down the field' has never been properly appreciated. It's one of the very best of Kipling's poems, although it is marred by a few lapses of taste. (p. 267)

But I am always revising my opinion of Kipling. I have changed my mind about him so often that I have no confidence in my critical judgment. That is one of the reasons why I do not like to criticise my American contemporaries.

Do you think . . . that this tendency to pay attention chiefly to the more sensational poets is as characteristic of our generation as of those that came before?

I think it applies particularly to our own time. . . . More than ever before oddity and violence are bringing into prominence poets who have little besides these two qualities to offer the world, and some who have much more. (pp. 267-68)

I think it is safe to say that all real poetry is going to give at some time or other a suggestion of finality. In real poetry you find that something has been said, and yet you find also about it a sort of nimbus of what can't be said.

This nimbus may be there—I wouldn't say that it isn't there—and yet I can't find it in much of the self-conscious experimenting that is going on nowadays in the name of poetry.

I can't get over the impression . . . that these post-impressionists in painting and most of the *vers libristes* in poetry are trying to find some sort of short cut to artistic success. I know that many of the new writers insist that it is harder to write good *vers libre* than to write good rhymed poetry. And judging from some of their results, I am inclined to agree with them. (p. 269)

Do you think . . . that the poetry that is written in America to-day is better than that written a generation ago?

I should hardly venture to say that. . . . For one thing, we have no Emerson. Emerson is the greatest poet who ever wrote in America. Passages scattered here and there in his work surely are the greatest of American poetry. In fact, I think that there are lines and sentences in Emerson's poetry that are as great as anything anywhere. . . .

Within his limits, I believe that A. E. Housman is the most authentic poet now writing in England. But, of course, his limits are very sharply drawn. I don't think that any one who knows anything about poetry will ever think of questioning the inspiration of *A Shropshire Lad.*

Would you make a similar comment on any other poetry of our time? (p. 270)

I think that no one will question the inspiration of some of Kipling's poems, of parts of John Masefield's *Dauber,* and some of the long lyrics of Alfred Noyes. But I do not think that either of these poets gives the impression of finality which A. E. Housman gives. But the way in which I have shifted my opinion about some of Rudyard Kipling's poems, and most of Swinburne's, makes me think that Wordsworth was very largely right in his attitude toward the judgment of youth. But where my opinions have shifted, I think now that I always had misgivings. I fancy that youth always had misgivings in regard to what is later to be modified or repudiated. (pp. 270-71)

[There] has been much discussion recently about the rewards of poetry, and Miss Amy Lowell has said that no poet ought to be expected to make a living by writing. What do you think about it?

Should a poet be able to make a living out of poetry? . . . Generally speaking, it is not possible for a poet to make a decent living by his work. In most cases it would be bad for his creative faculties for a poet to make as much money as a successful novelist makes. Fortunately, there is no danger of that. Now, assuming that a poet has enough money to live on, the most important thing for him to have is an audience. I mean that the best poetry is likely to be written when poetry is in the air. If a poet with no obligations and responsibilities except to stay alive can't live on a thousand dollars a year (I don't undertake to say just how he is going to get it), he'd better go into some other business.

Then you don't think . . . that literature has lost through the poverty of poets?

I certainly do believe that literature has lost through the poverty of poets. . . . I don't believe in poverty. I never did. I think it is good for a poet to be bumped and knocked around when he is young, but all the difficulties that are put in his way after he gets to be twenty-five or thirty are certain to take something out of his work. I don't see how they can do anything else.

Some time ago you asked me . . . how I accounted for our difficulty in making a correct estimate of the poetry of one's own time. The question is a difficult one. I don't even say that it has an answer. But the solution of the thing seems to me to be related to what I said about the quality of finality that seems to exist in all real poetry. Finality seems always to have had a way of not obtruding itself to any great extent. (pp. 272-73)

> *Edwin Arlington Robinson, "A New Definition of Poetry," in* Literature in the Making, by Some of Its Makers, *edited by Joyce Kilmer, 1917. Reprint by Kennikat Press, Inc., 1968, pp. 265-73.*

Scribner's Magazine (essay date 1919)

[*The following is a tribute to Robinson on his fiftieth birthday.*]

Edwin Arlington Robinson has reached the half-century mark, and those of us who are fortunate enough to know him and his work can fully appreciate how great has been his contribution to the literature of his country. He is essentially and above all else American, and at the same time cosmopolitan and of every country and age, as all great poets must be. The influence of Greece, of Elizabethan England, of France, and of modern England may all be felt in his verse, but the lines that are riveted in the memory are owed to no individual source but are as up-to-date as the *Medea* of Euripides or Rostand's *Cyrano.*

As shown in his poetry, Mr. Robinson's "philosophy of life"—to use a cant phrase—is basically vigorous and sound; there are the inevitable tragedy and sorrow, the periods of depression which come in greater or less degree to all when we feel with Luke Havergal's admonisher that "the dark will end the dark if anything," but the ever underlying conviction is expressed in **"Lingard and the Stars"**:

> When earth is cold and there is no more sea,
> There will be what was Lingard, otherwise
> Why lure the race to ruin through the skies?

There is ultimate justification of existence; there is to be no snuffing out; the torch is to be handed on, responsibility does not end there; we must not only justify existence to others, but first and last to ourselves.

Mr. Robinson's keen sense of humor is always sympathetic, it never degenerates into a mere exposition of the ridiculous or grotesque, it is never bitter or warped, and with it he relieves the inevitable sadness of life. Sometimes the whole poem is quizzically humorous, like the verses about Uncle Ananias, beginning:

> His words were magic and his heart was true,
> And everywhere he wandered he was blessed.
> Out of all ancient men my childhood knew
> I choose him and I mark him for the best.
> Of all authoritative liars, too,
> I crown him loveliest.

(pp. 763-64)

Mr. Robinson's humor is not the sort that makes you laugh aloud; you smile to yourself, and read the lines to someone with whom you can share your enjoyment. The words stick in your mind, and each time you think of them they appeal to you more strongly.

There was never a master poet who depended for his name less on any individual poem. In writing of Mr. Robinson verse after verse comes into one's head that would well emphasize some point that one has been making. The temptation is strong to continue quoting poem after poem. The technique is so perfect; there is everywhere such evidence of painstaking toil and refining of words. There are some who believe that geniuses do not need to work—there seems to exist a hazy belief that they produce their masterpieces with as little volition as a spider uses in spinning a web. As far as I have been able to ascertain, master minds are no more exempt from toil than the rest of us; the only difference is that with their work they can accomplish results that are beyond the possibilities and scope of ordinary mortals. Mr. Robinson writes and rewrites, chooses and eliminates; every word that is eventually printed has been weighed and considered over and over again, not once but many times. When we read one of his poems it is like looking on a masterpiece of painting; in the back of our mind we realize what infinite pains have been taken to perfect each detail, and the unthought-out realization only heightens our appreciation of the whole. Anyone who has read the poem on Lincoln called **"The Master,"** or that about Napoleon entitled **"An Island,"** will, I am sure, understand the completeness of the result of the painstaking fitting in of mosaics. Each word has been carefully tested and its value and fitness in the context considered at length, but as is the case with every great work of art, the labor that has gone to its fulfilment does not show upon the surface, for the whole has been so thoroughly blended. Rich has been Mr. Robinson's gift to his country, and much may be hoped for in the years of fruitful labor that lie ahead of him. (p. 764)

> *"An Appreciation of the Poetry of Edwin Arlington Robinson," in* Scribner's Magazine, *Vol. LXVI, No. 6, December, 1919, pp. 763-64.*

Babette Deutsch   (essay date 1920)

[*Deutsch was an American poet, fiction writer, translator, and critic. Her poetry has often been praised for both its intellectual and emotional qualities as well as its technical accomplishment. In the following excerpted review of* Lancelot, *she commends Robinson's ability to transform the legend of Arthur and Guenevere into a contemporary love story.*]

The chief distinction of Edwin Arlington Robinson, chief, that is, among the many astonishments of his genius, is his mingling of two strains: a Puritan austerity, and a discerning tenderness. He was ever one to see "a light behind the stars," and yet he is too keen a psychologist to measure men's worth by the distances between their intuitions and his own lucid vision.

An avowed traditionalist, it is perhaps natural that at a time when men grope for refuge from a broken world, Robinson should find his in a retreat to the dim Arthurian fields. But it is equally characteristic that his retreat has in it no shadow of surrender. Rather, he recreates the disillusion, the desolation, and the pain of our own period in the tragedy of this half-forgotten legend. *Lancelot* is finer than *Merlin* by as much as it is closer to Robinson. For what he has done in this latest work is to dramatize the griefs of Guenevere and of Arthur, of Gawain and of Lancelot, in such a way as to make them our contemporaries, and with such a fervor of insight as to body forth the very breathings and heartbeats, the very fire and dolorous rains of an age wherein men wronged each other and helplessly hurt each other in ways no different from our own. Throughout the poem shines undimmed the light that burned for the poet before he touched the story of the Grail, and therewith the old divining pity.

So one hears Guenevere:

> Knowing the world, you know
> How surely and indifferently that Light
> Shall burn through many a war that is to be,

> To which this war were no more than a smear
> On circumstance.

And later, Lancelot:

> The Vision shattered, a man's love of living
> Becomes at last a trap and a sad habit.
>
> (pp. 217-18)

What strikes one most forcibly perhaps is indeed the sharpness of the poem's reality. This is largely due to the strength of the dialogue. . . . There is also the eternal magic whereby Robinson's unique images gleam out of the sterner structure of the poem, as saints might gleam out of the simple aspiring architraves of some noble cathedral. So he speaks of

> The fading out of his three visitors
> Into the cold and swallowing wall of storm.
>   . . .

The piercing imagery of the leave-taking is typical as it is arresting:

> He crushed her cold white hands and saw them falling
> Away from him like flowers into a grave.

It is idle praise to crown a poet with premature immortality. But it is certain that any contemporary would be proud to have made this poem, and it is written that none but Edwin Arlington Robinson could have endured this ancient theme with so passionate a warmth and so kindling a light. (pp. 218-19)

> *Babette Deutsch, "A New Light on Lancelot," in* Poetry, *Vol. XVI, No. 4, July, 1920, pp. 217-19.*

Harriet Monroe   (essay date 1921)

[*In the following excerpt, Monroe discusses the character sketches in* The Three Taverns *and* Avon's Harvest.]

It is a relief to some of Mr. Robinson's admirers to find him once more in the U. S. A. instead of in Camelot; for, to tell the truth, he is much more at home here, and the figures he presents [in *The Three Taverns* and *Avon's Harvest*] are much more convincing. Although there are in *The Three Taverns* certain studies of historic or legendary characters—Hamilton and Burr, Rahel Robert, John Brown, Paul of Tarsus, Lazarus—both books are mainly in this poet's most characteristic vein, mainly studies of his gnarled and weather-beaten neighbors; of incomplete, unrounded characters in tragically ill-fitting human relationships.

Of these monologue or dialogue narratives *Avon's Harvest,* the longest, is perhaps the most distinguished. With true New England frugality, it weaves a closely knit, formidable tragedy out of meagre materials—a college antagonism, a blow, a long worm-eating revenge; and its creeping emotion of horror is all the more powerful, perhaps, because of the poet's restraint. Probably a psychoanalyst would diagnose Avon's case as insanity—delusions induced by fear of the serpentine, ruthless being whose offensive love had changed into consuming hatred. But such a gradual burrowing insanity was never more sharply and powerfully presented. The thing is done with a kind of cold thrift, as effective in its way as Poe's lush and shadowed eloquence; the music in the one case being slow and stern, and in the other rich and full of sombre color. *Avon* has a tonal, almost monotonous beauty:

> You need not ask
> What undulating reptile he was like,
> For such a worm as I discerned in him
> Was never yet on earth or in the ocean
> Or anywhere else than in my sense of him.

(pp. 273-74)

Last year's book, *The Three Taverns,* is mostly also dramatic narratives. I confess that certain ones interest me intellectually but bring little emotional thrill. The Hamilton-Burr dialogue, the monologues by Saint Paul and Rahel Robert and John Brown, are searching essays in character analysis, but they leave one cold. (p. 274)

There is no lack of fire in **"London Bridge,** a case of ill-assorted marriage in which the pair hurl swathed rocks of hatred at each other—these two are terribly alive. Also, in a marriage-case less violent but more perplexing, one is deeply moved by Nimmo of the "velvet eyes",

> At his bewildered and unfruitful task
> Of being what he was born to be—a man.

(p. 275)

But it is in Mr. Robinson's meditative poems that one tastes most keenly the sharp and bitter savor of his high aloof philosophy. He is not for Demos:

> Having all,
> See not the great among you for the small,
> But hear their silence; for the few shall save
> The many, or the many are to fall—
> Still to be wrangling in a noisy grave.

He offers no solution of the problem of creation, either in general or in detail, but he presents it in vivid lines:

> There were seekers after darkness in the Valley of the
> Shadow,
> And they alone were there to find what they were looking
> for.

(pp. 275-76)

Harriet Monroe, "Robinson's Double Harvest," in Poetry, *Vol. XVIII, No. 5, August, 1921, pp. 273-76.*

Louis Untermeyer   (essay date 1923)

[*Untermeyer was a contributing editor to the* Liberator *and the* Seven Arts, *and served as poetry editor of the* American Mercury *from 1934 to 1937. He is better known as an anthologist of poetry and short fiction. Notable among his anthologies are* Modern American Poetry *(1919) and* The Book of Living Verse *(1931). The following excerpt, taken from his book* American Poetry Since 1900 *(1923), Untermeyer offers an overview study of Robinson's verse up to the publication of* Collected Poems.]

At first glance, Robinson seems one of the least American of our poets. He uses, with surprisingly few variations, the traditional English forms; there are lines when he seems to be speaking with the accents of Robert Browning in the rhythms of W. S. Gilbert. But, beneath a superficial in-

debtedness, no living writer has achieved a more personal idiom or a more melodious speech—or a more indigenous one. His ironic studies of character are as incisive as (and far sympathetic than) those of Masters'; his New England backgrounds are as faithful as those of Frost's. Lacking a fundamental buoyancy, Robinson has other qualities which may be less national but are no less local. His shrewd appraisals, his constant questioning instead of placid acceptance, his reticence that screens a vigorous analysis—these qualities reveal the spirit of the early Puritan operating with the technic of the modern psychologist.

When most of the preceding generation were poeticizing in ornate and artificial numbers, Robinson was the first to express himself in that hard and clear utterance which became part of our present manner and, later on, was adopted as one of the chief articles in the creed of the Imagists. Unperturbed by the battles over new forms and metrical innovations, he has gone on, like every first-rate artist, making old forms distinctive and definitely his own. His rhymes are brought in with a masterly ease, showing what rhyme, at its best, should be: a natural, musical punctuation. They flow, like his lines, as smoothly and pointedly as a sharp conversation.

His precise and almost astringent tone is in itself a curious study. Robinson's idiom, though a simple one to read, is not always an easy one to understand. It is a simplicity that is sometimes deceptive and often circumlocutory. He speaks of a hypodermic needle as "a slight kind of engine"; billiard balls are referred to, in a sort of indirect irony, as "three spheres of insidious ivory." . . . It is not because Robinson is fond of words that he indulges in such roundabout rhetoric; it is the occasional mistake of an essentially direct mind in an effort to avoid baldness. Usually Robinson is not only economic but actually close-fisted with his clipped phrases; sometimes in his desire to get rid of excess verbiage, he throws away everything but the meaning—and keeps that to himself. He is often like a sculptor who takes an old statue, and, in order to give it fresh vitality, cuts away the insipid ornaments and floral excrescences that spoil a simple outline. But having removed the irritating fripperies, Robinson goes further. In an effort to get below the superficials, he occasionally cuts so far below the surface that he actually sacrifices the stark outline that he was most anxious to keep. (pp. 42-4)

In *Children of the Night* there are a few poems that illustrate how Robinson in an effort for the brightest clarity ends in a dazzling obscurity. Observe **"Fleming Helphenstine"** and several of the untitled sonnets. Or regard, for still better illustrations, such poems in the succeeding volume as **"Calverly's," "Leffingwell"** and **"Atherton's Gambit,"** and observe how everything is straight and simple except Robinson's thought. The words themselves are direct, the individual phrases are skilful and precise, the language is full of a rich intellectuality—but there has been so much pruning and paring that the story element often escapes. But it is not lost; it can be captured and held. Another reading usually brings it nearer, and a sympathetic effort to reach the matter through Robinson's manner will reward the reader with surprising flashes of a beauty that is none the less persuasive for being devious.

If from these sentences I give the impression that Robinson is difficult reading, I have written more clumsily than usual. It is, in fact, rare that he is quite so cryptic; rarer still that his poems withdraw into cloudiness. In the main, they are full of sunlight, sunlight so strong that we have to look two or three times before we can see all the details it plays upon. In the first volume we find at least half a dozen examples of such brilliance. [**"The Children of the Night"**] is a triumphant vindication of the spirit that questions, of the courageous self rising above darkness and doubt. Robinson has so often been charged with cynicism that such verses are needed as rebuttal. There is a sadness in his sagacity, but always he declares:

> It is the faith within the fear
> That holds us to the life we curse.

(pp. 44-5)

The most important things in this volume are Robinson's astringent character delineations which, with much greater artistry, suggest the portraits in Masters' *Spoon River Anthology* which they antedated by twenty years. But the most interesting technical feature is the way in which he has triumphed over his medium, particularly in the use of the old French forms and their English counterparts. He takes both ballad and ballade and, infusing a fresh energy of language, makes them as modern as his most intraverted studies. (pp. 45-6)

But it is in the etchings of personalities that Robinson is at his height. Few things could be more revealing in their very inconsequential tone than the swift glances of **"James Wetherell," "Cliff Klingenhagen," "Aaron Stark," "Luke Havergal," "Reuben Bright."** All of these are drawn with a sure and energizing touch. And none of the people in *Spoon River* (to which many of these characters bear a sort of avuncular relation) is pictured more surely and unforgettably than [**"Richard Cory"**]:

> Whenever Richard Cory went down town,
> We people on the pavement looked at him:
> He was a gentleman from sole to crown,
> Clean favored, and imperially slim.
>
> And he was always quietly arrayed,
> And he was always human when he talked;
> But still he fluttered pulses when he said,
> "Good-morning," and he glittered when he walked.
>
> And he was rich,—yes, richer than a king,—
> And admirably schooled in every grace;
> In fine, we thought that he was everything
> To make us wish that we were in his place.
>
> So on we worked, and waited for the light,
> And went without the meat, and cursed the bread;
> And Richard Cory, one calm summer night,
> Went home and put a bullet through his head.

(pp. 46-7)

One of the outstanding features of Robinson's work is his affection for . . . [the] "inferior wraiths." In an age which exalts the successful man, Robinson lauds or at least lifts the failure. The *Collected Poems* are crowded with his tentative tributes to those "beloved of none, forgot by many"; his heart goes out to the proud-blind mother of the mediocrity in **"The Gift of God"**; his sympathy stops us from laughing out loud at the bewildered **"Miniver Cheevy,"** lost in the modern world; he makes us share the ironic pathos of **"Bewick Finzer."** If Robinson had written nothing but these intimate portrayals, his title to first rank in our literature would still be secure.

As for the long title-poem, **"Captain Craig"** is an eighty-four page account of the decline of a picturesque old vagabond, his four young friends and the interminable letters he writes them. For all its technical sprightliness and dialectic repartee, there is something a bit owlish in its unblinking seriousness (it, also, is an example of Robinson's glorification of failure), even in its irony. Captain Craig himself seems less a character-study than a peg on which to hang a great quantity of brilliant, sometimes beautiful but finally tiresome talk.

The succeeding poem is a far more eloquent affair. In **"Isaac and Archibald"** we have not only one of the poet's kindest analyses but one of Robinson's few glimpses of his boyhood. The drawing of the two old men, each separately confiding in the lad their fears for each other and, unconsciously, for themselves, is one of the most touching (as it is one of the most native) pictures in the gallery of American art. (pp. 49-50)

The next volume, *The Town down the River,* shows an ever surer and and more versatile turn of speech than the previous volumes. This is Robinson's second-best and probably his most generally admired book. It begins splendidly with a poem to Lincoln [**"The Master"**] in his terse, epigrammatic style, a style that seems at first to be almost too dry and close-packed, but which mellows gradually into something quite different than its hard contours. Of all the tributes to the great emancipator, this is one of the few that maintain a genuine nobility and practically the only one that does not try to show the man's intimate humanity by some reference to rail-splitting and the use of "Honest Abe." Without descending from his austere level, Robinson actually comes nearer Lincoln than any of his compatriots. (p. 51)

The long monologue of Napoleon on Saint Helena [**"An Island"**] is frankly disappointing; it is neither tragic nor vivid, merely petulant. And, what is worse, it is almost dull—one of Robinson's few uninteresting passages. A few pages further on we come, with an abrupt contrast, to one of Robinson's liveliest moments. Just as, in the sonnets, he condensed dramatic portraiture in a way to make the classical form seem surprisingly new, so his flawless quatrains—without departing from the pattern to the extent of an added grace note—are indubitably his own. In the whimsical appraisal of **"Miniver Cheevy,"** Robinson achieves a fresh triumph; in these lines describing the shiftless romanticist the poet has permanently etched a character with strokes that are lightly drawn but go deep as life. (p. 53)

All three of these volumes, excellent in themselves, seem little more than a succession of preludes for the dynamic volume which was to establish Robinson in the respect of a larger public. Meanwhile, he published two plays (*The Porcupine* and *Van Zorn*), the first in 1914, the second in 1915. Both of them show clearly that Robinson is far more dramatic as a writer of ballads than as a dramatist.

The following year Robinson published his fullest and most representative work; a fusing of all his gifts. In *The Man Against the Sky* we not only have all of Robinson in one hundred and fifty pages; we have him unfalteringly at his best. I have already said that the preceding volumes were, for all their penetrative vigor, only preparations for this intellectually robust and far more varied work. Here the human sympathy is deepened; the epigrammatic turns are sharper; there is even a more definitely lyric note in such poems as the eloquent **"Flammonde,"** the highly dramatic scene ironically entitled **"The Clinging Vine,"** the delicately satiric **"Bokardo"** and . . . [**"The Gift of God"**, a] more gentle piece of disillusion and sympathy. . . . (pp. 54-5)

In this volume we notice with greater emphasis how strict and simple are the forms Robinson uses and how much he is at home in them. Even the rhyme-schemes are free of the slightest twist or innovation. He takes patterns that are anything but unusual and, without an effort to change the shape, makes them somehow as original as if they had been devised by him. In fact, some of the most intense and serious lines he has written are cast in the identical light-verse stanzas of Austin Dobson, C. S. Calverley and Locker-Lampson. These poems are, in themselves, a complete refutation of the still persisting theory that nothing psychological, nothing probing or intimately sensitive—in short, that nothing "new"—can be expressed in the old forms (*vide* Mr. Edward Storer), that rhyme and a regular rhythm will, in a few years, be practically obsolete. Such brilliant and analytic verse as Robinson's completely explodes the fallacy that (I quote Mr. Storer's conclusion) "a poet who wishes to give expression to realities in modern life . . . will find that he is confined for his literary expression to the two media of prose and free verse." Page after page in this collection refutes this exceedingly impressionistic dictum. Observe the intricate mental processes revealed in one octo-syllabic eight-line stanza (a favorite medium of Robinson's) as regular as this from **"Flammonde"**:

> How much it was of him we met
> We cannot ever know; nor yet
> Shall all he gave us quite atone
> For what was his, and his alone;
> Nor need we now, since he knew best,
> Nourish an ethical unrest.
> Rarely at once will nature give
> The power to be Flammonde and live.

Or note how the "realities in modern life" are made still more pointed in evenly-rhymed poems like **"Old King Cole,"** with its mellow nonchalance, the obviously scientific diagnosis in **"Eros Turannos"** with its unexpected picturesque climax, the Freudian analysis of repressed desire in **"Llewellyn and the Tree."** And what could be more surprising than the way Robinson achieves modernity of thought through a medium as old as the ballad form? [**"John Gorham"**] is, surely, one of the most remarkably turned dialogue-ballads of this generation. . . . (pp. 56-7)

There are two other poems in this volume that call for more extended notice than I can possibly give here. One is the title-poem [**"The Man Against the Sky"**] that brings the book to a high and splendid *finale;* the other is **"Ben Jonson Entertains a Man from Stratford."** Here, in spite of the four hundred lines of blank verse (or should one say because of them), Robinson's firm pencil does not waver; he has succeeded in drawing the clearest and most human portrait of Shakespeare that has been attempted by any one, not even excepting the full-length prose studies of Georg Brandes and Frank Harris. Even in the trivialities of conversation (where Jonson is sketched almost as un-

erringly as his friend and master) the interpretive power rises. (p. 60)

Merlin and *Lancelot* are adaptations or rather revaluations of the Arthurian legend, two long poems which, upon first reading, suffer by comparison with the original as well as with similar variations on historic themes by Lascelles Abercrombie. But, on closer examination, both (and especially the former) burn with intellectual heat. Robinson has surrounded the old romance with gorgeous color and a flashing vocabulary; his shrewd philosophy plays through it and transforms the tale into a complexity of spiritual cross-purposes. In both, Robinson has pictured the downfall of an order, a world in ashes, a disintegration through the very qualities which, at another time or from other standards, might have been rescuing heroisms. *Merlin,* the more vivid of the two, depicts the ruin of Arthur's kingdom when it is forsaken by its wise leader; *Lancelot* presents the final crash, the toppling of old orders and ideals. Definitely symbolic, the two poems have various implications. Whether the leading theme is the crumbling of beauty and idealism, a civilization destroyed by the intrigues that brought about the European war, or whether it is a parable of the conflict between "Woman and the light that Galahad found," the struggle between the forces that impel desire and action is eloquently projected. As units, the poems suffer from a lack of variety, a lack that seriously limits their very vitality. The characters all speak the same thoughtful speech, even the lesser figures intone it in the same slow idiom, and the heavy air of allegory makes many of the passages distant and indistinct. In the midst of lengthy recitatives, however, there are individual bits of great beauty, such as the scene where Merlin goes to Broceliande, his meeting with Vivian, and the half-lyrical, half-whimsical conversation when they first talk together. (pp. 62-3)

It is an absolutely individual and supple blank verse that Robinson has perfected, a blank verse that rises to magnificence in the climax of Guinevere's speech in *Lancelot* or sinks to a grave *adagio* at the end of *Merlin.*

> Fiercer now,
> The wind was like a flying animal
> That beat the two of them incessantly
> With icy wings, and bit them as they went.
> The rock above them was an empty place
> Where neither seer nor fool should view again
> The stricken city. Colder blew the wind
> Across the world, and on it heavier lay
> The shadow and the burden of the night;
> And there was darkness over Camelot.

The Three Taverns and *Avon's Harvest* followed rapidly—almost too rapidly. The latter poem which the author has called "a dime novel in verse," is a study of a fear-haunted, hate-driven man disguised as a mystery story which suffers toward the end from a cumulative cloudiness. *The Three Taverns,* though on a somewhat lower plane than *The Man Against the Sky,* has much of its spirit. The sonnets are firmer than ever, such monologues as **"Nimmo," "John Brown," "Lazarus,"** impress the most careless reader with a high seriousness. And if the book contains such errors as **"On the Way,"** which is unrelievedly tedious, and **"London Bridge,"** in which Robinson has attempted the impossible task of setting a tragic theme to a lightly galloping meter, it also contains dramas as poignant as **"The Mill"** and a lyric [**"The Dark Hills"**]

which is the very epitome of Robinson's musical condensation.

> Dark hills at evening in the west,
> Where sunset hovers like a sound
> Of golden horns that sang to rest
> Old bones of warriors under ground,
> Far now from all the bannered ways
> Where flash the legions of the sun,
> You fade—as if the last of days
> Were fading, and all wars were done.

All of Robinson's books already mentioned may be found,
with the addition of a dozen new poems and an improved
revision of **Avon's Harvest,** in the comprehensive single
volume, **Collected Poems**. . . . This splendid collection,
in its arrangement as well as its scope, discloses, more
sharply than any of the individual works, Robinson's importance—and his limitation. His language is unusually
indirect, but it is not that which brings his poetry to a halt
at the very peak of greatness. It is not that he is devious
in the way he gives himself, but that, in the sense of complete abandon to an emotion, he never gives himself at all.
The reader feels this lack of surrender, and it is this insufficiency which keeps Robinson from joining the small company of those whose lines not only smiled their ironies in
cryptic meditation or sang their loveliness beneath the
breath, but also leaped and raged and bled and suffered
with their creator.

But though Robinson exercises too Puritan a restraint
upon his characters as well as upon his passions, although
much of his later work seems to have been written in the
chill of autumnal moonlight, his performance occupies a
leading place in American literature—a place not confined
to this particular period. With his extraction of wisdom
from knowledge, his hundred or more passages of profound but never pompous philosophy, his brilliantly
turned phrases and mastery of a form beyond technique,
he shares with Frost twin summits of our poetry—
eminences to which no American poets, since Poe and
Whitman, have ever attained. (pp. 64-6)

> *Louis Untermeyer, "Edwin Arlington Robin-
> son," in his* American Poetry Since 1900,
> *Henry Holt and Company, 1923, pp. 40-66.*

Marianne Moore   (essay date 1924)

[*Moore was an American poet, translator, essayist, and
editor whose poetry is characterized by the technical and
linguistic precision with which she reveals her acute observations of human character. In the following excerpt,
Monroe praises Robinson's insights into various human
emotions.*]

Reserved though he is, and non-committal in respects in
which the psychoanalysis-infected poet is not, Mr Robinson is entirely explicit in trusting the reader with his beliefs, tastes, and judgements; and his intuitively dramatic
expanding of a theme carries conviction even in respect to
"the success of failure," a subject which he repeatedly
presents, and without collapse of interest develops at
length as in **The Man Who Died Twice.** In it as in his other
work, the triumph of truth is galvanically thrilling. In its
pursuit, he declares, you may not untroubled enjoy "the
perennial weed Selfishness": "No doubt you call it Love";

on the other hand, "hell shall have . . . No laughter to vex
down your loyalty." His inability to think selfishly with
blind aboriginal zeal, differentiates him from the sybarite
or mere connoisseur; and in this basic spiritual sensitiveness, he recalls Hardy, although one feels no consanguini-
ty of dogma between these poets, Hardy's tenacious incredulity and Mr Robinson's persistently tentative credulity
being obversely helpful. It is in an extra-normal sense of
responsibility that one feels a resemblance—in the capacity for suffering and the incapacity intentionally of inflicting it; in a sense of "the eternal tragedies" that render as
Mr Robinson says, "hope and hopelessness akin": this fidelity to experience leading him to visualize "sunlit labyrinths of pain" as it has actuated Hardy to uphold in his
"pleasing agonies and painful delights" with titanic inevi-
tableness, a concept of romance which in its superiority to
actuality, is surely deathless.

Mr Robinson deplores "the brain-waste of impatience,"
and as a concomitant of deliberate, searching scholarship,
we perceive in his work, the dominance without protest,
of humility. With an acuteness of perception and of speech
which are the attributes of a truly sentient view of life, he
shows us Fernando Nash, now "disintegrated, lapsed and
shrunken,"

> The king who lost his crown before he had it,
> And saw it melt in hell,
>
> Pounding a drum and shouting for the lost.

Yet Mr Robinson seems not to be immune from the aggressive superficiality of critics who share least, the basic
quality of his reserve; and at a time when

> The ways of unimaginative men
> Are singularly fierce . . .

wise craftsmanship must suffer not the ridicule but the ridiculousness of final dictum as unsubstantial as a Hollywood substitute for mediaeval masonry when it affirms his
writing to be "aurad with the dim halo of futility." . . .
(pp. 168-70)

Mr Robinson's work is completely self-vindicating, however, in its sensitive, self-corroborating, rhetorically measured, elegant articulateness. It is true that in a capacious
treatment of large themes which embody more than one
climax, parts of the design must be subordinate and the
necessary line which is not emotionally inevitable, is sometimes a difficulty. In the poems **Merlin** and **Lancelot,** the
reader's imagined familiarity with the subject-matter puts
the author at the disadvantage of being more than adequately splendid, but Mr Robinson is at all times a poet—
at all times circumstantially exact, the actuality of his
treatment of characters in the Bible and in history making
it difficult to think of him as restricted to one place or to
an epoch. His intuitively aesthetic use of experience is notably embodied in the fluently sustained, aristocratic manipulating of what passes for casual talk in the play, *Van
Zorn;* and in **The Man Who Died Twice,** there is the actual
sound of

> . . . those drums of death, which, played by Death
> Himself, were beating sullenly alone.

This tale of Fernando Nash with its "flaming rain," and
the "competent plain face of Bach" as its presiding influence, exhibits that personal attitude of Mr Robinson's—of

care for humanity and for art which makes his work stand out with a self-sustaining stiffness which is not mere exterior North American correctness, and gives it an aspect of solitary, mystical security of possession. *Captain Craig*'s biographer says: "I felt the feathery touch of something wrong," and in a day of much shallowness, muddy technique, and self-defended mystery, one is grateful for this highly developed obedience to a sensibility which is a matter not only of the nerves, but of the whole man. (p. 170)

> Marianne Moore, "The Man Who Died Twice," in The Dial, Chicago, Vol. LXXVII, August, 1924, pp. 168-70.

James Daly   (essay date 1925)

[*The following excerpt is taken from a review of* Dionysus in Doubt.]

Two of the poems in Mr. Robinson's latest book [*Dionysus in Doubt*] are based on a theme that has always fascinated him—the human triangle. **"Genevieve and Alexandra,"** the first of them, is a dialogue between two sisters in which gradually is revealed the fact that Genevieve's husband, to Genevieve's torture, is feeding "his hungry mind" on Alexandra. On the whole it is a poignant piece of work, one in which Mr. Robinson uses to fine purpose his power of shadowed implication. **"Mortmain,"** the other psychological study, appeared in *Poetry* under the title of **"Avenel Gray."** It tells, in blank verse handled with mastery, how "a ghost," Avenel's dead brother, has power to defeat "an understanding . . . between the laws and atoms" that two lives "together were to be a triumph." (pp. 40-1)

In both poems Mr. Robinson proves again his power of deft characterization and psychological insight. And again he shows himself the dramatist. Reading him, I have often found myself wishing he would write us, in verse, a play for the theatre. Though complete and moving as it stands, **"Genevieve and Alexandra"** is also the seed of what might be a great drama.

The sonnets, and the two long poems featuring Dionysus, remain to be spoken of. **"Demos and Dionysus,"** the second of the two, seems to me so unutterably beneath Mr. Robinson's usually distinguished level that I cannot put in strong enough terms my regret for its publication. The fact that it is spaced on the page as blank verse does not save it from being dull prose. It is, for me at any rate, a laborious social tract in iambic pentameter. I cannot find an inspired line in it; nowhere, I believe, does it rise to poetry. Fortunately the title-poem, **"Dionysus in Doubt,"** does not fall so far short as the other of the expectations which the splendor of its title arouses; but it also does fall short. (pp. 41-2)

But not so with the sonnets—in them the wisdom pulses. Some of them are tragic, some cryptically ironic, some dramatic; but there is beauty in all of them. (p. 43)

In dignity and austere loneliness Edwin Arlington Robinson is an unmatched figure among American poets; he is of those who have "kept their watch and word." Much of this dignity and this loneliness are in his latest book; especially are they in the sonnets. If he were totally unknown these sonnets would win for him a high distinction. As it is they can but augment and confirm a long-held eminence. (p. 44)

> James Daly, "The Inextinguishable God," in Poetry, Vol. XXVII, No. 1, October, 1925, pp. 40-4.

Conrad Aiken   (essay date 1927)

[*An American man of letters best known for his poetry, Aiken was deeply influenced by the psychological and literary theories of Sigmund Freud, Havelock Ellis, Edgar Allan Poe, and Henri Bergson. In reviews noted for their perceptiveness and barbed wit, Aiken exercised his theory that "criticism is really a branch of psychology." In the following excerpt taken from his review of* Tristram, *Aiken asserts that Robinson fails as an adapter of Sir Thomas Malory because, he contends, "[Robinson] is curiously unable to deal with a hero as 'man of action'."*]

To his two preceding poems dealing with themes from the Arthurian cycle, Mr. Robinson now adds a third, this time courageously venturing on a new treatment of the Tristram and Isolt story: courageously, because more than any other tale from Malory has this been drawn upon by poets. Wagner, Swinburne, and Arthur Symons have all had their turn at it; and it is to Mr. Robinson's credit that, despite the crystallization, or conventionalization, of the theme, which has inevitably resulted from this repeated handling, he has again, as in *Merlin* and *Lancelot,* made the thing remarkably his own. Whatever his merits or defects as a narrative poet, Mr. Robinson never fails to saturate his theme with his own character. . . . These Merlins and Tristrams and Isolts and Lancelots are modern and highly self-conscious folk; they move in a world of moral and emotional subtlety which is decidedly more redolent of the age of Proust than of the age of Malory; they take on a psychological reality and intensity which would have astonished, and might have shocked, either Tennyson or William Morris—whose aim, in dealing with the same material, was so largely decorative.

Mr. Robinson's method [in *Tristram*] lies half way between the tapestry effect of Morris and the melodrama of Wagner. Its chief excellence is an excellence of portraiture. And, again like James—of whom he is in many respects curiously a poetic counterpart—he particularly excels in his portraits of women. Merlin was not so good as Vivian, nor Lancelot as Guinevere; and in *Tristram* it is again true that the heroines are much more sharply and sympathetically realized than the hero. For the full-length portraits of the two Isolts—Isolt of Ireland and Isolt of the White Hands—one can have only the highest praise; both of them are as admirable and subtle as they can be; and in Isolt of the White Hands especially, Mr. Robinson has created a figure of extraordinary loveliness and pathos, as deeply moving, in its way, as the figure of Milly Theale.

To realize, beside these, the comparative failure of Mr. Robinson with his Tristram, is to realize also his chief weakness as a narrative poet; and, in particular, his weakness as an adapter of Malory. For he is curiously unable to deal with a hero as "man of action." Mr. Robinson's heroes think and feel—they think and feel almost inordinately; but they do not act. Every one of them is a kind of helpless introspective Hamlet; and not only that, but a Hamlet shorn of all masculine force. One cannot much respect this melancholy Tristram—one even feels that he is rather a namby-pamby creature; and without a forceful hero, how can one possibly have an altogether forceful poem? Mr. Robinson avoids "action" as he would avoid the plague. Such action as takes place in the present poem at all takes place off-stage, soundlessly and briefly. This contributes to one's feeling that the poem is too long—perhaps twice as long as it needed to be; but there are other factors as well. One cannot safely, in a poem two hundred-odd pages long, restrict oneself wholly to analytic dialogue and romantic description, with interlardings of lyricism. The lyricism is sometimes very beautiful, though perhaps not as beautiful as certain passages in *Merlin;* the analytic dialogue is often acute; but there is a great deal too much of both.

With this diffuseness in the narrative itself goes a corresponding diffuseness in the verse. Mr. Robinson's habit of ironic elaboration has grown upon him. An excellence in the short poems, where it was kept within bounds, it has now become, or is at any rate becoming, a dangerous mannerism. In the dialogue, especially, Mr. Robinson too often gives himself up to a sort of overwrought verbalistic *playing* with an idea: as if he were bent on saying the same thing three times over, each time more complicatedly and abstractedly and involutely than before. Sometimes these tortuous passages conceal a subtlety worth the pain of extraction—and sometimes they do not. On at least one occasion, Mr. Robinson becomes so involved in his own involutions that he forgets to finish his sentence—losing himself, as now and then Henry James did, in a maze of inversions and parentheses. This elaborate obscurity, with its accompanying absence of tactile qualities in the language and of ruggedness in the blank verse, too frequently makes these pages hard and unrewarding reading. It is the more regrettable as Mr. Robinson has given to his poem great beauty of design. And that it contains many pages of extraordinary loveliness and tragic force goes without saying.

> Conrad Aiken, "Tristram," in The New Republic, *Vol. LI, No. 651, May 25, 1927, p. 22.*

Louis Untermeyer   (essay date 1929)

[*In the following excerpt, Untermeyer comments on Robinson's mastery of characterization in* Cavender's House.]

It is a curious circumstance that Edwin Arlington Robinson, who is New England—and contemporary New England—to the granite bone, should so frequently be contrasted with two nineteenth century English poets. His manner has been likened to Browning; his matter (particularly the Arthurian themes) to Tennyson. The comparison to Browning, though superficial and inaccurate, is at least comprehensible. The author of *Merlin,* like the author of *Sordello,* delights in subtly psychological portraiture, in the half-withheld inner drama, in the shift of suspensions and nuances of tension. But here the resemblance ceases. Where Browning is forthright, Robinson is tangential; where Browning is lavish with imagery and flaring interjections, Robinson is sparse in metaphor and so niggard

with words that almost every phrase is twisted forward, backward, and tied into verbal knots before he discards it. But the principal dissimilarity lies in their *Weltanschauung;* here they are diametrically opposed. Where Browning regards the universe compact of sweetness and light, Robinson observes a scheme whose chief components are bitterness and blight; the realm where "God's in his heaven, all's right with the world" becomes (as in the significantly entitled **"The Man Against the Sky"**) a place where:

> He may go forward like a stoic Roman
> Where pangs and terrors in his pathway lie—
> Or, seizing the swift logic of a woman,
> Curse God and die.

Robinson's characters are, it is obvious, the projection and amplification of his characteristics. They are his philosophy made flesh. One can no more imagine Browning the creator of Bewick Finzer, Richard Cory, Miniver Cheevy, Roman Bartholow than one can imagine Robinson creating Pippa, Hervé Riel—or Marianna of the Moated Grange. Even Robinson's Arthurian figures are as unlike the parfit, gentil knights and stained glass ladies of the "Idylls of the King" as they are unlike the eloquent, self-dramatizing *dramatis personae* of "Men and Women." *Tristram* showed Robinson was anything but a converted Tennyson; *Cavender's House,* which (the critics to the contrary) might have been built on the same Cornwall cliffs, shows he is no inverted Browning.

Cavender's House is a double story, or rather it is two stories, one coiled darkly within the other. The "outer" narrative concerns a man (Cavender) who has come back to a house "where no man went," revisiting the scene because of a compulsion that is also conscience. Thus murderers return to the scene of their crime—and Cavender, it is plain, is a murderer. In that half-teasing, half-tortuous manner, reminiscent of the early *Captain Craig,* the narrator discloses the futility of the crime with its hideous aftermath: its physical finality and its unresolved perpetuity. Cavender in a nightmare of uncertainty, has killed his wife Laramie—and the dead Laramie, or her wraith, is the most living part of Cavender. It is here that the second story, the psychic parallelism, begins. Cavender's anguish or his memory summons Laramie and they converse. But it is an altered woman who holds out the few bitter "drops of hope" in that room where "midnight was like a darkness that had fingers," where the barren house was alive with triumph, "but none of it was his." It is no longer the pale ghost of a patient woman who alternately fires and freezes him, who asks:

> Why are we made
> So restless and insatiable in change,
> That we must have a food that is not ours.
> And having poured the vinegar of suspicion
> On food that once we found so appetizing,
> Why in the name of heaven are we amazed
> To find it not so sweet.

Gradually the reader is aware that this agonizing dialogue is no dialogue at all, or rather that is a conversation conducted by one person. Laramie, thrown violently out of his life, has entered Cavendish and is in complete possession; "she was the part of him that he had left and wandered from, and, wandering, had starved for." Yet it is not Laramie whose voice he thinks he hears; the ghostly apparition is hers, but the accents are his own. The questions—particularly the one question—hurled against her compel no answers, for she, being his own frustration, cannot tell him what he does not know. The end is no spectacular finale; there is no crying curtain, only—

> a peace that frightened him
> With wonder, coming like a stranger, slowly
> Without a shape or name, and unannounced—
> As if a door behind him in the dark,
> And once not there, had opened silently,
> Or as if Laramie had answered him.

So much for the intricate structure. But, rewarding as the unfolding of the tale may be, it is the sheer poetry of it that compels and convinces. (p. 995)

Cavender's House reveals Robinson's restless, uncertain but persistent search for moral values. This quest—and questioning—of ultimates runs through the story, as it seems to be running through an age no longer satisfied with skepticism. Even the brilliant discoverer of The Wasteland cannot live in the limbo he explored; it is significant that the same year should disclose Eliot turning to a faith beyond intellect and Robinson driving past reason to find

> . . . there must be God; or if not God
> A purpose and a law.

There is still, though less disturbingly than usual, the grammatically involved Robinson, the Robinson who seems to have a perverse pleasure in writing sentences as contorted as:

> There might be so much less for us to learn,
> That we who know so little, and know least
> When our complacency is at our best,
> Might not learn anything.

But this is an exceptionally calisthenic construction and, for the most part, the new poem proceeds without such verbal back-somersaults. Less panoplied than *Tristram,* less dramatic than *The Man Who Died Twice, Cavender's House* is simpler but no less characteristic of its author. It is, in accent and authority, essential Robinson, one of his major creations and one which has the deep breath of permanence. (p. 996)

> Louis Untermeyer, "Essential Robinson," in
> The Saturday Review of Literature, Vol. V,
> No. 42, May 11, 1929, pp. 995-96.

Horace Gregory (essay date 1930)

[*Gregory is a highly regarded American poet, critic, and translator. In the following excerpt, he comments on the technical features of* The Glory of the Nightingales.]

Indirectly there is scarcely a poet living in America today who does not owe something to the early work of Edwin Arlington Robinson. It was he, long before the poetry revivals of 1910 to 1915, who brought to the writing of poetry the dignity of serious performance. If we remember that *Captain Craig,* perhaps the most important of his longer poems, was written back in 1902, we realize at once that his intimations of human weakness and mortality have a prophetic ring and that the study of the great American failure began in the halcyon twilight of the Mauve Decade.

Sometime between the publication of *Captain Craig* and the arrival of *The Man Who Died Twice* in 1924, Robinson became completely converted to the tenets of his own faith. His mind was already fixed and secure; all that remained for him was a matter of technical perfection and the physical labor of setting words down upon paper. . . . Robinson, today, at sixty, may have the satisfaction of looking back over a thousand pages of closely printed verse in which he has never compromised his own particular attitude toward life. Like Hardy, his honesty of purpose is above reproach or question. He has tested the validity of his own dogma in three distinct divisions of his work: the semi-dramatic narratives, of which *Captain Craig* is the first and *The Glory of the Nightingales* is the latest; the Arthurian legends reworked in modern terms; and a sizable quantity of short blank-verse narratives and miscellaneous lyrics, including a fairly large collection of sonnets. The great bulk of this work is composed within what we have come to recognize as Robinson's own standard of excellence. Again, like Hardy, he has developed a principle of self-criticism which has prevented him from committing any of the grosser errors evident in the work of such contemporaries as Edgar Lee Masters and Vachel Lindsay.

From this large background of technical experience and his considerable ability, Robinson presents us his narrative poem, *The Glory of the Nightingales.* It is perhaps unfortunate that this latest book did not fall into the hands of a book club, an accident that steered *Tristram* into the best-seller class, for *The Glory of the Nightingales* is easily read and almost as easily forgotten. Given a wide distribution, the story with its subdued gun-play and delicate moderation of melodrama could become popular in a worthy sense and serve as an attractive introduction of Robinson to people who merely know him as a name discussed in "literary" company.

Superficially the poem has all the high polish and slickness of a well turned detective story. We are introduced to Malory, bitter and frustrated, who is on his way, gun in hand, to settle a score of hatred against an old friend and enemy, Nightingale. Nightingale, a dying man in a wheel chair, receives his desperate visitor. The poem launches into a brilliant dialogue between two highly civilized men, both attempting to justify his hatred for the other, each realizing that their lives are at the point of suicide and natural death, bound together by the personality of a woman and their own frustrated ambitions and ideals. It seems almost unfair to tell how Nightingale outwits Malory in his decision to fire off his tidy little gun and spoil their conversation. Robinson is so adroit in managing the scene that we very nearly forget the artifice at work behind the footlights. The play speeds on to the futile but inevitable death of Nightingale by his own hand; he selects the very gun that Malory gave him in surrender to a glib tongue and an agile mind.

Robinson has never shown the mere technique of his narratives to better advantage. His blank verse has become a flexible medium indeed, with stops and pauses that reflect the tempo of our speech; and it is almost unnecessary to add that there are no heavily dramatic gestures in the phrasing of individual lines. (pp. 303-04)

In relation to the main body of his work, *The Glory of the Nightingales* merely proves again that Robinson has already said very nearly everything he has to say. We think of Nightingale and Malory as first cousins of Richard Cory and Captain Craig or Bewick Finzer. Even the Arthurian heroes have the familiar gestures that we recognize at sight as belonging to Robinson's fraternity. If *The Glory of the Nightingales* contributes little or nothing to the advance of Robinson's fully recognized reputation, most certainly it verifies the opinion that he is an artist of remarkable ingenuity. (p. 304)

> Horace Gregory, "The Glory of the Nightingales," in The New Republic, Vol. LXIV, No. 830, October 29, 1930, pp. 303-04.

Percy Hutchinson   (essay date 1931)

[*In the following excerpt, Hutchison offers a positive assessment of* Matthias at the Door.]

One often wonders, in following these closely involved dramatic poems of Robinson, just what must have been the poet's own method in fabricating them. It would appear that Mr. Robinson's method, like Conrad's, is first to take a simple story, involving few characters and slight of plot, and then so to penetrate to possible causes that the resulting product becomes an intricate organism of psychological and ethical values. At least *Matthias at the Door* bears out such a hypothesis.

There are but four characters in the drama: Matthias, the egotist; Timberlake, the full-made man; Natalie, the wife of Matthias, and "Garth." Before the poem opens, and before his marriage to Natalie, Matthias saves Timberlake from being burned to death, and because of this the latter stifles his love for Natalie, who, it would seem, had preferred him to the man she married. An unpleasant mentor for an egotist is the remaining character, "Garth," whose name is here placed in quotation marks for the reason that, the living man having killed himself, his presence in the action is in reality but a figment of Matthias's imagination, his voice the pricking voice of Matthias's conscience. The "door,"

> A dark hole in a dark rock,

in a vale as weird as any in Xanadu, from its resemblance to a tomb, is also the symbol of the gateway to death. Indeed, in the opening canto "Garth" leads Matthias to this rock, where a colloquy ensues on the subject of life and death. The really dead, as it was insisted in the Gospels, are those who, having eyes and living, see not. This is the key to the poem, and it is the first shaft that has pierced the egotism of Matthias, whose appearance is such when he returns to his wife that she inquires in alarm whether he has been seeing demons. . . .

The entry of Timberlake into the drama is the signal for the egotism of Matthias to reassert itself. He sees Natalie blossom and bloom in the presence of Timberlake as she had not done with him. Robinson allows his verse a moment of free rein and opulence (though an opulence restrained) in the encounter between Timberlake and Natalie, then, like a man calling a dog to heel, he brought the drama back to Matthias. The latter has spied on Natalie and Timberlake, and, despite the fact that it has been in the main an innocent tryst that they have held, Matthias

feeds his jealousy upon it until Natalie is driven to suicide. She kills herself in the valley, by the "door."

Although in scores of isolated lines, on scores of phrases scattered here and there, Robinson has instilled into the reader an immense sympathy for the starved and pathetic Natalie, he does not, now that she is dead; make the mistake a lesser artist might have made and give us a sympathetic Matthias. If the husband is apparently broken-hearted his sorrow is principally for himself. . . .

However—and this shows the subtlety of Robinson, both as an analyst of men and women and also as an artist—the reader, although made aware of Matthias's egotism even in the hour and presence of death, is not without some pity for Matthias, for Robinson has seen to it earlier that his reader shall not be without something of pity. True, the poet has created a protagonist who is egocentric, spiritually anemic, unlovely and unlovable; but, like any physical congenital marring, the soul's perversion was not of Matthias's own doing. If Robinson harps on free-will, he also makes concession to destiny. . . . (p. 2)

Hence, pity has been built up for Matthias (against the time when he should need pity) by such earlier lines as,

> Matthias
> Saw facing him the picture of a woman
> No longer his. Her body and her face
> Would always be as fair to see as ever,
> And only fair to see. The woman herself
> Was not for him, and never had been for him.

Matthias finally is goaded, not only by remorse but by wounded pride also, to seek the "door," hoping, as had "Garth" and Natalie, to end it all. But as he nears the rock he finds the way blocked by "Garth," who is now made the mouthpiece for both the metaphysical and the ethical purport of the drama. (pp. 2, 18)

Matthias's sin has been that of omission: he has not heeded the commandment, "Seek, and ye shall find," by applying it to himself.

> There's more of you for you to find, Matthias,
> Than science has found yet, or may find soon.

Thus Matthias, who wants not life, finds that he is not wanted in the realm of the dead. He "must be born" before he can die. Strange idea! There is nothing said of the kingdom of heaven, and of entering in. Whether it will be heaven, or what it will be, Robinson does not even ask. The point is that Matthias, moving, breathing, taking to himself a wife, amassing wealth, has not yet lived. It is not a second birth that must be accomplished—it is the first birth, one not yet achieved. . . .

Time was when Edwin Arlington Robinson was called an imitator of Robert Browning, and he has always been regarded as something of a disciple of that English poet. But following on his early tutelage, the American poet marked out his own individual way. *Matthias at the Door,* even though it may stem from Browning, is Robinson, and nobody else. Indeed, it may not be too much to say that it is the crowning achievement in the poet's career, by which is meant that it is the sort of thing Mr. Robinson has been striving to do and has not before so completely accomplished in every particular. As a soul-tragedy, as precisely that shuffling of life-in-death and death-in-life with which

Robinson has so repeatedly concerned himself, as a soul-story with the heart-break lighted by the morning-glow of at least partial revelation and atonement, it is the reading of life Robinson has been endeavoring to convey to us. If we insist that no one other than Edwin Arlington Robinson could so mystically have combined all the multifarious weavings that are the rich tapestry of his magnificent *Tristram,* there are several who might have wrought this or that portion of the design, attained this or that degree of its final beauty. *Matthias at the Door,* is at every point so irrefutably individualistic of its author that compact within its total of lines is everything that is the poet Robinson. Whether it be all in all, what one would like for a poet's crowning work does not matter. Mr. Robinson, from the first, clearly has sought to be an ethical teacher as well as a poet. In the present work he superlatively attains that combined purpose. (p. 18)

> Percy Hutchinson, "Robinson's Dramatic Poem, 'Matthias at the Door'," *in* The New York Times Book Review, *October 4, 1931, pp. 2, 13.*

Allen Tate   (essay date 1932)

[*Tate was an important critic, editor, and poet who is closely associated with two critical movements, the Agrarians and the New Criticism. The Agrarians were concerned with political and social issues as well as literature, and were dedicated to preserving traditional Southern values. The New Critics, one of the most influential critical movements of the mid-twentieth century, did not subscribe to a single set of principles but agreed that a work of literature should be examined as an object in itself through close textual analysis and maintained that a literary work could not be evaluated in the general terms of any nonliterary discipline. Tate, however, believed that literature is the principal form of knowledge and revelation which restores human beings to a proper relationship with nature and the spiritual realm. In the following excerpt, first published in the* New Republic, *Tate offers a brief discussion on the tragic elements in Robinson's poetry.*]

Edwin Arlington Robinson, most famous of living American poets, was born at Head Tide, Maine, on December 22, 1869. [After this paper had been prepared for the press, Mr. Robinson died of a lingering illness on April 5, 1935]. He attended Harvard from 1891 to 1893, but left college without taking a degree. In 1896 he printed privately his first book of verse, *The Torrent and the Night Before,* which was followed a year later by *The Children of the Night,* a volume little noticed at the time but one which marks the beginning of a new era in American poetry. In the next fourteen years he published two more books, *Captain Craig* (1902) and *The Town Down the River* (1910). But it was not until 1916 that he attracted wide attention and won a notable fame. For with *The Man Against the Sky* Mr. Robinson stepped quickly into the front rank of American poetry. In his early years he wrote some of the finest lyrics of modern times: these are likely to be his permanent claim to fame.

Able critics have thought otherwise. Not only, they say, are Mr. Robinson's long narrative poems his best work; they are the perfect realization of a "tragic vision." But

Front cover of The Children of the Night.

hear Mr. Mark Van Doren, a distinguished critic whom I do not like to disagree with:

> His vision is essentially tragic in that it stresses the degeneration of ideas, the dimming of the light, when these become implicated in the rough action of the world.

> Passion has its victories no less than reason. The tragic picture would be incomplete without either of these. It is because Mr. Robinson's picture is fairly complete that he deserves the rare title of major American poet.

I should be the last person, I hope, to dispute Mr. Robinson's right to that title. Nor should I contend for a moment that Mr. Robinson lacks the "tragic vision," but I am convinced that Mr. Van Doren's qualifying word, *essentially,* is accurate. For Mr. Robinson writes, I believe, less from the tragic vision than from the tragic sentiment; and the result is the pathetic tale of obscure ambition or thwarted passion; not tragedy.

It is true that he deals with the degeneration of ideas. The question that Mr. Van Doren does not ask, it seems to me, is this: what is the exact significance of the ideas? Is their ultimate reference to a religious or philosophical background, a realm of ideas possessing at least for their time and place the compulsion of absolute truth? Or are they the private ideas of modern persons, the personal forms of some egoistic thrust of the will? In other words, is Mr. Robinson a true tragic poet, or is he a modern poet like other modern poets, whose distinguished gifts are not enough to give him more than the romantic ego with which to work? (pp. 193-94)

In *Talifer* there are four characters, two men and two women. The woman Althea—the name is a dry piece of irony—is in love with Talifer; she is woman domestic, sensitive, but commonplace and child-bearing. Talifer himself is an ordinary person, but he talks of his "tradition," carries himself well, and expects of life more than his inner quality entitles him to: so he imagines that he is in love with the other woman, Karen, who is beautiful, treacherous, cold, and erudite, dividing her time between inscrutable moods and incredible reading in the ancients. But she is vaguely conceived by the poet, and the motivation of the hero's action remains obscure.

Talifer has been fatuous enough to say that with Karen he expects to find Peace. Life becomes, after a year or two with her, intolerable. Then, one day in his ancestral forest, he meets Althea, who still loves him, and he decides to leave Karen. Now all this time, the other man, Doctor Quick, could have been in love with either of the women; he is too skeptical to push his desires; and his place in the story is that of commentator. He explains the confusion to the other characters, and affords to the poet a device by which the real actors become articulate. The story ends with the reappearance, after a couple of years, of Quick: in the meantime Talifer has married Althea, who has by him a child. Although Quick himself has tried to participate in life by taking Karen off to a "cottage in Wales," his return witnesses his failure. But he is not much affected by it. He proceeds to analyze for Althea and Talifer the true basis of their love, which is thoroughly commonplace after a good deal of romantic pretense.

Mr. Robinson's style in the new poem is uniform with the style of its predecessors; it is neither better nor worse than the style of *The Glory of the Nightingales* or of *Cavender's House.* It requires constant reviewing by Mr. Robinson's admirers to keep these poems distinct; at a distance they lose outline; blur into one another. They constitute a single complete poem that the poet has not succeeded in writing, a poem of which these indistinct narratives are partial formulations.

We get, in them all, a character doomed to defeat, or a character who, when the tale opens, is a failure in the eyes of his town, but who wins a secret moral victory, as in *The Man Who Died Twice.* But Talifer, whose ego betrays him into an emotional life that he cannot understand, is not quite defeated. The tragic solution of his problem being thus rejected by Mr. Robinson, and replaced by a somewhat awkward bit of domestic irony, Talifer at first sight appears to be a new kind of Robinsonian character. Yet the novelty, I think, lies in the appearance. For Talifer is the standard Robinsonian character grown weary of the tragic sentiment, accepting at last the fact that his tilt at fate had less intensity than he supposed, and

> with grateful ears
> That were attuned again to pleasant music
> Heard nothing but the mellow bells of peace.

That is the Tennysonian end of the poem. (pp. 195-97)

Mr. Robinson's genius is primarily lyrical; that is to say, he seldom achieves a success in a poem where the idea exceeds the span of a single emotion. It is, I think, significant that in his magnificent **"The Mill"** the tragic reference sustains the emotion of the poem: his narrative verse yields but a few moments of drama that are swiftly dispersed by the dry casuistry of the commentary upon them. The early **"Richard Cory"** is a perfect specimen of Mr. Robinson's dramatic powers—when those powers are lyrically expressed; similarly **"Luke Havergal,"** a poem in which the hard images glow in a fierce intensity of light, is one of the great lyrics of modern times:

> No, there is not a dawn in eastern skies
> To rift the fiery night that's in your eyes;
> But there, where western glooms are gathering
> The dark will end the dark, if anything . . .

Mr. Van Doren is the first critic to appreciate this peculiarly Robinsonian legerdemain with figures of light.

It is probable that the explanation of the popular success of *Tristram,* and of most of Mr. Robinson's narratives, lies in the loss of the dramatic instinct by the contemporary public. It is a loss increasingly great since the rise of middle-class comedy in the eighteenth century. Since then, in the serious play, instead of the tragic hero whose downfall is deeply involved with his suprahuman relations, we get the romantic, sentimental hero whose problem is chiefly one of adjustment to society, on the one hand, and, on the other, one of futile self-assertion in the realm of the personal ego. Mr. Robinson's Talifer exhibits both these phases of the modern sensibility: he plays with his ego in the irrational marriage with Karen, and he later sees his difficulty strictly in terms of a social institution, or of social adjustment, in the marriage with Althea, who, of course, represents "truth."

The dramatic treatment of the situation Mr. Robinson permits himself to neglect; for the dramatic approach would have demanded the possession, by the hero, of a comprehensive moral scheme. He would have applied the scheme with perfect rigor to his total conduct, with the result that it would have broken down somewhere and thrown the hero into a tragic dilemma, from which it had been impossible for him to escape. The story as it is told is hardly more than anecdotal; Mr. Robinson turns his plot, at the end, into an easy joke about the deliquescent effects of marriage upon the pretensions of human nature.

It is one of the anomalies of contemporary literature that Mr. Robinson, who has given us a score of great lyrics, should continue to produce these long narrative poems, one after another, until the reader can scarcely tell them apart. We may only guess the reason for this. Our age provides for the poet no epos or myth, no pattern of well-understood behavior, which the poet may examine in the strong light of his own experience. For it is chiefly those times that prefer one kind of conduct to another, times that offer to the poet a seasoned code, which have produced the greatest dramatic literature. Drama depends for clarity and form upon the existence of such a code. It matters little whether it is a code for the realization of good, like Antigone's; or a code for evil like Macbeth's. The important thing is that it shall tell the poet how people try to behave, and that it shall be too perfect, whether in good or in evil, for human nature. The poet seizes one set of terms within the code—for example, feudal ambition in Macbeth—and shows that the hero's faulty application of the perfect code to his own conduct is doomed to failure. By adhering strictly to the code, the poet exhibits a typical action. The tension between the code and the hero makes the action also specific, unique; the code is at once broken up and affirmed, the hero's resistance at once clarified and defined by the limits thus set to his conduct. Macbeth asserts his ego in terms of the code before him, not in terms of courtly love or of the idealism of the age of Werther: he has no choice of code. The modern character has the liberty of indefinite choice, but not the good fortune to be chosen, as Macbeth and Antigone had.

Mr. Robinson has no epos, myth, or code, no suprahuman truth, to tell him what the terminal points of human conduct are, in this age; so he goes over the same ground, again and again, writing a poem that will not be written.

It has been said by T. S. Eliot that the best lyric poetry of our time is dramatic, that it is good because it is dramatic. It is at least a tenable notion that the dramatic instinct, after the Restoration and down to our own time, survived best in the lyric poets. With the disappearance of general patterns of conduct, the power to depict action that is both single and complete also disappears. The dramatic genius of the poet is held to short flights, and the dramatic lyric is a fragment of a total action which the poet lacks the means to delineate.

It is to be hoped that Mr. Robinson will again exercise his dramatic genius where it has a chance for success: in lyrics. Meanwhile it would be no less disastrous to Mr. Robinson's later fame than to our critical standards, should we admire him too abjectly to examine him. Let him then escape the indignity of Hardy's later years when such a piece of bad verse as "Any Little Old Song" won egregious applause all over the British Isles. That Mr. Robinson is unable to write badly will not excuse us to posterity. (pp. 197-201)

> *Allen Tate, "Edwin Arlington Robinson," in his* Reactionary Essays on Poetry and Ideas, *Charles Scribner's Sons, 1936, pp. 193-201.*

> **"I think it is safe to say that all real poetry is going to give at some time or other a suggestion of finality. In real poetry you find that something has been said, and yet you find also about it a sort of nimbus of what can't be said."**
> **—Edwin Arlington Robinson, 1917**

Padraic Colum (essay date 1933)

[*An Irish-born American poet, dramatist, novelist, and nonfiction writer, Colum was a central figure in the Irish Literary Renaissance. He first gained recognition in 1902 as one of the founders of the Irish National Theatre, later known as the Abbey Theatre. Throughout his works, Colum sought to expand international recognition and appreciation of Irish literature. In the excerpt*

below, Colum examines the theme of moral defeat and ruin in Nicodemus.]

The word most frequently used in Edwin Arlington Robinson's poetry is "ruin;" I can recall many significant passages in which it occurs. But I recall, too, that bare ruin is never the subject of any of his poems:

> There may be room for ruin yet,
> And ashes for a wasted love,
> And like one whom you may forget,
> I may have meat you know not of

says Old King Cole in an earlier volume. The lives of his characteristic creations appear to be laid in ruin, but these men and women are able to make an assertion of freedom; they have at least broken with the routine and the complacency of the undefeated. The Prodigal Son in [*Nicodemus*] puts the matter humorously to his unstraying brother:

> You will be glad enough when I am gone,
> But you will know more of what's going on,
> For you will see more of what makes it go,
> And in more ways than are for you to know.

Ponce de Leon, dying of his arrow-wound, talks to his physician who knows that there are voices beyond the marching and the carnage, and finds in the old man's eyes an assurance of this. The Nicodemus of the first poem will be a ruin presently; it will be as Caiaphas tells him it will be; he will be faithful to the established order and "wary of Messiahs" henceforth. (p. 256)

The inattentive reader might think he found in Edwin Arlington Robinson's monologues and dialogues a likeness to Browning's. To me it seems that Robinson's method is akin to Henry James's—that is to say, it comes out of New England introspection and psychological awareness. Henry James I had not read for many years until the other day when I opened *The Wings of the Dove*. I said to myself as I read the first chapter, the scene between the English girl and her father, "This is E. A. Robinson in prose." Another phase of New England is in this poetry—the sense of something deserted, emptied, ruined, the classic expression of which is for us in *The House of the Seven Gables*. In *Nicodemus* only one of the longer pieces deals with the New England scene and character. **"The March of the Cameron Men"** is a long dialogue which has the careful soundings of motive and character that are in a Henry James dialogue. A woman and a man talk together after the man has released the woman from a dreadful husband:

> We did not kill him. We have let him die.

She saves both from ruin by leaving him:

> Her smile was like a blow
> Dealt softly on his heart and staying there
> For time to cool and heal.

Of short pieces there are only three or four in the present collection. This is to be regretted. Edwin Arlington Robinson is a master of what might be called the psychological ballad—**"Flammonde"** in a previous collection is an unforgettable piece of this kind. Now when I read **"Annandale Again"** and **"Hector Kane,"** with their grimness and indulgence which makes an odd kind of humour, I feel that several more such pieces were due to us. (pp. 256-57)

Padraic Colum, "Edwin Arlington Robinson's

Poetry," in The Spectator, *Vol. 151, No. 5487, August 25, 1933, pp. 256-57.*

R. P. Blackmur   (essay date 1934)

[*Blackmur was a leading American literary scholar of the twentieth century. His early essays on poetry were immediately recognized for their acute attention to diction, metaphor, and symbol. Consequently, Blackmur was linked to the New Critics, who believed that literature could not be evaluated in the terms of any nonliterary discipline. He distinguished himself from the New Critics, however, by broadening his perspective through discussions which explored a given work's relevance to society. In the following excerpt, Blackmur gives a negative assessment of* Talifer.]

Talifer is a series of conversations, with a certain amount of transitional descriptive stage-direction, which together present a fable of modern love and the basis of human relationships. Talifer, a young man of wealth and sexual ambition, deserts his betrothed Althea, a girl of traditional solid virtue, to marry and find peace in the arms of Karen, who combines cold beauty with cold Greek. A year teaches him his mistake; the true life re-asserts itself, he divorces Karen, marries Althea, breeds a child, and finds his peace in the homely reality from which false ambition and glittering, but icy, prospects drew him away. Dr. Quick, who in the first part of the poem serves as interlocutor and chorus, later as the agent of the divorce, himself runs off with Karen for a few cold months in Wales, but returns in time to bless and interpret Talifer's domestic bliss.

Such a tale is inherently no more hollow and wooden then *Volpone* or *Women 'Ware Women;* but Mr. Robinson has neither, like Jonson, observed the surface of his experience, nor, like Middleton, explored its interior. The observation, of which there is a measurable amount in the poem, is suppositious in character; it may be presumed to apply to the persons indicated, but it does not flow from them, nor render them specific. Similarly, the interior life in the poem is not a specific image mirrored, but exists rather in the realm of hypothesis. It is not the substance of Talifer and his two women revealed in their reported words and feelings; it is rather a vague substance, labelled "interior life," in which by hypothesis the characters participate without either vivifying it or being themselves vivified.

These wants of the poem are perhaps not altogether unintentional on Mr. Robinson's part. The Faustian character of Dr. Quick, and especially his humor, are intended to make him both the substance and the agent of the poem. It is his business to bring the emotions of the others to the point of orderly consciousness, and then by his humor and wisdom to salt the ensuing action. Seen from this angle, Talifer and his women do not require necessitous character; it is enough if they can be moved, not like human beings, but like pawns; the meaning will reside in the player of the game, Dr. Quick, and will be merely illustrated in the movements of the pieces. For such treatment both wisdom and humor should have been firm and specific; on the contrary, both are adulterated, the one with kindliness and the other with verbiage, so that ultimately Dr. Quick has the force, not of a brimming reservoir of human character, but only that of a Dickensian "character." The lesson, if you want a lesson, is this: you cannot begin like Ben Jonson with the idea of combining the typical elements of character by the compelling force of a humor, and then add, as an easy and hasty solvent, constant doses of the Christmas Spirit; you cannot do this and make a poem, because as a rule, and in Mr. Robinson's case certainly, the solvent is all you have left. And if you want proof by opposite example in Mr. Robinson's own work, you have only to re-read *The Man Who Died Twice,* where the conceptual strength alone is enough to hold the elements of character in undissolved combination.

It is the existence of a content such as that above described which vitiated the need for a solid sharp verse; there was nothing, that is, to require the tensile strength of a composed surface, and nothing, either, to require direct or implicit depth of feeling. Kindliness is the ruination of rhetoric, if only because it leaves so little to be definite about. What such a content did require, apparently, was a nerveless, flat and tenuous verse without a muscle to make it quiver or a body to make it still. The measure is blank verse of the colloquial dramatic order, and compared with Mr. Robinson's own earlier blank verse it is as bad as that of Massinger, say, compared with that of Shakespeare, or even Ford: it is not intimate with a living and necessary subject. (pp. 222-24)

> *R. P. Blackmur, " 'Verse That Is to Easie',"
> in* Poetry, *Vol. XLIII, No. 4, January, 1934, pp. 221-25.*

Eda Lou Walton   (essay date 1934)

[*Walton comments on the abstract nature of* Amaranth.]

Robinson, as a poet, has never used elaborate or personal imagery. His imagery is the offspring of reflection or thought. It is symbolic of certain universal conceptions and emotions. The sea is the sea of life. The hill against the sunset is man's ascent to death. The house on the hill is the house in which greatness of spirit has lived. Empty, decaying streets and houses are the abodes of those dead in spirit. The tavern is the scene of momentary forgetfulness, of self-betrayal. Drink is always a means of escaping petty self. In no sense is Robinson a nature poet. He uses physical nature only as the image of certain psychological states. Nor is he a city poet. City images are scarce in his poetry, industrial images practically non-existent. Primarily he is intent on analyzing the meaning of life. And particularly he has investigated the psychology of failure. To failure he has given value; in almost all the early work of Robinson the man who fails is the man who has had a transcendental vision, some idea of himself which, though never realized, has separated him from the herd. (p. 457)

In *Amaranth* Robinson deals with what seems for him a strange problem. The characters are people who have desired beyond themselves and are therefore lost. Each has heard the voice of Amaranth—inner truth, the flower that never fades—questioning him, making him doubt his capabilities. Those few who have looked into Amaranth's eyes—Time's judgment upon men's work—have either resigned themselves to their own smallness or killed themselves. Fargo is an artist who at thirty-five knows his shortcomings and gives up art for life, the real life of building pumps. At forty-five he looks at an old painting and the desire to be an artist revives. Thereupon Amaranth takes him into the town of the dead. He meets all the other failures, eternally deluding themselves. Evensong, the musician, has looked into Amaranth's eyes, knows he is a failure, but goes on composing small music. Pink, the poet, faces Amaranth and hangs himself. Fargo, however, neither lives in limbo nor commits suicide. He returns to actuality and the vision of inferno fades. In the end he breaks loose from his self-deceit and finds himself in a real world, in brilliant sunlight.

Robinson is examining here a delusion common to human beings, who, in order to believe themselves superior, retreat into a dream world. He implies what seems a partial contradiction of his old theme—that aspiration when it ends in failure has small glory in it. Nor does he state whether true genius knows definitely its own worth. Rather he hints that even the true artist, in life or in art, has his moments of doubt. Above all, *Amaranth* seems to prove that no man, least of all the artist, should leave reality. This is the most abstract in treatment of any of Robinson's narratives, the least dramatic, the least projected from the inner mind. But its theme is compelling. (p. 458)

> *Eda Lou Walton, "A Compelling Theme," in* The Nation, *New York, Vol. CXXXIX, No. 3615, October 17, 1934, pp. 457-58.*

Robert Frost   (essay date 1935)

[*Frost is among the most revered, honored, and popular of American poets. Emphasizing what he termed "sound of sense," his poems are often rendered in tight forms featuring rhyme, regular meters, and common sentence structure, effectively evoking a recognizably American voice. In the following excerpt taken from his introduction to* King Jasper, *Frost praises Robinson for maintaining his traditional style in an era of diverse experimentation in poetry.*]

The first poet I ever sat down with to talk about poetry was Ezra Pound. It was in London in 1913. The first poet we talked about, to the best of my recollection, was Edwin Arlington Robinson. I was fresh from America and from having read *The Town Down the River.* Beginning at that book, I have slowly spread my reading of Robinson twenty years backward and forward, about equally in both directions.

I remember the pleasure with which Pound and I laughed over the fourth "thought" in [**"Miniver Cheevy"**].

> Miniver thought, and thought, and thought,
>   And thought about it.

Three "thoughts" would have been "adequate" as the critical praise-word then was. There would have been nothing to complain of, if it had been left at three. The fourth made the intolerable touch of poetry. With the fourth, the fun began. (pp. x-xi)

There is more to it than the number of "thoughts." There is the way the last one turns up by surprise round the corner, the way the shape of the stanza is played with, the easy way the obstacle of verse is turned to advantage. The mischief is in it.

> One pauses half afraid
> To say for certain that he played—

a man as sorrowful as Robinson. His death was sad to those who knew him, but nowhere near as sad as the lifetime of poetry to which he attuned our ears. Nevertheless, I say his much-admired restraint lies wholly in his never having let grief go further than it could in play. So far shall grief go, so far shall philosophy go, so far shall confidences go, and no further. Taste may set the limit. Humor is a surer dependence. (pp. xi-xii)

I know what the man wanted of Old King Cole. He wanted the heart out of his mystery. He was the friend who stands at the end of a poem ready in waiting to catch you by both hands with enthusiasm and drag you off your balance over the last punctuation mark into more than you meant to say. "I understand the poem all right, but please tell me what is behind it?" Such presumption needs to be twinkled at and baffled. The answer must be, "If I had wanted you to know, I should have told you in the poem."

We early have Robinson's word for it:

> The games we play
> To fill the frittered minutes of a day
> Good glasses are to read the spirit through.

He speaks somewhere of Crabbe's stubborn skill. His own was a happy skill. His theme was unhappiness itself, but his skill was as happy as it was playful. There is that comforting thought for those who suffered to see him suffer. Let it be said at the risk of offending the humorless in poetry's train (for there are a few such): his art was more than playful; it was humorous. (pp. xii-xiii)

Miniver Cheevy was long ago. The glint I mean has kept coming to the surface of the fabric all down the years. Yesterday in conversation, I was using **"The Mill."** Robinson could make lyric talk like drama. What imagination for speech in **"John Gorham"**! He is at his height between quotation marks. (p. xiii)

"There are no millers any more." It might be an edict of some power against industrialism. But no, it is of wider application. It is a sinister jest at the expense of all investors of life or capital. The market shifts and leaves them with a car-barn full of dead trolley cars. (pp. xiii-xiv)

The guarded pathos of **"Mr. Flood's Party"** is what makes it merciless. We are to bear in mind the number of moons listening. Two, as on the planet Mars. No less. No more ("No more, sir; that will do"). One moon (albeit a moon, no sun) would have laid grief too bare. More than two would have dissipated grief entirely and would have amounted to dissipation. The emotion had to be held at a point.

> He set the jug down slowly at his feet
> With trembling care, knowing that most things break;
> And only when assured that on firm earth
> It stood, as the uncertain lives of men
> Assuredly did not . . .

There twice it gleams. Nor is it lost even where it is perhaps lost sight of in the dazzle of all those golden girls at the end of **"The Sheaves."** Granted a few fair days in a world where not all days are fair.

> Well, Mr. Flood, we have the harvest moon

Again, and we may not have many more;
The bird is on the wing, the poet says,
And you and I have said it here before.
Drink to the bird.

Poetry transcends itself in the playfulness of the toast.

Robinson has gone to his place in American literature and left his human place among us vacant. We mourn, but with the qualification that, after all, his life was a revel in the felicities of language. (pp. xiv-xv)

> *Robert Frost, in an introduction to* King Jasper: A Poem *by Edwin Arlington Robinson, The Macmillan Company, 1935, pp. v-xv.*

Richard Crowder   (essay date 1945)

[*In the following excerpt, Crowder examines the psychological profiles of Robinson's male characters.*]

Robinson's critics have been quite generally agreed on his abilities as a psychological explorer of some kinds of human experience. His method in general is to seize upon a situation, usually at its most telling moment, and to subject to minute examination the characters therein enmeshed. Such a system of exposition parallels the classical *in medias res,* except that the reader is not so often plunged into a whirlpool of action as into a well of careful, sometimes virtually picayune analysis. From his first Tilbury Town sonnets to his allegorical *King Jasper,* the number of his portrait studies is large enough to satisfy a very exacting scientist. The critics' numerous comparisons of Robinson with Henry James as a psychological novelist suggest that a typological review of Robinson's characters may be one means of approaching the poet's longer works. The fact that he wrote in smooth, though often difficult blank *verse* should not blind readers to his capacities as a writer of the novel (generally considered a *prose* form). To accept his medium of verse as a convention and to proceed to a consideration of his work as one would of a novel by Joyce or Gide, Howells or James, may be one way of reaching an understanding of a very controversial American poet.

Though Robinson, especially in the sonnets and shorter pieces, often confines himself to descriptive analysis of the immediate situation, there are many poems in which a way out is at least intimated, if not actually described. Some of the long narratives—**"Roman Bartholow,"** *Talifer, Cavender's House, Matthias at the Door, The Glory of the Nightingales*—show that there are at least potential remedies for the ailments of their heroes. (pp. 346-47)

This study proposes to look at Robinson's characters as representatives of specific psychic attitudes toward life. Eduard Spranger, the German psychologist, postulates six ideal types of individuality: first, the theoretic; second, the economic; third, the aesthetic; fourth, the social; fifth, the political; and sixth, the religious. To this list Gordon W. Allport would add a seventh category, the sensual (hedonist, vital) man. It should be emphasized, of course, that these are *ideal* types and cannot be completely exclusive, but will indicate only predominant tendencies and interests in any one personality. It is conceivable that a man's attitude may be an intricate union, for instance, of the po-

litical and the religious elements perhaps in balance. Granted such a man's personality would be highly complex (possibly even to the point of schizophrenia), still, careful testing and study would probably show the ascendancy—however slight—of one trait over the other.

Testing of fictional characters is, of course, an impossibility. A critic can use only so much information as an author has offered. A classification according to types, insofar as is practicable, may, however, be useful in determining the breadth of an author's interests and may provide one means of accomplishing the complex task of clarifying the intricacies of the author's genius. The seven types of men posited by Spranger and Allport offer a basis for the consideration of the principal male characters in Robinson's long narratives. Even if the common trait often be failure, some differentiation may be detected in the following categories.

If I read Robinson correctly, his theoretical men are few in number. Spranger describes this type as fundamentally intellectualist. While it is true that most of Robinson's characters exhibit an analytical bent, we must consider such a trait as a Robinsonian convention, not unrelated to the dramatic monologue, a form with which Robinson experimented. . . . Robinson's male characters are sometimes thought of as atypical in their loquacity and introspection, lacking the drive for masculine action. If one recollects Avon, the widely-traveled, money-making lawyer; Bartholow, who takes a robust pleasure in being out-of-doors; Cavender, the successful business man who, on impulse, travels halfway round the world to come home again; Jasper, the power-hungry industrial magnate; Fargo, the twice-born man turned pump-maker; Nightingale, first citizen of Sharon; Malory, the scientist who returns intending to murder his erstwhile persecutor; Nash, enthusiastically pounding Salvation Army drums; Tristram, "the loud-accredited strong warrior"; Lancelot, who valiantly rescues Guinevere from the flaming stake; Matthias, who "glowed with honors earned" and once saved Timberlake from death by fire; and many lesser Robinson characters—if one recollects these men, he will see that most of them are active in a very masculine sense. Their apparent introversion and their self-analysis may often simply be means by which Robinson himself seeks to vary his own method of detailing character types. If during the narrative proper there is a preponderance of self-searching—what Harriet Monroe called "X-ray talk"—the reader should consider the entire record and recognize that, even if not so pictured at the moment of the story, Robinson's men are often forthright and active. It is as if the character has simply paused to have his portrait painted. Many of the highly ramified ideas, much of the probing, most of the scalpel operations of the dialogue, should be thought of as Robinson speaking. If his characters seem at first glance to be introverts, their extroversions may have been temporarily disguised through the Robinson device of self-analysis.

Robinson, then, did not always intend that his characters be thought of as analytical or intellectualist. Spranger's theoretic man aims at organizing his knowledge in an effort to get at the truth. He is indifferent to the beauty or usefulness of objects, seeking only through observation and ratiocination to discover points of similarity and difference. The purely theoretic man would be most likely found among scientists or philosophers, though a complex personality combining, say, the aesthetic and the theoretic, is not inconceivable. One might, for example, think of Robinson himself as looking at life partly as a theorist, partly as an aestheticist. He was always interested in peeling away veneers to see the true wood beneath. But, on the other hand, he was also absorbed in the production of poetry—well-formed verse—to which he had early dedicated his life. Hence, there was in the man a professed aesthetic attitude—a feeling for beauty—which a pure intellectualist would lack. In the full-length narratives there are no examples of this type unless one except Umfraville, the loyal friend of Roman Bartholow.

If intellectualists are rare in the ***Collected Poems,*** the aesthetic men are no more numerous. Spranger assigns form and harmony as the foremost interests of this type; each experience is enjoyed for its own sake: interest in diversity rather than identities differentiates the aesthetic man from the theoretic. Rather than bewilderment, he feels repulsion at economic activity—big business, advertising, stocks and bonds, transportation of goods. His concern with variety and differences makes him more interested in individuals than in the welfare of the people as a whole. His tendency is towards self-sufficiency and development of his own individuality. In the matter of religion he is likely to be moved by beauty of ritual rather than by genuine religious experience. (pp. 347-50)

The sensual man is the man for whom pleasure is the highest value. In Robinson's long narratives, such an attitude may be discerned in two types: the lustful villain (King Mark and young Hebron) and the amorous adventurer (Gawaine, Penn-Raven, and Timberlake). Of these, Mark, Hebron, and Gawaine are made ugly by hate; Penn-Raven is made to seem a scoundrel; Timberlake alone is pictured sympathetically. Physical traits are—except in the case of Gawaine—illustrative of their pleasure-seeking attitude. Mark and young Hebron both have lewd, distorted faces: Mark's bloated by long indulgence, Hebron's frenzied and venomous with selfishness. Penn-Raven's face is square, with a heavy forehead, a large nose, and a soft mouth with lips too full. Timberlake's blue eyes shine with a kindly, though now dimming, sparkle. His brownish, leathery face, wrinkled not with age nor decrepitude, but with living, is softened by gentleness. Though not precisely described, Gawaine's urbane carriage implies his essential love of living.

With the exception of Timberlake, these men are all looked upon askance by Robinson: Mark and Hebron are undisguised in their evil; Gawaine, lightly passing from love to love, is eventually scarred by hatred; Penn-Raven's apparently generous helping hand is revealed as an ugly paw of animal desire. Robinson's kindness toward Timberlake is caused possibly by the man's restraint, his honorable bearing toward Matthias, his self-sacrifice. New England morality would applaud such uprightness. (pp. 350-51)

[Few] of Robinson's chief characters are predominantly religious. Lancelot, though deeply affected by what he saw while questing the Grail, is still interested in earthly love, centered in Arthur's queen, Guinevere. But, all the while, he is living "in two kingdoms." A man of energy and of great renown, he has followed Guinevere instead of the Light. At the fall of Arthur's kingdom, Lancelot sees the ephemerality of the world and leaves it—and Guinevere—for his pursuit of the Gleam. His mysticism has predominated at last.

Among Robinson's modern heroes, the well-to-do Roman Bartholow is at least a partial instance of the "immanent mystic." Having been rescued from a three-year spiritual darkness by the "omphalopsychite," Penn-Raven, he now finds tonic in out-door activity and hearty living. His attitude has been chiefly governed by his search in life and in love for the complete meaning of the world. Spranger explains that the religious man is subject to periods of darkness. So is it hinted that Bartholow will not always be in this present Light, but will return to his void. He has escaped once, however, and with persistence will probably be able to emerge again from the hell of no values.

Lancelot and Bartholow, if sometime erring, achieve spiritual success which would contradict any opinion that Robinson was wholly absorbed by a study of failure. For Bartholow and for Lancelot there are shown roads of escape from the Valley of the Shadow. Despair and disaster are not permanently theirs.

The economic man is the "practical" man, whose interest in the useful frequently conflicts with other values. It is more important to him to have amassed wealth than to have gained power (the political attitude) or to have been of service to the people (the social attitude). In his mind the concept of beauty (the chief concern of the aesthetic man) may be confused with luxury. Not a religious man, he still may hold to the God of tradition, thinking of Him as a general gift-giver.

In Robinson's longer works, Avon and Cavender, Fargo and Atlas represent the economic attitude. Fargo and Atlas, pump-maker and stevedore, are members of the working class. The others have gained wealth, Cavender in business, Avon in the law.

Cavender, before he murdered his wife, Laramie, had always thought of her as "an unmatched possession." While living with her, he had been very successful in business, thinking nothing of crushing a man who might be in his way, then justifying his action by charities. A man who believes in a God, a Purpose, a Law (not atypical of the economic attitude), a man who had done much to keep material promises to Laramie, a man possessed of great strength and will beneath a pleasant, playful surface, a man so cloaked by his own vitality that there was no finding out his soul, he would not brook even a suspicion of infidelity. Though he might treat his wife as a toy (he often bought her costly flowers) and would sometimes look elsewhere for the sake of variety, he killed Laramie in a fog of doubt which has not left him in twelve years of wandering. . . . His passion over Laramie had been the result of a possessive instinct: she was like the other things he owned. He did not want to run the risk of sharing anything that was his. His economic drive—his instinct for ownership—had put him in a darkness from which he could not escape into the light of truth and of a sympathetic understanding of his wife.

Fargo has now been free for ten years from the "servitude and error" of following the wrong profession. He was warned of his "wrong ambition" by Amaranth (the allegorical representation of the truth about oneself) and escaped from the "wrong world" to a more congenial occupation. He has been a painter of mediocre rank, actually not having much interest in art. Once he recognized the truth, he did not regret destroying his pictures. Having learned from Amaranth that suicide was not the solution to his problem, he became an excellent pump-maker, a realist, a "practical" man. He is no longer a pseudo-aesthetic man, but an economic man.

The political man, according to Spranger, is not necessarily interested in politics. Rather he wants power in some form—whether personal power, a broader influence, or simply fame. This desire is common to many people, but it is the elemental trait in some, its achievement their *summum bonum*. And these are the men to be classed as political.

In the long narratives Robinson's male characters illustrate various aspects of the political attitude. In **Tristram** King Howel and Andred demonstrate two sides to the desire for actual governmental influence. Nightingale, Matthias, and King Jasper achieve power through wealth. Avon's insulted schoolmate gains power through persistent haunting of Avon's very conscience. One group of characters are the familiar Robinsonian failures, whose desire for power, position, or fame has somehow been thwarted: Figg and Flax—in Fargo's nightmare—have learned that their professions were badly chosen; Garth and old Hebron have been held down by materially stronger men; and Nash's ambition has been defeated by his own impatience. (pp. 351-54)

Nightingale, Matthias, and Jasper are similar to economic men in that they have been activated by the desire for wealth. All three have wanted money, however, not for its own sake, but for the power which can accompany great fortune. Nightingale and Matthias maintain their material influence to the end; Jasper—unrealistic because symbolic—dies as his kingdom falls.

Nightingale illustrates the type. He recognizes early in life that he is to be

> a part of a small world
> Of traps and lies and fights and compromises

and hates himself for it, but he dares not turn away from success even at such a price. He restores the family "honor," which has been dissipated by the improvidence of his thriftless father; he does material good in the city of Sharon, though always with an eye to the profitable return; he becomes, as a matter of fact, Sharon's leading citizen, the man with the greatest influence. When Malory deprives him of Agatha, whom he needs to make his career complete, he becomes blind with malice, permits, through his own wilful negligence, Malory to suffer total economic privation, and so unwittingly brings about the death of Agatha. He has "healed" his soul by trying to believe that Malory, as a man of science, should be willing to suffer; his own bad advice was really not to blame for Malory's misfortune, for, after all, he had himself to provide for and could not be held responsible for others. More recently he has become cognizant of the falsity of this attitude, but he still maintains control in the crisis: his directing of Malory's scientific ambition toward public service in an endowed hospital constitutes the climax of his life of influence and power.

Another Robinson character—the life-long haunter of the conscience-ridden Avon—is successful in the achievement of a different kind of power: power over a man's soul. When at the age of sixteen he is knocked down by Avon for carrying malicious gossip, he warns him that he will always know where Avon is. At school he has been arrogant, somewhat cringing, and finally a little pitying towards Avon. Indolent, malignant, always too neatly dressed, he gives the appearance of uncleanness, no matter how many washings. At Avon's blow, vengeance and desolation come into his eyes. He has haunted Avon ever since, sending him a yearly card: "I shall know where you are till you are dead." Even after his drowning, his ghost returns one night to Avon, who finally dies of fear. The injured man has been successful: he has kept evil control over Avon's personality to death.

These are men who have succeeded in achieving the influence that has been the chief object of their lives. Power over many through government and capital is on a different level from power over one through insidious and relentless probing of the victim's weakness, but either type is representative of the political attitude carried through with vigor and determination. (pp. 354-56)

The cause of Fernando Nash's downfall is his very eagerness for renown. From the first, though constantly haunted by the "drums of death," he knew that he had genius which would blossom if he were patient. He was certain that his first two symphonies showed great promise. He was scornful of those who envied his genius, but he allowed doubts as to his ability to take hold of him until he turned to evil ways. For twenty years he has simply wandered in the Valley of the Shadow. At forty-five he curses himself and decides on starvation as a means of extinction. Hunger clears his brain so that the great symphony which would have been his third, and the fame-bearing masterpiece, comes flooding through his consciousness, but he is too weak to write it out. Later, on regaining strength, he becomes resigned to oblivion and devotes himself to the Salvation Army. Though he feels that God was just in taking away his talent, which he had thrown away by being too impatient, the last of his life, however humble, is colored by regret at not achieving renown, at not being able to take precedence, in the world's opinion, over those who, as young composers, were envious of his original genius.

Robinson's proverbial interest in failures, however, was counterbalanced by his interest in success. In this analysis, for instance, it becomes evident that the number of men who satisfy their ambitions virtually equals the number who, for one reason or another, fail. True, where Jasper, Matthias, and Nightingale have gained in affluence they have acquired also ruthlessness and irresponsibility, but they have been successful in accordance with their attitude of mind—the political. The converse cannot be said to hold. Figg and Flax, failing to achieve, are not spiritually virtuous either, but are mere nonentities. Garth and Hebron, lacking success, develop envious dispositions. Even Fernando Nash, who is re-born to spiritual salvation, cherishes a "grim nostalgic passion" for the unattained. What is Robinson saying? Is there any man who can be a total success? Robinson's "successful" men have paid out in honesty and integrity; his "failures" have not reached total wholesomeness of the soul. For the poet the problem remains unsolved.

The remaining attitude—the social—is the most complex

in Robinson. It may appear in a variety of forms. For the social man the only type of power is love: he is incompatible with the political man. Love may be directed towards one individual or towards humanity, but if that love dominates a man's life and mind, he is a social man. He is kind, sympathetic, and unselfish. In the extreme, his attitude approaches the religious.

Robinson's social men may be grouped in two large categories: those who think of others in large groups and those who are devoted to individuals. In the first class—the group-minded—come those characters who feel a responsibility to society and those who have a natural gregariousness, who love the company of others. Of these only Merlin, Captain Craig, and Lamorak are characters in the long narratives. The others are subjects of dramatic monologues or short portrait studies. Lamorak himself is only briefly glimpsed in *Merlin* as a man of action whose uppermost interest is the well-being of the state. Merlin and Captain Craig represent two phases of this kind of social attitude—service to the state and service to humanity in general.

In Merlin, Robinson pictures a man whose struggle is finally resolved in his leaving the woman he loves for the performance of duty to the government (his dilemma involving two aspects of the social attitude). He has no political ambition to be king, nor is he religious enough to see the Holy Grail, for, as he says, he has seen too much of life. He has made Arthur king that the world might see itself reflected in him. Once with Vivian in Broceliande, however, Merlin is in his grave, so far as the world goes. When first called back to Camelot by Arthur, he is restive until he can again return to Broceliande. Though he loves Vivian, he cannot avoid giving her the impression that states mean more to him than women. Having warned Arthur time and again of ruin if the state be neglected, after twelve years of love and life with Vivian he feels a compulsion to return to his duty to the world, which he recognizes is on the verge of ruin. Once again at Camelot, however, he knows that it is too late to see Arthur and save the kingdom. Nevertheless, in leaving Vivian, he has demonstrated his predominant life motive—service to the state.

Captain Craig is essentially a social man who has found his most satisfying experience in love of life and the world. Whereas he used to curse the afflictions of the unfortunate, he now feels a responsibility to mankind to be a leader toward the Light. Though poor and hungry, he is not bitter, nor ashamed, nor regretful. He is fundamentally beneficent, outward-looking, rather than dreary, grievous, discontented, or envious. Recognizing that he is a failure in terms of the world, he is nevertheless sure that he has something to bestow on mankind, and feels a "larger kind" of gratitude for what he has to give. In his will he bequeaths the universe to his young friends. In his great affirmation of the humor and wholesomeness of the world he would appear as an "immanent mystic," but his feeling of responsibility for drawing all men after him toward the Light would make his attitude predominantly social.

Merlin and Craig are both men of large vision. Their difference lies in the worldliness of the one and the mysticism of the other. Merlin's social attitude looks toward the political; Craig's toward the religious. In the Arthurian narratives are described men who are social through their ser-

vice and loyalty to individuals (as opposed to the group-attitude of Merlin and Craig). These include Blaise, Gouvernail, and Dagonet.

Despite differences of era and social organization, Talifer's friend Dr. Quick is related to these Arthurian characters, as a man who enjoys serving and advising individuals. He secretly loves Althea, but has treated her much like a daughter. She in turn trusts him and confides in him. Though forty years old, he has never found a woman who would marry him, in spite of his attributes—cheerfulness, conversational ability, attentiveness, kindness to animals, ability to dance, complete amiability, and skill at flattery. On the whole, he is unambitious. He is kind and sincere in time of trouble and is the confidant not only of Althea but of Talifer himself. When, after a season in Wales with a woman he cannot love, he returns to find Talifer and Althea comfortably married, he resumes his old rôle of loquacious observer-counsellor, enjoying the companionship of his friends.

Finally, Robinson's characters include those men who exercise the social attitude through love of woman. Many of Robinson's male characters are married or are attracted to women, but for the most of them the predominant attitude is not social: their main interests lie in other directions. (It should be understood, however, that the largest single group is that of the social man.) In the group who are shown by Robinson to be chiefly moved by love of a woman two distinct kinds of men are evident: those who are variously ineffectual, and those who exhibit forthright, positive, masculine qualities.

No love at all is part of the general futility in the lives of Evensong and Ipswich, dream characters in *Amaranth,* who regret that they have never known love, but have been sidetracked by fruitless careers. These two miscast individuals are inhabitants of a dream and so are not realistic characters, but their instinctive feeling of need for love and marriage is nonetheless valid. They are obviously spokesmen for Robinson. Other characters are married and are chiefly influenced by the love they hold for their wives, but they are undistinguished. Their mediocrity is a hurdle they cannot leap, even with devoted wives to support them. (pp. 356-60)

This analysis of male character in Robinson's narrative poetry points to several conclusions. In the first place, his treatment of economic man is often either pitying or acid in quality. In his letters he speaks of his "total lack of all commercial instinct" and his feeling of "the futility of materialism as a thing to live by." This attitude explains his unsympathetic manner of dealing with men whose principal goal is the amassing of fortune. Much the same may be said for his attitude towards sensual men: for the most part, his New England conscience must look with disapproval on the man whose chief aim is pleasure.

With only one or two exceptions, Robinson's religious men are either tramps or figures from the past—sketched in the shorter poems—a fact which leads to the conclusion that the poet reflected his age, in which the religious man was replaced in prevalence by the social, the political, and the economic man. That Robinson, further, should pay so little heed to the aesthetic man might find explanation in his conviction of the rarity of genius:

Only at unconjectured intervals . . .
A questing light may rift the sullen walls . . .

The predominance of studies in the social and political attitudes shows where the poet's chief interest lay. His frequent return to the investigation of social character would indicate possibly a sublimation of his own seeming diffidence. Never a "mixer," Robinson sometimes gave the impression of being haughty and unapproachable, where actually he enjoyed people and was a pleasant, witty companion. All his social men in the long narratives are uninhibited talkers; they may be so for the very reason that Robinson himself was generally laconic. The recurrence of the political attitude in his poetry, furthermore, may be interpreted as the probing of his own conscience, for he was constantly driven—like his Shakespeare—by the urge for attention from the people of his home town.

It is quite commonly agreed that the texture and tone of Robinson's later verse differs considerably from the quality of his early work. His last poems are more qualifying, less lyrical, more circumlocutory, somehow more cautious. The elements of comedy are maintained to the end—the elegance, the suavity, the turn of phrase, but often the poet overplays his hand, is merely wordy.

What relation is there between the quality of the verse and the choice of character type? I can see none. It is true that Robinson drops from his later long narratives the religious character—the type of Lancelot and of Bartholow, but not because of a change in verse quality, for the verse of **Roman Bartholow** (1923) is, in fact, very little different from that of **Cavender's House** (1929) or **The Glory of the Nightingales** (1930). On the other hand, the sensual, economic, political, and especially the social types are found in Robinson's work from beginning to end. It may have been his periphrastic literary habits which led him to the abstractions of his last two poems—**Amaranth** (1934) and **King Jasper** (1935), but the types of character even in these two poems are highly various—ranging through the entire catalogue with the exception of only the intellectualist and the religious types, both of which play only a small part in the whole body of the poetry. So one cannot say that the quality of the verse Robinson used from period to period influenced the types of men he chose to study—at least on the level of the Spranger-Allport categories.

Robinson's own complex attitude was a mixture of the theoretic, the aesthetic, the religious, the political, and the social: that is, he was analytical, sensitive to beauty, mystic, desirous of recognition, and deeply aware of man's relation to society. The men in his poetry no more exhibit pure attitudes than he. Conscious of the tensions in his own inner life, he found in his male characters similar complexities. The ideal type cannot be discovered more frequently in his narratives than in life.

Of the long narratives, eight are concerned with a love triangle, if one count the story of Annandale, who actually loved only one woman at a time, and **Cavender's House,** in which the "other man" may have been only imagined. The rest of the narratives center on other problems besides those of three-sided love: **"Captain Craig"** on philosophy and life attitudes; **Merlin** on the tension between love and duty to state; **"Avon's Harvest"** on persecution and fear; **The Man Who Died Twice** on ambition; **Amaranth** on the concept of resignation; and **King Jasper** on economics. It must be confessed, certainly, that except in **"Captain Craig"** and **The Man Who Died Twice** love of woman plays some part even in these poems. Merlin is drawn from Vivian by his sense of duty to Arthur's kingdom; Avon is prevented from having a free and normal existence with his wife by the terror which pursues him; two minor characters in **Amaranth**—Evensong and Ipswich—regret that ambition has stood in the way of their loving a woman; and King Jasper's son, wanting only to love Zoë, makes small impression in his world.

Of the "triangle" poems, excluding the Annandale series, all except **Talifer,** the last one, involve two men and a woman. The husbands vary in their attitudes: Arthur and Malory are social, being impelled by love of a woman; Bartholow is mystic; Mark is sensual; Cavender is economic; Matthias is political. The "other men" also are of varying types: Lancelot is mystic; Penn-Raven and Timberlake are sensual; Tristram is social; Nightingale is political. Apparently, Robinson was interested in studying the reaction of dissimilar characters to a similar situation. If there appear to be a unity among the characters of Robinson's longer works, I am inclined to believe that it is only a superficial affinity, suggested by the somewhat uniform continuity of situation throughout the narratives. The foremost problem in the poet's mind for many years was no doubt this problem of complex love; the gallery of diverse portraits he has left us grew from his unachieved desire to find the solution.

If frequency of recurrence has any significance, it may be concluded that for Robinson the most important problems were those of the social man, whereas the theoretic (intellectualist) and the aesthetic, being—with the "transcendental mystic"—farthest removed from the social, invited the least consideration. Robinson's preoccupation with the relationships between men and women testifies to their importance in his mind. The full story of his own experience with love may never be known, but it is evident that the whole problem was fundamental to his thinking. If Robinson was concerned with the plight of contemporary society, it may be added that he was no less concerned with man's part in it, both as public citizen and as private individual. "The elemental dualism of love and duty" is, from another point of view, a problem within the area of the social attitude—a problem which must have as many solutions as there are citizens and lovers. To such perplexing complication Robinson bore witness, as he returned again and again to the theme of love, like a restless, questioning stream seeking answer in some far-off, quiet sea. (pp. 363-67)

> *Richard Crowder, " 'Here Are the Men . . .':*
> *E. A. Robinson's Male Character Types," in*
> The New England Quarterly, *Vol. XVIII,*
> *September, 1945, pp. 346-67.*

Richard P. Adams   (essay date 1961)

[*In the following excerpt, Adams contends that Robinson's shortcomings as a poet stem from his failure to develop the consistent, romantic philosophy which, according to Adams, most suited his nature.*]

Edwin Arlington Robinson presents a difficult paradox. There is general agreement that he was, either actually or potentially, a great poet. But many good critics believe that he failed in some measure to achieve the greatness of which he was or should have been capable. I am disposed to agree more or less with both of these opinions, and to offer a formula which I hope will tend to reconcile the terms of the paradox.

The solution I wish to suggest is that Robinson was potentially a great *romantic* poet, but that he was bluffed out of greatness, except on a few occasions, by the inordinate popular prestige in his time of mechanistic materialism—a world-view which has been and is antagonistic to a strong, consistent development of romantic philosophy or romantic art. The failure, according to this formula, was of nerve rather than intellect; in fact, . . . Robinson recognized the conflict, identified the enemy, and placed himself in the camp of those whose writings had established the romantic tradition. But his morale was bad, and therefore he consistently failed to realize either the strength of his own position or the weakness of the opposing one. (p. 97)

The paradox of Robinson's attitude can be seen, from an extraliterary point of view, in his attitude toward commercial values and activities. He wrote on September 27, 1890, to his friend Harry Smith, "Dollars are convenient things to have . . . but this diabolical, dirty race that men are running after them disgusts me. . . . [There] is something to life outside of 'business.' Business be damned." Here we have the conventional romantic attitude, but hardly the usual romantic verve and confidence. On February 2, 1892, Robinson wrote to the same correspondent, "Every day that I live I realize more and more the existence of several elements or characteristics in my make-up that, unless they are put down, will be of decided disadvantage to me in the future. In the first place, I am and always was too much of a dreamer; I have no sympathy with the cold, matter-of-fact, contriving nature that has made the fortunes enjoyed by multitudes all around us . . . and this is a dangerous state to be in." But why should a poet have any sympathy with coldness, matter-of-factness, or contriving? Why should Robinson not have gone calmly and vigorously about his work, which was writing, and let who would make money? Why should he either hate or fear the commercial virtues?

Robinson tries to answer some of these questions in the same letter. "Another thing that troubles me," he admits, "is the knowledge that I am lacking to a considerable extent in self-confidence:—not exactly that, either—perhaps I had better say that [the] sight of success awakens a feeling painfully approaching envy, and I am inclined too much to look upon its achievement as a kind of destiny." Or perhaps, we might say, a kind of black magic. "But," he continues, "I am glad to say that I think that this is leaving me gradually, and [in] time I hope to have a fair chance of growing sensible." . . . Robinson did grow more sensible, especially after he began to have a little of the success he needed, not so much in making money as in getting his poetry published and his quality as a poet recognized. But in the early 1890's he was severely oppressed by the feeling that, having just attained his majority, he was still economically dependent, and that he had very little to show for the money his family spent to support him. (pp. 99-100)

The conflict between the poet's vocation and "business" was an aspect of the metaphysical war then raging be-

tween the incompatible world-views of romantic organicism and mechanistic materialism. It was in the heat of this larger conflict that Robinson's much-discussed philosophy was forged. Emotionally, his position was clear; his heart was thoroughly romantic. "I hope," he wrote to Smith on February 18, 1894, "that a time may come when we shall have a romantic spirit of our own, but perhaps we are too young. This may be the reason that there are no spirits in our ruins. All our romance is cen[tered] in the traditions of the red men, and there is a sad lack of human interest." The same complaint had been made by Irving, Cooper, Hawthorne, and Henry James, often in closely similar terms; and this was not mere nostalgia for a nonexistent American past, as we shall see. But the head, or intellectual side of Robinson's personality, was not so clearly or so firmly oriented.

He was himself well aware of this fact, and he tried more than once to minimize it. For example, he wrote to an admirer, Bess Dworsky, on December 7, 1931, "I am naturally gratified to learn that you are writing a thesis on my poetry, but I am rather sorry to learn that you are writing about my 'philosophy'—which is mostly a statement of my inability to accept a mechanistic interpretation of the universe and of life." And he repeated, "I still wish that you were writing about my poetry—of which my so-called philosophy is only a small part, and probably the least important. . . ." This is a legitimate defensive tactic, up to a point. Of course the critical focus should be on the poetry. But when the poetry deals with metaphysical problems, as Robinson admits his does, then the critic must play philosopher and judge the adequacy of the dealing, especially if it seems to him, as it does to me, that the poetry is not as good as it ought to be because the philosophy in it is weak and inconsistent. My impression is that Robinson's philosophy ought to have played a larger and more important part in his poetry than it did. . . . Robinson's weakness lies in the fact that he never found anything of sufficiently positive value to offer in place of a mechanistic interpretation of the universe. Mechanism was wrong, he knew; but what was right he never could tell. Moreover, because he had no strong positive belief, he was not even able to make his rejection of mechanism stick. Mechanism was the only intellectually respectable philosophy he knew, and, hate it as he might and did, it would come crowding into the vacuum. (pp. 100-01)

The character of the myth which Robinson both desired and let himself be constrained to deny is suggested by a pair of statements he made in the autumn and winter of 1896-7. In a letter to Smith he spoke of his "acceptance of life as a state of 'quiet desperation,' as Thoreau had it. All I can see to life, as an occupation, is a kind of spiritual exercise (or at least a chance for that) by which we may, if we will, put ourselves beyond it." He repeated the formula not long after in reply to an anonymous criticism to the effect that for him, in *The Torrent and the Night Before,* "The world is not beautiful . . . but a prison-house." Robinson denied the charge: "The world is not a 'prison-house,' but a kind of spiritual kindergarten, where millions of bewildered infants are trying to spell God with the wrong blocks." He was quoted, much later, as having commented, " 'I was young then and it was a smart thing to say.' " But he did not retract the substance of it. His point would appear to have been that he saw the material world as a condition to be transcended, but acknowledged at the same time that it was, for him at least, very hard to transcend. I take this to mean that he was a frustrated transcendentalist.

That is to say that the myth which Robinson desired was the romantic myth of a transcendent relation between the individual man and nature, on the one hand, and between the individual and other men in society, on the other. In this respect he was the disciple of many romantic writers, both English and American, but the character of the "myth desired" can perhaps be most clearly seen—as I think it was by Robinson himself—in Emerson. As Waggoner says, "The faith he longed for and at times thought he had was a sort of Emersonian romantic naturalism." The odd phrase "Emersonian . . . naturalism," however, indicates that Robinson was a disciple with a difference. He often said that he was an optimist, but he was never a cheerful one like Emerson. . . . (pp. 103-04)

The clearest abstract statement I have been able to find by Robinson himself of his philosophical position is in his answer to a letter from William T. Walsh, in which the usual criticism had evidently been made. "I am pleased with all you say of the other poems," Robinson says, after discussing *Nicodemus* and *Ponce de Leon,* "—though I didn't detect, or feel, anything like despair in my work. If it is there, it ought not to be, for it isn't in me. On the other hand, I doubt if there is in me a latent possibility of singing obvious hymns of joy. For while I see this life as only a contributory phenomenon in its relation to life itself, I'm afraid there is too much Adamic bile in me to permit an altogether different expression of my faith—which, in its way, is probably as strong as yours. I cannot see materialism, so-called, as anything but short-sighted damned nonsense." The elements of Robinson's philosophy, and of his attitude toward it, are all present in this statement: his opposition to materialism, his denial of despair, his belief in a life transcending life, and his usual inability to give a happy account of himself or of the world in which his own life was lived. Inevitably, he gave the impression of lacking any positive belief at all, and of being perhaps ripe for conversion to some faith such as Roman Catholicism which would provide one ready made. But this was not at all his real situation. He knew what he believed—or what he ought to believe—or at least what he wanted to believe— and a different belief would not have helped. What he needed, in order to believe effectively and in order to be the poet of his belief, was a good deal more confidence in his conviction. He spent too much of his time and energy opposing materialism; he had too little left to build an adequate positive understanding of the transcendentalism he was drawn to. His poetry, therefore, is the record of a courageous and dogged resistance to what he hated, not the sublime assertion of what he loved. But the greatest poetry is positive, and in its own context omnipotent. Within its limits, what it attacks is demolished past repair; what it asserts is established for all time. It does not apologize or look over its shoulder. It says what it has to say, and it is so. It creates its own world, better than the actual world because it is clearer, more permanent, and more beautiful. It does not have to defend itself, no matter how much battling there may be about it. It is above the battle; it has transcended the conflict, with all its losses and agonies, not by denying or ignoring losses and agonies—Robinson was right about that—but by asserting the value of the life that both engenders and suffers them, and of the human

character that emerges out of them, or develops through them.

That is what the great romantic poet—the Wordsworth, the Whitman, the Yeats—does, by virtue of his belief in the myth of transcendence. He is filled with the energy of his conviction that somehow, no matter exactly how, life is expanded and illuminated, and made worth living, by a complex relatedness that extends beyond the relations we know. The real world is bigger and more complex than any concept of it that we can grasp. Its bigness, its power, and its complexity are at once natural, human, and divine; it is altogether fascinating and overwhelmingly wonderful; it takes us out of ourselves and returns us more than ourselves. That is, if we have at least an intuitive sense of our own relation to all the huge and manifold relatedness around us, in us, and among us; and if we trust ourselves to it, even though it kills us. And we can be creators, artists, and poets if we have the courage as well as the talent to find symbolic patterns that will suggest the relations we only partly know, and will communicate the sense of the deep and powerful harmonies of which we are part, at the same time that we are also part of the conflict, the doubt, and the suffering that must be reconciled to make the harmony ring out. As with any other mode of metaphysical feeling, we must believe in order that we may know; the desire to believe is not enough. But with Robinson, the desire to believe was about the full extent of it. His knowledge, therefore, was sketchy, partial, and uncertain. He had the talent, but the kind of courage needed, the sublime confidence that enables a man to accept the responsibility of creating a better world than he or anyone else can ever know, he did not have.

This negative attitude appeared at the beginning of Robinson's career, as we have seen. It continued, with very little essential change, to the end of his life. (pp. 104-06)

These unkind strictures are worth making because Robinson did leave behind him a large body of poetry, some of which is extremely fine. It is the poetry, rather than the philosophy as such, by which he makes his claim—a very substantial one—to serious critical consideration. . . . It always has a certain interest, and sometimes, if not as often as we could wish, it rises to an electrifying intensity of point and beauty.

The pervasive theme in Robinson, as in most romantics, is that of personal growth or development. His characterization of the world as "a kind of spiritual kindergarten" provides a convenient keynote, and his further remark that in this kindergarten "millions of bewildered infants are trying to spell God with the wrong blocks" tells us how he felt about it. He was an optimist, since he would have it so, in his belief that growth or development was possible, but his overwhelming sense of the difficulty of life and learning made him always a tough-minded and often an exceedingly gloomy celebrant of this genial doctrine. Throughout his life and poetic career he was preoccupied far more often with failure than with success, and he tended always to be more eloquent about the wrongness of the blocks than about the possibility, vague and distant to his perceptions, of getting the spelling right.

Both the tough-mindedness and the vagueness are well exemplified in the sonnet **"Credo,"** which was first published in *The Torrent and the Night Before* (1896). . . . The speaker's courage, though negative, is commendable, and up to a point his doctrine is sound. He is embarked on the typical romantic quest, which, as with Whitman's open road and the journey of the Ancient Mariner, is endless. The growth which the romantic search represents is pursued for its own sake, for the pure adventure of searching. Its interest lies in the well founded hope that every new discovery will open up newer, more fascinating ways to be explored and ways of exploring. Any imaginable final goal would only be a letdown and a disappointment; finality is not something to be achieved, but something by all means to be avoided. The purpose of life is life, and the transcendence of life takes place in the discovery of more and greater life.

It is obviously correct to say that life is agony, and that the more intense it becomes, the more agonizing it must be. Emily Dickinson's comment, "I like a look of Agony, / Because I know it's true," is definitive. The difference between her attitude and Robinson's, however, is also definitive: she likes the agony of living, but he does not. She is a tougher-minded as well as more orthodox and positive romantic than he is, and she is a greater poet, partly because she more consistently and courageously faces the intolerable difficulties of life, change, and development than he does. His longing for a star to guide him toward "the coming glory of the Light" is a weakness, as is his sentimental supposition that the "angel fingers" that have woven the garlands of this life were unaware that some of us would receive them as "Dead leaves" rather than roses. He only thinks he knows "the far-sent message of the years"; he has got it wrong. . . . The compensation for the agony of life is to be found in the ecstasy of life, not in any distant and problematical music; and those who want garlands of living roses may weave their own. Robinson's pie in the sky is not convincing, and it is not what strong men want. They want action, here and now.

"But some are strong and some are weak," says Robinson in **"The Children of the Night"** (1897)—"And there's the story."

> And if there be no other life,
> And if there be no other chance
> To weigh their sorrow and their strife
> Than in the scales of circumstance,
>
> 'Twere better, ere the sun go down
> Upon the first day we embark,
> In life's imbittered sea to drown,
> Than sail forever in the dark.

Again the negative attitude, again the struggle toward some vaguely defined "other life," and again the suspicion, in my mind at any rate, that such a man as this would make a hell of heaven if he should ever have the misfortune to get there and find that it did not correspond to his sentimental expectations. (pp. 107-09)

Robinson, as many critics have said, is better in short character sketches and sharply drawn dramatic situations than in his explicitly philosophical pieces. The reason may be partly that his philosophy is less obviously inadequate when it is only implied than when it is more clearly stated; but it is also partly that people can be interesting even when their ideas are not. Robinson's anti-materialistic feelings are more attractively embodied, for example, in **"Richard Cory"** than in **"Credo"**; Cory's dramatic ges-

ture, so cleverly, so unexpectedly, so satisfactorily sprung on the reader at the end, leaves that reader free to decide, if he has his own courage to do so, that working and waiting and going without, and even cursing on occasion, may be a pretty good life after all. At least, in the poem, it is life, not death. Similarly, and more emphatically, **"Cliff Klingenhagen"** describes a gesture that is grimly convincing in its embodiment of the principle that the man who meets the agony of life head-on can break through to find the ecstasy. Housman's "Terence, This Is Stupid Stuff" presents the same idea; Emerson is even more positive about it in his "Mithridates."

"Captain Craig" (1902), along with a lot of loose talk, gives us a fine gesture too, when the Captain wills his friends "God's universe and yours," requiring in return the provision of a brass band for his funeral. The music here is neither "lost" nor "imperial," but rather that which, as the Captain says, can be heard

> in the fury and the clash
> Of battles, and the closer fights of men
> When silence gives the knowing world no sign . . .

Here the light is less distant, more of this world and this life; for the Captain has been reborn to see it, not above and beyond our world, but through and in it. (p. 110)

"Isaac and Archibald" (1902) is a story of the laying-on of hands, of a boy's inheritance of wisdom from his elders, partly by and partly beyond their intention. What [Isaac] learns is the same, at least in one aspect, as what Captain Craig has learned. . . .

The light, according to Archibald, is "behind the stars," but it is those "who have dared to live" in this world who see it. And the boy sees it all around him—perhaps, as he suggests, largely because he is still young and has thus far been able to live without having to dare very much—but he sees it, and he remembers it vividly as he tells the story years later: . . .

> So I lay dreaming of what things I would,
> Calm and incorrigibly satisfied
> With apples and romance and ignorance,
> And the still smoke from Archibald's clay pipe.
> There was a stillness over everything,
> As if the spirit of heat had laid its hand
> Upon the world and hushed it; and I felt
> Within the mightiness of the white sun
> That smote the land around us and wrought out
> A fragrance from the trees, a vital warmth
> And fullness for the time that was to come,
> And a glory for the world beyond the forest.
> The present and the future and the past,
> Isaac and Archibald, the burning bush,
> The Trojans and the walls of Jericho,
> Were beautifully fused; and all went well
> Till Archibald began to fret for Isaac
> And said it was a master day for sunstroke.

Aside from being good blank verse and better description, this is excellently sound philosophy. The elements of the romantic metaphysic are all essentially involved: the past-present-future sequence of time; the relation of the individual to nature and the universe, and to other men; and (in the reference to the burning bush) the immanence of God in both man and nature—and all are indeed "beautifully fused," not just because Robinson says so but because the symbolic overtones make them so. The focus, as in romantic narrative generally, is on the boy's growth, on his development of an ever-widening awareness of his relations, which is the essence of a romantic education; and into that focus all things come and become related. It is probably no accident that the key-word "fused" is one of Coleridge's favorites, or that the theme and situation are almost precisely parallel to those of *The Ancient Mariner*. . . . Robinson was never more thoroughly in the romantic tradition, and seldom more successful poetically, than in **"Isaac and Archibald."**

His lack of confidence is dramatized in **"Miniver Cheevy"** (1910), which probably, as critics have suggested, describes one aspect of the author's character. The important difference for Robinson was, of course, that he wrote good poetry. But he also fell into certain of the sentimental clichés that he so neatly satirizes in Miniver. He too "loved the days of old / When swords were bright and steeds were prancing"; he too "mourned Romance, now on the town, / And Art, a vagrant"; he too "scorned the gold he sought," and for a long time—much too long—he "kept on drinking." Miniver is not Robinson, but he probably owes his existence to some need on Robinson's part to purge himself of the faults that keep Miniver from being the kind of man Robinson wanted to be. Miniver, we might say, is Robinson's J. Alfred Prufrock or Walter Mitty, the element in the romantic character which, unable to cope with the mechanized complexities of modern technology or with its social and psychological effects, tries to "escape" into fantasy. There is nothing intrinsically wrong with sentimental fantasy, which can be very charming on occasion, or with escape from unpleasantness of any sort; the real trouble with the artist as Miniver Cheevy is that he fails to produce anything. Robinson did well to repudiate him and his lack of works, and might have done better yet if he had never had to think about him at all.

A good many other poems in the Robinson canon are concerned with art and artists, and with the relation of artists to the world and to other men. In some of his representative cases, the artists see and do too much—for example Shakespeare in **"Ben Jonson Entertains a Man from Stratford"** (1916). The trouble with Shakespeare, as Jonson sees it, is partly that he knows the world and men too well to be a happy member of society or even of the human race, and partly that he wants very much to be a solid, substantial, respectable citizen—or rather lord—of the realm. . . . The overpowering vision Shakespeare has had, we are told, is that of nature's indifference to man, and of man's mortality. . . . We see at once that this Shakespeare has been reading Herbert Spencer in the spirit of the social Darwinists of the late nineteenth century, and that what he sees is not what his original saw, and that it is not necessarily so. It is rather what Robinson saw when he read Spencer and feared that the social Darwinists might be right. Then we understand why Robinson was afraid of seeing too much and why, like so many others of his generation, he clung to what he regarded as life-giving illusions. If the truth led to death, the truth must be rejected. The artist must preserve his faith in life, against all reason, as the popular scientific mind saw reason, in order to go on living and doing his work. The objection to this metaphysical attitude is not that it is harsh—no view of life can be as harsh as life itself—but that it is wrong. It is naive, abstract, simplistic, and per-

verse; it is as far as possible from the concrete realities of experience with which art must deal if it is to mean anything of value. The most fundamental fact about life is the reality of life; anything which denies that cannot be true. The illusion in all this is not what gives life. The illusion is the pseudo-scientific assumption that life can be reduced to its material components, and thus completely explained. The effect is to explain it away, and that effect is what Robinson is really complaining about.

Another of Robinson's artists, in **"Rembrandt to Rembrandt"** (1921), wins his way through this negative attitude to a better one, though he still seems rather tentative about it. The poem is essentially an elegy, Rembrandt mourning the death of Saskia and meditating on the meaning and value of his own life and work. He is oppressed by the fact that his late style is not understood by his contemporaries, and by the corollary fact that his faith in himself is undermined. He is beset by a demon of doubt. . . . But there is another demon, this one of inspiration and faith, who says that the artist must go on living and working no matter whether or not anyone appreciates him or ever will. . . . Rembrandt accepts this advice, thereby achieving a kind of rebirth, and by painting another of his self-portraits he reassures himself of immortality.

The negative side of Rembrandt's situation is developed in a number of poems Robinson published from time to time deriding, often intemperately, American democracy as he saw it. The voice in **"Cassandra"** (1902) says,

> Verily,
> What word have I for children here?
> Your Dollar is your only Word,
> The wrath of it your only fear.

Like Melville in "Misgivings," Robinson seems to take a grim and vindictive pleasure in foreseeing trouble for these worshippers of the bitch goddess. . . . We have some reason to wish that Americans in 1902 had been more willing than they were to listen to such warnings and to accept the responsibilities their growing power entailed. Other warnings apply at least as well today as when Robinson first uttered them. In two poems published in 1920, he attacked the reactionary temper, which he liked no better than complacency. In **"The Wandering Jew"** the speaker describes the old man's wrath at seeing, apparently,

> New lions ramping in his path.
> The old were dead and had no fangs,
> Wherefore he loved them—seeing not
> They were the same that in their time
> Had eaten everything they caught.

"The Old King's New Jester" is addressed directly and polemically to those who "in vain would front the coming order," those to whom "the old wrong seems right." . . . Robinson was not one of those who fell into proto-fascist attitudes in the 1920's, though his attack was parallel at some points with theirs. He was not longing either for the agrarian past, with its aristocracy of land-owning horsemen, or for a future in which democracy would be suppressed by totalitarian dictatorship.

The point of his contention becomes more clear in **"Demos and Dionysus"** (1925), where Dionysus represents the free creative spirit of man as an individual and the opposing Demos is a false image, wrongly identified with mechanization and conformity. Dionysus, obviously

Robinson at the MacDowell Colony in Peterborough, New Hampshire.

speaking for Robinson, suggests that this false, collectivistic "democracy" is itself totalitarian in tendency. . . . As poetry this is pretty poor stuff, but it is good enough propaganda, and better for our time than for that of its first appearance, methods of brainwashing having improved so much and been so much more widely put into use. Now even more than in 1925 we need "a few that are peculiar," if only, as Dionysus says, to keep "the machine" from breaking down with disastrous results for all. Furthermore, as Dionysus tells the false Demos, with proper contempt for the organization man,

> You and your amiable automatons
> Will have no more the feeling or the fancy
> To prove or guess what ails it.

Dionysus hints, rather vaguely, of a real Demos who may come forward some day to clear away the wreckage of the machine and replace it with a social order more in harmony with human thought and feeling; but this theme remains undeveloped.

Beginning with **Merlin** in 1917, Robinson devoted his energies increasingly to long narrative poems, which his critics generally agree are not as good as his best short lyric and dramatic pieces. They are interesting in that they give the author a chance to display his theme in more detail than elsewhere, but the fact that he also betrays a certain meagerness of imagination is a measure of his failure to use this chance to the best advantage, and of his limits as a writer. The long poems are weak in structure, sparse in imagery, and monotonous in tone and style. Many a modern novel is, in the broad sense, more poetic in conception and execution: *Huckleberry Finn* for example, or *The Ambassadors,* or *The Red Badge of Courage,* or *The Great Gatsby,* or *The Sun Also Rises,* or *The Sound and the Fury.* In view of such prose narratives as these, I cannot entirely agree with Allen Tate's opinion concerning Robinson's failure. Tate blames the age, which, he says, "provides for the poet no epos or myth, no pattern of well understood behavior, which the poet may examine in the strong light of his own experience. . . . With the disappearance of general patterns of conduct, the power to depict action that is both *single* and *complete* also disappears. The dramatic genius of the poet is held to short flights, and the dramatic situation is a fragment of a total action which the poet lacks the means to delineate" [see Tate's excerpt dated 1933]. But why does the poet lack means that the prose writer evidently does not lack? I suspect that the dearth of good long poems might better be explained on the ground that good writers of long narratives mostly use prose, and Robinson's particular failure on the ground that he was not a very good writer of long narratives. (pp. 111-19)

The long narratives of Robinson consist of three poems using Arthurian materials and eight with modern settings. Those two classes had better be handled separately, though all eleven poems have more or less the same basic theme. The Arthurian titles are *Merlin* (1917), *Lancelot* (1920), and *Tristram* (1927). *Tristram* was much the most popular, on first publication, but *Merlin* seems to me the best, partly because it most adequately tells the whole story of which the other two are comparatively incomplete fragments.

Robinson's treatment of the Matter of Britain is distinctively his own. He does not hold, for instance, that the society of the Round Table is an ideal government overthrown by evil forces of greed and lust, but rather that it is one stage in the evolution of human culture, better than some that have preceded it and not so good as some that may be hoped for in the future. Merlin is the prophet who foresees it and does much to bring it into being, but he also sees beyond it, sees its defects, and sees the necessity of its giving way to newer developments, whether they appear, in the immediate context, as better or as worse. He is the protagonist of *Merlin,* who tries to withdraw from the turmoil and responsibility of Arthur's fall, but who is twice forced to return and participate, if only by offering futile and unheeded advice, in crucial events. He confesses to Vivian that there are "specks" in Camelot, which, in her sylvan refuge at Broceliande, where existence is timeless and carefree, he says he does not fear. But he realizes later that time has overtaken him. "For now to Merlin, in his paradise, / Had come an unseen angel with a sword," and he is driven back to the world of changing life. Arthur's own weakness and sin have prepared his downfall through the agency of Modred, his bastard son in the version of the story Robinson chooses to tell, and Merlin is in some degree responsible, and therefore unavoidably involved, even though there is nothing he can do to avert the kingdom's destruction or Arthur's death. At the end, he sets out on the brief remainder of his life's journey, away from Camelot but not toward Broceliande, with the fool, Sir Dagonet, as his only companion.

> Colder blew the wind
> Across the world, and on it heavier lay
> The shadow and the burden of the night;
> And there was darkness over Camelot.

So the poem ends.

The total effect is not so cold, dark, or desperate as the concluding lines might suggest. Camelot is doomed to destruction, but the power of life is not therefore evil; for, as it destroys, it also builds. Merlin's expulsion from paradise brings him, according to Sir Kay, " 'Out of his grave, as he would say it for us'," and his own observation is that " 'in the end / Are more beginnings . . . than men / Shall name or know today'." (pp. 122-23)

Lancelot leaves a bad taste in my mouth. The interlude in which Lancelot and Guinevere are together at Joyous Gard is an interlude of life and not of death, and the logic that persuades him to return her to Camelot is contrary to life. The opposing logic of her plea to stay with him seems at least equally sound: the king has forced him into rebellion; he has the means to fight for her and for his life

(he has to fight anyway, as things turn out); and yet he gives her up. Robinson tries to convince us that Guinevere's final abnegation when Lancelot tracks her down at Almesbury is motivated by religious devotion, but it looks rather more like despair at not finding even him capable of keeping her when he had her. The concluding formula, delivered by "a Voice within" Lancelot, is that

> Where the Light falls, death falls; a world has died
> For you, that a world may live. There is no peace.
> Be glad no man or woman bears for ever
> The burden of first days. There is no peace.

So Lancelot goes away "in the darkness . . . Alone; and in the darkness came the light." In this context the Light seems to mean death much more clearly than it means ensuing life; but, however interpreted, this Light and this Voice are pretty abstract goods compared to the living woman, and Robinson does not make them more attractive by spelling them with capital letters.

In *Tristram* death is plainly offered as a positive element in the final solution. When King Mark reforms, recognizes his error, and gives the lovers his blessing, Andred stabs Tristram; and Isolt of Ireland dies along with him. . . . Again there is no peace, except in death. Conversely, life is identified with change. King Howell tells his daughter, Isolt of Brittany, Tristram's widowed wife,

> When the dawn comes, my child,
> You will forget. No, you will not forget,
> But you will change. There are no mortal houses
> That are so providently barred and fastened
> As to keep change and death from coming in.
> Tristram is dead, and change is at your door.
> Two years have made you more than two years older,
> And you must change.

Light, in the image of the dawn, is here associated—when the king corrects himself—with change, which includes death because life includes death. Light and movement are strongly associated in the concluding image of the poem, as Isolt of Brittany looks out across the bright water and sees ["white birds everywhere, flying, and flying"]. . . . The impression of life going on is cryptic, perhaps even logically inconsistent, but it is much more convincing than in the ending of *Lancelot.*

During the period between the publication of *Lancelot* and that of *Tristram,* Robinson completed two other long poems, *Roman Bartholow* (1923) and *The Man Who Died Twice* (1924), in each of which a man passes through the symbolic cycle of death and rebirth, with somewhat equivocal results. For Bartholow, rebirth involves the loss of his wife, Gabrielle, because she falls in love with Penn-Raven, the man who brings about Bartholow's regeneration, and drowns herself in the river. We first see Bartholow, before he becomes aware of his loss, enjoying his new sense of life on a bright spring morning. . . . This feeling of renewal is proof against misfortune. After the loss of his wife and of his friend Penn-Raven, whom he sends away just before Gabrielle's body is found, Bartholow tells his other friend, the ugly scholar-fisherman Umfraville,

> I'm not saying . . .
>   why it is that nature baits for men,
> Between them and the pit, so many traps
> To save them with a poisoned obligation.
> Nature has ways, you say, not reasons. Well,

They lead us, if we find and follow them,
Strangely away from death.

Umfraville grumbles skeptically, " 'And into it— / As
often, or as likely'." But later he says, " 'You are going to
live, / At last, that more may live'." Bartholow concludes
that Gabrielle was "a woman doomed never to live," and
sells his house and goes away. What kind of life he has
thereafter we are not told, but we are clearly meant to believe that it will continue to lead "away from death."

Fernando Nash, in *The Man Who Died Twice,* is a musical composer of towering genius and equally towering
pride who, after writing two strikingly experimental symphonies and thereby earning the envy and condemnation
of critics and competitors, sinks into "the Valley of the
Shadow" of alcoholism. After a debauch intended to end
his twenty years of slow suicide, of listening to "drums of
death," he is brought back to his right mind by an orchestra of rats who file into his room through the keyhole and
play a symphony in which "those drums of death" are
dominant. Then he hears his true music, first in a shower
of "choral gold" which builds "a gay temple" for "the
Queen of Life;" then in the Poe-like image of

> The faint approach of slow, infernal drums
> That were not long in coming, bringing with them
> A singing horde of demons, men and women,
> Who filled the temple with offensive yells
> And sang to flight the frightened worshippers;

and finally in "a marching hymn" which brings back "All
the banished / Who had been driven from the house of
life" and overcomes death. . . . However, as he is rushing
out for paper on which to write the Third Symphony that
he is sure will make him immortal, he falls down the stairs,
and the resulting injury renders him incapable of composition.

Here we have the same general pattern as in the Annandale story, as completed, and frequently in Robinson's
handling of the death-and-rebirth structure: the protagonist, if he succeeds in completing the cycle, seems able
only to die or to depart, usually in darkness. Fernando
Nash insists to his old acquaintance, the narrator of the
poem, that " 'Mine are the drums of life' "; but the narrator finds him playing them in a Salvation Army band not
long before his death. It may be relevant also that Robinson had spent a number of years (particularly from about
1901 through the first half of 1905) in his own "valley of
the shadow" when he drank considerably more whiskey
than was good for him or his work, and after which he had
great difficulty getting back to the writing of poetry—as
the gap between *Captain Craig* (1902) and *The Town
Down the River* (1910) shows perhaps more eloquently
than anything else in the record. These years, when Robinson was in his thirties, ought to have been among his
most productive. What was lost we cannot know, but Robinson must have had some idea, and his recovery of creative power and his later critical and even popular success
must have come trailing clouds of irony. In **"The Valley
of the Shadow,"** published in the 1920 volume, he included among the valley's inhabitants "drinkers of wrong waters" as well as "pensioners of dreams" and "debtors of
illusions," in all which categories he seems to have felt that
he belonged; and he ended bravely but rather too pathetically by saying, "There are builders of new mansions in

the Valley of the Shadow, / And among them are the
dying and the blinded and the maimed." (pp. 125-29)

I have suggested that Robinson's failure, with which I
have been concerned for the most part so far, would not
be important if Robinson had not been potentially a very
great poet. I wish now to look rather closely at four poems
that seem to me to show his great potential either partly
or, within the narrow compass of his occasional brilliantly
successful short pieces, fully realized: **"Luke Havergal"**
(1896), **"The Man Against the Sky"** (1916), **"For a Dead
Lady"** (1910), and **"Eros Turannos"** (1916). These are not
all Robinson's best, by any means, but I believe they can
be made to show his most attractive aspects.

One of his earliest published works, **"Luke Havergal"** is
one of the most fascinating. . . . Critics have puzzled
much over this poem, wondering who the speaker is, who
"she" is, and whether or not Luke Havergal is going to
commit suicide. These questions, though relevant, may
not be primarily important. Probably Robinson here, like
Eliot in "Sweeney Among the Nightingales," is mainly
concerned to create an atmosphere rather than to tell a
story; however, in Robinson's piece much more than in
Eliot's, the atmosphere seems to depend on the reader's
explicit awareness of a situation arising in the course of
certain particular events.

In a letter to Smith, dated December 14, 1895, Robinson
referred to "a piece of deliberate degeneration called
'Luke Havergal,' which is not at all funny." He had been
reading Max Nordau's *Degeneration* in June, when he remarked to the same correspondent, with particular reference to Nordau's chapter on Zola, that "It is pretty good
work and sound, too, I think; only it is overdrawn and unnecessarily vituperative. . . . " His own sonnet on Zola,
first published in the 1896 volume, is much more favorable
than the account of Nordau, who classes Zola with the
worst of his "degenerates"—along with the English Pre-
Raphaelites, Baudelaire, Verlaine, Mallarmé, Wagner,
Tolstoy, Ibsen, and other leading moderns of the time. In
this context, we need not assume that Robinson would
consider "a piece of deliberate degeneration" to be necessarily a bad thing. *Degeneration* was an attack on both
symbolism and naturalism in literature, as well as impressionism in painting, and it left a latter-day romantic such
as Robinson very little to admire if he had to agree with
its thesis. A second clue links Nordau with **"Luke Havergal."** In another letter to Smith, dated October 6, 1895,
Robinson remarked, "I like the red leaves. Red leaves
makes me think of *Degeneration*. . . . " I have found no
reason for this association, unless it lies in the fact that,
according to Nordau, "degenerates" take a special pleasure in the color red because it is "dynamogenous," or
"force-producing."

Nordau characterized the "degenerate" mind as having a
"predilection for inane reverie" and "capricious and, as a
rule, purely mechanical associations of ideas and succession of images," as well as "weakness of will and morbid
susceptibility to suggestion." He admitted that Verlaine,
although extremely "degenerate," had written superb lyrics. "This," Nordau said, "is because the methods of a
highly emotional, but intellectually incapable, dreamer
suffice for poetry which deals exclusively with moods, but
this is the inexorable limit of his power. . . . [Poetry of
moods] has no need of a fundamental thought, or of a pro-

gressive exposition to unfold it. Verlaine often attains to astonishing effects in such poetry of moods." Robinson may have said to himself, in effect, that by Nordau's definition he might be considered "degenerate," but that if so he was in good company; therefore why not develop his "degeneration" in the hope of writing as good a lyric as some of Verlaine's? One critic has suggested, as a way of resolving or avoiding some of the troublesome questions raised by **"Luke Havergal,"** that perhaps "this poem should be regarded as an exercise in the manner, say, of the symbolists, not, of course, without serious overtones, but possibly without a great deal of specific meaning." But I believe that it has some specific meaning, and that its beauty depends partly on our understanding of it.

The most obvious meaning lies in the evident fact that it is an elegy, a poem about death, or, more precisely, about our attitudes toward death. Luke Havergal is being advised by a voice "Out of a grave" to adopt one attitude rather than another. He is to "Go to the western gate" in "the wall" which apparently separates this life from whatever is to come. The gate seems to represent death. . . . Luke is told that "the crimson leaves" of vines that "cling . . . on the wall" will say "dead words" to him, which, however, he will not be able "to riddle" or "to feel." But, says the voice, "if you listen she will call," and again, "if you trust her she will call." Luke is not to seek light in the obvious direction—"there is not a dawn in eastern skies"—but rather "The dark will end the dark, if anything. . . ." It may be significant, however, that he is instructed to go *to* the gate, not *through* it, and to listen for a call, not to join the caller. There is nothing in the wording of the poem that requires us to regard Luke's death as either imminent or desirable, and I prefer not to.

It is desirable that he confront the fact of death closely and face it uncompromisingly. He is promised that if he will do so—perhaps in the same spirit in which Cliff Klingenhagen drinks his wormwood—he will receive some message, presumably of truth and possibly of hope and cheer. But at the same time we have it, if we take the poem at face value, from one who knows, one who has died, that "the kiss" on Luke's forehead is to be quenched, because it blinds him to the way that he must go. I take these lines to mean that Luke is not to follow his sweetheart into death, but is to take a different way, which will be a better way to preserve the relation that death has interrupted. It will not be the way of either death or a sentimental-optimistic denial of death; it will be bitter, and will require faith. The logic is obscure, partly because it is not explicitly stated and partly, I suspect, because it is intrinsically difficult. But I believe that it is sound.

If we begin with the assumption that life is a process of continual change, and if we add that one of its kinds of change is the death of people we love, then I think we must conclude that, in order to go on living ourselves, we must undergo or bring about a change in the quality of our love. We must give up the body of it—the red leaves that fall—in order to keep the spirit. To maintain a relationship in a changing world is, inevitably, to change the relationship. If life is change, what does not change is dead. But if we can change our love enough, and in the right way, we can preserve it through the most appalling change of all, the death of those we love. We cannot succeed if we try to ignore the reality of death and loss, or pretend that they can

be repaired in any way whatever; instead, we lose the love we are trying so hard to keep. To deny death is to deny life, and that is suicide indeed. If this logic is correct, Luke Havergal is being advised against suicide. He is being urged not to die but to live, and to keep his love alive by accepting the bitter fact that his lover is dead.

There is also, I believe, a more general significance, or at least implication, in **"Luke Havergal"** and in its relation to Max Nordau's book. Nordau was talking not only about individual degeneration and degenerates, but about degeneration as a social or cultural phenomenon as well. "One epoch of history is unmistakably in its decline, and another is announcing its approach," he said. "Meanwhile interregnum in all its terrors prevails. . . . Men look with longing for whatever new things are at hand. . . . They have hope that in the chaos of thought, art may yield revelations of the order that is to follow on this tangled web. The poet, the musician, is to announce, or divine, or at least suggest in what forms civilization will further be evolved." Robinson, in the Arthurian poems and in others, accepted at least a part of this program. If he did not suggest very clearly what forms of civilization were to come, he emphatically suggested that the old order was passing and that something—preferably something better—would have to take its place. And he certainly felt the terrors of interregnum keenly, as the dark conclusions of *Merlin* and *Lancelot* make plain. The same feeling is evoked by **"Luke Havergal,"** a feeling appropriate not only to a man who has lost a lover (as Merlin and Lancelot have done), but to all living men, who lose all kinds of things as they gain other things. Growth always means loss or death of the old in development of the new: death always precedes or, logically, accompanies rebirth. We cannot have the one without the other, and that is the reason why romanticism, which is devotion to change, involves so much nostalgia. (pp. 129-34)

The structure of **"Luke Havergal"** is unusually regular, even for Robinson, who liked strict forms. The last stanza is a repetition, with only a little variation, quantitatively, of the first. Six of the eight rhymes are not only the same sounds but the same words. The resulting symmetry is reinforced by the similarity of the predominant rhyming sound in the second stanza to that of the third: "skies" and "this." These effects combine with the many repetitions within stanzas to develop a remarkably sustained and consistent tone of voice and feeling for the whole poem, a result which, as any poet will testify, requires the highest kind of technical skill to bring off successfully. I am not for a moment suggesting that the total impression is brought about by technique alone, but rather that the technical aspects are functional in carrying the quality of feeling that the poet meant to evoke. It is the quality of deep, earnest attention to an almost impossible-to-formulate idea, the reaching for something which cannot quite be grasped, but which faith must have in order for life to continue. I doubt if it can fully be explained; but anyone who has experienced the death of a person he loved more than himself will have had the feeling I believe Robinson was reaching for. At any rate, it is safe to say that the slightest slip or stumble in execution would have ruined the work.

This tone that Robinson so brilliantly sustains is one of mourning and even of despair. Luke Havergal, at least for the time being, is caught and pictured in a state of degeneration, not of regeneration. He hears the voice, but he is not yet able, if he ever will be, to accept and believe what I have interpreted it as saying. He is overcome by grief, which he is at present unable to assimilate or to transform into anything else, or to transcend. As Robinson remarked, the work "is not at all funny"; its dominant feeling, no matter how it may be read, is one of gloom rather than joy. But Robinson always maintained that he was an optimist, and I feel that the latent meaning of **"Luke Havergal"** bears out this contention.

The identities of characters in **"Luke Havergal"** remain, for me, problematical. The speaker, as Winters guesses, may possibly be Luke's dead lover, also referred to by the pronoun "she," though I think it probable that, as Winters also theorizes, the voice is not to be taken literally, but rather as something Luke imagines. I think it matters very little whether the message originates in the afterworld or in imagination, or, for that matter, whether the reader thinks the final result will be suicide or whether he supposes there will be an improvement in Luke's state of mind and feeling, leading to renewed and continuing life. The thing that matters, in the poem, is the quality of the message itself, rather than its supposed origin or result.

"The Man Against the Sky" is also a poem about death, in which several possible attitudes are proposed, compared, and rejected. The conclusion seems mainly negative, after Robinson's typical fashion. It is put in terms of a question: If we know for certain that there is no life after death, why do we live at all? The implication is that, since we do live, we must believe in life after death. A weakness of the strategy lies in the fact that Robinson rules out all the familiar, conventional, traditional beliefs concerning immortality without stating any belief of his own or any belief which he can recommend to his readers. There is also, to my way of thinking, a purely logical weakness. I would feel that, if this life is the only life we have, it must be all the more precious for that reason, and all the more to be lived to the fullest and richest possible degree.

In some respects **"The Man Against the Sky"** is an elegy, although both the speaker and the man he speculates about are almost completely anonymous. One way of judging it, then, may be to compare it to some of its predecessors in the elegiac tradition. I will take up two which seem to have some affinity to Robinson's effort: "Lycidas," because it has a closely similar verse form and because it was one of Robinson's favorite poems, and Wordsworth's "Ode: Intimations of Immortality," though it does not follow the usual pattern, because it deals with the traditional question, because the image of the man on the hill against the sunset was probably borrowed from Wordsworth, and because Robinson referred to the volume of which **"The Man Against the Sky"** is the title poem as "my latest intimations of mortality." What both of the earlier elegies have, and Robinson's poem lacks, is the formula by which the speaker positively assures himself and his readers that there is life after death. Though the two formulas are not the same, they both give definite promise of immortality. In "Lycidas" the traditional pattern is complete: the speaker learns that his friend is dead; he feels an initial shock of personal grief, horror at the realization that he too must die, and despair; he comforts himself "with false surmise" concerning flowers and

dolphins; and he ends by roundly declaring that "Lycidas . . . is not dead" but has been taken up into heaven, and also made a tutelary deity, thus having the best of two afterworlds, the Christian and the pagan. Its intensity of personal feeling and richness of imagery make "Lycidas" one of the greatest lyrics in the language; the degree to which these qualities are absent from **"The Man Against the Sky"** is a measure of its inferiority. The comparison hardly seems fair, but Robinson invited it by using the same verse form, which is not common in English, and by incorporating most of the same pattern. I believe that Robinson's typical failure of nerve prevented him from carrying the work to conclusion. It does not do what an elegy ought to do; that is, help the reader face his own inevitably coming death and live his meanwhile continuing life with proper courage and effectiveness. (pp. 135-37)

A more conventional and much finer elegy is **"For a Dead Lady,"** first published in *Scribner's Magazine* for September, 1909. Yvor Winters says that it is "an elegy unlightened by any mitigating idea or feeling . . . purely a lament for the dead. Robinson suggests no way of dealing with the experience except that we understand it and endure it." As I read the poem, Robinson does not suggest that we can hope to understand death, but, on the other hand, he does suggest some ideas which, though they do not mitigate sorrow, may keep the work from being "purely a lament." The question is the same as in **"The Man Against the Sky"**: How can we reconcile ourselves to death if this is a mechanistic world? (pp. 141-42)

The difference between **"For a Dead Lady"** and **"The Man Against the Sky"** is partly structural. After its promising beginning, **"The Man Against the Sky"** takes a wrong turn at the point where the speaker begins his diatribe against materialism, and it never recovers its tone. **"For a Dead Lady"** is more like **"Luke Havergal"** in that it never loses its tone. It begins by announcing the lady's death in a series of vivid, concrete images, and it returns in the last line to a concrete personification of Death, scythe in hand. Being short, it hardly has a middle; the announcement is played upon in various terms, and the conclusion, with its implied question, follows. Nevertheless there is development, or increment, in the series of statements, which do more than emphasize the fact of death by the manifold repetition of it. The lady's eyes—a favorite image for Robinson, in harmony with his emphasis on light—have lost their lustre, and there are no other eyes like them. Her movements, which were various and beautiful, are stilled, and her gracefulness is inadequately remembered. Her emotional involvement, perhaps with more than one man—the line "The laugh that love could not forgive" is cryptic but suggestive—is ended, the physical shape of her features has been lost in time . . ., and the color of life is gone from her bosom along with the movement of her breathing. All of these images and their qualities are then summed up in the word "beauty," which is immediately opposed to the mechanistic image of impersonal "laws." These laws, closely associated or even identified with time, as well as with the "inexorable cause" of the next to last line, have destroyed the lady's beauty and its responses to emotional relationships with admirers and with objects of solicitude such as sleeping children, and no explanation can satisfactorily account for the loss or reconcile lovers and students of beauty to the destruction.

The topic is Poe's favorite theme, the death of a beautiful woman; and something of Poe's technique is recalled by the repetition of the phrase "No more" in the first stanza and by the rhyme "lore"—"before" in the last. Robinson's technique, however, is much better than Poe's, if only because it avoids Poe's excesses. The form of **"For a Dead Lady"** is simple but subtle. Each stanza begins with the common quatrain consisting of octosyllabic lines rhyming abab; but this is not repeated in the last four lines, which instead consist of a couplet, with a new rhyming sound, followed by a return to the ab rhyme in the last two lines. The result is an eight-line rhyme scheme, ababccab. The effect is of development, suspension, and recapitulation or return. The form of each stanza reflects something of the total structure of the poem, which also follows a sequence of development, static tension, and recapitulation. The proportions are nearly the same, if we take the first two stanzas to be the development, the first four lines of the last stanza the suspension, and the last four lines the repetition. Each stanza has a heavy stop or pause at the end; the poem as a whole has an equally heavy conclusion. Both effects are reinforced by the use of feminine b-rhymes throughout, forcing a pause at the end of each b-rhyming line, at the end of each stanza, and particularly, at the end of the poem, before the reader can escape to any thought or feeling other than those the poet imposes.

The excellence of the poem, however, can be accounted for only partly on technical grounds; it is also partly or largely due to the superlative management of thematic imagery, and especially the images of life. Almost everything that is caught and summed up in the abstract word "beauty" in the last stanza has been concretely presented earlier in terms implying movement: "overflowing light" in the eyes, the "quiver" and "flowing" of "shifting" and "many-shaded" activity, the "rising" and "falling" of the "breast" which is the seat of the heart and which owes its color of "roses" to blood coursing through the veins. Beauty is the wonder and the grace of life as change and motion, elusive, mysterious, always welling up to our awareness, and always escaping the grasp of our conscious attention in the very moment of our attempt to seize it. It is because this sense of the ineffable beauty of life is so vividly and concretely evoked that the word "shattered" falls with such force in the first line of the last stanza, when the "laws / That have creation in their keeping" become the agents of destruction; and it is for the same reason that the word "vicious" cuts so deeply in the last line of the poem. If the sense of life were not so powerfully and attractively evoked in the first and second stanzas, the shock of death would not be so sharp in the last, nor would the sense of loss be so poignant throughout. A delicate but tense balance between the beauty of life and the pain of death seems to me to raise this poem far above the quality of **"The Man Against the Sky,"** with its merely negative theme, and above, though not so far above, **"Luke Havergal,"** the tone of which is so much more heavily and exclusively weighted with gloom and despair. In **"For a Dead Lady,"** although no explicit formula of comfort, reconciliation, or immortality is offered, there is real compensation for the thought of death. There is the beauty of life, and it is beautifully rendered.

"Eros Turannos," first published in *Poetry* for March, 1914, maintains a similar balance and strikes a rather more positive note, though it is still sufficiently grim to escape any charge of easy or sentimental optimism. . . . The form, particularly the stanza form, is similar to that of **"For a Dead Lady."** The rhyme scheme is ababcccb, identical with that of **"For a Dead Lady"** except that line seven rhymes with the couplet lines five and six instead of lines one and three; the b-rhymes are again feminine. The only other difference in stanza form is that the b-rhyming lines are trimeter instead of tetrameter. (pp. 142-46)

The total structure of the poem can most readily be defined, perhaps, in terms of the point of view. For the first four stanzas it is or appears to be objective; the anonymous speaker describes the little drama as it might strike a casual though fairly sympathetic observer. In the fifth he associates himself with other observers and shows how superficial such a view must be. In the last stanza sympathy predominates; the attitude of objectivity is abandoned, and we receive a sudden, penetrating insight into the clench of agony that must occur when the town point of view moves nearer that of the house and its blindly driven mistress. Again, as in **"For a Dead Lady,"** the structure of the whole poem is essentially the same as that of the individual stanzas. There is a building up of tension as we learn the story, then a held pause as the speaker shifts his ground, then the conclusion, which returns us to the story with a greatly heightened awareness of its meaning and importance.

Thematically, the tension arises most obviously out of the opposition of reason and emotion. The lady is, in a sense, under no illusion whatever; she knows she is making a fatal mistake. But she goes ahead and makes it anyway, because she is under compulsion by a power that neither she nor any other human being can have much change of resisting, or of wanting to resist. She is rather literally "by love possessed"; but this possession, as the speaker comes round in the end to telling us, is not so pure an evil as the town may suppose. It is, after all, a divine gift, not alone of suffering, but of life, the condition of which is always suffering but which nevertheless remains divine. One implication of the shift in point of view is that those who suffer little, as the townspeople seem to do, cannot live very fully either. The lady, having sacrificed her pride, having been overcome by the tyrannous god, and having made her home a refuge from public criticism, still has something her fellow citizens lack. The house may be a place where passion has died, as the neighbors believe, but passion has lived with her as it seems not to have done with them. The only thing wrong is that it has not overcome the gentleman in the case, whose motives are evidently social and economic. From what we know of him, he appears incapable of any intense emotion, whether of pain or of ecstasy; therefore the divine gift of love and life is given to her and not to him. The tension between reason and emotion is only a superficial indication of a profounder tension, which might be defined as stretching between life and not-life. Not, let us note, between life and death; for life implies death and includes death as one of its terms. The lady's mistake is fatal in much the same sense that all living things are mortal, precisely because they are living. Fate here is change, which is life, at the same time that it is what destroys life, and love, and happiness. In life, the condition of having anything is the inevitability of losing it. (pp. 146-47)

As in **"For a Dead Lady"** and, on a somewhat lower level

of excellence, in **"Luke Havergal,"** the technical quality of **"Eros Turannos"** is crucial, and it is so much more than merely adequate that the effect is of almost unbelievable beauty. Ellsworth Barnard has given a good brief analysis of the last four lines, pointing out "the tremendously effective use of assonance in the long-*a* sound," "the hammering recurrence of *d* in the last line," and the "steady acceleration" from the slow, spondaic fifth line up to the last line, which, Barnard says, measures "the heavy footfalls of Fate." The same kind of analysis might equally well be applied to many other passages to indicate the extremely subtle grace with which Robinson maintains the tone he needs throughout the poem to achieve the effect he wants the reader to carry away at the end. The third stanza seems particularly fine to me, with its *s* and *l* sounds building up a liquid sibilance, punctuated by a few stopped consonants, particularly the *t*'s in lines one and three and the *d*'s in the last four lines. There are also some dividends in the rhyme scheme, which has the effect of tying the second, third, fifth, and sixth stanzas lightly together, and making a formal division of the poem into two equal parts. These correspond to a thematic division between the process of courtship and its result, without interfering with what seems to me the more important structural divisions between the fourth and fifth stanzas and between the fifth and sixth. We might also note in passing the fact that in all but the first stanza, and particularly in the second, third, and fifth, the pause and turn of thought at the end of the sixth line reinforces both the stretching of the triplet rhyme and the heavily conclusive effect of the feminine b-rhyme at the end. The total result is an impression of elegance, economy, and precision seldom matched in English.

In **"Eros Turannos,"** if my reading is correct, Robinson brilliantly succeeds precisely where he fails in **"The Man Against the Sky"**; that is, in writing a poem which confounds the materialists and justifies his too often wavering faith in the qualities of life as opposed to those of mechanism—or, we might say, of any dead abstraction. What he tells us, in effect, is that from an "objective" point of view, human emotion is at once destructive and ridiculous. Extended, this means that life is destructive and ridiculous. Therefore the abstract, "objective" point of view is the wrong one to take. The more we abstract, the farther we get from the values of life. These values lie in concrete experience, which is personal, emotional, and even irrational, but which is first of all, and above all other considerations, *real*. Any utterance which denies these values is contrary to reality, no matter how logically it may be constructed or stated. The purpose of poetry, in this connection—the purpose, at least, of romantic poetry—is to affirm, demonstrate, and embody in concrete symbolic emotional terms the value of life and the reality of immediate personal experience. When Robinson does this, as he does in **"Eros Turannos"** but not in **"The Man Against the Sky,"** he is a great romantic poet. His failure consists in his inability to do it often enough throughout the body of his work. (pp. 149-51)

Richard P. Adams, "The Failure of Edwin Arlington Robinson," in TSE: Tulane Studies in English, *Vol. XI, 1961, pp. 97-151.*

"Any poetry that is marked by violence, that is conspicuous in color, that is sensationally odd, makes an immediate appeal. On the other hand, poetry that is not noticeably eccentric sometimes fails for years to attract any attention."
—Edwin Arlington Robinson, 1917

Radcliffe Squires   (essay date 1969)

[*An American poet, critic, and biographer, Squires is well known for his verse which draws from his extensive knowledge of Greek mythology to delineate problems and concerns of modern existence. In the following excerpt, he comments on Robinson's perseverance.*]

Time gives us two different ways of looking at the poetry of our contemporaries. In youth we read that poetry as the truth of the present as well as of the future, as reportorial as well as prophetic knowledge. We are taken up, if we are lucky, by the modes of language which create the ruminant spirit of our history whose facts often fail to survive the moment of their birth. The facts sag away, but we are borne by the spirit into dim but paradisiacal guesses into the life of the future. In maturity we stand partly in a friendly territory of a few confirmed guesses and partly in an enemy territory, the existence of which we could never have imagined. We are no longer then among *our* contemporaries: we are among other men's contemporaries. We look back through time at the poetry of our time. And it is different to us. What had seemed a vocabulary of audacity may seem only the slang of bravado. The forms and tones that once squirmed for very life in our embrace may seem as static as poor sculpture, as finished and set as the verse of Tennyson or Dryden or Chaucer. The time is an unhappy one, yet we compensate for sorrow by claiming for it "objectivity," by supposing that at this moment criticism may really begin. Criticism comes, true enough, but not in the state of cool objectivity that we hopefully suppose; rather in a state of dual subjectivities somewhat at war with each other, somewhat neutralizing each other. The impressions of the past remain nostalgically monumental, but the chaotic present is running like a flood over everything. Somewhat at war within, somewhat demobilized by neutrality, I find that in the centennial year of the birth of Edwin Arlington Robinson and thirty-four years after his death, I see him as a quite different poet from the one I knew in my youth.

The fact is I could not but neglect Robinson's virtues at the time I first became interested in poetry. The flood running in the 1930s was not one to pay much heed to Robinson. Homage to his technical assurance, yes, to his "plots," certainly; but in one major way he seemed remote and unexciting: he seemed too much dedicated to direct statement, and his statements seemed to belong to some previous century. The poetry which particularly enthralled me and my friends was that of T. S. Eliot and of Wallace Stevens. Eliot and Stevens are dissimilar poets but in one way they are alike. They do not *assert* meaning or theme; they do not *achieve* it, not really, from the materials of their poems. They *assume* theme, and their poetry is an elaborate design embroidered on the cloth of an assumption. Their poetry is result rather than consideration of cause. Both Eliot and Stevens could move gracefully into their respective fields of surmise because those fields had already been surveyed and mapped. For Eliot the withering away of an aristocratic eminence in society and the attendant flourishing of Apeneck Sweeney (or Flem Snopes) were both incontrovertible and, in a masochistic way, exhilarating. The evolutionary myths of progress were turning back upon themselves. Retrogression, sterility, pluralistic chaos had become the new myths. For Stevens the two sources of his poetry—the scientific and philosophical subjectivism of this century along with the artistic subjectivism of the various modes of impressionism—presented him with his basic concern with a sensuous epistemology. In the 1930s these large assumptions floated like cloudy fates, pervasive determinations. In a way they seemed like one fate. . . . In short, the fatal and sterile subjectivity assumed by T. S. Eliot, raged at by Robinson Jeffers, became in Stevens' poetry a kingdom of the mind. The wasteland, the perishing republic which punished us extravagantly, could also reward us sumptuously. But Edwin Arlington Robinson's poems, modestly confined to lives which themselves appeared too confined, gave no such punishment or reward, seemed trivial, almost sophomoric. That, at any rate, is an approximation of my feelings when I first read poetry seriously. It is not my feeling as I look back from a present scene and view Robinson's poems through the haze of poetry today. (pp. 175-77)

Others have commented with justice and brilliance on Robinson's style, and I have no hope of adding new insights. Nevertheless, with Robinson's style my re-evaluation must begin. It must begin with the observation that the apparent conventionality, the seeming timidity of his verse have come to seem more and more original, more and more brave. Perhaps Yvor Winters always knew this, but few of us could have known this so well at any earlier time, for most of us could not have known that experimentalism as preached and practiced by Pound or Eliot or Crane would some day blur into a convention. We feel it is convention because the poetry cannot surprise, if only for the reason that we know that it is intended to surprise. All of the packrat gleanings, the allusions, the prodigality of images contract before our eyes into something as expectable as one of Pope's couplets. And the symbol, the mother of modern subtlety, becomes not subtlety but obvious device. But Robinson's poetry exists almost without symbols; it offers few images; it does not seek to make God over in the image of language. Its immense surprise lies in its humble poetic fact. It is poetry that has primarily the ambition to be poem; the ambition to convert the artesian sub-pressure of creativity into that which is created; the ambition to make the half-known truly known in the way that only the strait geometry of form can make it known. We can never say of Robinson's poetry, as we might of Eliot's, that it is becoming obvious, for in always intending to be obvious it remains mysteriously obvious. We can never say that his contemplative lyrics become small, as we might of Hart Crane's once we understand them well enough to count just how many eggs there really are in the nest, for Robinson always made his poems as mysteriously irreducible as they could be made. But that is not to postulate that it would be impossible to expunge a word here or there from the verse; it is to postulate that no one in his right mind would want to. The reason is not far to seek.

The reason is the singular consistency of Robinson's language. As consistent as water. His poems do not occupy a page: they fill a vessel just to the top. To remove a few drops might not drastically alter the weight or substance. But one would know that the vessel was not quite used.

These are surface matters, but beneath the surface lies a very odd profundity: Robinson's remarkable modesty. It is as if Robinson, not wishing us to think he considered his insights superior to our own, politely refused to surround them with claims of brilliance. It is as if he suggests that his perceptions scarcely deserve anything more intense than the language of the polite essay. That one element of his poetry may in the long run turn out to be quite the most brilliant thing about it. Certainly, the calm susurrus of his "drab style," to borrow a phrase from Allen Tate, is not boring, but haunting; not tiring, but entreating. Yet the poems do not haunt to inspire terror, nor entreat to nail down our affection. They haunt and entreat because we are aware of their fine, natural courtesy, their unassuming intelligence. . . . The lines do not bargain with images, nor do they parlay an image into a "chain of images." In some way, however, the whole style, language and form, creates one large image, not solely auditory, of a speech sufficiently calm to be sure of its grief, sufficiently ordinary to secure the grief from the inevitable temptation of over-dramatization. Such poetry never recedes from its climaxes. It keeps a measured but firm pressure through all its parts. Only such poetry can create simultaneous qualities of pathos and acceptance, as, for example, in the first section of **"Romance"**:

> We were all boys, and three of us were friends;
> And we were more than friends, it seemed to me:—
> Yes, we were more than brothers then, we three. . . .
> Brothers? . . . But we were boys, and there it ends.

These four lines suggest that statement which is also understatement can obtain as much in the way of emotion and subtlety as can concrete images. The argument is not for doing away with images, of course, but for appreciating what can be obtained without them. Even beyond emotion and subtlety, one remarks that the bareness grants a grave honesty and a high confidence to the formal surface of the poems. It invests the rhythms with a quality of inevitability. It deputes a necessity to the rhymes. And those rhymes in Robinson's poetry close like hands about the ends of the lines. They hold on for dear life.

In a sense, then, the effect of this formal but drab style derives less from focusing attention on important predications than from refusing to distract from those predications. And so the substance comes forth in such a way that we call it clear rather than luminous, comprehensible rather than suggestive. (pp. 177-79)

Let us return to the observation that Eliot works from an assumption. His soliloquies, whether Prufrock's or the committee members' of *The Waste Land,* take place, like important soliloquies in Shakespeare's plays, after the dramatic situation has been established. These soliloquies do not make the dramatic condition: they exploit it. Thus we may say that Eliot's poems depend on a dramatic situation but do not create it. And Eliot's method is unquestionably appropriate to his aim. Never arguing the truth of his assumption, he compounds examples of it. His intent being to intensify the drama, he employs richness, reiteration,

...ex linguistic mirroring. He is not interested ...g the assumption. Nor would his technique be ap...opriate to proof. The opposite is true of Robinson's technique.

The nearly bare, the nearly gray properties of Robinson's verse demand that something happen, that dramatic change occur. Even more important, these properties, in contrast to Eliot's, *permit* the dramatic change. Eliot's technique of rich, metaphorical demonstration thus can only properly lead to an effect of pageant. Robinson's technique can only properly lead to an effect of dramatic change. Eliot's poetry demonstrates a condition. Robinson's poetry proves a condition. At this point I think one can see why Robinson's poetry has never been influential in the way that Eliot's or Stevens' has been: because it proves a case, it has seemed to lose too much to reason. At the same time, however, one must observe that poetry which depends upon an assumption, loses a good deal of its power when the assumption fades. The poetry that proves its case, poem by poem, remains what it has always been. Its substance continues because it is created within the poem rather than by an external climate. But what is it, this substance that is both demanded and permitted by the tone and procedures of the poetry?

Robinson's poems, the best of them and those that will last, emerge from an awareness that life is continuously menaced: that innocence and experience alike are threatened by the bland modular construction of society and the soulless press of industrialism. Not that Robinson continuously harps on the menace. The contrary is true. His specific mention of materialism or industry could not be called frequent, and where we do find mention, the language, while clear, is not strident. Still, the reader recognizes the corrosive presence of a puritanic and materialistic society as an ambience about much of the poetry and most of the lives he considers in that poetry. Even the idylls, such as **"Isaac and Archibald"**—seemingly remote and immune pastorals—are, like Wordsworth's "Michael," surrounded by a mundane ruthlessness only the more emphatic for being unstated. At this point, exactly here, Robinson's great theme appears. Oddly enough the theme has often been dismissed as being an "O. Henry ending," frequently as being "negative" or "bitter." Neither of these assessments is just. Neither is sensitive to the true deportment of Robinson's poetry.

Robinson is brusquely realistic about American social attitudes. He sees a life where emotion is not approved. He sees a life where imagination is suspect and where nonconformity expires early or evolves toward a painful eccentricity. Yet in the midst of these repressive proscriptions, Robinson saves life itself, for over and over again, he allows his Tilbury people to turn at bay and to fulfill themselves emotionally, imaginatively, and individually.

The word "individually" is of quintessential importance, for to accept this word is to reject the claim that Robinson was chasing after the melodramatic loot of surprise endings. The suicide of Richard Cory is not, or ought not to be, a surprise. It is an inevitability, predetermined by the subjugation of selfhood. Even more significantly, however, the subjugated self reclaims itself in the act of suicide. Not that the poem recommends suicide as a way of asserting individuality. Rather, it observes an extreme gesture in an extreme case. To see the poem in this way is to see it as

neither bitter nor negative, at least not entirely so. We read ill if we cannot see that Richard Cory is granted an oblique triumph at the end, for he has refused to suppose himself made happy by what "everyone" supposes will make everyone happy. In short, Richard Cory's self emerges neurotically perhaps; still it emerges triumphant over the imposed role of "success." (pp. 180-81)

"Miniver Cheevy" is usually described as a mocking self-portrait, but such an observation tells us little about the poem itself. Indeed, such phrases as "mocking self-portrait" are usually a means of dodging a poem. I suggest that one must ask why Miniver Cheevy (*not* Edwin Arlington Robinson) prefers an earlier, more "romantic" era than his own, what it is that he loses, if anything, by being out of phase with his time, and, finally, if his anachronistic attachment is virtuous or vicious. These questions burden an admittedly middle-weight poem and I shall not burden it further with specific answers. Still, does not the sum of reasonable answers amount to an impression that Miniver's escapism is really an effort to establish an individuality which a world of "progress" denies?

But possibly it will seem that I have added perversity to convenience. In that event one is directed to the poem **"Reuben Bright"** which is so unequivocal that no two readers are apt to differ greatly. And here we are definitely told that the world would prefer to ignore the essential capacity of a man for grief. But the poem continues on resolutely to detail not merely the delicately imaginative ritual of the butcher's grief, but most significantly to bring him to a gesture whereby he destroys the symbol of the world's idea of himself: he tears down the slaughterhouse. Reuben Bright's gesture is parallel to Richard Cory's suicide. But this gesture—which is also Robinson's primary theme, this stubbornly beautiful discovery of the self within, this ultimate insistence that individuality survives and in some devious way supersedes society—this gesture has also a parallel outside Robinson's poetry. It is the most important gesture in the American imagination, simply because it is the most necessary.

The acknowledgment that the self must create itself even as the railroad tracks unreel onto the land is the real meaning of Emily Dickinson's solitary room. The realization that the self must recreate itself—even if perversely and destructively in an inverted image of the Christian soul—is the real meaning of Poe's poem "Alone." All of Melville's "isolatos" are desperate, last-ditch preservers of self. His Bartleby has lost all will except one negative will—he "prefers" not to accommodate the vestigial soul to Wall Street. And even Whitman, the presumed celebrator of simple democracy, complicates his celebration. For even as he is touching everything, learning as an infant learns indiscriminately, he stops short to remind us from time to time that we cannot possibly learn him, that we cannot truly know *him*. He is not hiding a secret, he is saving a unique and finicky self.

But Edwin Arlington Robinson is not so hermetic as Emily Dickinson, not so upside down as Poe, not so renegade as Melville, nor so cryptic as Whitman. As soon as he had saved a soul from society he wanted to return it to society. And he did. He did this by the same means that Thomas Hardy—whom he admired—employed for a similar aim: he created a neutral, choral voice that murmurs above, below and through the lives of Tilbury Town. The knowledge of self, sacred grief, even of Faustian diabolism, is given through this choral voice to the town (New York City as much as Gardiner, Maine). It is given somewhat as a saint's life is given to be pondered by the conscience of the community of men, except that for Robinson, it was the sensibility rather than the conscience he wanted to affect. For this reason in his finest poem, **"Eros Turannos,"** Robinson drifts away in the last two stanzas from the tortured wife and the "secured" husband to the commentary of the town, to his chorus. The chorus cannot absorb all of the pain that is pressed into the one devastating image of "the foamless weirs / Of age," but the chorus can take in much of it, can modulate the water image in another, diminished water image. In this way the chorus mediates in the classical manner between tragedy and society. One remembers that in his youth Robinson labored with his friend Harry de Forest Smith on a translation of Sophocles' *Antigone*. Like that drama, much of Robinson's poetry contemplates the problem of how the self might separate itself from a rigid society, yet remain as a tutelary spirit. In the end Robinson's decision would seem to have been that this could best be done by eschewing the dramatic catastrophes—vengeance, martyrdom—and offering instead temperate ironies, cool understatements and a language calculated, like Wordsworth's, to heal. This decision, as one looks back now from the present with its poetry of scrimshaw, its poetry of sociology, requires one to say that Robinson chose not to write for any particular time, for "any particular time" likes to have salt in its wounds. Equally it requires that one say that Robinson wrote for all time, for "all time" wants to be made healthy and to survive. (pp. 181-83)

> *Radcliffe Squires, "Tilbury Town Today," in* Edwin Arlington Robinson: Centenary Essays, *edited by Ellsworth Barnard, University of Georgia Press, 1969, pp. 175-83.*

FURTHER READING

Barnard, Ellsworth, ed. *Edwin Arlington Robinson: Centenary Essays.* Athens: University of Georgia Press, 1969, 192 p.
> Collection of scholarly essays on Robinson's work, including a chronology of Robinson's life and a bibliography of biographical writings and criticism.

Benét, William Rose. "Round About Parnassus." *The Saturday Review of Literature* VII, No. 9 (9 September 1930): 142.
> Considers Robinson an innovator in modern verse; sees affinities with Robert Browning.

Bogan, Louise. "Tilbury Town and Beyond." *Poetry* XXXVII, No. 4 (January 1931): 216-21.
> Critical overview.

Cary, Richard. *Early Reception of Edwin Arlington Robinson: The First Twenty Years.* Waterville, Maine: Colby College Press, 1974, 321 p.
> Collects reviews, interviews, and essays about Robinson from 1896 to 1916.

Crowder, Richard. "Robinson's 'Talifer': The Figurative Texture." *Boston University Studies in English* (Winter 1960): 241-47.
> Discusses nature imagery in *Talifer*.

Dauner, Louise. "Avon and Cavender: Two Children of the Night." *American Literature* 14, No. 1 (March 1942): 55-65.
> Delineates symbols of light and dark in *Avon's Harvest* and *Cavender's House*.

Drinkwater, John. "Edwin Arlington Robinson." *The Yale Review* XI, No. 3 (April 1922): 467-76.
> Comments on Robinson's traditionalism in an era of great experimentation in verse.

Fussell, Edwin S. *Edwin Arlington Robinson: The Literary Background of a Traditional Poet.* Berkeley, Los Angeles: University of California Press, 1954, 211 p.
> Traces the influence of naturalism as well as classical, biblical, and English literature on Robinson's work.

Hagedorn, Hermann. *Edwin Arlington Robinson: A Biography.* New York: The Macmillan Company, 1938, 402p.
> Biocritical study.

Kaplan, Estelle. *Philosophy in the Poetry of Edwin Arlington Robinson.* New York: Columbia University Press, 1940, 162 p.
> Study of Robinson's philosophical thought through analysis of several of his poems.

Kreymborg, Alfred. "The Wise Music of Robinson." In his *Our Singing Strength: An Outline of American Poetry (1620-1930)*, 297-315. New York: Coward-McCann, Inc., 1929.
> Surveys Robinson's poetry up to the publication of *Cavender's House*.

Lowell, Amy. *A Critical Fable*, pp. 26-9. Boston and New York: Houghton Mifflin and Company, 1922.
> A light-hearted commentary on Robinson composed in verse.

Lucas, John. "The Poetry of Edwin Arlington Robinson." *Renaissance and Modern Studies* XIII, (1969): 132-47.
> Overview essay.

Monroe, Harriet. "Robinson as Man and Poet." *Poetry* XLVI, No. 3 (June 1935): 150-57.
> Tribute to Robinson published shortly after his death.

Primeau, Ronald. "Robinson and Browning Revisted: "Man against the Sky' and 'Childe Roland'." *College Literature* XII, No. 3 (Fall 1985): 222-32.
> Demonstrates that "The Man against the Sky" parallels Robert Browning's "Childe Roland to the Dark Tower Came" in thematic development and compares similarities and differences in treatment by the two poets.

Pritchard, William H. "Edwin Arlington Robinson: The Prince of Heartachers." *The American Scholar* 48, No. 1 (Winter 1978/1979): 89-100.
> Examines the fatalist aspects in Robinson's canon.

Scott, Winfield Townley. "To See Robinson." *New Mexico Quarterly* XXVI, No. 2 (Summer 1956): 161-78.
> Recounts a visit Scott made to Robinson at the MacDowell Colony in the summer of 1929.

Walsh, William Thomas. "Some Recollections of E. A. Robinson," Parts 1, 2. *The Catholic World* CLV, Nos. 929, 930 (August, September 1942): 522-31, 703-12.
> Memoir by a colleague of Robinson's at the MacDowell Colony.

ROBINS Poet and President." *The New England* ~ I, No. 4 (December 1943): 615-26.

W prints extracts of correspondence between Robinson and Theodore Roosevelt from 1902 to 1918.

Winters, Yvor. *Edwin Arlington Robinson.* New York: New Directions, 1947, 180 p.

The first book-length critical analysis of Robinson's work.